Microsoft® Office SharePoint Server™ 2007 Administrator's Companion

Bill English with the Microsoft SharePoint Community Experts

PUBLISHED BY
Microsoft Press
A Division of Microsoft Corporation
One Microsoft Way
Redmond, Washington 98052-6399

Library of Congress Control Number: 2006937020

Printed and bound in the United States of America.

4 5 6 7 8 9 QWT 2 1 0 9 8 7

Distributed in Canada by H.B. Fenn and Company Ltd.

A CIP catalogue record for this book is available from the British Library.

Microsoft Press books are available through booksellers and distributors worldwide. For further information about international editions, contact your local Microsoft Corporation office or contact Microsoft Press International directly at fax (425) 936-7329. Visit our Web site at www.microsoft.com/mspress. Send comments to mspinput@microsoft.com.

Acquisitions Editor: Martin DelRe
Developmental Editors: Karen Szall and Melissa von Tschudi-Sutton
Project Editor: Melissa von Tschudi-Sutton
Production: Custom Editorial Productions, Inc.

Body Part No. X13-24125

This book is dedicated to my lovely and gracious wife, Kathy,
my two children, David and Anna, who are growing up much too fast,
and my Lord and Savior, Jesus Christ.

Contents at a Glance

Part IV
Integrating Additional Server Platforms

Part V
Upgrading to Microsoft Office SharePoint Server 2007

Part VI
Extending Microsoft Office SharePoint Server 2007

Table of Contents

Part II

Administrating and Configuring Your Implementation

Part III
Search, Indexing, and Shared Services Provider

Part IV
Integrating Additional Server Platforms

Part VI
Extending Microsoft Office SharePoint Server 2007

Acknowledgments

The book that you're holding in front of you is the result of many people working long hours. As the principle author on this book project, I am indebted to those who worked so hard to make this book a reality. While my name is on the cover, my efforts pale in comparison to others who worked to make this book a reality.

First, I'd like to thank my editors at Microsoft Press for their hard work, persistence, and patience throughout this project. I think this is the fourth or fifth book project I've worked on with them since 2000, and all the Press editors have been outstanding people with whom to work. I'll start by thanking Martin DelRe, the acquisitions editor for this project. He and I started talking about a SharePoint Server 2007 book in mid-2005, and without his persistence, help, and wisdom in navigating the currents inside Microsoft, this book might not have happened.

Maureen Zimmerman lent her usual expertise in getting the project off to a great start. Karen Szall has seen this project through to completion and didn't ride my case when we were way behind getting chapters to her. Karen, thanks for knowing when to push and when not to—that's a mark of a great editor. Melissa von Tschudi-Sutton has been an incredibly great person with whom to work. She was my day-to-day point of contact at Press for this project and was timely, professional, and genuinely fun to work with. Melissa, I hope we can work together on another project in the future.

Needless to say, I didn't write all 31 chapters in this book. There were a number of coauthors and contributing authors. The coauthors on this book were Penny Coventry, Daniel Webster, Steve Smith, Milan Gross, Kathryn Hughes, and Nikkander and Margriet Bruggeman. The contributing authors for this book included Ben Curry, Laura Derbes Rogers, Brett Lonsdale, Andrew Connell, Chris McCain, Ken Sproule, William Jackson, Graham Tyler, Mark Schneider, and Rick Taylor. You can view their bios on the About the Authors page in the back of the book.

There were several advantages to working with such a talented group of individuals. First, I can say that this book is really an international effort. While it made for interesting timing on some e-mail messages and chapter deliveries, it was also great to be able to leverage the talent of great authors and thought leaders from across the globe for this book.

Second, each author was selected to write because she or he had a particular interest in the subjects they wrote on and demonstrated expertise in that subject area. There's no possible way I could have produced all of this quality material on my own. There is some really good content in this book, as you'll discover by reading it. Every author did a great job.

Third, there were times when I needed several authors to collaborate to ensure they weren't writing overlapping content. One of the big challenges in working with a large author crew like this is to ensure that we don't miss any major topics in the book, that we emphasize the right topics for the intended audience, and that we don't write overlapping content. Every time I asked these folks to work together to ensure the right content was being written in the right chapter, they jumped in without complaining and got the issue resolved. Not only is that a sign of true professionals, but also the mark of great individuals. Thank you all for being really great authors with whom to work.

There were also a number of people on the product team who offered significant assistance in answering questions via e-mail or in person at conferences. I'd like to thank the product team members, including Cheryl Jenkins, Arpan Shah, Avi Shmueli, Sid Shah, Dan Evers, Sage Kitamon, Luca Bandinelli, Daniel Kogen, Brenda Carter, Joel Oleson, John Norby, Keith Bankston, Samantha Robertson, Steve Tullis, Richard Riley, Brad Stevenson, Mike Fitzmaurice, Dmitriy Meyerzon, and Mircea Neagovici-Negoescu. I want to personally thank each of you because without your individual assistance at different times during this project, this book would not have the quality of technical detail that it has. Thank you all for giving us great assistance in writing this book!

I'd also like to thank Mitch Tulloch for doing a great job technical editing this book and Roger LeBlanc for copy editing this book. Catching mistakes and making us sound much better than we (natively) write, these two guys added significant value to this book.

I also want to thank the SharePoint MVPs for their continued participation in this exciting software product. I am truly honored to be numbered with such an outstanding bunch of people who are very talented and technically savvy. I've learned from reading your e-mails and posts during the beta cycle. I've picked up tips and tricks from you guys—some of which probably found their way into this book. I can't think of a better group of people from whom to learn. My challenge now is just to keep up with you all!

Also, I genuinely enjoy the process of writing and editing a book and I enjoy meeting those who read the book. One way for us to meet is by participating together in this book's Web site at *http://admincompanion.mindsharp.com*. It is run entirely on SharePoint Server 2007. At first, the site will be a read-only site, but we'll work to build interactivity into the site as soon as possible. I'll be visiting there too, so I look forward to seeing and meeting you (virtually anyway!).

Back here in the frozen tundra of Minnesota (where summer is the six best days of the year <grin>), I want to stop and give a special 'thank you' to my wife, Kathy. Writing is always time consuming—more so when the author travels as much as I do. I've learned that a good author needs a good support structure, and for me that support structure is my wife. Kathy, thanks for being a great friend, a life-long companion, and a person who loves me unconditionally.

I also want to mention several couples whose friendship I enjoy and depend on when times get tough: Mark and Marcia Schneider, Jay and Dawn Herman, Dave and Merle McGauvran, Rolf and Sandy Engwall, and Scott and Andrea Preissler. Life's greatest fulfillments are found in relationships, not technology, and I'm blessed to have you all in my life.

Contacting the Author

You're always welcome to contact me at any time by e-mail at *bill@mindsharp.com*. My (virtual) door is always open, and I will try to respond to your e-mail within 72 hours of receiving it. Thank you for reading this book. I hope you enjoy reading it as much as we enjoyed writing it!

Bill English
MCSE, MCSA, MVP
Maple Grove, Minnesota

November, 2006

Introduction

Welcome to the *Microsoft Office SharePoint Server 2007 Administrator's Companion*! If you're reading this introduction, chances are good that you're interested in Office SharePoint Server 2007 administration. As you might suspect, this book is filled with ideas, tips, "how-tos," and best practices on planning, deploying, and administrating a SharePoint Server 2007 farm.

But despite the title, we have not assumed that only administrators will pick up this book and use it. You might be a project manager, an information management specialist, a network or SharePoint architect, a developer, a Web designer, or a power user who wants to learn more about SharePoint Server 2007 administration, design, and best practices. We have written this book with a wide variety of interested readers in mind:

- **Architects** will find good information in these pages about how to design a SharePoint implementation.
- **Power users** will benefit greatly from reading about site administration, the site templates that are available, and the Web Parts that ship with this product.
- **Content creators** will learn how to use document libraries to their full advantage.
- **Project managers** will find this a handy reference when working with SharePoint-oriented projects.
- **Information management specialists** will find ideas about best practices for implementation when building taxonomies.
- **Compliance specialists** can learn how SharePoint Server 2007 works with record and document management with a view to meeting compliance requirements.
- **Web content managers** will learn how to publish a Web site from a staging area to a production area, even if multiple languages are involved in the process.
- **Developers** will be interested not only in the Microsoft Office SharePoint Designer and workflow information, but also in how to build sites using features.

As you can see, there is solid information in this book for a wide variety of professionals who will interface with SharePoint Server 2007.

How to Use This Book

This book contains not only great information about designing, deploying, and managing a SharePoint Server 2007 implementation, but also elements like tips, ideas, and best practices.

Look for book elements such as the following:

Real World

Everyone can benefit from the experiences of others. Real World sidebars contain elaboration on a theme or background based on the experiences of others who used this product during the beta testing period.

Note Notes include tips, alternative ways to perform a task, or some information that needs to be highlighted.

On the CD On the CD readeraids point to additional information that is provided on the book's companion CD.

Best Practices Best Practices provide advice for best practices that this book's authors have gained from our own technical experience.

Security Alert Nothing is more important than security when it comes to a computer network. Security elements should be carefully noted and acted on.

Planning As we stress throughout the book, proper planning is fundamental to the smooth operation of any network. These boxes contain specific and useful hints to make that process go smoothly.

Important Boxes marked Important shouldn't be skipped. (That's why they're called Important.) Here you'll find security notes, cautions, and warnings to keep you and your network out of trouble.

What's In This Book

Microsoft Office SharePoint Server 2007 Administrator's Companion is divided into six parts, as follows:

Part I: Planning Your Deployment and Installing Microsoft Office SharePoint Server 2007

Part I of this book contains five chapters. Chapter 1 introduces SharePoint Server 2007. Chapter 2 covers the architecture of SharePoint Server 2007. It discusses how Microsoft Internet Information Services (IIS) and SharePoint Server 2007 work together to provide a solid foundation for the features and benefits that ship with SharePoint Server 2007. In addition, it covers the core, supporting, database, workflow, and operating system services that underlie SharePoint Server 2007 and create the environment in which SharePoint Server 2007 can function effectively.

For those needing to understand how to design and architect a SharePoint Server 2007 deployment, Chapter 3 is the chapter you'll want to read. This chapter discusses the design and architectural choices that you should consider before you implement a SharePoint Server 2007 deployment. It covers defining objectives and requirements. You'll take a look at your current infrastructure and what this means to a SharePoint Server 2007 deployment. This chapter outlines the system dependences of SharePoint Server 2007 and then finishes with some security best practices for your SharePoint Server 2007 deployment.

Chapter 4 focuses on the multilingual architecture and planning considerations that you should think through if you're going to be working in a deployment that crosses multiple languages and localizations.

Chapter 5 is the chapter you'll need to read if you want to learn how to install SharePoint Server 2007. This chapter presents the product matrix and the hardware and software requirements you'll need to meet before you install SharePoint Server 2007. It also describes how to add and remove servers from your farm, the changes that SharePoint Server 2007 makes to your servers, and how to uninstall SharePoint Server 2007 too, in case you ever need to do that.

Part II: Administrating and Configuring Your Implementation

Part II begins with Chapter 6. There are two parts to Central Administration: operations and application management. This chapter covers the operations side of Central Administration. As part of this discussion, you'll look at the Home page in Central Administration and at the main administration and configuration areas such as topology management, security configuration, logging and reporting, global configuration, and data configuration.

Chapter 7 focuses on the application management side of Central Administration. This chapter looks at how to create new Web applications, what the best practices are, how to manage Web applications, and how to configure core farm services. It also discusses application security, workflow management, and external service connections.

Once you've finished with Central Administration and configuring core and farm services, you'll turn your attention to administrating personalization features and taxonomies in Chapter 8. You'll start by looking at what taxonomies are, and then discuss some of the best practices on how to build them. You'll also look at managing My Sites. This chapter also provides an extended discussion about the Knowledge Network software that can be downloaded and installed with the SharePoint Server 2007 platform. It finishes with a discussion about how user profiles and audiences work in SharePoint Server 2007.

The next two chapters focus on records and document management. Chapter 9 includes a robust discussion on enterprise records management, including an extended discussion on the records repositories in SharePoint Server 2007. It also discusses how to secure records repositories and how to submit content to a records repository.

Chapter 10 focuses on document management. It discusses document workflow, document metadata, document versioning, and how the Microsoft Office client fits into the overall picture. It also discusses the document management site template.

Chapter 11 shifts gears once again and discusses the staging and publication model for SharePoint Server 2007. This chapter illustrates and describes how to stage a "rough draft" Web site and then how to publish that Web site to the public. You'll also learn how to publish individual Web Parts and how to set publishing schedules.

Chapter 12 introduces the new Business Data Catalog (BDC). The BDC is a new feature that is heavily used by a number of other components in the SharePoint Server 2007 family. You'll learn how to create a BDC, how to manage data connections within the BDC, and how to use BDC's features. This chapter also offers some best practices when it comes to creating and using the BDC.

For readers who want information on Microsoft Operations Manager (MOM) 2005 and SharePoint Server 2007, Chapter 13 focuses on performance monitoring using MOM 2005. You'll learn what a Management Pack is and how to install it. You'll also learn about the performance monitoring basics and how to troubleshoot problems indicated by counters whose readings land outside of normal behavior. This is an important topic for any administrator.

Chapter 14, "Information Security Policies," is one that you'll be tempted to overlook. It is full of dry, boring stuff that you'll never use–until you need to help your managers figure out new information security policies in light of a SharePoint Server 2007 implementation. Because information security policies form the foundation for security in our environments, you should read this chapter and get up to speed on some of the policies that you should consider implementing when you deploy SharePoint Server 2007.

The last chapter in this section on administration and configuration is Chapter 15, which focuses on two new elements: content types and features. In this chapter, you'll learn what content types and features are, how to work with them, and how to use them effectively in a SharePoint Server 2007 deployment.

Part III: Search, Indexing, and Shared Services Providers

Part III of the book focuses on the core services provided by the new Shared Services Provider (SSP). Chapter 16 focuses on the enterprise search and indexing architecture. In addition, this chapter covers the core technologies on search administration, such as creating content sources, site path rules, site hit frequency rules, search scopes, management properties and other details to search administration.

Chapter 17 is a follow up to Chapter 16. It discusses search topology models, sample deployment scenarios, and using Search as a feature.

Chapter 18 focuses on the other administrative options for shared services, including interfarm shared services. It also discusses design and planning issues surrounding changing SSP associations and running multiple SSPs in a single farm.

Part IV: Integrating Additional Server Platforms

This part of the book focuses on integrating additional server platforms into SharePoint Server 2007. Chapter 19 is a robust chapter on displaying SharePoint Server 2007 technologies on mobile devices. Included in this chapter is a discussion of the Microsoft Office Project Server 2007 mission, its architecture, and how to install it in a SharePoint Server 2007 environment. In addition, you'll learn how to set up and use Office Project Server 2007 in your environment.

Another server platform that can be nicely integrated with SharePoint Server 2007 is Microsoft Office Excel Calculation Services, which is discussed in Chapter 20. This chapter explains how to install and configure Excel Calculation Services, provides an overview of the components, and discusses how the server interacts with spreadsheets–both those consumed over the Web and those published to the server. Moreover, you'll learn about the Dashboard Web Parts and performance considerations as you work with this server product.

Forms now becomes a core feature and component of SharePoint Server 2007, so an entire chapter is devoted to Microsoft Office Forms Server 2007. In Chapter 21, you will learn about the new features in this server product as well as how to create forms that will be useful to your environment.

Part V: Upgrading to Microsoft Office SharePoint Server 2007

Chapter 22 focuses on upgrading from previous versions of SharePoint Products and Technologies to the 2007 versions. This chapter discusses the tricky upgrade process to move from Microsoft Content Management Server 2001 or 2002 to Web content management on SharePoint Server 2007. It discusses how to prepare your site, how to create migration paths, and how to migrate your Web content. The chapter then outlines the post-migration tasks that should be performed to finish the migration correctly.

Chapter 23 focuses on Microsoft Windows SharePoint Services and looks at how to upgrade from version 2.0 to version 3.0. This discussion does not include information on how to upgrade from SharePoint Portal Server 2003 to SharePoint Server 2007 because those scenarios are covered in Chapter 24.

Because custom site definitions are a part of many deployments, the need to upgrade those site definitions will be high. So Chapter 25 discusses how to migrate site definitions to SharePoint Server 2007.

Part VI: Extending Microsoft Office SharePoint Server 2007

The final part of the book deals with extending SharePoint Server 2007. Chapter 26 starts this effort by looking at using features to build Windows SharePoint Services sites. Chapter 27 looks at how to use the SharePoint Designer 2007 to customize and brand sites in SharePoint Server 2007.

Chapter 28 drills down into the creation of workflows in SharePoint Server 2007. While the farm management of workflows is discussed earlier in this book, how to create workflows in the standard site UI and how to build them in SharePoint Designer are discussed in this chapter.

The next chapter is one that many have wished would have been written in the last set of books on SharePoint. Chapter 29 will focus on providing an overview of the more commonly used Web Parts that ship "in the box" with SharePoint Server 2007. You'll learn how to create and modify Web Part pages, how to add and remove Web Parts from a page, and how to configure the more common settings for Web Parts. In addition, the chapter provides a summary of over 30 common Web Parts that ship with SharePoint Server 2007.

Disaster recovery is always saved for the end of a book. It's a tradition, right? So Chapter 30 focuses on disaster recovery methods for SharePoint Server 2007. You'll learn how to use the built-in tools to both back up and restore a SharePoint Server 2007 farm, as well as about fail-over scenarios, IIS backup and restore procedures, and best practices when it comes to backup and restore.

Finally, Chapter 31 looks at a little-known issue that will grow in importance for administrators and that is Code Access Security (CAS). Increasingly, administrators will be asked to manage security for code just as they are tasked with securing information resources. Chapter 31 is the first chapter in an administrator's book that we know of that focuses completely on this topic from an administrator's perspective. Be sure to read this chapter. You'll need these skills in your toolbox moving forward.

System Requirements

The following are the minimum system requirements to run the companion CD provided with this book:

- Microsoft Windows XP, with the latest service pack installed and the lastest updates installed from Microsoft Update Service
- CD-ROM drive
- Internet connection
- Display monitor capable of 1024 x 768 resolution
- Microsoft Mouse or compatible pointing device
- Adobe Reader for viewing the eBook (Adobe Reader is available as a download at *http://www.adobe.com*)

About the Companion CD

The companion CD contains the fully searchable electronic version of this book, additional chapter materials you might find useful, as well as the book's glossary. We've also included several white papers we found useful while we were writing this book.

Support

Every effort has been made to the accuracy of this book and companion CD content. Microsoft Press provides corrections to this book through the Web at the following location:

http://www.microsoft.com/learning/support

To connect directly to the Microsoft Knowledge Base and enter a query regarding a question or issue that you may have, go to the following address:

http://www.microsoft.com/learning/support/search.asp

If you have comments, questions, or ideas regarding the book or companion CD content, or if you have questions that are not answered by querying the Knowledge Base, please send them to Microsoft Press using either of the following methods:

E-Mail:
mspinput@microsoft.com

Postal Mail:
Microsoft Press
Attn: Microsoft Office SharePoint Server 2007 Administrator's Companion Editor
One Microsoft Way
Redmond, WA 98052-6399

Please note that product support is not offered through the preceding mail addresses. For support information, please visit the Microsoft Product Support Web site at the following address:

http://support.microsoft.com

In addition, there is a community site dedicated to those who read this book at *http://admincompanion.mindsharp.com*. At this site, you'll find a place to collaborate with others about the contents and ideas in this book and see updated information about the book's contents and best practices. We'll also include an errata for the book so you can find the updated corrections about the book. An errata section will help us keep track of the corrections to the book because we wrote this book using the Beta 2 software and checked the content and screen shots against the Beta 2 Technical Refresh version. It is possible that some sections and some screen shots will have changed in the final version of SharePoint Server 2007, so referencing this errata section will be helpful to everyone reading the book.

Part I
Planning Your Deployment and Installing Microsoft Office SharePoint Server 2007

Chapter 1

Introducing Microsoft Office SharePoint Server 2007

Welcome to Microsoft Office SharePoint Server 2007!

This is, by far, the most exciting collaboration and information management product that Microsoft has ever released. There are 27 products that now exist under the Microsoft Office brand, and SharePoint Products and Technologies is taking center stage within the 2007 Microsoft Office system with the release of Microsoft Windows SharePoint Services and Microsoft Office SharePoint Server 2007. You'll find, in the coming years, that SharePoint will continue to be the platform of choice for Web application development as well as information sharing and presentation.

Office SharePoint Server 2007 is a robust, stable platform upon which you can build Web-based applications, collaborate with colleagues on important projects, comply with many Sarbanes-Oxley Act of 1992 (SOX) and Health Insurance Portability and Accountability Act of 1996 (HIPAA) requirements, and create a one-stop location to find all the information you and your users will need to be successful. SharePoint Server 2007 is built on the .NET Framework 3.0 and the Windows Workflow Foundation (WF) and can work with ASP.NET 1.1 and 2.0 Web Parts. In addition, SharePoint Server 2007 runs on the Internet Information Services (IIS) 6.0 or later platform and can work with either Microsoft SQL Server 2000 or SQL Server 2005. (Note that Microsoft SQL Server 2005 is required for the business intelligence features to run properly.)

Microsoft Office SharePoint Server 2007 Product Matrix

In Microsoft Office SharePoint Portal Server 2003, you were accustomed to thinking about a single-server product. The generic phrase "SharePoint Server" would often be equated to a single product: SharePoint Portal Server 2003. In SharePoint Server 2007, you'll find that the generic phrase "SharePoint Server" refers to a suite of server components under the "SharePoint" name. Those components and their features are listed in Table 1-1.

Table 1-1 SharePoint Server 2007 Feature Areas

Component area	Features
Portal	Enterprise Portal template
	Site directory
	My Site
	Social networking
	Privacy control
Search	Enterprise scalability
	Contextual relevance
	People and business data search
Content Management	Integrated document management
	Records management
	Web content management with policies and workflow
Business Forms	Web forms-based front ends
	Line-of-Business (LOB) actions
	Pluggable Single Sign-On (SSO)
Business Intelligence (BI)	Server-based Excel spreadsheets and data visualization
	Report Center
	BI Web Parts
	Key Performance Indicators (KPIs) and dashboards
Collaboration	Documents, tasks, and calendars
	Blogs and wikis
	E-mail integration
	Project management "lite"
	Outlook integration
	Offline documents and lists

Portal Services

Portal services in SharePoint Server 2007 are now available through the Corporate Intranet site template. This template automatically creates several sub sites, including a Sites Directory, Document Center, News page with Real Simple Syndication (RSS) capabilities, a Report Center, Search Center, and access to My Site. (See Figure1-1).

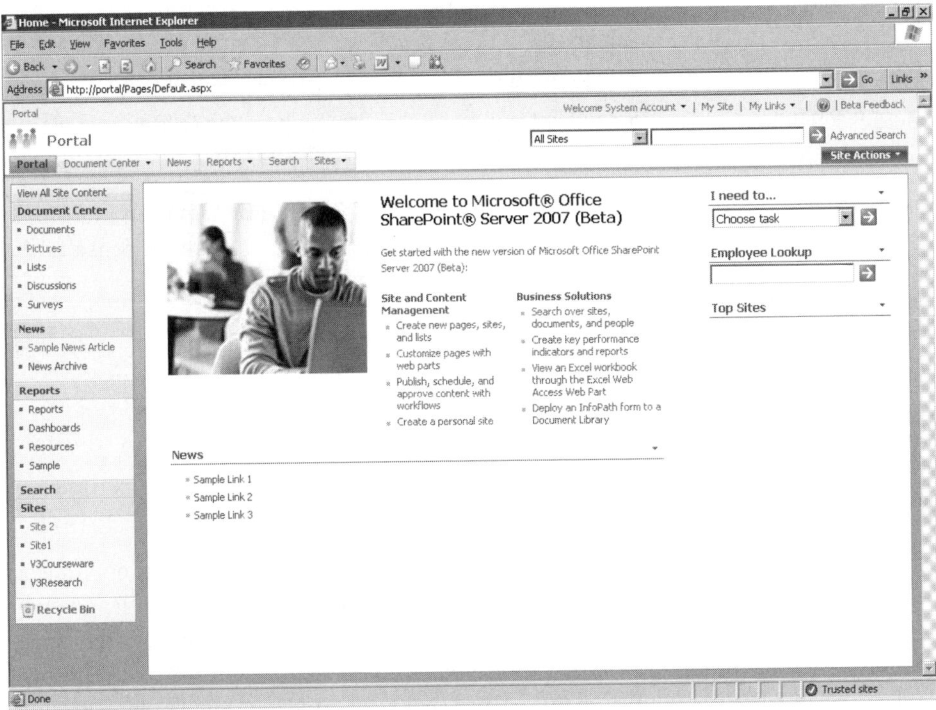

Figure 1-1 Default portal in SharePoint Server 2007

If you take a long step back from the actual page, you'll see that the portal is aggregating content from various locations and presenting that content to the user in a single view. The primary goal of SharePoint Server 2007 is to provide each of your users with a single location from which they can access or find all the information they need to do their jobs. The SharePoint Server 2007 portal goes a long way toward accomplishing that goal.

My Site

Included with portal services are the user's personal portals, called *My Site*. In SharePoint Server 2007, My Site serves three important functions. First, My Site forms part of a larger targeting picture that is rather compelling. SharePoint Server 2007 now allows information to be targeted to the user so that the user doesn't have to remember *where* the information resides. The ability to develop a robust targeting topology for end users is a nice feature in SharePoint Server 2007. Table 1-2 illustrates how the targeting topology can work.

Table 1-2 Targeting Information to Users Using My Site

Items that can be targeted	Where items can be targeted to	Where targeted items can show up
Any SharePoint list item	Rules-based SharePoint Audiences	Any SharePoint page
Web Parts	SharePoint groups	Any SharePoint page
Links for navigation	SharePoint groups	Links in the Office client file dialog box

Second, My Site can be used to allow the end user to aggregate information in a single location, employing nearly any organizational method that seems to make sense to the end user. Items that can be aggregated include the following:

- My documents, tasks, e-mail messages, and other SharePoint lists
- My SharePoint sites
- My Colleagues
- My Web/RSS feeds
- My Outlook Web Access

Third, using some interesting yet flexible privacy controls, end users are able to deliver information about themselves to the enterprise, to a predefined set of colleagues, or somewhere in between. For example, users can take the information about themselves that is imported from Active Directory—or any Lightweight Directory Access Protocol (LDAP) version 3.0-compliant directory—and make that information available to individuals and groups that they can define. In addition, they are able to provide information about themselves—such as skills, keywords, and other self-descriptors—for someone else's consumption.

Other information that can be distributed by end users includes organization profile information, such as common managers, colleagues, site memberships, and e-mail distribution lists.

Knowledge Network

Knowledge Network software does not ship with the SharePoint Server 2007 product, but you'll be wise to download and install it to enhance the social-networking capabilities of your users. Knowledge Network addresses the following familiar problems:

- Most information is not documented in a formal sense.

- It's often difficult to connect the information you have with the right person.
- "Weak ties" are not easily discoverable.

The term *weak ties* refers to folks who know people whom you know. They are usually secondary or tertiary contacts made through your family and friends. In an organizational sense, they are often people who work at your company but with whom you have only occasional contact. People whom your colleagues know are your "second degree contacts" or what we call your "colleagues' colleagues." The friends and contacts of your second degree contacts are your "third degree contacts." These second and third degree contacts form your "weak ties." In social networking theory, weak ties connect together cliques or subgroups, which can provide powerful connections to new ideas, information, and opportunities. An organization needs to have a deep social network and expertise profile for an individual if that profile is to have any worth. Automating the creation of that profile is the key to unlocking that person's tacit knowledge—that is, knowledge that is not readily available in a documented form.

Common Features

As you might expect, the taxonomy features of SharePoint Server 2003 have been retained in SharePoint Server 2007, so you still have a Sites Directory to organize sites across your organization, a News page to organize and present news and announcements that pertain to the consumers of the portal, and the ability to use the portal's home page as your intranet's home page.

Search and Indexing

Aggregated search and indexing is enhanced and extended in SharePoint Server 2007 from its predecessor in SharePoint Server 2003. Microsoft has implemented a common search engine across the entire SharePoint platform in such a way that it doesn't matter whether you install Windows SharePoint Services 3.0 or SharePoint Server 2007. Either way, you will get the same basic search and indexing engine. However, the version of search that ships with SharePoint Server 2007 has many more features than Windows SharePoint Services, including the ability to index nearly any type of content. The search engine for Windows SharePoint Services is able to search only content hosted in a SharePoint site.

In addition, Microsoft has made significant investments in relevance capabilities, which ensure that the right information (or the most relevant information based on the query) appears at the top of the result set.

Microsoft has also made the search result set more customizable and certainly more user friendly. For example, if you misspell a word in your search query, the Did You Mean (DYM) feature prompts you to repeat the search using the correct spelling.

Content Management

Under this broad umbrella are three very distinct and needed feature categories: Web content, records management, and document management. All three are now included in SharePoint Server 2007. In addition, you can both secure and privatize content by using a combination of permissions and Windows Rights Management Services (RMS).

Content management provides end users with the capability to author content on a Web site and publish that content to a public-facing Web site either manually or on a schedule. Embedded in the publishing model is workflow for approval routing. Auditing is included as part of this process so that security and regulatory compliance needs can be achieved using SharePoint Server 2007.

Web Content

The features and functionalities of what used to be known as Microsoft Content Management Server 2002 are now included with SharePoint Server 2007. As a product, Content Management Server (CMS) no longer exists. The Web content management feature essentially has become the publishing model for Web content using the CMS features and ideas from the CMS product line. Now users have a spot in which they can create new Web content, run it through an approval process, and then publish that content to another, public Web site. This staging feature covers not only Web content but also custom code and modifications to the site.

In addition, for developers, the solutions management features in SharePoint Server 2007 neatly eliminates the significant problem that existed in SharePoint Server 2003, wherein developers were tasked with writing code but did not have an acceptable method of moving that code from alpha to beta to production environments.

Records and Document Management

Records management is also provided by SharePoint Server 2007. By using content types, you can now manage bits of information, such as e-mail messages, that have traditionally existed across a wide range of repositories.

Document management allows an organization to create a single location at which finished documents can be placed for consumption by parties with the correct permissions. Inherent in this process is the ability to audit what happens to the document and place expiration dates on documents that should expire after a given amount of time.

Both records and document management allow an organization to leverage SharePoint Server 2007 as it attempts to comply with SOX regulations in the United States and similar types of legislation in other countries. What follows is an example of how SOX regulatory compliance can be achieved using SharePoint Server 2007.

- Legal Requirement (Paraphrased):
    - The signing officers of the corporation must certify they have reviewed the financial report by signing the report.
    - The officers' signatures certify they found the financial report to be accurate and the figures to be accurately derived.
- What this Requirement Means to IT:
    - Data used in the financial report must be of known origin and derivation, have correct formatting, and be used in the appropriate context.
    - The processes must have owners and the data must have owners.
    - Supporting and final documents must be managed under change control.
- Specific Collaboration Software Requirements:
    - Metadata to provide classification and context for the data.
    - Collaboration sites must share information in an ordered fashion between stakeholders.
    - Central document libraries must provide contributors with a single set of documents to use for editing purposes. Ultimately, the final documents will be published as authoritative change-managed documents.
    - Document change control must provide audit trails and controls for changes made to authoritative documents.
    - Central issues logs to provide a forum for contributors to officially draw attention to problems and issues that might have an impact on SOX compliance.
    - Workflow management.
    - Automatic alerts and notifications.
    - Authentication and access control.

Because many corporations and organizations operate in multilingual environments, SharePoint Server 2007 allows for documents to be translated and indexed across multiple languages. For example, a Microsoft Office Word document can be created using French and then opened in a German version of Word, appearing in the German language. The localization of content for users in different locations speaking different languages is one of the new, key features in SharePoint Server 2007.

Rights Management

In addition, RMS, which allows content to be privatized, is embedded in the SharePoint Server 2007 platform. The difference between permissions (who can access the resource) and privatization (the actions that can be committed by those who do have permissions to the content) is important. With SharePoint Server 2007, you'll be able to both secure and privatize content by using a combination of permissions and information rights management. If you're not accustomed to working with certificates, you'll need to ramp up on Public Key Infrastructure (PKI) because implementing RMS will require a working knowledge of PKI. For more information about PKI, see *Microsoft Windows Server 2003 PKI and Certificate Security* (Microsoft Press, 2004) and also review the topic "Designing a Public Key Infrastructure" found on the PKI TechCenter on Microsoft TechNet (*http://www.microsoft.com/windowsserver2003/technologies/pki/default.mspx*).

Business Forms

As part of the new suite of SharePoint Server 2007 server-side products, Microsoft is introducing Office Forms Server 2007. Office Forms Server 2007 allows companies to capture critical data in electronic formats and then automate processes for this information once it is captured. Web-based forms can be created and consumed across the enterprise using Forms Server 2007.

This means that you can extend data-gathering activities to anyone who has a browser and nothing more. Hence, you can make your forms-driven business processes accessible to customers, partners, and suppliers through a Web browser. By using the advanced browser-based form-rendering technology built into Forms Server 2007, you can design cool forms that provide a positive user experience.

In addition, you can create forms to act as front-end data-gathering tools for your Line-of-Business (LOB) applications. You can also connect multiple forms to existing data systems using Web services.

Some other features of Forms Server 2007 include the following:

- Advanced form functionality that can be created without having to write code
- Data validation at the time of entry
- Mobile device access to certain kinds of forms

Business Intelligence

Microsoft Business Intelligence (BI) is a focal area for Microsoft software in SharePoint Server 2007. Part of the premium content services, BI is focused on aggregating information into a report structure and presenting those reports in a report center. BI is much more than simple information regurgitation. BI is a prepackaged solution that combines SQL Server 2005, SharePoint Server 2007, and the 2007 Microsoft Office system client to help deliver the right information at the right time in the right format. Three main parts to this solution exist and can be used separately or in conjunction with each other.

The first part is the business scorecard solution, Microsoft Business Scorecard Manager 2005 (BSM). Also offered as part of the larger Microsoft Office PerformancePoint Server 2007 brand, this solution enables you to keep track of employee productivity. Office PerformancePoint Server 2007 offers scorecard capabilities that help users better understand what is happening in their business and align their actions with corporate strategy. Users can build and manage personalized scorecards without looping in IT as well.

Note There are three parts to BSM: the server, builder and client. BSM was written for the .NET 1.1 platform as well as Windows SharePoint Services 2.0. You can install BSM on a SharePoint Server 2007 platform, but you'll need to do some tweaking of the install process. Be sure to check out the blogs that are focused on BSM, such as Patrick Husting's blog at *http://bimvp.com/blogs/bsm/*.

In addition, you can learn more about PerformancePoint at *http://office.microsoft.com/en-us/assistance/CH101649551033.aspx*

The second main area of BI in SharePoint Server 2007 is the Microsoft Office Excel Calculation Services. Microsoft Office Excel has long been a favorite tool for analyzing information, and this product now delivers Excel functionality in a zero-client format if needed. In addition, Excel users gain a server-side component wherein the spreadsheet can be configured to maintain a persistent connection between their Excel spreadsheet and the data source. Moreover, new features include complete support for SQL Server 2005 Analysis Services, greatly expanded spreadsheet capacity, improved sorting and filtering capabilities, rich data visualization schemes in both Excel and Microsoft Office Visio, and enhanced PivotTables and PivotCharts.

The third main area of business intelligence is SQL Reporting Services and Analysis Services. These services allow you to aggregate granular information from multiple data sources using SQL Server Integration Services, build complex analyses of the data using Analysis Services, and then use Reporting Services to build accurate, easy-to-consume reports.

Collaboration

Rich collaboration features ship with Windows SharePoint Services 3.0 and are leveraged by SharePoint Server 2007. The number and depth of features is complex and varied and we'll be dicussing many of them later in this chapter in the section "Improvements to

Windows SharePoint Services 3.0." But at a high overview level, the collaboration features include elements such as blogs, wikis, e-mail integration, "lite" project management, Outlook integration, as well as v2 features that have been retained.

One of the main drawbacks of Windows SharePoint Services 2.0 was the lack of a security-trimmed user interface (UI). The UI in Windows SharePoint Services 3.0 is now security trimmed so that users will see only links to which they have permissions to perform actions or access resources. In concept, this feature stems from the Access Based Enumeration (ABE) with Windows Server 2003 Service Pack 1. The idea is that if a user can see, but not use, a resource, this is still a security problem. On file servers, this can be especially critical when a user can see the file names of files to which she does not have access. In SharePoint, the administrative links don't represent access to resources, but they do represent access to actions that users should not see if they can't perform the action. This keeps users from "wandering" a site, trying to perform administration actions that they shouldn't be trying to perform.

Other new features in Windows SharePoint Services 3.0 include the following:

- Large list indexing (via the SQL Full-Text Search engine, not the Microsoft Search engine)
- Versioning and per-item security for all list items in all list types
- Addition of multivalued lookup fields
- Ability to use list views from another Web
- Creation and consumption of Content Types across all lists
- Two-stage recycle bin for sites and site collections
- Auditing of user actions with application programming interface (API) to allow independent software vendors (ISV) to write auditing into their own applications
- Explicit login/logout
- Search scoped to "this site and down"

Improvements in Windows SharePoint Services 3.0

The client components of the 2007 Office system work with and use the server components in Windows SharePoint Services. Improvements in Windows SharePoint Services have resulted in new features and functionality at the client end. Let's start by looking at the data platform improvements.

Data Platform Improvements

One of the more common customer scenarios is a company that wants to store a large quantity of documents in a single document library and yet have the ability to quickly find and filter those documents. In addition, users want to host different document types with different schema inside the same document library and be able to sort and search against the differences in the document schemas. And users want to be able to retrieve documents after they have deleted them without having to go to IT personnel for a restore service. In Windows SharePoint Services, all this and more is now possible.

Storage Improvements

The largest area of improvement for this version of Windows SharePoint Services is in the data storage and query lookup features. The first feature that was added was large list indexing, which gives the user the ability to search across large lists (document libraries are included in this discussion) for specific information. For example, assume that you have a document library with one million documents in the library and you want to search for all the documents authored by Bill English. Windows SharePoint Services will allow you to do this quickly because there are now indexes stored on the data in fields for the list items. In this example, the author field has its own index that can be queried to enumerate quickly all the authors in the document library.

Multivalued Lookups

Another new feature is multivalued lookups. This feature allows your users to use a list that is a lookup to another list wherein the user can specify multiple values. For example, you have a central list that contains all the status types that you might want to assign to your documents across the enterprise. You want to find all the documents that have had a technical and copy editorial review but not a legal review. In this version of Windows SharePoint Services, you can execute this type of query and receive back all the documents that match your query for which you have permissions to see. The ability to have a one-to-many lookup from within one SharePoint list to another SharePoint list is a new, exciting feature that will provide endless possibilities for better content management and methods to find information.

Because you have the ability to do lookups from one list to another list, the product also introduced a link fix-up component that allows you to learn which lists and list items have dependencies in other lists across the enterprise.

Windows SharePoint Services will also include a slimmed-down version of the SharePoint Server 2007 search engine. Replacing the SQL Full-Text Indexing engine with the SharePoint Server 2007 search engine allows a similar fidelity of results at the site level that are enjoyed in the portal search results while also allowing users a more seamless upgrade to SharePoint Server 2007, should that be desirable at some point. The Windows

SharePoint Services version of this engine does not allow for the creation of external content sources, but it allows for a more consistent user experience across sites and portals in SharePoint Server 2007.

There is a change log that keeps track of changes to a library, list, or item that can be polled either via the change log API or Web services so that you can track what changes have been executed to a particular item.

Windows SharePoint Services includes a new feature called *AutoCopy*. This feature allows you to take an individual list item and copy it to one or more other locations on a regular, scheduled basis. The autocopy action can occur when an item is updated, when a document is updated, or when a document is published. This feature is a core feature in the new publishing model in Windows SharePoint Services.

Windows SharePoint Services includes a new transformation feature. Assume you need the ability to automatically save documents in PDF format. Now all you need to do is install the .doc to .pdf transformer, and that transformer will show up on all the menus for documents in Windows SharePoint Services so that it can be leveraged across the enterprise. This feature is installed and managed centrally, but it's consumed (potentially) across the sites in the enterprise.

Windows SharePoint Services supports more fields in a Web Part. In the previous version of Windows SharePoint Services, there was a limit of 64 columns or fields that could be made a part of that list. In this version, you can create up to 2000 fields for an individual list.

Overcoming the inability of the previous version of Windows SharePoint Services to enumerate large lists in the browser has been an ongoing effort for the product team. For example, assume you have a list with 15,000 or more items. Enumerating such a large number of items in one page in the browser can often overload the HTML engine and make it literally impossible to enumerate the entire list in the browser. Work-arounds to solve this problem continue to focus on using the Data View Web Part, using Views to filter the list, or placing the list items into folders to break up the list's enumeration. You can also build indexes around the metadata in the list and search for items in the list based on their metadata assignments.

List and Library Alignment

The Windows SharePoint Services team has also worked hard to ensure that there is list and document library alignment across all sites in the enterprise. For example, in the previous version of Windows SharePoint Services, document libraries had folders but lists did not. Version history on list items were not available, whereas version histories were available on documents. You could also assign permissions to individual list items, but you were unable to do this in a document library. Moreover, the Discussions Web Part implemented a complex folder scheme in which each discussion was housed inside a folder—one where each post in the overall thread represented a child list item in that folder.

Content Types

Content types is another new feature that has been added into Windows SharePoint Services. Content types are a set of fields that you group together to form metadata, behaviors, and workflow for a particular content item.

If you're a knowledge worker and you want to manage the metadata for documents inside of a SharePoint list, and if those documents are stored in multiple lists, maintaining a consistent metadata list can be difficult because you need to visit each list and ensure that it has the same column structure and naming convention as the others. In this version of Windows SharePoint Services, content types solve that problem. Content types allow you to centrally manage the individual metadata that is attached to a document across the enterprise.

For example, let's say that you want all the organization's press releases to have a copy edit and a legal review before being published and you want to enforce this across all document libraries in your enterprise. Content types will enable you to do this by configuring a Press Release content type that requires a document to have both a copy edit and a legal review before it can be published.

Content types can also be hierarchical. That is, you can set global content types that are managed centrally, create local content types that inherit their information from the global content type, and still have the freedom to add, remove, or modify characteristics and behaviors of the local content type that were inherited from the global content type. For example, you could create a content type called Public Documents and then create another one at a document-library level called Press Releases that inherits from Public Documents but also modifies in various ways the inherited properties of the Public Documents content type. You could also add behaviors, workflows, and characteristics to the Press Releases content type. This architecture allows for great flexibility in how schemas are defined, while still allowing centralized output of an initial schema for the enterprise.

Content types also facilitate the ability to do large list indexing because you know that the lists that are using a particular content type are all storing the data in that field (or set of fields) in the same way across all the lists, which enables easier, faster indexing of the content.

Data Restore

Probably the most anticipated new feature in this version of Windows SharePoint Services is the Recycle Bin. This bin is actually a two-stage recycle bin, which has its first stage at the library level and second stage at the site-collection level.

At the document-library level, the content owner is able to both delete and restore the document without the involvement of either the site collection owner or the system administrator. At the site-collection level, the site collection owners are able to restore documents without the involvement of the system administrator.

The site collection administrator is able to set policies for all the document library recycle bins, such as a clean-up interval of two weeks at the document-library level and three months at the site-collection level. As long as the deleted document is in either of these two bins, the document can be restored without the help of the system administrator.

The robust auditing features of Windows SharePoint Services will track when and who deleted the document, even if the document no longer exists. The audit trail for actions on a document is not stored with the document. It is stored separately from the document for future reference, even though the document might no longer exist or might have been renamed or repurposed in some manner.

Windows SharePoint Services also provides three types of backups: one is for catastrophic events, one is for individual sites and the third is for individual documents in a document library. Microsoft Office SharePoint Designer 2007 will give end users the ability to back up entire site collections and take them away from the network for offline use. This functionality is similar to that provided by smigrate.exe, but now it's at a site-collection level as well as at an individual-site level.

Catastrophic restores are provided by enterprise backups. These backups are provided by SQL backups as well as by a Volume Shadow Copy Service (VSS) writer so that they can participate in enterprise backup routines. Site backup and restores are provided by using the command-line tool, stsadm.exe. Individual documents can be deleted and restored because of the two-stage recycle bin feature.

Security Improvements

Security is another big area of improvement in Windows SharePoint Services. The most requested feature improvement from the last version of Windows SharePoint Services to this version was document-level permissions in a document library. That feature is now available in this version. Now you not only have item-level security in the document library, but you also have a security-trimmed user interface. The interface a user sees will expose only links to actions that the user has permissions to perform. Actions that a user does not have permissions to perform will not be displayed to the user.

Windows SharePoint Services now ships with a robust auditing engine that can audit every action a user performs within SharePoint. There is also a full auditing object model against which you can develop your own custom applications.

And each SharePoint Server 2007 site will have an explicit login/logout function. This function will not apply to Readers in the site, meaning that Readers will not be required to log in to the site to view the contents of the site. However, those who navigate to the site with elevated privileges will need to log in to use their elevated privileges. Because the user interface is trimmed for security, this means that the same site that hosts the development of documents can also present "finished" documents to the enterprise, providing those with read-only access the ability to read a document from that site without requiring a login to that site.

Administrator Platform Improvements

There were some key scenarios that the product team wanted to address. The most important scenario was the extranet scenario. In this scenario, administrators seek to collaborate with vendors, partners, and customers and control the authentication methods to their collaboration sites without having to add external accounts to their Active Directory. There were reverse proxy and perimeter network (also known as DMZ or demilitarized zone) configurations that the previous version of Windows SharePoint Services didn't support very well. In addition, not all administrators wanted to use NTLM authentication in their extranet scenarios.

A second common scenario that the product team wanted to address and improve upon was the process of upgrading from the previous version of Windows SharePoint Services to the current version of Windows SharePoint Services. This section discusses both scenarios, but first let's take a look at the new key components for the Administration Platform.

Key Components of the Administration Platform

This section discusses several key components and outlines what the product team has done to improve the overall Administration Platform in Windows SharePoint Services. These items include the following:

- The product team has taken all the configuration links for Administrators and placed them into a common location in Central Administration.
- An extensible time service has been implemented in this version of Windows SharePoint Services.

  Earlier versions had the timer service, but now it is extensible. The service, which must be running on each physical server in the SharePoint Server 2007 farm, is used to automatically pull all the configuration information out of the configuration database and update all the servers in the farm automatically. You'll also be able to register your own objects with the timer service and expose those in the administration interface so that you can run your own timer jobs on top of the built-in jobs in Windows SharePoint Services.

- The Central Administration tool has been greatly enhanced.

  All configuration changes are made under the Operations tab, and all Web site and virtual server activities will be managed under the Application Management tab. You'll also find that you can group administration activities together and customize the administration interface to meet you needs. The tool is extensible because the Central Administration tool is now just another Windows SharePoint Services site that is based on the Team Site template. Because the underlying code base allows for site extensibilities, these extensibilities are available to the administrator in Central Administration.

- The navigation structure has been improved and flattened in this version of Windows SharePoint Services.

- There is a new administration task list that appears as soon as you open Central Administration to inform you of the tasks that SharePoint believes are the most important tasks to be accomplished in your farm.

  This task list is literally just that—a Windows SharePoint Services task list that can be extended by you with recurring tasks or one-time tasks that can be assigned to you or other members of the farm administration team.

- There is a new Farm Topology information screen that will list each server in the SharePoint Server 2007 farm, along with the server's status and the services that the server is running.

  Also, you can manage the servers from this interface. One especially noteworthy feature is that if the status shows "error," you'll can click on the "error" link to bring up the logs from the remote server so that you can see what events are being recorded and learn about the problems associated with that server.

Extranet Scenario Improvements

The product team added support for more extranet configurations with the ASP.NET-pluggable authentication model. This means that form-based authentication and Web-based Single Sign-On (SSO) are now supported methods of authentication in Windows SharePoint Services. These two supported methods are not shipped "in the box" in Windows SharePoint Services, but they are supported and can be purchased from third-party sources or custom coded for your own environment.

Upgrade Improvements

The product team had four main goals related to upgrade paths and methods that they wanted to accomplish in this version of Windows SharePoint Services. First, they wanted to ensure that you could upgrade over time, meaning that you weren't forced into upgrading your entire SharePoint deployment all at once. The goal was to allow you to upgrade your current implementation in "weekend-size chunks" so that a disparate, discrete portion of your overall deployment can be upgraded and finished without having to upgrade other segments of your current deployment.

Second, the product team understood that most people can't take down their entire deployment all at once to perform an upgrade to the next version of Windows SharePoint Services. Having all your users sitting around, unproductive, while you're performing an upgrade is not the scenario that Microsoft wants you to experience. Therefore, the product team has assured that you'll be able to leave all parts of your deployment up and running while you take down a smaller part of your deployment for the upgrade action.

Third, the product team wanted you to be able to write your own upgrade code and plug it into the upgrade path provided by Microsoft. To accomplish this goal, they made the upgrade path itself extensible. When you adopt this approach, upgrade.exe will simply run your code along with its own code to ensure that all parts of your deployment are upgraded to the current version of Windows SharePoint Services.

Fourth, the product team wanted a consistent set of experiences between the previous version and the current version of Windows SharePoint Services, even during the upgrade efforts. This has been achieved by the product team.

Upgrade Approaches

There might be some reading this who will ask the following question: "Why didn't Microsoft write an upgrade path for everyone?" The answer is that this is, quite literally, impossible. At the time of this writing, there are over 20,000,000 team sites in production spread out over nearly every country in the world. There is no possible way that the product team could know the custom coding that everyone has performed on their sites. It is literally impossible to write an upgrade path whose starting point is not always known and whose end point might or might not be what the customer wants. It's really impossible to write an upgrade path that will take into consideration every possible permutation of customization that might have taken place and then ensure that all that custom code is preserved when the upgrade effort is completed.

Therefore, the product team opted to allow the upgrade path to be extensible. By doing this, administrators of environments who performed many customizations across many sites can write their own upgrade code to move their sites off of version 2.0 to version 3.0.

There are three main upgrade approaches. The first is an in-place upgrade, in which the administrator selects Upgrade when running the Windows SharePoint Services setup program and the program performs the upgrade without further intervention from the administrator. When the upgrade is completed, the administrator is informed and the users have been moved to the current Windows SharePoint Services platform. This method is ideal for single-server or small-farm implementations.

The second approach is a Gradual upgrade, which is intended to be used by medium or large farms. Characteristics of this upgrade approach include running version 3.0 code alongside your version 2.0 code on the same physical server. In addition, you'll get the version 3.0 farm up and running. You then select which site collections you want to migrate and perform the migration of those sites at a time that fits your schedule and pace. If you can do 10 site collections each night, that's what you'll do. If you want to do 1,000 site collections each weekend, you can do that too. Note that if you upgrade more than 100 site collections at a time, you'll need to use the command-line feature because the user interface will display only 100 site collection at a time.

A very nice characteristic is that the URL the user types in the browser doesn't change from version 2.0 to version 3.0. So, if they were typing *http://trainsbydave* in version 2.0, they'll still type *http://trainsbydave* in version 3.0 and receive the version 3.0 site after it has been upgraded.

Finally, let's assume you upgrade a site to version 3.0 and then realize you want the site moved back to version 2.0. You'll be happy to learn that you can revert sites back to version 2.0 on a per-site basis.

Microsoft Office FrontPage customizations in version 2.0 will be preserved when the site is upgraded to a version 3.0 site. You'll also have the option to convert the site's template from a version 2.0 template to a version 3.0 template, but if you choose to do this, you'll lose your version 2.0 FrontPage customizations.

The third upgrade approach is to build a new farm, upgrade the content databases, and manually reconfigure the entire farm and recode all the customizations you need in the new farm. This book contains three chapters that discuss upgrades from the present version of SharePoint Products and Technologies to SharePoint Server 2007.

Summary

SharePoint Server 2007 is a complex, maturing product that offers your organization solid potential in managing and working with your information in a better, faster, and smarter manner. This book attempts to offer a great deal of information in a short amount of space. There is much to learn about SharePoint Server 2007, so let's get started!

Chapter 2

Architecture for Microsoft Office SharePoint Server 2007

Before reading the details of how to design, deploy, and manage SharePoint Server 2007, you should understand the overall plan Microsoft used to develop it. Just as Office SharePoint Server 2007 helps turn raw data into meaningful information by providing a context, so this chapter will help provide a context for SharePoint Server 2007 itself. The rest of this book is about the details; this chapter is about the big picture of architecture.

Before Microsoft developed SharePoint Server 2007, it first developed a plan to build the platform. This plan, known in the industry as an *architecture*, described in detail how the 2007 Microsoft Office release and SharePoint Server 2007 would be organized—how all the components would work together. Microsoft's architectural plan for the Microsoft Office system goes further than this immediate product release. A good architecture plan is also a vision or strategy for future growth and development. The architecture plan, which guided the development of the 2007 release, provided an excellent platform for today while allowing room for some services and features to be matured and developed in later releases.

Architecture planning is the process of organizing a set of concepts and ideas that lead to repeatable and effective decision making. With a well-thought-out and thorough architecture, individuals are able to make independent decisions that fit with the overall technical design. A robust architecture also provides a set of tools that can be used to objectively assess the quality and fit of decisions made by others. These aspects of architecture are said to be *logical* rather than *physical*. This means that they define patterns of thought used in making technical decisions rather than the organization of physical technologies that are described in a physical architecture. Because they represent a method for organizing thoughts and decisions, logical architectures, by their nature, can be difficult to understand. They are conceptual and not concrete.

To make sure the logic of SharePoint Server 2007's architecture is easy to understand, this discussion begins with a concrete example from the past. As you'll see, once the technical jargon is removed, logical architecture planning is nothing new. To help understand the concepts of Microsoft's leading-edge architecture, a brief discussion of the American railway systems of the 1800s will prove useful. This particular discussion will focus on the railway of North America because it was an achievement brought about by a large number of people from many different countries. Working without common language, they were able to unify a wild continent with a well-designed railway system. The railway system worked because its architects had a plan.

Enterprise Architecture and SharePoint Server 2007

In creating SharePoint Server 2007, Microsoft developed an excellent enterprise architecture plan. This plan, although seemingly complex, has the following main concepts built into it.

Modularity and Reusability

The 2007 Microsoft Office system runs in the existing Microsoft Windows 2003 environment because it is designed with minimal dependence on any specific version of the Windows operating system. The Microsoft Office system is organized into independent and encapsulated services that are connected through a set of standards and rules known as the *provider framework*. To make administration, support, organization, and deployment easier, these services have been organized into the applications associated with the Microsoft Office system, including SharePoint Server 2007.

Extensibility

The SharePoint Server 2007 architecture also provides you with the ability to extend its capabilities and services without disrupting the core software platform. An example of this is Microsoft Office Project Server 2007. When installed, Project Server 2007 provides project teams with all the services they need to implement project management methods in the enterprise. Rather than create a competing and largely incompatible enterprise project management tool, Microsoft created a modular application that extends the capabilities of SharePoint Server 2007 to meet the demands of project management.

Scalability

Possibly the most meaningful advancement in SharePoint Server 2007 is its ability to scale. Need greater user interface capacity? Just add more first-tier Web servers. Need greater shared services capacity? Just add more second-tier application servers. Need to handle larger databases? Just add more third-tier database servers. SharePoint Server 2007 offers flexible and unlimited scalability in any tier of the architecture, without requiring a redesign and redeployment of the other two tiers.

Its scalability includes giving you the ability to scale out the SharePoint Server 2007 services as well. If you have a need to crawl and index large volumes of information, you can scale out the number of search servers to accommodate your needs. If user demand is very high for queries of your index, install more index servers. If your Excel calculation needs are high, consider installing more than one Excel Calculation server. SharePoint Server 2007 is scalable in any manner you want so that you can create any topology configuration that meets your needs and can adapt as those needs change.

Separation of Concerns

The architecture of SharePoint Server 2007 has been created to provide separation between the concerns and operation of the various architecture layers. In other words, the entire three-tier environment can be deployed to a single server or it can be deployed to any number of Web servers, application servers, and database servers, and in any combination. The SharePoint Server 2007 logical architecture is not tied to any particular physical deployment architecture because the various aspects of the architecture have been separated from each other. They are not intertwined in a manner that dictates how they are deployed, which frees administrators to make capacity planning, business continuity, and deployment decisions that are driven by the needs of the business organization and not by the constraints of the software.

The 2007 Microsoft Office System Logical Architecture

In the 2007 Microsoft Office System architecture, all applications enjoy compatible storage and retrieval operations because they all use the same storage and retrieval services. The same holds true for all common services throughout the enterprise. Security can be administrated uniformly across the organization because all applications make use of the same security services in the software infrastructure.

A Strong Move Toward Service-Oriented Architecture

The 2007 Microsoft Office release is a strong move toward true Service-Oriented Architecture (SOA). Office 2007 implementations reap the benefits of modularity, extensibility, scalability, and separation of concerns. Although most architecture experts agree that SOA is the next logical step in software evolution, it can present challenges for administrators. How does one monitor, manage, and administrate a whole environment full of independent services? To make SOA practical and to provide consistent support for system administrators, the services that compose the Microsoft Office system have been grouped into applications that serve specific purposes. This organizational strategy makes all the various services understandable and manageable without detracting from the benefits of SOA.

All SharePoint Server 2007–specific services can be accessed only through SharePoint Server 2007. They are still enterprise services, but they are located and accessed within the SharePoint Server 2007 container. All services specific to Internet Information Services (IIS) are similarly grouped and accessible within IIS.

The grouping of services into applications makes deployment, organization, training, and administration far easier and simpler. The 2007 release of Microsoft Office offers the best of both worlds. From the bottom up, its architecture is organized as a series of discrete and independent services. From the top down, it is organized into applications that serve as containers for those services.

SharePoint Server 2007 is the application that is responsible for providing document repository services, document workflow services, intranet sites, search indexing, and collaboration services.

The Services of the 2007 Microsoft Office System

Figure 2-1 represents a logical view of the service architecture for the 2007 Microsoft Office system. At the bottom of the diagram are the more fundamental services. Each succeeding layer then uses the services below it to build more specific services to support business operations. At the top level are specific business services that can be used independently or organized to support business applications and processes. A quick look shows that applications such as SharePoint Server 2007 are composed of discrete services located at various levels of this diagram. (See Figure 2-1.)

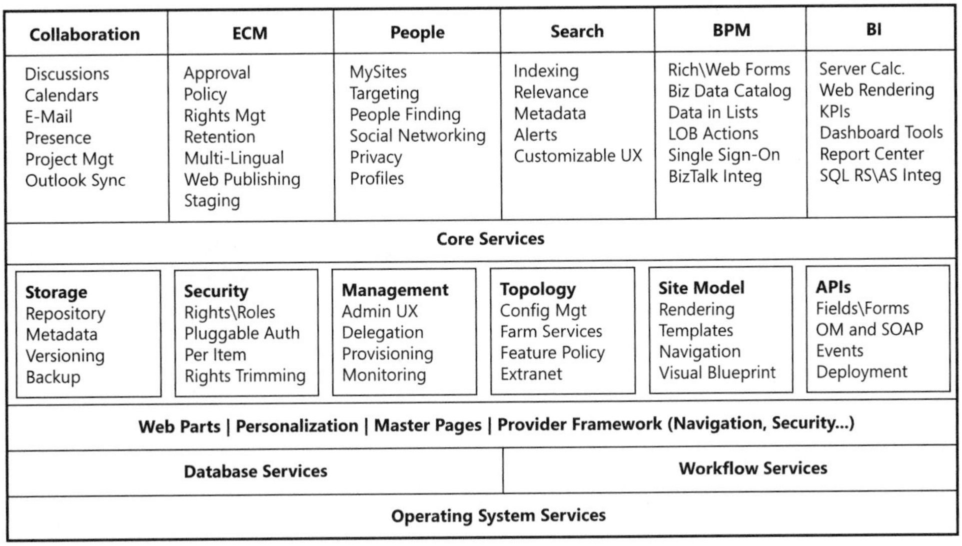

Collaboration	ECM	People	Search	BPM	BI
Discussions Calendars E-Mail Presence Project Mgt Outlook Sync	Approval Policy Rights Mgt Retention Multi-Lingual Web Publishing Staging	MySites Targeting People Finding Social Networking Privacy Profiles	Indexing Relevance Metadata Alerts Customizable UX	Rich\Web Forms Biz Data Catalog Data in Lists LOB Actions Single Sign-On BizTalk Integ	Server Calc. Web Rendering KPIs Dashboard Tools Report Center SQL RS\AS Integ

Core Services

Storage	Security	Management	Topology	Site Model	APIs
Repository Metadata Versioning Backup	Rights\Roles Pluggable Auth Per Item Rights Trimming	Admin UX Delegation Provisioning Monitoring	Config Mgt Farm Services Feature Policy Extranet	Rendering Templates Navigation Visual Blueprint	Fields\Forms OM and SOAP Events Deployment

Web Parts | Personalization | Master Pages | Provider Framework (Navigation, Security...)

Database Services | **Workflow Services**

Operating System Services

Figure 2-1 The 2007 Microsoft Office system logical architecture

What Are the Operating System Services?

You can see in Figure 2-1 that at the lowest level of the architecture is Operating System Services. This layer is responsible for directly managing the physical and logical devices that make up the physical infrastructure for the environment. Here are the drivers and administrative tools that can be used to manage, configure, and optimize the network, peripheral, and platform hardware. The architecture principle of "separation of concerns" means that the 2007 Microsoft Office system is isolated from the operating system to a large extent and is treated as a service. The 2007 Microsoft Office system is therefore able to run on Windows Server 2003 platforms as well as future releases of the operating system.

What Are the Database Services?

Microsoft SQL Server provides a common database service, shown in Figure 2-1, that is intended to meet all data storage, retrieval, modification, and destruction requirements across the enterprise for SharePoint Server 2007. By using one database platform, the Microsoft Office system removes the requirements of maintaining separate and often incompatible databases in the same environment. Because the storage services are isolated so that they are independent of the applications, you can modify, extend, or replace the database service without affecting applications and services that depend on it.

What Are the Workflow Services?

How do you know when a document is a final version or a draft? How do you know if a proposal has been accepted and approved? When is information official and when is it unofficial? Workflow services, provided by Windows Workflow Foundation (WF), shown in Figure 2-1, provide a method for formalizing, enforcing, recording, and auditing the progress of a document through formal work processes.

With workflow services, you can tell whether a document has been properly processed, reviewed, approved, updated, published, and destroyed. Each of these business processes can be defined, automated, enforced, recorded, and audited along with the document. With the advent of information control and quality standards such as the Health Insurance Portability and Accountability Act (HIPAA), Sarbanes-Oxley, and the various Department of Defense (DoD) regulations, it is becoming increasingly important to provide a metadata trail showing the execution of processes that led to the creation, modification, approval, publication, and ultimate destruction of a document. By leveraging workflow services in the architecture, it is possible to standardize and accumulate process metadata throughout the enterprise to govern the reliability and use of documents.

What Are the Supporting Services?

The supporting services for SharePoint Server 2007are pulled from the .NET provider framework and ASP.NET 2.0. Web Parts, Web Part pages, master pages, personalization, and other features of SharePoint Server 2007 are dependent directly on the services and architecture provided at this layer.

ASP.NET 2.0

ASP.NET 2.0 is a common and well-known developer platform. Building Windows SharePoint Services 3.0 to leverage the ASP.NET development platform ensures that there is a more solid developer platform for third-party integration and extensions, and it makes Windows SharePoint Services 3.0 more accessible to the ASP.NET developer community. Following are some examples of how Windows SharePoint Services 3.0 leverages features and built-in functionality in ASP.NET.

Page Rendering

ASP.NET has its own page rendering engine. Windows SharePoint Services 3.0 will get out of the business of rendering pages and trust ASP.NET to render the pages on its behalf. This means that Windows SharePoint Services 3.0 pages will run in ASP.NET direct mode.

No Compile Pages

ASP.NET has the ability to ensure that pages are not complied into a dynamic-link library (DLL) before Windows SharePoint Services 3.0 can use them. Instead, the page is parsed and the allowed controls in the control tree are rendered on the page. This means that administrators are be able to set at the application scope through the Web.config file which controls can be rendered on the page. In addition, ASP.NET allows you to override the application scope by allowing approved controls to be set on the individual page within the application. This helps you guard against malicious code being compiled into pages in Windows SharePoint Services 3.0. If needed, you can still give trusted developers the ability to author new code directly in pages.

Safe Controls List

Administrators have the ability to set permissions on ASP.NET controls via the bin directory on the server. Configuring control permissions at this level affects all applications and pages across the entire SharePoint farm. The errors that are given vary depending on where the control resides. For example, an unsafe control in a Web Part zone will mean that an error Web Part is rendered. An unsafe control outside a Web Part zone will cause the entire page to not render correctly. An "unsafe" control is one in which the control does not have sufficient permissions in the Safe Controls List to render properly.

More Info For more information on how to configure the Safe Controls List, please see Chapter 31, "Administrating Code Access Security."

Master Pages

The entire Web page that is rendered in the user's browser is actually a combination of two pages: a Master Page and a Content Page (or Page Layout). Master pages are associated with one or more content pages and are used to render the "chrome," such as the left Quick Launch bar and the top navigation bar. Master pages are built by developers whereas content pages are created and managed by end-users.

Master pages usually contain the branding and other features that needs to be consistent across multiple sites and site collections. ASP.NET 2.0 renders these pages for Windows SharePoint Services 3.0.

Web Parts

A Web Part and the Web Part framework are built into the core of the ASP.NET platform. A Web Part is a custom control assembly that uses a Web Part description file in either the Windows SharePoint Services 3.0 format (.dwp) or the ASP.NET 2.0 format (.webpart). The Web Part description file can be stored and referenced on any computer; it contains XML data that describes an instance of the Web Part. The Web Part .NET assembly is a DLL that must be installed and registered on each Windows SharePoint Services computer that uses the Web Part. The Windows SharePoint Services 3.0 architecture allows for backward compatibility with Windows SharePoint Services 2.0 Web Parts.

In SharePoint, data cannot be exposed or hosted outside a Web Part. All data is held ultimately either as a list item or as metadata to the list or a list item. Applications are also exposed using Web Parts, where functionality is broken up into Web Parts and the summation of the Web Parts forms the overall application.

Personalization

Personalization in SharePoint Server 2007 is rich and multifaceted. Users with appropriate permissions can drag and drop Web Parts onto a Web Part page and even create new pages within a site. They can target information to other users based on their audience group membership, Active Directory group membership, or e-mail group membership. In addition, users can expose information about themselves and then use the privacy controls to decide who gets to see which piece of information they have posted. Moreover, users have the ability to find out what social groups they are members of and then add members of those groups to their own social groups.

Master Pages

Master pages (.master) are a much improved concept over the ghosted pages concept, which in Windows SharePoint Services 2.0 was the way pages were shared between sites. Windows SharePoint Services 3.0 moves to the concept of master pages as the method of sharing pages between sites.

With master pages, a developer can specify all the shared elements in the .aspx pages in the master page, and have content pages that add the elements specific to the content page. In Windows SharePoint Services 3.0, there are regions on each page that are common to all pages, such as the navigation bar or title area. Using master pages to present the Windows SharePoint Services 3.0 sites makes sense because master pages can be used to create regions that are standard across all the instances of the page and create other regions that are uniquely editable in those same instances of the page.

You'll need to differentiate between master pages and page layouts. Master pages contain controls that are shared across multiple page layouts, such as navigation. Page layouts (sometimes referred to as *content pages*) control the content of a page. Each page layout has at least one associated content type that controls the kind of content that can be stored on the page. By default, there are three content types:

- Page
- Article Page
- Welcome Page

Each content type for page layouts contains columns that define content that can appear on a page along with the metadata that is associated with the layout page.

Content in a layout page is stored as SharePoint list items in the Pages document library. When users view or edit the page, content is pulled from the SharePoint list and displayed to the user.

Together, the master page and the layout page form a *page instance*, which is the look and feel of the page in the SharePoint site. Page layouts can be used by all page instances that are based on that page layout. Master pages can be used by all page instances in a site. Page instances based on the same page layout in different sites can use different master pages.

The root site for a site collection has a document library called the Master Page and Page Layout Gallery. All page layouts and master pages are stored in this document library. Like other document libraries, this document library supports versioning and workflow, so you can use those features when you need to create new master pages and page layouts.

Note There is a Master Page Gallery created for every site in SharePoint Server 2007, but you can only create new master pages with the page layouts stored in the Master Page Gallery of the top-level site in the site collection.

The SharePoint Designer 2007 is the preferred tool for creating and customizing master pages.

Provider Framework

All this talk about services and standards raises an important question: how in the world does it work? All services in the in the 2007 Microsoft Office system release and SharePoint Server 2007 environment have to communicate and operate within certain rules or guidelines in order to be used. Services are offered by providers that are governed by rules and standards called a *framework*. As an example, if a storage area network (SAN) manufacturer wants to market a new storage array to Microsoft Office system customers, the manufacturer must make sure that its storage software is designed to be a service that obeys the rules of the provider framework. If so, it will install smoothly into place and the software and services "above it" will have no idea that there has been a change. It will be transparent.

The framework that is used by Microsoft is called the .NET Framework. The .NET Framework is an integral Windows component that supports building and running the next generation of applications and XML Web services. The .NET Framework provides the following benefits:

- A consistent object-oriented programming environment regardless of where the object code is stored and executed

- A code-execution environment that does the following:
    - Minimizes software deployment and versioning conflicts
    - Promotes safe execution of code, including code created by an unknown or semi-trusted third party
    - Eliminates the performance problems of scripted environments
- Homogenizes the developer experience across different types of applications, such as Windows-based applications and Web-based applications
- Is compatible with industry standards to ensure that code based on the .NET Framework can integrate with any other code

There are two main components to the .NET Framework. The first is the common language runtime and the second is the class library. You can think of the common language runtime as an agent that does the following:

- Manages code at execution time
- Provides core services such as memory management, thread management, and remoting
- Enforces strict type safety and other forms of code accuracy that promote security and robustness

The concept of code management is a fundamental principle of the common language runtime feature. Code that targets the runtime is known as *managed code*, while code that does not target the runtime is known as *unmanaged code*.

The *class library*, the other main component of the .NET Framework, is an object-oriented collection of reusable types that you can use to develop applications ranging from traditional command-line or graphical user interface (GUI) applications to applications based on the latest innovations provided by ASP.NET, such as Web Forms and XML Web services.

Navigation

The Microsoft Office system provides standard navigation services that make sure there is one standard user interface for selecting common tasks and changing focus from one Web page to another. This helps provide the end user with a consistent set of choices for common tasks regardless of where they are being selected.

Security

Essential security operations such as encryption and authentication are provided as common low-level services. Using common services across the enterprise makes it easier to keep control over security issues, compliance, versioning, and testing.

Security settings are configurable throughout the entire product—from Central Administration all the way to each individual item. Through the Central Administration interface, you'll be able to create and set policies at the virtual server level that will affect all the sites, lists, and list items that are hosted by the virtual server. The security policies set at the Web application level replace the Security Rights Mask at the virtual server level in Windows SharePoint Services 2.0.

For example, if a particular user's account is granted Contributor access using a policy at the virtual server level, the user will have Contributor access to all the sites, lists, and list items that are hosted within that virtual server. If there is a conflict with a local setting, whether the right is granted or denied, the policy set at the Central Administration level will take precedence and override the local security setting. This architecture allows end-users to manage the day-to-day security of their information while allowing you to ensure that your corporate security policies are enforced correctly.

Each virtual server gets its own set of security policies in Central Administration. In addition, security policies cannot be shared across virtual servers; they must be created manually for each virtual server. Some of the more common uses for security policies include scenarios such as the following:

- Setting the default content access account to have read access to all objects within the Web application, even if users try to deny that account access to their information.
- The ability to deny access to content is a positive administrative action that helps certain businesses in certain vertical markets comply with legal requirements. In some instances, it is not enough to *not* include a group of users in accessing content; instead, it is expected that these users will be explicitly *denied* access to that content.
- Setting the Deny Write policy for All Authenticated Users on their extranet virtual server so that any changes made to the content in the read-only extranet must be made on the internal staging servers and then published to the extranet servers.

What Are the Core Services?

The core services are those services that must be functioning in order for SharePoint to run properly. What follows is an architecture overview of these services.

Storage Services

The database services stores information accurately, retrieve the strings quickly, and return them intact. Through the use of various data types, database services can even determine what kind of data is represented. A database can't, however, provide a context for interpreting the meaning of the data. If the database services return the currency number 500.00, what does it mean? Does it represent U.S. dollars or euros? Is it a receipt or an estimate? Is it a guess, or is it a firm number? Is it a secret, or is it public information?

The storage services offered as core services provide metadata and context to the raw data stored in the database. This makes the data more easily indexed, managed, interpreted, and published.

Metadata

Metadata is information about information. For example, information that records who originated the data and when, whether the data has been approved, what the security requirements are for the data, how it is to be represented when it is published, when the data is to be destroyed, and how the data is to be used.

Metadata provides context for data so that it can be interpreted and understood when it comes time to use it. Metadata also supports the ability to intelligently index and quickly search large databases by automating the classification and organization of like-kinds of information.

Versioning

Versioning services provide the ability to organize, track, and control the evolution of documents. Multiple contributors are vital to collaboration, but multiple contributors can also create confusion. Version control, as the name implies, is a core service that provides standard version control functions for documents and data within the Microsoft Office system.

Windows SharePoint Services 3.0 provides two types of versioning. One type of versioning was first available in SharePoint Portal Server 2001 and is called *major/minor versioning*. With major/minor versioning, only major versions can be published. Minor versions can be viewed by those who have the right to view the minor versions of the document or list item, but these versions cannot be published, nor can they be viewed by those who have only Reader access to this list.

The other type of versioning that was available in Windows SharePoint Services 2.0 is called *simple versioning*. With simple versioning, each version is a full copy of the document and the versions are numbered sequentially. Users will determine which type of versioning is used in each list. Simple versioning is also available in Windows SharePoint Services 3.0 along with major/minor versioning.

When used correctly, versioning gives the user a clear picture of the difference between major and minor changes to a document or list item. Both the document and its metadata can be versioned as well. At any given time, the same document might have any of the following three states, which dictate what can be done with the document and who can do it:

- **Checked Out** The user who has this document explicitly checked out is the only user who can make and save changes to this document or list item. This is the version of the document that is the latest version.
- **Draft (minor version)** The user or group of users who have permissions to see the document's minor versions can read and check out the document if the document is not already checked out.
- **Published (major version)** The user or group of users who have permissions only to read the document's major versions can consume the content in the major version, but cannot see or read the minor versions that might exist as the developing document history for the next major version.

Versioning and auditing are not the same concepts. Versioning allows the user to tell the system which changes are minor changes and which changes are major changes to a document. Auditing is the process of tracking which user made a change to a document, regardless of the importance of that change. Versioning is focused on allowing the user to assign a value to the change made to the document. Auditing is merely tracking that a change has taken place, by whom and when.

Personalization of a list item or a document is applied only to the published version.

Backup

By providing a common backup service, the 2007 Office system streamlines the administration of backup and recovery operations. If applications are designed to take advantage of common backup and recovery services, there is minimal need for special handling, scripting, and testing of backup operations.

The architecture for backup is improved in SharePoint Server 2007. When you take a step back and look at an overview of this product, you'll realize that SharePoint Server 2007 is actually held in several different locations:

- Content and metadata for crawled content is held in SQL content databases.
- The binaries for the program are held on the file server—by default, in C:\Program Files\Office SharePoint Server\Bin.
- The content indexes are held on the file server—by default, in C:\Program Files\Office SharePoint Server\Data.
- The Web application files are held on the file server—by default, in C:\Inetpub\wwwroot\wss\VirtualDirectories.
- The configuration information for the Web applications is held in the metabase.
- The farm configuration information is held in the SQL Configdb database.

The built-in backup tool that ships with SharePoint Server 2007 will back up all farm SQL databases (including the ConfigDB), provisioned Web applications and the index. This combination is a significant improvement from Spsbackup.exe, which only backed up the SQL databases and the indexes.

Backups and Disk Space

Most of you will use a third-party backup solution to back up your SharePoint implementation. Whether or not you use the built-in backup solution, it's important to remember that all backups initially are committed to disk and then can be copied to tape or a SAN. Because of this architecture, you'll find that your disk needs will grow as your SharePoint implementation grows.

At a minimum, you'll need to work with a 4 to 1 ratio of disk space (in your overall disk topology) to data hosted in SharePoint. Here is how the model works assuming 1 GB of data is held in SharePoint (keeping in mind that this is a model, not a formula):

- 1 GB of data will need 1 GB of disk space.
- Another 1 GB of free disk space is needed for SQL maintenance utilities to run properly. You should always have 100 percent free disk space relative to the size of your largest database.
- You'll be indexing this data, so assume your index is 20 percent the size of the content being indexed. White papers and experience point to actual figures ranging from as little as 10 percent up to as high as 40 percent. Using 20 percent as our number for this model is a bit conservative and doesn't take into account external content sources that might need to be crawled and that would add to the size of your index. In this example, assume you need one search server and two query servers, which means you'll need 400 MB of disk space because the index will be held twice, once on the search server and once on the query server.
- Your farm will need to be backed up. Your backup image, in this example, consumes another 1.2 GB of disk space. The index is backed up only once, even though it is held on multiple servers.

Overall, in this example, you will need 3.8 GB of disk space for every 1 GB of data that is hosted in your environment. This example does not account for external content sources that will need to be crawled, nor does it include a SQL backup (as opposed to using the built-in SharePoint backup tool). Your SQL database administrators (DBAs) will likely want to do their own backup of your SQL databases, which will increase the amount of disk space that you will need.

Farm backup is not the only feature that is improved in Windows SharePoint Services 3.0. Another major improvement is the two-stage Recycle Bin for users, where restores of individual documents and list items are driven by end users. The lack of per-item restore capabilities was one of the significant drawbacks of Windows SharePoint Services 2.0. Not only did several third-party vendors develop tools to address this shortcoming, but Microsoft found consultants building customized applications for individual customers that solved this problem. Clearly, this issue needed to be addressed in the new version of Windows SharePoint Services.

In the first stage of the Recycle Bin, the user deletes a document or list item and the item appears in the end-user and site collection Recycle Bins. The end user can restore or delete the item from this Recycle Bin. Deleted items in this stage count toward the site quota. Items in this Recycle Bin are automatically cleaned out after a preconfigured number of days. Items are sorted in descending order by data deleted.

The second stage is invoked when the end user deletes the item from her Recycle Bin. The item no longer appears in the interface for the end user, and it no longer counts toward the site quota. However, Site Collection administrators can see all second-stage deleted items and can restore deleted items from this stage.

The Windows SharePoint Services Recycle Bin functionality is similar to that of the Windows Recycle Bin. When an item is deleted, it is removed from its list and placed into the user's Recycle Bin. On the Recycle Bin page, the user has the option to restore or permanently delete any item.

Restoring a document moves the item from the Recycle Bin back into its original list—the process includes making sure that the file name doesn't conflict with existing files. In addition to using the basic Recycle Bin functionality, the site collection administrator has the option to set a cleanup service that will automatically permanently delete items that have been deleted for a specified amount of time. Deleted items and nondeleted items can have the same name, and there can be multiple deleted items that have the same name. Multiple nondeleted items that have the same name have the automatic iteration number "(x)" appended to them.

Only users who have permissions to delete and restore items are able to delete and restore items. In addition, Site Collection administrators have the ability to override individual user's decisions and restore items if needed. The life span of deleted items is decided by the farm administrators, and the configurations are set in Central Administration.

The Recycle Bins can be turned off at the virtual server level. If this feature is turned off, all the bins are emptied of any items they contain and any future delete actions will result in the items being permanently deleted. Turning off the Recycle Bin feature has the effect of implementing the delete architecture of Windows SharePoint Services 2.0.

Sites and site collections are not included in this architecture. The two-stage Recycle Bin feature applies only to documents and list items. In addition, items cannot be opened or viewed while deleted. The item must first be restored in order for the item to be viewed. Attachments to list items are treated as part of the list item.

This architecture has the benefit of giving users direct control over when and how to delete and restore individual items, as well as reducing maintenance costs by reducing the need to include IT personnel into the restore process.

Security

Regardless of which security standard is being implemented, security functions can be grouped into a small number of common security services.

Rights and Roles

The rights and roles services assign the role that the individual has in the organization. Rather than keeping track of unique rights for individuals based on their own lobbying efforts, the individuals are simply assigned one or more roles that dictate their rights and privileges throughout the enterprise.

A *role* is a collection of rights that is assigned to an object in SharePoint that can then be associated with a user or group. Roles are first defined, which means that the list of rights is enumerated and grouped into a role. Then roles are assigned, which means that the roles are attached to an object in SharePoint.

A *right* is an action that the user can perform within SharePoint. The action is usually explicit and well defined. For example, the action of deleting a document is a right. User and group accounts are never assigned rights directly. Rights are always grouped into roles, the roles are assigned to a SharePoint object, and then user and group accounts are associated with the role. This is the only architecture that is supported and available to users to gain rights to perform actions in SharePoint.

A *user* can be either an Active Directory user account or an external user account via pluggable authentication. The user's profile is scoped to the site collection.

Windows SharePoint Services 3.0 works with the access token, which contains the security identifiers (SIDs) of both the user's account and all the groups that the user is a member of. User accounts that are used via pluggable authentication have a much more simple access token because that account is not a member of any Active Directory domain security group.

SharePoint *groups* are a collection of user accounts. SharePoint supports both domain groups from Active Directory and SharePoint groups that are created within SharePoint itself. SharePoint groups can be used only within the scope of the site collection, whereas domain groups can be used anywhere in the SharePoint farm.

The inheritance model is such that each object within SharePoint can have its own set of permissions or inherit its permissions from its parent container. A modified or *combined* model is not supported. A combined model is one in which an object can inherit permissions from its parent object *and* have additional permissions added to the inherited set of permissions. In addition, you cannot configure an object to inherit permissions from any other object other than its parent object.

Pluggable Authentication

Pluggable authentication is an authentication service that any application can use to authenticate users and processes. This approach greatly simplifies regulatory compliance, as one set of processes can be configured to the compliance requirements for the entire organization. It also removes the burden on the administrators to manage a large number of security levels for specific applications.

For the end user, pluggable authentication provides for Single Sign-On (SSO) authentication. Once the end user opens a session and is authenticated, the system provides them with the correct access across the enterprise. There is no need to remember a different password for each system or application. In addition, many companies have already implemented an SSO solution other than the Microsoft Single Sign-On service. As an alternative to maintaining and mapping two sets of credentials, SharePoint Server 2007 allows you to specify an alternative SSO provider to the standard SSO provider in SharePoint Server 2007.

Replacing the default SSO provider in SharePoint Server 2007 involves implementing the Microsoft.SharePoint.Portal.SingleSignon.ISsoProvider interface, installing it into the global assembly cache, and registering the new SSO provider with SharePoint Server 2007.

You can register only one SSO provider for SharePoint Server 2007. Registering a new SSO provider replaces the default SpsSsoProvider class in SharePoint Server 2007. Because only one SSO provider can be in use at a time, it is recommended you stop the Microsoft Single Sign-On service when using a custom SSO provider.

Per Item Security

Sometimes you need to prevent a single individual from seeing or changing one data field in a record or database. The Microsoft Office system provides *per-item security*, which enables access privileges to be granted for each individual data element.

SharePoint's security model can work with either users or groups. When you are thinking about individual sites, keep in mind that you can add users individually to SharePoint sites. But if thousands of users are added to the site, performance might degrade because the enumeration of thousands of users' SIDs for SharePoint to reference might consume an inordinate amount of resources. Adding individual users to team sites or Web Parts doesn't scale well, so it is recommended that larger installations that need to add thousands of users to sites or Web Parts use Active Directory security groups.

Rights Trimming

The end user should not be able to see what she can't have access to or actions she cannot perform. Once an end user is authenticated and her rights are applied, any pages, buttons, functions, data elements, windows, or instructions that she doesn't have access to are automatically removed from her configuration. This helps limit confusion and is a security best practice.

Rights trimming affects several parts of SharePoint Server 2007. The content in lists is trimmed so that users see only the content that they have permissions to see. The page links are rights trimmed so that users see only links for which they have permissions to navigate. This includes links to add and edit content, such that users can access only links to Web Parts that allow them to edit content for which they have permissions. Actions are also trimmed so that the user sees links only for actions that they have rights to perform.

In Windows SharePoint Services 3.0, a *link* is considered any part of the user interface that takes a user from one Web page to another Web page. To accommodate link trimming for anonymous users, Windows SharePoint Services 3.0 gives the user explicit login and logoff. When a user accesses a Web site anonymously, most of the user interface links will not appear because anonymous users usually have minimal permissions to the site. By providing explicit login and logoff, user's who have first accessed the site anonymously will have the opportunity to explicitly log in and gain greater access to the site's functionality.

Management

Imagine a world where administrative functions and processes are consistent throughout the enterprise. Microsoft did imagine this and built it right into the product architecture. All administrative services that are accessed through the operating system and the applications are presented through a common service that organizes and standardizes the administrator user experience.

Many, but not all, management actions can also be scripted using the stsadm.exe command-line tool. In most cases, any action you can commit using the command line can also be undone using the command line.

Admin UX

Admin UX stands for "Administrator's User Experience." System administrators are the backbone of any IT organization, and Microsoft has focused considerable time and effort in simplifying and unifying the tools and interfaces used by system administrators. This service provides commonality and integration for administrative functions throughout the 2007 Microsoft Office system.

Central Administration is divided into two main areas: operations and application management. If you're configuring the farm or making farm-wide configurations, you'll use the Operations page of Central Administration. If you're working with a Web application or executing configurations for a Web application, you'll use the Application Management page.

Provisioning

One of the strengths of SharePoint Server 2007 is its ability to dynamically and automatically create and provision Web sites based on templates and master pages. SharePoint Server 2007 has unified the provisioning process so that all such pages are created and provisioned in the same manner, rather than through separate creation and provisioning services. This arrangement makes it simpler and safer to create, modify, manage, and remove SharePoint Server 2007 sites and Web pages.

The provisioning services also provide for the workflow management of Web sites and content using workflow services. This ensures that content is properly reviewed, approved, staged, and published according to the organization's policies and procedures.

SharePoint Server 2007 unifies three disparate site provisioning models. If you look at the predecessors to SharePoint Server 2007, you'll find that there were three distinct ways to create a Web site using Microsoft products:

- Windows SharePoint Services 2.0
- SharePoint Portal Server 2003
- Content Management Server 2003

Each product had the ability to create and provision a Web site. SharePoint Server 2007 unifies these approaches and gives the end user the ability to provision new sites, regardless of whether they are content management-oriented sites, collaboration sites, or new portals. As part of the provisioning aspect, administrators can set a farm-wide Sites Directory to capture metadata about newly created sites. Whether or not site metadata is captured to the farm-wide sites directory, it is always captured to the local sites directory for each site inside the site collection.

To help you understand the provisioning process, here are a few items to consider:

- New Web applications are created in Central Administration and must be executed by an IT administrator.

- A new top-level site (TLS) (also called a *root* site), which is the first site in a new site collection and is created in a managed path, can be created either in Central Administration or by using the Self-Service Site Creation (SSSC) feature. These new TLSs can be created either by administrators or end users with sufficient permissions.
- Sub-Web sites are created inside site collections and are usually created by end users who have sufficient permissions to create new sites.

Monitoring

Simply stated, "That which can't be seen, can't be managed." The only accurate and effective way to monitor systems and applications is to build monitoring services into the environment from the beginning. Monitoring technology is not something that can be successfully retrofitted into the environment. The monitoring services provide integrated system, exception, and performance monitoring that is available to all applications in the Microsoft Office system.

Topology

Topology services provide for the physical deployment of the 2007 Microsoft Office system and the SharePoint Server 2007 environment into a variety of platform and networking configurations. This deployment allows the administrator to optimize and revise the physical infrastructure for efficiency and performance without requiring a change to the logical software architecture or its deployment.

The topology services include tools for viewing, analyzing, and administering server farms. Also included are services that define and administer the policies that govern the use of various features and services by applications and end users. The topology model is also extensible, allowing for support of extranet connections and services beyond the organization's boundaries.

The Services on Server page in Central Administration allows you to turn on and off services for each server in the SharePoint farm. Although all the binary code is installed on each server, the Topology Manager ensures that each server has "turned on" or "turned off" those portions of the code that are required or not needed for the server to fulfill its assigned duties in the farm.

Windows SharePoint Services 3.0 provides the base topology services for SharePoint Server 2007. Any code or configurations that are installed on one Web Front End (WFE) server should also be installed on the other WFE servers in the farm. This includes Web Parts and Web services.

The topology for SharePoint Server 2007 is scalable, flexible, maintainable, and reliable. Any tier within the farm topology can be scaled to any need just by adding servers to the farm and making the proper configurations in Central Administration. Servers can also change roles just by starting and stopping services, which makes them flexible in their role assignment. Each server can be maintained either individually for patches and upgrades, or they can be maintained as a group by using Windows Server Update Services. In addition, if you have multiple servers servicing a single role in the farm topology, servers can be brought down individually for maintenance without bringing down the entire farm or causing an interruption of services. Because multiple servers can be installed in a redundant fashion for farm services, you can achieve high availability in your farm, ensuring that users rarely, if ever, experience downtime from your SharePoint implementation.

Site Model

SharePoint Server 2007 provides common site models to guide the generation and provisioning of SharePoint Server 2007 pages and sites. The Site Model organizes site-rendering services, templates, and navigation services into a coherent and consistent site architecture without requiring code changes.

APIs

Standardized services supported by a standardized provider framework require a standardized application programming interface (API).

Fields and Forms

The Microsoft Office system API provides standard support for data entry through common forms and embedded fields. Forms and embedded fields allow the entry of information embedded in a document, which establishes the context and meaning of the information being entered. The Microsoft Office system services can be used to infer context that can be used to drive metadata, which in turn drives search indexing and metadata. Because these services are standard and centralized, they can be used consistently across the enterprise without programmatic changes.

Object Models and SOAP

The services and features have been created using object-oriented software development techniques. This means that the features are encapsulated in self-contained software packages that communicate with each other using messages. Object models and Simple Object Access Protocol (SOAP) services provide the Microsoft Office system with consistent tools to use in managing and using software objects.

Deployment

Although logical architecture is the heart of the Microsoft Office system architecture plan, software needs a physical place to run. Although the logical architecture is intangible, it becomes tangible when it is actually installed and run in a physical environment. This expression of logical architecture according to a physical architecture plan is known as *deployment.* The deployment services provide for the location and use of the Microsoft Office system services in a physical computing environment or platform, without disrupting the organization of the logical architecture. The deployment services know how to map the Microsoft Office system to real-world physical architecture configurations when it is installed.

The SharePoint Server 2007 logical architecture can be physically deployed to a single machine serving as all three tiers in the three-tier environment, or on any number of machines serving one or more of the tiers cooperatively. Figure 2-2 is an example of this three-tier environment.

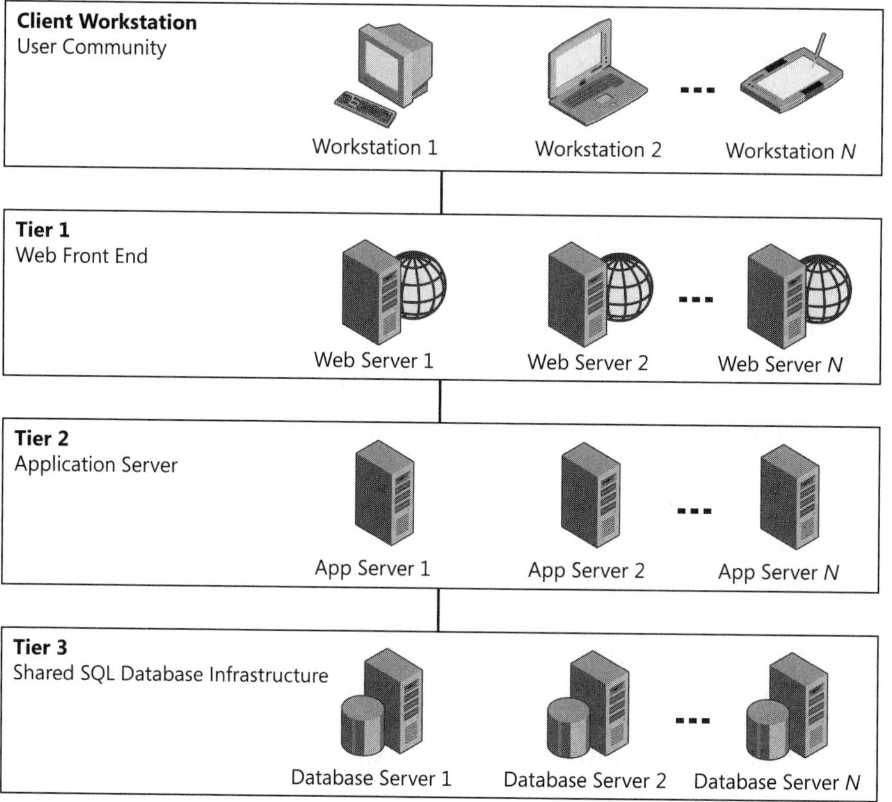

Figure 2-2 Three-tier server farm deployment options with the Office SharePoint Server 2007 physical architecture

The general deployment architecture for SharePoint Server 2007 is made up of the following three tiers:

- **Tier 1: Web Front End** Static Web content and services on the corporate portal, business unit portal, sites directory, and My Sites host
- **Tier 2: Application Server** Dynamic content processing and application services, including search, indexing, audiences, user profiles, Excel Services, and BDC
- **Tier 3: Shared SQL Database Infrastructure** Shared database infrastructure

Keep in mind that the strength of the underlying architecture plan for the Microsoft Office system is that the logical architecture can be deployed to a variety of physical architectures, to one machine or many.

Application Pools and SharePoint Server 2007

Software programs run best when they run on their own dedicated servers. This arrangement eliminates much of the worry about resource contention between programs. On the other hand, protecting program execution through the use of dedicated hardware is a very expensive solution. To provide integrity for resource allocation to individual programs, and to minimize unforeseen consequences due to program interaction, SharePoint Server 2007 structures its Web applications into Internet Information Services (IIS) application pools.

IIS application pools are software containers that function as virtual hosting environments for program instances. A program instance and its allocated resources are known as processes within the Microsoft Windows environment. System resources are allocated to each application pool and then shared between the program instances that are hosted within the pool.

This model provides for the sharing of resources between pools, and between processes within a pool. However, it isolates the processes in one pool from interaction with the processes in another pool. The application pools do not, however, map directly to any hardware configuration; they are not bound to a single CPU or set of CPUs. One CPU can support multiple application pools, and a single application pool can span multiple CPUs. So the application pools isolate applications from applications outside their application pool. They also isolate the application from interaction with the hardware. Therefore, SharePoint Server 2007 Web applications bind to application pools that serve as a virtual hosting environment for processes that result from instantiations of the Web applications.

By default, the Central Administration UI in Microsoft Office SharePoint Portal Server 2007 asks you to create a new application pool each time you create a new Web application. Should you do this? Should each new Web application run inside its own application pool?

One benefit to having each Web application run inside its own application pool is that each Web application enjoys the *worker process isolation* that each application pool offers. This feature gives your deployment maximum stability, especially if many of your Web applications are running homegrown code that could potentially bring down a Windows SharePoint Services–based application. In addition, any security exploits that would bring down a Web application would need to be replicated across each application pool to be effective in bringing down your entire farm.

To understand the relationship between application pools and Web applications in SharePoint Server 2007, take a look at the application pool architecture.

Application Pool Architecture

A *worker process* in an application pool is really a single thread that the subsystem uses to process all the pages in the Web applications. A *thread* is an entity within a process that Windows schedules for execution. It is the smallest unit of code that can be run by itself. A thread includes the contents of a set of CPU registers representing the state of the processor, two stacks (one for the thread to use while executing in kernel mode, and one for executing in user mode), a private storage area for use by subsystems, runtime libraries, DLLs, and a unique identifier called a thread ID. These elements, when combined, are called the thread's *context.*

In an ideal world, each thread would have its own processor exclusively for its own use. But we don't live in an ideal world, so we have to share multiple threads between one or more processors. The feature of sharing threads across multiple processors is called *multitasking* and is the operating system's way of sharing a single processor between multiple threads of execution. If the computer has more than one processor, it can process as many threads simultaneously as it has processors. The Windows operating system, by default, can run all threads across all processors, meaning that one processor is not dedicated exclusively to running one or more threads. This is known as *symmetric multiprocessing* (SMP).

Windows can be configured to assign one or more threads to run on a specified processor. This is known as *processor affinity* In either case, the memory space for the threads that are run is shared across all the processors, so having multiple processors does not increase the amount RAM (in a virtual sense) on your system, nor does it imply a more efficient use of RAM on your server.

At this point, you need to understand the difference between user mode (UM) and kernel mode (KM) to understand how memory is mapped. These two modes are set up primarily to protect the operating system components from being damaged or hindered by applications that run on top of the operating system.

User application code runs in user mode, whereas operating system code runs in kernel mode. UM applications that call for system services must run through a subsystem .DLL to make their calls for resources. The KM processes retrieve the resources for the UM application. If the UM application needs to manipulate the hardware, such as repainting the screen, the call is proxied to the hardware by KM processes. At no time do UM applications talk directly to the hardware, whereas KM process can and do manipulate hardware directly. KM is a mode of execution in a processor that grants access to all system memory and all CPU instructions. These threads of execution have a higher processing priority than threads that run in UM. KM operating system and device driver code have complete access to system space memory and can bypass Windows security to access objects.

A *program* is a static sequence of code instructions. A *process* is a container for a set of resources that are used when executing an instance of the program. A process can be run in either UM or KM, but it will contain all the supporting environment structures that a thread needs to run. Other supporting environment elements that need to be in place when a process runs a thread include items such as communication ports, files, and semaphores. (A *semaphore* is essentially a counter that allows a maximum number of threads to access the resources of the process that are protected by the semaphore.) A process also contains a set of virtual memory addresses that the process can use, a process ID (seen in Task Manager), and at least one thread of execution.

It is important to understand that every thread within a process shares the process's virtual address space, meaning that all the threads in a process can write to and from each other's memory. The overall size of the virtual address space varies for each hardware platform, but for 32-bit, X86 systems, the maximum is 4 GB. By default, Windows allocates half of this address space to UM processes and the other half to KM processes.

If you have 4 GB of RAM, you can boot the server (Windows 2000 Server with SP2 and later) with the /3GB switch and the /USERVA switch. The net effect of using the /3GB switch is that 3 GB of the memory address spaces are reserved for UM processes, leaving 1 GB for KM processes. The advantage of using the /USERVA switch is that you can specify a value between 2048 and 3072 and that amount of RAM will be given to UM and the balance left for KM. The /3GB switch must also be used, but you can throttle the UM memory space to be 2.5 GB, for example, instead of having to choose between 2 GB or 3 GB when booting the system. These switches are applied to the boot.ini file.

One of the attractive things about running in a 64-bit environment is that the overall address space for processes increases from 4 GB to 7152 GB. If you're running in a 64-bit environment (and more SharePoint servers are these days), Windows Server provides a way to map the 32-bit memory spaces to a 64-bit virtual environment. This feature is called *Address Windowing Extensions (AWE)*, and it allows a 32-bit application to allocate up to 64 GB of physical memory and then map views or windows into its 2-GB address space. Note that IIS 6.0 has a Large Memory Support feature that enables you to cache up to 64 GB of memory on a traditional x86 system.

An application pool will have, by default, one process assigned to run in UM. You can increase the number of worker processes that will be run and configure a Web garden. A *Web garden* is an application pool that uses more than one worker process. But don't let the word "pool" fool you: each process will get its own set of supporting elements that it needs to be a complete, independent process, including its own memory space. The main advantage of a Web garden is that each process provides independent access to the Web application. This means that if one process is either busy (for example, servicing a backup request) or blocked, the other processes can answer calls and give the clients access to the Web application. This increases the stability of the Web application, but it also uses more memory because each process gets its own memory address space as part of its context.

Discussion of Application Pool Architecture and SharePoint Server 2007 Integration

Now that you've gone through a bit of operating system architecture, come back to the question of how many Web applications can you associate with a single application pool.

First, you need to do some performance monitoring of the process that runs your SharePoint threads. This will be the worker process (w3wp.exe) that is associated with the application pool hosting your Web applications. You need to know how much memory these processes are consuming on average. There will always be spikes and valleys, but the overall average is what you're after.

Next, you need to decide if you're going to run the /3GB switch and perhaps the /USERVA switch to allocate more of the 4-GB address space to UM, which is where SharePoint runs. Because application pools run in UM, you can easily conclude that SharePoint Server 2007 also runs in UM. Increasing the amount of RAM that is available to the application pool also increases the user demand that each application pool can handle via increased maximum memory limit configurations in the properties of the application pool.

Finally, if you've never run SharePoint and are trying to predict the future without any past history, make an educated guess based on performance monitoring of other Web sites you might have that have experienced similar demand.

Here are some tips for designing your SharePoint implementation:

- Do not run more than 10 Web applications per application pool until you have some performance monitoring experience behind you and you can point to your own numbers, which tell you that your application pools can handle more virtual servers.

- Do not plan to run more than 20 Web applications on a single physical server without adding a second Web server (or more) in your farm. The reason for this is because if you're running 20 virtual servers, you've got a growing, busy farm and chances are good that you should scale out before you scale up.
- Always purchase servers with 4 GB of RAM to give yourself maximum flexibility in memory allocation for your application pools.
- Make each application pool a Web garden with two or three worker processes associated with it. When stsadm.exe runs, it locks one of the threads for its own use. Having other threads available to service calls during backup/restore operations or other scripted operations using stsadm is necessary in most environments. In addition, if a thread becomes very busy, the other threads can pick up the slack.

Summary

From the big picture perspective, SharePoint Server 2007 can't really be understood apart from the architecture of the 2007 Microsoft Office system. With the release of the 2007 Microsoft Office system, Microsoft created a logical architecture plan that makes use of the best concepts in architecture planning available today. Each service is intended to stand on its own as an independent software component. These services are grouped into cooperative sets that then form applications within the Microsoft Office system. SharePoint Server 2007 is one of the core applications of the 2007 Microsoft Office system. By building all the applications out of the same set of services, Microsoft is driving toward universal compatibility among all of its products and applications. Using a common set of services within Microsoft Office system as application building blocks drives those applications toward simplification and compatibility.

Keep in mind that Microsoft's architecture plan is still a work in progress, as software always is. Microsoft is pursing compatibility among all of its applications, but it isn't quite there yet. The 2007 Microsoft Office release is a giant leap toward this goal, but it is not the whole journey. It is, however, a wonderful leap.

Chapter 3

Design Considerations and Deployment

Microsoft Office SharePoint Server 2007 is a robust, flexible solution that can scale to almost any organizational size or requirement. Many of the limitations of Windows SharePoint Services 2003 and SharePoint Portal Server 2003 have been lifted. With the new release, administrators have practically unlimited design options using many new features, but with new features and flexibility comes an additional layer of complexity. In this chapter, we will build the framework for successfully implementing Office SharePoint Server 2007 and map it to everyday business requirements.

The Windows SharePoint Services 3.0 foundation provides platform and collaboration features, such as document libraries, calendars, contacts, wikis, blogs, and lists. SharePoint Server 2007 adds and integrates rich functionality such as search, indexing, Excel Calculation Services (ECS), My Sites, process management, content management, and Business Intelligence. Although the SharePoint Server 2007 feature set is the primary focus of this chapter, a properly designed Windows SharePoint Server 3.0 implementation is required and salient points will be covered on it as well. Keep in mind the goal here is not to cover installation or administration of SharePoint Server 2007, but rather to understand how each of the product features will affect your design choices.

Before You Begin

System administrators often insert the installation media and install the software product before considering the ramifications of the software they are installing. When upgrading an existing system, for example, care must be taken to ensure compatibility with legacy systems and custom code. This level of caution is especially important considering the ASP.NET 2.0 integration with SharePoint Server 2007. You should consider a top-down approach to your SharePoint Server 2007 design and implementation. Take the time to study the design possibilities and reach a deliberate, educated decision.

Understanding the Design Life Cycle

Some administrators and architects might use their own organization's specific life-cycle guidelines. If you are one of them, you will still find useful information in this section. If you have not been exposed to design life cycles, you should consider using them in your SharePoint Server 2007 implementation. Most major published design life cycles are similar, but they do not always mesh well with deploying collaboration solutions. This section gives you an example of a design life cycle you can use when deploying SharePoint Server 2007 solutions. Figure 3-1 is an overview of the design life cycle.

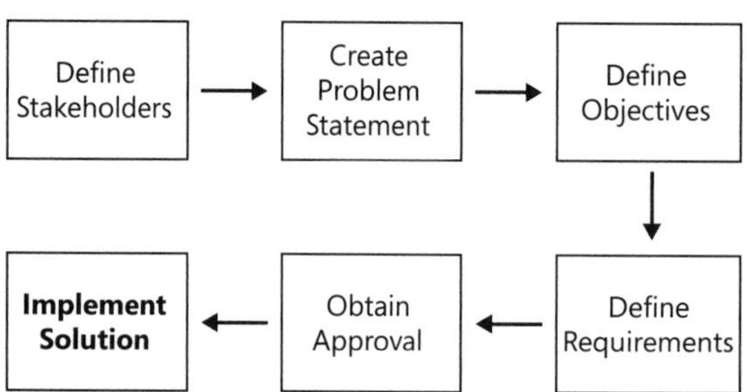

Figure 3-1 SharePoint Server 2007 design life cycle

Defining the Stakeholders

The term *stakeholder* in the information technology (IT) realm has come to mean those who have the final decision, fund projects, or are in a position to benefit from implementing a new system. One of the most difficult tasks as an IT professional is convincing management to spend time and money to effectively architect solutions. Many solutions are hastily designed and then later fail because a solid, scalable foundation wasn't laid. A well-designed SharePoint Server 2007 solution takes investment of both time and money from the stakeholders.

Ask yourself how your implementation will help your stakeholders, and then educate them on the increased profit and productivity they will receive. Stakeholder involvement will be essential in building a solid SharePoint Server 2007 platform that can grow with your business. Take the time to think through your design, and don't rush to install or upgrade. Time spent asking questions, testing applications, and using test groups will save you substantial administration effort down the road. Always get written approval from senior management before embarking on a new project.

Creating a Problem Statement

You cannot perfectly execute an SharePoint Server 2007 implementation without a clear definition and understanding of the business reasons for implementing SharePoint Server 2007 in the first place. Work closely with the stakeholders to define a problem statement and objectives to solving that problem. The following are examples of business, functional, and security problems.

- **Business problems** Helpdesk trouble ticketing and disposition, workflow issues, inventory control, document management, records management, portability and accessibility of data, duplication of effort, content management
- **Functional problems** Overworked IT staff, dispersed geographical management of servers and data, organizational boundaries, multiple subsidiaries, multiple contractors
- **Security problems** Legal issues, regional laws and regulations, federal mandates and regulatory guidelines, protection of intellectual property, integrity of data, disaster recovery, continuity of operations

Security Alert It is important to consider security in each phase of your design. Study how your objectives, requirements, and implementation plan affect the safekeeping of your data. This effort will save you significant time and energy in the future. Include your IT Security staff in all phases of your design.

After consulting with your stakeholders and other interested parties, you develop the problem statement, which will look similar to the following statement:

Data is scattered throughout the enterprise on personal computers, e-mail folders, Web servers, thumb drives, compact discs, content management solutions, databases, and file servers. It is very difficult and time consuming to locate previously authored documents, and employees waste time and money finding the correct resources. Frequently, the IT department must get involved to locate, copy, or authorize access to data. There have been issues with hardware failures preventing access to data. Management would also like data owners to authorize user access to content, ensuring that users access content on a need-to-know basis.

Defining Objectives

Objectives should show value specific to solving your business, functional, and security problems, but they should not include details for development and implementation. From your problem statement, you clearly define the objectives:

- **Objective 1** Consolidate as much information as possible to a central location and lower the total cost of ownership.
- **Objective 2** Install an indexing capability for searching all content that is centrally and remotely located.
- **Objective 3** Create a way to share ideas and information within a team while allowing and promoting interaction between teams. This information should be indexed, searched, and consumed by an audience defined by the data owner.
- **Objective 4** Implement a highly available solution.

This section outlines a few of the design considerations you need to take into account early in the design life cycle so that you can accurately define your objectives and requirements.

Establishing an Administrative Model

As you work through your design, keep in mind how you will administer all the different pieces. Many organizations are geographically dispersed or departmentally separated, and a well-thought-out administrative model is important to success. If you are planning a multifarm SharePoint Server 2007 topology, it can be difficult maintaining a secure and consistent implementation.

Enterprise Administrators

Multifarm installations should have an enterprise administrator with administrative access and control over all farms. An enterprise administrator is responsible for the overall architecture including security, deployment, and customization of all SharePoint installations. In this model, day-to-day administration is carried out by administrators dedicated to their individual SharePoint Server 2007 server farm.

If your organization has a centralized IT department, you might need to plan for remote server administration. For example, you may need to open certain firewall ports in order to be able to access Central Administration from anywhere on your network.

If you have distributed IT support for your infrastructure, you might want to create groups by division or geographic location, following your Active Directory organizational unit (OU) design, to manage your SharePoint Server 2007 server farms.

Identifying Hardware and Software Costs

When designing your SharePoint Server 2007 installation or upgrade, create a detailed spreadsheet defining what your costs will be. Here are a few items to get you started:

- **Legacy hardware** Will your current hardware support the additional load placed on it during and after the upgrade? SharePoint Server 2007 will inevitably increase the hardware usage of existing servers.
- **New hardware** Plan for sharply increased usage of the system once users see the advantages of SharePoint Server 2007. Enterprise implementations of My Sites have a rapid adoption rate, and large enterprise-class solutions will do well to have dedicated hardware.

> **More Info** For more information on hardware requirements, visit *http://www.microsoft.com/sharepoint/default.mspx*.

- **Software** Contact your Microsoft sales representative for licensing costs for SharePoint Server 2007, Windows Server 2003 R2, Windows Server Code Name "Longhorn," and Microsoft SQL Server 2000 or 2005. Remember that each person accessing your SharePoint Server 2007 servers must have a client access license (CAL).

Defining Service Level Agreements

In the modern IT world, you have no doubt been exposed to service-level agreements (SLAs). *SLAs* are agreements between two or more parties that describe the deliverables, support, and communication that will be provided by each party to the agreement. You might be asked to define the SLA for your SharePoint Server 2007 implementation. Draft these documents carefully, and request the appropriate funding for your scenario. If you do not directly manage all components of your installation, consider having SLAs with owners of your particular installation components–SQL Server, server hardware, switches, routers, firewalls, and so on.

> **Planning** If you are asked to provide high availability, many variables must be considered. These variables will be covered later in this chapter and in Chapter 30, "Microsoft Office SharePoint Server 2007 Disaster Recovery."

Defining Requirements

Objectives are commonly formed by IT staff in conjunction with the stakeholders, while requirements are usually formed with little assistance from the stakeholders. Requirements derived from your example objectives might look like this:

- **Requirement 1** Implement a small, three-server SharePoint Server 2007 server farm to consolidate corporate data, and allow remote access using Secure Sockets Layer (SSL) to discourage the use of thumb drives and local personal computer storage.
- **Requirement 2** Customize the search and indexing functions in SharePoint Server 2007 to search current data in Microsoft Exchange servers, file servers, Web servers, third-party content management systems, and previous versions of Microsoft SharePoint Server.
- **Requirement 3** Implement self-service site creation and administration to reduce the overhead of the IT department. This will allow faster service for customers, as well as lower the total cost of ownership of the service.
- **Requirement 4** Implement a multiserver, load-balanced solution that will ensure availability of data in the event of hardware failure.

Although your problem statement, objectives, and requirements will vary greatly, always research and test before implementation. Be sure to take into consideration multiple time zones, languages, customs, and legal and security issues before you begin.

Obtaining Approvals and Implementing the Solution

After you have defined a solid set of requirements, you need to present these requirements to the stakeholders, and your peers, in a design review. Design reviews offer an excellent opportunity for all involved parties to recommend changes and approve of your design. Provide an implementation plan at your design review, and begin scheduling any technical resources you will need.

Understanding Your Current Environment

Understanding your current environment is critical in the planning and implementation of any new system. When designing your SharePoint Server 2007 installation, plan on many documents being migrated while indexing the remainder. Try to get a comprehensive view by thoroughly documenting the location, type, and quantity of content in your enterprise.

Determining Staffing Needs

One commonly overlooked component of a successful implementation is staffing. Architects and administrators usually do a good job creating a bill of goods for hardware and software, but they often forget to secure funding for personnel to adequately develop and maintain a new system. SharePoint Server 2007 can consume a large amount of human resources if used to its full potential. Understand what types of dedicated personnel are required in the beginning, and start getting stakeholders' support immediately. Table 3-1 offers a suggested staffing schedule for you to consider. (Note: F = One full time person and P = One part time person.)

Table 3-1 Suggested Staffing Recommendations

Staff position	Small farm	Medium farm	Large farm	Multiple farms
System administrator	F	F	F F	F F
Search administrator	P	F	F P	F F F
Site designer	P	F	F F	F F F
Software developer	N/A	P F	F F	F F F
Software tester	N/A	P	F	F F
SQL DBA	P	F	F	F F

Keep in mind these are minimum recommendations and will vary based on how deep and wide your SharePoint Server 2007 implementation will be. For example, if you connect to line-of-business systems or use multifarm content deployment, you will require a much larger IT staff. A common shortfall of SharePoint Portal Server 2003 implementations was the lack of dedicated personnel for search/indexing and SQL Server SharePoint database administration. Medium and large SharePoint Server 2007 implementations will require at least one full-time person for each of these tasks. Don't forget that software testers can easily pay for themselves with decreased Helpdesk and IT staff support calls, as well as increased user productivity.

Surveying Current Content

A common reason that a company implements SharePoint Server 2007 is because its information currently exists in disparate data islands that are disconnected and the company lacks any method of finding critical data across these islands. With new SharePoint Server 2007 features, organizations can host or index the majority of their information and connect content from these disparate data islands. Following is a list of common content locations and suggestions for how you can move or index that content using SharePoint Server 2007:

- **File cabinets** Scan in and archive these documents using the Records Repository.
- **Web servers** Migrate and upgrade from Content Management Server 2002.
- **File shares** Migrate documents to Document Libraries, and index the remainder.
- **Personal computers** Move data to SharePoint Server 2007 My Sites and Team Sites.
- **Exchange public folders** Migrate data and use SharePoint Server 2007 Forms Server.
- **Outlook personal information stores and Exchange Server inboxes** Use SharePoint Server 2007 discussion lists to store e-mail threads and capture tacit knowledge (know-how). Also, store content in Document Libraries and send hyperlinks instead of entire documents.
- **Line-of-business systems** Index popular ERM systems.
- **Third-party document management and archival systems** Move this content to SharePoint Server 2007, and use native Document and Records Management.

If you decide to move large sets of content, plan your migrations to reduce the impact on the end user. Attempting to move all data simultaneously can be an impossible challenge—take it one step at a time.

Documenting the Network Infrastructure

Gaining a detailed understanding of the network infrastructure and implementing thorough documentation are necessary components in a solid system design. It is important to know all connection points, traversal paths, and personnel responsible during your implementation. Several network infrastructure components are used in medium and enterprise-scale SharePoint Server 2007 implementations. Consult with the network administrators to understand any nuances, such as maintenance windows, that you need to be aware of. Here are some examples of network infrastructure components and considerations:

- **Switches** Port speed, Duplex, virtual LANS, media type
- **Routers** Restrictions, wide area network bandwidth and latency
- **Storage area networks** Type, capacity, SAN HBA compatibility
- **Firewalls** Restrictions, configuration control, screened subnets

Meticulous documentation of these components up front will save time and energy as you progress through your design.

Choosing Server Platforms

When deploying an SharePoint Server solution, you need to choose sufficient hardware to support your requirements. Hardware that is insufficient for your services will cause your solution to perform slowly, delaying access to content and thus increasing the total cost of ownership. With the recent popularity in virtual machine (VM) technology, many organizations are implementing VMs to reduce server sprawl and CPU waste. Experience has shown that medium and large implementations are not likely to run well on most VM implementations.

Whether you choose physical or virtual machines, be mindful that modern processor architectures favor CPU-intensive applications or high I/O throughput, but usually not both.

Physical Machines

Most servers running today are physical, single-solution machines. Many SharePoint Server 2007, SQL Server 2000, and SQL Server 2005 systems will be unaffected by the trend toward virtualization; these servers usually require all resources the hardware has available. A small SharePoint Server 2007 installation might be run on a single machine, but most SharePoint Server 2007 installations will require several machines.

Virtual Machines

Many organizations are moving commodity servers to virtualized platforms. In SharePoint Server 2007 implementations, virtual machines are beneficial in saving development resources along with easing the transition of content from development to test systems. Small organizations, or large organizations with unique legal or regulatory requirements, might find it useful to host some components of their SharePoint Server 2007 implementations on virtual machines. If you decide to use virtual machines, be sure to test your implementation before production deployment to ensure acceptable performance.

Identifying Infrastructure Dependencies

Your new or upgraded SharePoint Server 2007 solution will depend on many pieces of IT infrastructure. Most of these will be covered here, but there is always the possibility your unique implementation, such as Line-of-Business (LOB) system integration, will require additional components.

Windows Server Software

SharePoint Server 2007 can be installed on Windows Server 2003 with Service Pack 1 or higher. Installing all updates prior to installing SharePoint Server 2007 is recommended.

Active Directory

Most SharePoint Server 2007 implementations will use Active Directory for authentication. This arrangement is fairly straightforward, and most administrators will find it simple to use. Be sparing when using Active Directory groups exclusively to authenticate SharePoint Server 2007 users, otherwise certain features such as Task Lists and Contacts might not function as desired. SharePoint 2007 provides a new list view called By My Groups, but users might overlook that functionality.

There is a second method to authenticate against an Active Directory, and it is often used by Internet service providers. Active Directory account creation mode is selected during the initial installation of SharePoint Server 2007 and cannot be reversed. When a user account is created in SharePoint Server 2007, an account is also created in Active Directory. Although this approach works fine for ISPs whose Active Directory is single-use, it is unfavorable for most organizations with an existing Active Directory. Unlike its predecessor, SharePoint Server 2007 does not require Active Directory. It can authenticate access against local system accounts or external data sources using pluggable authentication. This functionality is acceptable in a workgroup environment or implementations with extranet accounts.

Domain Name System

Domain Name System (DNS) will play a small but critical role in your SharePoint Server 2007 deployment. If you are not the DNS administrator in your organization, be sure to include the administrator in the very early stages of your design. In a single-server installation, you need a single entry (A record or CNAME) for your server name. In a load-balanced deployment, you will need a CNAME record for the cluster node IP address, as well as for each individual network interface card IP address.

Security Alert Many implementations will have Internet-facing servers publishing the same data with different security controls in place. As a security best practice, it is important to publish only the external IP addresses in DNS and not the intranet addresses.

E-Mail Servers

To use alerting, discussion groups, and other functionality of SharePoint Server 2007, you need to have an e-mail server correctly configured for SharePoint Server 2007. SharePoint Server 2007 provides the ability to allow inbound mail to document libraries and discussions. Correct functionality requires the following minimum configuration:

- **SMTP relaying** SharePoint Server 2007 cannot authenticate to an outbound Simple Mail Transfer Protocol (SMTP) connection. Your SMTP solution must allow relaying based on an IP address.
- **Single SMTP host** SharePoint Server 2007 does not provide a method to use multiple SMTP servers. Large organizations can implement round-robin DNS for SMTP high-availability.

Any SMTP server can be used to send and receive e-mail for a SharePoint Server 2007 implementation. Check with your e-mail administrator for further details.

SQL Server

SharePoint Server 2007 is heavily dependent on a well-running SQL Server back end. Except in the most limited deployments, you should not use SQL Express for your long-term database solution. SQL Server hosts the content and configuration databases, forming the foundation to SharePoint Server 2007.

Carefully plan your SQL Server installation to provide the level of service required by your SharePoint Server 2007 deployment. Although SQL Server 2000 Service Pack 3a (SP3a) or later will support SharePoint Server 2007, SQL Server 2005 will give a definite performance increase and has an improved feature set, including enhanced transaction log shipping and database mirroring. In addition, some of the Business Intelligence (BI) features in the Excel Calculation Services require SQL Server 2005.

Because there are many possible SQL Server configurations, it is wise to include your SQL database administrator (DBA) from the very beginning. The simplest configuration is a standalone Microsoft SQL Server for SharePoint Server 2007. Although this is an acceptable solution for organizations that are already using Microsoft SQL Server, it doesn't provide fault tolerance. Configurations based on a single SQL Server will not function if a SQL Server failure happens. If availability or performance requirements introduce multiple Web front-ends, it is time to consider a clustered SQL Server back end.

More Info You can find more information about high-availability SQL Server solutions at *http://www.microsoft.com/sql/technologies/highavailability/default.mspx.*

Identifying Other Design Considerations

There are many different ways to design and implement SharePoint Server 2007. Although the majority of design choices will depend on your specific implementation, many need to remain constant across all SharePoint Server 2007 installations. Note that configurations contrary to best practices can resist scaling, ease of administration, performance, and availability.

Deploying Web Front-End Servers

The SharePoint Server 2007 Web front-end (WFE) server renders Web content to the end user. The Web front-end server runs Internet Information Services (IIS) and provides the user interface via a Web browser. Using a Web browser simplifies many things, such as client software, firewall rules, customization and portability. Simply open TCP Port 443 (HTTPS) on your firewall and your users will have rich, secure document sharing. This approach alleviates the need for open Server Message Block (SMB) and NetBIOS ports, and eliminates the possible vulnerabilities that are associated with them. Keep in mind that WFEs do not store content–content is stored on SQL Server

Important Although most popular Web browsers function with SharePoint Server 2007, full functionality cannot be realized without Internet Explorer 6.0 or higher.

Deploying Query and Indexing Servers

An index server crawls data from many sources, and a query server consumes that content index to search for data. Users interact with the query server, not the index server. Searching and indexing are a large component of SharePoint Server 2007 and are covered in Chapter 16, "Enterprise Search and Indexing Architecture and Administration," and Chapter 17, "Enterprise Search and Indexing Deployment."

Note If you have a large environment and crawl very little external content, use a dedicated Web front-end server for indexing your SharePoint Server 2007 content. The dedicated WFE can be the indexing server itself (legacy functionality of SharePoint Portal Server 2003) or a standalone machine. This approach can significantly increase user-side WFE performance when indexing your SharePoint Server 2007 databases. The down-side with this implementation is *all* indexing will proxy through this WFE and could present a bottleneck. Using a standalone, dedicated WFE is illustrated in Figure 3-2.

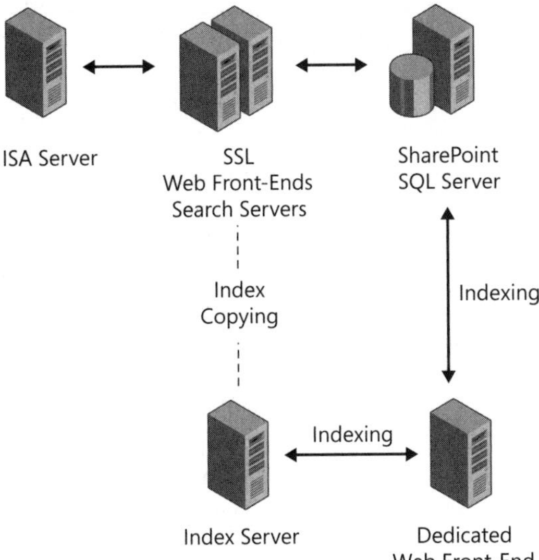

Figure 3-2 Using a dedicated Web front-end server for indexing content

Deploying Excel Calculation Services

A new feature in SharePoint Server 2007, Excel Calculation Services, includes a number of features found in the desktop Office application. Excel Calculation Services can be used by the full desktop client, Web browser, or custom application. Although Excel Calculation Services are easily scaled, it is best to have your calculation requirements defined before the production rollout. In calculation-intensive environments, you might have several Excel Calculation Services servers, with the possibility of scaling further by moving the query service to its own hardware.

Note Excel Calculation Services does *not* allow authoring in the browser or handle multiuser Excel authoring.

In SharePoint Services 2003, the functionality of lists was less than perfect for most organizations. SharePoint Server 2007 allows for most Excel functions to be embedded in your Web pages, allowing for a clutter-free and user-friendly Web site. More information on Excel Calculation Services can be found in Chapter 20, "Excel Services and Building Business Intelligence Solutions."

Ensuring Availability and Performance

Many things can affect the performance of SharePoint Server 2007, such as server processor speed and type, bus speed, network speed, disks and many other factors. All these things must be carefully considered when designing your SharePoint Server 2007 implementation. Web front-end servers, for example, are input/output (I/O) intensive applications, while application servers, such as Excel or index servers, are processor-intensive applications. This is another place to make informed, deliberate decisions about processor types in your farm. Remember that the bulk of your data, including all document libraries and lists, is stored on the SQL Server server specified in Central Administration. SharePoint Server 2007 can benefit greatly by a well-tuned and maintained SQL Server installation.

Note Medium and large SharePoint Server 2007 implementations might require a full-time DBA.

Implementing Web Front-End Load Balancing

Many times SharePoint Server 2007 deployments are a critical part of the day-to-day operations of an organization. In these instances, multiple Web front ends are useful to balance large network traffic loads and provide a layer of fault tolerance. All front-end Web servers need to be identical in their SharePoint Server 2007 configuration options.

Microsoft Windows Server includes functionality to create Network Load Balancing (NLB) clusters. This is an administrator-friendly and inexpensive way to add performance and fault tolerance to your SharePoint Server 2007 implementation. Although most implementations will use a hardware NLB solution, the Windows NLB component works fine for implementations that need a reliable, basic NLB solution.

More Info For detailed information on NLB and hardware compatibility, visit *http://www.microsoft.com/windowsserver2003/technologies/clustering/*.

Implementing Search and Query Server Load Balancing

Technically, you won't load balance either the search or query servers. However, implementations that rely heavily on search and indexing will benefit from multiple search servers if you can't get all the content sources indexed in a timely fashion using one search server. Multiple search servers can provide access to many content sources. Start your design with one search server, and let your business requirements drive you to multiple servers if necessary. For most small to medium organizations, a single search server is sufficient.

There might or might not be a direct relationship between the number of queries your users will submit on a daily basis and the number of content sources you'll be crawling. You can implement many query servers to help service the query load if needed. Start with one query server and scale up as demand increases.

Note Medium and large SharePoint Server 2007 implementations require at least one full-time search and indexing administrator.

Scaling Excel Calculation Services

Rarely does a new feature provide the robust scalability that Excel Calculation Services provides. In the very first version, Microsoft has provided the ability to scale ECS to any calculation requirement and connect to many common database types. Refer to Chapter 20 for more information on Excel Calculation Services. Figure 3-3 shows the potential granular design scalability for ECS.

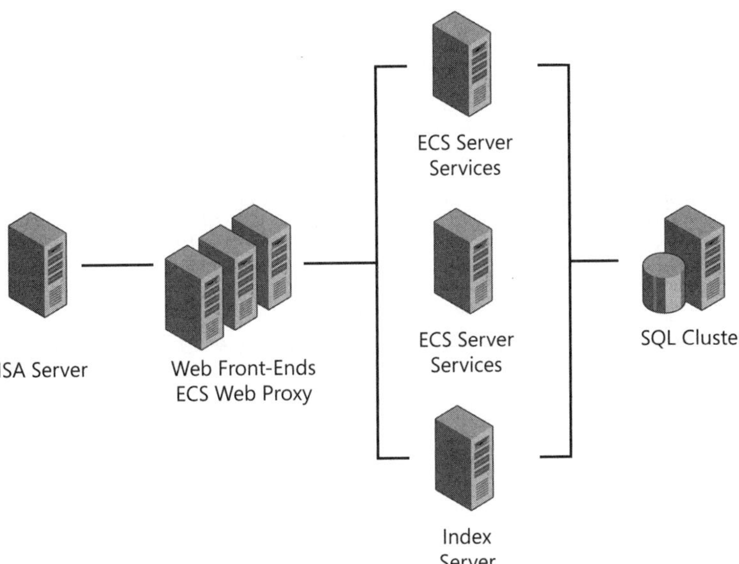

Figure 3-3 Granular breakout of Excel Calculation Services

Designing a Network Infrastructure

There is not enough room here to cover all the network performance issues that might arise, but here is a list of the most common issues:

- **Port speed and duplex** 100-megabit Ethernet is considered the minimum wire speed for any component of SharePoint Server 2007. Your SQL Server and application servers will benefit significantly from a gigabit Ethernet connection.

- **Wide area network (WAN) bandwidth** If users will be accessing your server farm from geographically separated locations, bandwidth must be carefully calculated. Bandwidth will vary greatly based on the type of data, SharePoint Server 2007 services used, and frequency of use. An enterprise My Sites solution can consume an enormous amount of bandwidth. Remember to justify the expense with the huge gains in productivity realized by My Sites.
- **Routers and firewalls** Routers and firewalls that are already routing and filtering large amounts of data might degrade your SharePoint Server 2007 performance. Check with your firewall and network teams to determine capacity for your installation.
- **Storage area networks** Many organizations are moving to storage area networks (SANs) for SQL Server databases. SANs can add significant performance gains as well as features to increase resistance to disasters. Check with your IT management team to see what options are available.

Considering User Location

Your design can vary significantly depending on the location of your users. If you are in a large, geographically dispersed organization, you might want to consider more than one SharePoint Server 2007 server farm. Using the Shared Services capabilities of SharePoint Server 2007, you can localize as much traffic as possible while still leveraging a single area for search, indexing and personal portals. With the advent of inexpensive and large bandwidth wide area networks (WANs), many organizations can consolidate Windows SharePoint Services 2.0 and SharePoint Portal Server 2003 installations.

Planning Consider creating a single SharePoint Server 2007 server farm, and let your business and functional objectives drive your requirements to create multiple server farms.

Performing Capacity Planning

SharePoint Server 2007 has grown into a very flexible solution, and capacity planning has become an individualized task. We will cover the basics here, but be sure to use and reference the SharePoint Server 2007 Planning and Deployment Guides for detailed planning. The general rule is to plan for 1 RPS (requests per second) per 1000 users. A medium server farm with two front-end Web servers can serve about 200 RPS on the minimum recommended hardware; a small farm can serve about 100 RPS with a single front-end Web server. Your capacity will vary greatly based on several things:

- Corporate and personal portals have mostly static content, and caching can be a benefit when serving content.

- Team Sites are very dynamic, and caching will be of little benefit. Plan on more resources for highly collaborative environments.
- Static Web portals generally use the fewest resources for a given number of users.
- Custom Web Parts should be properly tuned. Microsoft recommends re-using existing code when possible.
- Location of users is very important. Having too many remote users can overload WAN links.
- Specialized processing, such as Excel Services and indexing, can consume large amounts of hardware resources and network bandwidth.
- The minimum hardware suggestions might not be sufficient if your environment requires high performance and availability.

Commercially available load-testing tools, monitoring tools, and Windows Server Performance Monitoring can be used to fine-tune your hardware requirements. In addition, Microsoft Visual Studio .NET includes the Application Center Test (ACT) tool that can be useful for load testing.

Organizing Your Content

Reducing the total cost of ownership (TCO) is the goal of any organization. SharePoint Server 2007 has several new features to lower TCO when organizing and managing content. Use this section as a guide for designing new or upgraded installations of SharePoint services.

Reorganizing and Consolidating SharePoint Services 2003 Content

With the highly anticipated features released in SharePoint Server 2007, many organizations will consolidate document libraries, lists, site collections, subsites, and even entire portals. The following sections present ideas for consolidating content when upgrading from SharePoint Services 2003 and migrating from other platforms such as Exchange Public Folders, file shares and third-party document management systems.

Multiple Content Types in a Single Document Library

SharePoint Services 2003 allowed a single content type per document library. This limitation necessitated many top-level document libraries to handle multiple types of metadata associated with documents. Windows SharePoint Services 3.0 native functionality allows several content types and predefined templates in a single document library. This functionality can give you and your site administrators the ability to group content by business, security, and other organizational requirements.

Per-Item Security and Benefits for Consolidation

One of the most exciting enhancements to SharePoint Server 2007 is the ability to have granular permissions–similar to NTFS permissions–on any document, document library, or list. In SharePoint Portal Server 2003, many organizations had to create multiple document libraries to control access to content. Early adoptions of SharePoint Server 2007 are seeing document library consolidations of as much as 20 to 1 with the ability to change permissions on a per-item level.

Using Enterprise Content Management Services

SharePoint Server 2007 now includes full Enterprise Content Management (ECM) functionality. SharePoint Server 2007 ECM benefits content consolidation by allowing a variation of multiple languages, security policies, and content archival. Go to Chapter 11, "Web Content Management and Publishing Features," for more information on Web content management.

SharePoint Server 2007 document management eases the management of large document libraries and increases their usability. In Windows SharePoint Services 2.0, document libraries with hundreds or thousands of documents were difficult to navigate and manage. SharePoint Server 2007 natively supports document and records management that can be integrated with workflows and third-party archival solutions. When planning for consolidation and migrations, remember that you can have only one records management repository per site collection. Refer to Chapter 9, "Document Management," and Chapter 10, "Records Management in Microsoft Office SharePoint Server 2007," for more information.

Deploying SharePoint Portals

When it comes to Web portals, much has changed with this version of SharePoint Services. SharePoint Portal Server 2003 was very different from Windows SharePoint Services 2003. New administrators always struggled with the different management interfaces and areas structure. In contrast, SharePoint Server 2007 simply extends the management of Windows SharePoint Services 2007 while simplifying the customization and addition of portals.

Deploying Corporate Portals

A corporate portal is a central Web location to aggregate and distribute organizational information. With SharePoint Portal Server 2003, you created a single portal per IIS Web application. The process of customizing SharePoint Portal Server 2003 was also very different than Windows SharePoint Services 2.0. SharePoint Server 2007 has greatly simplified portals by making them a site template rather than having them always be the root of a site collection. Gone are the limitations and nuances of SharePoint portals, such as areas and bucket Webs.

Planning Most organizations will create a site collection at the root of a namespace, such as https://portal.contoso.msft, and apply the Corporate Intranet Site template there. This approach produces the common look and feel of legacy SharePoint portals. Remember, this version is highly customizable, and there might be instances where you have several portals in a single namespace.

Deploying Personal Portals (My Site)

Another type of portal in SharePoint Server 2007 is a *My Site*, or personal, portal. A My Site portal provides a feature-rich, one-to-many collaborative area for each user. Examples of the features available are Private and Public document libraries, blogs, wikis, rollup views, custom links, and many others. A great selling point for My Sites is that users can use their My Site instead of thumb drives, personal Web mail, and other disconnected storage for content. This functionality encourages centralized storage that can be captured and indexed, reducing the loss of tacit knowledge. When designing your My Site's framework, be sure to consider the default size limitation of My Sites, bandwidth requirements, and access control. Large personal portals are becoming more feasible with the downward trend in storage costs. Enterprise-class organizations will require dedicated hardware serving MySites content.

Managing Your Content

SharePoint Server 2007 provides several new and old features to help manage content that will influence you design decisions. Organizing content is only the first step in a successful SharePoint Server 2007 implementation. You also need to devise a plan to manage and access it.

Using Site Collections

When creating a new Web application in Windows SharePoint Services 2007, you are actually creating the environment to create a new site collection that can contain many subsites, document libraries, lists, and all other SharePoint Server 2007 and Windows SharePoint Services 3.0 content types. Think of a *site collection* as a container for sites and other SharePoint content, as shown in Figure 3-4.

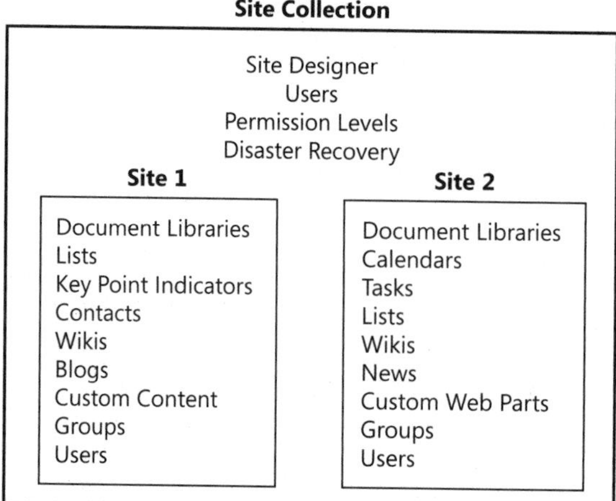

Figure 3-4 Site collection container view

Deploying Self-Service versus Administratively Created Sites

When readying your SharePoint Server 2007 server farm for production, you must decide how sites will be created. There are two options: administratively created sites and Self-Service Site Creation (SSSC). Administratively created sites is the default, but because this setting is a Web application setting, you can combine the two approaches with multiple Web applications. There are obvious advantages to Self-Service Site Creation, such as reduced labor by IT staff and immediate site creation. However, the SSSC approach also has drawbacks, such as a lack of control and accountability for site management.

Understanding Self Service Site Creation

Self-Service Site Creation enables users to create sites without the intervention of the IT administrative staff. This flexibility results in a user-friendly and highly collaborative environment. If SSSC is chosen, be sure to manage and expire content based on policies. The absence of these policies can lead to a plethora of outdated sites and content.

Understanding Administratively Created Sites

When site creation is limited to site designers or administrators, there is more control over the content and structure, but obvious delays in site creation and administration occur. Administratively created sites often have larger numbers of subsites, which can affect performance. Administratively created sites have the advantage of organizational control and might be necessary in some geographic or business areas to meet legal and regulatory guidelines. Keep in mind that administrative control and effective collaboration are inversely proportional.

Best Practices Most deployments will need a combination of both administratively created sites and user-created sites. A hallmark of a highly collaborative environment is that it provides the ability for the end-user to create new collaboration spaces that have a low transaction cost. The ease and flexibility of creating new sites by end users without having to involve IT staff is a key component to a successful deployment of SharePoint. Now, I know this runs counter to your need for control. Most IT administrators are high-control people; it's a necessary part of the job. And a talented administrator will control that which needs to be controlled, such as site creations for departments, divisions, new servers, content sources, new search scopes, and other centrally administrated and controlled farm, server, and site configurations. That same administrator won't try to control tasks that users can do themselves. The distributed administrative architecture of this product leads to a distributed architecture for creating new sites. Give your users a place to create new sites, and don't worry too much about a loss of control.

Using Administrative Delegation

Whichever site creation model you choose to implement, allow site administrators to delegate the level of access to content. In many organizations, the person who controls access to particular content is referred to as the *data owner* and is responsible for the dissemination of that content. The data owner will have a better understanding of required permission and can shorten the time a new user waits for access. A carefully planned migration can allow data owners to grant permissions on files and folders easily.

Using the Two-Stage Recycle Bin

With Windows SharePoint Services 2007 comes the addition of a Recycle Bin. This is a much anticipated addition and can drastically reduce the phone calls to restore data from tape. It is referred to as a *–two-stage Recycle Bin* because it consists of the user stage and the site administrator stage. It works much like the Windows Server Recycle Bin. Users can empty their Recycle Bin, but the administrator can also restore the deleted file within a configurable time limit set in Central Administration. This feature reduces the involvement by server operators and drastically lowers the TCO from SharePoint Services 2003.

Implementing Mobile Access

Be sure to plan and allow for access to your SharePoint Server 2007 implementation for remote users. SharePoint Server 2007 allows for offline files either in Office Outlook 2007 or in a My Documents drafts folder. Publishing your site via Secure Sockets Layer (SSL) or allowing access through a virtual private network (VPN) can solve most remote access issues. Keep in mind that Outlook calendars, contacts, and tasks are editable on either the SharePoint site or Outlook client. This flexibility increases the need for seamless remote connectivity to your server farm.

Connecting to External Data Sources

SharePoint Server 2007 comes with connectors to Line-of-Business (LOB) systems and SQL Server Reporting Services. The Business Data Catalog (BDC) integrates business data from LOB applications into SharePoint Server 2007 sites without the need for extensive custom programming. This functionality is useful for extracting sales, manufacturing, or other financial information and putting it into a user-friendly format.

Using the Reporting Site template, in conjunction with SQL Server Reporting Services and Excel Services, organizations can create Business Intelligence (BI) portals dedicated to providing real-time visuals into the health of the company. SharePoint Server 2007 has built in functionality for Key Performance Indicators (KPIs), SQL Server reporting tools, custom Excel Calculation Services, and many other BI tools that can be incorporated into a BI portal. Go to Chapter 20 for detailed information on Excel Calculation Services and Business Intelligence.

Note A BDC source connection need only be configured once; it can then be available to all farms in an intrafarm or interfarm topology.

Planning Security

This section is not meant to be exhaustive because system security is very dynamic. It is provided as an overview to securing SharePoint Server 2007. Security can always be improved, but too much security can affect the usefulness of the product. This section assumes you have already secured your Windows servers and are installing updates regularly.

More Info For more information on securing Microsoft products, visit *http://www.microsoft.com/security/default.mspx*.

Planning and Implementing Security Accounts

SharePoint Server 2007 was designed with security in mind by isolating the three tiers of administration: Central Administration, Shared Services Provider Administration, and Site Administration. This process isolation requires several security accounts to authenticate and connect services such as SQL databases, Web content, and Shared Services. Proper creation and permission settings are critical in protecting your SharePoint Server 2007 server farm from intentional or accidental intrusions. Provide these accounts with least privilege, and escalate those privileges only when necessary.

Note After creating Shared Services Providers (and My Site if a separate Web application), you must add the administrators manually in Central Administration, under Application Management. This prevents accidental unauthorized access.

The following list details the security accounts used by SharePoint Server 2007:

- **Microsoft Office SharePoint Server 2007 Setup User Account** This account must be an administrator on all servers in the farm.
- **Server Farm Account** The farm account is used by the Central Administration Web application and SPTimer service. (SPTimer is responsible for sending notifications and scheduling tasks.) This account must be an administrator on all servers in the farm and have Database Creator and Security Admin rights on the SQL Server server.
- **SharePoint Admin Account** The admin account is defined as *'localsystem'* on all servers and is used to propagate changes and administrative tasks across servers in a farm.
- **Shared Services Provider Process Account** The Shared Services Provider (SSP) process account is used by the SSP Web administration application. It has full access to the SSP configuration database and must be secured. It cannot be Network Service (default) in a farm configuration.
- **Shared Services Provider Web Content Account** The SSP Web content account provides the access to consumers of Shared Services. It requires the Network_Service logon type.
- **Web Application Process Account (Sites)** The Web application process account provides for isolated IIS application pools and content database access. A best practice is to have a Web application process account for each Web application created, providing application isolation.
- **Search Content Access Accounts** You must define a default content access account when enabling an indexing service. This should be an account with broad access and the password should not expire. You may also need to define content access accounts when crawling any data the default content access account cannot successfully authenticate and is authorized to view. You may define as many additional search content access accounts as required, but only one may be defined per crawl rule.
- **User Profile and Properties Access Account** If you need to import users from a 3rd party LDAP or another Active Directory Domain, you will need to specify the import connection account in SSP Administration when creating the data connection.

- **Excel Calculation Services Unattended Process Account** If you need to connect to external data sources with Excel Calculation services, you will need to define an additional account in SSP Administration. By default, the above defined SSP Process account will be used.
- **Office Web Server Process Account** This account runs under the Network Service user context and does not have to be changed.

SharePoint Server 2007 creates and connects to several SQL Server databases. Several of your existing security accounts will require permissions to access SQL Server databases. Table 3-2 details the permissions required.

Table 3-2 SQL Permissions

Account Name	Configuration Database	Central Admin Content Database	SSP Configuration Database	SSP Content Databases	Web Content Databases
Farm Account (SQL Server Database Creator and Security Admin)	DBO	DBO	DBO	DBO	DBO
SSP Process Account	R	R/W	R/W	DBO	R/W
SSP Web Content	R	R/W	R/W	R/W	R/W
Web App Account	R	R/W	R/W	R/W	DBO *

DBO=Database Owner

R=Read

W=Write

* R/W for all other Web Application Content Databases

Securing Internet Information Services

Securing Internet Information Service (IIS) is critical to meeting your organizational goals of data integrity and availability. SharePoint Server 2007 allows you to assign an IP address to all IIS Web applications, except Office Server Web Services. Assigning each Web application an IP address mitigates the risk of an intruder accessing your administrative interfaces via a public IP address. For example, if you don't assign IP addresses to Web applications and leave TCP ports open to a public Web site on the same box as Central Administration, that Web site's IP address can be used to access Central Administration remotely. Using a single IP address for multiple Web Applications introduces complexities when isolating web traffic on firewalls and intrusion detection systems.

More Info Visit *http://www.microsoft.com/technet/prodtechnol/WindowsServer2003/Library/IIS/* for more information about security and IIS 6.0.

Several authentication mechanisms are available to you as a SharePoint administrator. How you choose from among these mechanisms will vary depending on your network topology and business requirements.

Anonymous Authentication

Anonymous authentication allows unprompted access to your SharePoint Server 2007 content. This authentication type uses the IUSR_*computername* system account to allow access to NTFS files and SharePoint Server 2007 content. Public Internet sites often use anonymous authentication, but using it for collaborative sites is a bad idea. Routine audits for IUSR_*computername* file access and vulnerability scans are considered best practices by the majority of the security community when using anonymous authentication.

Security Alert Don't allow unauthenticated public access to a fully enabled collaborative SharePoint Server 2007 farm. Your farm could be vulnerable to hackers, and any information published could be compromised.

Integrated Authentication

Integrated authentication allows users access to sites with their currently logged-on username and password. This is the preferred method for authentication because it reduces the frequency of username/password errors that require Helpdesk assistance. Integrated authentication can use Kerberos or NTLM authentication mechanisms.

Kerberos is the preferred authentication type for internal-facing SharePoint Server 2007 implementations, and it can be used in conjunction with integrated authentication. Keep in mind that the client and IIS server must be able to see the Kerberos Distribution Center (KDC) to successfully authenticate. Kerberos and NTLM are secure, but NTLM passwords sent over HTTP are considered insecure unless the password length is more than 14 characters.

Enabling Kerberos Authentication

Kerberos authentication requires special configuration. When creating a Web application in Central Administration, choose Kerberos as your authentication mechanism and configure a service principal name (SPN) for your Web application pool process account identity.

Configuring an SPN

Using the Setspn.exe tool from the Windows Server 2003 Support Tools, type the following at a command prompt:

```
setspn.exe -A HTTP/ServerName CONTOSO\UserName
```

ServerName is your IIS system name; *CONTOSO* is the name of your Active Directory domain; and *UserName* is the identity of the Web application's application pool.

Configuring an Existing Web Application

If you need to enable Kerberos after the initial creation of a Web application, you must configure an SPN and enable Kerberos for your Web application. First, verify your current NTAuthentication Providers. At the command prompt, type the following:

```
cscript c:\inetpub\adminscripts\adsutil.vbs get w3svc/7898/root/
NTAuthenticationProviders.
```

The output should look like this:

```
NTAuthenticationProviders : (String) "NTLM"
```

If the output is `"Negotiate,NTLM"`, your IIS Web application is already configured to use Kerberos. Note that *7898* is our sample IIS virtual server ID (Web Application). The default Web site is *1*, and you can find the ID for your Web application by opening the Web Sites folder in IIS Manager and looking in the Identifier column.

To enable Kerberos for this Web application, type the following at a command prompt:

```
cscript c:\inetpub\adminscripts\adsutil.vbs set w3svc/7898/root/
NTAuthenticationProviders "Negotiate,NTLM"
```

This will allow IIS to authenticate users with Kerberos or NTLM authentication. Do not remove NTLM or Kerberos-only users that cannot see the KDC or have unsynchronized clocks will not authenticate.

Basic Authentication

Many organizations will deploy SharePoint Server 2007 in a large, enterprise environment that is facing the Internet and is well protected by firewalls. In addition, highly compartmentalized organizations might not allow the required ports to enable Kerberos or NTLM authentication over routers. These scenarios require basic authentication to be enabled. The primary flaw with basic authentication is that the username and password are sent in clear text. Because of this, authentication traffic is easily compromised. Implementing SSL is considered a best practice for all public-facing SharePoint Server 2007 implementations, but it's mandatory when using basic authentication.

.NET Forms-Based Authentication

.NET Forms-based authentication provides a method for authenticating users at the application level instead of the at the operating-system level. This arrangement saves processing power and allows extreme scalability.

Important Forms-based authentication is sent in clear-text, secure using SSL.

Pluggable Authentication

SharePoint Server 2007 supports the ASP.NET provider model, allowing authentication to any database using pluggable authentication. By using a standalone database, you can keep extranet accounts out of your internal Active Directory.

Understanding Critical Services Placement

Most system administrators today are using screened or dual-screened subnets in securing Internet-facing services. The following topics assume you have a screened subnet using firewalls or routers. If you do not have these in place and are considering an Internet-facing solution, you should consider implementing them.

Securing the Central Administration Interface

The SharePoint Technologies Central Administration interface is a very powerful tool. Securing the location of this interface is very important to the foundation of SharePoint Server 2007 security. Ideally, this interface is on a secured network, not facing the Internet and using SSL for administrative communications. If an intruder gains access to your Central Administration home page, it only takes a username and password to render your security efforts null and void. Protect your Central Administration home page with SSL and *never* publish the administration TCP port.

Note If you have several SharePoint Server 2007 server farms, you will find it beneficial to assign all your farms the same Central Administration TCP port number. Never publicly publish this port.

Securing SQL Server

A significant area of concern when securing your SharePoint Server 2007 server farm is SQL Server. A secure SQL Server server is paramount to system integrity and availability because the majority of your data is there. Use the least permissions required when securing all traffic to the database server, including that which is not related to SharePoint Server 2007. Securing your SharePoint Server 2007 traffic is of little use when another application is the root of a SQL Server server being compromised.

Best Practices We have all heard about and felt the pain from TCP 1433 vulnerabilities such as the "slammer worm." Within the computer industry, it is now considered best to block public traffic to your SQL Server server. This is accomplished by blocking TCP 1433 on firewalls and routers while using IPSec to encrypt data going to and from your Web front-end servers, as shown in Figure 3-5.

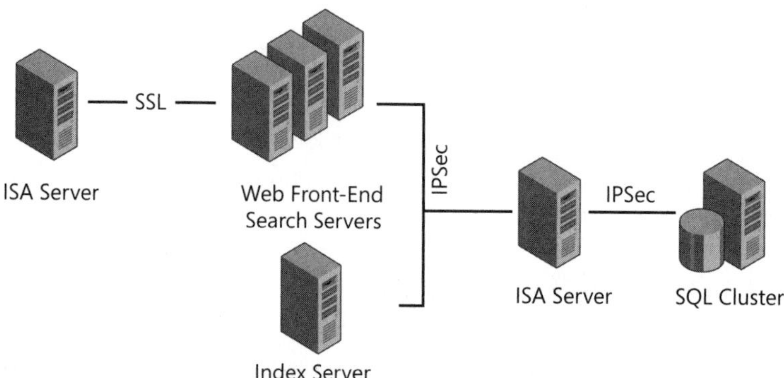

Figure 3-5 Securing SQL Server via IPSec

Securing Extranets and Internet-Facing Collaborative Solutions

Always use SSL to encrypt Internet-facing or extranet-facing SharePoint Server 2007 solutions. Allowing collaborative access to your SharePoint Server 2007 servers from the Internet can be very beneficial in keeping your data centralized and indexed, but using standard HTTP is an invitation to intrusion. Have a perimeter Active Directory with limited visibility into your organizational network for extranet accounts and service accounts. Establish a one-way trust, with your perimeter Active Directory trusting your internal Active Directory. This configuration allows your organization's users to access the extranet remotely with one username, and it provides for smooth content deployment.

Security Alert Never configure your internal Active Directory to trust your perimeter Active Directory.

Extending Existing Web Applications

SharePoint Server 2007 includes the ability to republish content databases with different Web applications using special security controls. Many organizations use Kerberos authentication internally while publishing the same Internet-facing Web application using basic authentication encrypted via SSL. An example of this is shown in Figure 3-6.

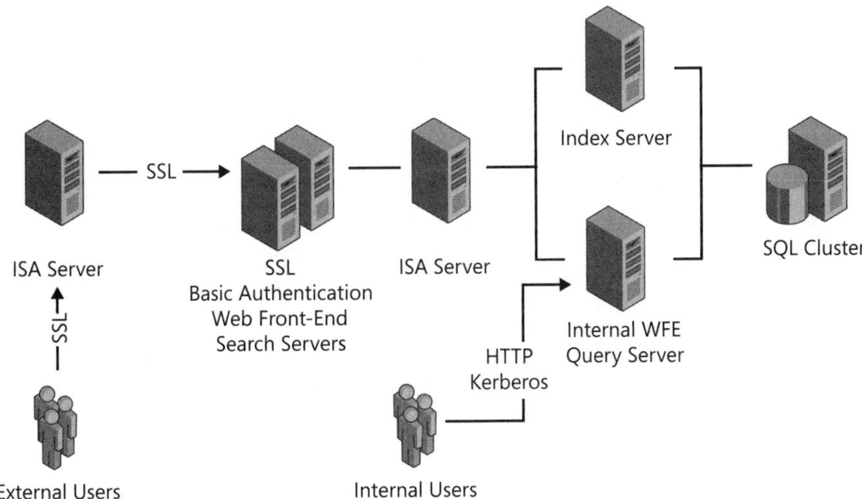

Figure 3-6 Extending an existing Web application

Deploying SharePoint Server Farms

You can choose from a multitude of farm deployment scenarios to include as part of your design. In this section, you'll become familiar with some of the more common scenarios and presented with a roadmap for deploying SharePoint Server 2007. The classifications given here to these farm topologies is rather arbitrary; none of the topologies are enforced in the user interface. You can craft any combination of server you want in a SharePoint Server 2007 farm. These classifications are for discussion purposes only, and you can use them as starting points for planning the right topology for your environment.

Single-Server Deployment

In a single-server deployment scenario (shown in Figure 3-7), a single server services all the client's needs and offers all the needed services to the network. This topology also uses the SQL Express database engine and installs it on this server. A single server is assigned all the farm roles, including the following ones:

- **Web front-end** The role to which users always connect to access all farm services, including search and indexing, Excel Calculation Services, collaboration, portals, and more
- **Query server** The role that allows users to query the index to find content
- **Search server** The role that crawls and indexes content from content sources
- **Excel Calculation** The role that hosts complex queries for end-user Excel spreadsheets and helps users maintain persistent connections to data points
- **Forms Server** The role that offers InfoPath forms to the users on your network
- **Web content management** The role that allows staging and publishing of Web content

Single-server roles are best suited for environments with a small user base or for testing labs.

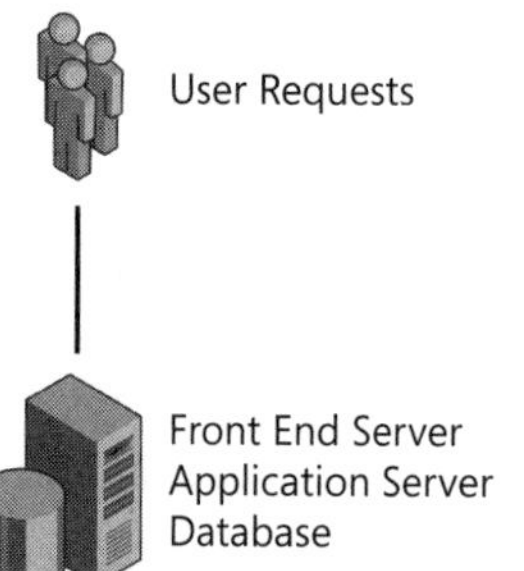

Figure 3-7 Single-server topology

Small Server Farms

A small-farm environment (shown in Figure 3-8) is a two-tiered environment in which one server is running SQL Server and the other server is running all the roles in the SharePoint farm.

If performance becomes an issue, you can always add another WFE server to the farm. If data redundancy becomes an issue, you can always cluster your SQL servers. If both increased performance and data redundancy are needed, you can add servers to your SharePoint farm as needed and cluster your SQL Server server. Both actions will help ensure that users can access their data quickly and easily.

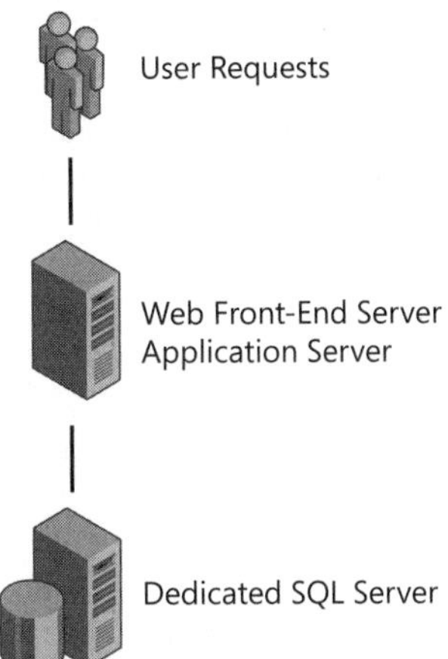

Figure 3-8 Small-farm topology

Medium Server Farms

We move to a three-tier topology with a medium server farm. This topology places the application services—such as search, query, Excel calculation, Office Forms Server and other services—on the middle tier (as shown in Figure 3-9). In this topology, two servers are dedicated to being WFE servers: one application server in the middle tier, and a clustered SQL Server deployment for data redundancy. The most likely reason you'd add a second server to the middle tier is to isolate the search function on a single server, because that activity is very processor and RAM intensive.

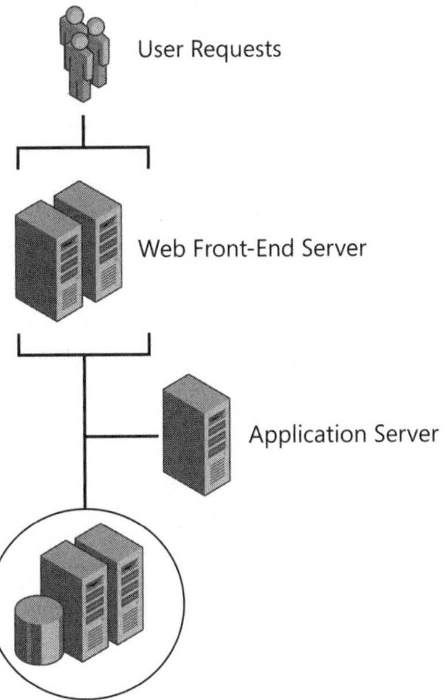

Figure 3-9 Medium server farm topology

In addition, by modifying this topology and adding another server to the middle tier, you can achieve maximum redundancy with the fewest number of servers, which is six. (See Figure 3-10.) Each tier has two servers offering the same services, thereby giving you the greatest opportunity for redundancy with the fewest number of servers. Most environments for small and medium servers will be similar to what I've described in this section.

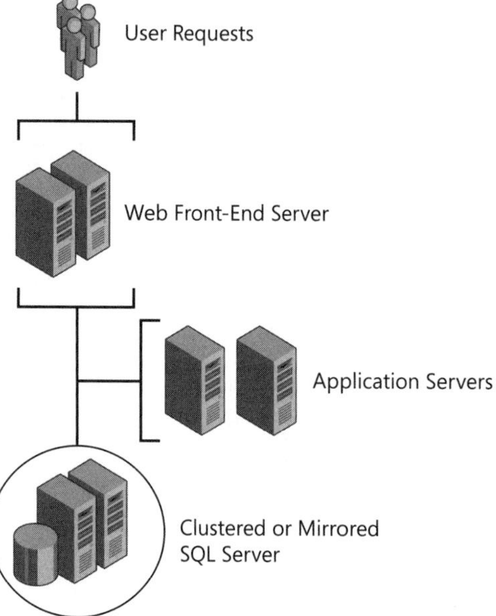

Figure 3-10 Medium server farm topology with redundancy

Large Server Farms

A large farm merely builds on the medium farm topology and allows us to scale out servers for any combination of services that are needed. Figure 3-11 offers one illustration of a large server farm for SharePoint Server 2007. Note that there is redundancy at each tier and for each service. Notice also that you're writing content to multiple SQL clusters. Finally, notice that as you need to, you can scale out any tier and service you need with additional servers. The only servers that need NLB are the WFE servers. All other servers merely have their services started or stopped and SharePoint Server 2007 does the rest to ensure they are all utilized properly.

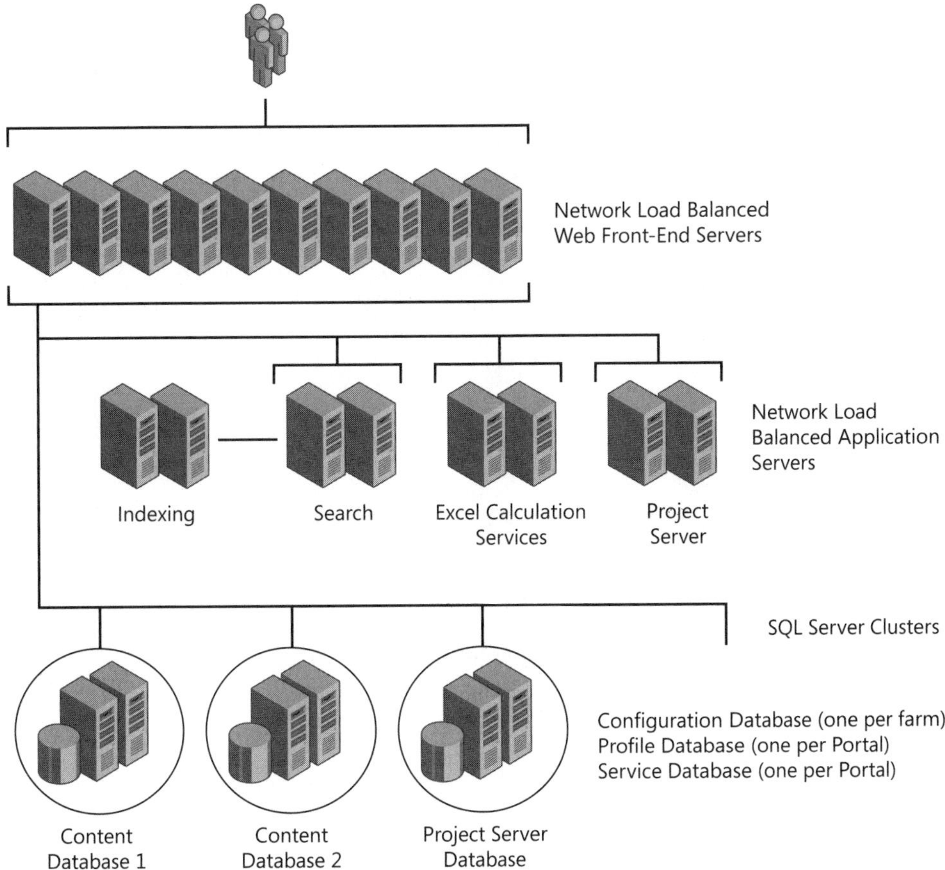

Figure 3-11 Large server farm topology

Multiple Farms

At times, you will find that multiple SharePoint Server 2007 server farms are required. (Figure 3-12 shows content deployment in a multiple-farm environment.) As an example, software development requires development, test, and production environments. SharePoint Server 2007 perfectly meets this need by using multiple farms, which allows development and test environments to be on intranets and schedules the publishing of production content to a screened subnet. Geographically dispersed organizations and implementations with unique legal and regulatory requirements will require multiple farms as well.

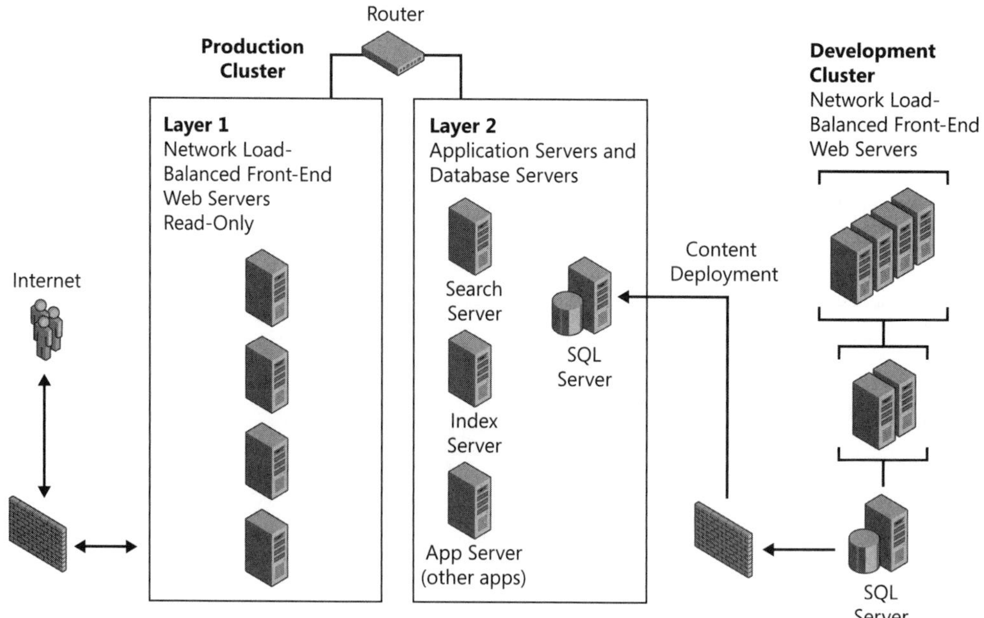

Figure 3-12 Content deployment in a multifarm environment

Using Interfarm Shared Services

If you have several SharePoint Server 2007 server farms, you should leverage SharePoint Server 2007 capabilities of interfarm shared services. Interfarm shared services reduce the administrative and operating overhead by limiting custom Shared Services development to one server farm. A single Business Data Catalog connector, a single MySites namespace, and centralized search and indexing are the most common reasons for a unified Shared Services implementation. There are some limitations to be aware of when designing this model, the most obvious being bandwidth limitations. Interfarm shared services are generally not supported over WAN links. Robust search and indexing, Business Data Catalog, and My Sites can require huge amounts of expensive bandwidth. However, with the advent of large, high-speed optical carrier (OC) backbones, an exception might be made in some large organizations. Refer to Chapter 18, "Administrating Shared Services Providers," for information on integrating interfarm and intrafarm Shared Services.

Note To avoid My Site URL collisions between multiple domains, be sure to select Domain and User Name when defining Site Naming Format.

Summary

This chapter presented you with an overview of the considerations involved in designing and deploying SharePoint Server 2007. Don't let the many features intimidate you–these are easily deployed with research, planning, testing, and peer reviews. Remember that SharePoint Server 2007 is very flexible, so you can change your mind if your original deployment isn't an exact fit. If you are in a small IT department or you are the only administrator, consider consulting with local technology users groups or the numerous newsgroups available for SharePoint Server 2007. There are many Microsoft MVPs (Most Valuable Professionals) and others with extensive experience ready to help you.

Chapter 4

Multilingual Planning, Deployment, and Maintenance

This chapter focuses on the new capabilities of Microsoft Windows SharePoint Services 3.0 and Microsoft Office SharePoint Server 2007 to host sites in different languages and present content in multiple languages within the same site collections. This new functionality and the flexibility of multilingual options presents new planning decisions prior to deployment, new deployment options, and new maintenance concerns. You'll find an in-depth discussion of the functionality of the Variation feature provided by Office SharePoint Server 2007 and how variations extend beyond the more common application of synchronizing content in multiple languages.

This chapter helps you understand the planning issues for content translation encountered in a multilingual scenario and the solutions provided by the translation workflow and variation packaging. It includes a discussion of the limitations or constraints in the variation processes, including issues with some Web Parts.

The tools provided to assist in managing the process of manually translating content are also covered in this chapter, with particular focus on planning issues.

Multilingual Support in Windows SharePoint Services 3.0 and SharePoint Server 2007

Windows SharePoint Services 3.0 supports hosting site collections, sites, and content in multiple languages on the same servers across your farm. This support is an enormous step forward from previous versions, which required the product to be installed in a specific language version that could host content only in that single language.

SharePoint Server 2007 extends this multilingual support with several features that simplify the implementation and maintenance for the administrators and the utilization for the users. Multilingual support does, however, create myriad planning decisions that should be addressed prior to implementing your farm. These decision points are introduced throughout the chapter in the discussions of the technology itself.

Preparing Front-End Servers for Multiple Languages

Before you install language packs on SharePoint farm servers, you must install the necessary regional and language files on at least your front-end Web servers. Because roles within your farm might change, installing and configuring these regional files on all members of your farm could prevent problems later on. All members of the farm should be configured with the same options, including having all the same regional and language files installed.

Regional and language files are used by the operating system to provide support for displaying and entering text in multiple languages. These files include keyboard files, Input Method Editors (IMEs), TrueType font files, bitmap font files, codepage translation tables, national language support (.nls) files, and script engines for rendering complex scripts. Most language files are installed by default on Windows Server 2003; however, you must install language files for East Asian languages and languages that use complex script or require right-to-left orientations. The East Asian languages include Chinese, Japanese, and Korean; the complex script and right-to-left-oriented languages include Arabic, Armenian, Georgian, Hebrew, the Indic languages, Thai, and Vietnamese.

Microsoft recommends that you install only the language files you need. The East Asian files require about 230 megabytes (MB) of hard disk space. The complex script and right-to-left languages do not use much disk space, but installing either set of files might cause some slowdown in performance when entering text.

Note You must be an administrator on the computer to install these language files. Once the language files are installed, the languages are available to all users of the computer. You need your Windows Server 2003 product disc to perform this procedure. Alternatively, you need to know the location of a shared folder that contains your operating system installation files. Restart your computer after supplemental language files are installed.

Installing Additional Language Files

To install additional language files, perform the following steps:

1. On your server, in Control Panel, select Regional And Language Options.
2. In the Regional And Language Options dialog box, click the Languages tab. In the Supplemental Language Support section, do one or both of the following:
   a. Click Install Files For Complex Script And Right-To-Left Languages (Including Thai) if you want to install language files for Arabic, Armenian, Georgian, Hebrew, the Indic languages, Thai, and Vietnamese.
   b. Click Install Files For East Asian Languages if you want to install language files for Chinese, Japanese, and Korean.
3. When prompted, insert your Windows Server 2003 product disc or provide the location of your Windows Server 2003 installation files.
4. When prompted to restart your computer, click Yes.

As this process indicates, the language files must be installed in the server operating system to be available to the SharePoint Technologies platform.

Selecting a Product Installation Language

After you install the necessary language files on your servers, you need to install Windows SharePoint Services 3.0 or SharePoint Server 2007 and run the SharePoint Products And Technologies Configuration Wizard.

Your first planning decision is the language you want to use for administering your farm. This will always be the language version of the product you install on all members of your farm. Only one installation language is supported per farm. All members of the farm must have the same language version of the product installed. To change the language used for administering the farm requires removing and re-installing the product on all members of the farm.

The product language does not have to be the same language as that of the operating system, but it probably will be in most cases. However, if your server administrators prefer English but your SharePoint farm administrators prefer a different language, install the appropriate language version of the operating system and add the necessary regional and language files on the server before installing SharePoint in the desired language. The operating system must provide the appropriate language support for the SharePoint product or even the installation dialog boxes cannot be displayed.

Understanding Language Template Packs

Language template packs allow site administrators to create SharePoint sites and site collections in multiple languages without requiring separate installations of Windows SharePoint Services 3.0. Language packs are installed on your front-end Web servers and contain language-specific resource files that support language-specific site templates. When you create a site or a site collection based on a language-specific site template, the text that appears on the site or site collection is displayed in the site template's language. Language packs are typically used in multinational deployments where a single server farm supports people in several different locations or in situations where sites and Web pages must be duplicated or hosted in one or more languages.

Language packs are also specific to Windows SharePoint Services 3.0 or SharePoint Server 2007 because of the number of extra templates included with SharePoint Server 2007. Table 4-1 lists the product language versions and language template packs scheduled to be available. Language packs for Windows SharePoint Services 3.0 or SharePoint Server 2007 are not currently bundled or grouped into multilingual installation packages.

Table 4-1 Product Languages and Language Template Packs

Language	SharePoint product	Language template pack
Arabic	X	X
Bulgarian		X
Catalan (LIP)		X
Chinese (Simplified)	X	X
Chinese (Traditional)	X	X
Croatian		X
Czech	X	X
Danish	X	X
Dutch	X	X
English	X	X
Estonian		X
French	X	X
German	X	X
Greek	X	X
Hebrew	X	X
Hindi		X
Hungarian	X	X
Italian	X	X
Japanese	X	X

Table 4-1 Product Languages and Language Template Packs

Language	SharePoint product	Language template pack
Korean	X	X
Latvian		X
Lithuanian		X
Norwegian	X	X
Polish	X	X
Portuguese (Brazil)	X	X
Portuguese (Portugal)	X	X
Romanian		X
Russian	X	X
Serbian (Latin)		X
Slovak		X
Slovenian		X
Spanish	X	X
Swedish	X	X
Thai	X	X
Turkish	X	X
Ukrainian		X

Installing Language Packs on Front-End Servers

After the necessary language files are installed on your Web front-end servers, you can install your language packs. They are available as individual downloads and must be installed on each of your Web front-end servers. You must install a specific language pack for each language you want to support. Also, the same language packs (and the same version of the pack) must be installed on all your Web front-end servers to ensure that each Web server can render content in the specified language.

Best Practices Install the language packs on any member of your farm that could be called into service as a Web front-end in the future.

Installing the language pack is simple and quick: Just run the Setup program. However, you must re-run the configuration wizard to modify the Config_db and register the new template support files. The steps are as follows:

1. Click Start, point to All Programs, point to Administrative Tools, and then click SharePoint Products And Technologies Configuration Wizard.

2. On the Welcome To SharePoint Products And Technologies page, click Next.
3. Click Yes in the warning dialog box that appears notifying you that some services might need to be restarted during configuration.
4. On the Modify Server Farm Settings page, click Do Not Disconnect From This Server Farm and then click Next.
5. If the Modify SharePoint Central Administration Web Administration Settings page appears, do not modify any of the default settings and then click Next.
6. On the Completing The SharePoint Products And Technologies Configuration Wizard page, click Next.
7. On the Configuration Successful page, click Finish.

Uninstalling Language Packs

If you no longer need to support a language for which you have installed a language pack, you can remove the language pack by using Add/Remove Programs in Control Panel. Uninstalling a language pack removes the language-specific site templates and resource files from your computer. All sites that were created with those language-specific site templates will no longer work. To return the functionality of the sites, simply re-install the language pack.

By default, sites and site collections are created in the language in which Windows SharePoint Services 3.0 was installed and you cannot remove that language option. In other words, if you installed the English version of SharePoint Server 2007 and then installed the French Language Pack, you cannot then remove English options. You can, however, uninstall French to remove the French option.

Hosting Sites in Different Languages

After installing one or more language packs, when a you create a site or site collection, you can choose an installed language for the site or site collection by choosing the Language-Country ID (LCID). This language ID determines the language that is used to display text and interpret text that is input on the site or site collection. For example, if you create a site in French, the site's toolbars, navigation bars, lists, and column headings appear in French. Or if you create a site in Arabic, the site's toolbars, navigation bars, lists, and column headings appear in Arabic. In addition, the default left-to-right orientation of the site changes to a right-to-left orientation to properly display Arabic text.

If it is enabled by the Shared Services Provider (SSP) administrators in the My Site configuration, users will be presented with a language selection option when first creating their personal sites. As with other sites, the language selection must be made prior to creating the site and cannot be changed afterwards. If you intend to permit personal sites to be created in various languages, the appropriate language packs should be installed and the option enabled prior to the creation of any personal sites by users.

Some user-interface elements such as error messages, notifications, and dialog boxes might not display in the language of the site because the supporting technologies—such as Microsoft .NET Framework, Microsoft Windows Workflow Foundation, Microsoft ASP.NET, and Microsoft SQL Server 2005—are localized into only a limited number of languages. Generally, these type of elements are generated for content creators and site administrators and not users.

Site Collection Administration will always be in the language of the template selected for the root site of the site collection. Subsites can be created in a language other than that of the Site Collection root site. Subsite Administration will be in the language of the subsite. If you choose to create a subsite in a language different from the parent site, the template picker changes to the language choice for the site you are creating.

> **Important** The language-specific template choice is a one-time, irreversible decision. This is *not* a choice that can be modified by adding and removing features or modifying the site definition. However, the locale of a site can be modified by the site administrator.

Creating a Variation Hierarchy of Web Sites

So what's the big deal about variations? Building on ASP.NET 2.0 Master/Layout pages and reusable content, the variation system simply creates multiple sites—similar versions of a primary or *source site*. Each variation (or *target site*) contains the same content as the primary site, only it is presented in different formats using different layout and master pages. The format change might be simpler pages for mobile devices; different chrome for intranet, extranet, and Internet users; or multiple languages for International corporations. If it is basically the same content but with a different presentation, it's called a *variation*. However, technically, to the variation system, even the source site is a variation. In the management interfaces variation sites are called Labels which is the term used in the remainder of this chapter.

Microsoft Content Management Server had the capability of linking different "channels" (*sites* in SharePoint Server 2007) so that when a page was created in the source and approved, a corresponding page was created in the target with the same content but using a different template. The SharePoint Server 2007 Variation feature extends and enhances that concept. With Content Management Server channels, the user had to go to the appropriate site. With SharePoint Server 2007 variation hierarchies, all users can go to the same root site and be redirected to the appropriate site with no user interaction. They are also presented with the option to pick a specific variation site via a field control available within the variation hierarchy.

Because, with Windows SharePoint Services 3.0 and SharePoint Server 2007, you no longer need to install different language versions of the product to support sites in different languages, language is frequently considered the focus of Variation hierarchies. Languages are, in fact, the default redirection logic. You can now support multiple languages within the same site collection.

The Variation hierarchy must be contained within a site collection and is limited to publishing content. However, it is not limited to just creating language labels of the same content. It could be based on any information about the browser, device, or user available in the page request.

Managing Variation Settings

All four pages used to configure the Variation feature are found in the Site Collection Administration column of the Site Settings page of the Site Collection. To access the Site Settings page, navigate to the root site in the site collection. Under Site Actions, select Site Settings, and then select Modify All Site Settings.

Following are the four configuration and management pages for the Variation feature:

- Variations: Configure The Variation System
- Variation Labels: Create And Manage The Variation Hierarchy
- Variation Logs: View Actions Of The Variation System, Both Successes And Failures
- Translatable Columns: Identify Content Requiring Translation

These pages will be shown and discussed throughout the following sections on planning, configuring, and managing the Variation feature.

Planning Considerations

The Variation feature works only on publishing sites, not collaborative sites. The site collection can have both publishing and collaboration features activated, but only publishing content will be pushed from source to target sites or labels. For instance, publishing subsites are created on target sites, complete with all features and resources defined in the site template for the target site language. This can include lists, document libraries, reusable content libraries, and even subsites. However, new lists, document libraries, and so on created on the source will not be copied to the target sites because they are not publishing content.

Variations must be planned—not added later to copy existing sites. Here are some important facts to keep in mind when planning variations:

- The site collection can have other content that is not part of the variation hierarchy. Variations are not replications; only content is copied, not master pages or page layout templates.
- This is a one-way push only function. Changes made in the target do not get reflected back to the source. Target sites might contain content originating at the target.
- The target workflow is respected, and the target site administrator does not have to accept the changes. Variations are not a relay race. There is only one source label, and the target of one source cannot be the source for another target. Neither the source nor target variation labels can point to existing sites.
- You do not have to create variations of everything that is published on the source site.
- The variation hierarchy publishing rules can include all available content, but the target label rules can limit what the target site accepts.
- You can create unique content, sites, workspaces, lists, and so on in the target sites. The variation system does not overwrite content on the target site with the same name as the source content if the target content was originally created on the target site.

The Variation System: An Example

The planning for variations is critical and the implementation is somewhat tedious. However, once variations are configured and working, actually using variations seems relatively simple. This summary provides a quick overview of the steps of the variation system pushing content from an English source site to a French target.

- **New content created on source site (English)** Either the English site content authors create new content (pages) or site administrators create new publishing subsites.
- **Workflow process completes for new content** The approval process for the new content is completed. Keep in mind that if there is no workflow, publishing happens instantly.
- **One-way replication to destination site (French)** The content is sent to the French site. By default, the variation system job checks every 20 seconds for new published pages and copies them to the target sites. Rules configured when creating the Variation Home specify whether reusable content is sent as a link or as a copy.

- **Chrome and layout are in French, content still English** Because the Master and Layout pages of the French site are in French, you do not overwrite those and the chrome and field controls show up in French. Great, but the text of the reusable content is still in English and the picture has the New York City skyline in the background.
- **Content translated as part of "human" workflow** Editors and translators must now get involved. A decision needs to be made as to whether it is appropriate to replace the picture, and the text needs translating. The translating can be accomplished in-house or sent out to specialists.
- **Upon approval, content appears in French on site** After the content is translated and the page meets everyone's approval, it appears in French on the French site according to the publishing rules of the French site.

Incorporating Variation Concepts into Planning

Target site administrators do not have to accept everything that is sent to the targets. And the targets can still create their own unique content, even subsite structure. Here's a summary of some of the concepts central to understanding and using variations:

- **Variations support unique security permissions** Like any other subsites within a site collection, variation sites support broken security inheritance so that each site can be the root of unique security permissions, such as members or roles.
- **Not just for languages** There is a tendency to always think of languages when Variations are mentioned. That certainly is the default use, but perhaps for your organization Variations can present a solution to other concerns. Variations can provide multilingual sites, multidevice sites, and multibranded sites with equal ease, although you must manually configure some redirection logic in the anchor site welcome page.
- **Pages must share content type, not layouts or master pages** Sharing Master or Layout templates across variation labels would defeat the purpose of Variations. For content to be pushed from source to target, it must share a content type. If the target site does not have a content type defined in common with the source, you will see an error message similar to the following in the variation log:

  "The variation system failed to pair up pages
  http://portal.contoso.msft/ENU/News/Pages/Default.aspx and
  http://portal.contoso.msft /JP/News/Pages/Default.aspx
  because their Content Types do not match. "

- **Separate approval process** The approval processes of all sites are respected by the process. The storage locations at the target should be configured so that the arrival of new content will automatically trigger a new workflow. However, in some scenarios, a workflow might not be required. For instance, if you are creating a variation simply to have a "cleaner" site for mobile users and no translation is involved, automatic publishing would be desired. If you were creating variations for your extranet or Internet site of some selected intranet content, perhaps no workflow is necessary.
- **Target pages start with source page content** The target pages start with the same content type and the same content in the same fields for the pages–they are just presented with different templates. Suppose that on the source site the page has a field control that displays corporate status reports from internal lists or databases and you do not want to display that on some target sites. Simple: do not put the field control on the master or layout page in the target site. The rest of the content will be displayed, but there is no presentation available to build or display the status reports.
- **"Flag Control" chooses variation for user** Here is the fun part! When the user hits the root site of the variation, information in the HTTP request header will identify certain characteristics of the browser, operating system, and user. One is the language of the browser. So if the "Flag Control" in the redirect page on the root site is set to identify language (because your variations are based on language), the request is redirected to the appropriate language site.

  The flag control does not have to be set to identify language; it can be any attribute of the browser or user. So, if the users are browsing from a Macintosh or Linux do you want to invest in a variation of your site that only supports their browsers? And if the user is browsing from his cell phone, maybe the stock ticker field control would not be a good implementation. Think about the possibilities.
- **Hide variation sites in navigation** By default, all variation sites will be displayed the Global and Current navigation field controls. However, the Site Collection administrator can choose to hide them in either or both locations in the Navigation settings page of Site Settings. Likewise, a link to the root of the variation hierarchy will be available for direct access by users who click on it in navigation, but it can be hidden just like the subsites. The root site can also be addressed by including the full path to a page that bypasses the variationroot.aspx, such as the original default.aspx.

- **No built-in translation tool** Neither Windows SharePoint Services 3.0 nor SharePoint Server 2007 provide a translation service to translate text from one language to another. However, SharePoint Server 2007 does provide tools to assist you in managing the translation process. See the "Managing Translations" section later in this chapter for a discussion of those tools.

Planning Variation Configurations

Now that you are familiar with the concepts of the variation system and some big-picture planning considerations, you need to determine the options to take when configuring your variation hierarchy.

Configuring the Variation System

Figure 4-1 illustrates configuration choices on the behavior of variations discussed in this section.

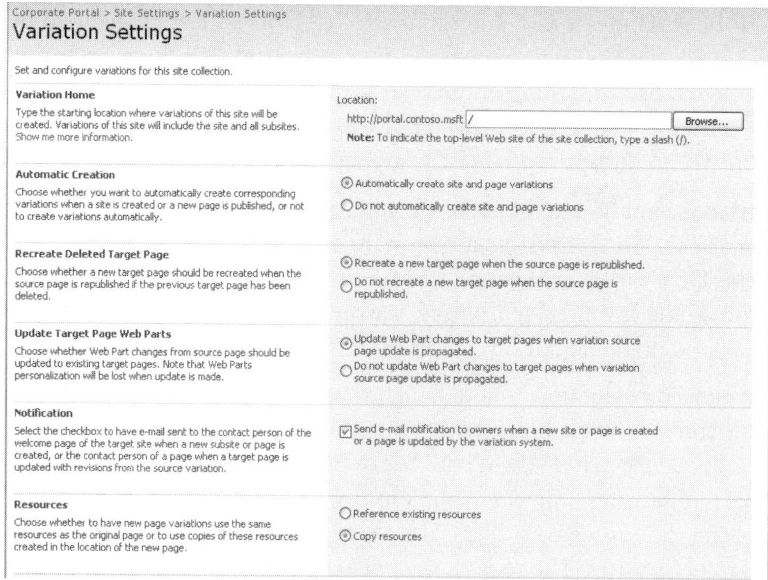

Figure 4-1 Variation process settings

Six planning decisions that are global to the variation system of the site collection must be made on this page:

- Variation Home
- Automatic Creation

- Recreate Deleted Target Page
- Update Target Page Web Parts
- Notification
- Resources

Variation Home

All variations must share a common root within the site collection. This root can be at any level, but the variations must all be at an equal level just below the root. This becomes a very important planning issue because users normally never see the root site of the hierarchy.

Once a site is designated as the root of the variation hierarchy, the default page is changed to a special page, variationroot.aspx, which contains the redirection logic to detect the browser language or mobile setting and redirect to the appropriate site. This decision cannot be changed later without completely rebuilding the variation hierarchy. This can be the root of a site collection or any location lower in the site collection tree. This home site should not be used for content other than the redirecting page and the default reusable content libraries because users will not normally access this site. This site can be a publishing site or a publishing and collaboration site. Other subsites of this variation home can still be used normally. To specify the root of a site collection, type a slash (/) in the dialog box (as shown in Figure 4-1).

Automatic Creation

Do you want content to be created on targets automatically or manually? *Manual publishing* allows the content editors and administrators of the source variation to control what is pushed to the target site or sites. *Automatic publishing* pushes all published content with a matching content type to all target sites. In both instances, however, the target site administrator or workflow approvers can reject content or modify the publication of content.

The moving of content can be configured to be either manual or automatic when publishing. Your business needs will drive this decision. If you select the Do Not Automatically Create Site And Page Variations option, you need to trigger the process manually or with a schedule.

To initiate the manual variation process, complete the following steps:

1. From the Action menu, select Manage Site Content And Structure.
2. The shortcut menu of the published object in the source variation contains the option to initiate a new variation as shown in Figure 4-2. For a site, select New, and then select Site Variation. For a page, select New Page Variation.

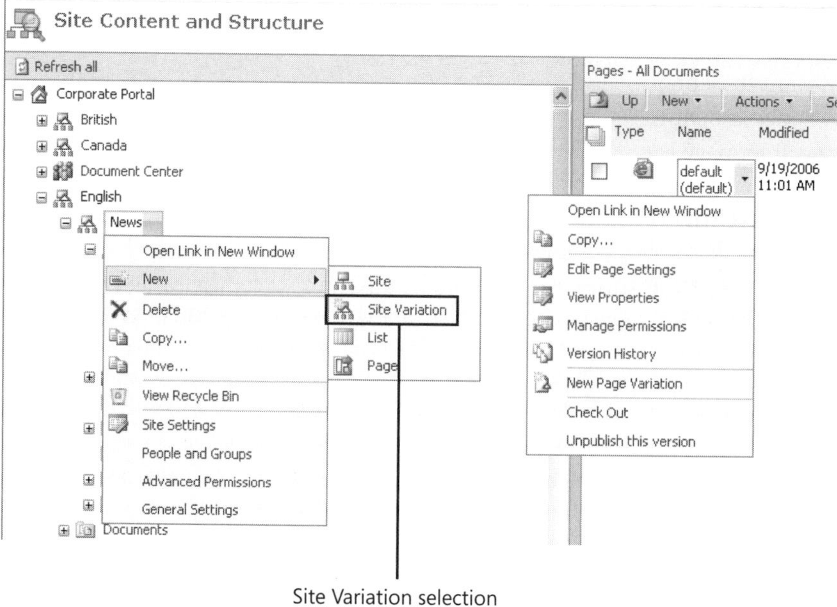

Figure 4-2 Manually initiating a new variation object

3. In the dialog box that opens, select the variation target and the name and location for the object in the target. While the automatic operation uses the same name on target variations as is used in the source variation, with the manual process you can use different names and URLs on each target and still maintain the variation relationships with the source.

Recreate Deleted Target Page

If the administrator of a target site decides that content is not needed on the target, she can choose not to publish it and to delete it. The default action, should the source content be republished due to content publication date changes, is to push the content to the target again. You can choose not to overwrite target choices. This option applies only to content that was deleted at the target site.

Update Target Page Web Parts

Do you want to overwrite Web Parts on target pages with those on source pages? A major consideration here is that Web Parts might need to be customized or rewritten for the language of the site where they are being used. These customizations and personalizations are lost when the Web Parts are overwritten by the variation system.

Notification

Do you want the variation system to notify the owners of the target site of any changes, or do you want to depend on the workflow process of the site? If a subsite is created, an e-mail message is sent to the owner of the parent subsite in which the new subsite is created. If a target page is updated as a result of a change made to its source variation, a message is sent to the owner of the site in which the page list exists.

Resources

Do you want the reusable content (resources) in the new pages to be links to centralized resources? You can choose whether the new page variations contain a link to the resources used in the original page or get a copy of the resources in the new page. Like all instances of links to resources, this choice permits changes in a single location to be instantly reflected throughout the sites. However, in a multilanguage scenario, the target owners might want to replace the content with pictures more appropriate for their audience or translated re-useable content.

Designating Source and Target Sites with Variation Labels

Next, you create a label for each site in the set of variations, including one that you designate as the source. Every other site becomes a target by default. Be careful here!

Important There is no method for correcting your choice once you create the variation hierarchy.

To create a variation label, open the Create Variation Label page shown in Figure 4-3.

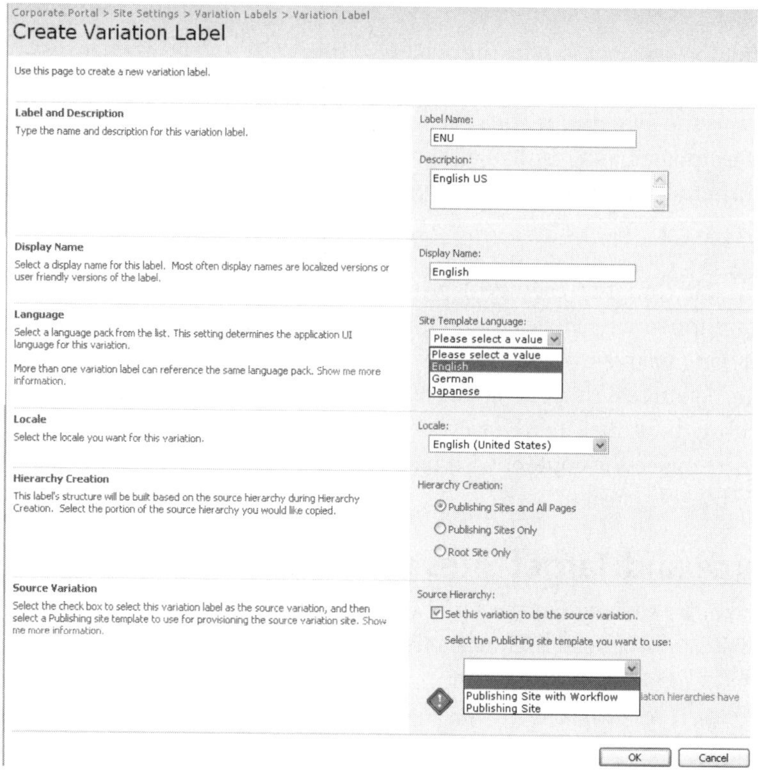

Figure 4-3 Configuring variation labels

There are several planning issues involved with creating variation labels. Consider each before creating the variation label. You'll need the information to complete each of the following sections on the Create Variation Label page:

- **Label Name** This unique name serves to identify the label in the database and in management tools, but it also identifies the site in the URL. It should be short but identify the language and the locale. For instance, to identify US English, you can use the standard language name abbreviation, ENU, or the language ID, 1033. Because users will rarely be typing this value, the value should be useful to administrators and support personnel.
- **Label Description** Normally exposed only in the management tools, this text box is used to further clarify the purpose of the site.
- **Display Name** Because the display name is used by both the Master Pages and the Navigation controls as the name of the site, it should be a short but descriptive name.

- **Site Template Language** The language selected represents the language ID, and the language ID determines the language that is used to display text and interpret text that is input on the site. This language selection determines the language pack templates and resources to use in creating the site. More than one site can reference the same language ID. SharePoint will support 36 languages at its release.
- **Locale** These settings reflect languages and cultural conventions as they are used in different parts of the world. These variations can occur within languages, such as "English US" and "English UK". The Locale ID controls the numbering, currency, sorting, calendar, and time formatting for the Web site. Locales expand the languages supported by SharePoint. SharePoint supports 135 separate locales. Although the language cannot be changed later, the locale can be changed by the site administrator in Site Settings. However, it cannot be changed in this interface.

> **Best Practices** Determine the language support you might need for your farm and establish a standard naming convention based on industry standards. For example, English might not be sufficiently distinctive because your farm could have 13 different English language sites serving the various English locales supported.

- **Hierarchy Creation** The three options here control only what portions of the source variation site will be used to create the target site initially:
    - **Publishing sites and all pages** This option specifies the entire site, including subsites and pages. This includes copying reusable content used in existing pages if the variation rules specify copying this content. However, if the reusable content of the source site is contained in nondefault document libraries, the containers must be manually created with the same names on the target sites before the content can be copied.

      Publishing sites are created at the target label using the site templates of the language specified for the label. The default content of the site is whatever is specified in the template, including the empty Default.aspx file for the sites. Therefore, if the source label has a customized Default.aspx file, the customizations of that page will not appear in the target variation until it has been modified again at the source or manually pushed to the target. Nondefault pages at the source will be pushed to the target as a separate operation once the site is created. Lists, document libraries, Web Parts, and features that have been created or activated on the source but that are not defined in the site template will not be created on the target.

- ❑ **Publishing sites only** The content of the source variation is not pushed to this target variation; only the publishing sites that exist on the source are created on the target. These sites are created according to the site definition contained in the corresponding site template of the language specified for the target or label. New content pages or modified content pages will be pushed to the target, as they are published at the source variation. Existing pages at the source can be manually pushed to the target later.
- ❑ **Root site only** Only the root site will be created at the target variation according to the site definition contained in the corresponding site template of the language specified for the target or label. Existing pages will not be pushed to the target variation.

  This selection is useful when creating a custom variation target that requires only certain subsites of a source variation. For example, the source variation contains subsite A, subsite B, and subsite C, but the variation needs only the tree structures of subsite A and subsite B. By selecting Root Site Only and then manually creating a site variation at this target for subsites A and B, all content (existing and newly published) will be pushed to the target. No content from source subsite C will be pushed to the target because no variation relationship exists for that subsite and this target. Other target variations for this variation system can be configured differently.

- **Source Variation** There can be only one source variation per hierarchy and only one variation hierarchy per site collection. Once this selection is made and the hierarchy is constructed, it cannot be changed without completely removing the hierarchy and reconstructing it. Only the source variation site presents the option to select the site template, and your choices are publishing the site with or without workflow. By default, only publishing sites can be created under this site. If you add collaboration features to a site or subsite, these features will not be copied by the variation system to target sites.

Important Of the choices available on this page, only the Display Name and the Description can be modified in this interface once the variation hierarchy is built. The locale can be modified in the Site Settings by the site administrator.

Building Sites with the Variation Hierarchy

Click the Create Hierarchies button shown in Figure 4-4 and SharePoint Server 2007 will build sites in the appropriate language with the template you chose. Because the source site is created as a new site during this process, you can choose to build the hierarchy with only the source variation label defined. This option permits you to complete the basic structure of your source site, test it, and obtain approval from your stakeholders before adding variation targets.

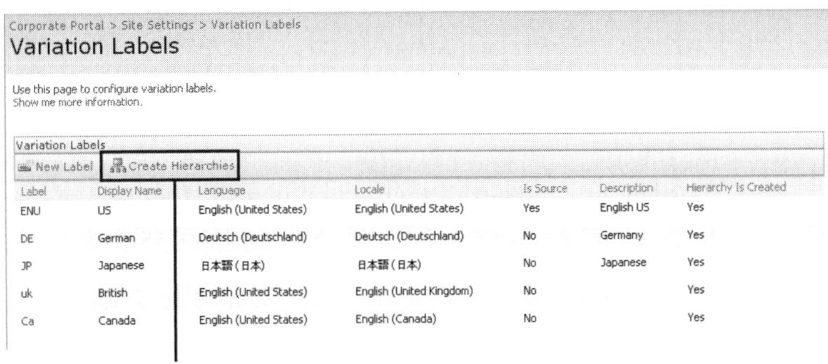

Figure 4-4 Managing the variation hierarchy

The variation hierarchy can be modified by adding or removing variation labels at any time. After you create the new Variation Label, click Create Hierarchies to create the new sites from the current source label.

Propagating Content from Source to Target Sites

Based on the choices you made on the page shown in Figure 4-4, when content is published in the source site, a variation of the content will be created in all targets. Depending on the workflow settings of those sites, the content will be published immediately, a workflow will be initiated first, or the content publishing will wait for a manual workflow to be started. With auto-replication enabled, the delay should not be more than one minute for moving the pages to the other variation sites.

Only publishing content published on the source site is pushed to the targets. Publishing content will include any sub-sites created on the source site which have the publishing feature activated. This publishing feature is available for activation on all sites created in SharePoint Server 2007 but is not activated by default on sites designed primarily for collaboration. If the publishing feature is activated on a sub-site, that site will be created on the appropriate target sites and any publishing content of the site will be pushed to the target(s).

Also, the site templates available by default for creating sub-sites of publishing sites are Publishing Site with Workflow and Publishing Site. Additional sites can be exposed in the Create Site page by adding them as follows: select Site Settings, then open the Page Layouts & Template Settings page of the root site of the Variation hierarchy.

Managing Variation Sites

Target sites are managed separately, with different users in the roles for the sites. What do the targets sites have in common? They have a Site Collection hosting the variation hierarchy, a root site that is redirecting traffic, Content Types, and content that is accepted by the other target sites. There are some issues to be managed either proactively or reactively.

Customize Web Parts for Variation Sites

Most Web Parts are not designed to be variation-aware, and for many types of Web Parts this is not an issue. Other Web Parts become dysfunctional if copied from one site to another. For example, the list Web Parts always reference lists using the site-level globally unique identifier (GUID), which is not modified when the Web Part is copied from one site to another. You can choose the option to not copy Web Parts as part of the variation system. Unfortunately, this is a global choice for all Web Parts, and you can't select it only for certain types of Web Parts.

Custom Web Parts can be written to be variation-aware in that they contain the logic to reset information and content during the variation process.

Managing Corrections

By default, the variation system cannot distinguish between a minor correction to a page and a major revision. It only recognizes that there is now a new major version published that needs to be copied to all target sites. By default, there is no process available to notify the target site administrator that the change consists only of a corrected spelling of a word in the source language, which has probably already been corrected during the translation process.

A solution is needed to avoid the unnecessary retranslation of pages. One solution is to create a custom Boolean column for the page content type that will be used by the content editors on the source site to mark new versions as "local corrections" not requiring republishing on target sites. On the target sites, a custom workflow is developed to check every new publishing page for that column and delete new pages where the attribute is set to True.

Customizing Search for Variation Sites

To enable users to conduct searches in their own languages, you can create a Search Center with Tabs site in the source site that will then be re-created in the target sites in the appropriate language. Or, target site administrators can individually create a Search Center on their site. You might then choose to hide the default search center. Your developer can modify the master page to remove the search box that appears on each page or simply redirect the advanced link to the local search center's advanced search page.

Note The Search Center template does not have publishing feature activated and therefore will not be pushed by the Variation process. The Search Center with Tabs does include publishing features and is pushed by the Variation process.

You might also need to set up different search scopes for your variation sites to limit the search to specific Language-Country IDs (LCIDs). Alternatively, your developer might be able to add special search criteria for languages on a custom search query. See Chapter 16, "Enterprise Search and Indexing Architecture and Administration," for more information on configuring search and on the resources provided to facilitate search and indexing in multilanguage scenarios.

Removing Variation Hierarchy and Sites

If you remove a site from the variation hierarchy, the following will be true:

- The site will no longer reflect any additions or changes made to the source variation.
- The site remains a fully functional site but must be accessed through normal navigation, as it is no longer listed in the redirection scheme.
- You cannot re-establish the site within the variation hierarchy because you have deleted the variation label. New variation labels cannot be pointed to established sites.
- If you delete the label for the source variation, the remaining sites still function and the redirection functions for all sites except the source. However, you cannot designate a new source variation, and any subsequent changes must be made manually at each site. There is a warning that you are deleting the source variation.

Removing a Site

To remove a site from the variation hierarchy, complete the following steps:

1. On the Site Actions menu choose Site Settings, Modify All Site Settings.
2. In the Site Collection Administration column, open Variation Labels page and in the drop-down menu for selected site's Label select Delete. You must confirm the deletion.

Removing a Variation Hierarchy

To remove the entire variation hierarchy, complete the following steps:

1. In the Site Collection Administration column, open the Variation Labels page, and delete all variation labels.
2. In the Site Collection Administration column, open theVariation Settings page, remove the root site designation and click OK. All sites now function independently.

Removing Redirection Functionality

To remove the redirection functionality, complete the following steps:

1. In Internet Explorer, enter the full URL for the root site including the name of the welcome page file in the URL. Normally, the Welcome page would be default.aspx.
2. From the Site Actions page, choose Site Settings, Modify All Site Settings, and then click Welcome Page in the Look and Feel column.
3. Reset the Welcome page to a page other than the Variationroot.aspx. You can delete or hide the Variationroot.aspx.

> **Note** Any site in the variation hierarchy cannot be deleted until the corresponding variation label has been deleted. Deleting the variation label does not remove the site or its content.

Managing Translations

In a multilanguage variation hierarchy, translation of content will be the prevailing management task and it certainly deserves special attention in this chapter. This translation task might involve documents as well as page content. Neither Windows SharePoint Services 3.0 nor SharePoint Server 2007 provide a translation service to translate text from one language to another. Your organization might have translation capabilities in-house or need to engage the services of an external provider. SharePoint Server 2007 has addressed both options.

Local Translation Management Tools

SharePoint Server 2007 provides three translation management tools designed to assist you in automating your local translation processes:

- **Translation Management Workflow** Manages the translation of a document into one or more languages. It creates and routes copies of a source document in a Translation Management Library to designated translators for translation. The workflow creates placeholder documents, and both assigns and tracks translation tasks for each language version of the source document. If the source document changes, the workflow assigns tasks to the appropriate translators to update the translation versions. This special workflow is available only for Translation Management Libraries and can be activated in site collection features.

- **Translation Management Library** A document library template available for SharePoint Server 2007 sites that is designed specifically to help organizations create, store, and manage translated documents.
- **Translators lists** Custom lists that provide information to workflows about the available translators and their language capabilities.

What Is a Translation Management Library?

The Translation Management Library helps organizations create, store, and manage translated documents by providing both views and specific features that facilitate the manual document translation process. The Translation Management Library is designed specifically to store documents and their translations. The library tracks the relationship between a source document (an original version of a document) and its translations, and it groups all these documents together to make them easy to find. Additionally, the library can be configured with one or more special Translation Management Workflows that are designed to help manage the manual document translation process.

The library has customizations that help organizations store and manage document translations:

- A required language property field for all documents saved or uploaded to the library ensures that all documents are identified by language.
- Columns in the default library view display information about a document's Language, Translation Status, Source Document Version, and Translation Workflow status.
- Users can create relationships between a translated document and its source document by specifying whether or not a document is a translation of an existing document in the library when they upload a document to the library.

Creating a Translation Management Library

To make the Translation Management Library template available for a publishing site, follow these steps:

1. On the Site Actions menu, choose Site Settings, Modify All Site Settings.
2. In the Site Administration column, open the Site Features page.
3. Click the Activate button next to Translation Management Library.

From the Create page, you can now create a Translation Management Library. This process includes the options of creating and adding a Translation Management Workflow to that library and creating a translators list to be used by the workflow. You must have the Manage Lists permission to create a Translation Management Library for a site.

Planning You might need more than one Translation Management Library. Although one library can support multiple workflows, you might have confidential or sensitive material that requires translation and must be managed in a more restricted environment.

To create a Translation Management Library, complete the following steps:

1. From the Site Actions menu, select View All Site Content, and then click Create to open the New page.
2. Under Libraries, click Translation Management Library. This starts a series of configuration pages for creating the library, the workflow, and, optionally, the translators list. The first of these pages is shown in Figure 4-5.

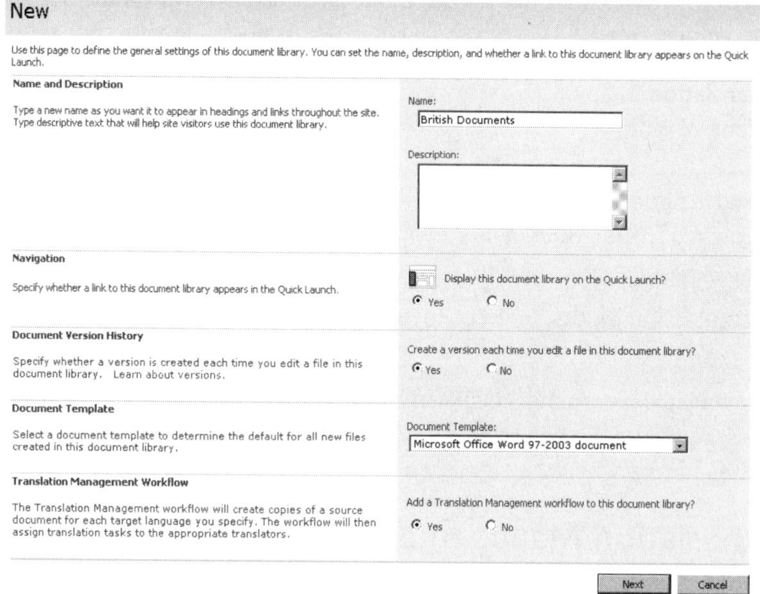

Figure 4-5 Creating a Translation Management Library

3. Complete the information on the New page:
   - **Name And Description** Required. You should have a naming convention defined for library names because they appear not only at the top of the library page but also in the URL and in navigational elements. This name should be short but unique and descriptive.

     Although a description of the purpose of the library is optional, it appears at the top of the library page, underneath the name of the library. If you plan to mail-enable the library, you might add the e-mail address of the library here to make it readily available to users.

- **Navigation** Indicate whether you want the library to appear on the Quick Launch menu.
- **Document Version History** Choose whether you want a version created each time a document is edited. You might or might not need a version each time a file is checked into the library. This decision can be revised if needed, and you can choose later whether you want to store both major and minor versions and how many versions of each you want to track.
- **Document Template** Click the type of default file that you want to be used as a template for files that are created in the library. You might have multiple Translation Management Libraries for different types of documents. Although this chapter has focused on sites and pages in various languages, many other documents stored in document libraries will need translation as well.
- **Translation Management Workflow** Click Yes to add a Translation Management Workflow to the library.

4. Click Next to configure the Translation Management Workflow and open the Add A Workflow page shown in Figure 4-6.

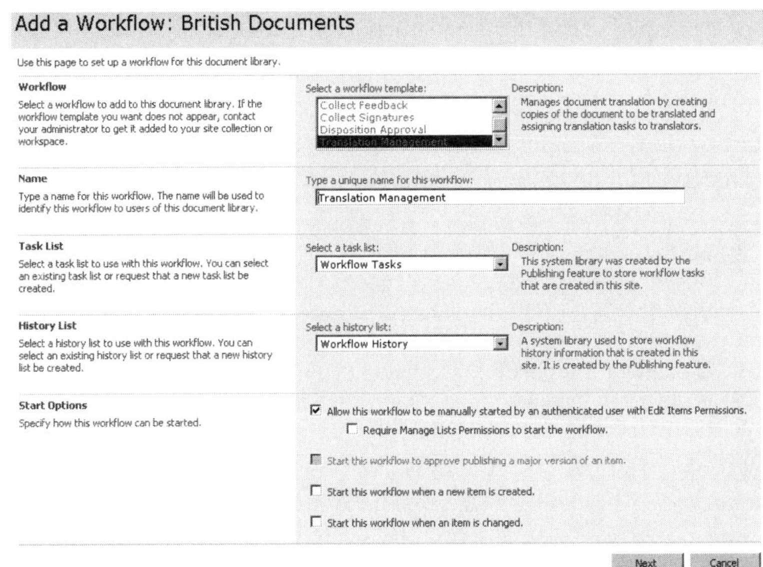

Figure 4-6 Configuring the Add A Workflow page

5. Configure the new workflow by providing the following information:

- **Workflow** Select a workflow to add to this document library. The default value is Translation Management, which has special functionality needed to select translators and assign tasks to the selected translators.
- **Name** You might have more than one Translation Management Workflow, so a naming convention should be planned and include a unique name for this workflow.
- **Task List** Specify a task list to use with this workflow. You can use the default, Workflow Tasks, or you can create a new one. If you use the default task list, workflow participants will be able to find and view their workflow tasks easily by using the My Tasks view of the Task List.

  However, if the tasks for this workflow will involve or reveal sensitive or confidential data that you want to keep separate from the general Task List, select Create A New Task List from the Select A Task List drop-down list.

  > **Note** Translation Management Workflows will probably involve numerous tasks, and you might have numerous Translation Management Workflows. You might want to create task lists for each workflow to simplify the task lists.

- **History List** Select a history list to use with this workflow. Because the history list displays all of the events that occur during each instance of the workflow, you might need more than one history list for the same reasons you need more than one task list.
- **Start Options** Deciding how, when, or by whom a workflow can be started is an important planning decision. This can be modified later.

  > **Note** Some options might not be available if they are not supported by the workflow template you selected or are dependent on the configuration of the library. For example, the option Start This Workflow To Approve Publishing A Major Version Of An Item is available only if support for major and minor versioning has been enabled for the library and if the workflow template you selected can be used for content approval.

6. Click Next.
7. In the Lists Of Languages And Translators section, you might have two options:
   a. If a translators list already exists for your site, you can click Use An Existing List Of Languages And Translators From The Site, and then select the list you want to use.

b. If no list exists, click Create A New List Of Languages And Translators For This Workflow, and give a unique name for the list in the List Name box based on your naming convention.

8. If you want to begin adding names to the new translators list when you finish customizing the workflow, select the Open The New Translators List In A Separate Window check box.

   These lists appear in the View All Site Content page and can be managed directly. In some organizations, the management of workflows might be separated from the management of translators lists. In these cases, you assign management of these lists to specific people who are knowledgeable about the capabilities of your translator teams and the person configuring the workflow will need to use an existing list.

9. In the Due Date section, the option to set a due date is available only if you chose to have the workflow start automatically when documents are either created or changed in the library. Business requirements will define the range of days within which workflow tasks should be completed for workflows that start automatically.

10. In the Complete The Workflow section, select the When The Source Document Is Changed check box if you want the workflow to be completed whenever all tasks are completed or someone changes the source document for the translation. If you do not select this option, a translator could continue to work on a document that has been replaced and no longer needs translating. By default, the workflow will be completed when all translation tasks are completed.

11. If you chose to create a new list of translators for use with this workflow and to have that list open in a new window, a separate window opens after you click OK, and you can begin adding names to the list.

12. You can add a Translation Management Workflow to an existing Translation Management Library at any time in the library settings, Workflow Settings. You might want to add multiple Translation Management Workflows to one library if you want to have separate translators lists for different source documents in the same library, or different translation rules for different source documents.

Uploading a Document

Now that you have the necessary components in place, you are ready to start your translation management process by placing a document in the library. When you upload a document to a Translation Management Library, you need to supply profile information about the language and translation status of that document. Documents that you upload to a Translation Management Library remain checked out to you until you fill out the required profile properties for the document.

1. In your Translation Management Library on the Upload menu, click Upload Document.

2. In the Upload Document section, click Browse to locate the document you want, and then click Open and then click OK.
3. On the properties page for the document, complete the Name and Title boxes if they have not already been populated with data.
4. If the document you are uploading is a completed translation of a source document in the library, type the version number of the source document in the Source Document Version box. This information will be set automatically if you use a workflow to manage translation.

   For example, if your document is a translation of the first version of the source document, type **1.0**. If the document you are uploading is not a translation, you should leave this blank.
5. In the Translation Status section, select the value that applies to your document. If the document you are uploading is a source document on which translations will be based, you should leave this blank. This information will be set automatically if you use a workflow to manage translation.
6. In the Language section, select the language property that applies to your document or click Specify Your Own Value, and then type the language you want.
7. If the document you are uploading is a translation of another document that already exists in the library, click Yes, and then select the source document for your document. If the document you are uploading is not a translation of another document in the library, click No.
8. When you check in the document, the workflow will be started if configured to start automatically. Otherwise, you need to start the workflow from the drop-down menu of the uploaded document.

Completing the Translation Management Workflow Process

The Translation Management Workflow works with a translators list, which lists the people responsible for translating documents into a specific language.

When the Translation Management Workflow starts on a source document, it creates a copy of the source document for every translator specified in the translators list for the source document's language. The workflow also sets the appropriate language property for each placeholder document and creates a relationship between the placeholder and the source document. The workflow then assigns a translation task to each of the translators. The workflow participants receive e-mail alerts about their workflow tasks.

After a translator completes a translation task, he marks it as complete. When all translation tasks in a workflow are completed, the workflow is marked as Complete.

The workflow can be configured so that it ends automatically and cancels all uncompleted translation tasks if the source document changes while the workflow is in progress.

Customizing a Translators List

When you start a translation workflow, the workflow creates a copy of the source document for each of the target languages specified in the translators list for the workflow. It then assigns the translation tasks to the translators specified for these languages in the translators list. If there is more than one translator specified for a specific type of translation (for example, for a translation from English to Spanish), each of these translators will receive a translation task.

The translators lists are custom lists with special columns used by the workflow. These lists appear in the View All Site Content page and can be managed directly. When adding translators to the lists, you will supply the user name of the translator, the original language of the source documents as the Translating From entry, and the desired translated language as the Translated To entry. You can browse for the user name or type it in directly, and you can pick languages from a list or enter the language directly.

When the workflow starts, it creates translation tasks for each of the qualified translators in the translators list. The tasks request that the source document be translated into the specified language. If e-mail has been enabled for the site, the workflow participants will also receive an e-mail notification of their translation tasks.

Forwarding to External Translation Services

The tools provided for translation management are designed for internal translation processes. However, your business capabilities and requirements might require that the content be shipped to external translation service companies.

To use an external translation service, three processes must be accomplished:

1. You identify, package, and ship the content to be translated to your translation service provider.
2. The translation service provider opens, translates, repackages, and returns the content to you.
3. You place the translated content back on your site without breaking the variation relationships established in your hierarchy.

The SharePoint Server 2007 Variation feature provides the tools described below that you can use to manage the external translation shipment processes.

Identifying Content Needing Translation

You can identify the portions of the objects needing translation in the Translatable Column Settings page, shown in Figure 4-7, which you access through the Site Collection Settings page. This tool uses your selections to produce a Manifest.xml file within the variation export packages that identifies the content within the package needing translation.

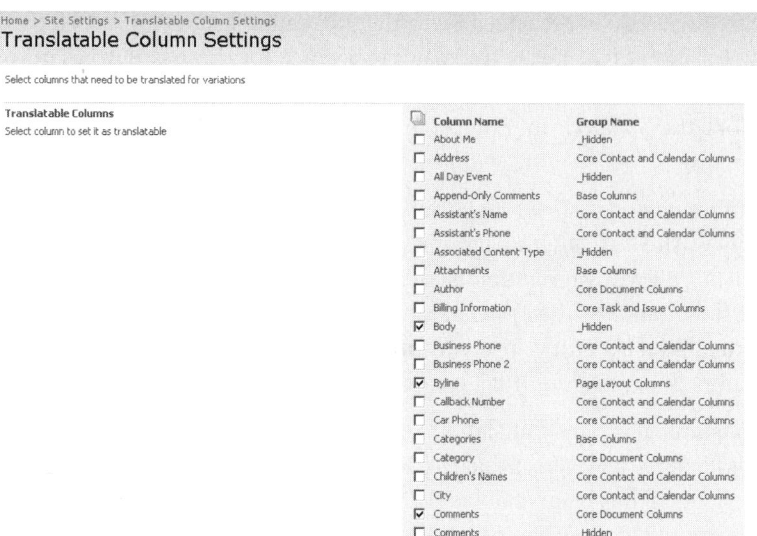

Figure 4-7 Translatable Column Settings page

Using Variation Packaging for Export and Import

The Variation feature adds two tools to the drop menu of target sites within your hierarchy: Export Variation and Import Variation. These tools, working with the translatable column settings, package the variation pages of an entire site along with a Manifest.xml file into a CAB file with a .cmp extension.

You can then ship this file to your translation service provider, and they will open it, identify the content needing translation as identified by the Manifest.xml, translate the content, and repackage it for return to you. You can choose to use a document library and SharePoint alerts to assist in the transfer process.

You access these tools on the Site Content And Structure page, as shown in Figure 4-8.

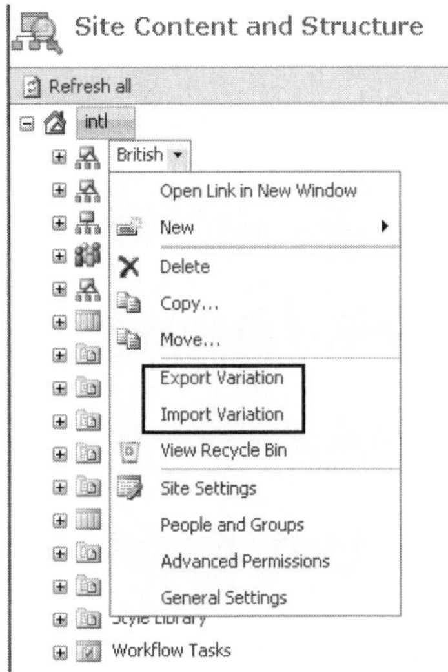

Figure 4-8 Export Variation and Import Variation menu options

These processes hook into the prime API in the object model. They are able to distinguish the variation publishing content, use the translatable content configuration, and build a Manifest.xml file during the content packaging process. This eliminates the need for packaging any site content that is not part of the variation process. The import function also works at the site level, and by importing at this level you can maintain the variation relationship of the imported content. Content that is checked out by users is not packaged during the export. The export package only contains page content since other site content such as master pages, layout pages, etc. are already in the appropriate language for the site.

If your variation target has subsites, you can export and import at any site level. For example, if you have created a News site at the source variation, you can export or import at the News site level of any target variation if that happens to be the only site with content needing translation.

Note Although SharePoint Designer has the capability of exporting a single page, it does not use the same API and cannot distinguish variation content. The package file that it creates is in a different format than the .cmp package and does not contain the Manifest.xml file identifying content needing translation. Improperly replacing a page on the variation target can break the variation relationship between the source and target pages.

Real World Solutions for External Translation Services

Third-party companies will offer external translation services for organization which do not have in-house translation capabilities. These services will need to provide applications that can provide the following processes:

- Download the Variation exported packages from published locations, probably SharePoint Document Libraries which can generate alerts. The application may have a workflow capability that can be triggered by an alert or may crawl the document library on a schedule.
- Open Variation exported packages and manage the human translation of the content requiring translation.
- Repackage translated content back into the appropriate format to be imported by your Variation process.
- Upload the package to the designated published location, probably a SharePoint Document library which can be configured with a custom workflow automatically initiated to manage the placement of the translated content in the appropriate location.

You would then initiate the process by packaging the site into a .cmp file with the accompanying Manifest.xml to identify what needs translating. You then place this file in a location that the external service checks periodically for new content. The service application will pick up the package, open it, and send the identified content to be translated by human teams. Their workflow should include checks to make certain that the source language sentence has not been translated previously to avoid duplicate translation efforts.

When the translation is approved externally, the service workflow repackages the returning translation with the remaining data back into a .cmp file and returns it to the designated location. You then import it into the appropriate site and continue your workflow process.

Deploying Content

Your content is ready and approved on your staging server. Now it's time to move this published content to your production servers which will probably be read only. SharePoint Server 2007 provides a feature evolved from Microsoft Content Management Server that will deploy content from one farm to another over the http or https protocol.

This feature, called *Content Deployment*, is covered in detail in Chapter 11, "Web Content Management and Publishing Features." This section focuses on how the choices you've made regarding languages and variations affect content deployment planning.

Your Web publication design may involve servers that are centrally located or dispursed around the world (geo-deployed). Content deployment can be used for both local and geo-deployed multilanguage sites when the various language sites are self-contained sites and not part of a variation hierarchy. The content deployment process is not language aware and deploys content in any language.

With local deployments from the staging process to production, content deployment is a useful tool for variation hierarchies because you are deploying the entire site collection. The Content Deployment feature can also be used in conjunction with the Variation feature to enable geo-deployed multilingual solutions. The goal of a geo-deployed solution would be to place the sites in various languages physically close to the largest user base of the language. However, this scenario does introduce some complications.

Although you might want to use variations to create the various language copies of the source site and then use content deployment to stage the individual sites to different servers around the globe (geo-deployment), this is not recommended.

The recommended method to implement a geo-deployment solution is to have Content Deployment jobs that deploy the entire site collection variation hierarchy rather than deploying only sites for specific languages. Some variation functionalities, such as picker controls, require the entire site collection to work properly. Using this approach, it's possible to have read-only instances of the same site collection distributed in multiple locations. Although using Content Deployment jobs will deploy more content than just an isolated site, it does assure functionality of the site collection.

If you are going to experiment with other content deployment scenarios, the treatment of reusable content should be considered in your trials. Also, remember that Content Deployment jobs only deploy content, not custom code; therefore, if you developed custom Web Parts or templates, they must be installed on the Content Deployment target sites.

Summary

This chapter has covered the multilanguage capabilities of Windows SharePoint Services 3.0 and SharePoint Server 2007, focusing on planning and maintenance issues revolving around hosting sites in multiple languages on a single SharePoint farm. The integration of Microsoft Content Management Server functions into SharePoint Server 2007 introduced a new Variation feature, which automatically creates content in multiple presentations (including languages) based on content created in a source site. This chapter covered the planning and design issues involved in implementing and maintaining a variation hierarchy.

Although SharePoint Server 2007 can create each variation target in a designated language, human translation of content is still required. This chapter covered the tools provided to help manage this manual translation process and to manage content for external translation service providers. Finally, this chapter addressed some of the planning and design considerations for using content deployment in both local deployments and geo-deployments.

Chapter 5

Installing Microsoft Office SharePoint Server 2007

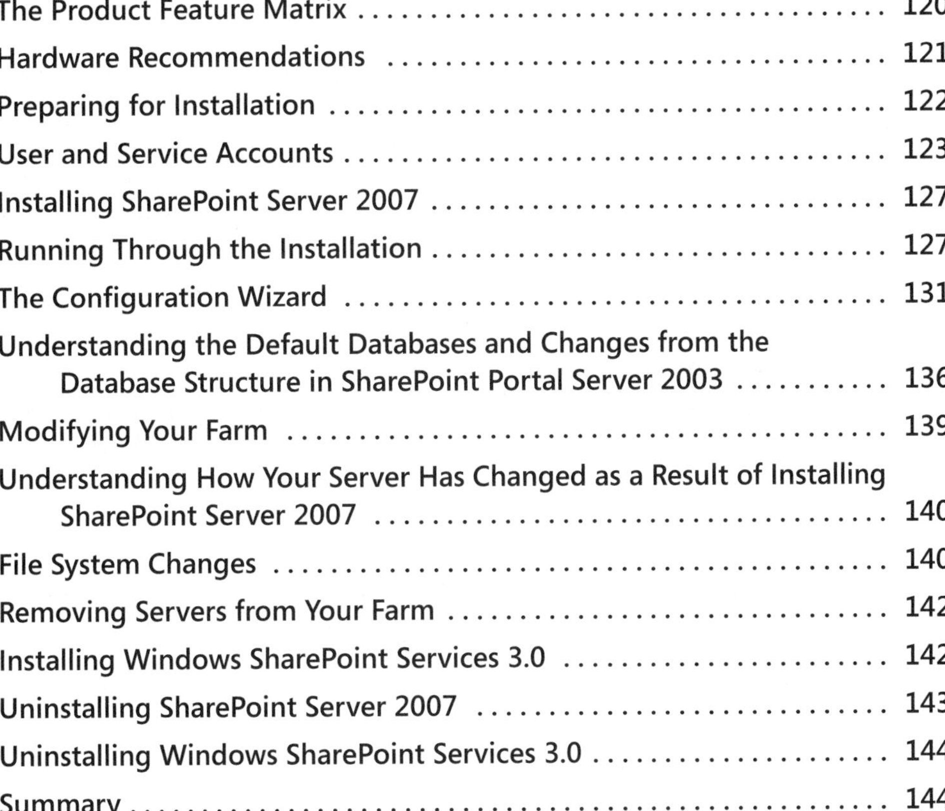

This chapter focuses on the installation of Microsoft Office SharePoint Server 2007. The goal of the chapter is to prepare you to plan for the installation of Office SharePoint Server 2007 and Microsoft Windows SharePoint Services 3.0. You will also learn how to add and remove servers from a server farm. This chapter also covers the process for uninstalling the products and items that are not removed during the uninstall process.

Installing SharePoint Server 2007 is a straightforward process, but some of the decisions you'll make are pivotal to your farm deployment. There's much to learn, so let's get started.

The Product Feature Matrix

The first installation decision you'll make is to select the appropriate SharePoint product for your implementation. In general, Windows SharePoint Services 3.0 offers only collaboration tools, but is covered by the operating system license. SharePoint Server 2007 is offered in two editions: Standard and Enterprise. The binaries installed are the same for both the Standard and Enterprise editions, but some features are disabled in the Standard edition. The same installation source is used for both editions, and the choice of Standard or Enterprise is determined by the Product Key entered during installation. An installation of Standard Edition can be upgraded to Enterprise in Central Administration without performing additional installation. To change from Enterprise to Standard however requires an uninstall and reinstall of the product. Table 5-1 provides a feature comparison of Windows SharePoint Services 3.0 and the two versions of SharePoint Server 2007.

Table 5-1 Feature Comparison

	Windows SharePoint Services 3.0	SharePoint Server 2007 Standard Edition	SharePoint Server 2007 Enterprise Edition
Services	Central Administration Site Administration Incoming Email Windows SharePoint Services 3.0 Search Windows SharePoint Services 3.0 Web Application	Web Content Services: Publishing, Content Deployment, Variations Portal Services: Profiles, Audiences, Personalization Document & Records Management Office Search Document Conversions	Excel Server InfoPath Forms Line Of Business Interoperability (Business Data Catalog)

Table 5-1 Feature Comparison

	Windows SharePoint Services 3.0	SharePoint Server 2007 Standard Edition	SharePoint Server 2007 Enterprise Edition
Features	Mobility Shortcut URL Team Collaboration Lists Standard Content Type Definitions Standard Field Definitions Issue Tracking Workflow Alerts Discussions RSS Feeds Data Connection Library	Document Center Enhancements Translation Management Library Publishing Slide Library Office Server Standard (User profiles, Search, Personalization, and so on) Workflows (Approval, Collect Signatures, Collect Feedback, Disposition, Translation Management) Reporting	Office Enterprise: Business Data Catalog, Forms services, Excel services, Key Performance Indicator and various Business Intelligence Web Parts
Site Templates	Blank, Team, Document Workspace, Wiki, Blog, Meeting Workspaces	Records Center, My Site Host, Document Center, Personalization, Site Directory, Report Center, Search Center, Search Center with tabs, Publishing Portal, Collaboration Portal, Publishing, Publishing with workflow	

Hardware Recommendations

Before you install and configure SharePoint Server 2007, make sure your servers have the recommended hardware and software. For a small server farm, you need at least one server performing all SharePoint roles and one server acting as a database server. The server computers should meet the following requirements:

- **Web server and application server** Dual-processor computer with processor clock speeds of 2.5 gigahertz (GHz) or higher and a minimum of 2 gigabytes (GB) of RAM.
- **Database server** Dual-processor computer with processor clock speeds of 2.0 GHz or higher and a minimum of 2 GB of RAM.

Field experience shows us that nearly everyone now is purchasing hardware with a minimum of 4 GB of RAM. This amount is preferred and should be considered a best practice in all but the smallest environments.

Preparing for Installation

Before installing SharePoint Server 2007, you'll also need to consider three different server roles: Web application server, database server, and Active Directory. These roles are described in this section. A detailed discussion of hardware and software requirements can be found in Chapter 3, "Design Considerations and Deployment."

Web/Application Server

The server hosting the SharePoint components must have the following minimum software configuration:

- Microsoft Windows Server 2003 (Standard, Enterprise, Datacenter, or Web Edition) with Service Pack 1 (SP1).
- Microsoft .NET Framework 3.0 installed, which includes Microsoft Windows Workflow Foundation
- Microsoft Internet Information Services (IIS) in IIS 6.0 worker process isolation mode, with Microsoft ASP.NET 2.0 installed and enabled. IIS 6.0 is in the correct mode unless you upgraded the Web server from Windows 2000 to Windows Server 2003. Upgraded Web servers default to IIS 5.0 mode and need to be changed to IIS 6.0 mode.
- NTFS file system.

Database Server

SharePoint requires SQL databases and prefers Windows Authentication. SharePoint is hardware agnostic, so the hardware configuration, physical location of the SQL server, and location of the databases–such as a storage area network (SAN)–is fine with SharePoint as long as SharePoint can communicate efficiently with its databases. SharePoint is unaware of any non-SharePoint databases on the SQL server. If you have multiple named instances of SQL, identify the instance you are using for SharePoint as part of identifying the SQL server.

Therefore, the SQL Server configuration characteristics are flexible and include the following:

- Any operating system version that supports Microsoft SQL Server 2000 or 2005.

- Microsoft SQL Server 2005 or Microsoft SQL Server 2000 with Service Pack 3 (SP3) or later.
- The database server does not have to be dedicated to SharePoint.
- Optionally, the database server can be an SQL cluster.

Active Directory

Planning is essential for every part of implementing SharePoint. A crucial part of preparing for installing SharePoint Server 2007 is planning the various Active Directory accounts that will be needed throughout your implementation, not just for the installation process. The time that you spend on this process will be appreciated when you do not have to modify the accounts later.

Accounts Requirements

SharePoint Server 2007 will require many dedicated accounts. These accounts are discussed in greater detail in the Security Accounts section of Chapter 3. Before beginning your installation, plan for and create these dedicated accounts with these considerations:

- Provide the appropriate rights and permissions so that they are available when needed.
- The dedicated accounts need to have passwords that do not automatically expire.

User and Service Accounts

It is strongly recommended that you use a dedicated account to log in and install Windows SharePoint Services and SharePoint Server 2007 servers. This account can also be used as the identity of the Central Administration site application pool, or it can be unique. By design, the Welcome menu displays "system account" if that account is used to log on to any application pool or Web site. This behavior continues even if the application pool identity is changed to the Network Service. This means your administrator account should not be used as an application pool identity or to install an SharePoint Server 2007 server.

Table 5-2 provides a detailed list of the accounts that are required by a SharePoint Server 2007 farm installation.

Table 5-2 Accounts Required by an SharePoint Server 2007 Farm Installation

Account	Purpose	Scope	Used by	Needed	Requirements
Setup User	User account that is used to run setup on each server.	Farm	Person installing	Setup	Member of the administrator group on each Web front-end (WFE) server and application server computer in the farm. Member of the following SQL Server groups with SQL Security administrator and database creator rights on SQL servers.
SQL Server Service	This is the security context used By Central Administration for creating databases and other SQL configurations.	Farm	MSSQLSERVER, SQLSERVERAGENT	Setup	Member of the administrators group on each server on which setup runs, administrators group on each SQL Server computer, database system administrator, and member of the SQL security administrator and database creator SQL Server groups.
Server Farm	This account is also referred to as the *database access account*.	Farm	Central administration site application pool identity	Setup	Member of administrators group on each WFE server and application server computer in the farm with SQL security administrator and database creator rights on SQL Servers. Database Owner (DBO) for all databases and additional permissions on WFE server and application server computers are automatically configured for this account when SharePoint is installed.
SSP App Pool		App	SSP App Pool Identity	SSP Creation	No configuration is necessary. The following permissions are automatically configured for this account when SharePoint is installed: DBO for the Share Service Provider (SSP) content database, read/write permissions for the SSP content database, read/write permissions for content databases for Web applications that are associated with the SSP, read permissions for the configuration database, read permissions for the central administration content database, and additional permissions on WFE server and application server computers.
SSP Service Account	Used to run timer jobs and for interserver communications.	Farm	SSP Timer service; SSP Web services	SSP Creation	Same as SSP App Pool Account

Table 5-2 Accounts Required by an SharePoint Server 2007 Farm Installation

Account	Purpose	Scope	Used by	Needed	Requirements
Windows SharePoint Services Search	Used as the service account for the Windows SharePoint Services Search service. There is only one instance of this service, and it is used by all SSPs.	Farm	Windows SharePoint Services 3.0 Search service	SSP Creation	Must be a domain account, but must not be a member of the farm administrators group. Permissions automatically configured for this account when SharePoint is installed include the following: read/write permissions for content databases for Web applications, read permissions for the configuration database, and read/write permissions for the Windows SharePoint Services Search database.
Search Default Content Access Account	The default account used by a specific SSP to crawl content. It is used when an account is not specified for a content source.	App	Windows SharePoint Services 3.0 Search service	SSP Creation	Must be a domain account, but must not be a member of the farm administrators group. It requires read access to external or secure content sources that you want to crawl using this account. Additional permissions for this account are automatically configured when SharePoint is installed.
Search Specific Content Access Account	This is an optional account that is configured to replace the default content access account to crawl a specific content source.	Rule	Windows SharePoint Services 3.0 Search service	Create a new crawl rule	Read access to external or secure content sources that this account is configured to access.

Table 5-2 Accounts Required by an SharePoint Server 2007 Farm Installation

Account	Purpose	Scope	Used by	Needed	Requirements
User Profile and Properties Content Access Account	Account used to connect to a directory service, such as Active Directory, a Lightweight Directory Access Protocol (LDAP) directory, Business Data Catalog (BDC) application, or other directory source and used to import profile data from a directory service. Note: If no account is specified, the Search Default Content Access account is used. If the Search Default Content Access account does not have read access to the directory or directories that you want to import data from, you will need to specify a different account. You should plan for one account per directory connection.	App	Profile Import	SSP Creation	Read access to the directory service. For an Active Directory service connection that enables Server Side Incremental, the account must have the Replicate Changes permissions for Active Directory directory services provided by Windows 2000 Server. This permission is not required for Windows 2003 Active Directory. Manage user profiles right. View rights on entities used in Business Data Catalog import connections.
Excel Services Unattended Service Account	Excel Calculation Services uses this account to connect to data sources that require user name and password strings for authentication. The SSP App Pool account is used if none is specified. For security, plan to use a low-privileged account that does not have the database privileges of the SSP App Pool Account.	App	Excel Services Service	SSP Creation	Read/write access to the Excel data sources.

Table 5-2 Accounts Required by an SharePoint Server 2007 Farm Installation

Account	Purpose	Scope	Used by	Needed	Requirements
App Pool Identity	Used to access content databases associated with the Web application. Plan one for each application pool.	App	Web Applications	App Pool Creation	No configuration is necessary. SQL Server privileges that are automatically assigned to this account are member of Database Owners Group for content databases associated with the Web application, read/write access to the associated SSP database only, and read permission for the configuration database. Additional privileges for this account on WFE servers and application servers are automatically configured by SharePoint.

Installing SharePoint Server 2007

SharePoint Server 2007 installation is much more modular than previous versions. The installation walkthrough involves the following processes that can be accomplished by different individuals or roles in production environments:

- Installation process
- Run the Configuration Wizard
- Assign services
- Create the corporate intranet portal

Running Through the Installation

To begin the installation process for SharePoint Server 2007, complete the following steps:

1. Log in to your computer using the installation account that was previously created.
2. Start the SharePoint Server setup program from your source files, which are located on either a network or CD.
3. Enter your product key on the Enter Product Key page. Note in Figure 5-1 that the page confirms the correct key before permitting you to proceed.

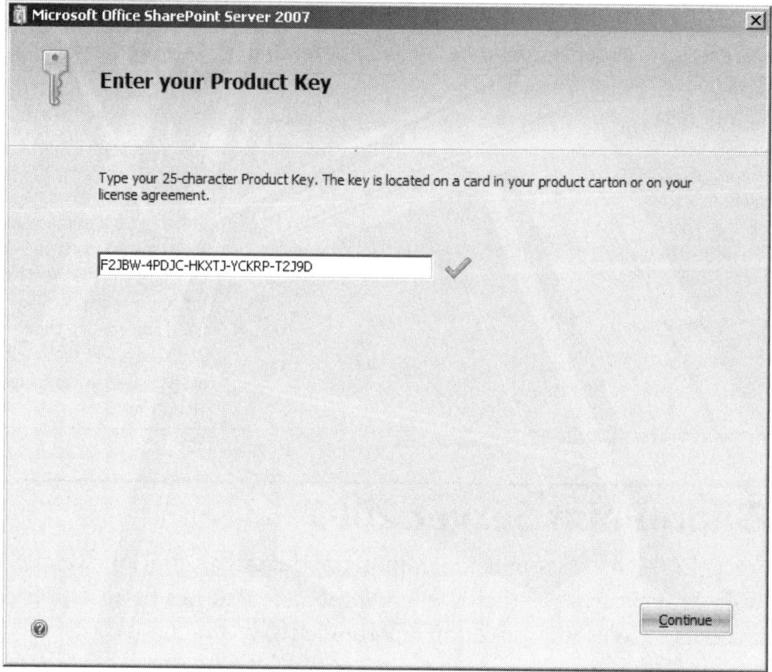

Figure 5-1 Enter Product Key page

4. Accept the end-user license agreement (EULA) on the End-User License Agreement page.

5. Next you need to decide which installation type is required for your system. (See Figure 5-2.) Your decision will determine the number of configuration pages you see during installation, as well as the installation process and results.

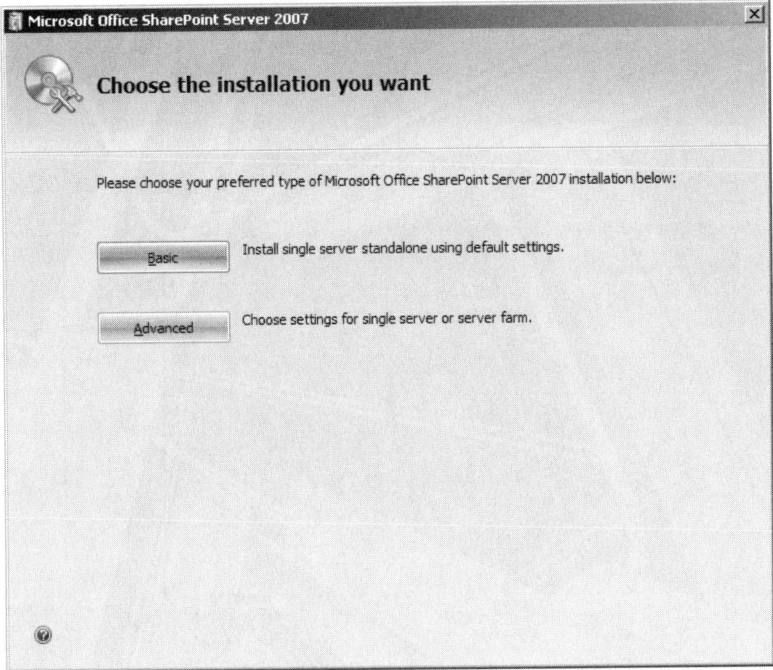

Figure 5-2 The Installation Types page

The Basic, or single-server, option installs the product on a single server with no options of later adding other servers or building a farm. This limitation exists because this option installs and uses Microsoft SQL Server 2005 Embedded Edition. A basic installation does not present any opportunity to change from the default options. Use the basic installation only when you know your deployment will not grow very large and will not ever need to scale out with additional servers.

Advanced Options

If you choose the Advanced option, you are presented with a page that has three tabs: Server Type, File Location, and Feedback. (See Figure 5-3.) We'll discuss your options on each of these three tabs in this section.

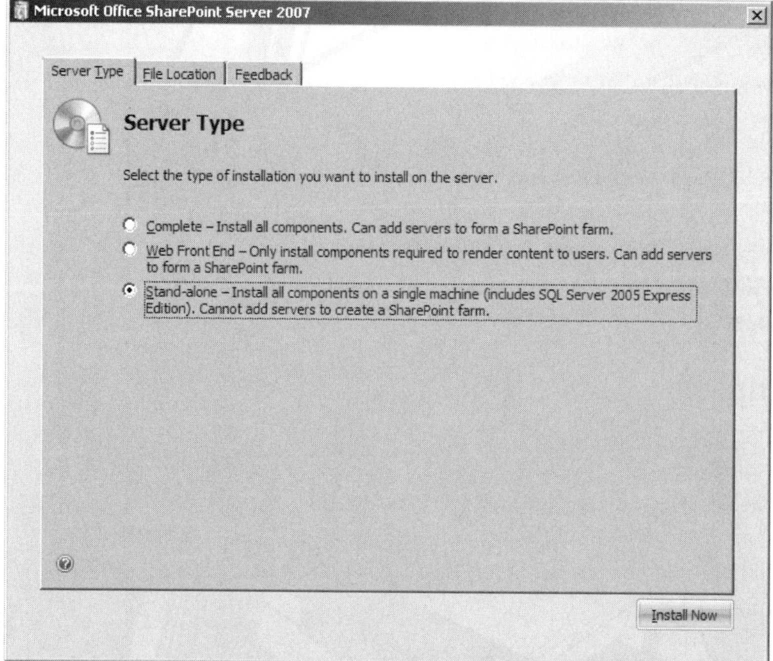

Figure 5-3 The first of the advanced options tabs

The Server Type tab presents three installation options. The first option we'll mention is the Stand-alone option. This option is the same as Basic on the previous page except that you now have the options on the other two tabs to configure along with setting up a basic server. The second option is the Web Front End option. This option installs only the services required for Web services and features. This option will require a reinstall if you need to support other services on this server later. You should have a Complete installation on one server before starting a WFE installation so that the Shared Services Provider (SSP) services will be available for the WFE.

Note In most cases, you'll not want to choose the Web Front End option because it limits your ability to quickly change a server's role without reinstalling the SharePoint binaries on the WFE server.

Finally, the Complete installation option installs all the SharePoint binaries on the server necessary to perform any or all roles and to deploy either a Standard or Enterprise edition of this product in your environment. Services and features can be turned on and off as needed on each server that has a Complete installation when you expand or shrink your farm.

Both Web Front End and Complete will require the selection of an SQL server, preferably a remote server. For a small environment or for test purposes, you can install SharePoint

Server 2007 on a server that is running as a domain controller, SQL server, and Exchange Server services. But except in rare circumstances, it is not a best practice to do this.

The remaining two tabs can be used to customize your installation as follows:

- **File Location** Allows you to choose alternate locations for your binaries. Choices made on this tab will not affect the installation location of the common files, which will be discussed later in this chapter during the review of installation changes to your system.
- **Feedback** Allows you to choose whether or not to participate in the Microsoft feedback program.

Installation Complete

This will be the first indication that, to permit separation of roles, this product is very modular in its installation and configuration. At this point, you have only installed the binaries. No databases have been created, and no modifications have been made to IIS. In your environment, another team might be involved in configuring the server. If this is the case, that team will run the Configuration Wizard later. However, for the purpose of this chapter, it is assumed that you are responsible for all tasks.

The Configuration Wizard

The Welcome page (shown in Figure 5-4) explains the information you will need to provide during the configuration.

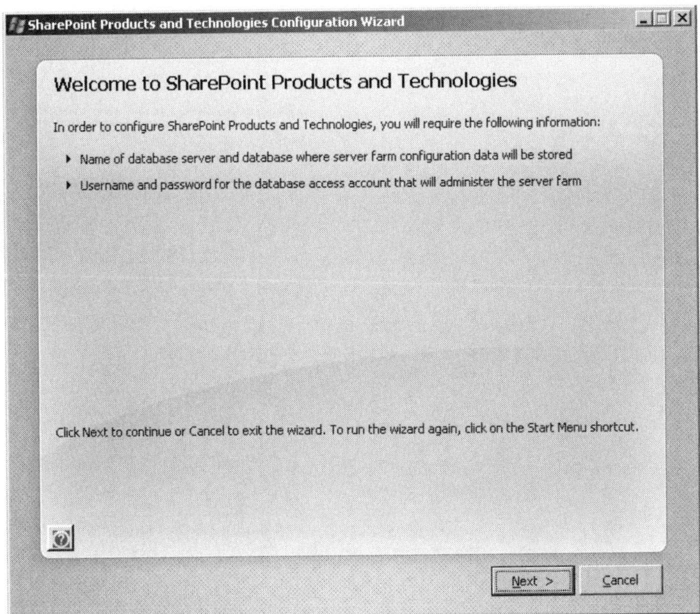

Figure 5-4 Configuration Wizard Welcome page

When you click Next, a warning dialog box is displayed explaining that some services will need to be restarted during the configuration. This does not present issues if you are working with a new, dedicated Web server. However, if your server is currently serving other Web sites, restarting the Web services will disrupt services, which might be unacceptable during certain time periods. If this is the case, you'll need to perform this action during off-hours. Also, it is highly recommended that you check network connectivity and DNS resolution from the server to the SQL server prior to running the wizard.

Server Farm Connection

Farm membership is defined by servers that are registered with the same configuration database. To join an existing farm, the server must use the same configuration database that the other servers are using. (See Figure 5-5.) If you want to set up a new farm, you need to create a new configuration database. You also need to know the SQL service account and password to join it to the farm. As was discussed earlier, in most instances this will be a domain account.

Best Practices Best practice is to always use domain accounts to install, configure, and secure your SharePoint deployment. If you use local server accounts and then later want to move to a domain environment, all your accounts in the farm and the Web applications need to be reassigned to domain accounts. This can be a challenging activity that can be avoided by simply using domain accounts initially.

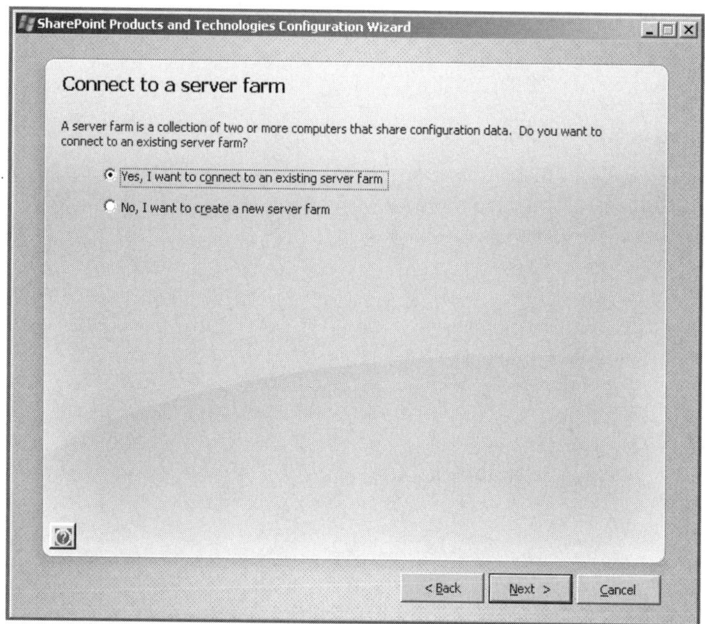

Figure 5-5 Farm connection choices

Create a New Farm

When you configure a new farm, you must specify a SQL Server instance and a new configuration database name. (See Figure 5-6.) At this point, you should have a naming convention in place not only for the configuration databases, but also for the other databases that will be configured later. You also need the SQL account username and password that has db_creator and db_security admin permissions on your SQL server. If this is your first SharePoint deployment, you need to ensure this account is also a member of the local Administrator's group on the SharePoint server. (See Table 5-2.)

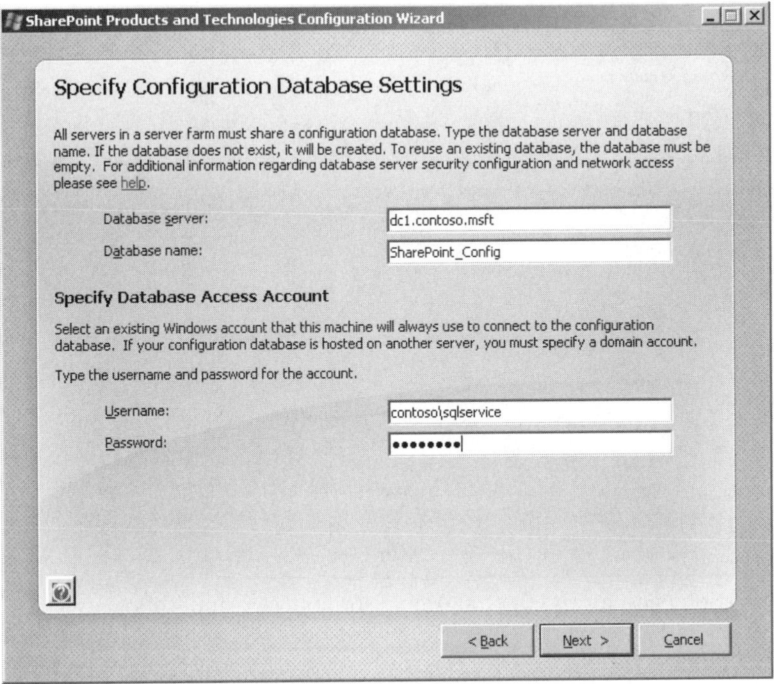

Figure 5-6 Specify Configuration Database Settings page

The username being requested on this page also will be used by the application pool in the Central Administration Web site. This is the same application pool account that was discussed earlier that has the appropriate rights on the SQL server and on all members of the farm. This is the security context for central administrative functions in SQL. In other words, all the system calls between the SharePoint servers and the SQL server will be committed within the security context of the Central Administration application pool account.

Note Remember that in SharePoint, user accounts should always be entered as domainname\username to distinguish them from local accounts.

Create the Central Administration Web Application

On the next page (shown in Figure 5-7), you instruct setup to create the Central Administration Web application. On this page, you can use the randomly generated port number or specify your own port number. In addition, you can choose if you want the Central Administration Web site to use Kerberos or NTLM authentication.

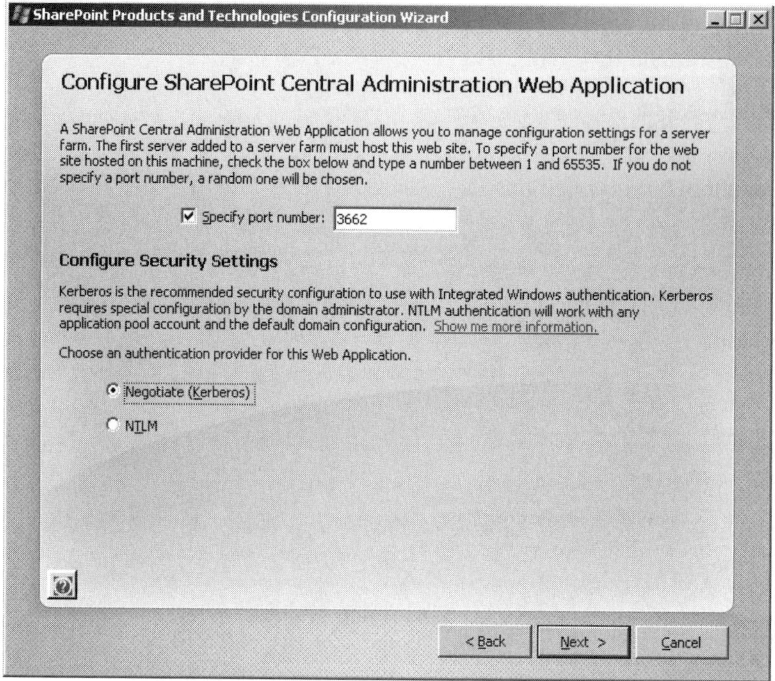

Figure 5-7 Configuration page for the Central Administration Web application

---

Important Choose your port number carefully. You cannot change the port number for Central Administration after SharePoint is installed.

The choice between Kerberos and NTLM authentication is important. In most cases, you will use NTLM because even though Kerberos authentication is more secure and more efficient, it must be supported throughout your environment. The Kerberos option will require you to configure service principal names (SPNs) for your accounts used as application pool identities. The Negotiate (Kerberos) option will allow IIS to authenticate users with Kerberos or NTLM authentication if the user's machine cannot access the KDC (Key Distribution Center) or has an unsynchronized clock.

Enabling Kerberos Authentication

Kerberos authentication requires special configuration. When creating a Central Administration Web application, choose Kerberos as your authentication mechanism and configure an SPN for your Web application pool process account identity by using the setspn.exe tool from Support.cab in the Support folder of your server install CD or the Windows Server Resource Kit. Enter the following at a command prompt:

```
setspn.exe -A HTTP/ServerName Contoso\UserName
```

In this example, *ServerName* is your IIS system name, *Contoso* is the name of our Active Directory Domain, and *UserName* is the identity of the Web application's application pool.

For more information about configuring Kerberos, see Microsoft Knowledge Base article 832769, "How to Configure Windows SharePoint Services to Use Kerberos Authentication," found at *http://support.microsoft.com/default.aspx/kb/832769.*

Complete Wizard Input

At this point, the Configuration Wizard has sufficient information to begin. Review the accuracy of the information (shown in Figure 5-8) before you click Next. If necessary, back up and make changes.

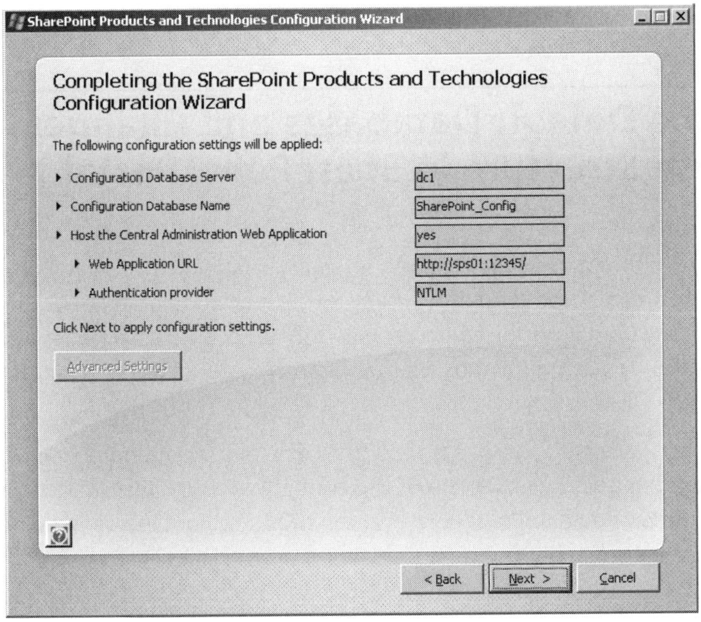

Figure 5-8 Completing the wizard

Once you click Next, a progress screen displays while the following actions are taken:

1. Initialize SharePoint products and technologies configuration.
2. Create configuration database.
3. Install Help collections.
4. Secure SharePoint resources.
5. Install and register SharePoint services.
6. Install and register SharePoint features.
7. Provision the SharePoint Central Administration Web application.
8. Install Web application files.
9. Finalize SharePoint products and technologies configuration, followed by IIS reset.

Moving to Central Administration

When the installation has been successfully completed, the wizard presents a report on its actions. When you click Finish, you are directed to the SharePoint Central Administration Web page. To open the Central Administration page, you need to add it to your Trusted Sites zone in Internet Explorer. The default settings of Internet Explorer require authentication for all Trusted Sites. To pass through your current logon credentials, you need to either modify the settings for Trusted Sites zone in Internet Explorer or add the Web site to the Local Intranet zone using the Sites button. If you are using a proxy server to access the Internet, ensure that your local sites are listed as local addresses in the Bypass Proxy Server For Local Servers dialog box.

Understanding the Default Databases and Changes from the Database Structure in SharePoint Portal Server 2003

The installation of SharePoint Server 2007 implements many changes to the database structure, particularly when compared to SharePoint Portal Server 2003. As part of the reduction in resource overhead of a portal, setup creates only one content database for each Web application, unlike the three databases that were created for each portal in SharePoint Portal Server 2003.

The Configuration database, which was always central to a farm, has taken on many new important roles. One major shift you will see is that the configuration database must be backed up for disaster recovery. In SharePoint Portal Server 2003, the configuration database was rebuilt "on-the-fly" during a recovery operation. In SharePoint Server 2007, the configuration database is restored from backup. However, members of the farm still must check the configuration database constantly to see whether their role in the farm has changed, as well as to check where all the other roles within the farm are located. By default, each server in the farm checks with the configuration database every 30 seconds.

The Job Server role in SharePoint Portal Server 2003 has been eliminated in SharePoint Server 2007. The configuration database now stores information on the various jobs, their parameters, and their schedules. In addition, many SharePoint settings formerly stored only in an individual member's registry are now also stored in the configuration database, as well as the IIS metabase configurations and file system changes on the WFE servers. When new applications are "created" in Central Administration, the information is first placed in the configuration database and then all WFEs complete the appropriate actions on their servers. This new centralized storage enables quick duplication when a new WFE is added to the farm, and it allows for replication of local changes on the WFE members. This also means that changes to a Web application's configurations in IIS Manager made after the Web application has been created are not written to the configuration database. Best practice is to not make configuration changes to this Web application using the IIS Manager after the Web application has been created.

In addition to the configuration database, the following databases are created as part of the installation and configuration of SharePoint Server 2007:

- **Admin_content database** Stores the information related to lists, document libraries, tasks, and so on of the Central Administration site. You can add information and documents to the site.
- **SSP database** Each SSP requires a database for service-specific data. The SSP database stores any nonsearchable data that needs to be accessed by multiple sites. This data includes, but is not limited to, the following:
  - User information imported from Active Directory or another directory–for example, people profiles
  - Calculated audiences and organizational hierarchies
  - Security information needed for the rights for the administrative delegation of the SSP site
  - Business Data Catalog (BDC)–related imported data
  - Business application data such as Service Advertising Protocol (SAP)
  - Business Intelligence (BI) methods
  - Site usage data
  - IPFS session state information

- **SSP search database** Separated from the SSP database primarily to ease the management of these databases. The SSP search database also enables a database administrator to back up other Office Server databases at a more granular level. One SEARCH database is created per SSP. The search database contains frequently changing search-related data that is created during the search indexing process, such as crawl properties, document properties, and propagation properties. This is similar to the metadata information stored in the Embedded Database Engine (edb) database by the search service of SharePoint Portal Server 2003. The SEARCH database serves as the data store for the following:
    - Search metadata (also called the *property store*)
    - History log
    - Search log
    - Calculation tables for crawl statistics
    - Links tables and statistical tables

  These SSP databases do not contain the index created by the gatherer service.
- **Content databases** Used for site collections to store all Office Server data, including the following data:
    - All site details
    - Structure details
    - User content
    - Files
    - Security information
    - InfoPath form server templates
    - Excel server data

A significant change in database structure is the creation of content databases for each application regardless of the application's function. So although we no longer get the extra _serv and _prof databases for each portal as we did in SharePoint Portal Server 2003, we do get content databases for the Shared Service Provider (SSP) application, the Web Services application, and the Central Administration application. These content databases serve the same functions as those of every other Web application's content database.

Modifying Your Farm

Technically, your farm exists as soon as you create the configuration database with the first Complete installation type. Depending on your design, you can immediately begin to expand your farm with additional servers to support WFE or other functions. You might need to move search, index, personal sites host, Excel services, and other services to separate hardware to reduce workload on the WFE.

Alternatively, your farm can continue for some time as a single server hosting all services (other than SQL Server) until performance monitoring indicates a need to expand. We recommend that the SQL server always be on a separate server except in very small production implementations or development and staging implementations.

Adding Servers to Your Farm

The installation process is the same for additional servers as for the first server in the farm except for the installation type selection that you make. Your only options are Complete or Web Front End. You can choose to always use Complete and turn off services not required for the WFE server when installing a WFE so that you retain the flexibility of changing roles later. If you use the WFE option and choose to add other services to the server later, you must reinstall SharePoint Server 2007 to add the new functionality to the server.

When you run the Configuration Wizard, however, you must choose to join the farm by picking the appropriate configuration database that defines the farm. The information in the configuration database will be used to configure SharePoint Server 2007 on the new server. The existing configuration database names can be retrieved after you identify the database server.

After the Configuration Wizard completes, you will define the role of the new server in Central Administration by starting and stopping services. If you're coming from a SharePoint Portal Server 2003 background, you'll find that there is no server selection screen with clean check boxes. Instead, starting and stopping services in Central Administration on each server is the method you'll use to assign server roles in the farm. This is much more granular in defining roles, and the hard-coded farm structures of SharePoint Portal Server 2003 are gone.

Understanding How Your Server Has Changed as a Result of Installing SharePoint Server 2007

Sometimes, especially for troubleshooting purposes, you'll need information on how the SharePoint installation changed your server. In this section, we will review how the installation of SharePoint Server 2007 modifies the following:

- File system
- Registry
- IIS 6.0
- Databases

File System Changes

The binaries were installed in the location specified during installation. The default location is C:\Program Files\Microsoft Office Servers\12.0. Here you will find global files for the installation and applications. For instance, the C:\Program Files\Microsoft Office Servers\12.0\Data\Applications\(instance ID)\Config folder contains global configuration files used by the search engine, like the language-specific noise word and Thesaurus files along with the Thesaurus schema xml file. Other folders are also installed as follows:

- **Projects** This is the location for the various indexes.
- **Single sign-on** Common files are installed to C:\Program Files\Microsoft Shared \Microsoft Office 12\ Single Sign-on.
- **Global executables** C:\Program Files\Common Files\Microsoft Shared \OFFICE12 contains the dll's used globally.
- **1033** This folder is used for US English. Other folders will appear as you install additional language packs.
- **Setup files** Critical setup files that might be needed later for re-running certain aspects of the setup and Configuration Wizard are placed at C:\Program Files\Common Files\Microsoft Shared\SERVER12.
- **Web services** Common files are installed to C:\Program Files\Microsoft Shared\Web server extensions\.
- **The new "12 hive"** C:\Program Files\Common Files\Microsoft Shared \Web server extensions\12 is the equivalent of what we affectionately called the "60 hive" in SharePoint Portal Server 2003.

Some files that you find here are global, some are language specific (En-us or enus is US English), and some are application (Web site) specific.

In addition, there is a hierarchy to many of the files. For instance, in C:\Program Files\Common Files\Microsoft Shared\Web server extensions\12\Data\Config, you will find another set of noise word and thesaurus files that supersede those discussed previously. In the C:\Program Files\Common Files\Microsoft Shared\Web server extensions\12\Data\Applications\SPS2\Config folder, you will find a set of noise word and thesaurus files that are specifically for the SPSv2 application. Under this folder, you will also find other search files and logs specific to this application.

In the C:\Program Files\Common Files\Microsoft Shared\Web server extensions\12\TEMPLATE\LAYOUTS folder, you will find the administrative pages address by the _layouts relative path on your sites. Also, in the C:\Program Files\Common Files\Microsoft Shared\Web server extensions\12\TEMPLATE\images is the _images relative path for images addressable anywhere in your sites.

Registry Changes

The Configuration Wizard makes hundreds of registry entries as it installs and registers dlls, services, and features. For example, the installation of SharePoint Server 2007 adds several entries to the registry under HKEY_LOCAL_MACHINE\Software\Microsoft\Office Server and HKEY_LOCAL_MACHINE\Software\Microsoft\Shared Tools\Web Server Extensions\12.0.

The creation of the first SSP adds 48 keys to the registry, many of which have up to 36 entries within the key. These changes are found in a file named RegistryBlob.reg located in the SSP: C:\Program Files\Microsoft Office Servers\12.0\Data\Office Server\Applications\(Site GUID) directory.

Configuring the Search and Index server adds 186 keys to the registry, many of which have up to 53 entries within the key. These changes are found in a file named RegistryBlob.reg located in the C:\Program Files\Microsoft Office Servers\12.0\Data\Applications\(site GUID) directory. These registry changes are also stored in the configuration database so that other WFEs can replicate them.

Web Sites and Application Pools

No changes were made to IIS during the installation of SharePoint Server 2007. However, the Configuration Wizard made several changes, including the following ones:

- The following two application pools were created:
    - SharePoint Central Administration v3 using the SQL service account specified during the wizard
    - OfficeServerApplicationPool using the Network Service account

- The Central Administration Web site was created using the SharePoint Central Administration 3.0 application pool.
- The Office Server Web Services Web site was created using the OfficeServerApplicationPool.

With SharePoint Server 2007, new Web sites and new application pools, such as Corporate Portal, must be created from within Central Administration so that the process includes storing the configuration in the configuration database. Also, modifications to IIS configuration, with the exception of adding more host headers, should be made with Central Administration.

Removing Servers from Your Farm

How you remove a server from the farm will depend on the future use of the server. In both instances, if you have other members of the farm, you should modify the roles of the members before removing a server that supports a critical role.

If you want to move a server from one farm to another, run the Configuration Wizard and choose to disconnect from the configuration database. You can now run the wizard again and connect to another configuration database to join the new farm or create a new configuration database for a new farm. If you are going to uninstall SharePoint Server 2007 from the server, you do not need to run the Configuration Wizard, as the uninstall program will remove the appropriate configuration database settings. (See the "Uninstalling SharePoint Server 2007" section later in the chapter.)

Installing Windows SharePoint Services 3.0

The Windows SharePoint Services 3.0 installation prerequisites and process are the same as for SharePoint Server 2007 with only a limitation of options. Other than their titles, the screens look exactly like those in the SharePoint Server 2007 installation and Configuration Wizard with some limitations unique to Windows SharePoint Services 3.0.

Running Through the Installation

The first page with options presents the same Basic and Advanced choices as before with essentially the same results. The Basic option installs on the server using SQL Express with no installation options and no capability of expanding into a farm later.

Figure 5-9 presents the Advanced page that differs from SharePoint Server 2007. There are only two options: Web Front End and Stand-alone.

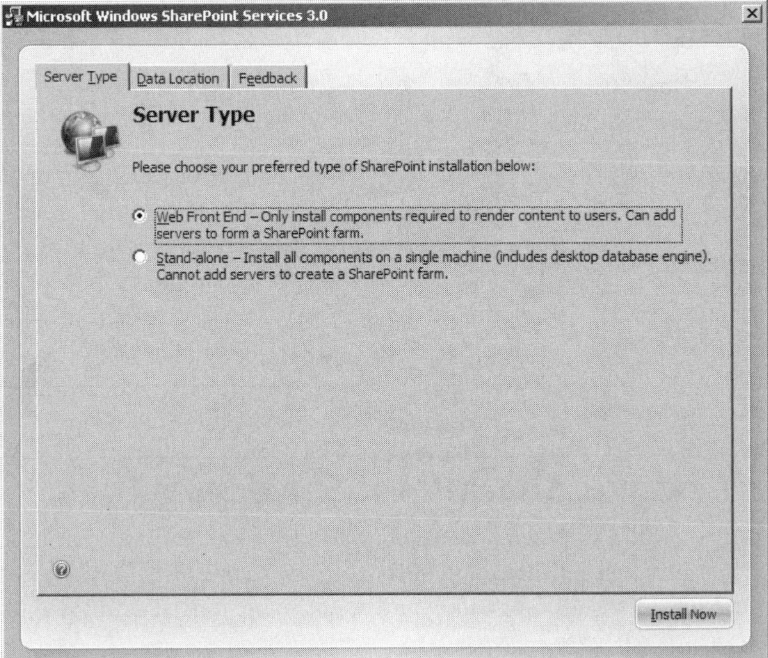

Figure 5-9 Advanced page of the Windows SharePoint Services 3.0 installation

WFE Installation

Because Windows SharePoint Services 3.0 provides only Web services, the WFE choice is similar to the Complete option with SharePoint Server 2007. This option uses a remote SQL database and has the option to expand the farm to have multiple load-balanced servers.

Stand-Alone Installation

As with SharePoint Server 2007, this option installs SQL Embedded and cannot be expanded.

Uninstalling SharePoint Server 2007

To remove SharePoint Server 2007 from the server entirely, simply uninstall the product using Add/Remove Programs in Control Panel. The setup program that uninstalls the program modifies the configuration database and reverses other modifications accomplished during the installation, including changes made to IIS 6.0. In the case of a Basic or Stand-alone installation using SQL Embedded, SQL Embedded is uninstalled as well but the SQL client tools remain.

With Add/Remove Programs, the product is uninstalled, including all program files except for those that might contain custom information. The following program files however are not removed:

- Noise word and thesaurus files
- Webconfig files for applications
- Index files
- Database files, including the configuration database

These files remain in their original locations, so the directory structure remains as well. This allows the farm to be rebuilt using another server and the same databases, files, and index.

Uninstalling Windows SharePoint Services 3.0

As with SharePoint Server 2007, use Add/Remove Programs to uninstall Windows SharePoint Services 3.0 from your server. This will remove all changes to IIS but leave the log files, the web.config for Central Administration and Site Administration, and the databases, including the search database.

Summary

This chapter covered the installation and farm configuration for both SharePoint Office Server 2007 and Windows SharePoint Services 3.0. In many instances, these will be ongoing processes, so the chapter also included the preparation steps and a summary of decisions required before beginning installation, modifying the farm by adding and removing servers, making changes to the servers during installation, and removing the services. Some of the best practices from this chapter were as follows:

- Except in very small implementations, use a separate server to provide SQL Server services.
- Use domain accounts if there is any possibility of having more than one member of the farm or if you are using SQL Server services on a separate server.
- Create accounts and determine naming conventions prior to beginning installation.
- Choose a Complete installation for Web front-end servers to provide more flexibility in modifying farm roles without requiring a reinstallation.

Part II

Administrating and Configuring Your Implementation

Chapter 6

Performing Central Administration and Operations Configuration

In Chapter 5, "Installing Microsoft Office SharePoint Server 2007," you installed Microsoft Office SharePoint Server 2007, and now you need to configure the farm and the operational components. Central Administration provides the interface for these tasks. The Central Administration interface contains three separate pages for this purpose: the Home, Operations, and Application Management pages. In this chapter, you will work with the Central Administration Home page and the Operations page to perform the core administrative functions required to configure your new farm. You will also see how to configure the farm when you add SharePoint Server 2007 servers and create a medium farm topology. Then, in the next chapter, you will learn about how to use the Application Management page.

In earlier Microsoft products, the installation of the binaries and the initial configuration of the product were combined into one, long administrative action. Ultimately, this design proved to be inflexible and led to dissatisfaction for those who wanted to commit simple configuration changes but were forced to go through longer administrative actions than they felt was necessary.

SharePoint Server 2007 separates the installation and configuration processes. Setup.exe installs the binaries onto your server. Then, either immediately after installing the binaries or at some point in the future, you can run the SharePoint Products and Technologies Configuration Wizard, which will allow you to configure the server.

SharePoint Server 2007 configuration is accomplished via two tools: the SharePoint Products and Technolgies Configuration Wizard and Central Administration. You learned about the wizard in the previous chapter. In this and the following chapters, you'll learn about (what is sometimes called) the Post Setup Configuration (PSC) options in Central Administration.

Introducing Central Administration

The Central Administration Home page is the starting point after installing SharePoint Server 2007. The Home page for Central Administration is available only as a Web page and is not available as a Microsoft Management Console (MMC) snap in. By default, the Central Administration site is configured and enabled only on the first SharePoint Server 2007 server in a farm. However, you can enable the Web site on additional servers if you need to. This is demonstrated later in this chapter in the discussion about configuring a medium farm.

Each Central Administration site has its own application server Web site, known in SharePoint Server 2007 as a *Web application*, and its own application pool. If any other configured Web sites or Web applications shut down or become corrupt, they will not affect the Web application hosting the Central Administration site. Figure 6-1 shows the SharePoint Central Administration Web application in Internet Information Services (IIS) Manager.

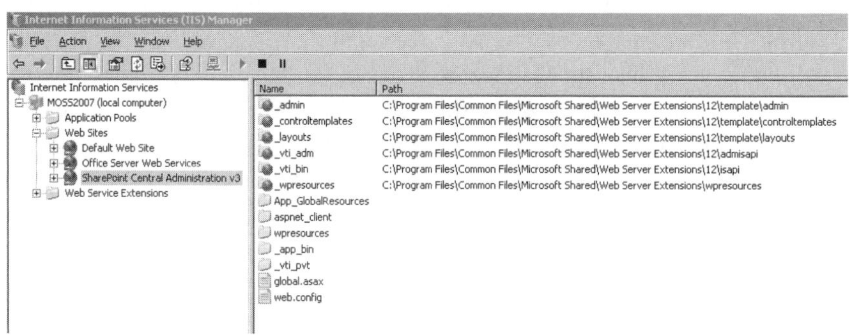

Figure 6-1 The Central Administration Web site in Internet Information Services (IIS) Manager

More Info For more information about Web applications, see Chapter 7, "Application Management and Configuration."

There are two options for launching the Central Administration Home page:

- Via the Administrative Tools
- Via the default URL and port number, as configured during the installation

To manage the Central Administration settings, you need to be logged on either as a member of the server's local Administrators group or as a user configured as a SharePoint administrator. Once you are logged on to the server, follow these steps to access the Central Administration Home page:

1. On the Start menu, point to All Programs and then click Microsoft Office Server.
2. Click SharePoint 3.0 Central Administration.

Best Practices For enhanced security, you can choose to add a Secure Sockets Layer (SSL) certificate and use https:// to access the Central Administration Web page. This helps to secure all traffic, including authentication, across the network. Refer to Microsoft Knowledge Base article 299875 found at *http://support.microsoft.com/default.aspx/kb/299875/* for more information on configuring SSL on your Web sites.

Once you've entered Central Administration, it's time to start configuring and administrating your SharePoint Server 2007 farm.

Using the Central Administration Home Page

When the Central Administration Home page first loads, you are presented with a simple page-to-navigate interface. There are two core management Web Parts on the page and one Web part for creating links:

- The Administrative Tasks Web part
- The Farm Topology Web part
- Resources Web part

Navigational aids are on the quick launch section of the page and the Site Actions menu for managing the page and team site, as shown in Figure 6-2. Note that Central Administration is exposed via a Windows SharePoint Services team site configured or provisioned to be the Central Administration site for your SharePoint Server 2007 deployment.

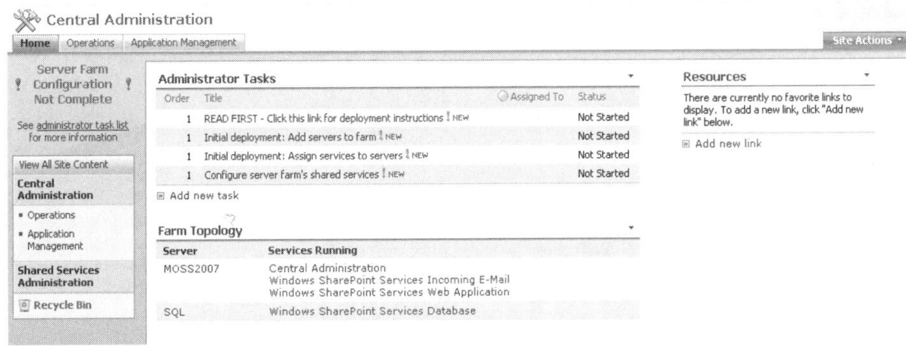

Figure 6-2 The Central Administration Home page

The three Home page Web Parts are preconfigured during installation but will change as servers are added to the farm or as tasks are added, completed, or deleted.

On the left side of the page is the "quick launch" menu, which has links to the pages in Central Administration and also to the Shared Services Administration page for each Shared Services Provider (SSP). There is a Recycle Bin as well, which is used to enable the administrators to restore deleted items from the site.

Performing Administrative Tasks

The Administrative Tasks list is a prebuilt list of recommended tasks. Consider this a checklist of actions to be performed after an installation and before any other tasks. The tasks list includes each task name and optional fields such as Assigned To and % Complete, as shown in Figure 6-3.

Central Administration > Administrator Tasks

Administrator Tasks

An Administrator Tasks list is created by the system to contain actions required of Farm Administrators.

New ▾ Actions ▾ Settings ▾ View: **All Tasks**

Type	Title	Action	Associated Service	System Task	Assigned To	Status	Order	Due Date	% Complete
	READ FIRST - Click this link for deployment instructions ! NEW	Read the Quick Start Guide		Yes		Not Started	1		
	Initial deployment: Add servers to farm ! NEW	Initial deployment: Add servers to farm		Yes		Not Started	1		
	Initial deployment: Assign services to servers ! NEW	Initial deployment: Assign services to servers		Yes		Not Started	1		
	Configure server farm's shared services ! NEW	Configure server farm's shared services		Yes		Not Started	1		
	Incoming e-mail settings ! NEW	Configure Incoming E-Mail Settings	SMTP	Yes		Not Started	2		
	Outgoing e-mail settings ! NEW	Configure Outgoing E-Mail Settings	SMTP	Yes		Not Started	3		
	Create SharePoint Sites ! NEW	Create new Web application	SPWssService	Yes		Not Started	4		
	Configure Workflow Settings ! NEW	Configure Workflow Settings		Yes		Not Started	4		
	Configure Session Throttles for InfoPath Forms Services. ! NEW	Configure InfoPath Forms Services		Yes		Not Started	4		
	Check services enabled in this farm ! NEW	Check services enabled in this farm		Yes		Not Started	10		
	Diagnostic logging settings ! NEW	Configure diagnostic logging		Yes		Not Started	15		
	Add anti-virus protection ! NEW	Configure anti-virus settings	SPWssService	Yes		Not Started	18		

Figure 6-3 The default Administrative Tasks list

Not all of the tasks will be relevant to your configuration–for example, configuring the Excel Calculation Services–but you should review all the default tasks to make sure you do not miss anything. The initial list is generated by the system based on the services that you have started or stopped on the server. However, you can add new list items and assign these new tasks to SharePoint administrators. In addition, you can edit the tasks or configure the task list properties. To add and configure the task list, follow these steps:

1. Launch Sharepoint Central Administrator from the Administrative Tools.
2. Click New on the options bar.

3. Complete the description and action for the task as well as the person assigned the task. The order number assigned to a tesk determines how high it is listed in the Administrative Task list. Finally add a start and end date if required. Click OK.

Administrators can also manage the Administrative Tasks by using the Actions available from the list. The actions available are:

- Edit In A Datasheet
- Export To A Spreadsheet
- View As An RSS Feed
- Receive An Alert For Changes

Note The ability to edit and configure the Administrative Tasks list provides the benefits of centralized administration, in order for a company to track who managed those tasks in SharePoint Server 2007 includes auditing and workflow policies.

See Figure 6-4 for the settings available in a task list, which can be displayed by clicking Settings and then clicking List Settings.

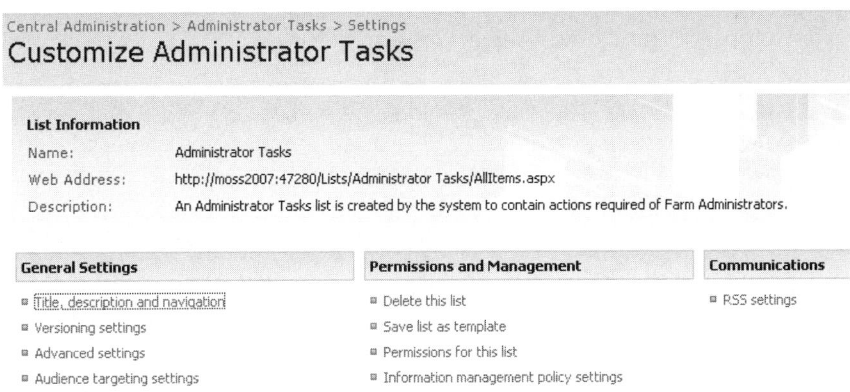

Figure 6-4 List Settings for the Administrative Tasks list

Not all of the tasks listed need to be configured immediately, and some might not be required at all. Some tasks require additional software, such as antivirus software, to be installed on the SharePoint server. To identify the relevance or priority of tasks, the Order column (shown in Figure 6-3) contains values that range from 1 through 18, with 1 being the most important task. When you launch a task, you see the hyperlink to its management page if it has one. For example, in Figure 6-5, when configuring the Add Servers To Farm task, the item in the Action row is a link to the management page for this task. After finishing the task, the Administrative Tasks list will be updated and the task will be removed from the list.

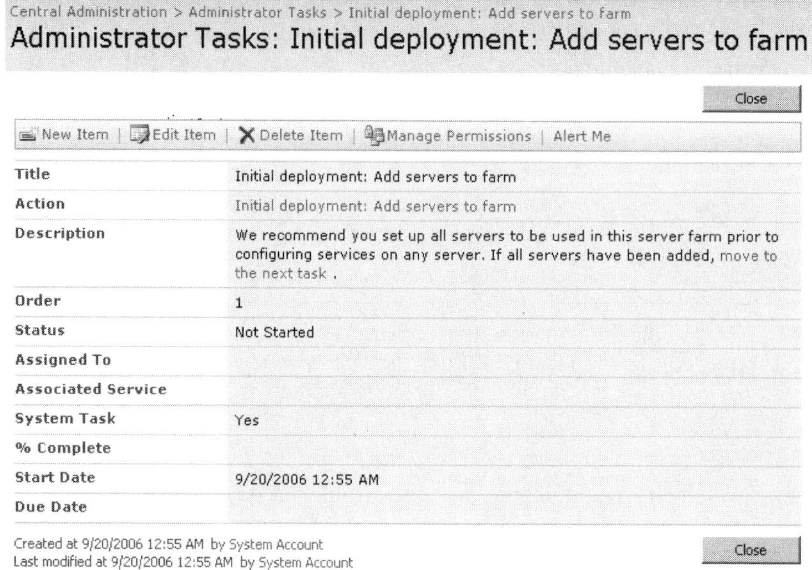

Figure 6-5 Task properties for the Add Servers To Farm task

> **Tip** Your design might not require all tasks to be performed. To avoid confusion, delete any unnecassary tasks from the default task list after installation and always clear the tasks after they have been completed.

Table 6-1 lists some common tasks that you might want to configure soon after installing your first SharePoint Server 2007 server. This list does not include all possible tasks included with the product, but these are certainly tasks you should consider early on in your deployment.

Table 6-1 Common Administrative Tasks Available in SharePoint Server 2007

Task name	Description
Outgoing E-mail Server	This task is required for users to receive alerts and notifications, such as an invite to a site.
Configure Farm's Shared Services	Although installed by default, Shared Services require additional configuration. This task will link you to your Shared Services Provider management page.
Central Administration Application Pool Should Be Using A Unique Account	To avoid conflicts and issues with site Web application pools, you should configure a unique Windows account for the central administration application

Table 6-1 Common Administrative Tasks Available in SharePoint Server 2007

Task name	Description
Add Servers To Farm	When adding servers to the farm, you can manage each service provided by the servers.
Check Services In Farm	If required, additional services (such as the Excel Calculation Services) can be enabled on servers in the farm.
Add Antivirus Protection	This task is important to configure prior to documents being imported into SharePoint.
Incoming E-mail Server	This task is required if you want your lists to receive e-mail directly with their own e-mail address.
Run Best Practices Analyzer Tool	This task is for checking the configuration of your servers and farm.

Understanding the Farm Topology View

The Farm Topology view, shown in Figure 6-6, is also found on the Central Administration Home page. Before using this view, you need to understand the relationship of servers and services in SharePoint Server 2007.

Farm Topology

Server	Services Running
MAIL	Windows SharePoint Services Outgoing E-Mail
MOSS2007	Central Administration Windows SharePoint Services Incoming E-Mail Windows SharePoint Services Web Application
SQL	Windows SharePoint Services Database

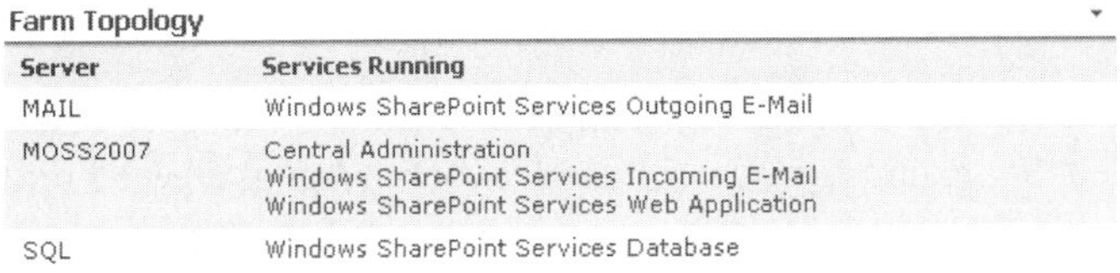

Figure 6-6 Viewing the services running on each server

How Many Servers?

If you have only one server in your farm, all services are under one server in the view. Some of these services (such as Search or Excel Calculation Services) are directed at users, whereas other services (such as Single Sign On) run in the background and are often transparent to the users' experience.

As you add servers to your SharePoint farm, they can all take part in providing services. When you add a server to the farm, the server is added to the list in the Farm Topology view. Notice that other servers appear here, such as the server hosting the databases and the e-mail server (if you configure the outgoing e-mail settings from the Administrative Tasks list).

Using Multiple Servers

When planning on using two or more SharePoint Server 2007 servers in your farm, it is important to decide which server will provide which services. Build multiple servers in order to offload resources from a single server and also to enable resilience in the farm. By enabling a server to have a specific role in the farm you can support many more concurrent users by having dedicated application servers for services such as the Excel Calculation Services and Search Service. Resilience can be achieved by adding additional Web Servers that can also be load balanced so that even if one Web Server goes down there is still a second accepting requests from the users. For small to medium companies these servers do not have to be such powerful servers as the resilience spreads the workload as well. For larger companies multiple Web Servers could help spread the load of heavily customized pages and Web Parts.

Flexibility is also provided when considering multiple servers. If your company decides to start with only one or two servers and then scale out when financial budgets permit then this is also possible and servers can be added to the farm at any time and associated with a specific role if required.

The type of install you choose will affect the default services turned on for that server and the binaries that are installed. For example, you might select your server as a Web Front-End (WFE) server, in which case only the services and binaries needed to fulfill this server role will be installed and enabled. However, if you select a Complete installation, all the binaries are installed but not all the services will be initially started.

When planning how many SharePoint Server 2007 servers you need in your design, one factor you might consider is the amount and type of services you want to provide. A single server can easily run out of server resources if it is running all the services for a large number of users. For example, Excel Calculation Services enables SharePoint Server 2007 to render Excel workbooks straight into an HTML page for users to view the data without having the Excel client installed locally on their machine. By enabling this service when there were many Excel workbooks to render, the resources required to do this task might be too much for one server to manage.

Choosing Server Roles and Services

After a server is added to the farm, you can choose one of the five default options for providing services. To see or change the available services, left-click the server name in the Farm Topology view to launch the Services On Server page, as shown in Figure 6-7.

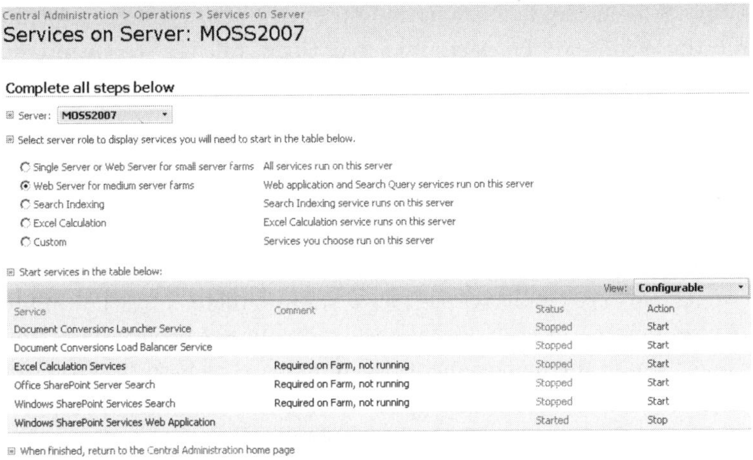

Central Administration > Operations > Services on Server

Services on Server: MOSS2007

Complete all steps below

Server: MOSS2007

Select server role to display services you will need to start in the table below.

Single Server or Web Server for small server farms — All services run on this server
Web Server for medium server farms — Web application and Search Query services run on this server
Search Indexing — Search Indexing service runs on this server
Excel Calculation — Excel Calculation service runs on this server
Custom — Services you choose run on this server

Start services in the table below:

View: Configurable

Service	Comment	Status	Action
Document Conversions Launcher Service		Stopped	Start
Document Conversions Load Balancer Service		Stopped	Start
Excel Calculation Services	Required on Farm, not running	Stopped	Start
Office SharePoint Server Search	Required on Farm, not running	Stopped	Start
Windows SharePoint Services Search	Required on Farm, not running	Stopped	Start
Windows SharePoint Services Web Application		Started	Stop

When finished, return to the Central Administration home page

Figure 6-7 Choosing the services running on the server

The upper part of the Services On Server page lists the roles that are available for the server. Table 6-2 lists the five roles available for the servers in your farm and describes the services that are associated with each role.

Table 6-2 Five Default Services Roles

Role name	Service description
Single Server Or Web Server For Small Server Farms	Turns on all core services on this server, as it is assumed that you have only one server at this time or that the server will be a WFE server in a farm with a low number of concurrent users.
Web Server For Medium Server Farms	Tells this server to act as a WFE server in a multiserver farm. It also enables the server to provide search query results using the indexing server.
Search Indexing	Allows the server to provide an Index file and search mechanism for Shared Services Providers to consume from, and thus provide aggregated search abilities from the portal sites for users.
Excel Calculation	Enables the server to provide Excel Calculation Services to users for rendering Excel workbooks into HTML.
Custom	Allows you to choose your own services to provide from the selected server.

When you select a role on the upper part of the page, the default services associated with that role are highlighted in the list of services in the lower part of the page. Services that require starting in order to comply with the role selected will have a comment in red stating that it is required on the farm but not running. This helps you identify services that are not yet started but are associated with the server role. Enable or disable each service by clicking either Start or Stop in the Action column to the right of the service name. In Figure 6-7 for example, the Web Server For Medium Server Farms role is selected and the Excel Calculation services are not started.

If you have more than one SharePoint Server 2007 server in your farm, you can easily switch between servers by selecting a server from the drop-down list above the list of services. The list refreshes to show the status of the services for that server.

Configuring Services

Some services listed on the Services On Server page have links on them. These links indicate that additional configuration is necessary either before or after the service starts running. The hyperlink takes you to the management page for that service so that you can perform the necessary configuration. For example, before starting, the Office Sharepoint Server Search service requires a location for the creation of the index file. After completing the index file configuration, you can start the Search service.

Using the Central Administration Operations Page

Once you've completed the tasks on the Home page, your next step is to configure the global options for your server farm. Global configuration options affect all servers that you add to the farm. You use the Operations page to complete the tasks associated with the global configuraton options. On the Home page, select the Operations tab to open the Operations page shown in Figure 6-8.

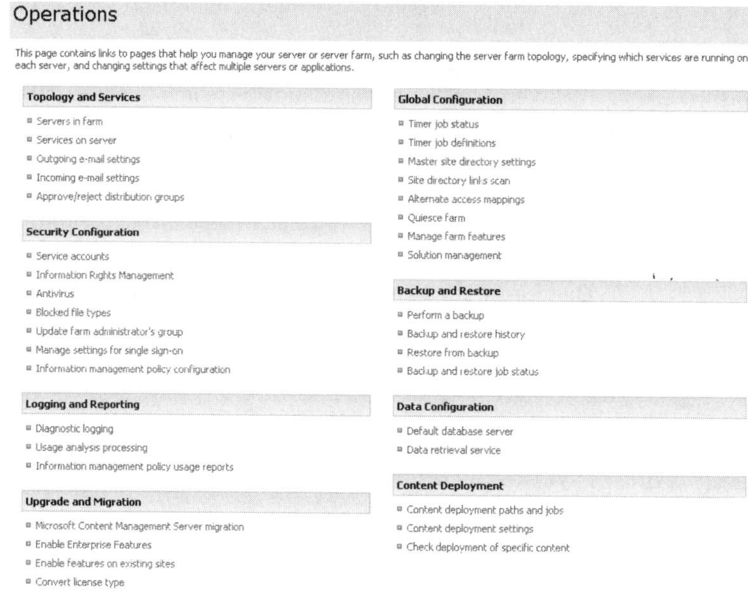

Figure 6-8 The Central Administration Operations page

Important Make sure you have a working backup of your farm before making global changes. Some options, such as Remove Server, can have catastrophic consequences if the server you've removed was providing needed services to the network.

There are eight defined sections on the Operations page and each section is grouped to represent a common set of tasks. The eight sections are as follows:

- **Topology And Services** Configure servers in the farm and E-mail.
- **Security Configuration** Manage farm accounts, Single Sign On (SSO) farm wide security policies and global document management settings.
- **Logging And Reporting** Configure for use across the farm.
- **Upgrade And Migration** Manage server upgrades and adding new features to the farm. Also used to configure migration from Microsoft Content Manager Server.
- **Global Configuration** Many unique settings such as site collections links management and bringing the farm offline in a managed state (Quiesce). There is also alternate access mappings for multiple zone and URL support and managing deployed farm wide solutions packages.
- **Backup Restore** Managing all farm backup and restore jobs down including all Web applications and databases associated with the farm.
- **Data Configuration** Change the default database location and also configure data retrieval services.
- **Content Deployment** Configure the deployment of site collection content in the same farm or between farms to other site collections using multiple paths and scheduled jobs.

Some management tasks on the Operations page will be covered in other chapters in this book. This chapter covers e-mail configuration, security configuration, data configuration, and content deployment tasks.

Farm-Level Server Management

The Topology And Services section has five configuration options, and some of the options for managing servers in the farm and configuring services on the server can also be accessed via the Central Administration Home page, as described earlier in this chapter.

- Servers In Farm
- Services On Server

- Outgoing E-Mail Settings
- Incoming E-Mail Settings
- Approve/Reject Distribution Groups

Servers In Farm

The Servers In Farm page, shown in Figure 6-9, is a more advanced version of the Farm Topology view that you saw on the Central Administration Home page. On the Central Administration home page, you saw the services that were configured to run on the servers. On the Servers In Farm page in Operations you can also see the installed binaries version number and the option to the remove the server from the farm. Servers are sorted by server name on this page. In addition, this page is helpful if an administrator ever removes the Farm Topology Web Part on the Central Administration home page.

Note If a Web Part has been removed from the Central Administation Home page, you can add it back as an administrator by going to Site Actions and Edit Page to add the Web Part back. If you do not see the Site Actions tab on the page, you do not have the necessary administrative rights on the page.

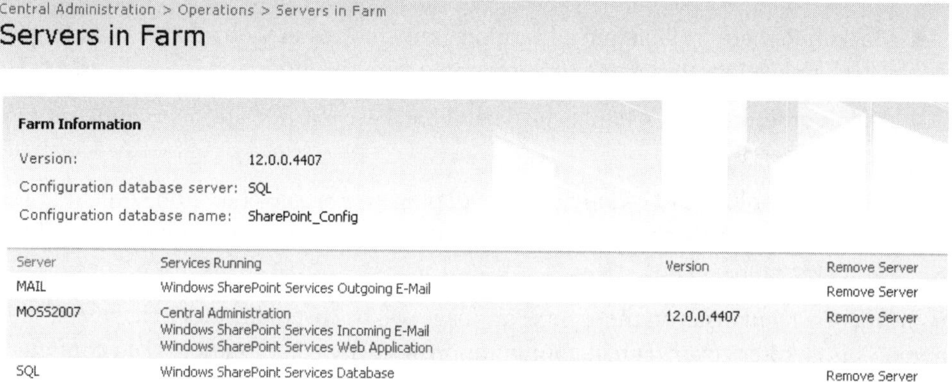

Figure 6-9 Additional options for servers in the farm

Important If you select Remove Server for a server on this page, you are removing the server from the farm's configuration database. Once it is removed, it will not be available to provide any services to other farm servers or users. Therefore, it is important to have a backup of your farm and databases before proceeding with this option. See Chapter 30, "Microsoft Office SharePoint Server 2007 Disaster Recovery," for more information on backup and restore.

Services On Server

The Services On Server option takes you to the same configuration screen shown in Figure 6-7, where you can configure the services on the servers in the farm that you were able to access from the Farm Topology Web Part on the Central Administration Home page. The status of the services running is pulled from the configuration database. You will need to refresh this page to capture updates to services that have occurred since the page was initially rendered.

Outgoing E-Mail Settings

For any messages to be sent out of SharePoint Server 2007—such as alerts, notifications, and site invitations—you need to configure an SMTP server that will be responsible for routing the messages. This server can be any SMTP-compliant server, and you must be able to connect to this server using port 25 from the SharePoint Server 2007 server.

> **Note** Firewalls in between the SharePoint Server 2007 server and the mail server can cause outgoing mail to fail, so make sure that SMTP traffic is allowed through your firewalls.

When configuring the mail server settings, you can use different *from* and *reply* addresses for your mail so that you could, for example, have mail sent to recipients as Office SharePoint Server 2007@constoso.msft but have the reply address for the mail be spsadmin@contoso.msft.

Incoming E-Mail Settings

A new feature for SharePoint Server 2007 is the ability to allow e-mail messages to be routed directly to a list in a site and therefore have the actual .eml e-mail message appear in the list or library as well as any attachment it has. The process is very simple: you create a new list or library in a Team site and mail enable it. By doing this, you create a new contact in Active Directory using the SharePoint Directory Service and enable people to send mail to the contact's mail address. When an e-mail is sent to this address, it is routed to the configured drop folder on the SharePoint Server 2007 server. After it arrives in the drop folder, the message will wait until the SPTimer service next polls the folder. The SPTimer service then re-routes the mail into the list configured with that e-mail address in a site.

Setting Up Key Components

When setting up incoming e-mail, you need to configure several key components that allow this process to complete. To do this, follow these steps:

1. On the Web front-end server where you want to route mail, ensure the Simple Mail Transfer Protocol (SMTP) service is installed and running by opening the IIS management console in Administrative tools.

2. In Active Directory, create an organizational unit (OU) in which the new distribution or contacts will be created.

> **Important** The domain account configured to run the Central Administration Application Pool must have write access to the organizational unit created in Active Directory.

Configuring Incoming E-Mail Settings

Once you've completed the preparatory steps described above, the next thing you need to do is to configure your incoming e-mail settings using Central Administration (Figure 6-10). To do this, follow these steps:

1. Click Incoming E-Mail Settings on the Operations page under the Topology And Services section.
2. Select Yes to enable incoming e-mail in the Enable Incoming E-Mail section. Leave the Settings mode as Automatic.

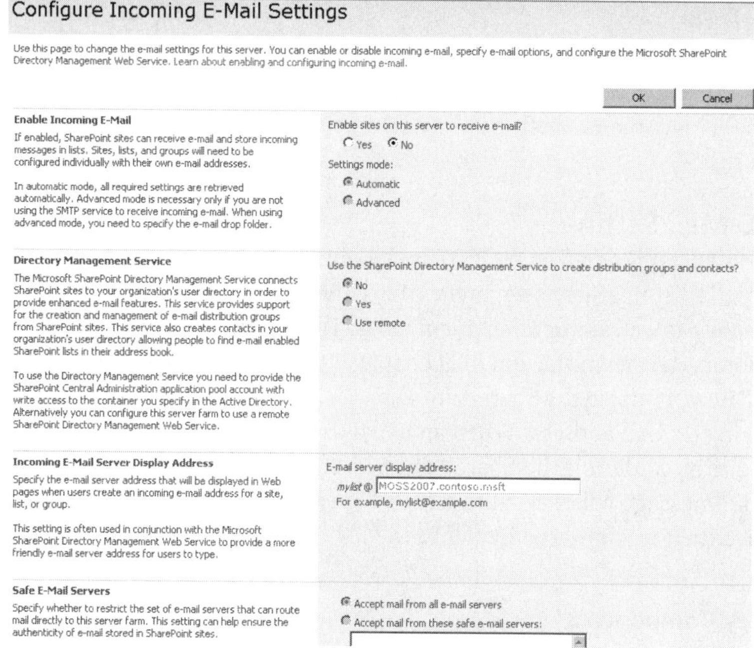

Figure 6-10 Configuring incoming e-mail

3. Configure the SharePoint Directory Management (DirMan) service. There are several options for configuring the DirMan service. See Table 6-3 below for a detailed

explanation for each option. (For more information about this service, see the "Collaboration and DirMan" sidebar.)

Table 6-3 Configuring the Directory Management Service

Setting name	Choice description
Use The DirMan Service To Create Distribution Groups And Contacts	❑ No – Allows you to use only the local SMTP service for mail delivery. No Objects are created in Active Directory. ❑ Yes – Requires that you define the container in the Active Directory where you wish the Contacts and Distribution Lists to be created. For example OU=SPContacts,DC=Contoso,DC=MSFT ❑ Remote – Lets you specify the DirMan Service URL on another farm to provide the connection to the Active Directory. For example, *http://mossserver:portnumber/_vti_bin/sharepointEmailWS.asmx*
SMTP Mail Server For Incoming Mail	Lets you specify the SharePoint Server where the SMTP service has been configured. The mail will be routed to this SMTP server for delivery to the list or library, for example moss2007.contoso.msft
Accept Messages From Authenticated Users Only	Used for reducing the amount of relayed junk mail that is received by the SMTP service.
Allow Creation Of Distribution Groups From SharePoint Sites	Selecting yes allows sites and site groups to be given their own distribution group and mail address in Active Directory. After selecting yes, you must choose what level auditing is required for creating and managing the objects in Active Directory. The four choices are ❑ creating a distribution group ❑ changing the group's e-mail address ❑ changing the title and description ❑ deleting the distribution group Once configured, an object will remain in the approval state awaiting approval. In order to approve an item follow these steps: 1. On the Operations page click View All Site Content on the left hand quick launch bar. 2. Click the List Call Distribution Lists. 3. Select the item to approve or reject from the drop down arrow next to the item.

Table 6-3 Configuring the Directory Management Service

Setting name	Choice description
Incoming E-Mail Server Display Address	Lets you assign a friendly e-mail address name to the list (for example, contoso.msft). Every e-mail enabled list name will then include this mail address after the list name (for example, helpdesk@contoso.msft).
E-Mail Drop Folder (only available if you selected advanced settings mode)	Lets you define the folder where mail will be dropped by the local SMTP service to await pick up by the SPTimer and delivery to the list or library (for example, E:\spsmail\drop). If you selected Automatic mode the drop folder will be the SMTP service folder (by default, C:\Inetpub\mailroot\drop).

Collaboration and DirMan

The SharePoint Directory Management (DirMan) service provides a way for Windows SharePoint Services to mail-enable discussion groups and SharePoint groups. The reason this service has been created is because in the previous versions of SharePoint Products and Technologies, users were forced to choose between collaboration using e-mail and collaboration using team sites. With the advent of DirMan, you no longer need to make an exclusive choice.

In addition, most organizations have rich, mission-critical information encapsulated in e-mail messages. The DirMan service allows users to more fully integrate this rich information into the SharePoint collaboration process, while also allowing the content of the e-mail messages to be indexed and queried.

The DirMan service is installed as part of the Shared Services Provider (SSP) in SharePoint Server 2007. It is not a service that you'll see in either the Service page in Central Administration or the Services Control Panel for the operating system. Instead, it is a Simple Object Access Protocol (SOAP) service that is exposed when the SSP is created and configured, and it is called by Windows SharePoint Services to perform e-mail services. For the DirMan service to work properly, you must have installed Active Directory and Exchange Server 2000 or later. Because SSPs can be federated across farms, this topology flows through to the DirMan service.

Configuring Sites to Receive E-Mail

Now that you have configured the server side, you can go to your lists or libraries in SharePoint Server 2007 sites and configure them to receive mail and specify which e-mail address to receive mail items from. To configure these settings, follow these steps:

1. Open any site such as a custom site named Helpdesk that you created for your organization.
2. Click Shared Documents in the quick launch section of the page.
3. Click Settings and select Document Library Settings.
4. Select Incoming E-Mail Settings under Communications to open the Change E-Mail Settings page shown in Figure 6-11.

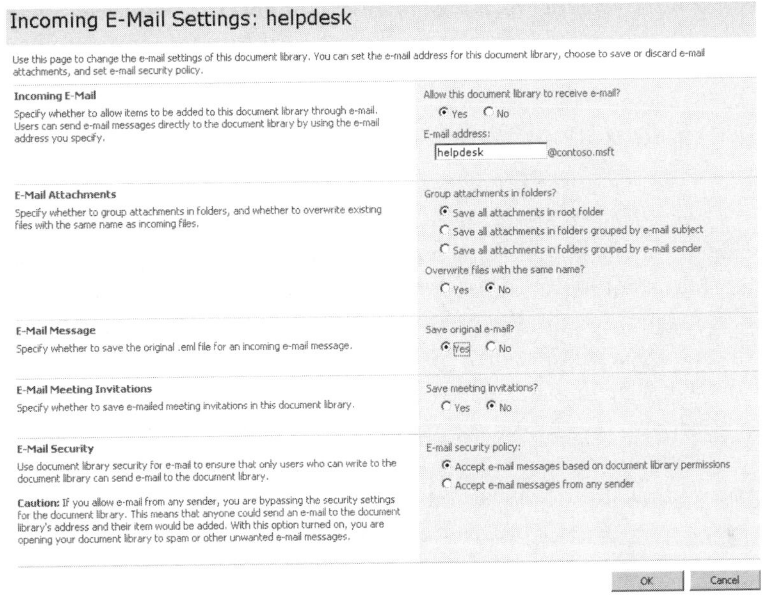

Figure 6-11 Configuring the document library to receive e-mail

You now have several options to configure for the incoming e-mail:

- **Incoming E-Mail** Select Yes to enable e-mail on the library, and choose the e-mail address you want to give the library.
- **E-Mail Attachments** Choose how you want mail attachments to be grouped when received in the library. The default is to save all attachments in the root of the folder.

- **E-Mail Message** Choose Yes to have the original .eml mail message saved in the document library as an attachment.
- **E-Mail Meeting Invitations** Choose Yes if you want this library to receive and show meeting request e-mail messages.
- **E-Mail Security** Select the level of security on the document library to determine who can actually add items. By default, only senders who have write access to the library will be able to send mail items to that address; however, you can change this setting to allow all senders of mail to populate the library.

After completing the e-mail settings process, a contact is created in the specified OU in Active Directory using the directory service manager. If you want to add more e-mail addresses to that contact to support external mail addresses, for example, you can use the Active Directory management tool for users and computers and add more e-mail smtp addresses.

Real World Using Incoming E-mail

As a real-world example of the process detailed in this section, suppose that you have created a document library in an SharePoint Server 2007 site called *helpdesk*. You have enabled the incoming e-mail settings and assigned an e-mail address to the list in the SharePoint Server 2007 site—for example, helpdesk@contoso.msft. A contact is created in the Active Directory OU using the directory management service, and you can now have the e-mail messages sent to the e-mail address of helpdesk@contoso.msft. The messages are then sent to the drop folder configured on the SharePoint Server 2007 incoming mail server. The SPTimer service picks up that mail, and it puts the mail itself into the helpdesk document library. You can now set up a workflow on the document library and a notification mechanism so that the helpdesk query can be processed by the right helpdesk member.

Security Configuration

SharePoint Server 2007 includes several security options that enable global configuration for better control of security. Start with the Security Configuration section of the Operations page (shown in Figure 6-8) to configure security. Changes to many of the options in this management section will have a global effect on all SharePoint Server 2007 servers in the farm, so it is important to understand the available options:

- Service Accounts
- Information Rights Management

- Antivirus
- Blocked File Types
- Update farm Administrator's Group
- Information Management Policy Configuration
- Manage Setting For Single Sign-On

Service Accounts

When SharePoint Server 2007 needs to communicate with other applications, it will use the service accounts you configured here. There are three Windows service accounts that can be configured:

- Conversions launcher service
- SSO administration service
- Conversion load-balancer service

In addition to these Windows services, you can configure the accounts used by the various Web application pools that you create for hosting the shared service providers and site collections. If you choose to change the service accounts configured here, you also need to make sure the new service account name and password have access to the relevant databases that were configured when setting up the actual Web applications. The minimum rights required are Read and Modify database rights.

Information Rights Management

Security is always on the mind of system administrators and management alike. Even though SharePoint Server 2007 has file security built into the document libraries, you still might need an additional layer of protection in terms of privacy. Information Rights Management (IRM) is built on top of a certificate-based infrastructure, and it allows users to restrict access to a document not just by name but also by their certificate. Information rights management requires both client-based and server-based add-on software to work, and there are additional client access licence (CAL) costs involved.

The difference between IRM and security is important to understand. *Security* has as its focus regulating who can see which content. *IRM* has as its focus what can be done with the content when it is accessed by the user. Some have used the terms "security" and "privacy" to differentiate between the two, with privacy being the feature offered by IRM. Those who work extensively in the security field don't like the *privacy* term, but nevertheless, they are good terms to help you remember the difference between security and IRM.

More Info See the online documentation at *http://www.microsoft.com/windowsserver2003/technologies/rightsmgmt/default.mspx*.

Antivirus

Before you can enable antivirus settings, the required antivirus software needs to be installed on the SharePoint Server 2007 server. Antivirus software does not come with SharePoint Server 2007, so you need to purchase an SharePoint Server 2007–specific antivirus package. After the software is installed, go to the e-mail settings and enable the level of scanning that you want. You can choose from the following four options:

- Scan Documents On Upload
- Scan Documents On Download
- Allow Users To Download Infected Documents
- Attempt To Clean Infected Documents

More Info Microsoft has an antivirus solution called Microsoft Antigen for SharePoint, available at *http://www.microsoft.com/antigen/default.mspx*.

Blocked File Types

Any files trying to be uploaded into SharePoint Server 2007 with the file extensions listed here will be automatically blocked. You can modify this list with new extensions or remove any of the default extensions.

This list will apply not only to the uploading of documents, but also to extension changes of documents once they are in the list. For example, by default, .exe documents are blocked. If you zip up an .exe file, upload it with a .zip extension, and then try to unzip it in the document library, you'll find that the document will not extract because SharePoint will block the hosting of any document with an .exe extension. To configure blocked file type, follow these steps:

1. Go to Central Administration.
2. Click the Operations page.
3. Click Blocked File Types under the Security Configuration section.
4. Scroll to the bottom of the list and add your new file extension by typing in the box, for example **zip**.
5. Click OK.

Update Farm Administrator's Group

This option allows you to add users or groups to become administrators in the SharePoint Server 2007 farm and to remove users or groups from the list of administrators in the farm. You should always use an Active Directory security group because it enables you to swap out users in a group without affecting security in SharePoint. To add a new administrator, follow these steps:

1. Go to Central Administration.
2. Click the Operations page.
3. Click Update Farm Administrator's Group under the Security Configuration section.
4. Click New.
5. Add the new user or group account account, for example CONTOSO\SPSADMINS
6. Click OK.

Note Being an administrator in SharePoint Server 2007 does not give the user the right to create Web applications in IIS; that still requires local administrator rights on the server.

Information Management Policy Configuration

Policies are a new feature in SharePoint Server 2007. You can configure four farm-level policies that are available for lists, libraries, and content types used throughout the farm. Table 6-4 describes these default policies. By default, all policies are enabled and available throughout the farm.

Table 6-4 Information Management Policies

Policy name	Policy description
Labels	Gives users the ability to view and add metadata labels in a document. These labels can be printed along with the document, and they can also be a searchable attribute.
Auditing	Allows list and libraries to audit users' actions, such as modify and delete, that take place within the list or library.
Expiration	Assigns an expiration setting to content, possibly through a workflow for archiving.
Bar Codes	Allows unique bar codes to be inserted in documents that can then be printed with the document or searched for.

With policies such as auditing, it is a case of enable or disable, but for the expiration policy there several settings that can be configured including a manual launch of the process. To configure the expiration policy, follow these steps:

1. Go to Central Administration.
2. Click the Operations page.
3. Click Information Management Policy Configuration under the Security Configuration section.
4. Click Expiration.
5. Change the schedule to weekly and choose a day and time.
6. If you wish to run a manual process cleanup of expired content click Process Expired Items Now.
7. Click Save.

Manage Settings for Single Sign-On

If you plan to use the Single Sign-On (SSO) service, you need to configure certain farm-wide settings first. The Single Sign-On service is a user credential mapping service that enables a user to access Office SharePoint Server 2007 sites using one account and also get access to, say, his Service Advertising Protocol (SAP) account without continuously providing another set of credentials. Before you can configure the Single Sign-On, you must ensure that the Single Sign-On service has been started on the server–use the Services console in Administration tools to start this service, and change the Startup type for the service from Manual to Automatic.

Note You must configure the Single Sign-On service account with a domain user account that has Create and Modify database permissions, because the service account will be used in the creation of the single sign-on database and in communications with it. The service account is configured on the logon tab in the properties of the Single Sign-On service accessible through the services console in the Administration tools.

Once the service has been started, you need to configure the server settings for single sign-on before you can manage the other options. Here you will configure the account used for single sign-on and also the name and location for the single sign-on database, see Figure 6-12. When these tasks have been completed, you can finish the configuration by setting the encryption level and enterprise definitions that determine how the Single Sign-On service will log on and authenticate users with various applications. To configure the server settings, follow these steps:

1. Go to Central Administration.
2. Click the Operations page.
3. Click Manage Settings For Single Sign-On under the Security Configuration section.
4. Click Manage Server Settings.
5. Configure the following settings on the Manage Server Settings for Single Sign-On page.
   a. Single Sign-On Administrator AccountMust be a domain user or group account from the same domain where the single sign-on service account is from.
   b. Enterprise Application and Definition Administrator AccountMust be a user or group account from the same domain wher the single sign-on service account is from.
   c. Database SettingsDefine the location of the database server and also the name for the SSO database.
   d. Time Out SettingsDefine time out in minutes for SSO connection sessions and also number of days that the SSO audit logs are kept for.
6. Click OK.

You can now proceed to configure the encryption key if required and also the application definitions that have been applied to the SSO service.

Central Administration > Operations > Manage Single Sign-On > Manage Server Settings for Single Sign-On

Manage Server Settings for Single Sign-On

Use this page to manage the server settings for single sign-on.

* Indicates a required field

Single Sign-On Administrator Account In the **Account name** box, type the name of the group or user account that can set up and manage the single sign-on service. This account must be a member of the same domain to which the single sign-on service account belongs. Learn about managing Single Sign-On	Account name: * CONTOSO\ssoadmin Example: DOMAIN\group name or DOMAIN\user name
Enterprise Application Definition Administrator Account In the **Account name** box, type the name of the group or user account that can set up and manage enterprise application definitions. This account must be a member of the same domain to which the single sign-on service account belongs.	Account name: * CONTOSO\ssoadmins Example: DOMAIN\group name or DOMAIN\user name
Database Settings In the **Server name** box, type the name of the database server that stores the settings and account information for single sign-on. In the **Database name** box, type the name of the single sign-on database.	Server name: * SQL Examples: computer name or computer name\SQL Server instance Database name: * SSO
Time Out Settings In the **Ticket time out** box, type the number of minutes to wait before allowing a ticket to time out. In the **Delete audit log records older than** box, type the number of days to hold records in the audit log before deleting.	Ticket time out (in minutes): * 2 Example: 2 Delete audit log records older than (in days): * 10 Example: 10

Figure 6-12 Configuring the Single Sign-On service

More Info To learn more about the architecture of SSO and pluggable authentication, refer back to Chapter 2, "Architecture for Microsoft Office SharePoint Server 2007."

Logging and Reporting

When troubleshooting or information gathering, you should always have as many logs and listed events as possible to track down problems or trends over time. The Logging And Reporting section on the Operations page (shown in Figure 6-8) has several features that you can enable to help with the information gathering process:

- **Diagnostic Logging** This feature sets the thresholds at which SharePoint Server 2007 will log and report errors as they occur for certain types of user activity. If you do not want to receive a lot of alerts for a certain type of event, you can set the trigger to send an event to the event log to Error rather than Warning, as shown in Figure 6-13. By doing this, fewer entries would be submitted. If you need to monitor activity in maximum detail, set the logging method to Verbose, which captures everything. Do not leave the Verbose setting turned on permanently because this will have a detrimental effect on performance.

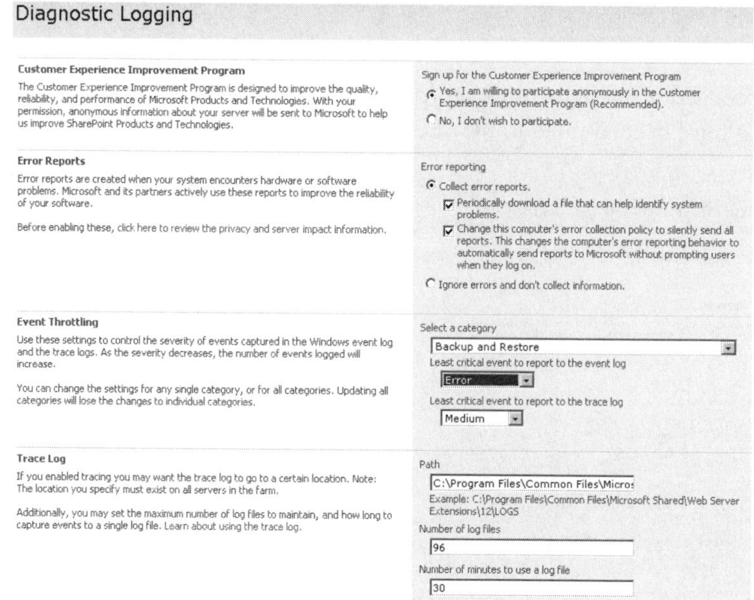

Figure 6-13 Setting the backup job to send only error events to the log

- **Usage Analysis Processing** This useful reporting tool for site administrators gets information on what is happening with their site. Before a site administrator can view the usage reports, you must enable it here. Choose the location and quantity of the log files created and also the time of day to generate them.
- **Server Event Logs** You can use the Server Event Logs interface to view the error events generated from the Diagnostic Logging settings. You can also use Event Viewer via the administrator tools.
- **Information Managment Policy Usage Reports** Earlier in this chapter, we looked at configuring information management policies such as auditing or expiration. You can create reports on this information by using the information management policy usage reports. By default the report will use the default reporting template for the reports or you can direct your reports to a customized report template created for you using the templates URL address.

To set up Policy Usage Reports, follow these steps.

1. Go to Central Administration.
2. Click the Operations page.
3. Click Information Management Policy Usage Reports under the Logging And Reporting section.
4. In the Web Application section, select a Web application from the drop down menu to run the reports for.
5. In the Schedule Recurring Reports section, either specify the time and occurence that the reports are generated or force a manual creation of the report by clicking the Create Reports Now button.
6. Specify the Report File Location using the URL to the site collection to host the reports.

   Note You can use URL \ to send the reports to the root of the site collection or you could send the report directly to a reports list on the reports page by using the URL /Reports/ReportsLibrary/. The new report will be generated in this list using an XML file format.

7. In the Report Template section, use the default template for the reports or select a URL pointing to a customized report template.
8. Click OK.

Upgrade and Migration

Use the Upgrade And Migration options on the Operations page (shown in Figure 6-8) for managing your farm migration and upgrade from SharePoint Portal Server 2003 and Content Management Server 2002. You can see the various stages of the upgrade process as well as finalize the upgrade when all servers are on SharePoint Server 2007. You can also enable additional services on your SharePoint Server 2007 farm by enabling premium features. See Chapter 23, "Upgrading from Microsoft Windows SharePoint Services 2.0," and Chapter 24, "Microsoft SharePoint Portal Server 2003."

Global Configuration

The Global Configuration options on the Operations page (shown in Figure 6-9) can be grouped into common tasks for management.

Job Service

The options available under Job Service are:

- **Timer Job Status** Provides a quick view of all jobs running on the farm. The jobs displayed are taken from the Timer Job Definitions page.
- **Timer Job Definitions** Enables you to view currently configured job definitions that can be disabled and in some cases deleted. For example, you may run a backup job that fails and the only way to run a new job is to delete the current running Backup/Restore Job definition.

Site Management

The options available for Site Management are:

- **Master Site Directory Settings** When users create new sites in the sites directory, you can configure categories for the sites to belong to. These categories enable users to find sites by a logical grouping on the site directory home page. The Master Site Directory Settings page allows Administrators to specify the URL of the site directory and also the choice to make all new sites created by users belong to at least one or all site catagories. Making these categories mandatory ensures that sites belong to at least one category grouping.
- **Site Directory Links Scan** Runs a scan and checks known site URLs for site dead links that either do not exist or have moved in the site directory. As users create, delete and move sites it is possible that links in the site directory will not reflect the correct URL to the site as when a site URL changes the site directory does not change dynamically to reflect this change. Choosing to update site properties will auto-correct the dead links in the site directory to reflect the new or deleted URL's of the site links.

Farm Settings

The options available for Farm Settings are:

- **Alternate Access Mappings** Alternate Access Mappings (AAM) allows administrators to add and manage URL namespaces and associate those URL's with a Web application and its content databases. The AAM also manage the zones for the incoming requests. There are five Zones available for defining where the URL mapping is coming in from or going out to.
  - Default
  - Intranet
  - Internet
  - Custom
  - Extranet

  For example, A new Web application is created that extend and maps to an existing site collection. This new web application has Anonymous authentication and will be used for internet users accessing the published site. The AAM is configured with a new Public URL using the Internet URL namespace using the Internet zone and also an Internal URL specifying the internal namespace for the site collection. SharePoint Server 2007 will return requests to the user with the correct URL based on them coming from the internal or internet namespace, including alerts and search results.
- **Quiesce Farm** Stops the farm from accepting new user connections and gradually brings any long-running applications offline without causing data loss. There are three stages of Quiescing:
  - **Normal** Active state handling all requests.
  - **Quiescing** The farm only handles existing requests but denies new requests.
  - **Quiesced** The farm does not allow any new sessions to start.
- **Manage Farm Features** Allows you to deactivate or activate features on your farm, such as deactivating the Excel Services feature or spell checking. Once deactivated, the feature will not be available to any site collections in the farm. Additional features can also be managed here that have been added manually, such as third-party add-ons. By default, all features for the farm are active.
- **Solution Management** A grouping of SharePoint components that can be registered in the Solution Store and then deployed to the Web servers for use in the site

collections. The components that can make up a solution can include one or more of the following:

- Feature Definitions
- Site Definitions
- Web Part Package

This enables developers and administrators to centrally manage and deploy complete customized packages across the farm from a single page. The contents of the solution can be sent to a specific virtual server and also deployed to the Bin or GAC on the servers receiving the package. Solutions are deployed using the Solutions Management page. Once a solution is available for deployment, it enables administrators to send the same solutions to new Web servers when they get added to the farm. Solutions are added to the management page using the stsadm—addsolution command.

Backup and Restore

Disastor recovery should always be right near the top on any administrators to-do list. The Backup And Restore options on the Operations page (shown in Figure 6-8) are for farmwide jobs that can also include Web application and site-collection backups. You can also view the backup jobs in this location and their associated job status.

More Info See Chapter 30 for more information on configuring Backup And Restore options.

Data Configuration

Use the Data Configuration options on the Operations page (shown in Figure 6-8) to identify the default database server and data retrieval service.

- **Default Database Server** The SQL server configured here is the default location where all new content databases will be created by default. However, when you create a new Web application on the Application Management page, you can specify a database server other than the default.

  More Info See Chapter 7 for more information on creating and managing Web applications.

- **Data Retrieval Service** Data retrieval services are XML Web services that return XML data from various data sources such as an SQL database. For example, Web

Parts can use the data retrieval service to query the data source to return data in a list. When any connections in SharePoint Server 2007 require the use of data services such as SOAP, OLEDB, XML-URL, and Windows SharePoint Services, the data retrieval services must be enabled. By default, the Data Retrieval service is enabled but OLEDB update query support is not, so if you have any data connections requiring this function, make sure that you enable the Data Retrieval services first. The services can be set on a global basis affecting all Web applications or on a per-Web application basis.

Tip If the data retrieval service is trying to connect to a remote SQL server that is configured to use Windows authentication, then you should configure all the servers and clients involved in the process with Kerberos authentication. This includes the client sending the request, the server initiating the service request (SharePoint server), and also the remote SQL server receiving the request.

Content Deployment

In SharePoint Server 2007, content deployment is a feature of Web Content Management (WCM), which allows multifarm topologies for deploying content from sites or site collections to remote sites or site collections. The ability to transfer content in this manner can, for example, be used in a staging environment where you have an authoring environment that then needs to go to a staging environment and finally on to a production environment.

Note Content Deployment paths are only one way. You create a source and a destination.

This flexibility of content deployment can be used in both intranet sites as well as Internet-facing sites. Because the content is being deployed from site collection to site collection, it can be used between sites on the same server as well as by sites on completely different farms. Having multiple farms might well be a setup configuration you will have in an Internet-facing scenario for Web page hosting, where the other farms could be living in a screened subnet, for example. Use the Content Deployment options on the Operations page (shown in Figure 6-8) to set up this feature.

With content deployment, you push the content one way, so this is not a two-way synchronization tool. You configure a path and job that define a source site or site collection and also a destination site or site collection that the content will be pushed to. The site collections can be in the same farm or different farms. You can push content via a schedule and specify only content that has changed since the last deployment. To set up content deployment, you need to configure two primary sections on the Operations page in Central Administration.

Content Deployment Settings

Before you can create deployment jobs and paths, you must first enable the import and export feature in the farm to allow deployment jobs to be both sent and received by servers in the farm. In the Content Deployment settings page, as shown in Figure 6-14, there are six settings that need configuring. Follow these steps to configure the settings:

1. Go to Central Administration.
2. Click the Operations page.
3. Click Content Deployment Settings under the Content Deployment section.
4. On the Content Deployment Settings page complete the following sections:
    - **Accept Content Deployment Jobs** Needs to be enabled for the farm to receive any incoming jobs
    - **Import Server** The server chosen will require enough disk space for all incoming content and must also be a server that has an administration Web application for the farm.
    - **Export Server** The server chosen will send all outgoing jobs and will require enough disk space for the content and must also be an administration Web application for the farm
    - **Connection Security** Defines whether to use https for encrypting the traffic between source and destination farms. By default it is enabled, if you decide to use only http then the username and password of the authenticating account between farms will be sent in clear text.
    - **Temporary Files** The location where all content deployment files will be stored. This folder location must have sufficient free disk space for all possible deployment content.
    - **Reporting** Specify how many reports you wish to keep until the first one is overwritten. By default 20 report jobs are kept.

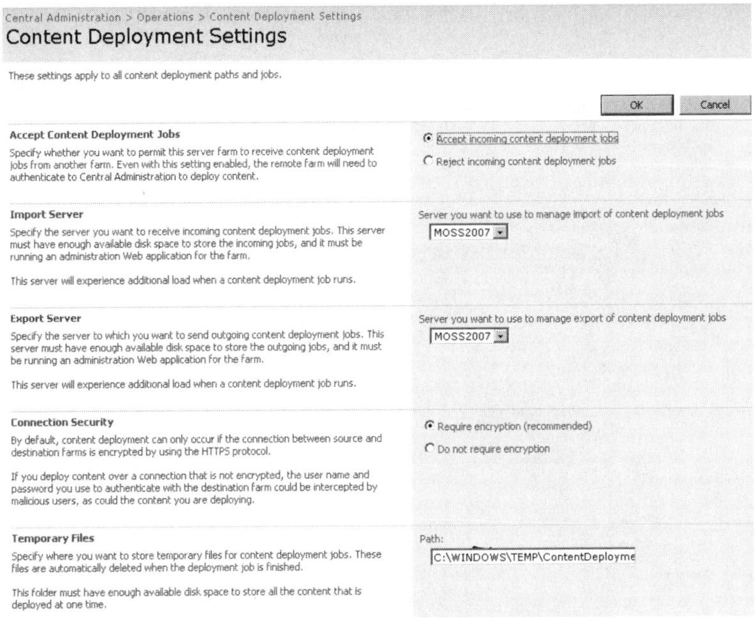

Central Administration > Operations > Content Deployment Settings

Content Deployment Settings

These settings apply to all content deployment paths and jobs.

OK Cancel

Accept Content Deployment Jobs

Specify whether you want to permit this server farm to receive content deployment jobs from another farm. Even with this setting enabled, the remote farm will need to authenticate to Central Administration to deploy content.

Accept incoming content deployment jobs

Reject incoming content deployment jobs

Import Server

Specify the server you want to receive incoming content deployment jobs. This server must have enough available disk space to store the incoming jobs, and it must be running an administration Web application for the farm.

This server will experience additional load when a content deployment job runs.

Server you want to use to manage import of content deployment jobs

MOSS2007

Export Server

Specify the server to which you want to send outgoing content deployment jobs. This server must have enough available disk space to store the outgoing jobs, and it must be running an administration Web application for the farm.

This server will experience additional load when a content deployment job runs.

Server you want to use to manage export of content deployment jobs

MOSS2007

Connection Security

By default, content deployment can only occur if the connection between source and destination farms is encrypted by using the HTTPS protocol.

If you deploy content over a connection that is not encrypted, the user name and password you use to authenticate with the destination farm could be intercepted by malicious users, as could the content you are deploying.

Require encryption (recommended)

Do not require encryption

Temporary Files

Specify where you want to store temporary files for content deployment jobs. These files are automatically deleted when the deployment job is finished.

This folder must have enough available disk space to store all the content that is deployed at one time.

Path:

C:\WINDOWS\TEMP\ContentDeployme

Figure 6-14 Configuring content deployment settings

Note Make sure you have plenty of disk space on the temporary storage location folder, because some deployment jobs could be very large in size if the deployed site has large amounts of content in its lists and libraries.

Reports can also be created to follow the progress of the jobs as they transfer between the site collections.

Content Deployment of Paths and Jobs

After a farm is enabled to accept incoming jobs, you can create the path between the sites and specify the jobs that use those paths. A path in content deployment is a relationship between two specific site collections that must be configured. The path must also specify the authentication method to use when connecting the site collections. To accomplish this, follow these steps:

1. Go to Central Administration.
2. Click the Operations page.
3. Click Content Deployment Paths And Jobs under the Content Deployment section.

4. On the Manage Content Deployment Paths And Jobs page, click New Path (see Figure 6-15).

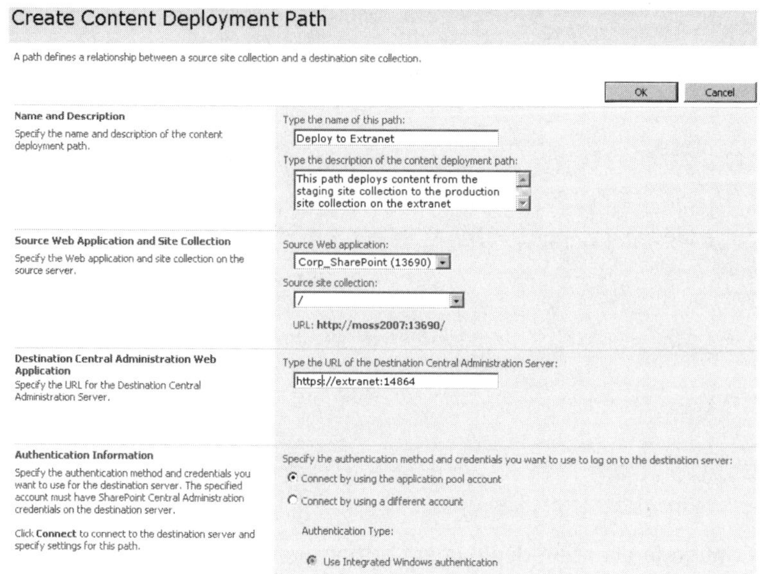

Figure 6-15 Creating a new Content Deployment path

5. On the Create Content Deployment Path page, complete the following sections on the page:

   a. Type a name and description.

   b. In the Source Web Application And Site Collection section, select a source Web application and then choose a site collection or a site from the drop-down arrows.

   c. In the Destination Central Administration Web Application section, specify the URL of the destination Central Administration site that will receive the incoming deployment jobs. Ensure this has been enabled for receiving incoming deployment jobs in the Content Deployment Settings page.

   d. In the Authentication Information section, decide how the authentication will be handled when connecting to the destination server. You can either use the application pool account or specifiy a unique account. You must also connect to the remote Central Administration site that you just configured before you can specify the destination site.

e. In the Destination Web Application And Site Collection section, specify the destination Web application and then choose the site collection or site to send the deployed content to.

f. In the User Names section, select whether to deploy user names with the deployed content.

> **Note** Deploying a user name could be useful in a situation of publishing blog entries but would not be useful if it was published content for an Internet facing site where the financial manager had added some yearly financial figures for the site.

g. In the Security Information section, decide if you want to send any security information such as roles or memberships along with the content.

> **Note** If you were sending content to a screened subnet in another farm in a different Active Directory forest, for example, there would be no benefit to sending the security information as the destination farm would be handling its own membership and role structure for access to the published content.

6. Click OK to complete the page.

After a path is defined, multiple jobs can be associated with the path to use the relationship between site collections. You can set up the jobs you create to deploy only certain sites in the site collection, and you can also choose a schedule for when the job will run. To accomplish this, do the following:

1. Go to Central Administration.
2. Click the Operations page.
3. Click Content Deployment Paths And Jobs under the Content Deployment section.
4. On the Manage Content Deployment Paths And Jobs page, click New Job (see Figure 6-16).

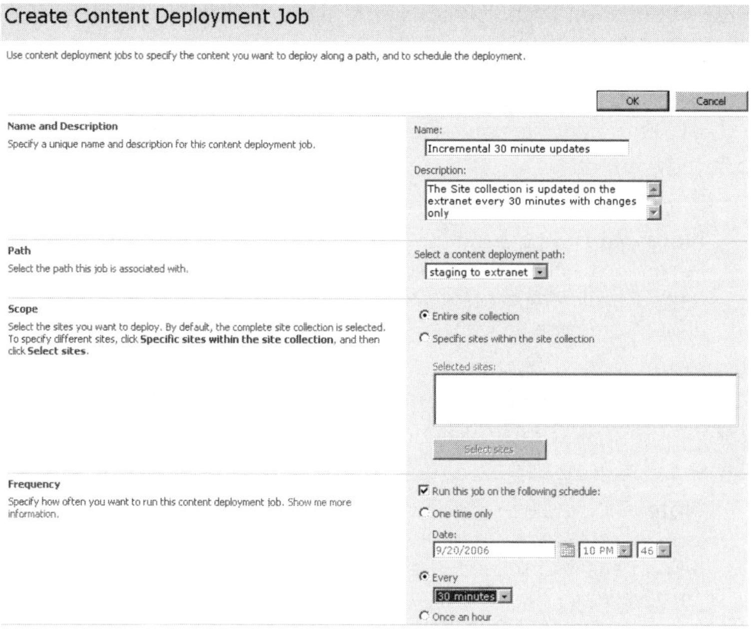

Figure 6-16 Creating a new Content Deployment Job

5. On the Create Content Deployment Job page, complete the following sections on the page:
   a. In the Name And Description section, type a name and description.
   b. In the Path section, select a path to use for the job. A job can be associated with only one path.
   c. In the Scope section, select a scope that is either the root of the site collection to be deployed or a specific site within the site collection. If you select the root of the site collection, all sites and content in the site collection will be deployed to the destination.
   d. In the Frequency section, select a schedule for when the job should run. You have many options for the frequency of the job timings. If you want to just run it once, there is no need to configure a schedule.
   e. In the Deployment Options section, select if you want to deploy all the content every time the job runs or just deploy the changes to the content since the job last ran. For regularly scheduled jobs, you should deploy the changes only.
   f. In the Notification section, select how notifications are sent for job success or failure and which e-mail address will receive the notification.
6. Click OK to complete the page.

Scenario: Expanding a Server Farm

Finally, in the following scenario we'll look at expanding an SharePoint Server 2007 small farm into a medium farm by adding a Web server and using the existing server as a back-end application server. By doing this you'll see how servers are managed in Central Administration and also how to configure the services running on each server in a farm.

More Info This scenario does not cover fully installing the SharePoint Server 2007 binaries. For more information on how to install SharePoint Server 2007, see Chapter 5.

Configuring the Server Farm

When installing SharePoint Server 2007, you choose the type of server to install. After typing in your product key code, you must select Advanced. You are then presented with a dialog box, as shown in Figure 6-17. Because you are building a medium farm and already have a complete installation that will be your back-end application server, you now need to add a Web server that will be responsible for the users' requests for Web services and also for search requests.

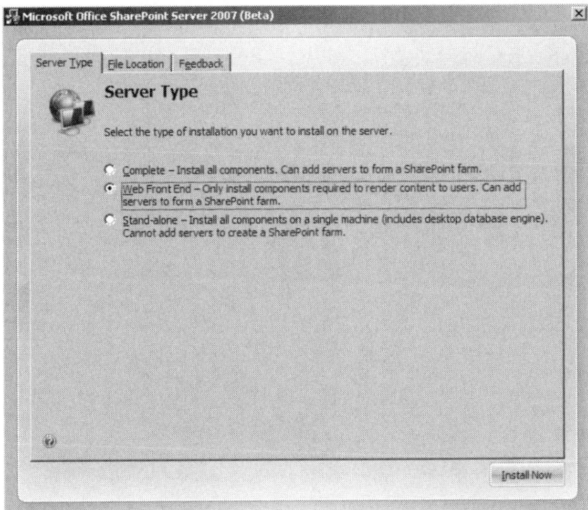

Figure 6-17 Choosing the install type for a Web front-end server

After the binaries have been installed, you are presented with the SharePoint Products And Technologies Configuration Wizard. Because you already have a farm and database server configured, you need to make sure you follow the process of joining the existing farm. Let's look at the settings required:

1. Select Yes, I Want To Connect To An Existing Server Farm. Click Next.
2. On the Specifiy Configuration Database Settings dialog box, shown in Figure 6-18, in the Database Server box, type the name of the server that is running your SQL database. Because you have already configured the first server, click Retrieve Database Names and select the name of the configuration database created when you installed the first SharePoint server. By default, the database name is SharePoint_Config.

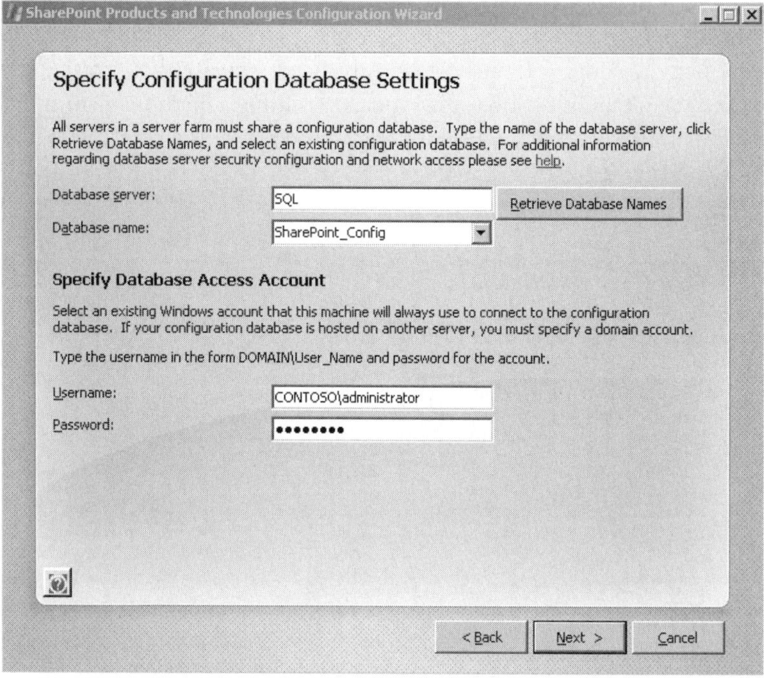

Figure 6-18 Specifying an existing configuration database

3. Specify the user name and password for the user account being used to connect to the SQL server. Click Next.
4. Because you already have the Central Administration site configured on the farm, you can go straight to the next page. Click Next.

5. You now need to select the method of authentication you want to use on your Web application. The default is NTLM, but if your environment supports Kerberos authentication, you can switch to Kerberos.
6. When the wizard has successfully completed, click Finish.

Configuring the Farm Services

Now that the Web server is joined to the farm, you need to configure the services that will run between the two servers in the farm. The services running on servers in the farm are configured from Central Administration using the Farm Topology tool. The services you need to configure will be based on that topology and on how many servers you have in your farm. In your topology—with only one Web server—you should enable the Share-Point Server Search service. If you had more than one Web server, you could choose to have the Search service enabled on all Web servers or just on one of them. Because this server will be the Web server, select at least the role of Web server and start the associated services as shown in Figure 6-19.

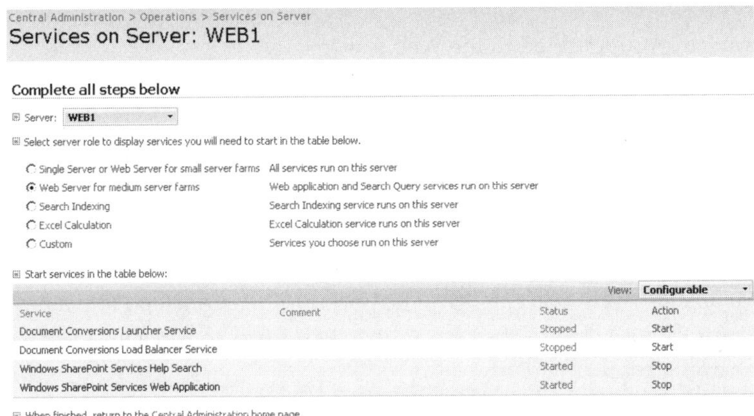

Figure 6-19 Configuring roles and services on a medium farm

A new feature of SharePoint Server 2007 is that Web applications are replicated to all servers configured in the farm. By joining the Web server to the farm, the Web applications already created on the Application server will already have been replicated to the Web server and will appear in IIS Manager. The only thing that has changed is the server name that users will use to connect to that Web application on the Web servers. In Figure 6-20, you can see that the Web applications and Application pools are now visable in the IIS Manager on Web1, the Web server.

Note If your application server was using *http://Office SharePoint Server 2007:43543* as a URL to connect to a site collection when the Web application was replicated to the new Web server, you would use the Web server name in the URL to connect via the new Web server. For example *http://web1:43543*.

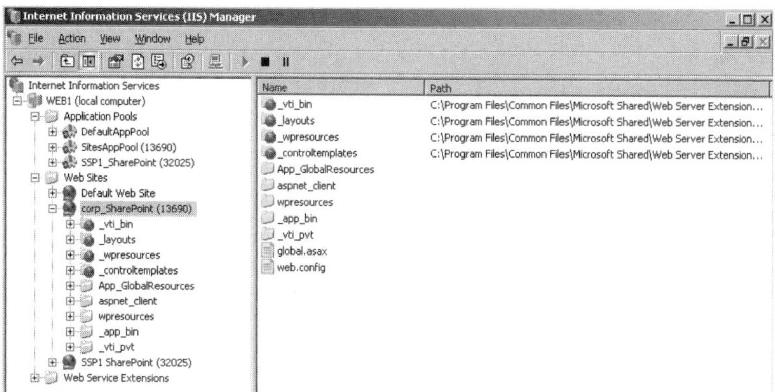

Figure 6-20 Web applications replicated to the Web server

Now that the server has been configured as a Web server, you can define how users will connect to that server from the network. Most users will connect to the server using the server name on port 80. This is usually a good idea as users generally don't like to have to remember how to connect to a site using a server name and random port number—DNS names make it easier for them. To have users connect using port 80, you can go into the Web application hosting the site collection and change the port used to 80 and use a specific IP address, or, alternatively, you can leave the port number alone and add a new host header and use port 80 with the host header. Follow these steps to add a host header and port 80 to a Web application:

1. Go to Start, Administrator Tools, Internet Information Services (IIS) Manager.
2. Expand Web Sites and right click the Web site you want to add the host header to.
3. Select properties of the Web site.
4. On the Web Site tab, click Advanced.
5. In the multiple identities for this Web Site section, click Add and complete the following fields:
   - **IP address** Leave as All Unassigned.
   - **TCP port** Type **80**.
   - **Host Header value** Type the name that users will type when accessing the Web site. For example, **portal.contoso.msft**.

6. Click OK, then click OK again, and then click OK again to leave the Properties page.

All that remains now is for the Administrator for DNS to add the new host header name to DNS for the contoso.msft domain and the correct IP address to the network card on the Web server, and any requests for that URL will be redirected now by IIS to the correct Web site.

Configuring Network Load Balancing

You now have successfully installed and configured a medium server farm. From here, you can add greater resilience to the Web server by adding another Web server and configuring Network Load Balancing on the operating system. Doing this will enable IIS to use load-balancing requests across the two Web servers for users' requests. After you implement this arrangement, if one of the Web servers goes down, all users' requests are routed to the one Web server that is still available. By setting up network load balancing, you also offload some of the work load for generating the Web pages. Two servers sharing this load can handle a lot more concurrent users connecting to the same content sources than one server can. Let's have a look at how we set this up.

The first step after adding your second Web server to the farm is to configure network load balancing. It is better to configure this from a server that is not one of the Web servers.

1. Launch Network Load Balancing Manager from the administrative tools.
2. Right-click Network Load Balanced Cluster and select New Cluster.
3. On the Cluster Parameters page, specify the new IP address, subnet mask, and full Internet name for the cluster. Use the Internet DNS name you want to use for your users (for example, portal.contoso.msft). This host name and IP address need to have been set up in DNS prior to completing this step.
4. On the same page, select the Cluster Operation mode.
    a. If the Web server has a single network card, select Multicast.
    b. If the Web server has two network cards or more, select Unicast.
5. Click Next.
6. On the Cluster IP Address page you can add additional cluster IP addresses to be used by the load balanced servers. Accept the default and click Next.
7. On the Port Rules page, click Edit and select None for the Filtering Mode Affinity setting.
8. Click OK.

9. Click Next.
10. On the Connect page, add the first Web servers IP address as the first host to be added to the cluster in the Host field section. Click Connect.
11. Ensure the Interface card name for the Web server is displayed. If you have two network cards on the Web servers, select the inteface that the users will be connecting to.
12. Click Next.
13. On the Host Parameters page, accept the defaults and click Finish.

The Web server should now be configured in the Network Load Balancing Manager screen, as shown in Figure 6-21.

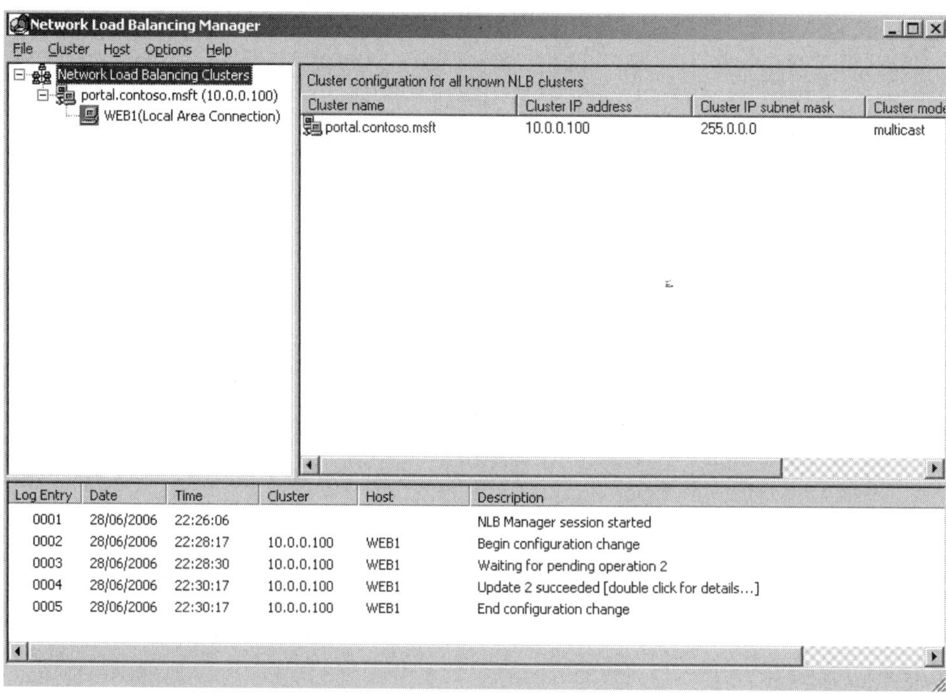

Figure 6-21 Configuring Network Load Balancing

To configure the second Web server follow these steps:

1. In the Network Load Balancing Manager screen, right-click the network load balancing cluster that you created in the previous steps, and select Add Node To Cluster.

2. Repeat steps 1 through 7, selecting the correct network interface card and ensuring that the priority is set to 2, and then click Finish. You should now see both nodes configured in the Network Load Balancing Manager and their status should show as Converged, meaning that the configuration is satisfactory, as shown in Figure 6-22.

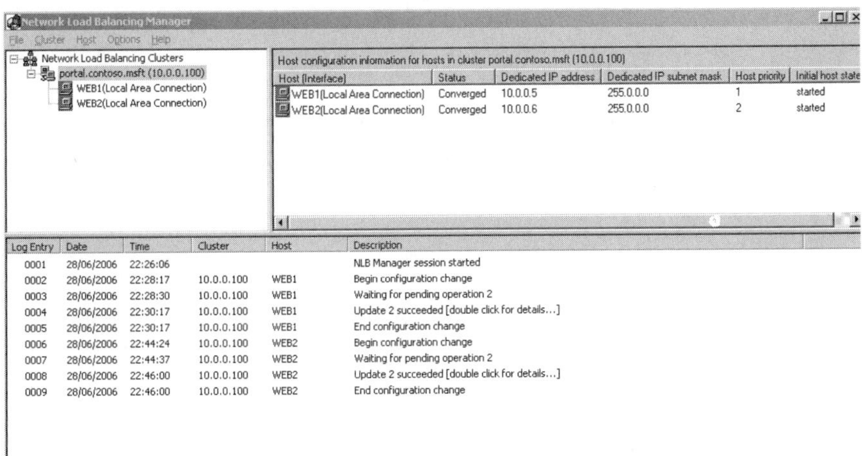

Figure 6-22 Configuring Network Load Balancing with both servers converged and load balanced

3. To test the cluster, open a command prompt and ping the IP address of the cluster's IP you configured in step 3. Also, after adding the cluster's fully qualified domain name to DNS, ping that as well.

More Info You can find more information on configuring network load balanced clusters at *http://technet2.microsoft.com/WindowsServer/en/library/98d46a24-96d8-412c-87d8-28ace62323d21033.mspx?mfr=true*.

Now that the cluster is set up, you now have resilience and load balacing set up on your Web servers. As you can see from Central Administration in SharePoint Server 2007, you now have three servers: one is configured as a back-end application server, and two are Web servers, as shown in Figure 6-23. If you want to scale this out further, you can do so by adding more servers into the load-balanced cluster manager and adding the servers as Web servers in the SharePoint Server 2007 configuration.

Farm Topology

Server	Services Running
MAIL	Windows SharePoint Services Outgoing E-Mail
MOSS2007	Central Administration Excel Calculation Services Office SharePoint Server Search Windows SharePoint Services Help Search Windows SharePoint Services Incoming E-Mail Windows SharePoint Services Web Application
SQL	Windows SharePoint Services Database
WEB1	Windows SharePoint Services Incoming E-Mail Windows SharePoint Services Web Application
WEB2	Windows SharePoint Services Incoming E-Mail Windows SharePoint Services Web Application

Figure 6-23 Central Administration with two Web servers in the Farm Topology view

Summary

This chapter concentrated on the options available to you on the Central Administration Home page, such as configuring administrative tasks and defining the services and roles that are provided by the servers in the farm topology. You also looked at the Operations interface in Central Administration and saw how most of the configuration options in this page were farmwide and had a global impact on all servers configured in the farm. This chapter did not cover all the sections on the page because other chapters in this book go into those topics in detail.

Finally, you looked at adding more Web servers to an SharePoint Server 2007 farm, expanding out to a medium farm, and configuring the services and roles that each server provides in that topology. To add resilience to the Web servers, you added Network Load Balancing. By doing this, requests from your users were spread between the two Web servers. You also saw how you needed to configure both the host header and DNS properties to make the name resolution work correctly by pointing to the load-balanced cluster's fully qualified domain name.

In the next chapter, you will look at the final part of Central Administration, which is the Application Management interface.

Chapter 7

Application Management and Configuration

In the previous chapter, you learned how to configure and manage the Central Administration Home page and the Operations page. Now you are going to learn about the third management page in Central Administration, which is the Application Management page. Don't confuse application management with *Web* application management however. Even though you configure Web applications on this page, it is only one section of the configuration options available. Many of the applications that can be configured in Microsoft Office SharePoint Server 2007 are optional, and you might not want to configure everything that is presented on this page. However, this chapter addresses all the available options and points out certain options, such as the Shared Services Provider (SSP), that are important to the successful initial deployment of your farm.

One improvement made in Office SharePoint Server 2007 is the ability to create and manage Web applications that exist in Internet Information Services (IIS) 6.0. In the previous version of SharePoint, you had to create Web sites (virtual servers) and configure them prior to extending them with SharePoint. With the new Web application management tools, you can now do this from Central Administration. You will also be learning about site management tools, such as quota templates, that enable you to configure and manage site collections and even configure an auto-site deletion rule.

There are eight sections on the Application Management page (see Figure 7-1), and in this chapter, you will learn about the following five sections:

- SharePoint Web Application Management

- SharePoint Site Management
- Application Security
- External Service Connections
- Workflow Management

The remaining three sections are covered in the following chapters:

- Search: Chapter 16, "Enterprise Search and Indexing Architecture and Administration," and Chapter 17, "Enterprise Search and Indexing Deployment"
- InfoPath Forms Services: Chapter 21, "Administrating Office Forms Server 2007 in Office SharePoint Server 2007"
- Office SharePoint Server Shared Services: Chapter 18, "Administrating Shared Services Providers"

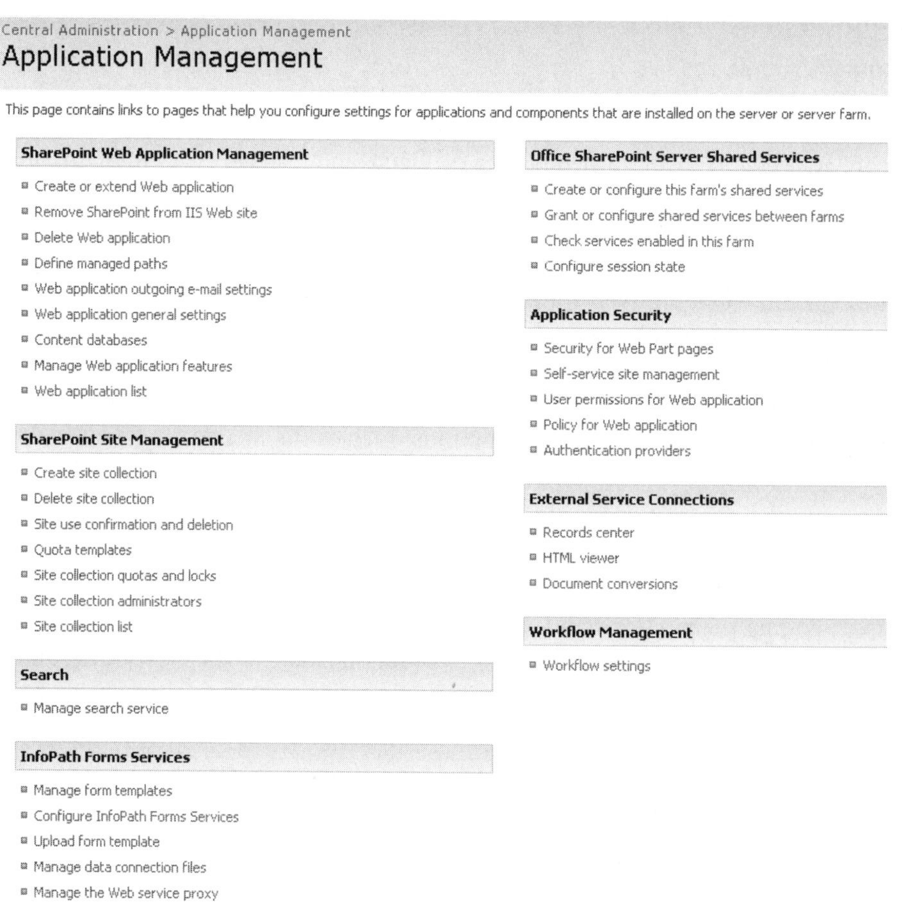

Figure 7-1 The Application Management page in Central Administration

SharePoint Web Application Management

After your servers have been installed and configured with SharePoint and your farm topology has been created, the next step is to create and manage the Web applications that will be used by the SSP and site collections. A *site collection* is a group of Web sites on a virtual server; the Web sites have the same owner and administrative settings. An SSP is a collection of farm services, such as profiles, search, and audiences, that are made available and consumed by the associated Web applications and site collections.

More Info For detailed information on SSPs, refer to Chapter 18.

This section covers creating, deleting, and managing these Web applications and establishes why Web application management knowledge is critical to the successful running of your farm's services and applications.

Hosting a Web Application

To host site collections and SSPs, you need to have a hosting application to manage those services. This hosting application for SharePoint Server 2007 is IIS 6.0. Although "Web applications" is the term we use to describe this functionality in SharePoint Server 2007, you might have heard Web applications referred to by other names, for example:

- An IIS administrator might refer to them as "Web sites."
- A SharePoint Portal 2003 administrator might refer to them as "virtual servers."

IIS 6.0 is a set of software services that enables Microsoft Windows Server 2003 to host Web sites, Simple Mail Transfer Protocol (SMTP) servers, File Transfer Protocol (FTP) sites, and Network News Transfer Protocol (NNTP) services. The type of Web sites that IIS 6.0 can host depends on the software that is installed and enabled on top of IIS. In the case of SharePoint Server 2007, you have installed the .NET Framework which includes Windows Workflow Foundation. With these two components installed on top of IIS, you have a very feature-rich set of components with which to create the Web applications and SSPs.

More Info See Chapter 5, "Installing Microsoft Office SharePoint Server 2007," for more information on the installation procedure for the .NET Framework and Windows Workflow Foundation.

Creating a Web Application

A Web application is defined by a port number or host headers, or both, and includes an application pool and authentication method. As part of the creation process, a database is also created that is used for storing the content from the sites associated with the Web application. (You will learn about each of these options in the "Creating a New Web Application" section.) Once a Web application has been created, you can do one of three things:

- Extend it to create a new site collection.
- Extend and map it to an existing site collection.
- Leave it as is to be used for hosting an SSP.

Each of these options will be covered in more detail later in this chapter, in the "Provisioning a Web Application" section.

Note When creating a new SSP, if you do not have a free Web application, there is a link to create a new Web application as part of the configuration screen.

Extending a Web Application

If you choose to extend the Web application and create a new site collection, you can associate the top-level site with a template such as a corporate portal or team site. By creating multiple Web applications and extending them with different templates, you can create standalone site collections that are all associated with a single SSP. All the sites in these Web applications can consume the available services from the SSP, such as profiles, audiences, and search. Within SharePoint Portal Server 2003, it was not possible to have standalone site collections and have them participate in shared services. This feature is a big step forward for Web applications.

Shared Service Providers

An SSP is required before you create Web applications that will host site collections. This is because the Web application hosting a site collection needs to know which SSP it is associated with in order to consume the services provided by the SSP. The services that can be configured in an SSP and consumed by a Web application include some or all of the following:

- Profiles and My Sites
- Audiences

- Search
- Business Data Catalog
- Excel Services
- Usage Reporting

For more detailed information on configuring and managing the SSP, see Chapter 18.

In SharePoint Server 2007, you can also create multiple SSPs, which can then provide different services to any Web applications associated with them. This enables administrators to choose which Web applications belong to which SSPs, and therefore, what services are provided to the sites housed by the Web application.

Why Use a Separate Application Pool for Each Web Application?

When creating Web applications, you need to decide whether you want to associate each Web application with its own application pool in IIS. There are several reasons to consider this issue:

- Each application pool runs in its own memory space using a worker process, which means that if an application pool fails, it does affect other Web applications using their own application pool.
- Each application pool requires additional resources and can easily consume up to 100 MB of physical memory without any connected users. This extra resource use is offset by the advantage given by running each Web application in its own memory process.
- Multiple worker processes can be associated with a single application pool for resilience.

Creating a Database for Each Web Application

A final reason for creating multiple Web applications is that you can create a database for each one. This helps with database management size and in situations such as performing disaster recovery and SQL maintenance jobs.

More Info For a detailed discussion of how application pools work with Web applications, see Chapter 2, "Architecture for Microsoft Office SharePoint Server 2007."

Creating a New Web Application

After completing your initial Central Administration tasks and configuring the server farm, the next task is to create a new SSP.

> **Note** An SSP is required before additional Web applications and site collections can be created because the Web applications that host site collections need to be associated with an SSP.

As part of this process, you must create a new Web application either through the Application Management section of Central Administration or during the creation of an SSP.

Both methods take you to the Create New Web Application page (shown in Figure 7-4) in Central Administration. This section shows you both methods for accessing this page, and it describes the choices available to you for creating your Web application. If you need to create a new site collection or extend a Web application, use the Application Management page. If you are creating a new Web application for an SSP, use the New Shared Services Provider page.

> **Note** A good reason for creating the Web application from the SSP page is if creating a Web application from the SSP creation page it will take you back to the SSP creation page once the new Web application has been created.

> **Note** Unlike previous versions of SharePoint, SharePoint Server 2007 automatically replicates Web applications to all SharePoint servers in your farm so that there is no need to re-create the Web applications on all front-end servers and extend them.

Creating a New Web Application Using Application Management

To create a Web application through the Central Administration Application Management tab, complete the following steps:

1. On the Central Administration Home page, select the Application Management tab.
2. On the Application Management page (shown in Figure 7-1), in the SharePoint Web Application Management section, select Create Or Extend Web Application to open the Create Or Extend Web Application page, shown in Figure 7-2.

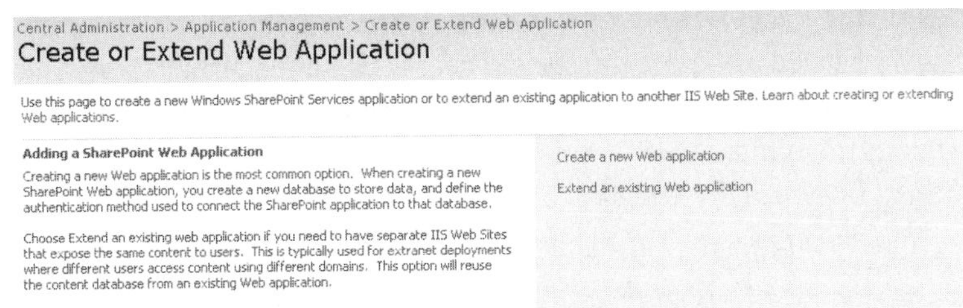

Figure 7-2 Creating a new Web application on the Application Management page

3. Select Create A New Web Application to open the Create A New Web Application page.

Creating a New Web Application Through SSP Creation

To create a Web application when you create a new SSP, complete the following steps:

1. On the Application Management page in Central Administration, in the Office SharePoint Server Shared Services section, select Create Or Configure This Farm's Shared Services to open the Manage This Farm's Shared Services page.
2. To create an SSP, select New SSP.
3. On the New Shared Services Provider page (shown in Figure 7-3), assign a unique identifier to the provider in the SSP Name box, click Create A New Web Application, and click OK to open the Create New Web Application page.

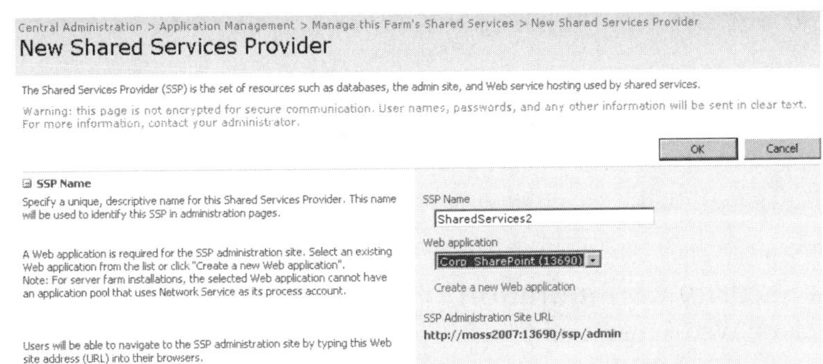

Figure 7-3 Creating a new Web application when creating the SSP

Assigning a Port Number or Host Header

On the Create New Web Application page (see Figure 7-4), your application is automatically allocated a random port number, a description, and a folder location in the default local path. By default, this path is C:\Inetpub\wwwroot\wss\VirtualDirectories *portnumber*. You are not, by default, given a host header value. Therefore, add it in the

Host Header box if you want to use a fully qualified domain name, such as http://portal.contoso.msft, as well as a port number to access this Web application. Therefore, in order to connect to the Web application using the random port number, you would use http://portal.contoso.msft:46189. You must ensure that this host header URL is resolved by your users. Normally, this is achieved by adding an entry into DNS pointing the URL to the Web server.

Note If you want to use port 80 and host headers for your Web applications, make sure you leave the IIS IP settings set to All Unassigned.

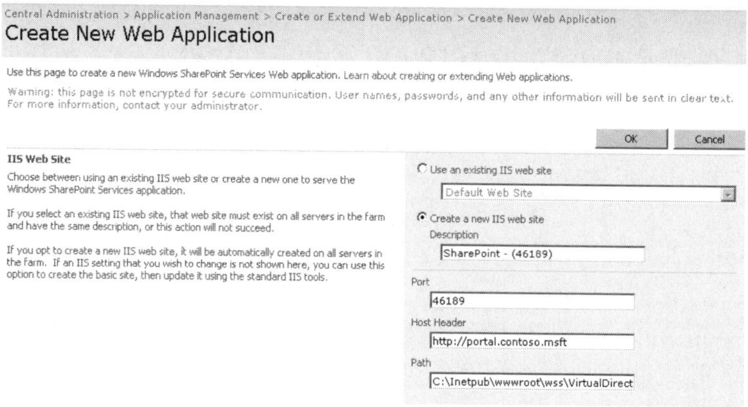

Figure 7-4 Choosing a port and host header

Best Practices Name your Web application descriptions and paths with a logical naming convention to easily identify them in the folder structure and in IIS. For example, instead of using "SharePoint (9845)" as the description, use "Corporate Portal (9845)", and do the same for the path.

Choosing a Security Configuration

On the Create New Web Application page, there are two authentication protocols available for a Web application: Kerberos and NTLM. By default, it is set to NTLM authentication for maximum compatibility with mixed-domain models and user account permissions, as shown in Figure 7-5. Web applications use these security mechanisms when they communicate with other servers and applications in the network, such as when communicating with the Microsoft SQL server hosting the databases.

Security Configuration

Kerberos is the recommended security configuration to use with Integrated Windows authentication. Kerberos requires the application pool account to be Network Service or special configuration by the domain administrator. NTLM authentication will work with any application pool account and the default domain configuration.

If you choose to use Secure Sockets Layer (SSL), you must add the certificate on each server using the IIS administration tools. Until this is done, the web application will be inaccessible from this IIS Web Site.

Authentication provider:

Negotiate (Kerberos)

NTLM

Allow Anonymous:

Yes

No

Use Secure Sockets Layer (SSL):

Yes

No

Figure 7-5 Security configuration options for a Web application

Kerberos authentication is more secure than NTLM authentication, but it requires a service principal name (SPN) for the domain account that SharePoint is using. This SPN, which must be added by a member of the domain administrators group, enables the SharePoint account to use Kerberos authentication.

More Info For more information on configuring a Kerberos service principal name for the domain user account, refer to the Microsoft Knowledge Base article located at *http://support.microsoft.com/?id=832769.*

When you choose NTLM authentication, it does not matter which domain account is being used by the Web application to communicate with the application pool because the application pool will run as long as it has the required permissions to access the SQL server and the Web server. The required SQL permissions for a Web application account are configured in the Security Logins page on the SQL server's Enterprise Manager console. The required roles are as follows:

- Database Creator Role
- Security Administrator

Also in the Security Configuration section of the Create New Web Application page, you can enable anonymous access on the Web application, which enables users to gain access to the sites hosted on the Web application without authenticating. You must, however, also enable anonymous access on the site itself because enabling it on the Web application only gets the users past IIS authentication. This is a useful configuration for any Internet-facing sites, such as a company Web site. To enable Anonymous access in a site, follow these steps:

1. Click Site Actions.
2. Click Site Settings.
3. Click Modify all Settings.

4. Click Advanced Permissions.
5. Click Settings.
6. Click Anonymous Access to define the access rights for Anonymous users.

For added security, you can also enable Secure Sockets Layer (SSL) certificates on the Web application. You can choose to use certificates from both your internal certificate authority or from an authorized certificate authority such as Thawte or VeriSign. You must install the SSL certificate, however, on all servers where users will be accessing the Web application or their access attempt will fail.

More Info For more information on creating an SSL certificate, see the Microsoft Knowledge Base article located at *http://support.microsoft.com/kb/299875/en-us*.

Creating a Load-Balanced URL

When you configure a load-balanced URL, it becomes the default URL with which users access the sites hosted on this Web application. To add a load-balanced URL, complete the following steps:

Note Adding a host header automatically populates the load-balanced URL.

1. On the Create New Web Application page, scroll down to the Load Balanced URL section, shown in Figure 7-6.

Figure 7-6 Creating a load-balanced URL

2. Add your load-balanced URL by using the fully qualified domain that will be used by your users–for example, http://portal.contoso.msft.

A load-balanced URL is used when configuring multiple front-end servers that are load-balanced using the Windows Server 2003 Network Load-Balancing Service. The Network Load-Balancing Service enables administrators to create a cluster IP address that will be shared by all front-end servers' network cards configured in the load-balancing configuration. See Chapter 6, "Performing Central Administration and Operations Configuration," for more information on configuring the Network Load-Balancing Service. For your users to connect to the clustered IP address, however, you should also define a load-balanced URL both here in the Web application and on your DNS servers so that the name resolutions match.

The load-balanced URL uses the default zone for user access, and this zone is matched to the URL mappings that are configured for the default zone configured in Central Administration. To configure the URL mappings, complete the following steps:

1. On the Central Administration Home page, click the Operations tab.
2. On the Operations page, click Alternate Access Mappings in the Global Configuration section to open the Alternate Access Mappings Management page.
3. Click Add Incoming URLs.
4. Select the Web application hosting the load-balanced URL.
5. Add the load-balanced URL to the incoming URL.
6. Leave the zone set to Default.
7. Click Save.

More Info See Chapter 6 for more information on Alternate Access Mappings and Zones.

Configuring the Application Pool

An application pool is used to configure a level of isolation between different Web applications and their hosted sites. Each application pool is serviced by its own worker process (w3wp.exe). This means if one worker process hangs it will not affect other worker processes hosting different application pools.

Planning You do not need to create a new application pool for every Web application because Web applications can share application pools, and each new application pool can easily consume 100 MB and more of physical memory once users start connecting to Web sites hosted on the Web applications. Only create new application pools when a site collection must have higher levels of resilience and its own physical set of memory resources.

What type of install you have chosen determines how many application pools are created by default. Unless you have created a Standalone (Basic) installation, you will need to create at least one application pool for hosting the SSP and one for hosting the first Web application and its associated sites. When creating a new application pool, use a meaningful descriptive name to make it easy to identify in IIS. This naming strategy is especially useful in a disaster recovery scenario when you might have multiple application pools and random port numbers.

When selecting a security account that will be used by the application pool, you can either choose a predefined local or network service account, or you can create and assign your own service account, as shown in Figure 7-7. In most cases, you will want to create and assign your own service account because it gives you the most flexibility for scaling out a server farm:

- *Local Service* is an account that has low-level access rights on the server and is useful when you do not need to connect to resources on remote computers. This is suitable only on a standalone installation with SharePoint and SQL Server on the same server.
- *Network Service* is also a low-level access rights account, but it also has the ability to connect to remote resources.
- *Configurable* allows you to assign a domain user account you created as the service account that will be used by the application pool to access the necessary services and servers, such as an SQL database. This account should be configured with the following rights:
  - Naming format of domainname\username
  - Local Administrator on the SharePoint server
  - SQL database creator and security administrator server role

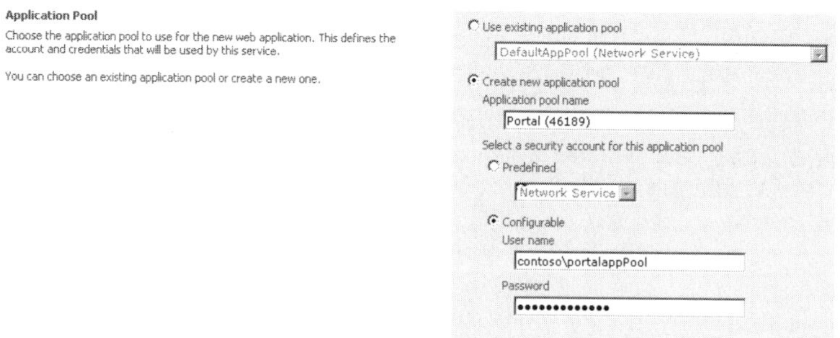

Figure 7-7 Creating a new application pool

Reset Internet Information Services

Select Restart IIS Automatically so that an iisreset is performed on all Web servers after the new Web application has been replicated. See Figure 7-8.

Warning If you do not select restart IIS automatically, then you will have to manually go to each Web server and run iisreset /noforce before the new sites are available to be used.

Reset Internet Information Services

Use this section to allow SharePoint to restart IIS on other farm servers. The local server must be restarted manually for the process to complete. If this option is not selected and you have more than one server in the farm, you must wait until the IIS web site is created on all servers, and then run "iisreset /noforce" on each Web server. The new IIS site will not be usable until that is completed.

Figure 7-8 Reseting Internet Information Services on the Web servers

Database Name and Authentication

By default, the database server name presented is the SQL server configured in Central Administration and is the one used when you first installed the product and configured your farm. It is possible to specify a different SQL Server instance for a Web application. To configure the database name and authentication method, complete the following steps:

1. Scroll down the Create New Web Application page to the Database Name And Authentication section, shown in Figure 7-9.

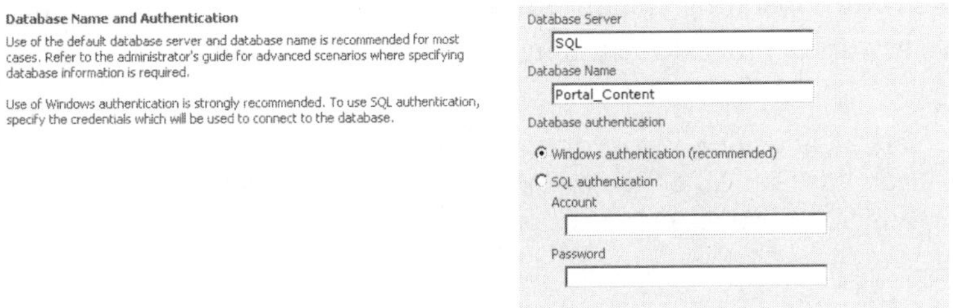

Figure 7-9 Specifying the database server and name

2. Change the Database Server if it is different than the default.
3. Choose a name for the new database, and type it in the Database Name box.
4. Select a Database Authentication method. The default is Windows Authentication.

Best Practices Always name your databases with a useful description so that you can easily identify the database in backup and restore situations. For example, if this Web application was going to manage the My Corporate Portal site, you could call the database Corp_Content rather than the default of WSS_Content.

When configuring the database account, use Windows authentication and, by default, your SQL server will be set to accept only Windows authentication for security purposes. This account must have Create and Modify database rights in the SQL server and use the format of *domainname\username*.

Search Server

As shown in Figure 7-10, a Web application will use the search server that has been configured for the Office SharePoint Server Search service that is configured on the Services On Server page, as discussed in Chapter 6.

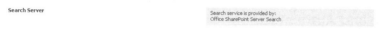

Figure 7-10 The search server using the Office SharePoint Server Search service

Assigning Additional Worker Processes to an Application Pool

A simple way to add resilience and enhance performance for an application pool is to create additional worker processes associated with that application pool. All Web applications and their sites will benefit from this additional availability of resources. In IIS 6.0, an application pool configuration that is supported by multiple worker processes is known as a *Web garden*. Creating additional worker processes creates additional w3wp.exe processes running in your operating system. You can see in Figure 7-11 that currently there are two w3wp.exe worker processes running on the SharePoint Server 2007 server.

Note Create an additional worker process per 600 MB of physical memory. For example, if you have 1.5 GB of free memory at peak use of the server, you could create two additional worker processes on the server.

Windows Task Manager

File Options View Help

Applications | Processes | Performance | Networking | Users

Image Name	User Name	CPU	Mem Usage
ctfmon.exe	Administrator	00	2,268 K
IEXPLORE.EXE	Administrator	00	2,696 K
w3wp.exe	Administrator	00	92,396 K
w3wp.exe	Administrator	00	5,384 K
taskmgr.exe	Administrator	05	3,516 K
explorer.exe	Administrator	02	11,648 K
wuauclt.exe	Administrator	00	4,616 K
mssearch.exe	Administrator	00	5,736 K
wsstracing.exe	LOCAL SERVICE	00	5,036 K
svchost.exe	LOCAL SERVICE	00	5,132 K
svchost.exe	LOCAL SERVICE	00	1,172 K
svchost.exe	NETWORK SERVICE	00	2,952 K
svchost.exe	NETWORK SERVICE	00	3,880 K
msdtc.exe	NETWORK SERVICE	00	3,756 K
wmiprvse.exe	NETWORK SERVICE	00	6,956 K
System Idle Process	SYSTEM	89	16 K
System	SYSTEM	02	220 K
smss.exe	SYSTEM	00	428 K
csrss.exe	SYSTEM	02	3,312 K

Show processes from all users   End Process

Processes: 35 | CPU Usage: 11% | Commit Charge: 336M / 2069M

Figure 7-11 Two worker processes

To create a Web garden and see the effect it has on the amount of available w3wp.exe processes, complete the following steps:

1. Open Internet Information Services Manager from your administrator tools on the SharePoint Server 2007 server where you want the additional worker processes to be created. This should be the server your users are connecting to, such as a front-end server.
2. Expand Application Pools.
3. Right-click the application pool to be configured and select Properties.
4. Select the Performance tab, shown in Figure 7-12. Under the Web Garden section, set the Maximum Number Of Worker Processes to 4.

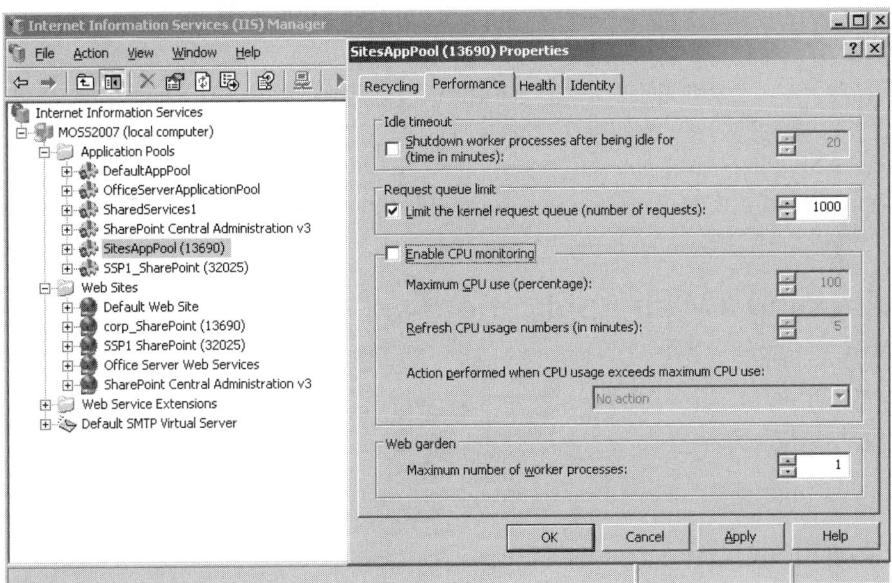

Figure 7-12 Adding more worker processes

5. Click Apply and then click OK.
6. Close the IIS Manager.
7. Open a command prompt and type **IISRESET**.

Configuration is now complete. When the Web application that uses the application pool has multiple connections associated with it, multiple worker processes will be launched up to a maximum of four, as shown in Figure 7-13.

Note The fifth worker process shown is for the application pool running Central Administration.

Windows Task Manager

File Options View Help

Applications Processes Performance Networking Users

Image Name	User Name	CPU	Mem Usage	Handles
wuauclt.exe	Administrator	00	4,652 K	111
wsstracing.exe	LOCAL SERVICE	00	5,060 K	80
WSSADMIN.EXE	SYSTEM	00	13,652 K	345
wmiprvse.exe	SYSTEM	00	4,792 K	148
wmiprvse.exe	NETWORK SERVICE	00	6,912 K	192
winlogon.exe	SYSTEM	00	11,140 K	671
w3wp.exe	Administrator	00	102,048 K	769
w3wp.exe	Administrator	00	102,832 K	783
w3wp.exe	Administrator	00	5,356 K	119
w3wp.exe	Administrator	00	100,604 K	761
w3wp.exe	Administrator	00	90,056 K	832

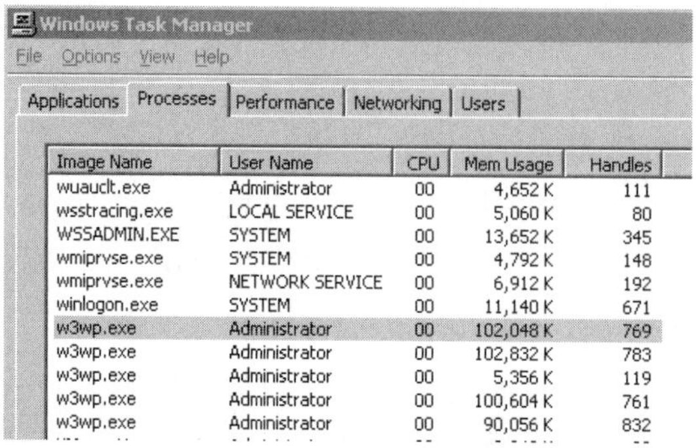

Figure 7-13 A Web garden with four worker processes running

When a Web garden is running, each process is allocated its own memory space. This means that if you allocate 800 MB of memory to the application pool and then set up a Web garden with three processes, the application pool will divide the memory usage of 800 MB between the three processes.

Provisioning a Web Application

After you create a Web application, you have three options for provisioning it:

- **Option 1** Extend the Web application, and create a new site collection.
- **Option 2** Return to Central Administration, and create a new SSP.
- **Option 3** Extend the Web application, and map it to an existing site collection.

Creating a New Site Collection

Creating a new site collection allows you to select a template and extend the Web application with a site template. There are many new templates included with SharePoint Server 2007, and they are divided into four tabbed choices. Table 7-1 describes each of the tabs. To create a new site collection on a free Web application and choose a template, complete the following steps:

1. Go to Central Administration, and select the Application Management page.
2. Select Create Site Collection in the SharePoint Site Management section.
3. Give the site collection a title, URL, and administrator account.

4. Choose a template from the available four tabs (described in Table 7-1), and click OK.

Table 7-1 Site Collection Template Choices

Tab name	Template choices
Collaboration	Team Site, Blank Site, Document Workspace, Wiki Site or Blog
Meetings	Basic Meeting Workspace, Blank Meeting Workspace, Decision Meeting Workspace, Social Meeting Workspace, Multipage Meeting Workspace
Enterprise	Document Center, Records Center, Site Directory, Report Center, Search Center with Tabs, My Site Host, Search Center.
Publishing	Collaboration Portal, Publishing Portal

Creating a New SSP

Creating a new SSP allows you to configure and provide a new set of services to Web applications associated with that SSP. The new SSP will have its own management page. To create a new SSP on the Web application, refer to Chapter 18.

Mapping a Web Application to an Existing Site Collection

If you choose to extend and map the Web application, you select an unused Web application, and by extending the Web application, you are able to redirect requests made to that Web application to another Web application already provisioned with a site collection. This allows you to change the authentication mechanism on the new Web application to Basic authentication for example, with an SSL certificate to support external users connecting from the Internet. This method enables both Windows authenticated users and Basic authenticated users to access the same site collection and content, but to do so by using unique URLs from both internal and external networks.

Additional Web Application Management Settings

After a Web application has been created, several additional management settings are available to configure. These options allow fine tuning of the Web application or even removing SharePoint altogether from the Web application. To configure the additional Web application settings, go to Central Administration and click the Application Management page. The following management options are listed under the SharePoint Web Application Management section:

- Remove SharePoint From IIS Web Site
- Delete Web Application
- Define Managed Paths
- Web Application Outgoing E-Mail Settings

- Web Application General Settings
- Content Databases
- Manage Web Application Features
- Web Application List

This section describes each of these management options.

Remove SharePoint From IIS Web Site

This management option allows you to unextend the Web application and remove SharePoint Services from using the Web application in IIS. The Web application itself is not deleted and can be used for reprovisioning a new site collection or SSP at any time. To use this option, complete the following steps:

1. Go to Central Administration, and click the Application Management page.
2. Click Remove SharePoint From IIS Web Site under the SharePoint Web Application Management section.
3. On the Unextend Windows SharePoint Services From IIS Web Site page, select a Web application by clicking the Web Application Name drop-down arrow and choosing to change the Web application.
4. Confirm the Web site and zone to be unextended.
5. If you want to delete the Web site from IIS and the IIS metabase, select Yes.
6. Click OK.

Delete Web Application

This management option allows you to delete the Web application and also the databases associated with it. Before deciding to delete a Web application, make sure you have a working backup. To use this option, complete the following steps:

1. Go to Central Administration, and click the Application Management page.
2. Click Delete Web Application under the SharePoint Web Application Management section.
3. On the Delete Web Application page, select a Web application by clicking the Web Application Name drop-down arrow and choosing to change the Web application.
4. Select Yes to delete the content databases from the database server.
5. Select Yes to delete all the IIS Web sites and IIS metabase entries associated with the Web application.
6. Click OK.

Define Managed Paths

This management option lets you identify the managed paths that indicate which parts of the URL namespace are managed by each Web application in IIS. On the Define Managed Paths page, shown in Figure 7-14, you can also define a taxonomy within the namespace by creating new sites and associating them with specific namespaces such as customers or projects.

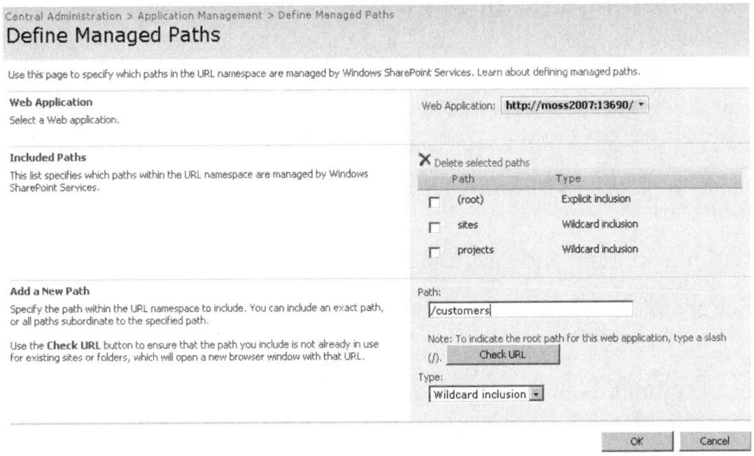

Figure 7-14 Adding a new managed path

There are two types of managed paths: explicit and wildcard. Use an *explicit* managed path to allow only a particular namespace, such as /customers, or use a *wildcard* managed path to include that namespace and all URL namespaces that come after it, such as /customers/*.

> **Note** For example, if you create a new managed path for customers, the URL will become http://portal/customers. With this new mapping, when a new site or site collection is created, it can be associated with the new managed path, such as http://portal/customers/customerA, instead of using the default managed path of sites.

To define managed paths, complete the following steps:

1. Go to Central Administration, and click the Application Management page.
2. Scroll to the SharePoint Web Application Management section, and click Define Managed Paths.
3. On the Define Managed Paths page, select a Web application by clicking the Web Application Name drop-down arrow and choosing to change the Web application.

4. Add the new path by typing the name in the Path box. If the new path is to be at the root of the Web application, start the path with a forward slash (/).
5. Click Check URL to ensure that the path is not already in use for the selected Web application.
6. Click OK.

Web Application Outgoing E-Mail Settings

By default, a global e-mail server for outgoing mail is defined on the Operations page of Central Administration. You can, however, also specify a unique outgoing mail server for each Web application. This could be useful in a situation where a Web application that is hosting an extranet-facing site collection needs to use an SMTP server that resides within the screened subnet rather than on the internal network. To update the e-mail settings, complete the following steps:

1. Go to Central Administration, and click the Application Management page.
2. Scroll to the SharePoint Web Application Management section, and click E-mail Settings.
3. On the Web Application E-Mail Settings page, select a Web application by clicking the Web Application Name drop-down arrow and choosing to change the Web application.
4. Specify the Outbound SMTP server using the fully qualified domain name.
5. Choose a From and Reply To SMTP address.
6. Choose a localized character set.
7. Click OK.

Web Application Settings

Each Web application has individual settings that affect all the sites that are being hosted by the Web application. Table 7-2 describes each of these settings. To access the Web application settings, complete the following steps:

1. Go to Central Administration, and click the Application Management page.
2. Scroll to the SharePoint Web Application Management section, and click Web Application Settings.
3. In the Web Application Settings page, select a Web application by clicking the Web Application name drop-down arrow and choosing to change the Web application.
4. Use Table 7-2 for information on each available field for the Web application settings.

Table 7-2 Web Application Settings

Property name	Description
Default Time Zone	All sites created on all Web applications take the time zone from the farm's global settings. Here you can change the default time zone for all sites created on just that specific Web application.
Default Quota Template	This property allows you to create and assign a specific database quota limit on the total amount of content allowed to be stored for all site collections associated with that Web application. Multiple quota templates can be created and used by different Web applications.
Person Name and Smart Tag and Presence Settings	When users browse a site, they can see details of other users' online status with instant messenger clients, including their presence status. If you prefer this information not to be available, you can disable the option. By default, it is enabled for all Web applications.
Maximum Upload Size	Fixes the size of content that users can upload to a site in any single procedure. By default, this is 50 MB. Any file or group of files that a user tries to upload above this limit is rejected.
Alerts	By default, alerts are enabled that allow users to create their own alerts on all sites they have access to on the specific Web application. You can also limit the amount of alerts a user can set up. By default, this is set to 500 per user.
RSS settings	A Really Simple Syndication (RSS) feed allows users to subscribe to lists and libraries in Sites. To allow RSS feeds from the lists and libraries, this option must be enabled. The default is enabled.
Blog API settings	This property enables you to turn off the Blog API. Alternatively, if you choose to keep it enabled, it can be set to allow user names and passwords to be sent via the Blog API.
Web Page Security Validation	After a session has been established to the sites, this property will automatically cease the session if the session is idle for the specified amount of time, which by default is 30 minutes. If a user tries to access the page after this time of being idle, she will have to refresh the page or re-establish the connection.
Send User Name And Password In E-mail	This property allows administrators to create or change a user's details in the site and have the user's new details sent via e-mail to the user. For additional security, you could choose to disable this functionality.
Backward-Compatible Event Handlers	By default, event handlers are off, so users cannot use an event handler operation for a document library.

Table 7-2 Web Application Settings

Property name	Description
Change Log	After 15 days, entries are deleted from the change log. You can change the length of time in days or set it to never delete entries.
Recycle Bin	The Recycle Bin allows users in sites and administrators in sites and site collections to restore deleted items from lists and libraries. Here you can specify how long these items are stored in the Recycle Bin in their site and also how long the items remain in the site collections Recycle Bin. The site collection Recycle Bin is a second-level Recycle Bin that captures all deleted content from site recycle bins.

Content Databases

You can associate multiple databases with each Web application. By default, only one database is displayed here, and this is the one specified when creating the Web application. The default content database is limited to 15,000 top-level sites that can be created within it.

Important A user's My Site portal is also a top-level site in the database.

By creating additional databases, however, you are able to control the database growth by spreading the quantity of sites across the databases. You can then limit the total amount of sites each database can hold, even as low as one site per database.

Configuring Additional Content Databases

You can give each top-level site its own database or group top-level sites by database. For example, if you have 20 top-level team sites, you can give each site its own database or put five sites together in each database. For this to work effectively, limit each new database for the site collections to one site, and create the new site collection after its associated database has been created. By doing this, you can name each database with its respective site collection—for example, projects_db for the project's team site. You will also benefit from creating additional content databases for the Web application hosting users' My Sites. It is recommended to have a dedicated Web application for hosting My Sites. Alternatively, you could store the users' My Sites portals on another Web application.

To configure the database settings for a Web application, complete the following steps:

1. Go to Central Administration, and click the Application Management page.
2. Scroll to the SharePoint Web Application Management section, and click Content Databases.
3. On the Manage Content Databases page, select a Web application by clicking the Web Application Name drop-down arrow and choosing to change the Web application.
4. To modify an existing database, click the database name in the list of available database names. For each database, you can modify the following settings:
    a. Change the database status to offline or ready.
    b. Change the number of top-level sites that can be created in the database and the number of sites at which a warning event is generated.
    c. Select the Windows SharePoint Services search server.
    d. Choose to remove the content database and all data in it.
5. Click Add A Content Database, and configure each of the following options for the new database:
    a. Select a Web application for the new content database.
    b. Choose a database server to host the content database.
    c. Select the Authentication method to access the database server. The default and recommended method is Windows authentication. If you are using SQL authentication, add the SQL account name and password.
    d. Define the total number of top-level sites that can be created in the database and the number of sites that can be created before a warning event is generated.
6. Click OK.

Manage Web Application Features

You can disable any of the available features on a Web application that have been enabled by default. This enables an administrator to restrict all the sites associated with that Web application from using a standard feature, such as the ability to convert a document for publishing from .docx to HTML. If you also have premium-level features available, such as the Business Data Catalog (BDC), you can choose to disable these features on a Web application as well. To manage Web application features, complete the following steps:

1. Go to Central Administration and click the Application Management page.

2. Scroll to the SharePoint Web Application Management section and click Manage Web Application Features.
3. On the Manage Web Application Features page, select a Web application by clicking the Web Application name drop-down arrow and choosing to change Web Application.
4. Next to the feature, click Deactivate or Activate to enable or disable the feature.

Web Application List

The Web Application List allows you to get a quick view of all your configured Web applications and the associated URLs and port numbers for each Web application.

SharePoint Site Management

On the Application Management page, the Site Management section gives the administrator the ability to manage all aspects of a site collection. You can remotely add new sites to existing Web applications that have been provisioned with a site template or configure a quota limit that applies to the content on a Web application's site collection. This remote management facility gives administrators an easy way of centrally configuring sites and site collections that exist on all available Web applications on the farm. It is therefore important to make sure you are making changes to the right Web application. You might, for example, inadvertently add a low quota limit to a Web application that hosts a site collection with content that already exceeds that quota limit and, therefore, prevent users from adding any new content to their document libraries or lists.

There are seven management options that can be configured under SharePoint Site Management on the Application Management page in Central Administration:

- Create Site Collection
- Delete Site Collection
- Site Use Confirmation And Deletion
- Quota Templates
- Site Collection Quotas And Locks
- Site Collection Administrators
- Site Collection List

Create Site Collection

New top-level site collections can be created in two ways. One way is to create a site collection from an existing site, such as a corporate portal home page, and then create a new site collection using the Site Directory, as shown in Figure 7-15.

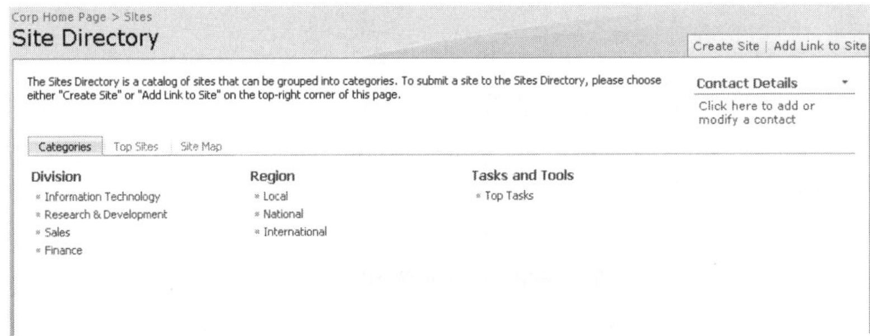

Figure 7-15 Creating a site through the site directory on a corporate portal

The second way to create a new top-level site for a Web application is to use the Create Site collection from this management screen. You can create a top-level site collection either by using the root URL of an unextended Web application or by using a managed path such as /sites, which is the default, or by adding your own managed site. (See the "Define Managed Paths" section for information about configuring a managed path.) To create a new site collection, you need to provide the following information:

- Title
- Web Site Address, using either the root of the Web application or a URL path
- A Primary Site Collection Administrator and secondary administrator if required
- A quota limit template if required
- A site template for the new site collection to be created with, as mentioned in Table 7-1

Planning If you want to create a site hierarchy based on a URL mapping for projects, you could create a new managed path called "projects" for a Web application. Then create each new top-level site collection using the /projects URL path and add each new project as its own sub-URL of /projects, such as http://servername:54635/projects/ProjectAlpha, as shown in Figure 7-16.

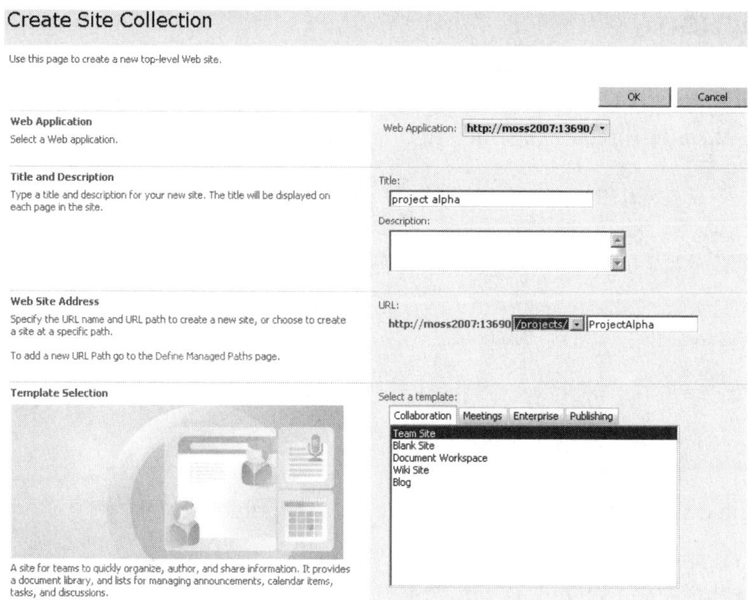

Figure 7-16 Creating a top-level site collection site from site management

Delete Site Collection

In the same way that you can create top-level site collections, you can also delete a site collection from here. By selecting a Web application, you are presented with all the available top-level site collections for all URL paths, as shown in Figure 7-17. By selecting one of the site collections, you have the option to delete it, as shown in Figure 7-18.

Important When you delete a site collection, all content is deleted with it. Therefore, you should make a backup of the site collection before performing the deletion.

Select Site Collection

URL Search | Web Application: http://moss2007:13690/

URL
/
/projects/ProjectAlpha

URL	http://moss2007:13690/projects/ProjectAlpha
Title	Project Alpha
Description	
Primary administrator:	CONTOSO\administrator
E-mail address:	Administrator@contoso.msft
Database Name	Corp_Content

OK Cancel

Figure 7-17 Selecting a site collection URL

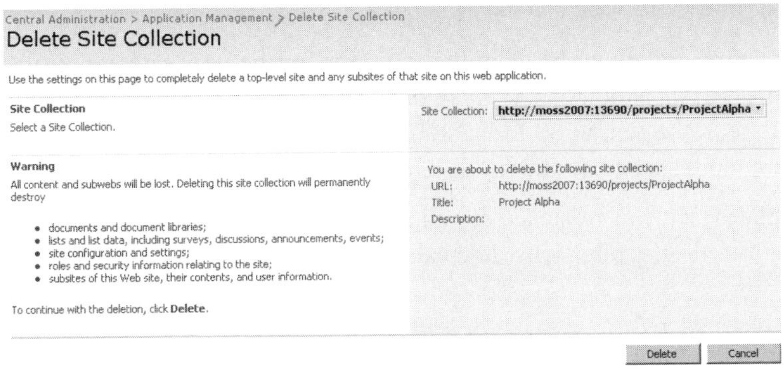

Figure 7-18 Confirming a site collection deletion

Site Use Confirmation And Deletion

By enabling site use confirmations, you can have an e-mail sent to all site collection owners of a Web application asking them whether they are still using their sites. There are two parts to configuring the site use confirmation e-mails. First, you need to enable the option for sending the notifications and provide the time frame for the first notification to be sent; the time frame is based on the time the site was created or first used. By default, the first e-mail notification will be sent 90 days after the site is created or first used. In order for the unused sites to be detected, you also need to configure the schedule to check for unused site collections. This schedule can be daily, weekly, or monthly.

The second part of the configuration is indicating if and when the site collection is automatically deleted. You can set an automatic deletion of a site collection based on a predetermined number of unanswered confirmation requests that are sent to the administrator of the site collection. If the administrator does not confirm the site collection is still in use, you can choose to automatically delete the site collection and all its content. By default, the configuration is to send four notifications to the administrator before the site collection is deleted. This means that by default every 90 days a notification will be sent out. After four attempts with no reply from the administrator of the site collection, the site collection will be deleted–this is a total of 360 days before actual deletion.

Important Ensure that your site collection administrators are aware of the consequences of not confirming the e-mail notifications they receive if you are going to enable the automatic site deletion option.

Quota Templates

There is one quota template defined by default and that is for the user's personal sites (My Sites). This quota is set to a total of 100 MB of data for each user's My Site; a warning e-mail notification is set to be sent at 80 MB. You can change this quota or create additional quotas that are more specific to the needs of the site collection.

The site quota templates that you create are stored as a central pool and are available to all Web applications and all site collections. To create a new quota template, complete the following steps:

1. Select Create A New Quota Template, as shown in Figure 7-19.

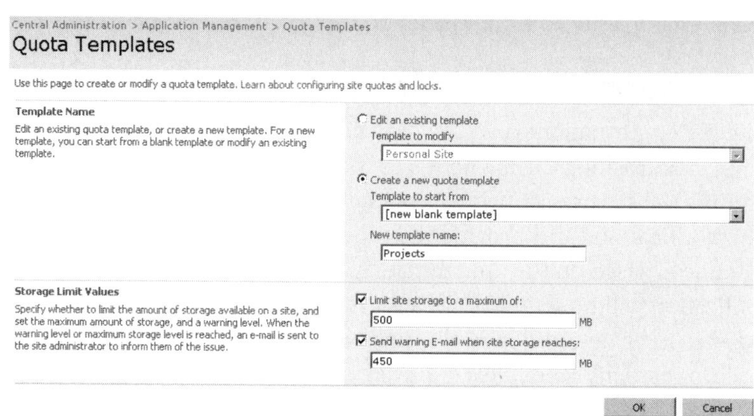

Figure 7-19 Creating a quota template

2. Select a template from the Template To Start From list; the default is New Blank Template.
3. Type a name for your new quota template.
4. Select a maximum storage limit for the quota in megabytes.
5. Select a warning size limit to notify the site administrator when the storage reaches a certain size in megabytes.

Site Collection Quotas And Locks

After you have created your quota templates, you are able to apply them to your site collections. Another option is to put a lock on the site collection to prevent certain types of use on the site. First, select a site collection that you want to configure. This can be on any Web application in the farm. Once the site collection is selected, you can choose to set a lock on the site collection or apply a quota template to it, or both.

Applying a Site Collection Lock

You can only lock a site collection; there is no option for choosing only a site. There are four choices for locking a site collection:

- Not Locked is the default option, and it has no restrictions on the site collection.
- Adding Content Prevented stops all contributors from saving or uploading content to the site collection.
- Read Only prevents deletion of content and stops contributors from adding or editing content.
- No Access stops all users from accessing the site collection.

Applying a Quota Template

After you create a new template, it is added to the Template To Start From list on the Quota Templates page. (See Figure 7-19). Now, on the Site Collection Quotas And Locks page, select the site collection to which you want to apply the template, and then select your chosen quota template. The predefined quota limits for the template are applied and appear dimmed, as shown in Figure 7-20.

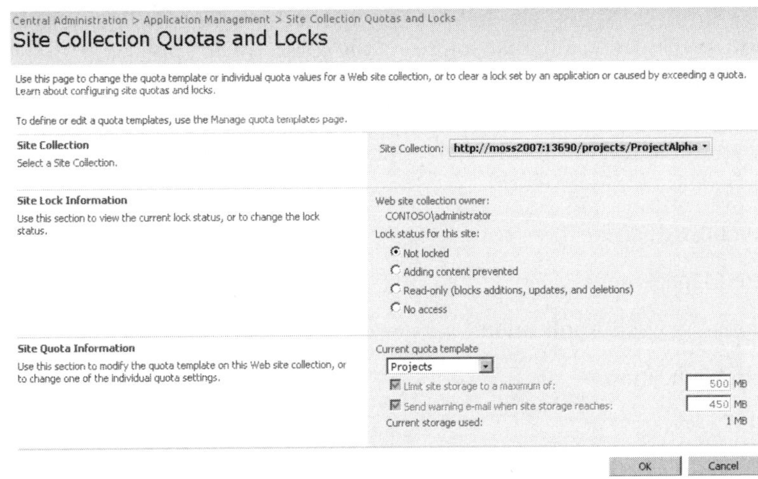

Figure 7-20 Applying a quota template to a site collection

Site Collection Administrators

When you first create a new site collection, you must identify a primary site collection administrator and, optionally, add a secondary administrator. The Site Collection Administrators page lets you define a new primary and secondary administrator if there is a need to change those settings.

Site Collection List

This management page allows you to view all sites that are hosted on a Web application. It includes the root of the site plus all sub sites. By clicking any of the sites, you are able to view information about that specifc site. This information includes:

- The URL
- Site Title
- Site Description
- Primary Administrator
- E-Mail Address
- Database Name

Application Security

In the Application Security section, you have the ability to define permissions, rights, and policies for individual Web applications that can restrict the rights the users have throughout the Web application and all its associated sites. Like everything with the security configuration, you must ensure that you select the correct Web application in the management control; otherwise, you might stop valid users from performing their required roles. There are five configurable security options and each plays a different role in applying security at different levels in the Web application. The five options are as follows:

- Security For Web Part Pages
- Self-Service Site Management
- User Permissions For Web Application
- Policy For Web Application
- Authentication Providers

Planning Before configuring any of these security options on a Web application, plan and test the configuration first. Many of the settings, such as the user rights for Web applications, can benefit from being implemented before users are added to the site for general access.

Security For Web Part Pages

Web Parts contain Web content such as text and images. *Web Part zones* are groupings of Web Parts. Web Part zones can also be grouped to form a Web Part page.

Most of the time, the Web Parts serve a single purpose, such as a document library or an announcements list. It is possible, however, to have Web Parts connected to each other to manipulate the data returned by one or several of the Web Parts viewed on the page. This connection enables a user, for example, to select a customer name in one Web Part and then have information only about that customer displayed in the second Web Part. By default, users can create Web Part connections on a page; however, if you do not want this to be possible, you can disable this capability in this screen.

Planning There is a performance increase on the Web server when generating views based on connections between Web Parts. Take this into consideration when planning and testing these Web Part connections.

Important By preventing Web Part connections, you are preventing all sites associated with the selected Web application from creating connections between Web Parts.

The second option for security in Web Part pages is for accessing the online Web Part gallery. When you want to add a Web Part to a page, you are presented with a default gallery view. However, as a user, and if all galleries are enabled, you can use the advanced view to see all four of the available galleries The online Web Part gallery includes Web Parts such as the MSN weather and stock news, but it does affect the performance of the page when adding Web Parts because the gallery has to go to the online sites to retrieve the list of available Web Parts. If your users do not need access to these Web Parts, it might be worthwhile to disable this option because it speeds up the Web Part gallery retrieval. Also, look at access in terms of security. You might not want the users of a particular Web application to have access to the Internet gallery for security reasons and, therefore, preventing such access can be a security benefit.

Note If you do want to use the online gallery but are unable to connect to the site, you might need to configure the outgoing proxy server settings in Central Administration, which informs SharePoint which route to take (such as a Microsoft ISA server) when accessing the Internet for the gallery.

Self-Service Site Management

By default, users cannot create subsites from a top-level team site. This policy gives the site collection administrators the ability to control the growth of top-level sites. When necessary, the site collection administrators can give users the right to create subsites at a lower level only. This control is not always necessary, though, and by enabling the Self-Service Site Creation correctly, you can allow users to create new sites at any level below the site collection top level. Once self service has been enabled, a message is displayed in the announcements list on the home page of any new top-level site collections to inform users that Self-Service Site Creation has been turned on for that site collection.

Note Make sure your site collection home page has an announcements list available. Not all site templates have the announcements list by default. Create the announcements Web Part and then enable the Self-Service Site Creation right.

All sites that are created will default to the defined managed path, which is /sites. You can create additional managed paths, however, by using the Define Managed Paths page, which is discussed in the "Define Managed Paths" section in this chapter.

Planning It is an important design decision early on to plan which site collections will require the Self-Service Site Creation right and those that will not. It might also have an effect on how many Web applications need to be created, because this right is enabled on a per-Web-application basis.

User Permissions for Web Applications

Three different sets of rights with individual permissions are applied by default to every new Web application created. Every site collection and site created in that Web application inherits these user rights. The user rights are used when creating or editing the rights of a site group. The three available sets of rights are as follows:

- *List permissions* include the standard rights of a user for viewing, adding, or deleting a list item. The site groups you belong to determine which list permissions you get. A reader, for example, gets the view-item-only right, whereas a contributor also gets the ability to edit and delete items. After a user has been added to a group with contributor rights, these default Web application rights would be applied.
- *Site permissions* deal with the rights available on sites throughout a site collection, and they include rights such as the right to apply a theme to a site. You might not want any individual who can access your Web application and its sites to have the ability to change a theme to a site, such as changing the site appearance away from

the corporate branded theme. By removing the right to apply a theme at the Web-application level, you are able to prevent even the site administrators from having the right by removing the right from all groups in the site collection and sites.

- *Personal permissions* are rights associated with a user being able to add Web Parts that are specific to the user, such as Web Parts that are available for the My Sites of users. By removing these rights, you could create a uniformed view for all the pages and sites in the Web application that users are not able to personalize or change with their own private content.

Important When removing user rights from a Web application, remember that it also affects the administrators of the site collection as well. You cannot choose to have the user right affect only a select group of users in the Web application.

Policy for Web Applications

Policies are a new management tool in SharePoint Server 2007. This tool enables administrators to create a centralized policy mechanism that will affect all top-level site collections and sites configured in the Web application. An administrator creates a centralized policy mechanism to determine the level of rights a user gets when accessing the particular Web application from a certain zone. If a user is accessing a site from the Internet and the Internet zone is set for All Users Full Read, then even if a user has write access to the site, he is restricted from doing so because of the zone he has come through to access the site.

Note *Zones* in a Web application refers to the zones associated with the Alternate Access Mappings. Zones include Default, Intranet, Extranet, Internet, and custom. See Chapter 6 for more information on Zones and Alternate Access Mappings.

Real World Configuring Web Application Policies

Suppose that you have a group of users who work remotely, and they need read-only access to the sites in a Web application. These users will be accessing the Web application from the Internet and, therefore, they will be in the accessing from an Alternate Access Mapping that is defined in the Internet zone. Other users on the local area network (LAN) will be in the Default zone because they are accessing the Web application using the internal URL which is mapped to the Default zone. Using the policy configuration, you can create a new policy for the remote users and configure the necessary permissions. You can choose from the following permissions to apply for the selected zone:

- Full Control
- Full Read
- Deny Write
- Deny All

To configure a policy for users on a Web application, complete the following steps:

1. Select the Web application to which you want to apply the new policy.
2. Choose the zone that the policy is to be applied to. For all users who use Windows authentication, you can select All Zones. In this case, select the Internet zone.
3. Click Next.
4. Type the user, group name, or e-mail address for the policy to be applied to. In this case, you would specify the remote users.
5. Select the specific permission to be applied to the group that matches the zone type—for example, Full Read.

   The final option is to have the user account masked as a system account. This means all actions carried out by the user would be registered as a system account entry rather than the actual user account. A good example of this is if an administrator fixed an issue on a public-facing Internet site and you wanted the account that made the change to be shown as System rather than the actual user's name.
6. Click Finish.

You can create as many policies as you require and therefore control the level of access for many different groups of users accessing the Web application from multiple zones.

Authentication Providers

The authentication provider allows you to change the method with which users are authenticated against the Web application. The default is to authenticate all users using Windows authentication; however, SharePoint Server 2007 now supports multiple authentication provider mechanisms:

- Windows
- Forms

- Web Single Sign-On (SSO)
- Anonymous Access

You can switch your IIS authentication mechanism to either Windows or Basic authentication. When choosing Windows authentication, you also have the option to enable the more secure option of Kerberos instead of NTLM. However, your environment must be able to support this. The final option for configuration here is to disable client integration, which stops certain client applications from launching when connecting via this particular Web application. When client applications are disabled, users have to save their work locally and then use the upload function to add the document to the library.

Configuring Authentication Providers

SharePoint Server 2007 does not let you use two authentication mechanisms on the same Web application. If you require two methods of authenticating to the same content, such as might be needed by external users, you can do the following:

1. Extend and map a new Web application to an existing Web application hosting the content.
2. Change the new Web application to the new authentication mechanism–for example, Forms or Anonymous Access if the content is to be published to all external users.
3. Set publishing rules on your firewall to point to the new Web application for the external users.

To provide a more robust and secure publishing environment, you could use a Microsoft ISA 2006 server in your screened subnet that has the ability to support both forms-based authentication and single sign-on authentication.

External Service Connections

There are three configurable options for external connections, each of which has a unique role in the SharePoint Server 2007 environment. By default, none of the services are enabled but each can be enabled individually.

Records Center

The records center is a global farm configuration setting that allows users to send documents from document libraries in all Web applications and site collections to a central official file site. For more information about configuring records management, see Chapter 9, "Document Management."

HTML Viewer

The HTML Viewer service enables an administrator to configure a server with IIS installed to render Microsoft Office system documents to users who are trying to view the documents but do not have the Microsoft Office products installed on their client machine. For example, this could occur if a user is accessing the site from the Internet by using a public Internet machine. To set up the service, you need to install the HTML Viewer service for Windows SharePoint Services, which is available from the Microsoft download center at *http://www.microsoft.com/downloads*. It is not advisable to have the HTML Viewer service running on the same server as the SharePoint front-end servers because of the strain that can be put on the servers' resources when rendering the Office documents into HTML.

After you have installed the server side of the HTML Viewer service, you need to configure the application management side. There are four configurable options available after enabling the service, as shown in Figure 7-21.

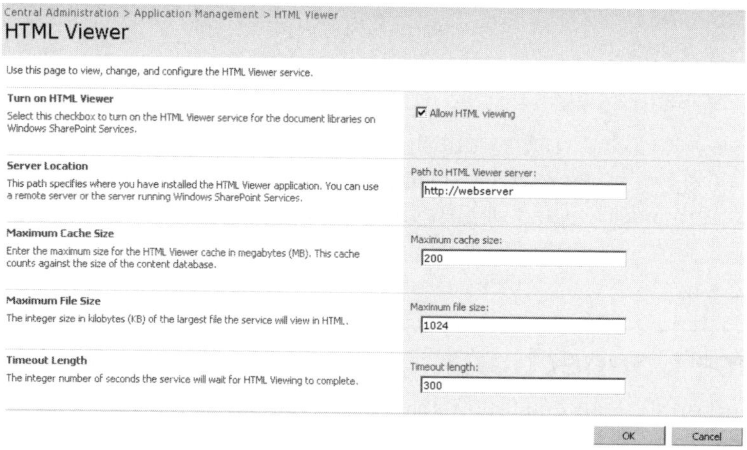

Figure 7-21 Configuring the HTML viewer service

The URL points to the Web server location where you installed the HTML Viewer service file, and the cache size is the amount of rendered HTML documents stored in the Web application. The maximum file size is configured in kilobytes (KB), and it defines the largest size of a file that can be rendered into HTML. The larger the file to be rendered, the more resources that are required by the Web server to render it. If the file is too large, it could time out while being rendered; setting the timeout length to a higher value enables the service to complete the process.

Document Conversions

This service allows users to select content from their sites and then convert it to a chosen format. Document conversion takes place on a per-Web-application basis and at a scheduled interval in either minutes, hours, or days. The types of documents that can be converted are determined by the installed converters. The default converters are as follows:

- Convert InfoPath Form To EMF Image
- Convert InfoPath Form To PNG Image
- Convert InfoPath Form To TIFF Image
- Convert InfoPath Form To Web Page
- Convert Word To Web Page
- Convert Word With Macros To Web Page
- Convert XML To Web Page

Once converted, documents can be used for many purposes, such as publishing to an external-facing site using content deployment. To help with the resources required for the conversion process, you can point the specific Web application at a load-balanced URL to spread the resource load over several front-end servers.

Workflow Management

Workflow is enabled by default, and it's enabled or disabled on a per-Web-application basis. When workflow is enabled, users can use workflow templates that have been created either by themselves or by workflow designers. Designers of workflows can use Microsoft Designer or Visual Studio 2005 for creating additional workflows for users to access and start a workflow model.

A second configurable option determines how a document workflow takes place if a user does not have access to the site where the actual document is stored. By default, if a document workflow is triggered in this situation, the person who is to receive the document is sent the document via e-mail as an attachment instead. For more information on configuring workflows, see Chapter 10, "Records Management in Microsoft Office SharePoint Server 2007."

Summary

In this chapter, you looked at the configuration options for application management at both a farm level and for individual Web applications. Although not all the available options are required, many of them are enabled by default for all Web applications. You will need to make a design decision to establish which services are required. The new features of Web application management make it easy to configure multiple mechanisms of security and authentication; combined with zone mapping for different user locations, this makes a very robust hosting and collaboration scenario.

One of the most important points to remember with configuring application settings is that a single change can have a cascading effect on many users and in sites housed within a single Web application. Wherever possible, these types of settings should be thought out and configured at an early stage, prior to the site collections and sites being created.

Chapter 8

Administrating Personalization and Portal Taxonomies

This chapter will cover the following three fundamental areas of architecting and designing your Microsoft Office SharePoint Server 2007 deployment:

- **Taxonomy** Refers to how you structure and categorize your content, and how users will find information throughout the sites.
- **Personalization** Refers to how you can effectively target information to the right users throughout your sites; configure My Sites, or personal sites, for users; and integrate Office SharePoint Server 2007 with directory sources, such as Active Directory, to include user profiles or user-specific information throughout your sites. By effectively using personalization you can enhance searches for people and your organization's ability to connect people with particular knowledge to people looking for that expertise.

- **Social networking** Enables your users to find other users throughout your organization with similar experience or interests and to connect with them. Social networking also dynamically connects users with their colleagues by leveraging personalization Web Parts, such as when one person is seeking other users who share the same distribution lists or SharePoint sites.

This chapter also introduces *Knowledge Network* (KN), an extension to the core social networking features of SharePoint Server 2007 that is being offered as an add-on to SharePoint Server 2007. KN will greatly enhance and extend the social networking aspects of your SharePoint Server 2007 deployment by tapping into key user resources, such as e-mail, to disseminate user interest, knowledge, and skills throughout your organization.

For instance, suppose you are researching a particular product within your organization and you want to locate other users in the organization involved in the same research. This is where KN will help. It enables you to perform custom and personalized searches on that information indexed throughout your SharePoint Server 2007 deployment so that you can narrow down users with expertise in that area or involved in similar discussions. Just as with the default social networking aspects of SharePoint Server 2007, users will also have the added advantage of choosing which information, such as certain e-mail folders, they want to have included in the KN indexing. This chapter shows you some key configuration and design considerations in deploying KN.

Key to configuring and administering personalization in SharePoint Server 2007 is the Shared Services Provider (SSP). SSP allows you to centrally manage all facets of personalization features, such as your users' My Sites, configure and import user profiles from a configured directory service, such as Active Directory, and create and configure custom audiences for content targeting throughout your SharePoint Sites. If you previously worked with SharePoint Portal Server 2003, you might already be familiar with the concept of Shared Services. The main difference between the Shared Services model of SharePoint Portal Server 2003 and SharePoint Server 2007 is flexibility. In SharePoint Server 2007, Web applications can easily be associated with any SSP configured in your farm and bound to personalization tasks, such as My Sites and alerts, configured in that SSP. In SharePoint Portal Server 2003, once you configured Shared Services, you could not change the *parent* portal or promote one of the *child* portals to become the new provider of personalization services. This chapter will show you the ease of centrally configuring the personalization and audience settings for Web applications using the SharePoint Server 2007 SSP model.

Understanding Taxonomies

Core to designing a successful SharePoint Server 2007 deployment, and one that will be readily adopted by your customer base, is factoring in the organization, or *categorization*, of your content and deciding how people will find that content. For instance, will you structure the design of your SharePoint sites on your company's organization chart, such as creating sites based on Department or Office location? Or will you structure it based on your company's products or product groups? Happily, with SharePoint Server 2007, you can build multiple, dissimilar taxonomies in the same interface so that users have a choice as to how they find information.

This section will help you to understand taxonomies and adoption of taxonomies for Web-site design, and it will provide some considerations for implementing taxonomies in SharePoint Server 2007.

What Is Taxonomy?

Taxonomy is effectively an information architecture that defines how you categorize or group content and *metadata* into a logical and easily identifiable structure for your target audience. Taxonomy architectures are important in designing taxonomies that have the following characteristics:

- Are suited to their intended purpose
- Can be maintained over time
- Provide strong application support to information applications in the new challenging Web environment

Taxonomy can be summarized by the following formula:

architecture + application + usability

There are four types of taxonomies:

1. Flat
2. Hierarchical
3. Network
4. Faceted

Important You can encounter problems when creating a taxonomy if you fail to identify which type of taxonomy should be used before the taxonomy is developed.

Flat Taxonomies

Flat taxonomies are merely a listing of items. They are best suited for 30 or fewer objects and do not require a complex design. More than 30 objects can be presented in a flat taxonomy, but only if the list items are intuitive to the users of the taxonomy. Flat taxonomies have the following characteristics:

- They group content into a controlled set of categories.
- There is no inherent relationship among the categories; they are equal groups with labels.
- The structure is one of *membership* in the taxonomy and can include the following:
    - Alphabetical lists of people
    - Lists of countries or states
    - Lists of currencies
    - Controlled vocabularies
    - List of security classification values

An example of a flat taxonomy would include an eCommerce site with a pull-down list of product categories and horizontal list of stores. In SharePoint, flat taxonomies are best for simple lists of items that don't need to be nested. The items can be links to sites or lists or libraries. Also, if you have a flat taxonomy that has large list of content items in a list, such as a large list of documents, you can use the filtering capabilities in custom views of the lists to ensure that users can find the content items they are looking for quickly. Finally, the filtering Web Parts can be used to help build a limited but flat view of a large list of items.

Hierarchical Taxonomies

A hierarchical taxonomy is represented as a tree architecture. The tree consists of nodes and links. The relationship between two linked nodes (the way they are associated with each other) will be based on meanings. The meanings define the hierarchical link depending on which direction you are going. For example, with Refrigerated>Drinks>Juice>Orange, the meaning of the link between Refrigerated and Drinks is drinks stored in the refrigerated section. Meanings in a hierarchy are limited in scope—for example, to group membership or type. In a hierarchical taxonomy, a node can have only one parent.

Hierarchical taxonomies have the following characteristics:

- Hierarchical taxonomies structure content into at least two levels.
- Hierarchies are bidirectional.

- Each direction has meaning.
- Moving up the hierarchy means expanding the category or concept.
- Moving down the hierarchy means refining the category or concept.

An example of a hierarchical taxonomy would be a Web site which includes a Web Site Directory categorized by subject hierarchy. In SharePoint, every site collection's Web structure is a hierarchical structure. In addition, this type of taxonomy is well suited for finding sites via your organizational chart, because those charts are hierarchical in nature and list key individuals and divisions or departments within the hierarchy.

There is more than one way to implement a hierarchical taxonomy in SharePoint Server 2007. For example, you can progressively disclose layers of the taxonomy across sites or pages. You can use cascading or expanding menus to present a hierarchical taxonomy. Or you can use category and subcategory labels in a multicolumn display. The Sites Directory is well suited for building nested, hierarchical lists.

Bear in mind that hierarchical taxonomies should have content at every level. Empty levels mean nothing to the end user. In addition, each level should have a clear and unambiguous reason for existing in the hierarchy. Each level should be related to the parent and child levels in clear, obvious ways. Best practice is to stay away from hierarchies that are more than four levels deep.

Network Taxonomies

Network taxonomy is a *plex* architecture. Each node can have more than one parent. Any item in a plex structure can be linked to any other item. In plex structures, links can be meaningful and weighted differently (meaning that their relative importance varies from link to link). You can think of this as a modified mesh topology, in which the relationships within the nodes of the taxonomy are different, both in weight and quality.

Network taxonomies have the following characteristics:

- They organize content into both hierarchical and associative categories.
- They combine hierarchy and star architectures.
- Any two nodes in a network taxonomy can be linked.
- Categories or concepts are linked to one another based on the nature of their associations.
- Links can have more complex meanings than you find in hierarchical taxonomies.

Examples of network taxonomies include the following:

- Complex thesauri
- Ontology

- Concept maps
- Topic maps
- Knowledge maps and knowledge representations

In SharePoint Server 2007, you can use the thesaurus to build expansion and replacement sets for query terms, as well as creating "dotted lines" between content items that appear in different layers of different, dissimilar hierarchical taxonomies.

Faceted Taxonomies

A faceted taxonomy looks like a plant start, where each leaf node is connected to the center node. A faceted taxonomy must be suited to its purpose, and the facets must be needed in the taxonomy. Each facet should have a distinct behavior or reason for existing. In addition, each facet should have a clear relationship to the central object around which the taxonomy is being built. Most faceted taxonomies, when explicitly presented, are built using a records or table format.

Faceted taxonomies have the following characteristics:

- Facets can describe a property or value.
- Facets can represent different views or aspects of a single topic.
- The contents of each attribute can have other kinds of taxonomies associated with them.
- Facets are attributes, and their values are called *facet values*.
- Meaning in the structure derives from the association of the categories to the object or primary topic.

For example, Metadata is one type of facet in a faceted taxonomy. Consider that the following list can be metadata about a single object type:

- Creator
- Author
- Title
- Language
- Publication date
- Access rights
- Format
- Edition

- Keywords
- Topics
- Security level

An example of a faceted taxonomy includes the Universal Description, Discovery & Integration of Business (UDDI), which you can find out more about at *http://www.uddi.org*. In SharePoint, every time we associate metadata with a content item, we're building a faceted taxonomy.

Industry Best Practices for Developing a Taxonomy

Building taxonomy is hard work and is more art than science. Experts say you should start with a well-thought-out blueprint that allows you to map out how you'd like your taxonomy to look. Keep in mind the following elements when designing a taxonomy:

- Users want options, but not complexity.
- The quality of metadata affects the quality of the taxonomy; ensure that you're using metadata that is rich and accurate.
- Scalability means that the quality of the metadata must increase as the taxonomy scales into millions of represented objects.
- Consistency of metadata is achieved better programmatically than by human intervention.
- Persistency of metadata is foundational to building a taxonomy that will persist over time.
- Enterprise taxonomies must take the following into account:
    - Functional architecture
    - Content types and locations
    - Technical requirements
    - Presentation aesthetics

Tools for Determining Taxonomies

A key factor in planning a successful taxonomy is the methodology you employ, which must be the most effective model and structure for your design. To avoid inheriting a singular view of content and deploying a Web site structure that falls well short of meeting your navigational needs, consider using some of the proven methodologies to determine your content structure. Two such methodologies include card sorting and Unified Modeling Language (UML).

Card sorting will help to identify taxonomies through user involvement. Users will be asked to place cards into the most relevant categories, or the best fit. For instance, you might create a primary set of cards that represents a suggested top-level navigational hierarchy and then have users place cards, representing subsequent hierarchical items, into those primary categories. From this, you'll be able to determine your secondary categories, tertiary categories, and so on, until all the cards can be matched against a category. This will often result in items being placed in more than one parent category or in using a category as both a primary and secondary category. This setup is shown in Table 8-1, where Drinks is a primary category but is also a secondary category to the primary category Refrigerated.

Table 8-1 Categories by Card Sorting

Primary category	Secondary category	Tertiary category
Refrigerated	Drinks	Juice
Drinks	Juice	

UML helps to identify taxonomies by placing *actors* in scenarios to determine how the actors interact with and navigate throughout a system. There are many papers available detailing UML methodologies.

Resources for Planning and Developing Taxonomies

The following references may prove useful in planning and developing your Web site taxonomy:

- *http://www.boxesandarrows.com/view/developing_and_creatively_leveraging_hierarchical_metadata_and_taxonomy*
- *http://www.ontopia.net/topicmaps/materials/tm-vs-thesauri.html*
- *http://www.boxesandarrows.com/view/card_sorting_a_definitive_guide*
- *http://www.uml.org/*

Taxonomy Considerations in SharePoint Server 2007

SharePoint Server 2007 includes a wealth of possibilities for structuring content and navigating throughout sites. Unlike its predecessor, SharePoint Portal Server 2003, SharePoint Server 2007 by default offers flexible navigational options, including the option to include tree view navigation throughout your sites. Figure 8-1 shows an example of tree view navigation in a SharePoint site's navigation.

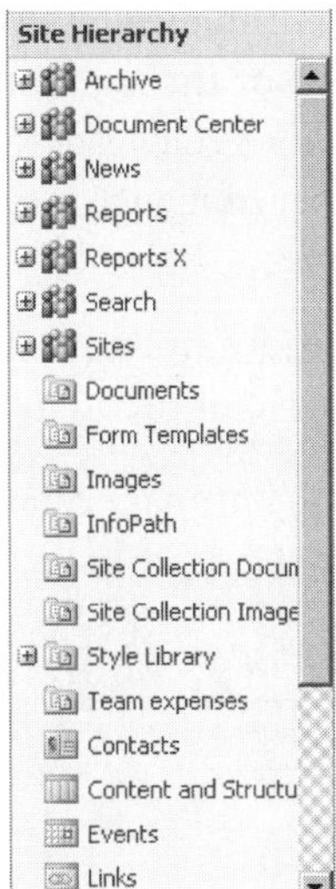

Figure 8-1 SharePoint Server 2007 tree view navigation

Another new navigational feature in SharePoint Server 2007 is the ability to edit the subsite navigational items through in-place editing via the user interface. This includes the ability to update item titles, links and audiencing on menu items. Figure 8-2 shows the navigational editing and sorting editor for the Fabrikam site.

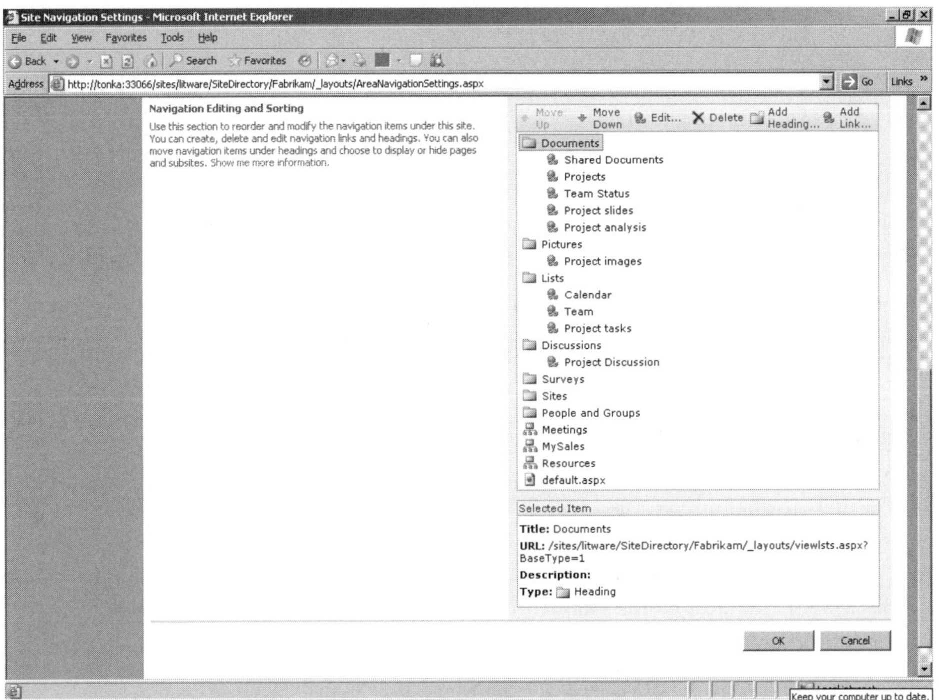

Figure 8-2 Navigational editing and sorting editor shown in user interface

Reciprocal navigation is offered through bread crumb navigation and is enhanced with the option to include the parent site tabbed navigation within sub sites, or throughout site collections. Where personalization is enabled, users will easily be able to navigate to their member sites through the My Links link in the personalization tier of navigation, which remains constant throughout site collections.

Figure 8-3 highlights the Home page of the Fabrikam site, which includes horizontal tabbed navigation from the parent site, vertical navigation, representative of the items within the Fabrikam site, and breadcrumb navigational path.

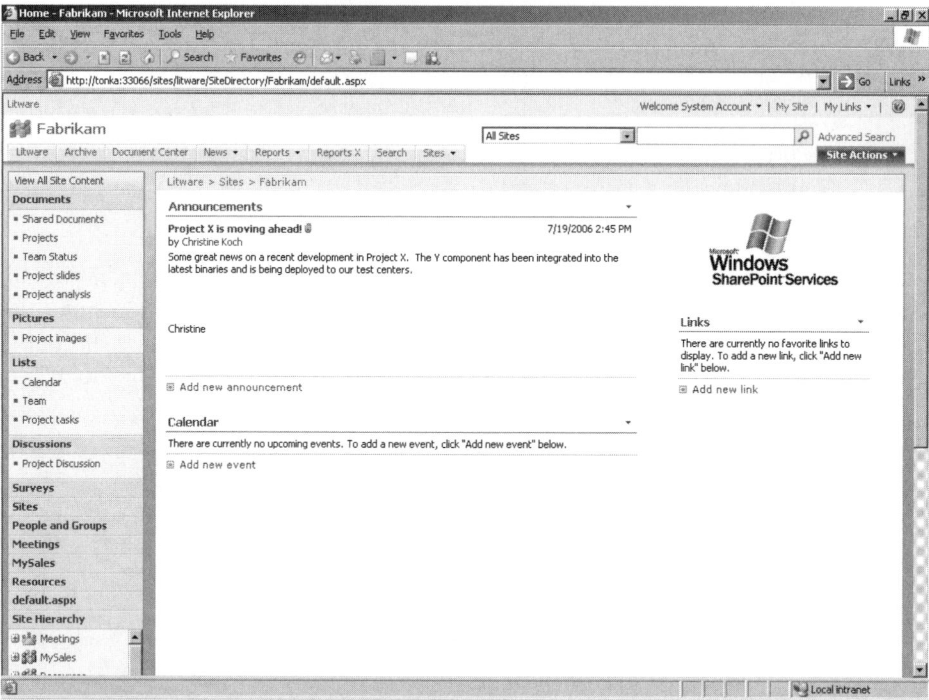

Figure 8-3 Home page navigational options

SharePoint Server 2007 also includes a customizable Site Directory where you can create and categorize sites. By default, Site Directory includes the categories Division, Tasks and Tools, and Region. But you can edit, or remove, these default categories and add your own categories to better match your business needs.

When you create a site from the Site Directory's Create Site link, you have the choice of associating that site with one or more categories, at the time of creating that site. You can also add links to existing sites and associate those sites with one or more categories. Figure 8-4 shows the default Home page of the Site Directory. An additional category, Global Projects, has been included.

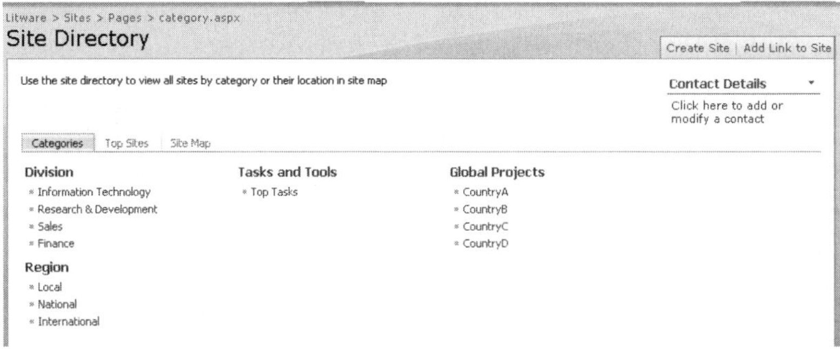

Figure 8-4 Default Home page of the Site Directory

Additionally, the Site Directory includes an option to list sites as Top Sites. For instance, you can nominate sites listed in the Site Directory to be included under Top Sites by selecting the Top Sites check box when adding sites to the Site Directory. The Site Directory also includes a configurable Site Map. Figure 8-5 shows a site map configured to display sites at the existing level, but you could have sites displayed three levels deep.

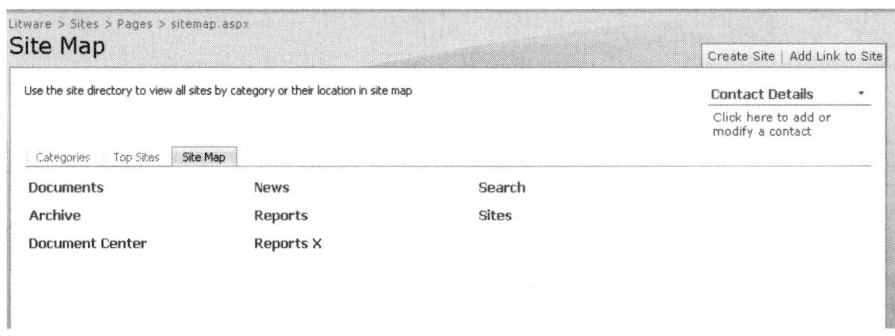

Figure 8-5 Site map

Navigation is one mode by which users will find content, and we've just provided an overview on how you can effect site level navigation using some of the built-in functionality offered through the user interface. Second to navigation, users will choose to locate content by using search. Using content types, you can define the metadata throughout your sites, site collections and lists. Designing effective metadata and leveraging metadata in your search means you can more granularly define search queries and search scopes. For more information on content types and metadata, including instructions on how you can use content types to enhance search, see Chapter 15, "Managing Content Types."

Real World Designing your SharePoint Taxonomy

Remember, that in designing your SharePoint Server 2007 taxonomy, you still need to consider the fundamentals of Web site design and plan on designing your SharePoint Server 2007 structure before going ahead with the implementation—don't assume that by simply implementing Office SharePoint Server 2007, your design needs will be met!

As a guide, you should consider reviewing and addressing the following during design phase:

- Existing business processes
- How employees currently store their documents
- Types of documents
- Existing naming conventions
- Presence of backend systems for integration

Most importantly, you should involve your users, or customers, in the design phase to ensure that navigational needs are addressed and to also to avoid unnecessary duplication. For example, a customer may cite a requirement for a knowledgebase for one group and an additional knowledgebase for another group, when in fact you may, through working with the customer and explaining options available within SharePoint Server 2007, discover that the knowledgebase needs to be a shared entity.

Workable taxonomy is a blend of communication and pre-deployment design. If you are planning for a large SharePoint Server 2007 deployment, you may also consider hiring an Information Architect to help structure your design.

Scale Considerations when Designing your Taxonomy

Following are limitations to consider when designing your taxonomy:

- 10,000,000 items in a library
- 100,000,000 items per search indexer
- 2000 sites per site collection
- 2000 lists per site
- 2000 items per folder
- 2000 items per view (after indexed filtering)

Personalization in SharePoint Server 2007

SharePoint Server 2007 includes a wealth of personalization features to help you to effectively bridge the gap between the users throughout your organization and the content throughout your SharePoint sites. Underpinning user personalization in SharePoint are two key features: user profiles and My Sites.

User Profiles

A personal profile about each user includes properties such as a user's title, e-mail, distribution list membership, and contact details. It is typically imported by SharePoint from a directory such as Active Directory, but it can also be manually created directly inside SharePoint. User profiles can be customized in SharePoint to include additional details, such as birthday and interests. Personal profile are used throughout SharePoint Server 2007 to disseminate or target information to users, help users locate colleagues with similar interests, and return search results on people.

My Sites

A My Site is a Windows SharePoint Services site collection that provides a centralized location for each user to store and share his or her information—such as photos and documents—with other users, set user alerts, and connect with and track other colleagues throughout the organization. My Sites are created when a user clicks on the My Site link on the main page of an SharePoint Server 2007 site.

Users will feel more in control with the new privacy controls introduced in SharePoint Server 2007 My Sites and will be able to more granularly target their personal information. Custom roll-up Web Parts enable users to easily review their sites and documents, and link directly to that content. The ability to easily connect with other colleagues throughout the organization using specialized My Site colleague Web Parts allows knowledge to be more readily exchanged, enabling users to connect to colleagues with similar interests.

Configuring Personalization Settings in SSP

The personalization administrative interface in the SSP allows administrators to centrally configure and manage personalization settings, including establishing the location and permission settings for My Sites, configuring user profile import and directory connections, and including additional user profile properties. Administrators can also affect the navigation of My Sites from the SSP by targeting and publishing links to users' My Sites. Table 8-2 details the SSP settings available for User Profiles and My Sites.

Table 8-2 **User Profiles and My Sites Administrative Settings in SSP**

Administrative function	Description
User Profiles and Properties	■ Add user profiles. ■ View user profiles—Access can be used to edit each user profile and manage existing user personal sites. ■ Configure profile import from a source directory, such as Active Directory or Lightweight Directory Access Protocol (LDAP), including scheduling subsequent imports ■ Configure import connections to directories, such as Active Directory or LDAP. ■ Start full or incremental profile import. ■ View import log—Displays the status of imports as success, warning, or error.
Profile Services Policies	■ Set the default privacy policies against each profile property, such as whether the property is required to be completed or is an optional property. ■ Specify who is the audience of the property—for example, everyone or just the user's colleagues. ■ Specify whether the user can override the policy settings for a given property.
My Site Settings	■ Set the default location for My Sites. My Sites can reside on a separate portal. ■ Set the location that will be used as the location parameter in the URL for a user to access the My Home page of her My Site—for example, http://server_name/personal/username. (The default location is *personal*.) ■ Set the Site Naming format. Choose whether to include the domain username in the My Site naming format—for example, Domain\username. Proper naming format helps you avoid conflicts in multiple domain deployments or in deployments where there are duplicate usernames. ■ Set Language options. These options allow users to choose the language for their personal sites. Selected languages will be determined by the language packs installed on the server hosting the My Sites. ■ Configure the Multiple Deployments settings. These settings enable full use of personal features where users' My Sites are hosted on remote servers in a multiple My Site deployment. ■ Set the default reader site group access. Account or accounts added to the default reader group as each My Site is created. The default group is the NT AUTHORITY\authenticated users group.

Table 8-2 User Profiles and My Sites Administrative Settings in SSP

Administrative function	Description
Trusted My Site Host Locations	■ List other My Site locations serviced by other SSPs. Audiences can be used to identify which users belong to which My Site locations.
Published Links to Office Client	■ Links added to this list are published to client Microsoft Office applications—for example, links published and inserted as objects in Microsoft Office PowerPoint 2007 slides or a link published and made available as a data connection object in Microsoft Office Excel 2007.
Personalization Site Links	■ Target links to users' My Sites using audiences. Links will appear in targeted users' My Sites as an additional link in the My Site navigation. For example, you could target a link to all users' My Sites that highlights an upcoming company event or to the My Sites of users in the sales organization alerting them to the location for the latest sales figures.
Personalization Services Permissions	■ Set permissions to create My Sites, use personal features, manage user profiles, manage audiences, manage permissions, and manage usage analytics. The default group is the NT AUTHORITY\Authenticated Users group, which includes permissions for creating My Sites, using personal features, managing permissions and managing usage analytics. If you wanted to remove the My Site link for all your users, you would do that by adjusting the permissions on the NT AUTHORITY\Authenticated Users group and removing the ability to create a My Site.

Configuring and Customizing User Profiles

User profiles make it easy for users to connect with and find other users and share information throughout your SharePoint Server 2007 sites. User profiles include information, or *properties*, specific to each user—such as contact details, areas of interest, and organizational reporting structure—and are used as the basis for users to create their personal sites, called *My Sites*. User profiles, combined with My Sites, form the backbone of social networking throughout your SharePoint Server 2007 by allowing users to easily connect with colleagues with similar interests and sets of skills throughout the organization.

Note User profiles are not used for authentication and are not user accounts like those in Active Directory.

User profile properties are both imported directly from Active Directory and created manually in SharePoint. The obvious advantage of importing user profile information is that the information already exists and can be updated from one central point. This assumes, of course, that you're richly populating your Active Directory user account properties. Properties, such as user account name and e-mail addresses, are imported from Active Directory and automatically distributed throughout all sites. This means, for example, that when a user wants to create an alert on a site, his e-mail address is already included and he is not prompted to manually enter his e-mail address to receive that alert.

Profile properties for each user can be mapped, or linked, directly to the Active Directory schema. For instance, if you extend your Active Directory schema to include an additional property unique to your organization, you can then map that property to the SharePoint user profiles and have it displayed in the user information in SharePoint. Conversely, if you create a new profile property in SharePoint, you can map that property to an existing user account property. You are not required to do this, but the option is available to you.

You can also further customize user profiles imported from Active Directory directly within SharePoint by creating SharePoint-specific profile properties, such as Skills and Interests. These properties are optional and are available in addition to the imported Active Directory prepopulated properties. User can then populate those additional properties through their My Site to display that information to other users throughout the organization. User profiles in SharePoint Server 2007 scale up to 5 million in number, compared to only 1 million in SharePoint Portal Server 2003.

Importing User Profiles

With SharePoint Server 2007, you can import user profiles and properties from the following four directory sources:

- Active Directory
- LDAP
- Business Data Catalog (BDC) application—for example, cost center from SAP
- Active Directory Resource

By default, SharePoint Server 2007 selects the main domain controller in the domain in which it is deployed and sets that domain controller as the default directory source for a user profile import. For example, Figure 8-6 shows the Contoso domain as the Current Domain selected on the Configure Profile Import page because the SharePoint server is deployed in the Contoso.msft domain.

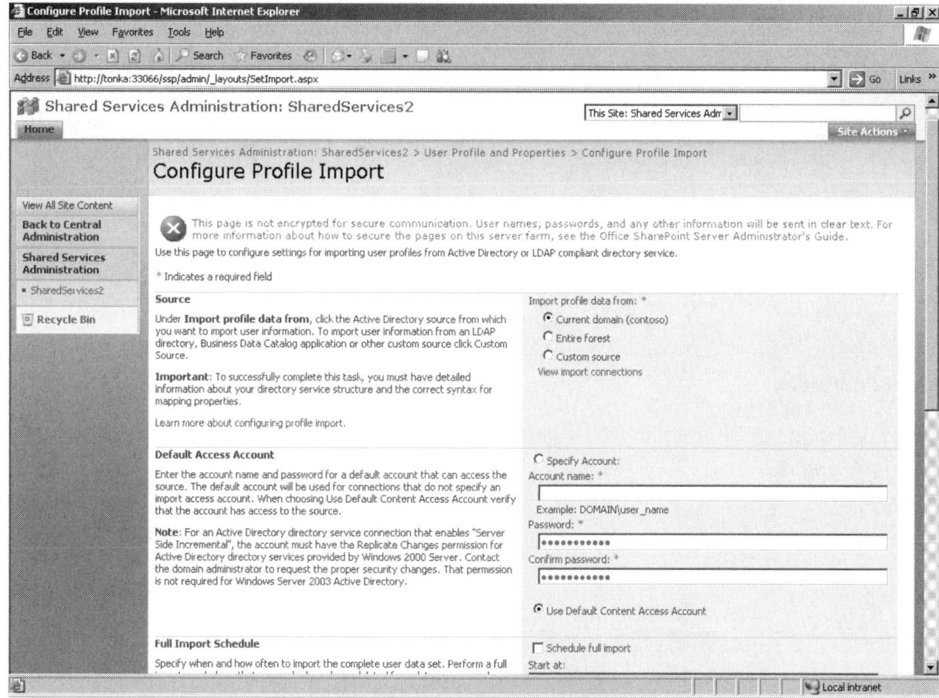

Figure 8-6 Default domain controller for a profile import

If you want to include additional connections to domain controllers or create a custom profile import using an LDAP query, or if you want to import a column from an associated BDC application (such as an SAP cost center), you need to configure import connections to those additional directories before profiles or profile properties can be imported from those connections.

To configure additional import connections, follow these steps:

1. On the SSP Home page, under the User Profiles And My Sites section, click on User Profiles And Properties.
2. On the User Profiles And Properties page, click on Import Connections.
3. On the Import Connections page, click on the Create New Connection link.
4. In the Connection Settings section, under the Type drop-down list, select the type of directory connection, as shown in Figure 8-7. After you have completed entering configuration details for the directory, such as LDAP search filters, click OK. See Table 8-3 for some examples of LDAP filters.

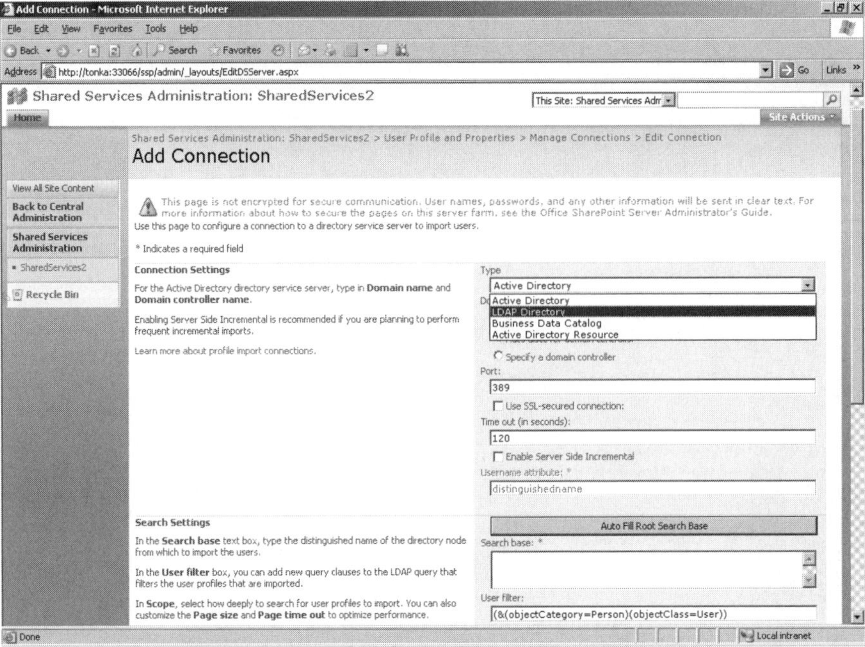

Figure 8-7 Choose directory connection type

The new connection will be saved and is accessible via the Import Connections page, shown in Figure 8-8.

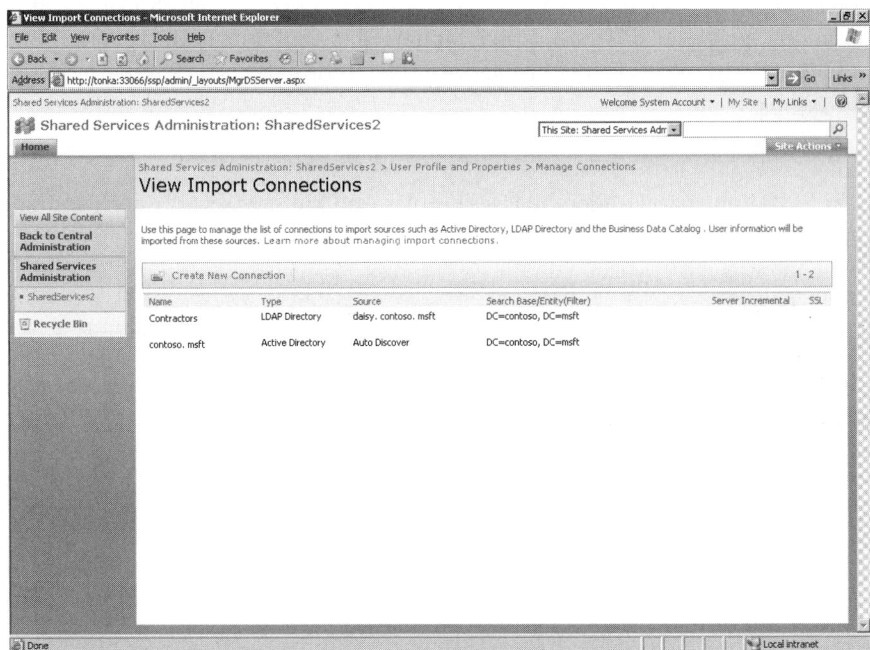

Figure 8-8 Custom import connections

New connections will be added and included in subsequent profile imports. The additional connections are denoted as a Custom Source on the Configure Profile Import page, as shown in Figure 8-9.

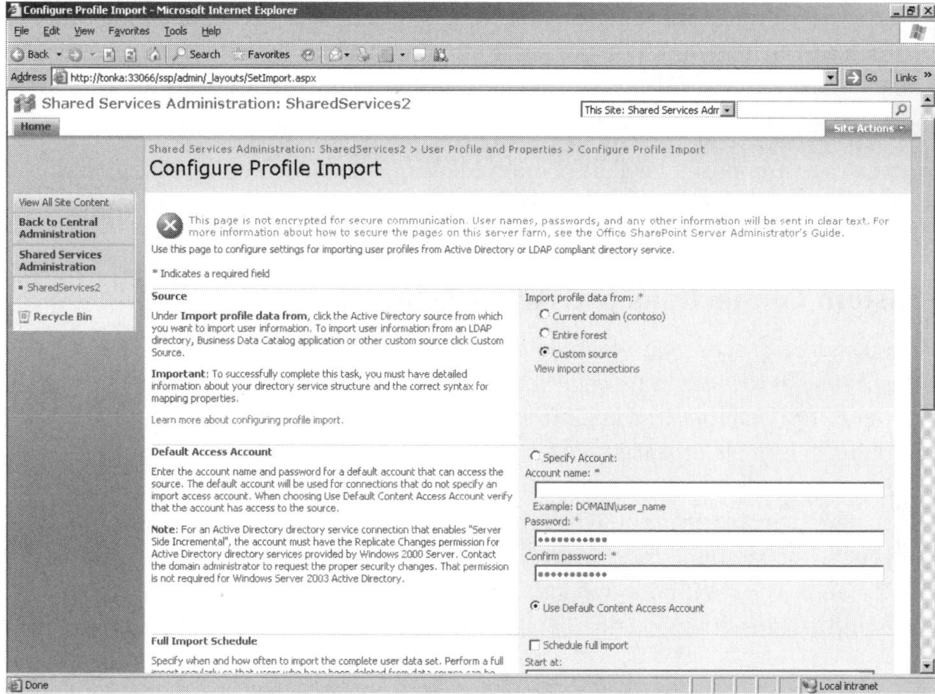

Figure 8-9 Custom Source profile import selection

Table 8-3 Examples of LDAP Search Filters

Search filter	Description
(objectClass=*)	All objects
(&(objectCategory=person) (objectClass=user) (!cn=amy))	All user objects but "amy"
(sn=sa*)	All objects with a surname that starts with "sa"
(&(objectCategory=person)(object-Class= contact)(|(sn=Purcell)(sn=Bezio)))	All contacts with a surname equal to "Purcell" or "Bezio"
(&(objectCategory=person) (objectClass=user) (!(userAccount-Control:1.2.840.113556.1.4.803:=2)))	Imports user profile information of only user accounts that are enabled

The Configure Profile Import page also includes the options to configure both full and incremental import schedules. A full profile import removes users who were deleted from a source directory from the SharePoint profile database. Incremental profile imports ensure updates are made to user information in the SharePoint profile database. Depending on the size of your organization, you could, for example, schedule a full import once per month and an incremental import once every two weeks. You also have the option to manually start either a full or incremental profile import in addition to scheduled imports.

Any updates to user profiles will be re-indexed by incremental crawls so that correct user information is returned in people searches and throughout sites, including My Sites.

Custom Connections and Active Directory

If you choose to set up one or more custom connections to your Active Directory, you need to have thought through your Active Directory design for user and group accounts. For example, let's assume that you place all your Active Directory service accounts in a single organizational unit (OU). Let's further assume that you don't want to import those accounts into the profile list in Office SharePoint Server 2007. To achieve this objective, you will have had to design your Active Directory so that all your service accounts exist in an OU. Hence, best practice here is to ensure that the accounts you want imported into SharePoint exist under one or more common OUs and accounts that you do not want imported exist under a separate OU.

Note SharePoint Server 2007 includes a profile import log, which will log successes and errors during profile imports. This will help you to troubleshoot any issues relating to importing user profiles. To access the import log, click View Import Log from the User Profiles And Properties page.

Viewing and Editing User Profiles

After you have successfully imported user profiles, you can view the list of user profiles by clicking the View User Profiles link on the User Profiles And Properties page.

On the View User Profiles page, you can search for users by E-mail Address, Account Name, or Preferred Name; you can also choose to show only active users or users missing from an import. Users missing from an import includes any user profiles previously imported but missing from the most recent import. You can also create a new user profile in addition to the imported user profiles. If you create a new user profile, you need to populate the user information, including the username and user e-mail.

On the View User Profiles page, user profiles can be edited by selecting profiles individually and choosing *edit* from the profile contextual drop-down menu, as shown in Figure 8-10. From this same menu, you can also delete user profiles and manage users' personal sites—for example, make changes to a user's alerts.

Note Before deleting a user profile, see the "Deleting User Profiles" section in this chapter.

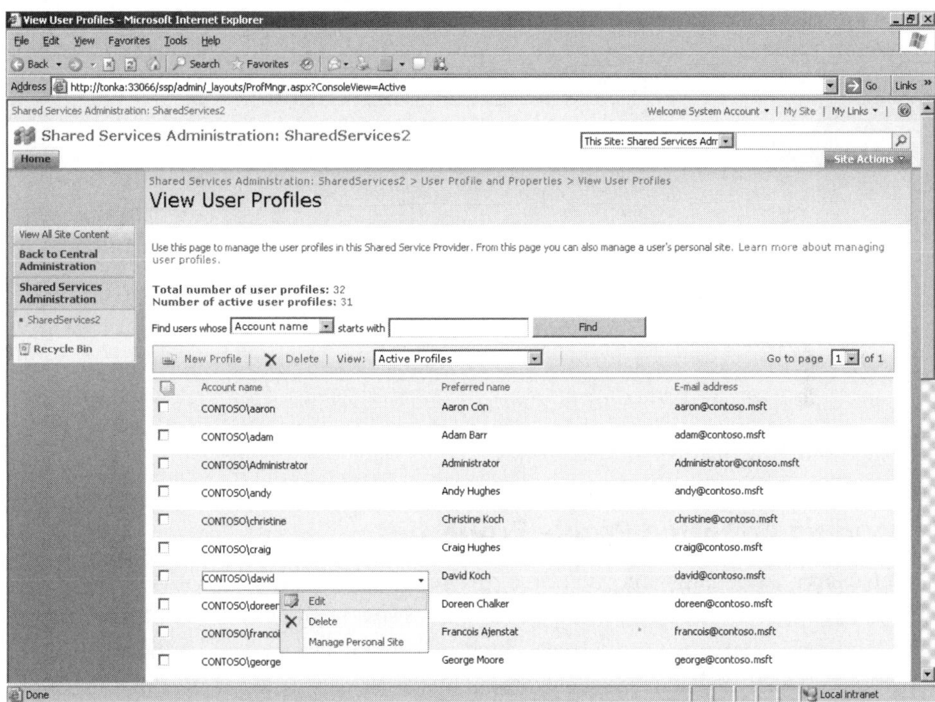

Figure 8-10 View User Profiles page in SSP

If you choose to edit a user profile, you are directed to the Edit User Profile page, shown in Figure 8-11. Here, you can choose to update any user information or override any existing information.

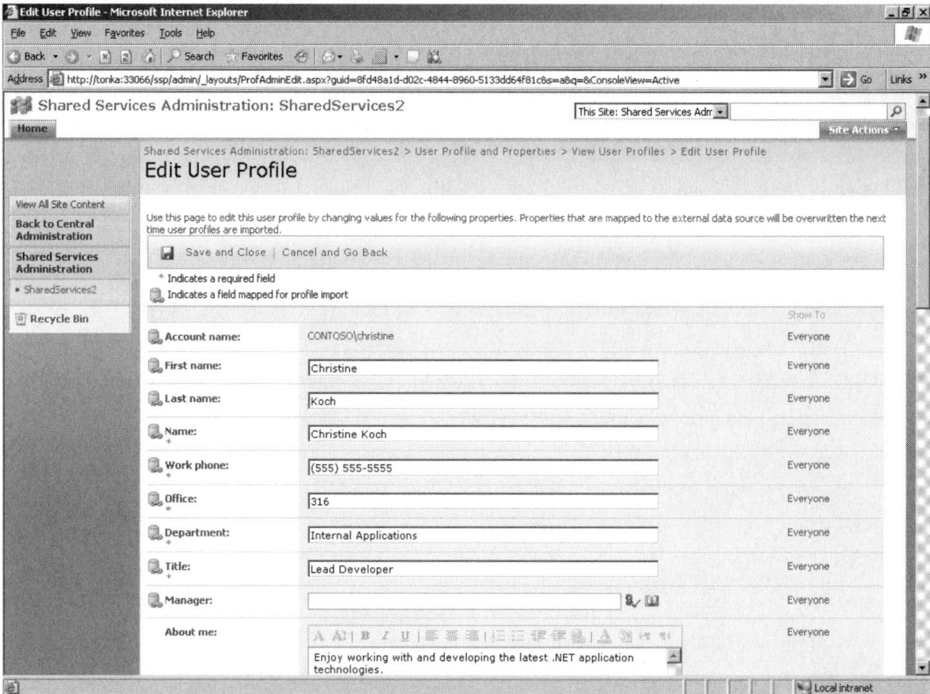

Figure 8-11 Edit individual user profiles in SSP

Changing Imported Profile Properties

If you override or change information or properties imported from Active Directory, those changes will be overwritten on the next user profile import—for example, the Name or Department properties, which are directly mapped and imported from the Active Directory schema. Best practice is to ensure that properties that are imported from Active Directory are not user-editable in their My Profiles page.

For instance, you might choose to update one of the SharePoint-specific properties on a user's behalf, such as Hire Date. Remember, as an administrator, you have rights to edit all editable properties on a user profile, whereas users only have rights to update their own profile properties via a My Site. Users have only limited editing rights, as determined by the administrator. For example, administrators can edit or override a user's First Name and Last Name properties on the Edit User Profile Page, whereas, by default, an end user will not have access to edit those properties.

Managing Profile Properties

SharePoint Server 2007, by default, includes approximately 46 user profile properties, 21 of which are mapped to common Active Directory properties, such as *givenName* and *sn* (surname). By *mapped*, we mean that there is a direct connection between some user attributes or fields defined in SharePoint and those already existing in Active Directory and exposed through the Active Directory schema, such as the user First Name, Last Name, and Work E-mail. SharePoint simplifies the population of its user attributes by mapping directly to user attributes in Active Directory and importing the prepopulated values during user profile import from Active Directory.

You can create additional profile properties either by mapping to existing fields in your Active Directory or other directory connection, such as a property from a BDC application, or by creating a SharePoint-specific profile property—that is, an unmapped property. For example, SharePoint Server 2007 includes a number of unmapped properties that can be optionally populated by the end users, such as Interests, Birthday, and Skills. You can also extend your Active Directory schema to expose additional fields and map to those fields from SharePoint.

An example of a situation in which you might want to create a new, custom mapped profile property in your SharePoint profile property store is if your organization includes multiple subsidiaries and you want the option to be able to search on people by company. Active Directory exposes by default a user attribute named Company, in the Organization tab of the user Properties window, as shown in Figure 8-12. In this case, the Company is Contoso, Ltd. SharePoint can map to and retrieve the value for the user's Company upon profile import.

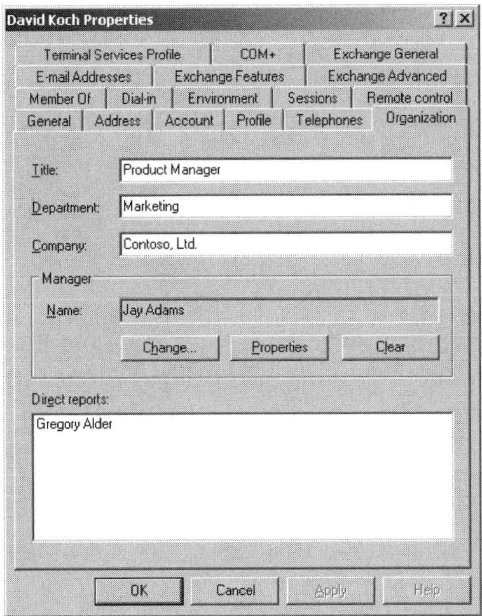

Figure 8-12 Including additional profile properties from Active Directory

To create a new user profile property for Company, follow these steps:

1. From the SSP home page, under the User Profiles And My Sites section, click User Profiles And Properties.
2. On the User Profiles And Properties page, under the User Profile Properties section, click Add Profile Property.
3. On the Add User Profile Property page, in the Property Settings section, give the profile property a name–in this example, *company*–and a Display Name of *Company*. (The Display Name is the name that will be displayed on the User Profile details page.) From the Type drop-down list, select the default value of *string*. Change the value in the Length field to 250. Leave the Has Multiple Values and Allow Choice List check boxes cleared.
4. Under the Policy Settings section, leave the Policy Setting field as the default value, *Optional*, and grant Default Access to *Everyone*. Leave the User Override and Replicable check boxes cleared.
5. Leave the settings in the Edit, Display, and Search sections as the default values. Note, by leaving the Search Settings section Indexed check box selected, the user company value will be included in the people search scope and available as a search option in the people search.
6. In the Property Import Mapping section, leave the Data Connection value as the default value, *Master Connection*. From the Data Source Field To Map drop-down list, select *company*, and click OK to save the new user profile property, Company.
7. Back on the User Profiles And Properties page, under User Profile Properties, click View Profile Properties.

Note The above steps assume that the Active Directory attribute of 'company' has not previously been added as a mapped profile property.

On the View Profile Properties page, scroll down to the bottom of the page to view the newly added user profile property, Company. You can use the up and down arrows to change the order of the property on the profile property details page, which is the order in which it will be displayed on the user's profile details page.

To populate the new Company value throughout your user profiles, you need to run a full profile import against your configured Active Directory store. After you have done this, any Company values retrieved from Active Directory are included in the Company property throughout your user profiles, as shown in Figure 8-13. Here the Company property has been populated directly from Active Directory with the value *Contoso, Ltd.*

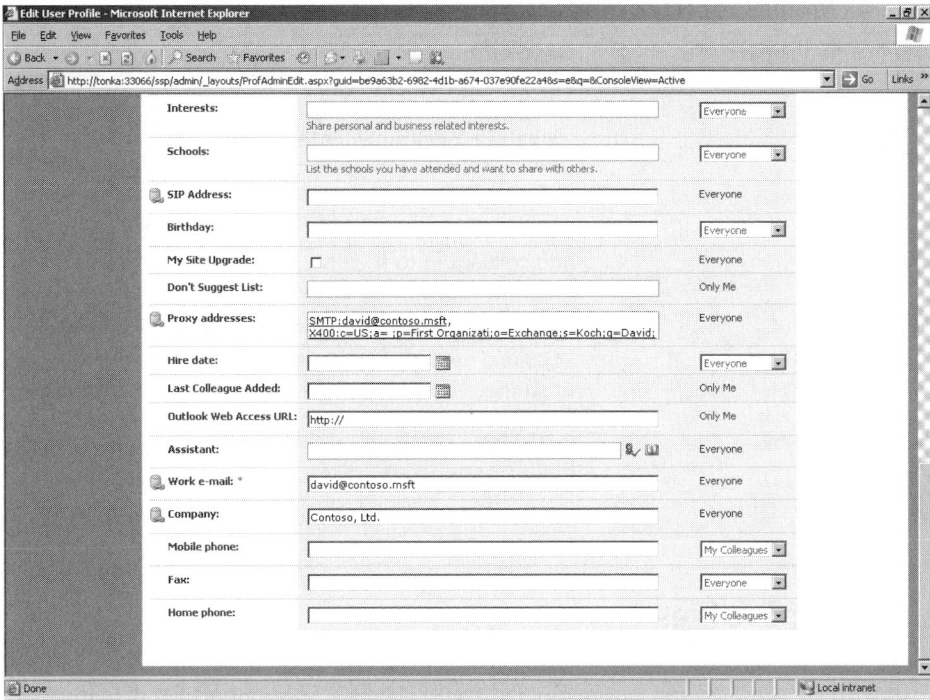

Figure 8-13 Additional profile property imported to the SharePoint profile database

Configuring Profile Property Policies

Profile Property Policies offer a means for you to centrally view, set, and modify the privacy and audience settings for profile properties. To view the Profile Property Policies, from the SSP Home page, click Profile Services Policies.

The policy settings also determine whether a user can override the settings for a given profile property on the user detail page in a My Site. For example, you can specify whether the user can change the visibility for the profile property from Everyone to a particular group. Additionally, you can configure a property to be a required or optional field. For example, the profile property *Manager* is set as optional and can be left blank, or it can be modified on the Edit User Profile page by the administrator.

Table 8-4 lists the options for setting visibility on profile properties. If the User Override policy option is selected for a policy property, the user will be able to select to whom they want to show that property.

Table 8-4 Profile Property Visibility Options

Show Profile Property To	Description
Only Me	The owner of the My Site.
My Manager	Dynamically assigned, as determined by the mapped profile property attribute—that is, the Manager entered in Active Directory and imported with the user profiles.
My Workgroup	A preconfigured group in each My Site. As My Site owners add colleagues to their My Sites, they can choose to also add those colleagues to the Workgroup group.
My Colleagues	Other user profiles that users can choose to add to their My Site. These profiles are either found by people search or suggested by SharePoint when a user might share common attributes with another user—for example, when they are members of the same site or sites or in the same Distribution List.
Everyone	All users with read access to the My Sites, such as the NT AUTHORITY\authenticated users domain group.

Deleting User Profiles

If you delete user profiles from the SharePoint user profile database and then want to reinstate those profiles, you can manually re-add profiles or re-import profiles from the source directory, providing the user accounts still exist on the source directory. One of the consequences of deleting a user profile from within SharePoint is that the user's My Site become inaccessible. Any custom profile property information that was added to the My Site before you deleted the user profile—such as About Me, Skills or Interests—is lost at the time of deleting the user profile. Any colleagues added to the My Site Colleague Tracker will also be removed. But any documents stored in the user's My Site Personal Documents and Shared Documents document libraries are reinstated after the user's profile is reimported and the user re-creates her My Site. If the user had previously created a personal blog, the blog will still exist and the link to the blog will be included under Sites in the left-hand menu on the My Home page.

Note You cannot delete a user profile where the user has created a My Site and has their My Site open in their browser.

If a deleted user profile has been previously added as a colleague to another user's My Site, that colleague reference will automatically be removed from the user's My Site Colleague list at the same time the user profile is deleted from SharePoint. Users will need to re-add the user to their Colleague list once the user profile has been reinstated. In deleting a user profile, assuming the user is still an active member in the source directory (such as Active Directory), permissions for that user will remain unchanged throughout site collections and the user will still be able to access sites where he is a member.

Each user profile is assigned a globally unique identifier GUID by SharePoint. If you delete a user profile, that profile is removed from the UserProfile table in the SSP database and added to the Profile DeletedUsers table. If you then reimport that user profile from Active Directory, SharePoint assigns a new user ID GUID to the user profile and adds the profile to the UserProfile table. Any references to the old user ID GUID should be updated with a content index crawl after the user profile has been reimported and any custom properties have been reapplied. Doing this also updates the user information throughout the associated site collections.

If a user account is disabled in the source directory, such as Active Directory, the equivalent user profile in SharePoint remains unchanged upon the next user profile import. If a user account is deleted from the source directory, such as Active Directory, the equivalent user profile in SharePoint is deleted upon the next profile import.

Managing My Sites

My Sites in SharePoint Server 2007 provide a means for users to centrally manage and link to their content and documents throughout SharePoint sites, monitor their memberships of SharePoint sites and distribution lists, create alerts, and link to their colleagues. My Sites also allow users to share their information, such as shared documents and user profile details, with other users. User profile details include information such as skills and organizational hierarchy.

Through My Site personal and public views, users can store their own private documents and also decide what information other users or groups of users can view. A user's default views of his My Site include two pages: My Home and My Profile.

The My Home page is the user's private page and the default page for the user's My Site. Here the user can integrate his personal Outlook folders, such as Inbox and Calendar; customize the page for his own personal folders, documents, content, and Web Parts; choose and track colleagues; and manage alert settings for SharePoint sites.

The My Profile page contains the user's information, or My Information, which will be made available to other users based on special controls, referred to as *privacy controls*. Using privacy controls, the My Site owner can choose which users to show information to, such as certain profile properties and memberships of distribution lists and SharePoint sites, links, and colleagues. The display options are as follows:

- Everyone (default, refers to authenticated users)
- My Manager

- My Workgroup
- My Colleagues
- Only Me

When other users navigate to a user's My Site, they will see a selective view of that user's My Site, entitled *My Site*. The view will be based on who the visitor is—that is, the visitor's user ID—as determined by the owner of the My Site. For example, if Content A on a user's My Site is made available only to *My Workgroup* and User A, a nonmember of My Workgroup who visits that user's My Site will not see Content A.

Table 8-5 summarizes the private and public My Site views.

Table 8-5 My Site Private and Public Views

Page title	View	Audience
My Home	Private	The My Site Owner
My Profile	Private/Only Me	The My Site Owner
My Site	Public—views determined by privacy controls	Users with read access —for example, NTauthenticated users and specific user views as determined by privacy controls

Planning My Sites Deployment

In planning your SharePoint Server 2007 deployment, you should include My Sites as part of your initial design strategy. You should consider the storage quotas for My Sites, such as whether you will allow your users the 100 MB of default storage, or increase or decrease this storage quota. Remember that these quotas are applied at the site-collection level, and each My Site is a separate site collection. Although you can adjust settings such as storage quotas after deployment, you should adequately plan for this from the outset.

You should also consider where in your farm you want to have your My Sites hosted. For instance, where there are multiple SSPs, you may choose one SSP to host My Sites, and remove the ability for users to create My Sites on other SSPs. Alternatively, in a geographically distributed scenario, you may choose to elect a dispersed model for My Sites and assign My Site creation across multiple SSPs to different groups of users.

Given that each My Site is in fact a site collection and includes features—such as incoming e-mail to lists and document libraries and workflow—that are enabled on Web applications and site collections on the SharePoint server or server farm, you might also want to plan for additional impact to your network and infrastructure.

This is especially true in a large organization where thousands of users are creating My Sites and generating additional e-mail addresses on your Exchange Server for the lists and libraries on each of their My Sites. For instance, you might want to establish a policy for naming standards on incoming e-mail in My Sites to denote those e-mail addresses as specifically for My Site usage and catalog those addresses accordingly in your Global Address List on Exchange.

A further consideration is to provide end-user training to ensure that your users understand how to effectively use their My Site and that the My Site features are fully realized. My Sites are much more than a simple document repository!

User Rights for My Site Creation

By default, the NT AUTHORITY\Authenticated Users group can create a My Site on a designated Web application. However, in some instances you will want to disable users or certain groups of users from creating My Sites. For example, if you are running several SSPs, which include common users, you might want those users to be able to create My Sites under only one of those SSPs, or you might want users from one part of your organization to create their My Sites under one SSP and have other users create them on a separate SSP. Or you might want to block contractors currently working for your organization from creating My Sites. You can do this by granting permission to users and groups from Active Directory.

To manage User Rights for My Sites, follow these steps:

1. On the SSP home page, click the Personalization Services Permissions link under the User Profiles And My Sites section.
2. On the Manage Permissions: Shared Service Rights page, note the existing groups, including the default group, NT AUTHORITY\Authenticated Users, as shown in Figure 8-14. You can choose to add more domain users and groups to this page to granularly add My Site permissions, such as adding and only allowing the Sales domain group to create My Sites.

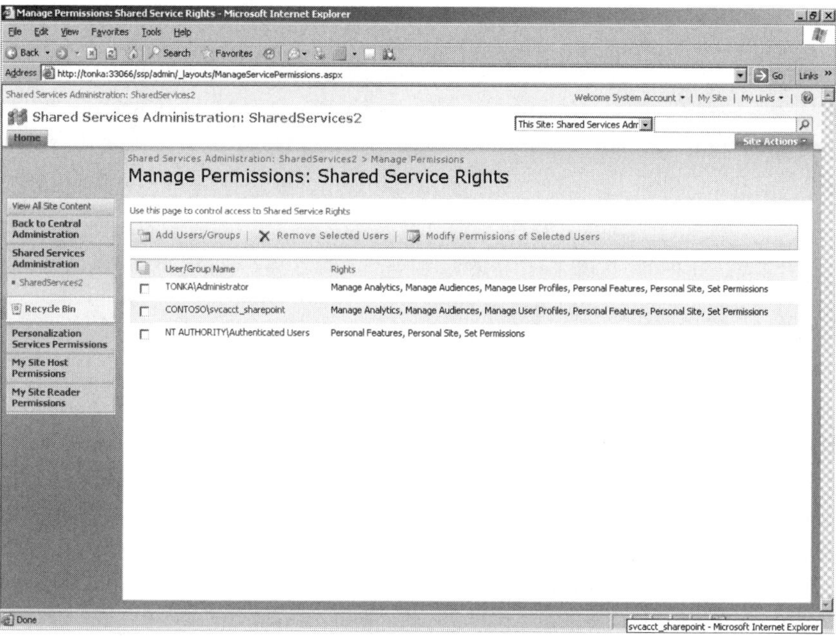

Figure 8-14 Domain groups with rights to create My Sites

3. To review default permissions, click on the NT AUTHORITY\Authenticated Users group to access the Modify Permissions: Shared Service Rights page, shown in Figure 8-15. Review the permissions for the NT AUTHORITY\Authenticated Users group.

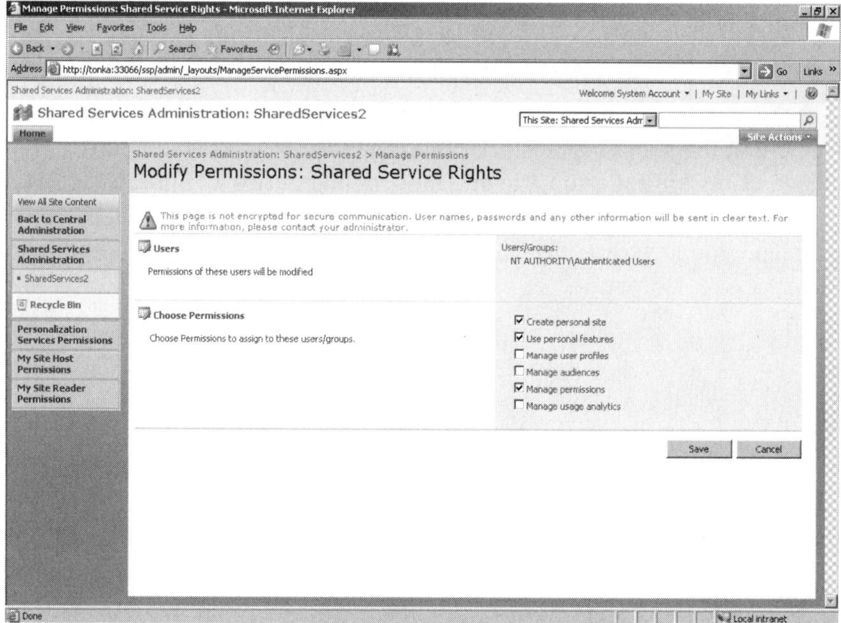

Figure 8-15 My Site creation permissions for NT AUTHORITY\Authenticated Users

If you want to remove the ability for *all* users to create and use My Sites, clear the Use Personal Features check box. This action removes the My Site link from appearing in the navigation of your site collection or collections, and those users who had previously created a My Site will no longer be able to access their My Site. Instead, those users will receive an access denied page.

If you clear the Create Personal Site check box, existing My Site users will still be able to access their My Site but the My Site link will no longer appear in the navigation of your site collection (or collections) and new users will not be able to create My Sites. Existing users and new users will still be able to use personal features, such as My Links to view their site memberships and centrally manage their links.

Creating My Sites

A basic, or non-collaborative, version of user My Sites is established in conjunction with creating or importing user profiles. As each user profile is created, a basic My Site is created that includes core user information imported from the directory source, such as user name, e-mail, title, contact information, distribution list membership, and organization hierarchy. This information is used as the basis for people searches.

Assuming the administrator has enabled the permission for users to create My Sites, each user's My Site is created the first time an authenticated user visits the SharePoint site and clicks the My Site link in the navigation of the SharePoint site. When a user clicks the My Site link on subsequent visits to the site, the user is directed to her existing My Site.

During My Site creation, the user is prompted with a dialog box to set the newly created My Site as her default My Site. The dialog text is shown here:

"Microsoft Office is attempting to set this site as your default My Site. Verify this is a location you trust as Microsoft Office connects with your My Site to offer it as a place to save your documents and share information. Do you want to set your default My Site to http://server_name/personal/username/?"

If the user chooses to not accept the My Site as her default My Site during the initial My Site creation, she still has the option to do so subsequent to her My Site creation by clicking on an additional tab– Set As Default My Site–on her My Home page. When the My Site is chosen as the user default My Site, two events happen:

- The My Site location is saved to a registry key on the user's client machine at HKEY_CURRENT_USER\Software\Microsoft\Office\12.0\Common\Open Find\Places\UserDefinedPlaces\PersonalSite. If this key is removed, it will be re-created when the user next selects her default My Site.
- The My Site location is written to the Active Directory, to the wWWHomePage attribute of the user account, as shown in Figure 8-16, where the wWWHomePage attribute is denoted by the Web Page field on the General tab of the user properties dialog box.

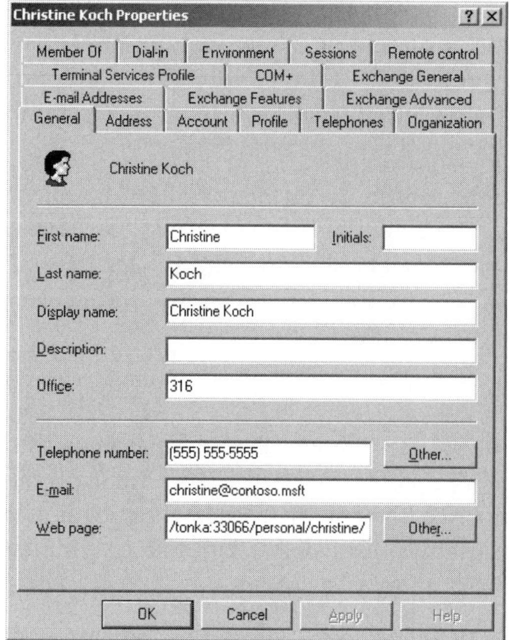

Figure 8-16 User My Site value written to the Active Directory wWWHomePage attribute

By selecting the default My Site, the user's My Site location will be included in the Save dialog boxes of applications, and any links published to Office clients, another feature of My Sites, will be included in the associated Office applications.

Note When a user creates a My Site, that user automatically becomes the site collection administrator of that My Site, with full control. This means that the user can choose to modify permissions on the My Site, including adding users and groups for specific access rights, such as contribute, and removing and deleting users and groups. If the user removes the default reader group, NT AUTHORITY\authenticated users, from the My Site, that user will still be found in people searches, but users other than those given specific rights to the My Site will not be able to access the user's My Site. Users attempting to access the My Site will instead receive an HTTP 403 (Forbidden) "You are not authorized to view this page" error.

If a user accidentally deletes the NT AUTHORITY\authenticated user group from her My Site, the user can reapply the group by adding the group back in under the Site Permissions for the My Site. The SharePoint Server 2007 administrator can also reapply users and groups to a user's My Site by selecting the user on the View User Profiles page and choosing the Manage Personal Site option from the user contextual drop-down menu.

Changing a User's Default My Site Location

If, after establishing an initial SSP and enabling users to create My Sites under that SSP, you create a second SSP and the users from the first SSP are granted access to that second SSP, including the ability to create My Sites, then your users could end up with duplicate My Sites. In this case, users will have the ability to set one of the My Sites as their default My Site for association with Office applications. A user can set a My Site as their default My Site by accessing the My Home page of the chosen My Site and clicking the Set As Default My Site link. In the case of a user clicking on the Set As Default My Site link on a secondary My Site, after having chosen that option on the initial My Site, a Configure My Site for Microsoft Office dialogue will be displayed notifying the user of the intended change in default My Site from the first My Site to the current My Site. The dialogue text is shown here:

"Microsoft Office does not recognize this site as your default My Site. Your default My Site should be a location you trust as Microsoft Office connects with you're my Site to offer it as a place to save your documents and share information. Do you want to change your default My Site from http://server_name/personal/username/ to http://server_name/personal/username/?"

An administrator can also change a user's default My Site, by launching the User Properties dialog box in Active Directory and changing the Web page, or wWWHomePage, URL to the desired My Site URL.

Moving My Sites

After deploying My Sites, you can choose to either move the My Sites location to another Web application within the same SSP or move the Web application currently hosting My Sites to another SSP. If you choose to keep your My Sites under the existing SSP but change the My Site host to a new Web application under that same SSP, you need to configure the Personal Site Provider URL under My Site Settings. You accomplish this from the User Profiles and My Sites section of your SSP home page. After you have updated the URL to point to the new Web application address, users will automatically be redirected to that new address when creating and accessing their My Sites.

Note If you move the My Site host to a new Web application, any existing My Sites remain at the old location and need to be manually moved to the new Web application.

If you choose to move the Web application currently hosting your My Sites to another SSP within your farm, you need to associate that Web application with the other SSP. To do this, click the Application Management tab from your Central Administration, and click Create Or Configure This Farm's Shared Services under the SharePoint Server Shared Services section. On the Manage This Farm's Shared Services, click the Change Associations link in the toolbar and change the Web application to the new SSP.

Note If you have the same users accessing Web applications across multiple SSPs, you should consider disabling My Site creation on those SSPs other than the SSP intended for My Site creation to avoid duplicate My Sites.

Customizing My Sites

My Sites, including user profiles, can be customized using the SharePoint Object Model. For example, using the object model, you could tap into the My Home page of users' My Sites and programmatically add more Web Parts or change the layout of pages for all users, such as including a preconfigured Real Simple Syndication (RSS) feed or custom list. You could also use the object model to retrieve users' My Site URLs and have those URLs displayed in a custom Web Part elsewhere in your Web application. For additional information on using the Object Model to affect My Sites, refer to the SharePoint Server 2007 Software Development Kit (SDK) documentation found at *http://msdn2.microsoft.com/en-us/library/ms550992.aspx*, specifically the Personalizing Your Portal topic.

Social Networking in My Sites

Through the use of My Site custom Web Parts, such as the Colleague Tracker Web Part, SharePoint Server 2007 helps bring people and knowledge together throughout an organization. Users can easily locate other users with similar interests and skills, and through My Sites, SharePoint Server 2007, they can also suggest other users for a user to connect with, such as users sharing common SharePoint sites and distribution lists. The Colleague Tracker also displays and highlights any changes to a user's connected colleagues, such as user profile changes and changes in user memberships.

The My Profiles section of this chapter will show you how you can leverage privacy controls to selectively expose user information, such as user skills and interests. The people search functionality throughout SharePoint Server 2007 will also leverage user-configured information, such as skills and interests, to further disseminate user information throughout an organization and help users to more effectively connect to one another.

The Knowledge Network (KN) section, discussed in the latter part of this chapter, delves further into the social networking aspects of SharePoint Server 2007 by explaining how you can extend the social networking aspects of SharePoint Server 2007 by installing and configuring KN.

Configuring My Home

My Home is the default page for a user's My Site and also the user's personal, or private, space for adding additional and custom Web Parts. From My Home, users can access the Site Settings for their My Site, set the site as their Default My Site, and create and add new lists, libraries, Web pages and sites (such as a blog) to their My Site. Users can also integrate their e-mail inbox and calendar, from Exchange Server 2003 and later, into the My

Home page by using custom Web Parts. Figure 8-17 shows some suggested Web Parts for the Middle Left Zone of the user's My Home page. Some Web Parts include dependencies, such as My Contacts, which require Exchange Server 2007.

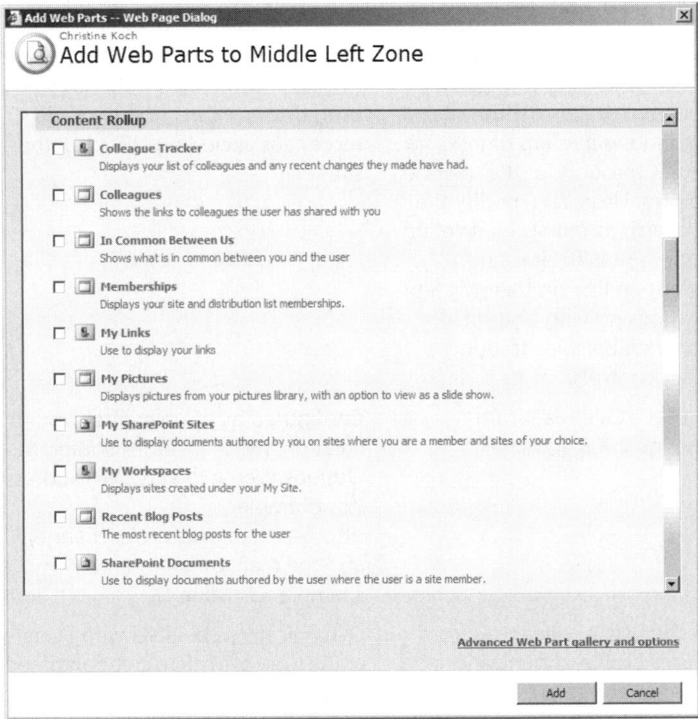

Figure 8-17 SharePoint suggested Web Parts for My Home

When a user first creates his My Site, the My Home page is populated with default Web Parts, as shown in Table 8-6.

Table 8-6 New My Site, My Home Web Part Population

Default Web Part Name	Description	Status at Time of My Site Creation
Getting Started with My Site	Includes reader aids to help the My Site owner configure his My Site, such as a *Describe yourself* and *Upload your picture* aid.	Textual instructions with hyperlinks to actions where appropriate
RSS Viewer	Add RSS feeds direct to the user's My Home page. RSS feeds are configured by opening the Web Part's tool pane and entering RSS feed URLs.	Unpopulated—configured by the user after My Site creation.

Table 8-6 New My Site, My Home Web Part Population

Default Web Part Name	Description	Status at Time of My Site Creation
SharePoint Sites	A rollup Web Part that displays the SharePoint sites the user is a member of, as well as any documents belonging to that user throughout each of those sites. It also shows a rollup of tasks for the user throughout the membership sites. Users can modify the Memberships details by deleting associations with sites and distribution lists on their My Site and choosing who to display those memberships to using privacy controls.	Unpopulated—dynamically populated by incremental search scope updates, by default every 14 minutes. Also configurable by the user; the user can choose to add more tabs, including URLs to other sites.
My Calendar	The user's Calendar, from Exchange 2003 and later.	Configured by the user after My Site creation, which includes adding the Outlook Web Access (OWA) address (for example, http://exchangeserver/exchange) and the mailbox user name (for example, Christine *).
Colleague Tracker	Lists the user's colleagues from the user profile, organizational hierarchy, and other information as chosen by the user. It also alertsthe user of changes to colleagues' properties and displays those changes (for example, if a colleague has joined one of the user's SharePoint sites, distribution lists, or updated user profile properties). Alerts on changes are configurable via the Colleague Tracker Web Part properties.	Dynamically populated with users at the time of My Site creation based on organizational hierarchy, as dictated by the user profile, such as Manager and Peers. User can choose to remove and add colleagues after My Site creation.
Recent Blog Post	Displays the most recent blog posts; each post is displayed based on user permission.	On My Site creation, blog site is created with an initial post, entitled "Welcome to your Blog!"

* You should include in your end-user documentation the instructions for configuring Web Parts, such as My Inbox and My Calendar, that involve adding the OWA address on your Exchange Server.

Just as in other SharePoint sites and site collections, users can add Web Parts to their My Home page by clicking on Site Actions, selecting Edit Page, and then clicking Add A Web Part in one of the Web Part zones on the My Home page. Users will have access to the

Web Parts deployed as part of the Web application hosting the My Sites. Available Web Parts can be viewed by accessing the user's Site Settings and clicking on Web Parts under the Galleries section of the user's My Site, Site Settings page.

Adding and Managing Colleagues

Colleagues are added to a user's My Site automatically as part of the user profile and My Site creation process, referred to as *My Colleagues*. Colleagues who are part of a user's hierarchical or reporting organization in Active Directory are dynamically populated in the Colleague Tracker on a user's My Site My Home page. Colleagues are also governed by the *privacy controls* in My Sites, and users can configure visibility on colleagues as well as the degree of their own information that will be shown to the added colleagues.

Colleagues are added as *interlinked colleagues*—that is, each colleague name a user adds is formatted as a hyperlink that links directly back to that user's My Site details. SharePoint includes special controls to dynamically reference linked colleagues to return any updates to colleagues on linked My Sites, such as changes to colleague profiles and colleague site and distribution list memberships. For example, in Figure 8-18 , Christine Koch's Colleague Tracker Web Part has been automatically populated with her peers from the imported Active Directory information and includes Greg Weber, Gregory Alder and Suzan Fine. You can see that Gregory Alder and Suzan Fine are new members of SharePoint sites and distribution lists that Christine Koch is also a member of–that is, Gregory Alder is a new member of the SharePoint sites Reports X, Litware and Archive, and Suzan Fine is a new member of the Project X distribution list.

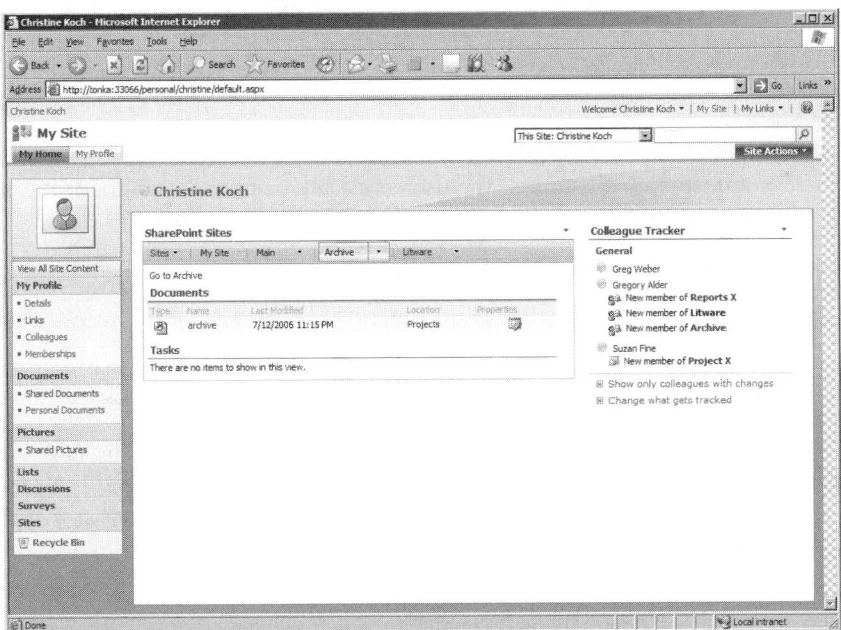

Figure 8-18 Dynamic population of Colleague Tracker on the My Home page

Clicking on Suzan Fine's name would redirect you to Suzan Fine's My Site shared view, which would show you the most recent changes to Suzan Fine. As shown in Figure 8-19, the most recent changes are denoted by a yellow highlight—in this case, the updated Memberships We Both Share Web Part.

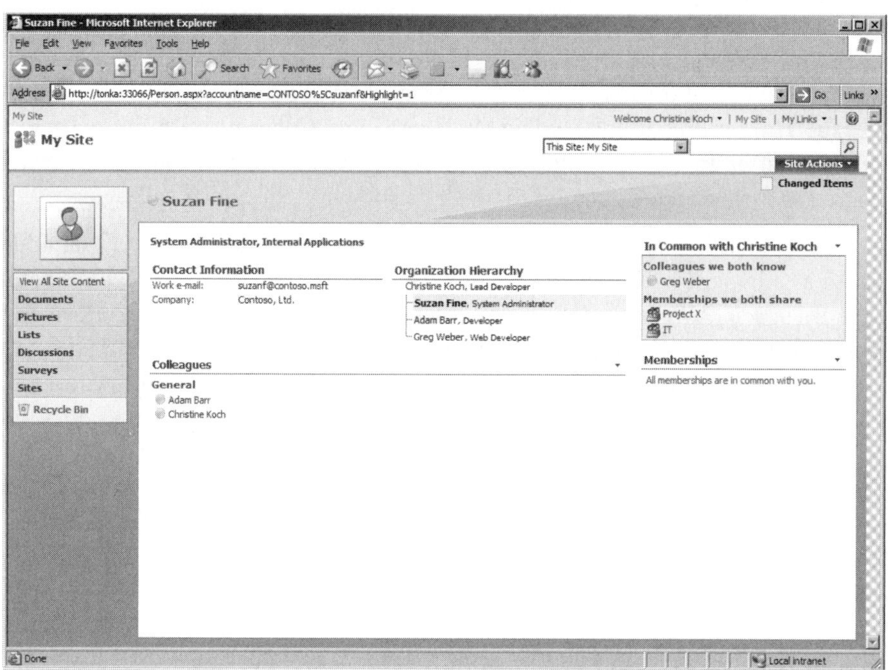

Figure 8-19 Interlinked colleagues—Memberships We Both Share

Adding Colleagues

Colleagues can be added to a user's My Site either by the user clicking on the Colleagues link under the My Information section of the user's My Site or by the user choosing to click on the Add To My Colleagues link returned in people search results.

To add colleagues from within a user's My Site, follow these steps:

1. Click the Colleagues link under the My Information section of the My Site lefthand menu.
2. On the My Colleagues page, click the Add Colleagues link in the tool bar.
3. On the Add Colleagues page, select colleagues either by clicking on the address book link to find users within the organizational directory or by selecting users listed in the Suggested Colleagues list, as shown in Figure 8-20. In the Privacy And Grouping section, you can define who you want to show colleagues added to your site to by selecting names from the Show These Colleagues To enumerated drop-

down list (also shown in Figure 8-20). The default value is Everyone, which means that all users with access to your My Site, such as the NT AUTHORITY\authenticated users group, will be able to view those colleagues.

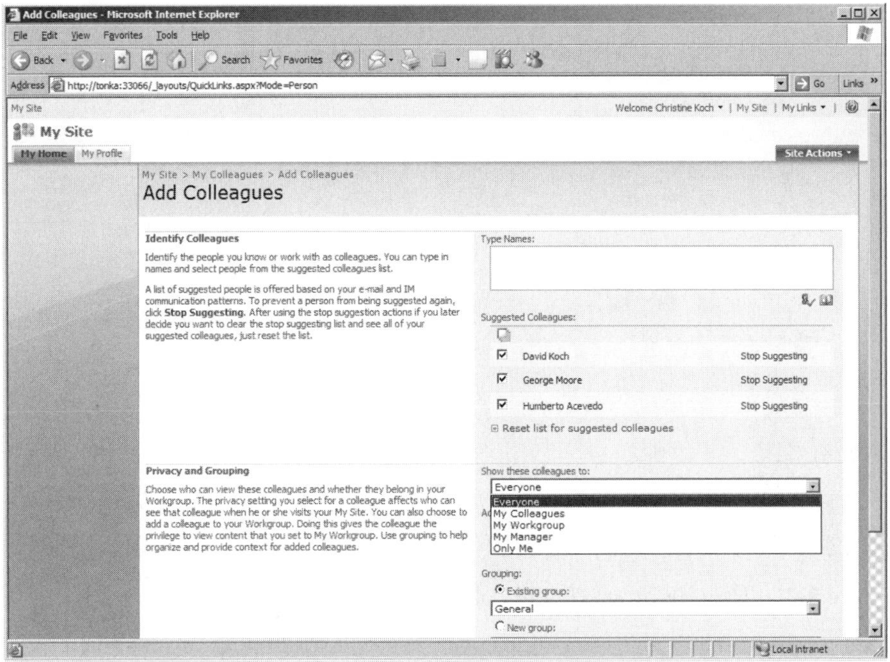

Figure 8-20 Adding colleagues to a My Site

When adding new colleagues, you can also choose, as part of the Privacy And Grouping section on the Add Colleagues page, to add those colleagues to your workgroup, *My Workgroup*. By adding colleagues to your workgroup, those colleagues have access to any other My Site information made available to the My Workgroup group, such as user profile properties made explicitly available to My Workgroup—for example, the My Site user's Birthday property. Along with adding colleagues to My Workgroup, you can also specify a New Group to add new colleagues to. For example, in Figure 8-21 two new users have been added to Christine Koch's colleagues in a new group named HR.

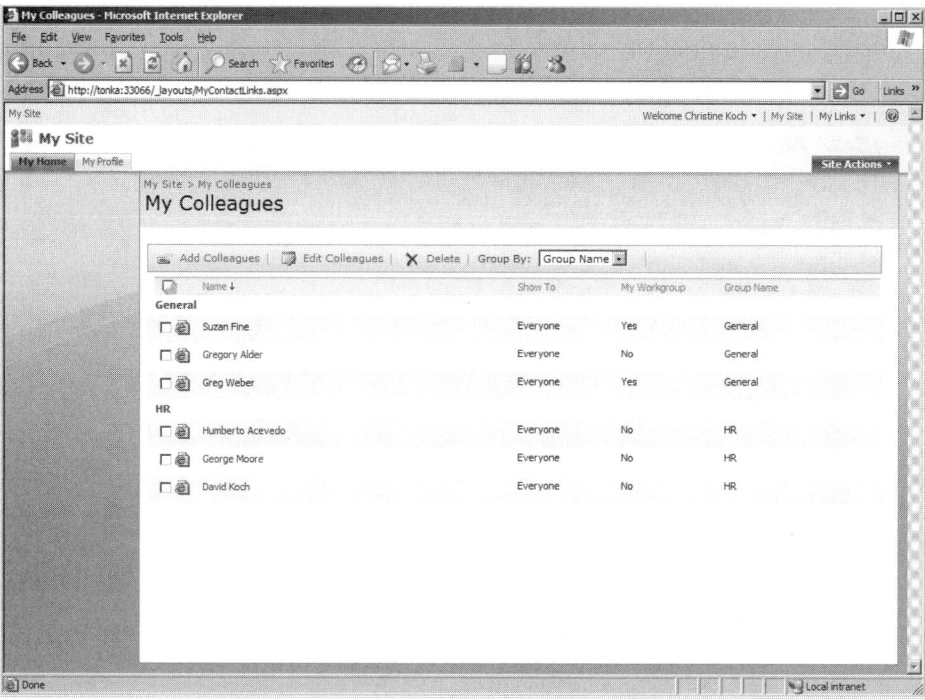

Figure 8-21 New HR group on My Colleagues page

Back on Christine Koch's My Home page, the additional HR group is shown in the Colleague Tracker Web Part. In Figure 8-22, you can see that the new group includes the two new colleagues.

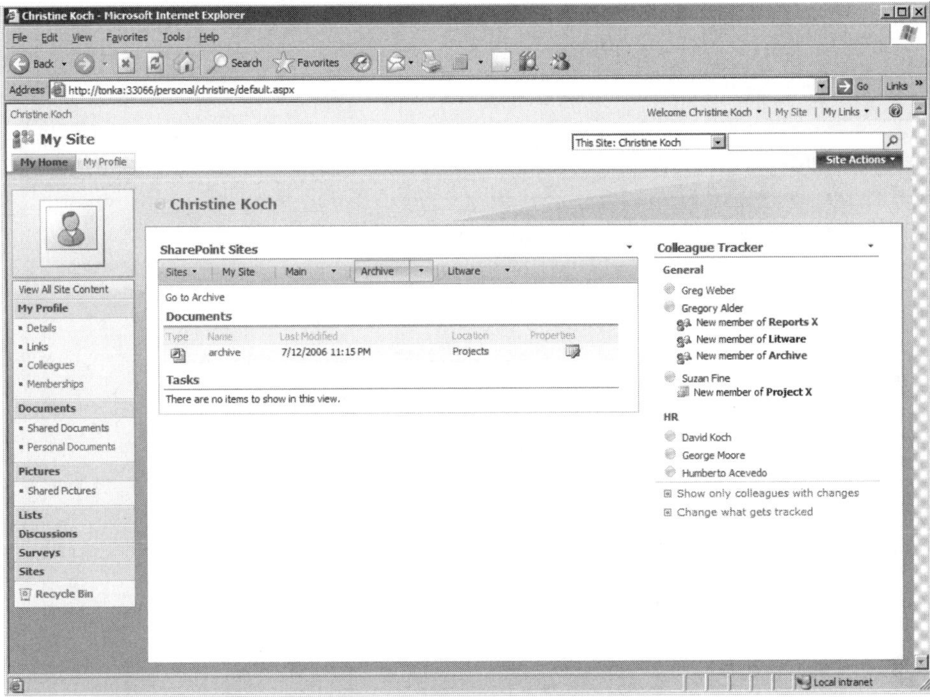

Figure 8-22 New colleagues added to Colleague Tracker on My Home

Colleague Alerts

My Site users can choose to show all colleagues in the Colleague Tracker or only show colleagues based on custom alert settings. For example, you can use a custom alert setting to show colleagues who have any membership changes to sites or distribution lists or who have changes to their blogs. To modify the colleague alert settings, click the Modify Alert Settings link under the Colleague Tracker Web Part on the My Home page of the user's My Site. Figure 8-23 shows the Colleague Tracker Web Part opened in edit mode and the configurable Alert Settings.

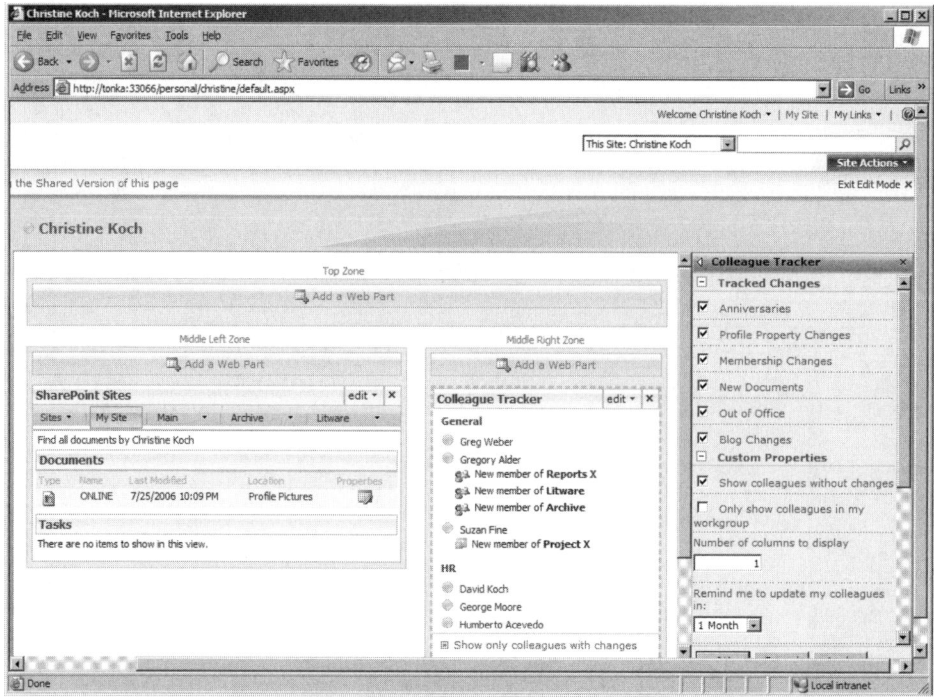

Figure 8-23 Configuring Colleague Tracker alerts

Configuring Memberships

Memberships are dynamically created by SharePoint, based on the My Site user's membership to SharePoint sites and distribution lists. The user membership configuration drives the display of the sites shown on the tabbed section of the SharePoint site's Rollup Web Part on the My Home page and also on the Document Rollup Web Part on the My Profile page. The user membership configuration also determines the display of the distribution lists in the In Common With Web Part on the user My Site My Profile page.

> **Note** If you have created and are accessing your My Site based on the SharePoint administrative account—that is, the account being used for the application pool—SharePoint views this account as the *System Account* and the SharePoint site's Web Part does not display any documents or tasks in the Rollup Web Part. This is by design. You should always work with My Sites using a non-system account, such as your domain user account.

If a My Site user decides to limit who can see her memberships, she can adjust the display properties by changing the privacy settings. To change the privacy settings for membership, click the Memberships link under My Information in the lefthand menu of the user's My Site, and then, on the My Memberships page, select from the SharePoint sites or distribution lists. For example, Figure 8-24 shows the Privacy And Grouping options available for the user's memberships—in this case, for the Litware SharePoint site. If the default value of Everyone is selected, all users with access to the user's My Site are able to see the Litware site as one of the tabbed sites displayed on the Documents tabbed interface on the shared or My Profile page of the user's My Site.

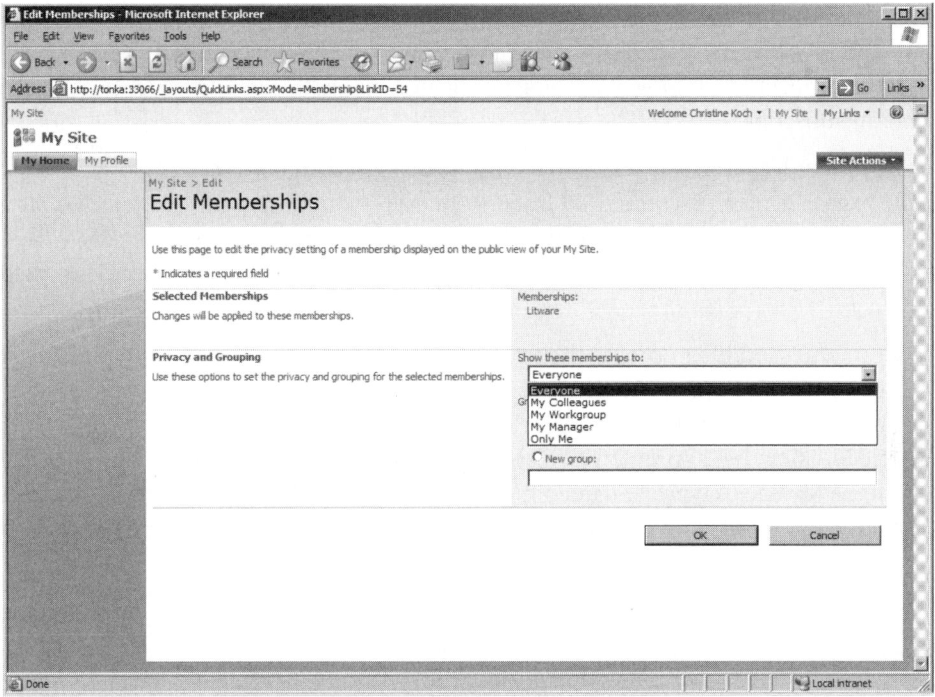

Figure 8-24 Editing Privacy And Grouping options for memberships

Creating Private Documents in My Sites

If you have previously worked with SharePoint Portal Server 2003 Personal Sites, you are familiar with the notion of private documents. The equivalent in SharePoint Server 2007 My Sites is the Personal Documents document library, By default, access to Personal Documents is limited to the My Site owner and administrators for the server. This means that when other users navigate to a user's My Site, such as NT authenticated users, those users will not see any documents stored in Personal Documents. A user can choose to modify the default Personal Document document library permissions but in doing so then opens up access, and exposure to, documents within Personal Documents.

The Shared Documents document library, also included on a user's My Site, is by default accessible to other users, such as NT authenticated users, browsing to the user's My Site. Users should add any documents they wish to share to the Shared Documents document library.

Creating a Personal Blog

The option to create a personal blog is created at the time of My Site creation, denoted by a *Create Blog* link in the upper right hand corner of the My Home page. After creating a personal blog, My Site users can create and edit new blog posts and set permissions against each post to their blog. Each blog post generates an RSS feed, to which authorized users can subscribe.

Blog post titles from the user's personal blog are displayed on both the My Home and My Profile pages, using a preconfigured Data Form Web Part entitled *Recent Blog Posts*. The blog post titles displayed in the Recent Blog Posts web part on the My Profile page will be displayed to other users browsing the user's My Site based on the user access to each post.

Users can also send blog posts to their private blog directly from Microsoft Office Word 2007. For example, Figure 8-25 shows a New Blog Account being configured for a SharePoint blog site. This means that a user can then publish any new blog postings from Word 2007 using that account, which also includes the URL parameter for the personal blog on the My Site. A typical SharePoint blog URL you can use to publish blog postings to directly from Word 2007 is depicted as *http://server_name/personal/username/Blog/*.

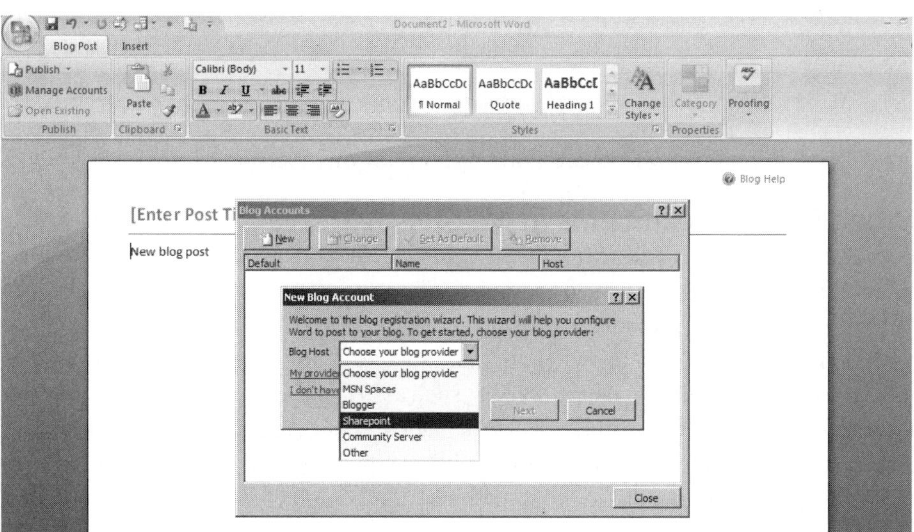

Figure 8-25 Configuring Word 2007 for publishing a blog post to a personal blog

Figure 8-26 shows the resultant Word 2007 blog post confirming the post has been successfully published to the user's My Site private blog.

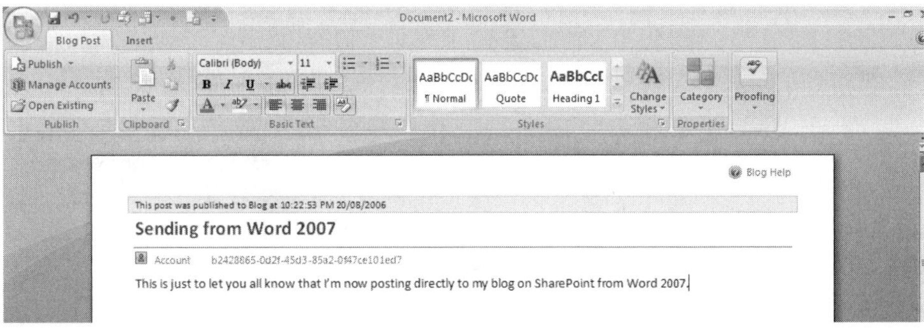

Figure 8-26 Blog Post successfully published to My Site personal blog from Word 2007

Configuring My Profile

The My Profile page is the public-facing page of a user's My Site. It includes custom controls and Web Parts to display information about the My Site user, based on the visiting user's credentials and association with the My Site user. It includes user profile information as imported from Active Directory, such as User Name and User Title.

When a user profile is created, a My Profile page for the user is also created to display that user's information. When a user creates a My Site, the My Profile page is further enhanced with custom Web Parts and filtered views based on user credentials. Figure 8-27 shows a user's view of his My Profile page, which includes the enumerated As Seen By drop-down list. The values in this drop-down list determine the view of the My Profile page that will be shown to visiting users. For example, the Everyone view shows all users with access to the My Site user information as determined by the My Site user. Some user profile properties—such as the My Site User Name, User Title, Work Phone and Work E-mail—are preconfigured for the Everyone group by the administrator and not configurable by the My Site user.

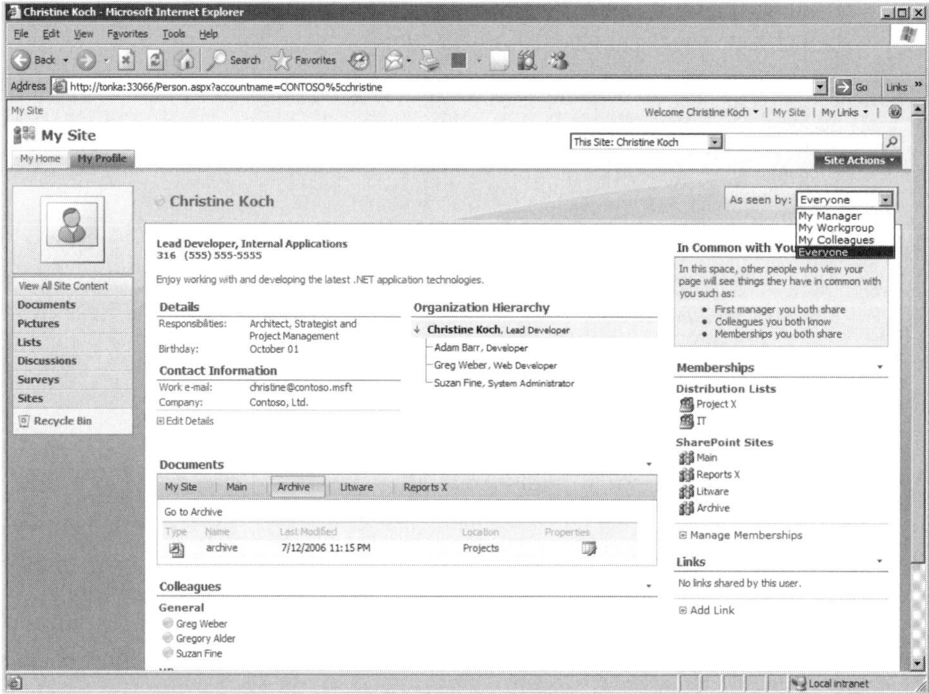

Figure 8-27 Privacy controls enumerated on the My Profile page

The My Profile page also includes an In Common With You Web Part. This is a custom Web Part that, when viewed by a visiting user, includes the My Site user's Memberships and shows memberships that the My Site user has in common with the visiting user. Only memberships that the My Site user has made accessible are displayed.

Configuring User Details

Users can modify some of the user profile properties on their My Sites to selectively display their information on the My Profile page. This includes targeting information to one of five selections, which includes Everyone (default, refers to authenticated users with access to My Sites), My Colleagues, My Workgroup, My Manager and Only Me.

Table 8-7 shows the default user profile properties in a user's My Site, including those for which the user can adjust visibility.

Table 8-7 User Profile Property Settings in My Site User Details

Property	Show To (Locked/Configurable)	Values
Name	Locked	Everyone
Title	Locked	Everyone

Table 8-7 User Profile Property Settings in My Site User Details

Property	Show To (Locked/Configurable)	Values
About Me	Locked	Everyone
Picture	Locked	Everyone
Responsibilities	Locked	Everyone
Skills	Configurable	Multiple All 5 selections
Past Projects	Configurable	Multiple All 5 selections
Interests	Configurable	Multiple All 5 selections
Schools	Configurable	Multiple All 5 selections
Birthday	Configurable	Multiple All 5 selections
Assistant	Locked	Everyone
Mobile Phone	Configurable	Multiple All 5 selections
Fax	Configurable	Multiple All 5 selections
Home Phone	Configurable	Multiple All 5 selections
Account Name	Locked	Everyone
Work Phone	Locked	Everyone
Office	Locked	Everyone
Department	Locked	Everyone
Work E-mail	Locked	Everyone

To edit the configurable profile properties on a user's My Site, follow these steps:

1. Click the Details link under My Information in the left-hand menu on the user's My Site.
2. On the Edit Details page, enter details and modify the visibility of the configurable profile properties by choosing them from the Show To drop-down list alongside each configurable property. For example, Figure 8-28 shows that the user Interests have been changed from the default of Everyone to My Colleagues and that the user Birthday has been changed to My Manager.

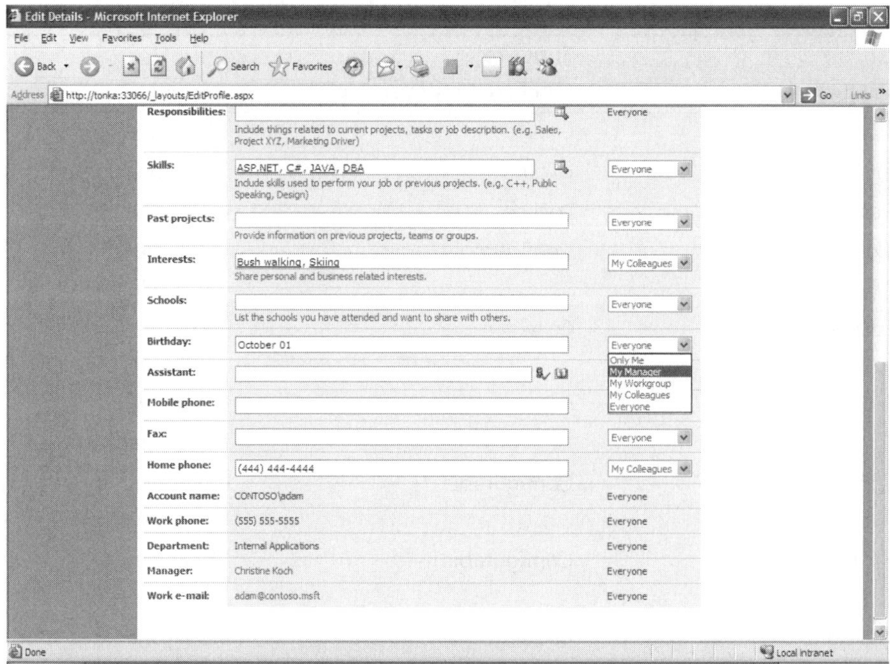

Figure 8-28 Editing user details on a user's My Site

The result of these changes is that users who are not part of the My Site user's My Colleagues group cannot view the user's Interests and only the My Site user's manager can view the My Site user's birthday.

Adding Responsibilities and Skills

When My Site users add values to the Responsibilities and Skills properties on the My Site Edit Details page, they have the option of freely entering text in the corresponding property text fields or selecting values from a populated list, as shown in Figure 8-29. To open a list and select from existing values, click on the plus sign icon to the right of the text field.

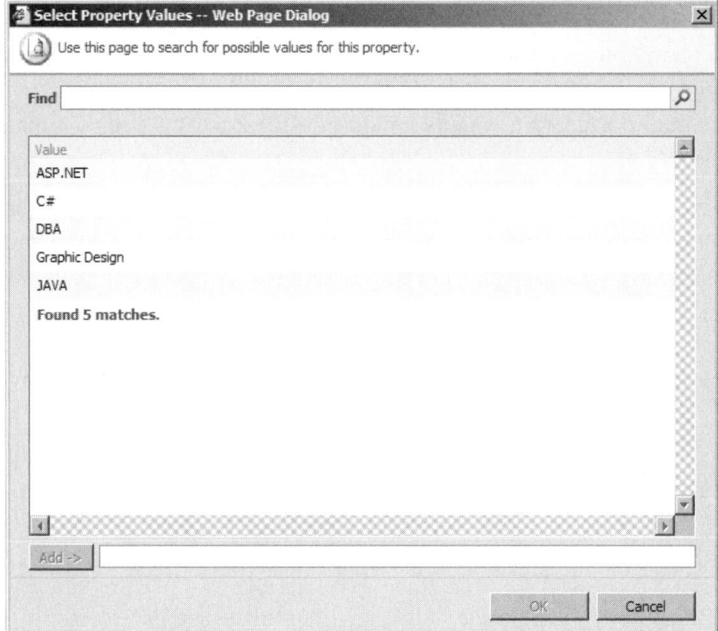

Figure 8-29 Adding user responsibilities and skills from existing values

Each time users enter new values into the text fields, those values are dynamically appended to the respective list. Otherwise, administrators can prepopulate, or edit, the lists as per the following:

1. Go to the SSP hosting the My Sites and click on User Profiles and Properties on the Home page of the SSP.
2. On the User Profiles and Properties page, navigate down to the User Profile Properties section and click on View Profile Properties.
3. On the View Profile Properties page, locate either Responsibilities or Skills and click on Edit from the contextual dropdown menu.
4. On the Edit User Profile Property page, scroll down to the section Choice List Settings. You can choose to Allow Users to Add to Choice List, which allows for dynamic list population as users enter new values against the Responsibilities and Skills profile properties on their My Site Edit Details page. You can also choose to Add A New Choice, Edit or Delete existing values, import values from an existing file, or export an existing list to a file.

Responsibilities and Skills are included as fields on the Search Options for People search form and users can choose to search against either of those properties. For example, entering JAVA in the Skills search field would result in a search on all people who had entered JAVA as one of their Skills.

Configuring User Alerts

Users can subscribe to SharePoint sites and lists and receive e-mail alerts when a document or an item is created, modified, or deleted. Alerts can be set at different frequencies, such as an immediate e-mail notification, a daily e-mail notification, or a weekly e-mail report.

Users can create and configure their alerts throughout sites in a site collection by clicking on the Welcome *Username* drop-down menu in the SharePoint top navigation pane and selecting My Settings. Alerts are set with respect to the current site location. For example, users working in the Litware site who decide to add an alert are presented with a list of available document libraries and lists within the Litware site on which they can then set alerts. This gives users a complete view of all site-specific alerts and saves users from having to navigate through a site's site settings to view and create alerts.

> **Note** You can centrally manage users' alerts with a third-party product, DeliverPoint. DeliverPoint, found at *http://www.barracudatools.com/*, also includes other features, such as the ability to centrally manage user permissions.

Navigating to Users' My Sites

Users can find other users through the SharePoint Server 2007 People Search or through the My Sites Add Colleagues option. If you search for and locate a user, you can also choose to add that user to your Colleagues list in your My Site by clicking the Add To My Colleagues link in the search results, as shown in Figure 8-30.

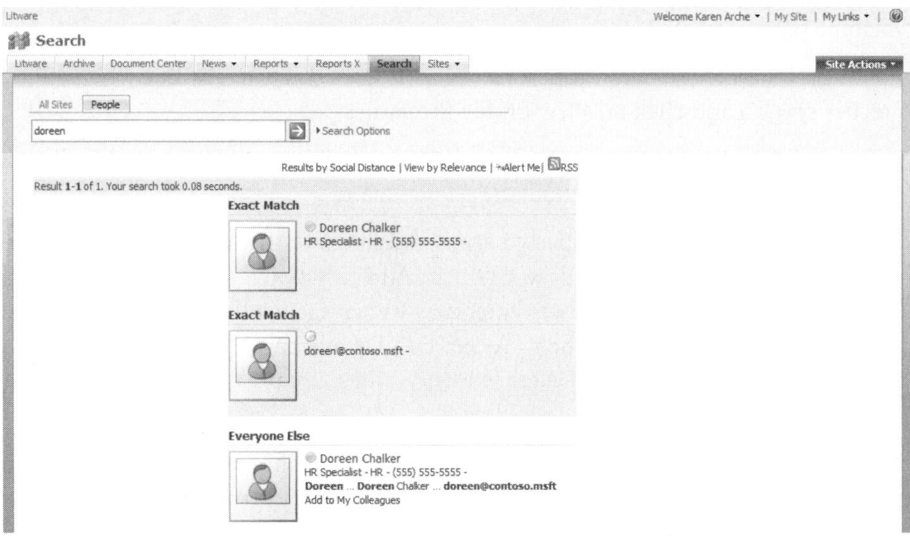

Figure 8-30 Adding to My Colleagues from People Search results

If a user has created a My Site and you know the username of the user, you can navigate directly to that user's My Site by entering the URL parameter http://server_name/personal/username. You will be redirected to the user's public view of the My Site.

Publishing Links to Office Clients

As part of My Sites deployment, you can publish links to users' Office applications to further streamline functionality between your SharePoint sites and those of other users. For example, you can publish a link from a SharePoint Data Connection Library, containing a specific data connection, to Excel applications of other users so that they can then access that data connection from directly within their Excel applications. They can then use that data connection to directly send data from Excel back to a database. Or you can publish a link from a SharePoint Slide Library so that other users can then add that link as an object directly to their PowerPoint applications as a link or additional slide.

Figure 8-31 shows a link that has been published from a SharePoint Data Connection Library that appears in the user's Excel workbook under the Existing Connections option in the Data Menu. It appears as one of the Connection Files on the network and is named Project Analysis.

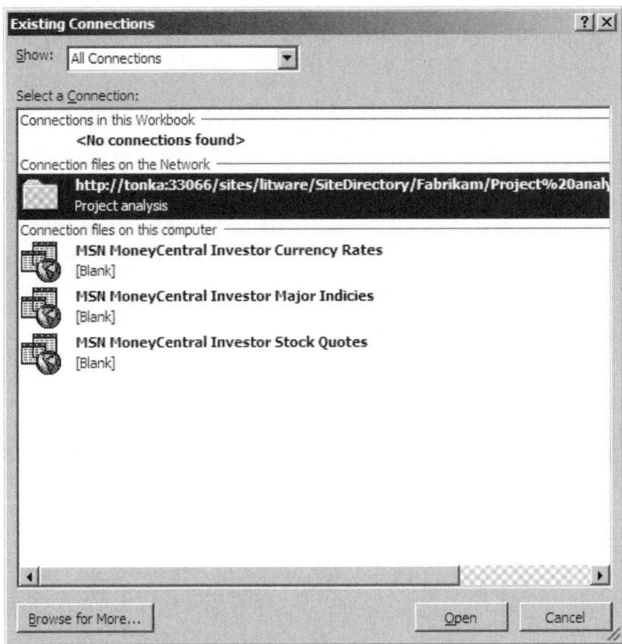

Figure 8-31 Published link to an Excel client

To add a published link, click the Published Links To Office Client link under the User Profiles And My Sites section of the SSP home page. On the Links Published To Office Applications page, add a new link to the SharePoint site containing the feature you want to have published. You can also set target audiences for the published links. For example, you can choose to publish only a particular data connection link to users in the Finance group of your organization so that only those users have that link available within their Excel applications. You can set target audiences either by selecting from an existing audience you have configured for SharePoint or selecting from a security group or distribution list in your Active Directory.

Note If you have changed your default My Site location to another SSP, any links pushed out from the old SSP remain in your Office applications.

Personalization Links

You can selectively target links to your users' My Sites by using personalization links. Personalization links appear as an additional navigational tab in a user's My Site. For example, you can choose to send a link to details for an upcoming company event to all users, or you can send links to different groups of users' My Sites, including links back to specific sites (such as a specific site collection or a link to all users' My Sites where the users are members of the Sales group).

You can create Personalization Links from the SSP home page by clicking on the Personalization Links link in the User Profiles And My Sites section. This will take you to the Personalization Links For My Site Navigation page, where you can create links for My Sites. Links are targeted to specific My Site users by selecting either from an existing audience or from a security group or distribution list. Figure 8-32 shows an additional tab, named Global IT Conference, that includes a link to the conference details and that has been specifically targeted to IT users throughout the organization.

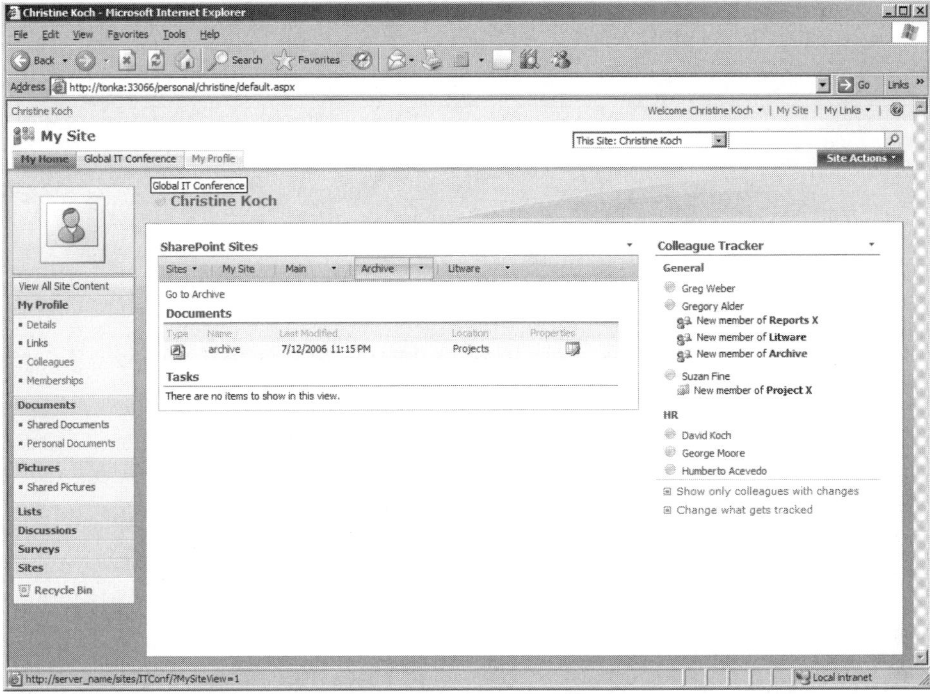

Figure 8-32 Published link added as an additional tab on a user's My Site

You can remove personalization links from My Sites by deleting the link from the Personalization Links For My Site Navigation page.

Using Personalization Links for My Site Navigation

Given that you can have many Web applications associated with a single SSP and users might have a different main intranet or Internet home pages, a novel way of leveraging personalization links is by *targeting* links to users' My Sites back to the respective main intranet or Internet home pages or to various Web applications. For example, User A sees a link back to his home page (A), while User B sees a link back to her home page (B).

Setting Quotas for My Sites

By default, My Sites are provisioned with a storage limit of 100 MB. This limit is defined in the *Personal Site template*. If you change this limit, any *new* My Sites will adhere to the new limit, but existing sites will not.

You can view the storage capacity for an existing user's My Sites by clicking the Site Actions link on the user's home page and selecting Site Settings. On the Site Settings page, under Site Collection Administration, click the Storage Space Allocation link. Figure 8-33 shows the default storage allocation on a user's My Site.

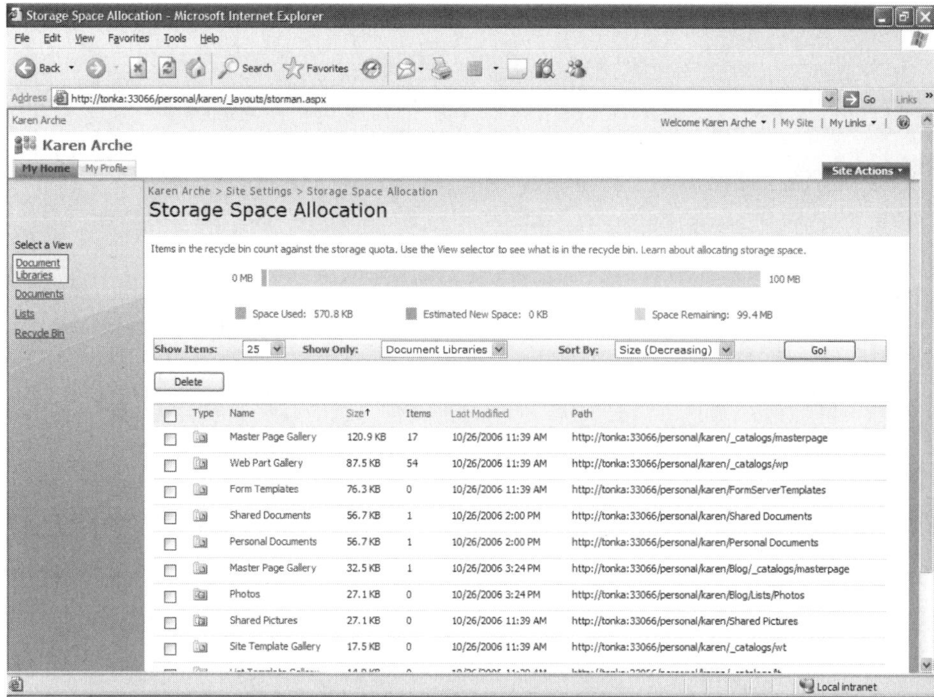

Figure 8-33 Default storage allocation for a user's My Site

You can change the storage quota for all *new* My Sites by clicking the Quota Templates link in the SharePoint Site Management section on your Application Management page in Central Administration. You can increase or decrease the maximum site storage.

To change the storage quota on an *existing* My Site, do the following:

1. Click on the Site Collection Quotas And Locks link in the SharePoint Site Management section on your Application Management page in Central Administration.
2. On the Site Collection Quotas And Locks page, you can choose the My Site from the Site Collection drop-down list and adjust the Individual Quota settings for the selected My Site.

Note Items in a personal site's Recycle Bin are counted in the total storage for that site.

Creating My Sites with Duplicate User Names

If your organization includes multiple domains or you are configuring access for both domain and local users, you might run into a situation in which a user attempts to access his existing My Site only to be met with the following error message:

"Your personal site cannot be created because a site already exists with your username. Contact your site administrator for more information."

This message is generated because the user is using the same username in another domain and logging in to a site from that domain, or the user is using the same name for a local server account. SharePoint will match the username but not the domain. You can correct this by changing the Site Naming Format from the SSP administration site. To do this, follow these steps:

1. From your SSP home page, click My Site Settings in the User Profiles And My Sites section.
2. On the resultant My Site Settings page, navigate down to the Site Naming Format section and change the naming format that you'd like to use to resolve conflicts.

Essentially, you have three choices: User Name (Do Not Resolve Conflicts), User Name (Resolve Conflicts By Using domain_username), or Domain And User Name (Will Not Have Conflicts). Examples of each choice are given in the interface. You need to select which type of conflict resolution you want.

Deleting My Sites

Each My Site is stored as a site collection. You can delete a My Site either through the SharePoint Server 2007 Central Administration interface or by using the command-line tool.

Note Deleting a My Site does not delete the associated user profile. The user can still be found in people searches and have access to all sites to which he or she has membership. Subsequent to deleting a My Site, you should run a full crawl to remove any references to the deleted My Site.

To delete a My Site using the Central Administration interface, follow these steps:

1. In Central Administration, click the Application Management tab.
2. In the SharePoint Site Management section on the Application Management page, click Delete Site Collection.
3. On the Delete Site Collection page, click the Site Collection drop-down list, and then select Change Site Collection.

4. On the Select Site Collection page, click the My Site you want to delete. The personal sites are denoted by the /personal/username parameter in the URL list on the left side of the page. Alternatively, if you have many personal sites, use the URL Search option to locate the My Site to be deleted. After you have selected the My Site to be deleted, click OK.
5. Back on the Delete Site Collection page, review the Site Collection to ensure it is the correct My Site. Also review the warning that you are about to delete the following site collection. When ready, click OK to delete the My Site.

To delete a My Site using the stsadm.exe command line, from your command prompt, enter the following text:

```
stsadm.exe -o deleteWeb -url http://server_name/personal/username
```

Personalization Sites

Aside from the personalization provided by My Sites, SharePoint Server 2007 includes a custom personalization site template that you can use to create personalization sites and have those sites targeted to different groups of users and also integrated into those users' My Sites. For example, you might create a personalized HR or Sales site and then have that site targeted and integrated into the My Sites of HR or Sales users. Personalization site templates include custom filters, such as a user filter and profile property filter. You can use these filters to set the visibility on content in the personalization site.

Personalization sites can be created anywhere in your site collection. To create a personalized site, create a new site and select the Personalization Site template from the Enterprise Template Section tab. When your users click the Personalization Site link, they will redirected to their My Site along with a custom view of the personalization site. For example, in Figure 8-34, a MySales personalization site has been created under the Fabrikam site, but it is integrated into the user's My Site.

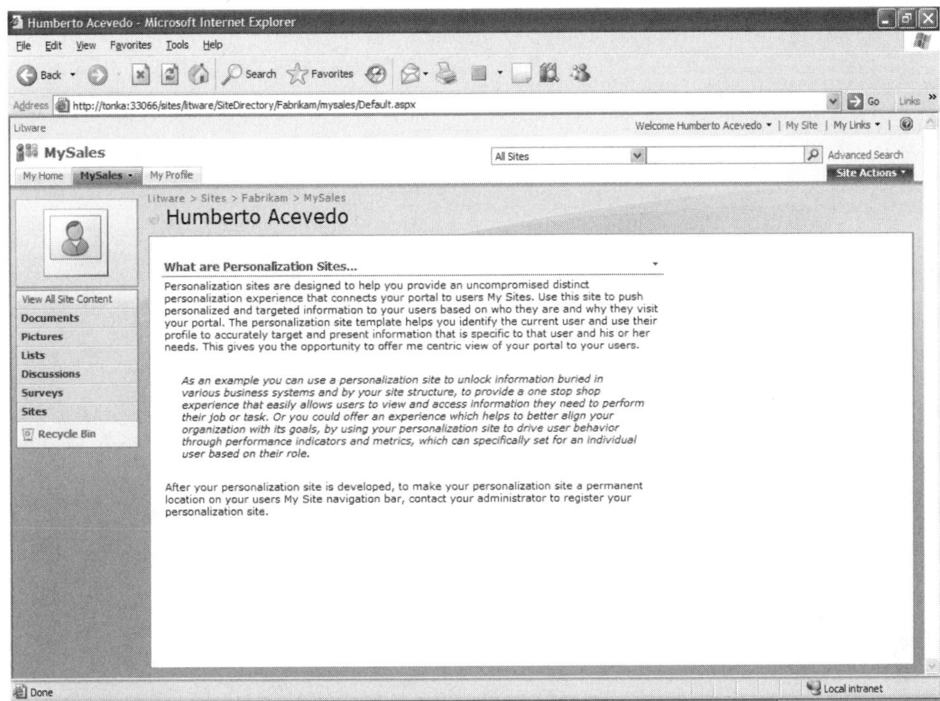

Figure 8-34 MySales personalization site integrated into a user's My Site

For ease of navigation, you can include the MySales site in users' My Sites as an additional navigational tab by adding the link to the list of links in the Personalization Links For My Site Navigation page. To access the Personalization Links For My Site Navigation page, go to the SSP hosting the My Sites, click on Personalization Site Links on the Home page of the SSP.

The creator, or owner, of the personalization site can edit the page and also set the filtering. Figure 8-35 shows the MySales personalization site in edit mode with the Profile Property Filter Web Part settings displayed to the far right side of the page. The default value for the Profile Property Filter is *Name*, but other user profile properties can be passed to a connected Web Part (such as a document library) for additional filtering.

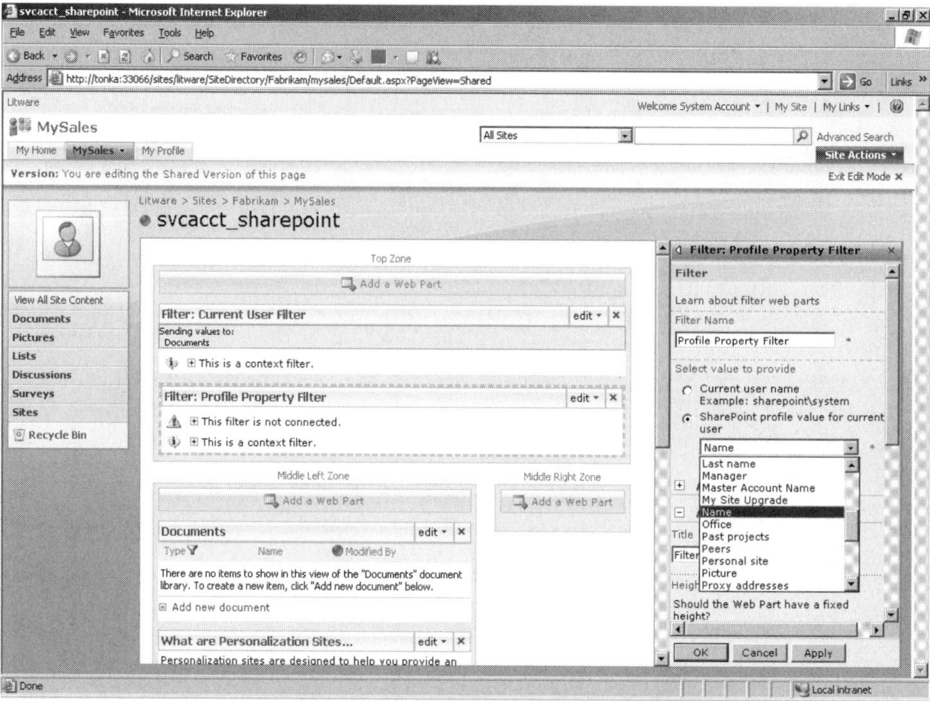

Figure 8-35 Personalization site filters and connections

Searching for People

After you've imported user profiles and SharePoint has crawled and indexed those user profiles, search is enabled on those user profiles and you can search on people. In other words, it is not necessary for users to have created My Sites to have People search enabled. But the search results on people where a My Site has not been created by a user will include minimal results. A basic My Site is generated as part of the user profile creation process, which includes user information added at the time of profile creation. This includes user information imported from Active Directory such as user name, title, e-mail, and hierarchical organizational structure. Incremental search crawls index any subsequent My Sites created by users, along with new content added to those My Sites, to enhance the people search results to include more user-specific information such as skills and interests. Incremental search crawls also index any updates to user profiles, following user profile imports, including any mapped properties in user profiles.

When you search on people, the default search result value is to Sort Results By Social Distance. This means that the results will include people with the least social distance in your My Colleagues list in the foremost section of the results, followed by related colleagues, My Colleagues, and then Everyone Else—that is, users not connected with you, the user performing the search. This arrangement lets you see where each person in the search results fits into your social space and reveals any relationships other people have to people included in your My Colleagues list. The names of people other than those in your My Colleagues list include an additional link named Add To My Colleagues. If you click the Add To My Colleagues link in search results, that user will be added to the Colleagues Tracker Web Part in your My Site. Figure 8-36 shows the search results for George, who is already in the user's My Colleagues, denoted by the My Colleagues heading and the absence of the Add To My Colleagues link.

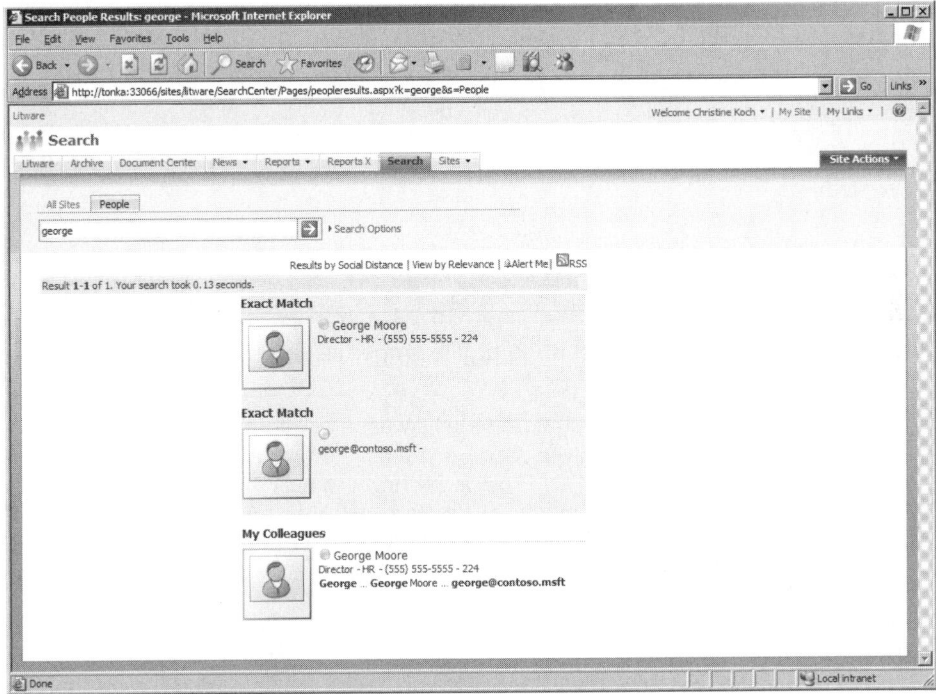

Figure 8-36 People search result by social distance and showing My Colleagues

You can also choose to use the People Search Options to search on specific areas such as Department, Title, Responsibilities, Skills, and Memberships. You can choose to add more profile properties to the Search Options to help locate people—for example, adding a SharePoint-specific profile property or an additional property you have mapped from your Active Directory. Figure 8-37 shows the default People Search Options.

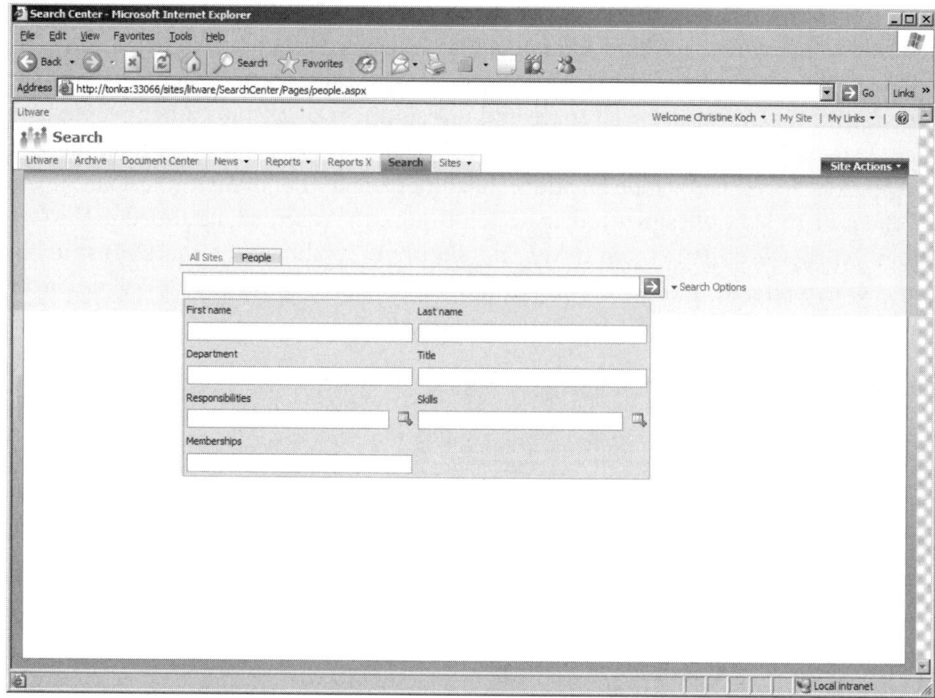

Figure 8-37 People Search Options using profile properties

Note User Details privacy controls determine what user information is returned in people search results for a given user. For example, if User A has selected to have only the profile property Past Projects as shown to only that user (that is, Only Me), any information added into Past Projects will not be returned in search results for the generic audience. If a user changes privacy controls for any user details, those changes will not be effective until the next incremental search crawl has updated the SharePoint indexes. In other words, even though User A has changed the privacy value from Everyone to Only Me, Everyone will continue to see the details of the changed property in search results until an incremental crawl has successfully completed.

Users can also search against their own or another user's details directly from within their My Sites. For example, if User A has Architect listed and shown as a Responsibility, the word Architect is formatted as a hyperlink under the Details section on the user's My Profile page. When the user clicks on the word Architect, *Architect* is passed as a parameter to the People search (such as Responsibilities:"Architect") and a search using that parameter is dynamically initiated. Any other people with the word Architect included and exposed as part of their profile are shown in the People search results.

Configuring and Managing Audiences

You create audiences in SharePoint Server 2007 to display and lock down content to certain groups of users, or even to just one user. Audiences can be used to target content in sites, lists, Web Parts, and Web Part pages throughout your SharePoint Server 2007 site collections. For example, you can create rules in your audience settings to only show content to users who meet a certain criteria, such as a profile property designating particular skills or a particular site, or to users who report under a certain manager or are part of a particular distribution list. Users meeting the criteria for an audience are referred to as *members* of an audience. Audiences embellish the personalization experience in SharePoint Server 2007 by delivering the right information to the right people. In this section, you will learn how to create audiences and specify the rules for those audiences to determine membership, and subsequently target content based on those audiences.

Creating Audiences

Audiences in SharePoint Server 2007 extend the ability to target specific information to users or groups of users. You can also target information to users by choosing security groups and distribution groups, but audiences can granulate the user targeting experience further by using the user profile properties. In SharePoint Server 2007, you can target Web Parts and list items to users throughout the entire site collection or collections. This section will demonstrate how you can create audiences and then associate those audiences to content throughout your sites.

Audiences are created and managed in the SSP. Any Web applications associated with that SSP are then able to take advantage of any of those audiences for targeting content to users throughout sites and site collections.

In this example, you will create four audiences: one for Human Resources, one for IT, one for Interns, and one for Marketing. You can then target relevant content throughout your SharePoint Server 2007 to each of those audiences.

To create an audience, follow these steps:

1. Go to the Home page of your SSP site, and click Audiences.
2. On the subsequent Manage Audiences page, shown in Figure 8-38, click Create Audience.

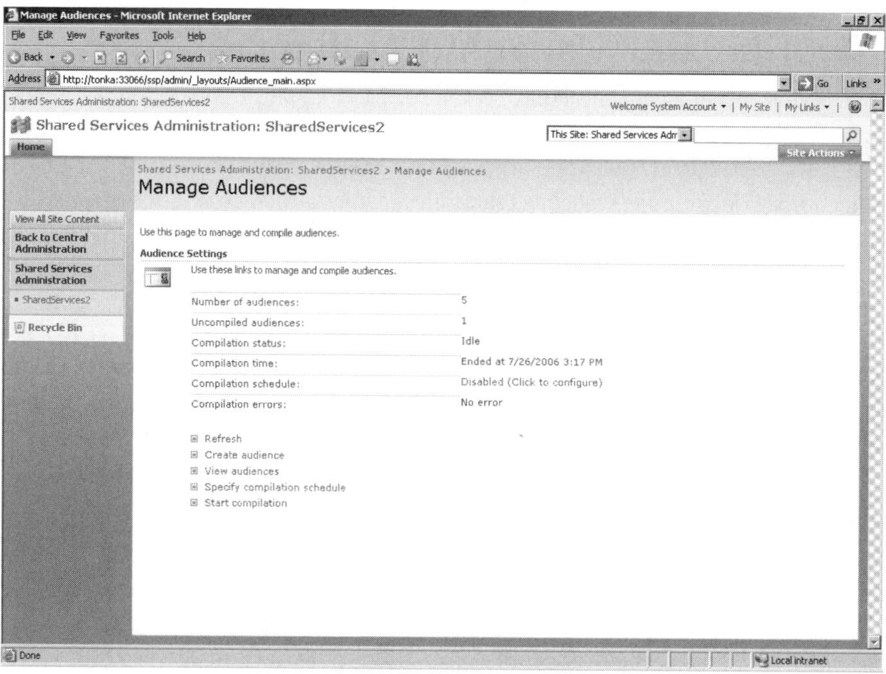

Figure 8-38 Manage Audiences page

3. On the Create Audience page, enter a Name for your audience. In Figure 8-39, we have used the name Human Resources. You also need to include an owner for the audience. Do this by either entering a username into the Owner field or by using the Add People Web Page dialog box by clicking on the address book icon alongside the Owner field. You can select which users will be included in the audience by choosing either the Satisfy All Of The Rules or Satisfy Any Of The Rules option for the criteria you set for the audience. If you choose Satisfy All Of The Rules, for each rule you create for the audience, the members will need to have satisfied each rule. This is the more restrictive way to build audiences. In this case, select the default Satisfy All Of The Rules option. Click OK.

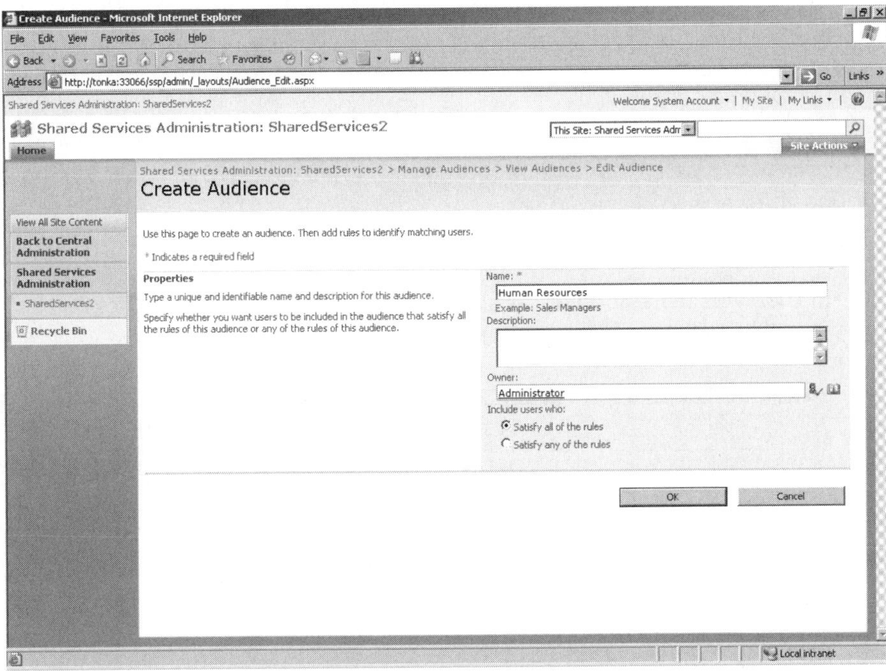

Figure 8-39 Creating an audience

You should now be on the Add Audience Rule: Human Resources page, where you can configure the rules and set criteria for determining the members for your newly created audience.

Set Audience Rules

On the Add Audience Rule: Human Resources page, you can choose which criteria you want to set for the Human Resources audience. There are two operands from which to choose. The User Operand enables you to select from one of two operators: Member Of and Reports Under. Using the Member Of operator, you can specify an existing security or distribution list from your configured Directory Services, such as Active Directory. Using the Reports Under operator, you can choose to include the direct reports for a particular manager, based on your organizational hierarchy. The Property Operand enables you to select from the profile properties configured in the current SSP scope, such as Account Name, Assistant, Skills, or Birthday. This list includes any custom properties you have added to the profile store.

Note When users create audiences at the list level, they also have the ability to specify a SharePoint group as a defining element of an Audience rule if the Member Of option is selected.

For this example, we'll demonstrate configuring a rule using the Member Of option. Use the following steps to create a rule.

1. Choose the User Operand, and select Member Of.
2. In the Value field, add **HR** (as shown in Figure 8-40), which is the corresponding distribution list from Active Directory. Click OK.

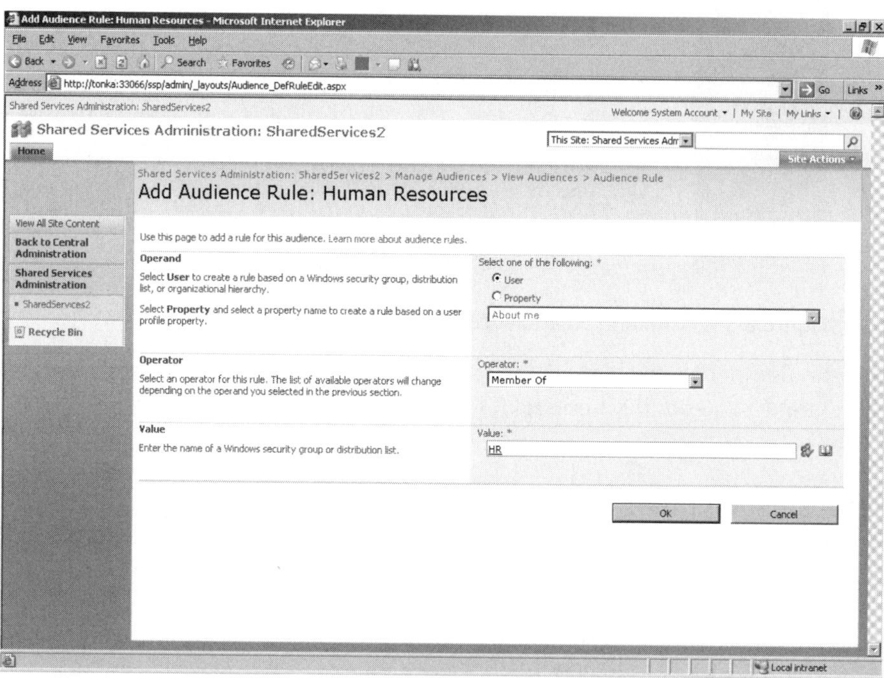

Figure 8-40 Adding an Audience rule

The resultant View Audience Properties: Human Resources page, shown in Figure 8-41, displays the properties for the Human Resources audience, including the rule. However, the audience will not be effective until you have compiled it.

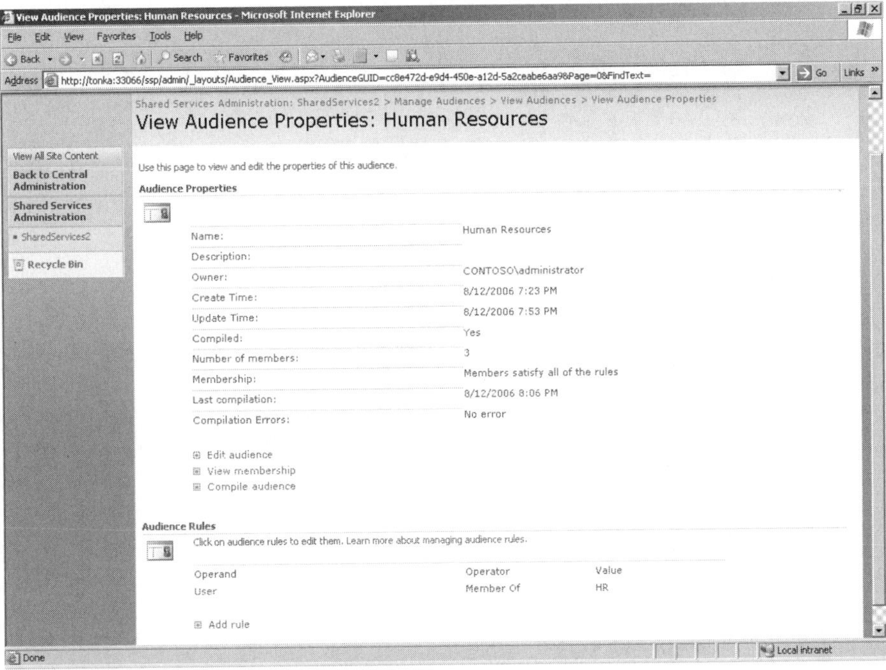

Figure 8-41 View Audience Properties page for a new audience

3. Click the Compile Audience link to compile the Human Resources audience and return to the Manage Audiences page.
4. On the Manage Audiences page, click the View Audiences link to view the existing audiences.

   Figure 8-42 shows the View Audiences page, which includes two audiences: All Site Users and Human Resources. The All Site Users audience is the default audience that is created when you install SharePoint Server 2007. Notice the Human Resources audience has three members, denoted by the number 3 in the Members column to the far right of the list.

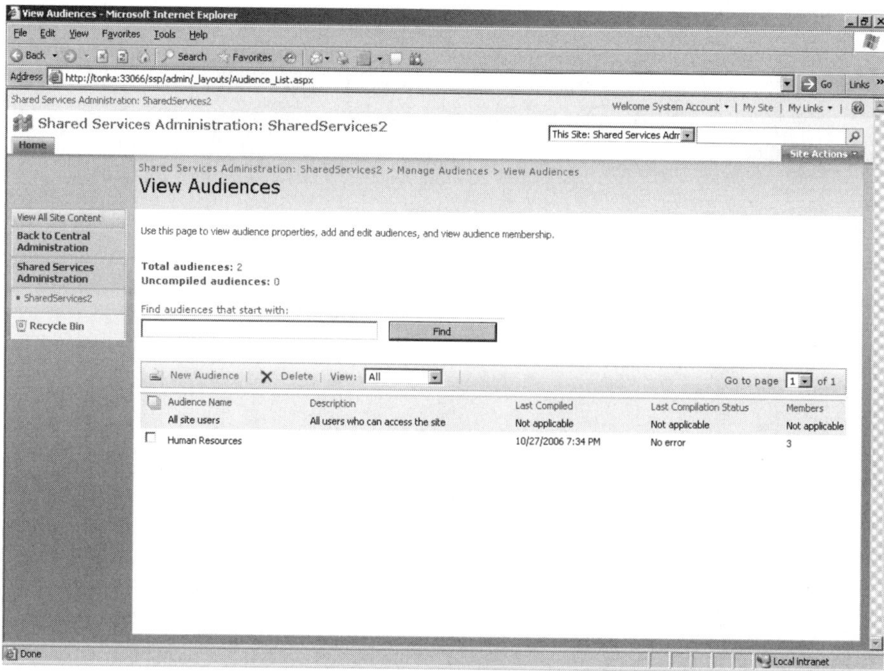

Figure 8-42 View Audiences

5. From the Human Resources contextual drop-down menu, select View Membership.

On the View Audience Membership: Human Resources page, shown in Figure 8-43, you can view the members for the Human Resources audience. These are the members of the HR distribution list that you specified under rules and selection criteria for the audience.

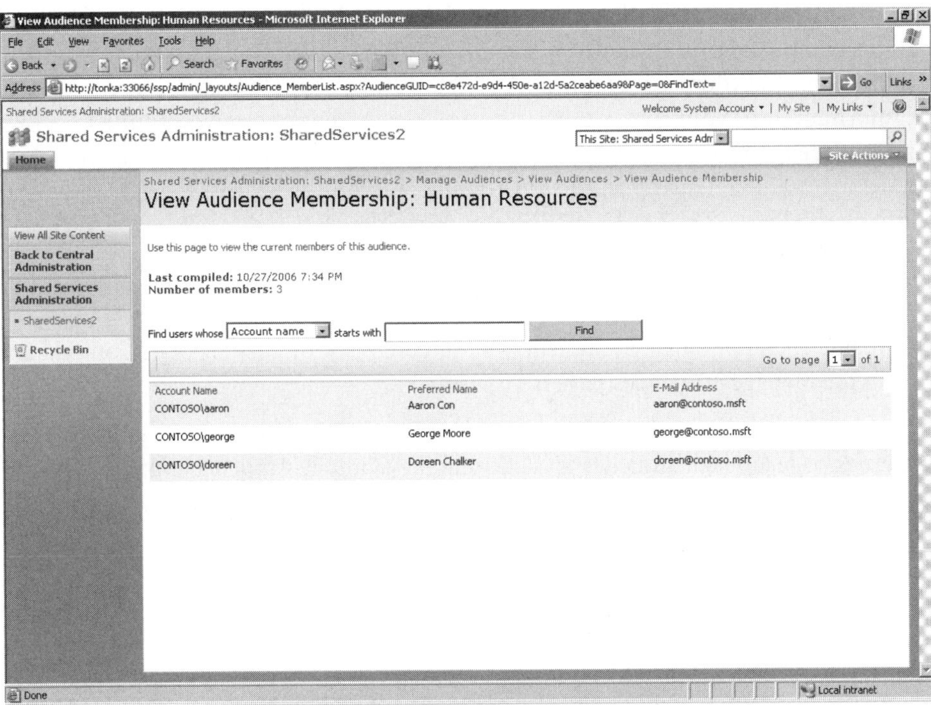

Figure 8-43 Viewing audience membership for a new audience

You can now use the HR audience to target content specifically to the members of that audience throughout your Web applications associated with the SSP in which you have configured the audience.

Table 8-8 shows some sample audience configurations, including the HR audience created above and three additional audiences: one for IT (which includes all members who report to the Lead Developer, Christine Koch), one for Interns, and one for Marketing (which includes members of the Marketing security group in Active Directory).

Table 8-8 Sample Audience Rule Settings

Audience	Operand	Operator	Value
HR	User	Member Of	HR (Active Directory Distribution Group)
IT	User	Reports Under	Christine Koch (Active Directory User)
Intern	Property Title	=	Intern (Mapped Active Directory Profile Attribute)
Marketing	User	Member Of	Marketing (Active Directory Security Group)

Note that if you create an audience that includes a profile property that is not yet populated, the compilation on that audience returns null results. If you subsequently update those properties in your Active Directory, you need to import the user profiles to update that information in your user profile storage *ahead* of compiling your audiences. An example is the Intern audience. Although we have created the Intern audience, we do not yet have any users in Active Directory with a title of Intern.

Setting Audience Compilation Schedule

You can choose from three options when compiling audiences:

- Manually compile all your audiences simultaneously, by clicking Start Compilation on the Manage Audiences page in the SSP
- Manually compile each audience separately by going into the View Audience Properties page for each audience and clicking the Compile Audience link
- Automatically compile all your audiences by setting a compilation schedule

To establish an automatic compilation schedule, follow these steps:

1. Click Specify Compilation Schedule on the Manage Audiences page to reveal the Specify Compilation Schedule page, shown in Figure 8-44.

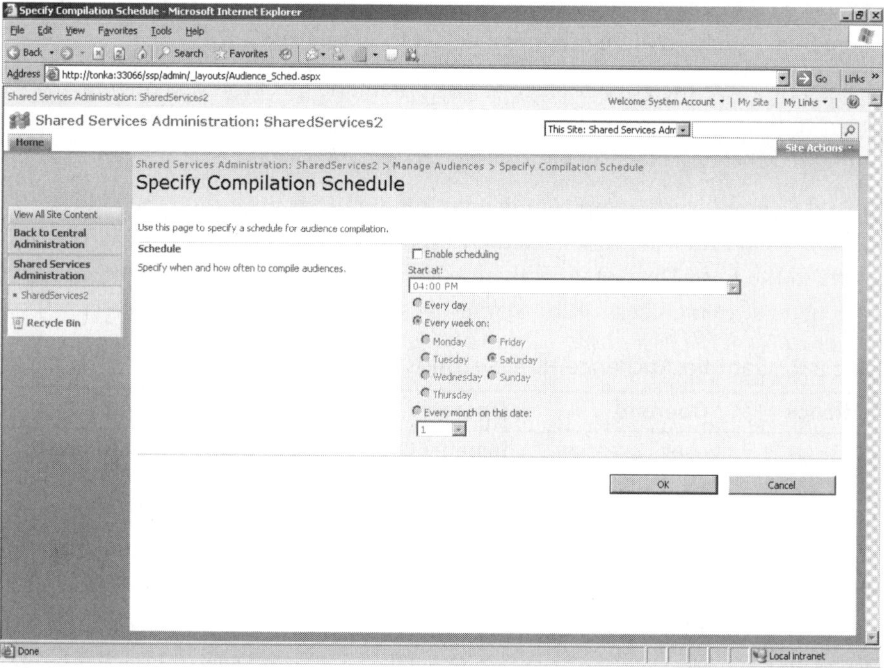

Figure 8-44 Audience compilation schedule

2. Select the Enable Scheduling check box, and then specify the time you want the compilation to begin by selecting from the drop-down options under Start At.
3. Next, select from either the daily, weekly, or monthly options to specify the frequency for the compilation to run. In this case, select the Every Week On option and then select Sunday. Click OK.

Note that you can choose to vary the frequency and timings of your schedules, depending on the number of audiences and the membership of each audience, to suit your business needs. For example, you can schedule compilation to occur outside of business hours to reduce any impact on server resources and avoid any degradation in performance. You might also want to synchronize audience compilation with your user profile import to ensure that any properties are updated in your profile store and reflected in your audience rules.

Updating Existing Audiences

You might want to update the membership for one of your existing audiences. For example, if you have an audience where the members are reporting to a manager who has left the organization, you need to update the rule for that audience to reflect the new manager and reporting structure.

To update an audience, follow these steps:

1. Ensure your user profile imports are up to date so that user information and organization hierarchy will be correctly updated in the SharePoint Profile database.
2. On the SSP Home page, click the Audiences link
3. On the Manage Audiences page, click the View Audiences link.
4. On the View Audiences page, click the Audience Name to be changed, and then select View Properties from the contextual drop-down menu.
5. On the View Audience Properties: Audience page, you can either choose to edit the audience to change the rule frequency or click the existing audience rule to edit that rule. Click the existing audience rule.
6. On the Edit Audience Rule: Audience page, change the Operand, Operator, and Value properties as required. Click OK.
7. Compile the audience to affect the update and push changes out to existing instances of the audience throughout the site collections.

Targeting Content Using Audiences

In Office SharePoint Server 2007, you can target Web Parts and list items to users or groups of users throughout your site collection or collections. In addition, users with the correct permissions can target information to other users without having to involve IT in the process.

Targeting Web Parts

To target a Web Part to an audience, you need to have administrative rights to the page or site to open the Web Part properties in shared view. To target a Web Part to an audience, follow these steps:

1. Select the Web Part against which you want to apply an audience, and open the Web Part in shared mode, Modify Shared Web Part.
2. In the Web Part properties, navigate down to the Advanced section and expand Advanced.
3. Scroll to the bottom of the Web Part's Advanced section until you see Target Audiences. Click the address book icon alongside the Target Audiences field, shown in Figure 8-45

Figure 8-45 Adress book icon alongside the Target Audiences field

4. In the Select Audiences dialog box, against Find, make sure Global Audiences (the default value) is selected and enter the name, or part thereof, of your audience. Then click the magnifying glass symbol for SharePoint to search and retrieve your audience.

5. Select the audience from the retrieved results, and then click Add. Click OK to acknowledge the audience and close the Select Audiences dialog box. Then click OK again to save the changes and close the Web Part properties.

Targeting List Items

Before you can set an audience against a list item, you need to configure the list for audience targeting. To do this, follow these steps:

1. Select the list against which you want to apply an audience.
2. From the Settings drop-down list, select List Settings.
3. On the Customize List page, under General Settings, click the Audience Targeting Settings link.
4. On the Modify List Audience Targeting Settings page, select the Enable Audience Targeting check box. Click OK.

Your list is now audience enabled, and you can target any item in the list to an existing audience. This process also applies to documents in document libraries as well. You can carry the granularity offered through audiences throughout your sites.

Introduction to Knowledge Networks

The word "network" has a myriad of similar meanings. Simply put, it means connecting separate pieces together to form a single or contiguous piece. When we talk about a network of knowledge, we mean connecting separate pieces of information together. The concept of Knowledge Networks dates back to the work of Mark Granovetter. His most famous work in networks theory can be found in an article called "The Strength of Weak Ties." The basic argument is that your relationship to family members and close friends ("strong ties") will not supply you with as much diversity of knowledge as your relationship to acquaintances, distant friends, and the like ("weak ties"). In other words, in the world we live in, there is information that we know and information that we must go somewhere to get. Sometimes we must go to another person to either have them give us the knowledge or show us where to go next to obtain the knowledge. If we were to do this and document how often the information existed physically for consumption or whether the information existed in the mind of another person, we would be surprised to find that the majority of the information (knowledge) we seek is found in the latter case. This is where Knowledge Network for SharePoint Server 2007 helps.

Knowledge Network is focused on enterprise social networking, automatic discovery, and sharing of undocumented knowledge and relationships. If we were to divide people into two groups—Information Seekers and Information Repositories—the software helps connect Seekers to Repositories with the objective of helping the Seekers obtain the information they desire. The Seekers then become Repositories themselves. Knowledge Network for Office SharePoint Server 2007 enables you to quickly locate who knows whom and who knows what within your organization.

Overview of Knowledge Network for SharePoint Server 2007

Knowledge Network for SharePoint Server 2007 is the first commercial offering from a new group at Microsoft called the Information Worker Greenhouse (IWG). The software has two parts: a client piece and a server piece.

The client piece is installed locally and indexes e-mail content to create a profile of keywords and contacts specific to that user. By creating this profile, the user becomes a Repository. The user then publishes the profile, and it is uploaded to the server. All the published profiles are then aggregated in the Knowledge Network server and then the SharePoint Server 2007 search service indexes the information created by the aggregated profiles so that it can be returned within search results. The more profiles that are published, the bigger the network and the more Repositories there are to reach out to. When a Seeker searches for information (knowledge), the search results will return Repositories. The results are also ranked by relevance and relative "distance" to the Seeker.

Of course, unless there are some restraints on what Repositories are available to the Seekers, we have potential privacy issues. A user can choose what type of information to include or exclude in his or her profile. There is also an "opt-in/opt-out" feature that administrators can configure. And probably the best piece of privacy protection in the software is that only APPROVED information by the Repository gets sent to the server.

Installing and Configuring Knowledge Network for SharePoint Server 2007

You need to be aware of certain prerequisites before installing and configuring Knowledge Network. Before beginning the installation procedure, make sure that you have done the following:

1. Installed SharePoint Server 2007 in your environment. For more information, see the SharePoint Server 2007 setup and install procedure earlier in this book.

2. Configured the outgoing e-mail settings by using the Operations menu in Central Administration.
3. Configured SharePoint Server 2007 with a Shared Service Provider running a corporate intranet portal.
4. Completed the import of User Profiles from Active Directory or other data sources to SharePoint User Profile. For more information, see the SharePoint Server 2007 setup and install guide.
5. Configured Search Center Portal along with My Sites enabled on the Server Farm, and confirmed that People search is working. For more information, see the Office SharePoint Server 2007 setup and install guide.
6. You must set up a Microsoft Outlook e-mail account before installing and running Knowledge Network. To create your profile, Knowledge Network needs access to your Microsoft Outlook folders. Therefore, you must set up a Microsoft Outlook e-mail account with an Exchange mailbox configured prior to installing and running Knowledge Network.

There are also some issues of which to be aware. Before installing Knowledge Network for SharePoint Server 2007, take care to address the following issues:

- When uninstalling the Knowledge Network Server, a few data entries are not cleaned up completely from the SSP databases. This issue can cause some warnings and minor exceptions to be raised in the SharePoint event log. To take care of this problem, you need to execute the following SQL script in each of the SSP databases where you provisioned Knowledge Network. This statement needs to be performed only once per SSP.

```
delete from MIPScheduledJob where [Assembly] like 'Microsoft.Office.Server.
SocialNetwork%'
delete from MIPObjects where Xml like '%spsDataPublishJobId%'
```

- The Knowledge Network Client does not run on 64-bit Windows.
- If your organization reuses e-mail aliases, unfamiliar contact names might appear in your Colleagues list. If your organization recycles e-mail aliases, you might find unfamiliar contact names in your list of colleagues. For example, an employee named Samuel Smith used an e-mail alias of SSmith. After Sam left the organization, a new employee named Sharon Smith assumed the alias of SSmith. If you had exchanged e-mail messages with Samuel Smith, Sharon Smith's name will now appear in your Colleagues list. You can delete Sharon Smith's name from your Colleagues list if she is not one of your colleagues.

Other issues can be found in the "known issues" readme text file.

Installing Knowledge Network

1. Start the installer by clicking KNServer.msi.
2. In the Knowledge Network window, click Start.
3. In the End-User License Agreement window, read the license agreement and then click I Accept.
4. In the Server Type window, click Install and allow the application to finish.
5. After installation is complete, click Close.
6. Repeat steps 1 through 3 on every server in the Office Server Farm.

Configuring Knowledge Network Server for Office SharePoint Server 2007

To configure the Knowledge Network Server, complete the following steps:

1. From the Windows Start menu, click SharePoint 3.0 Central Administration.
2. In the Farm Topology section, click the name of your Knowledge Network server.
3. For detailed information about the different types of topologies, see Suggested Topologies in the Microsoft Knowledge Network Deployment Guide.
4. On the Services on Server page, do the following:
   a. If this server is a Web Front End server, start the Knowledge Network Application Service (if it isn't already started). Go to the SharePoint Services Administration Home Page for the Shared Service Provider, click the Data Management link in the Knowledge Network section, and make sure the Database Status says Database Successfully Created. It might take some time for this status to appear, and you won't be able to click into any of the text boxes until the database has been created successfully as displayed in Figure 8-46.

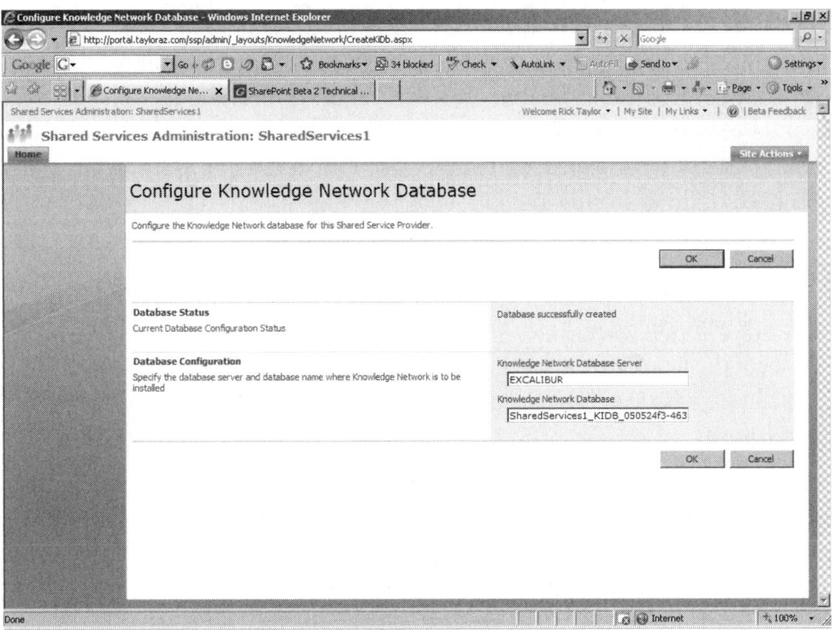

Figure 8-46 Illustration of the KN configuration

b. If this server is the intended Knowledge Network Application Server, start the Knowledge Network Search Service.

5. Perform step 4 for each server in the Office Server Farm. Note that the database verification in step 4a needs to be done only once. Also note that both the Knowledge Network Search Service and Knowledge Network Application Service need to be started on a farm (on any of the computers across the farm) in order for the product to function correctly.

Knowledge Network defaults all of its configuration requirements out of the box and does not need any further administrative actions. Your Knowledge Network Installation is now complete.

If you want to configure Knowledge Network for a Shared Service Provider, follow these steps:

1. On the left navigation bar of the Central Administration Home page, click Shared Services Administration.
2. Click the link with the name of the Shared Service Provider on which you would like to configure Knowledge Network. This is the Shared Service Provider that you created as part of the SharePoint Server 2007 installation.

Knowledge Network Database Configuration

The good thing about the Knowledge Network application configuration is that it automatically configures its database server location so that it is the same as the default database server for the SharePoint Server 2007 Farm. There are good reasons to configure a separate database instance for this application, and if you want to change this location, you need to do the following:

1. In the SharePoint Services Administration Home page for the Shared Service Provider, in the Knowledge Network [prerelease] Version 1.0.0.0 section, click Data Management.
2. On the Configure Knowledge Network Database page, make sure that the Database Status says Database Successfully Created. It might take some time for this status to appear.
3. If you want to change the name or location of the Knowledge Network Database configuration from its default settings, you can edit the Knowledge Network Database Server and/or the Knowledge Network Database and click OK. Note that Integrated Authentication is assumed between the SSP administration account and the specified database server. The process of configuring the database takes a few minutes.

Knowledge Network Job Configuration

You will notice that Knowledge Network runs several background tasks as scheduled jobs through the Office Server Jobs infrastructure. The jobs have preset recommended schedules. If you want to change these settings, follow these steps.

1. In the SharePoint Services Administration Home page for the Shared Service Provider, in the Knowledge Network [prerelease] Version 1.0.0.0 section, click Timer Jobs. The Microsoft Knowledge Network Job Status page displays the various tasks and their schedules.
2. To change a task, click the corresponding job in the list. The jobs could be switched to Full or Incremental for the next run, or their schedules could be altered. The Schedule syntax is similar to the Office Server Jobs syntax.

Important Make sure that Knowledge Network Portal Upgrade says Succeeded. This is critical for completing the upgrade of your existing Search Center and Profile Center on the Shared Resource Provider.

Knowledge Network Manage Members Configuration

Now that we have Knowledge Network installed and configured for use, we need to configure it for the purpose of connecting Seekers to the Repositories.

In the SharePoint Services Administration Home page for the Shared Service Provider, in the Knowledge Network [prerelease] Version 1.0.0.0 section, click Manage Members, as shown in Figure 8-47.

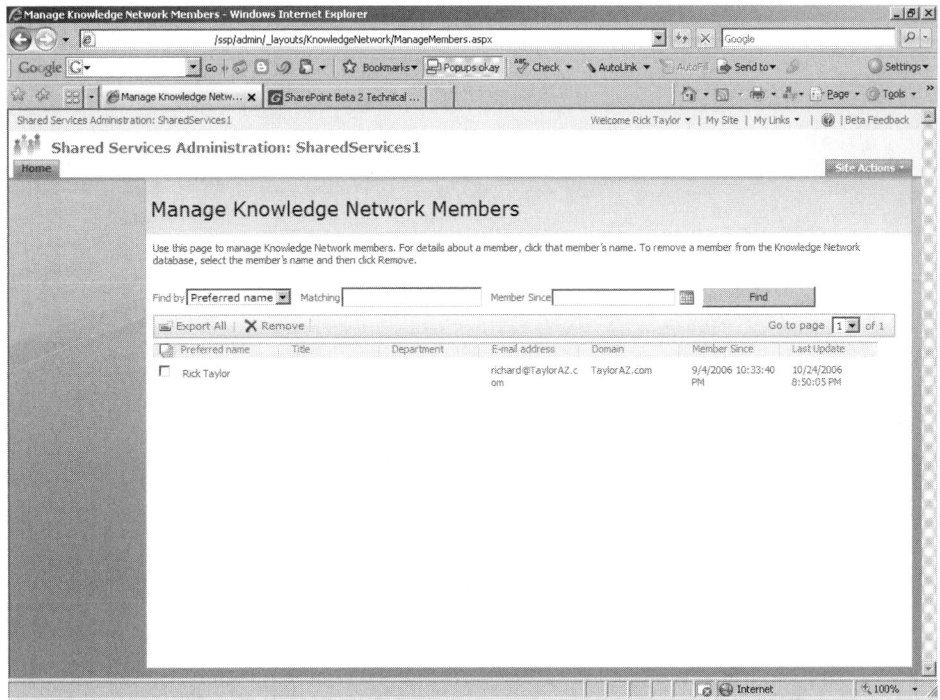

Figure 8-47 Illustration of the KN manage members configuration

From this interface, an administrator can configure a number of filters to be able to search for members (Repositories). For members who want to be removed as Repositories, an administrator can select the member and simply click Remove.

For Repositories that are external to your organization, the configuration is similar. In the SharePoint Services Administration Home Page for the SSP, in the Knowledge Network [prerelease] Version 1.0.0.0 section, click Manage External Contacts, as shown in Figure 8-48.

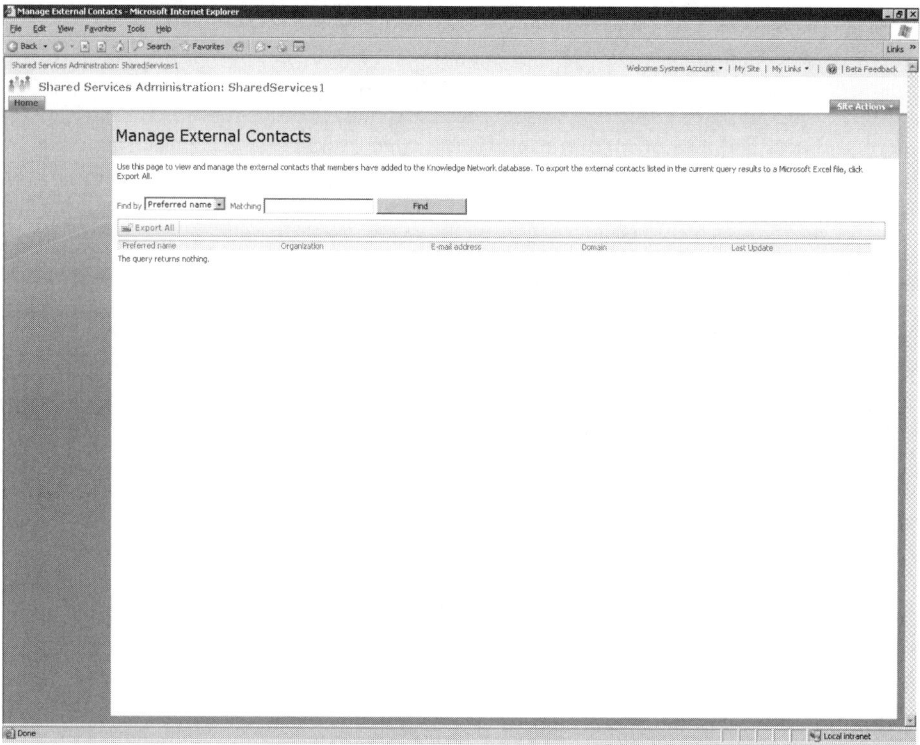

Figure 8-48 Illustration of the KN manage external contacts configuration

Knowledge Network Portal Feature

Even as powerful as the search feature is in SharePoint Server 2007, the Knowledge Network application enhances the features in the Search Center. By default, this enhancement is visible only on the Personal Site Provider and Preferred Search Center specified in the My Site Settings on the Shared Service Provider Home page. To activate or deactivate these features in other Search Centers or Personal Site Providers, or on the default Personal Site Provider or Preferred Search Center, follow these steps:

1. Navigate to the Personal Site Provider public site, and then on the Site Actions menu, point to Site Settings, and then click Modify All Site Settings.
2. On the Site Settings page, in the Site Administration List, click Site Features, as shown in Figure 8-49.

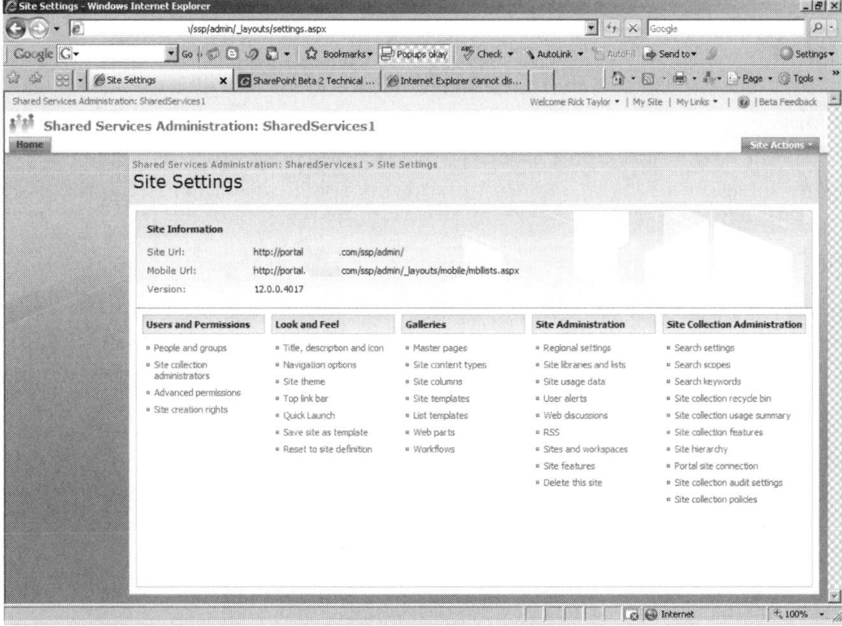

Figure 8-49 Illustration of the KN manage portal features

3. In the Site Features list, in the Knowledge Network Profile Center line, click either Activate or Deactivate as illustrated in Figure 8-50.

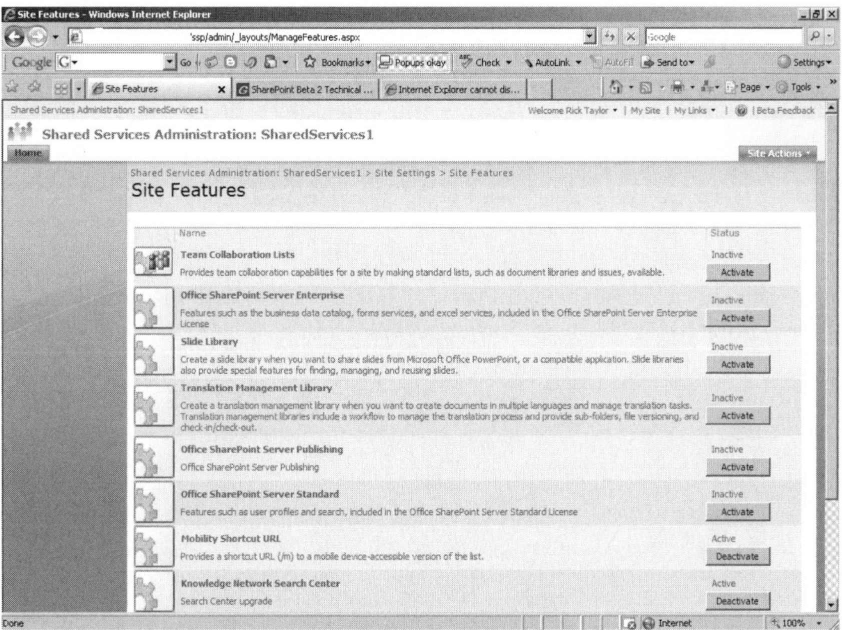

Figure 8-50 Activating features in the KN Profile Center

Summary

In this chapter, you learned about the personalization and social networking features of SharePoint Server 2007. You also gained an understanding of taxonomy and the relevance of taxonomy in designing your information infrastructure. You were also presented with some considerations in applying taxonomy specifically to your SharePoint Server 2007 design and deployment.

The chapter also demonstrated how you can configure personalization features, such as colleagues and privacy controls, to enhance your knowledge management and people search. Audience targeting in SharePoint Server 2007 has been extended to include audience targeting on list items, and configuration has been demonstrated so that you can readily adapt audience targeting in your lists.

You also learned how you can leverage the SSP to centrally configure all your personalization features and extend those features to include publishing links to Office clients and target links to users' My Sites throughout your organization.

Knowledge Network for SharePoint Server 2007, a powerful tool to allow people to connect to repositories of information, has also been introduced. Knowledge Network is focused on enterprise social networking, which empowers users to collaborate more effectively, giving them a rich user interface with which to create, manage, and consume resources.

Chapter 9

Document Management

This chapter is the first of two chapters dedicated to helping you understand how to implement a formal method of managing documents using Microsoft Office SharePoint Server 2007. This chapter focuses on document management. The next chapter focuses on records management. Chapter 11, "Web Content Management and Publishing Features," will focus on Web content management. Together, these three topics form what Microsoft calls Enterprise Content Management (ECM). ECM is one of the main investment areas for Microsoft in this release of Office SharePoint Server 2007.

The document tracking and editing features of SharePoint Server 2007 provide you with a rich set of tools for managing documents within your organization. This chapter explores the capabilities of SharePoint Server 2007 as a collaborative system for creating, managing, and revising documents.

Understanding Informal and Formal Communications

The Sarbanes Oxley Act of 2002 requires that a corporation clearly distinguish between its formal and informal communication. To avoid problems and remain compliant, corporations need separate workflow processes that govern formal and informal communications. For example, if informal communication channels are used for formal communications about financial information, corporate policies, and other critical interactions, factual and conjectural information could easily be commingled in critical financial reports. The information in this section explains how to differentiate between informal and formal communication.

The flurry of activity around collaboration software is being driven, in part, by the need to meet the formal and informal communication needs of geographically dispersed corporations, without bogging the workforce down in bureaucratic policies and procedures. In the world of collaboration software, the following can be a useful way to define these terms:

- Informal Communication, also known as collaboration
- Formal Communication, sometimes described as publication workflow

Informal Communication

Informal communication, which is also known as collaboration, occurs when information is shared spontaneously between individuals who work for or are associated with a corporation. Informal communication occurs in hallways, meeting rooms, and over lunch as individuals share ideas, resolve disputes, alert coworkers to pending issues, and discuss strategies in the course of a normal work day. Because most large corporations are geographically dispersed, informal communications can also take the form of e-mail, voice mail, telephone conferences, Webcasts, and other electronic communication channels. The availability of electronic forms of informal communication means everyone can be continually connected to everyone else in the workplace. This means the average decision-maker is often buried under a huge volume of e-mail messages and information. Problems occur when these decision-makers cannot quickly separate meaningful informal communication from formal communication or communication that is just plain noise.

As workers pursue a formal goal, they need to be able to share information, ask questions, gather thoughts, debate, encourage, argue, joke, and speculate. It is important that workers feel they are "being heard." They also need to know their informal communications will not be mistaken for formal communication or factual information. If workers are not given appropriate ways to communicate and work through socialization processes, they will find inappropriate means to do so.

Formal Communication

Formal communication, which is usually referred to as publication workflow, is often the result of collaboration that creates information that is more crystallized and somewhat final. As crystallization begins to take shape, work groups narrow down options and then collectively start creating a document or product that fulfills their stated goal. The tools provided to work groups need to help them achieve the goal being pursued whether it is a financial report, white paper, project specification, or marketing brochure. When the group achieves the stated goal, the document is submitted into a publication workflow that has been established by the corporation. At this point, the team has crossed the line from informal to formal communications. The publication workflow, using the workflow tools available to the users, usually involves review by senior leadership, feedback, rewrites, and other methods to make sure the final document meets the criteria for publication as a formal document.

When the document is formally approved by the policies and procedures enforced by the workflow management tool, it is placed under change control methods and is distributed according to policy. After the document is released, the team that created it no longer owns it. Instead, the document stands on its own merits unless the appropriate workflows are invoked to change the document and republish it under a new version number.

An efficient document workflow and publication system will have only one master copy of the published document in a central location, which reduces confusion and storage costs. Instead of sending copies by e-mail to the audience when changes occur, the workflow system sends *alerts* that direct interested parties to the centrally located document. Individuals interested in the document can post questions, complaints, corrections, and other action items in a centrally located issues log or task list. When the issues log contains a number of issues or issues of sufficient importance, the change control process can be invoked to pull the collaboration team together again to revise the document. The revised document is then resubmitted for publication, and the workflow processes govern its revision and release.

The Importance of Document Libraries

The document library is the standard list for storing documents and files in SharePoint Server 2007. Documents can be stored as attachments in other kinds of lists, but a document library is the only place in SharePoint Server 2007 where documents themselves are the main list item.

In Figure 9-1, you can see a typical document library with a variety of Microsoft Office system documents stored in it. It is theoretically possible to store almost any type of file in a document library, including scanned images, Zip files, audio files, and video media. However, you will find that there are both file type and size limitations that will enforce a pragmatic limitation on which files users will upload or create in a document library.

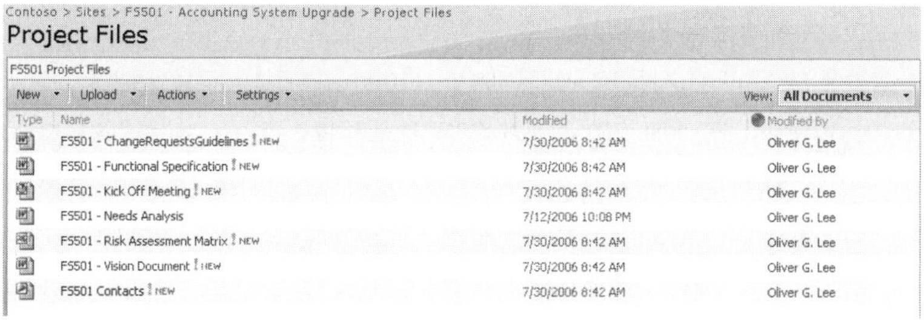

Figure 9-1 A SharePoint Server 2007 document library

Your users will "live" with a number of different document libraries across multiple sites. Because document libraries will play an increasing role in where mission-critical documents are stored, you'll need to be aware of several factors that will influence how document libraries are implemented in your organizations.

First, bear in mind that there are some scalability considerations. The Microsoft SQL Server database tables that store SharePoint Server information can potentially hold millions of documents, but that would result in a user interface that would be difficult, at best, to browse. To achieve best viewing performance with libraries, Microsoft recommends that each library hold no more than 2000 files and folders in the root of the library and that each folder hold no more than 2000 files and folders. Although these figures do not represent hard limits, you can expect to experience gradual performance degradation as you exceed these thresholds. In addition, 2000 folders will end up being a poor user interface (UI) experience for your users.

Best Practices Train users so that they understand how creating multiple document libraries can deliver an optimal user interface experience.

Second, remember that your users will naturally want to treat the document library the same as or similar to the file system that they are accustomed to seeing within their My Documents folder or using a mapped drive. Because a document library is not a replacement for a file system—even though there are similarities—it is important to educate your users about how to appropriately manage a document library.

The most common mistake users make is viewing SharePoint as a replacement for your file servers. Although there are some who advocate moving all your documents into SharePoint, this is not always a wise course of action. Clearly, SharePoint Server 2007 is a strong move in the direction of a document management system. But an individual document library should not be viewed as a Web-based file system that can replace a file server hosting hundreds of thousands of documents. Not only will the upload times for a large set of documents present a challenge, but the ability to traverse the library quickly and easily will be elusive.

Document Libraries versus File Shares

Shared folders on file servers and document libraries in SharePoint 2007 sites have both advantages and disadvantages when it comes to document storage and management. Document libraries provide greater flexibility and accuracy in managing versioning than Shadow Copies of Shared Folders on a file server. In addition, SharePoint 2007 document libraries allow users to undelete files that they have accidentally deleted without requiring the intervention of an administrator. Shared Folders, on the other hand, allow users to quickly and easily browse files in a tree-view layout and navigate through multiple-nested folders containing thousands of documents. It is also easier for administrators to restore individual documents from file system backups than from SharePoint 2007.

Working with Document Libraries

Working with document libraries involves tasks like the following:

- Adding a document to the library
- Checking out a document so you can edit it
- Checking the edited document back into the library
- Managing versioning for documents stored in the library
- Using permissions to control what users can do with versions
- Marking documents as final when you're finished working with them

This section will examine how to perform these various tasks.

Opening a Document Library

Before you can work with documents stored in a SharePoint document library, you first need to open the library. Do this, follow these steps:

1. Log on to the SharePoint site where the document library you want to work with is located.
2. If the document library you want to open is listed under Documents in the quick launch section, click the link to the library to open its page. If the document library is not listed under Documents, continue with the next step in this procedure.
3. Click the Documents link in the quick launch section to display a page showing all the document libraries on the site.
4. Click the link for the specific document library you want to open.

You can also click View All Site Content for any SharePoint site to display all libraries, lists, discussion boards, and other types of information available on the site.

Once you've opened a document library you can perform various actions on the documents stored in the library. Note that most of the commands you can use to work with documents in a library are available only through the All Documents view, which is the default view applied when you open a document library.

Adding Documents to the Library

Once you've opened the specific library you want to work with, you can add documents to the library using several different methods:

- Using the upload commands
- Using Explorer View
- Using WebDav

Adding Documents by Using the Upload Commands

There are several ways available to you to add documents to a library. The two most common methods used are the Upload Document and Upload Multiple Documents options, which are available from the main Upload menu, as shown in Figure 9-2.

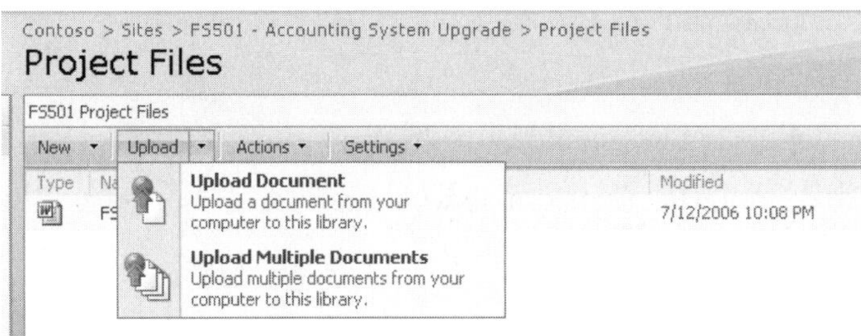

Figure 9-2 Uploading commands

The Upload Document command allows you to upload a single file at a time and, if you have versioning turned on, to add a version comment to the file. This page recognizes any custom columns created on the document library and will present the user with a data entry form to populate any required values.

Selecting the Upload Multiple Documents command opens the Upload Document page with an embedded tree view control that allows you to upload multiple files from the same folder and appears as shown in Figure 9-3. A limitation of the control is that it does not support uploading entire folders or uploading files from multiple folders. This page makes use of the Microsoft Office Multiple Upload Control (STSUPLD.DLL), an ActiveX control that is installed with the Microsoft Office system. Therefore, the command will not normally be available if you are using the Web browser on a machine that does not have Microsoft Office 2003 or the 2007 Microsoft Office system installed.

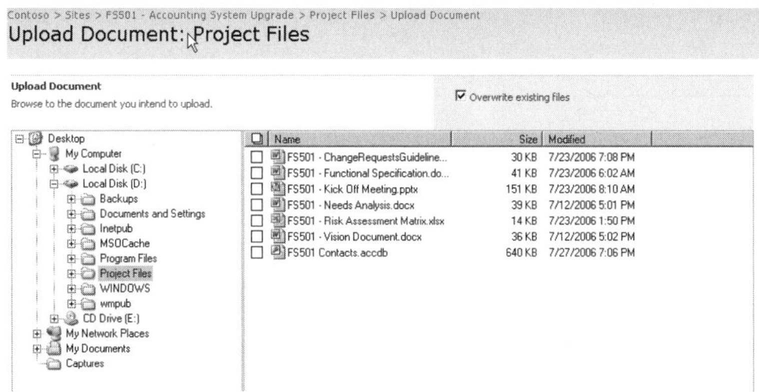

Figure 9-3 Upload Multiple Documents command

Internet Explorer security settings can also affect the behavior of this control. If the Script ActiveX Controls Marked Safe For Scripting option (found under Tools\Internet Options\Custom Level) is set to Disable, SharePoint removes the command from the Upload menu of the document library because it would not be able to load on the page displayed to the user. One disadvantage of this ActiveX control is that it is not aware of custom columns in SharePoint libraries, and as a result it will not prompt you to fill in these values during the upload. The columns will either be populated with default values or remain blank. You will have to go back to the library after the documents are uploaded and retroactively update the metadata.

Important If you have custom columns that are marked as "required," warn users about using any of the multiple document upload techniques because they will not be prompted to enter the required data during upload.

Adding Documents by Using Explorer View

The Explorer View, shown in Figure 9-4, is available from the View menu on the right side of the document library and provides another way of uploading documents to the library. In Explorer View, users can drag files from the file system on their local computer and drop them into the library. Explorer View requires that the client computer has installed Internet Explorer 5.0 or later and Web Folders, which are installed by default on Windows XP Professional and all versions of Microsoft Office beginning with Microsoft Office 2000.

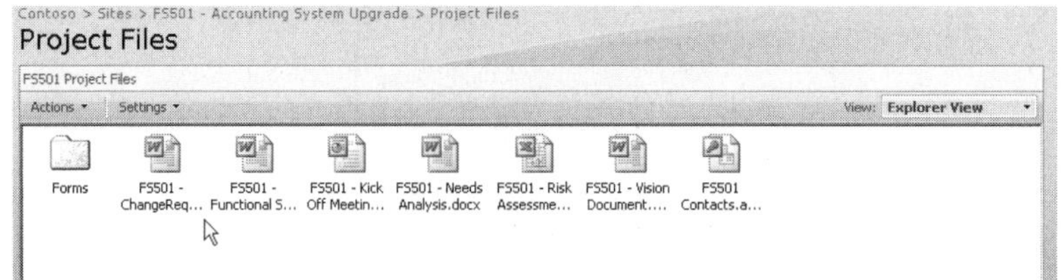

Figure 9-4 Explorer View

Note The Explorer View also supports many drag-and-drop features, allowing users to move and copy documents between folders as they would in Windows Explorer. To fully use these features, the security settings in Internet Explorer must be modified and the Launching Programs And Files In An IFRAME option must be set to Enable.

Choosing an Upload Method

One consideration in selecting which technique to use for uploading large numbers of files would be how the interface responds to copy errors. The Multiple Upload ActiveX control will stop uploading the moment it encounters an error, and there is not a mechanism to automatically resume where the upload left off. You will usually have to attempt to determine the last file uploaded and start the upload from that point or start the upload from the beginning. When using the Explorer View or WebDAV link, you will get a pop-up error message for each document that fails to copy, and the upload will pause until you click the OK button to continue. The upload will then skip the problem file and continue on.

Another consideration is the relative performance of the upload process. Uploading files through the Explorer View or WebDAV interfaces will support an upload rate of 1 MB per second and sometimes more. Using the Upload Multiple control results in an upload rate only slightly slower on average. However, uploading individual files with the Upload Document command may take 50 percent longer than the other methods. The actual performance you can expect will depend on the server workload and available network bandwidth.

Adding Documents by Using WebDAV

The Windows Explorer also provides a built-in method for connecting to SharePoint libraries through the WebDAV (Web Distributed Authoring and Versioning) protocol. This is the same protocol used by the Explorer View. WebDAV is natively supported by

SharePoint Server 2007 and allows you to view and work with the documents in the library as if they were folders on the file system.

The easiest way to invoke a WebDAV connection is to select the Open With Windows Explorer command from the Actions menu of the document library. The window that appears will look much like the Explorer View window, but it is no longer embedded inside the Internet Explorer browser.

One of the features integrating SharePoint Server 2007 and Windows is that you will usually find, after accessing a document library through either Explorer View or the Open With Windows Explorer commands, that a shortcut to that library has been created for you under My Network Places. If you want to create a shortcut manually, follow these steps:

1. Open Windows Explorer, and click My Network Places.
2. Double-click Add Network Place.
3. Click Next.
4. Select the Choose Another Network Location option, and click Next.
5. Type the URL to the document library in SharePoint Server 2007 (for example, **http://contoso.msft/projects/documents**), and click Next. (You might be prompted for a user name and password.)
6. Type in a name for the connection, and click Next.
7. Click Finish.

In addition to creating a shortcut under My Network Places, you can also use WebDAV to map a network drive to a library. This is particularly useful for allowing document imaging and processing software to write to a target drive that deposits the files directly into SharePoint. To map a network drive to a document library, follow these steps:

1. Open Windows Explorer.
2. Click Tools, and then click Map Network Drive.
3. Select a drive letter from the drop-down list.
4. In the Folder box, type the path to the site and document library in the following format:

   \\server_name\site_name\document_library
5. Click Finish.

A new window opens that displays the contents of the document library.

Naming Web Folder Client Connections

It is highly possible that your users will end up working in many different document libraries throughout the life of your deployment. Because of this, we recommend that you consider implementing a naming convention for your document libraries.

The Web folder client's name is built using the following convention: <document_library_name> on <site_name>. If your users regularly use the default "Shared Documents" library, then they can expect to have duplicate iterations of "Shared Documents on <site_name>" in their My Network Places, which really doesn't help them know, intuitively, *which* Shared Documents library they are trying to connect to.

Because the Web folder client name is built off of the document library's object name, changing the display name in the properties of the document library will not solve the problem of users having duplicate Web folder client names.

Best practice, then, is to ensure that your site templates don't create document libraries called "Shared Documents" and that users are forced to create new document libraries based on a naming convention that makes sense for your organization. This way, the Web folder client names will not only make sense, you'll have very little, if any, duplication.

Working With Documents in the Document Library

Once you've added documents to the library, you can work with them in various ways including:

- Checking them out to edit them
- Checking them back into the library
- Managing versioning and permissions
- Marking documents final

Checking Out and Editing Documents

Document libraries support two modes of file locking: explicit and implicit. *Explicit locking* occurs when you select the Check Out command from the document drop-down list, as displayed in Figure 9-5. The icon next to the file in the library changes to display a green arrow, and no other user can edit the document until it is checked in. *Implicit locking* occurs when you open a document for editing by selecting the Edit In [program] command from the document menu without explicitly checking out the file. The file will automatically be locked by SharePoint, thus preventing others from saving changes to the file. Although both forms of locking prevent other users from saving changes while the document is open, explicit check out has the following advantages:

- **Identification** The Checked Out To column of the library can be used to see which documents are currently locked by another user and who to contact if the documents need to be unlocked.
- **Privacy** While a document is explicitly checked out, changes made to the document, and new versions of it uploaded to the server, will not be seen by other users until the document is checked in again.
- **Offline Sandbox** Checking out a document puts a copy of it in the SharePoint Drafts folder in the user's My Documents directory. Changes made to the document are saved to the local file until it is checked into SharePoint again, at which point the changes are copied to the server and the draft is deleted. The location for files to be cached to can be changed by opening the 2007 Microsoft Office system application Options dialog box and selecting the Save tab. The folder location can be edited in the Server Drafts Location box.

Checking In Documents

When you have completed modifying a document and uploading it to the document library, you need to use the Check In command to remove the exclusive lock on the file and allow others to see your changes. Some programs, such as Microsoft Office Word 2007, prompt you to check in your document when you close the application after saving the document to the library. If a user leaves a document checked out, any user with the Override Check Out list right can either force the document to be checked in or discard the check out. By default, the permission levels that have this right are Full Control, Design, Approve, and Manage Hierarchy. Discarding the check out will cause any changes that have been saved to the file in the document library since the last check in to be lost.

Requiring Check Out

Because explicit check out is such a valuable feature of SharePoint, there is an option to force an explicit check out any time a user edits or updates a document. This option is found on the Versioning Settings page of the Document Library Settings, and it applies to all changes to the file regardless of how it is accessed. Any time a user attempts to open a document, he will be prompted to choose between Read Only and Check Out And Edit. (See Figure 9-5.) If the user chooses Read Only, most edit commands available in the document are disabled and the document cannot be saved back to the document library.

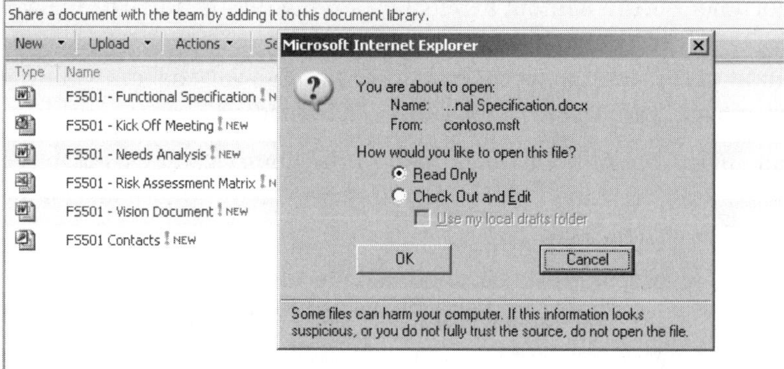

Figure 9-5 The Check Out option

When the document is open, the user will see an option on the Document Actions bar to check out the document for editing, if it isn't already checked out. If the Require Check Out option is not enabled, SharePoint will place an implicit lock on the document that is exclusive to the user who opens the document. Other users will not be able to overwrite the document while it is locked, but there will be no indication in SharePoint that the document is locked until another user tries to open it.

Managing Document Versioning

SharePoint Server 2007 offers several options for versioning, as displayed in Figure 9-6. These settings can be controlled separately for each document library and are located on the Versioning Settings page under Document Library Settings. A best practice is to configure the site templates for your organization to have predefined document libraries with the versioning setting already set according to your organization policies.

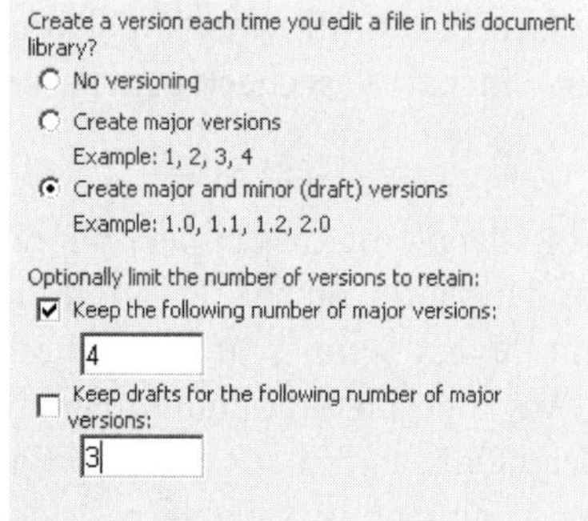

Figure 9-6 Versioning settings

Understanding Major and Minor Versions

Major and minor versioning was part of the workspace in SharePoint Portal Server 2001. Microsoft removed this feature in Windows SharePoint Services 2.0 but has brought it back as part of the collaboration feature set in Windows SharePoint Services 3.0. Major versions are intended to be "published" versions, while minor versions are intended to be "in draft" versions. You can have a major version published, such as version 2.0, and be working on a new draft for the next published version. New drafts for the next published version are incremented as 2.1, 2.2, and so forth. The following settings are found on the Version Settings page:

- **None** No previous versions of the document are saved. When a new copy of a document is uploaded or saved to the server, it overwrites the existing copy of the document. This option is useful for conserving space on the server, as only one copy of the document is saved. When other versioning options are used, a copy of the entire document will be saved with each new version, increasing the storage requirements of the SQL Server database.
- **Major Versions Only** All versions are saved with a simple numbering scheme (for example, 1, 2, 3, and so on). No distinction is made between draft versions and published versions, so every time a new version of a document is saved to the server it is viewable by all site users. To conserve space, you can set a limit on the maximum number of versions that will be saved on the server.
- **Major And Minor Versions** Versions of documents are numbered using a decimal notation scheme (for example, 1.0, 1.1, 1.2, 2.0, 2.1, and so on). Versions ending with .0 are major versions, and all others are draft versions. When the Major And Minor Versions option is selected, all users with Read permissions can access major versions of documents and you control which categories of users can view the minor versions–either those with Read permissions, those with Edit permissions, or only those with Approve permissions.

You can use the versioning feature of SharePoint Server 2007 to preserve the change history of a document as it moves through its life cycle of edits and revisions. To view previous versions of a document, select Version History from the document drop-down menu. From the Version History page, you can view and delete individual past versions of documents. You can also use the Restore command to roll back to a previous version of the document by making a copy of it and setting it as the current version.

Setting Version Limits

It is important to realize that SharePoint stores a complete binary copy of every version of your document in the SQL Server database. To illustrate, if you have a document that is 250 KB in size and you create three past versions of it along with the current version, a total of 1000 KB will be stored in the database along with appropriate metadata for each version. This formula applies equally to both major and minor versions.

> **Important** If the Require Check Out option is not enabled and a user forgets to check out the document first, a new version will be created every time a user saves the document to the server. This can lead to hundreds of versions of a document over time.

If the document is checked out before it is edited, all changes will be saved to the same checked-out version. To conserve the amount of space used by the content database, it might be a good idea to restrict the number of versions that will be saved over time. You can specify how many major and minor versions will be retained in a document library as users make changes to documents. The setting for minor versions does not limit the number of drafts that will be kept for each major version; it limits the number of major versions that will retain their draft copies. That is, if you have minor versioning enabled, an unlimited number of minor versions will be retained for each major version, but you can limit how many major versions will retain the draft copies with them.

Comparing Versions

While working with the current version of a document, you might want to know how it compares with a previous version of the same document. Word 2007 has been enhanced to include an integrated comparison tool to allow you to quickly view the differences between documents. The comparison feature uses the document's connection to the SharePoint document library to retrieve information about previous versions so that users don't have to browse to the file location. By default, the comparison appears in a new document with the original and revised documents displayed in side windows and the changes identified by formatting marks. There are five comparison options:

- **Compare With Most Recent Major Version** This option provides a quick comparison between the current document and the last major (published) version on the server.
- **Compare With Most Recent Version** This option provides a comparison with the last minor (draft) version on the server.
- **Compare With A Specific Version** This option allows the user to select which previous version to compare with the current version.
- **Compare Two Versions Of A Document (Legal Blackline)** This option is an all-purpose comparison that allows the user to view a comparison between two different documents.
- **Combine Revisions From Multiple Authors** This option takes changes from multiple documents and merges them into one document.

To begin comparing documents, complete the following steps:

1. Open the document that you want to compare with another version.
2. Click the Review tab in Word 2007.
3. Click Compare. If the document you have open has a connection to a SharePoint document library, you will see all five comparison options. Otherwise, you will see only the last two.
4. Choose the comparison method you want to use.
5. Select the Comparison settings you want to use. These settings allow you to specify exactly which types of changes you want to compare, such as Comments, Formatting, Case Changes, and so on.
6. Select the Show Changes settings you want to use. These settings define whether the comparison will be performed at the word or character level and whether the resulting comparison will appear in the original document, the revised document, or a new document.

Approving and Publishing Documents

The document approval process built into libraries allows you to place all documents into a Pending status until they are approved by a user with the Approver permissions. When content approval is enabled, any changes made to documents are considered to be in a draft state and are not visible to users who have only Read permissions. When an Approver approves the changes, all users can view the approved version. The approval process can be used without document versioning, but when combined, they create a powerful mechanism to formalize document change management in your organization. The Versioning settings, described in the following list, control how the approval process works:

- **No Versioning** SharePoint makes a copy of the document when changes are saved so that users with Read permissions can still access it, and the document is marked as Pending. When the new version of the document is approved, the old version of the document is discarded and all users can view the approved version.
- **Major Versioning Only** When a document is edited and saved to the server, it is placed in a Pending state and only the previous version is available to users with Read permission. When the document is approved, the current version becomes available and the previous version is retained.
- **Major And Minor Versioning** Under this model, all changes to documents are automatically saved as draft (minor) versions with an incrementing decimal in the version number. To start the approval process, you must select the Publish A Major

Version command from the document drop-down menu. Only the most recent minor version can be promoted to a major version. An Approver can then approve the major version, making it available to all users.

Using Permissions to Control Viewing of Versions

By default, all users with Read permissions for a document library can view all versions of a document, both major and minor. The Draft Item Security setting on the Versioning Settings page under Document Library Settings allows you to restrict the view of versions so that only users with Edit permissions can view minor versions. Users with only Read permissions are then automatically shown the most recent major version of a document when they open it. If Content Approval is enabled in the document library, a third option becomes available that allows you to restrict viewing of drafts to only the author and those with Approve permission.

Marking Documents As Final

When you have completed all edits, revisions, and approvals of a document and it has reached its final version, you can use a new Word 2007 feature—designating a document as Final—to indicate to other users that you are finished with it. When you mark a document as Final, it becomes read-only and all the edit commands are disabled. Additionally, all revision marks stored when Track Changes is enabled are removed. This setting is a property of the document that is designed to help users avoid accidentally modifying a document that has already been finalized. The Final status can be removed by any user with Edit permissions, so it will not function as a form of security. To mark a document as Final, perform these steps:

1. Open the document in Word 2007.
2. From the File menu, select Prepare, and then click Mark As Final.
3. Click OK to make the change.

Using Document Management Site Templates

Two site templates in SharePoint Server 2007 are specifically designed with document management in mind.

Table 9-1 Document Management Site Templates

Job service	Description
Document Center	A site template designed to allow users quick and easy access to large numbers of documents
Document Workspace	A site template designed to be used for team editing of a single document

Document Center

The Document Center template is new to SharePoint Server 2007, and it provides users with a more document-centered layout. The site includes only three default lists (Documents, Announcements, and Tasks), and the default navigation is set to Tree View mode for faster navigation. The site includes an instance of the new Relevant Documents Web Part, which displays, by default, all documents that you have created, checked out, or were the last one to modify. The Document Center site has been preconfigured to take advantage of the new features of SharePoint 2007. By default, the document library list has the Require Check Out feature turned on and versioning is set to track both major and minor versions.

Document Workspace

The Document Workspace site template creates a site much like a standard Team Site but with a unique built-in publishing feature. Although the Document Workspace can be used in place of a Team Site, it is typically created as a subsite under a parent project or Team Site by selecting Send To, Create Document Workspace on the drop-down menu of a document in the parent site's document library. This command creates a new subsite with the name of the document as its title and URL, and it copies the document into the new site for further editing. When editing is complete on the copy of the document, you can select Send To, Publish To Source Location from the drop-down menu of the document in the Document Workspace site to copy the document back to the parent site. Caution should be used when publishing the document, as this will overwrite the document in the parent site.

Managing Documents and Workflow

SharePoint Server 2007 makes available several features that allow you to implement sophisticated document management processes. Metadata, policies, workflows, and templates are among the powerful features that can be associated with a document library. These features can also be associated with content types, which are discussed in Chapter 10, "Records Management in Microsoft Office SharePoint Server 2007," and covered thoroughly in Chapter 15, "Managing Content Types." In this section, we will explain how these features work in the library context as part of a basic document management architecture.

Creating Metadata

When you want to store additional information about a document in the document library and make it available to users to sort and filter by, you create custom columns, also referred to as *metadata*. These custom columns, once defined, can then be updated by users when they upload and edit documents to provide meaningful information about the status, schedule, budget, ranking, or any other aspect of a file that might be useful to an organization. As a result of performance improvements made in SharePoint Server 2007, the practical number of custom columns that a document library can have has been greatly increased.

Creating a New Document Library Column

To create a new document library column, complete the following steps:

1. From the document library's Settings menu, click Create Column.
2. In the Column Name box, type the name of the metadata.
3. Select the data type for the column.
4. Optionally, type a description for the column as well.
5. Complete the additional column settings.
6. Click OK.

Choosing Column Data Types

When creating a custom column in a document library, you have a variety of data types to choose from, as shown in Figure 9-7. Table 9-2 describes each data type that is available.

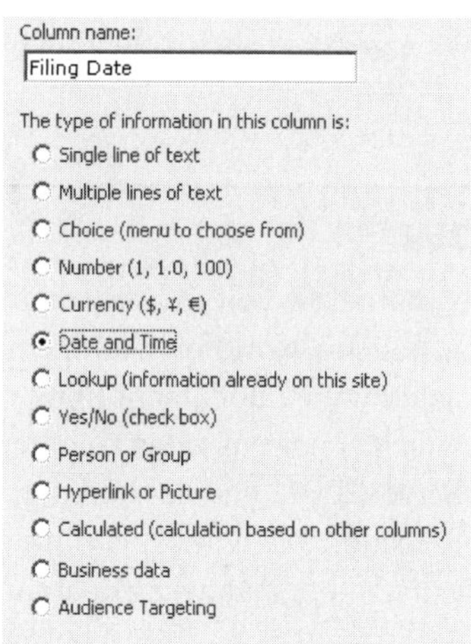

Figure 9-7 New column data types

Table 9-2 Column Data Types

Data type option	Description
Single Line Of Text	A basic text entry field with a maximum length of 255 characters.
Multiple Lines Of Text	An advanced text entry field that supports text entered on separate lines and with carriage returns. The field has a default maximum character limit of 255. Setting the Allow Unlimited Length In Document Libraries option to Yes removes this restriction. The Number Of Lines For Editing property specifies how long the text in the entry box should be in the HTML pages, up to a maximum of 1000 lines. The text box will automatically provide scroll bars to access text that exceeds the number of display lines.
Choice (Menu To Choose From).	Presents the user with one of three types of selectable fields: drop-down menu, radio buttons, or check boxes. Of these three, the check boxes option is the only one that allows multiple items to be selected. The items a user chooses from are entered manually at the time the field is created.
Number (1, 1.0, 100)	Validates the data as numeric, and requires that it contain only digits or numeric formatting (for example, a period or comma). You can specify a minimum and maximum range of values and display the number with a percent (%) sign as part of the formatting. This option does not convert a number to a percentage, so entering "1234" will display as "1234%" not "123400.00%" as it does in Microsoft Office Excel. You can also limit the number of decimal places of accuracy to store in the field. Note that this is not just a formatting setting. Setting the decimal places to "2" and entering a value such as "2.345" will round the value when it is saved and store it as "2.35".
Currency ($, ¥, €)	Similar to the Number (1, 1.0, 100) entry field, with the additional feature of including a formatting pattern on the data that rounds numbers to two decimal places and applies the chosen denomination character. The currency setting will not change the standard decimal and thousands separators used (for example, 1.234,56 versus 1,234.56). To change this setting, use the Regional Settings page under Site Settings.
Date And Time	Supports storing either a date or a date and time together within the valid range of 1/1/1900 to 12/31/8900. Dates and times must be entered in the format defined in the Regional Settings of the site.
Lookup (Information Already On This Site)	Allows you to link the data in this field to data from a field in another list on the same site. When you edit the value of this field for a document, you will be presented with a drop-down list displaying the values from the other field. An advantage of this data type is that the selected value itself is not stored in the lookup field; instead, it's stored to a link back to the selected value in the source list. If the source list is later changed, the selected value in the lookup column also changes.

Table 9-2 Column Data Types

Data type option	Description
Yes/No (Check Box)	A basic Boolean entry field that supports the values of Yes and No.
Person Or Group	A special field new to SharePoint Server 2007 that allows you to use the standard SharePoint user lookup tool to select a user from Active Directory or from a list of users in a specific SharePoint group. The user entering a value for this field must know the user name, first name, or last name of the user being selected. The Show Field property determines which attribute of the selected user will be displayed.
Hyperlink Or Picture	A specialized column that will display in entered URL as either a clickable hyperlink or an image. The URL must either begin with a valid protocol reference (HTTP, HTTPS) or be a relative URL beginning with a forward slash (/), which will be replaced with the root site reference.
Calculated (Calculation Based On Other Columns)	Allows you to use a calculated column to display the results of arithmetic or textual analysis on another column in the same list. Calculations begin with an equal sign, and column names should be enclosed in square brackets. For example, if the list contains the columns Cost and Revenue, you create a calculated column called Profit using the formula =[Revenue] - [Cost] to display the net gain. Other useful functions include the following: **Day** Use to return the day of the month of a date. For example, =Day("2/16/2006") returns "16". **Month** Use to return the month number of a date. For example, =Month("2/16/2006") returns "2". **Year** Use to return the year number of a date. For example, =Year("2/16/2006") returns "2006". **Dollar** Use to format a number as currency by putting a currency sign in front and adding a specified number of decimal places. For example, =Dollar("50", 2) returns "$50.00". **Concatenate** Use to combine multiple text strings into one string. For example, =Concatenate("The Quick Brown ", [Animal1], " Jumped Over the Lazy ", [Animal2]) used with column values of "Dog" for Animal1 and "Fox" for Animal2 returns the following: "The Quick Brown Dog Jumped Over the Lazy Fox".
Business Data	A new field type in SharePoint Server 2007 that allows you to add data from business applications registered in the Business Data Catalog to a document library. (For more information on the Business Data Catalog, see Chapter 12, "Administrating Data Connections.")

Table 9-2 Column Data Types

Data type option	Description
Audience Targeting	Another new field type in SharePoint Server 2007 that allows you to choose a specific audience, distribution list, or SharePoint group to target the document to. Adding this column displays an audience picker control that you can use to browse the audience, distribution list, or SharePoint groups and select one or more to filter the list by for your users.

Setting Metadata Values

When a custom column is added to a library, the values for the column will be blank for any existing document and will need to be populated retroactively. When a new document is added to a library, the user will be prompted to enter data for the custom columns, depending on which method is used to upload the document. Methods available include the following:

- Created as New from a library template. The user will see the Document Information Panel at the top of the page, allowing them to fill in the properties.
- Upload a single document. The user will be presented with a Properties page after the file is uploaded. Required properties need to be populated before the document can be checked in.
- Upload multiple documents, either through the Multiple Upload control or a drag-and-drop operation in Explorer view. No page is provided for populating columns. Properties must be set after the documents are uploaded.

Editing the Existing Metadata of a Document

You can directly edit the metadata of a file in SharePoint Server 2007, as shown in Figure 9-8, by following these steps:

1. Click the drop-down menu for the document.
2. Click Edit Properties.

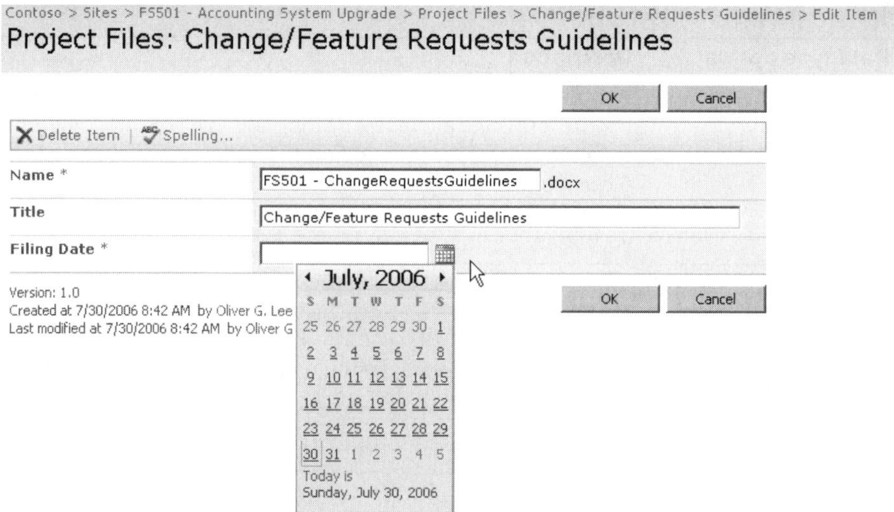

Figure 9-8 Document metadata—editing metadata

Document Information Panel

Custom columns are fully integrated into the 2007 Microsoft Office system as well as the SharePoint Server 2007 pages. When you open a document for editing in Word 2007, for example, a Document Information panel similar to the one shown in Figure 9-9 is displayed at the top of the screen so that authors using Word 2007 and other SharePoint-compatible clients can edit metadata columns defined on the server. If the panel does not appear at the top of a 2007 Microsoft Office system window, you can open it by clicking the File menu, selecting Prepare, and then clicking Properties.

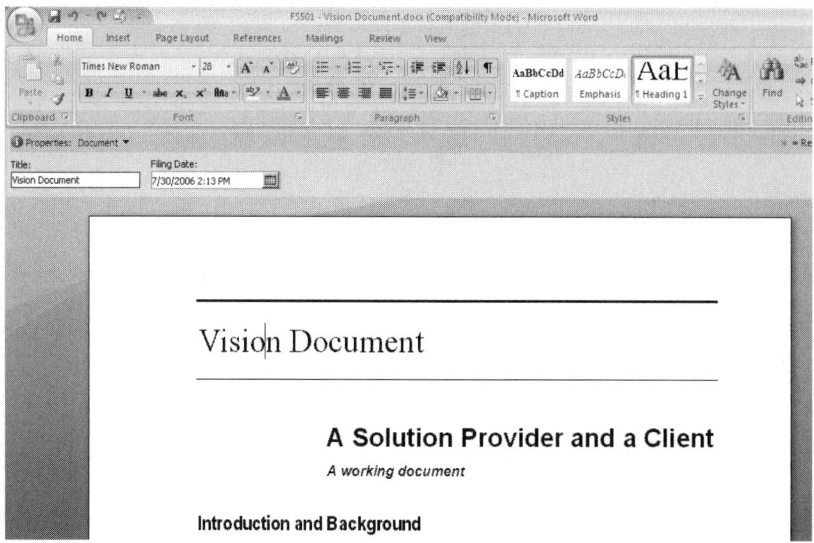

Figure 9-9 Document information panel in the 2007 Microsoft Office system

Creating Site Columns

About the time you discover the value of using custom columns in your libraries, you will also realize that you want to use the same column in more than one library. You don't have to re-create the column multiple times; instead, you can define the column once as a Site Column and then re-use it anywhere in the site.

Creating a New Site Column

To create a new site column, complete the following steps:

1. On the Site Actions menu, click Site Settings.
2. Under the Galleries section, click Site Columns, and then click Create.
3. Define the name and attributes of the column, and click OK.
4. Follow the procedure below to add the new site column to a document library.

Adding an Existing Site Column

After you have defined the column at the site level, you can add the column to each of your document libraries. When you open the Add Columns From Site Columns page, you'll see that a large number of site columns are built into the product, as shown in Figure 9-10. Searching through the list of existing columns, you might find that the metadata you want to track has already been defined.

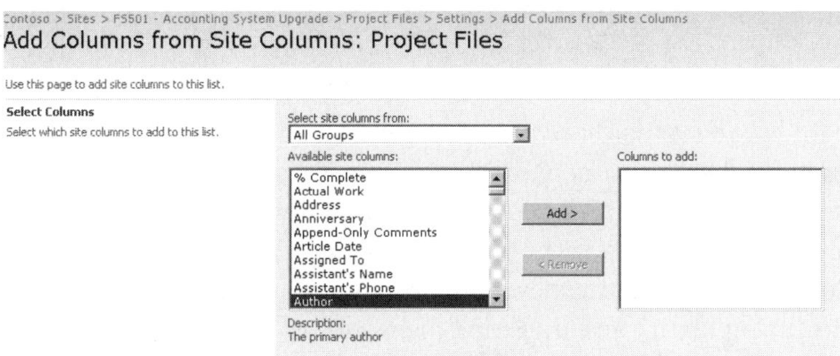

Figure 9-10 Document metadata—adding site columns

To add a site column, complete the following steps:

1. On the library settings menu, click Add Columns From Site Columns.
2. Select the existing site column to apply to the library, and click Add.
3. Select or deselect the option to add the column to the default view.
4. Click OK.

Note If you have enabled Content Types in the library, you will have an additional check box option to add the site column to all of the content types.

Defining Workflow

You use workflows in SharePoint Server 2007 to define how documents will be handled to conform to standardized business processes in your organization. Workflows are covered extensively in Chapter 28, "Implementing Microsoft Windows Workflow Services," so we will provide only an overview of this subject here. You can create customized workflows in SharePoint Server 2007 and associate them with a document library so that they can be applied to any document in the library. When you launch a workflow, it generates status entries for each of its stages in a Tasks list and the workflow's progress is recorded in a workflow history list.

A vital part of the life cycle of a document is the series of steps it needs to pass from creation, through approval, cataloging, and finally disposition. Until now, the most common way to pass a document through these steps has been to send it via e-mail to a distribution list or an individual for processing. As simple as this approach is, it usually requires manual effort to initiate the process, track the status of a document, and move the document to a final storage location when it is finished. It also has the disadvantage of creating multiple copies of the file as it is sent from one person to another. In SharePoint 2007, you can define a document workflow to automate these operations and ensure that the handling of the document conforms to standardized business processes in your organization.

For example, you might have a standardized performance evaluation that managers need to prepare on each staff member they supervise. The requirements are that the document must be created from a specific template and that when it is submitted by a manager, a serial approval process begins that must include a senior manager and the manager of the Human Resources department. You can achieve this in SharePoint 2007 by creating a custom workflow in a document library and triggering the workflow to start when the evaluation is published as a major version.

Standard Workflows

SharePoint Server 2007 includes several standard workflows that are ready to be applied to your document management processes. Here are the types of workflows available:

- **Approval** Routes a document to one or more site members who are designated as Approvers. The tasks that are generated notify each user in turn and ask them to approve or reject a document. If one user rejects the document, the workflow ends. Otherwise, it proceeds until all assignees have approved the document. By default, Approval is a serial workflow wherein Approvers are assigned their task in a sequential order specified by the workflow author.

- **Collect Feedback** Routes a document for review by one or more members of the site chosen by the workflow author. The Collect Feedback workflow is defined as parallel by default so that all reviewers receive e-mail notification and are assigned a task at the same time. Participants can optionally delegate their tasks or decline to participate.
- **Collect Signatures** Routes a document to a set of participants who must sign the document. This workflow is configured on the document library on the server, but it is initiated in the 2007 Microsoft Office system client by selecting Start Workflow from the File menu.

Creating a Document Workflow

To create a typical workflow, such as an employee evaluation, complete the following steps:

1. Browse to the site and document library where the workflow will be defined. In this case, the library is called Staff Evaluations.
2. Select Document Library Settings from the Settings menu.
3. Click Workflow Settings under Permissions And Policies. If this is not the first workflow in the library, click Add Workflow. The page will appear as shown in Figure 9-11.

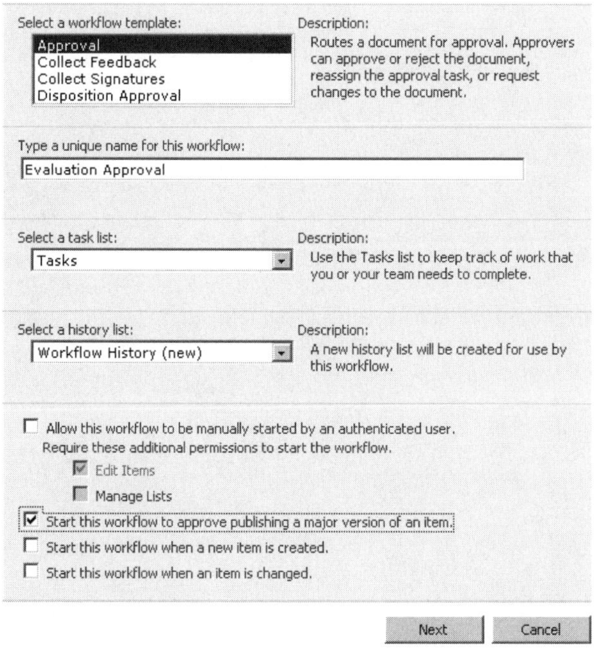

Figure 9-11 Creating a new workflow

4. From the Select A Workflow Template list, choose the type of workflow–in this case, Approval.
5. In the Type A Unique Name For This Workflow text box, specify a workflow name that will be used to identify it in reports. In this case, we will call it Evaluation Approval.
6. Select which tasks list will be used to store the task items for each user assigned an action in the workflow. You can choose to use an existing tasks list or have SharePoint Server create a new one for you for this workflow by clicking the listbox and selecting New Task List.
7. Select which list will be used to track the history of actions and operations that take place in the workflow. You can choose an existing list or have SharePoint Server create a new one for you for this workflow by selecting Workflow History (New).
8. Select which events can automatically start this workflow and whether a user can start the workflow manually. Because we want to control when this workflow begins, we will select only the Start This Workflow To Approve Publishing A Major Version Of An Item option. (The option to start the workflow when a major version has been published is available only if Document Approval has been enabled under the versioning settings.)
9. Click Next and the next page will appear as shown in Figure 9-12.

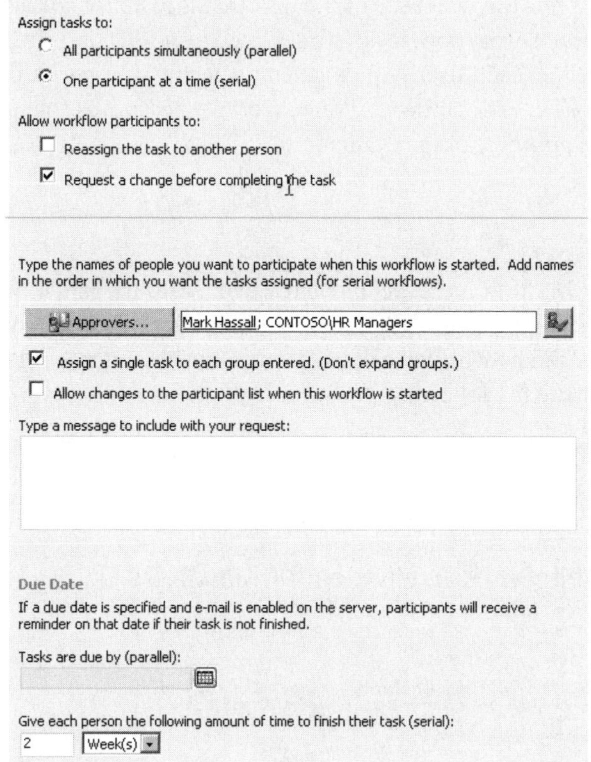

Figure 9-12 Document workflow—creating a new workflow, second page

10. You can choose to assign the workflow tasks to all users at once, which constitutes a parallel workflow, or to each user in turn, which is a serial workflow. In this case, you want to route the document only after the previous user has approved it, so you will select the One Participant At A Time (Serial) option.

11. You can also allow users to make changes to the workflow by either reassigning the task to another person or requesting a change to the document before approving it. In this case, we will select only the Request A Change Before Completing The Task option.

12. In the next section on the page, you can specify which users the document will be routed to for approval. In this case, we will route it first to the senior manager in this department (Mark Hassall) and finally to the Active Directory Domain group HR Managers. Because there might be more than one member of HR Managers, we will also select the option Assign A Single Task To Each Group Entered option so that all members of the group will receive the task at once rather than serially.

13. The last setting we will set is the Due Date of the task that is assigned to each user in the workflow. In a parallel workflow, tasks are assigned a specific date. In a serial workflow, such as this one, each user will be given a specific number of days or weeks to complete his or her task in the workflow. We will specify 2 as the number of weeks for review and approval of the evaluation.
14. Click OK.

Completing the Workflow

After you have defined your workflow, it will be initiated when a user triggers it through the specified actions or by starting it manually, if that option was allowed in the workflow definition. In this case, the workflow will start when a user publishes a major version of the evaluation, which will initiate the following steps:

1. When a user publishes an evaluation, the Start page for the workflow will open as shown in Figure 9-13. At this point, we can simply start the workflow and it will automatically generate the first task.

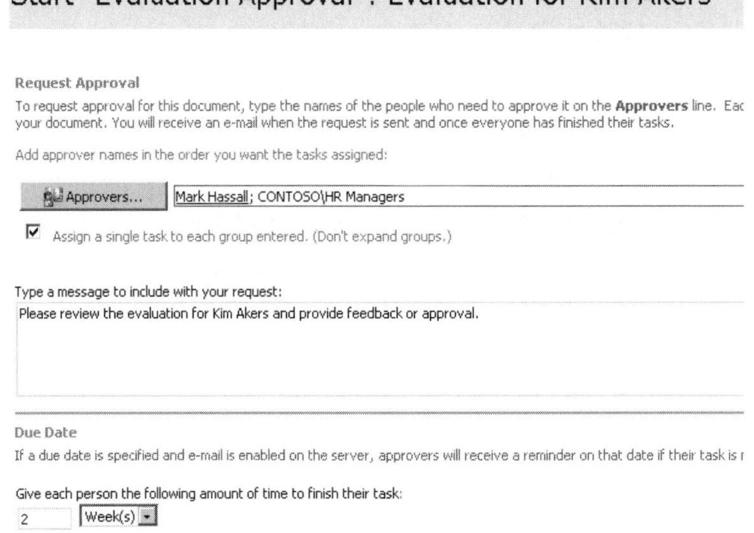

Figure 9-13 Document workflow—Workflow Start page

2. The first action in our workflow creates a task for Mark Hassall to approve the evaluation and sends him an e-mail with a link to the task. He can approve the evaluation either from within the e-mail in Microsoft Office Outlook or from the SharePoint Server 2007 site. The e-mail also contains a link to the document for approval.

3. After Mark Hassall has approved the evaluation, his task is marked as 100% completed and a new task is generated to the HR Managers group for its approval. After the document has been approved by a member of HR Managers, the workflow routing is complete and the document is marked as Approved.

Monitoring the Workflow

While the workflow is in progress, you can view a report of the current status of the workflow. To view the Workflow Status page, which displays the history of users who have acted on the workflow and the current user the workflow is assigned to, follow these steps:

1. Click the drop-down list for the document.
2. Select Workflows.
3. Click on the workflow you want to review under Running Workflows.

Workflows are also tightly integrated into the 2007 Microsoft Office system client applications, allowing users to easily participate in them from within the client program. For example, the following tasks can be performed either from the Web site or a 2007 Microsoft Office system application:

- Viewing the workflows available to run on an item
- Initiating a workflow
- Viewing and launching a workflow task
- Completing a workflow task, and filling the task completion form

Using Document Templates

The New drop-down menu in a document library gives users the option to create a file from a template stored in the Forms folder. By default, document libraries have one default template that all new files are created from. The default template is selected from the list of standard built-in templates at the time the document library is created and can be changed later.

You can change the default template for any document library to use a different starting file by following these steps:

1. Create a customized file in Word 2007, Excel 2007, or another client program written to work with SharePoint Server 2007 and copy it to your clipboard
2. From the Actions menu, select Open With Windows Explorer.
3. Double-click on the Forms directory and paste your customized file into this directory.

4. Click the Back button twice to return to the main view of your document library.
5. From the Settings menu, select Document Library Settings.
6. Click Advanced Settings under General Settings.
7. In the Document Template box, enter the relative URL of the new template, including the name of the document library—for example, Documents/Forms/Leave Request.docx.

Converting Documents

SharePoint Server 2007 provides a means to allow you to automatically convert documents from one format to another. For example, you can use this feature to convert a Word 2007 document into a Web page for viewing by users who do not have Word 2007 installed. Conversions can be set to run programmatically, as in a workflow, or they can be initiated by the user. Two services are installed with SharePoint Server 2007 that handle the conversion process: the Office Document Conversions Launcher service and the Office Document Conversions Load Balancer service.

The Load Balancer Service

By load balancing conversion tasks across SharePoint servers in the server farm, this service ensures that requests for document conversions do not overwhelm any single server. When a document conversion is started, SharePoint Server 2007 passes the request to the Load Balancer service, which identifies which SharePoint server will be used to perform the conversion. The Load Balancer service then connects to the Launcher service on that server through .NET Remoting and passes it the conversion settings information.

The Launcher Service

This service is called by the Load Balancer service and is responsible for queuing and initiating the conversion request. The Launcher passes the specified document to the appropriate document converter, which generates the converted file. SharePoint Server 2007 then loads the converted copy, performs post-processing on it, and uploads it into the document library where the original file was.

SharePoint Server 2007 maintains metadata in the document library to track the relationship between the original document and the converted document, and it retains the relationship as long as both documents remain in the same document library. Through this metadata on the converted document, SharePoint can identify the original document, but it does not work the other way around. Moving or deleting either of the files will break the conversion relationship, but copying or renaming the files does not.

Configuring Document Conversion

To configure document conversion, complete the following steps:

1. In Office SharePoint Server 2007 Central Administration, browse to the Operations tab and click Services On Server.
2. Start the Document Conversions Load Balancer Service.
3. Start the Document Conversions Launcher Service.
4. Select the Load Balancer server to associate the Launcher service with.
5. Specify a unique port number for the Launcher service to use when communicating with the Load Balancer service.
6. Browse to Application Management, and click Document Conversions under External Service Connections.
7. Click Yes to enable document conversions on the application. Choose the Load Balancer server to use, and select how often the Document Conversion timer job will run. Click OK.

Performing a Conversion

In some cases, document conversion can be configured to occur automatically, such as with the Form Conversion For Archiving feature discussed in more detail in Chapter 10. Otherwise, users can invoke this conversion manually by doing the following:

1. Browse to the document that you want to convert. If the document supports a converter, a Convert Document command will appear in the document drop-down list in the document library.
2. Click Convert Document, and select the converter to execute. An example of converting a Word document to a Web page is shown in Figure 9-14.
3. Follow the steps on the conversion page.

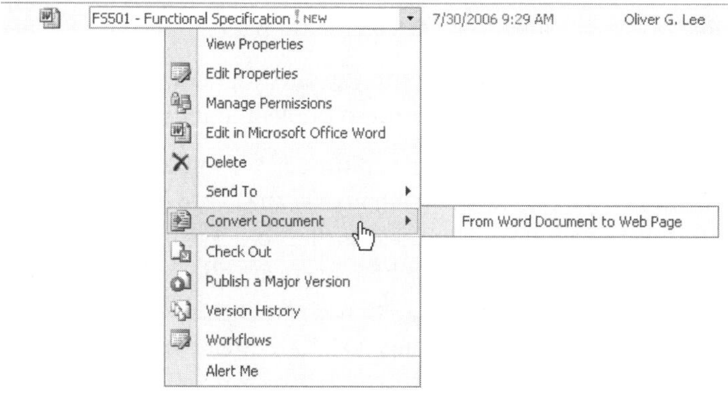

Figure 9-14 Convert Document option

Integrating with 2007 Microsoft Office System Clients

To better integrate your users' activities with SharePoint into their desktop environment, you can customize the Open and Save dialog boxes in 2007 Microsoft Office system to point to document libraries on the server. Doing so adds sites to the My Places bar next to the Open and Save dialog boxes so that users can easily select locations without having to enter URLs to SharePoint sites or go to the site to upload documents.

You make new site locations available to users through a SharePoint Server 2007 Web service that provides a list of sites targeted to a specific set of users based on their roles or site membership. Applications in 2007 Microsoft Office system can automatically discover the Web service through the user's My SharePoint Sites. The new locations then appear as new entries in the My Places bar in the Open and Save dialog boxes.

Administrators can use Group Policy and a Microsoft Active Directory directory service template provided in the 2007 Microsoft Office system Resource Kit to set registry keys on the client that will add specific sites to the My Places bar. You can install and configure the My Places settings through the following steps:

1. Start the Group Policy Object Editor on the domain controller.
2. Expand the User Configuration object.
3. Right-click Administrative Templates, and then click Add/Remove Templates.
4. Click the Add button.
5. Browse to the Office12.adm file, and then click Open.
6. Click Close to exit the Add/Remove Templates dialog.
7. Expand the "Microsoft Office 2007 system" folder.
8. Expand the "File Open/Save dialog box" folder and click Places Bar Locations.
9. Double-click Places Bar Location 1 in the right-hand pane.
10. Click Enabled and enter the Name to display in the My Places bar along with the URL Path to the document library you want to publish to users.

As an additional means to get users to save files on the server, you can use Group Policy settings to limit the locations that organization members can save to using the Save dialog box. For example, you can restrict the ability to save files to desktops and force users to save content in a document library. Limiting where users are allowed to browse to save their documents is one way to encourage users to use server-side locations rather than their local hard drives. The Group Policy settings for 2007 Microsoft Office system will even let you target the limitations to one or more Microsoft Office applications. For example, you can restrict Save locations in Excel 2007 while allowing other Microsoft Office applications to save elsewhere. To configure these settings, follow the steps above to install the Office12.adm template and navigate to the Restricted Browsing folder under File Open/Save dialog box. First, edit the Activate Restricted Browsing setting to enable browsing restrictions for any or all 2007 Microsoft Office system applications. Next, edit the Approve Locations setting to specify the list of locations that will be available in the Save As dialog box.

Working with Document Security

The 2007 Microsoft Office system introduces a new XML-based file format with new security features for protecting your document content. The Microsoft Office system now supports separate formats for different types of files: the "x" format (for example, docx), a secure file format that cannot contain macros or ActiveX controls, and the "m" format (for example, docm), which is a format that can contain active content. When you attempt to save a document containing macros as a Microsoft Office file with an "x" extension, the application will warn you that the macros will be removed and suggests saving the file as a macro-enabled file type instead.

When a document is opened that contains potentially unsafe content, such as an ActiveX control or a macro that has not been digitally signed, the default in the Microsoft Office system is to disable the content. Microsoft Office will display the Message Bar with a security alert identifying the content that has been disabled and providing options to enable the content and open the Trust Center. The Trust Center provides access to settings that control the behavior of macros, ActiveX controls (shown in Figure 9-15), and other content controls. The Trust Center can also be accessed directly via the Options button under the File menu.

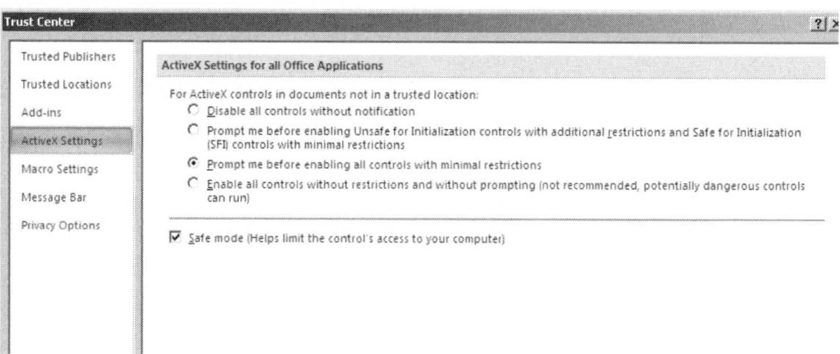

Figure 9-15 Trust Center settings

Using Document Inspector

One of the final steps in the document preparation and publishing process is to remove any personal or private information from the file before it is released. In some cases, this is information, such as comments and revision marks, that results from the collaboration process. In other cases, this is information that might have been hidden temporarily and then forgotten about. Hidden information in the document might not necessarily constitute a security risk, but it might not be information you want to distribute in the final version of the document. Word 2007 introduces a tool called the Document Inspector, which can identify and purge unwanted information.

The Document Inspector can find and remove the types of information listed Table 9-3.

Table 9-3 Content Removed by Document Inspector

Content	Application	Description
Comments and annotations	Word, Excel, PowerPoint	Side comments added to the page or ink annotations inserted using a pen tool
Revisions and version information	Word	History information logged when the Track Changes feature is enabled or comments are inserted
Document properties and personal information	Word, Excel, PowerPoint	Metadata stored in the document (such as title, subject, and author), as well as personal information (such as e-mail headers, routing slips, and template names)
Custom XML data	Word, Excel, PowerPoint	Custom XML data that might have been inserted into the file
Headers and footers (including watermarks)	Word, Excel	Information in headers and footers that might be hidden
Hidden text and invisible content	Word	Text that might have been formatted as hidden but could be revealed by another user
Hidden rows and columns	Excel	Rows and columns that have been hidden
Hidden worksheets		Worksheets that have been hidden
Invisible on-slide content	PowerPoint	Objects that have been set to be invisible
Off-slide content	PowerPoint	Objects that have been moved off the visible slide area
Presentation notes	PowerPoint	Information in the Notes section of the slides

To use the Document Inspector, complete the following steps:

1. From the File menu, select Prepare, and then click Inspect Document.

2. Clear the check boxes next to any items you don't want the inspector to scan for, and then click Inspect.
3. A results page will display the types of items found and a Remove All button next to each type of item to clear it from the document.

Using Digital Signatures

Word 2007 and Excel 2007 applications introduce enhanced support for digital signatures applied to the contents of a document. Digital signatures can be used in place of physical signatures to allow you to provide verifiable approval for a document without the need to print and fax it. Following is a list of the major benefits of digital signatures:

- **Authenticity** Assures that the identity of the author is valid
- **Integrity** Assures that the content has not been modified since it was digitally signed
- **Nonrepudiation** Assures that authors cannot later deny their use of a digital signature

Enabling Support for Digital Signatures

The first step in working with digital signatures in your documents is to establish your credentials through a digital certificate. Although you can create a self-issued certificate and sign documents with it, this approach will only help you make sure no one has tampered with your own documents.

To validate the authenticity of another user's digital signature, you must have access to the same certificate authority (CA). A CA is an organization that issues and revokes digital certificates and that can be used to validate a certificate as authentic. A CA can be a third-party company that provides certificates to users in your organization or it can be an internal IT group that generates the certificates.

Whether or not you need to use certificates from an outside company depends on who you will be exchanging documents with. If only users within your organization will be signing and validating documents, an internal certificate authority will be able to validate every transaction. However, if documents will be transferred to users in other companies or organizations and the digital signatures need to be validated, you might need a third-party certificate that can be validated by an external authority.

Using a Signature Line

With the digital signature feature in the Microsoft Office system, you can now create a signature line in a document where you want someone to sign and then send the document to the person, who can then sign it digitally. When a user signs a document digitally, she uses a digital signature to encode the file so that others can validate when and by whom the document was signed. A user also can either enter her name or use a graphical image with her hand-written signature in it to display in the document. Digital signature placeholders can be inserted into both Word 2007 and Excel 2007 files, but they cannot be used in PowerPoint 2007 or Access 2007 files. However, any user with a digital certificate can sign a Word 2007, Excel 2007, or PowerPoint 2007 file without using a signature placeholder. In these cases, the entire document is digitally signed.

Creating a Digital Signature Placeholder

To insert a placeholder into a document to receive a digital signature, follow these steps:

1. Click the line in the file where you want the signature to appear.
2. Click the Insert menu.
3. In the Text group on the Ribbon, click the Signature Line button.
4. Type the signer's information (using the suggested information that follows) in the Signature Setup dialog box, as shown in Figure 9-16:
   - **Suggested Signer** Type the intended signer's name.
   - **Suggested Signer's Title** Type the intended signer's official position in relation to the document being signed.
   - **Suggested Signer's E-mail Address** Type the intended signer's unique e-mail address.
   - **Instructions To The Signer** Type any additional instructions.
   - **Allow The Signer To Add Comments In The Sign Dialog** Select this option to provide an area for the signer to enter comments when he signs.
   - **Show Sign Date In Signature Line** Select this option to display the date signed as part of the signature line.
5. Click OK.

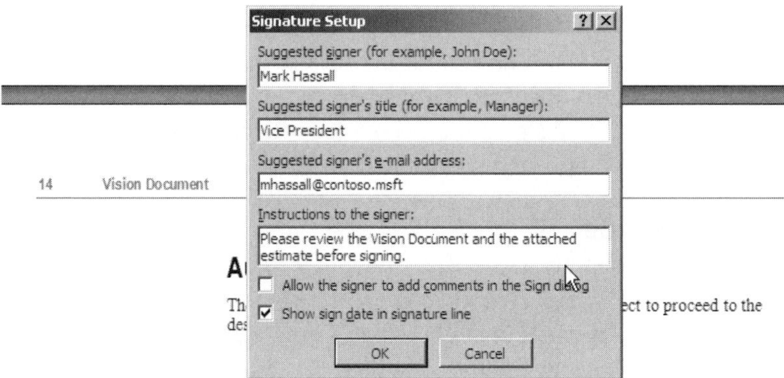

Figure 9-16 Inserting a signature placeholder

Digitally Signing a Document with a Placeholder

To digitally sign a document that has a Signature Line placeholder, complete the following steps:

1. Double-click the Signature Line to open the Sign dialog box, as shown in Figure 9-17.

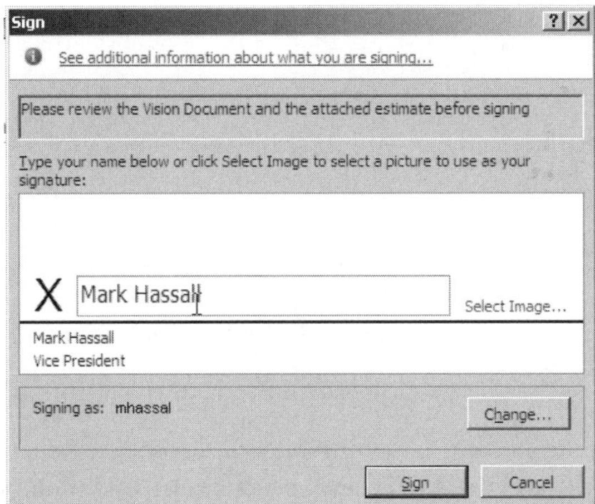

Figure 9-17 Signing a document

2. Type the signer's name, or select a prepared hand signature image to use by clicking Select Image, which will let you browse for an image file on your hard disk.
3. Click the Change button to select the digital signature to use to sign the document, then click OK.
4. Enter a purpose for signing the document (optional).
5. Click Sign.

Digitally Signing a Document Without a Placeholder

To digitally sign a document without a Signature Line placeholder, complete the following steps:

1. Click the Office menu.
2. Select Prepare, and then click Add A Digital Signature.
3. Click the Change button to select the digital signature to use to sign the document, then click OK.
4. Enter a purpose for signing the document (optional).
5. Click Sign.

Viewing Digital Signatures

To view digital signatures in a document, complete the following steps:

1. Click the Office menu.
2. Select Prepare, and then click View Signatures
3. In the Signatures pane, click the drop-down menu for a signature and select Signature Details.

Item-Level Permissions

SharePoint Server 2007 introduces the ability for you to set item-level security on documents in document libraries. You can individually secure documents so that only specific users and groups can read or edit them.

> **Note** By default, the item-level permissions of documents inherit from the permissions settings of the document library. Setting permissions on an individual file breaks the permissions inheritance.

In general, you might find it easier to manage large numbers of documents by creating several document libraries, each with unique library-level permissions, and then placing documents into the appropriate library to assign them permissions. By default, the permissions of libraries and documents can be assigned by the Site Owner, but any user who is assigned Full Control over the library can set permissions on individual documents within it.

To set permissions on a document in a library, complete the following steps:

1. Browse to the document library.
2. Click the drop-down list on a document, and select Manage Permissions.
3. Click the Actions menu, and select Edit Permissions.
4. Click OK to break the permissions inheritance.
5. Select the check box next to any users or groups from the parent library that you do not want to have permissions on this document. Then click the Actions menu, and select Remove User Permissions.
6. Select the check box for any other users or groups for which you want to change permissions, click the Actions menu, and select Edit User Permissions.
7. Click the New menu, select Add Users to add users, and grant them permissions.

Rights Management Services

The item-level permissions supported by SharePoint Server 2007 assist in securing documents that reside in document libraries, but what if you need even greater control over what users can do with documents? For example, anyone who has the right to read a Word document in SharePoint generally has the right to print the document. In addition, after a user has downloaded the document from SharePoint, you no longer have any control over it. If you want to apply more specific controls to documents and ensure that these controls are enforced anywhere the document resides, you need to implement Rights Management Services (RMS).

RMS is designed to protect Microsoft Office documents used within your organization from unauthorized use, and it applies to documents both inside and outside of SharePoint. RMS goes beyond SharePoint protections by encrypting the document and applying the security restrictions directly to it so that even if the document is removed from the SharePoint server or the network, the security restrictions are retained. Essentially, after the file is encrypted using RMS, only users authorized by the RMS server can access the document. All others users are blocked, and even if they attempt to open the file in another application they will see only the illegible encrypted version.

RMS is designed for organizations that need to persist data protection with the documents themselves to protect sensitive information, such as product design plans, medical records, credit card lists, and personal client data (such as Social Security numbers). RMS allows organizations to protect data through a set of usage rights and conditions that are applied to the document and protect any binary format of the file so that the usage rights apply to the document regardless of how it is transmitted.

RMS permissions are administered through the definition and application of Rights Policy templates. A Rights Policy template describes the specific permissions and conditions that will be assigned to users of a given type of content. A user with permissions to apply RMS policies then secures a document by assigning a Rights Policy template to it. The rights policy assigned to a document becomes part of the publishing license for that information, which also includes the list of users who can access the content. The following is a list of the rights that can be assigned to a Rights Policy template:

- Full Control
- View Rights
- Export (Save As)
- Save
- View
- Print

- Extract
- Edit
- Allow Macros
- Forward
- Reply
- Reply All

Summary

In this chapter we covered the new and enhanced features of SharePoint 2007 that support advanced document management. We began by introducing the differences between informal and formal communication and the importance of identifying their roles in the organization. We then explored the new features of document libraries in SharePoint 2007, including uploading and accessing documents as well as configuring document versioning. We next discussed how to add custom columns to document libraries to support additional metadata for documents, and we looked at incorporating workflows into your document management system. We also examined ways in which you can manage the user experience of browsing document libraries in the Open and Save As dialog boxes by Group Policy Administrative Templates. Finally, we discussed new security features of the 2007 Microsoft Office system such as digital signatures and item-level permissions in document libraries. In the next chapter, we will expand on these concepts by examining the new records management features of SharePoint 2007.

Chapter 10

Records Management in Microsoft Office SharePoint Server 2007

New to Microsoft Office SharePoint Server 2007 is Enterprise Content Management. Enterprise Content Management includes three major sections: Web content management, records management, and document management. The focus of this chapter is records management.

Organizations today are increasingly subject to state and federal regulations governing which electronic records they must retain, how long the records should be retained, and how readily the records should be made accessible to regulators. Some of these regulations, such as the Health Insurance Portability and Accountability Act (HIPAA), are industry specific, while others regulations, such as the Sarbanes-Oxley Act (SOX), apply to a wide range of industries. Organizations have found that defensive business practices call for good data management to protect the company during litigation. Organizations are often required to produce copies of documents and files deemed to be relevant to a lawsuit or prosecution. In some cases where an organization could not produce the requested documents, courts have ruled that the documents are assumed to have been relevant and would have supported the plaintiff's arguments. Organizations can no longer afford to not have control over their documents and e-mail messages.

In this chapter, you will learn how you can use Office SharePoint Server 2007 to automate and systematize the process of managing information records for regulatory compliance. You will examine the technology and review possible strategies you should discuss with your legal counsel to determine which ones best apply to your compliance needs.

Introduction to Enterprise Records Management

Records management enables an organization to effectively manage a content item, or record, from inception to disposal in accordance with applicable laws. A *record* is a physical or electronic document, an e-mail message, or some other form of digital information (such as an Instant Message transcript) that serves as evidence of an activity or transaction performed by the organization. *Records management* is the process by which an organization defines what type of information it must classify as a record, how long it must retain the information, and how it will manage the information throughout its life cycle. Part of the challenge of records management is to track information items that are legally or economically vital to the business. For example, an e-mail message that contains some reference to financial information about the company or a client might be considered a record. The other part of the challenge is to purge and filter out items that are not required to be stored as records. For example, an exchange of e-mail messages in which two employees of the organization decide where to have lunch might not be considered record material.

Although setting a policy that declares everything to be a record might seem like a safe approach, it can, in fact, be almost as harmful as not declaring anything a record. For example, if a lawsuit requires that an organization deliver approximately 100 e-mail records that pertain to a case, and the best that the IT department can do is narrow it down to 10,000 e-mail messages sent within a determined time frame, a court might rule that delivering the relevant items buried within a mass of irrelevant data is a form of obstruction. An additional benefit of not storing everything as a record is that it can improve the ability of users to perform targeted searches, avoiding the accumulation of irrelevant data.

Representative Regulations

In the United States for example, five prominent sets of laws and regulations are currently presenting a records management challenge to organizations. This section provides a brief overview of each set, as outlined in the following list:

- **Sarbanes-Oxley Act** This act applies to publicly traded companies and requires that they put in place extensive policies and procedures to control their financial information and prevent fraud. It also requires that executives certify the validity of company financial statements and that independent auditors verify the financial controls put in place.
- **Gramm-Leach-Bliley Act (Financial Institution Privacy Protection Act of 2003)** This act sets up requirements for companies holding private personal financial information and dictates their responsibility to secure these records and, once the records are no longer needed, to permanently destroy them.
- **Healthcare Insurance Portability and Accountability Act of 1996 (HIPAA)** This act requires that organizations that have access to personal health information adopt security policies to safeguard the confidentiality of the data. Organizations must also monitor and control access to the data and maintain an audit trail that is available to regulators.
- **National Association of Securities Dealers 3010 & 3110 (NASD 3010 & 3110)** This set of regulations specifies that member firms must implement processes to retain all correspondence involving registered representatives, broker-dealers, and professional securities traders.
- **Department of Defense Rule 5015.2-STD** This rule defines the requirements for U.S. military branches to follow systematic processes for recording official documents and files.

The Records Management Plan

A well-designed records management plan is essential for your data-retention policies to mesh with your data-management processes. For example, if a retention policy specifies that a document should be purged and destroyed after one year, backups should be designed so that no backup older than one year has a copy of the file on it. On the other hand, for example, a retention policy that dictates that a document must be readily available for review for a period of three years requires that a live copy of it be kept in a storage location from which it can be pulled without restoring it from backup. These requirements dictate that organizations not only develop the appropriate policies but implement and enforce them as well. There have been cases in which organizations have not followed their own policies and were required to retrieve selective data from archive backups and restore it onto their network—a very time-consuming process.

A records management plan should contain the following elements:

- A compliance requirements document that defines the policies that the organization must implement to ensure compliance with legal and regulatory requirements, along with the practices that employees must adhere to be in compliance with the policies.
- A chart that identifies who will be responsible for the different roles involved in the records management process.
- A file plan that identifies what types of information are considered records, where the records are stored, the permissions and policies that govern the records while they are active, and how and when the records will be disposed of.

Note These elements are described in detail in this section.

The Compliance Requirements Document

The compliance requirements document explains the purpose of a compliance program and describes its benefits and its essential components. It identifies the legal and business criteria to which the compliance plan must adhere, as well as the metrics or other objective criteria that will be used to measure the effectiveness of the compliance plan. The compliance requirements document includes the formal policies that represent the organization's internal statement of the regulatory rules it must follow. The compliance requirements document should also include specifications for ongoing training for employees at all levels and guidelines as to the role and involvement by senior management in the compliance process. Although it might not be practical for every organization, a formal compliance audit should also be carried out at regular intervals to ensure that the records management plan is meeting its objectives.

Records Management Roles

When developing the records management plan, it is important to consider who will fill the various roles that are involved in the creation and implementation of the plan. Because SharePoint Server 2007 is a content-rich application, some of these roles will include the SharePoint administrators, content and records managers compliance officers, and information workers.

SharePoint Administrators

Administrators are responsible for the installation and configuration of the SharePoint Server 2007 servers that provide records management services to the enterprise. They create the Web applications and the Records Repository site and configure the connection to the official file that allows users to submit documents to the Records Center.

Compliance Officers

Compliance officers are usually associated with an organization's legal department and are often lawyers. They are responsible for understanding and interpreting the regulations and rules with which the organization must comply. They develop the formal compliance policies the company will implement, and as a result, they are the primary authors of the compliance requirements document and perform internal monitoring and auditing to ensure that the organization closely follows the records management plan.

Records Managers

Records managers are responsible for developing the file plan that applies the compliance requirements document to the different types of information items the organization produces. The records managers can also be members of the organization's legal department, or they can be senior administrative staff who have a thorough understanding of the organization's business practices and workflow. After the SharePoint administrators have created the Records Center site, records managers are in charge of configuring the document libraries and retention rules in the site. Records managers should be consulted at all points in the design of the records management system.

Content Managers

Content managers work on the teams that create information items that will be designated as records. Content managers configure team sites with the appropriate content types and workflows to facilitate documents being effectively and efficiently categorized so that they can be routed to the appropriate repository library.

Information Workers

Information workers are the employees in an organization who create new documents and e-mail messages that need to be classified and routed to the Records Repository for safeguarding. The goal of a reliable records management system should be to make it relatively easy for information workers to classify information accurately, or even automatically, as it is produced.

The File Plan

The file plan is a written document or set of documents that list all the types of information an organization receives or produces and details how it should be classified and handled. Some information will be classified as a record when it is created. Other information will be treated as a record only when it reaches a certain stage in its life cycle. Then there will be information that is either temporary or unimportant enough that it is not considered a type of record. The criteria used to classify a record will come from the compliance requirements document that is produced by the compliance officer.

Note As part of your effort to train and educate your users about their use of SharePoint technologies, be sure to instruct them on how to differentiate among document types. Users need to know when a document or record moves from being unofficial communication to being official communication, and they also need to know how official records are consumed and disposed of.

Although the details of what enters into the file plan depends on the type of information your organization manages, there are usually some common elements in most plans. As shown in Table 10-1, these elements include a list of record types and the key information that must be associated with each record for it to be filed. Once an information item is classified as a record, it is copied or moved into a SharePoint Server 2007 site based on the Records Center site template. This site serves as the storage area for both active and inactive documents that must be readily available as an information resource for staff or as evidentiary material in litigation.

Active documents are those that are still in use as part of a project or an ongoing e-mail discussion. These documents might continue to be updated over time, and new versions will be submitted to the Records Center as they are generated. The file plan will specify whether older versions of the same document are retained and for how long. Inactive documents are those that have reached their final version or have been submitted formally to an agency. Although there are not expected to be any further versions of the document, the last version must be retained as an official record of the transaction.

Table 10-1 File Plan Elements

Plan element	Purpose
Record type	The classification of the information item. Each Record Type corresponds to a set of typical documents or messages that need to be tracked and managed in the same way.
Required fields	Any additional information that will be required when the document is submitted to the Records Center.
Expiration	How long the document will be retained.
Disposal	How the document will be handled when it expires.
Audit	Whether access to the document will be tracked and logged.

At this point, it is important to distinguish between documents that are retained as records and those that are retained in an archive. Archived information either is not classified as a record or the period for which it needs to be retained as a record has expired. It is usually written off to tape, or printed out, and placed in long-term storage with the expectation that it will be kept mainly for historical purposes. Archived data is generally not readily available for search and retrieval; therefore, it is inappropriate for research and legal discovery.

In Table 10-2, you see an example of a standard file plan filled out for several record types in an organization. As you can see, different document types have different record management requirements. Whereas financial statements are kept indefinitely in archival storage because of their historical value to the company, e-mail correspondence is considered in this case too voluminous and of too little value to archive long term.

Table 10-2 Sample File Plan

Record type	Required fields	Expiration	Disposal	Audit
Financial statements	Statement Date (date field)	Retain for seven years after Statement Date	Archive and delete on expiration	Audit View events only
Invoices	Delivery Date (date field)	Retain for five years after Delivery Date	Archive and delete on expiration	None
E-mail correspondence	Subject (string property, single line of text)	Retain for three years from date created	Delete on expiration	None

Setting Up Records Management in SharePoint Server 2007

To configure records management in SharePoint Server 2007, you begin by defining the content types that will be used to classify records throughout your enterprise. You then create a site based on the Records Center site template and configure the methods you will use to route documents to this site after they have been classified. Finally, you create information policies within the Records Center site to apply the rules dictated in the file plan. The following is a summary of the steps you will follow:

1. Create content types, and deploy them as site content types or features.
2. Create a separate Web application to host the Records Repository.
3. Create a new site collection in the Web application using the Records Center site template.

4. Create a new document library in the Records Center site for each record type or set of similar record types.
5. Define required fields (columns) on the document libraries.
6. Define Information Management Policies to implement the file plan rules.
7. Configure the series entries in the Record Routing list to route documents to the correct document library in the site.

The following sections provide more details concerning these steps.

Creating and Managing Content Types

A *content type* is a data element plus a pre-defined set of metadata. In this discussion, you can think of a content type as a collection of settings that can be applied to a document to categorize its content. Content types are essential to the proper functioning of your Records Center because documents submitted to the Records Center are automatically organized by filing them into a specific document library according to their content type. To ensure that all records are routed correctly, you must configure your enterprise content types strategy before implementing your Records Center.

In a traditional file plan, record classifications are tracked by using identification keys or codes that organize the records files for easy browsing. For example, a file could be given a "record locator id" such as IT-05-DOC-001, which could be understood as: file number "1" of the "DOC" format in department "05" in the "IT" division. These classification designators are often used to create a hierarchical structure of folders into which files can be organized. In SharePoint Server 2007, the recommended classification approach is to apply a specific content type to each document before it is submitted to the Records Center.

For every record type in your file plan, you'll likely need a corresponding content type that users can apply to the documents. You'll want to create a document-to-content type mapping database so that you will know which record types use which content type. In a large environment, it is very conceivable that you'll have thousands of content types.

Content types support inheritance, allowing you to base a new content type on an existing content type. In this way, you can define a single content type with specific attributes and create a derived content type based on it. You can then add new attributes to the new content type to extend the definition. In some cases, you might want to create several derived content types from the same parent type to distinguish different documents that otherwise have the same attributes. For example, the content types Financial Statement and Fiscal Report might be two sub-types of the parent type Finance Document that were created to distinguish the two types. Each type could then be routed into a different document library in the Records Center, or they could be grouped together.

Inheritance for content types works only within site collections, not between them. You can create parent and child relationships between content types either within the same site or between a parent site and a child site. However, if you have several source sites that will submit to the Records Repository, you need to re-create the content types in every site collection. A more efficient approach might be to develop the content types as SharePoint Server 2007 features that can be deployed to the server and made available in every site collection. A *feature* is a set of files and configuration settings that can be installed on a server so it can be available as an optional feature in every site collection. When a content type is defined in a feature, it can then be enabled or disabled in individual site collections as needed. This ensures that content types are uniform across the environment and are deployed only in the appropriate site collections.

More Info For more information on content types and features, see Chapter 15, "Managing Content Types."

For content to be correctly routed and stored in the Records Repository, users must apply the appropriate content types to documents before they are submitted to the Records Repository. If users upload existing documents to a document library and the library is configured with multiple content types, users will have the option to select a content type for the document on the document properties screen, as shown in Figure 10-1.

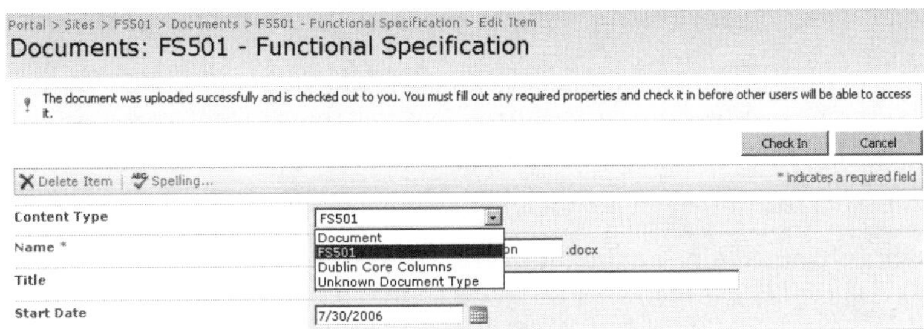

Figure 10-1 Selecting a content type for an uploaded document

Alternatively, users can create new content directly from Content Type templates by selecting the content type from the New menu in the document library. In both cases, the user must provide values for any required data fields associated with the content type. Content managers in each site collection should periodically review documents to ensure that they are being assigned the appropriate content types, as defined by the file plan.

Creating the Records Center

The Records Center site is used in conjunction with content types in SharePoint Server 2007 to implement a file plan. The Records Center site has been designed for use as the storage location for the official copies of all records in your organization. That does not mean that the file will be the only copy—there might be other copies of a document in other sites, but the copy in the Records Repository should never be changed.

It is recommended that you create the Records Repository site on a separate Web application, with the Repository template selected for the root site collection. One reason for adopting this approach is that it ensures complete security separation between the Records Repository site and any other sites. The security on the Records Repository site should be more restrictive than on other sites, with very few users having edit privileges. Another advantage of using a separate Web application is that it uses a separate SQL Server database for all data stored in the application. This approach allows you to back up and restore the Records Repository on a different schedule from other sites. Additionally, having the Records Repository in a separate application makes it easy to set up indexing of content on a separate schedule.

Although you can create multiple sites based on the Records Center site template, you can configure only one target site for each Web application as the default destination for users to send records to. Therefore, if you have configured multiple Web applications in your SharePoint farm, you can configure each application to submit files to a different Records Repository or you can have them all send files to one Records Center. Configuring multiple repositories in your farm is appropriate for situations where the documents in one records store must remain isolated from those in other record stores. In most other scenarios, it is much easier to manage your records, place holds on them, and generate reports if they are all in one site.

The Records Center contains a number of specialized features that make it easy to use as a records management site. Figure 10-2 shows a new site created from the Records Center site template that contains the following features:

- A document library named Unclassified Records, which will act as the default location for any file that does not match a routing record.
- A Record Routing list, which contains rules that define which document library a file is routed to when it is sent to the Records Center. This list has a default entry for the Unclassified Records library.
- A Missing Properties document library, which serves as the entry point for users to fill in missing metadata in submitted files.
- A Records Pending Submission library, which serves as a temporary storage location for records that are missing required metadata.
- A Holds list, which is used to create and manage overrides that suspend expiration policies on records.

- A Submitted E-mail Records list, which is used to temporarily store received e-mail records.
- A built-in reference to the Records Repository Web Service, which is used to submit files from other sites to the Records Center.

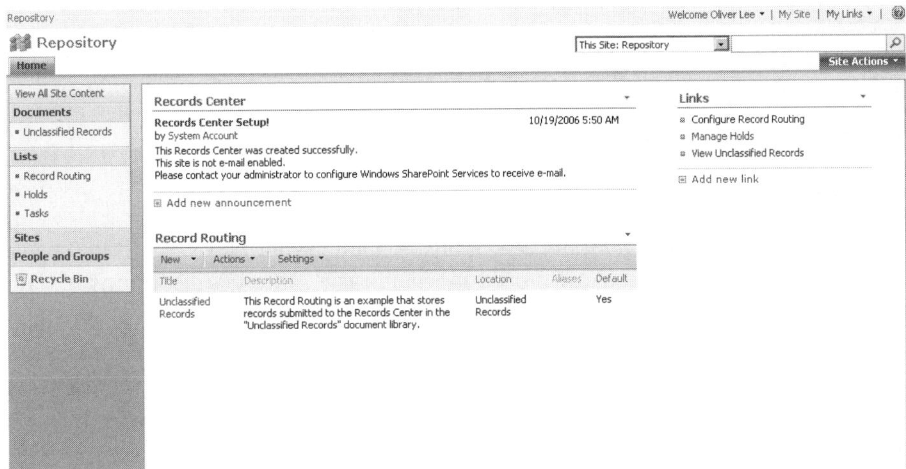

Figure 10-2 A new Records Center site

Creating Document Libraries

Document libraries serve as the storage locations for files in the Records Repository. Although you can configure only one target repository for each Web application, you can configure multiple document libraries to receive files. Each library can hold one type of file or many different types, depending on how you want to group files for browsing and navigation. Files will be automatically routed into the document libraries based on the locations you configure in the Record Routing list. Although you can create folders within document libraries, they cannot be used as destination locations in the record routing entries. Files can be routed only to document libraries, not to folders within the libraries.

> **More Info** For more details on creating document libraries and list columns, see Chapter 9, "Document Management."

You do not need to enable versioning in the document libraries in the Records Repository site. The Records Repository Web Service, which copies documents to the Records Repository, automatically creates new versions when they are submitted and appends a randomly generated identifier to distinguish them. For example, if two versions of the file

"FS501 – ChangeRequestsGuidelines.doc" are sent to the Records Repository, they will be stored with unique names, as shown in Figure 10-3.

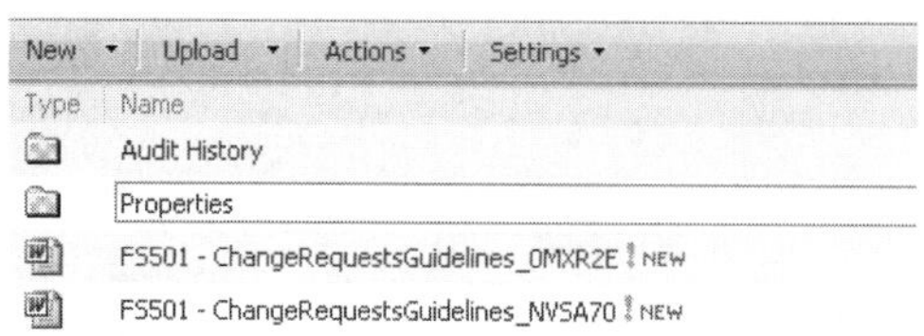

Figure 10-3 Automatic versioning of records

Defining Metadata

When you plan the document libraries to create, consider what types of metadata you want to track for documents that are stored in the library. If there are columns of data already associated with a document in the source site, you should create the same columns on the destination document library in the Records Repository. Otherwise, the metadata will be copied into the library but it will not be accessible through the Web site pages. You can also create additional columns to track metadata that is required by your file plan but which might not be present on the original document. For example, you might want to assign to the file an identification number that is generated by an external document tracking system. The user would then be prompted for this number when she sends the document to the Records Repository.

When a document is submitted to the Records Repository, the Record Routing list is queried to determine the series type (the routing rule, described later in the chapter in the section titled "Configuring the Record Routing Document Library") that identifies which document library the file belongs in. That library is then queried to retrieve a list of columns that constitute the metadata that will be associated with the file. Existing document metadata that matches columns in the document library is automatically promoted and stored in the library columns. If there are metadata columns that are not already populated with data, the user is presented with the Missing Properties page to provide the missing values, as shown in Figure 10-4. If the user fails to provide any required values or clicks Cancel on the Missing Properties page, the file is not sent to the Records Center but record entries are placed in the Records Pending Submission library and the Missing Properties library in the Records Center site. The entry in the Records Pending Submission library identifies the source file and the target library it should be routed to and the Missing Properties entry indicates the column values that still need to be populated.

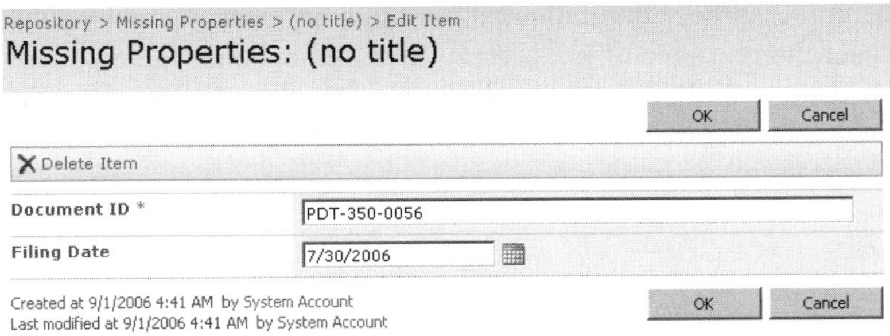

Repository > Missing Properties > (no title) > Edit Item

Missing Properties: (no title)

OK Cancel

Delete Item

Document ID *	PDT-350-0056
Filing Date	7/30/2006

Created at 9/1/2006 4:41 AM by System Account
Last modified at 9/1/2006 4:41 AM by System Account

OK Cancel

Figure 10-4 The Missing Properties page

> **Note** Although you can configure the document libraries in the Records Repository site with the same Content Types that the source libraries have, the content type association is not carried over to the Records Repository site.

Defining Information Management Policies

Information management policies are sets of rules that govern the automated management of documents, such as how long a file should be retained or which actions on the file should be audited. Each rule in a policy is a *policy feature*. Policies in a records management system are configured by records managers to reflect the file plan requirements. The value of storing files in separate document libraries becomes obvious when you start designing the information management policies that you will apply to each library.

There are two recommended approaches for implementing policies in the Records Repository: create individual policies for each document library if the requirements are unique to the content in each library, or create Site Collection policies to cover an entire set of record types and apply them to several document libraries as needed. You can either apply one policy for the entire document library or, if you configure the document library to allow multiple content types, you can apply a separate policy to each content type. The following section describes the policy features that are available in SharePoint Server 2007.

Expiration

The Enable Expiration policy feature allows you to specify how long a document is retained in the Records Center and to control what happens to it at the end of its life cycle. When you select the Enable Expiration policy feature, as shown in Figure 10-5, you have the option to set an expiration time based on when the file was created (that is, when it was copied into the Records Center) or last modified. You can specify values that range from 0 through 500 years, from 0 through 6000 months, or from 0 through 182,500 days from the date selected. Alternatively, you can choose to have the expiration date set either by a custom application or through a workflow process running on the document itself. You can define what action SharePoint will take on the document once the expiration date has passed. An action could be to delete only the document or to delete the record and submission information, or to initiate a workflow to gather input as to how the document should be disposed of.

Enable Expiration

The retention period is:

A time period based on the item's properties:

Created + 5 years

Set programmatically (for example, by a workflow)

When the item expires:

Perform this action:

Delete

Start this workflow:

Approval

Figure 10-5 The Enable Expiration policy feature

Auditing

The Enable Auditing policy feature allows you to feature log events and operations performed on documents and list items. The auditing feature not only tracks operations performed by users but also those of SharePoint itself and any custom code or Web services that access the document programmatically. See Figure 10-6 for the types of operations that can be audited.

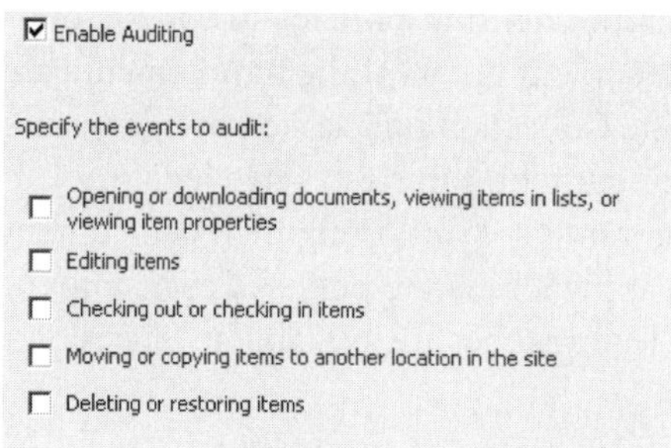

Figure 10-6 The Enable Auditing policy feature

To view the audit log, open the Site Settings of the Records Repository site (or the root site in the site collection if the Records Repository is a subsite). In the Site Collection Administration section, click the Audit Log Reports link. Doing this displays a page that lists each of the audit reports produced. You can click the Run A Custom Report link to manually specify the parameters for a report, or click on any of the predefined reports to generate a Microsoft Office Excel–based report of the audit log data.

Labeling

The Enable Labels policy feature enables SharePoint Server 2007 to automatically generate searchable text areas that are based on a formula that can include static text and document metadata. This feature allows you to insert a line of text or an external value into the document as an image in much the same way that a label is affixed to a document for filing. For example, an organization might want to attach a label to a project document that includes the document ID number and the date it was filed. You define the formula that generates the label by using metadata-based identifiers in conjunction with descriptive text, and SharePoint creates the label for each document added to the document library.

To enable the label feature, select the Enable Labels feature and enter a formula by combining text with valid column names inside curly brackets, as shown in Figure 10-7.

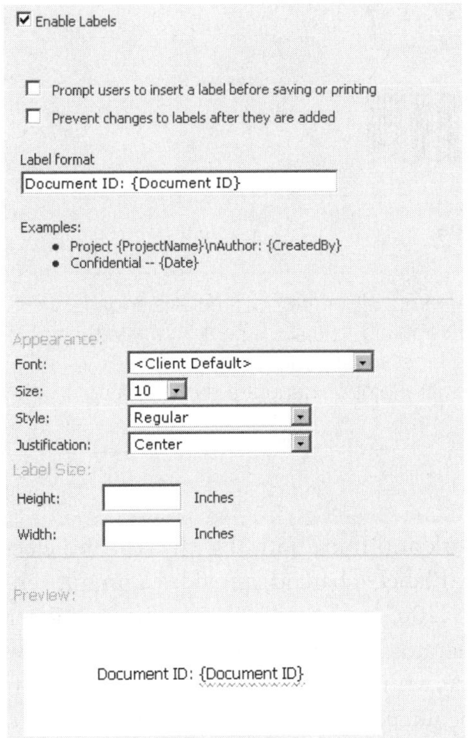

Figure 10-7 The Enable Labels policy feature

In this example, the formula Document ID: {Document ID} generates the label Document ID: IT-05-DOC-001 (as shown in Figure 10-8), where the custom column Document ID holds the value IT-05-DOC-001. When you select the Prompt Users To Insert A Label Before Saving Or Printing option (shown in Figure 10-7), users are given the option to insert the label into the document when they save or print the document. If the label is intended to become a permanent feature of the document, use the Prevent Changes To Labels After They Are Added option (also shown in Figure 10-7) to keep the label from changing in the document. If the label is not inserted into the document, it is still visible from the document properties window when a user selects View Properties from the document drop-down menu in the document library.

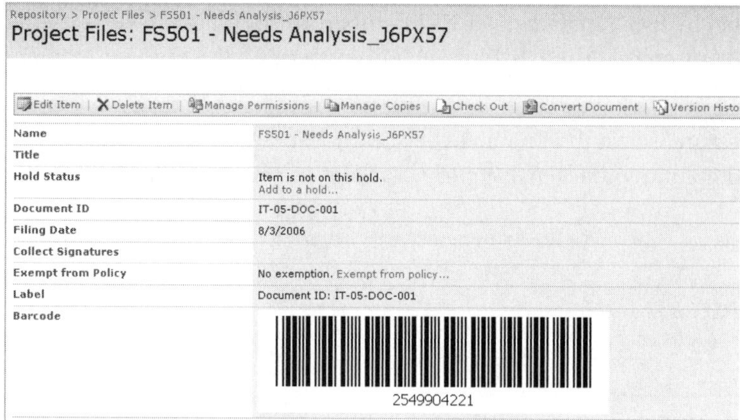

Figure 10-8 Records Center—label and barcode

Important Labels and barcodes are generated when the document is added to the document library. If these policies are applied to a document library with existing documents, they will not display the label or barcode. Making changes to the document or to its properties triggers SharePoint to generate the label and barcode.

Barcoding

The Enable Barcodes feature can help you mark and track both the physical and electronic versions of a document. Instead of a text label, a barcode provides a unique ten-digit identifier generated by SharePoint Server 2007 and rendered as an image. (Refer back to Figure 10-8.) After the barcode is generated, you can view it by selecting View Properties from the document context menu. As with the Enable Labels feature, you can prompt users to insert the barcode into the document when they save or print the document. The barcode component that ships with SharePoint Server 2007 generates barcodes compatible with the "Code 39" barcode symbology (formally known as ANSI/AIM BC1-1995). SharePoint Server 2007 provides an extensible plug-in model for barcode components that can be used to add custom barcode generators.

Best Practices A best practice when using labels and barcodes is to place them in either the header or footer of the document so that they appear on every page and don't cover existing text.

Form Conversion for Archiving

Enable Form Conversion For Archiving is a policy feature that generates an image of a completed form for permanent archiving. This feature is used primarily with InfoPath forms to convert the XML format into a fully rendered document that is no longer dependent on active style sheets or a specific XML parsing engine. To use this policy feature, you must first enable the Document Conversions Launcher Service and the Document Conversions Load Balancer Service. For details on these services, see Chapter 9. When you enable archiving in the policy, you must also select an image format for the output, as shown in Figure 10-9. The format options are PNG, EMF, and TIFF.

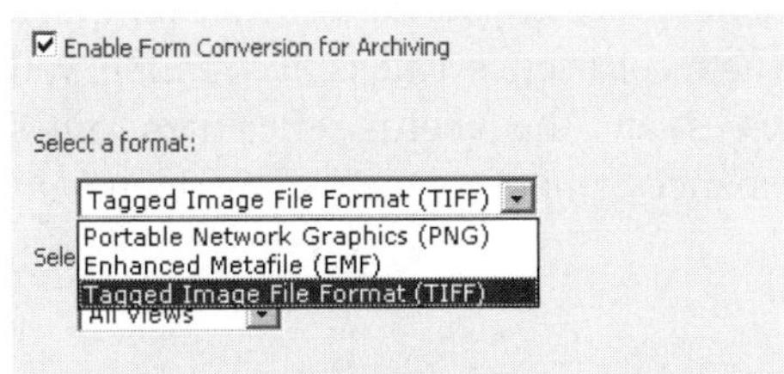

Figure 10-9 The Enable Form Conversion For Archiving policy feature

Configuring the Record Routing Document Library

The Record Routing document library is a special-purpose list in the Records Repository that evaluates every document sent to the site and routes it to the appropriate document library. Each item in the list is called a *record series* and acts as a business rule that evaluates the content type of the document and directs it to a single document library. The record series allows records managers to configure the Records Repository so that records are automatically organized as they are sent to the site. You can make changes to the routing rules and repository structure without needing to make changes to the originating document sites or content types.

When a document arrives in the Records Repository, its content type is matched to the names and aliases defined in the record series entries in the record routing table. Only the content type name is used in this matching, not the name of the file or any other metadata. If no match is found for the content type name, the routing series inspects the inheritance tree of the content type and attempts to find a match with the name of the parent content types of the document. Therefore, you can create record series that target base content types or derived content types of documents, depending on how granular the library structure of your repository is.

To create a new record series, open the Record Routing document library and click New on the menu bar. A new Record Routing page appears, as shown in Figure 10-10. You populate this page with the following information:

- **Title** The record series title matches the name of the content type or any parent content type.
- **Description** This is a short description of the record series entry that appears in the list. It helps records managers document the series.
- **Location** This is the target document library that the document will be routed to. This must be only the relative path name of the library and cannot include the names of folders in the path. For example, if all documents of a given content type will be stored in the Project Files document library, you enter **project files** in the Location text box.
- **Aliases** If you want to use the same record series to route documents of several different content types that aren't related by inheritance, you can list the additional content types as aliases. For example, if the record series Title is Accounting, you can enter **Finance/Billing** into the Aliases list and the records series then routes any documents with a content type of Finance or Billing to the same document library as those of Accounting.

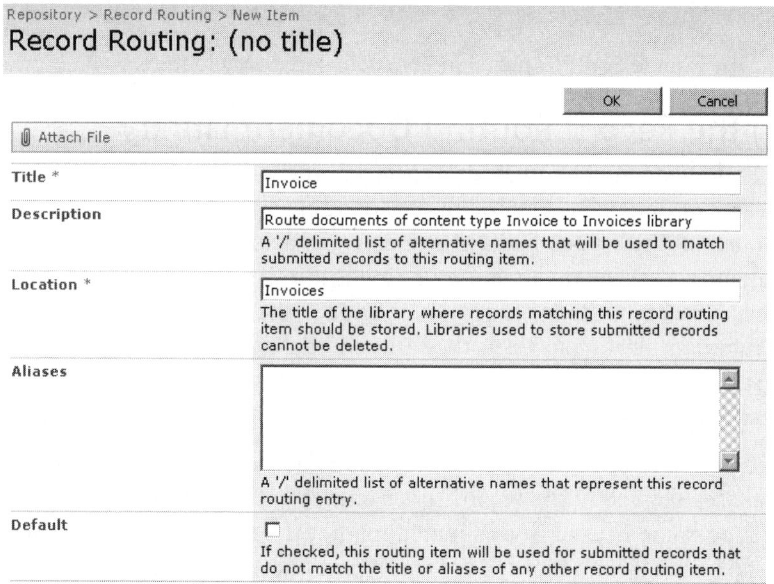

Figure 10-10 New record series

If the content type of the document does not match any record series entry, the document is routed to the library designated by the Default record series. There is always one—and only one—Default record series in the Record Routing list. The Records Center site template includes the Unclassified Records document library and a record series of the same name with its Default set to true.

Managing Documents in the Records Center

One of the most important aspects of a records management system is how easily it allows records managers to identify and mark documents that are required for an investigation, an audit, or litigation that involves the organization. For example, a financial audit might require that all documents pertaining to the financial state of the organization be produced for the past five fiscal years. If the policy applying to those documents set them to expire and be deleted after five years, the documents might start to be purged while the audit is ongoing. This policy would hamper the audit and possibly result in fines and penalties for the organization.

Placing a Hold on Documents

The Records Center site contains a Holds list that is used to place policy locks on sets of documents in the repository, preventing them from expiring or being deleted while on hold. When an item is placed on hold, all automated expiration policies are suspended for that item and users are prevented from deleting the item. Creating a hold involves creating a new item in the Holds list, as shown in Figure 10-11.

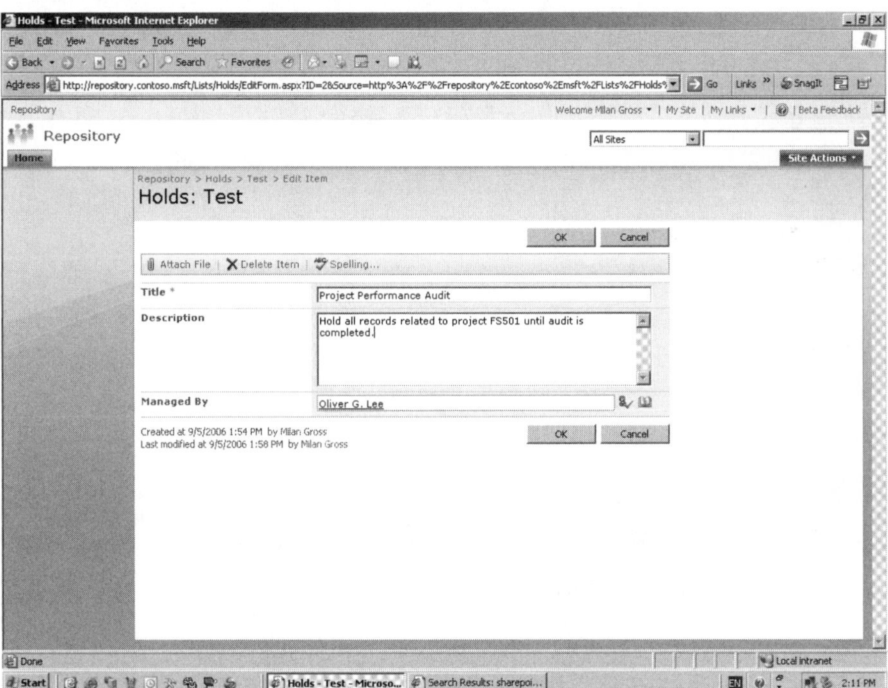

Figure 10-11 Creating a new hold

To create a new hold order, follow these steps:

1. Open the Records Center site.
2. On the quick launch bar on the left, click Holds.
3. Click the New button on the menu.
4. Enter the title and description, which will be used to identify the purpose of the hold. Optionally, in the Managed By section, enter the domain account of the user who is responsible for administering the hold. Click OK.

Note When you create a new hold, it initially has no documents associated with it.

There are two ways you can apply an existing hold to a document. One way is to search for files using the Search For Items To Hold page and assign them all at once to the hold, as shown in Figure 10-12.

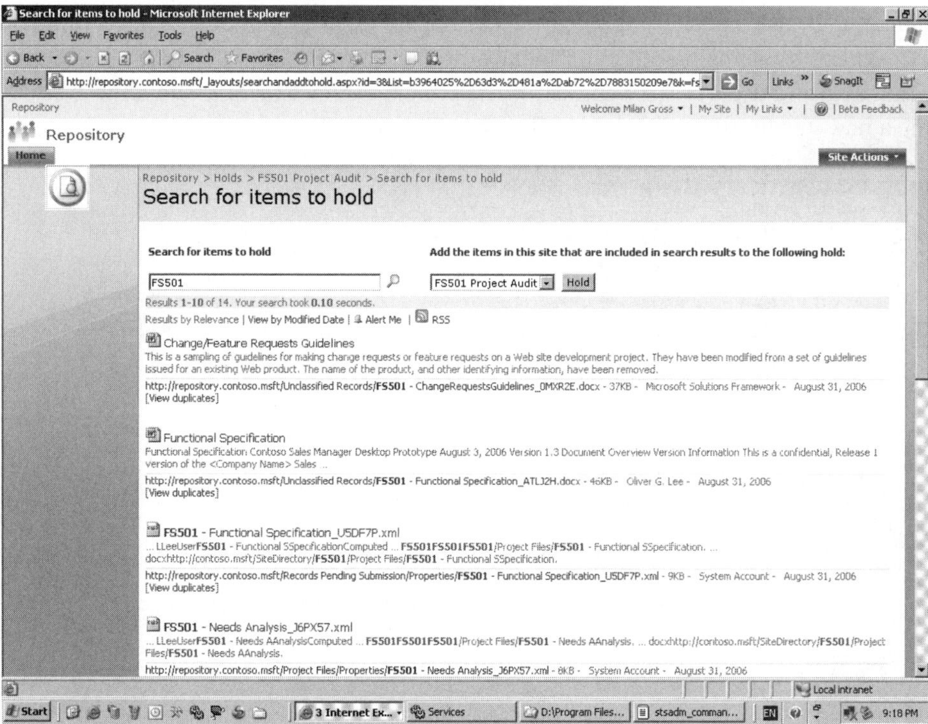

Figure 10-12 Searching for documents to hold

To search for files and assign them all at once, follow these steps:

1. From the Hold list, click Search For Items To Hold.
2. Enter a content keyword in the Search For Items To Hold text box, and then click the magnifying glass.
3. Review the search results to determine whether they correctly match the requirements for inclusion in the hold. If so, select the items to hold from the list on the right and then click the Hold button.

Alternatively, you can add individual documents to the hold one at a time, as shown in Figure 10-13.

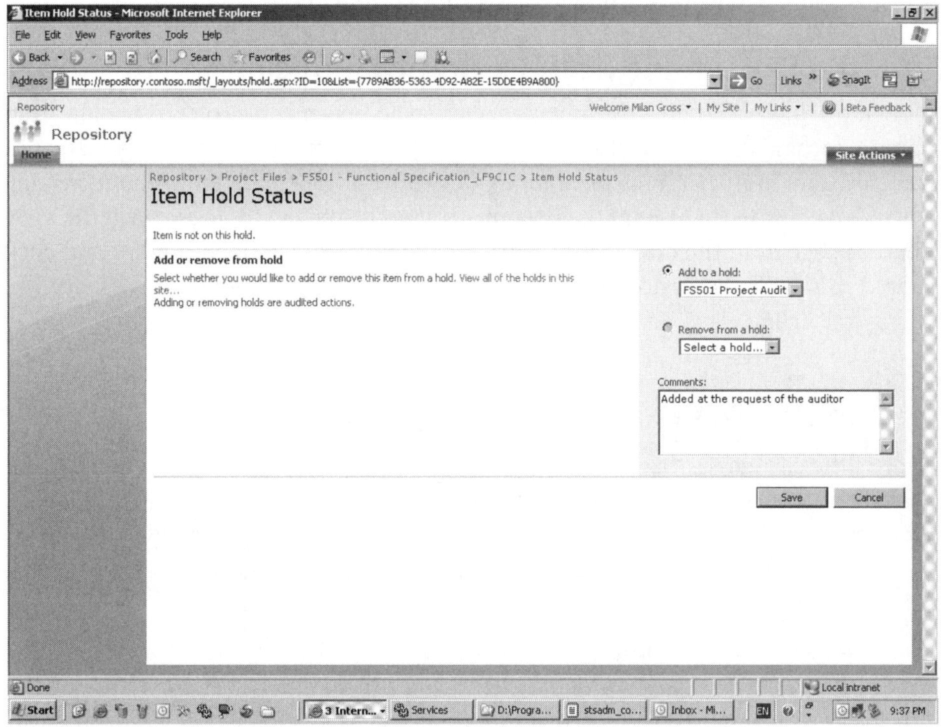

Figure 10-13 Adding individual documents to hold

To do this, follow these steps:

1. Click the drop-down list arrow for the document you want to place on hold, and select Manage Holds.
2. Select the option Add To A Hold, and from the drop-down list below that option, select the hold to associate the document with. Click Save.

Holds cannot be deleted like regular list items can. To delete a hold, SharePoint must guarantee that all documents associated with that hold are first released. Once SharePoint has released all the documents from the hold, it automatically deletes it from the Holds list.

To release a hold, follow these steps:

1. From the Holds list, click the hold you want to delete. This will open the View Properties page.
2. In the Hold Status section, click the Release Hold link.
3. On the Release Hold page, click Release Hold.
4. The hold now displays Pending Release in the Hold Status column.

Exempting a Document from Expiration Policy

Although placing a hold on a document is one way to prevent an expiration policy from purging a document, doing so also prevents users from deleting the document manually. If you only want to suspend the expiration policy on a single document without creating a separate hold, you can exempt the document from the policy. To do so, open the View Properties page from the document's context menu in the document library and click Exempt From Policy. This does not exempt the document from other policies, such as auditing or labeling.

Real World Designing a Records System Taxonomy

One of the challenges that large organizations face is mapping a traditional folder-based file plan to a SharePoint Server 2007 Records Repository implementation. Let's take a look at how we might approach this problem for a company with a file plan that covers over 100 record types that will be used throughout an estimated 300 site collections and in more than 1000 document libraries.

The company has an existing records management model in which files are classified by being placed into a specific folder within a hierarchical directory structure; the folder a document resides in determines its record type. The problem with the company's current system is that the company has no way to search the directory structure for metadata not contained within the document, such as the fiscal year to which the document applies and the client organization to bill the work to. For this purpose, the company has to maintain a separate database that tracks each document and includes metadata about the file.

For its SharePoint Server 2007 deployment, the company applied its folder-based file plan to content types and created a hierarchical classification system, taking advantage of inheritance as shown in Figure 10-14.

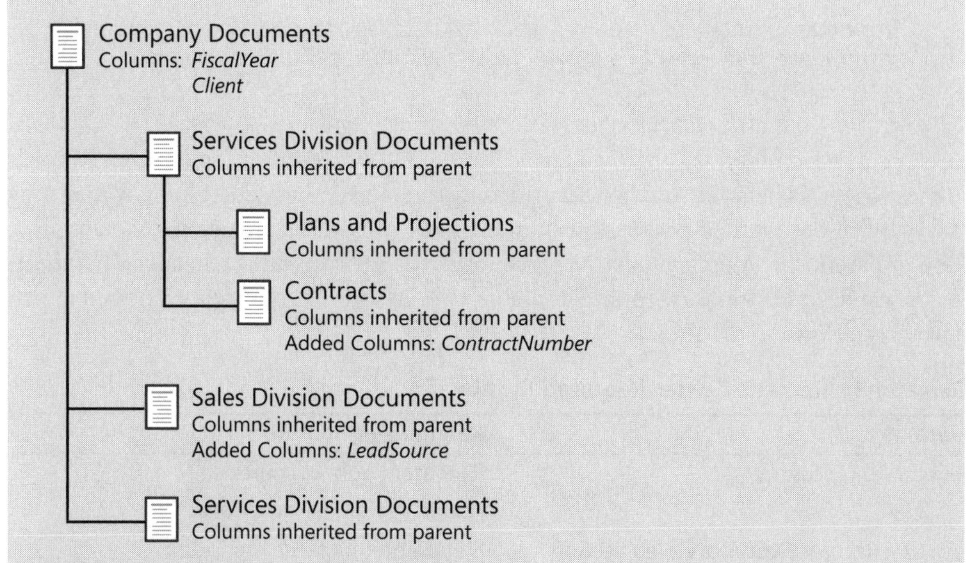

Figure 10-14 Content types taxonomy

The Company Documents content type is the parent type for all other documents in the organization and has two metadata columns in its definition that will be inherited by all child types. Each of the lowest tier documents, such as the ones under the Sales Division, will have customized templates assigned to the content type so that users can create new documents directly from the template and have the content type automatically associated with the file. By deploying the content types to every server as SharePoint Server 2007 features, they will become available in every Web application, and by creating custom site templates for each division, the appropriate content types will be made available in each site and document library.

Configuring Security on the Records Center

The security settings for the Records Center site are even more critical for your enterprise information management environment than security on other SharePoint sites. Once a repository is defined and users begin submitting documents to it, they will expect that those documents are safe, secure, and immutable until the documents expire and are purged. If documents in the repository can be edited or deleted outside of the defined file plan rules, the Records Repository site loses its value as a records store. For this reason, you should design and implement a much stricter set of security settings on the Records Repository site than might be necessary on most SharePoint Server 2007 sites.

Important The Records Center site template does not have a higher intrinsic security level than other SharePoint Server 2007 sites. It is up to you to craft a tight security environment.

It is highly recommended that you create a separate Web application for each Records Repository. This helps ensure that security is maintained at the highest level by removing any implicit or inherited permissions that might be present on an existing Web application or parent site. After creating the repository Web site, you must consider what rights users will need to interact with the site. Table 10-4 lists the various rights required to perform operations on the site.

Table 10-3 Records Center Required Rights

Task	Required right
Submit to repository	Read Item right in source site Add Item right in repository
Call the Records Repository Web Service	Edit Item right in the repository
Manage records	Edit Item right in repository
Create record series entries	Add Item right in Record Routing list
Create holds	Add Item right in Holds list
Manage and release holds	Edit Item right on file that is on hold View Item right on Holds list
View documents in search results	Read Item right in repository

Configuring User and Group Permissions

In most cases, documents will be submitted directly to the Records Repository by users who are responsible for the content of the document. They will use a menu item on the Send To menu (discussed in the "Submitting Content to the Records Center" section) to send a copy of the document through the Records Repository Web Service. The Send To command executes the call to the Web service under the Application Pool Identity account associated with the source site's Web application. This architecture allows users to submit documents without having permissions to add items directly to the Records Repository site. The recommended approach is to grant only the Application Pool domain accounts the right to add items to the repository.

The Records Center site automatically creates the "Records Repository Web Service Submitters for [site name]" user group and gives it permissions to submit records to the site using Web Services. You can use this group to grant limited rights to Application Pool accounts to add documents to the site. Other rights that you will have to assign to users will be Read rights for users who need to search for and retrieve documents from the repository for research or historical review purposes. Records managers in the Records Repository site need to have Edit Item rights to manage the documents that have been submitted and Create Item rights in the Record Routing and Holds lists. In general, a best practice is to set the security level to give most users the correct permissions across the site, and then grant selected users or groups elevated permissions where necessary. You might also need to restrict permissions on some items even further. Although there is no explicit "deny" right at the list level, you can remove specific groups from document libraries that should have restricted access.

Best Practices Configure all users to have Read permissions on the Records Repository for search and retrieval purposes. Configure a smaller group of records managers to have Edit permissions on the Records Repository.

Configuring Policy Settings in Central Administration

In Central Administration, administrators can control the settings that apply to all policies across the server farm. To access these settings, open the Operations page in SharePoint 3.0 Central Administration and click the Information Management Policy Configuration link under Security Configuration. For each of the policy features (Labels, Auditing, Expiration, Forms Conversion For Archiving, and Barcodes), the administrator has the option to make the policy available (the default setting) or to deactivate it for all future uses of the policy. To disable the policy, the administrator can select the Decommissioned option, which leaves the policy feature available for any sites that currently use the policy but prevents any new uses of the policy. Decommissioning a policy actually removes the policy setting from the Edit Policy page for any newly defined information management policies.

From the Central Administration page, you can configure the schedule on which Expiration policies are processed and force the processing of expiration policies. The default schedule for expiration processing is once every 24 hours, starting at 11:00 PM, as shown in Figure 10-15. Because expiration processing places additional load on the server, you should change the start and end times so that they do not overlap with data-backup or content-indexing operations. In cases where it is not mission-critical that documents be purged immediately, and where it is difficult to schedule a daily time slot for the processing, you can configure the processing to run on a weekly or even a monthly basis. SharePoint Server 2007 will process all documents that have expired since the last processing run. Be sure to allow the server a longer period of time between the start and end times so that it can complete the processing of all documents marked to expire.

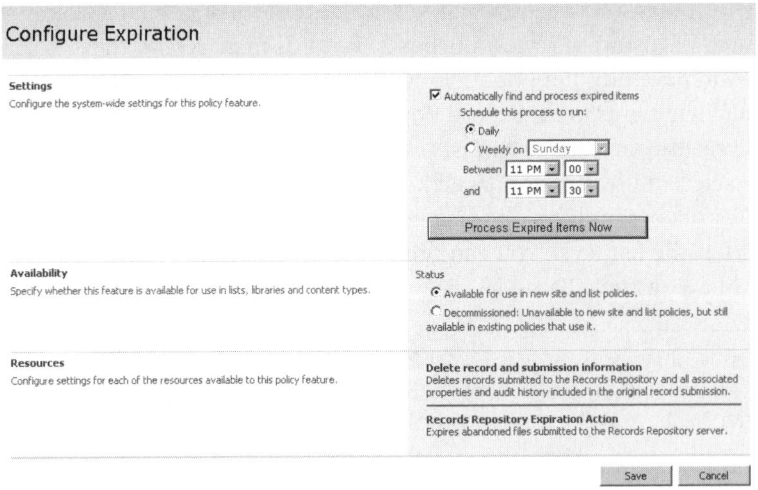

Figure 10-15 Configuring the expiration policy

The other policy that allows for additional customization is the barcodes policy. If you have installed one or more custom barcode generators, you can choose one in Central Administration using the Barcode Style list. By default, only one style is available, which is the ANSI/AIM BC1-1995 (Code 39) style. For the default style, you can also choose whether the barcode should be generated with only numbers (0 through 9) or with both numbers and letters (A through Z). The 10-digit format used by SharePoint Server 2007 for generating barcodes results in 10 billion combinations when using the numeric-only format. Normally that would be enough, but for greater randomness and variation, the alphanumeric format provides 4.8 quadrillion possible values.

Creating Policy Templates

As you have seen so far, an information management policy is a set of rules that can be applied to a document library to govern data auditing, retention, and disposal. If your repository has only a few document libraries, it is generally not a problem to configure each library with its own unique set of policies. If, on the other hand, you need to configure dozens or hundreds of document libraries in the Records Repository, it is more practical to create policy templates with common settings and apply them to multiple document libraries. Policy templates are created at the site-collection level and can be used on any list in the site collection.

To create a site collection policy, follow these steps:

1. From the Site Actions menu in the top-level site, select Site Settings.

2. Under Site Collection Administration, click Site Collection Policies.
3. Click Create, and define the policy settings. Then click OK to create the policy.

To apply a site collection policy, follow these steps:

1. Browse to the document library where you will apply the site collection policy.
2. From the Settings menu, select Document Library Settings.
3. Under Permissions And Policies, click Information Management Policy Settings.
4. Click the Use A Site Collection Policy option, and select the policy to use from the drop-down list, as shown in Figure 10-16. Click OK.

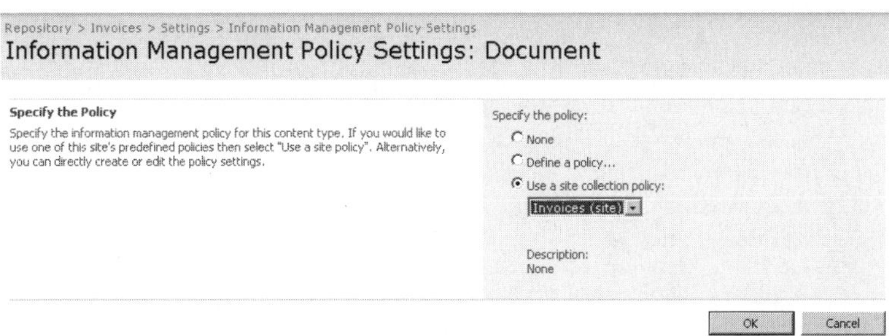

Figure 10-16 Assigning a site collection policy

Submitting Content to the Records Center

You can provide users with several ways to submit their documents to the Records Repository. The most common technique used to submit files to the Records Repository uses the Send To menu on the document context menu to provide a custom menu item, which will call the Records Repository Web Service and pass to it the binary version of the file along with metadata and audit history. For each Web application in your SharePoint Server 2007 environment, you can configure only one record repository Send To menu command. This menu command will appear in all document libraries in all sites within the Web application. The Send To command is available to all users who have Read rights on the document being submitted to the Records Repository.

To configure the Send To command, follow these steps:

1. Open SharePoint 3.0 Central Administration, and click Application Management.
2. On the Application Management page, under External Service Connections, click Records Center.

3. Select the Connect To A Records Center option, and configure the URL to contain the address of the Records Repository site followed by /_vti_bin/officialfile.asmx. For example, the URL entered for the Contoso Records Repository would be http://repository.contoso.msft/_vti_bin/officialfile.asmx.
4. Enter a Display Name, which will appear for this link.

A new menu command will now appear under the Send To context menu of every document in every site in the Web application, as shown in Figure 10-17. The menu will show the Display Name you entered and will initiate the submission to the Records Repository. When a user clicks this menu command, the Records Repository Web Service is invoked to send a copy of the file to the repository, where it will be routed to a document library based on the Record Routing list rules.

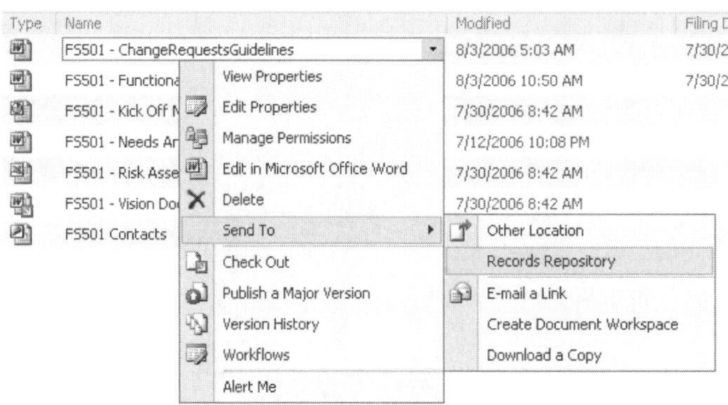

Figure 10-17 Records Submission—Send To menu

SharePoint Server 2007 is optimized for accommodating large volumes of documents submitted to the Records Repository. To facilitate this, SharePoint Server 2007 automatically generates folders within each document library in the Records Center to store the submitted files. The names of the folders are randomized to ensure uniqueness and new folders are created on an as-needed basis. The process of folder creation is built into the records submission feature of the Records Center and cannot be configured or customized.

The first time you send a file to a document library in the repository, SharePoint Server 2007 creates two folders in the library: Audit History and Properties. When a document is submitted to the repository, any audit information and metadata values are packaged by SharePoint into XML files and submitted along with the document. The audit information XML file is stored in the Audit History folder, and the metadata XML file is stored in the Properties folder. Although the properties are transferred along with the file, they will be merged into the metadata in the document library itself only if a corresponding column is created on the library to hold the value.

Submitting Content from Microsoft Exchange and Outlook

Using Microsoft Office Outlook 2007, users can submit e-mail messages as files to the Records Repository to store them as records. Administrators need to configure the Outlook 2007 client by assigning the location of the Records Repository to the user through an Active Directory Group Policy setting. The approach used with file submissions for routing documents to document libraries will not work with e-mail because messages do not support content types. Rather than submitting the e-mail messages to the Records Repository for routing, users can drag and drop e-mail directly into folders that represent each of the destination document libraries in the Records Repository site. Outlook 2007 calls the Records Repository Web Service and passes it the document file as data in the same way as a SharePoint site calling the Web service. When there are additional columns of metadata required by a document library in the Records Center, Outlook 2007 displays a page on which the user can fill in the information for the record.

The structure of the registry key that will be configured is as follows:

HKCU\Software\Microsoft\Office\12\Outlook\Official File Folders\[folder display name]

String Value: SendToURL : [URL]

String Value: DocLibURL: [target document library]

Submitting Content Using Managed Mail Folders

Exchange 2007 introduces a new feature called Managed Email Folders that allows it to work directly with SharePoint Server 2007 to enhance its records-management capabilities. In Exchange 2007, administrators can configure an Exchange folder to support policies that are similar to those in SharePoint Server 2007, such as content expiration or automatically forwarding a copy of an e-mail message to a SharePoint site through Simple Mail Transfer Protocol (SMTP). To users, the managed e-mail folder appears as a folder in Outlook that they can drag e-mail into to submit to a remote site. Alternatively, administrators can configure the managed folder to automatically move messages into folders based on their subject line, for instance.

Submitting Content Automatically Through Custom Workflow

An ideal method for submitting content to a Records Repository would be through a Workflow action. Unfortunately, SharePoint does not provide an out-of-the-box record submission worklflow. The solution is to write a custom workflow action using Microsoft Visual Studio 2005 and install it on the server running SharePoint Server 2007 and to use SharePoint Designer 2007 to configure the action as part of a workflow. A custom workflow can be created to automatically copy a file to the Records Repository. The submission could be based on the status of the document to be submitted as the final step in a series of review and approval operations. The workflow could also be based on the expiration of a document in the originating document library. For example, a policy could be defined with an expiration set to 10 days after the document is created. The expiration action could then be set to copy the document to the Records Repository and delete it from the current site. For more information on creating and using custom workflow actions, see Chapter 28: "Implementing Microsoft Windows Workflow Services."

Submitting Content Programmatically Using the Records Repository Web Service

SharePoint Server 2007 is designed to provide an extensible, programmable interface to records submission that supports both built-in and custom approaches to records management. The Records Repository Web Service is exposed by SharePoint Server 2007 to allow developers to integrate file transfer into a Records Repository from any external application or file store. The Records Repository Web Service provides methods to submit a file as a record along with two additional XML files containing the metadata and audit history associated with the file. Through this Web service, files can be sent to a SharePoint Server 2007 Records Center from any document management system. The Web service has been designed as an open and generic interface that can accept input from any source that can communicate through the Simple Object Access Protocol (SOAP) and Web Services Description Language (WSDL) protocols.

As an example of how this service could be used, consider the challenge of importing a large number of files from a file server into a SharePoint Server 2007 Records Repository. Although you saw in Chapter 9 that copying large numbers of files into a site is generally not a problem through a WebDAV connection, this drag-and-drop approach does not help us organize the files in the repository. The challenge is to examine the folder names that the files are stored under, map these to the document library storage locations in the Records Repository, and transfer the file directly to the correct target library. A potential solution to this problem is to create a Windows application to scan and iterate through every document in the shared folder on the file server and construct an XML file with any values for required columns on the target document library. The application would then call the Records Repository Web Service to transfer each file into the repository along with its metadata. Table 10-5 lists the methods of the Records Repository Web Service.

Table 10-4 Records Repository Web Service Methods

Method	Description
SubmitFile	Submits a file as a given record routing type, along with its metadata and, optionally, its audit history
GetRecordSeriesCollection	Obtains the properties of all record routing types for a Records Repository, as well as the metadata schema for each

Table 10-4 Records Repository Web Service Methods

Method	Description
GetRecordSeries	Gets the properties of a given record routing type, as well as its metadata schema
GetServer	Gets information on an implementation of the Records Repository

Configuring Document Retention and Disposal

When you create an expiration policy to apply to documents, you must choose what action SharePoint will take when the expiration date is reached. One of the options available is Delete, which moves the document to the Recycle Bin as a normal user delete action would. However, this option hides the file so that it is not visible to users. Administrators will still see the file listed in the Site Collection Recycle Bin and can restore it from there. When an expired file is restored, it is automatically marked as exempt from expiration policies to prevent it from being deleted again. Once the exemption is removed, it is once again subject to the expiration policy and will be deleted during the next expiration processing.

Although this option provides a safety net for documents that have been configured to expire, it might not meet the requirements of some regulations that specify that the content must be immediately and irretrievably purged from the online system. For this purpose, you can choose the Delete Record And Submission Information option, which deletes the document from the site and purges it from all recycle bins. This is a permanent delete action and cannot be undone.

Using the Disposition Approval Workflow

In many cases, your objective will be to permanently delete files that have expired, but records managers might be concerned about the unmonitored deletion of files. To alleviate this problem, you can configure the expiration policy with the option to start a workflow to invoke approval for the deletion instead of deleting the file directly. When a Disposition Approval workflow is used, the document is placed in an In Progress status when it expires and is held until a records manager reviews the event. The records manager can either confirm the deletion, at which point the document is permanently removed from the system, or elect to keep the file, at which point the document is marked as exempt from expiration policies.

To use the disposition approval workflow, begin by creating an instance of it as follows:

1. Browse to the document library where the expiration policy is applied.

2. Select Document Library Settings from the Settings menu, and click Workflow Settings.
3. Click Add A Workflow, and the Add A Workflow page appears, as shown in Figure 10-18.

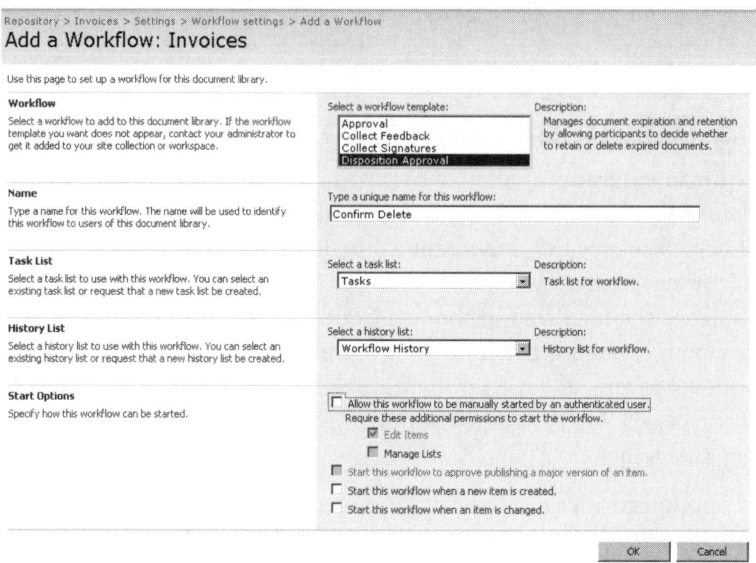

Figure 10-18 New disposition approval workflow

4. In the Select A Workflow Template list, select the Disposition Approval workflow template. In the Type A Unique Name For This Workflow text box, enter a unique name for the workflow. It is also a good idea to clear the Allow This Workflow To Be Manually Started By An Authenticated User option because it should be managed only by expiration policies. Click OK.
5. Click the Settings link to return to the Site Settings page.
6. Click Information Management Policy Settings, and then click Define Policy.
7. Under Expiration, select the Start This Workflow option and select the new workflow you just created. Click OK.

Configuring Information Management Policy Reporting

To determine whether your records management solution is actually meeting the requirements defined in your file plan, you want to monitor the operations in the Records Repository. SharePoint Server 2007 includes extensive auditing and reporting tools for tracking the documents submitted to the repository as well as the actions taken on the documents after they are copied. A critical question that records managers must answer is what number of documents are being sent to each document library through the automatic routing of records that reside in the repository. The Auditing Log Reports help you to determine whether the record series entries are correctly recognizing all the content types and whether users are correctly applying content types to the source documents. If you discover that too many documents are being routed to the Unclassified Documents folder, some content types might not be getting assigned to record series entries or users might not be applying the correct content types before submitting documents to the repository.

Administrators and records managers will also want to review how many policies are in place in a Web application and how many documents are affected by them. This information can help administrators identify which sites are using policies and which are not. It might also help compliance officers determine how effectively the compliance guidelines that have been formulated into the file plan are being implemented. For example, if it becomes apparent that no policies are being applied to a particular document library in the repository, data in that library might not be getting purged in a timely manner. This reporting feature is available in the Information Management Policy Usage reports feature of Central Administration, which is discussed later in this chapter in the "Information Management Policy Usage Reporting" section.

Configuring Audit Log Reports

SharePoint Server 2007 provides reports at the site-collection level that allow administrators to view the detailed activity results from auditing policies active within the site collection. To access these reports, open Site Settings for the top-level site in the site collection and click Audit Log Reports under Site Collection Administration. The reports are grouped into four sections, as shown in Figure 10-19.

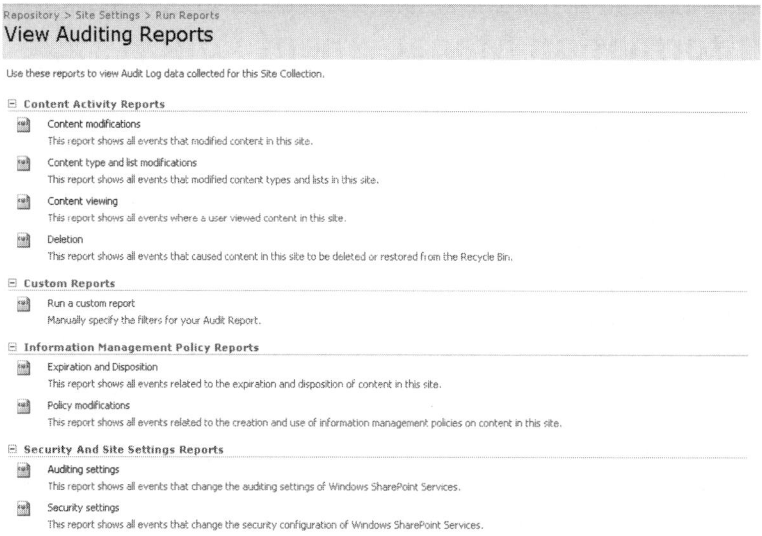

Repository > Site Settings > Run Reports

View Auditing Reports

Use these reports to view Audit Log data collected for this Site Collection.

Content Activity Reports

Content modifications
This report shows all events that modified content in this site.

Content type and list modifications
This report shows all events that modified content types and lists in this site.

Content viewing
This report shows all events where a user viewed content in this site.

Deletion
This report shows all events that caused content in this site to be deleted or restored from the Recycle Bin.

Custom Reports

Run a custom report
Manually specify the filters for your Audit Report.

Information Management Policy Reports

Expiration and Disposition
This report shows all events related to the expiration and disposition of content in this site.

Policy modifications
This report shows all events related to the creation and use of information management policies on content in this site.

Security And Site Settings Reports

Auditing settings
This report shows all events that change the auditing settings of Windows SharePoint Services.

Security settings
This report shows all events that change the security configuration of Windows SharePoint Services.

Figure 10-19 View Auditing Reports page

The Content Activity Reports and Information Management Policy Reports sections display information gathered as a result of Audit Policy settings applied to content types, document libraries, or the entire site collection. The Security And Site Settings Reports section shows data on changes to auditing policies and security settings throughout the site collections. The tracking of auditing policies and security settings is automatically enabled in SharePoint so that these reports can be run regardless of any other auditing that is turned on. The other report type is the Custom Report, which allows you to define a report that can be limited to a single list in a site, filtered by a date range, or restricted to the activities of a single user. This type of report also allows you to choose which of the auditing events monitored by SharePoint Server 2007 to include in the report. Certain audited events, such as searching site content, workflow events, and custom events can be viewed only through the custom report.

Configuring Site Collection Auditing

In addition to defining audit policies at the document-library level as we have discussed so far, you can also enable audit policies for all sites within a site collection. To access the site collection auditing page, open the Site Settings page for the top-level site in the collection and click Site Collection Audit Settings under Site Collection Administration. The first set of auditing options, under Documents And Items, shown in Figure 10-20, are the same as the options available within Information Management Policies. The second set of options under Lists, Libraries, And Sites are available only within the site collection auditing settings and include Editing Content Types And Columns, Searching Site Content, and Editing Users And Permissions.

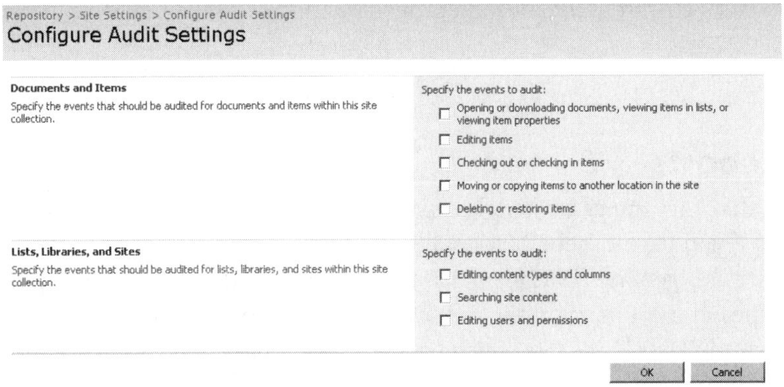

Repository > Site Settings > Configure Audit Settings

Configure Audit Settings

Documents and Items

Specify the events that should be audited for documents and items within this site collection.

Specify the events to audit:

- Opening or downloading documents, viewing items in lists, or viewing item properties
- Editing items
- Checking out or checking in items
- Moving or copying items to another location in the site
- Deleting or restoring items

Lists, Libraries, and Sites

Specify the events that should be audited for lists, libraries, and sites within this site collection.

Specify the events to audit:

- Editing content types and columns
- Searching site content
- Editing users and permissions

OK Cancel

Figure 10-20 Configuring audit settings

Note Processing audit data for the events across the entire site collection can add to the process overhead on the Web server and might affect performance. If you plan to implement site-collection monitoring throughout your SharePoint sites, you should factor the performance penalty into your hardware scaling estimates.

Configuring Information Management Policy Usage Reporting

To obtain information on which policies are being applied throughout your organization, you can configure Information Management Policy Usage reporting to generate periodic reports on policy behavior. These reports are generated as XML files that render as reports in Excel 2007 or that can be downloaded to a separate application for further extraction and processing. Policy usage reporting is enabled in Central Administration and generates separate files for each site collection in the selected SharePoint Server 2007 Web application. The reports are generated and placed in a designated SharePoint Server 2007 site location such as a document library. Policy usage reports can also be generated using an alternate report template that must be available through a URL that you provide.

To enable Information Management Policy Usage Reporting, follow these steps:

1. Browse to the Operations tab in SharePoint 3.0 Central Administration.
2. Under Logging And Reporting, click Information Management Policy Usage Reports.
3. If you want to generate schedule reports, select the box to enable recurring reports and specify the report schedule.
4. In the Report File Location text box, type the relative URL address for the document library where the reports will be placed. For example, if the reports will appear in a document library called Policy Reports in a top-level site in the site collection, you enter **/Policy Reports**.

5. If you want to use a custom template, enter the URL address to the template in the Report Template box.

You can also click Create Reports Now to generate a one-time report.

Viewing Policy Reports

To view the reports after they are generated, browse to the library location you provided and click the report. If you have Excel 2007 installed, it should open in that application or else in the browser as a generic XML file. Each report contains different information depending on the type of report that you are viewing. Audit Log reports generally contain two tabs of data: the Audit Data-Table tab, which provides a summary of the total number of events tracked for each list or document library in the report, and the Report Data tab, which lists each individual event including the date and time, the list it occurred in, and the user who performed the action. Information Policy Usage reports generally have four tabs: the Introduction tab, which lists the site collection the report is for and the date it was generated; the Report PivotTable tab, which provides a summary of the number of items in each site and list that are subject to each policy; the Policies tab, which lists each policy by name; and the Usage tab, which provides detailed data on the lists in each site as well as the number and percentage of items in each list.

Summary

In this chapter, you examined the new records management features SharePoint Server 2007 offers to organizations that have legal or regulatory compliance requirements. The chapter began by discussing the concept of document management from a high-level view and emphasizing how critical a document management plan is for organizations that deal with large numbers of electronic documents. You reviewed the major elements of a document management plan, including defining the key roles in the organization, defining compliance requirements, and writing a file plan. You then looked at the process of implementing the file plan in SharePoint Server 2007, beginning with the creation of content types and a Records Center site. You learned how to configure policies on the documents in the Records Repository and how to create and release holds in response to regulatory or legal needs.

You then considered the issue of security in the Records Repository site and the importance of defining a more restrictive set of permissions than in most other sites. You took a look at the steps required to enable users to send documents to the Records Repository directly from other sites and through Outlook 2007. You then considered the different mechanisms for deleting documents when they had reached their expiration date and how to retain them if it became necessary to do so. Finally, you looked at the various reporting options available in SharePoint Server 2007 for viewing audit logs and policy usage patterns.

Chapter 11

Web Content Management and Publishing Features

Chapter 1, "Introducing Microsoft Office SharePoint Server 2007," briefly mentioned that Microsoft Office SharePoint Server 2007 includes a new set of publishing features and controls that enable site owners to host content-centric sites on the SharePoint platform. These capabilities were adopted from another Microsoft product: Microsoft Content Management Server 2002 (CMS). Microsoft has decided to not continue evolving CMS as a separate product; instead, it has incorporated the rich content authoring experience, site branding, and publishing controls as Web Content Management (WCM), which is included in Office SharePoint Server 2007. WCM, along with records management, document management, and policy management, make up what Microsoft refers to as Enterprise Content Management (ECM), which is part of SharePoint Server 2007.

Managing a content-centric Web site can be a daunting task for an organization. Typically, the only people who have the rights to make changes to a company Web site are the IT staff of Web developers. Content owners send their updates to the Web developers, who then incorporate them into the company Web site, formatting the updates to match the site's navigation tools, organization, look and feel, and standards.

This process can result in bottlenecks because everything must route through the IT staff. Most likely, the IT staff isn't just managing the company Web site, but instead they are tied up with other projects. WCM addresses this problem by providing a platform that gives site developers and designers the capability to define the branding, look and feel, and organization with templates, as well as establish publishing rules within the site.

Content owners can then make their changes directly in pages based on the templates within specific areas the development team has carved out to allow for content. After content owners save their changes, the page can initiate workflows that follow the company Web site publishing guidelines, such as getting approval from the legal department before posting new content. After the page progresses through all the necessary workflows, it is published and made available on a public version of the Web site.

A site that uses the WCM features is called a *publishing site*. A publishing site is typically a SharePoint site, but it is one that has had the Publishing feature activated.

Understanding Web Content Management Sites

The SharePoint products and technologies are primarily positioned to be a collaboration platform. However, Internet-facing, content-centric sites are not typically collaborative; rather, they are usually static and provide a read-only view of the content to site visitors. This read-only experience is an obvious difference from how a typical SharePoint site is intended to be used. The addition of WCM solves this problem because it leverages all the capabilities that SharePoint Server 2007 has to offer while implementing a different experience for content consumers of the site. And it does all this while providing a rich and robust platform for content owners to manage the site.

> **Note** Because a publishing site is just another type of SharePoint site, this chapter will focus only on the publishing aspects of a publishing site. For example, management of permissions, site creation rights, themes, and features are not covered in this chapter because these topics are general topics that are covered in other chapters.

Because WCM is part of SharePoint Server 2007, which is built on top of Microsoft Windows SharePoint Services 3.0, publishing sites have access to all the native features that Windows SharePoint Services and SharePoint Server 2007 provide. These features include lists, the Recycle Bin, integrated workflow, integrated enterprise search, Real Simple Syndication (RSS) feeds, the Web Part framework, pluggable authentication, alerts, versioning, content deployment, audience targeting, and more. In addition to supporting all these features, WCM extends SharePoint Server 2007 by adding a rich Web-based authoring experience for site content owners, as well as extensive hooks into the 2007 Microsoft Office system for an even more robust authoring solution that leverages Microsoft Office Word 2007 and InfoPath 2007.

WCM adds a few additional default security groups that apply directly to managing a content-centric site. For site developers and designers, WCM adds a template mechanism that enables developers to specify a set of templates that content owners can use when creating new pages. These templates are used to enforce the common look and feel of a site, as well as the company branding and navigation tools. Finally, many companies also need to publish their sites for multiple devices (Web browsers, phones, and so on) and in multiple languages. To address these needs, WCM includes a feature called *variations*, which helps you manage separate versions of your site. Let's take look at each of these areas in more detail.

New Permission Levels and Security Groups

SharePoint Server 2007 includes five default permission levels (Full Control, Design, Contribute, Read, and Limited Access) and three default permission groups (Members, Owners, and Visitors) with all sites. The Publishing feature builds on this list by adding four new permission levels and five SharePoint groups. A *permission level* groups granular permission settings into a manageable collection that can be assigned a name and description. These levels are then used by permission groups to assign rights to users (who are members of the group). (Refer to the section "Assigning Security Groups and Permission Levels" later in this chapter for more information.) These additions give site administrators and owners more granular control of delegating capabilities and responsibilities over their content-centric sites than the permission levels and groups built into SharePoint Server offer.

Separating Content and Presentation

In a content-centric site, it's very important to have a clear separation of the presentation and branding code that implements the global look and feel of the site from the actual site content. This separation not only facilitates the easy and rapid creation of new content, but it also makes the process of rebranding an entire site much easier. The SharePoint Publishing feature fully supports this process of keeping the look and feel of the site separate from the content.

Site branding and design is implemented using ASP.NET 2.0 master pages and page layouts (ASPX pages). The *master page* is used to define the elements that make up the common branding of a site, such as the header, footer, and navigation tools. *Page layouts* are used to define the arrangement of the main content part of the page; a page layout is the template for a content page. When combined at runtime, the master page and the page layouts define the look and feel of the requested page.

This combination is managed by the site developers and designers; they will build and provide the various page layouts that content owners can pick from when creating new pages. Page layouts must conform to a content type that derives from the Page content type. The Page content type contains columns such as the name, title, and description of the page, as well as publishing schedule and contact information. Designers designate specific parts of the page layout files as locations where content owners can add and edit content. Each part of a page that contains the editable content is called a *field control*. Each of these fields is associated with a column defined in the content type the page layout is based on.

More Info For detailed information on content types, please see Chapter 15, "Managing Content Types."

When a new page is created on the site, the page's content and properties are stored as a new list item within a special SharePoint document library named Pages. When a site collection has the Publishing feature activated, all sites within the collection will have their own Pages document library. Administrators can control who has rights to create and edit pages by managing the permissions on the Pages document library. Because a publishing site usually consists of many sites within a site collection, each site can have unique permissions (or inherit permissions from its parent site), allowing administrators to delegate the content ownership and management to one team for one site while having a completely different permission structure for another site within the collection.

Using Variations

Many organizations don't want to limit use of their content-centric sites to only users with the most common Web browsers. However, creating separate versions of their content for each type of Web browser can be very challenging, as everything must stay synchronized. This is also true for organizations who want to publish their Web site in multiple languages. The Publishing feature solves these problems by introducing a new concept called variations. *Variations* allow administrators to define multiple versions of a site. SharePoint Server 2007 handles most of the work of keeping the variations of a site synchronized, although some manual tasks will likely be involved, such as translating content from one language to another. Variations will be discussed in greater detail later in this chapter.

Administering Web Content Management Sites

A publishing site is just another type of SharePoint site. Because of this, most common tasks associated with managing a publishing site are identical to those of managing a typical SharePoint site. However, some key differences and additions should be addressed. Take a look at these publishing-specific administrative tasks:

- Creating publishing sites
- Configuring the Welcome page

- Configuring master page settings
- Managing the Master Page And Page Layout Gallery
- Managing site content and structure
- Configuring navigation settings
- Assigning security groups and permission levels

Creating Publishing Sites

To enable the Publishing feature on a SharePoint site, you can either create a new site and pick one of the publishing site templates (as shown in Figure 11-1) or activate the Publishing feature from the Site Collection Features page, which is available from any site's Site Settings page. In fact, creating a site using one of the publishing site templates automatically activates the Publishing feature.

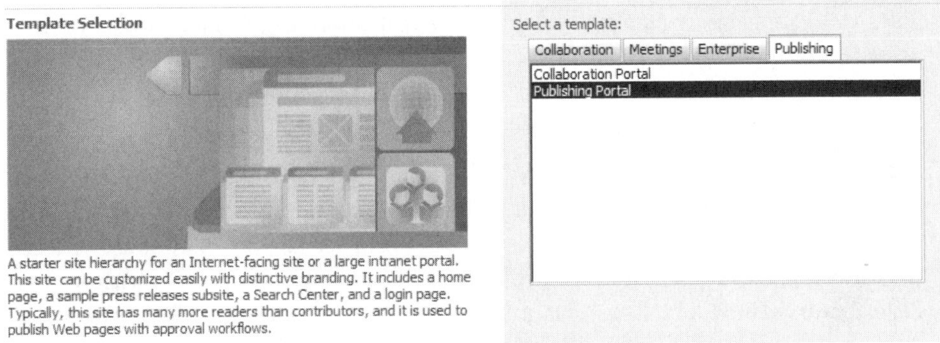

Figure 11-1 Site template picker on the Template Selection page

Configuring the Welcome Page

When you navigate to a site without requesting a particular page, the Publishing feature automatically redirects you to a specific page designated as the Welcome page. A site's Welcome page can be any page or document within the site or any document within the site collection.

To select or change the Welcome page, follow these steps:

1. Click the Site Actions menu, select Site Settings, and then click Modify All Site Settings.
2. On the Site Settings page, in the Look And Feel column, click the Welcome Page link.

3. Click the Browse button, and select a page or document from the current site, or select a document from the site collection using the Select A Link dialog box. Click OK.
4. To save your changes, click OK on the page named Site Welcome Page.

When you navigate to a site and request a particular page, SharePoint finds the page list item in the appropriate site's Pages library. This list item contains the page layout ASPX file that will be used to render the page. The page layout ASPX page is then combined with the site's master page, and the data within the list item is inserted into the field controls that have been specified in the page's content type and placed in specific locations within the page layout ASPX page.

The Structure of a Publishing Site

As with other SharePoint sites, all content within a publishing site is contained within a site collection. (Refer to Chapter 7, "Application Management and Configuration," for more information on site collections.) This content includes not only the master pages and page layouts that define the site branding as well as the pages, but also all the images, styles, and documents referenced within the page.

Subsections of a site–such as sections typically named About Us, Products, or News–are organized into separate publishing sites that are subsites to the root site in the site collection. Each of these sites has its own Pages document library where the actual page content is stored. Each page is represented as a list item within the Pages library. This hierarchical relationship between the site collection, sites, and Pages document library is illustrated in Figure 11-2.

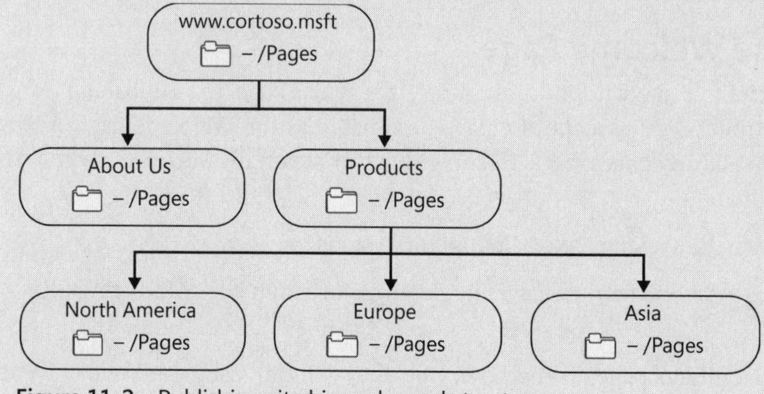

Figure 11-2 Publishing site hierarchy and structure

Page designers and developers carve out specific areas within a page layout (the ASPX file that's used to implement a template design of the site to enforce a common look and feel) by using field controls. Each field control is mapped to a column within the Pages document library within each site. The mapping is enforced using content types in the following manner:

- A content type that inherits from the root Page content type (installed when the Publishing feature is activated) is associated with the Pages document library.
- When creating a new page layout, you specify which content type it will be associated with.

One side benefit to the requirement of associating a page layout with a content type is that you can then build and design multiple page layouts that are all associated with the same content type. After a page has been created, the content owners can change the page layout that the page is associated with as long as it's of the same content type. Using this mechanism, site designers and developers can provide multiple rendering options to the content owners, allowing them to select which one best suits their needs.

Configuring Master Page Settings

When developers and designers build page layouts, they aren't given the option to specify the master page the ASPX file will use when it's rendered. This is because the master page is set at a site level and not at the individual page-layout level. You can configure all sites within your site collection to use the same master page as the top-level site, or you can optionally configure them to use a specific master page.

To change the master page used by all pages in a site, follow these steps:

1. Click the Site Actions menu, select Site Settings, and then select Modify All Site Settings.
2. On the Site Settings page, in the Look And Feel column, click the Master Page link.
3. In the first section Site Master Page, you'll see that you can either inherit the master page settings from the site's parent site, or you can select a specific master page.

   Note Below the master page preview image, you can optionally select a box to reset all subsites to inherit the change. Each of the sections on this page has this capability.

4. In the second section, System Master Page, you can select a different master page that will be used in all view and form pages within the site.

5. Once you've made the desired changes, click OK at the bottom of the page.

Managing the Master Page And Page Layout Gallery

Page layouts and master pages are stored in the Master Page And Page Layout Gallery in the top-level site of the Publishing site collection. (Note that this gallery appears simply as "Master Page Gallery" on many of the user-interface screens in SharePoint and that's the term we'll use most often in this chapter.) The Master Page Gallery is just a SharePoint document library, so you can use all the features available to libraries, such as versioning, workflow, approval, alerts, and managing permissions. To control who has access to create and edit a master pages and page layouts, edit the permissions on this document library just as you would for any other list. By default, the Publishing groups Approvers and Hierarchy Managers have Read permissions to this list, while the Designers group has Design permissions.

There are two ways to access the Master Page Gallery through the browser user interface (UI):

- Use the Site Actions menu. From the Site Actions menu select Manage Content And Structure. When the Site Content And Structure page loads, select the Master Page Gallery from the tree on the left-hand side of the browser. This tree is shown in Figure 11-3.

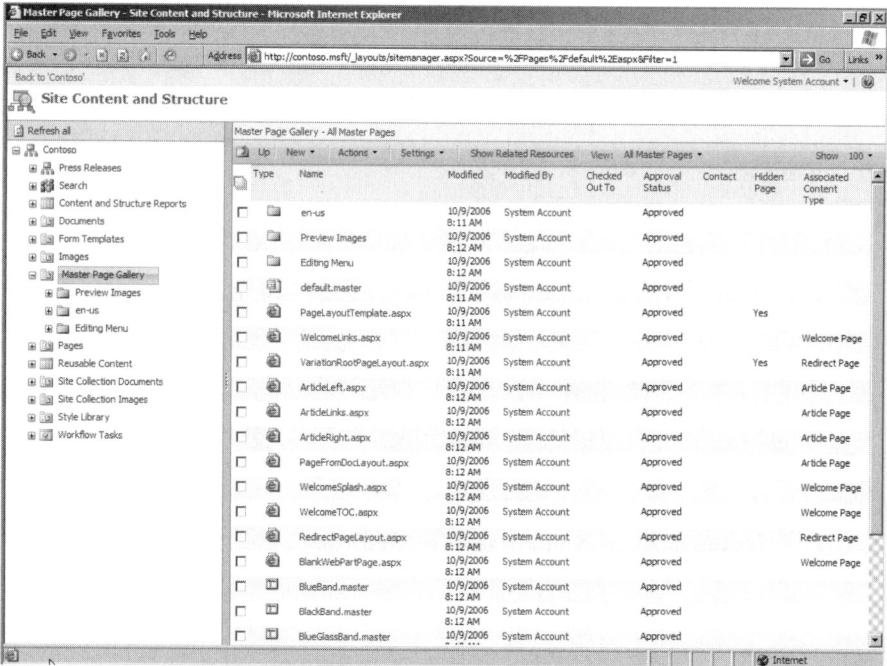

Figure 11-3 Accessing the Master Page Gallery via the Site Content And Structure page

- Use the Site Settings page. On the Site Settings page, under the Galleries column, click the Master Pages And Page Layouts link to open the Master Page Gallery, as shown in Figure 11-4.

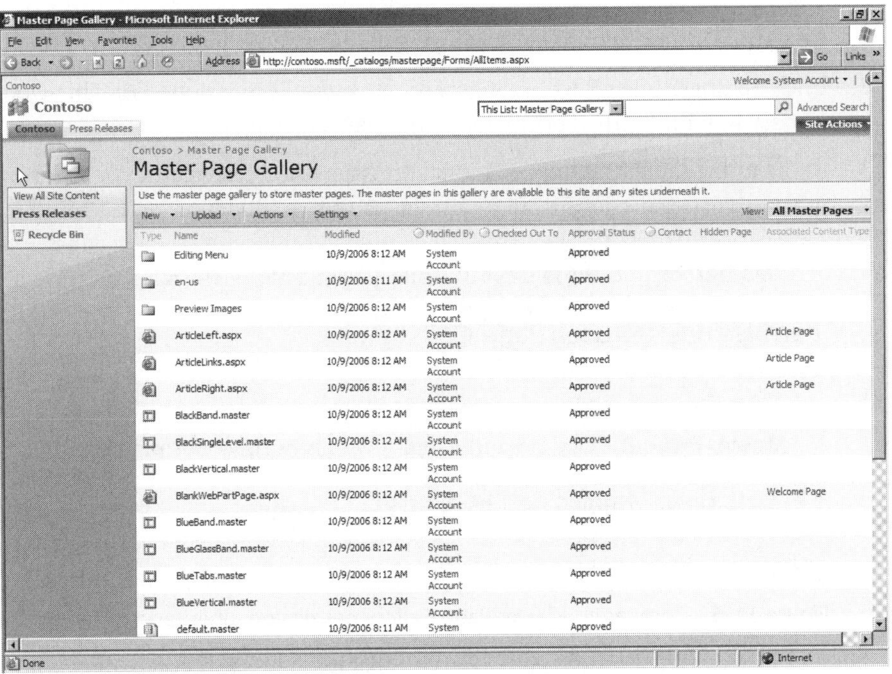

Figure 11-4 Accessing the Master Page Gallery via the Site Settings page

---

Note The Site Content And Structure page, available from the Site Actions menu as shown in Figure 11-3 or from the Site Settings page, is your one-stop shop to access all the lists and libraries in a publishing site. From this page, you can easily click through to child sites and view their lists and libraries as well. We'll take a more in-depth look at the Manage Content And Structure page in the section "Managing Site Content and Structure."

Depending on the method you use to reach the Master Page Gallery, the user interface might look slightly different. (When accessing it from the Manage Content And Structure page, you have an additional tree view of all libraries, lists, and subsites in the Publishing site collection.). However, both views have the same functionality and capabilities.

Configuring Master Page Gallery Permission Inheritance

Master page settings can be inherited from a parent site, or they can be unique to each site. To determine whether the Master Page Gallery inherits the permissions from its parent, follow these steps:

1. Go to the Master Page Gallery using one of the two methods previously mentioned.
2. Click Settings, select List Settings, and click the Permissions For This Document Library link under the Permissions And Management column.
3. At the top of the list, an informational message indicates whether or not the library inherits the permissions from its parent, as shown in Figure 11-5.

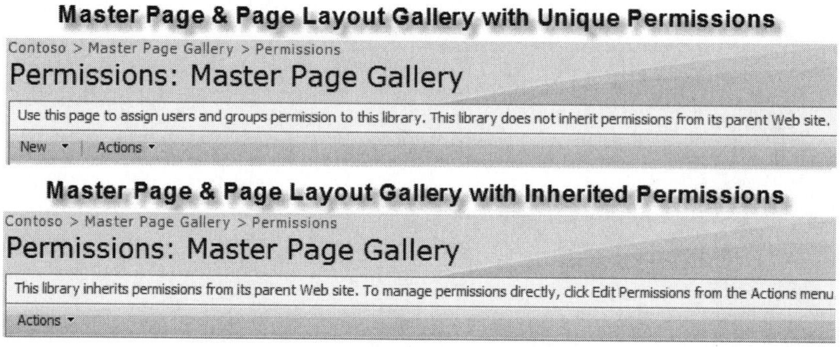

Master Page & Page Layout Gallery with Unique Permissions
Contoso > Master Page Gallery > Permissions
Permissions: Master Page Gallery
Use this page to assign users and groups permission to this library. This library does not inherit permissions from its parent Web site.
New | Actions
Master Page & Page Layout Gallery with Inherited Permissions
Contoso > Master Page Gallery > Permissions
Permissions: Master Page Gallery
This library inherits permissions from its parent Web site. To manage permissions directly, click Edit Permissions from the Actions menu
Actions

Figure 11-5 Comparing Master Page Gallery permission inheritance settings

a. To reset the Master Page Gallery so that it inherits its permissions from its parent site, click the Actions menu and select Inherit Permissions. Click OK in the confirmation box that appears.

b. To specify unique permissions on a Master Page Gallery that's inheriting from the parent site, click the Actions menu and select Edit Permissions. Click OK in the confirmation box that appears.

Managing Site Content and Structure

The Publishing feature adds a new page for administrators to manage their site's taxonomy and content. This page, Site Content And Structure, is accessible either from the Site Actions menu (where it is listed at the bottom of the menu as Manage Content And Structure) or from the Site Settings page found under the Site Administration column as Content And Structure. The Site Content And Structure page is shown in Figure 11-6.

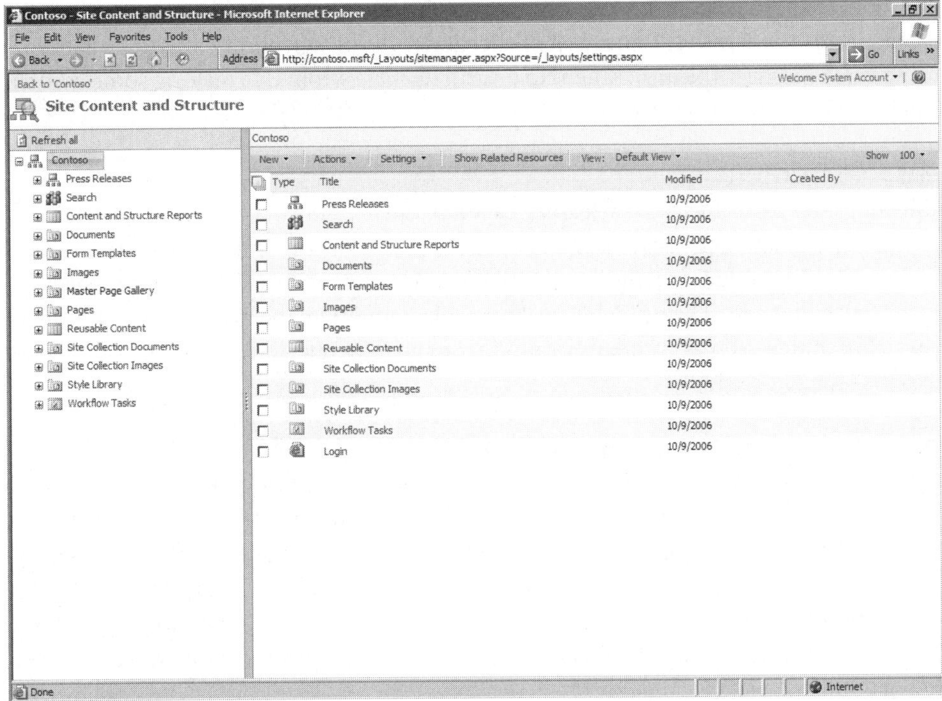

Figure 11-6 Site Content And Structure page

From the first glance, you can see that this page contains a significant amount of information. Using the navigation tree on the left side of the browser window, you can quickly access just about every list, document library, and site within your entire site collection.

Two topics that were already discussed in this chapter, the Master Page And Page Layout Gallery and Pages document library, can be seen in the tree navigation. (The Master Page And Page Layout Gallery is listed only as the Master Page Gallery for display reasons.) The Style Library contains all the cascading style sheets (CSS) used throughout the site, as well as the XSLT files used to render the XML output from some publishing-specific Web Parts such as Table of Contents, Summary Links, and Content By Query Web Parts.

One thing you'll notice is that both the top-level site and Press Releases subsite contain their own Documents and Images libraries, but the top-level site contains two additional related libraries: Site Collection Documents and Site Collection Images. What's the difference? The Documents and Images libraries are available to content owners at their current site scope. For example, if a content owner was editing a page within the Press Releases site, only images within the Press Releases' Images library would be available; images within the top-level site's Images library would not be available. The difference between the Documents and Images libraries and the Site Collection Documents and Site

Collection Images libraries is that items within the Site Collection libraries are available to content owners across the entire site collection. This design allows site administrators and owners to restrict specific content to a particular site while also making some content available to all sites within the site collection.

Reusable Content

Publishing sites introduce a new feature called *reusable content*. Site and content managers with appropriate permissions can now create pieces of content, managed in a central location (the Reusable Content library), that content owners can add to pages throughout the site collection. The availability of reusable content enables site administrators to ensure that things such as company or product names are referred to in a consistent manner across the entire site.

Content and Structure Reports List

Another feature of publishing sites is the Content and Structure Reports List. The *Content and Structure Reports List* contains a collection of reports that will help site administrators and content owners find content that meets certain criteria. Not only are the reports available from the Site Content And Structure page, but they have also been added to the Site Actions menu (available only when browsing content pages). The following reports, which are an included part of the SharePoint Server 2007 product, are available to you when a publishing site is created:

- Checked Out To Me
- Last Modified By Me
- Pending Approval
- My Tasks
- All Draft Documents
- Going Live Within Next Seven Days
- Expiring Within Next Seven Days

Publishing reports are nothing more than saved queries written in Collaborative Application Markup Language (CAML). CAML is an XML-based declarative language used to define sites, lists, fields, and views. It is also used to issue queries against SharePoint and render pages. The following code sample shows the CAML code for Report: Checked Out To Me.

Report: Checked Out To Me

```
<Where>
<Eq>
<FieldRef Name="CheckoutUser" LookupId="TRUE"/>
```

```
<Value Type="int"><UserID/></Value>
</Eq>
</Where>
```

In this code sample, the CAML query is requesting all pages and documents within the site collection where the *CheckoutUser* field is equal to the current *UserID*.

Note For more information on CAML, refer to the Reference section in the Microsoft Windows SharePoint Services 3.0 Software Development Kit: *http://www.microsoft.com/downloads/details.aspx?familyid=05e0dd12-8394-402b-8936-a07fe8afaffd&displaylang=en.*

You aren't limited to using only the reports that are provided as part of the SharePoint Server 2007 product. To create a new report, add a new item to the Reports List, give the report a name and description, and specify the CAML query. After you save the report, it will be available to all site administrators and content owners on the site (as long as you didn't specify a target audience when creating the report) through the Report List or the Site Actions menu as previously discussed.

Configuring Navigation Settings

SharePoint allows users to toggle the Quick Launch menu on or off from the Site Navigation Settingspage, via the Tree View link which is found under Look And Feel on the Site Settings page, as well as toggle a Tree View navigation of all lists and libraries in the site. However, regardless of the selections made on the Site Navigation Settings page, nothing changes in a publishing site because it implements its own navigation.

Publishing sites have additional features and controls with respect to navigation beyond what a typical SharePoint site has. Under the Look And Feel column on the Site Settings page, the Publishing feature adds a new link: Navigation. This link takes you to the Site Navigation Settings page as shown in Figure 11-7, where you can have granular control over the navigation within your publishing sites.

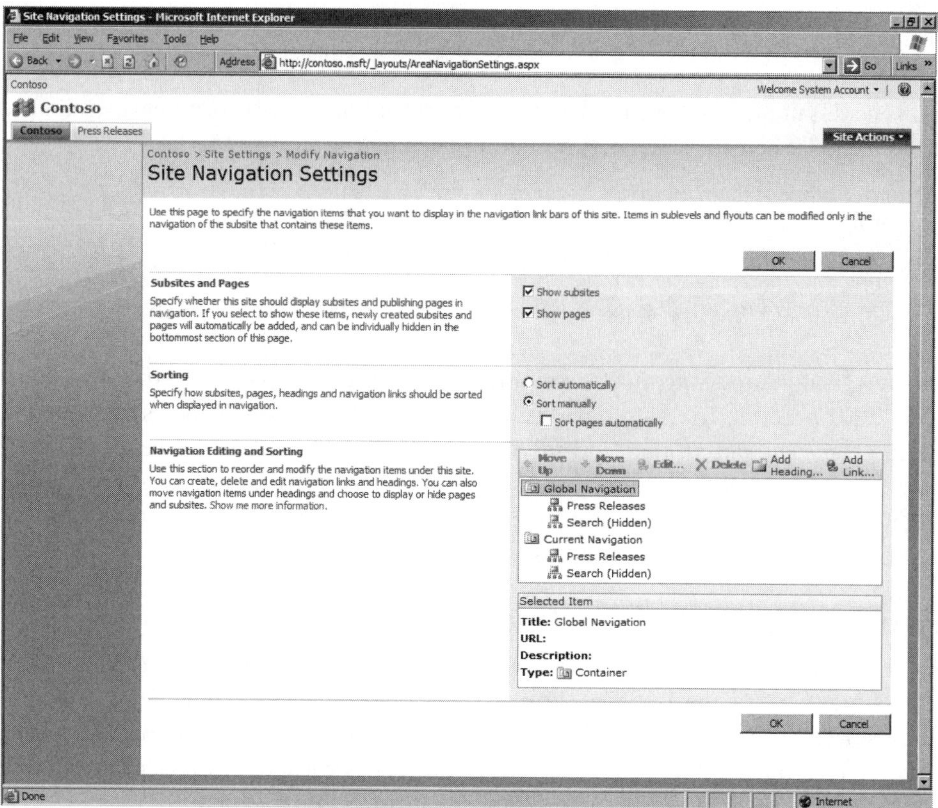

Figure 11-7 Site Navigation Settings page

From the Site Navigation Settings page, you can elect to have either sites and pages or just sites show in the navigation by selecting or deselecting the Show Pages In Navigation check box. You also have the ability to let SharePoint sort your navigation automatically, or you can take control and sort the sites listed in your navigation manually. The second option of manually sorting the sites in the navigation has a suboption that will enable SharePoint to sort the pages automatically within each site or allow you to take control over that aspect as well. Any automatic sorting selections, as well as the sorting order, are configurable on whichever field you want to sort on (title, created date, or last modified date).

The last section on the Site Navigation Settings page, Navigation Editing And Sorting, provides site administrators the most control over their navigation for a publishing site. Using the tools provided, you can manually re-sort navigation items, edit links, hide subsites, add headings (also known as *groupings*), or even manually add your own links. Selecting a navigation item will display the details of that item in a small informational window below the navigation view on the Site Navigation Settings Page.

Assigning SharePoint Groups and Permission Levels

As an administrators or site owner, you can control your publishing sites by delegating different management responsibilities to various team members. You exercise this control through permission levels and SharePoint groups. For example, one person can be delegated to manage the topology of the site, one can be delegated as the approver of new content while restricting content owners from pushing new pages into production without review, and so on. When the Publishing feature is activated, four new permission levels are created and five new security groups. The following two tables describe the new permission levels (Table 11-1) and groups (Table 11-2) available within publishing sites.

Table 11-1 Additional Permission Levels in Publishing Sites

Permission levels	Description
Approve	Can edit and approve pages submitted for approval, as well as list items and documents
Design	Can edit lists, documents, and pages
Manage Hierarchy	Can create and manage sites and pages, as well as list items and documents
Restricted Read	Can read pages and documents, but cannot view previous versions or rights information

Table 11-2 Additional SharePoint Groups in Publishing Sites

SharePoint groups	Description
Approvers	Granted Approve and Limited Access permission levels.. These users can edit and approve pages, list items, and documents submitted for approval.
Designers	Granted Design and Limited Access permissionlevels. These users typically create your site's master pages and page layouts. (We'll talk more about these later in the chapter.)
Hierarchy Managers	Granted Limited Access and Manage Hierarchy permission levels.. These users can create and edit sites, pages, list items, and documents.
Quick Deploy Users	Granted Limited Access permission levels. These users have the capability to schedule Quick Deploy jobs to urgently move content through the deployment process without waiting for existing schedules (for example, when publishing an urgent press release).
Restricted Readers	Granted Limited Access and Restricted Read permission levels. These users are typically anonymous visitors of the site and are only be able to see the published version of pages and documents. Previous versions and permission information are not available to users that are a member of this group.

You aren't limited to just these permission levels and groups. If you want, you can easily create additional level and groups just like you would in any other SharePoint site. The Publishing feature does not add any other administrative pages for security and permissions; everything is contained within the People And Groups page, which is accessible from the Site Settings page on each site. However, authenticated and authorized users can skip the Site Settings page, as the Publishing feature has made the People And Groups page accessible from anywhere in the site through the Site Actions menu under the Site Settings submenu.

Smart Client Content Authoring

SharePoint's Publishing feature enables content owners to create and edit pages directly though a Web browser. This is not the only vehicle for adding pages to a publishing site. Microsoft has added a new capability called Smart Client Authoring that enables users to author pages in certain document types and let SharePoint Server 2007 automatically convert those documents into Web pages. This processing of pages from documents is implemented with document converters. SharePoint Server 2007 includes four document converters:

- Microsoft Office Word 2007 DOCX to Web page
- Microsoft Office Word 2007 DOCM to Web page
- Microsoft Office InfoPath 2003 or 2007 to Web page
- XML files to Web page (via XSL supplied by the user that transforms XML to HTML)

Configuring Document Conversion Services

The document conversion services in SharePoint Server 2007 are not configured and started by default. This section looks at how you get these services up and running. First, you must start a pair of services on an SharePoint Server 2007 server and then configure your publishing site to allow document conversions:

1. Open a Web browser, and browse to SharePoint Central Administration.
2. Click the Operations tab to open the SharePoint Central Administration Operations page.
3. Under the Topology And Services grouping, select Services On Server.
4. In the Action column, click the Start link for the Document Conversions Load Balancer Service.

5. In the Action column, click the Start link for the Document Conversions Launcher Service. This loads the Launcher Service Settings page.
6. On the Launcher Service Settings page, select the server to run the launcher, the load balancer server, and the port number for the Document Conversions Launcher Service.
7. Go to SharePoint's Central Administration Application Management page by clicking the Application Management tab in the top horizontal pane.
8. Under the External Service Connections grouping, select Document Conversions.
9. On the Configure Document Conversions page (as shown in Figure 11-8), specify the Web application and the Yes option to enable document conversions for the specified Web application, the load balancer server, and scheduling details. Notice how you can customize the individual document converters from this page as well. For now, just click OK.

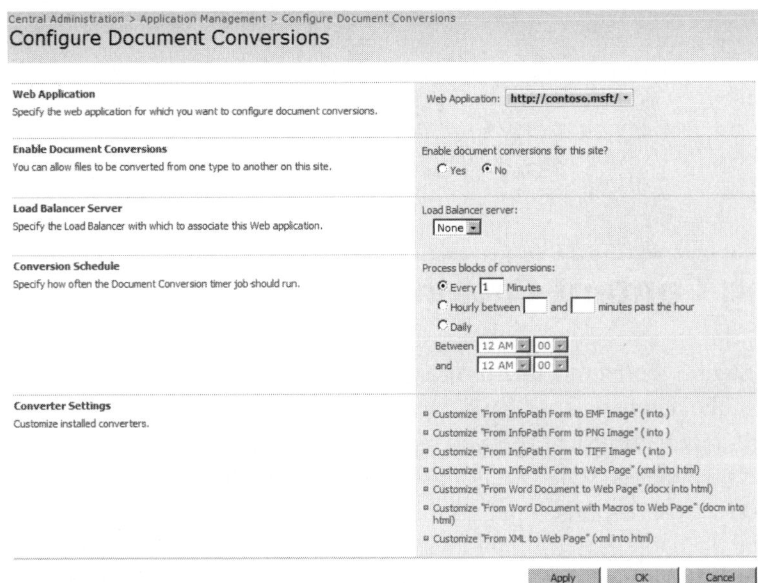

Figure 11-8 Configure Document Conversions page

Now that the document conversion services are configured and your publishing site is enabled for document conversion, your site will allow you to upload files to a document library for conversion to a Web page. After a file with one of the accepted file types (for example, .docx) is placed in a document library, you'll see a new option in the Edit Control Block (ECB) menu called Convert Document. If the file extension is .docx, the Convert Document menu option exposes another option: From Word Document To Web Page.

After a publishing site has been enabled for document conversions, site administrators will be able to configure each content type to specify how it will behave in the document conversion process. You can access these settings by going to the Site Settings page for the publishing site, selecting Site Content Types under the Galleries column, selecting a content type, and clicking the Manage Document Conversion For This Content Type from the Content Type Details page.

Document Converters

SharePoint Server 2007 ships with four document converters, which convert only Microsoft Office Word 2007 file formats (.docx and .docm), InfoPath files, and XML files. What if you have other types of files you'd like to run through the document conversion process to create Web pages from? SharePoint Server 2007 fully supports custom document converters that you build with custom code.

More Info Refer to the Microsoft Office SharePoint Server 2007 Software Development Kit (SDK) for more information on creating custom document converters: *http://www.microsoft.com/downloads/details.aspx?familyid=6d94e307-67d9-41ac-b2d6-0074d6286fa9&displaylang=en*.

Configuring Content Caching

One common theme across all SharePoint sites, including publishing sites, is that virtually all the content is stored in a Microsoft SQL Server database. The only content that's not included in the database is the JavaScript, CSS, images, and some ASPX files that are common to all sites (such as the pages you see linked from Site Settings). For a publishing site, this means all images, style sheets, custom JavaScript files, and documents will be stored in SQL Server. Every time a page is requested, SharePoint will go back to the database to retrieve the content. This is an obvious detriment to the performance of the site because fetching data from SQL Server compared to pulling it from memory or off the local hard disk of the SharePoint server takes considerably longer.

So how do you get around this bottleneck? Caching! Thankfully, SharePoint has advanced and granular configuration settings that give site administrators complete control over the level and type of caching available to publishing sites. SharePoint provides two types of caching mechanisms:

- **Page output caching** The process of persisting the compiled page in memory on the SharePoint server, eliminating the need to go back to the database for any subsequent requests for the same page.
- **Disk caching** Static content, such as images, CSS, and JavaScript files are persisted to the hard disk of the SharePoint server after they are retrieved from the server. Subsequent requests for these resources will result in SharePoint pulling them off the disk and returning them back to the requester rather than making another call to the database.

In a publishing site, cache settings are defined in profiles. These profiles are then available to the entire site collection, but each site can either inherit the cache configuration of the parent site or override the parent and define its own profiles.

Configuring Cache Profiles

The cache profile administration interface is available by clicking the Site Collection Cache Profiles link under the Site Collection Administration column from the site collection's Site Settings page. When a publishing site is created, the following four profiles are created by default:

- **Disabled** This profile disables caching.
- **Public Internet (Purely Anonymous)** This profile is configured to do no authentication checks and will be the fastest option; However, it should be used only when it's acceptable that everyone can view the same page.
- **Extranet (Published Site)** This profile is configured to cache only major versions of pages and always check permissions when content is requested.
- **Intranet (Collaboration Site)** This profile is configured to always check permissions when content is requested and cache major as well as minor versions of pages.

To create a new profile, click the New button on the list toolbar. As you can see in Figure 11-9, you have plenty of configuration options when creating a policy. Using these options, you can specify whether you want to check for permissions on each object request, choose from numerous Vary By options (custom parameter, HTTP header, query string parameters, and rights), specify whether users with Edit rights can view the items in cache, or specify whether the page is always pulled from the database and bypasses cache. The options aren't explained in detail here because a good description is listed with each field.

Contoso > Cache Profiles > New Item

Cache Profiles: (no title)

OK | Cancel

Attach File

Title *	
Display Name	Display name is used to populate the list of available cache profiles for site owners and page layout owners.
Display Description	Display description is used to populate the list of available cache profiles for site owners and page layout owners.
Perform ACL Check	Using the ACL check (checked) ensures that all items in the cache are appropriately security trimmed. Skipping the ACL check (unchecked) provides additional speed but should only be applied to sites or page layouts that do not have information that needs security trimming.
Enabled	If the cache profile is enabled (checked) then caching will take place. If the cache profile is not enabled (unchecked) then caching will not take place anywhere this profile is selected. This is useful for troubleshooting the rendering of all sites and page layouts associated with this cache profile. Remember to leave this enabled (checked) when troubleshooting is complete.
Duration	Duration in seconds to keep the cached version available.
Check for Changes	Using check for changes (checked) will validate on each page request that the site has not changed and will flush the cache on changes to the site. Skipping check for changes (unchecked) allows for better performance but will not check for updates to the site for the number os seconds specified in duration
Vary by Custom Parameter	As specified by HttpCachePolicy.SetVaryByCustom in ASP.Net 2.0.
Vary by HTTP Header	As specified by HttpCachePolicy.VaryByHeaders in ASP.Net 2.0.
Vary by Query String Parameters	As specified by HttpCachePolicy.VaryByParams in ASP.Net 2.0.
Vary by User Rights	Vary by user rights (checked) will ensure that users must have identical effective rights on all SharePoint security scopes to see the same cached page as any other user.
Cacheability *	As specified by HttpCacheability in ASP.Net 2.0.
Safe for Authenticated Use *	This should be checked only for those policies that you wish to allow to be applied to authenticated scenarios by administrators and page layout designers
Allow writers to view cached content	Enabling this will bypass the normal behaviour of not allowing people with edit rights to have their pages cached. This should only be enabled in certain scenarios where you know that the page will be published, but will not have any content that may be checked out or in draft (for example, a content by query web part).

OK | Cancel

Figure 11-9 Cache Profile creation page

Enabling Page Output Caching

Page output caching in SharePoint is similar to ASP.NET 2.0 output caching. Essentially, this edge form of caching enables Web front-end (WFE) servers to store the rendered output of the controls on a page and persist them in memory. When page output caching is enabled, the following occurs:

- When a page is requested, SharePoint retrieves all necessary information from the database and compiles the page, storing the resulting objects in memory.
- The next time the page is requested, SharePoint checks to see whether the page exists in memory. If it does, SharePoint retrieves the objects from cache and uses

them in rendering the response to the requester. If the objects aren't in memory, it repeats the first step.

- After a specified time has elapsed (configurable within the cache policy), the objects in cache are invalidated and purged. This feature prevents any stale information from being returned to the users.

To enable page output caching for a publishing site, complete the following steps:

1. Click the Site Actions menu, select Site Settings and then select Modify All Site Settings.
2. Under the Site Collection Administration column, click the Site Collection Output Cache link. If output caching is not enabled, you'll see a single check box to enable the cache. Selecting this check box refreshes the page, yielding additional configuration settings. As shown in Figure 11-10, you'll see that you can select a cache profile, created earlier, as the anonymous and authenticated profile. You can also optionally specify different policies for page layout designers. These options can be helpful because your designers can always be sure they are seeing their latest changes and not some cached changes from before.

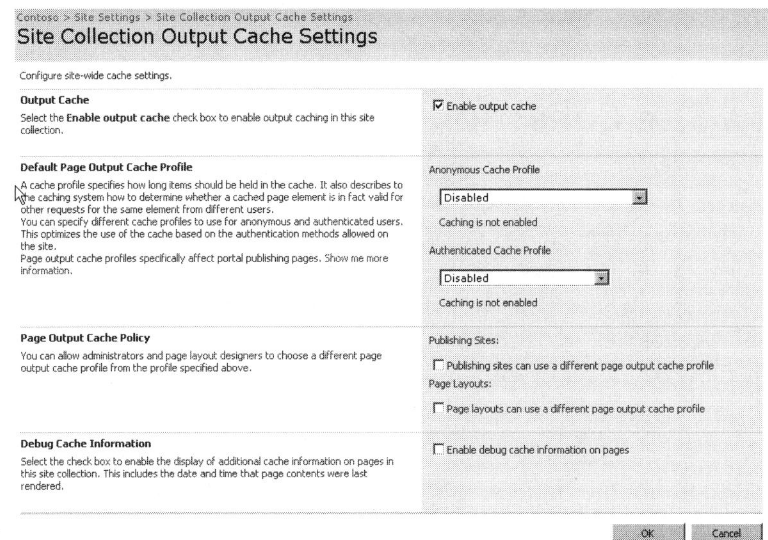

Figure 11-10 Site Collection Output Cache Settings page

SharePoint also gives site administrators the ability to specify how many objects are stored in cache, as well as forcing a flush of the object cache on a server-by-server basis or across the entire farm. These actions can be performed from the Object Cache Settings page, which is available via the Site Collection Object Cache Settings link on the Site Settings page under the Site Collection Administration column.

Enabling Disk Caching

Another type of caching that SharePoint Server 2007 offers is disk-based caching. This is the process of persisting specified file types to the physical disk of the WFE server when they are initially retrieved from the database, making future database requests unnecessary and resulting in a significant performance increase. Typically, you would want to persist only static files to the disk, such as images (*.gif/*.jpg/*.png), movies (*.wmv), media (*.swf), style sheet files (*.css), and JavaScript files (*.js).

Enabling disk caching for a publishing site is very simple even though there is no browser UI as with page output caching. To enable disk-based caching:, open the publishing site's web.config file located in the Web Application's root directory and search for the *<blob-cache>* node. Using the attributes in this node, you can turn on disk caching on the WFE (attribute: *enabled*), specify the location where files will be persisted (attribute: *location*), specify the type of files that will be persisted as a regular expression (attribute: *path*), and specify the maximum size the disk cache can reach in GB (attribute: *maxSize*).

Although there is no browser UI provided to save the disk caching settings, you can use the same administration page you used for the page output cache to flush the disk based cache: the Site Collection Object Cache Settings link on the Site Settings page under the Site Collection Administration column.

Publishing a Site Collection

In this section, we'll demonstrate how to publish a site using SharePoint Server 2007. The most common reason for doing this is to create a public site that has a staging site in which the content is first created. Because an Internet-facing site represents your enterprise to an external audience, it will be the focus of management concern over content, design, and presentation. SharePoint has increased the power of the user to create not only content, but sites as well, and this increased power enables end users to publish content directly to a public Web site without having to involve system administrators or developers.

Consistency, standards, and control might seem to be in conflict with artistry in creating Web pages and sites, but they have been the backbone of art historically and they are essential in Web sites today. Every business entity has policies to control business processes. Today Web site content and structure is a business process. It might be safe to say that the structure of your Web presence has an equally important impact on your business structure just as your business structure has on your Web site. With the flexibility and openness of SharePoint, it is essential that you have the correct technology in place to enforce your organization's business policies with regard to information flow.

Another reason to use WCM in SharePoint Server 2007 is for its ability to reuse content. What you need to increase efficiency is pre-approved text and pictures that you know will not create problems, will reflect the organization's standards, and can be used in more than one location on your Web. You might be thinking of stock photos and boilerplate text at this point. However, bear in mind that having reusable content created by personnel who are dedicated and trained in that area continues the separation of the technology of building Web pages from the creative of content creation and ensures that content reuse is leveraged effectively.

Finally, branding is a key reason for having a staging and publishing site in SharePoint Server 2007. Branding, or the consistent look and feel of a Web site, was not a big issue when a small group of developers had to code each page. However, the task of standardizing large numbers of sites and Web pages so that they have the same look and feel needs to be controlled by a technology that makes creating the content easy and maintaining the branding automatic. In addition, you need sources of content for Web pages and sites that are easy to locate and replace throughout your implementation when they need to be updated.

Real World An Installable Feature: Publishing

Although pure Windows SharePoint Services site templates (Blank, Team, Workspaces, Wiki, and Blog) do not support WCM by default, publishing is a feature that can be activated on any site or portal based on SharePoint Server 2007. The Publishing feature activation is what enables the publishing processes, not the template of the site. Features are discussed at length in Chapter 26, "Introducing Features."

If a particular feature is not available for your site collection, you can extend that features to all sites at by opening Central Administration under the Operations tab and then, inside the Upgrade And Migration section, selecting the Enable Features On Existing Sites link. You might need to use STSADM.EXE to install just one feature on a particular site collection. You can examine the available features in C:\Program Files\Common Files\Microsoft Shared\Web Server Extensions\12\Template\Features.

The command line for installing the publishing site feature is as follows:

```
STSADM.EXE -o activatefeature -filename Publishingsite\feature.xml
-url http://<sitename>
```

This command line will also install the Publishing Layouts and Publishing Resources features that are required for a publishing site.

Note that although STSADM.EXE is not in your default path for executables, STSADM.EXE knows the location of the features folder and, thankfully, does not require the full path.

After the feature is installed in the site collection, use the Site Features link on the site's Site Settings page to activate the Publishing feature.

Installing and activating the publishing site feature creates the standard lists needed for publishing (Documents, Images, Pages, Site Collection Documents, Site Collection Images, Cache Profiles, Style Library, Reports List, Reusable Content, and Workflow Tasks) and populates the Master Page And Page Layout Gallery with the 13 additional master and layout pages used in publishing sites. It also adds 14 new management links in Site Settings.

You might need only sub-Web sites configured as publishing sites, not sites higher in the hierarchy. This arrangement is possible, but features are scoped to the site collection, not to the site level. If your site collection started as a Windows SharePoint Services 3.0 template, first use STSADM.EXE to "activate" the Publishing Resources and Publishing Layouts features at the site-collection level, but do not activate Publishing in the features listed at the Top Level Site Settings.

Then use STSADM.EXE to activate the Publishing Web feature on the sub-Web-site URL, and in the Site Settings for that site, activate Publishing. You will now have a publishing site at a lower level but a team site above it. Command-line examples are as follows:

```
STSADM.EXE -o activatefeature -filename publishingresources\feature.xml
-URL http://extranet/sites/SiteCollection2/
STSADM.EXE -o activatefeature -filename publishinglayouts\feature.xml
-URL http://extranet/sites/SiteCollection2/
STSADM.EXE -o activatefeature -filename publishingweb\feature.xml
-URL http://extranet/sites/SiteCollection2/SubWeb1/
```

Some of you might be coming from a Microsoft Content Management Server (MCMS) 2003 background. If so, you'll need to learn the new terminology for WCM in SharePoint Server 2007. Table 11-3 outlines the terminology changes from MCMS 2003 to WCM.

Table 11-3 Publishing Terminology Changes

When this is said:	You remember:
Windows SharePoint Services Sites	Channels (or areas, in SharePoint Server 2003)
Pages	Postings
Page layouts or master pages	Templates
Field control	Placeholder
Content type	Template definition
Master Page and Page Layout Gallery	Template Gallery
Images, document, site collection images, or Site Collection document library	Resources Gallery
Images or reusable documents	Resources

Enable the Publishing Feature on the Farm

Before you can create deployment jobs and paths, you must enable the feature in the receiving farm to accept incoming connections. The pecking order works like this: enable the feature, set up a path, and then create one or more jobs for each path. The path will inform WCM which site is the staging site and which one is the public site. The jobs will inform WCM about the schedule and other elements of getting the content from the staging site to the public site. When you enable publishing in the farm, you'll be configuring the following elements:

- In the content deployment setting, you can enable the farm to accept incoming jobs, even if it is the same as the farm that is the sending farm.
- Determine which servers will be responsible for importing, exporting, or both.
- Enable encryption for better security between the sending and receiving servers.
- Configure a temporary storage location for files involved in the deployment process.
- Create reports to follow the progress of jobs between the sites.

So, here are the steps to publishing a staging site to a public site. First, be sure that you've created a staging site by using a site template. The public site should be a publishing site that has the same template applied.

Next, in Central Administration, navigate to the Content Deployment section in the Operations tab and click on the Content Deployment Settings link. Doing so will bring you to the Content Deployment Settings management page (shown in Figure 11-11).

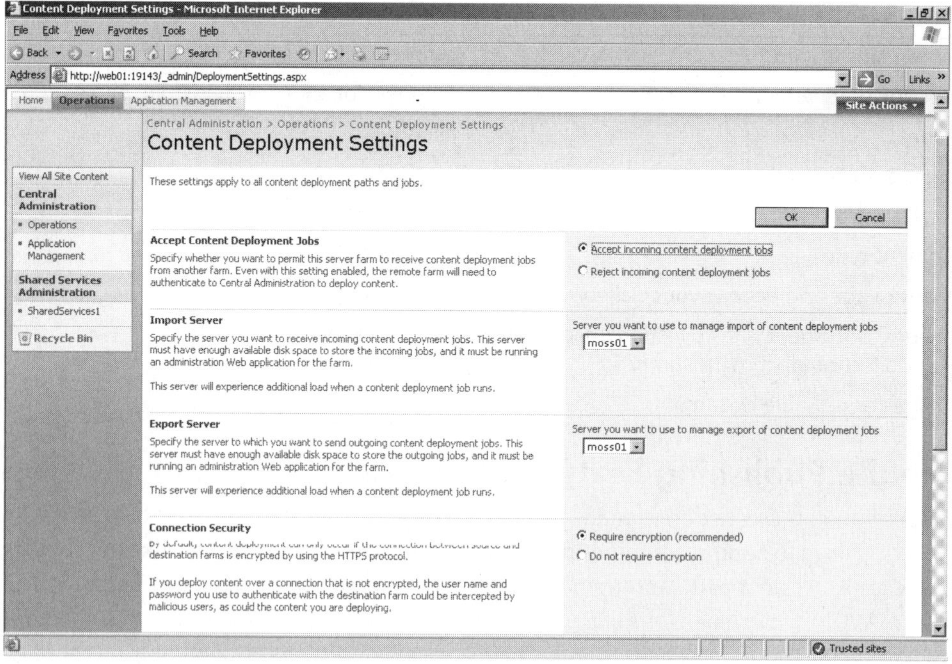

Figure 11-11 Content Deployment Settings management page

On the receiving farm, or if this is the only farm you have and both your staging and public sites are in the same farm, select the Accept Incoming Content Deployment Jobs radio button. Until you select this radio button, your deployment jobs won't work. You'll also need to select your import and export server and specify whether or not you want to use encryption. Then specify the temporary file location and how many reports you want to maintain, and click OK.

After clicking OK, you'll be taken back to the Central Administration Operation page. Now it's time to click on the Content Deployment Path And Jobs link. This will take you to the Content Deployment Paths And Jobs management page. On this page, you'll have the opportunity to create a New Path, a New Job, or both. A *path* is how you define the staging (source) site collection and the public (destination) site collection for publishing. A *job* is how you define the schedule and other configurations regarding how and when publishing will take place along the *path*.

When you click the New Path button, you're presented with the Create Content Deployment Path page (shown in Figure 11-12). On this page, you'll enter a path name and description. If you plan on publishing a number of different sites, be sure to create a naming convention for the various paths you plan on creating. You'll also need to select the source Web application (and use a good naming convention here, too) and the source site collection within the source Web application. This allows you to select a site collection inside a managed path if desired. You'll also need to type the destination Central Administration URL for the farm that will host the destination site. If you're publishing within the same farm, enter the local Central Administration URL. If you're publishing to a different farm, enter the remote Central Administration URL.

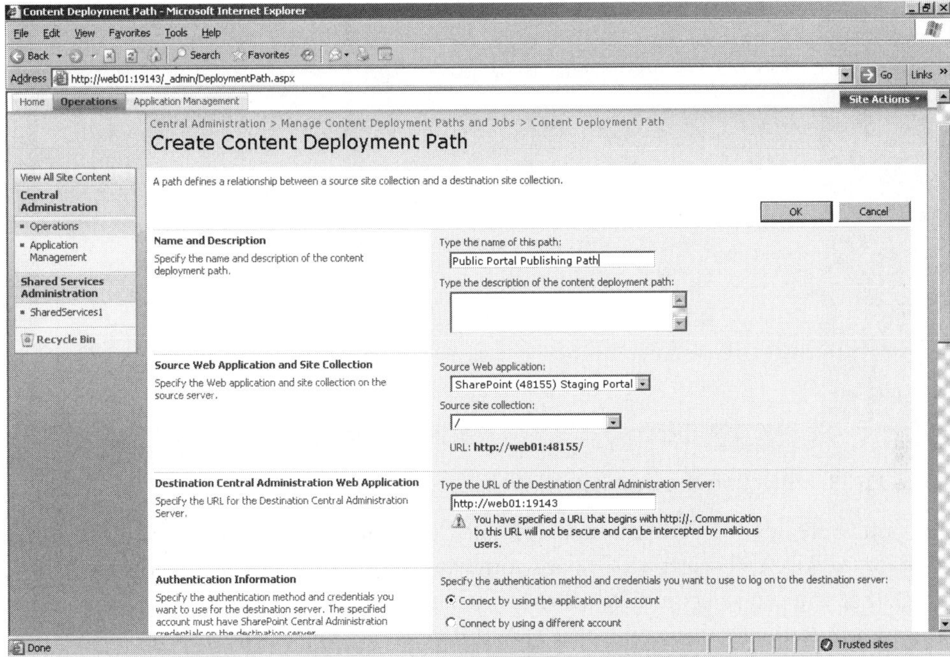

Figure 11-12 Configuring the connection for the publishing path

Next, you'll need to specify the authentication account information that has Write access to the destination site collection. Then, as part of the configuration efforts on this page, you'll click the Connect button. Until you can get a successful connection, you won't be able to finish configuring this management page.

Error messages at this stage will be embedded in the page and will be context sensitive. Be sure to read them to help you troubleshoot the connection if the connection attempt fails.

After the connection attempt has succeeded, you can select the destination Web application and site collection (as shown in Figure 11-13). You can also select whether or not to deploy user names and security information. After you have configured these options, click OK and the path will be created.

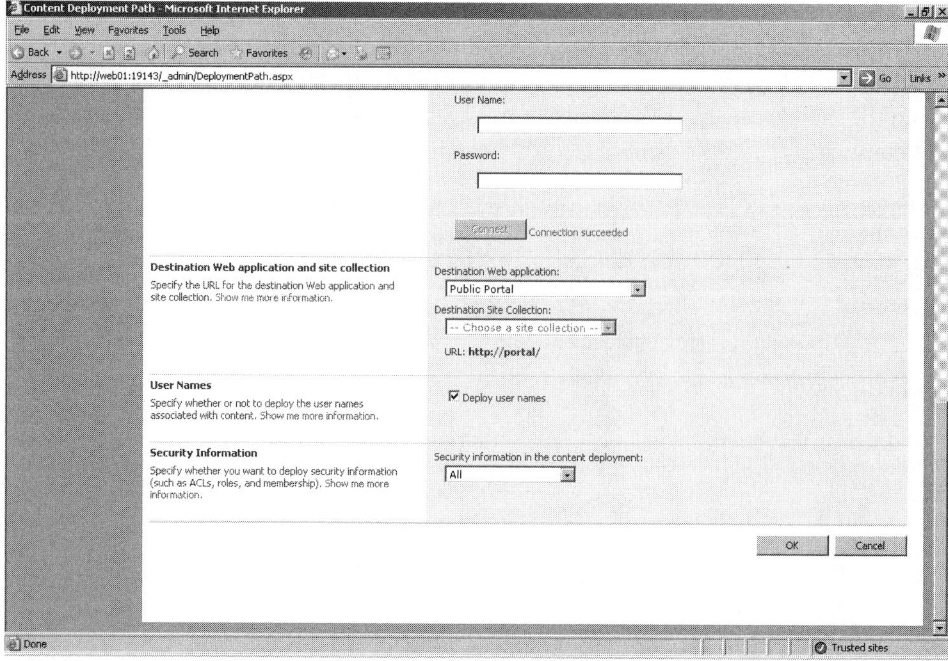

Figure 11-13 Selecting the destination Web application and site collection

After you've created the path, it's time to create the job for that path. Click New Job, enter a title for the job, and select which path you want this job to apply to (see Figure 11-14). Notice that you can select individual sites within the site collection you want to publish *on this schedule*. Remember, you might have different sites within the collection that need to be published on different schedules. To attain this type of setup, you create different jobs for the same path, selecting different sites within a single site collection.

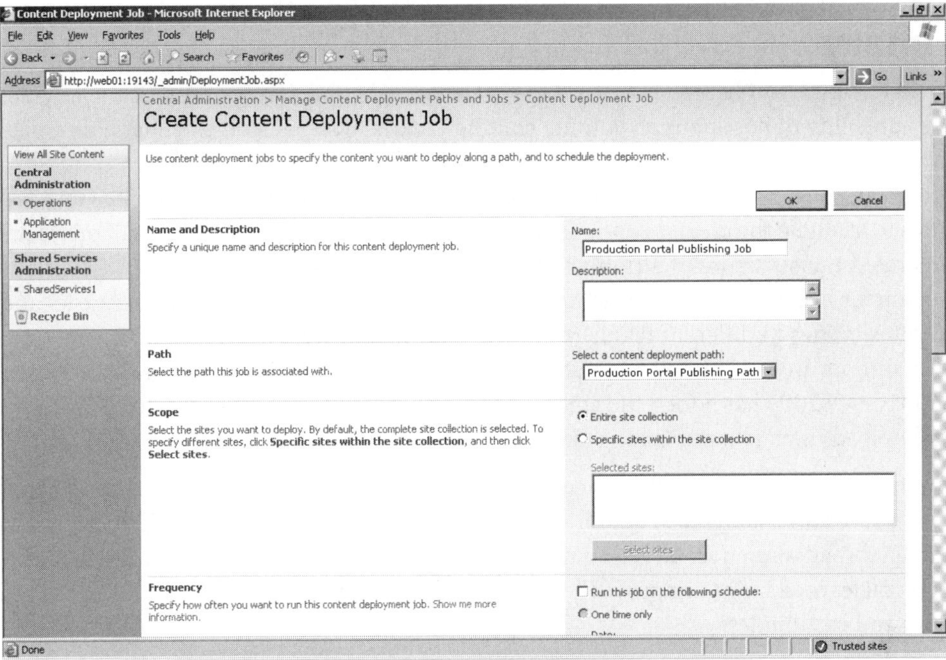

Figure 11-14 Creating a new content deployment job

Under the Deployment options on this page (not illustrated), you can select (essentially) either an incremental publishing schedule by selecting the Deploy Only New, Changed Or Modified Content radio button or a full publishing schedule by selecting the Deploy All Content radio button. Ensure you've selected the notification options that you would like and then click OK.

At this point, the staging and destination site collections have been configured and the scheduling job has been created. Now your content should be copied over on schedule from the staging site to the production sites.

To ensure that the job will run correctly, click the down arrow next to the job on the Manage Content Deployment Paths And Jobs page and select Test Now. This will run a test of the job along the path you have selected to ensure that future jobs will run correctly.

Summary

In this chapter, you've seen how the addition of WCM in SharePoint Server 2007 provides the capability of hosting high-volume content-centric Web sites on the SharePoint platform through the use of publishing sites created via the Publishing feature. Although a publishing site is just another type of SharePoint site, it has additional settings and features to facilitate the creation and management of content-centric sites. The chapter demonstrated the structure of a publishing site in WCM and how you can use the various document libraries and permissions unique to a publishing site to delegate tasks and responsibilities to different teams responsible for managing a content-centric site. Content authors are not limited to creating and editing pages in a browser interface. SharePoint Server 2007 has added the ability to author pages in Word 2007 and InfoPath 2007 and upload them to a publishing site for conversion to HTML pages.

You have also learned the differences between a publishing site and a typical SharePoint Server site. This chapter also demonstrated how you can configure your publishing site to reach a broad audience, targeting multiple devices and languages by using variations. And you learned how to improve the performance of your site by using various cache settings and capabilities.

Chapter 12

Administrating Data Connections

With Microsoft Windows SharePoint Services 2.0 and Microsoft Office SharePoint Portal Server 2003, the only way to interact with business applications and display data on a SharePoint site was either to use the Data View Web Part (DVWP), now known as the Data Form Web Part (DFWP), or to develop custom Web Parts. With Windows SharePoint Services 3.0, you can interact with business applications using the same methods as before; however, by using Microsoft Office SharePoint Server 2007, you can leverage a number of new features that allow business data to be exposed from dissimilar back-end applications in the same dashboard. These features also provide prebuilt Web Parts, which display information from these data sources without the need for coding. Some of these features aggregate and transform the data before displaying the information to the user; others are primarily designed for connecting, mapping, and fetching data. The feature that falls into this last category, and which is described in this chapter, is the Business Data Catalog (BDC), so named because it consists of a catalog of data connections to business applications that are used to present the data items in a SharePoint list or Web Part.

Note Other features introduced by Office SharePoint Server 2007 that relate to data connections include Excel Calculation Services (which is covered in Chapter 20, "Excel Services and Building Business Intelligence Solutions") and Forms Server (which is covered in Chapter 21, "Administrating Office Forms Server 2007 in Office SharePoint Server 2007"). In addition, Microsoft has published detailed information about this topic in the *Microsoft Office SharePoint Server 2007 Software Development Kit* (*http://msdn2.microsoft.com/en-us/library/ms400563.aspx*), which is excellent reading for both developers and administrators.

This chapter attempts to describe some key elements of the BDC from an administrator's perspective. You'll learn about the BDC and how to use it. You'll look at the architecture of the BDC, including the security options. Then you'll take a look at managing the data connections and using the BDC features.

What Is the Business Data Catalog?

The BDC is a shared service of SharePoint Server 2007 Enterprise Edition that bridges the gap between the various applications (from Siebel, Customer Relationship Management (CRM), and SAP to SharePoint sites, lists, search functions, and user profiles) that an organization uses for key business data. The Information Bridge Framework (IBF) provided a standard way to integrate business application data with Microsoft Office desktop programs, using the smart tag and smart document functionality. IBF is targeted at users of Microsoft Office desktop applications and requires developers to define both the method of displaying the business data, as well as its format. Therefore it is complex to implement. The BDC is the next evolution of IBF and provides an alternative method of exposing business data using SharePoint Server 2007 through the BDC application program interfaces (APIs). SharePoint Server 2007 provides a browser interface and a number of related Business Data Web Parts and therefore is not as complex to implement or deploy. The BDC is Microsoft's strategic integration technology, and it plans to expand BDC further. .More information on IBF can be found at *http://msdn.microsoft.com/office/tool/ibf/default.aspx* and information on Line of Business Interoperability (LOBi) for Office SharePoint Server 2007 can be found at *http://msdn.microsoft.com/office/tool/OBA/default.aspx*.

By using BDC, an organization can accomplish the following objectives:

- Reduce or eliminate the code required to access Line-of-Business (LOB) systems.
- Achieve deeper integration of data into places where a user works.
- Centralize deployment of data source definitions. An organization typically will not define all the data it uses, only the most important data in the BDC.
- Reduce latency to data, because once a data source is defined in the BDC it will be immediately available on the Web farm.
- Centralize data security auditing and connections.
- Perform structured data searches.

Understanding the Business Data Catalog Architecture

The BDC uses ADO.NET, OLEDB, or ODBC drivers to connect to practically all popular databases, and it can also use Web services to connect to business applications that support that method of retrieving data. For example, using the BDC, you can display data from SAP or Siebel applications using Web services.

Before the business data can be used within SharePoint Server 2007, it must be declared. A single XML file details the data connection and data formats, known as *metadata*, for a data source or business application—that is, the metadata describes the APIs of the data source or business application. Administrators use this XML file, known as the *application definition file (ADF)*, to register the data source in the BDC. Thereafter, SharePoint Server 2007 uses the declared APIs to access data from the data sources or business applications.

> **Note** The BDC is not the only Microsoft technology with which you use an ADF file. You use an ADF to build a notification application on the SQL Server 2005 Notification Services platform. Each ADF at the moment conforms to a different schema.

The BDC is a shared service—ust as user profiles, My Site, audiences, and Excel Services are—and therefore, it stores the metadata defined in the ADF within a set of SQL Server tables in a Shared Services database. All the tables associated with the BDC are prefixed with the two characters *AR*, which stand for Application Registry, the initial name for the BDC. After the metadata is imported into SharePoint Server 2007, the LOB data is made immediately available to any Web applications associated with that Shared Services Provider (SSP) by using one of the following features:

- Business Data Web Parts, of which there are six included with SharePoint Server 2007.
- Business Data in lists and libraries.
- Business Data actions. This feature allows you to use the business application user interfaces and forms that you might already use and don't want to rewrite.
- Links to business data. Wherever business data is exposed, it is possible to display a link to it.
- Business Data search. SharePoint Server 2007 can index LOB systems registered in the BDC, and therefore, users can search from data held in any business application. This makes the search function more powerful without a great deal of work.
- Business Data in user profiles. For the very first time, with SharePoint Server 2007, you can now place enterprise data in the user profile store.

- Custom code developed by using the administrator or runtime application programming interfaces (APIs). If custom Web Parts are required, developers can develop code against the BDC API instead of a multitude of APIs.

Figure 12-1 shows the high-level interaction between the data sources, metadata, features, and applications.

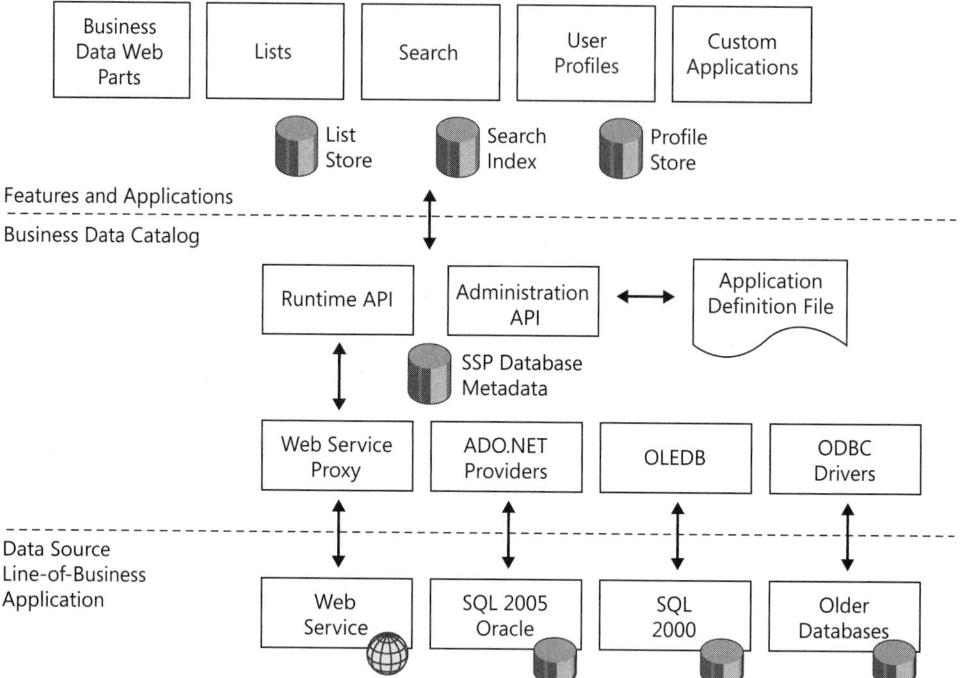

Figure 12-1 High-level architecture of the Business Data Catalog

Although this book is focused on administrator tasks, it is important you understand the administrative tasks in relationship to the other tasks that need to be completed for a successful solution based on the BDC. In the SDK, a development life cycle is described that involves four roles: a business analyst, metadata author, administrator, and developer. Administrators take over the ADF when a metadata author has finished creating and testing the ADF. They will also be involved with the developer if any applications, Web Parts, or formatting of search results are required. Therefore, administrators will need a high-level understanding of at least the metadata and the BDC APIs.

Metadata

Writing the metadata is a key activity. Metadata is usually created by a business analyst together with a metadata author, who can be the business analyst, a developer, or database administrator (DBA). Between the two of them, the business analyst and metadata author have knowledge of the business application or database as well as how the data will be used. They do not need to be able to code. After the metadata is defined, a user with administrator rights then imports the metadata into SharePoint Server 2007 at the SSP level.

One purpose of the metadata is to describe how the BDC shared service will obtain the data from the business system—that is, it describes the API. Another purpose of the metadata is to add meaning to the API and data. It describes what can be done with the API and the relationship between the data entities.

The metadata is described in an XML file, called the application definition file (ADF), and looks similar to that shown in Figure 12-2, which illustrates the main metadata object definitions. The administrative Web pages also use some of the same terminology, and therefore, you need to become familiar with them.

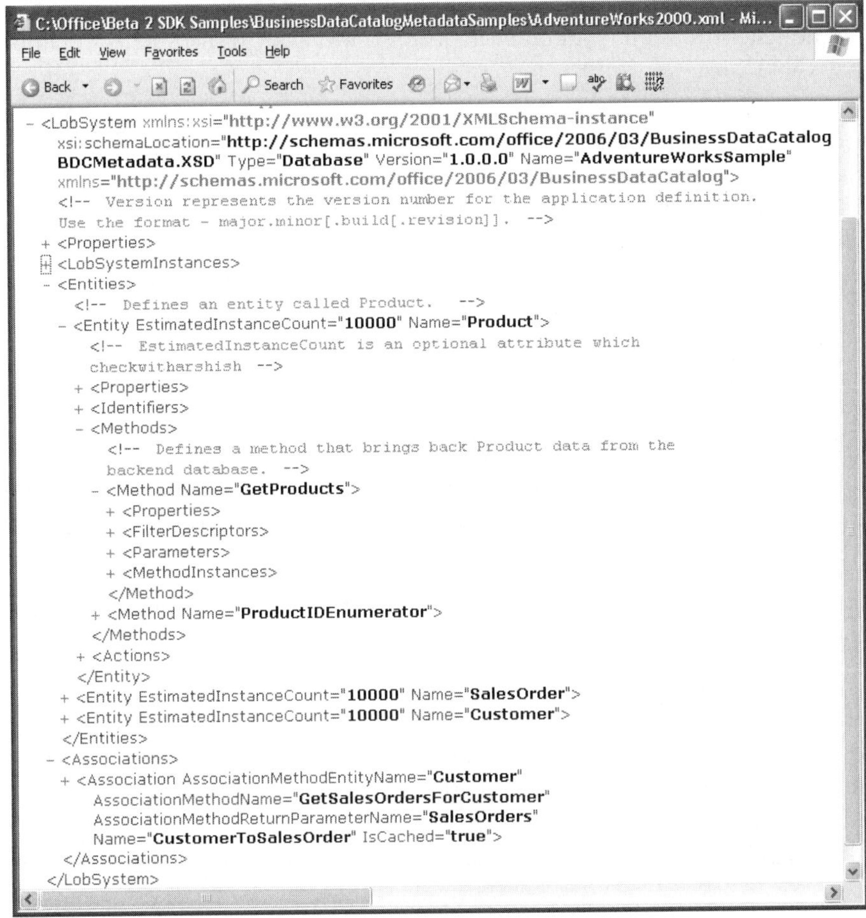

```
C:\Office\Beta 2 SDK Samples\BusinessDataCatalogMetadataSamples\AdventureWorks2000.xml - Mi...
File Edit View Favorites Tools Help
Back Search Favorites
- <LobSystem xmlns:xsi="http://www.w3.org/2001/XMLSchema-instance"
    xsi:schemaLocation="http://schemas.microsoft.com/office/2006/03/BusinessDataCatalog
    BDCMetadata.XSD" Type="Database" Version="1.0.0.0" Name="AdventureWorksSample"
    xmlns="http://schemas.microsoft.com/office/2006/03/BusinessDataCatalog">
    <!-- Version represents the version number for the application definition.
    Use the format - major.minor[.build[.revision]]. -->
  + <Properties>
  + <LobSystemInstances>
  - <Entities>
      <!-- Defines an entity called Product. -->
    - <Entity EstimatedInstanceCount="10000" Name="Product">
        <!-- EstimatedInstanceCount is an optional attribute which
        checkwitharshish -->
      + <Properties>
      + <Identifiers>
      - <Methods>
          <!-- Defines a method that brings back Product data from the
          backend database. -->
        - <Method Name="GetProducts">
          + <Properties>
          + <FilterDescriptors>
          + <Parameters>
          + <MethodInstances>
          </Method>
        + <Method Name="ProductIDEnumerator">
        </Methods>
      + <Actions>
      </Entity>
    + <Entity EstimatedInstanceCount="10000" Name="SalesOrder">
    + <Entity EstimatedInstanceCount="10000" Name="Customer">
    </Entities>
  - <Associations>
    + <Association AssociationMethodEntityName="Customer"
        AssociationMethodName="GetSalesOrdersForCustomer"
        AssociationMethodReturnParameterName="SalesOrders"
        Name="CustomerToSalesOrder" IsCached="true">
    </Associations>
  </LobSystem>
```

Figure 12-2 A sample application definition file

Note To get started with the BDC, you can find sample ADFs for mini-scenarios that use the Adventure Works SQL sample database in the Office SharePoint Server 2007 SDK. There are also two utilities that will help you create the XML tags for the ADFs, both unsupported. First, there is the SQL database metadata generator available with Codeplex, *http://www.codeplex.com/Wiki/View.aspx?ProjectName=DBMetadataGenerator*, which will produce a simple ADF. Second, there is the MOSS BDC MetaData Manager, which can be found at *www.mossbdcmetadatamanger.com*. Although dated, XML files for the pubs SQL sample database, can be found in the "B1TR Definitions" download at: *http://www.gotdotnet.com/codegallery/codegallery.aspx?id=5e078686-a05c-4a44-a131-88d75e550be8*. This site also has an active discussion forum.

The ADF contains a hierarchy of XML elements, each containing text or other elements that specify the application settings and structure. The ADF must conform to the standards for well-formed XML, so all element names are case sensitive. The ADF must also conform to the schema described in bdcmetadata.xsd, which is in the Microsoft Office Servers\12.0\Bin folder.

Note To configure Microsoft Visual Studio 2005 to use the bdcmetadata.xsd for IntelliSense, place a file named, for example, bdschema.xml in the folder *%ProgramFiles%*\Microsoft Visual Studio 8\XML\Schemas, with the following lines of code:

```
<SchemaCatalog xmlns="http://schemas.microsoft.com/xsd/catalog">
  <Schema href="file:\\C:\Program Files\Microsoft Office Servers\12.0\B
in\bdcmetadata.xsd"
   targetNamespace="http://schemas.microsoft.com/office/2006/03/
BusinessDataCatalog" />
</SchemaCatalog>
```

The metadata hierarchy can be seen by reviewing the XML tags of the ADF, which defines a single LOB system and consists of an XML root node, LobSystem. Following is a list of the main metadata XML tags: (For a list of all metadata tags, refer to *http://msdn2.microsoft.com/en-us/library/ms544699.aspx*.)

- **LOBSystemInstance** This object provides authentication and the connection string information.
- **Entity** This is the key object of the metadata. An entity relates to a real-world object, such as an author, a customer, a sales order, or a product. An entity belongs to a single LOB system and must have a unique name. Entities contain identifiers, methods, filters, and actions. Each entity should define two properties: an identifier (which, in database terms, is the primary key) and a default column. An *identifier* is used to uniquely identify a particular instance of an entity. In SQL terms, this is the

column designated as the primary key. Each entity also consists of a number of child XML element tags. Following is a description of the key components of or related to entities:

- **Methods** These are operations related to an entity. A *method* is a function that makes calls on the data source to locate an instance or instances of a particular entity. If the data source is a database, the method is a stored procedure or a SQL statement; if the data source is a Web service, the method is a Web method. The metadata must detail everything that SharePoint Server 2007 needs to know to call that method and, therefore, can be likened to interface descriptions. For each method, you should create at least two *MethodInstance* XML tags. A method instance defines the way to call the method plus default values for its parameters. Some systems, such as SAP, have methods that can be called in multiple ways, depending on the parameters passed. A method instance eliminates the need to duplicate the metadata. Using a method instance, you can define a method as a *Finder* method, which will return one or more instances of an entity, or as a *SpecificFinder* method, which will return a specific instance of an entity.

  If you want the data source to be indexed by SharePoint Server 2007, there must be a method of type *IDEnumerator*. This method allows the indexer to crawl all instances of the entity that are exposed by the *IDEnumerator* method. If an incremental crawl of the data source is also required, a *LastModifiedDate* property must be one of the return fields in the *SpecificFinder* method. This abstraction provides the ability to create generic business data Web Parts, business data searches, and user profiles; it also adds business data features such as lists and libraries.

- **Filters** These limit the number of entities returned from a method.

- **Actions** These provide a link to the back-end data source and can be used to provide write-back scenarios—for example, sending an e-mail, opening a Microsoft Office InfoPath form that writes back to the LOB application using a writable Web service, or opening a new browser window pointing to the LOB application's Web site. Actions are associated with an entity, and therefore, wherever the entity is displayed the action will be visible.

- **Associations** These link related entities within an LOB system. For example, if there are two entities, named Authors and Books, an association should be created to link authors to the books they have written.

Business Data Catalog APIs

The Business Data Catalog (BDC) provides two sets of APIs. Administrators need to have a high-level understanding of when these APIs are used, as that knowledge will help them predict network bandwidth usage. The built-in features of the BDC use the following two APIs:

- **Administration** This API creates, reads, updates, and deletes objects within the metadata. All of the SharePoint Server 2007 built-in features use this API. For example, the BDC Shared Services administration Web pages use this object model to import the ADF, as does the business data picker in any of the business data Web Parts. The BDC caches all the metadata objects, so most of the time a call to the Administration API will result in manipulating metadata objects from the cache instead of making round-trips to the Shared Services database. The caching of the metadata provides faster access to metadata. If the BDC sees a change to a metadata object, it clears and then loads the cache.

  Note After you change metadata, you must wait up to a minute for changes to propagate to all the servers in the farm. The changes take effect immediately on the computer on which you make them.

- **Runtime** This API abstracts the interface between the application solutions and the data sources. Therefore, developers need to understand only one object model to extract data from the business sources. The runtime object model calls the administration object model to find the location and format of the data so that it can call the appropriate provider, which in turn gets the business data. This process causes network traffic between the Web front ends and the business application server. Examples of the built-in features that use this API are business data Web Parts, the Retrieve data link, and the refresh icon in the business data column of a list or library.

Implementing BDC Security Options

This section introduces the security options that are available when you use the BDC—in particular, authentication, authorization, and access control. *Authentication* is the process by which you verify that a user is who he or she claims to be; *authorization* is the process of finding out whether the user, once authenticated, is permitted to access the data; and *access control* is how you will manage access to the business data exposed using the BDC.

To understand the BDC security options, it is important to understand the roles of the application pool and the search content access accounts. The following list summarizes key points to keep in mind about the BDC:

- When the business data is exposed through the BDC on a Web page, the BDC runs within the Internet Information Services (IIS) worker process (w3wp.exe), and therefore, it's using the IIS application pool user account.
- When the BDC is used for crawling to index content to which it is connecting, it runs in the filter daemon process (msadmn.exe), and therefore, it's using the search content source account. Unlike the NTFS file system, which consistently uses the same protocol for authentication and authorization, business applications will either use Windows authentication or a proprietary method of authentication and authorization. Hence, when the BDC indexes the business application, it cannot acquire security information from the back end. Therefore, if a business application is crawled, result sets from a keyword search will not take into account any access control.

The rest of this section details the BDC security options when data is exposed using the BDC APIs.

Authentication Methods

The two authentication models in BDC are as follows:

- **Trusted Subsystem** The SharePoint Server 2007 Web front-end (WFE) servers control authentication and authorization and retrieve data from the business application servers using a fixed identity. SharePoint Server 2007 servers primarily supports the trusted system model for access services and resources. In the trusted system model, a system account is used to access services and resources on behalf of all authenticated users so that administrators do not have to specify access for each user. The fixed identity is the application pool ID or a group ID retrieved from the Single Sign-On (SSO) database.
- **Impersonation and Delegation** In this authentication model, the business application delegates authentication to the WFEs and the application pool ID impersonates the user. The application pool ID then connects to the business application servers on the user's behalf by using Kerberos or SSO, or by passing the user's name as a parameter. Use this model if you want application-level authorization of the business data.

Security Alert In any system where credentials are sent between servers, an attacker can possibly compromise the security solution. Ensure that you secure your infrastructure appropriately—for example, by using Kerberos, Secure Sockets Layer (SSL), or IPSec.

Table 12-1 summarizes the reasons for choosing one authentication model over another.

Table 12-1 Authentication Models: Trusted Subsystem vs. Impersonation and Delegation

	Trusted subsystem	Impersonation and delegation
Connection pooling	Yes	No
Reduces licensing costs on the back-end LOB system	Yes	No
Less complex	Yes	No
Provides a single model for authorization	Yes	No
Support scenarios in which there is per-user authorization at the back end.	No	Yes
Enable auditing at the back end.	No	Yes

There are four authentication modes, which are defined on the *LOBSystemInstance* XML tag in the ADF:

- **PassThrough** The user's authentication information is passed through to the back-end server, which makes this the least desirable option from a security and administrator viewpoint.
- **RevertToSelf** If a user logs on with Windows authentication, the application pool ID is used to impersonate that particular account when using SharePoint Server 2007. RevertToSelf authentication allows SharePoint Server 2007 to revert back to the IIS application pool ID before requesting data from the back-end LOB system. This is the default option if no authentication mode is specified.
- **Credentials** If the data source is a database, SharePoint Server 2007 authenticates by using database credentials from the default SSO service. The XML tag *RdbCredentials* can also be used for this authentication mode. If the data source is a Web service, non-Windows credentials from the SSO are used for basic or digest authentication, depending on the configuration of the Web service.
- **WindowsCredentials** SharePoint Server 2007 authenticates by using Microsoft Windows credentials from its default SSO service.

Table 12-2 shows the relationship between the authentication models and authentication modes.

Table 12-2 Relationship Between Authentication Models and Modes

Mode	Trusted subsystem model	Impersonation and delegation model
PassThrough		X
RevertToSelf	X	
Credentials, Windows Credentials (SSO group account)	X	
Credentials, Windows Credentials (SSO user account)		X

Authorization

There are two methods of controlling user access to data managed by the BDC:

- Back-end authorization, if the business application can perform per-user authorization.
- Middle-tier authorization, which provides central security and auditing abilities using the BDC permission settings and SharePoint list/library security configuration options.

Central Security and Auditing

After the ADF is imported into the BDC, you can manage permissions centrally using the Shared Services Administration Web page to define permissions at the BDC level, application level, or entity level. You cannot define permissions at the entity instance level. If you add a business data column to a list or library, a copy of the data is placed in that list or library and you exploit the item-level security available in lists and libraries.

In the ADF, if an entity contains an *Audit* property set to true, an entry is written to the SSP audit log every time one of the entity's methods is executed. If a business data column is added to a list or library, the default auditing features in SharePoint Server 2007 are available to you.

Each object in the BDC hierarchy of metadata objects (*LobSystem*, *Entity*, *Method*, *MethodInstance*, and so on) has an access control list (ACL) that specifies which principals have which rights on the object. Out of the 13 metadata objects, only *LobSystem*, *Entity*, *Method*, and *MethodInstance* have their own individually controllable ACL. These objects are referred to as *individually securable metadata objects*. Other metadata objects inherit the ACL from their immediate parent and are referred to as *access-controlled metadata objects*.

Table 12-3 shows the rights that can be set by the administrator or someone with the Manage Permissions right.

Table 12-3 BDC Permissions

Permission	Applies to	Description
Edit	Access-controlled metadata objects	Person with this permission can perform the following actions: * Update * Delete * Create child object * Add property * Remove property * Clear property * Add localized display name * Remove localized display name * Clear localized display name
Set Permissions	Individually securable metadata objects	Person with this permission can manage BDC permissions
Execute (View)	*MethodInstance* objects	Person with this permission can execute the *MethodInstance* via various run-time API calls, that is, they can view the instances of a entity that are returned from a finder method.
Selectable in Clients	Application and *Entity* objects	Persons with this permission can use the business data picker to configure Web Parts and lists to use the BDC.

To set permission at the BDC level, follow these steps:

1. On the SharePoint 3.0 Central Administration Web site, in the left navigation pane, click the name of the Shared Services Provider where you want to import the metadata package.
2. In the Business Data Catalog section, click Business Data Catalog permissions, and then on the Manage Permissions: Business Data Catalog page, click Add Users/Groups.
3. On the Add Users/Groups page, shown in Figure 12-3, enter the appropriate users or groups and assign the appropriate permissions. You can configure rights to managing the BDC that are independent of the rights in the rest of the Shared Services Provider. Permissions set at this level can copied to any LOB system and entity imported into the BDC.
4. Click OK.

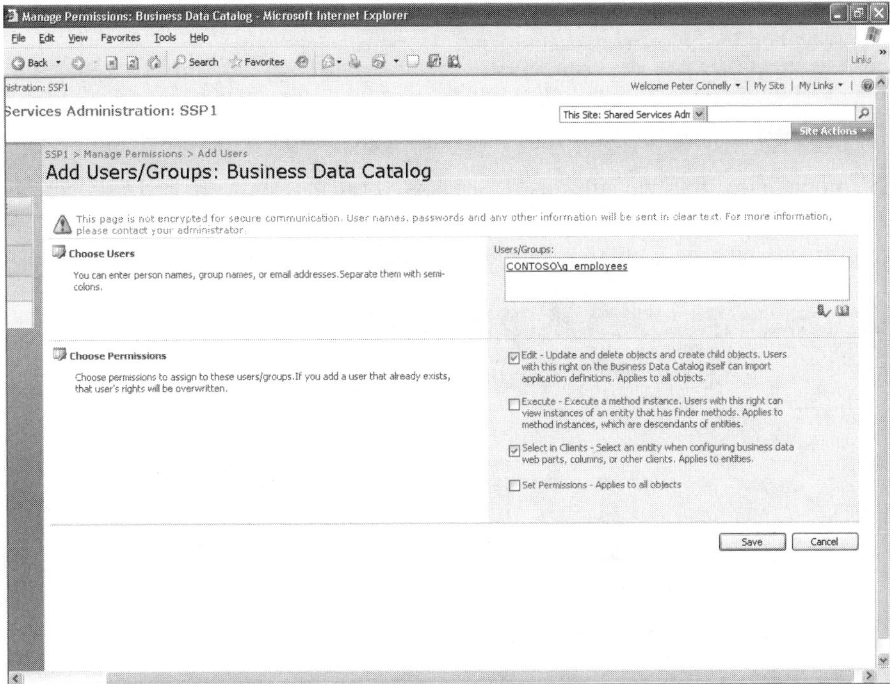

Figure 12-3 Add Users/Groups: Business Data Catalog page

Note When the SSP is created, the userid of the person who creates the SSP is given Edit, Execute, Selectable In Clients and Set Permission rights. Subsequently, if any users are given rights to the SSP Web site, by default they do not receive any rights to the BDC. Hence, only the SSP creator is able to manipulate the BDC or see data returned from the data sources. Therefore, using the procedure above, you should give appropriate BDC permissions to a group of users, who are to administer the BDC, and you should give the Execute (View) right to, for example, the Domain Users or some similar group. Ensure that your crawl account also has the Execute (View) right.

Managing Data Connections

The BDC allows you to connect your data sources to all Web applications without writing any code. To manage the BDC data connections, you need to perform the following administrator tasks:

- Deploy the metadata package.

- Set access permissions, auditing, and authentication settings. (Security was detailed in the previous section.)
- Configure Single Sign-On if required.
- Deploy custom business data solutions if any have been created.

To complete the first two administrator tasks, you will use the Shared Services Administration Web page, shown in Figure 12-4, to view, add, modify, and delete application definitions, as well as to configure permissions and edit the profile page template.

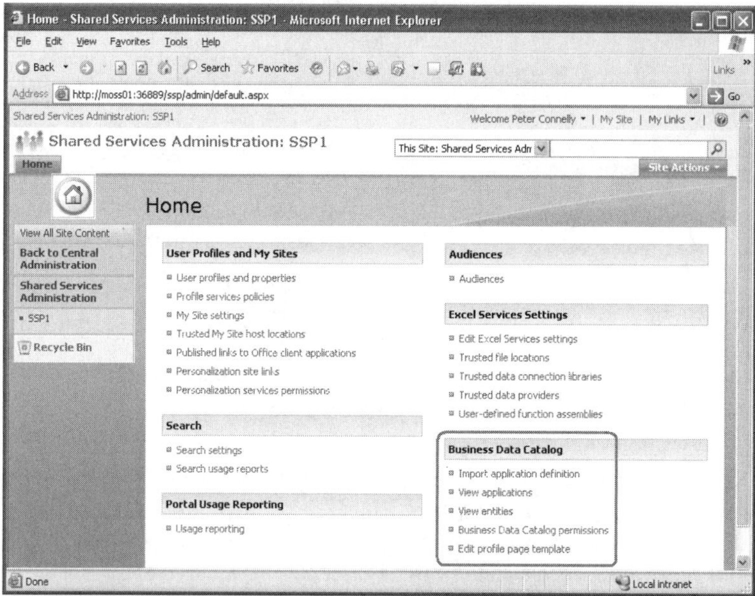

Figure 12-4 Shared Services Administration Web page

Note that the administrative interface describes business data sources as applications, although the metadata describes data sources as LOB systems.

Deploying Metadata Package

As already stated, the key to a successful solution based on the BDC is the metadata defined in the ADF, which you upload into a Shared Services database. The data then becomes available to all the Web applications. To import a metadata package, also known as adding an application definition, follow these steps:

1. On the Office SharePoint Server 2007 Central Administration Web site, in the left navigation pane, click the name of the Shared Services Provider where you want to import the metadata package.

2. In the Business Data Catalog section, click Import application definition to display the Import Application Definition page shown in Figure 12-5.

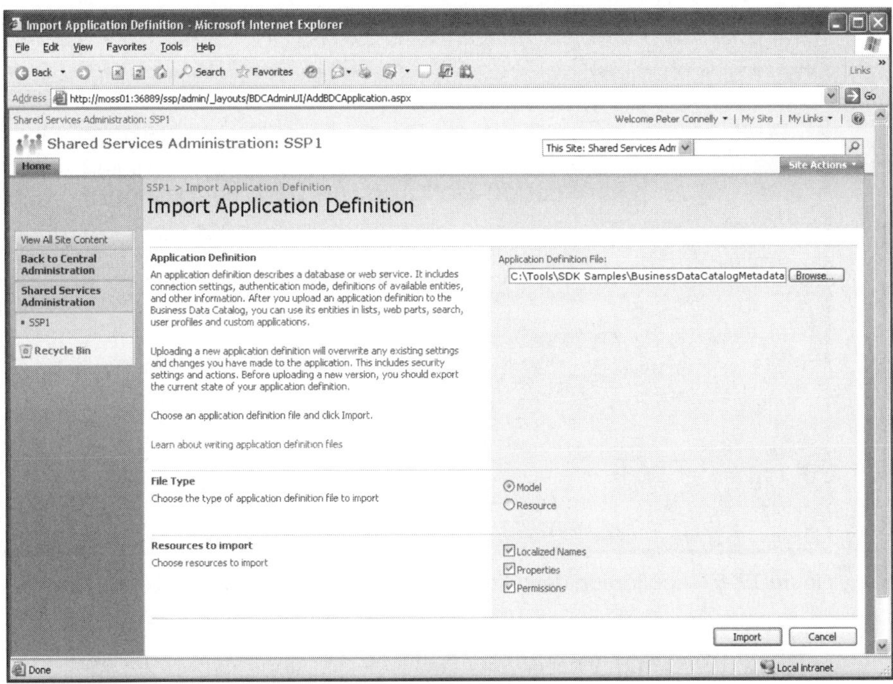

Figure 12-5 Import Application Definition page

3. Either click the Browse button to navigate to the ADF or type the location of the ADF in the text box and then click the Import button.

   The Application Definition importing Web page is displayed. The import process parses the file and validates it. If errors are found during the import process, the Web page will display additional information. Information can be found in the Windows event logs and the Windows SharePoint Services log file located at *%ProgramFiles%*\Common Files\Microsoft Shared\web server extensions\12 \LOGS, where the relevant messages will be in the Business Data category. You might have to pass this information back to the developer of the ADF. The SDK contains more information on troubleshooting metadata exceptions and interpreting the log files.

   A successful import will result in an "Application definition was successfully imported" message. The import process can identify deficits that the ADF may have, in which case, an "Application definition was successfully imported" message appears, together with any warnings issued, similar to the Web page shown in Figure 12-6.

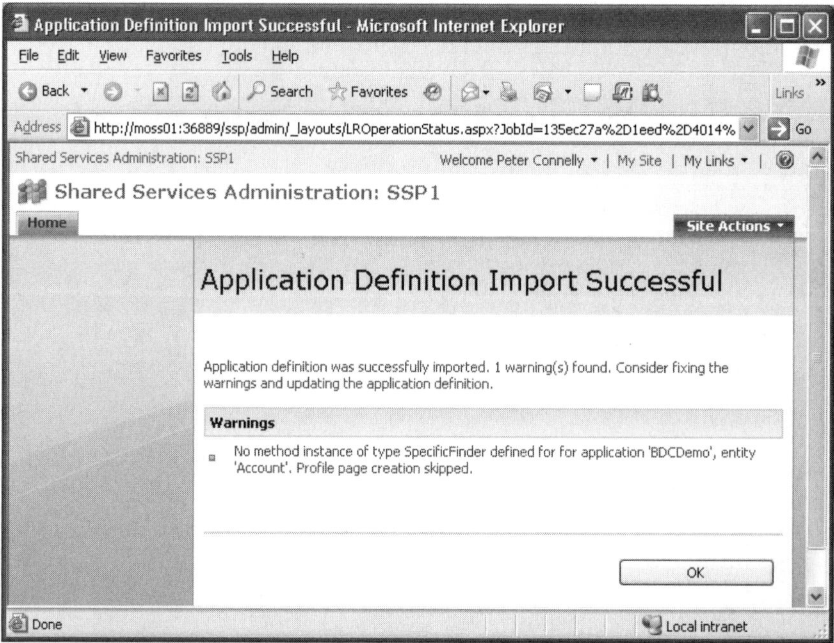

Figure 12-6 Application definition imported successfully with warnings

4. Click OK to display the View Application: <*application name*> Web page, as shown in Figure 12-7. On this page, you manage permissions, export the application definition, or delete the application.

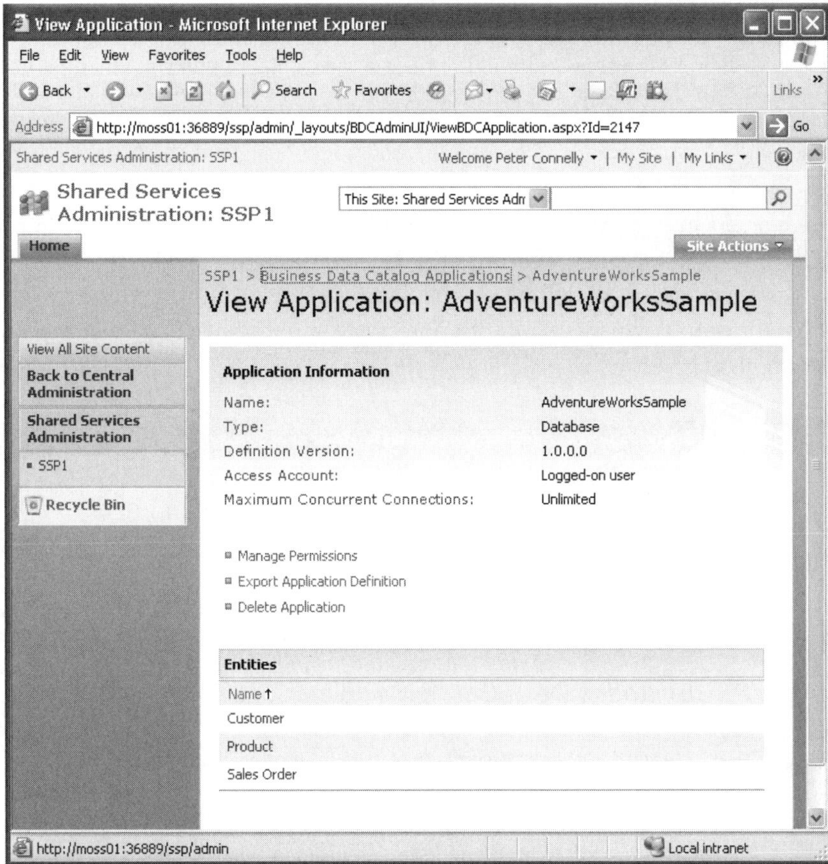

Figure 12-7 View Application page

After you have imported an ADF, you should view the entities and give appropriate access rights according to your requirements, especially if you have chosen at the BDC permission level to copy all permissions to descendants in the BDC.

When the ADF is imported, a profile page is created for each entity, which you can use to view an entity instance. A business data action will be added to any instance of an entity pointing to this profile page. See Figure 12-12, for an example of a profile page populated with data from an entity instance. These are virtual Web pages created from the business data profile template within the *Content* subsite of the Shared Services Administration Web site. The profile template can be customized by clicking the Edit Profile page template link on the Shared Services Administration Web page. By default, the profile page template contains one Web Part: the Business Data Item Web Part. For an entity profile page to be created, the metadata must have a *SpecificFinder* method for that entity.

Planning Because the profile page is exposed from a subsite of the SSP administration Web site, you should not use a random port number for the Web application that hosts the SSP, especially if you are implementing an Internet site. Firewalls are not usually configured to allow requests to Web sites on ports other than port 80.

If you have errors in your ADF and need to make amendments, before you re-import the ADF, change the version number within the ADF or delete the LOB application by first clicking the View Applications link on the Shared Services Administration Web page. Then, from the drop-down menu for the appropriate application, click Delete Application as shown in Figure 12-8.

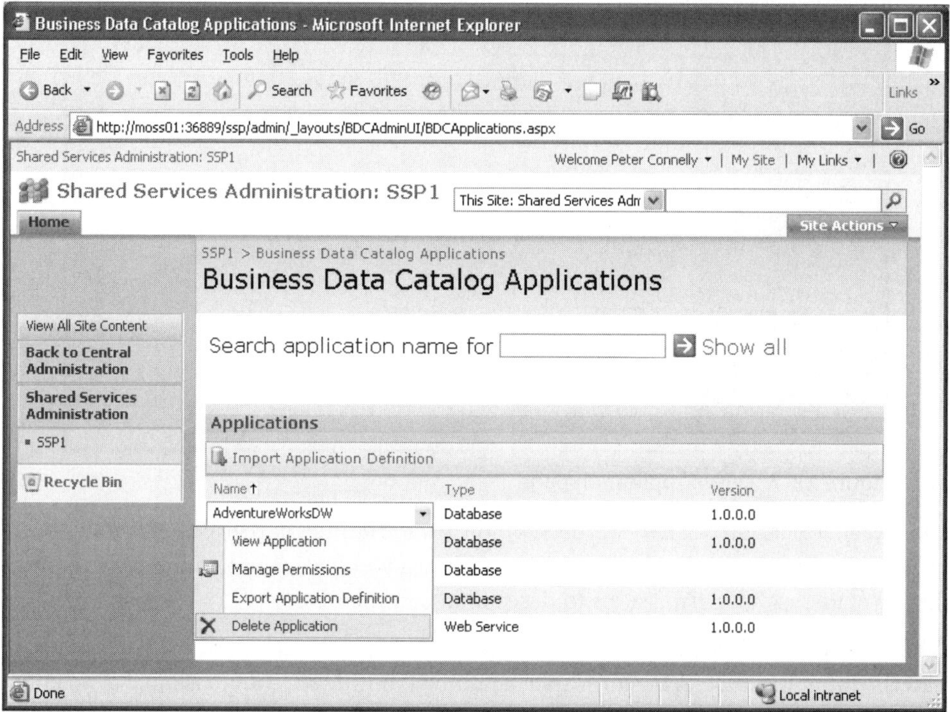

Figure 12-8 Deleting the business data catalog application

Best Practices You should not rely on the import process validation checks to identify errors in the ADF. You should check that the business data features—such as the business data Web Parts and business data actions—include a business data column in a list and that the crawl process can function correctly.

After the ADF is imported, you can change the following values at the application level, using the Administrator Web pages:

- Authentication mode, labeled as Access Account.
- Connection throttling–that is, you can limit the number of concurrent connections.
- For Web services business applications: Web Service URL, Web Service Definition Language (WSDL) Retrieval Account, and proxy server.
- For database business applications: Data Provider, connection *stringProxy* server address.

Business Data Actions

Actions provide a link to the back-end data source, usually for write-back scenarios. Actions are URLs that are usually defined in the ADF on a per-entity basis. You can add more actions, modify existing actions, or delete existing actions after you have imported the ADF, and you can do this without the need to delete the application and re-import the ADF. To add actions, follow these steps:

1. On the Shared Services Administration Web page, click View entities. The Business Data Catalog Entities Web page displays a list of all the entities imported into the BDC. From here, you can manage the permissions of an entity or view an entity.
2. From the drop-down menu for the entity for which you want to add a new action, click View Entity. The View Entity: <*Entity Name*> page is displayed as shown in Figure 12-9. Scroll down the page, and the existing actions are listed in the Actions section.
3. Under the Actions section, click Add Action.

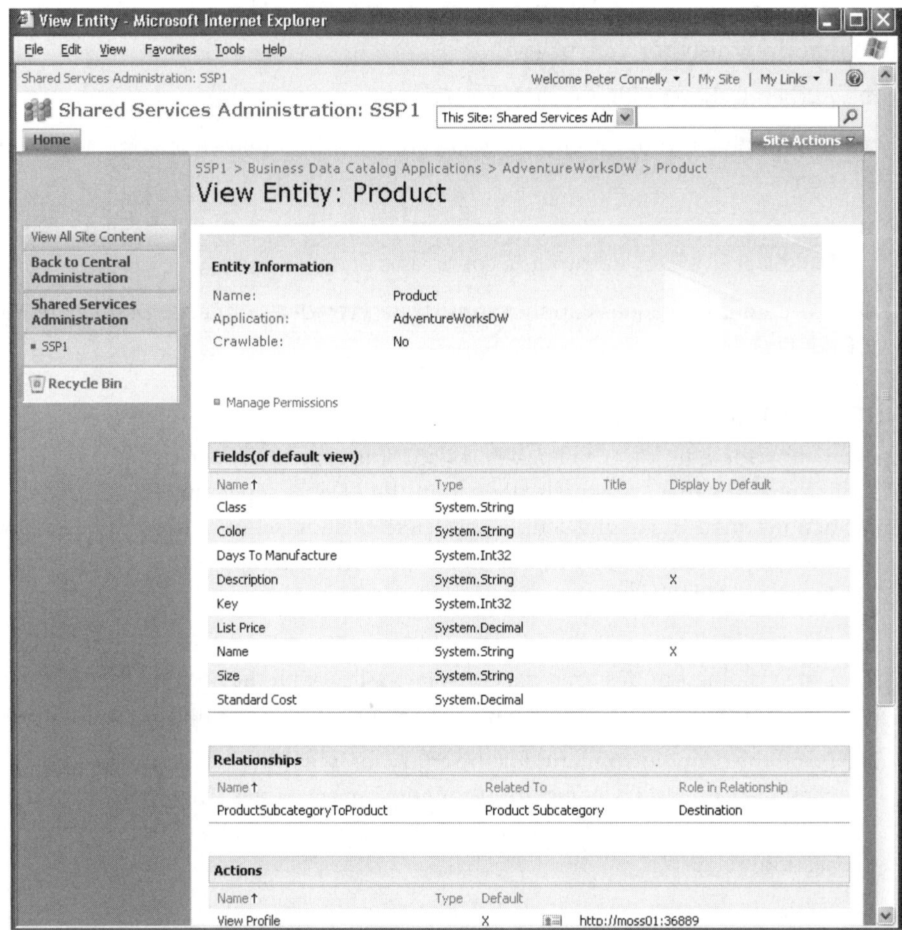

Figure 12-9 View Entity page

4. On the Add Action Web page shown in Figure 12-10, type a name for the action, type the URL, specify whether to launch the action in a new browser window or not (default), add parameters to the URL if required, and add the icon to display next to the action. You can choose from the Delete, Edit, or New actions, or you can choose your own image.

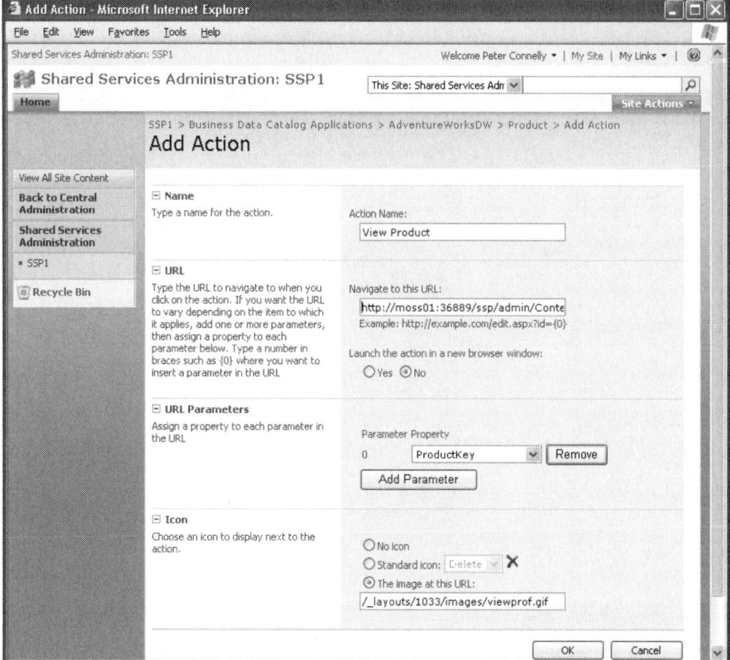

Figure 12-10 Add Action page

Wherever an instance of an entity is displayed, the actions will be visible and presented as a drop-down list of the default column. If a *SpecificFinder* method is defined for an entity, then the entity has at least one action: the action to display the profile page, as shown in Figure 12-11.

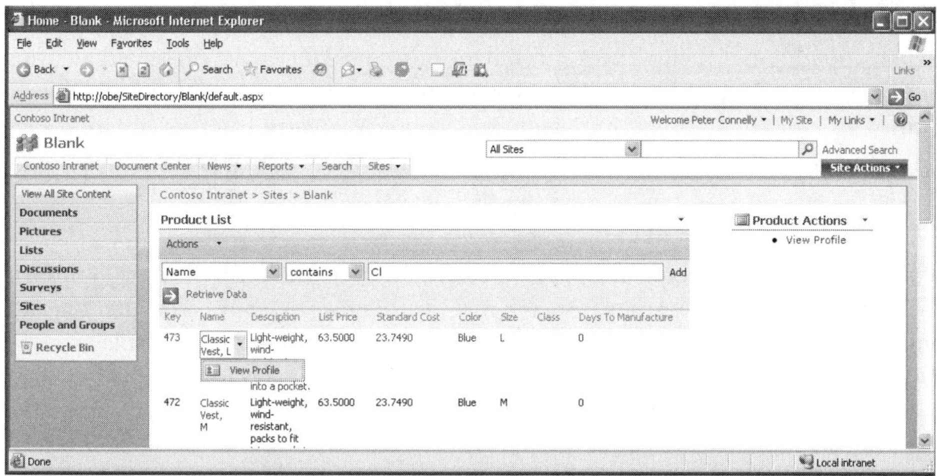

Figure 12-11 Business data actions

When the View Profile action is selected, the profile page is displayed, as shown in Figure 12-12.

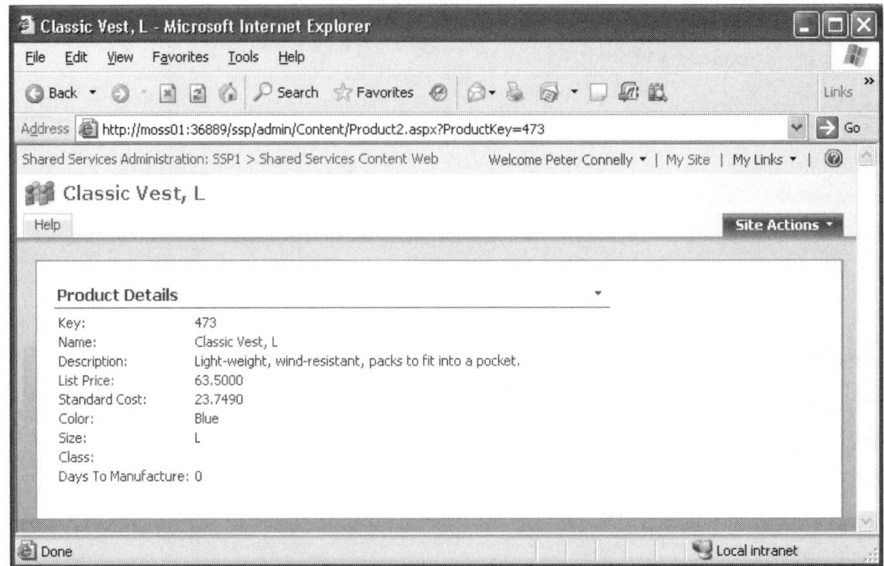

Figure 12-12 A populated generated profile page of an entity instance

Although actions are limited to a URL, you can open a client application from a URL. Two ways to do this are by either writing a Web Part that opens the client application using ActiveX or writing an Internet Explorer pluggable protocol handler.

How to Use Business Data Catalog Features

After an application is defined in the metadata, business data can be presented by using built-in business data Web Parts and incorporating business data columns in lists and libraries. You can then exploit the default behavior of Web Parts, lists, and libraries, such as defining an audience, targeting, filtering, and using Web-Part connections.

Business Data Web Parts

SharePoint Server 2007 ships with six generic Business Data Web Parts. These Web Parts can be used to display any entity from the BDC, without writing any code. After they are configured, they will automatically be named after the entity data they are displaying. The Web Parts that display data from the LOB systems query the metadata cached on each Web front-end server, and then the instance data is retrieved from the data source. The Web Parts are described in Table 12-4.

Table 12-4 **Business Data Web Parts**

Web Part	Description
Business Data Actions	Displays a list of actions associated with an entity defined in the metadata.
Business Data Items	Displays one instance of any entity that you register in the BDC. A filter must be defined in the metadata for this Web Part to be used.
Business Data Item Builder	The Web Part reads the URL of the page and sends the identifier to the other Web Parts on the page, using data Web-Part connections.
Business Data List	Displays a list of instances of any entity that you have registered in the BDC. A filter, if defined in the metadata, can be used to limit the number of instances retrieved.
Business Data Related List.	Displays a list of related entity instances, creating what is known as a master detail Web page. The description for this Web Part states to choose a type of data to display. In metadata terminology, you would say, "choose an entity to display." Microsoft believed that "type" was more user friendly for end-users than the term "entity." To use this Web Part, you do not need to understand the underlying database query, but you must know the relationships between the entities within an LOB system.
Business Data Catalog Filter	This Web Part is categorized as a Filter Web Part, which can be very useful on business intelligence site and dashboards. You can use this Web Part to filter the contents of connected Web Parts using a list of values from the BDC.

After these Web Parts are placed on a Web Part page, you will need to open the Web Part tool pane. See Chapter 29, "Microsoft Office SharePoint Services 2007 Web Parts," for detailed instructions on adding and customizing Web Parts. In the tool pane, click the Browse icon as shown in Figure 12-13.

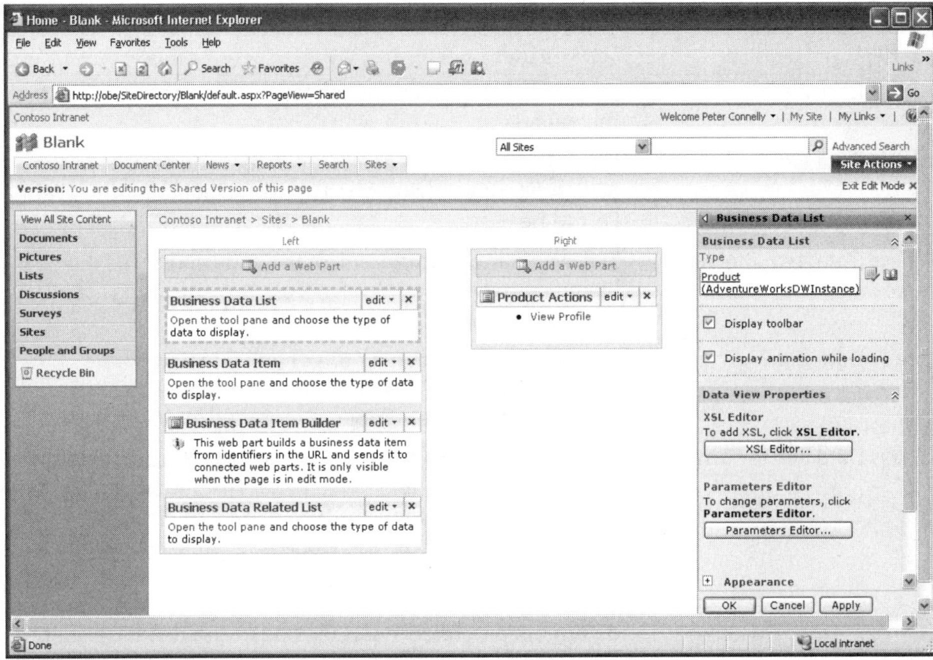

Figure 12-13 Business Data tool pane

The Business Data Type Picker dialog box is displayed as shown in Figure 12-14. It lists all the entities defined in the BDC and the data sources they come from.

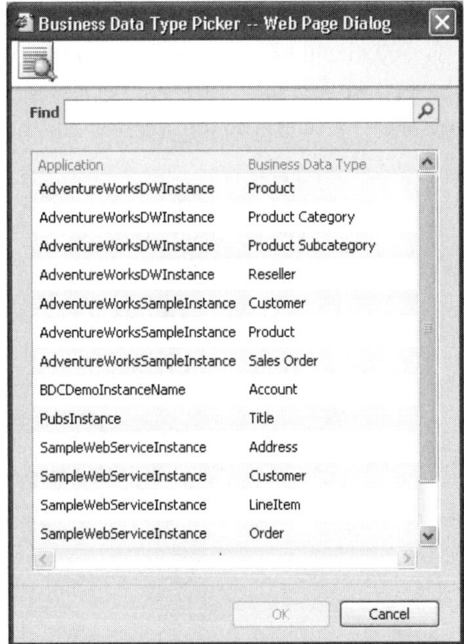

Figure 12-14 Business Data Type Picker

In Figure 12-13, you can see a Data Form Web Part section. All business data Web Parts are derived from the Data Form Web Part and, therefore, can be extensively customized using XSL or SharePoint Designer.

Business Data in Lists

SharePoint Server 2007 provides a new file type, *custom*, that you can use to make business data available to all lists and libraries in Web applications associated with the Shared Services where you have defined the business data. To add a business data column to a list, complete the following tasks:

1. Navigate to the list or library where you want to add the column.
2. On the list tool bar, below the list name, click Settings and then List Settings.
3. In the Columns section, click Create column.
4. In the Name And Type section, enter a column name and select the Business Data type. This column type can hold any entity data type. The page is redisplayed, and the Additional Column Settings section now contains business data Browse and Type Check icons.
5. Click the Browse icon and the Business Data Type Picker dialog box is displayed as shown in Figure 12-14. Choose the appropriate entity, and click OK. The dialog box closes, and the Additional Column Settings section contains a list of properties associated with this entity, as shown in Figure 12-15.

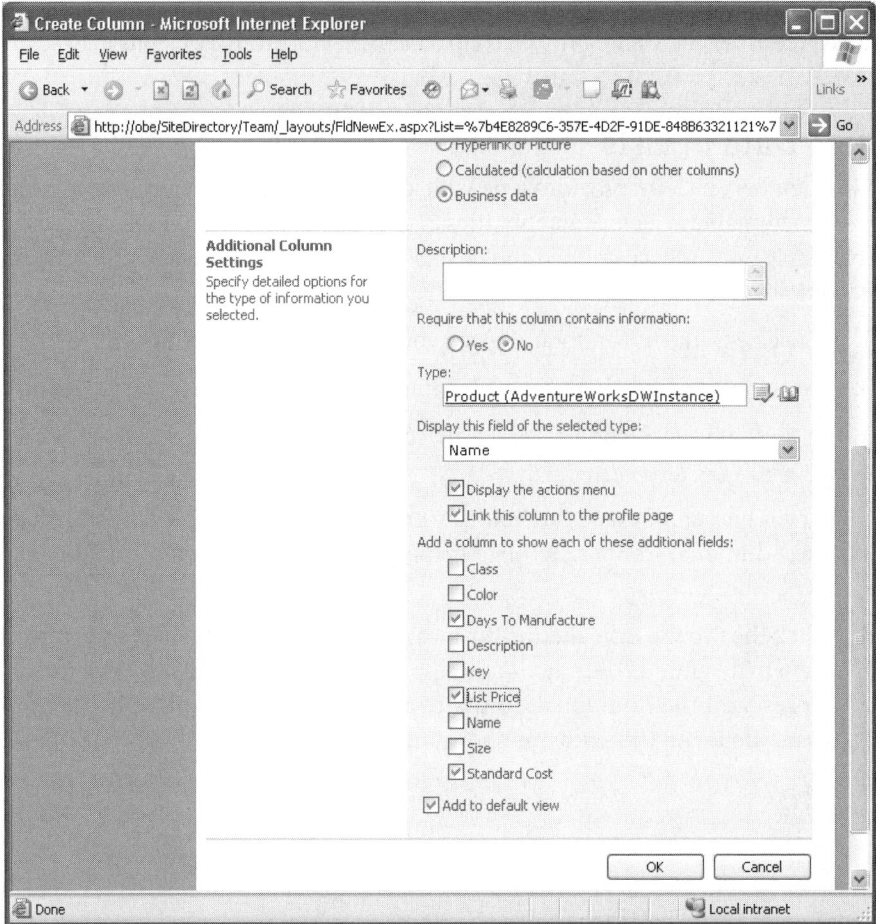

Figure 12-15 Business Data type additional column settings

6. From the Display This Field Of The Selected Type drop-down list, select a field and then click any related data you want to display. For example, you might choose to display a reseller's name together with the reseller's business type and phone number. You can choose to display the Actions menu and link the column to the Profile page.
7. Click OK.

When you create a new column, you can choose whether the column is added to the default view. If you select related data, those columns are also added to the default view.

Now when you add a new list item, you can use the business data Browse icon to display the Entity Instance Picker dialog box. Up to this point, only the metadata using the

Administrator object model has been used to retrieve the information from the cached metadata held in the Web front end. When the list is displayed, the runtime object model connects to the business data source, and it copies the identifier and the selected type, together with any related data, into the list, unlike the business data Web Parts, which contain only a link to the business data. To update the data in the list, you can click the Refresh icon in the selected type column name. A Web page is displayed that warns you that this operation could take a long time. If you click Yes, the data source is contacted to return the necessary data. By copying the business data in the list, the business data within the list has inherited all list type operations, such as view and filter.

Business Data and User Profiles

By default, SharePoint Server 2007 can import a list of domain users from the Active Directory directory service, LDAP server, or Business Data Catalog. SharePoint Server 2007 treats Active Directory and LDAP directories as master connections for importing user information–that is, it can use them as a source to create user profiles. This arrangement implies that, if a user is missing from the master connection, SharePoint Server 2007 assumes the user is no longer in the organization and removes the user from the user profiles database. However, SharePoint Server 2007 treats the business data sources only as a supplementary data source; it uses the data only to provide additional user information not available in the master connection. The Business Data Catalog data sources can not be used as the master user list. When an SSP is first created, no profile import is configured. To configure the profile import, navigate to the User Profile And Properties Web page, and click Configure Profile Import. On the Configure Profile Import Web page, which ever the source option selected, a master connection is created, based on an Active Directory or LDAP source. To add a user profile import based on the BDC, complete the process detailed below.

The use of the BDC with user profiles is a two-step process:

1. Import data from the BDC into the profile database.
2. Map the profile properties to the BDC data.

Importing Data from the BDC into the Profile Database

To import data from the BDC into the profile database, follow these steps:

1. On the Shared Services Administration Web page, click User profiles and properties.
2. Click View import connections, and then click Create New Connection.

3. On the Add Connection page, in the Type drop-down list, select Business Data Catalog. The page is refreshed and the Connections Settings section contains business data Browse and Type Check icons, as shown in Figure 12-16.

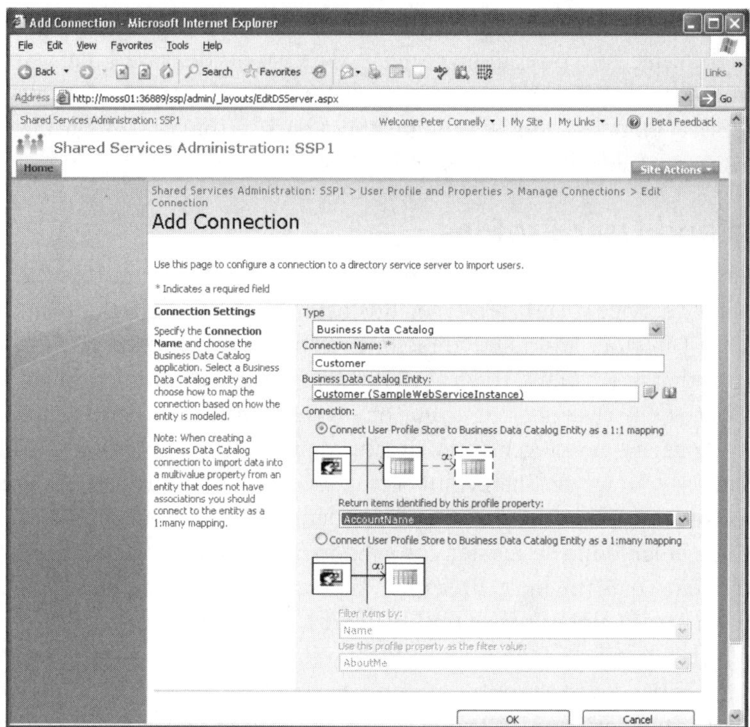

Figure 12-16 User Profile Import—Add Connection Web page

4. Type a name in the Connection Name text box, and click the Browse icon. The Business Data Type Picker dialog box is displayed (as shown in Figure 12-14). Choose the appropriate entity, and click OK to close the dialog box.

5. Choose either the 1:1 Mapping or 1:Many Mapping connection type.

Real World Mapping Business Data to User Profiles

Use the mapping connection type to map business source information specific to one user, such as when a SAP system contains a user's personal details. If your data source returns one row of personal data per user, then use the 1:1 mapping connection. In this situation, from the drop-down list, "Return items identified by this profile property", select the user profile property, such as, the *AccountName*. In the metadata, this information has to map to an *Identifier* property for the entity, with a matching *SpecificFinder* method. Both the user profile property and the identity type must match–for example, they both must be text; one cannot be defined as an integer and the other as a text string. If your data source contains more than one row per user, then use the 1:many mapping connection. From the drop-down list, "Filter items by," select the property in the entity that identifies the rows in the data source for a user, and then in the second drop down list, "Use this profile property as the filter value," select the profile property whose value can be used as the filter value.

Just as you can with an Active Directory import, you can schedule a process to synchronize the business data periodically.

Mapping Profile Properties to BDC Data

To map profile properties to BDC data, follow these steps:

1. On the Shared Services Administration Web page, click User Profiles And Properties to display the User Profile And Properties Web page.
2. If you do not have a profile property to map to in the User Profile Properties section, click Add Profile Property to display the Add User Profile Property Web page.
    a. Complete the Property Settings, User Description, Policy Settings, Edit Settings, Display Settings, and Search Settings sections according to your requirements.
    b. In the Property Import Mapping section, from the Data Connection drop-down list, choose the appropriate data source and map it to the required entity, as shown in Figure 12-17.

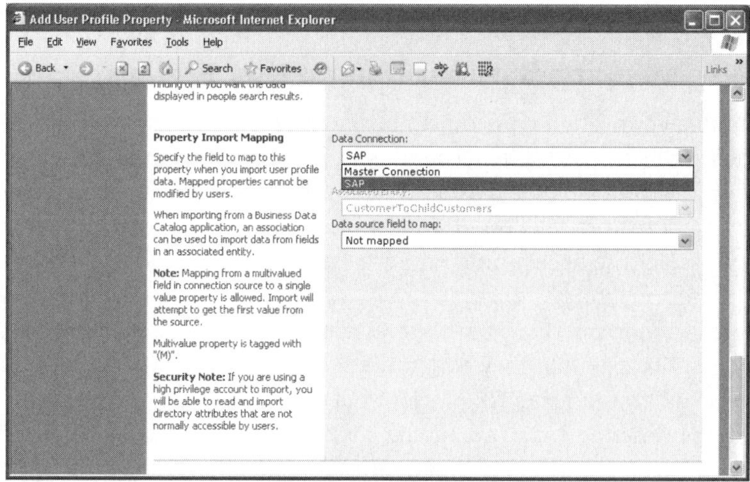

Figure 12-17 Property import mapping

3. If you have an existing property that you want to map to a BDC data source, in the User Profile Properties section on the Profile And Properties Web page, click View Profile Properties to display the View Profile Properties Web page.

   a. Find the required property, and from the drop-down list, select Edit to display the Edit User Profile Property page.

   b. Configure the Property Import Mapping section as described in part b of step 2.

Note In the Edit Settings section of the User Profile Properties page, you can allow users to edit a property. You should not allow users to edit profile properties that map to imported properties, as they will be overwritten when the next profile import is scheduled.

Business Data and My Site

After you have defined a business application in the BDC and configured the user profiles, you can use the existing features in SharePoint Server 2007 to personalize and target content to users, including the personalization features on My Site.

Connection Reuse in Excel, SharePoint, InfoPath, and Reporting Services

A new feature in Windows SharePoint Services 3.0, is the Data Connection Library (DCL), which provides a place to store, share, and manage connection files. The DCL connection files are designed for use with Excel, InfoPath, and Reporting Services. The connection files managed by the DCL are Office Data Connection (ODC) files that contain information and parameter needs to connect to a business application, such as server name, table name, and query. Therefore, they are very similar to the ADF. However, these connection files should not be confused with the ADF, which can be used only from the BDC. Now you no longer need to embed connection strings into each Excel workbook, you can save them centrally in a DCL.

To create a DCL, create a document library and select Microsoft Office Data Connection as the document template. Further information on this new feature can be found in Chapter 20 and Chapter 21.

Business Data Catalog and Search

The BDC comes with a protocol handler that enables SharePoint Server 2007 to index and provide full-text searches. However, defining data sources in the BDC does not make data automatically available within search. First, the data source must be registered with the BDC, and the metadata must have defined an *IDEnumerator* method, which is used in conjunction with the *SpecificFinder* method to return data from the data source. Then you must configure Enterprise Search for searching the business data. This section details this second activity, which consists of three steps:

1. Add a content source.
2. Map crawled properties.
3. Optionally, create a search scope, customized search pages, custom search queries, or all three.

Adding a Content Source

To include the content from a data source in the Enterprise Search, you must create content sources. For each content source, you have the choice of creating a content source for all the data defined in the BDC, for each LOB system, or for a combination of LOB systems. To create a content source for business data, complete the following steps:

1. On the SharePoint 3.0 Central Administration Web site, in the left navigation pane, click the name of the Shared Services Provider where you imported the metadata package.
2. In the Search section, click Search Settings to display the Configure Search Settings Web page.
3. Click Content Sources and crawl schedules to display the Manage Content Sources page.

4. Click New Content Source, type a name, and then in the Content Source Type section, click Business Data. The Add Content Source Web Part refreshes, and a list of all the LOB systems defined in the BDC is displayed, similar to the list shown in Figure 12-18.

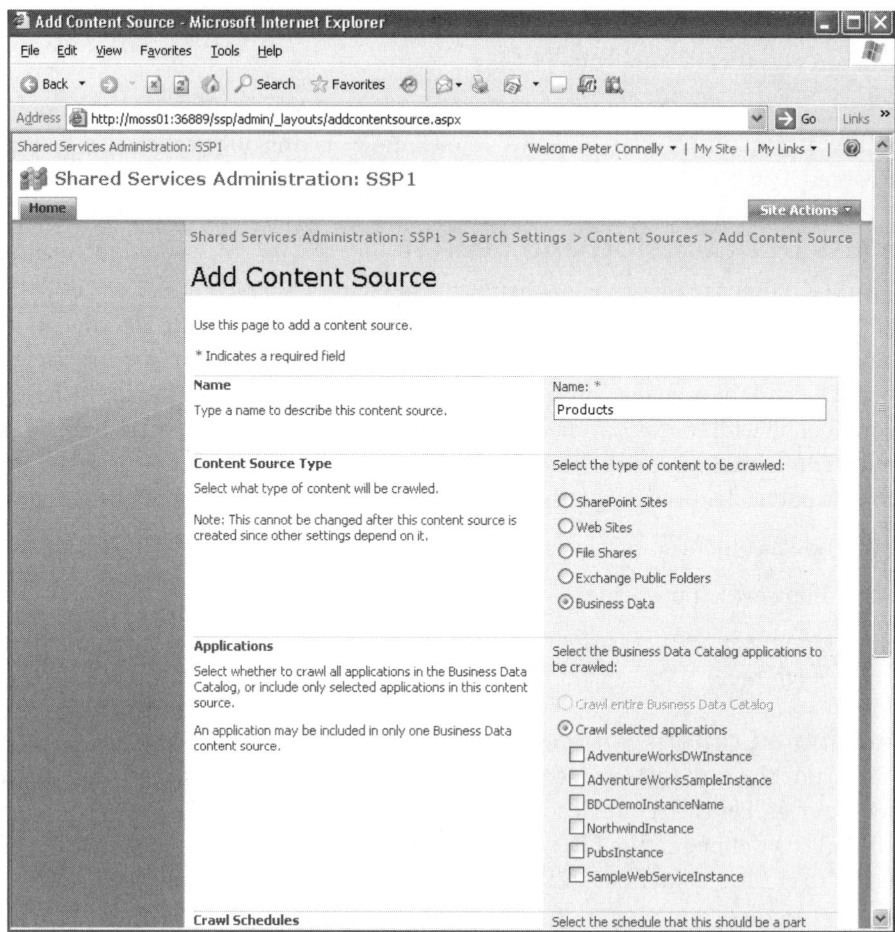

Figure 12-18 Adding a business data content source

You can set the crawl schedules for the incremental and full crawls at content source creation time or later. Incremental crawls are only possible if a *LastModifiedDate* property is one of the return fields in a *SpecificFinder* method for an entity. Similarly, you can start a full crawl immediately. See Chapter 17, "Enterprise Search and Indexing Deployment," for more information on the Search Settings options.

5. Click OK, and then if you haven't already done so, complete a full crawl.

Mapping Crawled Properties

In SharePoint Server 2007, the Enterprise Search feature is able to discover new properties, known as *crawled properties*. To make a crawled property available to a user, you need to make sure it is included in the search index and mapped to a managed property as detailed in the following steps:

1. Wait for a full crawl to complete on the new content source, and then on the Configure Search Settings Web page, click Metadata Property Mappings.
2. In the left navigation pane, click Crawled Properties. The Metadata Property Mappings page is displayed. If this is the first time you have crawled a business data content source, the Number Of Properties column for the Business Data category should not be zero if the crawl process was successful and your ADF was correctly defined.

> **Note** Keep track of the number of properties as you incorporate each business data content source so that, if the number does not rise, you can quickly identify issues with the *IDEnumerator* and *SpecificFinder* method definitions in the metadata.

3. Click the Business Data link in the Category Name column. The Metadata Property Mappings Web page is displayed, as shown in Figure 12-19.

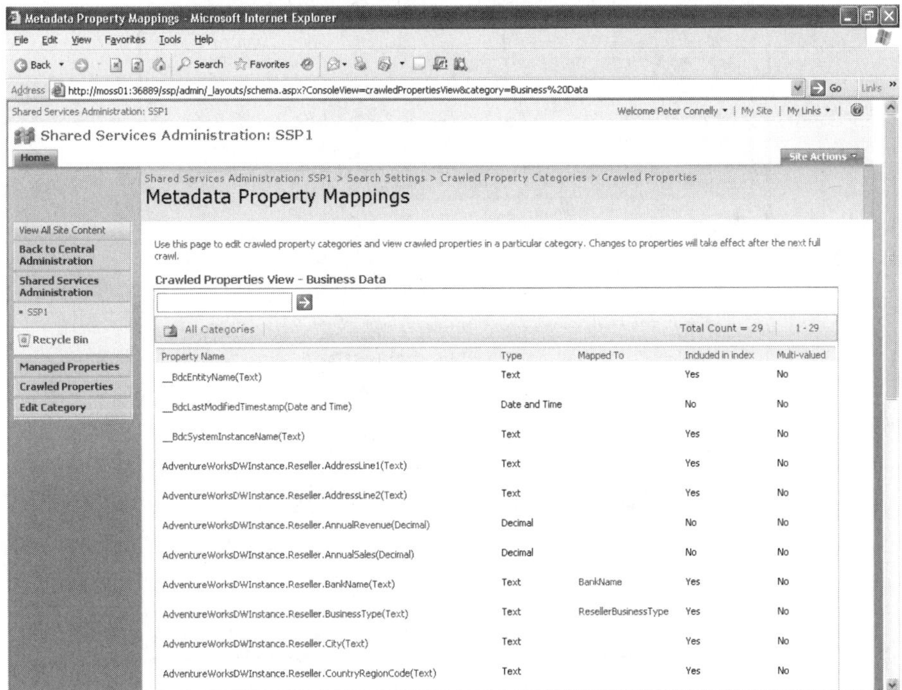

Figure 12-19 Metadata Property Mappings Web page

For each entity that has an *IDEnumerator* method, there will be at least one property name for each *TypeDescriptor* defined in the *SpecificFinder* method. Any property that has a Yes in the Mapped To Content column is already included in the search index. The default configuration, which you can amend, is to include only text properties in the search index.

4. To include a property in the search index—for example, one of the non-text properties—click the property name in the Property Name column. On the Edit Crawled Property Web page, in the Mappings to managed properties section, select the Include Values For This Property in the search index option and then click OK.

5. To map a crawled property, you can choose an existing managed property or create a new one. It is likely you will choose to create a new managed property as follows:

   a. In the left navigation pane, click Managed Properties, and then on the Metadata Property Mappings Web page, click New Managed Property. The New Managed Property Web page is displayed.

   b. In the Name and type section, enter a Property Name and select a type of information for the property.

   c. In the Mappings to crawled properties section, click Add Mapping. The Crawled Property Selection dialog box is displayed, as shown in Figure 12-20.

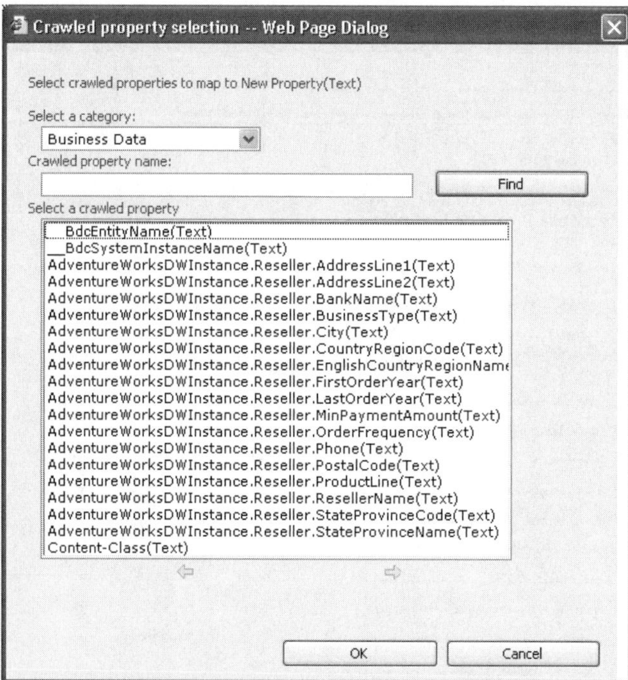

Figure 12-20 Crawled Property Selection dialog box

d. In the Select a category drop-down list, select Business Data. This dialog box will show only properties that are of the specified type and included in the index. If the number of properties available is greater than the dialog box can display, a yellow arrow is displayed. You can use the yellow arrow icons to scroll through the properties or, alternatively, you can use the Find feature.

e. Select the required property and then click OK. The dialog box closes, and the crawled property appears in the text box.

f. Select the Allow this property to be used in scopes option, to make the property available for use in defining search scoptes.

g. Click OK, and repeat this procedure for each crawled property you need to map to a managed property.

6. In the breadcrumb, click Search Settings, and then click Content sources and crawl schedules. For the appropriate content source you created, from the drop-down list select Start Full Crawl.

After steps 1 and 2 have been completed, you should be able to find data from the business data sources. The search results page provides links to the entity's profile page, as shown in Figure 12-21.

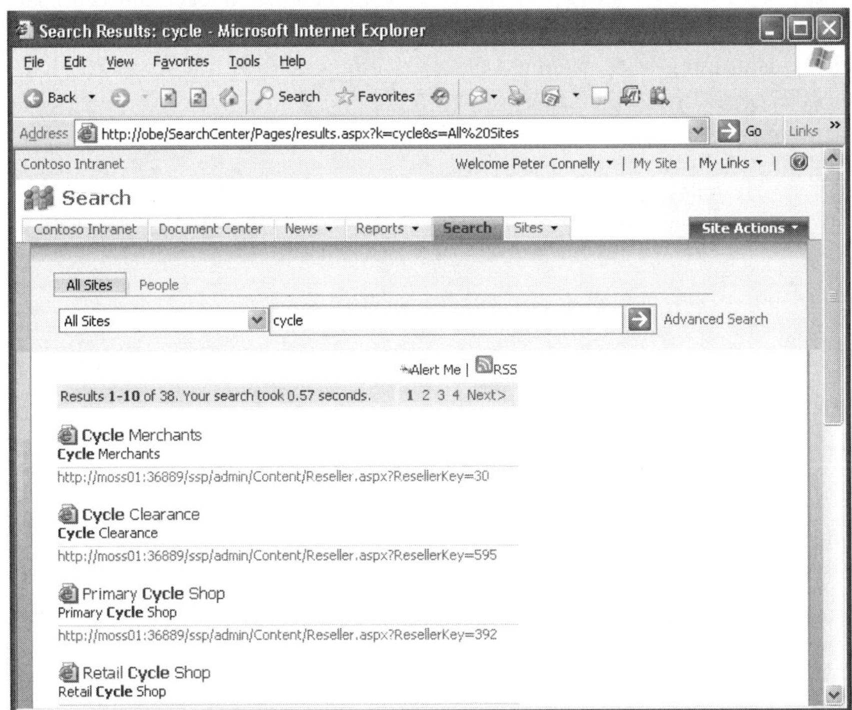

Figure 12-21 Search Center search business data result set

Customizing the End-User Experience

If you want users to limit the search for keywords to a specific business data source, you can create a search scope with a rule that specifies the content source you created. You could also create a new tab in the Search Center to display the search results associated with this content source. Please refer to Chapter 16, "Enterprise Search and Indexing Architecture and Administration" for information on configuring the user's experience in the Search Center.

Following are some important practices you should put in place:

- Expose your business applications as databases or as a Web service.
- Develop BDC-friendly *IDEnumerator Finder* and *SpecificFinder* methods.
- Simplify your custom integration code with the BDC runtime API.

Summary

In this chapter we've explored the Business Data Catalog, a feature of SharePoint Server 2007 that allows you to connect to business data using an application definition file. Once the business application metadata is defined, you can use the data from those systems using the provided Business Data Web Parts, search, business data column and user profiles. This reduces the need to write custom code to access business data and provides standard methods of integrating business data, with data held within standard SharePoint Server 2007 sites, lists and libraries.

Chapter 13

Performance Monitoring and Microsoft Operations Manager 2005

An often overlooked component of successfully implemented Microsoft Office SharePoint Server 2007 servers is performance monitoring. Performance monitoring should be an integral part of routine operations on every system—not just for Office SharePoint Server 2007 servers. However, this chapter will focus on performance monitoring for SharePoint Server 2007.

Ever-growing workload demands, shrinking schedules, and change of scope can cause server performance monitoring to be overlooked or completely ignored. Eventually, all complex systems will exhibit slowdowns of one severity or another for myriad reasons. This chapter will begin by identifying these potential bottlenecks and then give focused examples of how to resolve existing performance issues.

Of course, a contented SharePoint administrator is one whose server farm is operating well, with services that are meeting or exceeding the requirements of the business—and doing so with the least effort possible. The second part of this chapter will help SharePoint administrators get a little closer to that desired state by introducing Microsoft Operations Manager 2005—a product that can *automatically* monitor and report on the performance counters, event logs, and the health and availability of enterprise products and services from across the network, including SharePoint Server 2007. Monitoring system health closely is essential for spotting and addressing possible issues before they arise, quickly remedying problems that do occur, and understanding usage demands on the system to help predict future growth requirements.

The tool that most systems administrators find the easiest to use is the Microsoft Windows Performance tool (*%systemroot%*\system32\perfmon.exe). In previous versions of Windows Server, this tool was called Performance Monitor, or PerfMon. The default view of the Performance tool is called System Monitor. The Performance tool is always available, no matter which Windows Server system you work on. The Performance tool provides the required tools to diagnose virtually all performance issues on a Microsoft Windows Server system, regardless of the applications or products in use, with surprisingly little overhead. The Performance tool has the capability to monitor thousands of different counters, but it is best to identify possible bottlenecks and monitor only those. Trying to monitor too much will yield massive logs and essentially render the tool useless. For a potentially complex application, it is essential that the scope of monitoring be narrowed to effectively use the Performance tool.

Understanding System Monitor

Following are the four major pieces to the Performance tool:

- System Monitor
- Counter Logs
- Trace Logs
- Alerts

Each of these provides a different, but complementary, function in system monitoring.

System Monitor

Arguably the most utilized function of the four is System Monitor. This is the graphical representation of the counters that have been selected for monitoring. Counters are views into the core of the operating system that have been exposed to you as the system administrator for tracking. When a server such as Microsoft SQL Server or Office SharePoint Server 2007 is installed, new counters are installed that are specific to the server platform and that have been designed to provide performance information about that specific platform. A good example is with SQL Server. After installation, objects called SQLServer:Locks with various counters are added. Monitoring these counters will tell you if two or more SQL jobs are creating a lock on your SharePoint Server 2007 database and causing you to be unable to serve pages.

Figure 13-1 gives us a common view of System Monitor, illustrating operating system counters for Windows Server 2003.

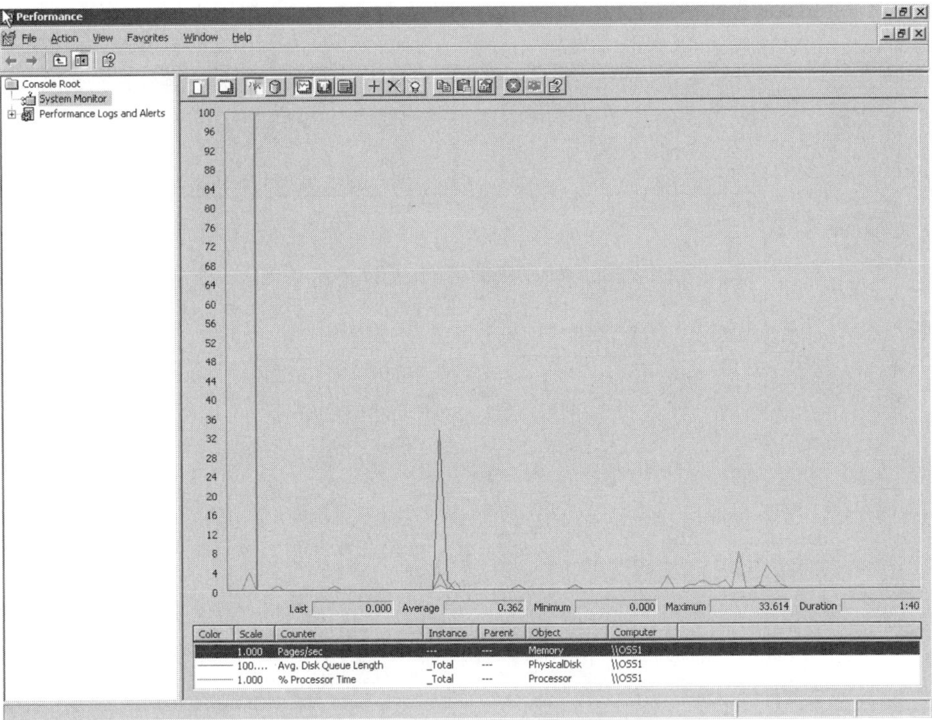

Figure 13-1 Windows System Monitor

Counter Logs

The next important function (and perhaps the most valuable) of the Performance tool is Counter Logs. With Counter Logs, you can create log files based on any counter in the Performance tool. This is extremely helpful when tracking issues over periods of time and outside normal business hours. Using this function of the Performance tool is the best way to establish the baseline the performance of a system. With Counter Logs, counters can be configured to record with a default interval (how often a snapshot of the value is taken) and to monitor for a specified period of time.

Another important component is how these logs can be recorded. The default format is a binary file, which is a good compact format that can be read by anyone with the Performance tool. Other ways to record these logs include using a text file (either tab-delimited or comma-delimited), binary circular file (which allows for setting a size limit so that the oldest point is deleted when the maximum size is reached), or SQL database. SQL data is the superior file type for long-term monitoring because it allows you to keep the data in a very compact format and allows for complex queries on your performance data. Figure 13-2 shows the Properties configuration screen for the default System Overview counter log in the Performance tool.

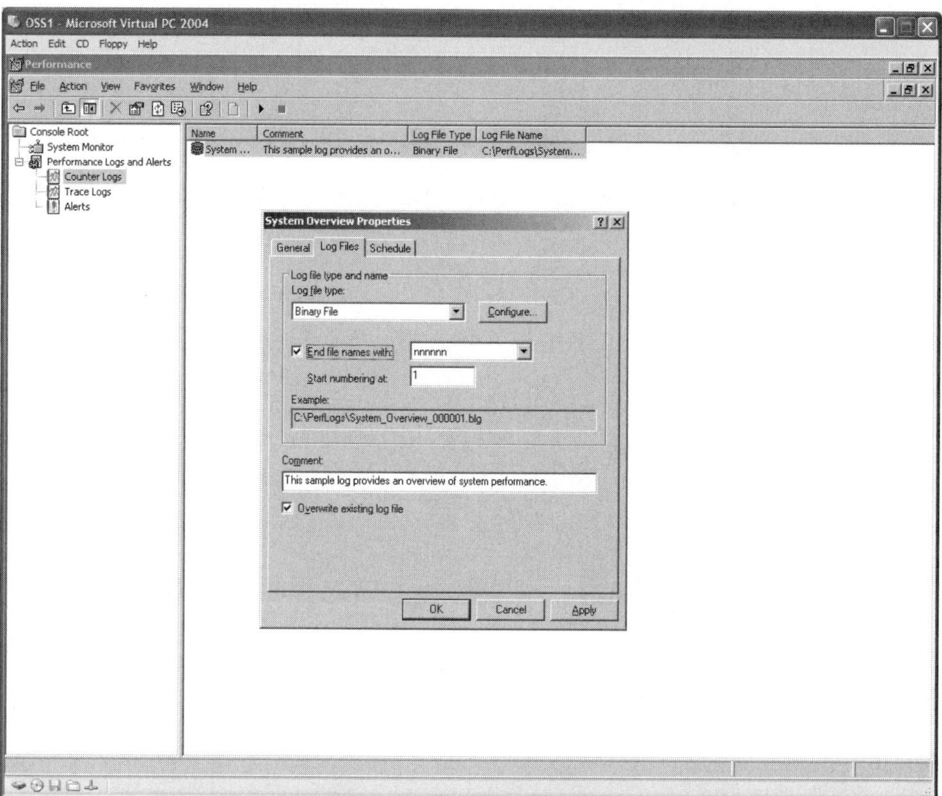

Figure 13-2 Counter Logs

Trace Logs

Trace Logs are a way to gather detailed data when certain system events occur. Instead of being used to record the measurements of specific counters as Counter Logs are used for, Trace Logs are used to record memory and resource events. Trace Logs are not readable by typical programs such as Notepad or Microsoft Office Excel, but rather require parsing tools that are used by developers, using the Trace Log application programming interface (API) from MSDN.

More Info More information on the Trace Log application programming interface can be found at *http://msdn.microsoft.com/library/default.asp?url=/library/en-us/DevTest_g/hh/DevTest_g/tracetools_f356ef23-eb23-48ab-a266-1f271339513a.xml.asp*.

Alerts

The last function of the Performance tool is Alerts. Alerts allow administrators to create a set of conditions with any available counter. (See Figure 13-3.) When this condition is met, such as % Processor Time > 95, an action occurs. The following actions are available by default in the Performance tool:

- Log an entry in the application log
- Send a network message
- Begin a Counter Log
- Execute a specific program

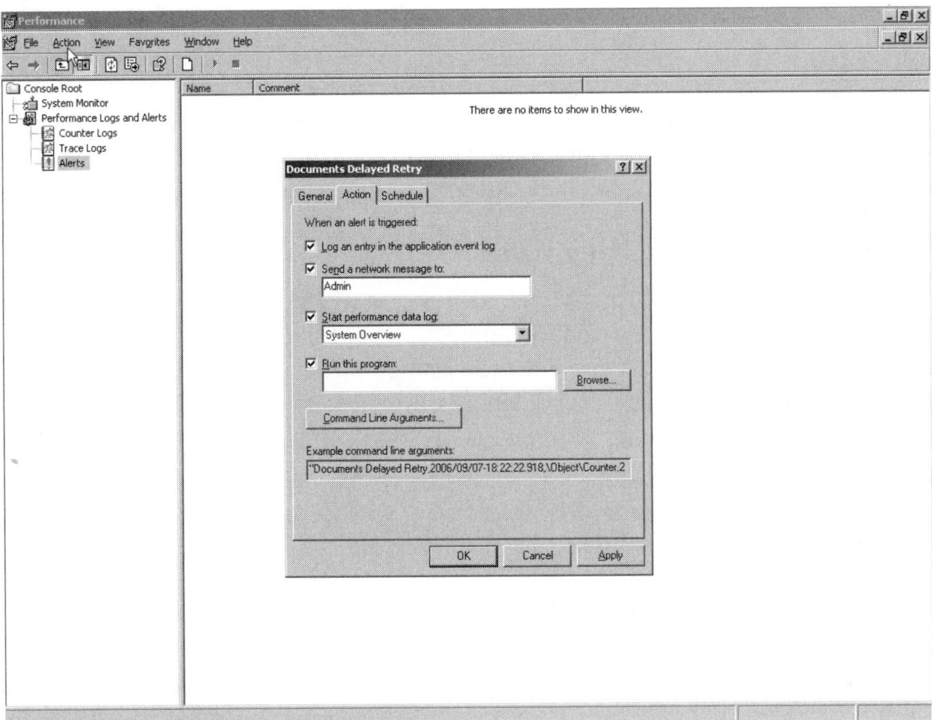

Figure 13-3 Example of Alert actions

More Info For more information on how to configure alerts using the Performance tool, see Knowledge Base article KB324752 found at *http://support.microsoft.com/default.aspx/kb/324752*.

The Performance tool allows you the flexibility of any combination of these actions, based on the list of counters. Alerts can also be scheduled. For example, you can turn off the alert for Physical Disk Queue length during the time at which a SQL Log Shipping transaction is running because high amounts of I/O will be generated for legitimate reasons. With SharePoint Server 2007, use the Office Server Search Search Gatherer\Documents Delayed Retry counter to alert you when a non-zero value occurs. This condition indicates a server is unavailable during crawling.

Preparing to Monitor Performance

The first required task is to understand what subsystems are critical to scrutinize. Begin with one or more of the following subsystems:

- Processor
- Memory
- Disk
- Network

Weaknesses in each of these areas can generate a significant bottleneck in one or more combinations of other areas. Looking at each one in detail will help determine what sort of impact might be incurred.

Monitoring Processor Utilization

The processor is the most obvious component that is critical to the performance of the system. But with a long list of potential counters, you need to pare down what is important to monitor and define the requirement for doing so. There are multiple counters that can be monitored for potential CPU bottlenecks, but the following three cover the majority of issues:

Note When we refer to an object, counter, or instance in this chapter, the format will be as follows: Object\Counter\Instance.

- **Processor\% Processor Time_Total** This counter shows the real-time utilization of the processor or processors. A value that is consistently above 50 percent demonstrates an emerging bottleneck at the processor. Consistent values at or above 75 percent require additional CPUs or farm servers to reduce the load on the processors being monitored.

- **System\Processor Queue Length\(N/A)** This counter measures how many items are waiting to be processed. A value based on the following formula (# of CPUs x 2) is the maximum this counter should read for an extended period. So in the case of a two-processor system, a value of four or less is acceptable. Sustained values above four (in this example) either require upgrading CPUs (additional L2 Cache), additional processors, or scaling out by adding more servers to the same farm role.
- **Processor\Interrupts/sec** This counter measures the average rate at which the processor must service system requests for hardware interrupts, such as network, hard drive, mouse, and system clock. This counter should be monitored over a longer period of time, looking for upward trends. Less than 1000 is acceptable for unhindered performance. Dramatic increases in this counter without corresponding increases in system use, indicate faulty hardware. Use your system vendor provided diagnostics to check for hardware anomalies.

Monitoring Memory Utilization

In many cases, system administrators are tempted to "throw memory" at the problem. This can work in the short term, but a correctly diagnosed problem will help you to avoid spending potentially thousands of dollars without actually resolving the issue. Monitoring memory counters can reap significant rewards.

- **Memory\Pages/sec\(N\A)** This counter measures the number of times per second that memory must either be written to or read from the hard disk. Consistent values above 150 to 200 typically mean the system is *hard page faulting*. This means the server is swapping content from memory to the pagefile on the disk or is thrashing for some other reason. Even the newest, fastest drives are still orders of magnitude slower than system memory, which can potentially cause a severe system impact. This counter should be monitored over a longer period of time, as normal activity can cause short periods of paging.
- **Memory\Pages Faults/sec\(N\A)** This counter measures the number of hard and soft page faults per second. Soft page faults, which means accessing other parts of physical memory for the memory pages needed, are not critical because modern processors are powerful enough to handle many thousands of them per second. Hard page faults, reading from disk, will create a serious bottleneck with even just a small number due to the very slow speed of disk compared to memory. The way to determine whether a system is experiencing hard page faults is to monitor Memory\Pages/sec in conjunction with PhysicalDisk\Avg. Disk Bytes/Read. Multiply the value of the PhysicalDisk counter by 4096, and if these values are approximately equal, the system is experiencing excessive page faults. To resolve this issue, increase the amount of physical memory.

- **Memory\Available Mbytes\(N\A)** This counter measures the amount of physical memory available to the system. Although this counter is something you should obviously monitor, it is often overlooked. You will find it helpful to monitor this alongside other predictors. A low value, such as less than 10 percent of total physical memory, over even a short period of time indicates a dire need for additional memory. The longer a low physical memory condition persists, the greater the impact on system performance due to the use of the pagefile.
- **Memory\Pool Nonpaged Bytes\(N\A)** The number of bytes that cannot be paged to disk and must remain in physical memory. This counter is not widely monitored but has a very drastic effect on system performance. Monitor it in combination with Available Bytes to determine whether there is an application requiring large amounts of memory that is unable to be paged. This condition could indicate either a need for additional memory or a poorly written application. This can be monitored directly by using Process\Pool Nonpaged Bytes\ for specific SharePoint Server 2007 processes. The most important processes are Office and Windows SharePoint Server Search (both called mssearch.exe), Windows SharePoint Services Timer (owstimer.exe), Windows SharePoint Services Tracing (wsstracing.exe), and Internet Information Services (IIS) (inetinfo.exe). The two largest consumers of memory will be the Server Search (Office or Windows) and IIS. If any combination of these processes claims 90 percent or more of the available nonpaged bytes, an interesting problem occurs. IIS will stop serving requests, but there will be no symptoms. To resolve the issue, restart IIS and then determine which items are causing the excessive use of nonpaged memory.

Monitoring Disk Utilization

There are two types of counters for disk: physical and logical. *Physical disk* refers to a disk without regard for grouping configurations, such as a concatenation of disks or RAID sets. *Logical disk* counters report only on the activity of the logical disk in a grouping. A great deal of performance benefit can be gained by tracking down and resolving disk issues. Because even the newest modern hard drives are orders of magnitude slower than memory or processor, even small gains will return large rewards. Note that if you are focusing your monitoring on disk-related issues, you should log your data to another server to ensure you are not adding load to your disk subsystem.

- **PhysicalDisk\% Disk Time\DriveLetter** This counter measures the percentage of time within the reporting window that the physical drive is active. If this counter consistently shows values above 80 percent, there is a lack of system memory or a disk controller issue. There are other counters you will use in conjunction with this one to determine the fault.

- **PhysicalDisk\Current Disk Queue Length\DriveLetter** This counter measures the number of requests waiting to be serviced by the disk at the instant of the poll. Disk drives with multiple spindles can handle multiple requests. If the value of this counter is over two times the number of spindles for a sustained period of time, along with a high % Disk Time, a disk upgrade is required in the disk subsystem. Typically, drives have only a single spindle. You should add to the number of disks available in the RAID set. Consider upgrading to a RAID 0 or RAID 5 configuration if this is a single drive.
- **PhysicalDisk\Avg. Disk sec/Transfer\DriveLetter** This counter measures the average number of disk transfers per second. The value for this counter should remain below 0.3. Higher values indicate possible failures of the disk controller to access the drive. If this occurs, confirm that the drive, as well as the disk controller, is functioning normally.

The counters just listed for physical drives pertain to logical disk as well, and in the same manner. Differences occur with RAID sets and dynamic disks. With a RAID set, it is possible to have greater than 100 % Disk Time. Use the Avg Disk Queue Length counter to determine the requests pending for the disks. When dynamic disks are in use, logical counters are removed. When you have a dynamic volume with more than one physical disk, instances will be listed as 'Disk 0 C:', 'Disk 1 C:', 'Disk 0 D:', and so on. In situations where you have multiple volumes on a single drive, instances will be listed as '0 C: D:'.

Storage Area Network Disk Monitoring

There are differences when monitoring disks on a Storage Area Network (SAN). A SAN is different than a physical disk in that you must be concerned with how many disks make up the logical unit number (LUN). Your SAN administrator will be able to provide that information. Most SANs will return a value to the Performance tool as if a physical disk is being monitored. This number is inaccurate because it is the additive value of all the disks. To determine the correct value, divide the Performance tool result by the number of disks in the LUN. Typically, physical disk counters and logical disk counters will return the same value on a SAN. It is a good idea to check with your SAN team before you start using the Performance tool, as tools specifically written for the SAN hardware generally give better information. It is likely this data will not be available in a usable format, and this is where the Performance tool can be very useful.

Monitoring Network Utilization

Many companies employ server administrators who must wear multiple hats. It is not uncommon for the person who maintains servers to also maintain personal computers and the network. Windows Server exposes some very good counters for helping to track network-related issues. If you must play the role of the network engineer in a smaller company, be aware that there are a multitude of helpful counters. In large companies with distinct network and server teams, these counters can be invaluable in coordinating with other groups to resolve complex challenges.

In most modern servers, the network card has a processor to handle the moving and encoding of network traffic. However, you might still administer systems that do not have server-level network cards. It is important to monitor processor and memory along with network statistics to determine the root cause of problems that arise. Unlike other counters previously covered in this chapter, network monitoring is done at different layers of the OSI model ranging from the Data-link layer up to the Presentation layer. Because most companies use Ethernet as the network medium and TCP/IP as the protocol, that will be the focus of this section. The TCP/IP layer model maps directly to the OSI model. All layers are monitored with different counters due to the unique nature of each.

More Info For more information on how TCP/IP is implemented on Microsoft Windows platforms, see the online book titled TCP/IP Fundamentals for Microsoft Windows found at *http://www.microsoft.com/technet/itsolutions/network/evaluate/technol/tcpipfund/tcpipfund.mspx*. For a map of the TCP/IP and OSI models, go to the following Web site: *http://www.microsoft.com/library/media/1033/technet/images/itsolutions/network/evaluate/technol/tcpipfund/caop0201_big.gif*.

Monitoring at the Data-Link Layer

The data-link layer is the bottom layer in the TCP/IP protocol stack. Even though the processes within the layer are dependent on the physical medium (Ethernet, SONET, ATM, and so on) and devices drivers, the information is passed on to the TCP/IP stack. It is crucial that you monitor these counters when exploring network-related bottlenecks.

- **Network Interface\Bytes Sent, Received and Total/sec** This counter measures the number of bytes sent, the number of bytes received, or the sum of both that pass in and out of the network interface per second during the polling period. These counters can be monitored individually or as a total. Typically, the total is the important counter, unless there is a specific application with heavy data flow in one direction. Monitor these counters for a longer period during normal production hours. This approach will help you chart a baseline for network activity so that you will be able determine whether the issues are network related.

A good rule of thumb for maximum expected throughput is ((Network Card Speed x 2) / 8) x 75%. Most network-use switches allow for full duplex (sending and receiving at the same time), which is why the speed is doubled in the formula. Divide the result by 8 to get the speed measured in bytes. The reason for only 75 percent of the listed speed is due to TCP/IP's and Ethernet's error checking and packet assembly/disassembly. For a 100-Mbit Ethernet card, you can expect a maximum throughput of 18.75 megabytes (MBs) per second. If applications or users are experiencing slow data-transfer speeds, confirm that your network cards are set to full duplex if you are in a switched environment. If you are not sure, set the card to auto-detect duplex or ask your network administrator for their requirements.

Monitoring at the Network Layer

This is the first layer that is independent of the physical medium. The network layer handles the routing of packets across a heterogeneous network. When referring to the OSI network model, this layer and its functions are referred to as *layer 3*.

- **Network Interface\Datagrams (Forwarded, Received, Sent, Total)/sec** As with the data-link layer, each of these counters should be monitored for a specified length of time during normal production hours so that a baseline can be established. The throughput of the datagrams through the network interface depends on a variety of factors. Most importantly, if a significant increase occurs, consider upgrading your network cards to server-class cards or upgrading the speed of your network. Problems with the network layer arise from the inability of the card and server to process the packets quickly. Server-class cards offload this functionality from the server.

Monitoring at the Transport Layer

The transport layer is responsible for ensuring packets arrive intact or are rtransmitted, congestion control, and packet ordering. This layer does a lot of the heavy work with regard to the network. Many of the problems with network issues can occur here, and therefore, this is one of the most critical layers to monitor.

- **Network Interface\Segments (Received, Sent, Total)/sec** Again, you should establish a baseline level of performance to look for with these counters to help assess future problems. Transport-layer work is handled by servers on each end of the communication and is not an intensive task for modern servers.
- **Network Interface\Segments Retransmitted /sec** If this value shows a sudden significant increase, check the status of your network card. Retransmissions occur when duplexing is set incorrectly or there are issues with a network route.

Monitoring at the Presentation Layer

This layer ensures that the information from the network layer is available in the correct format to the system. It ensures translation and encryption or decryption is performed before the data is passed.

There are two types of counters under this heading to be concerned with: server and redirector. The server object is specifically for monitoring the server or the machines serving the information. The redirector is used when monitoring client machines. Either or none of these machines could be a server in the hardware sense, but this refers to how they interact with each other in the client-server paradigm.

- **Server\Nonpaged Pool Failures** The number of times a failure occurs while attempting to read from the Nonpaged Pool. This is the memory that cannot be paged. After you have established a baseline for this counter, consider upgrading the memory in your system after a 10 to 20 percent increase.
- **Server\Work Item Shortages** The number of times during the polling interval the server had nothing to do or that a time slice could not be allocated for the request. This counter should remain unchanged, with a value under 3. If it does not, consider increasing the value of InitWorkItems or MaxWorkItems in the registry under HKEY_LOCAL_MACHINE\SYSTEM\CurrentControlSet\Services\LanmanServer. If the values do not exist, create them as REGDWORD with values in decimal format. InitWorkItems can range from 1 through 512, and MaxWorkItems can range from 1 through 65,535. For any value of InitWorkItems or MaxWorkItems, start with a value of 4,096, then double both values until the counter stays below 3.
- **Redirector\Server Sessions Hung** The number of sessions either hung or unable to be processed due to a server that is too busy. Any number above zero indicates some kind of bottleneck, but do not be concerned until the number is higher than one per second. If the number is higher, check the other counters for memory and processor on the server side to help trace the issue.

Note It is helpful to involve networking staff when tracking down possible network issues. Network engineers understand the network and are familiar with how it should respond. Be cautious when monitoring network counters without the cooperation of the network team.

Baselining Your SharePoint Server 2007 Install

There are many references to baselining in this chapter, but what exactly does it mean? *Baselining* means recording performance statistics for a relevant set of counters during normal usage times. Normal usage times should be during regular operating hours and off-peak times. Gathering statistics during timeframes with heavy, light, and no usage will help define what is normal for an individual system. There are quite a few options for you to choose from when monitoring your front-end SharePoint servers, but the most important ones are listed in Table 13-1.

Table 13-1 Monitoring Options

Object\Counter	Threshold/Description
Processor\% Processor Time_Total	<75%
System\Processor Queue Length\(N/A)	<# of CPUs x 2
Memory\Available Mbytes\(N\A)	< 80%
Memory\Pages/sec\(N\A)	<100
PhysicalDisk\% Disk Time\DataDrive	<80%
PhysicalDisk\Current Disk Queue Length \DataDrive	< #of Disks x 2
ASP.NET Applications\Requests/sec_Total	There is no hard limit. Determine this total by baselining.
ASP.NET\Worker Processes Restarts	Any number above zero can indicate that problems exist.
.NET CLR Memory\% Time in GC	Time spent on garbage collection. Thresholds depend on many factors, but a value over 25% could indicate there are too many unreachable objects.

Working with the Performance Tool

You need to have an understanding of what to monitor and how to perform that monitoring. Using the Performance tool can be daunting without first knowing how to choose your counters and the ways in which to choose them. To help understand how to use the Performance tool, please follow along on your own machine with the tool open. After opening the Performance tool, start by deleting the default items listed. You can do this by selecting the first counter, typically Memory\Pages/sec, and pressing the Delete key until all counters are deleted or clicking the "X" on the toolbar.

You can use the default counters, but deleting these confirms you will not be monitoring any extraneous items. Next, add a counter by pressing the plus (+) button beside the delete (X) button. A window will appear where you can select the counters to monitor. In Figure 13-4, Processor\% Processor Time_Total is selected, which is the total percentage of all processor capacity in use.

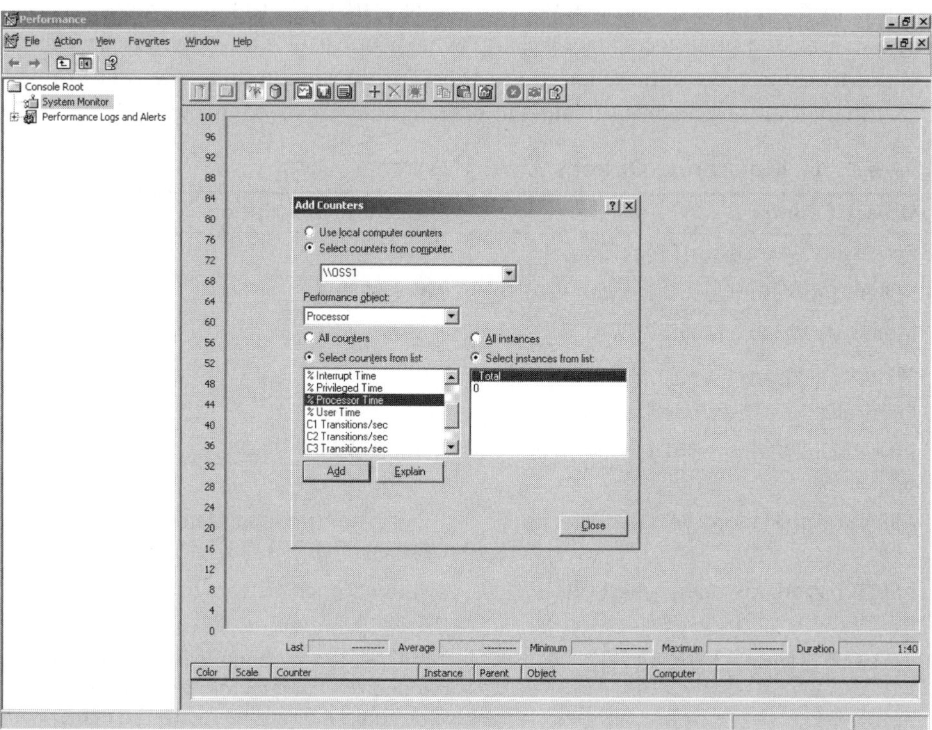

Figure 13-4 Selecting counters

In Figure 13-5, you can see where more counters have been selected. These counters are important to monitor general system performance and also to allow for demonstration of the capabilities of System Monitor. First, notice there are colored lines that represent each counter you have chosen. Colors are chosen for you, but you can change them. Examples of how to customize your counters are in the next section, "Customizing the Display." Below the graph there is a legend describing the color, scale, counters, and computer.

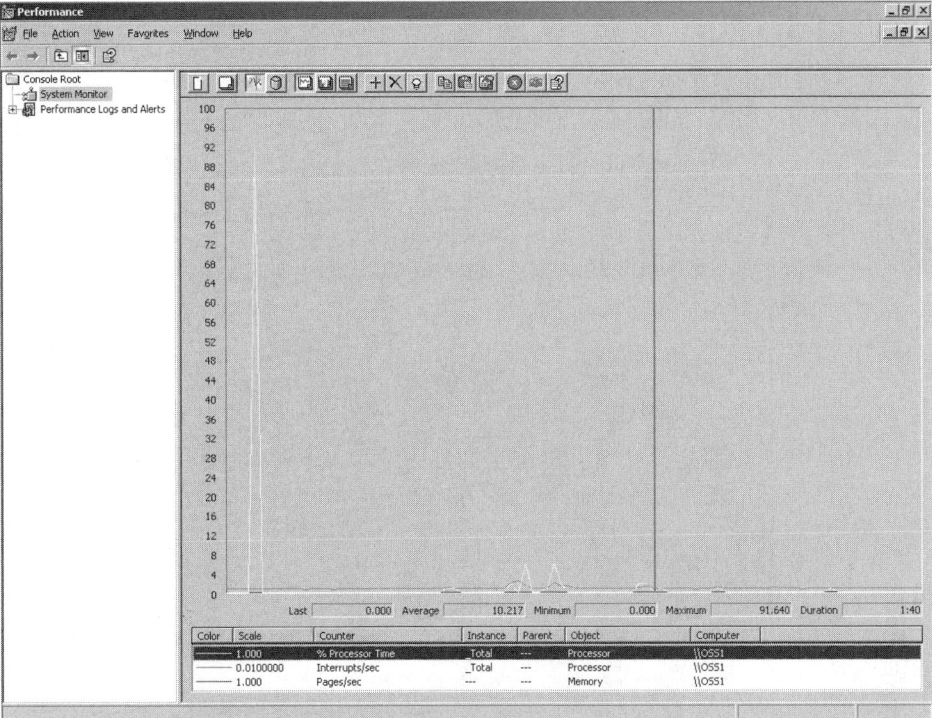

Figure 13-5 Example of System Monitor with multiple counters

The red, vertical line shows the point in time the graph is displaying. On the left of the red line is the most recently displayed performance data, while immediately to the right of the red line is the oldest data, which is about to be overwritten. The graph continually wraps as time progresses. Data collection can be paused by clicking the red circle with the small white x, which appears in the toolbar at the top of the graph. The right-hand axis shows the scale, which by default begins at 0 and ends at 100.

Customizing the Display

The display can be customized to your needs. Right-click the graph and select Properties. This opens the System Monitor Properties window. Figure 13-6 shows an example of System Monitor properties.

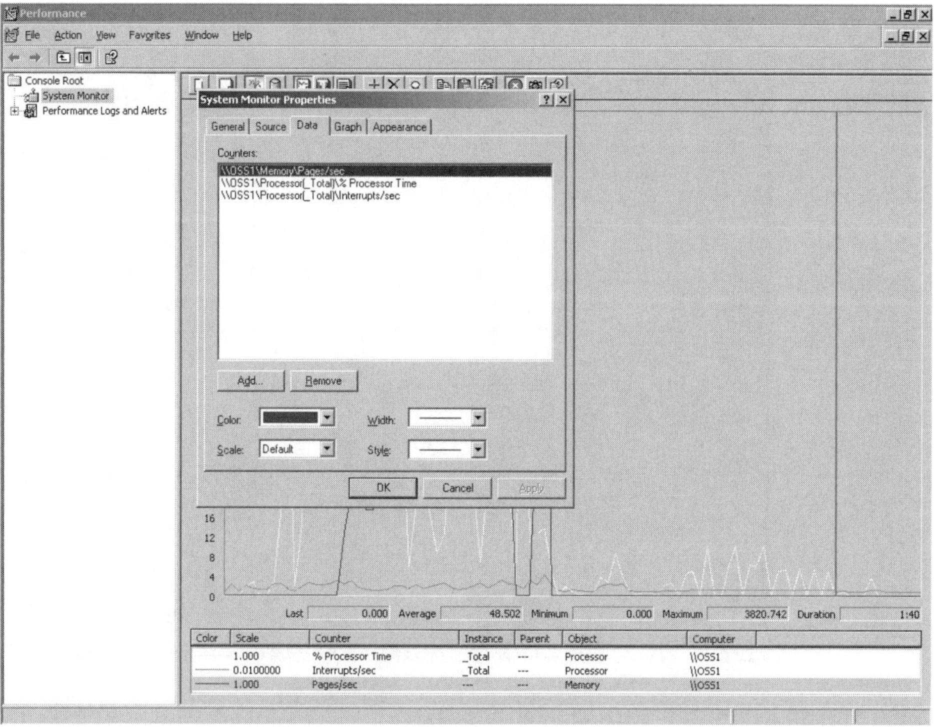

Figure 13-6 The Data tab of the System Monitor Properties window

By default, the Data tab is selected, which allows you to change the color, width, style, and scale of each counter currently displayed. Select the General tab to change items such as the View, Display Elements, and sampling rate. The sampling rate is set to one second unless you change it. Many times this is too high of a rate and can affect performance of an already taxed system. The sampling rate should be no less than 15 seconds unless you have some very good reasons to set it that low. In Figure 13-7, you see the General tab with examples of the various settings.

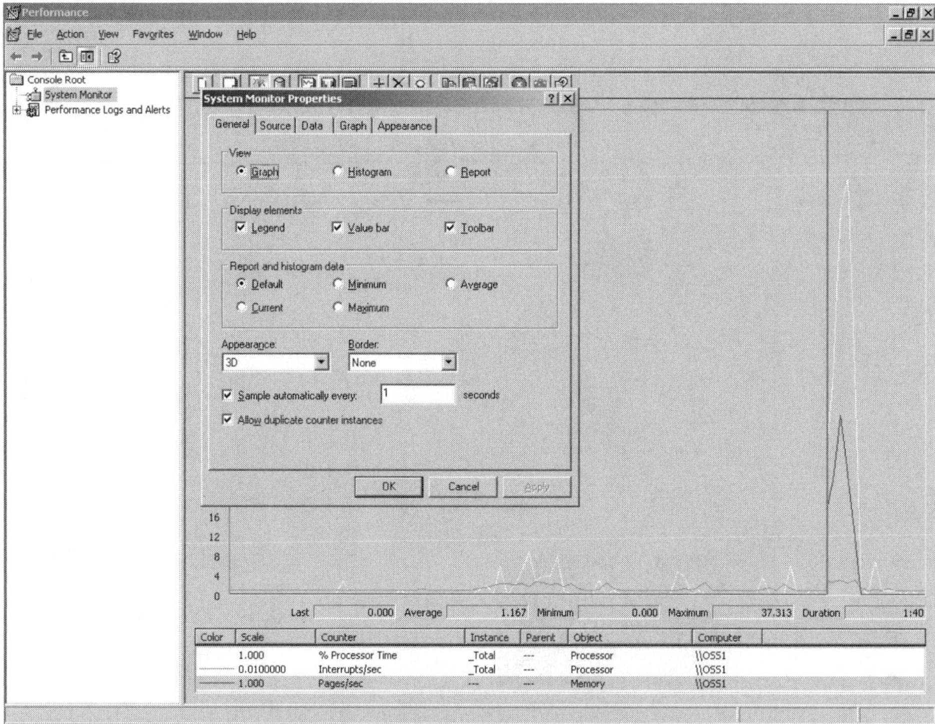

Figure 13-7 The General tab of the System Monitor Properties window

The Source tab allows you to choose your data source for displaying data. By default, Current Activity is selected for the counters chosen. The Source tab can also be used to change your input to previously logged Performance sessions, allowing you to review in detail counters you have logged to a file or database. In addition, a time range can be set so that you can focus more finely on the period of time desired. Lastly, the Appearance tab gives options to customize different aspects of System Monitor's color and font.

Additional Features

There are quite a few features of System Monitor that do not fit readily in a single category, and those will be covered in this section. From the main System Monitor window, click the View Histogram button to show a comparison of the data in real time. A *histogram* is a graphical representation, usually a bar graph, of the data presented. This is a good way for you to easily compare two or more counters at a moment in time. This feature, like any other counter within the Performance tool, can be used to track counters on a remote server. For example, when adding a counter, choose Select Counters From Computer (refer back to Figure 13-4) and type the Universal Naming Convention (UNC) path of the server you want to add counters from. Figure 13-8 shows an example of a histogram.

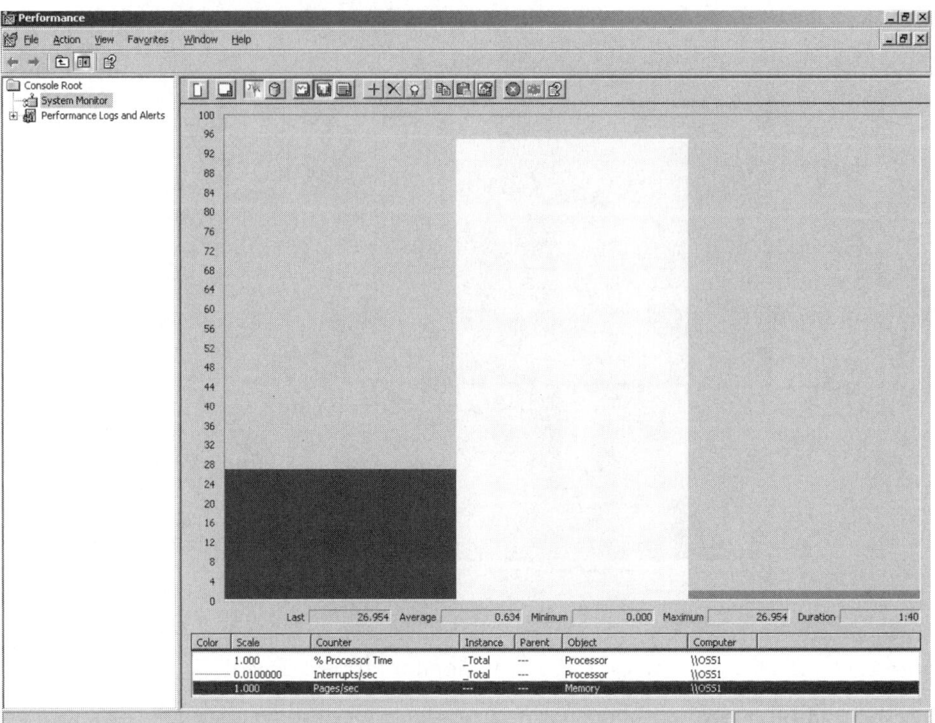

Figure 13-8 Example of a histogram

There is another option, called View Report, in the toolbar. It is denoted by the icon that looks similar to the NotePad icon. Clicking this icon displays the data in purely numerical format, also in real time. This is a very good way to watch for a certain high or low in your monitoring for a short period of time. If there is a need to monitor this over a longer period of time, consider using Alerts, which was previously covered. To the right of the Delete option (the black "X") on the toolbar is the Highlight option, which looks like a small light bulb. The Highlight option allows you to choose one counter to emphasize on your window.

Another very handy set of features is the ability to copy the properties of a Performance tool session as well as paste a counter list. Just to the right of the Highlight option is the Copy Properties button. Clicking this button copies the XML data from your monitor session to the clipboard. You can use this to track what you are monitoring or include it in a Web page. The Paste Counter List action lets you choose a list of counters from a text file and insert them into a monitor session.

The last miscellaneous options covered here is very helpful when you see a section of data you want to examine further. That function is the Freeze Display button, which looks like a red circle with a small white "x" in it. It stops monitoring while selected. Be careful with this option because it can skew your chart as monitoring is stopped. Clicking Update Data while the display is frozen causes the display to move only one time period, but that move is updated with the most current point. If you have frozen the display for 60 seconds, clicking Update Data moves the display ahead only one second if you are using the default sample rate. This does not, however, unfreeze the display..

There are a number of complex features of the Performance tool and many ways in which they can be applied. You are now armed with the knowledge of how to use the Performance tool and which counters you can use to track issues you might have. You will find that the more you use the Performance tool, the more you can learn from it.

More Info For more information on how to monitor server performance using the Performance tool, see the *Performance Guide* volume in the *Microsoft Windows Server 2003 Resource Kit* from Microsoft Press.

Microsoft Operations Manager 2005 and SharePoint Server 2007

Microsoft Operations Manager 2005 helps to centralize management of an IT infrastructure environment, reducing the complexity and costs of operation. Using Microsoft Operations Manager 2005, the status and performance of many products from across an enterprise can be automatically monitored, including infrastructure such as hardware or Domain Name Services (DNS); platform services such as Internet Information Services (IIS), SQL Server, or Active Directory (AD); and applications such as SharePoint Server 2007. SharePoint administrators can use these capabilities to monitor all the servers in a SharePoint Server 2007 farm, plus the critical platform services that directly affect SharePoint; view reports summarizing the performance and issues over time; and even perform management or troubleshooting tasks affecting those remote products and servers—all from a single desktop.

Using this central console, operators can view live and historical reports of the system status; they can drill into specific error messages or performance counters from any computer being monitored; and they can even run scripts or commands that affect those computers to make configuration changes. But rather than relying on the operators to spot problems after they occur and then spending time working out how to solve them, Microsoft Operations Manager 2005 can be always monitoring and ready to respond quickly. Thanks to preconfigured rules, performance thresholds, and best practice knowledge—provided either by the Microsoft product teams or customized and configured by the Microsoft Operations Manager 2005 operators at a specific organization—Microsoft Operations Manager 2005 can automatically detect that warning thresholds have been exceeded, whether problems have occurred, or if a failure seems *likely* to occur. Once something is detected, Microsoft Operations Manager 2005 can respond in a number of ways—from simply logging a performance issue for an operator to examine later, to sending an e-mail or paged alert message to an operator warning of an urgent issue, to executing troubleshooting scripts to immediately resolve well-known problems.

This capability provides a proactive means of troubleshooting issues before they affect users, and it reduces the time to detect and resolve failures. Fewer failures means fewer support calls, which means lower support costs, and ultimately achieves the goal of very contented SharePoint administrators.

Microsoft Operations Manager 2005 Architecture

There are two versions of Microsoft Operations Manager 2005 available: the full version of Microsoft Operations Manager 2005 and Microsoft Operations Manager 2005 Workgroup Edition. Microsoft Operations Manager 2005 Workgroup Edition is suitable for small organizations that need to monitor ten servers or fewer as all components are installed on a single server.

The full version of this product, called Microsoft Operations Manager 2005, is designed for larger organizations, and each of the main components can be separated and scaled across multiple computers, if required, to improve availability. However, administrators who plan to monitor fewer than 200 computers can choose to install all Microsoft Operations Manager 2005 components on a single computer that is appropriately sized and configured.

Note For more information on Microsoft Operations Manager 2005 scalability and sizing, refer to the Microsoft Operations Manager 2005 Deployment Planning Guide at

http://www.microsoft.com/technet/prodtechnol/mom/mom2005/Library/8331b1ef-ce28-4280-9952-ac3e067214b7.mspx.

Microsoft Operations Manager 2005 Components

Microsoft Operations Manager (MOM) 2005 comprises a number of components, which collectively are referred to as a *management group*. Although additional components are available for certain scenarios, we will examine the following core components of the management group:

- **Management Server** Used to configure monitoring and store operational data in the Microsoft Operations Manager 2005 database.
- **Managed Computers and Agents** Computers that are monitored by Microsoft Operations Manager 2005.

  Agents are the applications installed by Microsoft Operations Manager to collect operational data.
- **User Interfaces** The consoles available to administer and configure Microsoft Operations Manager 2005, and view reports on the status of monitored computers.
- **Management Pack** A collection of rules that define which information is important to monitor for a specific type of managed computer and how to respond to key events.

Microsoft Operations Manager 2005 Management Server

Microsoft Operations Manager 2005 Management Server collects event logging and performance information that is generated on the managed computers, stores this data in the central Microsoft Operations Manager 2005 database, and then filters and analyzes the data to focus on the most useful details. This data is typically already being generated on the managed computers before Microsoft Operations Manager 2005 is introduced, but you might need to review the audit logging configuration to ensure that the most useful data is being captured, ready for Microsoft Operations Manager 2005 to collect. This information can be collected from a number of existing sources on the managed computers, including the following ones:

- Any Windows Event logs (for example, Application, Security, and System)
- Trace logs
- Setup logs
- Performance counters
- Windows Management Instrumentation (WMI)

The specification defining which information to collect and the location of the required logs is contained within the Management Pack and then downloaded to the agent application that Microsoft Operations Manager 2005 deploys to gather the information.

> **Note** Microsoft Operations Manager 2005 Management Server requires either Microsoft Windows 2000 Server with Service Pack 4 (SP4) or later, or Microsoft Windows Server 2003. The Microsoft Operations Manager 2005 database requires Microsoft SQL Server 2000 with SP3a or later, or SQL Server 2005.

Managed Computers and Agents

To monitor a computer with MOM, it must be added to MOM's list of managed computers so that operational data can be collected. There are two methods of collecting the log and performance counter information from the managed computers: agent-managed and agentless. *Agent-managed* computers require a small, generic Microsoft Operations Manager 2005 agent application (around 3 MB in size) to be installed on the managed computer. The agent is then able to contact the management server, download the rules from the Management Pack specified for the managed computer, collect the required performance and event data locally, and send this data back across the network to the management server. The agents and the management server can be configured to communicate securely by using Kerberos for mutual authentication, and to sign and encrypt communications. Because the management server is merely receiving information in this scenario rather than crawling it remotely, the performance impact to the management server per additional managed computer is minimal; each individual management server is able to scale up to a maximum of 2,000 managed computers. However, be aware that the agents are sending data across the network; the more agents deployed and the more detail they are configured to collect, the more your network traffic increases.

Agentless monitoring does not require an installation on the managed computer, but an agent application is still required. However, it is installed onto the management server itself. This introduces an additional performance overhead to the management server because the server-based agents must subsequently crawl the managed computers and collect the information remotely. Microsoft Operations Manager 2005 is supported to host a maximum of only 10 agentless managed computers per management server due to the additional performance hit this introduces.

User Interfaces

There are three types of users who will use Microsoft Operations Manager 2005, and the user interfaces have been designed to cater to each of these groups:

- Administrators, who are responsible for configuring and maintaining Microsoft Operations Manager 2005
- Authors, who create custom Management Packs, manage alerts, change views, identify, diagnose, and fix problems
- Users—such as operators, IT staff, analysts, and managers—who are interested in seeing reports and historical analyses of operational data.

Users can connect to and use the management server from a console-based user interface, which typically will not be running on the management server itself, but on a standard desktop computer elsewhere. There are four main consoles provided, each of which is used to perform different tasks.

Administrator Console

The Administrator Console (shown in Figure 13-9) is a Microsoft Management Console (MMC) interface used by the Administrators and the Authors groups to manage and configure the Microsoft Operations Manager 2005 monitoring environment. These management and configuration tasks include the setup and configuration of management groups; adding and removing computers from management groups; deploying agents to managed computers; importing new Management Packs; and modifying the monitoring rules and criteria. The Information Center windows provide easy access to each of these areas.

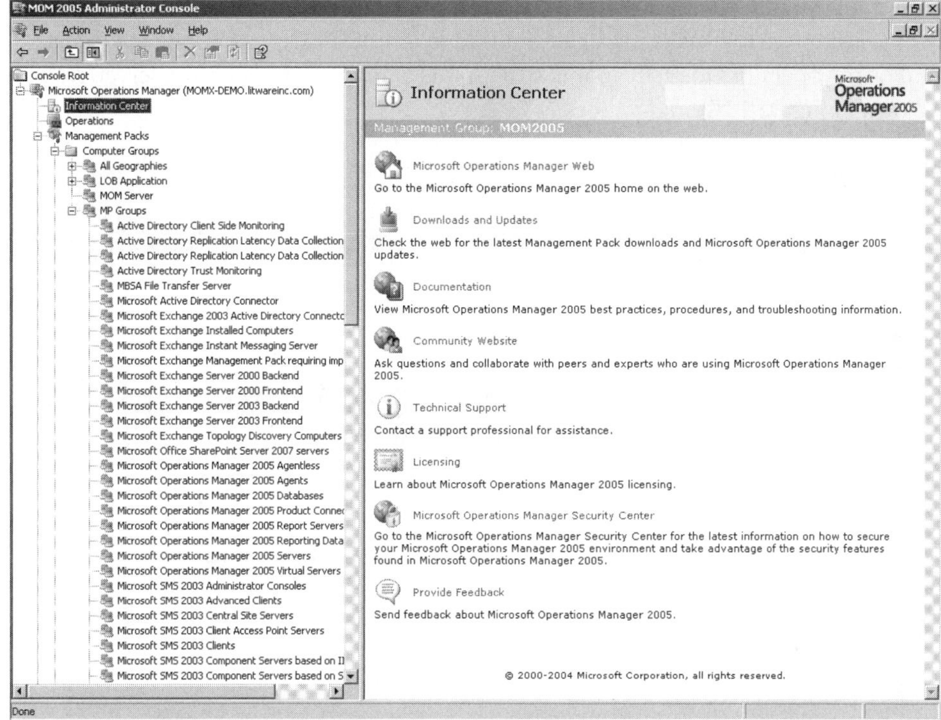

Figure 13-9 The Administrator Console

Operator Console

The Operator Console is used by the Administrators and the Operators groups to monitor the health of managed systems, discover solutions, and perform troubleshooting tasks using the range of tools that can be integrated with the console. This is where a lot of the power and the value that Microsoft Operations Manager 2005 delivers can be realized.

In a large organization, the operators might be delegated administrative responsibility for monitoring and maintaining the health of a specific type of server or line-of-business application—for example, the SharePoint server farms. Rather than require them to access the Microsoft Operations Manager 2005 server directly, you can install the Operator Console to the operators' desktops. Additionally, to reduce the amount of training required, the user interface has been designed to look similar to the familiar Microsoft Office applications, such as Microsoft Office Outlook 2003.

To make it as easy as possible for you to discover a solution, the Operator Console usually provides more than one route to follow through the user interface to find information, start a task, or change a configuration. Also, common tasks are usually automated using wizards and step-through dialog boxes to ensure that progress is made toward a goal.

The starting point for operators is to check on the aggregated views of alerts that have been received from the Microsoft Operations Manager 2005 agents on the managed servers, allowing operators to easily monitor the status of individual servers or server groups, as shown in Figure 13-10.

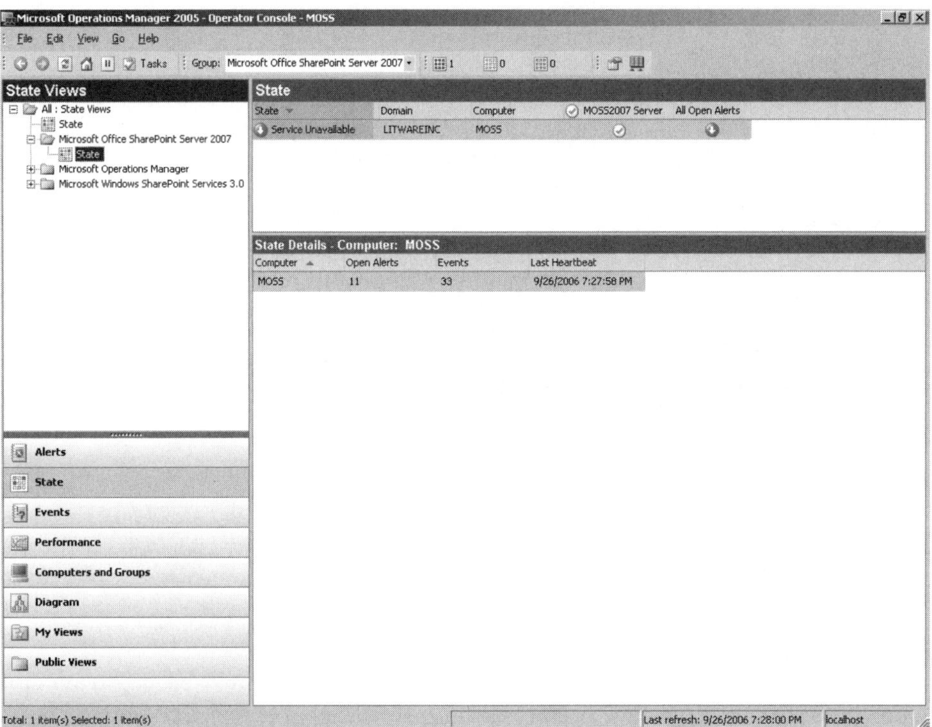

Figure 13-10 Operator Console showing the status of a managed SharePoint Server 2007 server

Any of the alerts can quickly be investigated by double-clicking the alert message in the list. This also displays detailed product knowledge and best practices that describe why the alert was sent, the probable cause if there was a problem, and advice on how to resolve the problem. Figure 13-11 shows an example of alert details concerning a problem with the Search service.

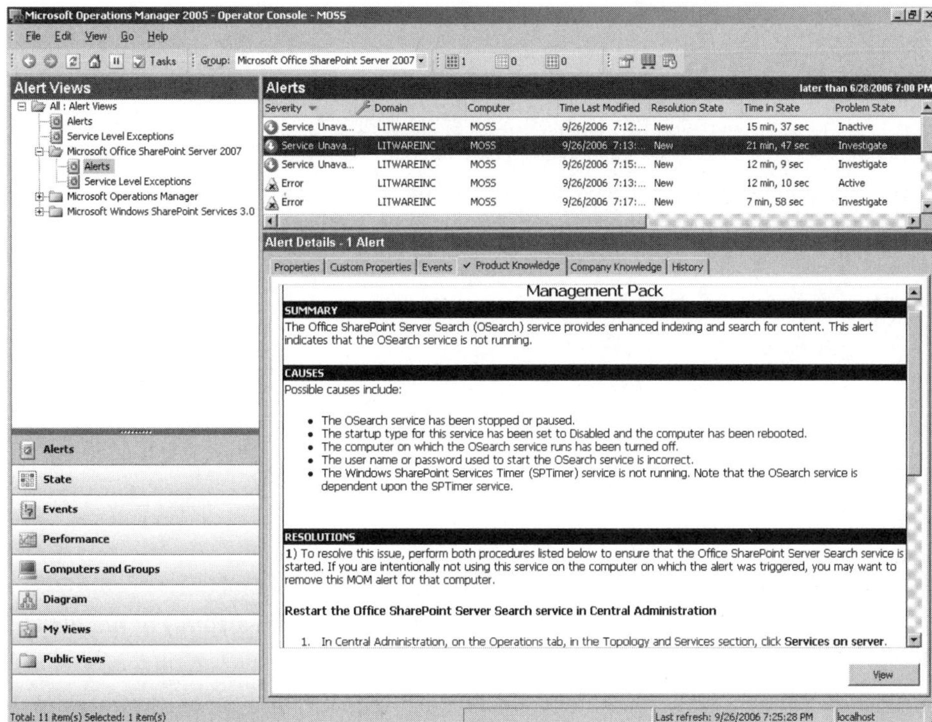

Figure 13-11 Alert details in the Operator Console

A large number of tools and scripts can be built in to the Operator Console Tasks pane, meaning that operators can immediately take action to resolve a problem by running a tool without leaving the console. Company-specific knowledge, tools, and scripts can also be added to tailor the Operator Console to each customer environment. An example of the troubleshooting tools that can be made available in the Tasks pane is shown in Figure 13-12.

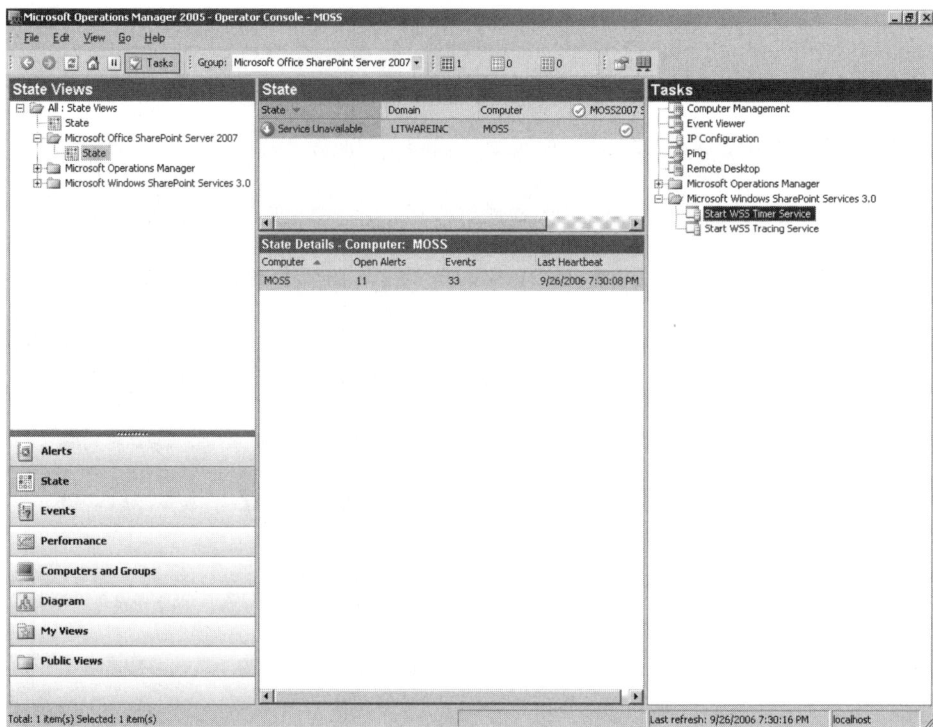

Figure 13-12 The Operator Console showing the Tasks pane with an array of troubleshooting tools

Figure 13-13 shows how the Operator Console can automatically generate network topology diagrams based on the live system. These diagrams can assist the operator in understanding the wider environment and the relationships between systems that could affect the managed computers that they are interested in. The diagram in Figure 13-13 shows the topology of the Active Directory servers as an example.

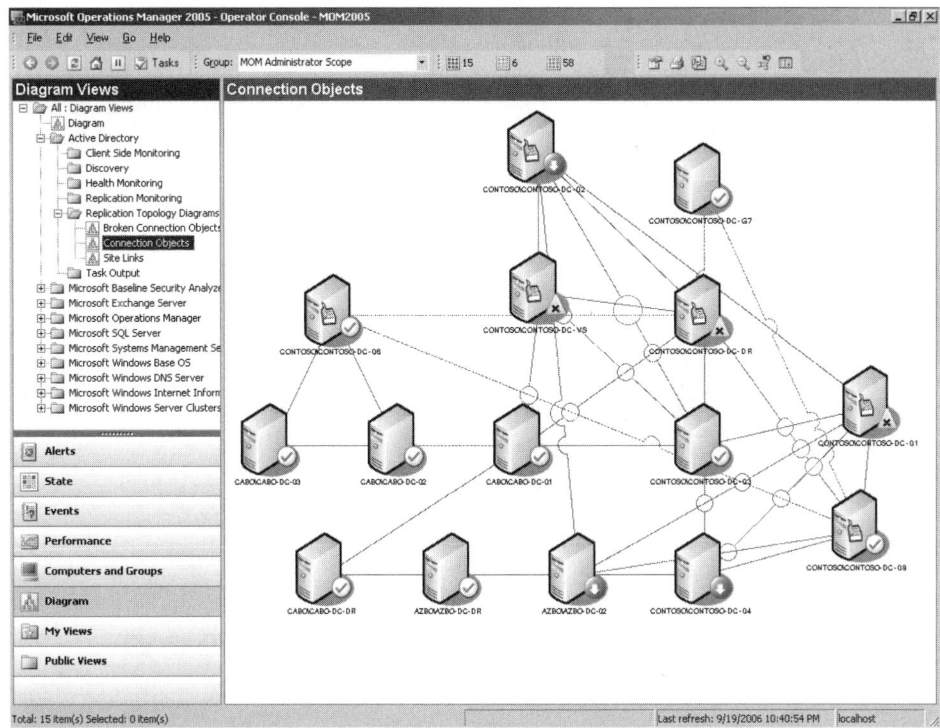

Figure 13-13 Operator Console showing an auto-generated Active Directory topology diagram

Reporting Console

An optional component of Microsoft Operations Manager 2005 is the Reporting Server. This feature requires that SQL Server Reporting Services be available, but the payoff is well worth it, as the range of predefined health and status reports you can generate using this component can represent great value to you in your monitoring efforts. Lists, charts, and graphs can be drawn based on a user-defined date range of historical status and performance data. The Reporting Console (shown in Figure 13-14) is Web-based, which means that the reports can be made available to a much wider audience—including IT staff, analysts, and managers—without needing to install a client to the desktop. The SharePoint Server 2007 Management Packs do not provide any additional SharePoint-specific reports, but existing report templates can be used to report on aspects such as bandwidth utilization and service availability for SharePoint servers and other systems that can affect SharePoint.

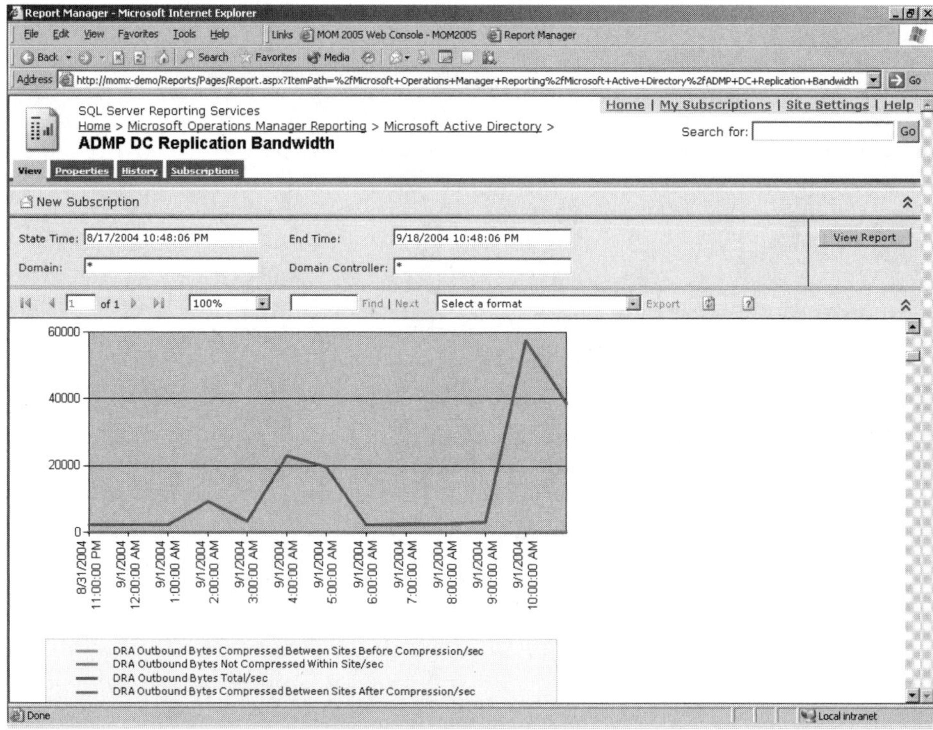

Figure 13-14 Reporting Console showing a bandwidth utilization report for a selected date range

Web Console

The core alert-monitoring features available through the Administrator and Operator Consoles can also be made available via a Web browser without installing the full console user interfaces—a nice touch that allows users the ability to use Microsoft Operations Manager 2005 even if they are away from their usual desktop computer. Figure 13-15 shows the Web Console running in Internet Explorer.

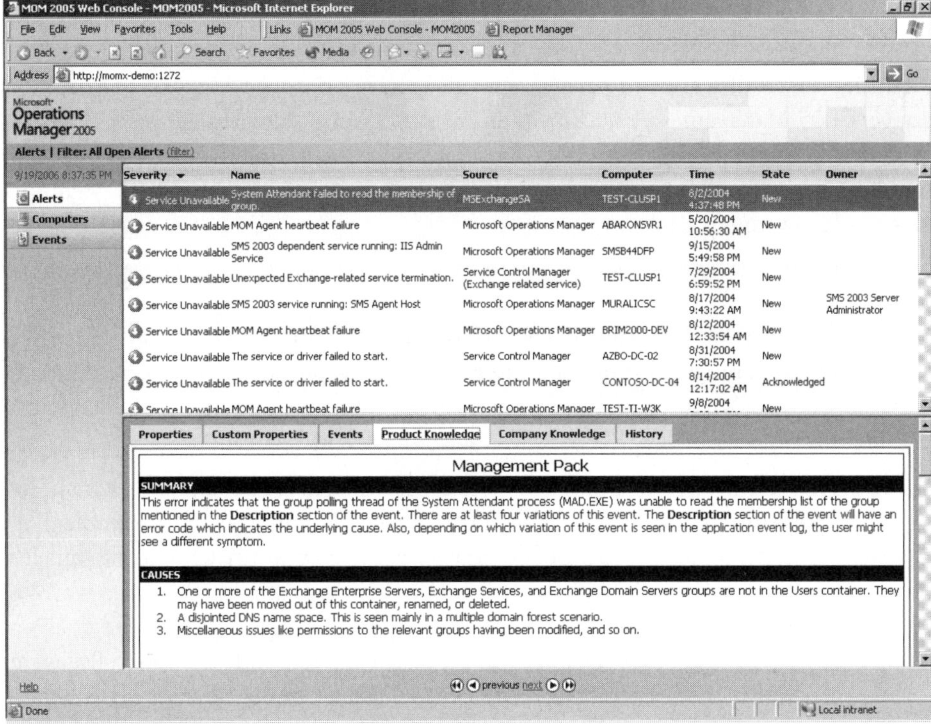

Figure 13-15 Web Console

Management Packs

After agents have been installed onto managed computers, a monitoring solution still would not be very useful if it simply collected every available piece of information. The operators would be drowned in data, and the useful information would be difficult to isolate. A MOM Management Pack is a collection of rules and product knowledge that elevates MOM from being an event log repository into an expert system able to deliver insight and analysis. We will examine Management Packs in more detail in the next section.

MOM Management Packs

To intelligently filter and analyze the event and performance data that has been collected, Microsoft Operations Manager 2005 requires an understanding of the system or application being monitored. This knowledge is transferred to Microsoft Operations Manager 2005 via the installation of a Microsoft Operations Manager 2005 Management Pack for each of the applications being monitored. Microsoft has a policy to produce Management Packs for all its enterprise products and has produced a Management Pack for Windows

SharePoint Services 3.0, plus another to monitor the additional capabilities that SharePoint Server 2007 provides.

Many third-party software and hardware vendors have produced Microsoft Operations Manager 2005 Management Packs for their own products. Management packs can also be customized, extended, or created from scratch by users to tailor monitoring to their own unique scenarios. In the following sections, we'll discuss each of the key components of a Management Pack.

Rules

A Management Pack contains a collection of rules that define which events and performance counters are most relevant to monitor for a given application. These rules filter out the unimportant information and bring out the most valuable and actionable data points. There are three types of rules: Event Rules, Alert Rules, and Performance Rules.

- **Event Rules** Event Rules define how Microsoft Operations Manager 2005 should react to events that have been logged on managed computers. For example, if an event occurs that matches a set of criteria, it might be appropriate to display an alert in the Operator Console; ignore the event as unimportant; or display a warning only if the event occurs multiple times. If an expected event is missing and does not occur at all, this might also be important to capture. Event Rules and Alert Rules can also generate alerts if a series of related events occurs over a period of time that, if taken together as a group, has a greater significance than each event individually.
- **Alert Rules** Alert Rules can be useful to ensure that the operator's attention is drawn to the most important events. Alert Rules can scan or filter the alerts that are being generated by the Event Rules, and they can perform a specific action only if, for example, a critical alert has been sent. The Alert Rule could, for example, send an e-mail message to a specific operator to ensure the operator sees the alert quickly.
- **Performance Rules** Performance Rules monitor performance counters and generate alerts if threshold values are exceeded. Additionally, they can collect data for historical performance reporting and analysis.

Alerts

Alerts are generated when a rule recognizes an event occurring that requires either the attention of an administrator or an automated task to be executed to resolve the problem. An alert can be sent to the administrator via a number of channels, including the Operator Console, an e-mail, or a message sent to a pager or similar device, depending on the nature of the emergency.

Knowledge

In addition to alerts or warnings about an impending problem or failure, the Management Packs allow Microsoft Operations Manager 2005 to serve up guidance about probable causes, possible solutions, and best practices written by the Microsoft product teams to help resolve the problem. This provides operators with a detailed understanding of system status from across their IT environment, and it assists with both reactive and proactive maintenance. Once the IT staff gains experience with the issues or problems they commonly encounter in their own IT environments, they can extend the Management Pack knowledge with advice specific to their enterprise.

Tasks

Tasks provide a way to execute commands from the Microsoft Operations Manager 2005 central console that take effect on the remote server being monitored. This allows Microsoft Operations Manager 2005 operators to immediately take action in response to an event without needing to visit the remote server separately. The Management Pack defines which tasks are most appropriate for the target managed computer.

Views

Views provide a filtered, targeted selection of the event and performance data from the monitored servers, enabling administrators to quickly understand the health of servers or server groups.

Note Regardless of the size of your enterprise, it is important to plan a deployment of Microsoft Operations Manager 2005 in advance. For further resources to assist with planning a Microsoft Operations Manager 2005 deployment, visit the Microsoft Microsoft Operations Manager 2005 Web site at *http://www.microsoft.com/mom*.

Using MOM 2005 to Monitor SharePoint Server 2007

Microsoft has released two separate Microsoft Operations Manager 2005 SP1 Management Packs for monitoring SharePoint Server 2007. The first is specifically for Windows SharePoint Services 3.0, and it can also be used in deployments that include only Windows SharePoint Services. Note that Microsoft Operations Manager 2005 SP1 is required if you want to use these Management Packs.

If SharePoint Server 2007 has been deployed in addition to Windows SharePoint Services, both the Windows SharePoint Services and the SharePoint Server 2007 Management Packs must be used to ensure all services are monitored. The Management Packs are not supplied with SharePoint Server 2007 but can be downloaded free of charge from the Microsoft Web site.

In addition to the Management Packs provided specifically for SharePoint, to adequately monitor SharePoint Server 2007 a number of additional Management Packs should be used to monitor the underlying services and technologies that SharePoint depends on. These supplementary Management Packs are covered in more detail later in this chapter in the "Supplementary Management Packs" section.

Microsoft has also released a Microsoft Operations Manager 2005 Management Pack for Microsoft Office Project Server 2007, a product that requires and builds on the Windows SharePoint Services platform. Any deployments that include Project Server 2007 will benefit from using both the Windows SharePoint Services Management Pack and the Project Server 2007 Management Pack.

Deploying the MOM 2005 Management Packs for SharePoint Server 2007

If you are deploying a new Management Pack, the best practice is to first install it into a test environment to gain an understanding of how it works, and to document the permissions and configuration settings that might need adjusting for your system. Once the tests are complete and the configuration has been documented, the Management Pack can be exported from the test environment and then imported into the live environment with a high confidence of success.

Before deploying a Management Pack, a number of elements of the target environment should be reviewed and configured correctly to ensure the installation goes smoothly. This section covers those pre-installation tasks.

Important This section assumes that you have already deployed a Microsoft Operations Manager 2005 server. Deploying Microsoft Operations Manager 2005 is outside the scope of this book. For assistance with deploying Microsoft Operations Manager 2005, refer to the Microsoft Operations Manager 2005 Deployment Guide on TechNet, at *http://www.microsoft.com/technet/prodtechnol/mom/mom2005/Library/b7b0c768-64d1-486e-b9ed-7292c9e545f9.mspx*.

Identifying Computers to Manage

First, you must identify the computers that need to be monitored. To ensure a high availability for SharePoint Server 2007, you should monitor every server in the SharePoint server farm. However, there are also services running elsewhere that SharePoint depends on, such as Active Directory, that SharePoint administrators should be closely monitoring.

Increasing the Size of Log Files

Microsoft Operations Manager 2005 relies on the event logs of the managed computers to monitor their health. If a problem stops the managed computer from logging events, this will remove a major source of information for Microsoft Operations Manager 2005 and might mean that the health monitoring picture is incomplete, which can lead to missed problems and degradation in availability for the managed computer. A common problem is that the logs quickly reach their maximum size limit and stop accepting new events. One important step to prevent this from happening is to increase the maximum size of the logs. Follow these general guidelines to increase the size of the logs:

- Increase the maximum size of Windows event logs (Application, System, Security) to at least 25 MB.
- Increase the size of other event logs (such as Directory Services, File Replication, and DNS) to at least 10 MB.
- Increase the size of any application logs, such as Internet Information Services (IIS) logs, to at least 10 MB.

Note Both the Windows SharePoint Services Management Pack and the SharePoint Server 2007 Management Pack focus on monitoring the Windows system event log and the Windows application event log, so ensure that these log sizes are increased.

You can also consider configuring the logs to overwrite events as needed. With this setting applied, as the logs fill up, the oldest entries are overwritten and the logs never run out of space. When changing log sizes, be sure to consider how much disk space is available, how quickly the computer is likely to generate events, and whether it is important to retain certain logs, such as the security logs, for longer periods of time.

Disabling Event Log Replication on Clustered Servers

By default, clustered servers replicate all events that occur on any node to every other node in the cluster. If any monitored components are installed onto clustered servers, each node must be monitored, but event log replication must be disabled.

Considering Slow or Expensive Network Links

If there are slow wide area network (WAN) links or expensive satellite links separating Microsoft Operations Manager 2005 from a group of servers, you might need to consider filtering the events that you are monitoring for these remote servers in order to reduce the traffic sent over the network. For example, noncritical events and performance data might be something that could safely be ignored.

Installing Microsoft Operations Manager 2005 Agents

The Microsoft Operations Manager 2005 agent should be installed onto every server that needs to be monitored. The agent can be easily installed, without needing to separately visit each of the target computers, by using the Install Agent Wizard from the Microsoft Operations Manager 2005 Administrator Console. This is the quickest option if you are trying out the SharePoint Management Packs in a test environment, and it can also be convenient in production environments. Microsoft Operations Manager 2005 can also be configured to identify new SharePoint servers as they appear on the network and install the agent automatically on behalf of the operator, but these methods take further initial setup.

Installing Management Packs

Management Packs are distributed as .akm files, which are imported using the Microsoft Operations Manager 2005 Administrator Console. There is a simple wizard-driven interface that steps through the import process. Once the Management Pack has been imported, the new rules appear in the rules tree within the Administrator Console, and Microsoft Operations Manager 2005 can begin to monitor the computers that you earlier identified to manage.

> **More Info** For more details on deploying Microsoft Operations Manager 2005 agents, Management Packs, and other step-by-step guides to assist with configuring a Microsoft Operations Manager 2005 environment, refer to the Microsoft Operations Manager 2005 Deployment Guide at *http://www.microsoft.com/technet/prodtechnol/mom/mom2005/Library/b7b0c768-64d1-486e-b9ed-7292c9e545f9.mspx.*

Supplementary Management Packs

In addition to the Windows SharePoint Services 3.0 and SharePoint Server 2007 Management Packs, the following additional Management Packs should be installed to monitor the underlying systems and technologies that SharePoint depends on:

- Microsoft Base Operating System

- Microsoft SQL Server 2000 or Microsoft SQL Server 2005
- Microsoft Internet Information Services
- Microsoft Web Sites and Services
- ASP.NET
- Microsoft Windows Active Directory
- Microsoft Operations Manager 2005

Note These Management Packs are all available to download from the Microsoft Management Pack Catalog at *www.microsoft.com/technet/prodtechnol/mom/mom2005/catalog.aspx*.

Real World Dealing with Cryptic Errors

Although Microsoft Operations Manager 2005 Management Packs generally do well to translate the errors and event messages picked up from managed computers into something meaningful and actionable by the operators, there are often just too many possible event messages that could occur to capture them all in one Management Pack. Therefore, Management Pack authors have to focus on covering the most important or most common events. Inevitably, there will be some error states or events for which the Management Packs will not include advice on how to resolve. This means in a real environment, Microsoft Operations Manager 2005 operators might encounter alerts with short, cryptic, or unhelpful error messages. There are at least two things that can help in this scenario.

The first is the event ID—the number that represents the event. This can be used to cross-reference and look up the event from other sources. A great source of this type of information is *www.eventid.net*—a Web site that collates and indexes event information for a huge range of products. By inputting the event ID number on the site home page, details of the error messages and a list of which products can generate the error are returned. Users of the site are able to input comments, advice on what causes these issues, and advice on how to resolve these issues, so the community helps to improve the service. Although some of the information requires a subscription to be accessed, much of the information is free to access, and you might find that the information is valuable enough to be well worth the subscription fee.

The second way to work around unhelpful event messages is to input your own help information! The Microsoft Operations Manager 2005 Operator Console allows operators to edit the Company Knowledge associated with the events in the

Management Pack. This means that as operators encounter new issues and solve them, they can capture the details back into Microsoft Operations Manager 2005 to ensure the problem won't take long to fix if it ever comes back again. This is a great way to customize the tools to better fit your own environment and help reduce the number of cryptic errors you are faced with.

Key Monitoring Scenarios

The SharePoint Server 2007 Management Pack monitors a number of key areas. Microsoft Operations Manager 2005 operators should be aware of the most important events to be ready to respond to them quickly. Table 13-2 lists each of these key areas, the services within the areas that are monitored, and summarizes some of the most important events that could affect overall availability of the server farm or specific service availability.

Table 13-2 Key Monitoring Scenarios

Key area	Elements monitored	Events to watch for
Business Applications	Business Data Catalog Web Service; Web Services for Remote Portlets; IView Web Parts	Runtime errors with the Business Data Catalog (BDC) or the BDC Web service could cause your line-of-business application integration and KPI indicators to fail.
Content Management and Publishing	Authoring Controls; Caching; Content Deployment; Document Conversion; Content Management Server 2002 Migration; Site Management	If the object or disk-based cache have issues, this can cause severe slowdowns, time-outs, or HTTP 404 errors.
Excel Services	Excel Calculation Services	If the Excel Calculation Service fails, or network connections fail between front-end Web servers and the server running Excel Calculation Services, users will not be able to use the Excel Services features.

Table 13-2 Key Monitoring Scenarios

Key area	Elements monitored	Events to watch for
InfoPath Forms Services		The most likely errors relating to InfoPath Forms Services are caused by poorly written business logic contained within InfoPath form templates, which can cause infinite loops and out-of-memory exceptions.
Search	Crawling and Indexing; Propagation; Query	Indexing will be stopped if the disk fills up, so check free disk space regularly. Microsoft Operations Manager 2005 will report if no disk space is available, and it also reports if index propagation fails or if search is configured incorrectly.
Single Sign-On Service		Watch for errors retrieving credentials; this can indicate that unauthorized users are attempting to access the system. Also look for problems with the Single Sign-On Service itself or auditing, both of which can prevent users from signing in.
User Profiles and Personalization		Errors in this group indicate problems with synchronizing User Profile properties, Audience Compilation errors, or problems in creating new My Sites.

Note Microsoft has announced that the next version of Microsoft Operations Manager is in development and is to be named System Center Operations Manager 2007. The name reflects the new alignment with the System Center family of products. At the time of writing of this book, the product was at the Beta 2 stage of development and available for trial from *www.microsoft.com/mom*.

Summary

This chapter outlined the importance of monitoring the health and performance of SharePoint Server 2007 and the underlying services and technologies that it depends on. Some of the available tools to monitor the health and performance were described, and you learned how Microsoft Operations Manager 2005 can be used to centralize and automate monitoring of whole SharePoint Server 2007 server farms from a single console.

Chapter 14

Information Security Policies

Note Sometimes, as an author, you find yourself writing on a topic that is both important and enduring. Information security policies is just such a topic. This chapter was originally written for the *Microsoft SharePoint Products and Technologies Resource Kit* (Microsoft Press, 2004). Since I was the principle author for that book as well as this book, and this topic is so important and the information has not changed much, I decided to use that chapter as the basis for this chapter and amend it where it seems appropriate.—*Bill English*

Information security policies are an essential part of any plan to help secure a network. Such policies are really business rules–rules that define acceptable and sometimes required behavior regarding your company's information. Information security policies continue to become more complex because the technologies that host an organization's mission-critical information are also becoming more complex every year, if not every month. From cell phones to laptops, from PDAs to servers, the access vectors and potential security holes are increasing as the technology complexity increases. Information security policies are one method of plugging many security holes by prescribing acceptable behavior as information is developed and stored.

The more an organization follows information security policies, the more dependent it becomes on these rules in a host of situations, such as guiding a manager on acceptable behavior about how information is accessed, informing a legal team as to whether a manager has performed due diligence, or using the policies as a guide to ensure a chain of evidence is retained during or after an attack on the network.

Information security policies (hereafter referred to simply as *policies*), in and of themselves, are just words on a page. They are essentially meaningless unless upper management both sees the need for such policies and possesses the will to enforce them. Ultimately, the enforcement of information security policies is a management responsibility.

Planning Some say that the problem with information security policies is that the rules are only as effective as the people who obey them. But the presence of information security policies in an organization is fast becoming a legal assumption: companies that operate *without* information security policies might be subject to the charge that reasonable care for an organization's information was not executed. Regardless of an organization's size, purpose, or location, effective information security is vital.

After the information security policies are set, it's time to set up governance guidelines. A SharePoint Governance Plan acts as a guidebook outlining the administration, maintenance, and support of your SharePoint environment. It identifies lines of ownership for both business and technical teams, defining who is responsible for each area of the system. Furthermore, it establishes practical rules for appropriate usage of the SharePoint environments that are based on the information security policies.

An effective governance plan ensures that the system is managed and used in accordance with its designed intent to prevent it from becoming an unmanageable system. The management of an enterprise-wide system involves both a strategic, business-minded board to craft rules and procedures for the use of the system. It also involves having a tactical, technically-competent team to manage the routine operational tasks that keep the system running. Users of the system will be empowered by a support and developer community sponsored by the business leaders.

This chapter outlines the types of policies that should be considered when implementing either Microsoft Windows SharePoint Services 3.0 or Microsoft Office SharePoint Server 2007. The purpose is not to write the policies for you or even to give you a sample set of policies from which to work, but rather to highlight the types of policies that will be affected when implementing Office SharePoint Server 2007.

Developing an Information Security Policy

Why is an information security policy so important? There are two main reasons such a policy is important and should be adopted:

1. **To provide a framework for best operational practice, so that the institution is able to minimize risk and respond effectively to any security incidents that might occur.**

   Security breaches, often involving prominent commercial organizations, are reported periodically in the press and often generate substantial publicity. Such incidents tend to fuel the popular conception that the major threat to information security comes from hostile attacks perpetrated via the Internet. Although there is some truth in this, the picture that it paints is highly oversimplified. Electronic information is at risk for a wide variety of reasons: natural disasters, failure of man-made equipment and services, and accidental as well as malicious acts by human beings.

   Because neither the systems themselves nor those who operate them can ever be totally reliable, the institution must be able to react promptly and appropriately to any security incident and restore its information systems to their normal operational state in an acceptable period of time.

   Investing in suitable security measures has a significant cost. Security concerns inevitably will consume considerable staff time, especially that of skilled IT staff, and in most cases there is likely to be security-related expenditure on hardware, software, and services as well.

   This investment can only be correctly judged if a policy exists: without a proper assessment of the value of the information assets to the institution, and the consequences (financial and otherwise) of any data loss or interruption to services, it is all too easy to fund this area inadequately or inappropriately with potentially serious effects should a security breach occur. Conversely, there is little point in spending money unnecessarily to protect data of little value or which can easily be re-created.

   Policies should define what behavior is and is not allowed, who is or is not allowed to do it, and in what circumstances these behaviors and permissions apply. A successful security policy will generate a high degree of consensus among all those involved and should foster a positive attitude toward security in terms of its benefits to the institution and the wider community of which it forms a part.

A useful concept in this context is that of a balance between privileges and responsibilities: making information and resources more freely available to members of an institution arguably places more responsibility on those members to behave responsibly. Some evidence is beginning to emerge that users of information systems would be willing to adhere to better security practices if they were more knowledgeable (that is, better trained) about what good practice actually involved.

Overall, the policy must define the role that information security plays in supporting the mission and goals of the institution. In a college or university, the security policy should be linked to (and should depend on) the information strategy, and it may well be drawn up by a subgroup of the body responsible for the information strategy. Even though much of the work on information security will be devolved to middle managers and technical staff, senior management should be committed to placing a high level of importance on information security and winning acceptance for the policy.

2. **To ensure that the institution complies with relevant legislation in this area.**

   With the advent of the Sarbanes Oxley Act of 2002 and other legal requirements, organizations are having to adopt a framework that provides suitable standards of security for all personal data held by the institution throughout their life cycle. All recognized benchmarks of good security practice specify a top-level security policy as the key requirement in such a framework.

   All organizations are strongly encouraged to adopt a recognized methodology for developing their security policies and plans: to do otherwise might leave them exposed in the event of a legal challenge. The choice of methodology is less critical: the issue of key importance is that sound policies should be drawn up and then embodied in effective operational security measures.[1]

Password Policies

Because SharePoint Server 2007 requires domain services for authentication, it is wise to have password policies in place for your network. If you have any policies in place in your organization, chances are good that you already have policies that address the issues listed in this section. However, the implementation of SharePoint Server 2007 is an

1 Adapted from Developing and Information Security Policy located at *http://www.jisc.ac.uk/index.cfm?name=pub_smbp_infosec.*

appropriate time to review those policies, because most of the information held in SharePoint Server 2007 can be compromised by obtaining a SharePoint-pervasive username and password combination.

Like most policy domain areas, there are subareas that should be addressed as the policies are written. Password policies are no exception. The following are some of the issues to be considered when developing your password policies:

- Minimum password length
- Password complexity and strength
- Prohibition of reusing old passwords
- Prohibition of written storage of passwords
- Prohibition against printing or displaying passwords
- Periodic forced change in passwords
- Method to manage expired passwords
- Authorized means to transmit new passwords to remote users
- Limits on consecutive attempts to enter a password
- Acceptance or prohibition of single sign-on services
- Prohibition of passwords sent through e-mail
- Requirement for encrypted storage of passwords
- Reliance on domain services for authentication
- Requirement for non-anonymous authentication before access to information is allowed
- Use of duress passwords (Duress passwords trigger scripts during a duress situation—that is, if a gun is pointed at your head and you are asked to log on to the server, a duress password would log you on, but because of the password entered, a script would be triggered to delete all predetermined sensitive data.)
- Requirement to change all administrative passwords if any have been compromised
- Password sharing prohibition
- User responsibility for all actions taken with his username and password combination
- Security notice in logon system banner
- Prohibition against leaving systems without logging off or locking the system

- Use of biometric devices required for logon to portal
- Use of smart-card devices required for logon to portal system

---

Note This chapter introduces issues that you should consider when writing your policies. Each issue introduced might or might not apply to your environment. For example, some organizations might have a strong password complexity policy, while another environment might not have one because of culture, industry, or other factors. The recommendation here isn't that each issue be implemented as presented, only that each issue be *considered* as the policies are written.

Most of these issues relating to password policies should be covered in your current information security policies, but one that directly affects SharePoint Server 2007 is the single sign-on policy. If your organization prohibits single sign-on capabilities, meaning that users must log on to each application that requires unique authentication, you will be unable to use the single sign-on feature in SharePoint Server 2007.

Important Also, the Active Directory Mode feature of Windows SharePoint Services needs to be considered in a Windows SharePoint Services–only installation. Given that this feature allows site administrators the ability to create new user accounts in Active Directory, if you are going to use this feature, you should have policies surrounding who can be a site administrator and under what circumstances a new user account can be created in Active Directory from a Windows SharePoint Services site.

In addition, if you are going to use SharePoint Server 2007 in an extranet environment—especially for its customer-relationship features—in which users outside your company will be authenticating in your domain to access their portion of the portal site, implementation of a policy specifying how you will securely transmit passwords to those users and whether or not e-mail can be used will have paramount importance.

Moreover, in situations in which you will be sharing sensitive information with other companies (maybe even competitors), you will probably want a robust set of password policies to be required by all parties to the agreement, necessitating the development of such policies before the project can begin.

As mentioned previously, much of the information in SharePoint Server 2007 is secured *only* through username and password combinations. The compromise of passwords in your environment could lead to sensitive information being exposed to the wrong people, and this, in most cases, would be disastrous.

Personal Use of Sites

It would be nice if there was no need to mention this, but it is possible that users will create their own Web sites, give only themselves permission to the site, and then use that site for private purposes. There have been times when a company's servers were used to set up Internet-based businesses without the knowledge of or the consent of the company's owners. Creating policies that prohibit personal use of company systems will help prevent this problem. Few things irritate system administrators more than the misuse of company systems for personal gain at the expense of system performance, storage space, and additional administrative effort.

Because it will be very easy—especially for the site administrators—to set up personal Web sites (this is not a reference to the My Site feature, but rather to rogue Windows SharePoint Services sites) for personal gain (which is possible if you have enabled Self-Service Site creation or if the user is already a member of the Administrator site group in a site), a strict prohibition should be approved by your managers and then communicated to your users as part of their training on the 2007 Microsoft Office system.

The following issues should be addressed in this domain:

- Use of SharePoint Server 2007 sites for personal use is strictly prohibited.
- Personal use of computers is prohibited.
- Incidental personal use of business systems is permissible. (Consider this issue only if your users are allowed to use company systems for personal use.)
- Storage of personal data is prohibited on company systems.

You might have noticed that the third bullet point contradicts the others. This point is included to emphasize that in certain situations, *some* personal use of computers and SharePoint Server 2007 is permissible. Some nonprofit organizations allow their employees to host in-kind Web sites to the organization's mission after gaining approval. Again, this list is not meant to dictate what should and should not be in your policies, but rather to alert you to the issues that should be considered when writing these policies.

Be careful to fully consider the use of My Sites in your environment when crafting your personal use policies. My Sites are designed to be a one-to-many collaboration path, which will also include *some* personal information. For example, the default use profile in a Shared Services Provider includes a field into which the user can enter his/her home phone number. Is this considered "personal use"? In some organizations, your policies may need to become detailed enough that such input fields are explicitly allowed or denied.

In addition, several other profile fields might be considered "personal use," such as the fields to enter a user's birthday or the schools the user attended. Again, personal use policies need to be well defined so that if you choose to use the social networking features of SharePoint Server 2007 and Knowledge Network, then you've already thought through the potential issues that might arise from the use of these features.

Real World Using Employee Pictures in SharePoint

When I teach administrators about SharePoint, I find a wide divergence of opinions and ideas about the use of employee pictures in a production environment. Some legal departments in some companies prohibit the use of pictures except for badges; others are fine with allowing employee pictures on the intranet Web sites. Before you try to do pictures of employees in your SharePoint implementation, be sure to check with your legal department for their opinion.

If your legal department allows employee pictures in your SharePoint implementation, then be sure that you can obtain consistent-looking pictures. Nothing is worse that having pictures with different color depths, resolutions and file types in your deployment. Best practice is to ensure that you are using jpeg files, with the same color depth and palette resolution along with the same cropping across all pictures so that the head size in each picture appears similar to every other picture in your deployment.

You'll also need a common Web site to host the pictures along with a naming convention that makes it easy for the users to enter the URL to their picture without having to ask an IT person what the URL is. For example, you could host these pictures in a SharePoint site that is the root site of a Web application and place the pictures in a library called "Name" and then name each picture using the person's firstname.lastname syntax. If the root site resolved to "Pictures", then the URL would be *http://pictures/name/<firstname.lastname>*. Nearly everyone can remember this URL, which makes it easier for users to use their picture in SharePoint.

In summary, the best way to ensure that pictures are used correctly is to do two things:

1. Ensure that your pictures are consistent in terms of size, cropping, pixilation, color depth, palette resolution, and file type.
2. Place the pictures in a location where the URL is very easy to reference by the end users.

Finally, when it comes to pictures, be sure to discuss the secondary effects of individuals being able to match names and faces with other individuals they don't interact with even occasionally. For example, people may experience harassment from other employees who surf the intranet, matching names, cubicle locations, and pictures. Stalking and other potentially criminal activities may ensue more easily because the predator can use your intranet to learn about a person with whom they would otherwise have very little interaction or method of learning personal and/or corporate information. While this possibility is remote, this scenario and other scenarios like it should be discussed up front with your legal and human resource department before you release employee pictures into your SharePoint deployment.

Information Storage Policies

Because increasing numbers and types of mobile devices—such as laptops, PDAs, and Tablet PCs (along with older technologies, such as floppy disks)—will be connecting to your SharePoint sites, you need to define what types of devices can permanently hold your mission-critical information. The last thing you want is a member of the Compensation Committee Site downloading sensitive information to an unsecured PDA and then leaving that device in an airport or hotel. It would be an understatement to say that this is an undesirable scenario for any organization. In addition, with SharePoint Server 2007 having mobile URLs for every list in the farm, the mobile capabilities of this product have increased over previous versions. Therefore, you should consider the following issues when determining how your mission-critical, private, secret, or sensitive information is stored:

- Outline acceptable use of mobile devices.
- Prohibit storage of sensitive information on mobile devices.
- Define what a mobile device is.
- Mobile devices must store all information in encrypted form.
- Mobile devices must be password-protected.
- Establish default permissions for all files on the network.
- Prohibit write-down permissions for company information.
- Information ownership must be assigned.
- Prohibit taking ownership of information without authorization.

Administrative Policies

In many organizations, often there is poor communication between the human resources department and the system administration people. Reasons for this vary from company to company, but it is common for the system administrators to be some of the last people to learn that a person has changed departments or has left the company.

In SharePoint Server 2007, when a user account is deleted in Active Directory, that deletion is not implemented in the user profile database in SharePoint Server 2007. Even though the account is marked for deletion in the user profile database, the account must still be deleted manually by a SharePoint administrator. If you need to remove a user's profile from the user profile database before it is removed through a full import, you need to propagate policies to this effect. In this domain area, here are some issues to consider:

- Worker status changes are sent to system administrators in a timely fashion.
- Users must inform system administrators about changes in status.
- Arrange for transfer of ownership of information after a user leaves the company.
- Specify a schedule of file deletion after a user leaves the company.
- User notifications need to be cleaned up by the SharePoint administrator.

Logging Events

One of the ways to troubleshoot any system is to have a robust logging system in place that can help you troubleshoot problems should they arise. One area to log for SharePoint Server 2007 is the Internet Information Services (IIS) platform. Because all the client calls come through IIS to the Windows SharePoint Services filter, you can capture who is connecting, when they are connecting, and which pages they are requesting. In addition, you can purchase third-party software that will give you more vigorous reporting capabilities.

Logging is also a security concern because you can track attack vectors that hackers might use to compromise your system. A robust logging system is essential for good security, and logging policies to be considered that relate to SharePoint Server 2007 include the following:

- Logs are required for all application systems that host sensitive information.
- Logs must support auditing requirements.
- Logs must provide accountability and traceability during an audit.

- Content of SharePoint Server 2007 logs must include specified information.
- Require a retention period for logs.
- Specify information to capture when a compromise is suspected.
- Require logging before a system can be placed in the production domain.
- Clock synchronization on all SharePoint Server 2007 servers with a master clock of all servers in production domain.
- Specify persons authorized to view logs.
- Logs must be reviewed on a regular basis by authorized personnel.

Authorized Web Parts and Applications

Because SharePoint Server 2007 is designed with a distributed administrative architecture, keep in mind that authorized users will be able to install Web Parts on a site. Authorized users can very easily download Web Parts that have been created on the Internet and then install those parts on their sites. Remember that site and portal administrators delegate the right to add Web Parts to a Web Parts page, and there are protections in place for the administrator to control how much a Web Part can do. Liberal delegation of this right might lead to compromised security in your SharePoint implementation. Unsuspecting users could download an infected or a compromised Web Part, install it, and expose your critical information to hackers on the outside.

Security Alert Because of this potential vulnerability, you should seriously consider restricting which software can and cannot be installed in SharePoint Server 2007.

Points to consider when creating policies in this area include the following:

- Prohibit downloading third-party software to your corporate systems.
- Require users to scan downloaded Web Parts before using them in a production system.
- Testing for viruses must be performed on a noncabled, stand-alone server.
- Multiple virus screenings must be performed on all downloaded software from the Internet to corporate systems.
- Virus scanning software must be employed on all SharePoint Server 2007 systems.
- Require that all third-party Web Parts be run in a test environment prior to deployment in a production environment.

Change Control

Because SharePoint Server 2007 will be hosting some of your most mission- critical and sensitive information, ensure that you have a strong change-control program in place for your servers. By controlling who can make administrative modifications to your system, you can maintain stability in your production environment and ensure that only authorized changes are made to your systems.

Pay attention to the Site Collection Use And Confirmation feature that allows SharePoint Server 2007 to automatically delete a site collection if site use is not confirmed by the site owners after a specified number of days. In many environments, automatic deletion of entire site collections is unacceptable. Factor into your policies the exact settings you want to have for this feature because an undesired configuration could result in the loss of a site collection.

This area actually touches a number of security policy areas, including backup and restore, information retention times, and change control. The topic is introduced here because the deletion of a site collection is significant, and the fact that this deletion can be automated makes this a more important consideration when you create your policies. Add to these considerations the fact that there is no method of archiving the site collection before it is deleted, and you'll quickly realize that controlling change management for this feature is rather important.

Considerations that will have particular interest to your SharePoint administrators include the following:

- Formal change control procedure is required for all administrative changes.
- System changes must be consistent with overall security architecture.
- Training is required before authorization will be given to administrate a site, portal, or server.
- Changes on supporting systems must be tested before introduction into production systems.
- Automatic deletion of content is prohibited.
- Automatic deletion of content is allowed only after content is backed up.

Information Privacy

Although it might seem obvious, you should spell out in your policies who actually owns content that is developed in your SharePoint Server 2007 systems and who owns the intellectual rights to that information. In most organizations, this has already been explained in a policy. But best practice is to include the SharePoint Server 2007 systems in that policy. If you have not done so, here are some topics to consider for inclusion in information privacy policies:

- Right of management to examine data on SharePoint Server 2007 systems
- Company ownership of all content developed on company-owned systems
- Right of company, without notification, to add system administrators to sites as administrators
- Permissible information to collect on employees when creating a contacts list
- Permissible information to disclose on self in the My Site area
- Expressions of personal views in My Site
- Prohibiting collection of information about children of employees
- Requirement of disclaimer when collecting information
- Existence of personnel records in SharePoint Server 2007 prohibited without proper security
- Disclosure of worker change of status notification
- Prohibiting marketing or promotion of employee-owned businesses on company systems

Data Classification Schemes

Different firms have different levels of confidentiality, but it is certainly worth assigning a security level to every document in your organization so that workers know how to handle the data. As the document is developed in SharePoint Server 2007, the security level of the document can become a defining (and indexable) piece of metadata. Most classification schemes use one or more of the following document categories: *public*, *confidential*, *secret*, and *private*. Each organization will have its own scheme, and our point is not that you should copy what is written here, but instead that you implement a classification scheme and then use that scheme as new information is developed. Because most content that is developed is automatically considered confidential, it might be important in your organization to spell that out to content developers. Doing so will ensure that they do not disseminate confidential information.

Note The Enterprise Content Management feature of SharePoint Server 2007 enables you to clearly communicate when informal communication becomes formal communication that is subject to regulatory and compliance issues. Propagating information security policies that clearly outline what constitutes informal or formal communication will help your users comply with auditing policies as well as know when their comments are "on the record" vs. "off the record."

Items to consider when developing this policy include the following:

- Data classification scheme is required for all company data.
- Labeling is required for all company data.
- Information is treated as confidential whenever the classification is unknown.
- Departments can create additional classifications if authorized.
- Content developers are responsible to assign data classification to all documents during development.
- Owner of content must meet classification requirements.
- Declassification of content must follow prescribed procedures.
- Co-presenting of different classified content is prohibited.
- Classified content must be hosted in SharePoint Server 2007 sites with required permissions.

Extranet Considerations

When users connect over the Internet, a whole new set of security issues is introduced. If you already have external connection security policies in place, chances are good that they will apply to SharePoint Server 2007 and cover a user's connection to the portal site. Port 80 is the most often attacked port, and even with the use of Secure Sockets Layer (SSL), external connections offer an obvious attack vector to a would-be hacker. Creating policies that detail acceptable behavior for your users when they connect to the portal site will help ensure that their connection is done securely.

If you do not already have such policies in place, consider the following:

- All Internet Web servers must be firewall protected.
- SharePoint Server 2007 servers must be in the perimeter network.
- Internet portal servers must be placed on a separate subnet.

- Connection to intranet portal servers from the Internet requires encryption and certificates.
- Employee-owned computers must meet minimum software requirements.
- Vendor connectivity to intranet from the Internet is prohibited.
- Customer connectivity to customer sites from the Internet requires encryption and certificates.

Summary

This chapter has presented information security policy considerations as they relate to SharePoint Server 2007. Remember that there is a host of other policies that should be written if you want to create an effective set of policies for your company. The introduction of SharePoint Server 2007 into any environment presents some unique security challenges that should be considered before you deploy SharePoint Server 2007 in your production environment.

- **Information security policy** One or more explict statements that formulate what to do or not do in a given situation.
- **Change control** The policies and methods employed to control when and how change occurs on a network or server
- **Personal use** The use of company computers that are not owned by the employee for the exclusive benefit of the employee's own interests, ideas, objectives and/or goals. These interests, ideas, objectives and/or goals are not job related nor are they part of the enumerated interests, ideas, objectives and/or goals of the company.

Chapter 15

Managing Content Types

Microsoft Office SharePoint Server 2007 extends document and content management with content types. A *content type* is a collection of settings that you can apply to a type or category of content. Content types allow you to centrally create and configure properties for sets of data, such as the metadata associated with a certain type of content. For example, you can centrally define the metadata for all pictures within a site collection by using a picture content type, regardless of where those pictures are stored in that site collection. Those pictures might be stored in a picture library on Site A or a picture library on Site B, but the metadata defined for the picture content type applies to either, or both, of those locations.

SharePoint Server 2007 also offers the flexibility to further customize content types at the site and list levels throughout an entire site collection. For example, it gives you the ability to create a new content type for a specific site or add metadata to a content type within a list or document library. You can define custom optional settings for each content type, such as a specific workflow or auditing, to further refine your reporting capabilities.

This chapter describes what content types are and how you can effectively manage your content and store documents using content types. It shows you how content types can be leveraged to extend content functionality, such as workflow.

Introducing Content Types

In SharePoint Server 2007, content types remove the dependency between content and lists that exists in SharePoint Portal Server 2003. SharePoint Server 2007 allows multiple document (or object) types in one list (or document library), each uniquely defined by a specific set of metadata and optional settings such as document templates. A document library simply becomes the container in which documents get stored. In SharePoint Portal Server 2003, each list is limited to a single set of metadata (or columns) and a single document template, which makes it hard to deal with heterogeneous documents in the same document library. If you want different metadata associated with your documents, you either use a custom or third-party solution or create a separate document library for each document type, which can lead to administrative overhead. SharePoint Server 2007 has remedied this by decoupling that dependency.

An example of content type usage in SharePoint Server 2007 is the creation of multiple content types in one document library and the application of different document templates for each of those content types. Figure 15-1 shows the differences between SharePoint Portal Server 2003 and SharePoint Server 2007 in the ability to apply different document templates for different content types to a single document library.

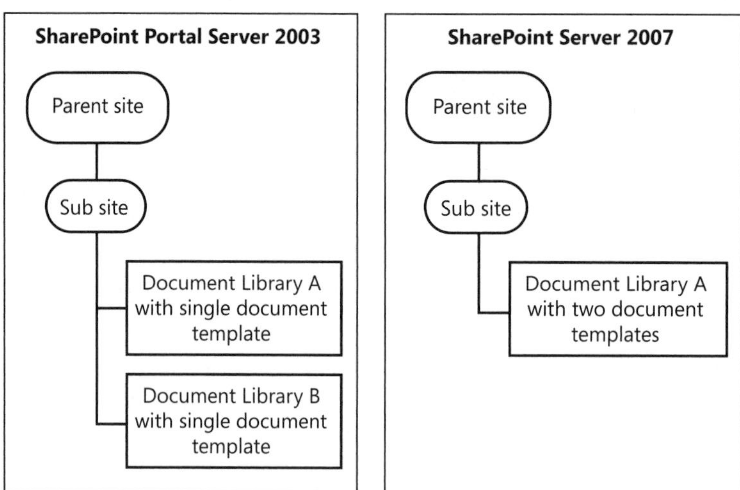

Figure 15-1 Multiple document templates per document library

Content types are defined by custom metadata, or list columns. Each content type within a document library has its own unique set of metadata bound to each content type.

Note *List columns* are the containers for the metadata defined for lists, document libraries, and content types throughout SharePoint Server 2007. See the "Configuring Columns for Content Types" section in this chapter for further details on creating and applying list columns to content types.

In addition to using custom document templates for content types, shown in Figure 15-1, you can customize content types further by adding custom settings, such as Workflow and Information Management Policy. Figure 15-2 shows the expanse of settings available to each content type stored within a document library.

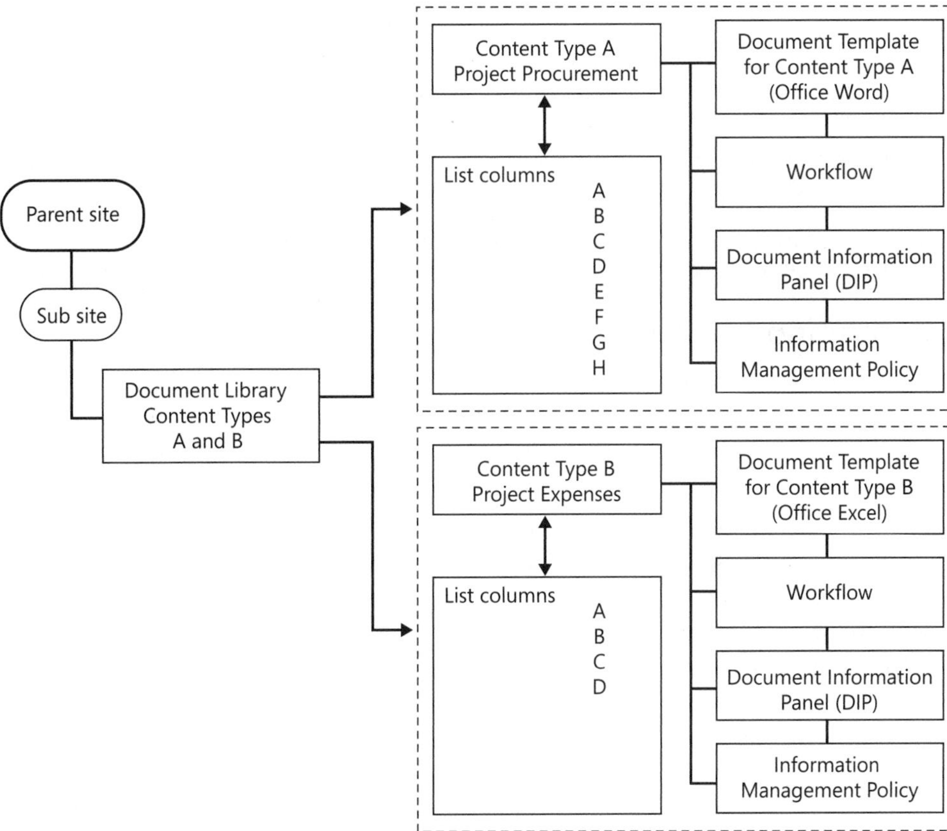

Figure 15-2 Content type configurations

Table 15-1 lists the configurable content type properties available through the administrative user interface.

Table 15-1 Content Type Configurations

Content type setting	Description
Document Template	The template associated with the content type—for example, Microsoft Office Word or Office Excel.
List Columns	Metadata assigned to the content type.
Workflow	The workflow built in to SharePoint Server 2007, such as approval, that is specific to the content type.*

Table 15-1 Content Type Configurations

Content type setting	Description
Document Information Panel (DIP)	The top panel, or properties area, of the associated client Office application, such as Word 2007 or Excel 2007, which displays the fields for the corresponding content type metadata when a document is created or modified. The DIP can be customized using Microsoft Office InfoPath 2007.
Information Management Policy	Records policy specific to the content type, such as expiration policy or auditing.

* Additional workflow can be created against content types using Microsoft Office SharePoint Designer 2007 and via the SharePoint object model using Microsoft Visual Studio.NET 2005.

Understanding Metadata

To work with content types, you need to understand what metadata is first. *Metadata* is a set of data that describes a piece of content or a document, and is included as part of that content or document storage. It can include core properties such as the author name, keywords, or comments, and can also include custom properties.

Metadata in SharePoint is applied to content types via *list columns*. These list columns can then be indexed by SharePoint, and powerful search and filtering queries can be built against the data stored in them. The metadata uniquely identifies and categorizes any document or content related to a content type—for example, expenses might include a list column of Department, while project procurement might include a list column of Project Name. A custom search can then be established to determine all expenses against Department X or on details relating to Project Y. Remember that list columns that are set as optional will not always be populated. If you want to enforce metadata population, set all list columns to require data. This includes any of the default metadata that is included with the default content types, such as Title. To learn how to enforce column data population, see the section titled "Configuring a Required Column" later in this chapter.

More Info For information on metadata in SharePoint Server 2007, refer to Chapter 9, "Document Management."

Default Content Types

SharePoint Server 2007 comes with a set of default content types. These default content types are installed at the time of provisioning a site collection and are accessible from the Site Settings Galleries page of the root site of the site collection. For information on how to access this page, see the section titled "Creating a New Content Type at the Site Level" later in this chapter.

Content types can be inherited by the child sites within a site collection and used throughout the document libraries and lists of those sites, or they can be used as the basis for creating new custom content types. Content types at the root level are referred to as the *global content types*.

Content types are stored and sorted by group. For example, the Document Content Types group includes the Document content type used by the default install of the document library. The Lists Content Types group includes the Announcement content type, used in the Announcements list. When creating a new global content type, you can add the new content type to one of the existing groups or create a new custom group and then add the new content type to your new group.

Table 15-2 shows the default content types and their respective groups, created at the time of provisioning a new site collection and accessible via the Site Content Type Gallery in the Site Settings of the root site.

Table 15-2 Default Content Types and Groups

Content type group	Content types
Business Intelligence	Dashboard Page
	Indicator Using Data in Excel Workbook
	Indicator Using Data in SharePoint List
	Indicator Using Data in SQL Server 2005 Analysis Services
	Indicator Using Manually Entered Information
	Report
Document Content Types	Basic Page
	Document
	Dublin Core Columns
	Form
	Link to a Document
	Master Page
	Picture
	Web Part Page
Folder Content Types	Discussion
	Folder

Table 15-2 Default Content Types and Groups

Content type group	Content types
List Content Types	Announcement
	Contact
	Event
	Far East Contact
	Issue
	Item
	Link
	Message
	Task
Page Layout Content Types	Article Page
	Redirect Page
	Welcome Page
Publishing Content Types	Page
	Page Layout
	Publishing Master Page
Special Content Types	Unknown Document Type

Each default content type is preconfigured with default list columns, or metadata. An example is the Document content type from the Document Content Types group. The Document content type is used each time a new document library is created. It includes two list columns: Name and Title.

Note Document content types cannot be used in lists, and list content types cannot be used in document libraries.

Understanding the Content Type Inheritance Model

The default content types, referred to as *global content types*, are located at the root site of a site collection. Content types are created and deployed throughout a site collection via an inheritance model—that is, content types are inherited from content types at the root site, or parent site, level by a child site and used in the site's lists and document libraries. In content type inheritance, the *parent content type* is the content type from which the new content type was inherited and the *child content type* is the resultant content type created from the parent content type.

In terms of modifications, each inherited content type is independent of the parent content type. Any custom list columns added to an inherited content type do not replicate back to the parent. For example, you could create a new content type in Site B based on the default Document content type in Site A, and then apply additional list columns to the Site B content type. Changes to that content type will be unique to Site B and can be inherited by any child sites, but not by the parent site, A. The default Document content type from Site A will still be available to all subsequent child sites in its original state.

This inheritance model is depicted in Figure 15-3. Site B is a child site. It inherits the default Document content type from Site A, which is its parent site. Site B creates a new content type, Project Procurement, which includes additional list columns and a custom document template. Site C is also a child site. It inherits the Project Procurement content type from Site B, which is its parent site. Site C then creates a new content type named Project Meetings, which is based on the Project Procurement content type. Project Meetings includes modifications to the list columns and custom document template. Site D is another child site. It inherits the default Document content type from Site A, which is its parent site. Site D then creates a new content type based on the Document content type, Project Expenses, which includes a custom document template. In this scenario, Site D had the option to inherit content types from Site A, its parent site. But if Site D had been a child site of Site C, then it would have had the option to inherit content types from Sites A, B, and C.

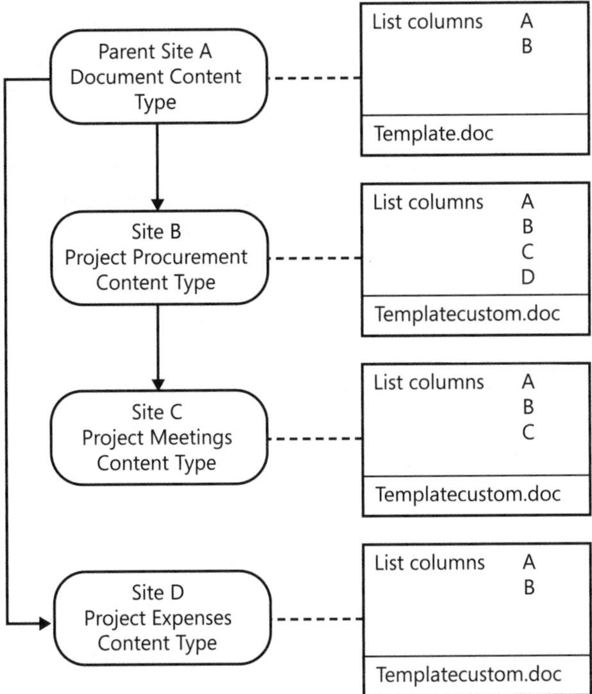

Figure 15-3 Inherited content type model

Planning If you make changes to the parent content type, you have the option of pushing those changes to any content types inheriting from the parent content type.

New content types are added to either one of the existing content type groups or to a custom group, as shown in Figure 15-4. In this example, the Litware group has been created in the Site Content Type Gallery on the Litware site to contain content types related to the Litware site collection. These include the Litware site, which is the root site, and the Fabrikam and Resources child sites.

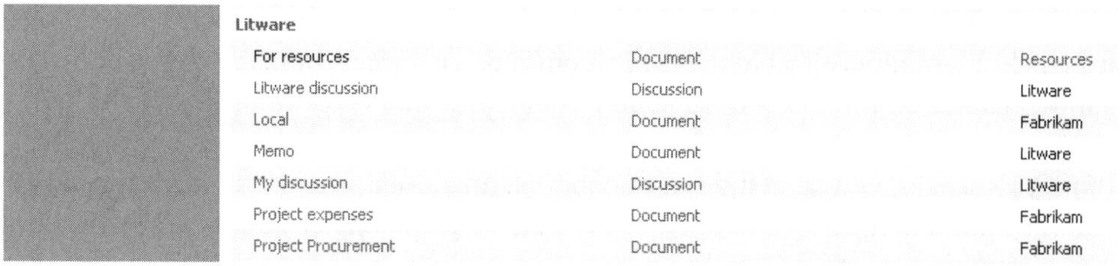

Litware		
For resources	Document	Resources
Litware discussion	Discussion	Litware
Local	Document	Fabrikam
Memo	Document	Litware
My discussion	Discussion	Litware
Project expenses	Document	Fabrikam
Project Procurement	Document	Fabrikam

Figure 15-4 Custom content type group

The location of each content type is shown in the *source column*, to the far right of the figure. This location indicates on which site the content type has been created and also the availability of the content type throughout the site collection. In the figure, the Resources location is grayed out and the For Resources content type is highlighted in blue in the *site content type column* on the left. This is because you are currently within the Resources site, which is a child site of the Fabrikam site. If you navigated back to the Fabrikam site, you would not see the For Resources content type in the Litware group in the Fabrikam Site Content Type Gallery because the Fabrikam site is a parent of the Resources site and content types can be inherited only from parent content types.

When content types are inherited and created on sites, they are within the site scope, referred to as site content types. Content types can also be inherited by the lists and document libraries on a site and modified within the scope of those document libraries and lists, independent of the content type site scope. Those content types are referred to as list content types, or list instances of a content type.

Note In describing the content type inheritance model, list content types, or list instances of a content type, should not be confused with the Lists Content Type group, as defined in Table 15-2.

For example, in Figure 15-3 you saw Site B inherit the default Document content type from Site A and create a new Project Procurement content type. The Project Procurement content type includes the default list columns inherited from the Document content type, but it also has some additional list columns. The Project Procurement content type is now available to the document libraries on Site B. In the document library on Site A, you can select the Project Procurement content type and add more list columns to this content type, but you can do so only within the scope of the document library. Changes made to the content type within the document library scope are not replicated back to the same content type in the site scope or other instances of that same content type used within other lists and document libraries on the same site.

Figure 15-5 shows the relationship between site content type and list content type inheritance. Document Library A and Document Library B have each inherited from the Site B Project Procurement content type. The Site B Project Procurement content type is the parent content type, and the Document Library A and Document Library B Project Procurement content types are both child content types, inherited from the Site B Project Procurement content type. Any changes made to the Project Procurement content type in Document Library A does not affect the Document Library B instance of the Project Procurement content type, and vice versa, and changes to either child content type will not flow back to the parent content type. In this case, the list columns for the Document Library A Project Procurement content type have been modified, leaving the Document Library B Project Procurement content type and Site B Project Procurement content type unchanged. At this point, you can choose to update the parent Site B Project Procurement content type and then push those changes to child equivalent content types.

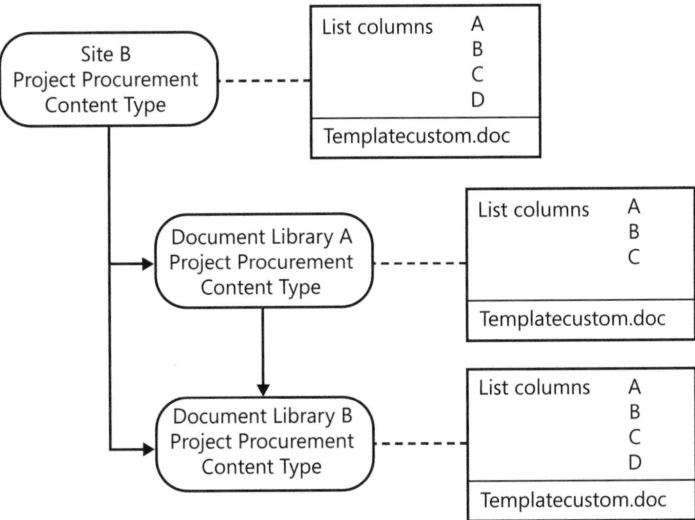

Figure 15-5 Site and List content type inheritance model

Understanding Content Type IDs

Each time a content type is inherited and a new content type is created, the new content type inherits the content type ID from the parent content type. All content types have a unique ID, denoted by a hexadecimal GUID. Content type IDs are limited to a maximum length of 512 bytes or 1024 characters.

You can find the GUID of a content type through the administrative user interface by clicking on a content type link under the Site Content Type column in the Site Content Type Gallery. The resultant URL includes a ctype= parameter. The GUID immediately follows the ctype= parameter and terminates at &Source, for example, ctype= **0x0101000BAD5FF495D8A8640BD3CC6E1D0EB8**&source.

The content type ID serves two purposes:

- It identifies the parentage and type of a content type.
- It avoids any duplication or collisions with existing content types—for example, content types created by a developer or third-party content types.

In reviewing the inheritance model of content type IDs, all content types inherit from the System content type, which is denoted by the content type ID *0x*. For example, the content type ID of the default Document content type is 0x0101. This number includes the Document content type ancestral relationship up to the System content type, with the prefix 0x. The appending numbers indicate the downward hierarchy, from parent to child. In the case of the Document content type, this includes the Item content type ID denoted by content type ID of 0x01. The default Document content type ID is a child of the Item content type and is uniquely identified by the appendage to the Item content type of 01. The Folder content type is also a child of the Item content type and is denoted by the appendage to the parent Item type of the unique number 20. This hierarchical breakdown for the default Document content type and default Folder content type is as follows:

System 0x, Item 0x01, Document 0x0101

System 0x, Item 0x01, Folder 0x0120

Note The System content type is sealed and is in a special group named _hidden. It cannot be modified either via the user interface or through the SharePoint object model.

If you create a new content type from the default Document content type, the new content type includes the default Document content type ID of 0x0101 and is suffixed with a unique hexadecimal GUID for the new content type. For example, in creating a Project

Procurement content type from the default Document content type, the ID for the Project Procurement content type includes the default Document content type ID 0x0101 plus a unique numerical appendage to uniquely identify the Project Procurement content type: 0009309DA06E3F4143B56078594040953C. Figure 15-6 shows the content type ID hierarchy in creating the Project Procurement content type, where each parent content type ID is appended to each subsequent child content type ID.

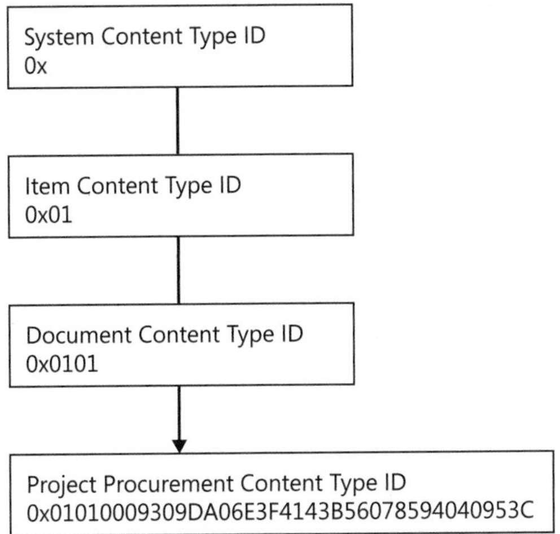

Figure 15-6 Content type ID inheritance model

Creating Content Types

You can create and deploy content types throughout SharePoint Server 2007 sites in the following three ways:

- Administrative user interface
- SharePoint object model
- As part of a Feature deployed to new or existing sites

This section focuses on the creation of content types through the administrative user interface. To learn more about deploying content types using the SharePoint object model, refer to the Windows SharePoint Services 3.0 SDK found at *http://www.microsoft.com/downloads/details.aspx?FamilyId=05E0DD12-8394-402B-8936-A07FE8AFAFFD&displaylang=en*. To learn more about deploying content types using Features, refer to Chapter 26, "Introducing Features," which includes an example of creating a content type Feature and demonstrates methods by which you can deploy Features to new and existing sites.

Permissions for Creating and Modifying Content Types

Table 15-3 shows the user access rights necessary for both creating and deploying content types at the respective levels throughout SharePoint Server 2007.

Table 15-3 Permissions to Create and Modify Content Types

Content type level	Action	Minimum access rights
Parent Site	Create for global site collection. All child sites can access this content type.	Manage Lists Add and Customize Pages
Child Site	Create for site. All lists on that site can access this content type.	Manage Lists Add and Customize Pages
List or document library	Add content type to specific list on site, and make modifications.	Manage Lists

Creating a New Content Type at the Site Level

Content types created through the administrative user interface are created at one of two levels within a site collection: the root site level and the child site level.

> **Note** This discussion is about the root site of the site collection. However, you can also have parent sites throughout a site collection. As you create new sites and subsites, sites become parent sites of subsites. As you create new content types throughout sites in your site collection, child sites might relate back to a parent site rather than to the root site of the site collection.

When a content type is created at the root site level, any child site can inherit that content type. However, root or parent sites cannot inherit from child sites. This section will demonstrate how to create a new site content type on the root site of the Litware site collection, Litware, and then inherit that content type on the Fabrikam child site.

Figure 15-7 shows the Litware site's Site Setting page. You can access a site's content types by accessing the Site Content Type Gallery. To access the gallery, click Site Content Types from under the Galleries section.

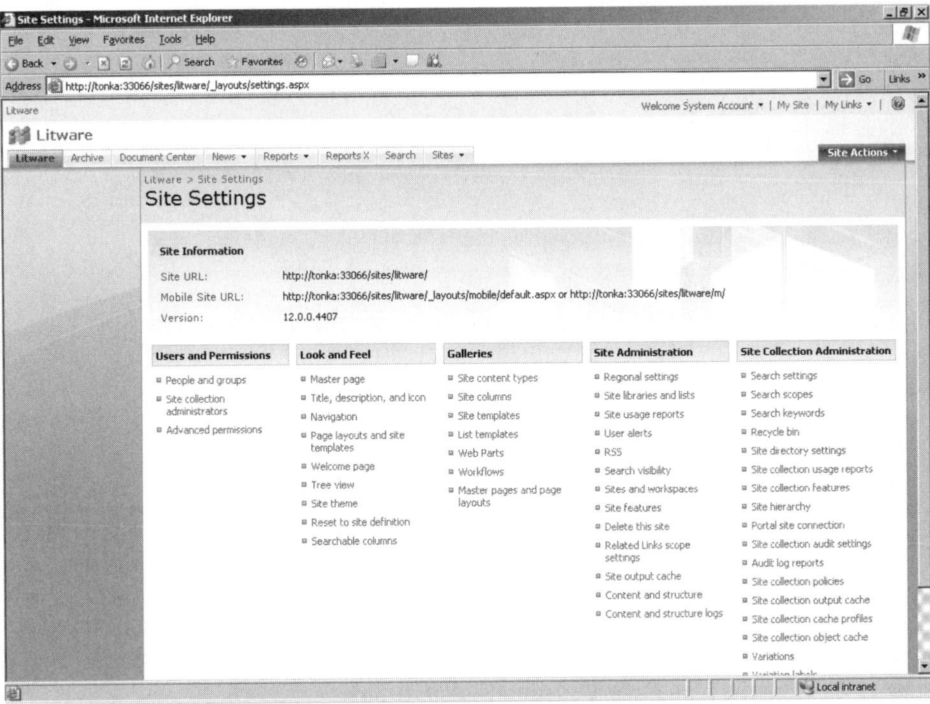

Figure 15-7 Site settings for access to content type gallery

Figure 15-8 shows the Site Content Type Gallery for the child site of Litware, Fabrikam. Notice the Source column to the rightmost of the page, which identifies the site on which the content type has been created, includes the sites Litware and Fabrikam. The parent site, Litware, is highlighted in blue, while the current site, Fabrikam, is grayed out. The leftmost column represents the Site Content Types and shows the custom content type group, Litware. The content types created on the current site (such as Project Procurement) are highlighted in blue, while the content types created on the parent site (such as Memo) are grayed out. Fabrikam content types will not be listed at all in the Site Content Type Gallery of the Litware parent site because child sites inherit content types from the parent site; the parent site does not inherit content types from the child sites.

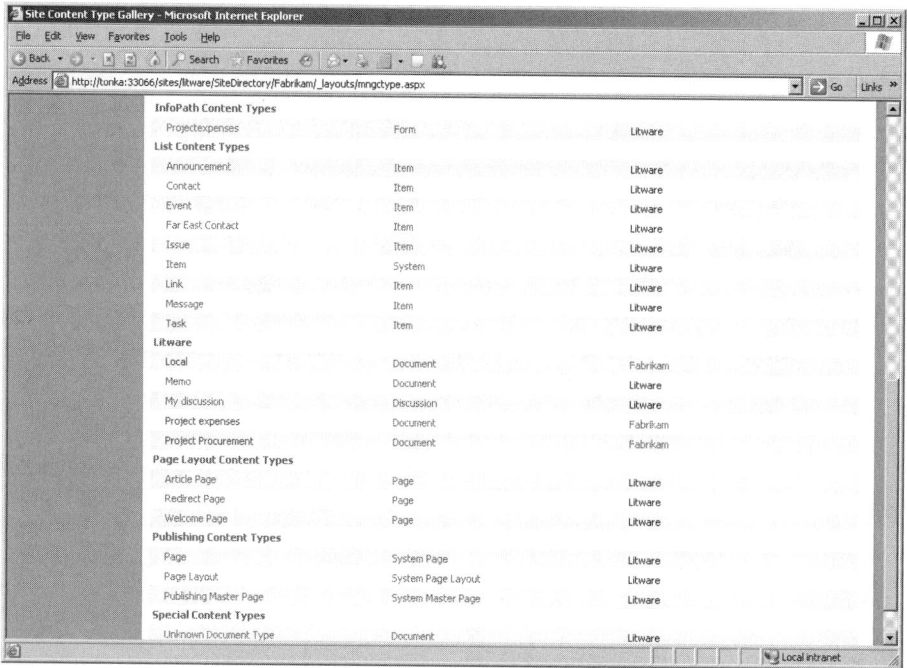

Figure 15-8 Content Type Gallery custom Litware group

To create a new content type for the Litware site, navigate to the Litware site and open the Site Content Type Gallery. Complete the following steps:

1. Click Create in the top tool pane to open the New Site Content Type page, as shown in Figure 15-9.

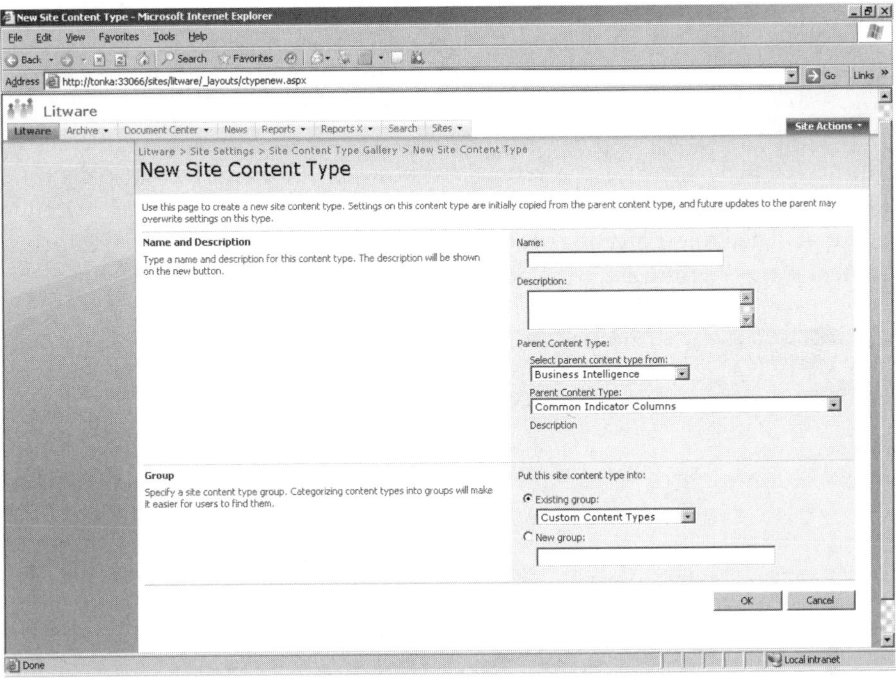

Figure 15-9 New Site Content Type page

2. Type **Project Meetings** in the Name text box to create a content type for Project Meetings.
3. In the Select Parent Content Type From list, select Document Content Types.

   This list enumerates all the existing Site Content Type groups within the context of the current site, including the default and custom content type groups. This includes Site Content Type groups created in the current site or the parent sites of the current site.
4. In the Parent Content Type list, select Document.

   This list contains the content types for the Site Content Type group you selected from the Select Parent Content Type From list.
5. In the Group section, under the Put This Site Content Type Into, choose the Existing Group option and then select the Litware group from the list. Click OK.

Note If you had not already created a custom content type group, you could at this point have used the built-in group of Custom Content Types to store your new content type or created a new group.

The new content type, Project Meetings, has been created on the Litware parent site in the Litware group. Figure 15-10 shows the configuration page for the Project Meetings content type. The Project Meetings content type configuration page also reveals the parent content type—in this case, the Document content type.

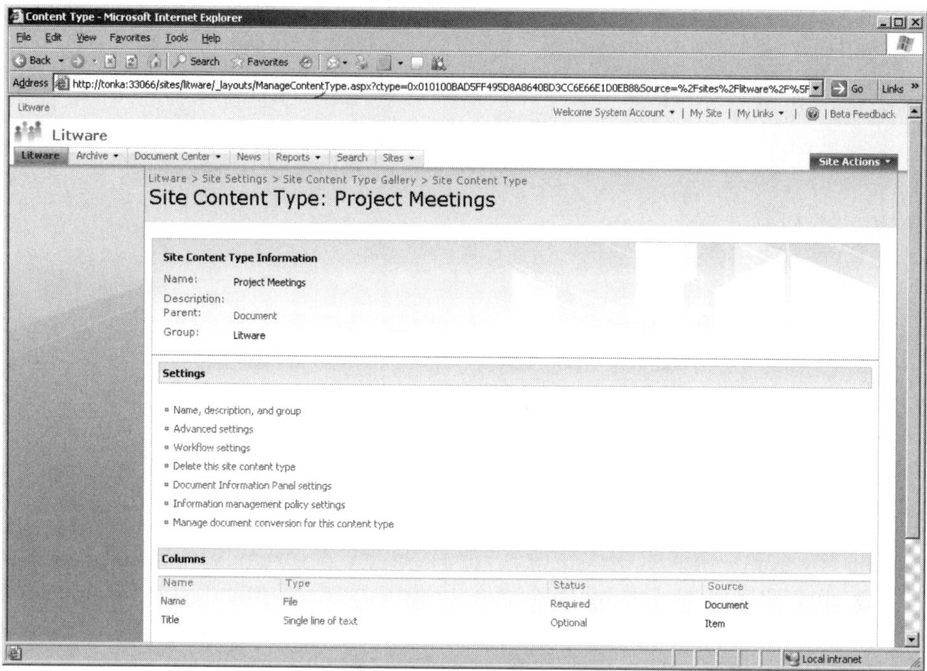

Figure 15-10 Content Type Configuration page

Also note the two default columns created as part of the Project Meetings content type, Name and Title. These two columns have been inherited from the parent content type, Document. You will now add some new columns to the Project Meetings content type to encapsulate the metadata specific to this content type.

Configuring Columns for Content Types

You can add new columns (metadata) to site and list content types. New columns can be added to site content types either by selecting from existing site columns or creating new site columns and associating those columns to a content type. When adding columns to list content types, for instance those content types used throughout a site's document libraries and lists, you can select from both existing site and list columns. To understand how to add columns to list content types, see the section titled "Adding Columns to a Content Type in a Document Library" later in this chapter.

To add a new column to the Project Meetings site content type from existing site columns, follow these steps:

1. From the Litware Site Content Type Gallery page, click on the Project Meetings content type you just created.
2. On the Site Content Type: Project Meetings page, scroll to the bottom of the page, and locate the Columns section.
3. Click Add From Existing Site Columns.

   A page with the option to add site columns to the Project Meeting content type will appear, as shown in Figure 15-11.

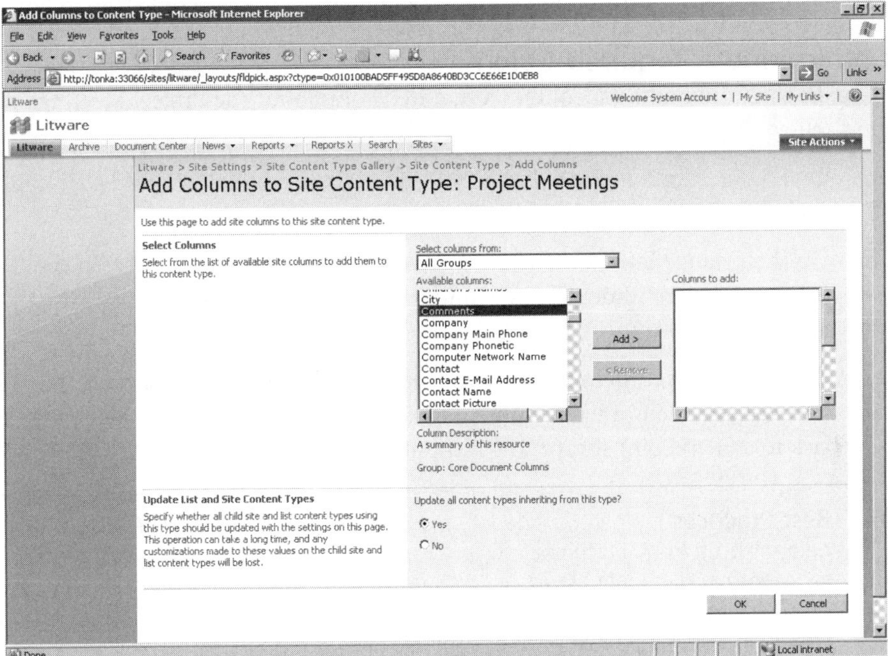

Figure 15-11 Add site columns to site content type

Note The available site columns are stored and sorted by group. If you wanted to create a new site column, you could also create a custom group in which to store all custom site columns or site columns for a specific content type.

4. In the Select Columns From list, select All Groups.
5. In the Available Columns list, select Comments and then click Add to add the Comments site column to the Project Meetings content type.

> **Note** With the Update All Content Types Inheriting From This Type option, any time you make changes to the content type list columns you can choose to push those changes to child sites where the content type is already being used. In this case, you'd choose not to update all content types because the Project Meetings content type is new and has not yet been deployed.

6. Select No and click OK.

The Comments list column has been added to the Project Meetings content type as an optional column, which means that the user will not be forced to enter information in that column when saving a document to a SharePoint site. If you make this a required column, it must contain information before a document can be saved back to SharePoint.

Configuring a Required Column

To make the Comments list column a required column for the Project Meetings content type, follow these steps:

1. On the Site Content Type: Project Meetings page, scroll down to the Columns section and click Comments.
2. On the Change Site Content Type Column: Project Meetings page, in the Column Settings section, under This Column is:, check the Required (Must contain information) radio button. Click OK.

By making the Project Meetings content type Comments column a required column, users will not be able to save documents associated with the Project Meetings content type back to a SharePoint site, or list, without populating the Comments column.

> **Best Practices** When configuring your content type columns, you should determine up front which columns are to be required columns. This is essential for capturing metadata associated with documents. However, you should also take care not to exaggerate the number of required columns for each content type and to limit required columns to that metadata essential to fulfilling your search criteria for given content types. Users will soon become fatigued at being overly prompted to enter data each time they attempt to save documents.

Configuring Document Libraries

In this section, you'll look at using the new Project Meetings content type in one of the existing document libraries, Projects, on the Fabrikam child site. You will also make some further modifications to the content type when you add it to the document library, including adding another column and associating a new custom template.

When a new document library is created, by default it includes the Document content type. Also, by default, document libraries are not configured for multiple content types. Therefore, the first step is to configure the document library to manage multiple content types so that you can add more content types to the same document library.

Configuring Document Libraries for Multiple Content Types

To configure the Projects document library for multiple content types, do the following:

1. Go into the Projects document library and click Settings
2. Choose Document Library Settings.
3. On the Customize Projects page, under General Settings, choose Advanced Settings.
4. On the Document Library Advanced Settings page, under Allow Management Of Content Types, select Yes and click OK to return to the Customize Projects page.

On the Customize Projects page, you now have a new section midway down the page called Content Types. This section is where you can add content types to this document library.

Also notice the Document content type under the Content Type column of the Content Types section. This was the default content type added at the time of creating the document library.

The Document content type can later be removed from the document library, but first you'll include your new Project Meetings content type.

Adding a Content Type

To add the Project Meetings content type to the document library, complete the following steps:

1. Under the Content Types section on the Customize Projects page, choose Add From Existing Site Content Types.
2. On the Add Content Types: Projects page, under the Select Site Content Types From drop-down list, select Litware. Litware is the custom Site Content Type Group created on the Litware site to contain custom content types for the Litware site collection.

3. From the Available Site Content Types list, select Project Meetings and click Add, as shown in Figure 15-12.

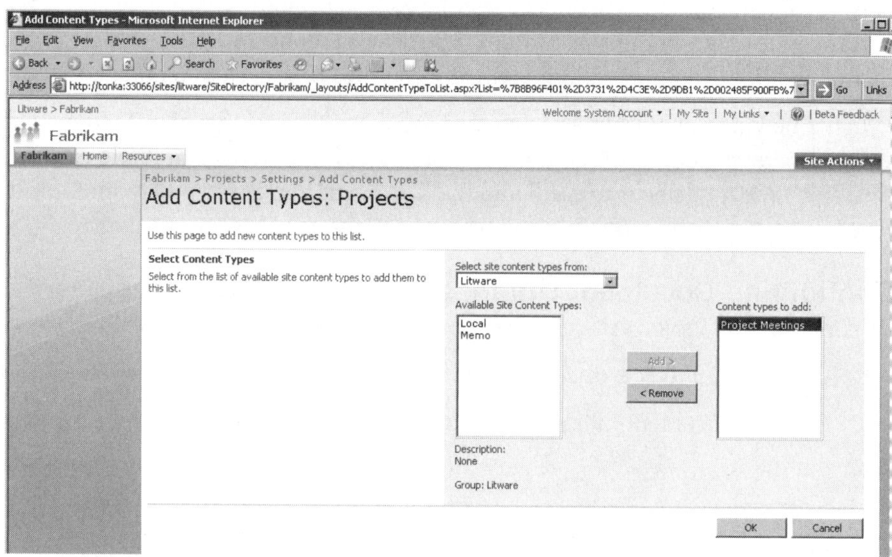

Figure 15-12 Adding content types to a document library

4. Click OK to return to the Customize Projects page.

Under the Content Types section on the Customize Projects page, note the additional content type, Project Meetings.

Planning You could also choose at this stage to add more content types to the same document library.

If you now navigate back to the default, or home, page of the document library and select from the New drop-down menu, you'll see the content types available to that library, denoted by the document templates associated with each content type. (See Figure 15-13.)

Note Clicking directly on the New button rather than on the drop-down arrow beside the New button will launch the default document template in the associated Office application. See the "Setting the Document Templates Order and the Default Content Type" section in this chapter for further discussion.

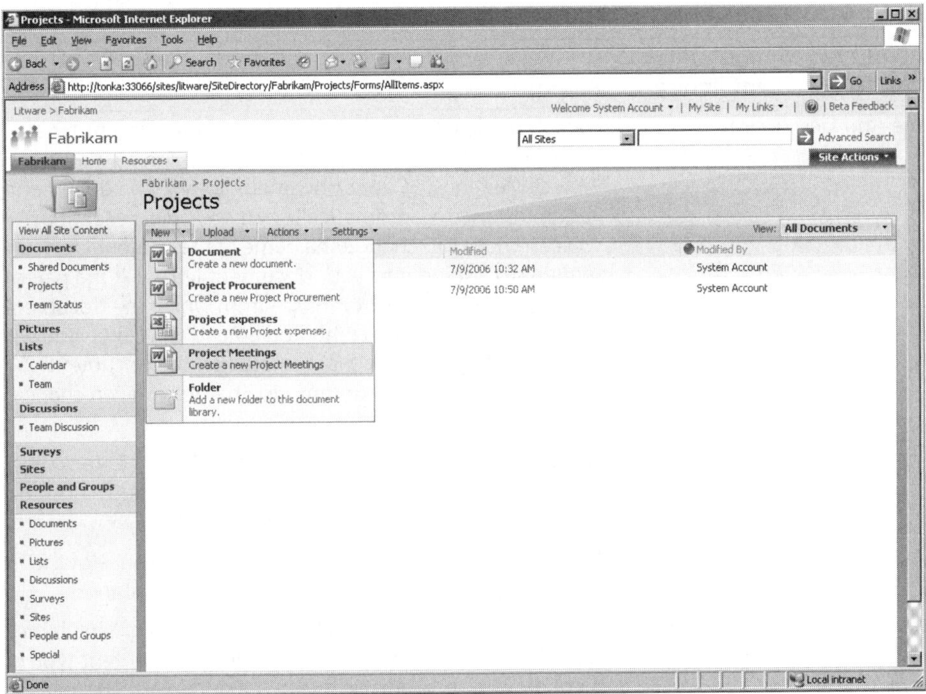

Figure 15-13 Selecting from available document templates in a document library

Changing the Template

In the case of the Project Meetings content type, the associated document template is a Word 2007 template. To change the document template associated with the document library instance of the Project Meetings content type, complete the following steps:

1. Go to the Customize Projects page and, under the Content Types section, click the Project Meetings content type.
2. Review the Settings section on the List Content Type: Project Meetings page. These are the settings available for the Project Meetings content type for the instance of the document library. Table 15-4 summarizes the settings.

Table 15-4 Content Type Settings

Content type configuration setting in document library	Purpose
Name And Description	Default name will be inherited from parent content type name. For instance, you chose to add the site content type, Project Meetings, to your document library. The document library instance is automatically named Project Meetings. You can choose to change the name of the content type subsequent to adding it to your document library. If the parent content type or site content type from which the document library content type was inherited is Read Only, then you will need to change the Read Only status on the document library instance of the content type before you can change the content type name.
Advanced Settings	Edit the existing template associated with the content type, or upload a new template instance. These settings include the option to make the content type Read Only.
Workflow Settings	Add or remove a workflow specific to the instance of the content type—that is, the document library instance.
Delete This Content Type	Remove the content type from the current document library. Note that you will not be able to delete the content type if there are currently documents in the document library associated with that content type.
Document Information Panel (DIP) Settings	Adjust the properties that get exposed in the associated template application—for example, the columns in a Word document. These settings also include the option to edit the existing DIP or upload a new custom DIP template. These settings include the option to always show the DIP when opening a document.
Information Management Policy Settings	Define a specific records policy against the content type in the document library instance, such as expiration date.

Note After you have allowed for management of content types on a document library, the Information Management Policy settings are no longer available at the library level but will apply to each content type in the library. You'll need to explicitly set information policy against each content type.

3. On the List Content Type page for Project Meetings, under the Settings section, click Advanced Settings.
4. On the List Content Type Advanced Settings page for Project Meetings, select Upload A New Document Template.

5. Browse to the location of the new document template, and upload a new template, as shown in Figure 15-14.

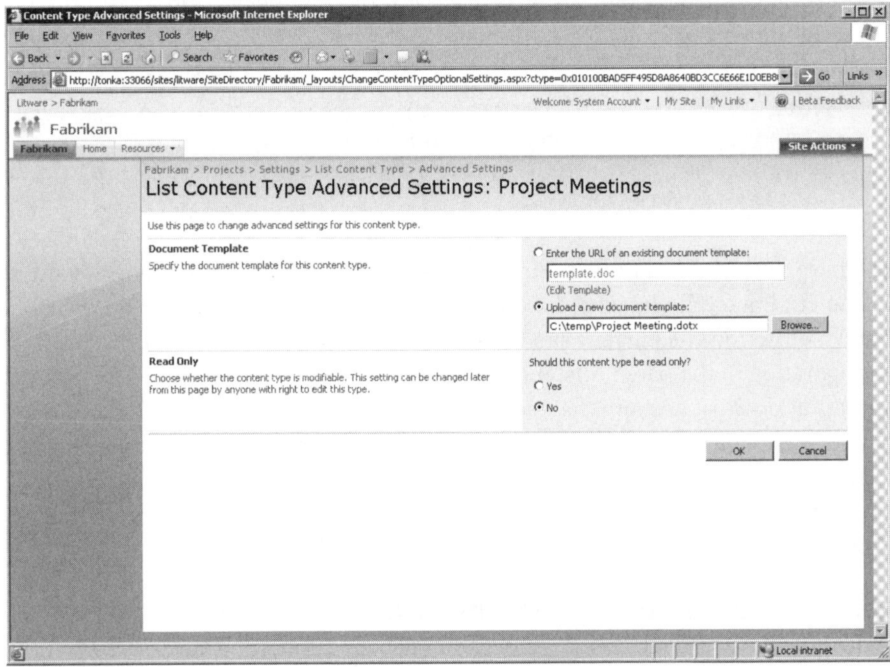

Figure 15-14 Uploading a new document template for a content type

6. Click OK to save the new document template, and return to the List Content Type For Project Meetings page.

Note Bear in mind that the Microsoft Office version of the template you use may determine the list column, or metadata, properties exposed in the DIP. For example, if you are using Word 2007 and use a template based on either Word 2007 or Word 97-2003 format, then the server side metadata will be shown in the DIP. Templates based on a version of Word pre Word 97-2003 format will not expose the metadata in the DIP. See the section "Associating Documents with Content Types" later in this chapter for a discussion on DIP views and properties.

Adding Columns to a Document Library Content Type

Next, add more columns to the document library instance of the Project Meetings content type by completing the following steps:

1. On the List Content Type: Project Meetings page, under the Columns section, click Add From Existing Site Or List Columns.

2. On the Add Columns To List Content Type: Project Meetings page, under the Select Columns From list, select All Groups.
3. In the Available Columns box, select Location and click Add to add the Location column to the Project Meetings content type.

Note When you create a new site column at the site level, you are asked if you want to apply that site column to all content types. This is an alternative way of adding columns to site content types and making those columns available to both site and list content types.

You have now updated the instance of the Project Meetings content type for the current document library. If you added the Project Meetings content type to another document library, either on the current site or another site within the site collection, the original configuration of the parent instance of this content type would apply. The new template and additional list column, named Location, would not be included. If you wanted to have all instances of the Project Meetings content type include these updates, you would need to update the global instance of the Project Meetings content type, located in this case on the Litware site, and then push those changes to all existing instances of the Project Meetings content type throughout the site collection.

Removing a Content Type from a Document Library

When you created your new document library, the default Document content type was automatically added. Because you've added your own custom content type, you can go ahead and remove the Document content type.

Note When you delete a content type, the list columns associated with that content type are not deleted and remain listed under Columns on the Customize Document Library page.

1. On the Customize Projects page, under Content Types, select Document.
2. On the List Content Type page for Document, under Settings, click Delete This Content Type.

   A warning dialogue appears, with the question "Are you sure you want to delete this list content type?".
3. Click OK.

Note You cannot delete a content type if that content type is being used. For example, if documents in the document library had already been associated with the Document content type, you would need to re-associate those documents with another content type before deleting the Document content type. To associate a document with an alternate content type, select Edit Properties from the document contextual menu. Then on the Edit Item page for the document, select a content type from the Content Type drop-down menu. As you select a new content type, the associated list columns, or metadata, for that content type will be displayed and you will need to populate any required columns before clicking OK to save and associate the document with the new content type.

Next, you can change the order of the content types.

Setting the Document Templates Order and the Default Content Type

The order of the content types determines the sequence in which the document templates from the New menu are shown on the document library home page. You can also set the default content type for the document library. The default content type is the one that is chosen if you click New instead of clicking the arrow next to New.

1. On the Customize Projects page, under Content Types, select Change New Button Order And Default Content Type.
2. On the Change New Button Order And Default Content Type page, shown in Figure 15-15, choose the order in which you want to have the content types sorted in the New drop-down list. The content type you select as the first will be the default content type for the document library.

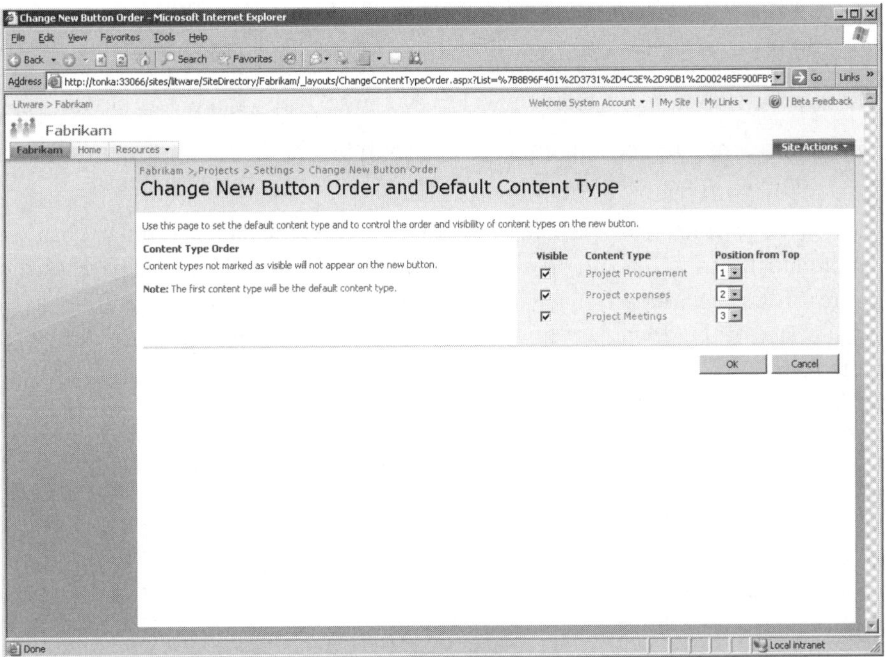

Figure 15-15 Changing the content type order, and setting the default content type

At this point, you could proceed to configure the additional settings for the Project Meetings content type, such as Workflow settings and Information Management Policy settings. There is a walk through on configuring workflow settings in the section titled "Attaching Workflow to a Content Type" later in this chapter.

Configuring Document Library Views for Multiple Content Types

When you add new columns to a content type, all the resultant list columns are exposed in the document library's default view. If you have multiple content types in the document library, by default all list columns are exposed and you could end up with one very busy default view page for the document library. One alternative is to create a view based on a content type. By default, a document library is configured with two views:

- All Documents view, which is the default view
- Explorer view

Because the content types give you additional columns of metadata, you might find that it's advantageous to create a view of this metadata. To create a new view for content types, complete the following steps:

1. Open the Customize Projects page.
2. Under the Views section, click Create View.
3. On the Create View: Projects page, select Standard View.
4. On the subsequent Create View: Projects page, type a name for the new view.
5. In the Group By section, under First Group By The Columns drop-down list, select Content Type and click OK.

The new view, which for this example you have chosen the name Summary, has been created and included under the Views section on the Customize Projects page, as shown in Figure 15-16. The Summary view is also available from the View drop-down list on the default page of the document library. You can also filter and sort your views based on content type.

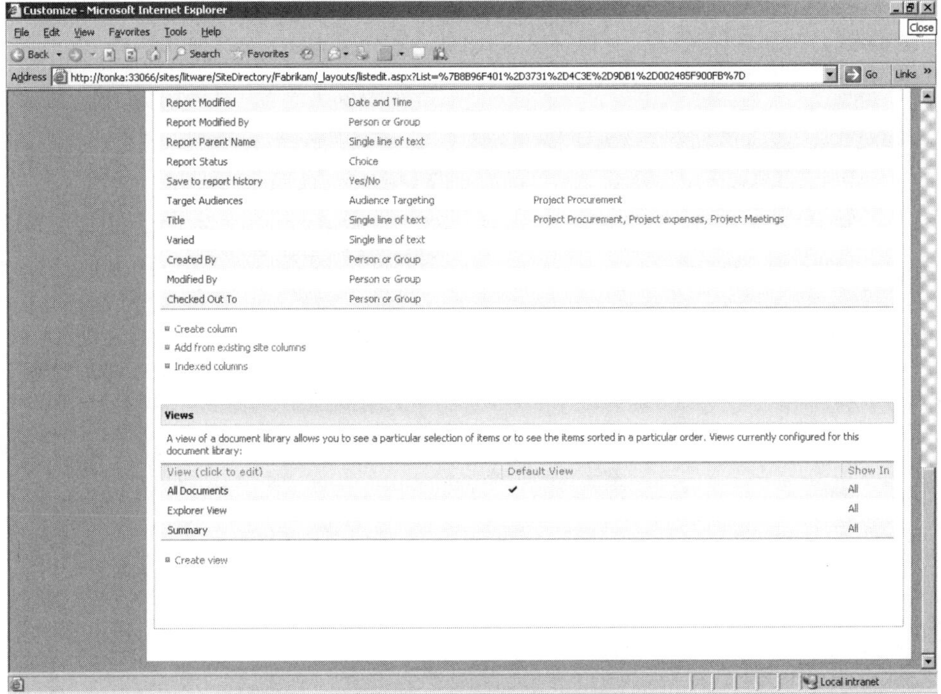

Figure 15-16 New document library View configuration based on content types

Associating Documents with Content Types

Assuming you have your document library configured to manage multiple content types and multiple content types are included, new and existing documents can be associated with one of those content types. For example, you might add existing documents to a document library and subsequently associate them with one of the document library content types if you are migrating your existing files from a file server or public folder store on your Microsoft Exchange server.

When creating a new document from the New menu in the document library, you can choose either the default content type or another content type, such as Project Procurement, Project Expenses, or Project Meetings.

External documents uploaded to a document library configured for multiple content types are associated with one of the content types at the time of uploading, as shown in Figure 15-17. In the figure, the message at the top indicates that an existing document has been successfully uploaded to a SharePoint document library configured for multiple content types. The Content Type list shows the available Content Types. The document can be associated with either the default content type, Project Procurement, or one of the other two content types. Depending on the content type, the associated list columns set as required, denoted by a red asterisk, will need to be populated before the document is checked in to the document library.

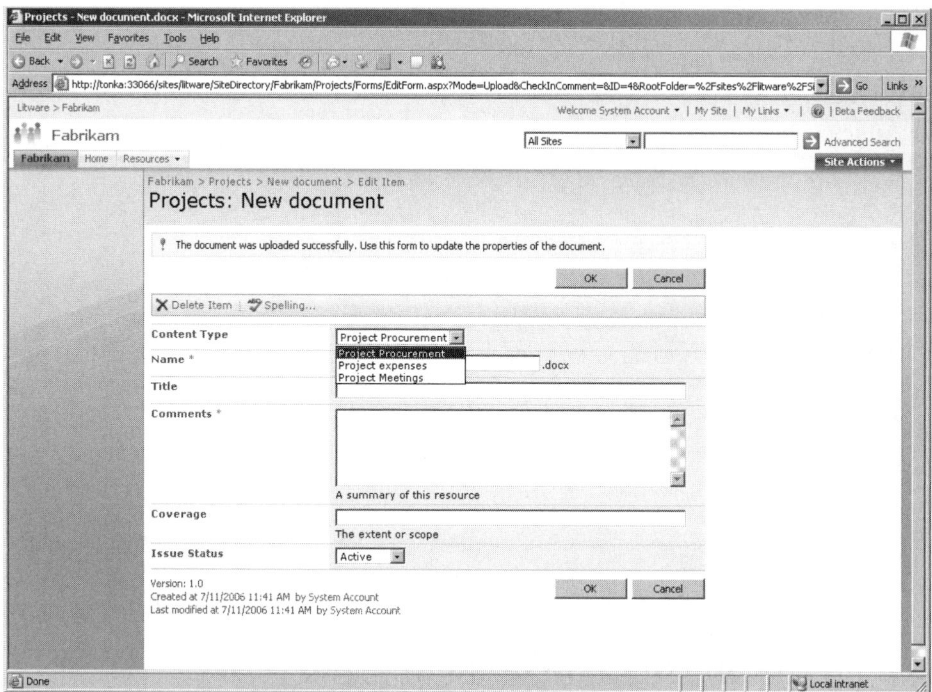

Figure 15-17 Associating external documents with existing content types

The metadata, or list columns, associated with the selected content type will be applied to the document on upload. If the document being uploaded, for instance a Word 2003 or Word 2007 document, includes any existing core document properties, such as title, comments, subject or keywords, then you can select the corresponding Content Type list column properties from the pre-defined Core Document Columns and those properties will be synched on file upload. This means that the original document property, such as keywords, will be exposed in the matching list column, keywords, and dynamically populated with the values from the original document. Any of the original document properties not exposed in SharePoint, such as custom properties, are retained in the document and can be viewed via the displayed properties in the associated Office application Document Information Panel (DIP).

In Word 2007, you will have the following three document property display options:

- Document library properties, which are the server properties, or those list columns assigned the content type
- Document properties, which includes properties included on the original document (such as Title, Subject, Keywords, Category, Status, and Comments)
- Advanced properties, which shows a popup of the properties window for the document (the window seen with the earlier versions of Word 2000 and 2003)

These options are shown in Figures 15-18 and 15-19.

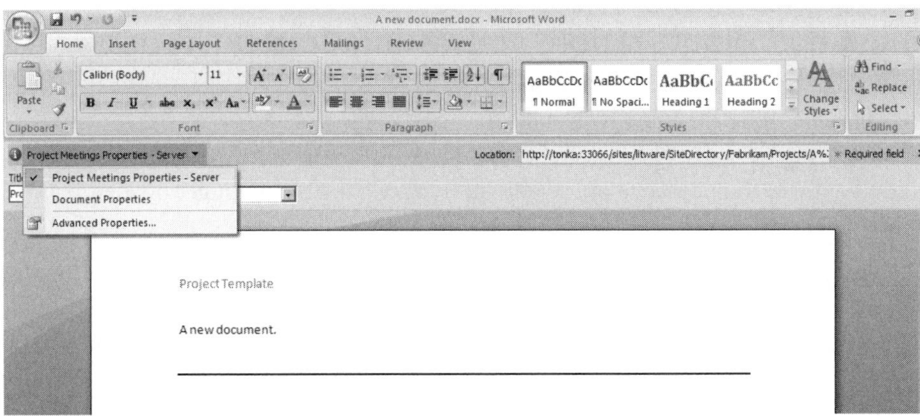

Figure 15-18 How to access content type metadata in Word 2007

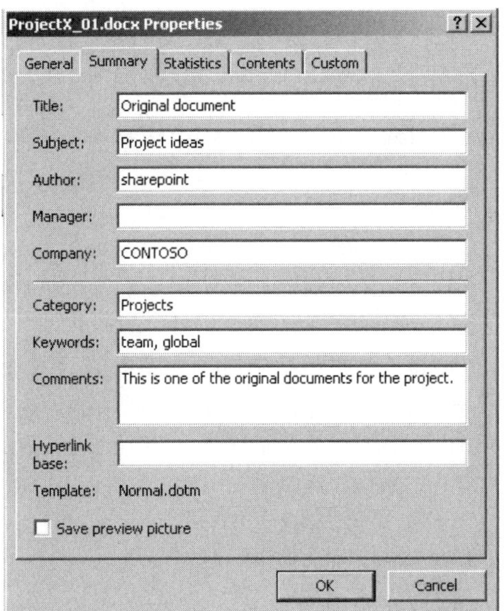

Figure 15-19 Word document original properties

Uploading Multiple Documents to a Multiple Content Type Document Library

You can choose to upload multiple documents either by using the Upload option on the tool pane on the default page of the document library or via the Explorer view, where you can drag and drop multiple documents into a document library.

When you upload multiple documents, those documents will be added to the document library, but they will be left as checked out to you or the person uploading the documents and won't be checked in until you populate the custom metadata, or actions, associated with the content types.

Versioning and Modifications to Existing Content Types

If you make modifications to a site-level content type, you are given the option to update all content types inheriting from this type. If you make modifications to a list content type (such as adding more list columns to a document library content type), those changes will apply only to that instance of the content type. Changes do not get pushed back to the parent content type.

If you change the list columns for a content type (for example, add a new site column to content type X on document library A), all existing documents in that document library using that content type will inherit the new column. If you delete a list column from a content type, SharePoint will remove that column from documents using that content type. This includes columns previously configured as required columns.

But what happens when you delete a document from a multiple content type list and then decide to restore that document from the Recycle Bin? If you restore a document from the Recycle Bin, the document and its content type association (and versions) are restored to the originating document library based on the content type at the time of deletion.

If you have versioning enabled and have at some point changed the content type association with a document in between versions and want to restore an earlier version, the version of the document you restore will be restored with the content type that was associated with it at the time it was versioned. So, if the current version of the document is of content type A and you restore version 2 of the same document, which is of content type B, content type B is the type restored with the document version.

You cannot delete a content type if it is currently being used throughout a site or site collection. This restriction also applies to the content types employed by the lists and document libraries on a site. You must either delete any associated instances of the content type or re-associate any documents using that content type to another content type. Associating documents with alternate content types is explained earlier in this chapter, in the section titled "Removing a Content Type from a Document Library."

When you delete a content type from a list, or document library, you are only deleting that instance of the content type. The content type will still be available from the site and global content types. If you delete a site content type, the content type will no longer be available to any lists on that site. If you delete a content type from the parent site or the global content type, it is no longer available to any sites in that site collection.

Real World Handling Global Content Types

Deleted content types do not get sent to the Recycle Bin! Best practice is to make global content types read-only to avoid unintended changes or deletion and also to standardize on content type configuration throughout your site collection. Global content types are created on the root site of a site collection and then are inherited by sites and lists, or document libraries, throughout the site collection.

If you set a global content type to read-only, then by default the inherited list instances of that content type will be set to read-only. For example, say you've created a Project Meetings content type on the root site of the Litware site collection, Litware, and you've added a custom workflow, custom columns, retention policy and template to that content type, and then set that content type to read-only. Then, on the Fabrikam site, a child site of the Litware site, you add the Project Meetings content type to your Shared Documents document library. The content type will include the settings applied to the parent but by default you will not be able to delete the content type, rename it or apply a custom template. It is possible to change the read-only status of the inherited, list instance content type, but you need to do this explicitly by accessing the list content type's Advanced Settings page and changing the Read Only status from Yes to No.

To set a content type to read-only, do the following:

1. Select the content type you want to set as read-only from the Site Content Type Gallery, for example, Project Meetings.
2. On the Site Content Type: Project Meetings page, under the Settings section, click on Advanced Settings.
3. On the Site Content Type Advanced Settings: Project Meetings page, in the Read Only section, check the Yes radio button, then click OK.

Back on the Site Content Type: Project Meetings page, the number of available Settings will be minimized to include only the Advanced Settings and Workflow Settings, and the content type will be denoted as read-only in the page title, that is, Site Content Type: Project Meetings (Read Only).

Creating Content Types when Deploying InfoPath Forms

A new feature of InfoPath 2007 is the ability to create an InfoPath form and save that form directly back to the SharePoint Server 2007 server as both an InfoPath template and as a new, or existing, content type.

On the CD A step-by-step tutorial on how to do this is included on this book's Companion CD.

Extending Content Types

Content types can be extended to enhance storage, format and expose content, and extend business processes. This section looks at associating workflows with content types both through the document library administrative user interface and also using SharePoint Designer 2007. It also looks at how you can leverage content types for managing e-mail records and formatting e-mail messages in lists and Web Parts throughout SharePoint Server 2007 sites.

Attaching Workflow to a Content Type

There are three ways to integrate workflow in SharePoint Server 2007:

- Through an administrative user interface
- With SharePoint Designer 2007
- With Visual Studio 2005

This section looks at adding workflows specifically to content types using the SharePoint built-in workflows, through the administrative user interface. It also looks at creating a custom workflow in SharePoint Designer 2007 based on content type.

Using the Built-in Workflows

You can add a workflow to either a site-level content type or a document library-level, or list-level, content type. If you apply a workflow to a global content type, all instances of that content type will include that workflow.

To add a workflow to a document library, or list, content type, complete the following steps:

Note In this scenario, you are only adding a workflow to the current list instance of the content type.

1. Go to the document library, in this case the Project document library, and select Document Library Settings.
2. On the Customize Projects page, browse to the Content Types section and click the content type against which you want to place the workflow.
3. On the List Content Type page, under the Settings section, select Workflow Settings.
4. On the Change Workflow Settings page, shown in Figure 15-20, the existing workflows are Approval, Collect Feedback, and Collect Signatures. These workflows are already associated with the global content type, Document, and are included here because this content type is a child of the Document content type. You can choose to edit these existing workflows or create new workflows.

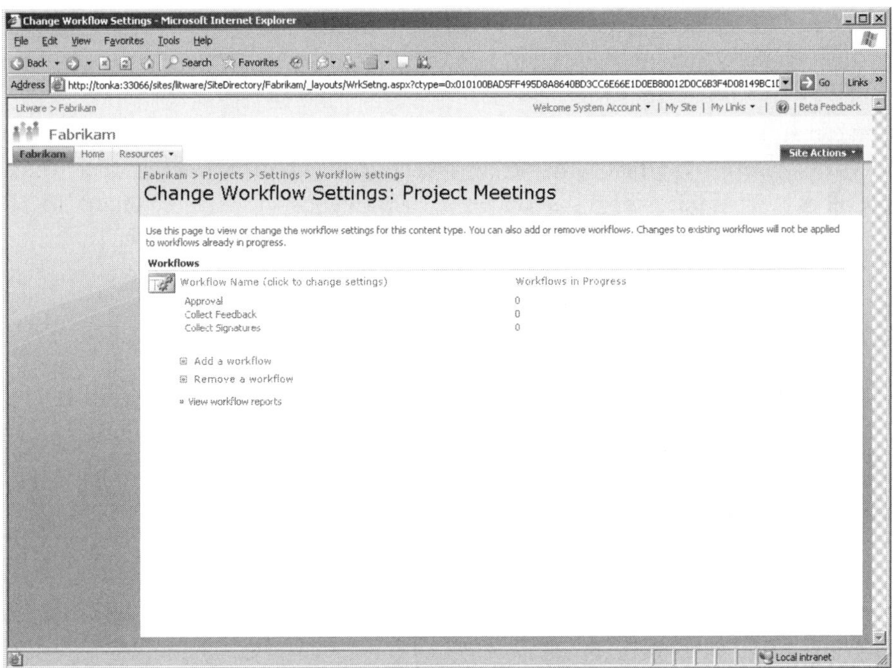

Figure 15-20 Changing workflow settings for the content type

5. Select Add A Workflow.

   There are four built-in, or default, workflows from which to choose and apply to the content type:

   a. Approval
   b. Collect Feedback

   c. Collect Signatures
   d. Disposition Approval
6. Choose Approval.
7. Add a name for the content type workflow, configure the rest of the settings, and then click Next.
8. On the Customize Workflow page, complete the configuration settings, add the users you want to have included in the approval workflow process, and then click OK to return to the Change Workflow Settings For Content Type page. You'll notice the addition of the new workflow you've just created. In this example, a new workflow called A Document Approval has been added to the document library instance of the Project Meetings content type.

The workflow assigned to the content type is unique to that content type; it is not available to the entire document library or to other content types in the same document library.

You can also start the workflow from within the associated Office application. For example, in Word 2007, on the File menu you can click Start Workflow and a dialog box showing all related workflows for that document type will be shown. (See Figure 15-21.) This dialog box includes any workflows specific to that document type, as well as any content types specific to the document library where that document is stored.

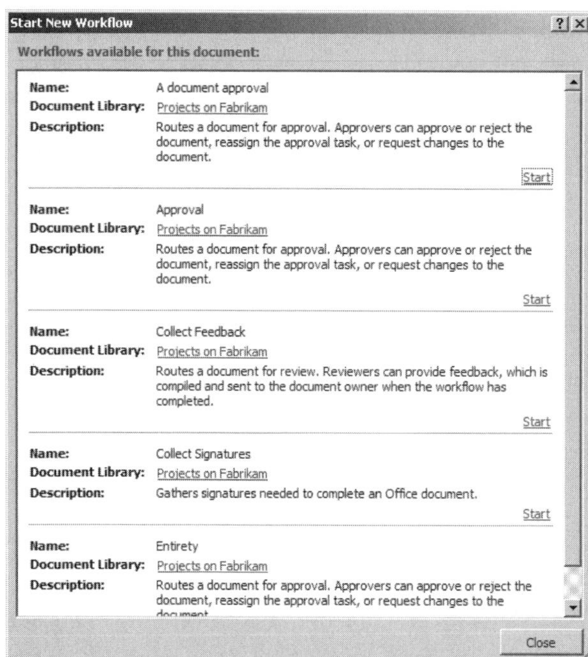

Figure 15-21 Start workflow from associated content type template

The obvious advantages of being able to apply both content-type-specific workflows and document-library-level workflows is that you might want to set a general approval workflow for all documents in the document library but only want to apply certain workflows to certain documents. For example, you might want to collect signatures for an expense report, or you might want to place an expiration date (Disposition Approval) on certain types of project documents. Or you might want different users or groups associated with one type of document workflow and not another.

Using SharePoint Designer 2007

We can configure workflows in SharePoint Designer 2007 using content type properties. SharePoint Designer 2007 allows us to take workflow a step beyond the built-in workflows just demonstrated by including the ability to add steps and conditions.

> **Important** To design and create a workflow using SharePoint Designer 2007, you will need to have installed the Windows Workflow Foundation on the same machine on which SharePoint Designer 2007 is installed.

To trigger a workflow on a multiple-content-type document library that sends e-mail to a user based on one content type and copy a document based on another content type, complete the following steps:

1. Open your site in SharePoint Designer 2007.

   > **Important** You need a minimum of Web Designer access to the site to access the workflow settings in SharePoint Designer 2007.

2. From the File menu, select New and then Workflow.
3. Define your new workflow, as shown in Figure 15-22. Give the workflow a name, and attach the workflow to a specific list (or document library) in the site. In this case, we've chosen the Projects document library on the Fabrikam site and named the workflow Project Workflow.

   > **Note** When you create a workflow in SharePoint Designer 2007, the workflow is specific to the list (or document library) you define. It is not available to other lists on the site, and it is not uniquely associated with a content type.

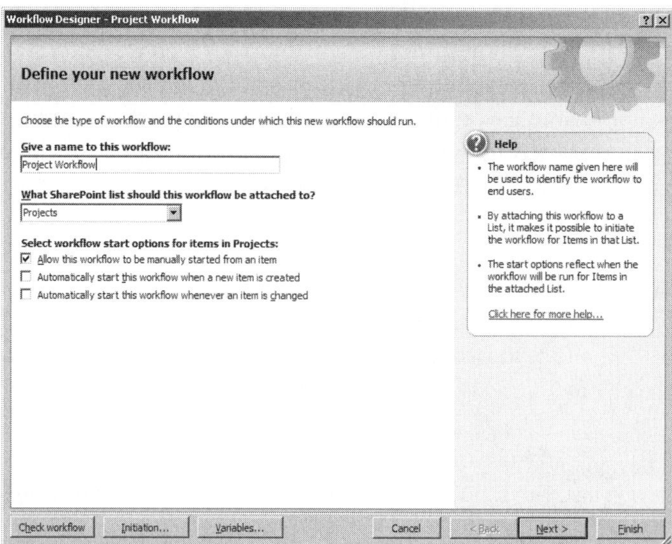

Figure 15-22 Defining a workflow

4. Still on the Define Your New Workflow page, under Select Workflow Start Options For Items In Projects, set the workflow to either start manually through end-user intervention only or to start automatically when a condition of the workflow is met. Click Next.

   The next screen prompts you for a step name. In SharePoint Designer 2007, you can include one or multiple steps in your workflows.

5. Optionally, give the step a name and then click Conditions.
6. From the drop-down list, select Compare Any Data Source.

   This results in the condition of:

   ```
   If value equals value
   ```

7. Click the first highlighted word *Value* and then click on the *fx* symbol (or *Display Data Binding*).
8. In the Define Workflow Lookup window, leave Source set as Current Item. From the Field drop-down list, select Content Type. Click OK.
9. Leave the *Equals* in the condition as *Equals*.
10. Click the next highlighted word, *Value*.
11. If the document library has multiple content types, they are listed in the drop-down list from *Value*.

12. Select the content type from the drop-down list, as shown in Figure 15-23.

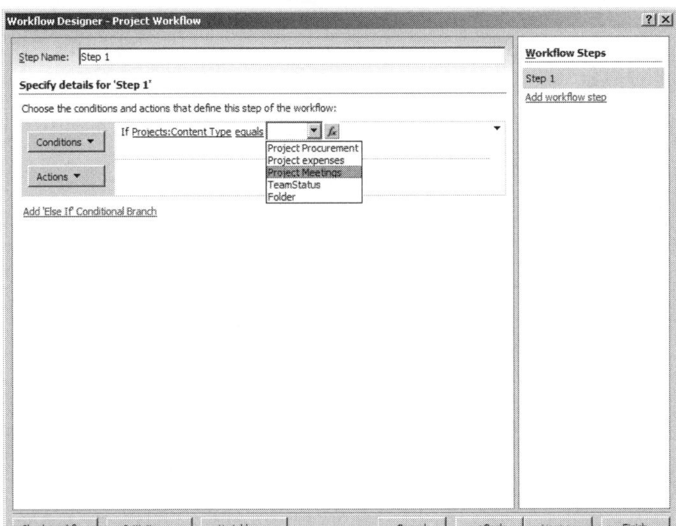

Figure 15-23 Selecting a content type

13. Next, select Actions.
14. From the Actions list, select Send An Email.
15. Click the highlighted words "This Message."
16. In the Define E-mail Message window, configure the e-mail settings and click OK.
17. Back on the Workflow Designer window, click Add Else If Conditional Branch link.
18. In the new conditional branch, click Conditions and select Compare Any Data Source.
19. Click the highlighted word *Value*.
20. Select the *fx* symbol.
21. In the Define Workflow Lookup window, leave Source set as Current Item.
22. From the Field drop-down list, select Content Type and click OK.
23. Leave the *value of equals* as *equals*.
24. Click the remaining highlighted word, *Value*.
25. Select one of the other content types from the value drop-down list, as shown in Figure 15-24.

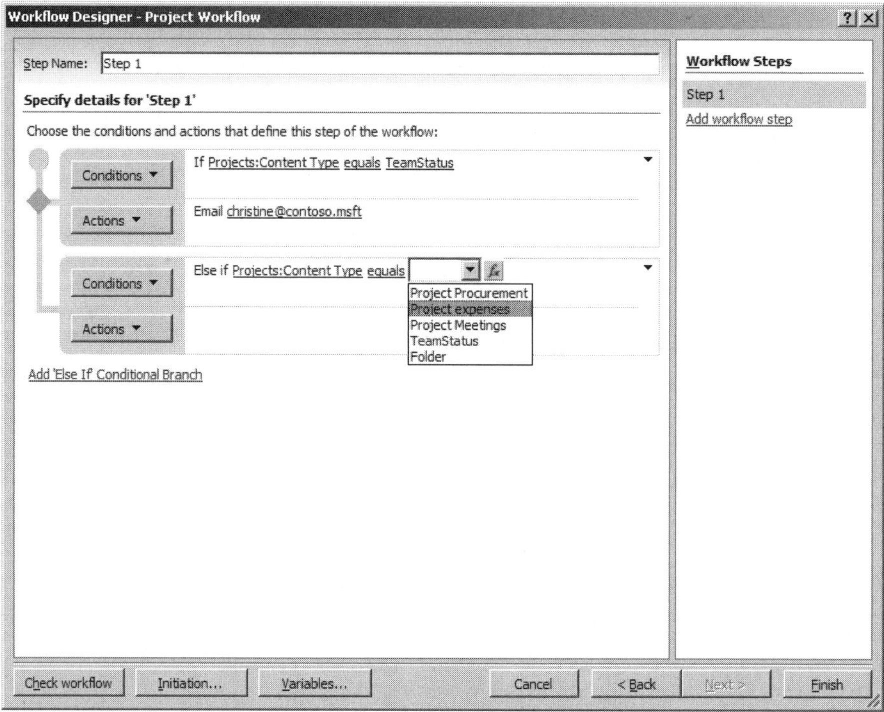

Figure 15-24 Selecting an additional content type for value

26. Next, while still working in the second conditional branch, click Actions and select Copy List Item.

27. In the resultant action Copy Item In This List To This List, select the first highlighted *this list* and choose Current Item.

28. Select the second highlighted *this list*, and choose an alternate document library, or list. Your workflow screen should look like Figure 15-25.

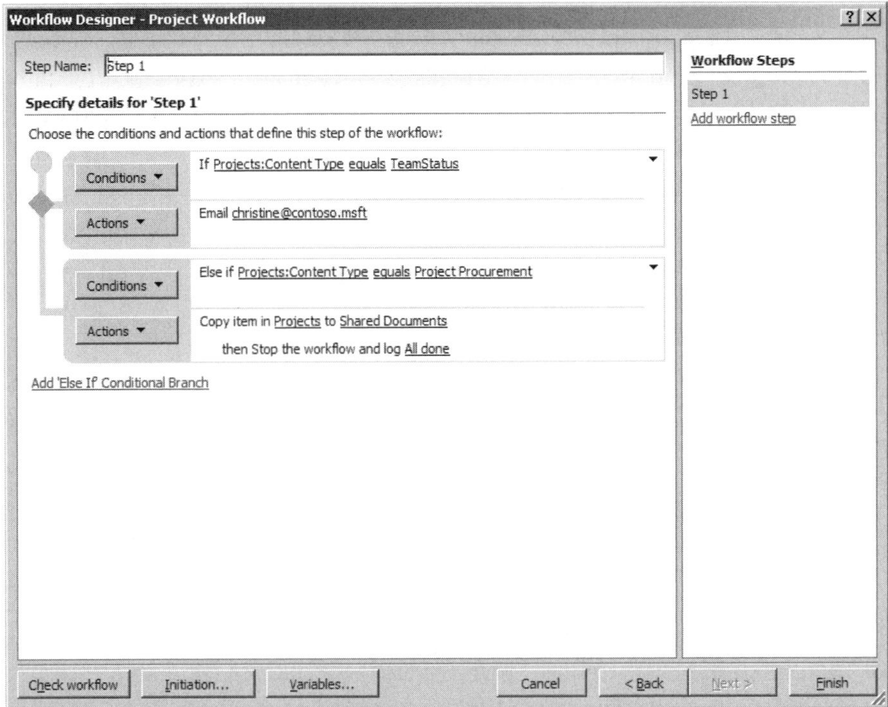

Figure 15-25 Completed workflow

29. Click Finish to save the new workflow back to the destination list (or document library).

Using the built-in workflows, you can assign a workflow to either a global content type instance or a list, or document library, instance of a content type. Using SharePoint Designer 2007, you can associate a workflow with a specific list, or document library, and you can set conditions and actions based on the content types within that list or document library.

Using Content Types to Format E-Mails

In SharePoint Server 2007, you can configure your lists and document libraries to receive incoming e-mail messages and attachments.

Note For instructions on how to configure incoming e-mail for SharePoint Server 2007, refer to Chapter 6, "Performing Central Administration and Operations Configuration."

How those e-mail messages are subsequently presented and stored in SharePoint Server 2007 can depend on the default content type of the targeted list or document library. For example, it can depend on whether the fields of your e-mail are exposed as columns, such as the E-mail sender and E-mail body, or whether there is a specific workflow or records policy set against the content type.

You can e-mail directly from your Microsoft Office Outlook client to document libraries, picture libraries, custom lists, announcements, calendars, and discussion boards. Document libraries are limited to Document content types, and lists are limited to List content types. E-mail messages will be presented and stored depending on the content type.

Note If you e-mail document libraries, or lists, where the default content type includes required columns, then those required columns will not apply to the e-mail and the sender will not be prompted to populate columns before the e-mail is checked in.

If you e-mail a document library, where the default content type is based on the Document content type, the e-mail message is stored as an EML file and any attachments are saved separately in the same document library. Both the e-mail message and attachment are saved with the default content type. For example, in Figure 15-26 an e-mail message has been e-mailed to a document library where the Project Procurement content type is the default content type. The e-mail message is stored as a file.

Note The default content type is that content type which has been set in order as the first content type in a document library configured for multiple content types.

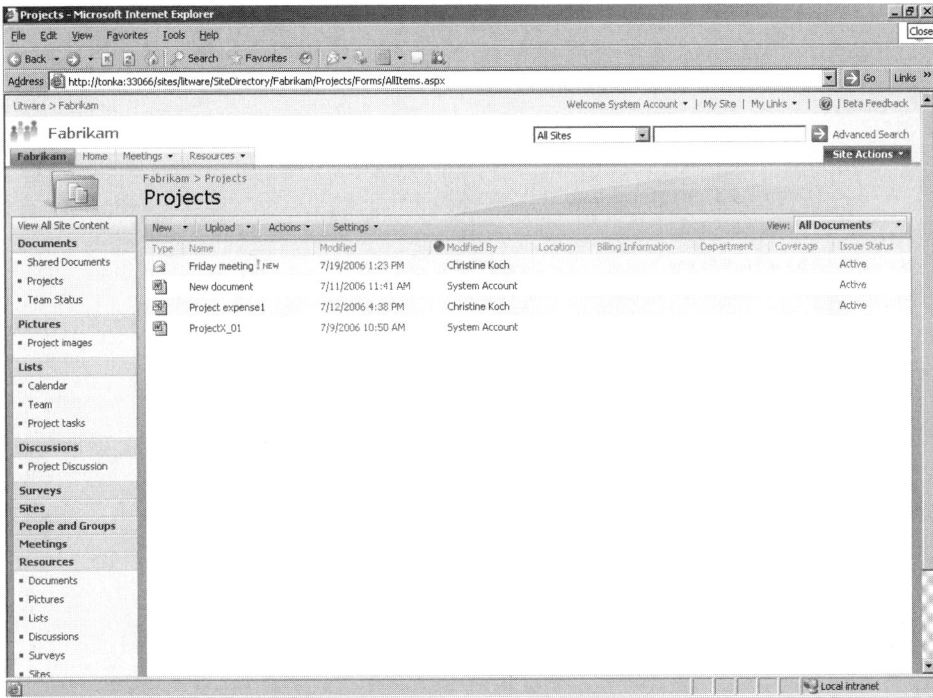

Figure 15-26 E-mail message stored using the default Document content type

If you open the e-mail file in the document library, the body of the e-mail is launched on a separate page. Viewing the e-mail properties confirms that the e-mail's content type is the Project Procurement content type.

Any received e-mail messages inherit any policies or workflow set against the default content type. For example, your company might have an e-mail retention policy whereby e-mail messages are deleted after a certain period of time. In the Information Management Policy Settings for a content type, you can enable expiration. So you could specify that all e-mail messages over three months old are to be deleted, or you could implement a workflow to alert users of the expiration period and copy e-mail messages to the Web application's record repository.

If you wish to have incoming e-mail properties stored in editable form, such as the title and body of the e-mail, then you can achieve this by configuring and leveraging the Announcement content type for those e-mails, as shown in Figure 15-27. In this case, an e-mail has been e-mailed to the Submitted E-mail Records list in the records repository and includes an Expiration Date.

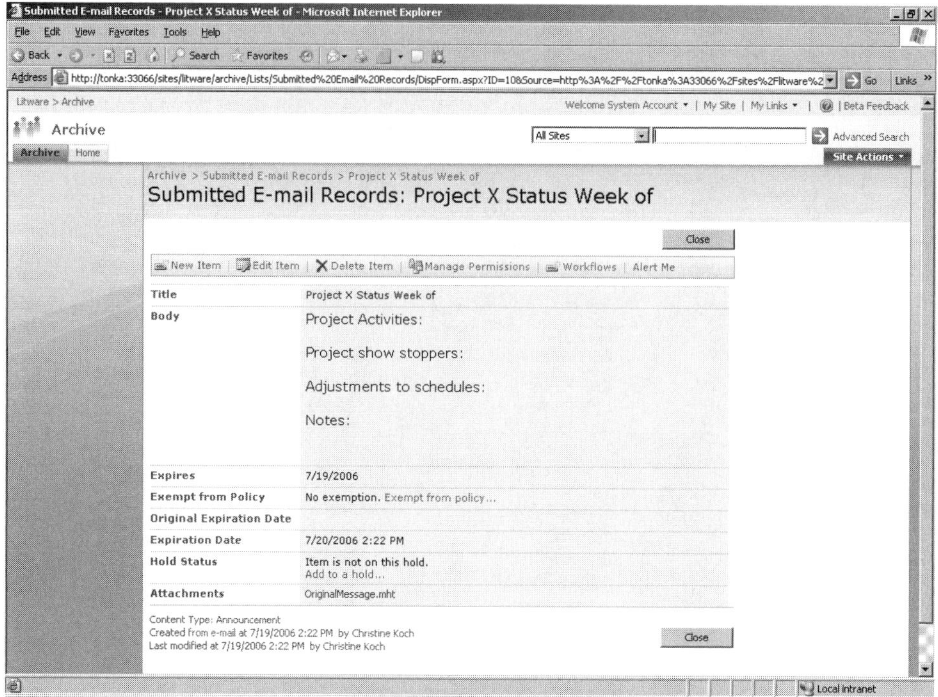

Figure 15-27 E-mail format in Announcement content type

By default, Team Sites include an Announcements Web Part on the home page. By configuring the associated Announcement list for incoming e-mail and e-mailing those lists, e-mail messages can be dynamically exposed as announcements in the Announcements Web Part.

One point worth mentioning here is the e-mailing capabilities of the SharePoint calendar. You can e-mail meeting requests from your Outlook calendar directly to a calendar in your SharePoint site. The meeting will be created and stored on the SharePoint calendar under the calendar's default content type, Event, as shown in Figure 15-28.

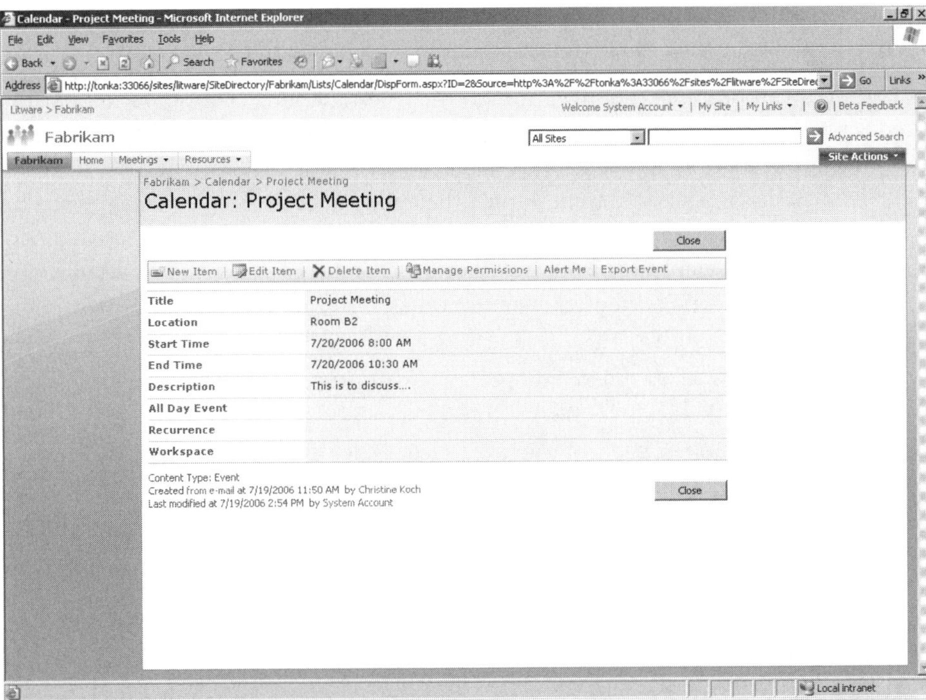

Figure 15-28 E-mail and the Event content type

If you make any changes to an e-mailed meeting on the SharePoint calendar, those changes will be automatically synchronized with the originating meeting planner.

You can also e-mail directly to a Discussion Board, which includes by default two content types, Discussion and Message. The e-mail message will be added as a new discussion thread.

As you can see, you can take advantage of the lists and contents types to both format and add custom actions to incoming e-mail messages in your SharePoint sites. You could also extend e-mail management by adding custom workflows to the content types associated with the document libraries or lists receiving e-mail messages using SharePoint Designer 2007 or Visual Studio 2005.

Searching by Using Content Types

You can use content types to establish search scopes. In SharePoint Server 2007, search scopes allow you to define and group a specific type, or source, of content to more granularly configure and categorize your search. For example, you could create a search scope in your site collection which includes content associated with the Document content type. Then, if you run a search query against that search scope, all content based on the content type of Document will be returned in the search results.

Search scopes can be created either through the Search Settings configuration page in Shared Services for an entire Web application or through the Search Scopes configuration on the root site of a site collection. For example, if you'd created a content type, Teamstatus, for Team Status reports and then wanted the ability to be able to search explicitly on Team Status reports for team members, you could establish a search scope for that content type. To create a search scope on the root site (Litware) of the Litware site collection and base the search scope on the Teamstatus content type, do the following:

Note You must be an administrator on the server to perform this action.

1. Open the Site Settings page for the root site and click the Search Settings link under Site Collection Administration.
2. Ensure that the Enable Custom Scopes And Search Center Features checkbox is selected as shown in Figure 15-29.

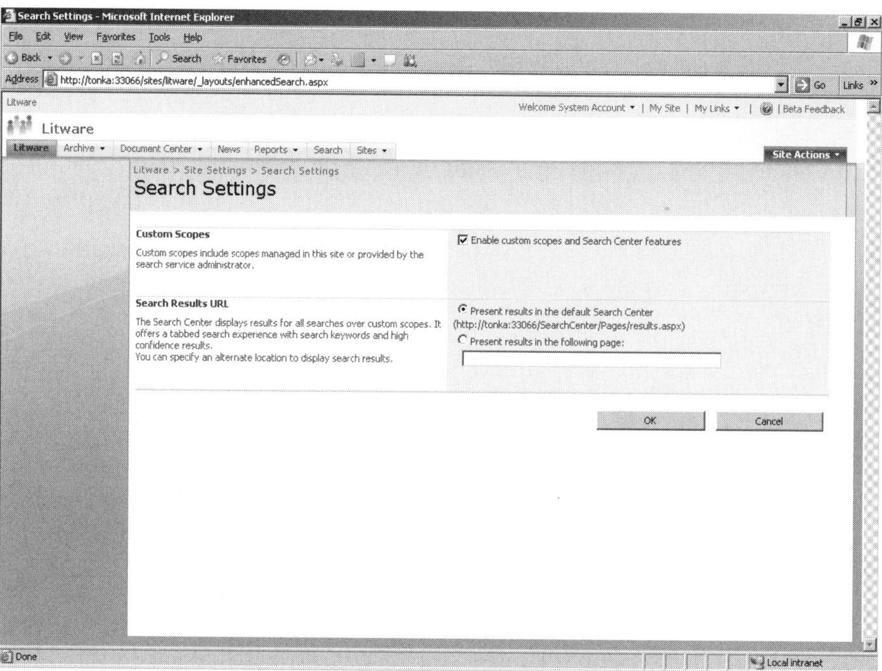

Figure 15-29 Enabling custom search scopes on a site

3. Go back to the Site Settings page and click the Search Scopes link under Site Collection Administration to open the View Scopes page.

4. From the toolbar on the View Scopes page, click New Scope.
5. On the Create Scope page, shown in Figure 15-30, type a name for the search scope in the Title box, in this case **Forms**, along with a description.

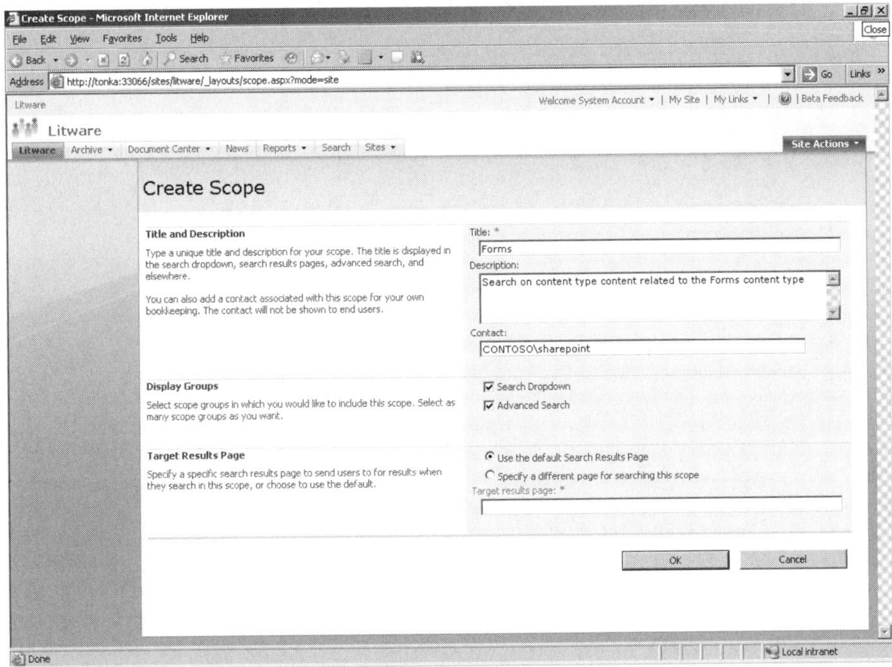

Figure 15-30 Create Scope configuration page

6. In the Display Groups section of the New Scope page, select both the Search Drop-down and Advanced Search check boxes.

   Selecting Search Dropdown includes the custom search scope name in the search drop-down list, as shown in Figure 15-31.

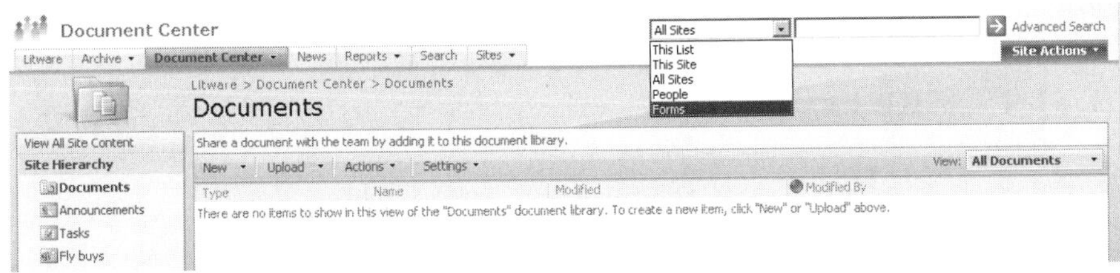

Figure 15-31 Search Dropdown including content type search scope

Selecting the Advanced Search option includes the custom search scope name on the Advanced Search page as an additional scope that you can use in your search queries, as shown in Figure 15-32, in this case Forms.

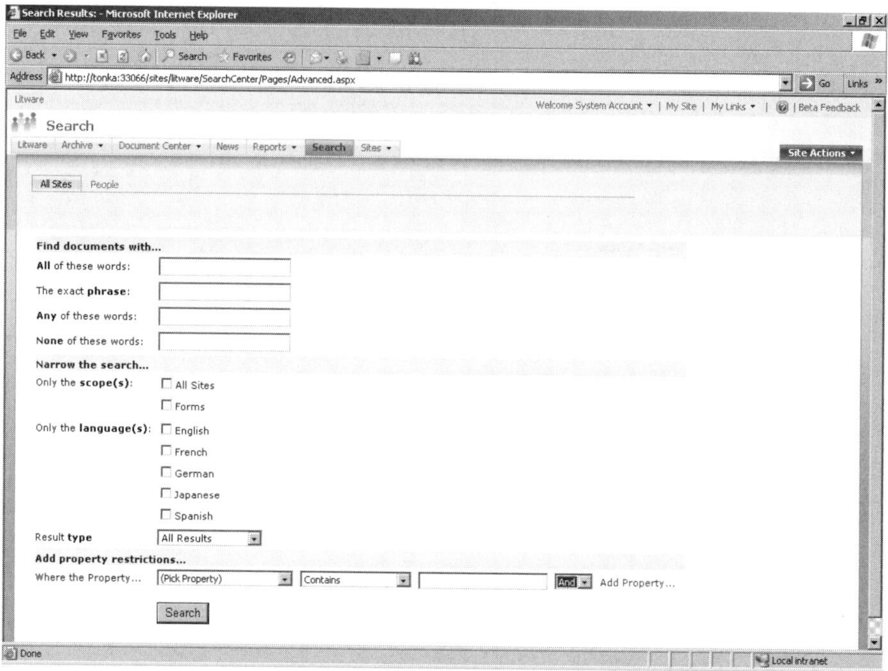

Figure 15-32 Advanced Search page including a content type search scope

7. Click OK to return to the View Scopes page.
8. Back on the View Scopes page, locate the Forms search scope and, from the Forms contextual drop-down menu, select Edit Properties and Rules.
9. On the subsequent Scope Properties and Rules page, click on New Rule.
10. On the Add Scope Rule page, in the Scope Rule Type section, select the Property Query option.
11. In the Property Query section under the Add Property Restrictions list, select ContentType, as shown in Figure 15-33.

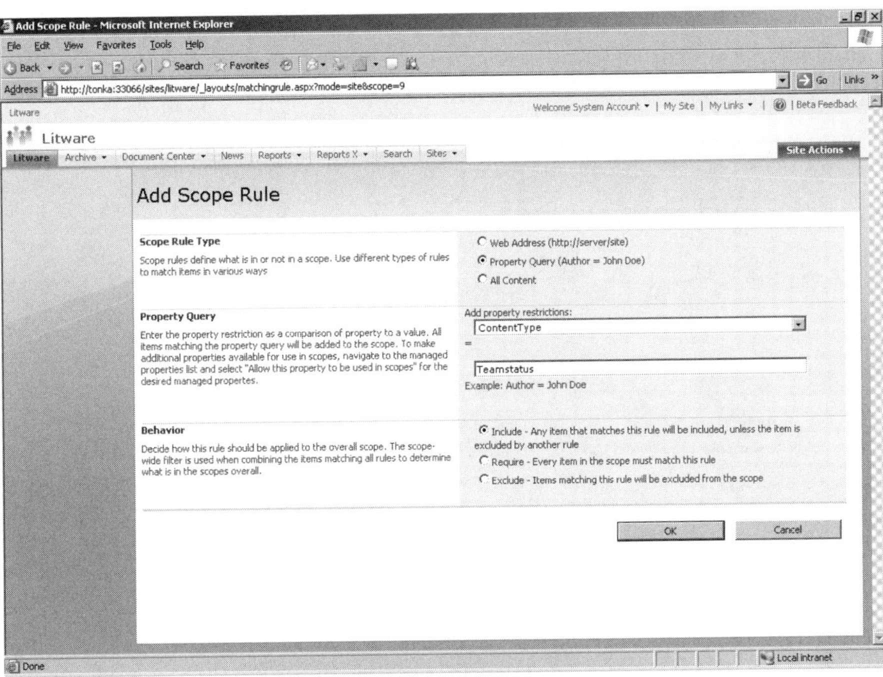

Figure 15-33 Select content type for a query parameter

12. In the Equal To field, type the content type you want to run a search against and then click OK. In this case, type **Teamstatus** so that you can search for Team Status reports entered by employees.

    SharePoint updates the new search scope and index content for that scope in the next scheduled crawl update.

13. Type the query on the Advanced Search page to run the search against the new Forms search scope.

> **Note** You can also run the search from the drop-down search box on the home page of the Litware site.

On the Advanced Search page, the new content type search scope, Forms, is included, and you can add search criteria against this new search scope.

14. In the All Of These Words box, type the name **Christine**.
15. Under Narrow The Search, Only The Scope(s), select the Forms search scope check box. Click Search.

The search returns two records, both of which are Team Status reports. One report has been submitted by Christine Koch; the other report has been submitted where Christine Koch is the Manager. (See Figure 15-34.)

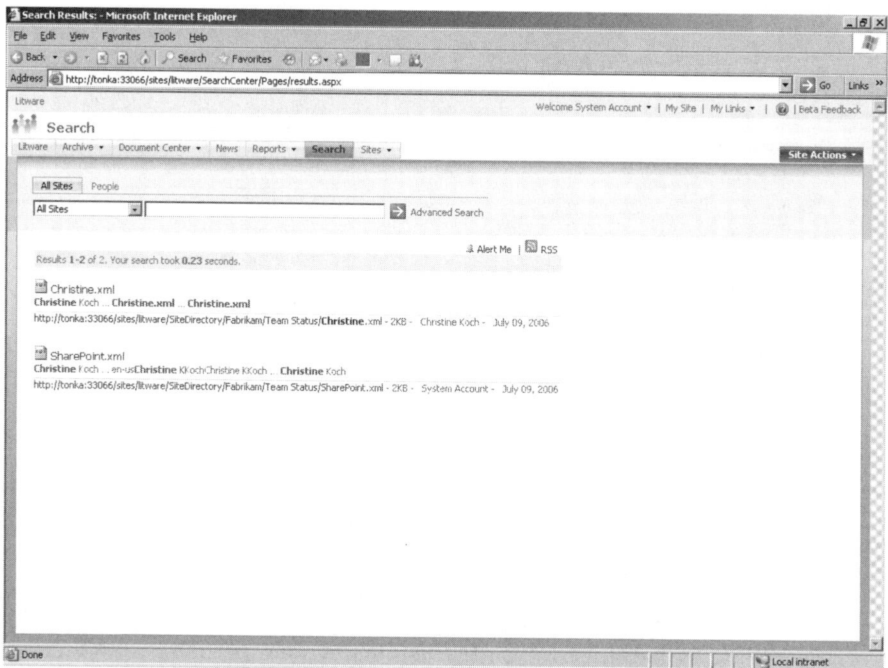

Figure 15-34 Search results based on a content type search scope

This example demonstrated how you can run search queries against content types. The Teamstatus content type was used to create a custom search scope and run a query on any forms associated with that content type. This is just one example of how you can use content types to enhance your search capabilities.

Summary

This chapter has provided an overview of content types and demonstrated how you can effectively create and implement content types to more effectively manage your content and documents. You have learned how to configure content types for use throughout SharePoint Server 2007 sites and lists, including associating custom metadata and custom settings to content types, such as workflow. You have also seen how content types can be used to manage e-mail messages and extend search functionality.

Part III
Search, Indexing, and Shared Services Provider

Chapter 16

Enterprise Search and Indexing Architecture and Administration

One of the main reasons that you'll consider purchasing Microsoft Office SharePoint Server 2007 is for the robust search and indexing features that are built in to it. These features allow you to crawl any type of content and provide improved relevance in search results. You'll find these features to be some of the most compelling parts of this server suite.

For both SharePoint Server 2007 and Windows SharePoint Services 3.0, Microsoft is using a common search engine, Microsoft Search (mssearch.exe). This is welcome news for those of us who worked extensively in the previous versions of SharePoint. Microsoft Windows SharePoint Services 2.0 used the Microsoft SQL Server full-text engine, and SharePoint Portal Server 2003 used the MSSearch.exe (actually named SharePointPS-Search) engine. The problems this represented, such as incompatibility between indexes or having to physically move to the portal to execute a query against the portal's index, have been resolved in this version of SharePoint Products and Technologies.

In this chapter, the discussion of the search and indexing architecture is interwoven with administrative and best practices discussions. Because this is a deep, wide, and complex feature, you'll need to take your time to digest and understand both the strengths and challenges that this version of Microsoft Search introduces.

Understanding the Microsoft Vision for Search

The vision for Microsoft Search is straightforward and can be summarized in these bullet points:

- **Great results every time.** There isn't much sense in building a search engine that will give substandard result sets. Think about it. When you enter a query term in other Internet-based search engines, you'll often receive a result set that gives you 100,000 or more links to resources that match your search term. Often, only the first 10 to 15 results hold any value at all, rendering the vast majority of the result set useless. Microsoft's aim is to give you a lean, relevant result set every time you enter a query.
- **Search integrated across familiar applications.** Microsoft is integrating new or improved features into well-known interfaces. Improved search functionality is no exception. As the SharePoint Server product line matures in the coming years, you'll see the ability to execute queries against the index worked into many well-known interfaces.
- **Ability to index content regardless of where it is located.** One difficulty with SharePoint Portal Server 2003 was its inability to crawl content held in different types of databases and structures. With the introduction of the Business Data Catalog (BDC), you can expose data from *any* data source and then crawl it for your index. The crawling, exposing, and finding of data from nontraditional data sources (such as file servers, SharePoint sites, Web sites, and Microsoft Exchange public folders) will depend directly on your BDC implementation. Without the BDC, the ability to crawl and index information from any source will be diminished.
- **A scalable, manageable, extensible, and secure search and indexing product.** Microsoft has invested a large amount of capital into making its search engine scalable, more easily managed, extensible, and more secure. In this chapter, you'll learn about how this has taken place.

As you can see, these are aggressive goals. But they are goals that, for the most part, have been attained in SharePoint Server 2007. In addition, you'll find that the strategies Microsoft has used to meet these goals are innovative and smart.

Crawling Different Types of Content

One challenge of using a common search engine across multiple platforms is that the type of data and access methods to that data change drastically from one platform to another. Let's look at four common scenarios.

Desktop Search

Rightly or wrongly (depending on how you look at it), people tend to host their information on their desktop. And the desktop is only one of several locations where information can be saved. Frustrations often arise because people looking for their documents are unable find them because they can't remember where they saved them. A strong desktop search engine that indexes content on the local hard drives is essential now in most environments.

Intranet Search

Information that is crawled and indexed across an intranet site or a series of Web sites that comprise your intranet is exposed via links. Finding information in a site involves finding information in a linked environment and understanding when multiple links point to a common content item. When multiple links point to the same item, that tends to indicate that the item is more important in terms of relevance in the result set. In addition, crawling linked content that, through circuitous routes, might link back to itself, demands a crawler that knows how deep and wide to crawl before not following available links to the same content. Within a SharePoint site, this can be more easily defined. We just tell the crawler to crawl within a certain URL namespace and, often, that is all we need to do.

In many environments, Line of Business (LOB) information that is held in dissimilar databases that represent dissimilar data types are often displayed via customized Web sites. In the past, crawling this information has been very difficult, if not impossible. But with the introduction of the Business Data Catalog (BDC), you can now crawl and index information from any data source. The use of the BDC to index LOB information will be important if you want to include LOB data into your index.

Enterprise Search

When searching for information in your organization's enterprise beyond your intranet, you're really looking for documents, Web pages, people, e-mail, postings, and bits of data sitting in disparate, dissimilar databases. To crawl and index all this information, you'll need to use a combination of the BDC and other, more traditional types of content sources, such as Web sites, SharePoint sites, file shares, and Exchange public folders. *Content sources* is the term we use to refer to the servers or locations that host the content that we want to crawl.

Note Moving forward in your SharePoint deployment, you'll want to strongly consider using the mail-enabling features for lists and libraries. The ability to include e-mail into your collaboration topology is compelling because so many of our collaboration transactions take place in e-mail, not in documents or Web sites. If e-mails can be warehoused in lists within sites that the e-mails reference, this can only enhance the collaboration experience for your users.

Internet Search

Nearly all the data on the Internet is linked content. Because of this, crawling Web sites requires additional administrative effort in setting boundaries around the crawler process via crawl rules and crawler configurations. The crawler can be tightly configured to crawl individual pages or loosely configured to crawl entire sites that contain DNS name changes.

You'll find that there might be times when you'll want to "carve out" a portion of a Web site for crawling without crawling the entire Web site. In this scenario, you'll find that the crawl rules might be frustrating and might not achieve what you really want to achieve. Later in this chapter, we'll discuss how the crawl rules work and what their intended function is. But it suffices to say here that although the search engine itself is very capable of crawling linked content, throttling and customizing the limitations of what the search engine crawls can be tricky.

Architecture and Components of the Microsoft Search Engine

Search in SharePoint Server 2007 is a shared service that is available only through a Shared Services Provider (SSP). In a Windows SharePoint Services 3.0-only implementation, the basic search engine is installed, but it will lack many components that you'll most likely want to install into your environment. Table 16-1 provides a feature comparison between the search engine that is installed with a Windows SharePoint Services 3.0—only implementation and an SharePoint Server 2007 implementation.

Table 16-1 Feature Comparison between Windows SharePoint Services 3.0 and SharePoint Server 2007

Feature	Windows SharePoint Services 3.0	SharePoint Server 2007
Content that can be indexed	Local SharePoint content	SharePoint content, Web content, Exchange public folders, file shares, Lotus Notes, Line of Business (LOB) application data via the BDC
Relevant results	Yes	Yes
Search-based alerts	Yes	Yes
Create Real Simple Syndication (RSS) from result set	Yes	Yes
The "Did You Mean....?" prompt	Yes	Yes

Table 16-1 Feature Comparison between Windows SharePoint Services 3.0 and SharePoint Server 2007

Feature	Windows SharePoint Services 3.0	SharePoint Server 2007
Duplicate collapsing	Yes	Yes
Scopes based on managed properties	No	Yes
Best Bet	No	Yes
Results removal	No	Yes
Query reports	No	Yes
Customizable tabs in Search Center	No	Yes
People Search/Knowledge Network	No	Yes
Crawl information via the BDC	No	Yes
Application programming interfaces (APIs) provided	Query	Query and Administration

The architecture of the search engine includes the following elements:

- **Content source** The term *content source* can sometimes be confusing because it is used in two different ways in the literature. The first way it is used is to describe the set of rules that you assign to the crawler to tell it where to go, what kind of content to extract, and how to behave when it is crawling the content. The second way this term is used is to describe the target source that is hosting the content you want to crawl. By default, the following types of content sources can be crawled (and if you need to include other types of content, you can create a custom content source and protocol handler):
    - SharePoint content, including content created with present and earlier versions
    - Web-based content
    - File shares
    - Exchange public folders
    - Any content exposed by the BDC
    - IBM Lotus Notes (must be configured before it can be used)
- **Crawler** The crawler extracts data from a content source. Before crawling the content source, the crawler loads the content source's configuration information,

including any site path rules, crawler configurations, and crawler impact rules. (Site path rules, crawler configurations, and crawler impact rules are discussed in more depth later in this chapter.) After it is loaded, the crawler connects to the content source using the appropriate protocol handler and uses the appropriate iFilter (defined later in this list) to extract the data from the content source.

- **Protocol handler** The protocol handler tells the crawler which protocol to use to connect to the content source. The protocol handler that is loaded is based on the URL prefix, such as HTTP, HTTPS, or FILE.
- **iFilter** The iFilter (Index Filter) tells the crawler what kind of content it will be connecting to so that the crawler can extract the information correctly from the document. The iFilter that is loaded is based on the URL's suffix, such as .aspx, .asp, or .doc.
- **Content index** The indexer stores the words that have been extracted from the documents in the full-text index. In addition, each word in the content index has a relationship set up between that word and it's metadata in the property store (Shared Services Provider's Search database in SQL Server) so that the metadata for that word in a particular document can be enforced in the result set. For example, if we're discussing NTFS permissions, than the document may or may not appear in the result set based on the permissions for that document that contained the word in the query because all result sets are security-trimmed before they are presented to the user so that the user only sees links to document and sites to which the user already has permissions.

  The property store is the Shared Services Provider's (SSP) Search database in SQL Server that hosts the metadata on the documents that are crawled. The metadata includes NTFS and other permission structures, author name, data modified, and any other default or customized metadata that can be found and extracted from the document, along with data that is used to calculate relevance in the result set, such as frequency of occurrence, location information, and other relevance-oriented metrics that we'll discuss later in this chapter under the section titled "Relevance Improvements." Each row in the SQL table corresponds to a separate document in the full-text index. The actual text of the document is stored in the content index, so it can be used for content queries. For a Web site, each unique URL is considered to be a separate "document."

Use the Right Tools for Index Backups and Restores

We want to stress that you need *both* the index on the file system (which is held on the Index servers and copied to the Query servers) and the SSP's Search database in order to successfully query the index.

The relationship between words in the index and metadata in the property store is a tight relationship that must exist in order for the result set to be rendered properly, if at all. If either the property store or the index on the file system is corrupted or missing, users will not be able to query the index and obtain a result set. This is why it is imperative to ensure that your index backups successfully back up both the index on the file system and the SSP's Seach database. Using the SharePoint Server 2007's backup tool will backup the entire index *at the same time* and give you the ability to *restore* the index as well (several third-party tools will do this too).

But if you only backup the index on the file system without backing up the SQL database, then you will not be able to restore the index. And if you backup only the SQL database and not the index on the file system, then you will not be able to restore the index. Do not let your SQL Administrators or Infrastructure Administrators sway you on this point: in order to obtain a trustworthy backup of your index, you *must* use either a third-party tool written for precisely this job or the backup tool that ships with SharePoint Server 2007. If you use two different tools to backup the SQL property store and the index on the file system, it is highly likely that when you restore both parts of the index, you'll find, at a minimum, the index will contain inconsistencies and your results will vary based on the inconsistencies that might exist from backing up these two parts of the index at different times.

Crawler Process

When the crawler starts to crawl a content source, several things happen in succession very quickly. First, the crawler looks at the URL it was given and loads the appropriate protocol handler, based on the prefix of the URL, and the appropriate iFilter, based on the suffix of the document at the end of the URL.

Note The content source definitions are held in the Shared Services Provider Search SQL Server database and the registry. When initiating a crawl, the definitions are read from the registry because this gives better performance than reading them from the database. Definitions in the registry are synchronized with the database so that the backup/restore procedures can backup and restore the content source definitions. Never modify the content source definitions in the registry. This is not a supported action and should never be attempted.

Then the crawler checks to ensure that any crawler impact rules, crawl rules, and crawl settings are loaded and enforced. Then the crawler connects to the content source and creates two data streams out of the content source. First the metadata is read, copied, and passed to the Indexer plug-in. The second stream is the content, and this stream is also passed to the Indexer plug-in for further work.

All the crawler does is what we tell it to do using the crawl settings in the content source, the crawl rules (formerly known as *site path rules* in SharePoint Portal Server 2003) and crawler impact rules (formerly known as *site hit frequency rules* in SharePoint Portal Server 2003). The crawler will also not crawl documents that are not listed in the file types list nor will it be able to crawl a file if it cannot load an appropriate iFilter. Once the content is extracted, it is passed off to the Indexer plug-in for processing.

Indexer Process

When the Indexer receives the two data streams, it places the metadata into the SSP's Search database, which, as you'll recall, is also called the *property store*. In terms of workflow, the metadata is first passed to the Archival plug-in, which reads the metadata and adds any new fields to the crawled properties list. Then the metadata is passed to the SSP's Search database, or property store. What's nice here is that the archival plug-in (formerly known as the Schema plug-in in SharePoint Portal Server 2003) automatically detects and adds new metadata types to the crawled properties list (formerly known as the Schema in SharePoint Portal Server 2003). It is the archival plug-in that makes your life as a SharePoint Administrator easier: you don't have to manually add the metadata type to the crawled properties list before that metadata type can be crawled.

For example, let's say a user entered a custom text metadata field in a Microsoft Office Word document named "AAA" with a value of "BBB." When the Archival plug-in sees this metadata field, it will notice that the document doesn't have a metadata field called "AAA" and will therefore create one as a text field. It then writes that document's information into the property store. The Archival plug-in ensures that you don't have to know in advance all the metadata that could potentially be encountered in order to make that metadata useful as part of your search and indexing services.

After the metadata is written to the property store, the Indexer still has a lot of work to do. The Indexer performs a number of functions, many of which have been essentially the same since Index Server 1.1 in Internet Information Services 4.0. The indexer takes the data stream and performs both word breaking and stemming. First, it breaks the data stream into 64-KB chunks (not configurable) and then performs word breaking on the chunks. For example, the indexer must decide whether the data stream that contains "nowhere" means "no where" or "now here." The stemming component is used to generate inflected forms of a given word. For example, if the crawled word is "buy," then inflected forms of the word are generated, such as "buys," "buying," and "bought." After word breaking has been performed and inflection generation is finished, the noise words are removed to ensure that only words that have discriminatory value in a query are available for use.

Results of the crawler and indexing processes can be viewed using the log files that the crawler produces. We'll discuss how to view and use this log later in this chapter.

Understanding and Configuring Relevance Settings

Generally speaking, relevance relates to how closely the search results returned to the user match what the user wanted to find. Ideally, the results on the first page are the most relevant, so users do not have to look through several pages of results to find the best result for their search.

The product team for SharePoint Server 2007 has added a number of new features that substantially improve relevance in the result set. The following sections detail each of these improvements.

Click Distance

Click distance refers to how far each content item in the result set is from an "authoritative" site. In this context, "sites" can be either Web sites or file shares. By default, all the root sites in each Web application are considered first-level authoritative.

You can determine which sites are designated to be authoritative by simply entering the sites or file shares your users most often visit to find information or to find their way to the information they are after. Hence, the logic is that the "closer" in number of clicks a site is to an authoritative site, the more relevant that site is considered to be in the result set. Stated another way, the more clicks it takes to get from an authoritative site to the content item, the less relevant that item is thought to be and the lower it will appear in the result set.

You will want to evaluate your sites over time to ensure that you've appropriately ranked sites that your users visit. When content items from more than one site appear in the result set, it is highly likely that some sites' content will be more relevant to the user than other sites' content. Use this three-tired approach to explicitly set primary, secondary, and tertiary levels of importance to individual sites in your organization. SharePoint Server 2007 allows you to set primary (first-level), secondary (second-level), and tertiary (third level) sites, as well as sites that should never be considered authoritative. Determining which sites should be placed at which level is probably more art than science and will be a learning process over time.

To set authoritative sites, you'll need to first open the SSP in which you need to work, click the Search Settings link, and then scroll to the bottom of the page and click the Relevance Settings link. This will bring you to the Edit Relevance Settings page, as illustrated in Figure 16-1.

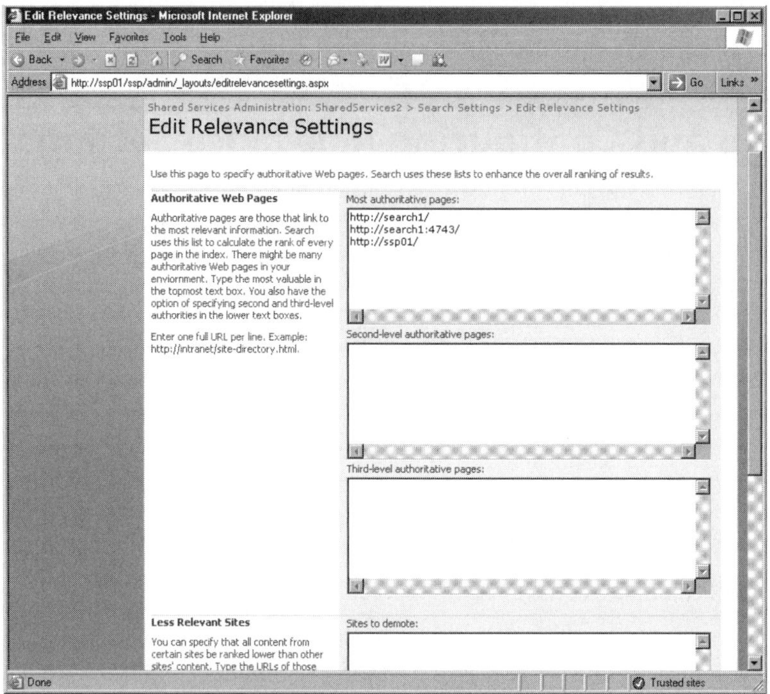

Figure 16-1 Edit Relevance Settings page

Note that on this page, you can input any URL or file share into any one of the three levels of importance. By default, all root URLs for each Web application that are associated with this SSP will be automatically listed as most authoritative. Secondary and tertiary sites can also be listed. Pages that are closer (in terms of number of clicks away from the URL you enter in each box) to second-level or third-level sites rather than to the first-level sites will be demoted in the result set accordingly. Pages that are closer to the URLs listed in the Sites To Demote pane will be ranked lower than all other results in the result set.

Hyperlink Anchor Text

When you hover your mouse over a link, the descriptive text that appears is called *anchor text*. The hyperlink anchor text feature ties the query term or phase with that descriptive text. If there is a match between the anchor text and the query term, that URL is pushed up in the result set and made to be more relevant. Anchor text only influences rank and is not the determining factor for including a content item in the result set.

Search indexes the anchor text from the following elements:

- HTML anchor elements
- Windows SharePoint Services link lists
- Office SharePoint Portal Server listings
- Office Word 2007, Office Excel 2007, and Office PowerPoint 2007 hyperlinks

URL Surf Depth

Important or relevant content is often located closer to the top of a site's hierarchy, instead of in a location several levels deep in the site. As a result, the content has a shorter URL, so it's more easily remembered and accessed by the user. Search makes use of this fact by looking at URL depth, or how many levels deep within a site the content item is located. Search determines this level by looking at the number of slash (/) characters in the URL; the greater the number of slash characters in the URL path, the deeper the URL is for that content item. As a consequence, a large URL depth number lowers the relevance of that content item.

URL Matching

If a query term matches a portion of the URL for a content item, that content item is considered to be of higher relevance than if the query term had not matched a portion of the content item's URL. For example, if the query term is "muddy boots" and the URL for a document is http://site1/library/muddyboots/report.doc, because "muddy boots" (with or without the space) is part of the URL with an exact match, the report.doc will be raised in its relevance for this particular query.

Automatic Metadata Extraction

Microsoft has built a number of *classifiers* that look for particular kinds of information in particular places within Microsoft documents. When that type of information is found in those locations and there is a query term match, the document is raised in relevance in the result set. A good example of this is the title slide in PowerPoint. Usually, the first slide in a PowerPoint deck is the title slide that includes the author's name. If "Judy Lew" is the query term and "Judy Lew" is the name on the title slide of a PowerPoint deck, that deck is considered more relevant to the user who is executing the query and will appear higher in the result set.

Automatic Language Detection

Documents that are written in the same language as the query are considered to be more relevant than documents written in other languages. Search determines the user's language based on Accept-Language headers from the browser in use. When calculating relevance, content that is retrieved in that language is considered more relevant. Because there is so much English language content and a large percentage of users speak English, English is also ranked higher in search relevance.

File Type Relevance Biasing

Certain document types are considered to be inherently more important than other document types. Because of this, Microsoft has hard-coded which documents will appear ahead of other documents based on their type, assuming all other factors are equal. File type relevance biasing does not supersede or override other relevance factors. Microsoft has not released the file type ordering that it uses when building the result set.

Search Administration

Search administration is now conducted entirely within the SSP. The portal (now known as the Corporate Intranet Site) is no longer tied directly to the search and indexing administration. This section discusses the administrative tasks that you'll need to undertake to effectively administrate search and indexing in your environment. Specifically, it discusses how to create and manage content sources, configure the crawler, set up site path rules, and throttle the crawler through the crawler impact rules. This section also discusses index management and provides some best practices along the way.

Creating and Managing Content Sources

The index can hold only that information that you have configured Search to crawl. We crawl information by creating content sources.The creation and configuration of a content source and associated crawl rules involves creating the rules that govern where the crawler goes to get content, when the crawler gets the content, and how the crawler behaves during the crawl.

To create a content sources, we must first navigate to the Configure Search Settings page. To do this, open your SSP administrative interface and click the Search Settings link under the Search section. Clicking on this link will bring you to the Configure Search Settings page (shown in Figure 16-2).

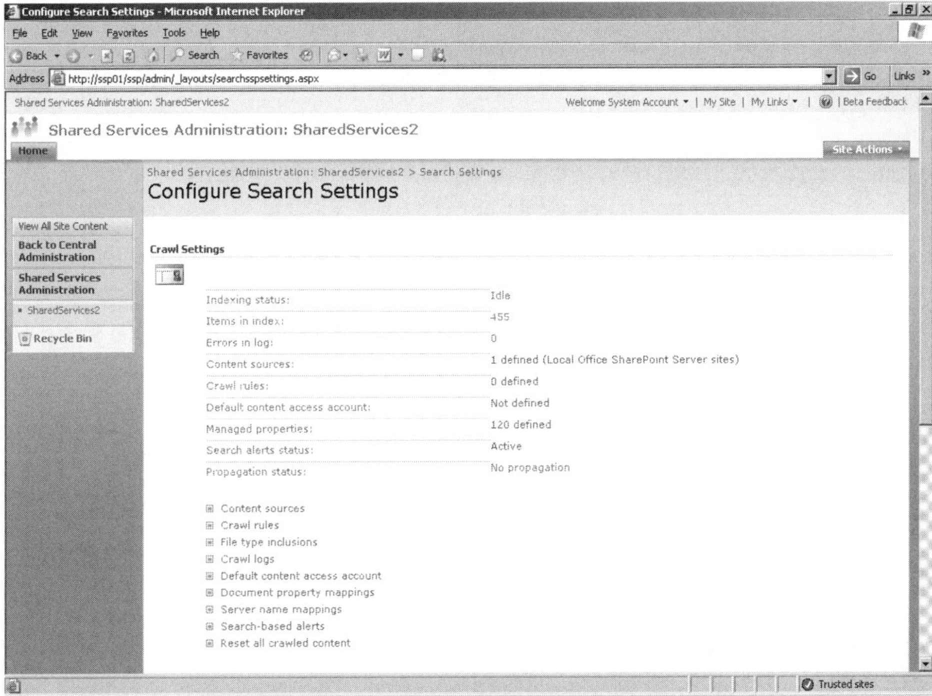

Figure 16-2 The Configure Search Settings page

Notice that you are given several bits of information right away on this page, including the following:

- Indexing status
- Number of items in the index
- Number errors in the crawler log
- Number of content sources
- Number of crawl rules defined
- Which account is being used as the default content access account
- The number of managed properties that are grouping one or more crawled properties
- Whether search alerts are active or deactivated
- Current propagation status

This list can be considered a search administrator's dashboard to instantly give you the basic information you need to manage search across your enterprise. Once you have familiarized yourself with your current search implementation, click the Content Sources link to begin creating a new content source. When you click this link, you'll be taken to the Manage Content Sources page (shown in Figure 16-3). On this page, you'll see a listing of all the content sources, the status of each content source, and when the next full and incremental crawls are scheduled.

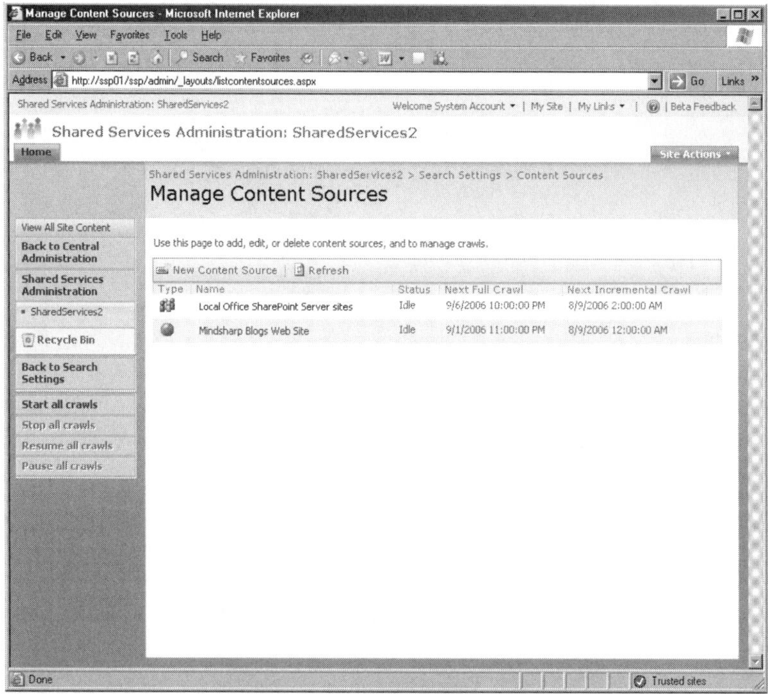

Figure 16-3 Manage Content Sources administration page

Note that there is a default content source that is created in each SSP: Local Office SharePoint Server Sites. By default, this content source is not scheduled to run or crawl any content. You'll need to configure the crawl schedules manually. This source includes all content that is stored in the sites within the server or server farm. You'll need to ensure that if you plan on having multiple SSPs in your farm, only one of these default content sources is scheduled to run. If more than one are configured to crawl the farm, you'll unnecessarily crawl your farm's local content multiple times, unless users in different SSPs all need the farm content in their indexes, which would then beg the question as to why you have multiple SSPs in the first place.

If you open the properties of the Local Office SharePoint Server Sites content source, you'll note also that there are actually two start addresses associated with this content source and they have two different URL prefixes: HTTP and SPS3. By default, the HTTP prefix will point to the SSP's URL. The SPS3 prefix is hard-coded to inform Search to crawl the user profiles that have been imported into that SSP's user profile database.

To create a new content source, click the New Content Source button. This will bring you to the Add Content Source dialog page (Figure 16-4). On this page, you'll need to give the content source a name. Note that this name must be unique within the SSP, and it should be intuitive and descriptive–especially if you plan to have many content sources.

Note If you plan to have many content sources, it would be wise to develop a naming convention that maps to the focus of the content source so that you can recognize the content source by its name.

Notice also, as shown in the figure, that you'll need to select which type of content source you want to create. Your selections are as follows:

- **SharePoint Servers** This content source is meant to crawl SharePoint sites and simplifies the user interface so that some choices are already made for you.
- **Web Sites** This content source type is intended to be used when crawling Web sites.
- **File Shares** This content source will use traditional Server Message Block and Remote Procedure Calls to connect to a share on a folder.
- **Exchange Public Folders** This content source is optimized to crawl content in an Exchange public folder.
- **Business Data** Select this content source if you want to crawl content that is exposed via the Business Data Catalog.

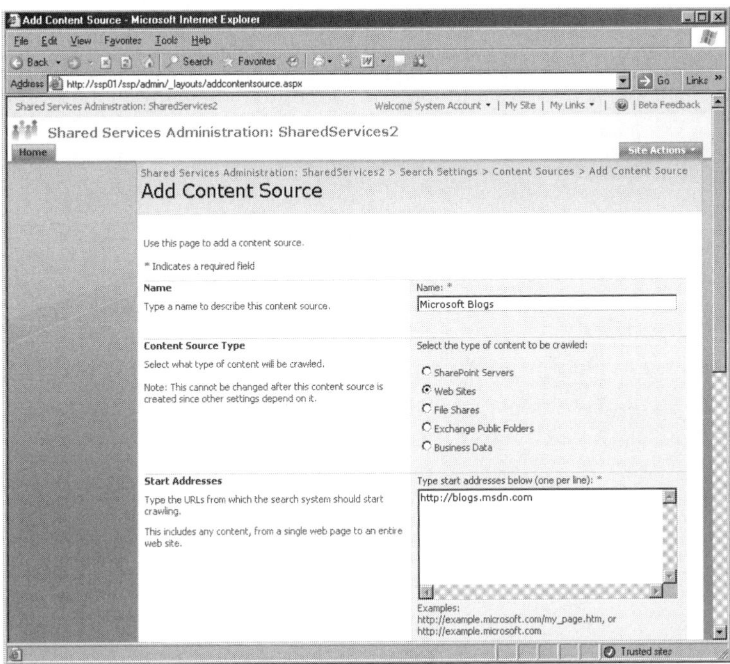

Figure 16-4 Add Content Source page—upper half

Note You can have multiple start addresses for your content source. This improvement over SharePoint Portal Server 2003 is welcome news for those who needed to crawl hundreds of sites and were forced into managing hundreds of content sources. Note that while you can enter different types of start addresses into the start address input box for a give content source, it is not recommended that you do this. Best practice is to enter start addresses that are consistent with the content source type configured for the content source.

Planning Your Content Sources

Assume you have three file servers that host a total of 800,000 documents. Now assume that you need to crawl 500,000 of those documents, and those 500,000 documents are exposed via a total of 15 shares. In the past, you would have had to create 15 content sources, one for each share. But today, you can create one content source with 15 start addresses and schedule one crawl and create one set of site path rules for one content source. Pretty nifty!

Planning your content sources is now easier because you can group similar content targets into a single content source. Your only real limitation is the timing of the crawl and the length of time required to complete the crawl. For example, performing a full crawl of blogs.msdn.com will take more than two full days. So grouping other blog sites with this site might be unwise.

The balance of the Add Content Source page (shown in Figure 16-5) involves specifying the crawl settings and the crawl schedules and deciding whether you want to start a full crawl manually.

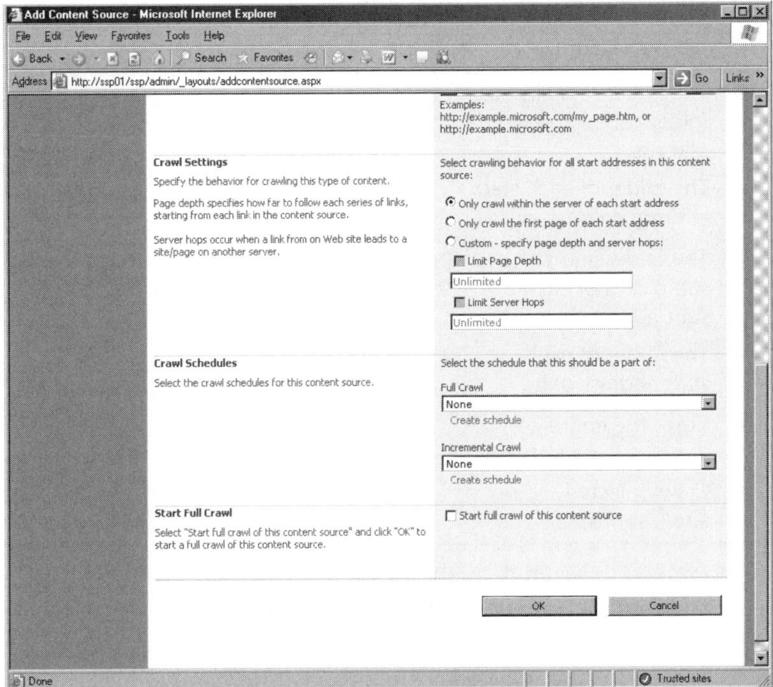

Figure 16-5 Add Content Source page—lower half (Web site content source type is illustrated)

The crawl settings instruct the crawler how to behave relative to depth and breadth given the different content source types. Table 16-2 lists each of these types and associated options.

Table 16-2 Content Source Types and Associated Options

Type of crawl	Crawler setting options	Notes
SharePoint site	■ Crawl everything under the hostname for each start address ■ Crawl only the SharePoint site of each start address	This will crawl all site collections at this start address, not just the root site in the site collection. In this context, *hostname* means URL namespace. This option includes new site collections inside a managed path.
Web site	■ Only crawl within the server of each start address ■ Only crawl the first page of each start address ■ Custom—specify page depth and server hops	In this context, *Server* means URL namespace (for example, contoso.msft). This means that only a single page will be crawled. *Page depth*" refers to page levels in a Web site hierarchy. *Server hops* refers to changing the URL namespace—that is, changes in the Fully Qualified Domain Name (FQDN) that occur before the first "/" in the URL.

Table 16-2 Content Source Types and Associated Options

Type of crawl	Crawler setting options	Notes
File shares	■ The folder and all sub-folders of each start address ■ The folder of each start address only	
Exchange public folders	■ The folder and all subfolders of each start address ■ The folder of each start address only	What is evident here is that you'll need a different start address for each public folder tree.
Business Data Catalog	■ Crawl the entire Business Data Catalog ■ Crawl selected applications	

The crawl schedules allow you to schedule both full and incremental crawls. Full index builds will treat the content source as new. Essentially, the slate is wiped clean and you start over crawling every URL and content item and treating that content source as if it has never been crawled before. Incremental index builds update new or modified content and remove deleted content from the index. In most cases, you'll use an incremental index build.

You'll want to perform full index builds in the following scenarios because only a full index build will update the index to reflect the changes in these scenarios:

- Any changes to crawl inclusion/exclusion rules.
- Any changes to the default crawl account.
- Any upgrade to a Windows SharePoint Services site because an upgrade action deletes the change log and a full crawl must be initiated because there is no change log to reference for an incremental crawl.
- Changes to .aspx pages.
- When you add or remove an iFilter.
- When you add or remove a file type.
- Changes to property mappings will happen on a document-by-document as each affected document is crawled, whether the crawl is an incremental or full crawl. A full crawl of all content sources will ensure that document property mapping changes are applied consistently throughout the index.

Now, there are a couple of planning issues that you need to be aware of. The first has to do with full index builds, and the second has to do with crawl schedules. First, you need to know that subsequent full index builds that are run after the first full index build of a content source will start the crawl process and *add to the index* all the content items it finds. Only after the build process is complete will the original set of content items in the index be deleted. This is important to note because the index can be anywhere from 10 percent to 40 percent of the size of the content (also referred to as the *corpus*) you're crawling, and for a brief period of time, you'll need twice the amount of disk space that you would normally need to host the index for that content source.

For example, assume you are crawling a file server with 500,000 documents, and the total amount of disk space for these documents is 1 terabyte. Then assume that the index is roughly equal to 10 percent of the size of these documents, or 100 GB. Further assume that you completed a full index build on this file server 30 days ago, and now you want to do another full index build. When you start to run that full index build, several things will be true:

- A new index will be created for that file server during the crawl process.
- The current index of that file server will remain available to users for queries while the new index is being built.
- The current index will not be deleted until the new index has successfully been built.
- At the moment in time when the new index has successfully finished and the deletion of the old index for that file server has not started, you will be using 200 percent of disk space to hold that index.
- The old index will be deleted item by item. Depending on the size and number of content items, that could take from several minutes to many hours.
- Each deletion of a content item will result in a warning message for that content source in the Crawl Log. Even if you delete the content source, the Crawl Log will still display the warning messages for each content item for that content source. In fact, deleting the content source will result in all the content items in the index being deleted, and the Crawl Log will reflect this too.

The scheduling of when indexes should be run is a planning issue. "How often should I crawl my content sources?" The answer to this question is always the same: The frequency of content changes combined with the level of urgency for the updates to appear in your index will dictate how often you crawl the content. Some content–such as old, reference documents that rarely, if ever, change might be crawled once a year. Other documents, such as daily or hourly memo updates, can be crawled daily, hourly, or every 10 minutes.

Administrating Crawl Rules

Formerly known as site path rules, *crawl rules* help you understand how to apply additional instructions to the crawler when it crawls certain sites.

For the default content source in each SSP—the Local Office SharePoint Server Sites content source—Search provides two default crawl rules that are hard coded and can't be changed. These rules are applied to every http://ServerName added to the default content source and do the following:

- Exclude all .aspx pages within http://ServerName
- Include all the content displayed in Web Parts within http://ServerName

For all other content sources, you can create crawl rules that give additional instructions to the crawler on how to crawl a particular content source. You need to understand that rule order is important, because the first rule that matches a particular set of content is the one that is applied. The exception to this is a global exclusion rule, which is applied regardless of the order in which the rule is listed. The next section runs through several common scenarios for applying crawl rules.

> **Note** Do not use rules as another way of defining content sources or providing scope. Instead, use rules to specify more details about how to handle a particular set of content from a content source.

Specifying a Particular Account to Use When Crawling a Content Source

The most common reason people implement a crawl rule is to specify an account that has at least Read permissions (which are the minimum permissions needed to crawl a content source) on the content source so that the information can be crawled. When you select the Specify Crawling Account option (shown in Figure 16-6), you're enabling the text boxes you use to specify an individual crawling account and password. In addition, you can specify whether to allow Basic Authentication. Obviously, none of this means anything unless you have the correct path in the Path text box.

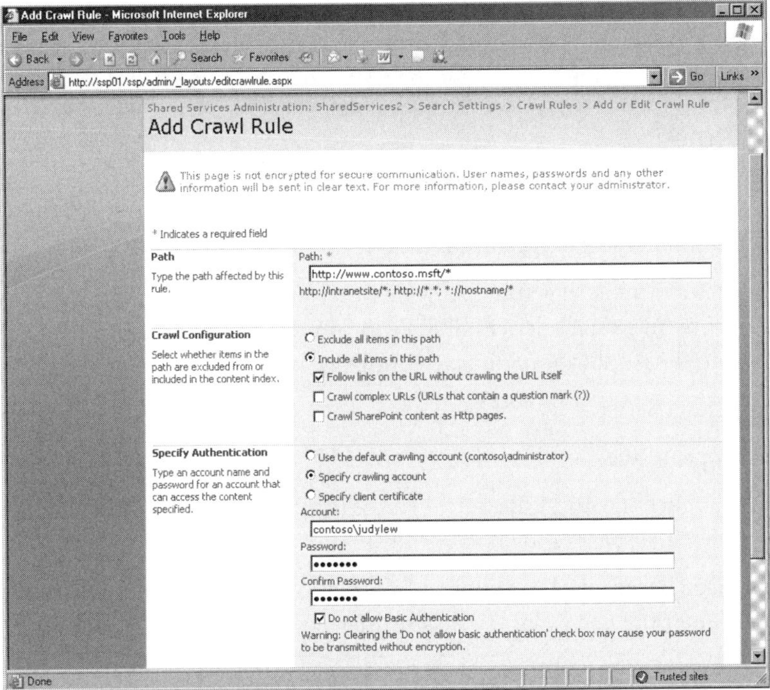

Figure 16-6 Add Crawl Rule configuration page

Crawling Complex URLs

Another common scenario that requires a crawl rule is when you want to crawl URLs that contain a question mark (?). By default, the crawler will stop at the question mark and not crawl any content that is represented by the portion of the URL that follows the question mark. For example, say you want to crawl the URL http://www.contoso.msft /default.aspx?top=courseware. In the absence of a crawl rule, the portion of the Web site represented by "top=courseware" would not be crawled and you would not be able to index the information from that part of the Web site. To crawl the courseware page, you need to configure a crawl rule.

So how would you do this, given our example here? First, you enter a path. Referring back to Figure 16-6, you'll see that all the examples given on the page have the wildcard character "*" included in the URL. Crawl rules cannot work with a path that doesn't contain the "*" wildcard character. So, for example, http://www.contoso.msft would be an invalid path. To make this path valid, you add the wildcard character, like this: http://www.contoso.msft/*.

Now you can set up site path rules that are global and apply to all your content sources. For example, if you want to ensure that all complex URLs are crawled across all content sources, enter a path of http://*/* and select the Include All Items In This Path option plus the Crawl Complex URLs check box. That is sufficient to ensure that all complex URLs are crawled across all content sources for the SSP.

Crawler Impact Rules

Crawler Impact Rules are the old Site Hit Frequency Rules that were managed in Central Administration in the previous version; although the name has changed to Crawler Impact Rules, they are still managed in Central Administration in this version.

Crawler Impact Rules is a farm-level setting, so whatever you decide to configure at this level will apply to all content sources across all SSPs in your farm. To access the Crawler Impact Rules page from the Application Management page, perform these steps.

1. Click Manage Search Service.
2. Click Crawler Impact Rules.
3. To add a new rule, click the Add Rule button in the navigation bar. The Add Crawler Impact Rule page will appear (shown in Figure 16-7).

You'll configure the page based on the following information. First, the Site text box is really not the place to enter the *name* of the Web site. Instead, you can enter global URLs, such as http://* or http://*.com or http://*.contoso.msft. In other words, although you can enter a crawler impact rule for a specific Web site, sometimes you'll enter a global URL.

Notice that you then set a Request Frequency rule. There are really only two options here: how many documents to request in a single request and how long to wait between requests. The default behavior of the crawler is to ask for eight documents per request and wait zero seconds between requests. Generally, you input a number of seconds between requests to conserve bandwidth. If you enter one second, that will have a noticeable impact on how fast the crawler crawls the content sources affected by the rule. And generally, you'll input a lower number of documents to process per request if you need to ensure better server performance on the part of the target server that is hosting the information you want to crawl.

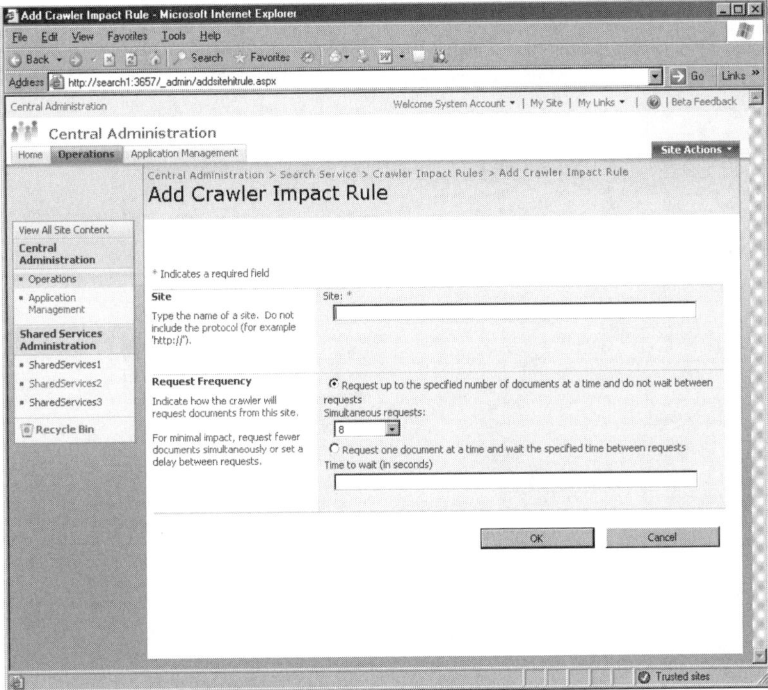

Figure 16-7 Add Crawler Impact Rule page

SSP-Level Configurations for Search

When you create a new SSP, you'll have several configurations that relate to how search and indexing will work in your environment. This section discusses those configurations.

1. First, you'll find these configurations on the Edit Shared Services Provider configuration page (not illustrated), which can be found by clicking the Create Or Configure This Farm's Shared Services link in the Application Management tab in Central Administration.

2. Click the down arrow next to the SSP you want to focus on, and click Edit from the context list.

3. Scroll to the bottom of the page (as shown in Figure 16-8), and you'll see that you can select which Index Server will be the crawler for the all the content sources created within this Web application. You can also specify the path on the Index Server where you want the indexes to be held. As long as the server sees this path as a local drive, you'll be able to use it. Remote drives and storage area network (SAN) connections should work fine as long as they are mapped and set up correctly.

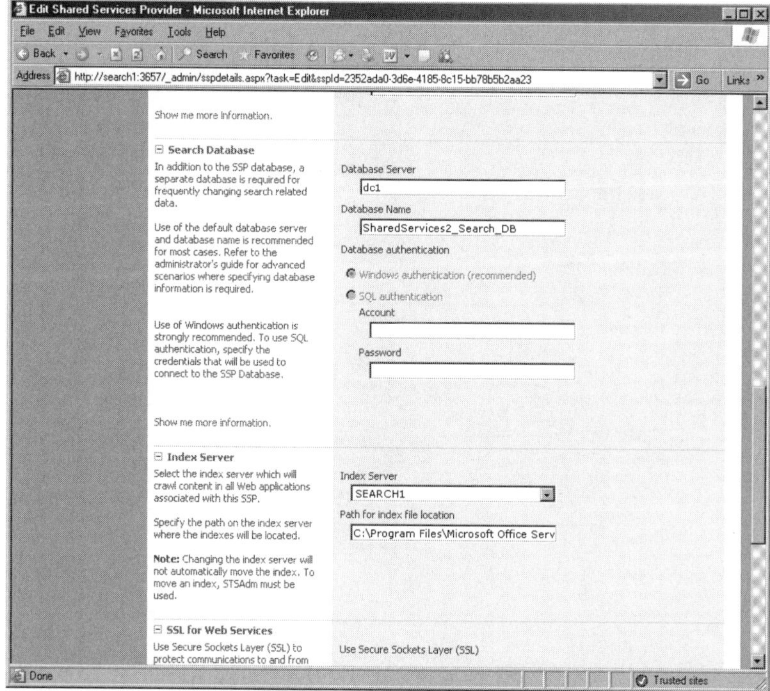

Figure 16-8 Edit Shared Services Provider page—lower portion

Managing Index Files

If you're coming from a SharePoint Portal Server 2003 background, you'll be happy to learn that you have only one index file for each SSP in SharePoint Server 2007. As a result, you don't need to worry anymore about any of the index management tasks you had in the previous version.

Having said that, there are some index file management operations that you'll want to pay attention to. This section outlines those tasks.

Continuous Propagation

The first big improvement in SharePoint Server 2007 is the Continuous Propagation feature. Essentially, instead of copying the entire index from the Index server to the Search server (using SharePoint Portal Server 2003 terminology here) every time a change is made to that index, now you'll find that as information is written to the Content Store on the Search server (using SharePoint Server 2007 terminology now), it is continuously propagated to the Query server.

Continuous Propagation

Continuous propagation is the act of ensuring that all the indexes on the Query servers are kept up to date by copying the indexes from the Index servers. As the indexes are updated by the crawler, those updates are quickly and efficiently copied to the Query servers. Remember that users query the index sitting on the Query server, not the Index server, so the faster you can update the indexes on the Query server, the faster you'll be able to give updated information to users in their result set.

Continuous propagation has the following characteristics:

- Indexes are propagated to the Query servers as they are updated within 30 seconds after the shadow index is written to the disk.
- The update size must be at least 4 KB. There is no maximum size limitation.
- Metadata is not propagated to the query servers. Instead, it is directly written to the SSP's Search SQL database.
- There are no registry entries to manage, and these configurations are hard-coded.

Propagation uses the NetBIOS name of query servers to connect. Therefore, it is not a best practice to place a firewall between your Query server and Index server in SharePoint Server 2007 due to the number of ports you would need to open on the firewall.

Resetting Index Files

Resetting the index file is an action you'll want to take only when necessary. When you reset the index file, you completely clean out all the content and metadata in both the property and content stores. To repopulate the index file, you need to re-crawl all the content sources in the SSP. These crawls will be full index builds, so they will be both time consuming and resource intensive.

The reason that you would want to reset the index is because you suspect that your index has somehow become corrupted, perhaps due to a power outage our power supply failur and needs to be rebuilt.

Troubleshooting Crawls Using the Crawl Logs

If you need to see why the crawler isn't crawling certain documents or certain sites, you can use the crawl logs to see what is happening. The crawl logs can be viewed on a per-content-source basis. They can be found by clicking on the down arrow for the content source in the Manage Content Sources page and selecting View Crawl Log to open the Crawl Log page (as shown in Figure 16-9). You can also open the Crawl Log page by clicking on the Log Viewer link in the Quick Launch bar of the SSP team site.

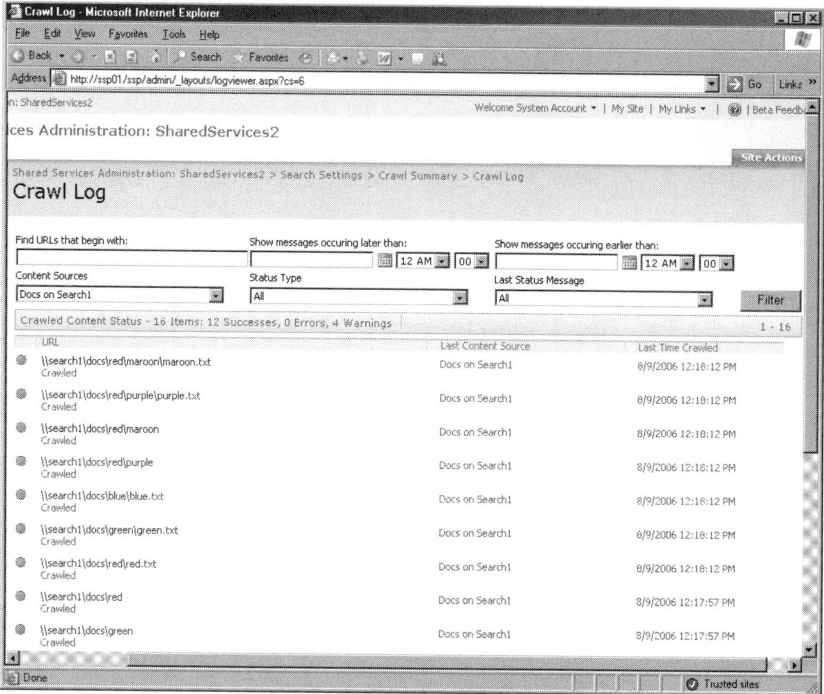

Figure 16-9 Crawl Log page

After this page is opened, you can filter the log in the following ways:

- By URL
- By date
- By content source
- By status type
- By last status message

The status message of each document appears below the URL along with a symbol indicating whether or not the crawl was successful. You can also see, in the right-hand column, the date and time that the message was generated.

There are three possible status types:

- **Success** The crawler was able to successful connect to the content source, read the content item, and pass the content to the Indexer.

- **Warning** The crawler was able to connect to the content source and tried to crawl the content item, but it was unable to for one reason or another. For example, if your site path rules are excluding a certain type of content, you might receive the following error message (note that the warning message uses the old terminology for crawl rules):

  ```
  The specified address was excluded from the index. The site path rules may
  have to be modified to include this address.
  ```

- **Error** The crawler was unable to communicate with the content source. Error messages might say something like this:

  ```
  The crawler could not communicate with the server. Check that the server is
  available and that the firewall access is configured correctly.
  ```

Another very helpful element in the Crawl Log page (refer back to Figure 16-9 if needed) is the Last Status Message drop-down list. The list that you'll see is filtered by which status types you have in focus. If you want to see all the messages that the crawler has produced, be sure to select All in the Status Type drop-down list. However, if you want to see only the Warning messages that the crawler has produced, select Warning in the Status Type drop-down list. Once you see the message you want to filter on, select it and you'll see the results of all the crawls within the date range you've specified appear in the results list. This should aid troubleshooting substantially. This feature is very cool.

If you want to get a high-level overview of the successes, warnings, and error messages that have been produced across all your content sources, the Log Summary view of the Crawl Log page is for you. To view the log summary view, click on the Crawl Logs link from the Configure Search Settings page. The summary view should appear. If it does not, click the Log Summary link in the left pane and it will appear (as shown in Figure 16-10).

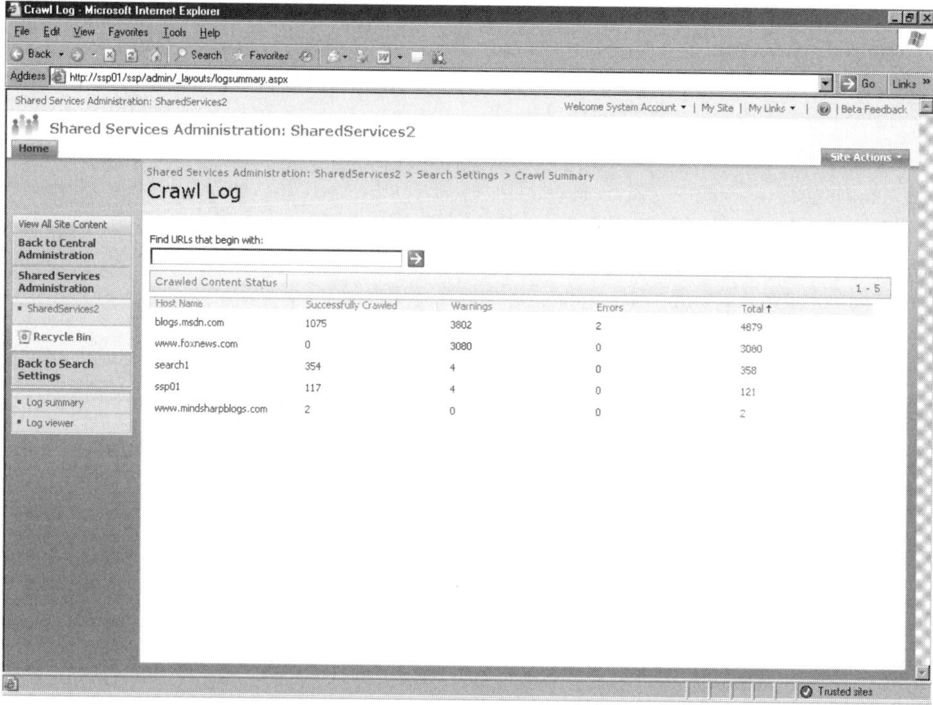

Figure 16-10 Log Summary view of the Crawl Log

Each of the numbers on the page represents a link to the filtered view of the log. So if you click on one of the numbers in the page, you'll find that the log will have already filtered the view based on the status type without regard to date or time.

Working with File Types

The file type inclusions list specifies the file types that the crawler should include or exclude from the index. Essentially, the way this works is that if the file type isn't listed on this screen, search won't be able to crawl it. Most of the file types that you'll need are already listed along with an icon that will appear in the interface whenever that document type appears.

To manage file types, click on the File Type Inclusions link on the Configure Search Settings page. This will bring you to the Manage File Types screen, as illustrated in Figure 16-11.

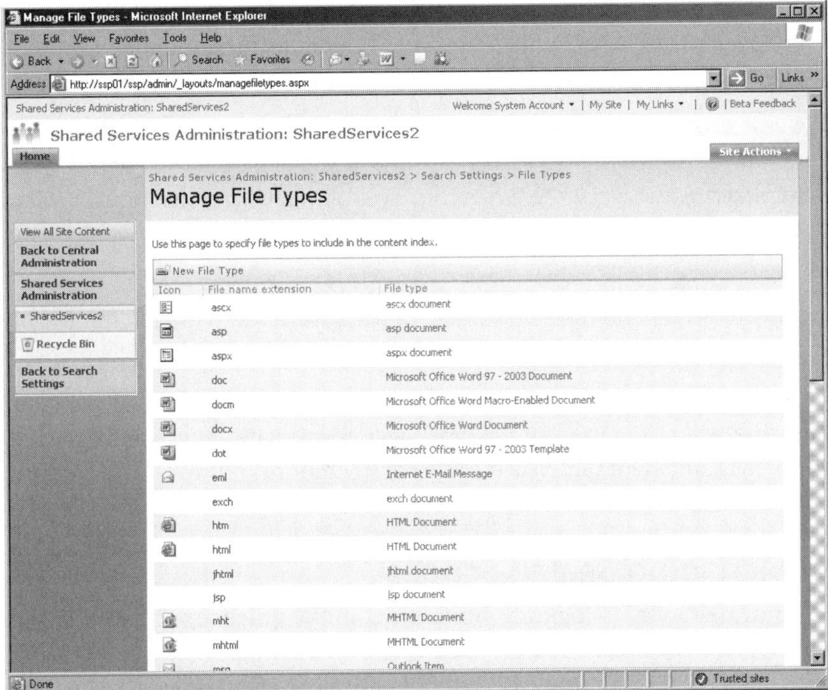

Figure 16-11 Manage File Types screen

To add a new file type, click on the New File Type button and enter the extension of the file type you want to add. All you need to enter are the file type's extension letters, such as "pdf" or "cad." Then click OK. Note that even though the three-letter extensions on the Mange File Types page represent a link, when you click the link, you won't be taken anywhere.

Adding the file type here really doesn't buy you anything unless you also install the iFilter that matches the new file type and the icon you want used with this file type. All you're doing on this screen is instructing the crawler that *if* there is an iFilter for these types of files and *if* there is an associated icon for these types of files, then go ahead and crawl these file types and load the file's icon into the interface when displaying this particular type of file.

Third-party iFilters that need to be added here will usually supply you with a .dll to install into the SharePoint platform, and they will usually include an installation routine. You'll need to ensure you've installed their iFilter into SharePoint in order to crawl those document types. If they don't supply an installation program for their iFilter, you can try running the following command from the command line:

```
regsvr32.exe <path\name of iFilter .dll>
```

This should load their iFilter .dll file so that Search can crawl those types of documents. If this command line doesn't work, contact the iFilter's manufacturer for information on how to install their iFilter into SharePoint.

To load the file type's icon, upload the icon (preferably a small .gif file) to the *drive:*\program files\common files\Microsoft shared\Web server extensions\12\template\images directory. After uploading the file, write down the name of the file, because you'll need to modify the docicon.xml file to include the icon as follows:

```
<Mapping Key="<doc extension>" Value="NameofIconFile.gif"/>
```

After this, restart your server and the icon should appear. In addition, you should be able to crawl and index those file types that you've added to your SharePoint deployment.

Even if the iFilter is loaded and enabled, if you delete the file type from the Manage File Types screen, search will not crawl that file type. Also, if you have multiple SSPs, you'll need to add the desired file types into each SSP's configurations, but you'll only need to load the .dll and the icon one time on the server.

Creating and Managing Search Scopes

A search scope provides a way to logically group items in the index together based on a common element. This helps users target their query to only a portion of the overall index and gives them a more lean, relevant result set. After you create a search scope, you define the content to include in that search scope by adding scope rules, specifying whether to include or exclude content that matches that particular rule. You can define scope rules based on the following:

- Address
- Property query
- Content source

You can create and define search scopes at the SSP level or at the individual site-collection level. SSP-level search scopes are called *shared scopes*, and they are available to all the sites configured to use a particular SSP.

Search scopes can be built off of the following items:

- Managed properties
- Any specific URL
- A file system folder
- Exchange public folders
- A specific host name
- A specific domain name

Managed properties are built by grouping one or more crawled properties. Hence, there are really two types of properties that form the Search schema: crawled properties and managed properties. The crawled properties are properties that are discovered and created "on the fly" by the Archiving plug-in. When this plug-in sees new metadata that it has not seen before, it grabs that metadata field and adds the crawled property to the list of crawled properties in the search schema. Managed properties are properties that you, the administrator, create.

The behavior choices are to include any item that matches the rule, require that every item in the scope match this rule, or exclude items matching this rule.

Note Items are matched to their scope via the scope plug-in during the indexing and crawl process. Until the content items are passed through the plug-in from a crawl process, they won't be matched to the scope that you've created.

Creating and Defining Scopes

To create a new search scope, you'll need to navigate to the Configure Search Settings page, and then scroll down and click the View Scopes link. This opens the View Scopes page, at which point you can click New Scope.

On the Create Scope page (shown in Figure 16-12), you'll need to enter a title for the scope (required) and a description of the scope (optional). The person creating the scope will be the default contact for the scope, but a different user account can be entered if needed. You can also configure a customized results page for users who use this scope, or you can leave the scope at the default option to use the default search results page. Configure this page as needed, and then click OK. This procedure only creates the scope. You'll still need to define the rules that will designate which content is associated with this scope.

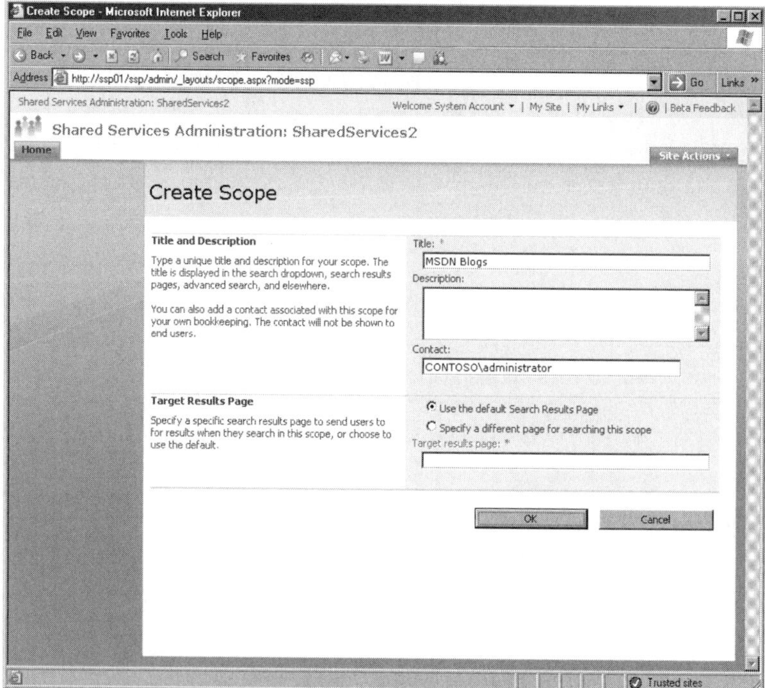

Figure 16-12 Create Scope page

After the scope is created on the View Scopes page, the update status for the scope will be "Empty – Add Rules." The "Add Rules" will be a link to the Add Scope Rule page (shown in Figure 16-13), where you can select the rule type and the behavior of that rule.

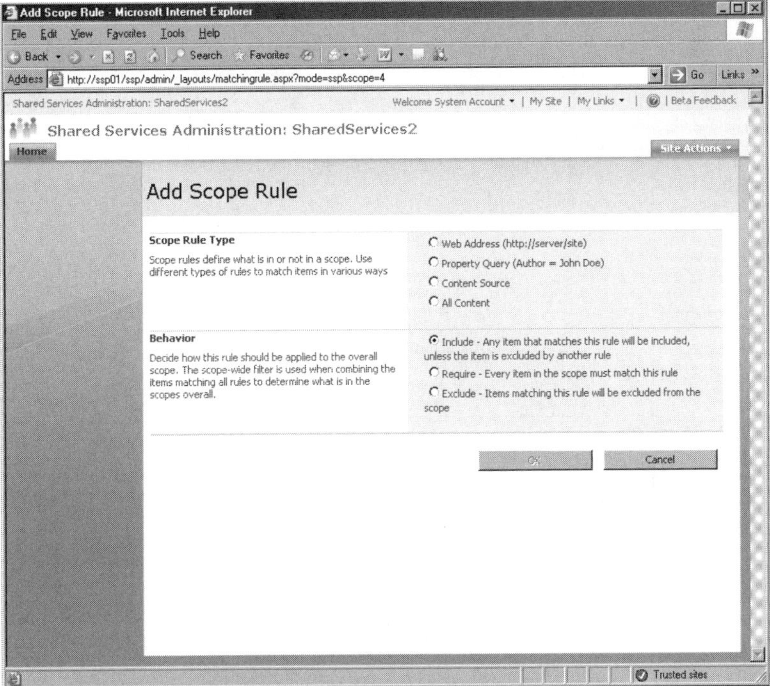

Figure 16-13 Add Scope Rule default page

Each rule type has its own set of variables. This section discusses the rule types in the order in which they appear in the interface.

Web Address Scope Type

First, the Web Address scope type will allow you to set scopes for file system folders, any specific URL, a specific host name, a specific domain name, and Exchange public folders.

Here are a couple of examples. Start with a folder named "Docs" on a server named "Search1." Suppose that you have the following three folders inside Docs: "red", "green" and "blue." You want to scope just the docs in the green folder. The syntax you would enter, as illustrated in Figure 16-14, would be file://search1/docs/green. You would use the Universal Naming Convention (UNC) sequence in a URL format with the "file" prefix. Even though this isn't mentioned in the user interface (UI), it will work.

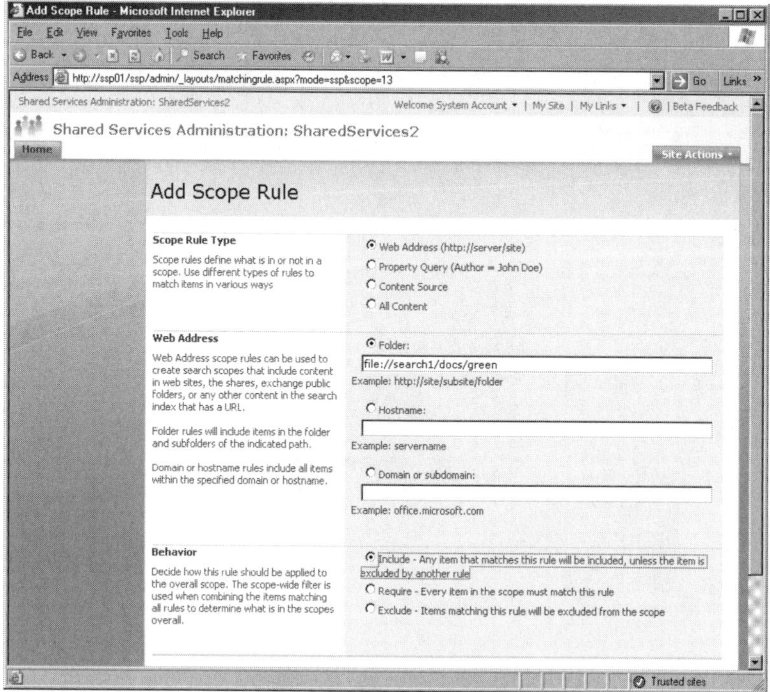

Figure 16-14 Configuring a folder search scope

Another example is if you want all content sources related to a particular domain, such as contoso.msft, to be scoped together. All you have to do is click to select the Domain Or Subdomain option and type **contoso.msft**.

Property Query Scope Type

The Property Query scope type allows you to add a managed property and make it equal to a particular value. The example in the interface is Author=John Doe. However, the default list is rather short and likely won't have the managed property you want to scope in the interface. If this is the case for you, you'll need to configure that property to appear in this interface.

To do this, navigate to the Managed Properties View by clicking the Document Managed Properties link on the Configure Search Settings page. This opens the Document Property Mappings page (shown in Figure 16-15).

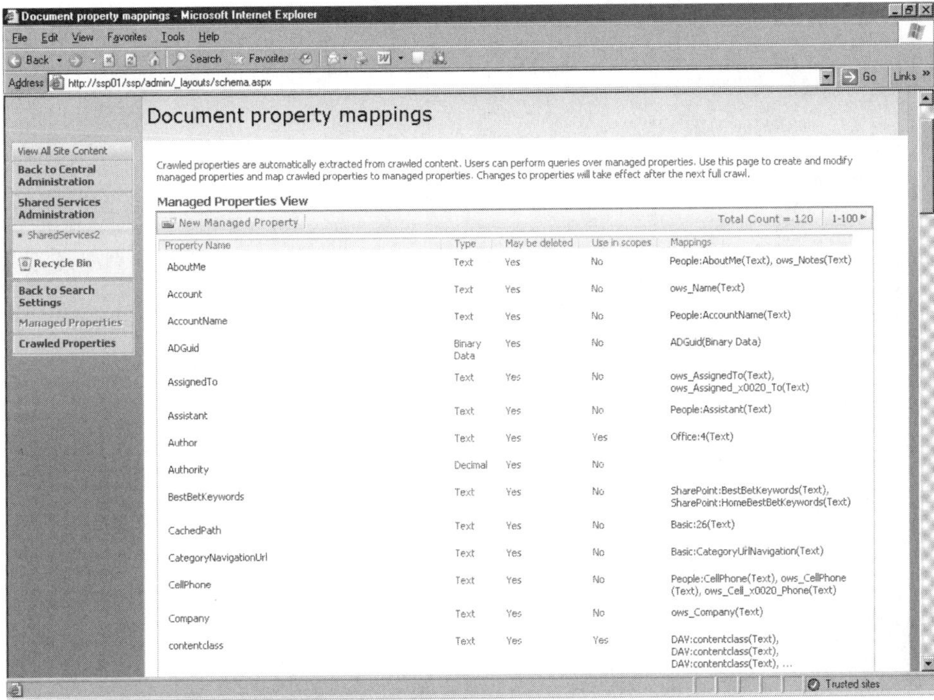

Figure 16-15 Document Property Mappings page

On this page, there are several columns, including the property name, the property type, whether or not it can be deleted, the actual mapping of the property (more on this in a moment), and whether or not it can be used in scopes. All you need to do to get an individual property to appear in the Add Property Restrictions drop-down list on the Add Scope Rule page is edit the properties of the managed property and then select the Allow This Property To Be Used In Scopes check box.

If you need to configure a new managed property, click New Managed Property (refer back to Figure 16-15), and you will be taken to the New Managed Property page (Figure 16-16). You can configure the property's name, its type, its mappings, and whether it should be used in scope development.

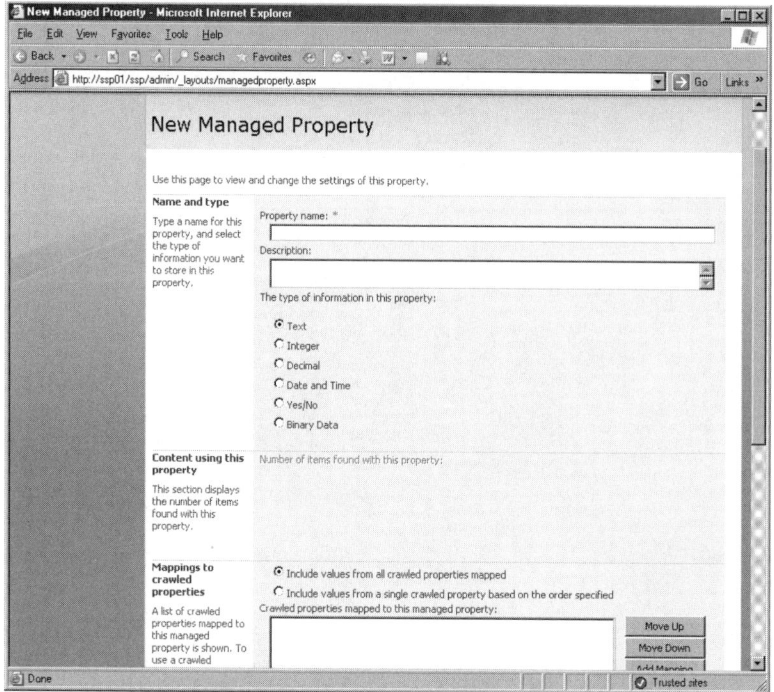

Figure 16-16 New Managed Property page

In the Mappings To Crawled Properties section, you can look at the actual schema of your deployment and select an individual or multiple metadata to group together into a single managed property. For example, assume you have a Word document with a custom metadata labeled AAA with a value of BBB. After crawling the document, if you click Add Mapping, you'll be presented with the Crawled Property Selection dialog box. For ease of illustration, select the Office category from the Select A Category drop-down list. Notice that in the Select A Crawled Property selection box, the AAA(Text) metadata was automatically added by the Archival plug-in. (See Figure 16-17.)

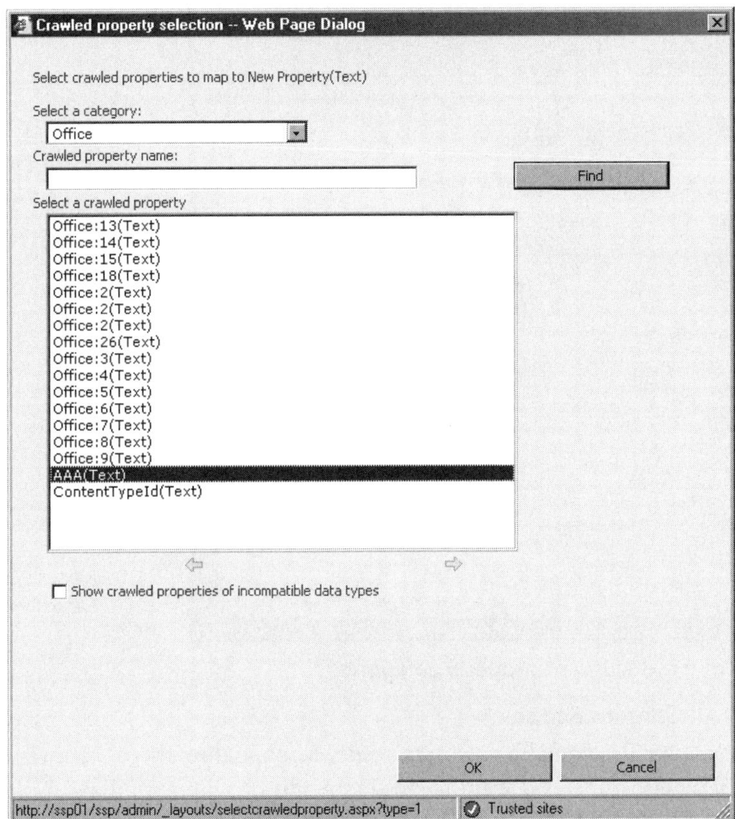

Figure 16-17 Finding the AAA metadata in the schema

Once you click OK in the Crawled Property Selection dialog box, you'll find that this AAA property appears in the list under the Mappings To Crawled Properties section. Then select the Allow This Property To Be Used In Scopes check box (*property* here refers to the Managed Property, not the crawled property), and you'll be able to create a scope based on this property.

If you want to see all the crawled properties, from the Document Property Mappings page, you can select the Crawled Properties link in the left pane. This takes you to the various groupings of crawled property types. (See Figure 16-18.) Each category name is a link. When invoked, the link gives you all the properties that are associated with that category. There is no method of creating new categories within the interface.

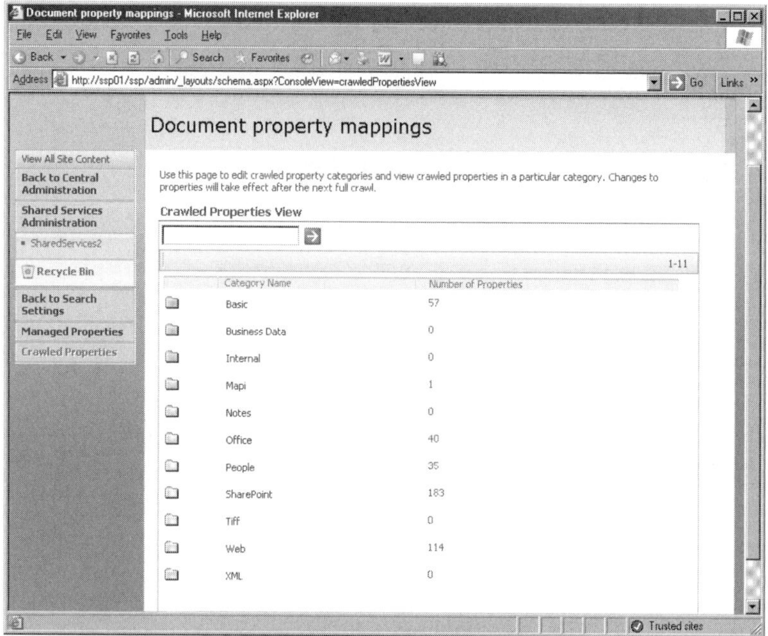

Figure 16-18 Listing of the document property categories

Content Source and All Content Scopes

The Content Source Scope rule type allows you to tether a scope directly to a content source. An example of when you would want to do this might be when you have a file server that is being crawled by a single content source and users want to be able to find files on that files server without finding other documents that might match their query. Anytime you want to isolate queries to the boundaries of a given content source, select the Content Source Rule type.

The All Content rule type is a global scope that will allow you to query the entire index. You would make this selection if you've removed the default scopes and need to create a scope that allows a query of the entire index.

Global Scopes

Thus far, we've been discussing what would be known as *Global Scopes*, which are scopes that are created at the SSP level. These scopes are considered to be global in nature because they are available to be used across all the site collections that are associated with the SSP via the Web applications. However, creating a scope at the SSP level does you no good unless you enable that scope to be used at the site-collection level.

Note Remember that scopes created at the SSP level are merely available for use in the site collections. They don't show up by default until the Site Collection Administration has manually chosen them to be displayed and used within the site collection.

Site Collection Scopes

Scopes that are created at the SSP level can be enabled or disabled at the site-collection level. This gives site-collection administrators some authority over which scopes will appear in the search Web Parts within their site collection. The following section describes the basic actions to take to enable a global scope at the site-collection level.

First, open the Site Collection administration menu from the root site in your site collection. Then click on the Search Scopes link under the Site Collection Administration menu to open the View Scopes page. On this page, you can create a new scope just for this individual site collection and/or create a new display group in which to display the scopes that you do create. The grouping gives the site collection administrator a method of organizing search scopes. The methods used to create a new search scope at the site-collection level are identical to those used at the SSP level.

To add a scope created at the SSP level, click New Display Group (as shown in Figure 16-19), and then you'll be taken to the Create Scope Display Group page (shown in Figure 16-20).

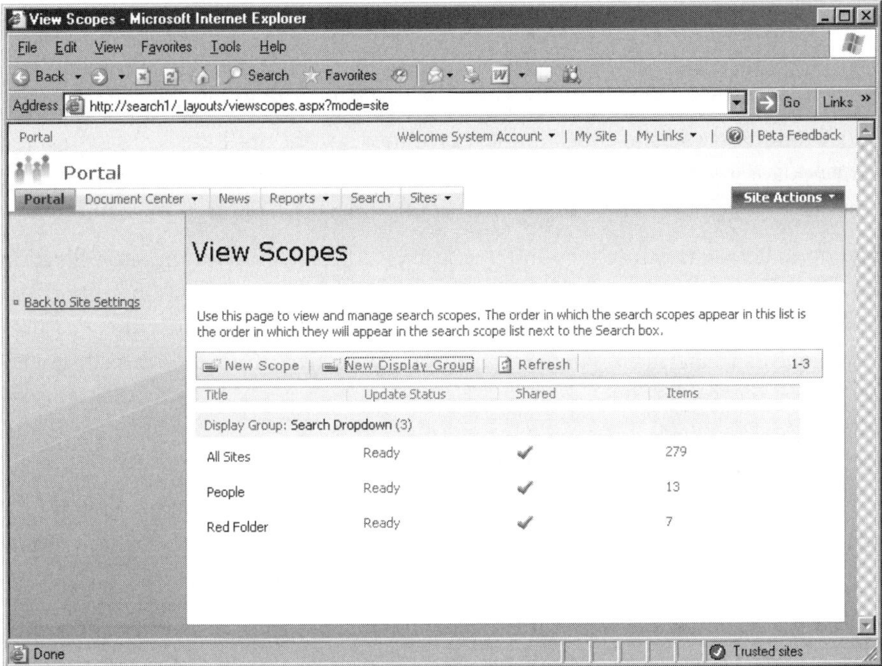

Figure 16-19 The View Scopes page

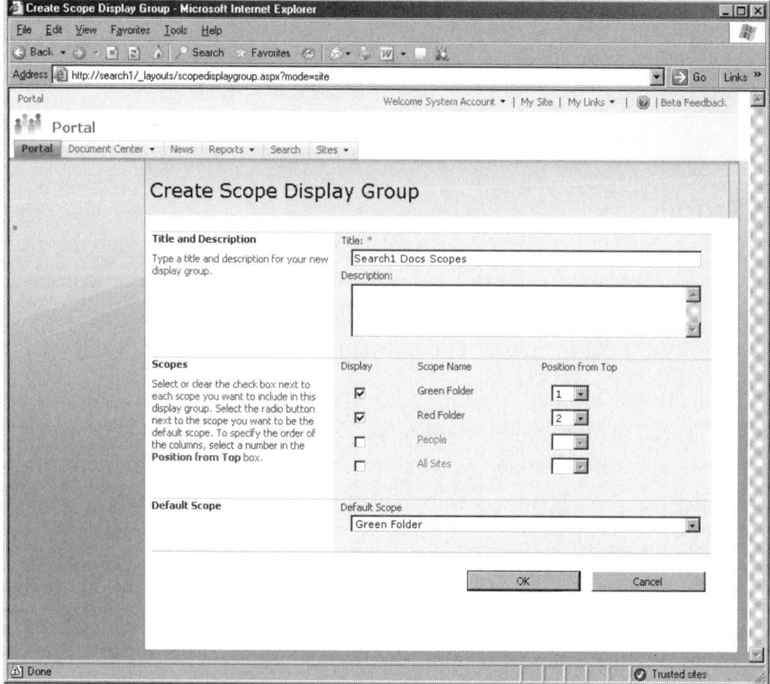

Figure 16-20 The Create Scope Display Group page

On the Create Scope Display Group page, although you can *see* the scopes created at the SSP level, it appears they are unavailable because they are grayed out. However, when you select the Display check box next to the scope name, the scope is activated for that group. You can also set the order in which the scopes will appear from top to bottom.

Your configurations at the site-collection level will not appear until the SSP's scheduled interval for updating scopes is completed. You can manually force the scopes to update by clicking the Start Update Now link on the Configure Search Settings page in the SSP.

If you want to remove custom scopes and the Search Center features at the site-collection level, you can do so by clicking the Search Settings link in the Site Collection Administration menu and then clearing the Enable Custom Scopes And Search Center Features check box. Note also that this is where you can specify a different page for this site collection's Search Center results page.

Removing URLs from the Search Results

At times, you'll need to remove individual content items or even an entire batch of content items from the index. Perhaps one of your content sources has crawled inappropriate content, or perhaps there are just a couple of individual content items that you simply don't want appearing in the result set. Regardless of the reasons, if you need to remove search results quickly, you can do so by navigating to the Search Result Removal link in the SSP under the Search section.

When you enter a URL to remove the results, a crawl rule excluding the specific URLs will also be automatically created and enforced until you manually remove the rule. Deleting the content source will not remove the crawl rule.

Use this feature as a way to remove obviously spurious or unwanted results. But don't try to use this feature to "carve out" large portions of Web sites unless you have some time to devote to finding each unwanted URL on that page.

Understanding Query Reporting

Another feature that Microsoft has included in Search is the Query Reporting tool. This tool is automatically built in to the SSP and gives you the opportunity to view all the search results across your SSP. Use this information to help you understand better what scopes might be useful to your users and what searching activities they are engaging in.

There are two types of reports you can view. The first is the Search Queries Report, which includes basic bar graphs and pie charts. (See Figure 16-21.) On this page, you can read the following types of reports:

- Queries over previous 30 days
- Queries over previous 12 months
- Top query origin site collections over previous 30 days
- Queries per scope over previous 30 days
- Top queries over previous 30 days

These reports can show you which group of users is most actively using the Search feature, the most common queries, and the query trends for the last 12 months. For each of these reports, you can export the data in either a Microsoft Excel or Adobe Acrobat (PDF) format.

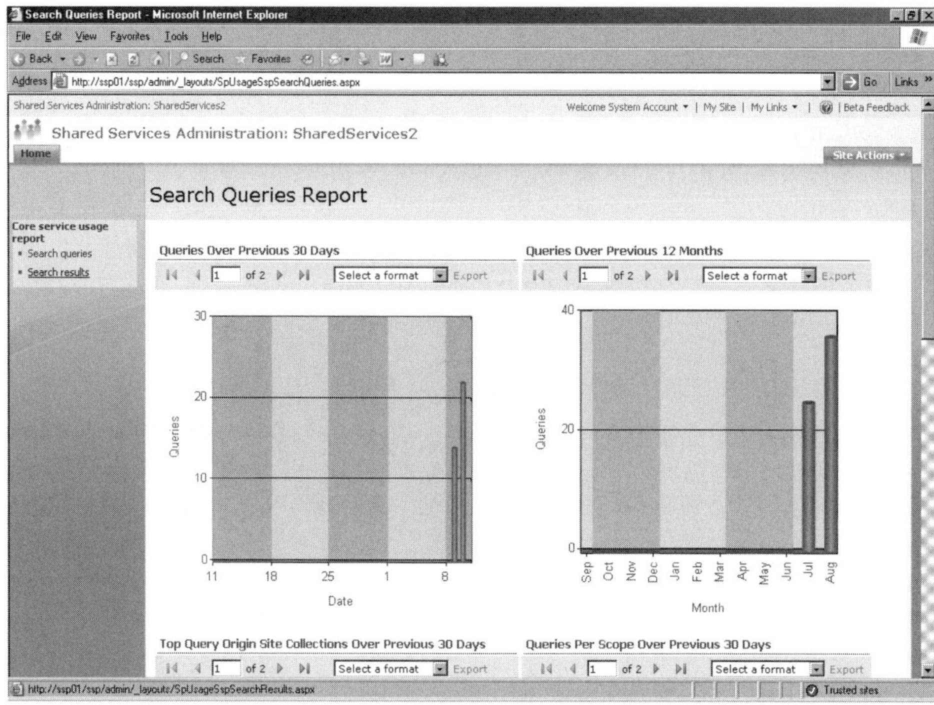

Figure 16-21 Search Queries Report page

In the left pane, you can click the Search Results link, which will invoke two more reports (as shown in Figure 16-22):

- Search results top destination pages
- Queries with zero results

Note These reports can help you understand where your users are going when they execute queries and inform not only your scope development, but also end-user training about what queries your users should use to get to commonly accessed locations and which queries not to use.

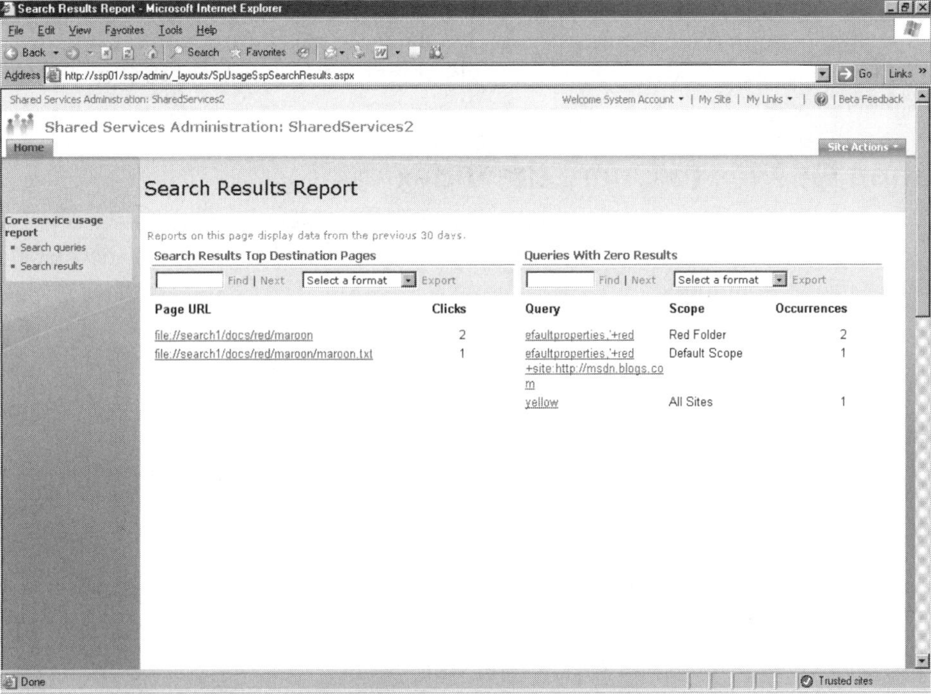

Figure 16-22 Search Results Report page

The Client Side of Search

End users will experience Search from a very different interface than has been discussed thus far in this chapter. They will execute queries and view query results within the confines of the new Search Center.

The Search Center is a SharePoint site dedicated to help the end user search the index. It includes several components, each responsible for a specific search task. The default setup for the Search Center includes the following components:

- Search Center Home
- Search Results
- Advanced Search
- People Search
- People Search Results
- Search Navigation tab

You can customize the Search Center by modifying these components or by creating your own version of these components. Because they are merely Web Parts, you can add them to the Search Center to extend its functionality or remove them to focus the Search Center's functionality.

Executing Queries to Query the Index

Search supports two types of queries: keyword and SQL. This section discusses only keyword search syntax because the SQL Server syntax is designed to be used by developers creating custom solutions.

You can use any of the following as keywords:

- Single word
- Multiple words
- Phrase (two or more words enclosed in quotation marks)
- Prefix (includes a part of a word, from the beginning of the word)

There are three types of search terms that you can use: Simple, Included, and Excluded. Table 16-4 describes your options.

Table 16-3 Overview of Query Terms and Usage

Name	Definition	Character	Example
Simple word	Search query word with no special requirements	N/A	Boots
Included term	Search query word that must be in the content items returned in the result set	"+"	+boots
Excluded term	Keyword that must not be in the content items that are returned in the result set		

The inclusion "+" mark means that each content item in the result set must contain at least this word. For example, if you were to search on "muddy boots" (without the quotation marks), you would see documents in the result set that contained the word *muddy*, the word *boots*, and both *muddy* and *boots*. The point is that if you wanted all documents that have the word *muddy* plus documents that have only *muddy* and *boots* but not *muddy* and *shoes*, your search phrase would be "muddy + boots" (without the quotation marks).

By the same token, if you wanted to exclude certain documents from the result set because of a certain word, you would use the "–" sign. For example, if you're looking for any type of boot except muddy, you would enter the query "boots – muddy" (without the quotation marks).

Note The query terms are not case sensitive. Searching on "windows" is the same as "windOWS." However, the thesaurus *is* case sensitive, by default, so if you enter "Windows" as a word in an expansion set and the user enters "windows" as a query word, the expansion set will not be invoked. If you want to turn off case sensitivity in the thesaurus, enter the following command at the beginning of the thesaurus file:

```
<case><caseflag="false"></case>
```

Query terms are also not accent sensitive, so searching for "resume" will return results for "résumé." However, you can turn on diacritical marks using the stsadm.exe command, such as:

```
stsadm -o osearchdiacriticsensitive
```

Managing Results

After a query is executed against the index, the browser is redirected automatically to the Search Results page. The results page can potentially contain the following types of results:

- Relevant results
- High confidence results
- Keyword and Best Bet results
- Query statistics

The layout of the information on the results page is a direct result of combining the search Web Parts for the results page. Because the results are passed from the index to the search results page in XML format, many of these Web Parts use XSLT to format the results. This is why you'll need to enter additional XSLT commands if you want to perform certain actions, such as adding another property to the Advanced Search drop-down list.

Adding Properties to Advanced Search in SharePoint Server 2007

To add a property to the advanced search Web Part, perform these steps:

1. Navigate to the results page and then click Edit Page from the Site Actions menu.
2. Open the edit menu for the search Web Part, and select Modify Shared Web Part to open the Web Part property pane.
3. Expand the Miscellaneous section in the properties pane, and find the property called “properties.” You’ll find an XML string that allows you to define what properties will be displayed in the advanced search. Best practice here is to copy the string to NotePad for editing.
4. Edit the XML string, and save it back into the property. You can save the XML in the format shown below. This XML is copied directly from the Web Part. You’ll need a profile property in the schema for the XML to hold any real value.

```
<Properties>
<Property Name="Department" ManagedName="Department" ProfileURI="urn:schemas
-microsoft-com:sharepoint:portal:profile:Department"/>
<Property Name="JobTitle" ManagedName="JobTitle" ProfileURI="urn:schemas-
microsoft-com:sharepoint:portal:profile:Title"/>
<Property Name="Responsibility" ManagedName="Responsibility" ProfileURI="urn
:schemas-microsoft-com:sharepoint:portal:profile:SPS-Responsibility"/>
<Property Name="Skills" ManagedName="Skills" ProfileURI="urn:schemas-
microsoft-com:sharepoint:portal:profile:SPS-Skills"/>
<Property Name="QuickLinks" ManagedName="QuickLinks" ProfileURI="urn:schemas
-microsoft-com:sharepoint:portal:profile:QuickLinks"/>
</Properties>
```

The elements that you’ll need to pay attention to are as follows:

- Property name
- Managed name
- Profile URI (Uniform Resource Identifier)

If you look at the URN (Uniform Resource Name) string carefully, you’ll see that the profile name is being pulled out of the profile URN. This is why you’ll need a profile property in the schema before this XML will have any real effect.

URI, URN, and URL: Brief Overview

URIs, URNs, and URLs play an important, yet quiet, role in SharePoint Server 2007. A Uniform Resource Identifier (URI) provides a simple and extensible means for identifying a resource uniquely on the Internet. Because the means of identifying each resource are unique, no other person, company, or organization can have identical identifiers of their resources on the Internet.

The identifier can either be a "locator" (URL) or a "name" (URN). The URI syntax is organized hierarchically, with components listed in order of increasing granularity from left to right. For example, referring back to the XML data for the advanced search Web Part, we found that Microsoft had at least this URN:

```
"urn:schemas-microsoft-com:sharepoint:portal:profile:SPS-Responsibility"
```

As you move from left to right, you move from more general to more specific, finally arriving at the name of the resource. No other resource on the Internet can be named exactly the same as the sps-responsibility resource in SharePoint. The hierarchical characteristic of the naming convention means that governance of the lower portions of the namespace is delegated to the registrant of the upper portion of the namespace. For example, the registered portion of the URN we're using in our running example is "schemas-microsoft-com." The rest of the URN is managed directly by Microsoft, not the Internet registering authority.

You will find URIs, URLs, and URNs throughout SharePoint and other Microsoft products. Having a basic understanding of these elements will aid your administration of your SharePoint deployment.

Modifying Other Search Web Parts

When you modify any one of the search Web Parts, you'll notice that a publish toolbar appears. This toolbar enables you to modify this page without affecting the current live page. You can then publish this page as a draft for testing before going live.

Server Name Mappings

Server name mappings are crawl settings you can configure to override how server names and URLs are displayed or accessed in the result set after content has been included in the index. For example, you can configure a content source to crawl a Web site via a file share path, and then create a server name mapping entry to map the file share to the Web site's URL. Another way to look at this feature is that it gives you the ability to mask internal file server names with external names so that your internal naming conventions are not revealed in the result set.

Thesaurus

The thesaurus is a way to manually force or deny certain types of query terms at the time the user enters a query in the Search box. Using the thesaurus, you can implement expansion sets, replacement sets, weighting, and stemming. This section focuses on the expansion and replacement sets.

The thesaurus is held in an XML file, which is located in the *drive:*\program files\office sharepoint server\data\ directory and has the format of TS<XXX>.XML, where *XXX* is the standard three-letter code for a specific language. For English, the file name is tsenu.xml.

Here are the contents of the file in its default form:

```
<XML ID="Microsoft Search Thesaurus">
<thesaurus xmlns="x-schema:tsSchema.xml">
 <expansion>
  <sub weight="0.8">Internet Explorer</sub>
  <sub weight="0.2">IE</sub>
  <sub weight="0.9">IE5</sub>
 </expansion>
 <replacement>
  <pat>NT5</pat>
  <pat>W2K</pat>
  <sub weight="1.0">Windows 2000</sub>
 </replacement>
 <expansion>
  <sub weight="0.5">run**</sub>
  <sub weight="0.5">jog**</sub>
 </expansion>
</thesaurus>
-->
</XML>
```

There are two parts to the code: an expansion set and a replacement set.

Expansion Sets

You use expansion sets to force the expansion of certain query terms to automatically include other query terms. For example, you could do this when a product name changes but the older documents are still relevant, if acronyms are commonly used as query terms, or when new terms arise that refer to other terms, such as slang or industry-specific use of individual words.

If a user enters a specified word, other hits that match that word's configured synonyms will also be displayed. For instance, if a user searches on the word "car", you can configure the thesaurus to force a search on the word "sedan" as a synonym for the word "car" so that the result set will include content items that include the word "car" but also the word "sedans", whether or not those "sedan" content items also mention the word "car."

For example, to use the car illustration, you create the following code:

```
<XML ID="Microsoft Search Thesaurus">
 <thesaurus xmlns="x-schema:tsSchema.xml">
  <expansion>
   <sub>car</sub>
   <sub>sedan</sub>
  </expansion>
 </thesaurus>
```

You can have more than two terms in the expansion set, and the use of any term in the set will invoke the expansion of the query to include all the other terms in the expansion set.

If you want multiple expansion sets created—say, one for "car" and the other for "truck"—your code would look like this:

```
<XML ID="Microsoft Search Thesaurus">
 <thesaurus xmlns="x-schema:tsSchema.xml">
  <expansion>
   <sub>car</sub>
   <sub>sedan</sub>
   <sub>automobile</sub>
  </expansion>
  <expansion>
   <sub>truck</sub>
   <sub>pickup truck</sub>
   <sub>SUV</sub>
  </expansion>
 </thesaurus>
```

You can see how each expansion set is its own set of synonyms. This file can be as long as you want, and expansion sets need not be topically similar.

Replacement Sets

You can use the thesaurus to create a replacement set of words by specifying an initial word or pattern of query terms that will be replaced by a substitution set of one or more words. For example, you could create a replacement set that specifies the pattern "book writer" with the substitution "author" or "wordsmith." In this example, when a user executes a query against the phrase "book writer," the result set returns documents that have the words "author" and "wordsmith," but *not* documents that contain the phrase "book writer."

You do this is to ensure that commonly misspelled words are correctly spelled in the actual query. For example, the word "chrysanthemum" is easily misspelled, so placing various misspellings into a replacement set might help your users get the result set they're looking for even though they might not be able to reliably spell the query term. Another example of using the replacement set is for product name changes where the old documents to the old product line are not needed any more or a person's name has changed.

Your code would look like this:

```
<XML ID="Microsoft Search Thesaurus">
 <thesaurus xmlns="x-schema:tsSchema.xml">
  <replacement>
   <pat>book writer</pat>
   <sub>author</sub>
   <sub>wordsmith</sub>
  </replacement>
 </thesaurus>
```

Creating replacement sets for each misspelling is more time consuming, but it is also more accurate and helps those who are "spelling-challenged" to get a better result set.

So how can you use this? Let's assume that you have a product-line name change. Use an expansion set to expand searches on the old and new names if both sets of documents are relevant after the name change. If the documents referring to the old name are not relevant, use a replacement set to replace queries on the old name with the new name.

Noise Word File

The noise word file, by default, contacts prepositions, adjectives, adverbs, articles, personal pronouns, single letters, and single numbers. You'll want to place any additional words in the noise word file that will not hold any discriminatory value in your environment. Further examples of words that don't highly discriminate between documents in your environment include your company name and names of individuals who appear often in documents or Web pages.

Managing Keywords

Keywords are words or phrases that site administrators have identified as important. They provide a way to display additional information and recommended links on the initial results page that might not otherwise appear in the search results for a particular word or phrase. Keywords are a method to immediately elevate a content item to prominence in the result set simply by associating a keyword with the content item. The content item, in this context, is considered a *Best Bet.* Best Bets are items that you want to appear at the top of the result set regardless of what other content items appear in the result set. For example, you could make the URL to the human resource policy manual a Best Bet so that anytime a user queries "human resources", the link to the policy manual appears at the top of the result set.

Keywords are implemented at the site-collection level. You'll create a keyword and then give it one or more synonyms. As part of creating the keyword, you'll need to enter at least one Best Bet. After you create the keyword, add the synonym. After associating at least one Best Bet, you'll find that when you search on the synonym, the Best Bet will appear in the Best Bet Web Part in the right-hand portion of the results page (by default).

Here is an example. Create a keyword by clicking the Search Keywords link in the Site Collection Administration menu. Then click the Add Keyword button. In the Keyword Phrase text box, type **Green**, and in the Synonym text box, type **Color**. Next, associate the keyword and the synonym with the Green folder in the Docs share as a Best Bet. (See Figure 16-23.)

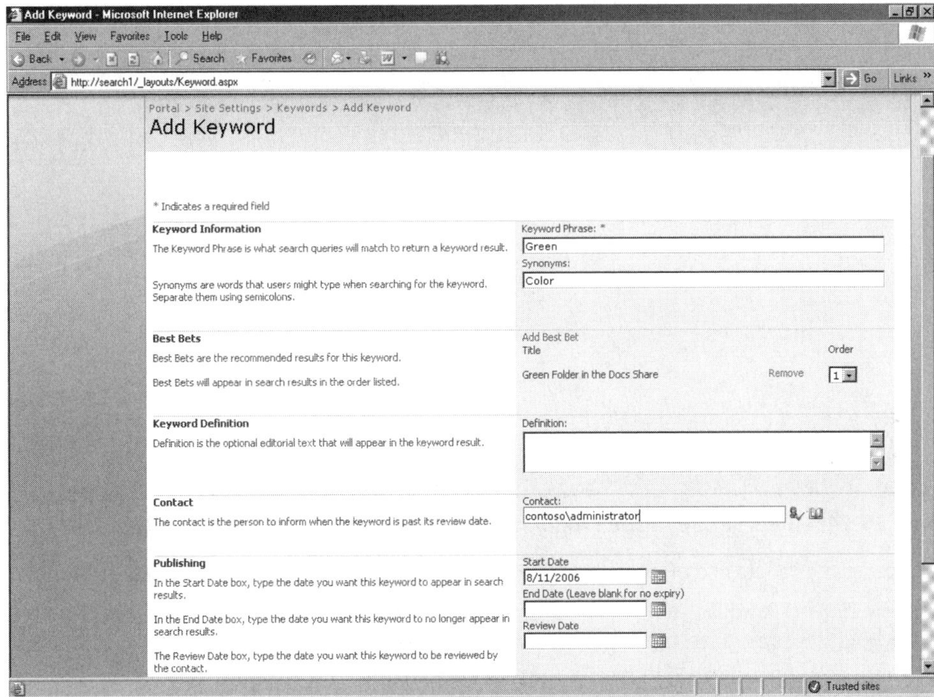

Figure 16-23 Creating the Green keyword Best Bet

After doing this, when you search on the word "color," you see the Green folder appear in the Best Bet Web Part to the right of the core result set. (See Figure 16-24.)

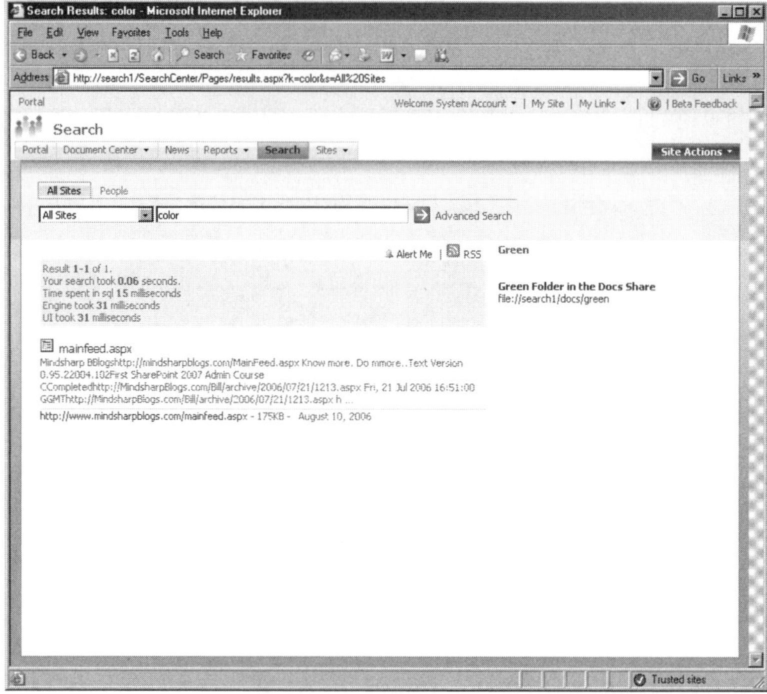

Figure 16-24 Green folder appearing in the Best Bet Web Part on the results page

Remember, Best Bets are merely a link to the information that is especially relevant to the keyword or its synonym. Be sure to look through your reports to find terms that are being queried many times, with users going to the same location many times. This is an indication that these terms can be grouped into a keyword with synonyms and these destinations become the Best Bet.

Working with the Result Set

The result set can be modified and managed in a number of ways. It will be impossible to fully cover every aspect of each Web Part in the result set, so this section highlights some of the more important configurations.

First, it is possible that there will be times when a user queries to find a document and receives a separate listing in the result set for each document in the version history of a document lineage. If this happens, try crawling the document library using an account with read permissions to the document library that isn't the same as the application pool account.

The application pool account has pervasive access to content in a way that is not displayed in the user interface and is not configurable by the site administrator. Regardless of the type of versioning that is turned on, if you crawl that library using the application pool account, all versions in the history of that document will be crawled and indexed and may be displayed in the result set for your users.

Secondly, it is important for search administrators (and anyone modifying the results page) to grasp is that a major portion of the configurations are pushed into the Web Part properties rather than being given links on an Administration menu page. This makes it a bit more difficult to remember where to go when trying to manage an individual element on the page. Just remember, you're really trying to manage the Web Part, not the page itself.

You modify Web Parts by clicking Edit Page under Site Actions. The page will immediately be placed into edit mode. Your actions from this point forward will not be seen by your users until you successfully publish the page.

The first thing that you'll notice you can do is add more tabs across the top of the page. If you click on the Add New Tab link (shown in Figure 16-25), you're taken to the Tabs In Search Results: New Item page. On this page, you can reference an existing page, enter a new tab name for that page, and enter a tooltip that will pop up when users hover their mouse over the tab (as shown in Figure 16-26). Remember, you're not creating a new Web page at this location. You're merely referencing a page that you've already created in the Pages library. You do this to map a new search results page with one or more search scopes.

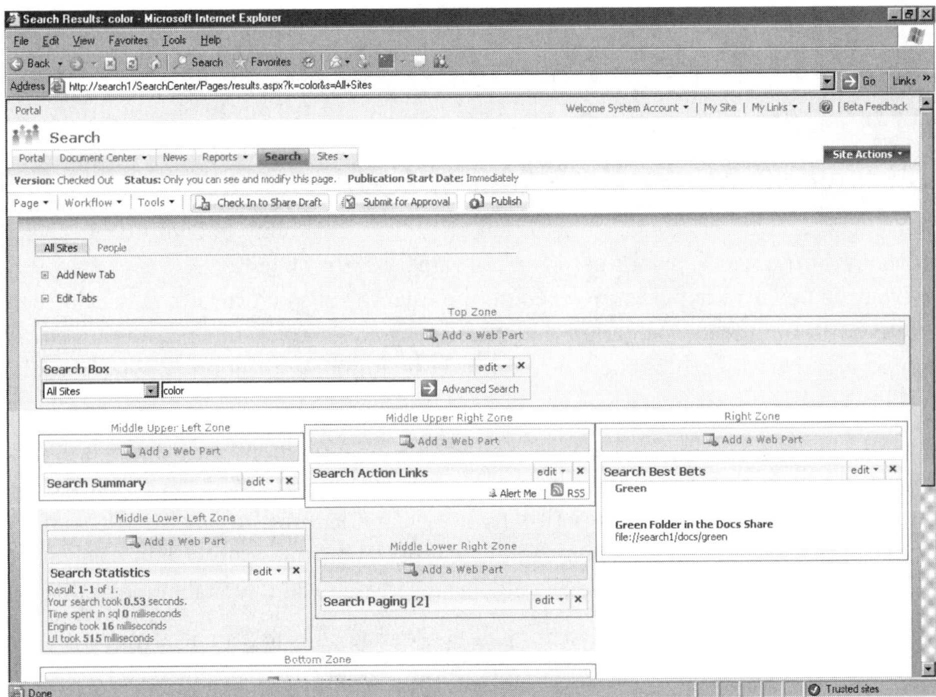

Figure 16-25 Add New Tab link in the Edit Page screen for the Search Center Result Set

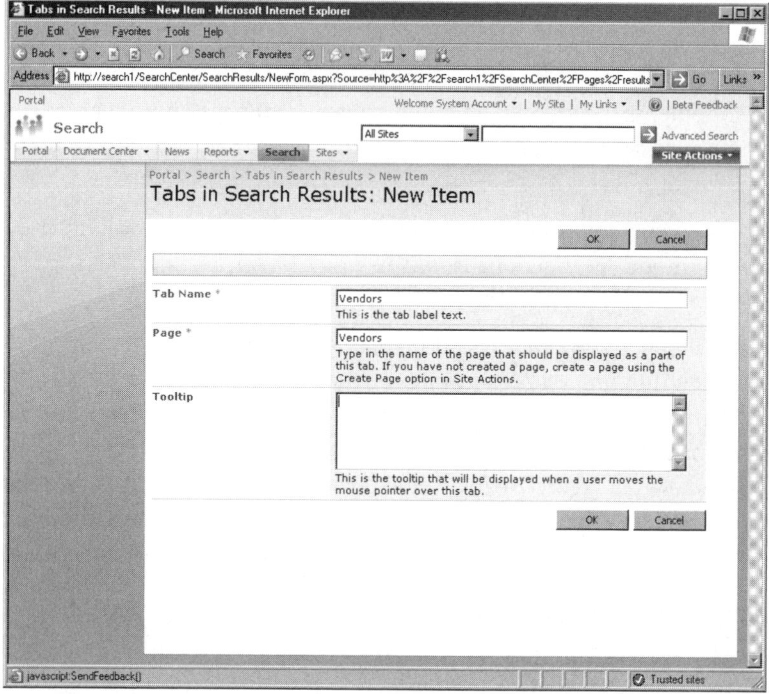

Figure 16-26 Tabs In Search Results: New Item page

Receiving Notifications from Search Results

When users receive a result set from Search, they have the ability to continue receiving notifications from search results based on their query. If they like the results of the query they've executed and expect to re-execute the query multiple times to stay informed about new or modified information that matches the query, users can choose to either create an alert based on their query or set up a Real Simple Syndication (RSS) feed to the query.

By using RSS, users can stay updated about new information in individual lists or libraries. The RSS feed will be automatically added to their Outlook 2007 client. (Earlier versions of Outlook do not support this feature.) In addition, to run the RSS client successfully, users will need to download the Microsoft desktop search engine. The desktop search engine will not be automatically installed: you need to install it manually.

If you need to remove the RSS link feature, first generate a result set and then under the Site Actions menu, click Edit Page. Navigate to the Search Actions Link Web Part, click Edit, and then click Modify Shared Web Part. Under the Search Results Action Links list, clear the Display "RSS" Link check box.

Best Practices Clear the Display "RSS" Link check box until you have deployed the Microsoft Desktop Search Engine. There is no sense in giving your users an option in the interface if they can't use it.

Customizing the Search Results Page

By default, the following Web Parts are on the Search Center's results page:

- Search Box
- Search Summary
- Search Action Links
- Search Best Bets
- Search Statistics
- Search Paging
- Search High Confidence Results
- Search Core Results

This section covers the management of the more important Web Parts individually. All of these Web Parts are managed by clicking the Edit button in the Web Part (refer back to Figure 16-25) and then selecting Modify Shared Web Part in the drop-down menu list.

Search Box

This is the Web Part that will allow you to select whether or not scopes appear in the drop-down list when executing a query. The Dropdown Mode drop-down list in the Scope Dropdown section offers you several choices. You can completely turn off scopes or ensure that contextual scopes either appear or don't appear. (See Figure 16-27.)

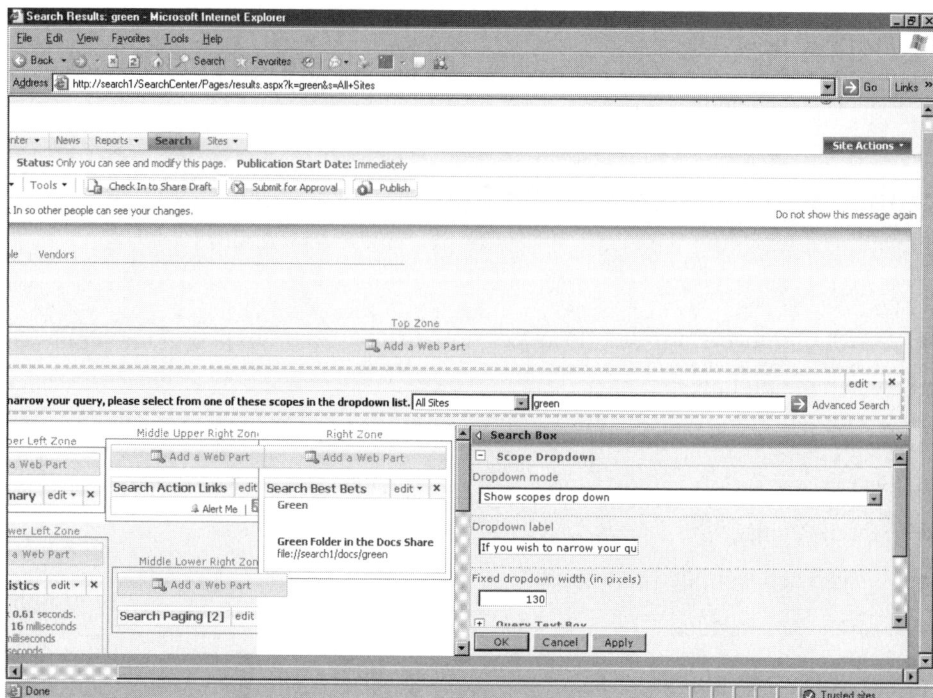

Figure 16-27 Scope configuration options

The "s" parameter can be used when the scopes drop-down is hidden. Note that you can enter the scope in the URL, if needed, as follows:

```
http://server/sites/results.aspx?k=thequrey&s=thescope
```

But if the scopes drop-down is hidden, the "s" parameter lets you indicate whether you want to default to the "contextual" scope, for example, "this site" or re-use the scope specified by a search box on the originating page, which is passed in the 's' parameter.

This is the mode used within the search center, allowing for the search scope to be carried through across tabs. It allows you to consruct a user interface where some tabs make use of the 's' parameter and others don't, but the parameter is preserved as the user navigates through the tabs.

For example, let's assume a user picks the scope "Northwest." After executing the query, the user is presented with the "northwest" results of the query in the search results page in the search center. On the search results page, the search box there has no scopes drop-down list displayed. So the user modifies the query slightly and re-executes the search. The search box re-uses the same scope for the second query, because it is specified in the 's' parameter.

In addition, you can enter a label to the left of the scope drop-down list that explains what scopes are, how the drop-down list works, or what each scope is focused on.

Search Core Results

The Search Core Results Web Part displays the result set. The rest of the Web Parts on the page can be considered helpful and supportive to the Search Core Results Web Part. In the configuration options of this Web Part, you can specify fixed keyword queries that are executed each time a query is run along with how to display the results and query results options.

Probably of most importance are the query results options. In this part of the configuration options (shown in Figure 16-28), you have the following choices to make:

- **Remove Duplicate Results** Select this option if you want to ensure that different result items of the same content item are removed.
- **Enable Search Term Stemming** By default, stemming in the result set is turned off, even though the indexer performs stemming on inbound words into the index. For example, if the crawler crawls the word "buy," the indexer will stem the word and include "buy," "buying," buys," and "bought." But in the result set, by default, if the query term is "buy," the result set will only display content times that contain the word "buy." If you select to enable search term stemming, then, in this scenario, the result set will contain content items that include the stemmed words for "buy."You'll want to enable this if you want the result set to include content items that might only have stemmed forms of the query terms.
- **Permit Noise Word Queries** This is a feature that allows noise words in one language to be queried in another language when working in a cross-lingual environment. For example, "the" in the ENG language is a noise word, but it's equivalent in another language might not be a noise word. So you enable the permit noise word queries so that a user who searches on "the" will obtain content items in other languages where "the" is not considered a noise word.
- **Enable URL Smashing** In this feature, we take the query and "smash" the query terms together and then see if there is a URL that matches exactly the smashed query terms. For example, if someone searches on "campus maps" and there is an intranet Web site with the URL http://campusmaps, then this URL will become the first result in the result set. This is different from URL Matching in that the smashed query terms must match exactly the URL, whereas in URL matching, the query terms only need to match a portion of the URL.

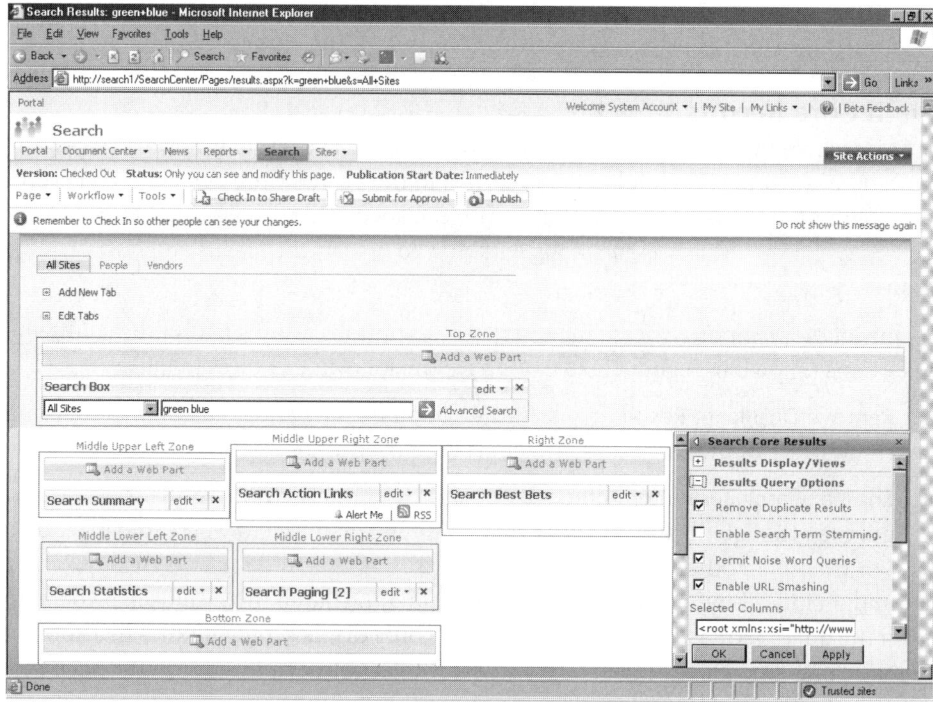

Figure 16-28 Configuration options for the Search Core Results Web Part

Results Collapsing

Search results frequently contain several items that are the same or very similar. If these duplicated or similar items are ranked highly and returned as the top items in the result set, other results that might be more relevant to the user appear much further down in the list. This can create a scenario where users have to page through several redundant results before finding what they are looking for.

Results collapsing can group similar results together so that they are displayed as one entry in the search result set. This entry includes a link to display the expanded results for that collapsed result set entry. Search administrators can collapse results for the following content item groups:

- Duplicates and derivatives of documents
- Windows SharePoint Services discussion messages for the same topic
- Microsoft Exchange Server public folder messages for the same conversation topic
- Current versions of the same document
- Different language versions of the same document
- Content from the same site

By default, results collapsing is turned on in SharePoint Server 2007 Search. Results collapsing has the following characteristics when turned on:

- **Duplicate and Derivative Results Collapsing** When there are duplicates in the search results and these are collapsed, the result that is displayed in the main result set is the content item that is the most relevant to the user's search query. With duplicated documents, factors other than content will affect relevance, such as where the document is located or how many times it is linked to.
- **Site Results Collapsing** When search results are collapsed by site, results from that site are collapsed and displayed in the main result set in one of two ways: content from the same site is grouped together, or content from the same folder within a particular site is grouped together, depending on the type of site (as described in the following sections).
- **SharePoint Sites** All results from the same SharePoint site are collapsed. No more than two results from the same SharePoint site will be displayed in the main results set.
- **Sites Other than SharePoint Sites** For Web sites that are not SharePoint sites, results are collapsed based on the folder. Results from the same site but from different folders within that site are not grouped together in the collapsed results. Only results from the same folder are collapsed together. No more than two results from the same folder for a particular site will be displayed in the main results set.

Finding People in the Search Center

Much of your organization's most important information is not found in documents or Web sites. Instead, it is found in people. As users in your organization learn to expose (or "surface") information about themselves, other users will be able to find them based on a number of metadata elements, such as department, title, skills, responsibilities, memberships, or a combination of those factors.

Use the People tab (shown in Figure 16-29) to execute queries for people. When you do this, the result set will list the public-facing My Sites for users whose names match the search query. In addition, the result set will default to sorting by social distance, so the My Colleagues Web Part will appear listing the users who fit the search query and who are also part of your colleague (or social) network.

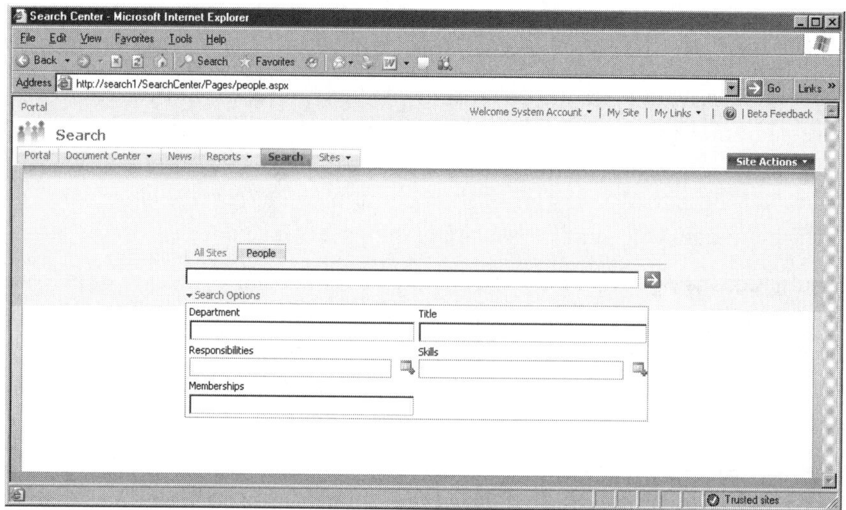

Figure 16-29 People tab for executing queries for people

If you want to view these results by relevance rather than by social distance, click the View By Relevance link and the result set will be displayed in rank order. If you want to change the default ordering of people to display by rank rather than by social distance, change the Default Results View setting in the Modify Shared Web Part properties of the People Search Core Results Web Part.

Real World Best Practices for Search and Indexing

It is difficult to read a chapter and be expected to remember all the best practices for implementing and administrating a feature set like this. This sidebar summarizes some of what I've learned over the last three years regarding search and indexing.

I'll start by mentioning some planning elements that often crop up when I work with customers in the field. After customers learn about the breadth and depth of what search and indexing can do, they realize that they need to take a long step back and ask two important questions:

Where is our information?

Which information do we want to crawl and index?

These are not inconsequential questions. One of the main reasons for implementing a software package like SharePoint Server 2007 is to aggregate your content. If you don't know *where* your content is, how can you *aggregate* it? The reason, often, that we don't know where our content resides is because it resides in so many different locations. Think about it. In most organizations, content is held all over the place, such as in the following places:

- Filing cabinets
- Web site
- Public folders
- E-mail
- .tiff files
- SharePoint sites
- Databases
- My Documents
- Local hard drives
- Mapped drives
- File servers
- People's heads

The exciting element about search and indexing in SharePoint Server 2007 is the existence of the Business Data Catalog and its ability to act as an abstraction layer between SharePoint and the different data interfaces so that we can finally aggregate content using SharePoint Server 2007.

But if you haven't take the time to genuinely understand where your data resides, you'll have a hard time knowing what data should be aggregated using search and indexing.

However, once you know where you data resides and you've decided which data will be indexed, you can begin the process of building your content source structure in way that makes sense. Most organizations have found that they can't "swerve" into success by creating content sources as the need arises. Most have found that it is very helpful to put some forethought and planning into the process of determining which content in their environment will be aggregated using search and indexing, as opposed to aggregating the content by either hosting it in SharePoint (which automatically gets indexed) or linking to the content (which might or might not index the content).

So, as you start your planning process, be sure to ask yourself some key questions:

- Where does the information reside today that is mission critical to my organization's success?
- Of that information set, what information should we index? (Presumably most, if not all, should be indexed.)

- How many content sources will be needed to crawl this information?
- Are there any crawl rules that will need to be established to help the content sources accurately crawl information?
- What is the schedule on which this information should be crawled? The more often the information changes relative to the urgency of that updated information appearing in the index will dictate how often the content source should be crawled.
- When should full index builds be run vs. incremental index builds?
- What search scopes will be needed to help the users commit effective queries?
- Are there any search results page modifications that we should configure?

Asking yourself questions like this will help you avoid mistakes when implementing a robust search and indexing topology. Some best practices to keep in mind include the following:

- Crawl a content source only when the target server is not being backed up or when it is not running any other resource-intensive activity. Scheduling is key here.
- Ensure that you've tested the crawls using a test server before implementing it in production. Nothing generates a help desk call more quickly than a user expecting to see a document in the result set and then not seeing it.
- Ensure that you've trained your end users well on how to execute queries, what the search scopes mean in your environment, and how to use the result set to their advantage.
- Don't crawl just everything that every user in your organization wants crawled. Build a set of criteria that can act as a business-case analysis for when new content sources get created and when they don't.
- Expand your horizons a bit and take a look at the range of information your users might need. For example, in a medical setting, don't be afraid to crawl and index medical journals or online research portals to help your staff stay up to date with their continuing education.

In larger organizations or in organizations with heavy search and indexing needs (say, 75 or 100 content sources or more), you might find that you need a full-time staff member just to manage this area. Consider your staffing needs as your content source topology grows and becomes more complex.

Summary

And this was just the overview! As you can see, search and indexing is a deep, wide technology that can provide significant value in your organization. In this chapter, you looked at the Search architecture, the many facets of search administration, and how to work and customize the Search Center and its results page.

The next chapter covers search deployment along with using Search as a feature. Much of the discussion of the Search functionality is behind you now, so it's time to move on to see how you can implement Search in your enterprise.

Chapter 17

Enterprise Search and Indexing Deployment

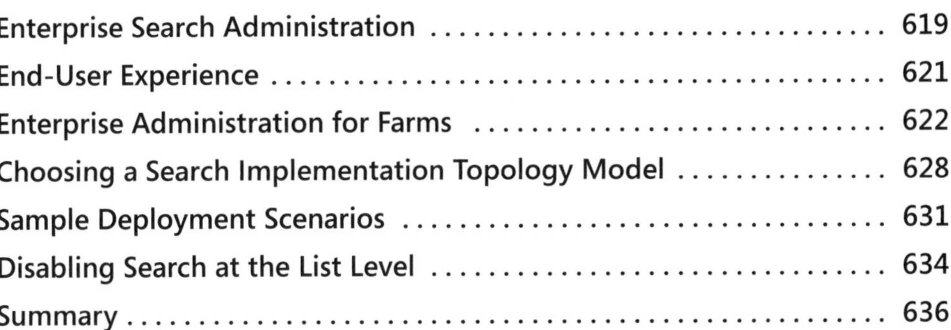

This chapter focuses on how to implement Search technologies in the enterprise, including how and when to scale out to more index servers, query servers, or both. The chapter will also cover the broader aspects of Search management across the enterprise. We'll look at the Search topology concepts, as well as three different (and hopefully common) scenarios. You'll also learn about the administrative aspects of Search at the farm level. The content of this chapter assumes you've read through the previous chapter, Chapter 16, "Enterprise Search and Indexing Architecture and Administration," and that you understand the search concepts and terms presented there.

Enterprise Search Administration

From a planning and training perspective, it is important to note that there are actually three levels of search administration:

- **Farm Level** Farm administrators will manage these elements:
    - Proxy settings
    - Time-out settings
    - SSL configurations
    - Crawler impact tules

  - Enabling or disabling services on one or more servers
  - Creation of new Shared Services Providers (SSPs) and configuring SSP-wide settings
- **SSP Level** SSP administrators will configure a plethora of settings, including the following:
  - Content sources
  - Crawl rules
  - Approved file types
  - Global search scopes
  - Click-distance settings
  - URL removals
  - Default content access account
  - Monitor gatherer and error logs
  - Install IFilters and protocol handlers
  - Create custom thesaurus
  - Monitor feedback and user activities
  - Create keywords and Best Bets
- **Site Collection Level** Site collection administrations will be able to do the following:
  - Display global search scopes in the site's interface
  - Create new search scopes for the site
  - Create, approve, and delete keywords and Best Bets
  - Create and display search scope groups for the search, advanced search, and site directories drop-down lists

Search technologies in Microsoft Office SharePoint Server 2007 have a distributed administrative architecture, requiring enterprise architects, Office SharePoint Server 2007 administrators, and site collection administrators to coordinate their plans and work together to deliver a solid, robust search solution to the users in the organization.

You'll want to seriously consider additional training for your site collection administrators when it comes to managing the search scopes at the site collection level. In addition, you will get questions regarding who is supposed to manage the Shared Services Provider

(SSP). It is recommended that an unusually technically oriented end-user manage an SSP, so best practice in most cases is that SSP administration should be executed by the SharePoint Server 2007 administrator.

End-User Experience

Sometimes, SharePoint Server 2007 administrators become lost in the details of implementing Search technologies and overlook the end users who interact and experience with the technologies administrators deploy. It is easy to forget that what you do at the server end has an impact on end users. And since first impressions tend to be lasting, it's important to ensure that you configure and deploy an impressive search technology right off the bat for end users.

There are a number of ways in which end users experience Search technologies:

- The Search box appears on every portal site page, with the exception of properties and settings pages. This includes InfoPath and Project Web Access pages. The Search scope drop-down list contains all the site-level and shared scopes that are needed for the entire site collection. As administrators, you have an impact on this part of the user experience by the number and type of search scopes you create and the content sources you crawl.
- When a user enters a query in the Search box, there is an implied OR for all queries. What this means is that, out of the box, the simple search Web Part will look for any or all of the words in the query. You can have impact on an increased positive experience by ensuring that the user has been exposed to training on how to enter proper queries.
- At the SSP level, the user's experience is affected by the content sources that you crawl as well as search scopes you create.The user can't query that which isn't in the index. As an administrator, you need to pay careful attention to the content that you crawl. You need to ensure that you crawl only that content users will want to see in their result sets. The more focused your efforts are on ensuring you only crawl content that needs to be in the index, the more helpful and focused the result sets will be for the end user. Few things are more frustrating than receiving result sets full of superfluous content items that match the query, but doesn't find the content for which the user is looking.
- Each Search Web Part has a link to advanced search, and the normal way to work with the Search and advanced Search Web Parts is to use the Search center. The Search center is a Search-specific area of the portal site activated by enabling the Search feature. As administrators, you can positively affect the user experience by

exposing managed properties that the users can use to focus and sharpen their query. In addition, you can help site administrators implement result set Web Part property configurations that help filter and craft the result set that end users see.

- The ability to find people or discussions in special search tabs is built in, meaning that site administrators do not need to go through the steps to configure a special tab just to find people in the Search center. As administrators, you can help users to have a more positive experience by teaching them how to use the people-finding technologies in the Search center and help them understand how the Knowledge Network features are connected.
- Site owners can create new types of searches using finder tabs/search tabs Web Parts using specific relevant properties that are configured in the Web Part's properties. In addition, site owners can customize the location and appearance of search results for customized needs. In this area, you can add value by training site owners how to configure the search Web Parts and the result set Web Parts, as well as helping them configure customized result set pages.
- With the Advanced search Web Parts, users can use additional logic for their queries, such as NOT or OR. In addition, users can select multiple-scope searches, execute language-restricted searches, and search by both content type and property, within a specified date range. Once again, education and training is the key to adding value for end users. You should teach them how to execute queries and how to use the content types for properties that you have exposed to their advantage when creating a query.

As you can see, in this version, many important search and query features are exposed to the end user. It is important to educate users if they will be using many of the features that are available to them.

Enterprise Administration for Farms

This section covers some of the Central Administration links that deal with administrating Search at the farm level. Within Central Administration, on the Application Management page, there is a single link, Manage Search Service, to manage farm-wide settings for Search. When you click this link, you're presented with the page shown in Figure 17-1.

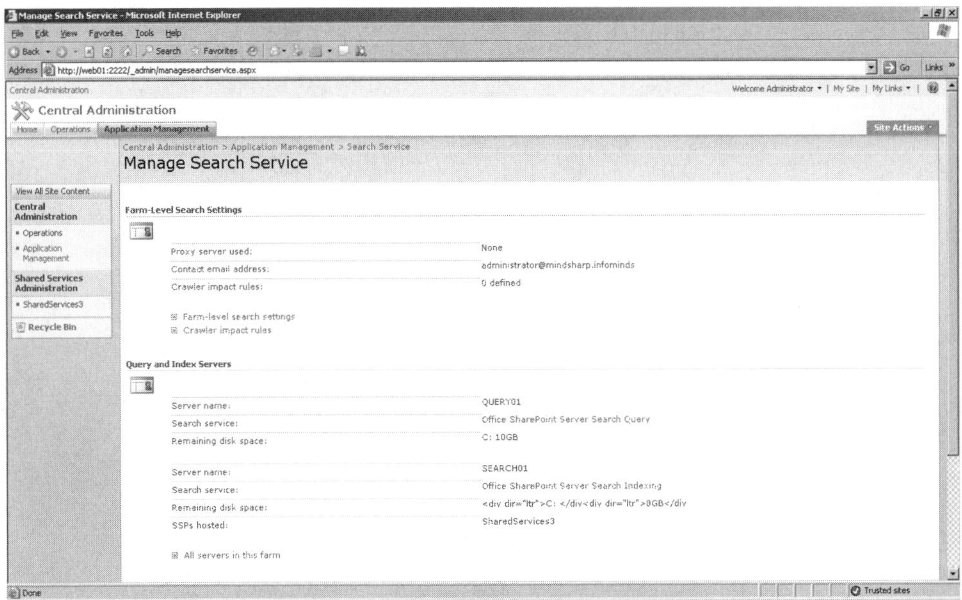

Figure 17-1 Upper portion of the Manage Search Service page

You'll note that on this page, there are three main sections:

- Farm-Level Search Settings
- Query And Index Servers
- Shared Services Providers With Search Enabled (not shown in Figure 17-1)

Let's discuss each section individually.

Farm-Level Search Settings

In the Farm-Level Search Settings section, you'll see two links. The first link, Farm-Level Search Settings, takes you to the Manage Farm-Level Search Settings page. (See Figure 17-2.) On this page, you can configure four elements. First, you can configure the the Search contact e-mail address. This account should be an active account that is checked regularly and has farm-wide permissions to make configuration changes for all search settings in the farm.

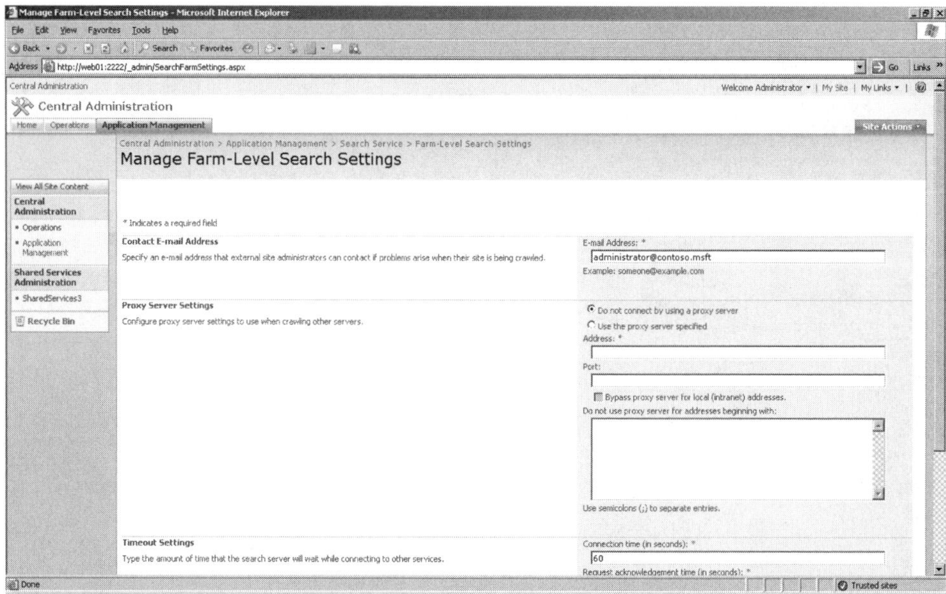

Figure 17-2 Upper portion of the Manage Farm-Level Search Settings page

The second configuration element is the proxy server settings you want search to use. Note that because this is a farm-wide setting, it will affect all SSPs in your farm and any child farms that are consuming shared services from your farm. Note also that because the Web front-end (WFE) servers actually crawl and index the content sources on behalf of the Indexing server, the WFE servers need to be on the "inside" part of your LAN and configured to connect out through your proxy server if you choose to enable proxy services.

The third configuration element of this page allows you to configure the Connection Timeout settings. The defaults are 60 seconds for both connecting to a content source and waiting for an acknowledgment from the target server. You can adjust these settings as necessary.

The fourth configuration element of this page allows you to configure the Secure Sockets Layer (SSL) Certificate Warning element. When this option is selected, the crawler will ignore SSL certificate warnings and continue crawling the content source over SSL. Best practice in most environments is to select this check box.

The second link in the Farm-Level Search Settings section on the Manage Search Service page is the Crawler Impact Rules link. This link will take you to the Crawler Impact Rules page. On this page, you can select to Add A New Rule, which will help configure the throttling of the crawler.

When you click the Add Rule link, you're presented with the Add Crawler Impact Rule page. (See Figure 17-3.) This page is used to throttle the crawler on a per-site (URL namespace) basis so that it doesn't overload either the content source's server, any routing hardware between the WFE servers and the target server, or bandwidth utilization.

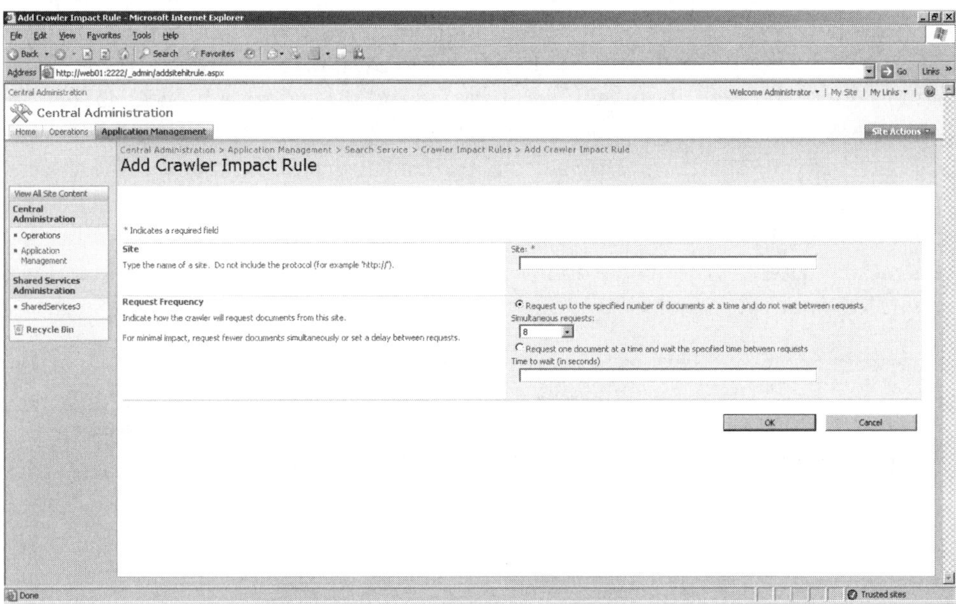

Figure 17-3 The Add Crawler Impact Rule page

Interestingly, you can enter global rules, such as ***.com** or *.*, or you can enter rules as specific as **domain.contoso.msft**. Regardless of how broad or narrow you configure your rule to be, you have one of two configuration choices for each rule. You can limit the number of documents downloaded per request (the default is eight), or you can enter a wait period between each download request (the default is zero).

Note If you're crawling a Web site, a document is considered to be an individual Web page regardless of the size of the page. By default, the downloads of documents occur pretty quickly, so if you really want to slow down the crawler, enter one second between requests. If you want to slow it down just a bit, scale back the number of documents that are downloaded per request.

The configurations on the Add Crawler Impact Rule page are directly related to the Indexer Performance settings on the Configure Office SharePoint Server Search Service Settings page and override these default settings for any give site configured in the Crawler Impact Rules. To find the Configure Office SharePoint Server Search Settings page, open Central Administration, then click the Index server link in the Farm Topology Web Part. Then click the Office SharePoint Server Search Service link. Then, on the Configure Office SharePoint Server Search Service Settings page (shown in Figure 17-4), in the Indexer Performance section, you can select Reduced, Partly Reduced, or Maximum. Select the Maximum setting if you want to crawl the content as fast as you can. Select the Partly Reduced setting if you want to slow down the crawling action some but not slow it to the slowest setting, which is the Reduced setting. Despite the interface verbiage, these settings aren't so much about SQL performance and the indexing process as they are about the SQL server's performance relative to other applications that are using the same SQL server as your SharePoint farm when Maximum is selected during the crawl process. Writing metadata to the SSP's Search Database in SQL can be an intensive process if you're crawling the content source at Maximum capacity, so slowing down the crawl process means that the write actions to the SQL database (Property Store) will slow down and be less intensive, thereby improving SQL Server performance for other applications.

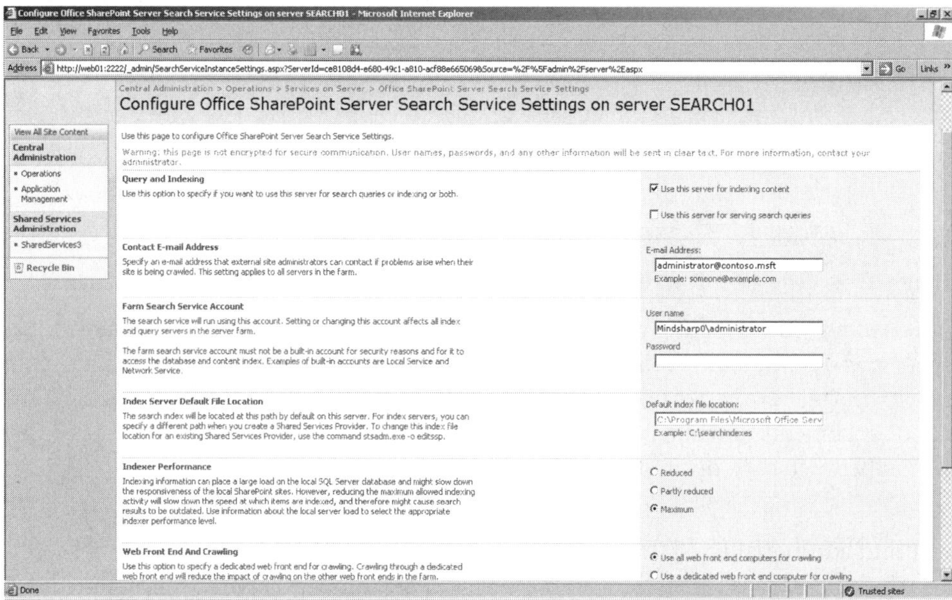

Figure 17-4 Indexer performance settings

Calculating Thread Usage for the Crawler

The Indexer Performance settings are the default value for the Search settings for the farm. The crawler impact rules override these default settings. The Indexer Performance settings are tied to the number of parallel threads that the crawler uses at any given time. Based on your hardware configuration, the crawler will calculate the number of threads it will use to crawl content. The maximum number of threads that the crawler will allocate to itself is 64, though even on quad processor servers, this will not likely be needed.

If you want the crawler to use a specific number of threads during the crawl process, you can modify the RobotThreadsNumber under the HKLM\SOFTWARE \Microsoft\Office Server\12.0\Search\Global\Gathering Manager registry key. If you see a zero "0" in this value, this means that SharePoint is using the default number of threads based on your hardware configuration. If you input a value other than zero, SharePoint will use the value that you explicitly input here.

The reason you'll increase the number of crawler threads is because content sources, especially Web sites, tend to not reply instantly, so a crawling thread is likely to be blocked on the network I/O. As you increase the number of threads, up to a point, there is a higher chance that some thread will actually get a reply back and will be able to consume the CPU by filtering and indexing some document. If the crawler is utilizing the CPUs at 100 percent, this means that the content source reply rate is quick enough to have all CPUs on the server utilized by unblocked threads. When this happens, increasing the number of threads won't improve performance.

Best practice is to ensure that your CPU utilization, during a crawl process, is utilized at the maximum capacity that you decide is acceptable to you. For example, if you want the CPU(s) on your server utilized at no more than 80 percent capacity during normal crawling operations, then ensure that you set the number of crawler threads to a level where CPU utilization is sustained at 80 percent, on average.

Query and Index Servers

On the Query And Index Servers section of the Manage Search Service page, you'll find a link named All Servers In This Farm that will open the Servers In Farm page where you will find additional links that will lead you to the Configure Office SharePoint Server Search Settings page for each server in your farm that has the Search Service started.

Shared Services Providers with Search Enabled

In the Shared Services Providers With Search Enabled section of the Manage Search Service page, you can view the status of the following Search activities for each SSP in your farm:

- Crawling status
- Items in the index
- Propagation status

Note that you cannot administer these parts of your Search deployment from here (you must go to the appropriate SSP for this), but you can use this as a type of information dashboard that reports on how your SSPs are functioning. For each SSP, you'll find a link to that SSP's administrative interface for convenient, fast access to managing the SSP.

Choosing a Search Implementation Topology Model

In this section, you'll learn about the different types of Search topologies that you can implement using SharePoint Server 2007. You'll find that your choices are both limited and expanded when compared to Microsoft SharePoint Portal Server 2003. Those of you coming from the SharePoint Portal Server 2003 platform will likely be pretty happy with the changes, overall. However, as with all systems, you'll encounter some considerations that need to be discussed and understood for your environment before you embark on a robust Search implementation.

Search is not that difficult to design in smaller environments. Many of you will find that you can implement a single Index/Query server in your farm and that will be sufficient to meet both your indexing and query needs.

However, those with larger environments (over 50 to 75 content sources multiple SSPs, or both) and those with unique security requirements will find that a more complex set of decisions need to be melded into a single whole for your farm. In this section, you'll explore those decisions, and the server roles will be the starting point for that exploration.

There are essentially three server roles that work together to form the complete Search topology and that execute the actions necessary to deliver a robust, aggregated search experience. Those three roles are the WFE server, query server, and index server. We'll start by looking at the index server role.

Role of the Index Server

The index server is responsible for executing the crawl process (which is described in Chapter 16). The index server is handed the URL from the SSP and ensures that the target location hosting the content you want to include in your index is crawled according to the rules you specify in the content source configuration and crawl rules. The index server works with the WFE server to ensure that the hosting target is crawled efficiently.

Role of the WFE Server

Most administrators have little idea of how important the WFE server is in the execution of the crawl function. When the index server initiates a crawl process for a content source, the URLs are passed to the WFE server from the index server, which is the server responsible for connecting to the location that hosts the content. It is the WFE server that actually crawls the content and retrieves both the metadata and content streams from the target hosting the content. The WFE then proxies those data streams back to the index server.

This is why you are given two choices about the incorporation of WFE servers into your Search topology. You can choose to dedicate a WFE server to be the only WFE server that the index server will use, or you can choose to have the index server use all the WFE servers in the farm. The design choice here is significant because you can assign only one index server to each SSP. The planning and design issues for a single SSP implementation are discussed briefly in the "Planning Your WFE Topology for Crawling Content Sources" sidebar.

Real World Planning Your WFE Topology for Crawling Content Sources

Both the index and WFE servers that are configured to participate in the crawling process will have a heavy load placed on them for memory, processor, and network subsystems resources during crawl times. You'll have only two basic choices:

- Route all your crawling activities through a designated, single WFE server.
- Route all your crawling activities through all the WFE servers in your farm.

One choice is not better than the other; each choice has associated pros and cons, as outlined here.

If you choose to route all the crawl processes through a single WFE server, and if you have a large number of content sources that consume a majority of a 24-hour period to complete, you should consider using a single WFE server *if* the server has the resources necessary to avoid becoming a bottleneck in the crawling process. Best practice is to adhere to the following guidelines:

- Do not allow the WFE dedicated to crawling activities to participate in being a member of any Network Load Balancing (NLB) cluster. This ensures that the WFE is fully dedicated to working with the index server to crawl the content sources, and it represents the most efficient use of this WFE server.
- Ensure there is reliable, high-speed bandwidth between the index server and the dedicated WFE server, because all the crawling processes will be routed through this WFE server.
- Configure the WFE server to have similar hardware capacity as that of the Index server since the load that is placed on the Index server will be repeated on the WFE server during the crawl process.

The upside of routing all the crawling through a single WFE server is that the other WFEs are free to service user requests for other farm services. The downside is that you now have a single point of failure in your crawling architecture, and this architecture is not scalable to a second WFE server. Remember, your choice is either a single WFE server or all WFE servers; you can't choose two out of five, or three out of eight, WFE servers for the index server to route calls through.

If you choose to route all your crawling activities through all your WFE servers, you need to understand that while those WFE servers are participating in helping the index server crawl a content source, they will also be participating in NLB clusters, helping users access data and other farm resources. The obvious, positive aspect of this configuration is that all the work (both user demand and crawling demand) is load balanced over the sum of the WFE servers in your farm. If you need additional resources, you can scale out with additional WFE servers.

How do you know whether you should devote a WFE to crawling activities rather than load balancing those activities over all your WFE servers? Here are some principles with which to work:

- If the number of content sources to crawl is increasing, user demand for other farm resources is constant, and your WFE servers are not heavily taxed by current user demand, consider load balancing your crawling activities over all your WFE servers.
- As client demand for other farm resources increases and the number of content sources remains constant, consider using a dedicated WFE server that will not participate in the NLB clusters but that can handle the crawling demand.
- If both client demand for farm resources and crawling demand for additional content sources increases, consider load balancing crawling activities across all your WFE servers and scale out by adding WFE servers to meet both needs.
- If you configure multiple SSPs in your farm, each with their own dedicated Index server, then route all crawling processes through all of your WFE servers and scale out your WFE topology if you need additional throughput. It is not recommended to route multiple Index servers through a single dedicated WFE server as this will likely turn that dedicated WFE server into a bottleneck. You could give each Index server its own dedicated WFE server, but since you're scaling out the WFE topology anyways, it seems logical to have all the Index servers use the entire set of WFE servers.

If you're deploying a multi-SSP environment, the design choices for using a single WFE server–rather than using all your WFE servers–for crawling activities becomes more complex. The complexity comes from the interplay of having multiple SSPs that might or might not crawl overlapping content and whose crawl schedules might or might not be aggressive. The way to address all this is to start by looking at what is the best content to crawl for each SSP, and then determine how much, if any, overlap there might be between the SSPs. Ideally, you'll have no overlap, but if there is overlap, you'll need to coordinate crawl schedules between the two SSPs.

For example, assume you have an SSP for your research division and another SSP for your sales and marketing division. Both divisions are likely to be interested in some common content, such as the corporate intranet site. To ensure that you don't overload the server (or servers) hosting the corporate intranet site, best practice is to stagger the crawl schedules of both SSPs so that they aren't crawling the intranet site at the same time.

Role of the Query Server

The query server fields user queries for the index. Users cannot query across multiple indexes (SSPs), so it is important to ensure that your users understand what content their SSP is crawling and that they have a way to communicate back to you other sources of content they would like crawled and included in the index.

Users can query the index by navigating to the Search center in the portal or by using the simple search Web Part to execute queries across their team sites. In fact, any time they are presented with a search Web Part, they are given the opportunity to query the index of the SSP that the Web application is associated with.

Role of the Database Server

The search database is held on the file system of the index and query servers in the path you specify when the SSP is created. The metadata is held in the SQL database (named *Search Database* in the interface) for the SSP. Unlike it was in SharePoint Portal Server 2003, the index is no longer associated with a portal; it is created and managed by the SSP.

Sample Deployment Scenarios

This section provides an overview of the various ways you can deploy Search technologies in your environment. These examples are merely illustrations of what you *can* do. Because there is no enforced, prescribed server matrix as in SharePoint Portal Server 2003, your design becomes both more simple and more complex. In this section, you'll see how this works in the various scenarios presented.

Collaboration Sites

The simplest deployment option is a Windows SharePoint Services 3.0-only deployment. This deployment is illustrated in Figure 17-5. Note that there is at least one, and perhaps more, WFE servers that offer NLB access to the content in the SQL databases. However, because a Windows SharePoint Services 3.0-only implementation cannot crawl any content outside the farm deployment, and because it lacks many of the aggregation and scoping features that ship with SharePoint Server 2007, you'll likely need only one server to crawl and index content.

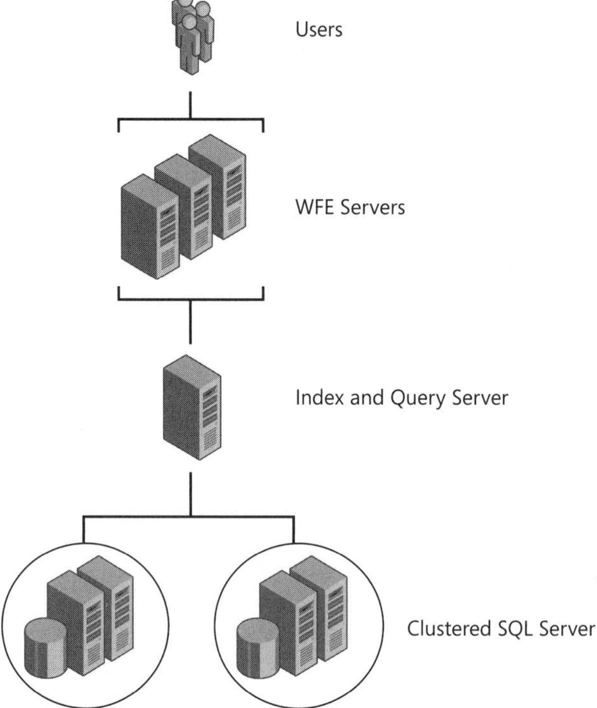

Figure 17-5 A Windows SharePoint Services 3.0–only search implementation

Enterprise Portal Deployments

There are different configurations that you can consider, but all can be reduced to two simple role combinations:

- Index and query roles on one server
- Index on one server, query on another server

Remember, the index role is the role that crawls content. The query role is the roles that executes user queries against the search database. You can run both of these roles on the same server, or you can split them onto different servers.

In a single SSP environment, this is certainly not difficult to design and deploy. Either install one server as an index/query server or install two servers—one as the index server and the other as the query server (assuming one SSP). The complexity occurs when you have multiple SSPs. If you have several SSPs, your server-to-role possibilities increase as the number of SSPs in your deployment increases. For example, if you have two SSPs, you can deploy any of the following combinations (and this is not an exhaustive list):

- Both roles for both SSPs on one server
- The query role for both SSPs on one server, and each indexing role for each SSP on another server
- The query role for both SSPs on one server, and each indexing role for each SSP on an individual server

Figure 17-6 illustrates two SSPs, each with their own index server and two query servers working together to field client requests for indexed content.

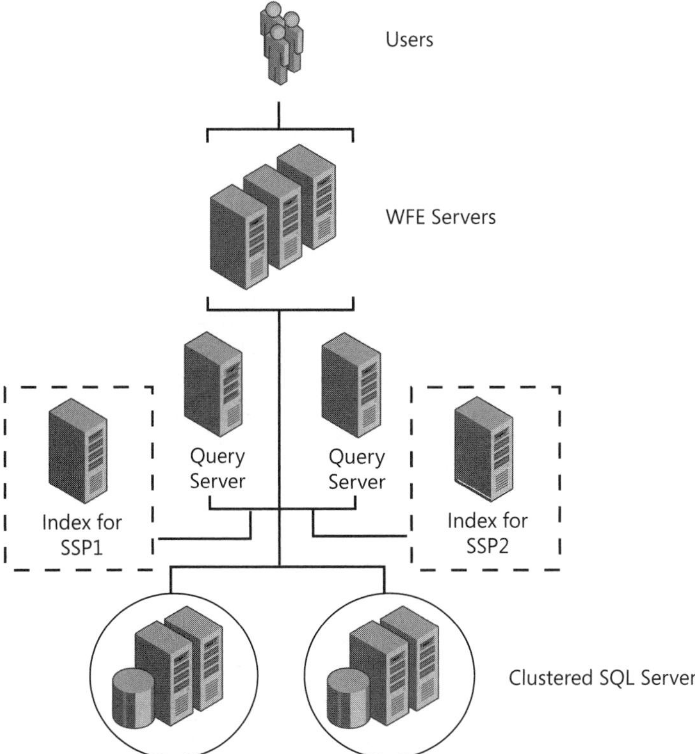

Figure 17-6 Multi-SSP, multi-server illustration

Note that the query role, unlike the indexing role, is not assignable to an SSP. So your query servers will handle all user search queries and will automatically know to which SSP to route the query. Because indexing and query demand will likely *not* be proportional or related (statistically speaking), you'll need to ensure that you have enough query servers to service peak demand for user queries. But don't worry about trying to ensure that you have one query server per SSP or any other type of query server-to-SSP mapping. That is not an issue in this version of SharePoint Server 2007.

Internet-Facing Site

Depending on the purpose of the Internet-facing site, you might find yourself offering search services to an undefined set of users (generically referred to here as the "Internet") or a predefined set of users who are known to you (generically referred to here as the "extranet").

You can certainly deploy farm that accepts requests from your intranet, extranet, and Internet zones. But in many deployments, the index that intranet users search will be different and distinct from the index that extranet or Internet users search. For Internet-facing sites, your concern is much more about index isolation–ensuring the content that Internet users can search does not include sensitive or protected information that your intranet users might be able to search.

The number of servers you'll need and their role assignment will become more clear to you as you work out the logical SSP and index topology for your overall environment. In most cases where there are extranet and Intranet users, you'll find yourself designing a multi-SSP topology. But don't automatically assume that you'll need one server per SSP. The number of servers you'll need is not related to the SSP topology as much as it is related to your overall crawling schedules for all of your SSPs and the number of user queries against all the SSP indexes combined. You'll need to ensure that you're monitoring your query and index servers to ensure they have sufficient resources to meet peak demand for your environment.

Disabling Search at the List Level

There might be times when the information that is held in a list is too sensitive to be included in the index. If the wrong persons were to find this information, the consequences would be too costly. Because of this, Microsoft has given the end-users the ability to remove a list from the index so that content items in the list are not indexed and thus, cannot appear in any result set. The end user can remove individual lists from the SSP's index by simply turning off indexing for that list. Users will not need to do this if their sole motivation is to ensure that the wrong people don't see the list's information in their result set. Users can turn off indexing for compliance reasons or because the information in the list is of such a sensitive nature that they don't want to take the chance that incorrectly secured information becomes available to the wrong users.

To disable searching on a list, navigate to the list's Settings, then to Advanced Settings, and then scroll down to the bottom of the page. There you'll find (as shown in Figure 17-7) that there is an Allow Items From This List To Appear In Search Results? option. Your site administrators will be able to make this selection without notifying you or your SharePoint team of their decision.

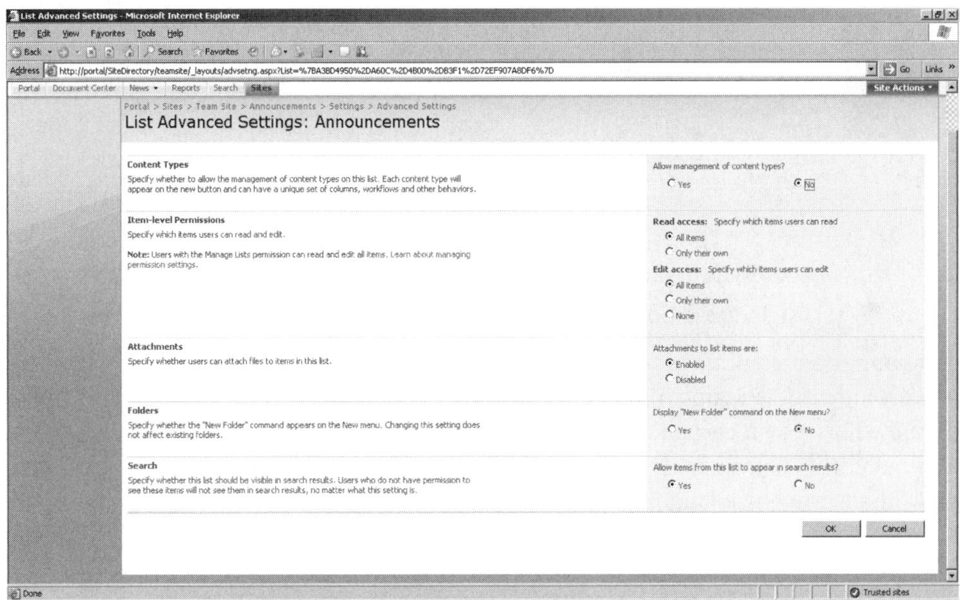

Figure 17-7 Disabling searching on a list

You can also select metadata to be indexed as part of a list to help build list views faster for large lists. This setting can be configured by entering the list's properties and then scolling down the page to the Columns section. In this section, you'll see a link called Indexed Columns (as shown in Figure 17-8). When you click this link, you're presented with a page to select the columns that you want to pre-index.

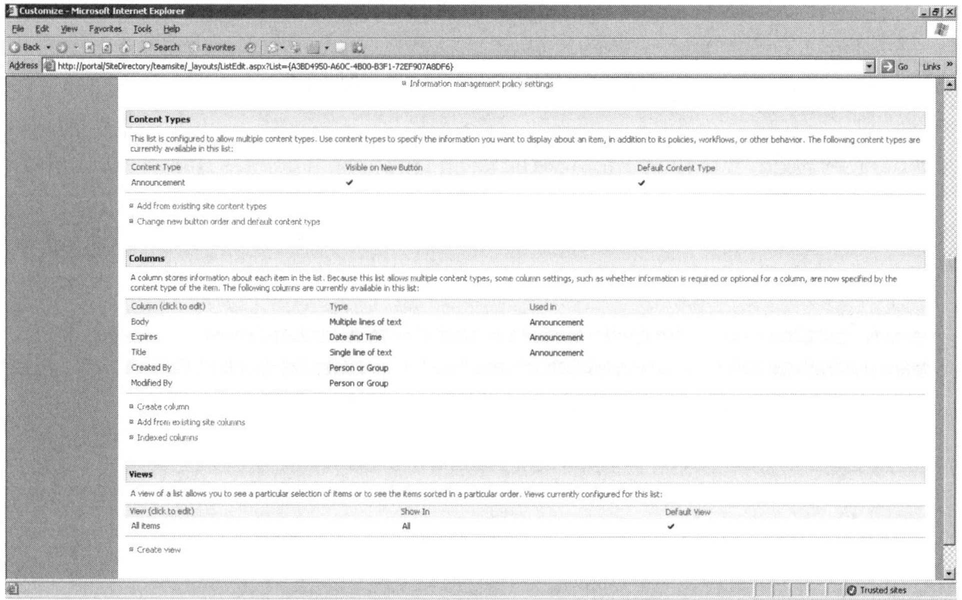

Figure 17-8 The Indexed Columns link

Indexing these columns does not make the content available because that content is already indexed by Search. What it does do is allow customized views that are configured to show or filter on certain columns to be rendered more quickly instead of having to enumerate, filter, or do both to the column's contents on the fly when the user clicks the view link in the quick launch pane.

Summary

In this chapter, you learned how to implement index and query servers at the farm level and how to make design choices based on whether you are using a dedicated WFE server or all the WFE servers to help proxy the crawl acitivities to the content sources.

You also explored the Indexer Performance choices and how to plan capacity for these choices. Finally, you considered implementing the server roles by reviewing three common scenarios.

Chapter 18

Administrating Shared Services Providers

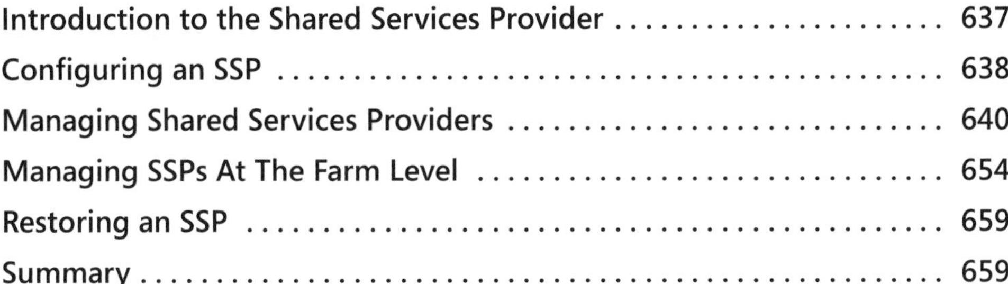

This chapter covers the configuration and management of the Shared Services Provider (SSP). First, you'll learn about management of a single SSP, and then you'll learn about creating additional SSPs and consider the reasons for using additional SSPs and implementations in your enterprise.

Introduction to the Shared Services Provider

An SSP is designed to provide a group of services that can be consumed or used by the associated Microsoft Office SharePoint Server 2007 sites created in the same farm. These services are centrally managed and highly configurable so that administrators can choose which component of each service they want to provide to all associated sites. If your design model requires providing different configurations of the same component to separate groups of users, additional SSPs can be created in the same farm to offer those services. Every time a new Web application is created in the farm, it can be associated with one of the SSPs. It will then consume the services offered, such as Audiences, Search, or a Profile database.

Planning For most companies, a single SSP should be sufficient, and a second SSP should be created only if the design and planning of the SharePoint implementation such as My Sites, Audiences, Profiles, and Search has been put into place first.

For larger companies with more than one farm, shared services can also be provided and consumed between farms. This functionality is provided by Inter-Farm Shared Services (IFSS) and enables companies to create aggregated information provided by the SSP component across an enterprise. This arrangement is similar in concept to how SharePoint Portal Server 2003 implemented shared services between farms.

An SSP also has its own databases that are used for storing the data of the services that it provides. The databases that are created by default for an SSP are as follows:

- A search database
- A service-specific database that holds information for the provided services. Some of the core data that is held by the SSP service-specific data includes the following:
  - User information imported from Active Directory or another directory
  - Audience information
  - Security information for access rights to the SSP
  - Business Data Catalog (BDC) data
  - Search Query data

The SSP itself requires a Web application and application pool that are hosted by Microsoft Internet Information Services (IIS). This supplies the resources and stability required for the services provided.

Note Dedicating a Web application and application pool for each SSP provides stability and resilience for the services offered by that SSP. You can also create IIS Web Gardens by adding IIS worker processes to the application pool for further reliability. Be aware, however, that doing this will require additional memory resources, so be sure you have enough resources to support your isolation and stability needs.

Configuring an SSP

Over time, you might need to alter the settings of your SSP, such as changing the credentials of the configured SSP service account because you want to change the password. To administer the properties of an SSP, you must first navigate to it. Follow these steps to access the page:

1. Launch SharePoint 3.0 Central Administration from the Administrative Tools menu.
2. Click the Application Management tab.

3. In the Office SharePoint Server Shared Services section, click Create Or Configure This Farm's Shared Services.
4. Hover your mouse over the SSP name so that the down arrow appears to the right of the SSP name. Click the down arrow, and from the drop-down menu, select Edit Properties, as shown in Figure 18-1.

Figure 18-1 Editing the properties of shared services

From this properties screen, you can make the configuration change to the SSP. The options available are described in Table 18-1. It is highly unlikely that you will need to alter any settings here once the SSP is created. However, these configurations are available if you need to change them. The page you will spend most of your time configuring is the default administrative page, and that's covered later in this chapter, in the "SSP Management" section.

Table 18-1 The SSP Property Options

Property option	Description
SSP Name	Enables you to change the descriptive name used for the SSP. You can also see the URL hosting the SSP administrative site. This property cannot be changed, but you can get redirected to the Shared Services Administration page by clicking the URL link.
My Site Location	This is the Web Application URL that is hosting the user's My Site for this SSP. If it is changed, any existing My Site needs to be migrated to the new location. It is recommended to host the My Site on its own Web application.
SSP Service Credentials	This account is used by the SSP to run local timer service jobs and also for interserver communication with the SSP Web services.

Table 18-1 The SSP Property Options

Property option	Description
SSP Database	This property lets you view both the database server hosting the database and the name of the database it is connecting to.
Search Database	A second SSP Database is used for search metadata; this option lets you view the location for the database server and the name of the database it uses.
Index Server	An SSP can use one index server, and all associated Web applications and content sources configured within this SSP are crawled by this Index Server. If you select a different index server, the index file is moved to the new index server. Make sure the new index server has sufficient space to hold the index file.
SSL For Web Services	You can enable SSL connections to the SSP Web Service by installing a certificate on each IIS Server that hosts an SSP administrative site.
Process Accounts With Access To This SSP	You can delegate additional access control rights to the SSP for users and Web applications by adding the domain account here. The usernames need to be in the format of *Domainname \Username*.

Managing Shared Services Providers

Because each SSP that you create provides its own services and you can create multiple SSPs in a farm, a Central Administration User Interface (UI) page exists so that you can configure these services on a per-SSP basis and also on a farm level for all SSPs. The SSP Management Interface is divided into two areas:

- SSP management
- Farm-level management of all SSPs

The remainder of this section covers the SSP management pages while the section following this one titled "Managing SSPs at the Farm Level" explains farm-level management of SSPs in a large enterprise environment.

The SSP management page has several key sections that enable you to easily configure and manage the services provided by the SSP. Although these components do not need to be configured prior to creating the new Web applications and sites associated with this SSP, you should configure any services that are to be consumed beforehand. As new Web applications are then associated with a particular SSP, they show up under the SSP name in the Manage This Farm's Shared Services administration page. To access the Manage This Farm's Shared Services page, follow the steps outlined earlier in the section for configuring an SSP. All Web applications listed under that SSP are consuming the services that the SSP provides. Figure 18-2 shows an example of this.

Figure 18-2 Viewing the associated Web applications

> **Note** As you can see from the list of associated Web applications in Figure 18-2, you must be sure to use well-planned naming conventions to easily distinguish one Web application from another. See Chapter 7, "Application Management and Configuration," for more information on creating Web applications.

Web applications are listed under the Default SSP even if they have not yet been extended with a site collection or mapped to another Web application. To reach the SSP administration page, click the name of the SSP you want to manage from the Manage This Farm's Shared Services page. Follow the steps outlined earlier in the section for configuring an SSP to get to this page. You will then be taken to the Shared Services Administration Home page, shown in Figure 18-3.

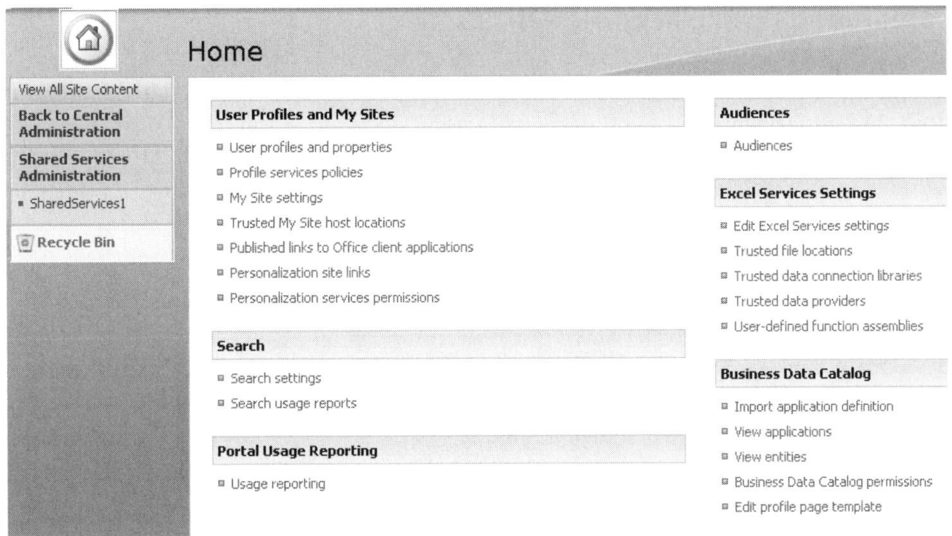

Figure 18-3 Shared Services Administration Home page

Note For quicker access to the Shared Services Administration Home page, in Central Administration, under Shared Services Administration, click the name of the SSP in the lefthand quick launch bar.

Configuring User Profiles, Audiences, and Personal Sites Settings

In the User Profiles And My Sites section on the SSP Administration Home page, the SSP is configured to provide services that deal with personalization, such as My Site; therefore, any changes you make to the personalization settings here affect all users who consume these services from their associated Web applications.

Configuring User Profiles And Properties

By clicking this link, you are presented with options that let you manage attributes and import configurations for our users' profiles. User profiles play a key role in the way you target content and set up social networking with other colleagues that you share common attributes with. When one user searches for information on another user, the profile information is used to help return the correct results from the search.

Note Configuring and managing profiles is covered in more detail in Chapter 8, "Administrating Personalization and Portal Taxonomies."

Configuring Profile Services Policies

The Profile Services Policies link enables administrators to configure which profile attributes are available to the user, which attributes the user is allowed to edit, and which attributes are viewable by which users when they are viewing the user's public My Site page.

More Info For more information on profile policies, see Chapter 8.

Configuring My Site Settings

Because the SSP can host more than one Web application, many site collections used by the same users all have links to their My Site. For this reason, the SSP allows you to configure which server holds all personal sites for the SSP. Therefore, when a user travels between different sites, he will always be redirected to the same My Site, regardless of which Web application he is working in. The same applies to the preferred Search Center option, which allows you to configure a centralized search page that all users are redirected to when they click the search center page from a portal.

More Info See Chapter 16, "Enterprise Search and Indexing Architecture and Administration," and Chapter 17, "Enterprise Search and Indexing Deployment," for more information on search.

To configure the location for personal sites and the preferred Search Center, click My Site Settings under the User Profiles And My Sites section and type the URL and port number for the Web application to host the My Sites in the Personal Site Services section.

If you do not want the URL of the My Site to include Personal, you can change the location name here. By default, the URL is set Personal so that a user's My Site address looks something like http://corpportal/personal/fred. However, you can change it by typing a new Personal Site location on the My Site settings page.

Important Any existing My Sites already created with the previous My Site location will not be affected and will continue to use the previous location. When the Web application that hosts My Sites is associated with a different SSP, the users profile and social networking information such as Colleagues and Site memberships will be generated by the new SSP. If you want to host multiple SSPs but have a centralized My Site Web application for all users, you can use Trusted My Site locations as described later in this chapter.

For enterprises that need to control the way multiple users with the same name are handled, there are three naming convention options that you can use to determine the actual name of the My Site associated with an individual:

- **User Name Only** This option does not resolve conflicting usernames.
- **User Name With Conflict Resolution** If two users exist with the same name in two different domains, the user name will appear after the domain name–for example, Contoso_fred.
- **Domain And User Name** The user's domain always comes before her domain name to avoid any potential conflict.

Therefore, if a company has more than one user named Fred across two domains—say one in the U.S. and one in the U.K.—instead of using the default URL http://corpportal/personal/fred, the company can use http://corpportal/personal/UK_fred. This approach is useful for avoiding name conflicts in large organizations. To alter naming conventions, click the My Site Settings link in the User Profiles And My Sites section, and select a naming format in the resulting dialog box (shown in Figure 18-4).

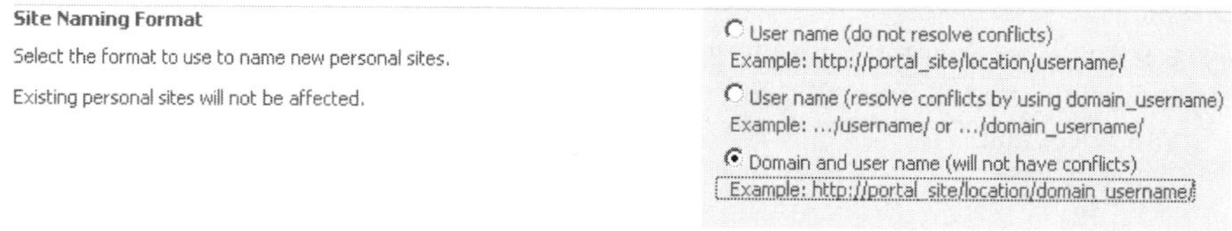

Site Naming Format

Select the format to use to name new personal sites.

Existing personal sites will not be affected.

- User name (do not resolve conflicts) Example: http://portal_site/location/username/
- User name (resolve conflicts by using domain_username) Example: .../username/ or .../domain_username/
- Domain and user name (will not have conflicts) Example: http://portal_site/location/domain_username/

Figure 18-4 Configuring a My Site naming format

If your organization also has users that use different language sets, select the option to allow users to choose their personal language. The language packs required must be installed on the server that hosts the users' My Sites. (See Chapter 4, "Multilingual Planning, Deployment, and Maintenance," for more information on how to install and manage language packs in Office SharePoint Server 2007.) To enable My Sites to support additional languages, select the Allow User To Choose The Language Of Their Personal Site check box in the Language Options section on the My Site Settings page.

From the My Site Settings page, you can also enable all personal features for remote users, which allows users whose My Site is located on a remote server to have access to adding and configuring specific My Site features, such as My Colleagues and My Links. Remote users can do this even if their My Site is hosted on a server at the end of a wide area network (WAN) link in a remote office. To enable My Sites to support global deployments, select the Enable All Personal Features For Remote My Site Users check box in the Multiple Deployments section on the My Site Settings page.

> **Note** If you are going to enable multiple My Site deployments to access all personal features, it is recommend that you replicate the profile information between the servers hosting the My Sites in the organization.

The final option on the My Site settings page provides you with the ability to change which users get read access to the public view of everyone's My Site. By default, the Windows authenticated users group is granted read access to every user's public My Site page. To change this group or add more groups, add the group name followed by a semicolon and then add the second group name. Names should be added in the format of *Domainname\Groupname* or *Domainname\Username* (as shown in Figure 18-5).

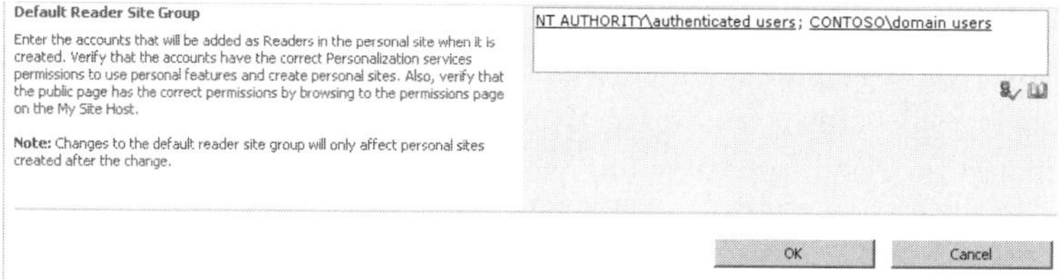

Default Reader Site Group

Enter the accounts that will be added as Readers in the personal site when it is created. Verify that the accounts have the correct Personalization services permissions to use personal features and create personal sites. Also, verify that the public page has the correct permissions by browsing to the permissions page on the My Site Host.

Note: Changes to the default reader site group will only affect personal sites created after the change.

NT AUTHORITY\authenticated users; CONTOSO\domain users

OK Cancel

Figure 18-5 Configuring group access to public My Site pages

After you add the group name, click the people picker lookup icon to verify the group. You can also add names by using the address book lookup icon, which will use the directory service to return local and domain groups and users. Any groups or users that are added will automatically be added to the Readers group in every user's My Site. Follow these steps to modify access to the public My Site view:

1. In the Default Reader Site Group text box, change or add the group or user by typing a name in the format of *Domainname\Groupname* or *Domainname\Username*.
2. After entering the name, click the people picker lookup icon, and then click OK.

Specifying Trusted My Site Host Locations

In a multiple SSP environment, there might be situations where users log on to sites hosted by different SSPs and from different geographic locations. In these situations, when they try to access their My Site, audiences and the URL of their correct My Site can be used to redirect them to the correct SSP that hosts their My Site as a trusted location.

Here are two scenarios in which you might want to use the Trusted My Site redirection functionality:

- **Rogue servers** To avoid rogue server URLs being used in this attribute, only URLs that are registered in the SSP properties and the Trusted My Site redirection list can be used. You can add multiple URL redirects, and to make sure a user gets the correct My Site URL you can use audiences to target the URLs. This approach ensures that no matter where the user is accessing her My Site from she is always redirected correctly.
- **Geo deployment** When companies have multiple locations hosting multiple SSPs yet still fall under a single organization, a user could be working on a site anywhere in that organization–for example, a U.S.-based project manager could be working on a project team site in Australia. When the project manager clicks on his My Site, he wants the action to take him to his My Site, which is located in his home location, and not to create a second My Site in the remote location he happens to be working in. You can also use profile replication, as mentioned earlier in this chapter, to make all the project manager's My Site features available even though he is accessing a site located in a remote office. This approach speeds up the display time for the content located on his My Site.

These are just two examples of using trusted My Site locations. To add a trusted My Site location to an SSP, follow these steps:

1. Click the name of the SSP you want to manage.
2. Click the Trusted My Site Host Locations link in the User Profiles And My Sites section.

3. On the Trusted My Site Host Locations page, click New in the list options.
4. Complete the URL field to the Web server hosting the My Sites.
5. Complete the Description field.
6. If required, add an audience and click the check names lookup icon to confirm the selection. If you prefer, you can click the directory lookup icon and find the audience via a search.
7. Click OK to add the new My Site trusted location.

Planning Where possible, add the required trusted My Site locations prior to creating a My Site. This will avoid duplicate My Sites being created unnecessarily.

Specifying Published Links To Office Client Applications

A published link is the ability to add features into a user's Microsoft Office client without the user realizing that SharePoint has added it. You target published links by audiences, and this enables SSP administrators to target office features by specific groups of users. For example, you could create a custom Microsoft Office Excel data connection and then publish this link to the Excel clients. When a user launches her Excel client on a site and goes to create a data connection, your published connection will be available to her in the available default connections. Follow these steps to add a published link to an office client:

1. Click the Published Links To Office Client Applications link in the User Profiles And My Sites section.
2. Click New on the options menu.
3. Fill in the URL field with the Web site address.
4. Enter a description.
5. Select a type for the link from the drop-down menu.
6. If required, enter an audience or look up an audience from the directory lookup icon. Click OK.

Configuring Personalization Site Links

Personalization site links enable administrators to add and target page links to audiences. Once added, each new link appears on the user's My Site Home page as an additional tab. When the user visits his My Site and clicks one of the links, it takes him to the URL of the link. Links can be any HTTP address and can point to any internal or external Web site. If when you add a new link you do not specify an audience or you choose the All Site Users audience, all users get the new tabbed link. See Figure 18-6 for an example of several personalization links as they appear on a user's My Site.

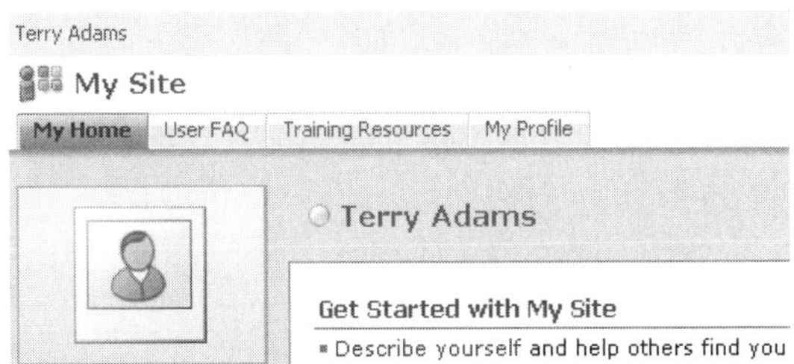

Figure 18-6 My Site showing additional tabbed links

Configuring Personalization Services Permissions

By default, all authenticated users have the ability to create personal sites and use personal features. However, this is not always practical, and there might be times when users of a particular SSP are required to have only restricted access to My Site or not have any access at all. By changing the permissions on this page, you are able to control this access and usage policy on My Site on a per-SSP basis.

Real World **Modifying Users' SSP Rights**

In some situations, companies might create more than one SSP—for example, to host a highly secure set of profiles and unique search index for a research and development department. When users work in sites associated with this SSP, you do not want any My Sites to be created or any personal features to be enabled. Also, because this is a highly restrictive group of sites, you also want to restrict the groups of users who are able to even have rights on the SSP. To fulfill this requirement, follow these steps:

1. Click the name of the SSP hosting the services you want to restrict.
2. Click the Personalization Services Permissions link in the User Profiles And My Sites section.
3. Select the check box for the NT AUTHORITY\Authenticated Users in the User/Group column, and click Remove Selected Users from the options bar.
4. Click Add Users/Groups on the options bar
5. Type the name of the security group or use the address book lookup icon to add the user group you want to give rights for to the SSP. When adding a domain group, use the format *Domainname\Groupname*.
6. Select the check boxes for the rights you want to give the users in the Choose Permissions section.
7. Click Save.

8. Add or remove additional users or groups as required.

You have now restricted the rights of users to perform certain tasks on the restricted SSP, yet the users still have all the additional rights on the SSP that is providing the services for users' everyday work.

Configuring Search Settings

When creating a new SSP, you must configure one server to provide the Index file for the SSP. This enables you to have all Web applications associated with this SSP consume the search services provided. In SharePoint Portal 2003, there was only one centrally configured search service in SharePoint Cap Central Administration. In SharePoint Server 2007, however, you can have a different set of configured search parameters on a per-SSP basis. For example, you could have one SSP that hosts all sites for company A and have another SSP that hosts all sites for company B. When users search for content in their sites, content will be returned only from their own sites associated with their SSP. You can change the Index server and file that an SSP uses, and you can do this in the SSP properties, as mentioned earlier in this chapter and described in Table 18-1. In the SSP, there are three settings for configuration:

- Search Settings
- Search Result Removal
- Search Usage Reports

More Info For more detailed information on configuring and implementing search, see Chapters 16 and 17.

Configuring Portal Usage Reporting Settings

Portal usage reporting is a way to control usage report processing across all Web applications associated with the SSP. Once it is enabled or disabled, portal usage reporting affects all sites that belong to those Web applications. There are two options available here to enable or disable, as listed in Table 18-3.

Table 18-2 SSP Usage Reporting Options

Reporting option	Description
Processing Settings	By default, this setting is disabled and needs to be enabled if you want to allow site administrators to run advanced usage reporting of how their site is being used. Once this option is enabled, a daily log is created that site administrators can access via the Site Settings menu on their site page. Because this is an SSP-wide change, all site administrators have access to the advanced usage reports.
Search Query Logging	By default, this setting is enabled and provides administrators and content managers with the ability to see search query reports based on how users have been using search queries. This enables administrators to see items such as the most commonly found word by query or, alternatively, which word has been queried the most but with no results. By using these reports, administrators and content managers can alter the way metadata is returned or targeted for certain keywords and phrases to avoid zero results issues for the content that exists in the index.

If a site administrator wants to get usage analysis reports, he must enable the processing settings, which are disabled by default. (See Figure 18-7.)

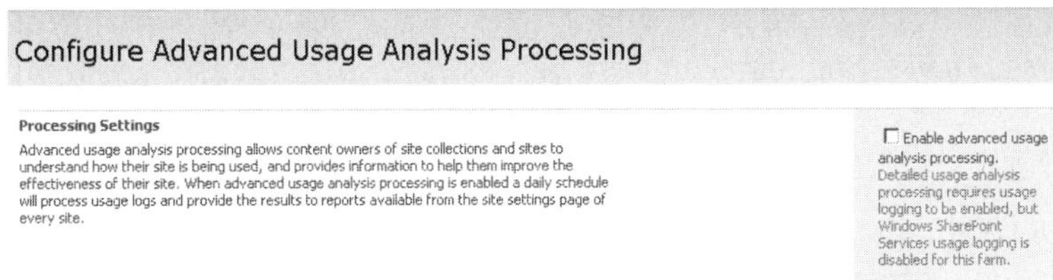

Figure 18-7 Configuring advanced usage analysis processing

If an administrator of a site tries to view the usage reports for the site and this functionality has not been enabled, or the first set of logs have not yet been generated (possibly due to a schedule not being configured), the administrator gets a generic error message, as shown in Figure 18-8.

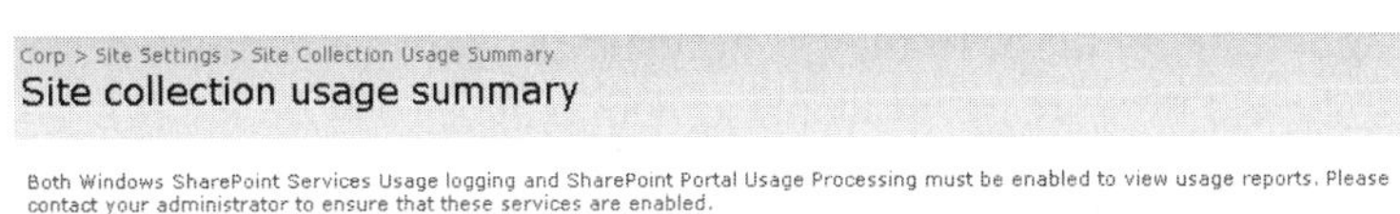

Figure 18-8 Site usage report, showing a report has not run

To enable the processing settings, follow these steps:

1. Click the name of the SSP you want to manage.
2. Click Usage Reporting in the Portal Usage Reporting section.

3. Select the Enable Advanced Usage Analysis Processing check box in the Processing Settings section, and click OK

Once the processing settings are enabled, the usage reports are available to every site once the logs have been processed. To view the reports, the site administrator can go to the Site Settings menu on his site via the Site Usage Data option. For site collection administrators, there is also a summary report for usage across all sites in the site collection. To view this report, administrators use the Site Collection Usage Summary link in the Site Collection Administration page in the top-level site.

Note Before you enable the processing settings, make sure you have first enabled the Windows SharePoint Services Usage Reporting option. To do this, in Central Administration, on the Operations page, select the Usage Analysis Processing check box in the Logging And Reporting section. When both Usage Analysis Processing and Processing Settings have been enabled, you can go to the site and view the usage reports.

Configuring Audiences Settings

Audiences is a very powerful feature of SharePoint Server 2007. It gives users the ability to target content to other users based on a common grouping, such as by department, region, or function. An *Audience* in SharePoint can be a rules-based audience, a distribution list from Active Directory, or a Windows SharePoint Services Group.

A *rules-based audience* is a group of users who meet a specific set of rules set by the audience configuration for a specific SSP in Central Administration. These rules can be based on a role-based selection process, such as "reports under," or an attribute-based selection, such as belonging to a certain department. For the audience rule to include attributes, the attributes themselves must exist in the profile database for this SSP and also include content. These attributes are normally configured in the Lightweight Directory Access Protocol (LDAP) directory first, such as an Active Directory attribute. Then, when the properties of the users from Active Directory are imported into the profile database, the matching attribute in the profile database is automatically populated. (See Chapter 8 for more information on importing profile attributes.) Alternatively, you can create your own fields in the profile database if they are not available in Active Directory.

Using Audiences to Target Content

Suppose that you have a page on a team site and you want to target certain information on that team site to two different groups of users. Some of the information is relevant to the marketing team, some information is relevant to the accounts team, and some information is relevant to both teams. In Active Directory, make sure that the attribute called

Department in the user property is correctly filled in for each user. You might need to speak with the Active Directory administrator for more information on configuring user object property fields. When the SharePoint Profile database import takes place, it populates the user profile in SharePoint with the same Department field attribute of sales or accounts. Follow these steps to manually configure a profile import:

1. Click the User Profiles And Properties link in the User Profiles And My Sites section.
2. Click Configure Profile Import, and select a source, such as Current Domain. Click OK.
3. Click Start Full Import to start the enumeration process for importing the user object attributes from Active Directory. This process might take a few minutes, depending on the number of users in your Active Directory.
4. Click the refresh button to ensure the enumeration is complete and set to idle.

You can now create three audiences in SharePoint for content targeting. First we need to create an audience based on one rule, which in our example will be to include users who have the property equal to Sales, as shown in Figure 18-9. Follow these steps to create a new audience:

1. Click Audiences in the Audiences section.
2. Click Create Audience.
3. Give the audience a name, and click OK.
4. In the Operand section, select the Property button, and from the drop-down menu, select Department from the attribute fields.
5. Leave the operator set to =.
6. Type **Sales** in the Value field, and click OK.
7. In the Audience properties, click Compile Audience. Wait for the compilation to complete.
8. Click View Membership to see the user accounts imported.
9. Click the Home tab to return to the SSP Administration Home page.

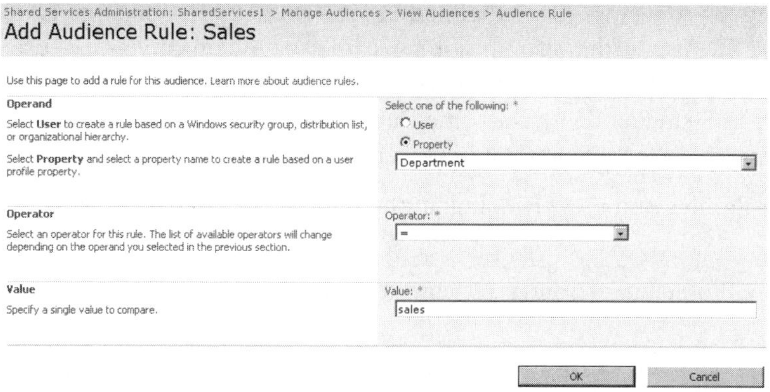

Shared Services Administration: SharedServices1 > Manage Audiences > View Audiences > Audience Rule

Add Audience Rule: Sales

Use this page to add a rule for this audience. Learn more about audience rules.

Operand

Select **User** to create a rule based on a Windows security group, distribution list, or organizational hierarchy.

Select **Property** and select a property name to create a rule based on a user profile property.

Select one of the following: *

User

Property

Department

Operator

Select an operator for this rule. The list of available operators will change depending on the operand you selected in the previous section.

Operator: *

=

Value

Specify a single value to compare.

Value: *

sales

OK Cancel

Figure 18-9 Creating a new rules-based audience

You can now create another rule with the property based on accounts, and you can then create a third audience that has two rules to include both departments. To ensure that both sets of users are included in this final rule, make sure that the audience allows memberships that satisfy any of the rules rather than all of the rules, as in this scenario a user is either in sales or accounts but not both. An example of how his audience property would look can be seen in Figure 18-10.

View Audience Properties: Sales

Use this page to view and edit the properties of this audience.

Audience Properties

Name:	Sales
Description:	
Owner:	CONTOSO\charles
Create Time:	9/9/2006 8:47 PM
Update Time:	9/9/2006 8:48 PM
Compiled:	No
Number of members:	Not compiled
Membership:	Members satisfy any of the rules
Last compilation:	Not compiled
Compilation Errors:	No error

- Edit audience
- View membership
- Compile audience

Audience Rules

Click on audience rules to edit them. Learn more about managing audience rules.

Operand	Operator	Value
Department	=	sales
Department	=	Accounts

Figure 18-10 Using multiple rules in a single audience

Users can now target content on a page, and the users will see only what is targeted at them through their audience membership. You can target Web Parts or individual list items, such as discussion threads, at audiences. To enable a discussion list, for example, to support list item audience targeting, follow these steps:

1. Go to the Home page of a team site.
2. Click the default Team Discussion list on the lefthand quick launch bar.
3. Click Settings to open the settings menu, and then select List Settings.
4. Click Audience Targeting Settings in the General settings section.
5. Select the Enable Audience Targeting check box to enable audience targeting, and then click OK.
6. Return to the discussion list, and click New to create a new discussion list entry.
7. Complete the Subject field and, optionally, add some body text.
8. In the optional Target Audiences field type "Sales," and then click the check names icon to the right of the field.
9. The "Sales" audience should now be underlined in the field as a recognized audience name. Click OK.

You have now targeted a specific list item at the sales audience, and any user who is not in the sales audience will not see any items targeted specifically at sales users. See Chapter 29, "Microsoft Office SharePoint Server 2007 Web Parts," for more information on configuring Web Parts.

Best Practices Always configure your audience compilation schedule to occur after your profile import schedule. That way the latest user profile changes will be taken into account when the audience membership is recompiled.

Configuring Excel Services Settings

Each SSP has the ability to host its own Excel Services environment. Excel Services allows Excel workbooks to be loaded, calculated, and rendered on the server and then presented to users via a Web page. The user can then view the rendered information and even update certain cells without the need for the users desktop to have the Microsoft Excel client installed locally. There are five configurable options for Excel Services:

- Edit Excel Services Settings
- Trusted File Locations
- Trusted Data Connections Library

- Trusted Data Providers
- User-Defined Functions

You do not need to configure all the options just listed. However, until you have added certain core requirements—such as a trusted file location or a trusted data connection library—users will not be able to use the features, such as publishing an Excel workbook to the Excel server.

More Info For more information on configuring and managing these services, see Chapter 20, "Excel Services and Building Business Intelligence Solutions."

Configuring Business Data Catalog Settings

The Business Data Catalog (BDC), a new feature in SharePoint Server 2007, is aimed at providing you the ability to connect various back-end business applications—such as databases, SAP, and Siebel—into SharePoint with minimal coding effort. Many connections are built into SharePoint Server 2007 with the XML code. Once the catalog is configured, the data can be used by Business Data Web Parts, SharePoint Lists, Search, Profiles, and additional Custom Solutions. Once a connection is configured, users can easily add the configured Web Parts, for example, onto their pages and start using the connection to the back-end system.

More Info For more detailed information on configuring and managing the BDC, see Chapter 12, "Administrating Data Connections."

Managing SSPs at the Farm Level

For most enterprise environments, a single SSP is sufficient. However, an enterprise occasionally will benefit from having a second SSP. An SSP provides a resource of services—such as Profiles, Search, Audiences, and the Business Data Catalog—for sites to consume. If you create a new SSP, all these configured services are lost to any Web applications and sites associated with the new SSP. That can, however, be just what is required to satisfy a business need. This section covers the following topics related to SSP in an enterprise environment:

- Creating a new SSP
- Changing Web application associations
- Granting shared services between farms

Creating a New SSP

Before you can create a new SSP, you must first create a new Web application that is not being used by other SSPs or sites. Also, it is recommended that for each Web application that is hosting an SSP, you also create a new application pool.

More Info For more information on creating Web applications and application pools, refer to Chapter 7.

This ensures that the SSP has its own worker process and memory space to run in. To create a new SSP, follow these steps:

1. Go to Central Administration.
2. Click the Application Management page.
3. Click the Create Or Configure This Farm's Shared Services link in the Office SharePoint Server Shared Services section.
4. On the Manage This Farm's Shared Services page, click New SSP on the options bar.
5. On the New Shared Services Provider page, complete the fields as described in Table 18-1.
6. Click OK to complete the process for creating the SSP.

To confirm that the new SSP has been successfully completed, return to the Manage This Farm's Shared Services page. You should see the new SSP listed under the default SSP. Notice also that no Web applications are associated with the new SSP. (See Figure 18-11.)

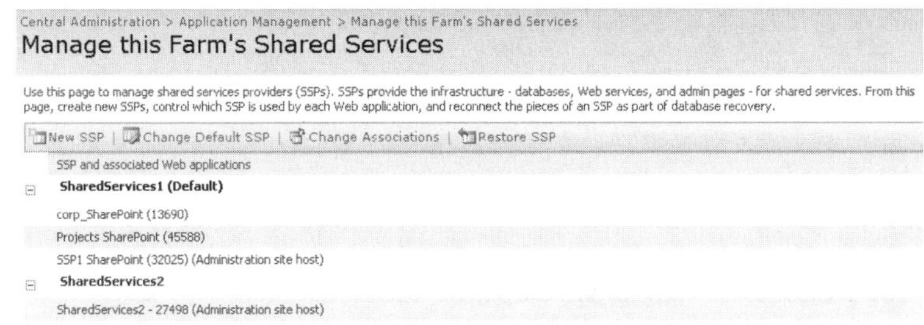

Figure 18-11 Viewing the new SSP

Note Because of limitations in system resources, it is recommended that you not create more than 20 SSPs.

Note You cannot delete the default SSP until all Web applications have been re-associated and it no longer has any Web applications associated with it. Once you have re-associated the Web applications to another SSP, click the Change Default SSP button to choose the new SSP. Then select the drop-down arrow next to the old SSP and choose Delete.

Modifying Web Application Associations

When you create a new SSP, any services that you configure on that SSP—such as search, audiences, and BDC—will be available only to Web applications that have been associated with that SSP. Therefore, all sites that are created in the Web application are only able to consume the available services configured from that SSP. When a new Web application is created, it is automatically placed in the default SSP. You can then re-associate it with any SSP.

Note A Web application can be associated with only one SSP. A single SSP has no limit to how many Web applications it can host.

A Web application can be re-associated at any time in Central Administration and, if required, multiple Web applications can be moved at one time. Once re-associated, the Web application will be displayed under the new Shared Services Provider hosting it, as shown in Figure 18-12.

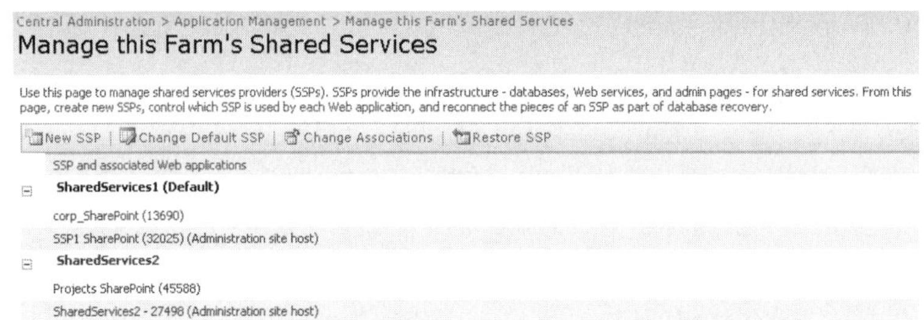

Figure 18-12 Web applications associated with separate SSPs

Planning Prior to re-associating Web applications, you need to plan your environment. Most of the topics covered in this chapter need to be addressed on both the old and new SSP hosting Web applications. These topics include profiles, Audiences, Search, and My Site Locations. Once a Web application has been re-associated, all sites in the Web application lose or gain new services, and these services need to be correctly configured prior to moving the Web application. An example of this is a My Sites in which a user creates a second My Site because the My Site Location has not been configured correctly in the SSP Management page to point to his correct Web application hosting the My Sites.

Changing associations is, however, very straightforward. To change SSP associations, follow these steps:

1. In the Manage This Farm's Shared Services page, click Change Associations on the options bar.
2. On the Change Association Between Web Applications And SSPs page, select the Shared Services Provider name from the drop-down list that you want to associate Web applications with.
3. In the Web Applications section, select the Web application you want to re-associate. Alternatively, choose Select All to re-associate all Web applications with this SSP.
4. On the Warning page, click OK.

Configuring Inter-Farm Shared Services

As mentioned earlier in this chapter, in an enterprise environment, you can have an SSP in one farm that provides services to an SSP in another farm, thus creating a parent/child relationship. This is known as Inter Farm Shared Services (IFSS). It works by selecting only one SSP from the farm, which then provides shared services to other farms. The farm that is providing the shared services is known as the parent, and all farms that consume from that parent are known as children. After you have prepared an SSP for providing services—such as the BDC, Profiles, and Search services—the child farms can consume those services for their own use. In Central Administration, you can identify a parent SSP because the word "Parent" is next to its name, as shown in Figure 18-13.

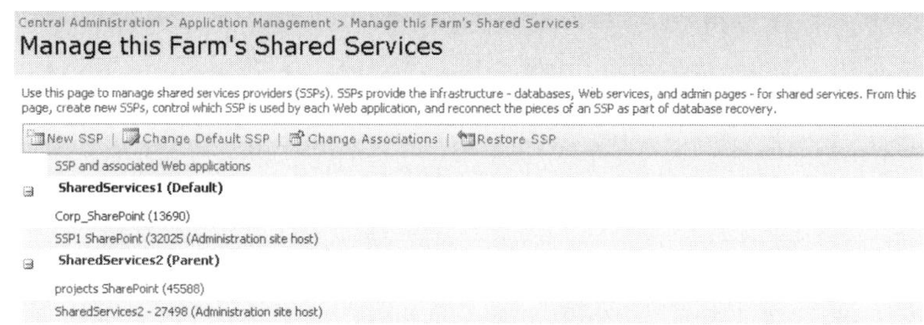

Figure 18-13 An SSP identified as the parent

To configure a farm to provide IFSS, follow these steps:

1. On the Manage Shared Services Between Farms page, select This Farm Will Provide Shared Services To Other Farms.
2. In the Provide Shared Services section, choose the SSP that will provide the services for child farms and add the users from the child farms who will be allowed to connect to this SSP. Click OK.

3. On the Success page, make a note of the parent farm database server and database name, as these will be needed when configuring the child farm. Click OK to complete the process.

Important Before a child farm can consume services from a parent, it must already have an SSP configured.

After a parent SSP has been configured and made available, other farms can start to consume the available services. The configuration of a child farm is also done in Central Administration. After a child farm is configured to consume services, an SSP is displayed and tagged as Remote in Central Administration. This Remote tag indicates that it is consuming services from another farm. You can now start associating Web applications with this SSP to consume its services. To configure a child farm, follow these steps:

1. From Central Administration, click the Application Management page.
2. Click Grant Or Configure Shared Services Between Farms in the Office SharePoint Server Shared Services section.
3. On the Manage Shared Services Between Farms page, select This Farm Will Consume Shared Services From Another Farm.
4. In the Consume Shared Services section, enter the database server, database name, and the user account that were specified earlier when creating the parent SSP.
5. If Excel Services are required, select the local SSP in the child farm that will be hosting Excel Services. Click OK.

There is no requirement for all SSPs to consume from the parent, and you can choose to have some farms not consume services at all from the parent. The parent/child relationship is also compatible with a SharePoint Portal Server 2003 Shared Services model. A child farm in SharePoint Portal Server 2003 can consume from the parent SSP in SharePoint Server 2007.

Planning As part of a migration strategy for a SharePoint Portal Server 2003 Shared Services model, you should upgrade your parent farm first and then the child farms.

Restoring an SSP

Although this is not a chapter on disaster recovery, this section covers the requirements for restoring an SSP if it becomes corrupted or is lost. The process to restore an SSP consists of two separate steps:

1. Restore the SSP Web application and its database.
2. Point the SSP at the restored Web application.

More Info For information on disaster recovery and the process used to restore a Web application and its databases, see Chapter 30, "Microsoft Office SharePoint Server 2007 Disaster Recovery."

After the Web application has been restored with its databases, you can then restore the SSP to use the Web application. Follow these steps to restore an SSP:

1. On the Manage This Farm's Shared Services page, click Restore SSP.
2. On the Restore The Shared Services Provider page, complete the required fields as if you were creating a new SSP. However, for the Web application and Database fields, select the restored Web application and database from your standard restore procedure. Click OK.

Note It does not matter whether you choose to give the restored SSP a new title name, but you must select the restored Web application and database as previously used.

Summary

In this chapter, you learned how to manage and configure the SSP and the services it provides to associated Web applications. You also learned how to create additional SSPs and re-associate Web applications with a new SSP. For most enterprises, a single SSP is all that is required. However, you saw how a second SSP can provide isolation for Web applications and their sites but still be within the same farm environment.

You also learned how SSPs can be configured in a parent/child relationship to enable multiple farms to consume services from a single SSP, a feature known as Inter Farm Shared Services. Finally, you learned how to restore a corrupt or missing SSP by restoring the Web application and database that hosted the SSP and then restoring the connection between them.

From a planning point of view, the SSP is a key part of a successful deployment. With proper planning, you can ensure that the associated Web applications and their site collections have the right services and resources to maximize their collaborative and management capabilities from a user's perspective.

Part IV
Integrating Additional Server Platforms

Chapter 19

Publishing SharePoint Server 2007 Data to Mobile Devices Through ISA Server 2006

At this point, it is certainly clear that Microsoft Office SharePoint Server 2007 focuses on the collection and distribution of data to a company's employees. Just as certain is the fact that it is only a matter of time before that data will need to be presented to mobile users. In support of the ever-growing mobile user community, Microsoft has made great strides in the development of the Windows Mobile platform. Now with its Windows Mobile 5.0 operating system, Microsoft has opened opportunities for instant access to user data including e-mail, contacts, calendar, and tasks. From a SharePoint perspective, Microsoft has included a new Mobile URL feature wherein the URL is generated automatically for each site to provide access to mobile device users. Rather than provide a picture-rich environment, a typical SharePoint environment for the mobile URL slims the page down to its most important List feature.

Windows Mobile 5.0 devices are available from all major cellular carriers and come in several different forms. Some devices use standard QWERTY keyboards to facilitate text input, while other devices use a normal phone-style number pad.

Windows Mobile 5.0 is split between two similar but different operating systems: Windows Mobile 5.0 for PocketPC and Windows Mobile 5.0 for Smartphone. Although these devices share a similar core operating system in Windows Mobile 5.0, there are differences in the feature set supported by each device. The PocketPC version of the Windows Mobile 5.0 platform includes functionality that makes these devices act more like a blend between phones and laptop computers. Windows Mobile 5.0 for PocketPC includes applications such as Mobile Word, Mobile Excel, Mobile PowerPoint, and even a Terminal Services client. In addition, devices that run Windows Mobile 5.0 for PocketPC have support for connecting to Wi-Fi networks to check e-mail or access Internet resources.

This chapter focuses on how to configure Microsoft Internet Security and Acceleration (ISA) Server 2006 to publish a SharePoint site to a Windows Mobile device.

Designing a Secure Mobile Infrastructure

Network engineers face a constant battle in today's network environments as demands for data and simplified communications continue to grow. They must find a way to manage the delicate balance between simplifying the delivery of information to end users with the ever present mindset of ensuring that the delivery will be secure. Without ensuring that data can maintain security levels as outlined in company security policies, it would not be wise to publish data to areas of the network that introduce widespread exposure to unauthorized individuals.

Real World Secure Access to SharePoint Server 2007 Sites

The decision to publish SharePoint data to the Web using ISA Server 2006 should only come after a good amount of time has been spent evaluating the data to be published and the depth of the security measures that should be in place. In some cases you may find that the data to be published does not pose any type of vulnerability to the company's intellectual property, brand, or personal privacy of the employees. In this case, publishing data without being overly concerned for data security is acceptable.

In many cases, however, data security is not a negligible piece of the deployment scenario. Rather, it is the key piece. In real-world implementations, the focus on security should never be absent from the task at hand. It is always best to error on the side of caution and work toward a solution that offers users access to pertinent information without jeopardizing company property. Microsoft's intention with the ISA Server 2006 product was to provide a means of facilitating the publication of internal resources to external users while still maintaining a blanket of security that protects the company and its property. The consistent challenge in real-world deployments is to find a happy medium between data security, ease of access, and ease of implementation.

In a situation such as this, you must always keep in mind that unmanaged devices such as Windows Mobile 5 Smartphones and Pocket PCs do not fall under the same constraints and restrictions of desktops and laptops that have been added as members of the domain. These devices, though manageable through the Microsoft

Exchange server deployment, are readily accessible to not only the employees who own them but also to the malicious individuals looking to obtain any piece of company information. As with any deployment that involves external roaming users, security awareness training for the end-user population is a major factor in the success of the deployment.

Understanding Firewall Configurations

Securing resources on the internal network can be accomplished using any of three common solutions: 1) the edge firewall solution, 2) the multi-homed firewall solution, and 3) the back-to-back firewall configuration. Figure 19-1 shows a simple comparison of these firewall solutions.

Note Although our discussions in the text will focus on understanding the back-to-back firewall configuration, the practice and procedure for configuring SharePoint is consistent across any of the three firewall scenarios.

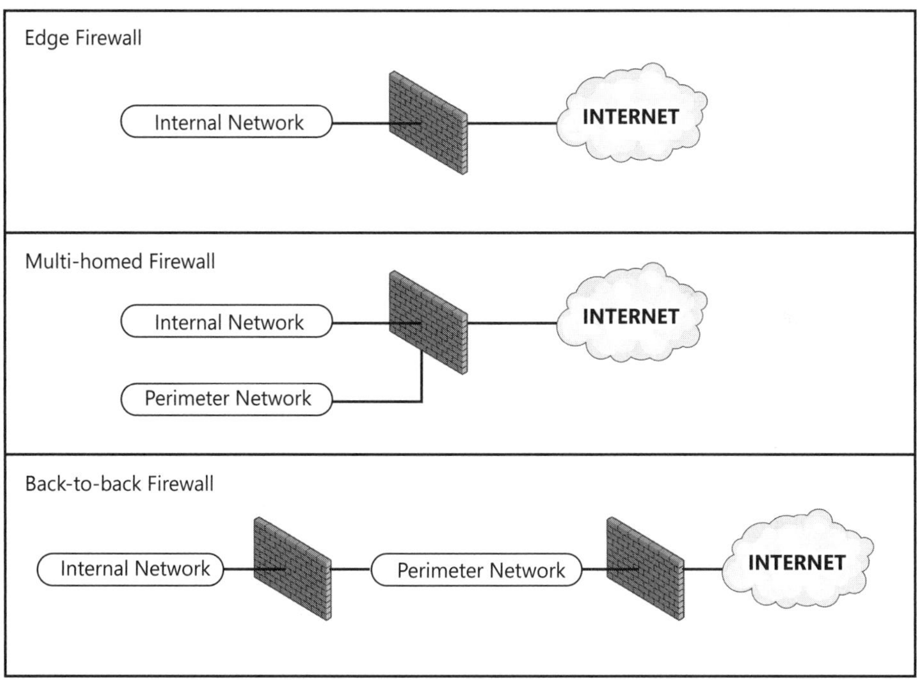

Figure 19-1 Comparison of the three common firewall security implementations

The edge firewall is by far the simplest and cheapest solution as it only involves a single firewall device that established a clear line between the internal network and the Internet. The down side is that there is a single point of attack and failure.

The multi-homed firewall, like the edge firewall, involves only one hardware device but it has at least one additional network card. The additional network card provides the opportunity to place resources on an external or perimeter network. However, there is still a single point of attack and failure in this topology.

The back-to-back firewall, as you might have guessed, is the most expensive one, but it is also the solution that affords the highest level of security and the lowest level of granularity with our access controls. Table 19-1 outlines the pros and cons of each firewall implementation.

Table 19-1 Pros and Cons of the Three Common Firewall Implementations

Firewall solution	Pros	Cons	Security rating	Notes
Internet Edge	Low cost	Not as secure	Moderate	Should never be member of a domain.
Multi-homed	Moderate cost	Not as expensive	High	Should never be a member of a domain.
Back-to-back	Easily scalable	High cost High knowledge level	Very high	Only internal firewall should be considered for membership in the internal Active Directory domain.

Before you learn about the infrastructure requirements for securely publishing SharePoint to Windows Mobile users, let's look at the network pieces that a corporation might already have employed in delivering a secure mobile messaging solution.

Solutions that involve the configuration of a perimeter network with two third-party firewall devices often include front-end servers placed into the perimeter network while the back-end storage servers are neatly tucked away on the internal network. The firewall configuration involves a loose set of firewall policy settings on the external firewall that allows traffic from any source terminating at the front-end servers. The internal firewall, on the other hand, protects the internal resources with a much more stringent set of firewall policy settings that allows traffic to pass through if the source of the traffic is a server in the perimeter network and the destination is a specific server on the internal network. This is illustrated in Figure 19-2.

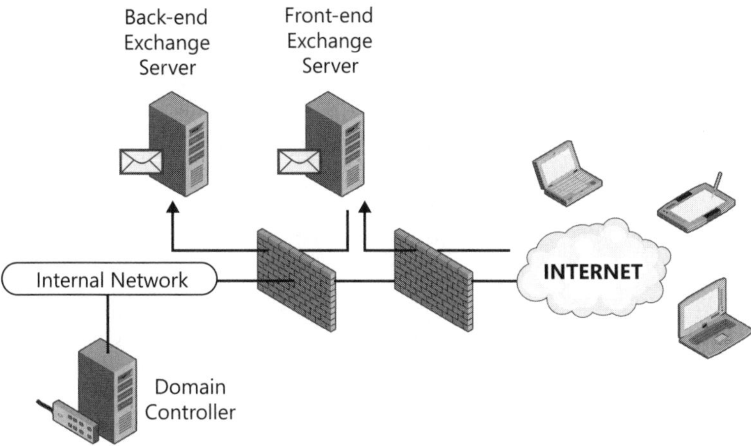

Figure 19-2 A messaging infrastructure deployed with two third-party firewall devices

Deploying SharePoint in this fashion would be very similar. In fact, the external firewall access policy would only need to be extended to allow incoming traffic over port 80, and possibly port 443, to the front-end SharePoint server or Network Load Balancing (NLB) device. The internal firewall, however, would require an additional rule to allow the front-end SharePoint server to communicate with an internal SQL Server 2005 server. The default port of 1433 would need to be permitted from a source of the front-end SharePoint server to the back-end database server. This is illustrated in Figure 19-3.

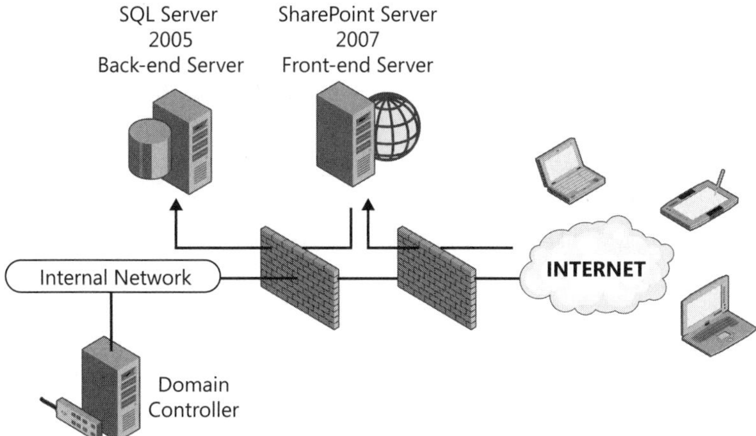

Figure 19-3 Deploying a SharePoint front-end server in a perimeter network with a back-end SQL server

If you're concerned with the idea of placing your SharePoint server in the perimeter network, then be assured that placing it on the internal network is even more unwise. The ramifications of placing it amongst the other internal resources are significant in that both the external and the internal firewall would have to be configured to allow Internet clients to pass through to the internal network. Indeed, unwise. So what should you do? Use Microsoft Internet Security and Acceleration (ISA) Server 2006 as the solution.

Using ISA Server 2006 with SharePoint Server 2007 Implementations

ISA Server 2006 comes in Standard and Enterprise Editions. The core difference in the editions lies in the scalability opportunities of Enterprise Edition. Standard Edition is limited to a single server with up to 4 CPUs and 2 GB of RAM. Enterprise Edition, on the other hand, has no hardware limitations and can scale as part of a Network Load Balancing (NLB) cluster with a maximum of 32 nodes. The combination of the size of the existing infrastructure and your projections for growth will determine which edition is right for you.

What ISA Server 2006 provides is a multi-tasking application that can exponentially enhance the security of traffic within, across, or directed to resources on your corporate network. ISA Server 2006 can function in one or all of three core roles:

- Web Access Protection
- Branch Office Gateway
- Secure Application Publishing

More Info You can read more about ISA Server 2006 at *http://www.microsoft.com/isaserver*.

The secure application publishing feature of ISA Server 2006 allows organizations to protect internal servers like Exchange, SharePoint, and other Web application servers. ISA Server 2006's publishing rules can be broken down into two forms: Web publishing and server publishing. Web publishing rules are distinguished from server publishing rules in that Web publishing rules are geared toward the traditional Web-based type applications like Web servers, mail servers, and ftp servers. Server publishing rules are used when publishing services like Terminal Services or Telnet. Since SharePoint is clearly one of the Web-based applications, we will focus on the use of Web publishing rules.

Web publishing rules provide a host of advantages including:

- Reverse proxy for internal resources
- Application layer inspection of connections to published services
- Path redirection
- Pre-authentication of traffic to published services

- Support for RADIUS, LDAP, SecurID, and more
- Publishing multiple sites to a single IP address
- URL re-writes
- SSL bridging and SSL tunneling
- Site publication scheduling
- Reverse caching of content for external requests

By the end of this chapter, you will see just how good things can be when ISA Server 2006 is part of your network infrastructure. Microsoft has done a great job of allowing administrators to secure deployments with an easy-to-use interface and a helpful set of wizards to facilitate application publishing.

Note It is a common debate among IT security professionals as to whether firewall applications such as ISA Server 2006 are as secure as hardware-based firewall devices. The raw answer to that debate is that a firewall is only as secure as it is configured to be. But if that isn't enough to satisfy your curiosity, please visit *http://www.microsoft.com/isaserver/hardware* to see how Microsoft has worked with several vendors to bring the ease of ISA packaged with a hardware platform as a security appliance.

Once you have decided that ISA Server 2006 should be a part of the network infrastructure, you must decide where and how you will deploy it. As a firewall product, ISA Server 2006 fits nicely into any of the three firewall deployment scenarios mentioned earlier; edge, multi-homed, or back-to-back. When a SharePoint site is published to the Internet using ISA, it is protected because the true name and IP address of the SharePoint server are never exposed to the external, requesting user. Users will submit their requests to the ISA server which, in turn, will authenticate the user if necessary and then forward the request to the SharePoint server.

For small organizations, and especially those built off of Microsoft Small Business Server 2003 Premium Edition, ISA is positioned to be the Internet edge firewall that provides a barrier of protection between the Internet and the intranet. As Figure 19-4 shows, ISA would be connected to the Internet and the intranet as it inspects all outbound and inbound traffic.

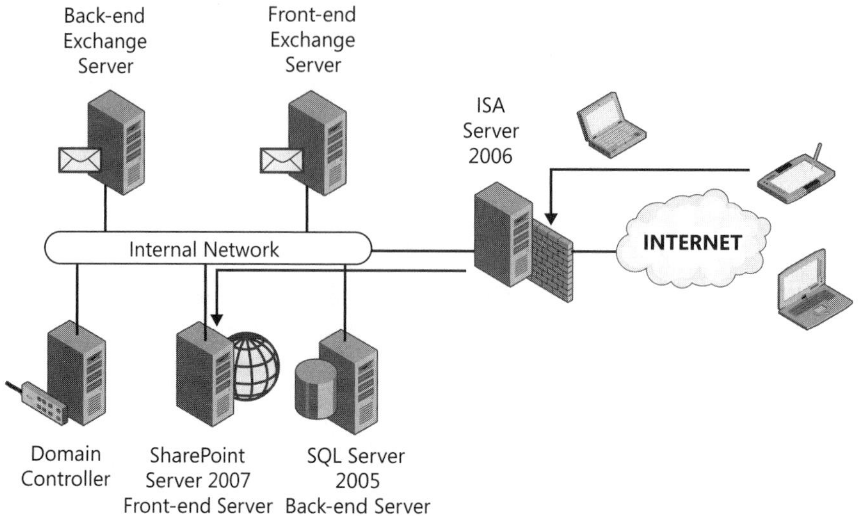

Figure 19-4 ISA Server as an edge gateway

Many large companies have already invested time, money, and manpower in building a secure network environment around the back-to-back firewall configuration. This does not preclude them from needing or wanting to use ISA Server 2006 in their infrastructure. As shown in Figure 19-5, ISA Server 2006 can slip nicely into an existing perimeter network.

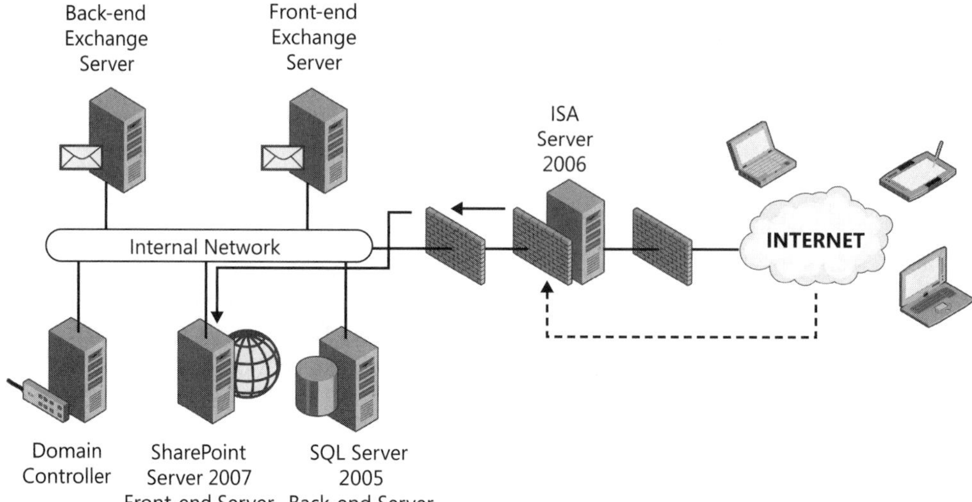

Figure 19-5 ISA Server 2006 as a compliment to an existing firewall configuration

This configuration minimizes the changes that are needed on the internal and external firewalls but adds all of the elements of security that ISA provides. All resources can now remain on the internal network. ISA Server 2006's reverse proxy features will introduce a "you wait and I'll go get it" method of handling traffic. ISA will receive the initial request as the internal firewall has allowed the passing of the traffic to ISA. ISA can then authenticate the user and proceed to retrieve the content on behalf of the authenticated user.

Another common practice in IT security is to deploy firewalls from different vendors in the front-end and back-end solution. If such is the case, it makes great sense to install ISA Server 2006 as the internal or front-end firewall, as shown in Figure 19-6.

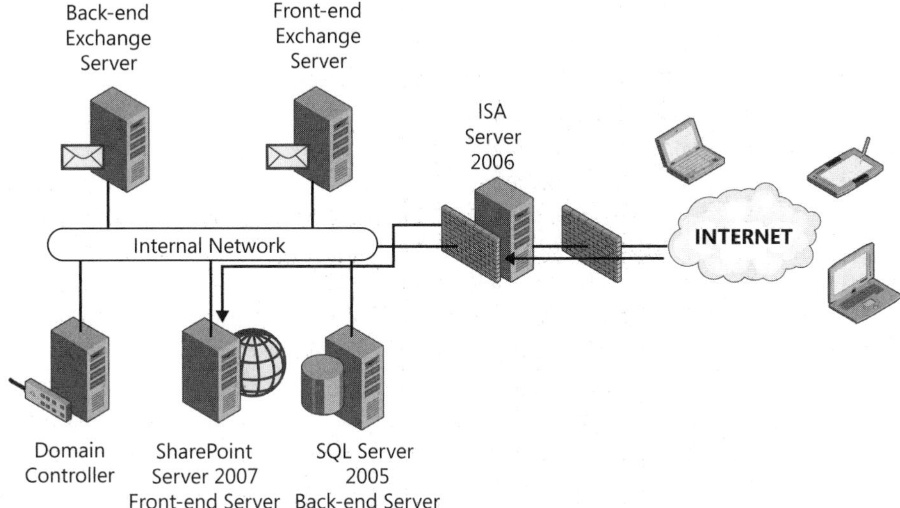

Figure 19-6 ISA Server 2006 as a back-end firewall

From small, low-budget organizations to large, well-funded organizations, there is a firewall deployment right for every situation. Whether it be a single firewall, multiple firewalls, third-party devices, or ISA, planning your infrastructure to support the publication of SharePoint data is a must.

Configuring Servers for Secure Mobile Access to SharePoint Data

After the design phase is over and the servers have been deployed into their respective places on the physical network, it is time to configure the servers to support the delivery of SharePoint data to mobile employees. Much as the design phase takes planning and consideration, the configuration phase requires careful considerations. Moving into implementation, you will need to answer questions such as:

- Do I have a single SharePoint site? Or an entire server farm?
- Is my SharePoint data accessed internally and externally?

- Do I need to use HTTPS? If so, do I have the appropriate certificates?
- What is the server information that we need to publish: IP address? Full qualified domain name (FQDN)?
- What type of authentication do I require? LDAP? Forms-based? Basic? None?

Having the answers to each of these questions will make the ISA configuration wizard much easier and will help ensure a smooth deployment. Since SharePoint is a Web-based service provided to the end user, it is most common to see users accessing information using fully qualified domain names like http://intranet.contoso.com. Alternate Access Mapping (AAM) is a feature of Windows SharePoint Services 3.0 (and thus Office SharePoint Server 2007) that provides users of multiple domains and even multiple networks to access the same set of content using unique URLs. SharePoint identifies the source of a request and matches that to a defined network (URL). This allows SharePoint to return a URL consistent to the FQDN provided by the user. For example, an external user referencing content from the URL http://companyweb.contoso.com should not receive a return URL of http://intranet.contoso.com. SharePoint uses zones as a means of managing URLs and authentication providers when accessing the same content from different networks. Figure 19-7 illustrates the use of alternate access mappings for SharePoint data.

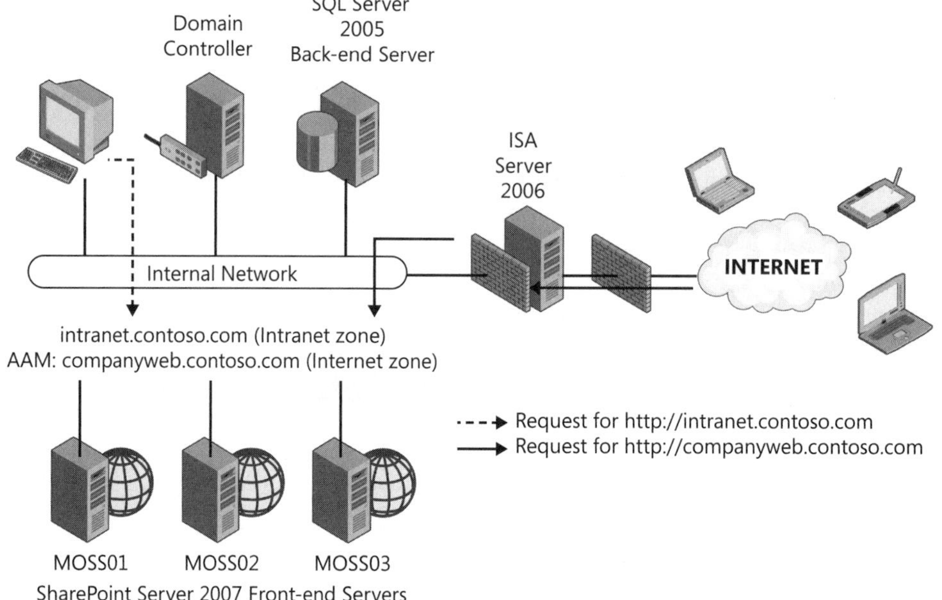

Figure 19-7 Example of alternate access mappings for SharePoint

The configuration in the diagram would allow users to access the content from multiple URLs including:

- http://moss01.contoso.com individual server name, defined on the Intranet zone
- http://moss02.contoso.com individual server name, defined on the Intranet zone
- http://moss03.contoso.com individual server name, defined on the Intranet zone
- http://intranet.contoso.com NLB cluster name for farm, defined on the Intranet zone
- http://companyweb.contoso.com Alternate Access Mapping to reference the NLB farm, defined on the Internet zone

When the SharePoint server receives a request for http://intranet.contoso.com, it assumes that the request is coming from a computer that is on the Intranet zone and will return the same URL. When the server receives a request for http://extranet.contoso.com, it assumes that the request is coming from the Internet zone and will return the same URL.

Note To support the scenario provided, DNS records would need to be created accordingly. The records for each server will most likely exist by default as a result of DNS Dynamic Update. The required Host (A) records for the intranet and company Web host names should be created manually.

Alternate Access Mappings are configured from the Global Configuration section of the Operations page in SharePoint 3.0 Central Administration, shown in Figure 19-8.

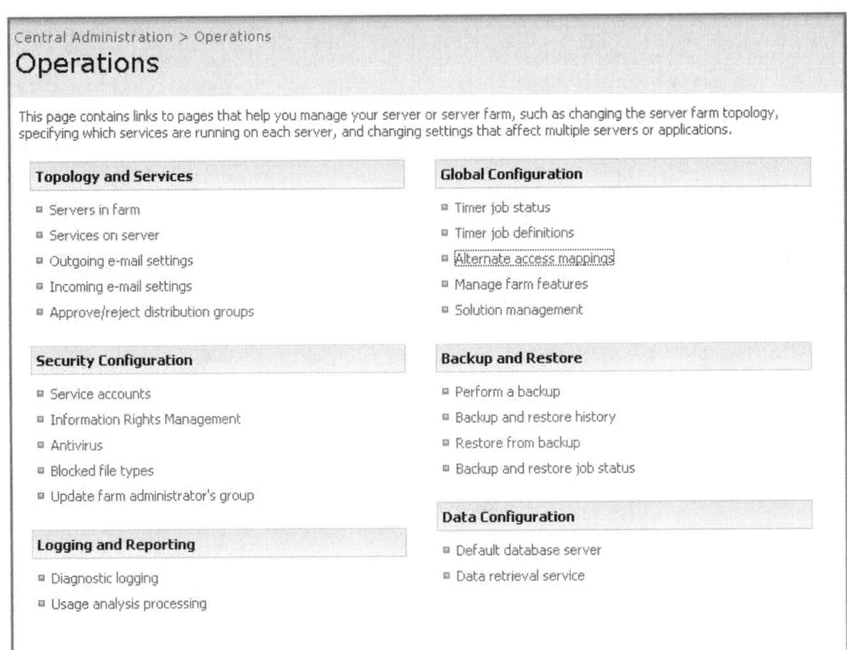

Figure 19-8 Alternate Access Mappings link in Central Administration

All currently configured URLs are listed on the Alternate Access Mapping page, as shown in Figure 19-9.

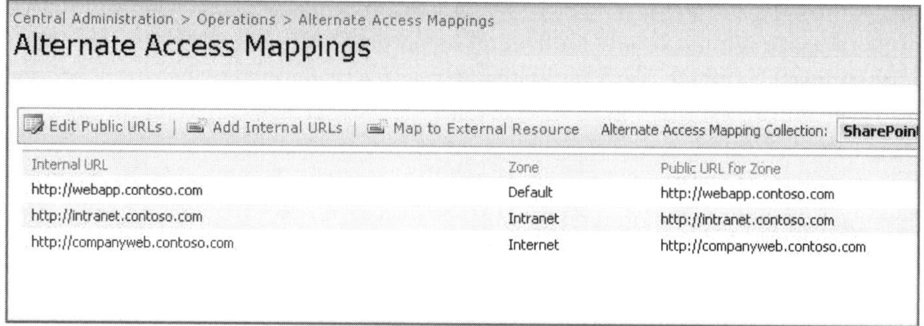

Figure 19-9 Alternate Access Mappings in SharePoint

New mappings can be defined by providing a URL and the appropriate security zone for the URL. The zone chosen is dependent upon the level of security required for the delivery of the data. In situations where information should be delivered to the requesting general public as part an Internet accessible site, the Internet zone would be best if Anonymous authentication is enabled. For scenarios where company employees need access to the data that perhaps is still the Internet zone but with a stronger security, a mechanism like Windows Integrated authentication would be in order.

With the Alternate Access Mapping in place, it will be possible for external user to access data using the http://companyweb.contoso.com URL. SharePoint is configured by default to allow mobile device access to the content using the http://companyweb.contoso.com/m URL (shown in Figure 19-9). Using the /m at the end of the URL identifies to SharePoint to return the less graphically intensive version of a SharePoint site.

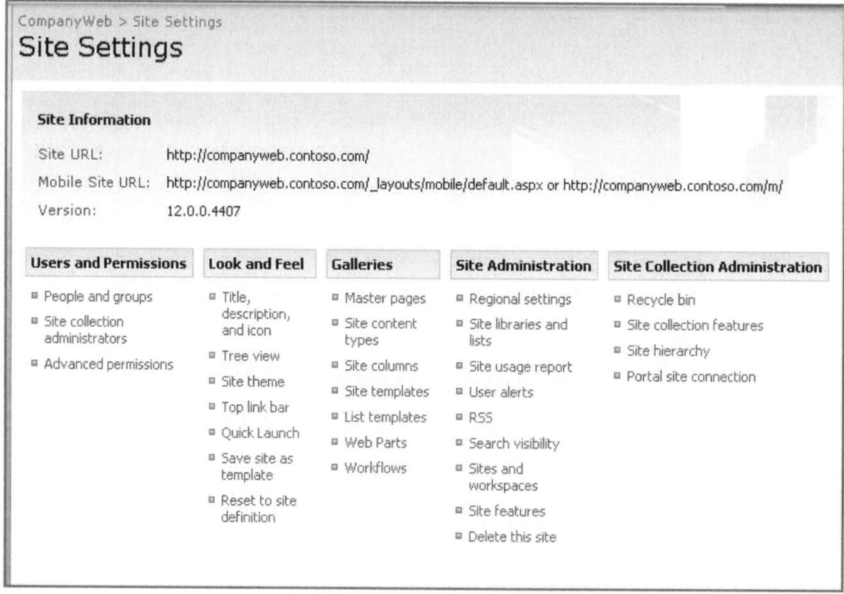

Figure 19-10 SharePoint mobile URL with the /m switch

Since we are dealing here with providing access to external users, it is critical that we consider the need for the encryption of traffic for connections between external mobile users and the SharePoint server. To configure SSL for the SharePoint site is similar to enabling SSL for any other Web site. A certificate must be obtained and installed on the SharePoint server. The certificate installed on the SharePoint server, and inevitably on the ISA server, can be obtained from either a certification authority (CA) on an existing internal Public Key Infrastructure (PKI) or it can be obtained from a publicly trusted certification authority. There will be some extra work involved to use an internal PKI as the devices running Windows Mobile will need to establish trust to the internal root server. On the other hand, there will be some extra money involved if a certificate is obtained from a publicly trusted PKI.

As shown in Figure 19-11, ISA supports two types of SSL deployments: SSL tunneling and SSL bridging. ISA server configured to perform SSL tunneling simply passes HTTPS information through to the Web front-end server itself. SSL bridging allows ISA to perform a stateful inspection of the traffic because the traffic is decrypted at the ISA server and re-encrypted as ISA makes the request to the SharePoint server.

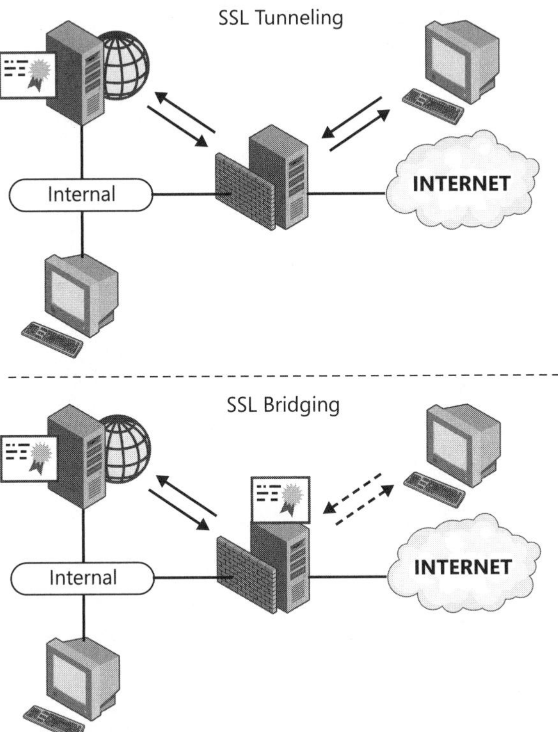

Figure 19-11 ISA Server 2006 and SSL tunneling

To configure the more secure SSL bridging option, two certificates are required. One certificate will be installed on the SharePoint server and one certificate on the ISA server. The certificate installed on the SharePoint server should have a common name equal to that of the server (for example, moss1.contoso.com). The second certificate will be installed on the ISA server and should have a common name that reflects the name of the site that users are connecting to (for example, companyweb.contoso.com). It is best practice to obtain the Web server certificate used on the ISA server from a trusted public certification authority since this is the server that users will directly query. Using a public certification authority prevents errors or warnings on the client system. For each URL that is accessed using SSL, you'll need a separate certificate installed on the ISA server and another certificate installed on the SharePoint server. The certificate stored on the SharePoint server can be obtained from an internal certification authority if one exists. However, the ISA server needs to be configured to trust the root certificate for the PKI that issued the Web server certificate to the SharePoint server.

Before purchasing a certificate from a public certification authority, review the list of certificates in the Trusted Root Certification Authorities on the mobile devices, shown in Figure 19-12.

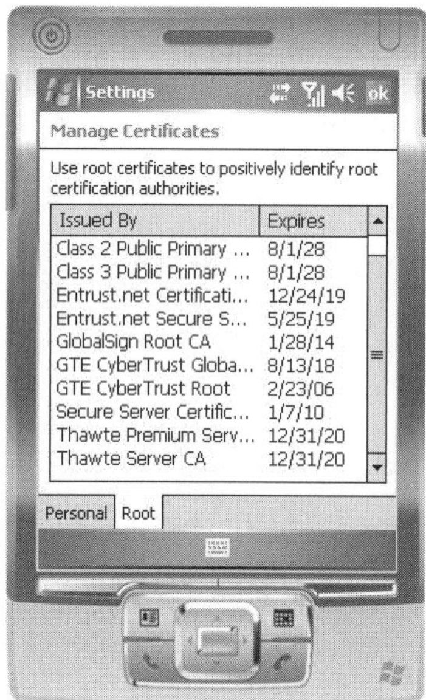

Figure 19-12 Trusted CAs on a mobile device

Once the certificates are in place, the ISA server can be configured with a Web listener and a publishing rule. A *Web listener*, as its name suggests, is an object that is created to specify a specific IP address and port to listen on. In addition, it defines the SSL requirements and the authentication mechanisms available to requesting clients that meet the outlined criteria. Web listeners can be created from the ISA toolbox.

Note Web listeners can be created during the Web Publishing wizard as well.

For providing access to SharePoint data, you will need to perform the follow steps to create a Web listener:

1. Configure the Web listener to use the Require SSL Secured Connection With Clients option, as shown in Figure 19-13.

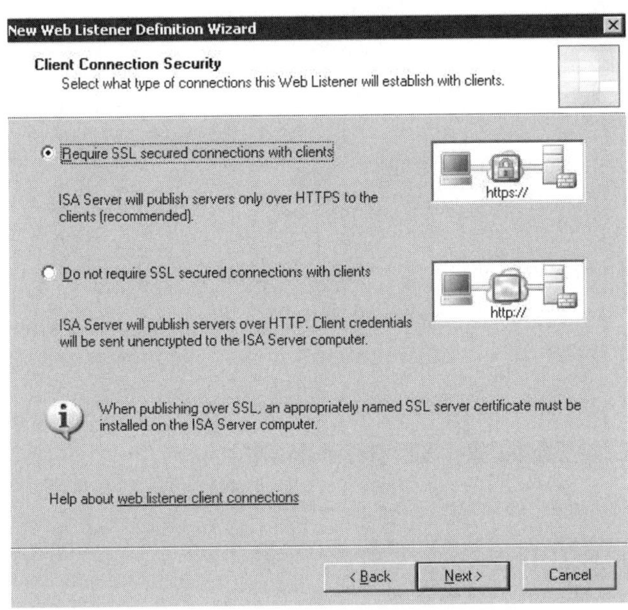

Figure 19-13 Illustration of the three available authentication methods

2. Assign an IP address to the Web listener. You can assign the entire pool of addresses from the External network or you can specify an individual IP address, as shown in Figure 19-14. If a single IP address is specified, you can provide unique certificates for each IP address.

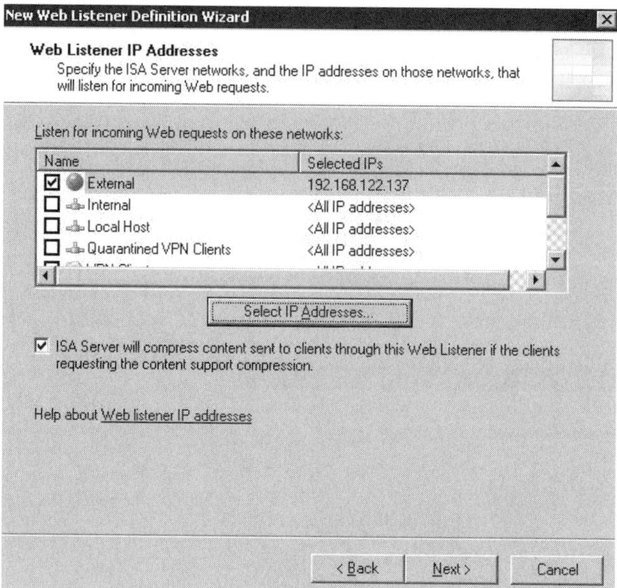

Figure 19-14 Configuring Web listeners for a specific network

3. Select an authentication mechanism for the Web listener. Figure 19-15 shows a typical configuration for Web listener authentication when publishing SharePoint data through ISA.

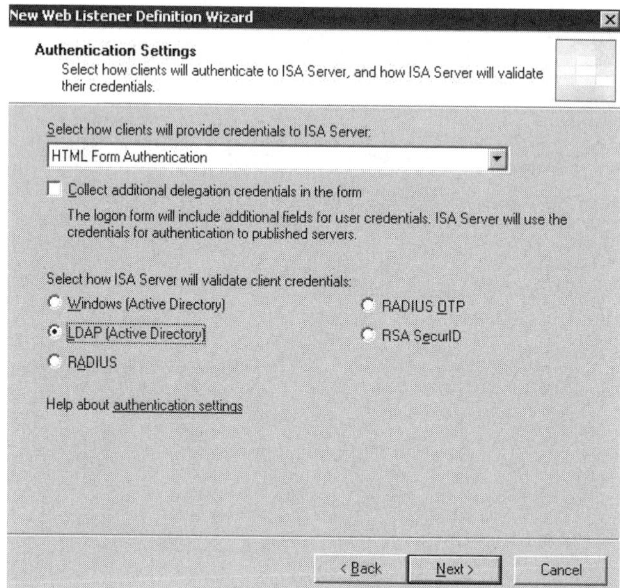

Figure 19-15 Selecting an authentication mechanism

The HTML Form Authentication option shown here will allow ISA to present a default HTML form to request authentication credentials. Clients could also provide credentials to ISA via SSL client certificates or they can use HTTP authentication types of Basic, Digest, or Windows Integrated. For situations in which no authentication is required, the Web listener can be set to allow no authentication.

Validating credentials involves determining how ISA will check the credentials provided through one of the methods mentioned in the previous paragraph. ISA provides several options including:

- **Windows (Active Directory)** Validates credentials against a Windows Active Directory domain. The ISA server must be a member of the domain.
- **LDAP (Active Directory)** Validates credentials against a Windows Active Directory domain. However, the ISA server does not have to be a member of the domain.
- **RADIUS** ISA can be configured as a RADIUS client that redirects requests to any RADIUS server specified.
- **RADIUS OTP** A RADIUS solution where password changes occur based on time or an authentication request counter, thereby a creating one-time-password (OTP).
- **RSA SecurID** An integration with the RSA SecurID authentication technology.

Choosing authentication servers is required when the authentication type that is selected requires validation against another server. Figure 19-16 shows the selection of validation servers for the LDAP (Active Directory) authentication method selected in the previous step.

Using Active Directory, RADIUS, or RSA SecurID will all require the configuration of the back-end servers that will perform the validation of the user credentials.

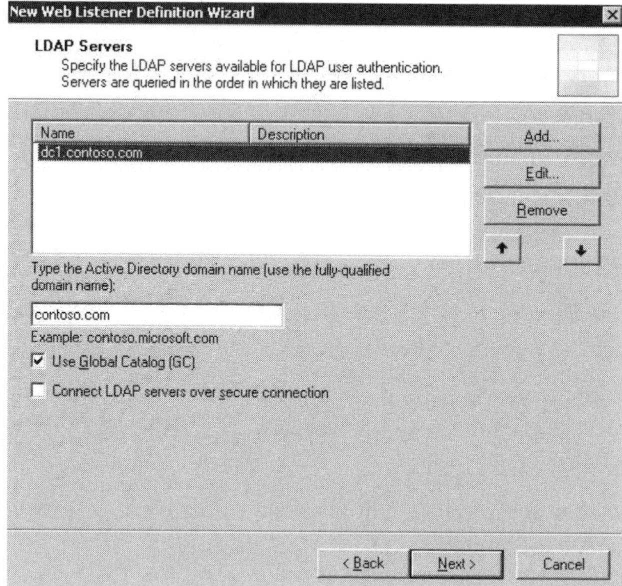

Figure 19-16 Selecting the LDAP authentication method

Once the Web listener is created, a publishing rule can be configured. The publishing rule, as noted earlier, is the core component to making resources available to the external network. Figure 19-17 shows the ISA Tasks option for easily instantiating a wizard to walk through the publishing of a SharePoint site.

Figure 19-17 ISA Tasks options

The Publish SharePoint Sites wizard involves several steps in which you specify much of the existing configuration and how it is going to be referenced by external requests. Once you have provided a name for the new publishing rule, you will need to provide information on the infrastructure that is being published. Figure 19-18 shows the options available at the beginning of the wizard.

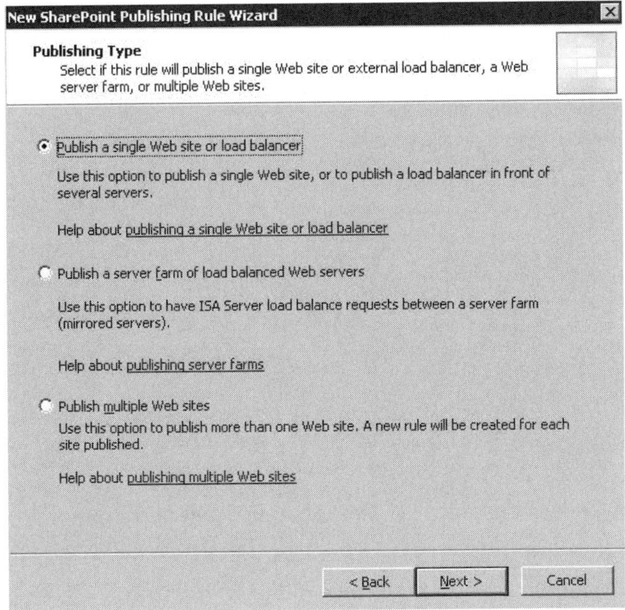

Figure 19-18 Publishing Wizard options

Creating the Web listener establishes the connection type that should exist between the ISA server and the clients. In our example above, we chose to use a secure SSL connection between Web listener and clients. Remember that the certificate with a common name for the Web site was added during the creation of the Web listener. This was to ensure the security of the data transmitted between the ISA server and the external client systems. However, the wizard that is used to publish the SharePoint site establishes the connection type that should exist between the ISA server and the SharePoint server hosting the site. Figure 19-19 displays the two options available for the connection type between the ISA server and the SharePoint server.

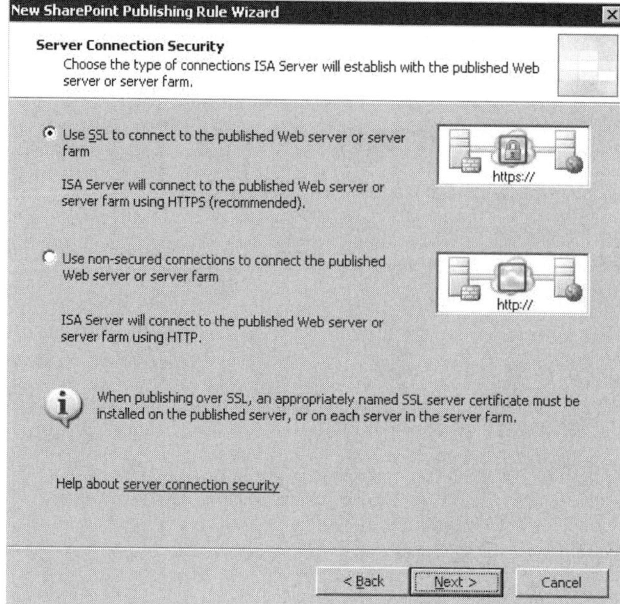

Figure 19-19 Server Connection Security page in the New SharePoint Publishing Rule Wizard

Using the SSL option to secure communication between the ISA server and the SharePoint server requires a certificate to be installed on the SharePoint server and that the ISA server trust the root CA that issued the certificate. If there are multiple SharePoint servers in a farm that is being published, the certificate must be installed on each server in the farm. It is not uncommon to use an internal Public Key Infrastructure to issue a certificate to the SharePoint server or servers. However, if this is the case, the ISA server will not have a native trust for this certificate. The ISA server will need to have the root CA certificate imported into the list of Trusted Root Certification Authorities. In a normal Internet scenario, if there is a lack of trust for a certificate, then the end user is prompted to accept the lack of trust and proceed with the request. Since this side of the publishing scenario involves two servers and no end users, there is no opportunity to accept the lack of trust. Therefore, the ISA server *must* be configured to trust the certificate.

Some network engineers might argue that using SSL for the communication between the ISA server and the SharePoint server is not even required. The argument for this case being that the communication between these two computers happens on a portion of the network that is not as vulnerable to attack. In situations where the ISA server is an edge firewall, a multi-homed, or the back-end firewall of a back-to-back scenario, the communication with the SharePoint server all takes place over the internal corporate network. Therefore the need to use SSL to encrypt data is not as significant unless you are in a highly secured environment. The decision to make between using HTTPS or HTTP for the ISA server is based solely on the desire for additional security since the performance hit on the Web front-end SharePoint servers is not significant.

The next step in the wizard, shown in Figure 19-20, is to provide information on the location of the internal site that needs to be proxied by the ISA server. There are a couple of important things to consider as you provide this information. The name of the internal Web site must match the common name on the certificate that was installed, if using HTTPS communication between the ISA server and the SharePoint server. The ISA server must be able to resolve the name of the internal Web site. This presents a problem in scenarios where the ISA server is not a member of the Active Directory domain and is not configured to use an internal DNS server. The wizard provides an additional text box to enter a computer name or IP address that the ISA server will be able to resolve.

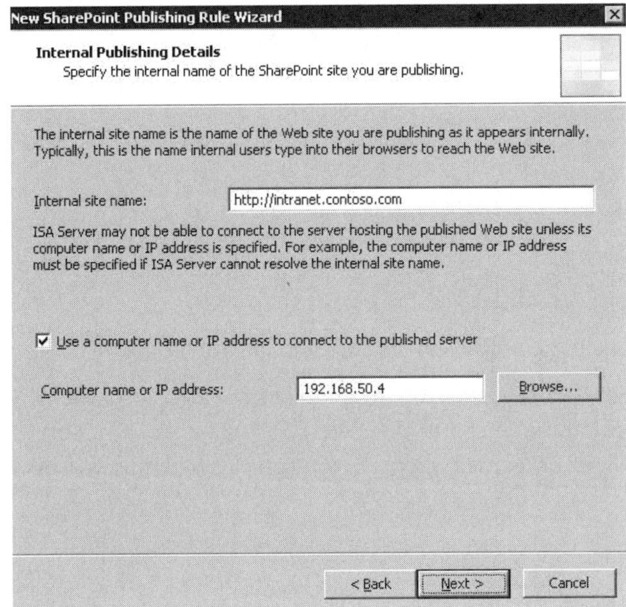

Figure 19-20 Internal Publishing Details page of the New SharePoint Publishing Rule Wizard

For security measures, it is most common not to include the ISA server in the Active Directory domain unless it is the back-end firewall in a back-to-back firewall scenario. Therefore it is important to specify the IP address of the internal SharePoint server that hosts the Web site.

Publishing a Web site by using ISA allows for the defining of the name of the public site that users type, as shown in Figure 19-21. An IP address can also be used, however, this is common only when name resolution methods are not available for a period of time or when testing the publishing of a site. The name that is specified must be resolvable on the Internet by having a Host (A) record created in the DNS zone database that is authoritative for your external domain.

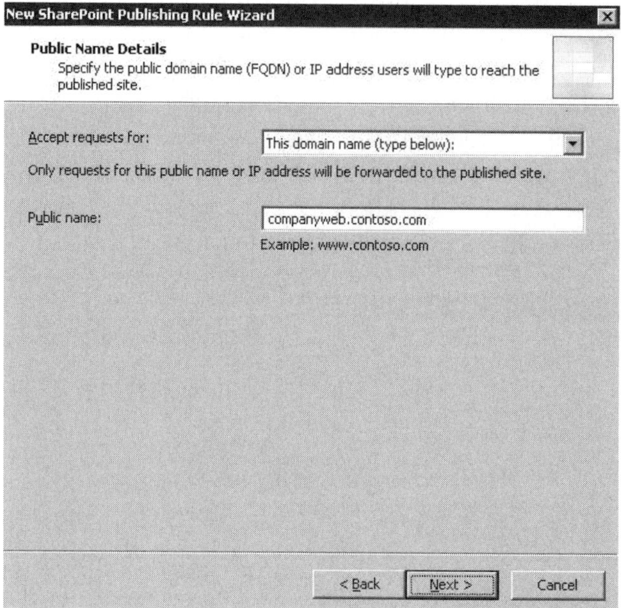

Figure 19-21 Public Name Details page of the New SharePoint Site Publishing Wizard

Next in the Publish SharePoint Site wizard is the configuration of the appropriate Web listener. Figure 19-22 shows the option for choosing an existing Web listener or creating a new one. Remember that a Web listener defines where the ISA server is listening and how authentication occurs.

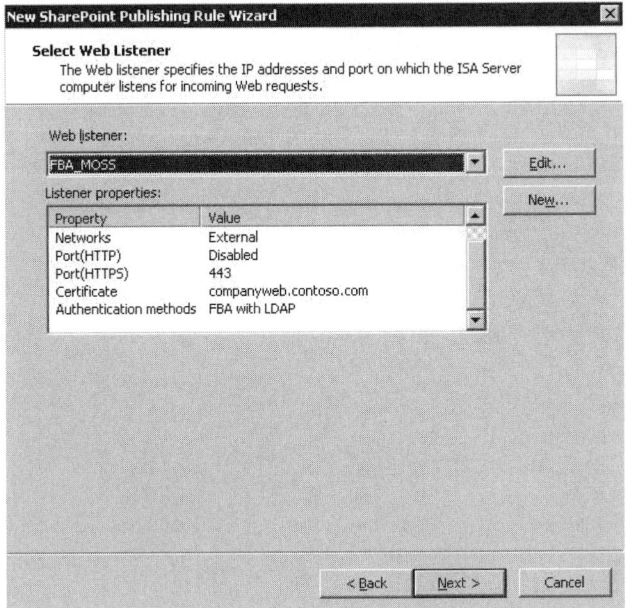

Figure 19-22 Select Web Listener page in the New SharePoint Publishing Rule Wizard

Since the ISA server needs to establish a connection to the internal SharePoint server, an authentication method must be configured, shown in Figure 19-23. The easiest selection to make for authentication of the ISA server to the SharePoint server is the option for NTLM authentication. NT LAN Manager authentication, or NTLM, is supported by all systems that are Windows Server 2003 operating systems and even some earlier versions of Windows. NTLM is used, in particular, to provide authentication between two Windows Server 2003 servers that are not part of the same domain. As we have noted on several occasions, here it is common to find that the ISA server is not, in fact, part of the Active Directory domain. It is more often a stand-alone server that belongs to a workgroup.

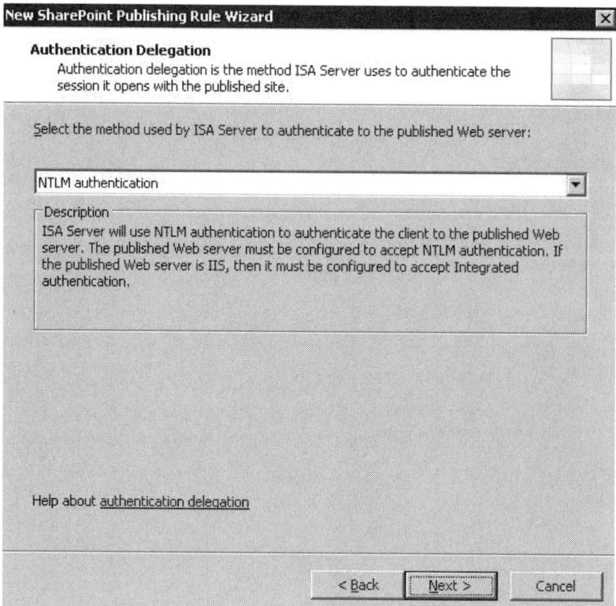

Figure 19-23 Authentication Delegation page in the New SharePoint Site Publishing Wizard

The ISA server needs to be configured to authenticate the client to the SharePoint server in order to retrieve content for the requesting user. The wizard provides several other options including:

- No Delegation, And Client Cannot Authenticate Directly
- No Delegation, But Client Can Authenticate Directly
- Basic Authentication
- Negotiate (Kerberos/NTLM)
- Kerberos Constrained Delegation

If the ISA server were a member of the internal Active Directory domain, it would be possible to select and configure the options that deal with Kerberos authentication. Using Kerberos for authentication requires some additional configuration steps. A service principal name (SPN) must be created to be used by the ISA server for the Kerberos authentication process. The Web server must be configured to accept Kerberos authentication and be configured to use Integrated Windows authentication in Internet Information Services (IIS).

The Kerberos Constrained Delegation option also requires that the ISA server be trusted for delegation. The Negotiate (Kerberos/NTLM) authentication option will try to use Kerberos as the first authentication method but will fall back to NTLM if and when the Kerberos authentication attempt fails.

As a true sign that this wizard is for SharePoint and not just any Web site, the next step in the wizard, shown in Figure 19-24, requires the acknowledgement that Alternate Access Mappings have been configured on the SharePoint server. Remember that Alternate Access Mappings allow the SharePoint site to be referenced by using multiple URLs.

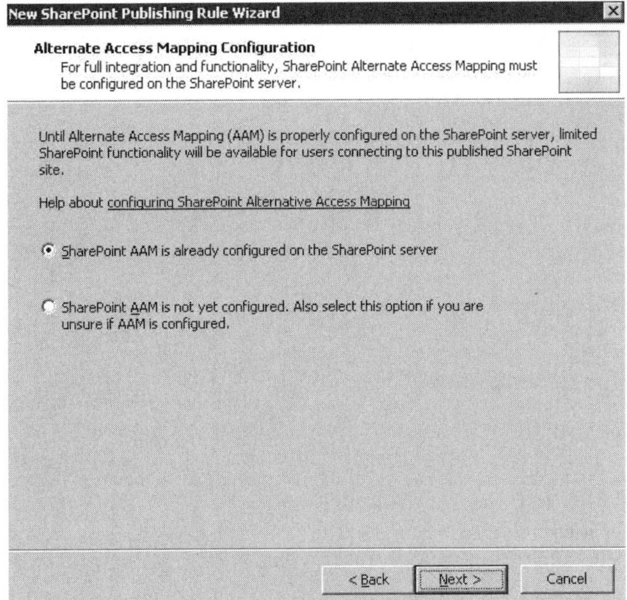

Figure 19-24 Alternate Access Mappings in the New SharePoint Site Publishing Wizard

The integration of ISA Server with SharePoint is undisputed when the a new wizard exists and that wizard request information particular to the SharePoint deployment.

The final step in publishing a SharePoint site to the Internet is to define the user set that this rule is applied to. Any SharePoint group can be added and removed at will. For situations in which all users should not have access to the published data, user-created groups can be used.

> **Note** Any changes to the ISA Server 2006 firewall policy or the system policy requires you to click the Apply button to complete the changes.

After completing the Publish SharePoint Site Wizard, the rule will be displayed in the Firewall Policy list.

Configuring Windows Mobile Devices to Access SharePoint

Once the SharePoint server and ISA server have been configured appropriately, there are some final configurations that need to be done on both the Windows Mobile devices and the infrastructure in general.

Windows SharePoint Services 3.0 has included a new default feature that creates a site URL specifically for mobile devices. As shown in Figure 19-24, the mobile URL is the same as the default URL with the /m characters added to the end.

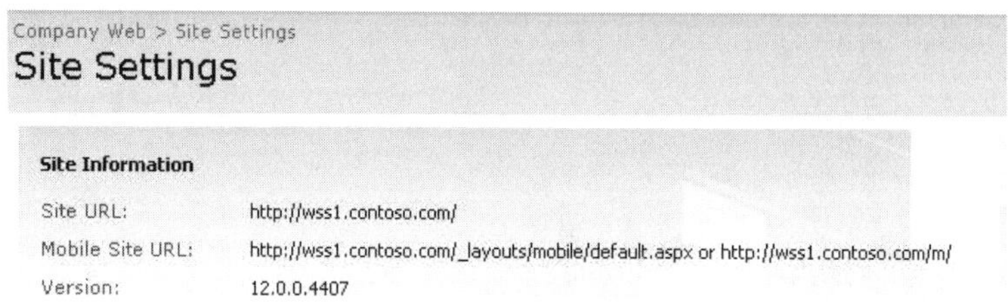

Figure 19-25 Mobile URL with the /m switch appended

If the ISA server was configured to use SSL to encrypt data transfers between clients and server using a certificate from an internal certification authority (CA), the clients should be configured to trust the root CA. The root CA certificate can be imported into the Trusted Root Certification Authorities list on each client. Without trusting the certificate, clients will consistently receive the warning message shown in Figure 19-26. If the certificate used by ISA was obtained from a certificate authority listed by default on the Trusted Root Certification authorities list of the Windows Mobile clients, then no further configurations will be necessary and no warning messages will appear.

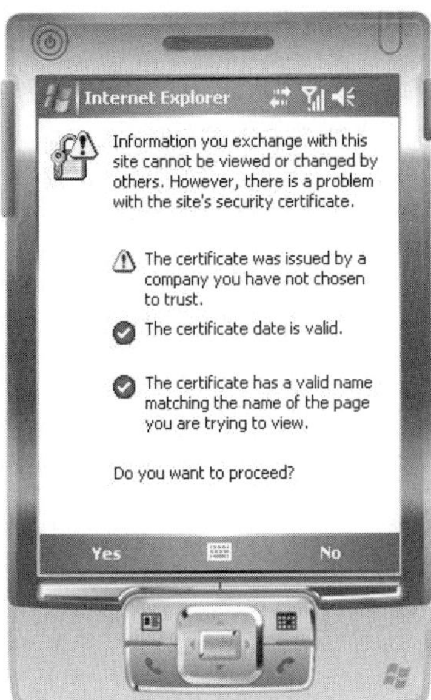

Figure 19-26 Certificate warning message in a mobile device

Once the user proceeds through the warning, if displayed, she will be presented with a logon form that is created automatically by the ISA server, shown in Figure 19-27. The form is presented when HTML form authentication is selected. The user is required to supply a username in the form of domain\user (for example, contoso\jlew) and the accompanying password. The ISA server, as configured, will forward the user credentials to an authentication server. Once the credentials are validated, the user will be presented with the reformatted page. Once on the page with the mobile device orientation, users can view and edit SharePoint lists.

Figure 19-27 Logon screen for mobile users

Summary

The ability of SharePoint Server 2007 to deliver data on demand to mobile devices while maintaining a secure communication stream is a powerful tool for today's telecommuters, remote workers, outside sales force, and much more. Couple the power of SharePoint Server 2007 and its data on demand with the Microsoft Exchange Server 2007 features of e-mail on demand, and the entire staff can be within reach of anything and everything that your typical and even atypical business day can throw at you.

Chapter 20

Excel Services and Building Business Intelligence Solutions

Excel Services are a key component in the Microsoft Business Intelligence strategy, which involves delivering key information, in real time, to the right audience, and in the format they can most easily work with. One of the challenges in complex organizations is the need to aggregate and display mission-critical information about the business pipeline—figures that help decision makers understand where the organization is succeeding in its stated objectives and where it is falling behind. Much of that information is often maintained in Microsoft Office Excel workbooks that are continuously updated by the information workers responsible for day-to-day operations in the organization.

The strength of Excel has always been the flexibility it gives users to create a data repository quickly and easily and to implement sophisticated data processing, charting, and analysis without the lengthy effort required to build a full-scale database application. The downside of the ease that Excel offers is that much of this data becomes spread throughout the organization in a disaggregated state, with no effective means to tie these workbooks into database-driven decision support systems.

Excel Services gives you the ability to integrate Excel workbooks into your information management architecture by consolidating them in common document libraries and publishing the spreadsheets, charts, and graphs on your SharePoint sites. Data can be combined with data from other databases and back-end systems and summarized into key performance indicators to give decision makers an "at-a-glance" view of the status of a project or business area.

It has always been possible to upload an Excel workbook to a Microsoft Windows SharePoint Services document library to make it available to others. However, users who wanted to view the data had to have Excel installed on their local machine and download the entire workbook to their system to open it. Excel Services will render the spreadsheet into HTML for display in a Web Part or in a full-screen browser, and you can control what parts of the spreadsheet users have access to. Only files produced in Office Excel 2007 can be submitted to Excel Services for rendering on the server, and only two file formats specifically are supported: XLSX and XLSB.

Understanding Excel Services Components

Excel Services consists of both the underlying services running on the server and a set of the Web Parts that are used to display them. In this section, you will look at each of the major components of Excel Services.

Excel Calculation Services

The Excel Calculation Services component is responsible for loading workbooks from Trusted File Locations, executing the calculations in the worksheet cells, and refreshing references to external data. Executing a calculation in a spreadsheet within Excel Calculation Services on the server produces exactly the same results as the same formulas executed in the Excel 2007 client. Excel Calculation Services manages security of the calculations in the workbooks, ensuring that no unauthorized external data source is called during recalculation. Excel Calculation Services is an application role that can be run on a separate server from the Web front-end components and can be load-balanced across multiple servers. The Excel Calculation Services component also manages caching of data related to workbooks for improved performance. The data cached includes the sheets and graphs, as well as the state of ongoing calculations and the results from external data queries.

Excel Web Access

Excel Web Access is the feature set that allows Excel 2007 workbooks to be rendered as HTML in a Web browser. Excel Web Access enables users to load entire workbooks in the browser and interact with them in much the same way as they could inside Excel, short of saving any changes to them. Excel Web Access requires no client installation beyond the browser and does not download any code to the user's workstation. The Excel Web Access Web Part is a standard Web Part that can be placed on any Web Part page and used to render all or part of an Excel workbook stored in a Trusted File Location.

Excel Web Services

Excel Web Services is the component of Excel Services that supports programmatic access to Excel workbooks stored on the server. Developers can write code to pass parameters to workbooks, refresh calculations, and retrieve results through Excel Web Services. This functionality allows organizations to remotely call server-side logic stored in workbooks in SharePoint for use in other applications without having to port or rewrite the code.

Excel Calculation Service Proxy

The Excel Calculation Service Proxy is responsible for coordinating requests for calculations from the Excel Web Access and Excel Web Services components to the Excel Calculation Services component. On a single-server machine, this is a simple hand-off operation. In a multiserver farm, the Excel Calculation Service Proxy is also responsible for load balancing requests between Microsoft Office SharePoint Server 2007 servers running the Excel Calculation Services component.

The Report Center Template

The Report Center template is the starting point for business intelligence portals in Office Server 2007. It provides a ready-to-use layout for organizing workbooks, reports, scorecards, data connections, and dashboards. A site based on the Report Center template can store multiple different sets of data focusing on distinct aspects of the organization or it can focus on displaying the progress results toward one specific goal.

Configuring Excel Services

Excel Services is installed as part of SharePoint Server 2007 but is not enabled by default. To make use of Excel Services, a few additional steps are required to configure it in an SharePoint Server 2007 installation.

To configure Excel Services, you must first install an instance of SharePoint Server 2007 in either the Complete or Web Server mode. Once it is installed, you need to create a Shared Services Provider (SSP). Excel Services is a shared service that is available only from an SSP. There are two parts to configuring Excel Services. First you need to enable Excel Services and then you need to configure a trusted connection.

More Info For details on configuring an SSP, see Chapter 18, "Administrating Shared Services Providers."

Enabling Excel Services

Excel Services are not enabled in a default installation of SharePoint Server 2007, so the first step is to enable the service on at least one server in the farm. In a server farm with one Web front-end server and one application server, you can enable the service on either server with the objective of using the server with the least load on it currently. If you have multiple Web front-end servers, best practice is to enable Excel Services on a separate application server that is available to all Web front-end servers. You can enable Excel Services on multiple servers in the farm to enhance redundancy and scalability. For instructions on how to do this, see the section "Scaling Excel Services." To enable Excel Services, follow these steps:

1. Open SharePoint 3.0 Central Administration.
2. Click the Operations tab.
3. Click Services On Server.
4. If the Status of Excel Calculation Services is Stopped, click the Start link to the right.

Configuring a Trusted Connection

Excel Services can only process data in workbooks that are stored in specifically authorized locations, known as *Trusted File Locations*. A Trusted File Location can be either a Windows SharePoint Services document library, a URL to an Excel file, or a path to a file in a shared folder. Controlling which locations Excel Services will recognize and render data from allows administrators to control who has permission to both publish and view Excel workbooks through Excel Services. For Windows SharePoint Services sites, you must create a new Trusted File Location for each document library by completing the following steps:

1. In Central Administration, on the left menu bar, under Shared Services Administration, click the link for the Shared Services Provider you are using for your Web application.
2. Under Excel Services Management, click Manage Trusted File Locations.
3. Click Add Trusted File Location.
4. On the Add Trusted File Location page, type the URL of the file location as follows (see Figure 20-1):

- **For Windows SharePoint Services** Type the full URL to a specific document library, for example: **http://mossserver1/sites/wsssite/doclib**.
- **For UNC** Type the path to an Excel file stored in a shared folder, for example: **\\server1\sharedfolder**.
- **For HTTP** Type the HTTP address to an Excel file stored on a Web site, for example: **http://webserver1/virtualdir**.

  Selecting the HTTP location type when referring to a document library, or vice versa, will cause the Excel Calculation Services request to fail. When loading a workbook from a Windows SharePoint Services site, permission checks are handled by impersonating the user account making the request, which cannot be done for UNC shares or HTTP Web sites.

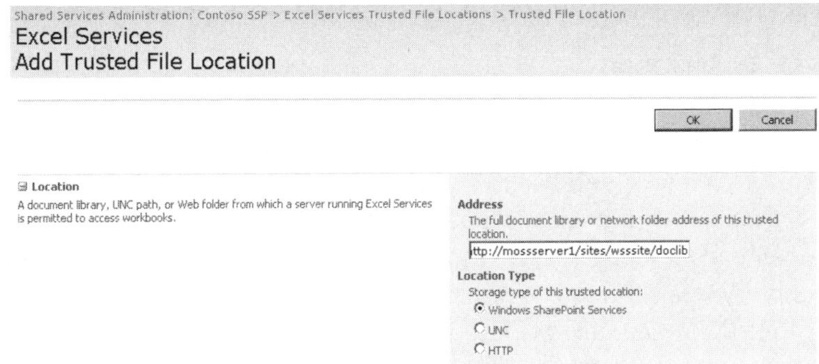

Figure 20-1 Add Trusted File Location

5. If the location you entered contains subfolders, they will not be trusted automatically. To specify that subfolders also be trusted, select the Children Trusted check box.
6. Under the External Data section, select the Allow External Data option if the spreadsheets you will be publishing have links to External data sources.

   External data sources include queries to databases through Office Data Connection (ODC) connections, which are supported by Excel Services only if this option is selected. Unless you select this option, you won't be able to use these data sources.
7. Click OK to add the Trusted File Location.

Real World Planning Trusted File Locations

When planning your Excel Services architecture, you need to decide how many Trusted File Locations to create within your farm. This is a complex question that can involve several possible approaches. Let's take a look at two possible approaches adopted by fictional companies.

A Small Organization

An organization with 300 users decided that their information needs were fairly specific and only a few users would be editing and published workbooks to the server. They concluded that they would need only one Trusted File Location for their intranet portal and sites. The decision was based partly on their interest in including the address to the Trusted File Location library in their training materials so that everyone who needed the feature would know where to go.

A Large Organization

An organization with several thousand users examined the same problem and came up with a different strategy. They realized that they would have several groups using Excel Services for different purposes and that that one size would not fit all. One department in the organization wanted to be able to put all its workbooks on the server and view any of them through the Web browser. For this group, a document library was configured so that everyone in the department had Edit permissions, but the maximum workbook size that Excel Calculation Services would process was set to 7 MB to reduce the overhead on the server. A different department had a limited set of relatively complex workbooks that generated cost projections for the department quarterly. At present, the department tracks large amounts of data in these workbooks, but it is considering moving the data into a back-end database and performing some of the calculations using User Defined Functions. For this group, a document library was configured with only a few users with Edit permissions, but which allowed workbooks up to 20 MB and allowed connections in trusted data connection libraries and user-defined functions.

Publishing Workbooks to Excel Services

Making an Excel workbook available through Excel Services begins with uploading an Excel 2007 workbook to a document library on a SharePoint Server 2007 site. You can upload an existing Excel workbook or create a new one directly within the document library. Any of the standard techniques for interacting with a document library will work to store an Excel file on the server, such as uploading it through the Web site or through the Explorer View. However, to take advantage of specific features of Excel Services, such as controlling which worksheets are visible and which cells can receive input, you must use the Publish feature within Excel 2007. None of the other methods of making an Excel 2007 workbook available through Excel Services (for example, storing it in a file share or non-SharePoint Web site) will provide support for restricting the visibility of sheets and defining input parameters.

To publish a workbook to Excel Services, follow these steps:

1. Open and edit the file in Excel 2007.
2. From the File menu, point to Publish and select Excel Services
3. For the Save As Type, select either Excel Workbook (.xlsx) or Excel Binary Workbook (.xlsb).
4. In the File Name box, type the full URL path to the document library along with the file name of the document—for example, **http://contoso.msft/sitedirectory/sales/forecasts/Q12007.xlsx**.
5. Click Excel Services Options as shown in Figure 20-2.

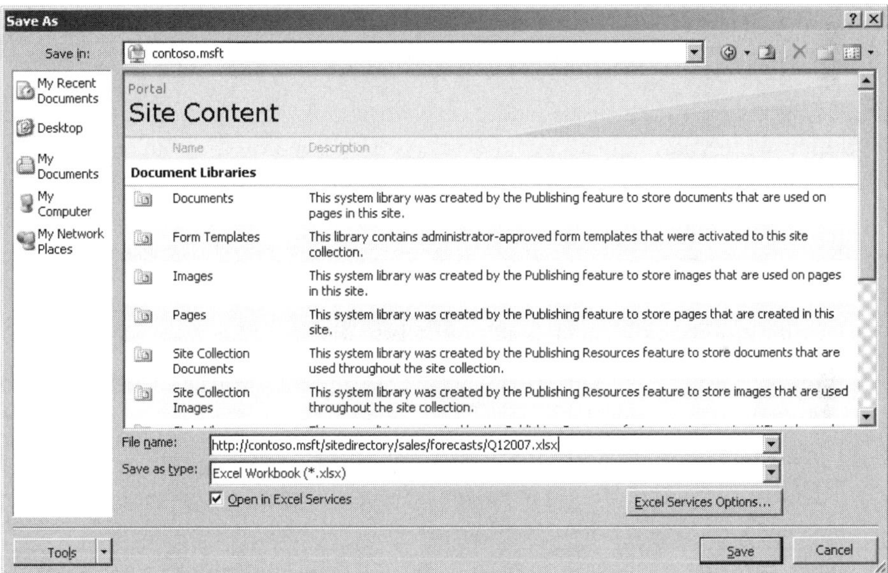

Figure 20-2 Publish Excel Workbook—Save As Dialog

6. If you want to hide any parts of the workbook, complete the following actions: On the Show tab, click the drop-down list and select either Sheets or Items In The Workbook. Then clear the check boxes for items that should remain hidden from viewers.

7. If you want to allow users to input new values into the spreadsheet at run time, complete the following actions: On the Parameters tab, click Add, and then choose the parameter cells.

> **Note** To use parameters, you must define named cells that can be updated with new values.

Publishing an Excel 2007 workbook stores it in a SharePoint Server 2007 document library, which allows you to take advantage of the document management features built into document libraries, such as version control, workflows, and life-cycle management, including information management policies and auditing. Users can publish workbooks to any document library for which they have Add permissions, but they will not be able to view the workbook through Web Access until you enable it as a Trusted File Location.

> **Note** Some organizations use the Workbook Sharing feature to allow multiple users to edit a spreadsheet simultaneously. If this feature is enabled in the file, Excel Services will not load or process it.

Limiting the Area That Can Be Viewed

One of the controls that can be placed on a workbook when it is uploaded to the server is to limit which parts of the workbook can be viewed by users in the Web browser. Although Excel Services loads and processes the entire spreadsheet when a user requests to view it, the author can specify which parts of the workbook are visible and which parts are hidden. Excel 2007 provides three options for controlling the visible area of the workbook:

- **Entire Workbook** The default option is to display all items.
- **Sheets** You can select specific sheets to display, but you cannot limit which items on each sheet are available.
- **Items In The Workbook** You can select from a list of named ranges, charts, tables, pivot tables, and pivot charts. In this case, you need to assign names to these objects before saving the workbook to the server.

None of these options affect the ability to view and edit items in a workbook when it is opened in Excel 2007, only when it is viewed through the Web browser. If the workbook contains many sheets of supporting data and calculations or charts that show different presentations of the results, you can choose to hide the parts of the workbook that are not relevant to the viewer. Any time you want to edit the workbook, you can open it directly in Excel 2007 and have full access to all the sheets and objects.

Defining Parameters

Excel Web Access renders workbook data in a read-only view, which allows users to navigate between the spreadsheet tabs but not edit any of the cells. You can enable selective user input to the workbook by naming specific cells and then identifying those cells as Parameters during the publishing process. To assign a name to a cell, right-click the cell in the workbook and select Name A Range. The dialog box shown in Figure 20-3 appears. Enter a meaningful name and a description that explains the purpose of the parameter.

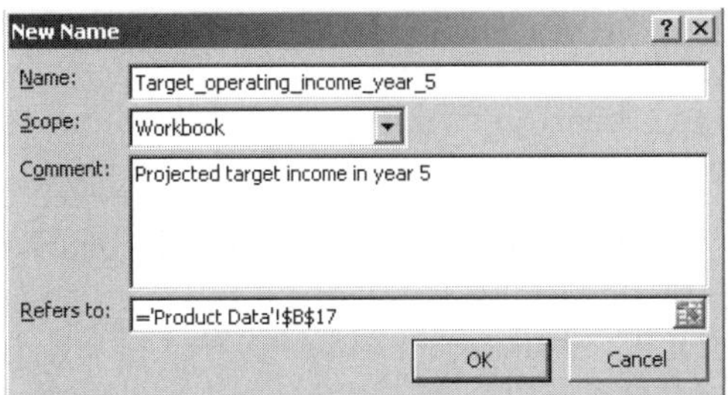

Figure 20-3 The New Name dialog box for defining parameters

Each parameter is a single value that can be changed by the user and will be updated in the workbook when the user applies the change. The changed value is preserved only for the individual session that the user is participating in, and all parameter changes are discarded when the user's session ends. Likewise, the parameters entered by one user are not visible to other users and do not affect the calculations in other users' sessions. You add and remove cells as parameters on the Parameters tab of the Excel Services Options dialog box, as shown in Figure 20-4.

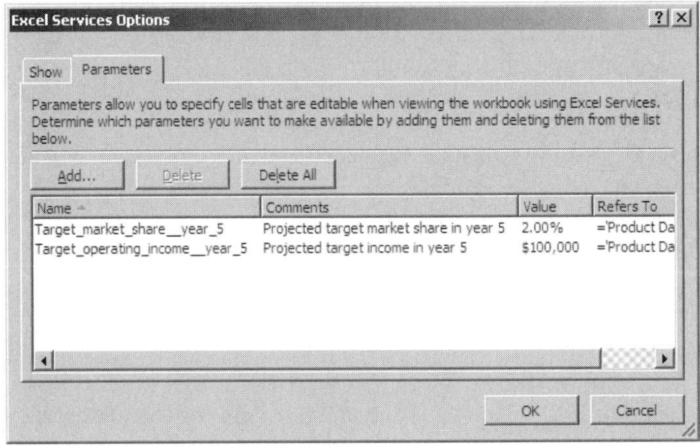

Figure 20-4 The Parameters tab

Note It is a good idea to use clear and easily understood names for the cells that will be used as parameters because the cell name appears as the parameter name in the Web browser.

There are certain requirements for a cell to be used as a parameter:

- The parameter can refer only to a single cell.
- The cell must be a named "cell."
- The cell cannot contain a formula.
- The cell cannot be in a pivot table, table, or chart.

A powerful aspect of the parameter feature is that a user can update a parameter even if the cell falls in a part of the workbook that is not marked as visible. Although the user might not be able to see the cell that is affected, the results of calculations linked to that cell value might be visible. This allows you to hide the underlying data set that produces results while still allowing users to update key values.

Working with Spreadsheets Through Excel Web Access

Excel Web Access allows users to interact with workbooks in two ways: opening a workbook so that it is completely rendered in the browser, and viewing a portion of a workbook within an Excel Web Access Web Part. All the features of Excel Web Access are available in both views, and the difference is primarily related to whether the data being displayed is important in the context of other indicators in the site or is self-contained within the workbook.

Viewing a Spreadsheet in the Browser

In some cases, the very power of Excel workbooks has become an encumbrance to users. In the past, large workbooks with complex calculations became difficult to use because they took time to load and the external link updating and formula recalculations had to be re-run by every user who opened the file. Sometimes a user only wanted to view a single chart or the results of one calculation. At other times, the user wasn't sure whether the workbook contained the information he was looking for, but he had to take the time to open it to find out.

When a workbook is published to Excel Services, you can configure the default settings of the document library so that a user can simply click the link to the file in the document library and SharePoint Server 2007 will redirect the user to a full-browser view of the workbook.

To specify that opening a file in the Web browser is the default action that occurs when a user clicks the link in a document library, modify the document library settings as follows:

1. Open the Document Library Settings page.
2. Click Advanced Settings.
3. Under Browser-Enabled Documents, click Display As Web Page and then click OK.

Alternatively, a user can select View In Web Browser from the document context menu, as shown in Figure 20-5.

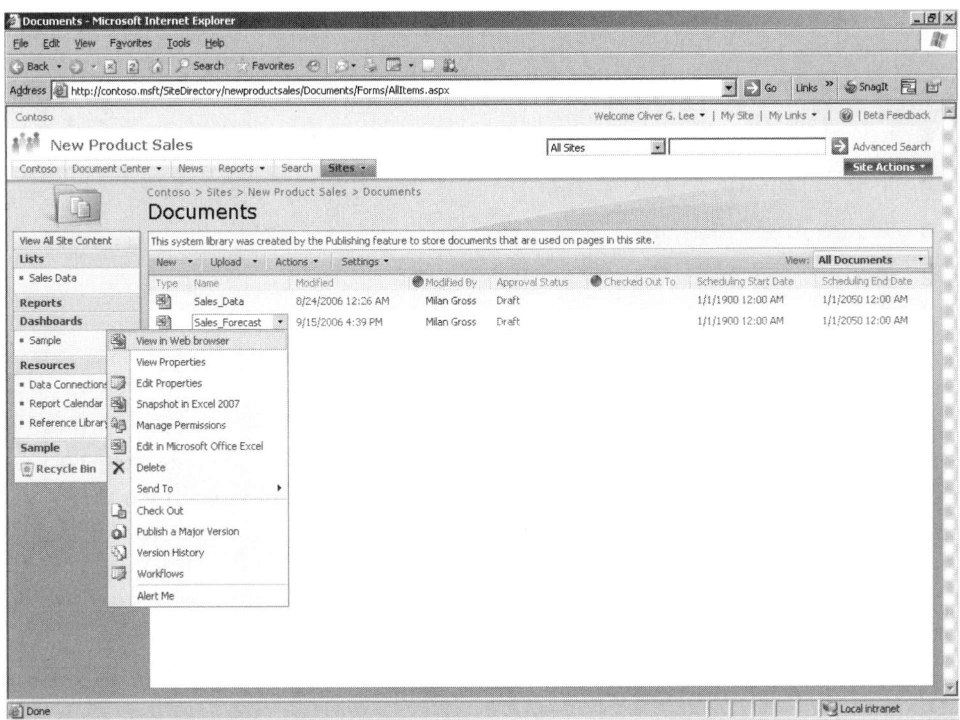

Figure 20-5 Viewing in a browser

This is different from the traditional method of opening an Excel file from a Web server, where the file is downloaded to the browser and Excel is loaded in place to provide the rendering. With Excel Web Access, Excel Services handles the processing and rendering of the workbook and returns only HTML to the Web browser. That means that large spreadsheets do not have to download to your workstation for you to be able to view them. Any sheets or objects that were hidden during the publishing process will be unavailable, and a parameters pane will appear to allow input of values into parameter cells.

Note Although you can view and interact with workbooks through the Web browser, you cannot edit them directly. To modify a workbook, you need to edit it in Excel 2007.

Commands Available Within the Browser

You will find that you are able to navigate around the workbook, changing sheets and scrolling to view cells or charts, in much the same way as in the Excel client. This section covers the following commands; however, other commands are also available within the browser:

- Open
- Open Snapshot
- Reload Workbook
- Refresh Selected Connection
- Refresh All Connections
- Calculate Workbook
- Find

Open in Excel 2007

Use the Open In Excel 2007 command to download the workbook to your local workstation and then open the workbook directly in Excel 2007. This command requires that you have sufficient permissions to load the workbook, including the Open Items and Edit Items list permissions. Using this command is not the same as opening the spreadsheet for editing directly from the document library. Although this command gives you complete access to all areas of the workbook, the workbook is opened as a copy of the file on the server and cannot be saved directly back to the server.

Open Snapshot in Excel 2007

A "snapshot" is a read-only copy of an Excel file produced by Excel Services for users who do not have the right to open the full spreadsheet. Use the Open Snapshot In Excel 2007 command to display the data and results from formula calculations, as processed by Excel Services, but not the formulas themselves. Only sheets and graphs that were made available in the workbook when it was uploaded are rendered in the snapshot. Excel Services generates the snapshot by opening the file on the server, requerying external data sources, recalculating cell values, and outputting the values and formats to the browser.

Reload Workbook

Use the Reload Workbook command to reset any parameter values that have been applied to the workbook, and reload the workbook from its file location. This command essentially requests the Web server to retrieve the original workbook file from its storage location and re-render it in the browser with all default values.

Refresh Selected Connection/Refresh All Connections

Use the Refresh Selected Connection command to refresh the external data from a single PivotTable with an external connection. Use the Refresh All Connections command to refresh the data from all external connections.

Calculate Workbook

Use the Calculate Workbook command to execute all calculations in the workbook without refreshing external connections. This can cut down the time that it takes to recalculate results compared to a full reload of the workbook.

Find

Use the Find command to perform a server-side search for a value and highlight the cell it is in. The standard browser-based Find command does not work in Excel Web Access because the workbook content is not rendered in the source HTML of the page.

Note Although you can view and interact with workbooks through the Web browser, you cannot edit them directly. To modify a workbook, you need to open it in Excel 2007.

Analyzing Data in the Browser

When users view a workbook through Web Access, they receive a copy of the data rendered as HTML in their browser. Although Web Access does not support updating data in the workbook, users can navigate through the sheets and change their view of the data. Users can perform analyses on the data by, for example, sorting and filtering data in a table, without affecting any other user's view of the data.

Working with Tables and AutoFilters

Workbooks that contain Excel 2007 tables defined on ranges automatically expose those features within Excel Web Access. You can use the drop-down menus on each column in the table to sort in ascending or descending order, to use numerical comparison and text filters depending on the data type of the column, and to use the multiselect filter to quickly select items based on discrete values.

Working with PivotTables

When you include a PivotTable in the workbook, you can also interact with it in the Web browser. Although you cannot restructure the pivot table in the browser, essentially all the other features available in PivotTables within Excel 2007 are also available in the browser view. You can expand and collapse levels, sort and filter, and apply quick filters such as "Top 10" (for numbers) and "Last Quarter" (for dates).

Unsupported Features

Excel Services can recalculate formulas embedded in cells, but there are several types of content that it cannot process. To ensure the security and stability of Excel Services, most external object references such as ActiveX controls and Excel Add-ins are not supported. Additionally, embedded code, such as macros written in VBA, are not supported, so any custom functions or procedures need to be rewritten as user-defined functions and compiled into assemblies.

More Info For more details on referencing external function assemblies, see the "User-Defined Function Assembly" section later in this chapter.

Following is a list of the various features that are not supported by Excel Services:

- Spreadsheets with code (includes spreadsheets with VBA macros, forms controls, toolbox controls, MS 5.0 Dialogs, and XLM Sheets)
- IRM-protected spreadsheets
- ActiveX controls
- Embedded SmartTags
- PivotTables based on "multiple consolidation" ranges
- External references (links to other spreadsheets)
- Spreadsheets saved in formula view
- XML expansion packs
- XML Maps
- Data validation
- Query Tables, SharePoint Lists, Web Queries, and Text Queries
- Spreadsheets that reference add-ins
- Spreadsheets that use the *RTD()* function
- Spreadsheets that use spreadsheet and sheet protection
- Embedded pictures or clip art

- Cell and Sheet background pictures
- AutoShapes and WordArt
- Ink Annotations
- Organization Charts and Diagrams
- DDE Links

Using Excel Services in Dashboards

The concept of aggregating decision-support data into a single place where the information can be seen side-by-side and reviewed at a glance has been emerging as a significant objective for information portals. The term *dashboard* has come to identify the place where a set of data views, possibly from different data sources, are brought together to facilitate business monitoring, analysis, and decision making.

The Excel Web Access Web Part

The Excel Web Access Web Part allows you to display data and charts from an Excel workbook and embed them into a SharePoint Server 2007 site or dashboard page. The Web Access Web Part presents the same display style as opening the workbook in a Web browser, but it offers additional features to allow better targeting of data. Within each Web Part, you can specify that only a single object in the workbook, such as a range of cells or a chart, be displayed, as shown in Figure 20-6.

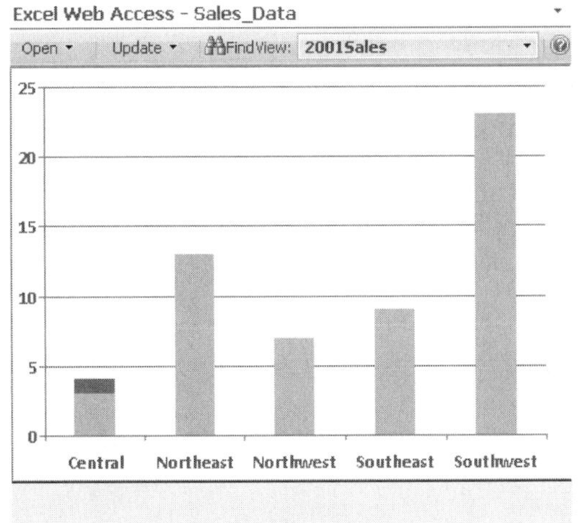

Figure 20-6 Web Access Web Part

To add the Web Part to the page, follow these steps:

1. Open the page in Edit mode.

2. Click Add A Web Part in the zone where you want to place it.
3. Scroll down the list to the Excel Web Access Web Part, select the check box next to it, and then click Add.
4. On the Site page, click the Click Here To Open The Tool Pane link.
5. In the Workbook To Display box, type the path to the workbook in its document library.
6. In the Named Range or Object To Display text box, type the name of the range of cells or chart objects to display in the Web Part. (If you leave this entry blank, the entire workbook is displayed.)
7. Click OK and the Web Part renders the Excel object.

Key Performance Indicators Web Parts

Key Performance Indicators (KPI) are scorecard values that provide visual information to enable users to communicate progress towards goals or standards. Although KPIs are not specifically an Excel Services feature, the Key Performance Indicator List Web Part is an important element for a business intelligence dashboard because it allows users to quickly get a sense of the status of key decision-making factors. KPI lists can retrieve data from Excel sheets or databases and can be configured to present the information as icons, check marks, traffic lights, or other graphical indicators.

To create a KPI display that is based on the data in an Excel workbook, you start by defining Indicators in a KPI List. To do this, follow these steps:

1. From the New menu in the KPI List, select Indicator Using Data in Excel Workbook.
2. Give the indicator a name, enter the workbook address, and enter the address of the cell that contains the indicator value.
3. Finally, identify the threshold values at which the status icon changes to a different color.

Once the list is populated with indicators, add a Key Performance Indicators Web Part to the site or dashboard page and associate it with the KPI List. The indicators then display it on the page and automatically update every time the page is refreshed, as shown in Figure 20-7.

Sales Performance Indicators

Indicator	Goal	Value	Status
Central	30	10	◆
Northeast	30	35	●
SouthEast	30	27	△
SouthWest	30	49	●

Figure 20-7 Key Performance Indicators Web Part

Filter Web Parts

Most data sets provide more information than you need to answer a given analytical question. The Filter Web Parts are used to target the information on a dashboard to allow viewing of more specific data and to focus on specific patterns. The Filter Web Parts can be added to a dashboard to enable users to filter all the content in other Web Parts quickly and easily without any code. Filters can be configured to allow users to select from a list of values, to filter on a value from an external database, or to filter on a value entered manually by the user.

Configuring Security

Excel Services provides you with the means to increase the overall level of security on workbook data and formulas without compromising ease of access and flexibility. Because Excel Services is built on top of SharePoint Server 2007, it offers all the same features for securing and managing workbooks as files, as well as a range of additional options that are specific to Excel Services. By allowing you to configure most users with read-only rights so that they can view only the version of the workbook rendered in the Web browser, you immediately reduce the risk profile by removing direct access to the workbooks themselves. This allows you, and the select users who author workbooks, to restrict the general visibility of proprietary equations and data that most users will not need to see.

Users who previously had to be given Read access to the physical workbook file on a file share might not need permissions to open the file at all. The ability to leverage server-side calculations means that most users will not need to run embedded queries and computations on their workstations, allowing you to deploy stricter client-side security policies.

File Access Security

When a user requests a workbook to view in the Web browser, or it is displayed within a Web Access Web Part, the user does not interact with the workbook directly. Instead, Excel Services loads the workbook on the user's behalf and performs all calculations and external data calls. Excel Services supports two modes for the service to access workbooks and back-end data sources: Impersonation, where Excel Services uses the Windows account of the user making the request; and Process Account, where Excel Services uses the identity account of the application pool associated with the Web application that the workbook is hosted in. This setting is controlled from the Excel Services Settings page available on the Shared Services Administration site.

The Process Account setting is the easiest to configure because it requires no additional steps beyond making sure that the Application Pool identity account has at least Read permissions on all files in all the Trusted File Locations it is configured for. It automatically has these permissions for workbooks hosted within document libraries, but it might not have permissions for workbooks in shared folders (UNC location) or other Web sites (HTTP location). Under this authentication model, a user can view data through Excel Web Access that she would not have permissions to view otherwise.

The Impersonation setting provides a higher level of security because Excel Services impersonates the account of the user and attempts to access the workbooks using that person's credentials. If the user does not have permissions to view the workbook in the folder or site it is on, Excel Services will not have permissions to load and render it. Using the Impersonation mode in a multiserver environment requires that Windows Kerberos authentication be used to allow the delegation of credentials between servers. The implementation of Kerberos requires that additional steps be taken to configure Active Directory accounts to support delegation.

More Info For more information on configuring Kerberos authentication, see the Microsoft Knowledge Base article at *http://support.microsoft.com/?id=832769*.

Data Access Security

Excel 2007 supports linking to external data by referencing an Office Data Connection (.odc) file stored in a data connection library on the server. When Excel Calculation Services loads and processes the file, it can refresh the data by using the ODC information to access the external data source. Within the configuration settings is a button for Excel Services Authentication Settings. The Excel Services Authentication Settings offers three options: Windows Integrated Authentication, SSO, and None as shown in Figure 20-8.

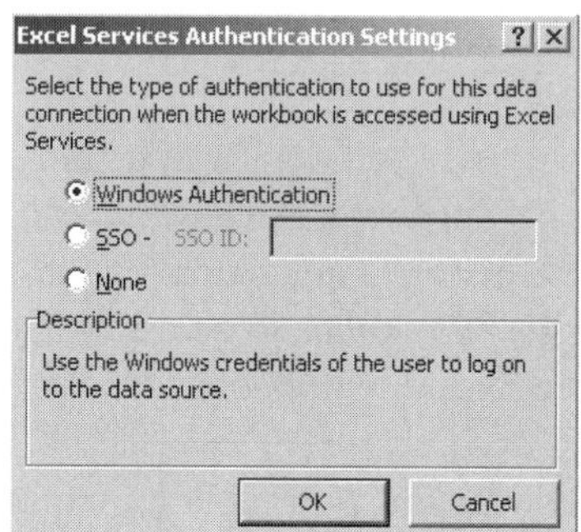

Figure 20-8 Office Data Connection—Excel Services Authentication Settings

More Info For more details on configuring external data connections, see the "Accessing Data from Other Sources" section later in this chapter.

When Windows Integrated Authentication is selected, Excel Calculation Services attempts to execute the external data query by impersonating the credentials of the user accessing the workbook. This setting requires that the user have sufficient permissions on the data source for Excel Calculation Services to execute the query. If the external data source is on a server separate from the Excel Calculation Server, Kerberos delegation has to be configured so that the account credentials can be passed to the data server.

Best Practices Implementing Kerberos delegation with Impersonation for communication between servers and Windows Integrated Authentication for communication with back-end data sources provides the highest level of security and is the recommended approach.

The SSO, or Single Sign-On, authentication option can be used for authentication against data servers that do not support Windows Authentication (for example, most UNIX and mainframe systems). In this case, Excel Calculation Services must submit a user name and password combination to the data server on behalf of the user for the request to be authenticated. To avoid storing the credentials permanently in the .odc file, and to avoid prompting the user for the credentials each time the data is refreshed, Excel Calculation Services can query an encrypted database where the credentials are stored. The SSO authentication method supports storing either a single set of credentials to be used by any user accessing the workbook (Group mapping) or separate credentials unique to each user (Individual mapping). In both cases, the credentials are stored in an encrypted format in a separate SSO database that is accessed by the Microsoft Single Sign-On Service running on the Web front-end and application servers. The credentials are all associated with an application identity (App ID), which identifies the external data server that is being queried. Individual mappings allow for more granular control over permissions and auditing, but Group mappings are easier to maintain and provide better performance.

The third Excel Services Authentication option of None specifies to Excel Calculation Services that the credentials used for the external data connection are either embedded in the .odc file itself or make use of a single set of default credentials configured on the server. Using this authentication method, you can configure the .odc file with a provider-specific connection string either by editing it directly on the Definition tab in the Connection properties in Excel or by opening the .odc file and editing it directly. If you choose to store the password in the connection string, Excel Calculation Services passes it along with the rest of the string to the data server for validation.

Security Alert The password will not be encrypted when it is stored in the .odc file, and if the file is stored in a Data Connection Library on the server, it could potentially be read by other users.

If the data provider supports Windows Integrated Authentication, the connection string can indicate that this mode be used for authentication, in which case no username and password are stored in the connection string. This authentication model also requires that you configure the Unattended Service Account setting found on the Excel Services Settings page available on the Shared Services Administration site. If the connection string specifies Integrated Windows Authentication, Excel Calculation Services attempts to authenticate using the Unattended Service Account. In this case, the account should be configured as a Windows domain account with permissions to access the data source. Otherwise, the account can be configured as either a domain account or a local account that is given network access to connect to the external data server. If a local account is used, it must be configured the same on every Excel Calculation Services application server.

User Access Security

The level of access that a user has to a workbook stored in Excel Services is determined by the permissions given to the user in the file storage location: the SharePoint Server 2007 document library, the Windows file share, or the Web site. In the case of the document library, the permissions are those assigned to the user within SharePoint 2007. In the case of the file share or Web site, access is controlled by share permissions and NTFS rights.

You might want to do the following:

- Limit some users to having read-only access to a workbook but still give them the ability to open it and view the formulas inside it.
- Give other users more restricted access to prevent them from viewing the formulas behind the cells.

If a user has the standard Read permissions on a site, the user can open and view the entire workbook, although she won't necessarily be able to save any changes. To restrict a user further, remove the Open Items permission and leave her with only the View Items permission. With only the View Items permission, the user can view the workbook in the browser and in the Web Access Web Part but can open it only as a snapshot in Excel. Setting this permission in the SharePoint document library will affect users' rights both through Excel Web Access and Excel Web Services, but it will not affect a user accessing a workbook referenced in a shared folder location or a URL.

Performance Considerations

Excel Services is designed to scale from a single-server installation up to an enterprise environment with multiple load-balanced servers. The flexibility in the Excel Services deployment model allows servers to be added to the server farm as the demand for Excel calculation processing grows.

Scaling Excel Services

For many organizations, the responsiveness and performance of Excel Services are critical factors in the deployment of the technology to the enterprise. Depending on the size, complexity, and number of workbooks hosted in Excel Services, a single application server might not be sufficient to meet your service level objectives. The component-based architecture of Excel Services allows you to allocate services across servers to relieve bottlenecks and optimize throughput. For example, if it appears that the processing of workbook calculations or external data calls are slowing down the delivery of data, you can enable the Excel Calculation Services role on more application servers. On the other hand, if the workbooks are calculating quickly but Excel Web Access is still sluggish in rendering results, you can add more front-end Web servers to reduce the rendering load.

Enabling Components

There are a number of variations possible for scaling Excel Services to meet your needs based on the number of users and the types of workbooks and data connections your farm will be handling. The architecture of Excel Services is divided between components that run on the Web front-end servers, which consist of Excel Web Access and Excel Web Services, and Excel Calculation Services, which runs on the back-end application servers. The relationship of these components is shown in Figure 20-9. At the core of the scalable architecture is the ability of Excel Services to load-balance calculation requests across multiple application servers running Excel Calculation Services.

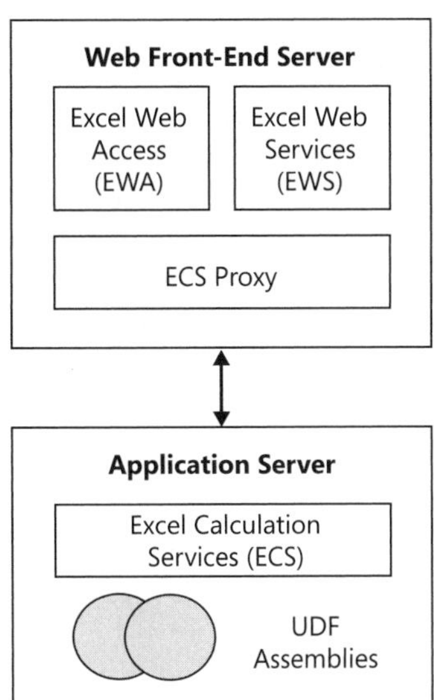

Figure 20-9 Excel Services components

Note Any user-defined function assemblies or dependency files that are used by Excel Services must be configured the same on every application server hosting Excel Calculation Services.

Enabling the Excel Calculation Services component on more than one server is simply a matter of starting the service on each of the servers that will provide calculation services. The component can either run exclusively on an application server or share the server with other SharePoint Server 2007 services. To configure a dedicated Excel Calculation Services server, open the Operations page in Central Administration and click the Excel Calculation role to highlight the components that should run on the server.

When multiple servers provide calculation services, Excel Calculation Services Proxy manages the requests from each Web front-end server and coordinates the distribution of requests to each of the calculation servers. Each server can handle the calculations for multiple workbooks at the same time and take advantage of multiple processor configurations by running requests on different threads. All the calculations for a single workbook are handled by one server and are not broken out across servers. Furthermore, once an application server has been designated to process calculations for a specific workbook, it continues to do so until the workbook is closed or the session ends. This arrangement allows Excel Services to improve performance by maintaining session state for a user interacting with a specific workbook.

Enhancing Throughput

To enhance throughput on both the front-end and back-end components, you can enable Excel Calculation Services on multiple servers to act in parallel. Figure 20-10 is an example of two servers acting in parallel. In this case, each server runs the Web Front End role, Search, and ECS, along with possibly other services as required. The Web servers themselves are load balanced through a device or service outside of SharePoint Server 2007, such as the Windows Network Load Balancing service. This arrangement allows users to make requests to a single URL and have the pages served up by either server, depending on priority and load. The workbook calculations themselves are load balanced by Excel Services between both available servers.

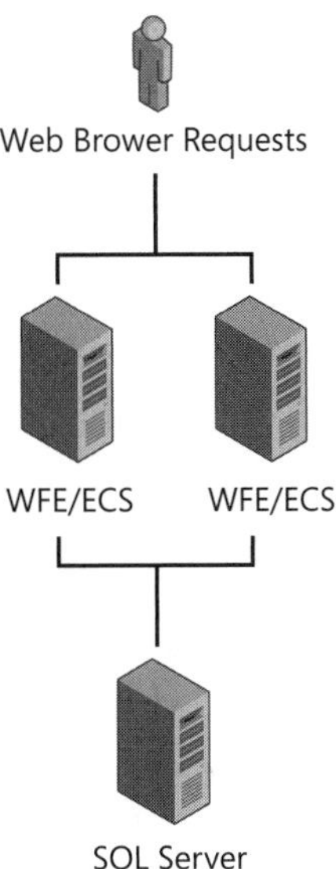

Figure 20-10 Scaling Excel Services by using multiple servers

If the heaviest usage in your farm is on the Web front-end servers, it might be more appropriate to have multiple load-balanced front-end servers but to have only one ECS server. For example, if your workbooks do not contain complex calculations with links to external data, a single application server might be able to perform all the calculations. At the same time, if your users are making heavy use of Excel Web Access Web Parts in many sites, the load might fall more heavily on the front-end server to render, cache, and refresh the Web Part displays. In this scenario, you can implement a farm configuration similar to the one shown in Figure 20-11, where two Web front-end servers both use a single Excel Calculation Server. This configuration also reduces the overhead that the Excel Services load-balancing feature would otherwise incur.

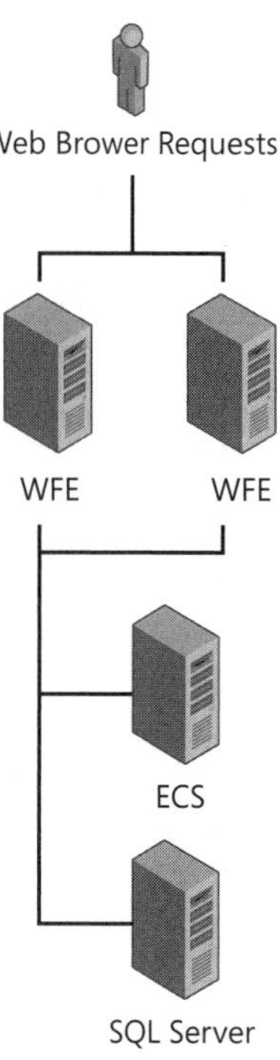

Figure 20-11 Scaling Excel Services by using a farm configuration with two Web front-end servers

A common scenario is one in which an organization needs to scale out its Excel Calculation Services components to take on a heavier load of workbook processing while the overall Web throughput is adequately handled by the Web front-end servers. This can happen as users become more aware of the capabilities of Excel Services and begin to feed in more sophisticated workbooks or to take advantage of User Defined Function assemblies on the servers. Figure 20-12 demonstrates a configuration that includes two Web front-end servers and two Excel Calculation Servers. This scenario illustrates how your Excel Services infrastructure can be expanded as the demand from your users expands. A server farm can start with only a single Excel Calculation Server and additional servers can be added as needed without having to re-architect the farm.

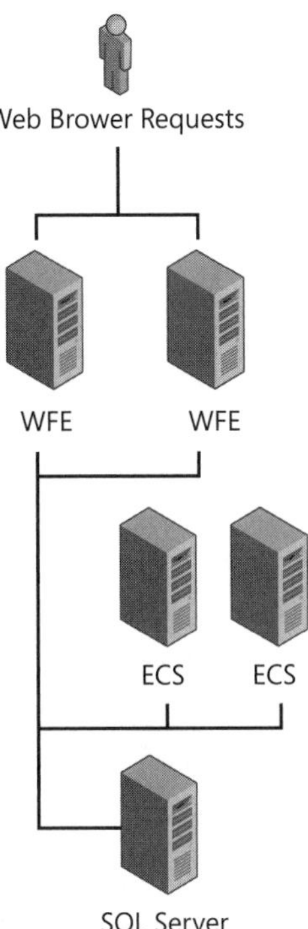

Figure 20-12 Scaling Excel Services by using two Excel Calculation Servers

Although performance scaling is one objective of adding multiple application servers to your farm, an added benefit is redundancy. By having multiple Web front-end servers and multiple Excel Calculation Servers, you also ensure that there will be no single point of failure in your server farm. If any one of the servers fails, there is always at least one server that can pick up its load temporarily. In a farm where there is only one ECS server and it fails, Excel Services will be unable to load and render workbooks and any dashboard Web Parts that use Excel data will not be available.

Modifying the Default TCP Settings

If you notice that Excel Calculation Services denies requests during periods of high usage, it might be due to a delay in releasing Transmission Control Protocol (TCP) session resources that is preventing Excel Calculation Services from receiving additional requests. By default, TCP maintains a closed connection for up to four minutes, which can result in closed or active sessions tying up all available ports and TCP control blocks. To modify the default TCP settings, you can change the *TcpTimedWaitDelay* value from 240 seconds to 30 seconds, which should still give all packets time to clear before the port is reused. Use the Registry Editor to edit this value under the following key:

HKLM\SYSTEM\ControlSet\Services\Tcpip\Parameters

Limiting the Number and Duration of Open Sessions

By default, users are allowed a maximum of 25 open Excel Services sessions. A new user connection is created each time a user opens a workbook in the browser and for each instance of a Web Access Web Part on a site page. For example, if a user opens a dashboard page that has four Web Access Web Parts each displaying a portion of a workbook, the user has consumed four sessions. When the maximum number of sessions has been reached, any additional Web Part instances fail to load and display Excel 2007 content. To change this setting, use the following steps:

1. Open SharePoint 3.0 Central Administration.
2. Under Shared Services Administration, click the Shared Services Provider hosting Excel Services.
3. Under Excel Services Settings, click Edit Excel Services Settings.
4. Under Session Management, edit the Maximum Sessions Per User setting.

The length of time that an Excel Services session remains active is determined by the Session Management settings defined on each Trusted File Location. Reducing the number of sessions that a user can start can result in Web Parts failing to load properly and frustrations for some users. To facilitate recycling unused sessions, you can adjust the Session Management settings Session Timeout and Short Session Timeout.

The Session Timeout setting controls the maximum time (in seconds) that an Excel Services session remains open after the last user interaction with the workbook through Web Access. The Short Session Timeout setting is similar and is used to configure the timeout interval for sessions that are opened but have no interaction from the user. For example, if a user opens a page with three Excel Web Access Web Parts on it, all three sessions normally expire at the end of the Short Session Timeout interval. If the user navigates to a different sheet in one of the workbooks before the Short Session interval expires, that session will not expire until the Session Timeout interval has passed. While a session is active, any interaction with the workbook is done through the existing session, thereby minimizing the need to open new sessions. If the Short Session Timeout expires and the user then begins interacting with workbook, Excel Services opens a new session. To change the Session Management settings, follow these steps:

1. Open SharePoint 3.0 Central Administration.
2. Under Shared Services Administration, click the Shared Services Provider hosting Excel Services.
3. Under Excel Services Settings, click Trusted File Locations.
4. Click the Trusted File Location you want to configure.

5. Under Session Management, edit the Session Timeout or Short Session Timeout settings.

Important Web Part sessions are not preserved following a browser refresh. Using the Refresh button in the browser to reload an entire SharePoint Server 2007 site page that has Excel Services Web Access Web Parts on it causes new sessions to be opened for every Web Part.

Accessing Data from Other Sources

Data Connection Libraries are SharePoint libraries that are similar to document libraries and are used as shared repositories for Office Data Connection (.odc) files. The .odc files were introduced in Excel Services in Microsoft Office XP as a means of storing the connection information needed by Excel to access back-end databases. Users create .odc files when they connect to an external data source, such as a SQL Server database. These files are stored, by default, in the My Data Sources folder on the user's local drive. This arrangement prevents them from being easily shared with other users.

By creating a Data Connection Library and populating it with the standard .odc files that your users are most likely to need access to, you can simplify the challenge of reusing these data connections. Your users can then browse to the library when creating an external connection and select from the available .odc files. The next time a change occurs on the network that affects the connection, such as a change in the name of a database view, the modification can be made one time in the .odc file on the server and all user connections will automatically receive the update the next time they refresh the connection.

You can create a Data Connection Library in any Web site that users will have permissions to access. To add an .odc file, upload a predefined file from the My Data Sources folder on your local drive, or direct other users to do so. To use the shared data connections in Excel 2007, click the Existing Connections button under the Data menu and click Browse For More to open the Browse dialog box. Type the address to the Data Connection Library on the server, and select the .odc file to use. You will then be offered the choice of displaying the data as a Table, Pivot Table Report, or Pivot Chart and Pivot Table Report. The Data Connection Library feature of SharePoint Server 2007 can be used independently of Excel Services. In this way, users can take advantage of shared connection settings without publishing their workbook to a SharePoint document library.

Data Connection Library

You can make it even easier for users to connect to a Data Connection Library by pushing the library listing to users through the Published Links To Office Client feature of SharePoint Server 2007. You can find this command under the User Profiles And My Sites section on the Shared Services Provider administration page. Add a new link and provide the URL to the Data Connection Library along with a description that users can recognize.

For security reasons, Excel Services does not automatically trust .odc files stored in all Data Connection Libraries. Excel Services allows workbooks to use only connections that are stored in Trusted Data Connection Libraries. To identify a Data Connection Library as trusted, follow these steps:

1. Open the Shared Services Provider page.
2. Under Excel Services Management, click Trusted Data Connection Libraries.
3. Click Add Trusted Data Connection Library.
4. Type in the URL address of the Data Connection Library you want to add and, optionally, add a description, as shown in Figure 20-13, and then click OK.

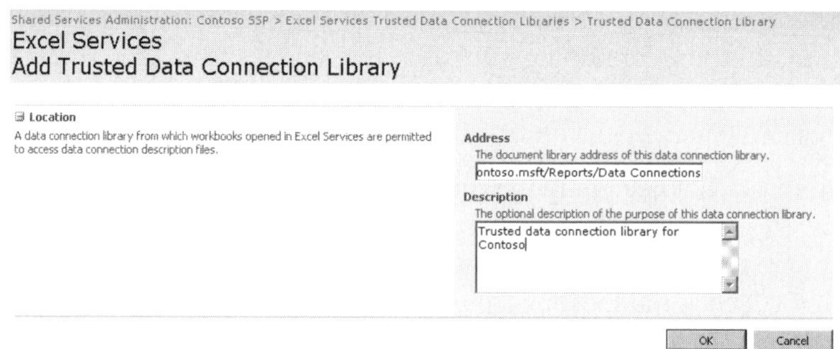

Figure 20-13 Adding a Trusted Data Connection Library

Important Excel Services does not support viewing spreadsheets in the Web browser if they have connections to standard database tables (referred to as query tables) or pivot tables. Only connections to SQL Analysis Services cubes are supported.

Trusted Data Providers

Excel Services restricts access to external database providers used in workbooks that it processes. Only database providers that it is explicitly configured to trust can be accessed from data connections in the workbook. If a connection attempts to access a nontrusted data provider, Excel Services will not load the workbook. To add a data provider as a Trusted Data Provider, follow these steps:

1. Open the Shared Services Provider page.
2. Under Excel Services Management, click Trusted Data Providers.
3. Click Add Trusted Data Provider.
4. Type in the identifier for the data provider you want to add.
5. Select one of the following provider types:
   - **OLE DB** Use for most Microsoft and many third-party drivers that have been written to use the current OLE DB interface.
   - **ODBC** Use for drivers that confirm to the Open Database Connectivity standard used by most database manufacturers.
   - **ODBC DSN** Use to identify a reference to a Data Source Name on the local server that contains connection string information for an ODBC driver.
6. Click OK.

User-Defined Function Assembly

For complex server-side calculations or to call scalable middle-tier code libraries, Excel Services supports custom user-defined functions . Only user-defined functions written as managed code in the Microsoft .NET Framework version 2.0 assemblies are supported directly by Excel Services. This architecture provides Excel Services with the security and stability advantages of the .NET Framework common language runtime, and it allows the deployed code to be subject to .NET Framework code access security policies. User-defined functions written for earlier versions of Excel Services and those written to run in the Excel 2007 client cannot be used by Excel Services unless they are called from within a .NET Framework 2.0 library, or *wrapped*, so that they are not exposed directly to SharePoint Server 2007.

For user-defined functions to be loaded and run by Excel Services, you have to register the assembly as a Trusted Assembly on the Excel Services server. When installing user-defined functions, you can place them either in a local directory, in a network share, or in the Microsoft .NET Framework global assembly cache (GAC). Any directory can be used for storing a local copy of the assembly as long as the Excel Services process account has permissions to access the folder. If a local path is used, the file must be placed in the same directory on every Excel Services server and any updates to the assemblies need to be copied to every server. Using a network share allows for one common code base to be used across all servers, but doing so might lead to errors if the network connection to the share fails. Registering the assembly in the GAC allows you to keep all versions of the assemblies in one place and facilitates applying code access security policies. Once the file is installed on the server, use the following steps to register it with Excel Services:

1. Open the Shared Services Provider page.
2. Under Excel Services Management, click User-Defined Function Assemblies.
3. Click Add User-Defined Function Assembly.
4. Under the Assembly field, enter the unique identifier for the UDF file.

   For a local file, type the full path–for example:

   ```
   D:\ExcelUDFs\CustomFunctions.dll
   or \\ExcelServer\ExcelUDFs\CustomFunctions.dll
   ```

   For an assembly in the GAC, type the Strong Name–for example:

   ```
   CustomFunctions, Version=1.1.0.0, Culture=Neutral, PublicKeyToken=d7012336c6
   ae8fd27
   ```

5. Select the Assembly Location option that corresponds with the path–either GAC or Local File–and then click OK.

Summary

In this chapter, we have examined the new Business Intelligence capabilities available in SharePoint Server 2007 through Excel Services. We began with a discussion of how to configure Excel Services on servers where Office SharePoint Server 2007 has already been installed. We identified the basic steps required to enable Excel Services and to configure a Trusted File Location, which will allow workbooks to be processed on the server. Next we reviewed the roles of the major components of Excel Services–including Excel Calculation Services, Excel Web Access, Excel Web Services, and the Excel Calculation Service Proxy. We then explained how to publish workbooks through the Publish command in Excel 2007, including how to hide sheets and define parameters that affect the way users interact with the workbook. We then looked at the ways that users can work with workbook data through Excel Web Access and Web Access Web Parts. In the next section, we described ways to control security on workbooks accessed by Excel Services. We discussed performance considerations with Excel Web Services, including controlling the number of sessions and the timeout duration for each session. Finally, we looked at ways that workbooks can access external data sources from within Excel Services.

Chapter 21

Administrating Office Forms Server 2007 in Office SharePoint Server 2007

This chapter examines Microsoft Office Forms Server 2007. Office Forms Server 2007 works with Microsoft Office InfoPath 2007 to form a complete forms solution for your enterprise deployment. Numerous features allow administrators and developers to work both in the enterprise and with local teams using InfoPath forms, while using Forms Server 2007 to make those forms available on demand. Office Forms Server 2007 and Office InfoPath 2007 are closely related in that InfoPath is used to create forms and the Forms Server is used to provide browser access to those forms. In fact, the InfoPath program and Office Forms Server 2007 are so closely related that it would be impractical and misleading to discuss one without mentioning appropriate features of the other.

Forms Server by Popular Request

An enterprise develops and deploys hundreds, if not thousands, of forms throughout its corporate facilities. Many companies wanted to take advantage of Microsoft InfoPath 2003 because it was a forms-building program that produced .xml files natively, allowed easy editing of the form itself, and allowed easy integration with Microsoft SharePoint Portal Server. However, it was not possible in InfoPath 2003 to fill out InfoPath forms using a Web browser. Having such a powerful technology that functioned fully only on the desktop led to requests by many to make InfoPath forms available over the Internet so that they could be filled in by anyone with a Web browser.

Although InfoPath 2003 had a Web solution, that solution offered just read-only access to the forms. InfoPath 2003 was intended to become SharePoint Portal Server 2003's forms solution. Because the appeal of both SharePoint Portal Server 2003 and InfoPath 2003 would be broadened by adding the ability to work with InfoPath 2003 forms from a browser, Microsoft created Office Forms Server 2007.

Office Forms Server 2007 Features and Enhancements

Office Forms Server 2007 makes available to the end user InfoPath 2007 forms, whether the client is a Microsoft Office system client or only a browser. Office Forms Server 2007 provides several benefits, two of which are particularly important. First, Office Forms Server provides a consistent, secure, and robust mechanism to more easily handle *n*-tier solutions. Second, Forms Server 2007 provides what has been called the *reach experience*. This allows people who do not have the InfoPath 2007 client software installed on their machines to fill out and view Office InfoPath forms using their Web browser. This ability is called *zero footprint form fill-in*. With the addition of Forms Server 2007, InfoPath is poised to become the new de facto standard for generating and filling out forms in an enterprise.

Forms Server 2007 is built on top of Microsoft Windows SharePoint Services 3.0. This underpinning allows Forms Server 2007 to supply several valuable abilities to the 2007 release of the Microsoft Office system. Its most notable feature is the ability to fill in forms on a remote computer using only a Web browser, including Internet Explorer, FireFox, and Apple Computers Safari. In addition, InfoPath 2007 forms can contain Microsoft .NET-managed code that performs a wide variety of valuable functions, such as automatically totaling prices on a purchase order or invoice.

Security Alert If it is not checked, the .NET-managed code can be a security risk. However, Forms Server 2007 helps keep the work place secure by allowing administrators to explicitly authorize the execution of custom managed-code business logic contained in InfoPath forms.

Here is an expanded list of Forms Server 2007 benefits:

- Allows explicit administrative authorization of custom business logic

- Promotes designing of forms once for both the InfoPath client and Web browser
- Helps improve security by the use of C# and Microsoft Visual Basic .NET to implement custom business logic
- Helps you comply with Sarbains-Oxley Act requirements, because it leverages the powerful digital signature-handling capabilities of InfoPath 2007
- Provides administrative control over the data connections an InfoPath form can use
- Uses InfoPath 2007 forms on personal digital assistants (PDAs) and other mobile Web devices
- Includes a backup and restore feature
- Hosts an InfoPath form in either an ASPX page or a Windows application
- Archives forms in a fixed format for legal and long-term retention purposes
- Prechecks a form's design and its features to ensure that it will function correctly when deployed to a SharePoint Portal Server document library
- Allows access to the same InfoPath 2007 form using a Web browser from multiple URLs
- Includes a powerful administrative command-line interface

Office Forms Server 2007 Architecture

Forms can contain custom business logic programmed in either C# or Visual Basic .NET. Moreover, forms can be deployed using a process called *administrative deployment*. In fact, forms must be administratively deployed if they contain custom business logic or managed code. Initially, this process places references to these forms in the Windows SharePoint Services 3.0 configuration database. When the process is complete, the form itself is placed into the Windows SharePoint Services 3.0 content database of the hosting site. You can upload forms to a central location and then list and manage them in the Central Administration site in the Application Management's InfoPath Forms Services section.

The Web browser accesses the form using a URL with the following syntax:

```
http://contos0.contoso.msft:39250/sites/ori/_layouts/
FormServer.aspx?XsnLocation=....wdata2.xsn&SaveLocation=...
url_to_Form_Library&Source=...AllItems.aspx&DefaultItemOpen=1.
```

FormServer.aspx accesses the Forms Server, which in turn accesses the needed content from the content database. FormServer.aspx then presents the form to the user after checking with the configuration database to make sure it's marked as safe. InfoPath forms are packaged in a file with an .xsn extension. The primary files contained in the .xsn file are listed in Table 21-1.

Table 21-1 Files Inside an InfoPath .xsn File

Extension	Name	Description
.xsf	Form Definition	Specification for an entire application. It is the application's conceptual manifest and can be customized.
.xsd	Schema Files	Holds type definitions for .xml files and connections.
.xsl	Transform Files	Each view is visually produced by applying a transform file to the appropriate underlying .xml files (for example, the template.xml and sampledata.xml files).
.xct	Component Template	Holds editing controls used to work with your forms (only in pre–version 1.0 .xsn files).
.js, .vbs	Script Files	Hold custom logic, event handlers, and so on.
.dll, .exe	Custom COM	Hold custom business logic.
.htm and others		Miscellaneous resource files used in the form application.

These files are parsed when run by the InfoPath client and are used to transform the .xml files into .html files for display in the InfoPath client. The .xsd schema files are used to validate the form data and structure, whether coming from a saved InfoPath .xml form file or from a database connection, .xml file, Web service, or SharePoint list.

> **Note** There will be one XML transformation file (*.xsl) for each InfoPath View that produces an appropriate file for display. The .xsl files can produce any type of file, but for Web purposes, they are generally .tlm, .asp, and .aspx files.

The Forms Server must take these various files, as shown in Figure 21-1, and convert them into corresponding .aspx, .css, and .js files for rendering in browsers such as Apple Safari, FoxFire, and Internet Explorer.

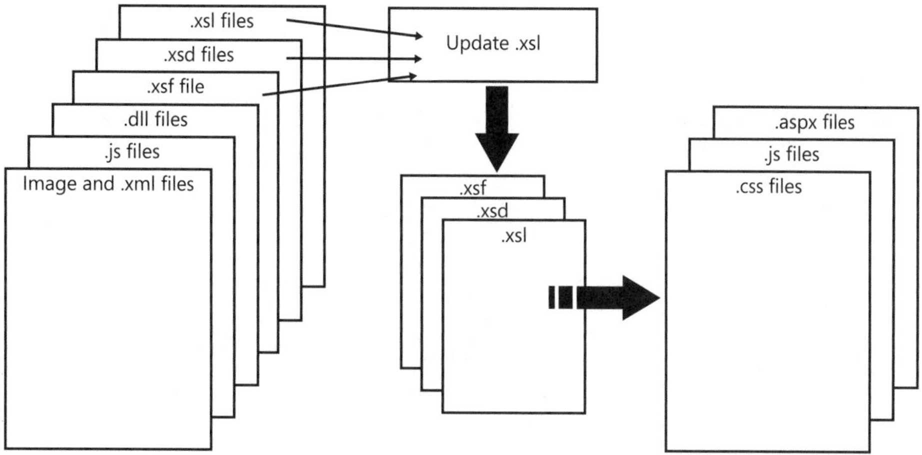

Figure 21-1 The Update.xsl file updates the view .xsl, .xsf, and .xsd files if necessary

Configuring Office Forms Server 2007

Forms Server 2007 is available in Microsoft Office SharePoint Server 2007 as a feature and needs to be made accessible to your various site collections. You must have at least one Shared Services Provider (SSP) configured and associated with the Web application to which you intend to publish InfoPath forms.

> **Note** You can check the association of an SSP to a Web application by going to Central Administration, Application Management and, in the Office SharePoint Server Shared Services section, selecting Manage This Farm's Shared Services.

To ensure that forms services will work properly in a given site collection, you need to enable the Office SharePoint Server Enterprise feature. To do this, complete the following steps:

> **Note** To use the Forms Server with InfoPath browser-enabled forms, you need to create your site collection at the root (/) of your Web application, not under "/sites."

1. Navigate to your site, and select Site Settings from the Site Actions drop-down menu.
2. In the Site Collection Administration column, select the Site Collection Features link to open the Site Collection Features page.

3. Locate and activate the Office SharePoint Server Enterprise Site Collection Features, as shown in Figure 21-2.

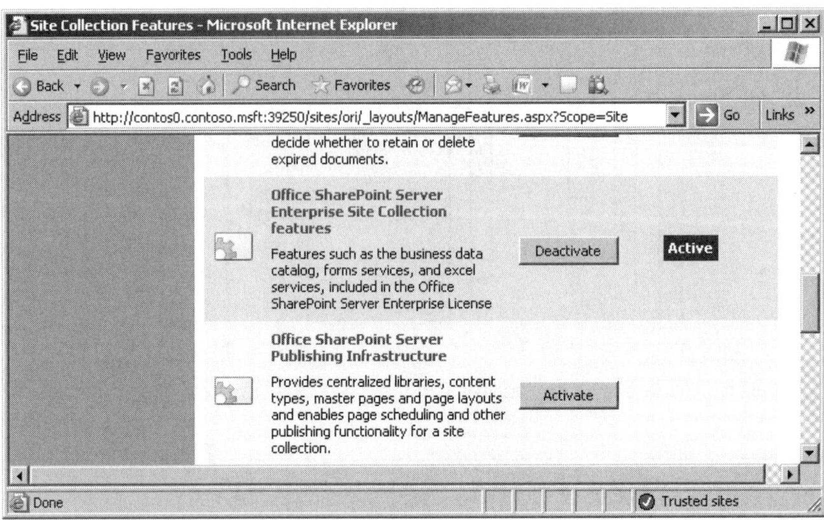

Figure 21-2 A list of site collection features

Important Office Forms Server 2007 requires a premium client license. If you haven't already activated Premium features, go to the Operations tab in Central Administration. In the Upgrade And Migration section, select the Enable Premium Features link.

4. After you activate this feature, return to the Office SharePoint Server Central Administration site and click the Application Management tab.
5. In the InfoPath Forms Services section, select Configure InfoPath Forms Services to open the page shown in Figure 21-3.

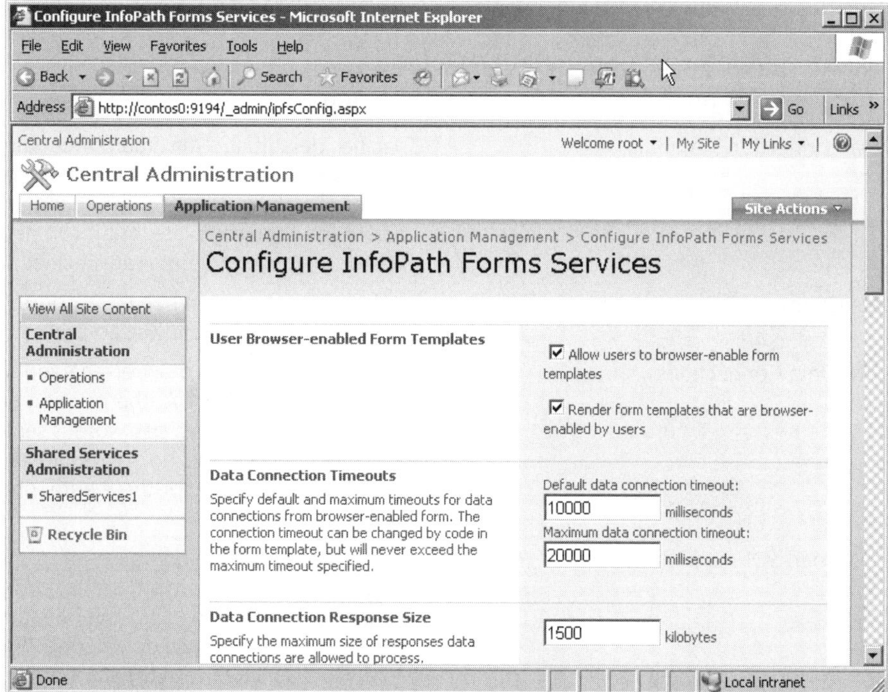

Figure 21-3 Configuring InfoPath Forms Services

On this page, you have several configuration options:

a. If you clear the Allow Users To Browser-Enable Form Templates check box, the following message is displayed whenever a user attempts to publish an InfoPath 2007 form to a form library:

   This form is browser-compatible, but it cannot be browser-enabled on the selected site.

b. Selecting the Render Form Templates That Are Browser-Enabled By Users check box prohibits the form from actually appearing even if the Allow Users To Browser-Enable Form Templates" check box is selected.

c. The Allow Cross-Domain Data Access For User Form Templates option addresses data access. However, when working with InfoPath Forms that might also contain ActiveX controls, keep in mind that Internet Explorer has zone security configurations. For example, Internet Explorer treats URL prefix changes, such as changing HTTP to HTTPS, as domain changes.

Refer to Table 21-2 for a description of other available configuration options.

Table 21-2 Additional Configuration Options

Configuration option	Description
Data Connection Timeouts	Specifies default and maximum timeouts for data connections from a browser-enabled form. The connection timeout can be changed by code in the form template, but it can never exceed the maximum timeout specified.
Data Connection Response Size	Specifies the maximum size of responses that data connections are allowed to process.
HTTP Data Connections	If data connections in browser-enabled form templates require Basic Authentication or Digest Authentication, a password is sent over the network. Select this box to require an SSL-encrypted connection for these authentication types.
Embedded SQL Authentication	Forms that connect to databases can embed a SQL username and password in the connection string. The connection string can be read in clear text in the universal data connection (UDC) file associated with the solution or in the solution manifest. Clear this box to block forms from using embedded SQL credentials.
Authentication To Data Sources (User Form Templates)	Data connection files can contain authentication information, such as an explicit username and password or a Microsoft Office Single Sign-On Application ID. Select this box to allow user form templates to use this authentication information.
Thresholds	Specify the thresholds at which to end user sessions and log error messages.
Form Session State	Form session state stores data necessary to maintain a user session. File attachment data in the form receives an additional 50 percent of session state space.

The Form Session State option, which is the final option listed in Table 21-2, needs a little more explaining. It has two radio buttons:

- Session State Service (best for low-bandwidth users)
- Form View (reduces database load on server). If form session state is larger than the specified value, the Session State Service will be used instead.

The Form View choice houses the forms information to be preserved during the roundtrip to the server in a hidden *html* control. Although it is true that this reduces the load on the back-end database server, the tradeoff is that it will increase the load on the front-end Web server.

Authentication, Security, and Forms Server 2007 Web Services Proxy

The overall architecture of a Forms Server 2007 and InfoPath 2007 implementation can quickly take on a three-tier or *n*-tier structure, which can complicate security and authentication. When the user (layer 1) requests a form from his Web browser, he accesses Internet Information Services (IIS) (layer 2), which passes the request to the Forms Server (layer 3). The Forms Server then loads and converts the InfoPath 2007 form, which might attempt to access a Web service (layer 4) to supply some of the detail it will return to the user. All these layers or tiers require authentication credentials to be passed along to the next layer, or tier.

For security reasons, Web services often require separate authentication. Under normal circumstances, the Forms Server can pass on only the user's credentials. However, these credentials often do not have the necessary permissions to access the Web service. You need to use the Forms Server Web Services Proxy Configuration option, which you can access by going to Central Administration and clicking the Manage The Web Service Proxy link in the Application Management section. This option allows users to access forms that, in turn, access Web services on behalf of the user without that user needing to enter her security credentials multiple times. As administrators and planners, you need to be aware of this potential problem and how to configure Forms Server 2007 and InfoPath 2007 to work securely.

A user authentication occurs either through the InfoPath client or the Web browser connecting through the Forms Server. This causes the Forms Server itself to attempt to connect to the various Web services, without having any way of supplying correct authentication credentials to the Web services. This problem is referred to in various documents as *multihop authentication* and is quite common in a variety of distributed application situations.

Real World **Alternate Authentication in Addition to the Proxy Settings**

Because a form might need to use multiple Web services—each requiring different credentials–Forms Server 2007 works with user-created universal data connection (UDC/UDCX) files to streamline the security processes across multiple tiers.

To manage the Web proxy services, you first need to go to Central Administration, Application Management, InfoPath Forms Services, Manage The Web Service Proxy, and select the Enable check box in the Enable The Web Service Proxy section, as shown in Figure 21-4.

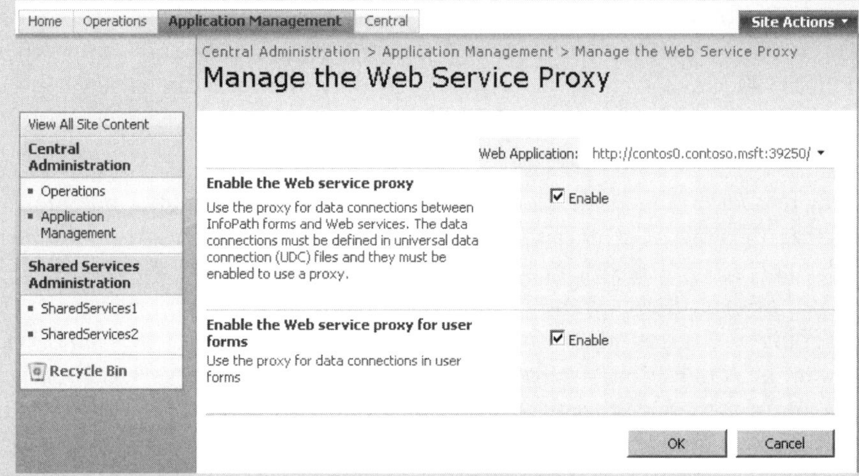

Figure 21-4 Managing Web proxy configuration settings

The text accompanying the check box explains that there needs to be a UDC file for the form's data connection. You can also enable the service for user-deployed forms on this page.

In the real world, this setup might be too restrictive. If you find it necessary to use multiple authentications based on different users and it is not appropriate to always use the Web application's account, you can use the *<UsernameToken>* passed to the Web service to programmatically impersonate whatever account necessary to accomplish your goal.

By default, this proxy connects to the Web service using the Web application pool account. This means that *all* Web service connections made in this entire Web application will authenticate using the Web application pool account. If you decide to use a UDC file, it needs to reside in a Data Connection library in the Web application the proxy is set to use, and the form library using the proxy needs to be encapsulated in the same Web application.

In the following sample code, there is an .xml element named *UsernameToken* that contains a child element named *Username*. This information is passed in the WS-Security header sent to the Web service. The header is set up in the UDC file and is used by the InfoPath form. The Forms Server using the Form Converter processes the InfoPath form and emits an HTML/ASPX file that is set up to use headers as prescribed by the UDC file. When the form connects to a Web service, the header is passed on, from the browser to the Forms Server and onto the Web service. Here is what the code looks like:

```
<!-- No Password -->
<UsernameToken>
   <Username>Bob</Username>
</UsernameToken>
```

This information can then be extracted and used inside the Web service programmatically to authorize this user as needed by impersonating, if necessary, the application pool account with sufficient permissions for access. Using the UDC file, an administrator can set this scenario up and then request that a programmer use this information from within the Web service to allow the needed specific user access.

To actually get the InfoPath form to communicate with the Web service and pass this information to it, you need to edit the UDC file as follows:

1. Locate the *ServiceUrl* XML element.
2. Set this element's *UseFormsServiceProxy* attribute to "1" (*UseFormsServiceProxy="1"*).

Deploying Forms Server 2007

In this section, we'll discuss and illustrate how to deploy Office Forms Server 2007 in your SharePoint Server 2007 deployment. We'll start by discussing how to plan for your deployment, with a focus on security. Then we'll move to a discussion on forms types and the different methods that can be used to publish forms in your environment. Along the way, you'll learn the steps you need to take to fully deploy forms in your environment.

Planning Deployment

Before deploying a form, you must first plan where you will deploy it. The deployment location of a form depends on several factors, but each factor, in one way or another, revolves around security considerations. For example, forms cannot be browser-enabled if they contain ActiveX controls.

Forms that perform certain operations, such as executing application programming interfaces (APIs) that InfoPath designates as level-3 security risks, require the Full Trust security level set on the form. You set the security level for a form in the InfoPath program while in Design mode by using the Form Options page, shown in Figure 21-5. This is done either by the person designing the form or an administrator at some point after the form is completed. One way to find the Form Options page is by navigating to the Info-Path form template (.xsn) using Windows Explorer. Then right-click the .xsn file, and choose the "design" selection. When the InfoPath program opens, navigate to Tools, Form Options, and then Security And Trust.

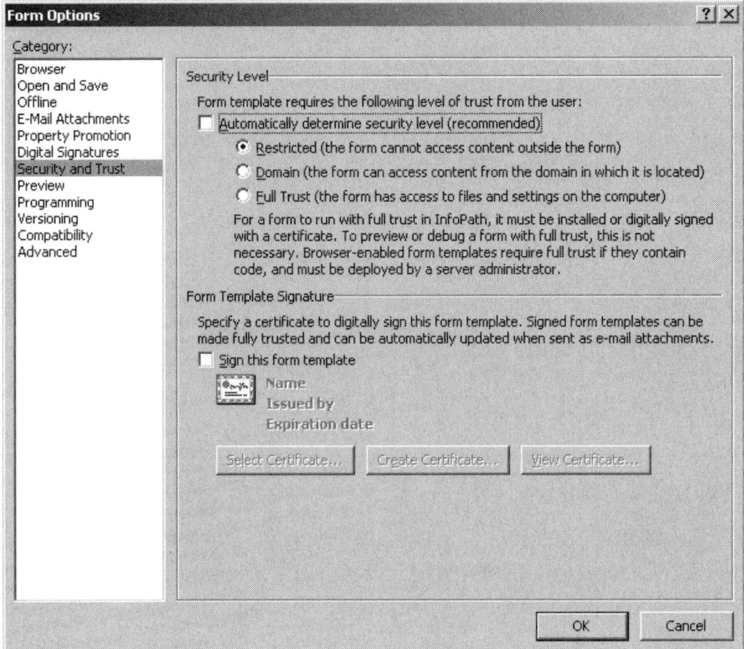

Figure 21-5 InfoPath security-level settings

A fully trusted form can be physically deployed in two general locations: either on the end user's machine or in a Windows SharePoint Services 3.0 form library. If installed directly on the user's machine, the form need not be digitally signed. However, a digital signature is required if the form is placed in a form library.

Real World Security in Forms Server 2007

As a planner involved in setting up an InfoPath project or an administrator with knowledge that such a project is being planned, you need to be aware of at least the following seven security models:

1. InfoPath's own security model, which divides its universe into three security levels: Restricted, Domain, and Full Trust. Each InfoPath API is given a security-level designation. These designations represent the security risk assessment of the individual method or property and range from 0 through 3, with 1 being reserved. The InfoPath 2007 *save* method is an example of a level-3 API that requires the form to be at the Full Trust level.
2. The Internet Explorer concept of security zones, which corresponds roughly to the InfoPath 2007 security levels. Internet Explorer uses Internet, Intranet, Trusted, and Restricted zones. The InfoPath form has to comply with both the Internet Explorer security requirements and the InfoPath security model to operate correctly. For example, the presence of both an InfoPath form of the *save* method and an ActiveX control that accesses the filing system brings both security models into operation.
3. The operating system's own security model, which needs to be accounted for. Can the user access a form that is installed on his hard drive, a UNC share, or a Web server?
4. The Windows SharePoint Services 3.0 security model, which might not allow a user to access a certain form library.
5. The Office SharePoint Server 2007 security model, which might not allow a user to find the form she wants by using search.
6. The Office Forms Server 2007 security model, which might prohibit a user from accessing information across a domain.
7. External interacting systems, such as the kind your user might need to authenticate and access the form from a Unix/Linux box using a Java-based security system. Also, you might want the form to be accessible to a PDA or other mobile device.

It should be evident at this point that setting up a client server project such as InfoPath in today's world is something that requires a good understanding of the various security layers and their interactions that are transparent at the desktop. Before you implement a Forms Server 2007 solution, the first thing you need to do is have a clear understanding of your enterprises security policies. These security policies must be documented in writing, and someone in authority must sign off on them. A general understanding concerning what is allowable, although quite common in the real world, is not good enough. In fact, it is a prescription for disaster.

Without a clear understanding of your security requirements, you don't even know where you can deploy the form once it's designed. Neither do you know what InfoPath APIs you can use, because enterprise security policy might prohibit either their use or the location for deployment these APIs might dictate. Gather together the interested parties—which might include upper management, project and team leads, and InfoPath-savvy senior developers—and hash out exactly what you want to accomplish with your solution, who needs access to it, where you want to deploy it, and how you want to deploy it. And, above all, agree to exactly what your enterprise security policies are.

Form Types and Forms Server 2007

There are two form types in InfoPath 2007:

- Browser-accessible forms called *InfoPath browser forms*
- Client-accessible forms called *InfoPath client forms*

Office Forms Server 2007 is concerned with the browser-accessible forms, so we will deal only with browser-deployable forms. Within the browser forms family, there are two types of deployment:

- User-deployed forms
- Administrator-deployed and administrator-approved forms

Regardless of the deployment mechanism used, the user initiating the process needs permissions to create lists and libraries on the farm or site collection, whichever is the target of the deployment.

For an InfoPath form to be browser viewable, it must be marked to be so in the InfoPath application at form design time. A form can be marked as browser viewable and available for use by selecting the Design Checker link in the InfoPath task pane and then selecting Change Compatibility Settings, which opens the dialog box shown in Figure 21-6.

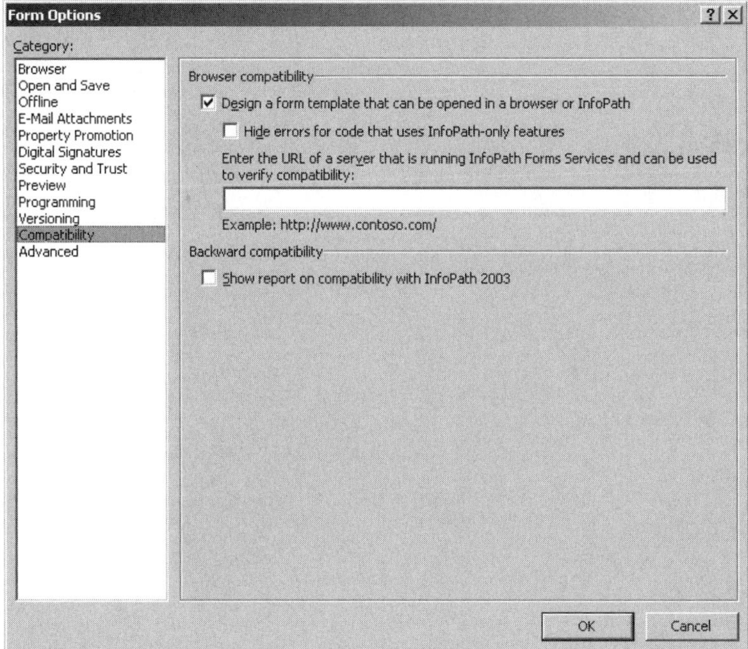

Figure 21-6 InfoPath browser-compatibility settings

If the Design A Form Template That Can Be Opened In A Browser Or InfoPath check box is not selected, the form cannot be used with Forms Server 2007.

Understanding User-Deployed Forms

Two form characteristics distinguish the user-deployable form from an administrator-deployable form:

1. It must have Domain Security Level as the form's trust level.
2. It must have only declarative features—that is, no custom code. Also, the forms server must be set up to allow users to Web-enable forms.

Publishing a form is generally a task performed by the InfoPath form designer, although it can be done by an administrator after a form is already finished being designed. It is true that administrators do not publish user-deployable forms as a general rule. When a user publishes a form to a form library directly or as a content type to a site collection and subsequently associated with a form library, the form is in a practical sense deployed without administrator intervention. However, administrators might be asked to work with forms that are not properly set up for them to work with, and in these cases, a general knowledge of the user-deployable publishing process will prove extremely helpful.

To begin the publishing process, invoke the InfoPath Publishing Wizard. This wizard has a link to it on the task pane of the InfoPath application. Figure 21-7 shows the initial page of this wizard.

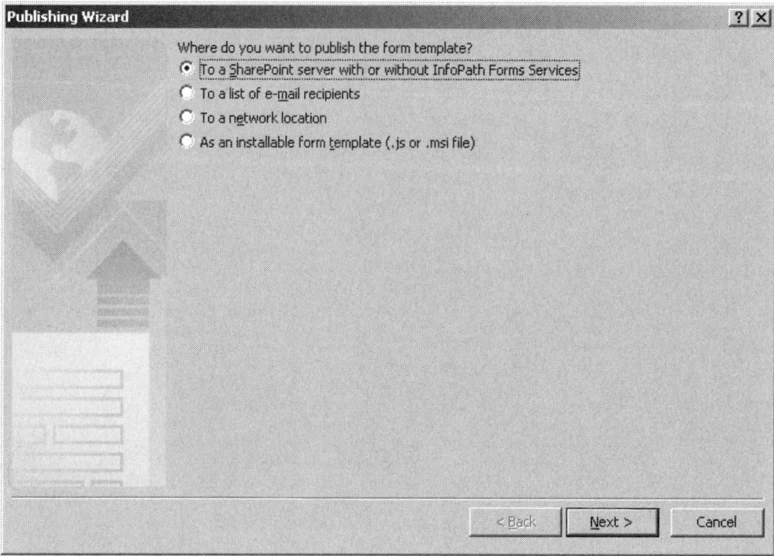

Figure 21-7 Initial InfoPath Publishing Wizard page

Select the To A SharePoint Server With Or Without InfoPath Forms Services option. On the next page (shown in Figure 21-8), enter the URL to your SharePoint site.

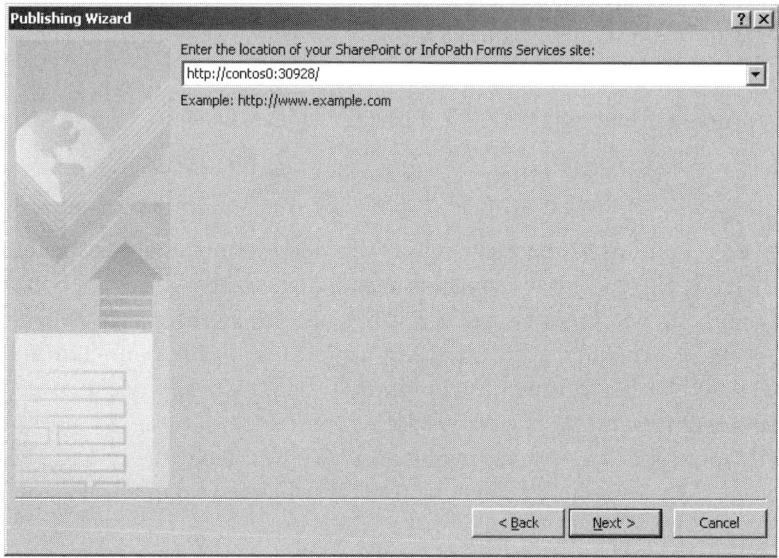

Figure 21-8 InfoPath Publishing Wizard URL text box

Note If you keep getting a dialog box no matter what URL you try stating that your URL is invalid, you might try opening Services from Administrative Tools and disabling System Event Notification and see if that will solve your problem.

On the next page (shown in Figure 21-9), choose one of the following three mechanisms to use in deploying Web forms:

- Document Library
- Site Content Type (Advanced)
- Administrator-Approved Form Template (Advanced)

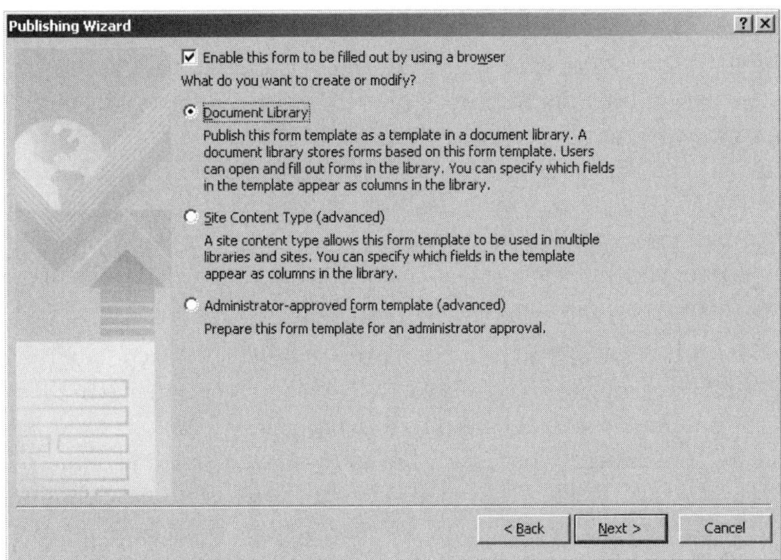

Figure 21-9 InfoPath Publishing Wizard deployment choices

We mentioned earlier in the "Form Types and Forms Server 2007" section that a form must be specially marked to be used with the Forms Server. Yet, here again, in this dialog box, we see a similar check box. These two configuration options are not the same but work in tandem. This check box can disable a form from being used with Office Forms Server at publishing time versus design time. This means that the form can be published to one location as a browser-viewable form and to another location as only viewable in the InfoPath client application. However, if the form is not originally set up for use with the Forms Server, selecting the Enable This Form To Be Filled Out By Using A Browser check box in this wizard page cannot make it browser compatible.

If the check box for browser usability is not selected, the Administrator-Approved Form Template (Advanced) option button will be dimmed. This particular option is useful if the actual user who wants to publish a form does not have sufficient permissions to do so. In that case, the user can publish the form to a location that both she and an administrator have access to. The administrator can then complete the process.

These choices represent three availability scopes:

- **Form library** Accessible forms usable only in a specific Form library in a specific site
- **Site collection** Accessible forms usable by only a specific site collection
- **Farm-accessible forms** Usable by all site collections and Web applications

Farm-accessible forms are really InfoPath form templates that are treated as content types. Although it might not be immediately obvious from looking at the wizard page, farm-accessible forms are part of the Administrator-Approved Form Template (Advanced) option. These forms are content types like the site collection–accessible scoped forms; however, these are available farm wide, not just to a specific site collection. We will talk more about content types and forms as we go on. Content type forms that are available and have been uploaded to the farm for farm-wide use can be listed by going to Central Administration, Application Management, and then clicking the Manage Form Templates link. (For more information, see Chapter 15, "Managing Content Types.")

Site collection–accessible forms are limited to a specific site collection. This type of form is also really an InfoPath form template that is treated as a content type. Content type forms that are available to a specific site collection can be listed by going to your site's Site Settings, and clicking the Site Content Type Gallery link in the Galleries section of the Site Settings page of a site in a particular site collection of a particular Web application. *Form library–accessible* forms are normal InfoPath form templates that are published directly to a specific site's specific form library.

As a content type, your form can be used in a form library as one of its library templates. (A form library can have multiple templates.) A form that has been designated as a content type can be linked to site collections in one of two ways:

- Directly to a single site's site collection by selecting the Site Content Type (Advanced) option
- To any site collection in any Web application on your farm by using the Administrator-Approved Form Template (Advanced) option

Choosing a Where to Deploy Forms

You might be wondering when to use one of the above deployment choices rather than another. Table 21-3 offers a concise outline of your choices and provides some guidelines for choosing where to deploy your forms.

Table 21-3 Form Deployment Choices

Category for identification purposes only	Deployment location	Form characteristics	Actor
A	Deploy to a specific form library using the Document Library option	Form has: Only declarative additions and Domain Level security	User with create list/library permissions.
B	Deploy a form as a content type to a specific site collection (can be used in multiple sites or form libraries) using Site Content Type (Advanced) option	Form has : Only declarative additions and Domain Level security	User with create list/library permissions. (See the "Single Site Collection Content Type—User Deployment" section.)
C	Deploy a form as a content type to a specific site collection (can be used in multiple sites or form libraries) using Site Content Type (Advanced) option	Form has one or more of the following characteristics: 1. Requires Full Trust 2. Data Connection Administrator controlled 3. Has managed form code*	User can initiate this by publishing the form in InfoPath to a specific site collection using the InfoPath deployment Wizard's Site Content Type (advanced) radio button option OR by using the method outlined in the Actor column in "D" immediately below.
D	Deploy a form as a content type to the farm (Central Administration) for use in many site collections (use in multiple Web applications, site collections, sites, or form libraries in each site collection) using Administrator-Approved Form Template (Advanced) option.	Form has one or more of the following characteristics: 1. Requires Full Trust 2. Renders on a mobile device 3. Data Connection Administrator controlled 4. Has managed form code	User can initiate this by publishing the form in InfoPath to a site collection and saving the actual form to a location an administrator can verify, upload, and activate. (See the "Farm Wide Content Type—Administrative Approved Deployment" section.)

Note The difference between A and B in Table 21-3 is whether the form is to be used in a single form library or made available to multiple form libraries in a single site collection. The difference between C and D is whether the form is to be used in a single site collection or made available to all site collections in all Web applications on the farm.

The managed form code characteristic can be confusing because older Visual Basic Script and Visual Basic for Applications scripting code can be included in a form. It is true that the form can only be administratively approved and deployed, but it will only run in the InfoPath client, not a Web browser. However, the discussion here is about Microsoft Forms Server 2007 and browser forms, *which must have only managed code.*

Single Site Collection Content Type—User Deployment

The Directly To A Single Site's Site Collection option of the InfoPath Publishing Wizard shown in Figure 21-9 makes the form template accessible only to a particular site collection. However, that site collection might have numerous sites, each of which might have several form libraries that could all use the form designated as a content type. What follows is a pictorial step-by-step guide. It shows how to deploy a form as a content type to a specific site collection. The form being deployed is a form that a user can deploy rather one that could only be administratively deployed because it contained characteristics of categories C and D in Table 21-3.

On the InfoPath Publishing Wizard page shown in Figure 21-9, select the Site Content Type (Advanced) option. Figure 21-10 shows the next page.

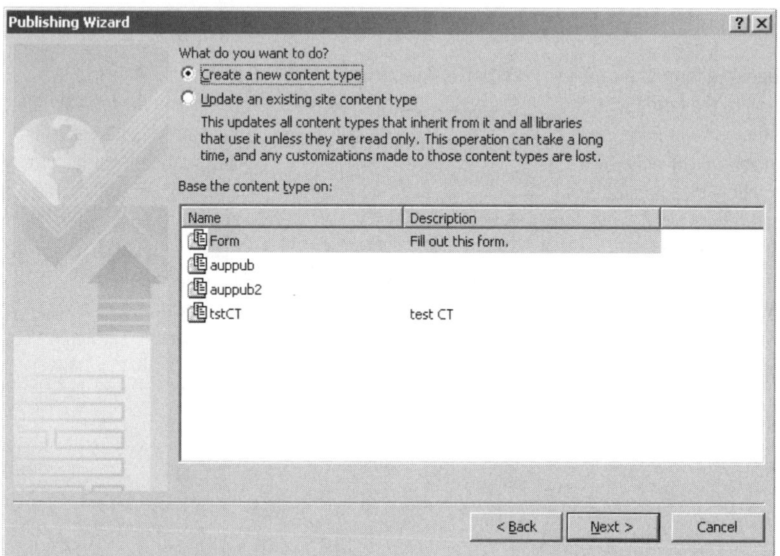

Figure 21-10 InfoPath Publishing Wizard page for selecting content type

On this page, you can decide to create a new content type (the default) based on an InfoPath form (the default) or update an existing content type. If you choose to create a new content type, the page shown in Figure 21-11 displays, asking you for a name and description for the new type.

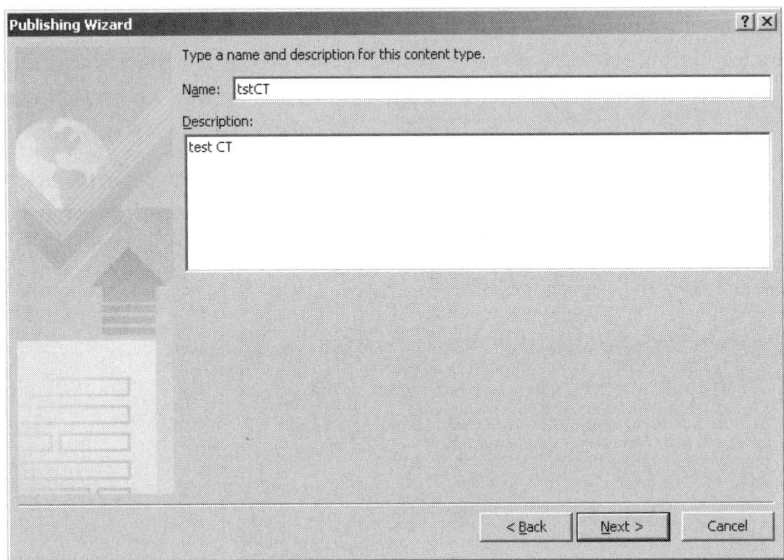

Figure 21-11 InfoPath Publishing Wizard new content type name page

On the page shown in Figure 21-12, you are asked for a location and file name for the new content type form template. Clicking the Browse button gives you a file save dialog box tailored for Web sites.

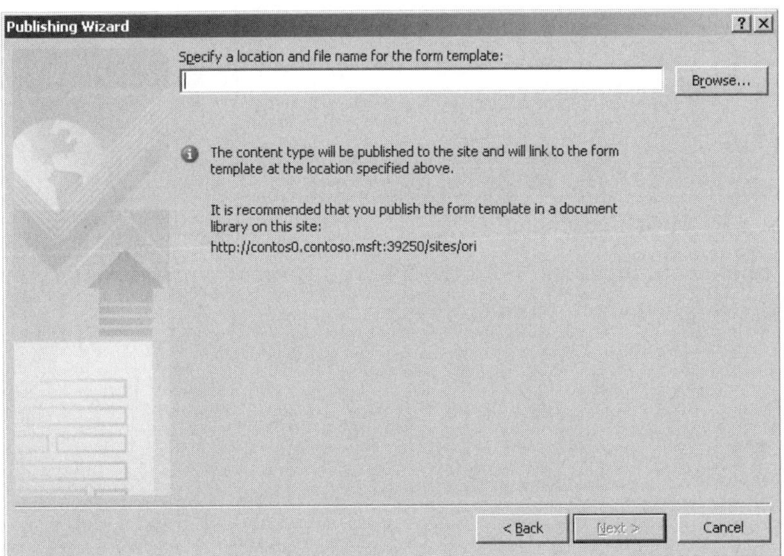

Figure 21-12 InfoPath Publishing Wizard file name and location page

You need to specify an existing form or document library in which to place your form template that will be treated as a content type. Click Next, which will bring you to a page allowing you to add columns to the SharePoint Form library. After clicking Next one more time, click Publish to finish the publishing phase of this process. Then click Close on the final page of the Publishing Wizard. The result of completing this process is that this form is seen as a content type, but only in the site collection you have published it to. You can view the new content type by going to your site's Site Settings and clicking the Site Content Type Gallery link in the Galleries section of the site where you saved your content type.

Now that our template is seen as a content type on a site collection, you can set it up to be the form template or one of the form templates for a form library. To do this, enter the Documents library and click the Settings link. Then select Form Library Settings (as shown in Figure 21-13) to open the library's settings.

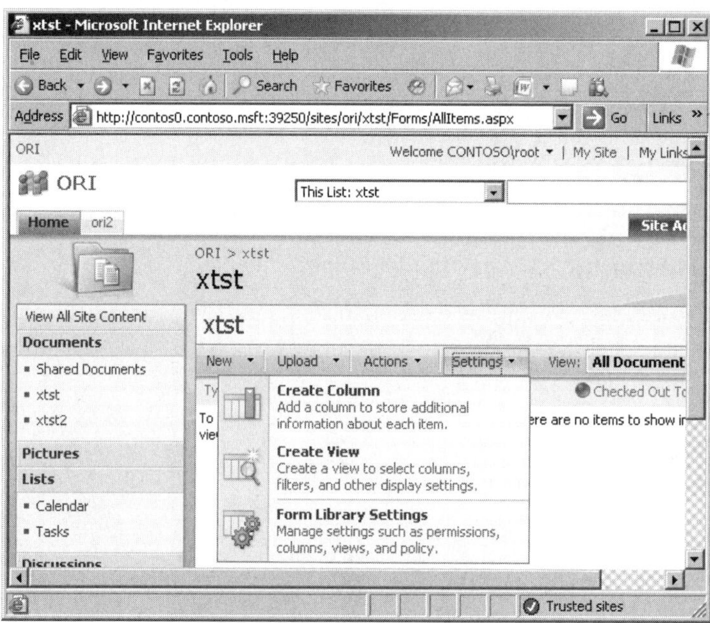

Figure 21-13 Form library Settings menu

On this page is where you can access both the library's content types as well as the Advanced Settings (shown in Figure 21-14).

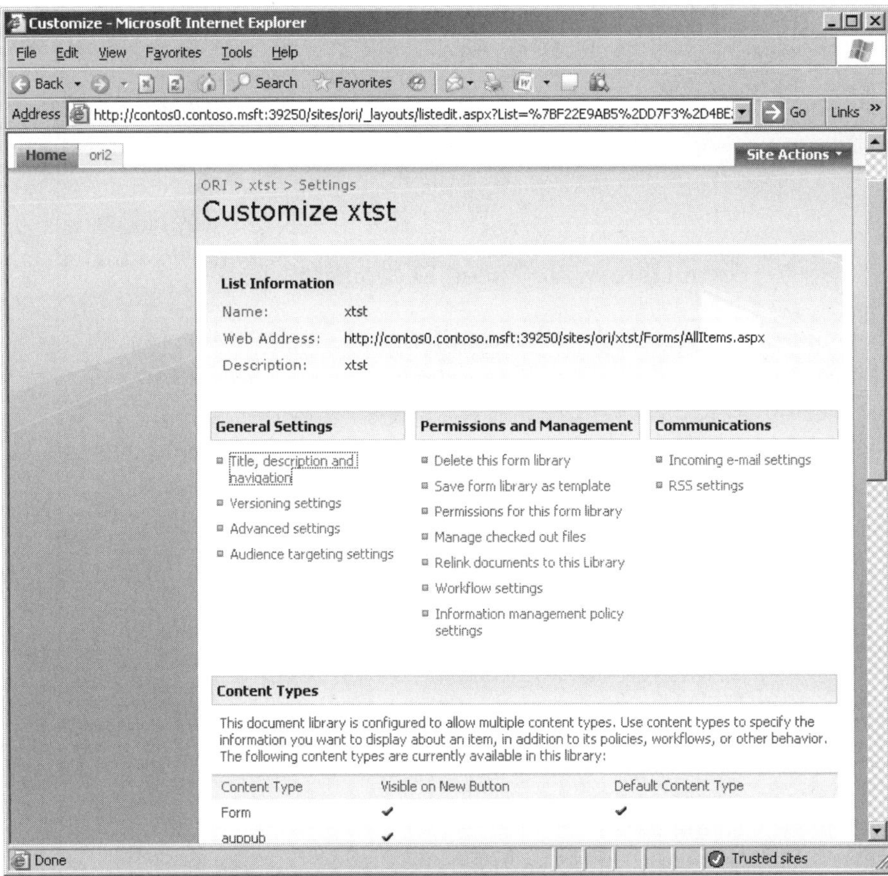

Figure 21-14 Form library Settings page

After selecting Advanced Settings, you can allow multiple content types in your form library and also ensure that these content types are accessible only as Web forms. If you click the Advanced Settings link, you'll be able to select the Yes radio button for Allow Management Of Content Types setting. This is illustrated in Figure 21-15.

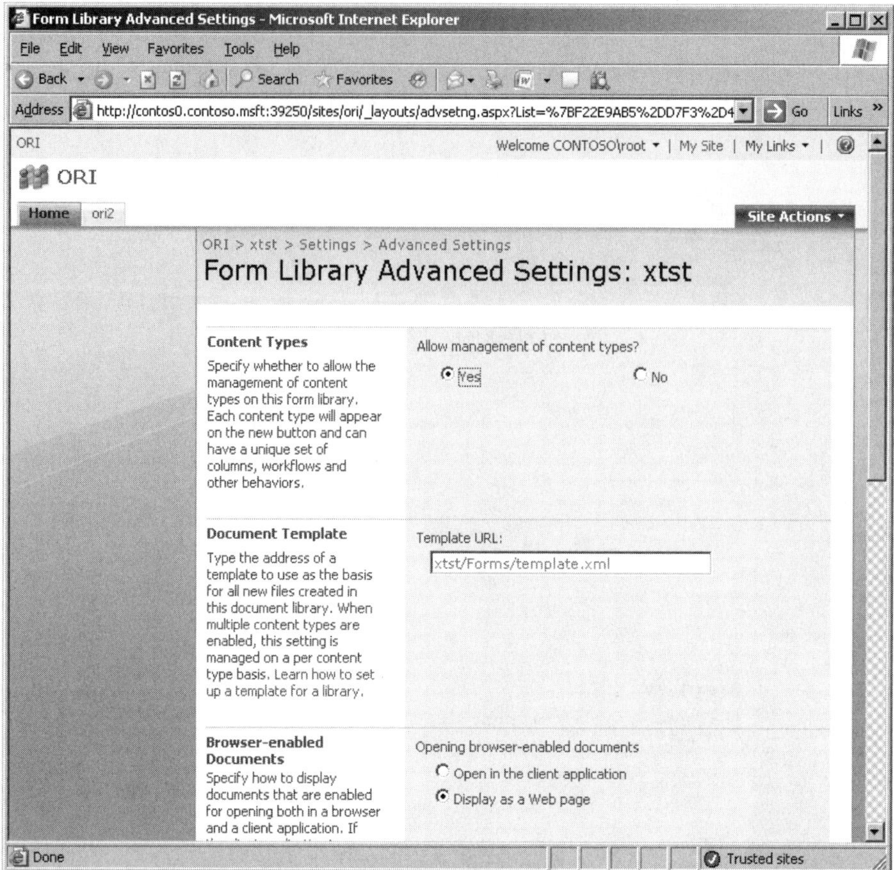

Figure 21-15 Form library Advanced Settings page

Note the Browser-Enabled Documents configuration, which states, "Specify how to display documents that are enabled for opening both in a browser and a client application. If the client application is unavailable, these documents will always be displayed as Web pages in the browser." Make the appropriate selection for your situation. You need to select Display As A Web Page if you want the forms to be browser enabled.

Now you can assign your particular content type form to this form library by selecting the Form Library Settings, Content Type Section, and clicking the Add From Existing Content Type link to open the Add Content Types page shown in Figure 21-16.

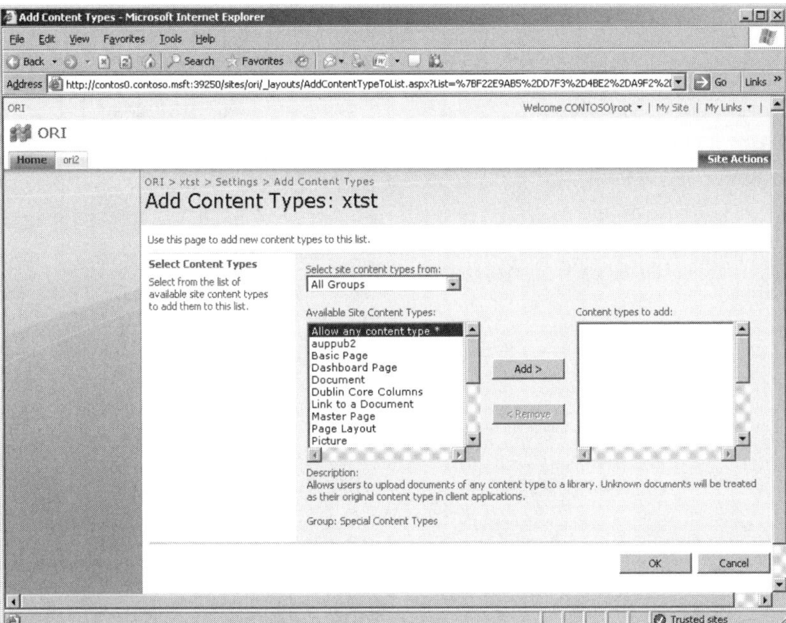

Figure 21-16 Adding existing content to a form library

This gives you a form selectable as one of the choices in your form library when you click on the New selection on the toolbar. All the forms in this form library can be viewed and filled-in only by using a Web browser if you selected the Display As A Web Page option in Advanced Settings.

Farm Wide Content Type—Administrative Approved Deployment

This type of deployment entails a three-step process:

1. Verify that the form is compatible with the server.
2. Ensure that the appropriate content type is available.
3. Activate the form on one or more site collections.

To make our form farm accessible, you need to publish it to a location that is globally accessible on your farm. To do so, complete the following steps:

1. In Central Administration, click the Application Management tab.
2. Under InfoPath Forms Services, click Manage Form Templates to open the page shown in Figure 21-17.

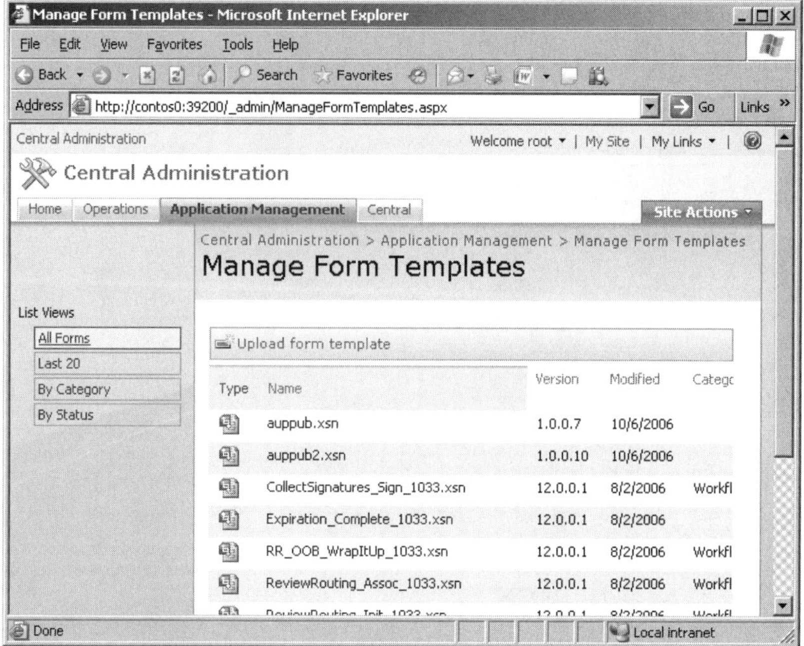

Figure 21-17 Managing form templates

The largest advantage to this type of deployment is that the same content type (form) can be used in many site collections farm wide.

Verifying and Uploading the Form

Because we are discussing administrative deployment, it is assumed that a form template suitable for such deployment is available. In the InfoPath Publishing Wizard, we stepped through earlier the third page (shown in Figure 21-9), which contained the Administrator-Approved Form Template (Advanced) option. If that option had been chosen in our User Deployed Form section instead of the Site Content Type (Advanced) option, the next page in the wizard would have asked you for a location for the form template, as shown in Figure 21-18.

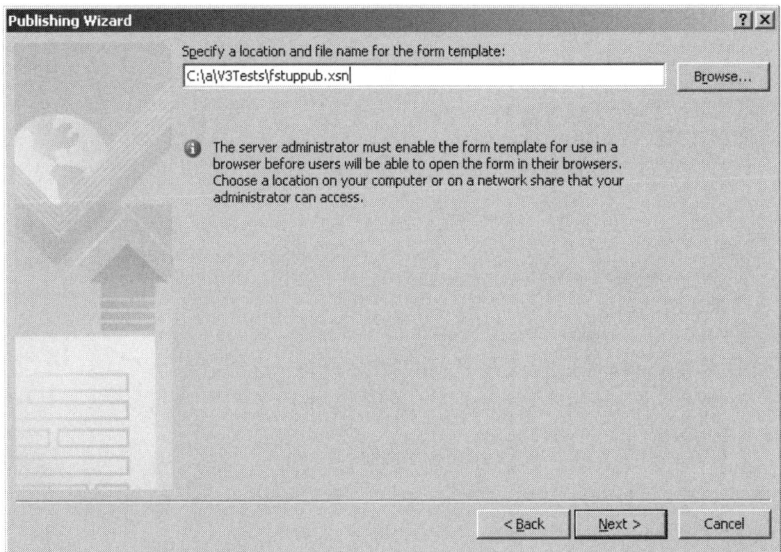

Figure 21-18 InfoPath Publishing Wizard location for administrator-approved form

This location is a physical directory location that an administrator has access to so that they can complete the rest of the steps discussed below. For deployment purposes, you can simply take the defaults for the rest of the InfoPath Publishing Wizard pages.

Making the form available requires both verifying and uploading. (In fact, you can upload without verifying, but you should always do both.) Administrators should first verify that the form is compatible with the server.

Important Verification is especially important if you are re-uploading the form, because someone might have altered the form. An administrator should always verify a form before uploading it, even though it is possible to upload the form while bypassing the verification step. Over time, the requirements for a form being compatible with various versions of Microsoft Forms Server might change and forms previously verified might be incorrectly assumed to work properly. An exception might be a developer with administrative rights who has just previously verified the form directly in InfoPath.

You can verify that the form is compatible with the server in two places. While designing the InfoPath form itself, you can navigate to Tools, Form Options, Compatibility, and type the URL to the Forms Server. It can also be accomplished from the InfoPaths task pane through the Design Checker link. Navigate to Central Administration, Application Management, InfoPath Forms Services, and click Upload Form Template. This link displays the Upload Form Template page, shown in Figure 21-19, where you can browse to your form and then verify it. A report on the suitability of the form is then generated and displayed.

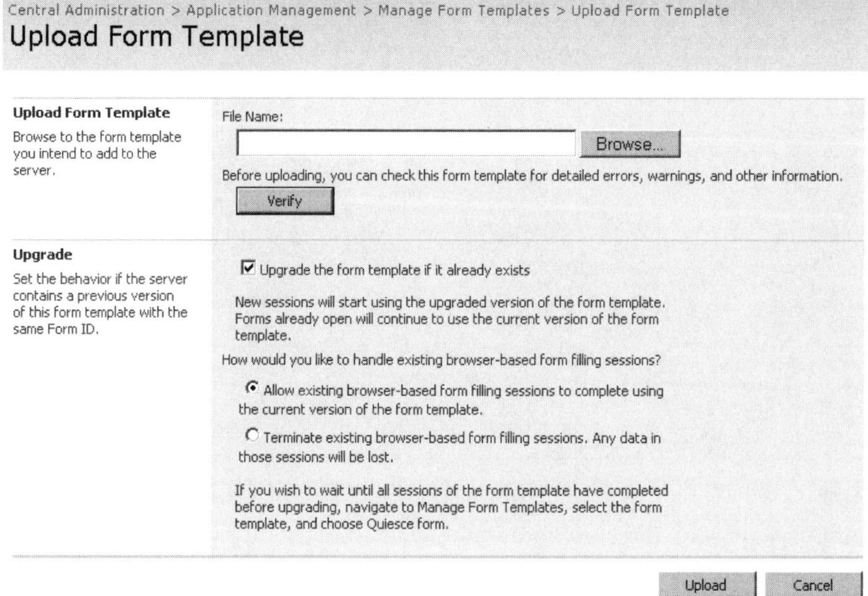

Figure 21-19 Upload Form Template page

Correct any problems and then upload the form. If you are changing an existing form and it is imperative that your changes take effect immediately, you can use the Upgrade section of the Upload Form Template page to force existing sessions offline. For example, you might have received an emergency correction to the form that corrects a problem in calculating the total price on an invoice form and want to implement the correction immediately.

Activating the Form to a Site Collection

After you upload the form, it is available on the Manage Form Templates page (shown in Figure 21-20).

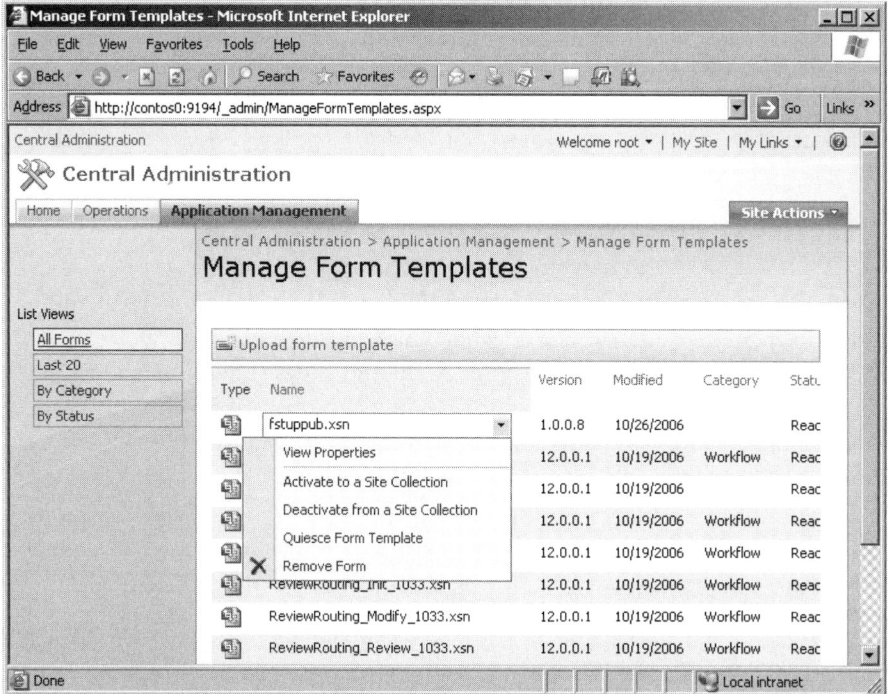

Figure 21-20 Activating the form

In the drop-down list above The Activate To A Site Collection option allows the form to be used in any Form library in that site collection. To activate the form, open the drop-down menu for the form and select Activate To A Site Collection. Next, go to the target site collection and follow the steps in the "Single Site Collection Content Type—User Deployment" section of this chapter to use the form content type in a form library.

Understanding Security Permissions

Even though this chapter treats permissions and deployment separately, you must treat them in practice as one inseparable topic. This section and the previous section on deployment (as they relate to permissions and form features allowable in Web-based forms) are extremely important for planning purposes. Make sure you have a firm grasp on these subjects before you start implementing forms or you will very likely waste a lot of valuable time.

Some Common Rules

First, a couple of rules apply universally to all Web-accessible forms and InfoPath client-accessible forms regarding accessing data that is outside the local domain:

- Web-accessible forms cannot access data outside the local domain boundaries, which is a security measure.
- The InfoPath client, although subject to a security prompt, can access data in other domains.

These basic rules are important because if your form is a Web-accessible form and you can not get a form to access data correctly when it previously worked fine, you can waste a lot of time attempting to adjust permissions. If you find yourself in this situation, determine whether the form was previously simply an InfoPath client-accessible form accessing cross-domain data and was re-deployed as a Web accessible form. If this is the case, then adjusting permissions will not help because this behavior is built in to the Forms Server.

Important Be careful when re-purposing InfoPath client-accessible forms to be Web accessible. You can easily develop forms using the client that you intend to use in the Forms Server that will not function because of the Forms Server 2007 cross-domain data access limitation.

Using Forms that Contain Code

A term that is commonly encountered since the advent of the .NET technology is managed code. Managed code is, in the broadest terms, simply newer .NET code. There is also an older coding technology called Common Object Model (COM). As administrators, you don't need to know how to code InfoPath forms, but you need to be aware of the security and deployment implications of the two coding technologies that might or might not exist in InfoPath 2007 forms you intend to use with Forms Server 2007. The two broad categories of code-bearing InfoPath solutions are InfoPath managed code-based solutions and InfoPath COM-based solutions.

Planning Administrators and planners need to have a general understanding of how the code contained in an InfoPath form will relate to its security level and ultimately affect both where and how the form can be deployed. It might be advisable to have an administrator present at some point in the planning stages of your Forms Server 2007 solutions.

Classic COM-Based Code—InfoPath COM-Based Solutions

InfoPath COM-based solutions run in both InfoPath 2003 and InfoPath 2007 if they do not use controls that are specific to InfoPath 2007. InfoPath COM-based solutions will not run in a Web browser using the Forms Server, but they will run in the InfoPath 2003 or InfoPath 2007 client. If you are unable to get an InfoPath form deployed using Forms Server 2007, be sure to ask whether this form is a COM-based or .NET managed code form.

Note For InfoPath 2003 forms, you can find out whether a form is compatible with Forms Server 2007. In Design mode in the InfoPath client, navigate to Tools, Form Options, and select Compatibility. Select the Show Report On Compatibility With InfoPath 2003 check box.

Managed Code Forms—InfoPath Managed Code-Based Solutions

As an administrator, you might get caught with some scenarios that perplex you because you are not a coder. Although you are not expected to be a developer, you need to recognize certain deployment problems and at least be able to ask the developers a couple of questions to help clarify why you can't get certain things working.

InfoPath forms can be designed to work in the older managed code programming model of InfoPath 2003 if they do not implement any of the newer Microsoft Office InfoPath 2007 managed code objects. However, these InfoPath 2003 forms will not run in Forms Server 2007. The newer 2007 managed code model can run in Forms Server 2007. Therefore, if you can get things working and you've been assured that the form has managed code in it, ask whether it's the 2003 or 2007 managed code, because the older code will not work.

Forms with managed code can be *partially* deployed by users who possess at least contributor permissions. However, it will require an administrator to verify, upload, and activate InfoPath managed code-based solutions.

Best Practices If you intend to keep your forms in service from one version to another, it is suggested that you convert your managed code to the 2007 managed code object model. This will not only allow you to take advantage of the new capabilities if you chose but will also give you a consistent code version base. Should it become absolutely necessary to upgrade your forms to a future version, it will be easier if you do not have to span multiple version changes at once. This strategy will also let you amortize your upgrade costs over a longer period of time.

Managed-code solutions using Forms Server 2007 depend on using some of the new .NET Framework 2.0 and Windows SharePoint Services 3.0 programming classes to achieve their flexibility. To create the InfoPath form in a browser, the infrastructure translates the InfoPath .xml form into a byte stream compatible with Web browsers. In this process, it brings the form to life using the new Windows SharePoint Services 3.0 *AppDomain* object, which is a new .NET Framework 2.0 derived creation. The result is the new .NET security model as adapted in SharePoint Server 2007 and Microsoft Forms Server 2007.

More Info For more information on this, see Chapter 31, "Administrating Code Access Security."

Using InfoPath Forms in Custom ASP.NET Pages

There is an *XmlFormView* control that allows a programmer to display an InfoPath form inside the *XmlFormView* control on his own Web page. This is more properly an InfoPath 2007 feature versus a Forms Server 2007 capability and is mentioned here because one of its limitations relates to detecting the type of client browser the aspx page is running in.

Forms Server 2007 is capable of detecting its client and will format things accordingly. This benefit is lost when using the *XmlFormView* control found in the *Microsoft.Office.InfoPath.Server.Controls* namespace which means your form might not be paginated properly when displayed in different Web browsers.

Controls Available to Forms Server Forms

If you cannot get a form deployed or working correctly, incompatible controls on the form is another possible avenue to look into. Only a certain subset of controls available to an InfoPath 2007 form are usable with Forms Server 2007. Table 21-4 provides a list you might use to inquire of the developers whether any restricted controls were inadvertently used on a form you are trying to use with Forms Server 2007. For example, the form might not originally have been thought of as a form that would be filled in from a Web browser, so it was not designed for the Forms Server.

Table 21-4 Forms Server Controls

Available to forms server forms	Not available to forms server
Standard Controls	Standard Controls
Text box	ComboBox
Rich-text box	Repeating and Optional
Drop-down list box	Horizontal Repeating Table
List box	Master/Detail
Date picker	Bulleted List
Check box	Numbered List
Option button	Plain List
Button	Multiple-Selection List Box
Section	File and Picture
Repeating and Optional	Picture
Optional section	Ink Picture
Repeating section	Advanced Controls
Repeating table	Vertical Label
File and Picture	Scrolling Region
File Attachment	Horizontal Region
Advanced Controls	Choice Group
Hyperlink	Repeating Choice Group
Expression Box	Choice Section
	Repeating Recursive Section
	Custom Controls
	All

Understanding Browser Compatibility Issues

The whole purpose of Microsoft Forms Server 2007 is to allow end users to fill in and view forms using a Web browser. Microsoft has identified four levels of Web browser compatibility, ranging from fully compatible (level 1) to not supported (level 4). Table 21-5 is an outline of browser-supported features that might be helpful to you when working with forms in the browser.

Table 21-5 Browser Support Level Feature Notes

Compatibility level	Supported features
1	Provides full fidelity and the best experience with the online form.
2	Provides a fully functional experience. However, certain features, such as a date picker, might not be available on some browsers.

Table 21-5 Browser Support Level Feature Notes

Compatibility level	Supported features
3	Does not provide full fidelity. Certain features might not work, and rendering will differ significantly between browsers.
4	No support and possible blocking (page might be prevented from loading).

Table 21-6 outlines a browser support matrix that can be useful when needing to troubleshoot Office Forms Server 2007 and your client browser interactions.

Table 21-6 Browser Support Matrix Based on Table 21-5 Levels

Browser support matrix	Operating system	Browser
Level 1: Windows SharePoint Services Forms Administration	Windows 98, Windows Me, Windows 2000, Windows XP, Windows Server 2003	Internet Explorer 6.x and Internet Explorer 64-bit version
Level 2: Internet, Windows SharePoint Services Site Administration, Form Filling for a majority of users	Windows 98, Windows Me, Windows 2000, Windows XP, Windows Server 2003	Internet Explorer, FireFox, Netscape 7.2 (moving to 8.x)
	UNIX/Linux	
	Mac OS X	FireFox, Safari 1.2
Level 3: Limited support	UNIX/Linux/Windows (versions other than above)	
Level 4: No support	Everything else	Everything else

Data Connections Used with Forms Server

When comparing Forms Server 2007 forms with the InfoPath client, there are some limitations when using data connections. It is common to use ADO.NET DataSets to pass database table information back and forth in InfoPath 2007 forms. Similar to three-tier/*n*-tier classic ADO.NET applications when returning a recordset from the back-end database to a client application in a simple client-server scenario, the recordset keeps an internal duplicate copy of all data. When changes are subsequently made to the data and then resubmitted to the database, the underlying data on the physical database is compared with the internal copy and if the current values in the raw database do not match the saved copy, a concurrency error is thrown. However, when passing the same recordset back from the middle tier to the client in a three-tier scenario after updating the physical database, the changes—that is, the internal duplicate copy made of the data—are lost. A similar situation happens with Forms Server 2007 forms using ADO.Net DataSets when changes are made to a dataset through a Web service; the changes are not automatically tracked and retained. You can think of what InfoPath calls a DataAdapter as simply a connection to some sort of data store.

As an administrator, you deploy a form that had been working as expected and all of a sudden it stops working. If the part that stops working is obviously a problem related to a data store connection, you might want to consider the following:

- InfoPath design-time DataAdapters become read-only when used on the Forms Server.
- On a Forms Server, Human Work Flow services adapters are not supported.

Except for the limitations just noted, the following Data Connection types are supported on Forms Server 2007:

- Database
- E-mail
- Http Post
- SharePoint (native API for same domain data connections, DAV for cross-domain)
- SharePoint List
- Web Services
- XML File

Forms Server 2007 Compatibility with InfoPath 2003

The day has arrived when coders cannot be completely unfamiliar with administrative tasks and be effective. Likewise, although not expected to code InfoPath forms, administrators need to be familiar with some of the tasks and concepts used in the development cycle. Because of the way the InfoPath forms and administrative tasks interact with each other (for example, during deployment), a knowledgeable administrator is a valuable asset to have at the project planning stage.

Microsoft Visual Studio Tools for Applications (VSTA) is the new programming development environment for working with Microsoft Office InfoPath 2007, Forms Server 2007, and SharePoint Server 2007. In relationship to InfoPath 2007 forms, these are the managed-code classes and infrastructure used for writing custom business logic. Because both Forms Server 2007 and SharePoint Server 2007 implement substantially the same functionality regarding InfoPath forms, you can use both browser-enabled forms and client forms to fill in and submit InfoPath forms.

Compatibility with Existing InfoPath 2003 Forms

SharePoint Services 2007 includes built-in compatibility with existing InfoPath 2003 forms regardless of whether they use manage code or the classic COM object models. These forms use the Microsoft.Office.Interop.InfoPath.SemiTrust.dll and its programming objects.

These forms do not run in the Microsoft Office Forms Server 2007, but they will run in the InfoPath client application. Programmers can continue to work with InfoPath project files created using either InfoPath 2003 (Microsoft Office InfoPath 2003 Toolkit for Visual Studio .NET) or InfoPath 2007 (Visual Studio 2005 Tools for the Microsoft Office System and VSTA).

Note The end user needs .NET Framework 2.0 to run forms compiled with Visual Studio 2005 Tools for the Microsoft Office System and VSTA for InfoPath 2007.

For forms compiled with the Microsoft Office InfoPath 2003 Toolkit for Visual Studio .NET, .NET Framework 1.1 needs to be installed on the client machine.

Using New InfoPath Forms

New forms can be created by using Visual Studio 2005; these forms will run in either InfoPath 2003 or InfoPath 2007. If you want to create an InfoPath 2007 form, go to InfoPath's design GUI under Tools, Form Options, Programming and select the InfoPath 2003 code compatibility option.

Although the classic COM interfaces, such as those found in the MSXML2 dll and the InfoPath-compatible Microsoft.Office.Interop.InfoPath.SemiTrust.dll, are available for use, Forms Server 2007 does not support their use. Therefore, you will not be able to browser-enable your COM code-based forms.

Summary

Microsoft Office Forms Server 2007 is a much needed addition to Office SharePoint Server 2007. It works in conjunction with InfoPath 2007 to bring remote filling in of InfoPath forms to an enterprise. It is powerful and robust, and it's positioned to propel InfoPath to the forefront as the "go to" solution for forms in the Microsoft Office system suite of products.

Part V
Upgrading to Microsoft Office SharePoint Server 2007

Chapter 22

Migrating from Content Management Server 2002 to Microsoft Office SharePoint Server 2007

Microsoft Content Management Server is a solution that can resolve many of the pain points associated with hosting a content-centric Web site. It facilitates the content authoring, template development, site management, and content deployment between two or more environments. Content Management Server stores all the content objects–such as pages, user roles and permissions, images and other media, and metadata–in the Content Repository. The Content Repository is persisted as a Microsoft SQL Server database. Microsoft does not recommend or support developers accessing or making changes to the content objects directly in the database. Instead, developers use the Publishing Application Programming Interface (PAPI), a Microsoft .NET library that Microsoft provides with Content Management Server.

Chapter 11, "Web Content Management and Publishing Features," describes how Microsoft Office SharePoint Server 2007 introduces to SharePoint capabilities that are similar to what Content Management Server provides for hosting and managing content-centric sites. Microsoft has decided to not continue developing Content Management

Server as a separate product; instead, it has incorporated the rich content authoring experience, site branding, and publishing controls into an Office SharePoint Server 2007 feature known as Web Content Management (WCM).

Although SharePoint Server 2007, which is built on Windows SharePoint Services 3.0, stores data in a SQL Server database like Content Management Server, the two databases are not compatible. Furthermore, the API included with Windows SharePoint Services 3.0 is very different than, and incompatible with, the Content Management Server Publishing API. As a result of this significant technology shift and Microsoft's decision to not continue developing Content Management Server as a separate product, site administrators need to decide whether they will continue to maintain their existing Content Management Server sites or migrate their sites to SharePoint Server 2007.

Why Migrate?

There are four main reasons to consider when deciding whether to migrate your Content Management Server Web sites to SharePoint Server 2007:

- End users can do more without developer assistance.
- Out-of-the-box features replace customizations.
- SharePoint has more built-in capabilities.
- Customization in SharePoint is less intensive.

This section covers each of these reasons.

End Users Can Do More Without Developer Assistance

Many of the tasks that required developer involvement in Content Management Server can now be done by information workers using SharePoint Server 2007. These tasks include customizing site navigation capabilities, creating pages containing summary links to other pages within the site, and deploying content from one installation to another. The SharePoint Server 2007 installation provides an additional navigation administration page to a WCM Site Settings page that allows administrators to implement simple customizations to the site navigation capabilities, such as sorting alphabetically or manually and adding headings and links, as shown in Figure 22-1.

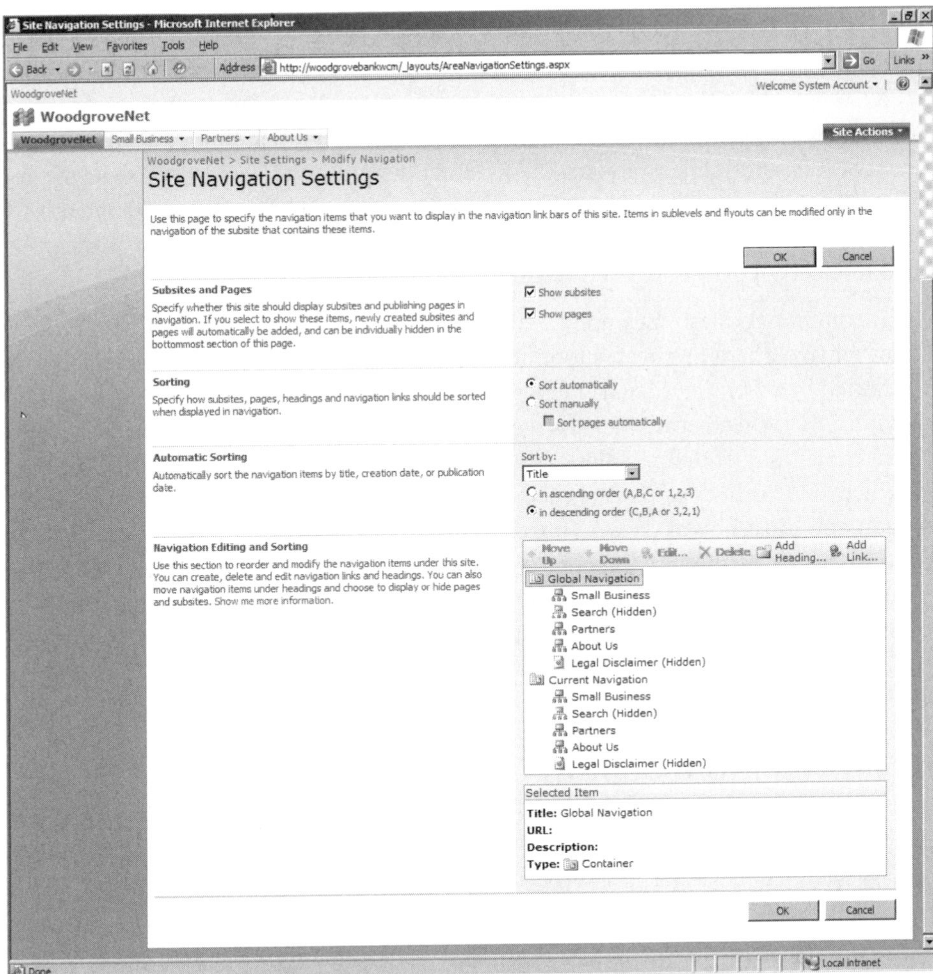

Figure 22-1 Site Navigation Settings page for the migrated Woodgrove Bank sample Content Management Server 2002 application

Content Management Server developers were required to create custom solutions to display links to pages within the site that might not be exposed through standard navigation. WCM addresses this developer task by introducing two new Web Parts: the Summary Link Web Part and the Table Of Contents Web Part. The Summary Link Web Part is used to display links on a page that a content author can group, style, or organize using typical drag-and-drop techniques. The Table Of Contents Web Part displays the navigation hierarchy on a page of your site.

Out-of-the-Box Features Replace Customizations

SharePoint Server 2007 addresses many tasks that required developers to write custom code in Content Management Server solutions. Content Management Server does not include any search mechanism out-of-the-box. To implement search for a Content Management Server solution, developers had to either integrate a third-party product to provide search capability or develop a custom solution. SharePoint Server 2007 includes a robust search mechanism available to all WCM sites, and no developer involvement is needed to incorporate it into a WCM site.

Another common request in Content Management Server solutions is to add e-mail notifications when content has been submitted for approval. Unfortunately, this capability is not included in a Content Management Server installation, so developers were required to provide it. However, because all storage containers are based on lists in SharePoint and each list provides user-defined alerts, this functionality is included out-of-the-box; content owners and authors can create their own alerts to be notified when specific content has been submitted or updated. In Content Management Server, site owners were required to have console access to a production Content Management Server Web server to manage the structure of the site, permissions, and to import or export content. However, this level of access is no longer required in SharePoint Server 2007, as all administration tools and tasks are exposed in browser-based interfaces accessible from the site owner's desktop.

SharePoint Has More Built-In Capabilities

SharePoint Server 2007 provides additional capabilities to WCM sites that were not possible in Content Management Server. Most important of these is the robust workflow engine provided by the .NET 3.0 Framework: Windows Workflow Foundation. Content Management Server provided a simple three-stage workflow that was not very extensible. Authors would create new content, they would submit it for approval to a content editor who would either approve or decline it, and finally approved content would be published by a site moderator. Content Management Server sites with more advanced workflow requirements needed a third-party workflow solution. However, SharePoint Server 2007, built on top of Windows SharePoint Services 3.0, includes a robust and very extensible workflow engine that information workers can leverage by creating custom workflows with Microsoft Office SharePoint Designer 2007. More advanced workflows can be created by developers using Microsoft Visual Studio 2005.

Customization in SharePoint Is Less Intensive

Site owners should consider migrating Content Management Server Web sites to SharePoint Server 2007 because WCM sites, overall, require less custom code than their Content Management Server equivalents. The three previous sections address various situations where Content Management Server custom code solutions have been replaced by an out-of-the-box component or feature in SharePoint Server 2007. The reduction in required custom code solutions in SharePoint Server 2007 is a good thing for site owners because less custom code means fewer changes need to be made for unforeseen bugs and less code maintenance needs to be done, freeing up developers for other tasks. But even when you do need to customize a content site in SharePoint Server 2007, those customizations will be less intensive and require less development than they would have required in Content Management Server 2002.

Understanding the Two-Part Migration Process

The migration of a Content Management Server Web site to SharePoint Server 2007 is unlike the upgrade of Windows SharePoint Services 2.0 to Windows SharePoint Services 3.0 or a SharePoint Portal Server 2003 site to SharePoint Server 2007 in that an extra step is required. Migrating a Content Management Server Web site involves two very distinct phases: content migration and code migration. This additional step–code migration–is required because any custom code in a Content Management Server Web site has been written against the Publishing API to interact with the Content Management Server Content Repository. SharePoint Server 2007 and Windows SharePoint Services use a completely different storage mechanism and API than what Content Management Server used. Furthermore, the Publishing API has not been modified to work with the SharePoint API; instead, it has since been retired. It is because of this technology shift that custom code written for Content Management Server Web sites will most likely not be compatible after a migration, and thus, an extra step to migrate the code is required.

Content Migration Phase

In the content migration phase, the migration of content is managed by SharePoint Server 2007 using migration paths that are created by site owners. There are three different types of content migration:

- Side-by-side
- In-place
- Incremental

What constitutes content in a Content Management Server Web site? Content Management Server *content* includes the actual pages in a site, site structure, permissions, templates, site metadata, and resources such as the following:

- Channels
- Postings

- Placeholders
- Resource galleries and resources
- Template galleries and templates
- Custom properties
- Security rights groups and users

Once the content in a Content Management Server Web site has been migrated to SharePoint Server 2007, you are left with a functioning site with no branding or look and feel applied. The Content Management Server template objects are migrated as unbranded page layouts in SharePoint Server 2007 so that you have a working, but unbranded, site. The next step is to migrate the code and implement your site's branding.

Code Migration Phase

In the code migration phase, the custom code in a Content Management Server Web site solution is written against the Publishing API, which is not supported in SharePoint Server 2007. Therefore, it's likely that all the code written for a Content Management Server Web site will have to be rewritten for SharePoint Server 2007. However, because many things that required custom code in Content Management Server, such as search and navigation customizations, are provided out-of-the-box in SharePoint Server 2007, you should not have to migrate 100 percent of the code in the Content Management Server solution.

As previously mentioned in the "Content Migration Phase" section, migrating the content in a Content Management Server Web site results in a plain, unbranded SharePoint site populated with content. The content migration process creates a page layout for each Content Management Server template, but it applies no branding. No code is migrated from the Content Management Server Web site solution. Once the content migration step has been completed, developers must address each page layout as well as create master pages to apply the desired site branding. In addition, any custom controls written for the Content Management Server Web site must be addressed.

The most common elements that need to be addressed are any custom placeholder definitions and controls that were included in the Content Management Server Web site. Although some placeholder controls–such as the HTML Placeholder Control and Single Image Attachment Placeholder Control–will migrate to SharePoint Server 2007 without issue, others have no SharePoint Server 2007 equivalent to migrate to. The XML Placeholder Control is the most common of these placeholders that do not have a SharePoint Server 2007 equivalent. Each XML Placeholder Control must be addressed by a developer after the migration and likely redeveloped as a *field control*–a new type of control used in page layouts.

Understanding Migration Options

The options for migrating a Content Management Server Web site to SharePoint Server 2007 are similar to those for upgrading a Windows SharePoint Services 2.0 or SharePoint Portal Server 2003 Web site to Windows SharePoint Services 3.0 or SharePoint Server 2007. However, because migrating a Content Management Server Web site to SharePoint Server 2007 is a significant change to the underlying platform, you should carefully consider each option prior to beginning a migration.

More Info For detailed information on the different upgrade options, please see Chapter 23, "Upgrading from Microsoft Windows SharePoint Services 2.0," and Chapter 24, "Upgrading from Microsoft SharePoint Portal Server 2003."

Side-by-Side Migration Option

The side-by-side migration option involves hosting both Content Management Server and SharePoint Server 2007 on the same hardware and using the same SQL server. In this option, you use existing hardware, and thus the need for procuring new hardware is eliminated. This option is ideal for customers whose existing Content Management Server Web sites are meeting business needs and who are not in a rush to migrate to SharePoint Server 2007.

Note The side-by-side option might be the most appealing to customers who have very large Content Management Server Web site implementations where multiple development groups are involved in the support of the site. Using this option, portions of the Content Management Server Web site can be migrated to SharePoint Server 2007 based on the availability of the different development and content owner groups.

In Place Migration Option

The in-place migration option migrates an entire Content Management Server Web site to SharePoint Server 2007 in one process. This will probably be the least used option because it allows the least amount of interaction in the process, eliminating the ability to address issues as they occur. Instead, any issues must be addressed at one time, which could potentially lead to significant downtime.

Note The in-place option might be appropriate in only the smallest Content Management Server Web site implementations, where there would be few post-migration issues resulting in minimal downtime.

Incremental Migration Option

The Incremental migration option is likely to be the most used option. With this option, content can be migrated from Content Management Server Web sites to SharePoint Server 2007 WCM Web sites gradually and repeatedly, allowing site owners to run two versions of the same site at one time, under the two products (Content Management Server and SharePoint Server 2007), and enabling developers to check their progress as they create and customize the target site's master pages, page layouts, and custom controls. As content is migrated, the existing Content Management Server Web site remains accessible to users, which limits downtime.

> **Note** The Incremental migration option is the preferred option of the three because it minimizes downtime and permits developers to migrate sections of a site one by one as they are ready for migration. This approach allows site owners to verify everything has migrated and is working correctly before migrating completely off Content Management Server.

Understanding the Different Types of Migration Tasks

The process of migrating a Content Management Server Web site to SharePoint Server 2007 can be separated into two different types of tasks: administrator-oriented tasks and developer-oriented tasks.

Administrator-Oriented Migration Tasks

Migration tasks performed by administrators typically are those surrounding the content migration. Site administrators perform tasks such as creating migration profiles in SharePoint's Central Administration Web site and running analyses on the profiles. Any content, structural, or organizational related warnings or errors reported in the analyses should be addressed by site administrators before executing the migration profile.

Some warnings and errors will not prohibit the successful execution of a migration profile, nor will you be required to resolve all of them prior to execution of the migration profile. In these instances, site administrators should review each issue identified by the analysis of the migration profile and determine a course of action either before or after execution of the migration profile.

Developer-Oriented Migration Tasks

Developers will likely have the most significant tasks in the migration of a Content Management Server Web site to SharePoint Server 2007. This is primarily because the custom code in a Content Management Server Web site has been written against the Content Management Server Publishing API, which is no longer available in SharePoint Server 2007. Therefore, most of the custom code in a Content Management Server Web site solution will need to be addressed and likely rewritten.

Microsoft recognizes that redevelopment of custom code written for Content Management Server Web sites will be a significant task. In an effort to assist developers with this task, Microsoft has released a free utility, the CMS Assessment Tool, which assists developers in identifying parts of their Content Management Server Web site solution that could lead to migration problems, as well as in determining the scope of the migration effort. We'll discuss this tool in depth later in this chapter in the "CMS Assessment Tool" section.

In addition to using the CMS Assessment Tool, analyzing the generated reports, and rewriting custom code, developers will also be involved in adding some of the new included features of SharePoint Server 2007 into the migrated Content Management Server Web site. These include tasks such as developing custom workflows and document converters, as well as incorporating the SharePoint Server 2007 search components and capabilities into the new site.

Note Because many of the tasks that required custom development in Content Management Server 2002 are included in SharePoint Server 2007, developers should not have to rewrite 100 percent of the custom code in the migrated Content Management Server Web site.

SharePoint Server 2007 Content Migration

The migration of content from a Content Management Server Web site to SharePoint Server 2007 is handled by the creation of migration profiles in SharePoint's Central Administration Web site or by using the SharePoint object model. Migration profiles contain all the information required to import content from a Content Management Server Web site to a SharePoint Server 2007 WCM Web site such as the Content Management Server Content Repository source database, the target SharePoint Server 2007 WCM site collection, user and system security credentials, and an e-mail address (or addresses) to notify administrators of a successful or failed execution of the migration profile.

When a migration profile is executed, it first runs an analysis job of the content being migrated. If the migration profile analysis stage identifies any errors that would prohibit the execution of the profile, such as duplicate Content Management Server template names, it logs the errors that require resolution prior to the execution of the migration profile.

Creating Migration Profiles

The creation of a migration profile requires access to the Content Management Server 2002 database. This database contains the content to be migrated and a Web application containing a site collection created using the Blank Site template to import the Content Management Server 2002 migrated content into. If an empty Web application does not exist, you must create it prior to creating a migration profile.

More Info For instructions on how to creating a new Web application and site collection, see Chapter 7, "Application Management and Configuration."

Migration profiles are created in SharePoint's Central Administration Web site. To create a migration profile, complete the following steps:

1. On the Central Administration Home page, select the Operations tab.
2. On the Operations page, in the Upgrade And Migration section, select Microsoft Content Management Server Migration, shown in Figure 22-2.

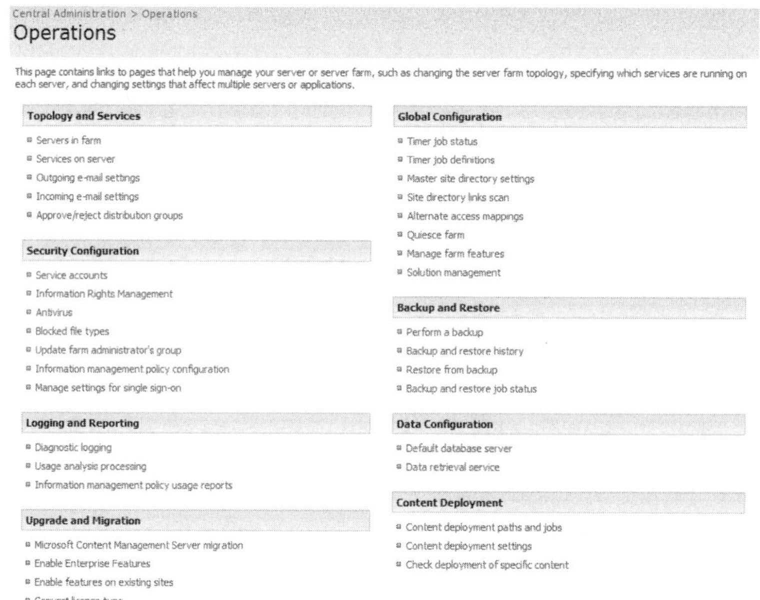

Figure 22-2 Microsoft Content Management Server Migration link

3. On the Manage Microsoft Content Management Server Migration Profiles page, select New Migration Profile.

4. On the Create Migration Profile page (shown in Figure 22-3), enter the following information:
   - **Name And Description** These fields are used to help distinguish this migration profile from others used in the future. None of the information here is used in the actual migration.
   - **Source Database** Enter the necessary information for SharePoint Server 2007 to connect to the Content Management Server 2002 database containing the content to be migrated.
   - **Destination** Select a destination Web application and site collection to migrate the Content Management Server 2002 data to.
   - **Top-Level Site** Select the top-level channel from within the Content Management Server 2002 Content Repository that will be the top-level site for the destination site collection.
   - **Security Information** Select the Migrate ACLs check box to migrate the access control lists from Content Management Server 2002.
   - **Language** Select the language to use for the migrated sites.
   - **Notification** Select the Send E-mail When The Migration Job Succeeds check box to be notified when the migration profile job completes with a successful migration, or select the Send E-mail If The Migration Job Fails check box to be notified if there are any failures in the execution of the migration profile. Finally, enter an e-mail address to send notifications to if either of the previous options are selected.

Central Administration > Operations > Manage Microsoft Content Management Server Migration Profiles > Migration Profile

Create Migration Profile

Use this page to create a migration profile.

Warning: this page is not encrypted for secure communication. User names, passwords, and any other information will be sent in clear text. For more information, contact your administrator.

Name and Description
Specify the name and description of this migration profile.

Name:

Description:

Source Database
Specify the connection information for the database that contains the content you want to migrate. It must be the database for an installation of MCMS 2002.

Click **Connect** to connect to the database server, and then choose the database that contains the data you want to migrate.

Database server name:

Authentication type:
Windows authentication
SQL authentication

Account information:
User name:

Password:

Connect

Database name:
-- Select a database --

Destination
Select the Web application and site collection to which you want to migrate data. Show me more information.

Web application:
-- Select a Web application --

Site collection:
-- Select a Site Collection --

Top-Level Site
Select the site you want to be the top-level site for the destination site collection. Only the content in and below the selected site will be migrated. Show me more information.

Site you want to migrate as the top-level site:
-- Select a channel --

Security Information
Specify whether or not to migrate ACLs from MCMS 2002.

Migrate ACLs

Language
Choose the language you want to use for the migrated sites.

English

Notification
When the migration job is finished, send notification to these e-mail addresses. Use semicolons to separate multiple e-mail addresses.

Send e-mail when the migration job succeeds
Send e-mail if the migration job fails
Type e-mail addresses:

OK Cancel

Figure 22-3 Create Migration Profile page

Running Content Migration Jobs

Once you have created a migration profile, you can execute an analysis to check for any issues prior to running the migration process. To analyze a migration profile, on the Manage Microsoft Content Migration Server Migration Profiles page, select the name of an existing migration profile and select Analyze from the menu.

The analysis initializes the migration profile and then runs a premigration analysis process. At the completion of the analysis process, you can select the name of a migration profile to display a drop-down menu of actions, select View History from the list of available actions, and finally select one of the migration history entries on the Migration History page. Each migration history reports the duration of the migration job and detailed errors and warnings encountered during the analysis.

Note If any errors are reported by the migration profile premigration analysis job, administrators and developers should address these issues prior to executing the migration profile.

After you have executed a migration profile premigration analysis job and resolved any issues, you can schedule and execute the migration job. To execute a migration profile, on the Manage Microsoft Content Management Server Migration Profiles page, select the name of an existing migration profile and then select Run from the menu.

SharePoint immediately triggers the execution of the migration profile job. To determine the status of a migration profile job, refresh the Manage Microsoft Content Management Server Migration Profiles page. Once the job is complete, the Status column displays Succeeded to indicate a successful migration.

CMS Assessment Tool

As with any project involving migrating from one solution to another, the migration of a Content Management Server Web site to SharePoint Server 2007 WCM is a process that requires analysis and some preparation. By assessing the readiness of your Content Management Server Web site solution as well as identifying and resolving potential issues prior to migration, you can greatly reduce the complexity and the number of problems that might arise during the migration process.

Running the CMS Assessment Tool will not make any changes to your Content Management Server Web site solution; it is a read-only tool that simply analyzes your Content Management Server environment and produces reports based on the analysis. One of the analysis steps the CMS Assessment Tool performs is identical to the analysis that the content migration profile performs within SharePoint's Central Administration Web site. The generated reports are viewed in a special Microsoft Office Excel workbook (provided with the CMS Assessment Tool) that contains information on the following areas of a Content Management Server environment:

- Information about the current Content Management Server 2002 infrastructure, which is helpful in determining whether the current hardware will support a side-by-side migration.
- Information about the current Content Management Server 2002 Content Repository, including channels, postings, resources, and security roles and users.

- Detailed information on all template files implemented in the current Content Management Server 2002 Web site solution and on which Content Management Server features each template file is using.

Because template files are very important to the implementation of a Content Management Server Web site, collecting detailed metrics on them is a helpful step in planning your migration process. In addition, many of the reports address where custom code is leveraging the Content Management Server Publishing API. All this information is very valuable prior to a migration, as it assists in determining exactly how much work will be involved in the migration process.

Installing and Running the CMS Assessment Tool

The CMS Assessment Tool is freely available from the Microsoft Download Center at *http://www.microsoft.com/downloads/details.aspx?FamilyId=360D0E83-FA70-4C24-BCD6-426CAFBCC627&displaylang=en*. After you download the CMS Assessment Tool, you must install it to begin the analysis. The only requirement for installing the CMS Assessment Tool is that it must be installed on a server that already has Content Management Server 2002 installed because it uses the Content Management Server Publishing API during the analysis.

To install the CMS Assessment Tool, follow these steps:

1. Run CmsAtSetup.msi.
2. On the Welcome To The CMS Assessment Tool Setup Wizard page, click Next.
3. On the License Agreement page, select I Agree and then click Next.
4. On the Select Installation Folder page, select Browse. Then select the folder to install the CMS Assessment Tool to, or accept the default location. Finally, choose whether the CMS Assessment Tool will be installed for Everyone or Just Me, and then click Next.
5. On the Confirmation Installation page, click Next.
6. On the CMS Assessment Tool Information page, read the Readme file and then click Next.
7. On the Installation Complete page, click Close.

Note The CMS Assessment Tool generates reports providing detailed information on a Content Management Server 2002 Web site solution, the Content Repository, and the infrastructure hosting the application. You should install the CMS Assessment Tool on a development or nonproduction server unless you need to determine whether your existing production hardware is suitable to support a side-by-side migration.

The installation of the CMS Assessment Tool creates a new program group in the Start menu: All Programs\Microsoft Content Management Server\Assessment Tool. The new program group contains the following two items:

- **CMS Assessment Tool** This is the actual tool that will analyze the Content Management Server 2002 Web site solution and generate reports based on its findings.
- **Content Management Server Assessment Tool Report Workbook** This is the Microsoft Office Excel workbook used to review and print the reports generated by the CMS Assessment Tool.

After you install the CMS Assessment Tool, you need to run it to generate the analysis reports. To run the CMS Assessment Tool, follow these instructions:

1. From the Start menu, select All Programs, Microsoft Content Management Server, Assessment Tool, and finally select CMS Assessment Tool.
2. On the Welcome To The CMS Assessment Tool page, click Next.

   More Info The CMS Assessment Tool has the capability to run using predefined options. For information on how to configure the predefined options, refer to the MSDN white paper "Assessing and Analyzing Your MCMS 2002 Application for Migration," which is located at *http://msdn.microsoft.com/office/server/moss/2007/migration/default.aspx?pull=/library/en-us/dnmscms02/html/CMSAssessAnalyzing2002Application.asp*. Specifically, read "Appendix B: Assessment Tool Configuration File."

3. On the CMS Area To Analyze page (shown in Figure 22-4), select the desired areas to analyze and then click Next:
   - **Application Code** Selecting this option configures the CMS Assessment Tool to analyze the Content Management Server 2002 custom application code.
   - **CMS Repository** Selecting this option configures the CMS Assessment Tool to analyze the Content Management Server 2002 Content Repository. Selecting this option automatically selects the following three options.
   - **Gather Inventory** Selecting this option configures the CMS Assessment Tool to collect an inventory of all assets within the Content Management Server 2002 Content Repository.
   - **Collect Statistics** Selecting this option configures the CMS Assessment Tool to collect statistics on the Content Management Server 2002 Content Repository.

- **Run Pre-Migration Analyzer** Selecting this option configures the CMS Assessment Tool to run the same premigration analysis process that the SharePoint Central Administration's migration profile execution process runs.

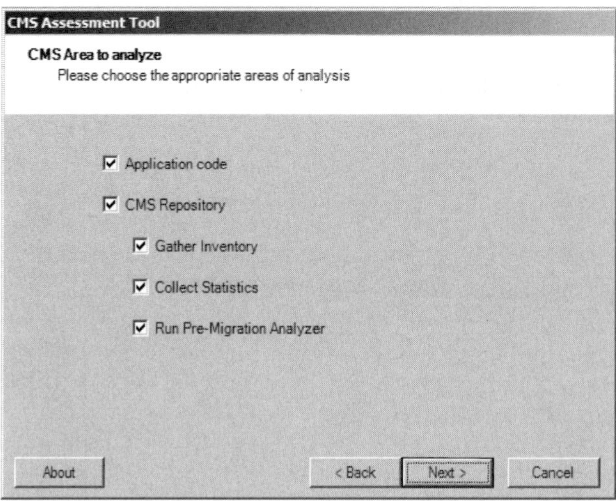

Figure 22-4 The CMS Area To Analyze page

4. On the Select Source Code Files page, shown in Figure 22-5, select one of the following three options and then click Next:
   - **Directories** Selecting this option allows you to select specific directories to analyze. Select Add to add a directory to the list.

     > **More Info** If electing to use the Directories option in the Select Source Code Files dialog box, you can select the Separate Report For Each Directory check box to generate a separate XML report file for each directory specified.

   - **IIS Virtual Directory** Selecting this option configures the CMS Assessment Tool to run the analysis on the same server where Content Management Server 2002 is installed. Select Browse to specify the virtual directory containing the Content Management Server Application to analyze.
   - **Visual Studio .NET Solution** Selecting this option configures the CMS Assessment Tool to run the analysis against a Visual Studio .NET solution containing one or more projects.

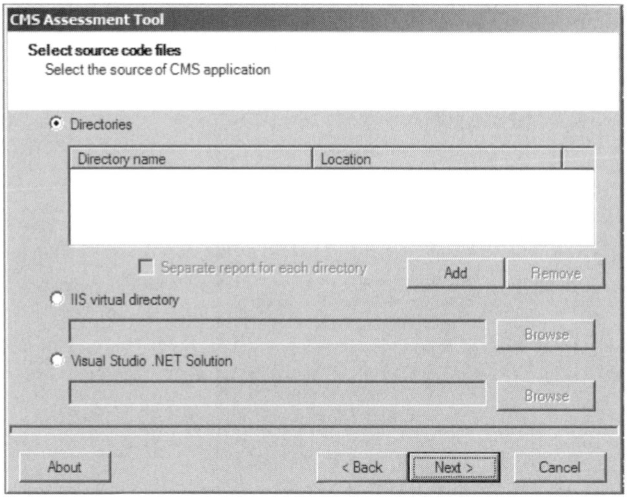

Figure 22-5 The Select Source Code Files page

More Info If a directory, IIS virtual directory, or Visual Studio .NET solution selected does not contain a debug build with .pdb files for the application code, the source column in the reports will be blank and the code line number column will display -1. A debug build with .PDB files is required for detailed source code analysis and reporting.

5. On the Choose Projects To Analyze page (shown in Figure 22-6), select the Visual Studio .NET projects to analyze and then click Next.

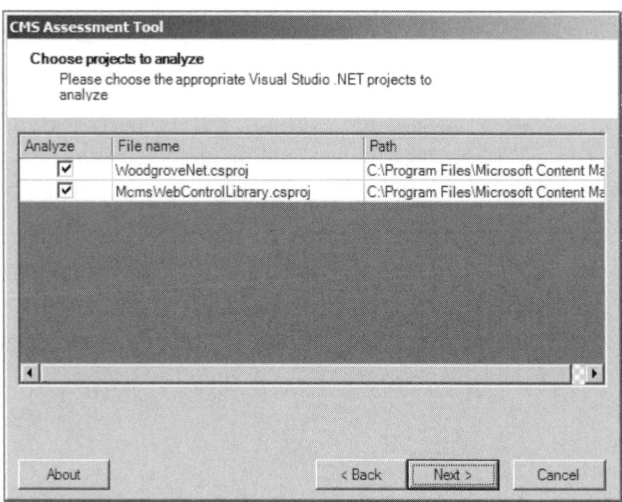

Figure 22-6 The Choose Projects To Analyze page

6. On the Choose ASP.NET Files To Analyze page (shown in Figure 22-7), select the template files the CMS Assessment Tool should analyze and then click Next.

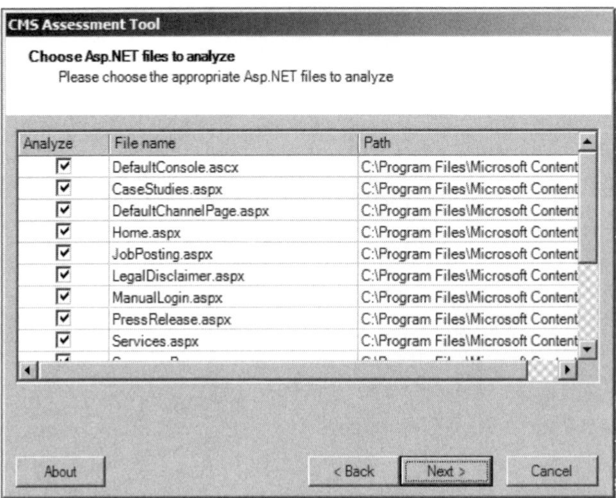

Figure 22-7 The Choose ASP.NET Files To Analyze page

7. On the Set User Information For CMS Repository page (shown in Figure 22-8), specify the following options and then click Next:

   - **Collect Posting Data** Select this option to collect and analyze information on each posting in the Content Management Server 2002 Content Repository.
   - **Authentication** The CMS Assessment Tool will, by default, use the current user's credentials to connect to the Content Management Server 2002 Content Repository; optionally, the CMS Assessment Tool can be configured to use a different user's credentials by selecting Change.
   - **Root Channel** The CMS Assessment Tool will, by default, start the analysis at the /Channels channel; optionally, the CMS Assessment Tool can be configured to analyze a different channel by selecting Change.
   - **Template Galleries** The CMS Assessment Tool will, by default, analyze all templates and galleries within the /Templates gallery; optionally, the CMS Assessment Tool can be configured to analyze only specific template galleries by using the Add and Remove buttons.

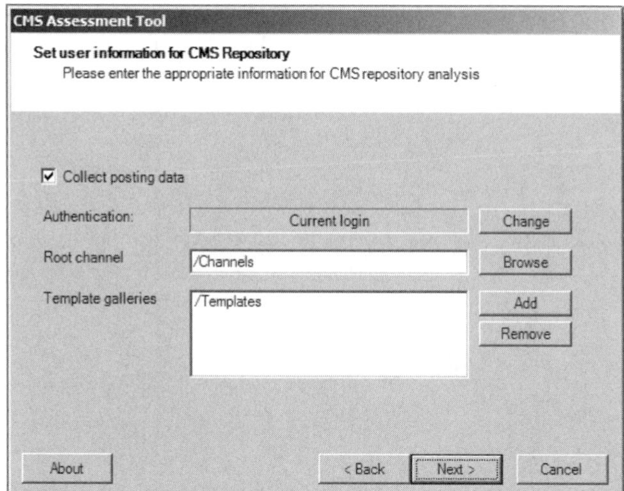

Figure 22-8 The Set User Information For CMS Repository page

8. On the CMS Site Analyzer page (shown in Figure 22-9), select one of the following options from the Information To Be Collected drop-down list and then click Next:

   - **Full** This option configures the CMS Assessment Tool to collect information on the server Content Management Server 2002 is installed on and from the Content Management Server 2002 Content Repository.
   - **Machine Only** This option configures the CMS Assessment Tool to collect information on the server Content Management Server 2002 is installed on.
   - **Database Only** This option configures the CMS Assessment Tool to collect information from the Content Management Server 2002 Content Repository.

> **Note** By default, the CMS Assessment Tool uses the current user's credentials to connect to the Content Management Server 2002 Content Repository. Select Change to configure the CMS Assessment Tool to use a different user to use to connect to the Content Management Server 2002 Content Repository.

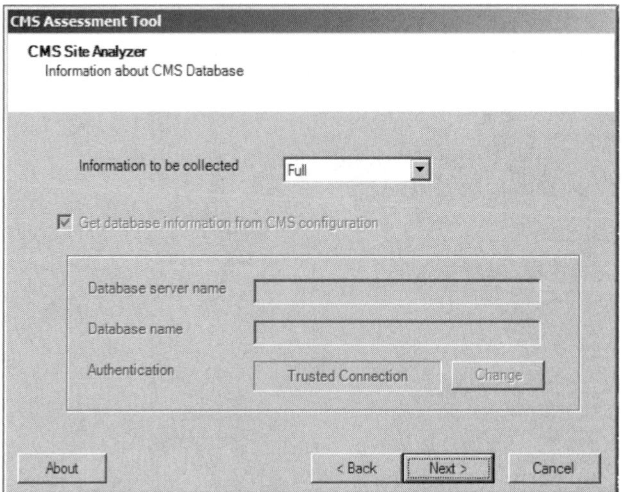

Figure 22-9 The CMS Site Analyzer page

9. On the Pre-Migration Analyzer page (shown in Figure 22-10), select Get Database Information From CMS Configuration to configure the CMS Assessment Tool to read the database information from the server's registry. Clearing this option requires that you specify a Database Server Name, Database Name, and user credentials.

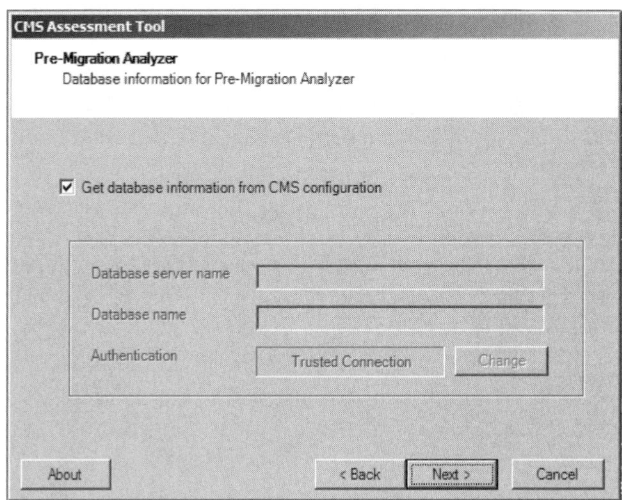

Figure 22-10 The Pre-Migration Analyzer page

10. In the Report Directory Selection page (shown in Figure 22-11), select Browse to specify a directory where the generated report output files will be saved, and then click Next.

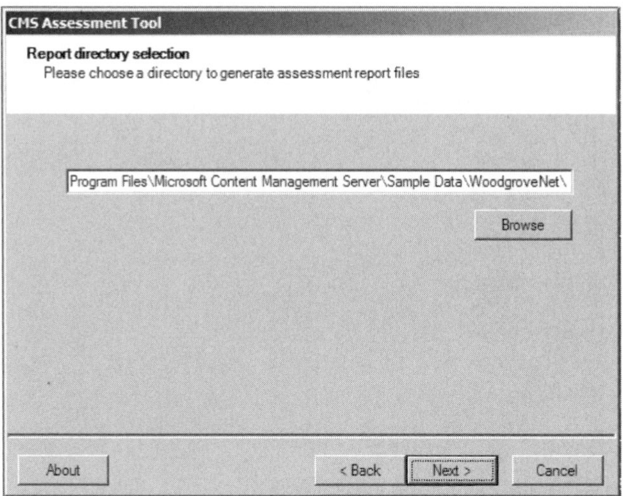

Figure 22-11 The Report Directory Selection page

11. In the Ready To Analyze page, click Next to start the analysis process. After the CMS Assessment Tool runs, it displays a summary of the results, as well as links to an error log.

Reviewing CMS Assessment Tool–Generated Reports

After running the CMS Assessment Tool, the next step is to open the generated reports using the provided MCMS Assessment Tool Report workbook. The workbook is a customized Microsoft Office Excel 2003 workbook that can load and easily navigate the various reports. Each report is presented as a separate worksheet.

To open the reports generated by the CMS Assessment Tool, complete the following steps:

1. On the Start menu, select All Programs, select Microsoft Content Management Server, select Assessment Tool, and finally select MCMS Assessment Tool Report Workbook. This will launch Office Excel and automatically open the MCMS Assessment Tool Report workbook, as shown in Figure 22-12.

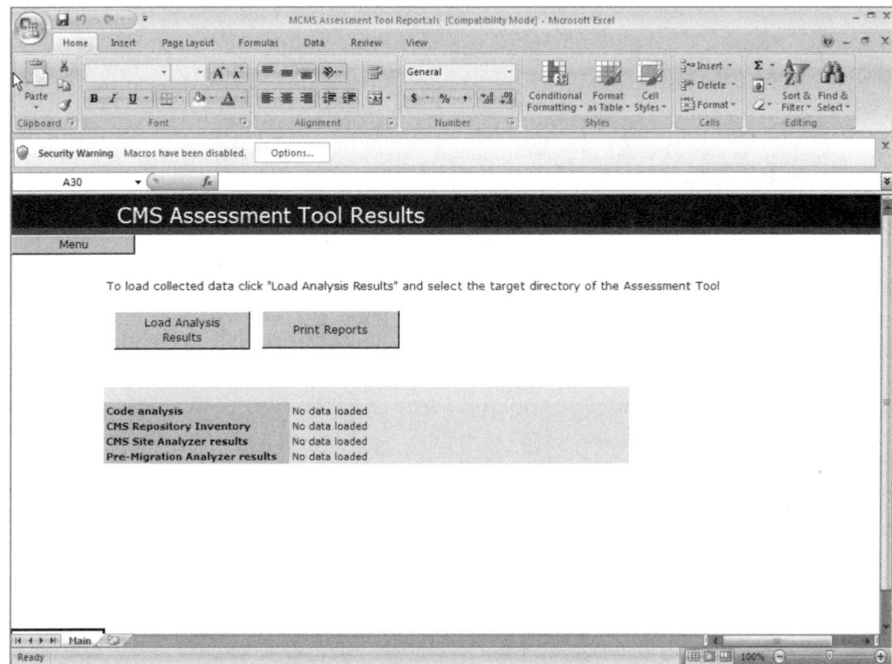

Figure 22-12 MCMS Assessment Tool Report workbook

Note The MCMS Assessment Tool Report workbook contains macros. Depending upon the configuration of Office Excel, it might or might not be configured to enable macros. If Office Excel is configured to disable macros, they must be enabled prior to loading the reports. To enable macros in Office Excel 2007, got to the Security Warning panel and select Options. In the Security Alert – Macro dialog box, select Enable This Content and click OK. Referring back to Figure 22-12, you can see this Security Warning just above the CMS Assessment Tool Results blue bar.

2. On the MCMS Assessment Tool Report workbook, click the Load Analysis Results button.
3. On the Select Folder With The Assessment Tool Output page, browse to the folder where the reports were saved as specified during the execution of the CMS Assessment Tool and then click OK.

After you select the folder that contains the generated reports, the MCMS Assessment Tool Report workbook creates a separate worksheet tab for each generated report. To view the reports (as shown in Figure 22-13), click the Menu button on the Main worksheet or select the appropriate worksheet tab at the bottom of the workbook. In the following sections, we'll give a brief overview of each report that the assessment tool generates.

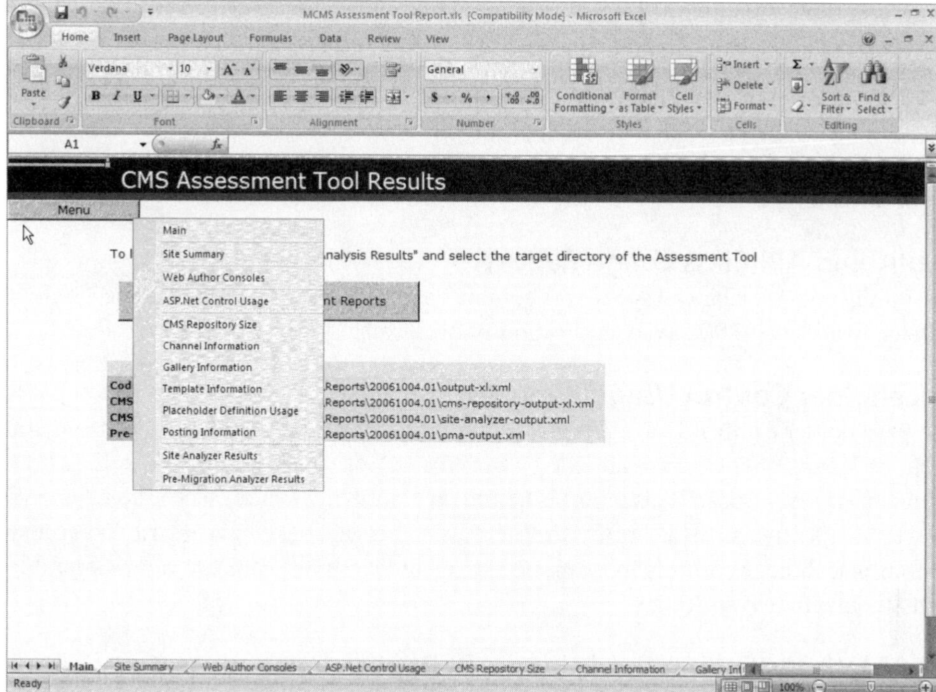

Figure 22-13 CMS Assessment Tool Results—navigating the reports

Note Figure 22-13 represents only a sample of the available reports that are generated by the CMS Assessment Tool. It is not a complete list of all reports listed in this chapter.

Site Summary Report

The Site Summary report contains a snapshot of the Content Management Server 2002 Web application project. It contains a list of all the classes, methods, properties, ASP.NET Web pages, Web controls, and assemblies used by the Web application project. This report is helpful in determining the scope of the migration effort when it is time to convert the Content Management Server 2002 Web application project to a WCM publishing site.

Publishing API Usage Summary Report

The Publishing API Usage Summary report contains a list of all the methods the Content Management Server 2002 Web application project calls in the Content Management Server Publishing API. This report is helpful to determine whether the Web application project uses any Content Management Server custom properties by applying a filter to the Class Name column for Posting or Channel and then applying another filter for *CustomPropertyCollection* or *CustomProperties* to the PAPI Method Name column.

In addition, this report is helpful in determining whether the Web application project contains any custom placeholders by applying a filter to the Class name column for *BasePlaceholderControl* and then applying another filter for *BasePlaceholderControl* to the PAPI Method Name column.

Publishing API Class Usage Report

The Publishing API Class Usage report contains a list of all the PAPI classes the Content Management Server 2002 Web application project is using.

Placeholder Control Usage Report

The Placeholder Control Usage report contains a list of all the placeholder controls the Content Management Server 2002 Web application project contains, as well as how many times they are used. This report is helpful in identifying which placeholder controls need to be rewritten as field controls or Web Parts. They will need to be rewritten because custom placeholder controls in Content Management Server 2002 are not compatible with SharePoint Server 2007.

User Methods Calling Publishing API Report

The User Methods Calling Publishing API report contains a list of the methods that contain calls into the Publishing API within the Content Management Server 2002 Web application project.

Methods Returning Publishing API Report

The Methods Returning Publishing API report contains a list of the methods in the Content Management Server 2002 Web application project that return a Publishing API object or receive one as an argument.

Classes with Publishing API Fields Report

The Classes with Publishing API Fields report lists all the classes that contain calls into the Publishing API Content Management Server 2002 Web application project.

Workflow Event Handling Report

The Workflow Event Handling report contains a list of all instances of publishing event handlers in the Content Management Server 2002 Web application project. SharePoint Server 2007 contains a different publishing and workflow engine than what Content Management Server 2002 uses. Event handlers written for Content Management Server 2002 need to be rewritten for SharePoint Server 2007 and Windows Workflow Foundation.

User Classes with Publishing API Parents Report

The User Classes with Publishing API Parents report lists all classes in your Content Management Server 2002 Web application project that are derived from classes in the Publishing API. This report is helpful in identifying any custom placeholder controls or custom Web Author actions contained in the Web application project. To find custom placeholder controls in the Content Management Server 2002 Web application project, apply a filter to the PAPI Class column, limiting it to the following results:

- *BasePlaceholderControl*
- *HtmlPlaceholderControl*
- *SingleAttachmentPlaceholderControl*
- *SingleImagePlaceholderControl*

To find custom Web Author actions in your Content Management Server 2002 Web application project, filter to the PAPI Class column for the following results:

- *BaseAction*
- *BaseNewWindowAction*
- *BasePostbackAction*

Placeholders per Template Report

The Placeholders per Template report contains a list of all the placeholder names and controls, as well as the number of times they are used on each template. This report is helpful in determining which templates contain custom placeholders that will need to be rewritten because they are not comparable with SharePoint Server 2007. In addition, this report also helps you identify which templates are using XML placeholders that need to be rewritten for SharePoint Server 2007 because there is no equivalent control for the Content Management Server 2002 XML placeholder control. To find the XML placeholder controls used in the Content Management Server 2002 Web application project, apply a filter on the Placeholder Control Type column for *Microsoft.ContentManagement.Publishing.Extensions.XmlPlaceholder*.

Template vs. Placeholder Control Report

The Template vs. Placeholder Control report contains a list of all the templates in the Content Management Server 2002 Web application project and the placeholder controls found in each template. This report helps to identify templates that do not contain any placeholders or templates that are used only for summary links.

Web Author Consoles Report

The Web Author Consoles report contains a list of all custom controls and templates in the Content Management Server 2002 Web application project that implement the Web Author console. This report helps in identifying whether the Web application project has implemented multiple instances of the Web Author console.

Http Modules Report

The Http Modules report lists all the Http modules the Content Management Server 2002 Web application project is using as they are listed in the project's web.config file. Many Content Management Server 2002 Web sites use custom Http modules to improve site performance, implement SSL support, and provide URL rewriting. Because these custom Http modules are used by the Content Management Server 2002 Publishing API, they have to be rewritten to use the new object model in SharePoint Server 2007.

Output Cache Settings Report

The Output Cache Settings report contains a list of all templates in your Content Management Server 2002 Web application project that are configured to use ASP.NET output caching. To find the templates using output caching, apply a filter for non-blank values on the following columns:

- Duration
- Location
- VaryByHeader
- VaryByParam
- VaryByCustom

SharePoint Server 2007 includes robust support for caching but does not permit setting the *OutputCache* attribute in the Page directive of each page layout. Instead, cache settings are managed using the browser-based administration tools. Because of this, any cache settings defined at the template level need to be removed when migrating the Content Management Server 2002 Web site to SharePoint Server 2007.

Project Line Count Report

The Project Line Count report contains the number of lines of code in the Content Management Server 2002 Web application project. This report is helpful in determining the scope of the code-migration task. Keep in mind that not all custom code will need to be rewritten, as many elements that required custom code in Content Management Server 2002 are not included in SharePoint Server 2007.

ASP.NET Control Usage Report

The ASP.NET Control Usage report contains a list of all the custom controls used in the Content Management Server 2002 Web application project. This report is helpful in determining the Content Management Server 2002–specific controls that will need to be rewritten for SharePoint Server 2007.

A sample ASP.NET Control Usage report, generated by running the CMS Assessment Tool against the Woodgrove Bank sample Content Management Server 2002 site, is shown in Figure 22-14.

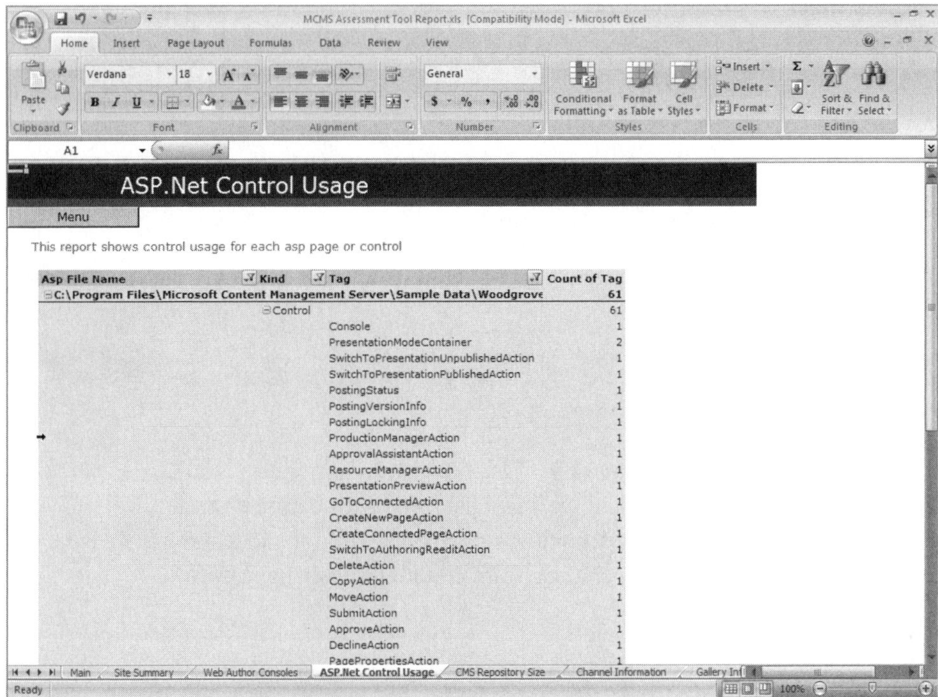

Figure 22-14 An ASP.NET Control Usage report

CMS Repository Size Report

The CMS Repository Size report contains the total number of channels, postings, template galleries, templates, resource galleries, and resources in your Content Management Server 2002 Content Repository.

A sample CMS Repository Size report, generated by running the CMS Assessment Tool against the Woodgrove Bank sample Content Management Server 2002 site, is shown in Figure 22-15.

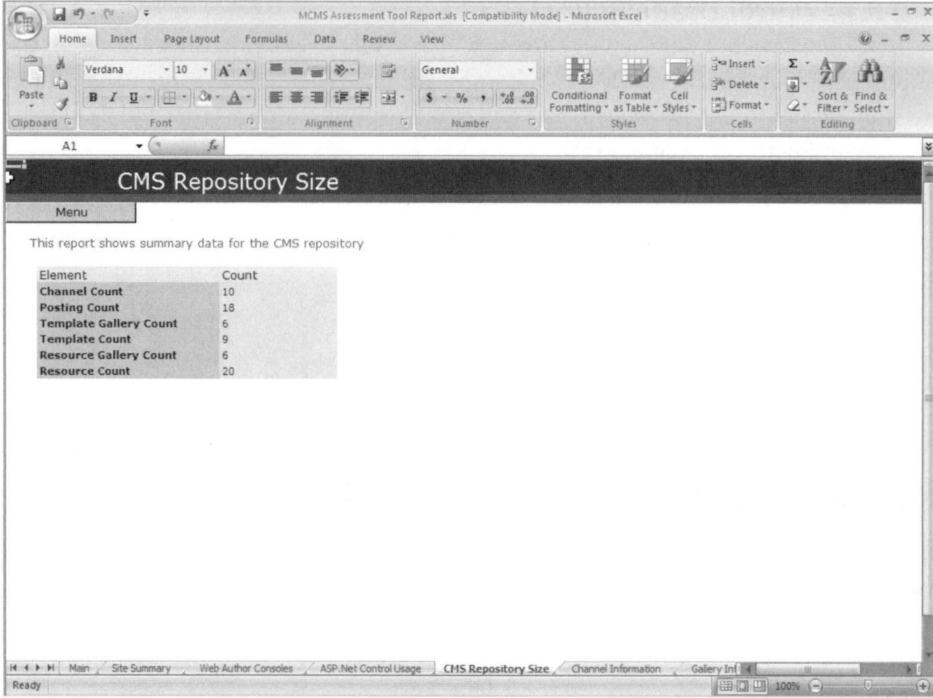

Figure 22-15 A CMS Repository Size report

Channel Information Report

The Channel Information report contains a list of all the channels in the Content Management Server 2002 Web site and many of the properties for each channel. This report is helpful in determining which channels use channel-rendering scripts.

Gallery Information Report

The Gallery Information report lists all the template galleries and resource galleries in the Content Management Server 2002 Content Repository, including the number of items in each gallery.

Template Information Report

The Template Information report lists all the templates in the Content Management Server 2002 Content Repository, including the ASP.NET file associated with the template and the number of postings dependent upon the template.

Template Property Definition Report

The Template Property Definition report lists all the custom properties for each template in the Content Management Server 2002 Content Repository.

Placeholder Definition Usage Report

The Placeholder Definition Usage report lists all the placeholder definitions used in the Content Management Server 2002 Web application project, as well as the number of times each one is used throughout the project.

Posting Information Report

The Posting Information report lists all the postings in the Content Management Server 2002 Content Repository and the major properties of each posting. This report helps identify any connected postings in the Content Management Server 2002 Content Repository, as these will need to be addressed because SharePoint Server 2007 does not support connected postings.

Posting Custom Properties Report

The Posting Custom Properties report lists all the custom properties for each posting in the Content Management Server 2002 Content Repository.

Duplicate Posting Names Report

The Duplicate Posting Names report lists all postings that have duplicate names. SharePoint Server 2007 does not support two postings with the same name in the same site, so this issue needs to be addressed before migrating the content from the Content Management Server 2002 Content Repository to SharePoint Server 2007.

Site Analyzer Results Report

The Site Analyzer Results report lists information about the hardware the Content Management Server 2002 Web site is hosted on, as well as various metrics for the Content Repository, such as user and role information and metrics on Content Management Server 2002 content not covered in other reports.

Pre-Migration Analyzer Results Report

The Pre-Migration Analyzer Results report identifies issues that might arise during migration from Content Management Server 2002 to SharePoint Server 2007. Potential issues include broken links, checked-out items, depreciated placeholders, invalid HTML objects, and objects with invalid names.

This report produces the same results generated when executing the analysis step on a migration profile in the SharePoint Central Administration Web site.

Summary of Migration Steps

You will successfully migrate a Content Management Server 2002 Web site to SharePoint Server by following four unique and very important stages: planning, preparing, upgrading, and testing/deployment. Each stage builds on the preceding stage and makes the next stage as streamlined and easy as possible.

Best Practices The primary goal for all Content Management Server 2002 to SharePoint Server 2007 migration projects should be to migrate your site with all existing functionality before attempting to add features, add capabilities, or implement customizations.

Planning the Migration

In this first stage in the migration of a Content Management Server 2002 Web site to SharePoint Server 2007, the goal is to develop a solid plan for the complete migration process. It is here where any potential problems are identified, and those that can be addressed ahead of time are resolved or mitigated. The following tasks will assist in composing a plan for the migration.

Run the CMS Assessment Tool

Obtaining a complete and comprehensive report form the CMS Assessment Tool should be the first thing you do during the planning stage. The report will help you to understand the scope of the migration project by using its many analyses. It should be fairly easy to identify trouble areas–such as heavily used templates and custom placeholders that need to be rewritten as field controls–by analyzing the various reports generated by the CMS Assessment Tool. Some of the issues identified using the CMS Assessment Tools can be addressed prior to migration–such as postings with duplicate names in the same channel, which is not supported in SharePoint Server 2007–making the process of upgrading less error prone.

Stop Current Development and Determine Site Migration Order

If the Content Management Server 2002 Web site that is the subject of the migration project is currently under active development, this should stop while the migration process is determined and a plan is put into place. Otherwise, actions such as changing template definitions and rearranging channel hierarchies could have a dramatic effect on the scope of work and analysis the migration plan is based on.

Run the SharePoint Server 2007 Content Migration Tool

The last step in planning for a migration of a Content Management Server 2002 Web site to SharePoint Server 2007 is to create a content migration profile in SharePoint Central Administration and run it against your Content Management Server 2002 Web site. The content migration task in SharePoint Server 2007 allows for multiple content migrations following an initial migration. This also will help in identifying any content issues that might arise during the migration process. If any errors are found, they should be addressed and resolved prior to migration.

Preparing for Migration

The second stage in the migration of a Content Management Server 2002 Web site to SharePoint Server 2007 involves updating your environment to the latest available version of Content Management Server 2002. In addition, if time permits, you can perform certain development tasks on the Content Management Server Web application solution that could reduce the amount of time required during the code-migration phase of the process. One example of this is if any business logic is included in the code behind of a template file in the Content Management Server Web application that contains calls to objects in the Publishing API, developers could refactor this code to put the Publishing API–specific calls into an abstraction layer that is separate from the template file.

Upgrade Content Management Server 2001 or 2002 to Content Management Server 2002 Service Pack 2

To migrate to SharePoint Server 2007, the Content Management Server Web site must be running the latest version of Content Management Server: Content Management Server 2002 Service Pack 2. If your Web site is running Content Management Server 2001, the server must first be upgraded to Content Management Server 2002 and then patched with Service Pack 1a, followed by Service Pack 2.

Note Content Management Server 2002 Service Pack 1a is cumulative, including Service Pack 1. However, Content Management Server 2002 Service Pack 2 is not cumulative, and therefore, Service Pack 1a must be installed prior to installing Service Pack 2.

Upgrade Content Management Server Web Site Application to ASP.NET 2.0

If the migration to SharePoint Server 2007 is not planned for the immediate future or active development is still being performed on the Content Management Server Web site, and the site has not been updated to leverage some of the new features provided in ASP.NET 2.0 (for example, Content Management Server 2002 Service Pack 2 adds

ASP.NET 2.0 support to Content Management Server 2002 Web application solutions), it can be advantageous to incorporate some of the ASP.NET 2.0 features into the solution in an effort to make the code migration task easier and shorter.

Master Pages

SharePoint Server 2007 heavily leverages ASP.NET 2.0 master pages in the implementation of the common user interface components. A Content Management Server 2002 Web site that already leverages ASP.NET 2.0 master pages typically takes less time to migrate than an equivalent Content Management Server 2002 Web site that does not. This is because a WCM site not only requires a master page to be specified, but page layouts use them as well. If the source Content Management Server 2002 Web application project already implements master pages, porting them to SharePoint Server 2007 will take less time than creating them from scratch.

Navigation Providers

Similar to master pages, SharePoint Server 2007 uses the ASP.NET 2.0 navigation provider model in all the navigation controls found in SharePoint sites, including WCM sites. A Content Management Server 2002 Web site that already leverages the ASP.NET 2.0 navigation provider model in its navigation controls typically takes less time to migrate than an equivalent Content Management Server 2002 Web site that does not. This is because after migration if the original Content Management Server 2002 Web application project used navigation controls that conformed to the navigation provider model, the only work required in the code migration phase will be to connect the navigation controls with the provided SharePoint navigation data sources. Otherwise, developers are forced to redevelop the navigation controls in the original Content Management Server 2002 Web application as controls that conform to the ASP.NET 2.0 navigation provider model.

Refactor Business Logic from Templates to Class Libraries

The last step is to move as much of the business logic out of Content Management Server 2002 templates. Any direct calls to the Content Management Server 2002 Publishing API in the template code-behind files will require a developer address the template after migration because the Content Management Server 2002 Publishing API is not compatible in SharePoint Server 2007. Ideally, if possible, all calls to the Content Management Server 2002 Publishing API should be moved to a separate set of classes, providing an abstraction layer that can be addressed and making the underlying framework (Content Management Server 2002 or SharePoint Server 2007) transparent to the templates or page layouts.

Perform Test Migrations

Running test migrations in the preparation stage will help you to identify and resolve any content issues that might arise during the final content migration.

Migrating Content Management Server 2002 to SharePoint Server 2007

Now that the migration of a Content Management Server 2002 Web site to SharePoint Server 2007 has been planned and prepared, the next step is to execute the migration. As previously covered in this chapter, the process of migrating can be divided into two types of tasks: content migration and code migration. The content migration task is likely to take the least amount of time considering that code migration requires a significant amount of developer interaction.

When you review the code migration process in the following steps, it should be evident that investing the time to prepare and upgrade the Content Management Server 2002 Web application project to leverage ASP.NET 2.0 capabilities such as master pages and navigation providers was not a waste of time, as it will make the migration process much simpler.

Run the SharePoint Server 2007 Content Migration Tool

To migrate a Content Management Server 2002 Web site to SharePoint Server 2007, first migrate the content. The content must be migrated first because without it, developers will not have a site to test the development of master pages and page layouts against for the new SharePoint Server 2007 Web site. Create and execute a migration profile within SharePoint Central Administration as outlined previously in this chapter.

Apply Master Pages for Site Branding

Once all the content has been migrated to SharePoint Server 2007 from the Content Management Server 2002 Content Repository, the next step is for the developers to create one or more ASP.NET 2.0 master pages to implement the site branding and user interface. Depending on the size of the site that is being migrated, developers might need to create just one master page for a small Web site, or many master pages if the migrated site is quite large. The master pages will then be leveraged by the unbranded page layouts to implement the site branding.

Upgrade Unbranded Page Layouts

When the migration profile is executed in the first step of the migration process, an unbranded page layout is created for each template definition found in the Content Management Server 2002 Content Repository. At this point, developers should address each unbranded page layout, associate it with one of the master pages created in the previous step, and apply any necessary additional modifications to implement the site branding.

Note The page layouts that correspond with the most used templates in the migrated Content Management Server 2002 Web site should be addressed first. Implementing the site branding to the most used page layouts results in the most sweeping changes, allowing developers and testers to evaluate the migration and branding process to make the necessary modifications early in the migration process.

Migrate Custom Placeholders and Other Controls

At this point, the migrated Web site will resemble the same branding as the equivalent source Content Management Server 2002 Web site; the next step is to address each of the custom placeholders that require attention. Some of the Content Management Server 2002 placeholders will migrate to new controls included in SharePoint Server 2007. However, it is likely that many Content Management Server 2002 placeholders will not have been automatically updated to equivalent SharePoint Server 2007 controls, such as the XML placeholder control. Developers should revisit each page layout and address any custom placeholders that did not map to a SharePoint Server 2007 control. Some of these placeholders might need to be rewritten as WCM field controls.

Other custom controls written for the original Content Management Server 2002 Web site might not work in SharePoint Server 2007. Each of these controls needs to be analyzed and addressed by a developer to determine whether they need to be rewritten for SharePoint Server 2007. Keep in mind that many controls that required custom code in Content Management Server 2002 Web sites might be replaced by controls included in SharePoint Server 2007.

Update Navigation Providers

Next, the navigation controls in the migrated Web site need to be addressed. If the source Content Management Server 2002 Web application leveraged the ASP.NET 2.0 navigation provider model in its navigation controls, the process of upgrading them to SharePoint Server 2007 should be fairly straightforward. In this case, developers simply need to modify the navigation controls to use the SharePoint navigation data sources instead of the Content Management Server 2002 data sources.

However, if the source Content Management Server 2002 Web application was not leveraging the ASP.NET 2.0 navigation provider model, developers need to rewrite navigation controls to utilize the SharePoint navigation data sources.

Migrate Data Abstraction Layer Code

Finally, the last step in the migration process prior to testing is for developers to rewrite the data abstraction layer from the Content Management Server 2002 Web application that used the Content Management Server 2002 Publishing API to instead use the SharePoint object model. The creation of a data abstraction layer was a common practice with many Content Management Server 2002 developers because it masked calls to the Content Management Server 2002 Publishing API from the site templates and custom controls.

If a data abstraction layer was not part of the source Content Management Server 2002 Web application, this step in the migration is unnecessary.

Testing and Deployment

Once all the content has been migrated from the Content Management Server 2002 Content Repository, master pages and page layouts have been modified to reflect the desired Web site branding, and the Content Management Server 2002 Web application code has been modified to work with the SharePoint object model, the next step is to perform thorough tests of the entire site, ensuring everything is functioning just as it was in the migrated source Content Management Server 2002 Web site. If any issues are found, they should be addressed accordingly until all problems have been eliminated or mitigated.

Once testing is complete and all issues have been addressed, the migration of the Content Management Server 2002 Web site to SharePoint Server 2007 can be considered complete.

After a successful migration of a Content Management Server 2002 Web site to SharePoint Server 2007, the next step is for developers to take advantage of some of the new features and capabilities in SharePoint Server 2007 that were not available in Content Management Server 2002, such as advanced and extensible workflow solutions, customizing the Page Editing toolbar, and implementing search features, among other things.

Summary

In this chapter, you learned what is involved in migrating a Content Management Server 2002 Web site to SharePoint Server 2007. There are two steps in the migration process: content migration and code migration.

SharePoint Server 2007 addresses the content migration task by creating and executing migration profiles from within SharePoint's Central Administration Web site. Prior to executing a migration profile job, administrators can run an analysis of the migration in an effort to identify any errors or warnings that might cause the migration process to fail.

Once the content has been migrated, developers get involved to address the various incompatibilities between the Content Management Server 2002 Web application project and SharePoint Server 2007. The most significant change is that the Content Management Server 2002 Publishing API is not compatible with the SharePoint Server 2007 object model. This incompatibility typically requires a significant amount of manual coding and rewriting of custom code contained in the original Content Management Server 2002 Web application project.

Microsoft recognizes that the migration to SharePoint Server 2007 from Content Management Server 2002 is not a trivial task. To assist in the preparation, planning, and assessment of the migration process, a free utility, the CMS Assessment Tool, is provided as an additional download to help developers and site owners obtain a clear picture of their existing Content Management Server 2002 Web site, determine the scope of the migration process, and identify key bottlenecks or errors in the migration process.

Chapter 23

Upgrading from Microsoft Windows SharePoint Services 2.0

If you have been using Microsoft Windows SharePoint Services 2.0, you have several Web sites that you might decide to upgrade to Windows SharePoint Services 3.0. This chapter will focus on how to upgrade a Windows SharePoint Services 2.0 installation to Windows SharePoint Services 3.0. If you need to upgrade from Microsoft Office SharePoint Portal Server 2003 to Microsoft Office SharePoint Server 2007, refer to Chapter 24, "Upgrading from Microsoft SharePoint Portal Server 2003."

Before you upgrade, it's best to read the relevant material. Fortunately, Microsoft has published a body of good, detailed information concerning the topic of upgrading your Windows SharePoint Services 2.0 installation, which you should read. Here are a few good starting points:

- Microsoft Windows SharePoint Services in Windows Server 2003 TechCenter found at *http://www.microsoft.com/technet/windowsserver/sharepoint/default.mspx*
- Deployment for Windows SharePoint Services 3.0 Technology found at *http://technet2.microsoft.com/Office/en-us/library/b9490b1a-45de-45fd-9f4c-754dab1383e61033.mspx*

Whichever upgrade option you choose, there are four stages that you need to complete for the upgrade to be successful:

- Planning the upgrade

- Pre-upgrade tasks
- The upgrade process
- Post-upgrade tasks

In this chapter, you'll learn the most significant aspects of each part, which will allow you to formulate the extent of the task you are undertaking and plan for the upgrade process. This chapter focuses on the administrative tasks that you will complete using the SharePoint 3.0 Central Administration Web pages and the tools you can use during the upgrade process.

If you have a highly customized Windows SharePoint Services 2.0 installation, you should read this chapter in conjunction with Chapter 25, "Upgrading Site Customizations and Custom Site Definitions to Microsoft Windows SharePoint Services 3.0." If you want to automate the upgrade process, refer to Chapter 24, which covers the use of the command-line tool stsadmn.exe in the upgrade process.

Note If you took part in the beta program and want to upgrade pilot environments to Release to Manufacturer (RTM) Windows SharePoint Services 3.0, you must upgrade to Beta 2 Technical Refresh (B2TR), refer to the Microsoft TechNet article "Installing Windows SharePoint Services 3.0 for Beta 2 Technical Refresh": *http://technet2.microsoft.com/Office/en-us/library/b3e52231-16bf-4a46-a7e8-cb31b814627a1033.mspx?mfr=true*.

Microsoft does not intend to provide tools to upgrade from SharePoint Team Services 1.0 (STS) to Windows SharePoint Services 3.0. If you have STS Web sites, you must migrate to Windows SharePoint Services 2.0 before upgrading to Windows SharePoint Service 3.0.

Understanding Your Upgrade Options

There are three approaches to upgrading a Windows SharePoint Services 2.0 implementation to Windows SharePoint Services 3.0:

- In-place upgrade
- Gradual upgrade
- Content database migration

An *in-place upgrade* is used to upgrade all SharePoint sites at once. This approach is the easiest and is best suited for single-server or small-volume deployments. A *gradual upgrade* installs Windows SharePoint Services 3.0 side by side with Windows SharePoint Services 2.0, and it allows you granular control of the upgrade process by allowing one or more site collections to be upgraded at a time. You also have the ability to revert the upgraded site back to a Windows SharePoint Services 2.0 Web site. Both in-place and gradual upgrades take place on the same hardware used by your Windows SharePoint Services 2.0 installation. A *content database migration* allows you to move your content to a new farm or onto new hardware, and therefore requires a greater number of servers to implement than the other two approaches. You could also use a database migration approach to gradually upgrade your Web sites to Windows SharePoint Services 3.0, keeping one set of servers–a Web farm–for Windows SharePoint Services 2.0 and a Web farm for Windows SharePoint Services 3.0.

Note For larger deployments, the gradual upgrade is a better option than in-place upgrade because it allows the administrator performing the upgrade to control how many site collections to upgrade at one time. In this way, large deployments can be upgraded gradually over time while continuing to host the previous version sites. This is possible because you can continue to host the sites that have not yet been upgraded on the same server as the upgraded sites.

In-Place Upgrade

Using the in-place upgrade option, the Windows SharePoint Services 2.0 implementation is upgraded in place (overwritten) with Windows SharePoint Services 3.0 and the SQL content databases are updated. Because of this, an in-place upgrade is an irreversible process; therefore, you should ensure that you have a tried and tested backup solution that you can use to restore the Windows SharePoint Services 2.0 solution.

The original sites are upgraded in-place, and you cannot view the previous versions of the sites after upgrade. This means you have no easy method of comparing or testing the upgraded Windows SharePoint Services 3.0 with the original Windows SharePoint Services 2.0 sites to verify that the upgrade process was successful. You have only your memory, documentation, or screen shots. If you use either the gradual or data migration approaches, you still have the Windows SharePoint Services 2.0 sites that you can use to verify that the upgrade process was successful.

Important Because you are using your existing implementation, you inherit the security settings of your Windows SharePoint Services 2.0 configuration. Therefore, ensure you review the security settings of your Web applications before the in-place upgrade process. For more information on this, see Chapter 14, "Information Security Polices."

The SharePoint Web sites are not available to site visitors during the upgrade process. The outage window for all users is the full time it takes to upgrade the entire server or server farm, plus the time required to check the results of the upgrade.

The advantage with this approach is that the site visitors continue to use the same URLs after upgrade. This approach is useful if you do not have another server available on which to install Windows SharePoint Services 3.0.

Gradual Upgrade

Using the gradual upgrade approach, Windows SharePoint Services 2.0 sites coexist with Windows SharePoint Services 3.0 sites on the same hardware until you are ready to uninstall the old version of the software. You can upgrade a site collection or a group of site collections one at a time. The upgrade process copies the data from the original SQL content database to a new SQL content database. The data in the new content database is then upgraded. The original data is maintained in the original database until explicitly deleted by the server administrator. Because of this, upgraded site collections can be easily rolled back to the previous version if necessary.

The gradual upgrade approach is best suited to organizations that want to stage the upgrade over a period of time either because of the time it will take to upgrade the Windows SharePoint Services 2.0 installation, because some feature (such as a language pack) is not yet available, or because they are waiting on some development work, such as a new site definition.

Most Windows SharePoint Services 2.0 sites are available to site visitors during the upgrade. Only site collections that are currently being upgraded to Windows SharePoint Services 3.0 are offline. (Note that the previous version sites are marked as updates only after they have been copied in preparation for upgrade.)

When the upgrade process is completed, the original URLs point to the upgraded version of the sites. This way, users can continue to use the same URLs they used before the upgrade.

Content Database Migration

Content database migration is also known as the *advanced upgrade process* because it is complex and requires many manual steps, especially if you want to retain the original URLs for the sites. It is like an in-place upgrade, performed on new hardware on a copy of the content, but it doesn't retain anything from your current installation other than the content itself. If your current hardware is outdated or your current farm has just outgrown the hardware, this might be a scenario to consider. You do not have to migrate all your content databases at the same time. Therefore, it is similar to a gradual upgrade with the unit of upgrade being a content database, which can contain one or more site collections. As with the gradual upgrade approach, you can choose to maintain both Windows SharePoint Services 2.0 and Windows SharePoint Services 3.0 deployments. However, in this approach, the two versions of the software product are on different hardware. In a content database migration, you perform the following tasks:

- Install Windows SharePoint Services 3.0 on a new standalone or server farm installation.
- Make a copy of all databases except for the configuration database to the Windows SharePoint Services 3.0 installation.
- Attach the databases to the Windows SharePoint Services 3.0 installation. This forces an upgrade process, which upgrades the data in place.

As in the gradual upgrade approach, the original data is untouched in the original databases. Because of this, you can quickly reinstate the Windows SharePoint Services 2.0 sites if necessary.

You must use the content database migration approach if you have a scalable hosting mode implementation, you have enabled an Active Directory directory service account creation, or you want to switch between 32-bit and 64-bit hardware.

Planning Your Upgrade

Because of the downtime involved and the risk that the upgrade might take longer than expected or that some sites might need some rework after upgrade, it is critical that the server administrator plan the upgrade process, communicate this plan to site owners and users, and communicate what to expect during the process. Use the following list as a check list:

- Understand each approach.
- Review supported topologies. (See Table 23-1 for a list of the supported topologies.)
- Review system requirements for Windows SharePoint Services 3.0.

  You should refer to other chapters within this book that cover planning and installation. In addition, you will need extra resources for the upgrade process, in particular the space required on the SQL server, because the transaction logs will grow enormously during the upgrade process. The amount of space you require is also dependent on the upgrade option you choose–for example, gradual and content migration will need more resources than the in-place approach.
- Identify the Windows SharePoint Services 2.0 sites and workspaces that are no longer used or are no longer required.

  In large installations, this analysis can reduce the number of sites you must migrate by a considerable amount. You might want to restructure your site hierarchy, sometimes known as the site taxonomy. Do not assume you will just duplicate your old structure. You might find that this is the perfect opportunity to reorganize your Windows SharePoint Services implementation now that you have worked with it for some time. Initial installations of Windows SharePoint Services—especially those that did not go through a structure prototype and pilot stages—resulted in chaotic usage. This could be your chance to add logic to your installation.

- Review that all the settings of your Windows SharePoint Services 2.0 sites are the way you want them to be in Windows SharePoint Services 3.0.

  For example, by default in Windows SharePoint Services 2.0, members of the Local Administrators Group on the server running Windows SharePoint Services 3.0 can access any Windows SharePoint Services site (and all its content). In Windows SharePoint Services 3.0 this does not happen, so if your user ID is placed in the local administrator's group, and you are not explicitly given access rights to Windows SharePoint Services sites, you might find that you are denied access after the Windows SharePoint Services 2.0 sites are upgraded.

  The security requirements in your organization might dictate that all members of the local Administrators group should not have global access to all Windows SharePoint Services Web site. However, to fulfill your administrative duties, your Active Directory userid might still need access to all Web sites, therefore, ensure you have explicit access to the Windows SharePoint Services 2.0 Web sites, before you upgrade them.

Table 23-1 Supported Topologies

Source topology (Windows SharePoint Services 2.0)	Supported destination (Windows SharePoint Services 3.0)	Unsupported destination
Single server using WMSDE	Single server using Microsoft SQL Express	Farm
Single server using SQL 2005 or SQL Server 2005	Single server using SQL 2005 or SQL Server 2005	Standalone server using SQL Express, Farm
Farm	Farm	Single server using SQL Express, SQL Server 2000, or SQL Server 2005.

If you cannot log on to a site after the upgrade process, log on as the system account, which is usually the Web application's Internet Information Services (IIS) application pool identity.

> **Note** A fix was included in Windows SharePoint Services 2.0 Service Pack 2 (SP2) that allowed you to remove full access rights for users who are members of the local Administrators group. See Microsoft Knowledge Base article number 892295 found at *http://support.microsoft.com/default.aspx/kb/892295* for details of the stsadm.exe command to enable this fix.

- Review your current Windows SharePoint Services 2.0 infrastructure, and decide whether you want to modify it, such as by reducing the size of your content databases, upgrading from SQL 2000 to SQL 2005, or using 64-bit technology.
- Estimate how long the upgrade process will take and the amount of space needed. Microsoft provides worksheets to determine how much disk space you need to perform the upgrade and how long the upgrade process might take.
- Understand how the URL redirects are handled during the gradual upgrade approach. During the upgrade process, each Windows SharePoint Services 2.0 Web site is moved to a new temporary URL. The new Windows SharePoint Services 3.0 Web site uses the old URL. During the upgrade process, users can still use the old URL and are redirected to the Windows SharePoint Services 2.0 Web site. When the site is upgraded, the redirect is deleted. More details of this can be found in the section "The Upgrade Process" later in this chapter.

> **Important** During the gradual upgrade process, certain client software, such as Microsoft Office client applications, cannot use these types of redirects. As part of your communication plan, you need to inform users of this and let them know they need to use the new temporary URL during the upgrade process.

- Perform a trial upgrade to find potential issues. This trial should take place in a non-production environment. If your production implementation contains a great deal of content, so will your trial environment. Performing this task enables you to estimate the amount of additional resources you need for the upgrade and the time it will take. This information is very important for the planning process.
- Test custom Web Parts with ASP.NET 2.0. Most Web Parts will work post upgrade. However, your developer will have to rebuild the custom Web Parts if he or she used ASP.NET 1.1 "obfuscation" tools or used application programming interfaces (APIs) that are removed from Windows SharePoint Services 3.0.
- Develop new and upgraded custom site definitions files. (See Chapter 25.)
- Determine how to handle customizations. (See Chapter 25.)
- Create a communication plan. You do not want your users to learn about the upgrade process while it is occurring.

Microsoft FrontPage Customizations

Although using Microsoft FrontPage 2003 makes it easy to change Windows SharePoint Services site Web Part pages, it does have a significant consequence. Initially, all Windows SharePoint Services Web Part pages are based on ASP.NET Web pages located on the file system in site definition folders; they are not stored in the content database. When these pages are first referenced, they are cached on the Web server. When a page is requested, the content database is searched for specific content, which is incorporated with the cached Web page and rendered to the user. This provides fast response time. The Web Part pages that are based on site definitions and cached in memory are known as *ghosted* (uncustomized) pages.

When a Windows SharePoint Services site is modified in FrontPage, these modified and now unique Web Part pages are stored in the content database. When a modified page is requested, it is not cached in memory and is known as *unghosted* (customized) pages. There are many disadvantages with unghosted pages–for example, unghosted pages are slower to render, and they are forced through the SafeMode parser and therefore cannot contain inline code. Additionally, changes to the underlying site definition Web Part pages do not percolate through to Web Part pages modified by FrontPage 2003.

If your Windows SharePoint Services 2.0 implementation contains no customized Web Part pages, or includes only small customizations of features–such as navigation bars, images outside Web Part zones, and Data View Web Part (DVWP)–your upgrade process might be relatively straightforward. However, if your Windows SharePoint Services 2.0 implementation has included more than a light degree of customization–such as drastically changing the look and feel, making changes to the default site definitions (which is not supported), or the heavy use of site definitions–you need to refer to Chapter 25, because you'll have some re-customization work to perform before upgrading to version 3.0.

Organizing and Resizing Content Databases

Many organizations might not have considered the size of their site hierarchy when they designed their Windows SharePoint Services 2.0 implementation; so, before you upgrade to Windows SharePoint Services 3.0, you should review your storage and database sizes. Although there is no hard-coded limit to the size of the databases, SQL Server best practices recommend that databases be no larger than 30 GB. Beyond that limit, performance can slowly degrade. Windows SharePoint Services 2.0 documentation recommends a size of less than 50 GB. However, a properly configured Windows SharePoint Services 3.0 and SharePoint Server 2007 installation should be able to handle terabyte-sized content databases. So the issue is not what SharePoint can support, but instead comes down to backup and restore, high availability and disaster recovery solutions. Many organizations have limited the sizes of their Windows SharePoint Services database, so that they can achieve their service level agreements. Databases will grow over time and therefore the time taken to back up and restore, which is dependant on the infrastructure in use, can increase to the point where it can endanger an organization's service level agreements.

As part of the upgrade planning process, ensure that your databases are smaller than 50 GB. This will make your upgrade easier to manage no matter which of the three upgrade approaches you choose. In fact, it is recommended that you not use the in-place upgrade approach if your database is larger than 30 GB. By not keeping to these size recommendations, the upgrade process can fail.

To reduce the size of your databases, you need to move Web sites or site collections to new content databases, either using smigrate.exe or stsadm.exe. There are also third-party tools such as SPSiteManager, found at *http://www.microsoft.com/sharepoint/downloads/components/detail.asp?a1=724*, that can help you divide your databases and can automate the process. This tool can also help to identify the site collection owners, which is really useful when you formulate your communication plan. Note that SPSiteManager is an unsupported tool from Microsoft.

Pre-Upgrade Tasks

Whichever upgrade approach you decide to use, you must perform a number of pre-upgrade steps or your upgrade process might fail. Once you have completed the pre-upgrade tasks, you can commence your chosen upgrade approach. The pre-upgrade tasks are as follows:

1. Ensure your Windows SharePoint Services 2.0 deployment is working correctly.

   Note The upgrade process will not resolve any problems you might have with your implementation. However, any outstanding problems might cause the upgrade process to fail, and depending on the point where it fails, it might leave your Windows SharePoint Services 2.0 implementation in an unusable state. This is particularly true if you are using the in-place upgrade approach. You will then have to restore your Windows SharePoint Services 2.0 environment before you can attempt the upgrade process again. The SharePoint Configuration Analyzer can analyze your Windows SharePoint Services 2.0 implementation and report a wide range of configuration errors. You can download the tool from *http://go.microsoft.com/fwlink/?LinkId=25438&clcid=0x409*.

2. Run and test a full backup of your SQL databases, and make sure you have copies of any customizations (such as site definitions), Web Parts and other files you would need to re-create your Windows SharePoint Services 2.0 environment. See the Microsoft TechNet article, "Backing Up and Restoring Web Sites Created with Windows SharePoint Services," at *http://www.microsoft.com/technet/prodtechnol/office/office2003/maintain/bureswss.mspx*.
3. Install Windows SharePoint Services 2.0 SP2.

More Info For more information about installing Windows SharePoint Services 2.0 SP2, see *http://office.microsoft.com/en-us/assistance/HA011607881033.aspx* and Microsoft Knowledge Base article number 875358, "You must update all the Web servers that are running Windows SharePoint Services in a Web farm," found at *http://support.microsoft.com/default.aspx/kb/875358*. This Knowledge Base article lists the version numbers of Windows SharePoint Services 2.0 and how to check and update a virtual server if the service pack did not update them correctly.

4. Ensure all Internet Information Services (IIS) virtual servers on each Web front-end server are at the same service pack and that all servers in the farm have the same security updates installed.

   You can check the version number of your virtual servers by completing the following procedure:

   a. From the Administrative Tools start menu, click SharePoint Central Administration.

   b. On the Windows SharePoint Services Central Administration Web page, under the Virtual Server Configuration section, click Configure Virtual Server Settings.

   c. The Virtual Server List is displayed. Check that each virtual server is at version 6.0.2.6568 or above, as shown in Figure 23-1.

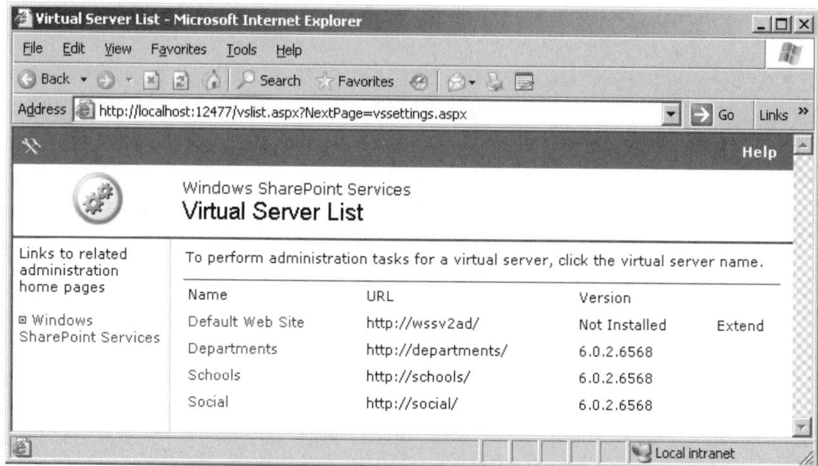

Figure 23-1 Windows SharePoint Services 2.0 Virtual Server List

5. Check again that your Windows SharePoint Services 2.0 installation is working as normal. Resolve any problems that the service pack or security updates might have introduced.
6. Perform a backup of your environment.

> **Note** Windows SharePoint Services 2.0 SP2 changes the database schema. Therefore, any backups that you made when the server was running the original release version of Windows SharePoint Services 2.0 or Windows SharePoint Services 2.0 SP1 cannot be restored to a server that has Windows SharePoint Services 2.0 SP2 installed.

7. Install Microsoft .NET Framework 2.0 plus any security updates. This allows the use of ASP.NET 2.0 Web service extensions in IIS. That is, both ASP.NET version 1.1 and version 2.0 will execute side by side, but it does not automatically upgrade your existing IIS virtual servers to use ASP.Net 2.0. You can run your Windows SharePoint Services 2.0 Web sites on .NET Framework 2.0 after you have installed Windows SharePoint Services 2.0 SP2. This will allow you to test your custom Web Part on .NET Framework 2.0 prior to running them on Windows SharePoint Services 2.0.
8. Increase the ASP.NET runtime executionTimeout. You can specify this at the machine, site, application, and subdirectory levels—that is, alter the *<httpRuntime>* element in your machine.config or the web.config. For more information, refer to *http://msdn.microsoft.com/library/en-us/cpgenref/html/gngrfHttpRuntimeSection.asp*.
9. Install Windows .NET Framework 3.0 (formerly known as WinFX). There are separate versions for x86-based computers and x64-based computers. Ensure you use the correct version for your server.
10. Deploy upgraded definition files and new site definitions. Existing sites created from a custom Windows SharePoint Services 2.0 site definition should work in Windows SharePoint Services 3.0. However, to take advantage of much of the new functionality and to create new sites from your Windows SharePoint Services 2.0 custom site definitions, these must be upgraded. For more information, see Chapter 25 and the Windows SharePoint Services 3.0 SDK.
11. Communicate outage details to your site owners and users. To help your planning process and to find who to target your communications to, you need to analyze your current Windows SharePoint Services implementation. You can use SPSiteManager (found at *http://www.codeplex.com/Release/ProjectReleases.aspx?ProjectName=SPUS* on the Releases tab) and SPReport (*http://www.gotdotnet.com/workspaces/workspace.aspx?id=8eb2bfa3-aac8-4b5a-b3a2-5accb29970eb*). Once the product is

released to manufacturing, the features from the SharePoint Configuration Analyzer, SPSiteManager, and SPReport may be merged depending on customer needs.

12. If you are planning a gradual upgrade approach, decide on your temporary domain names for your Web applications. For example, if the pre-upgrade URL for a Windows SharePoint Services 2.0 Web site is http://departments.contoso.msft, the new URL could be http://departmentsold.contoso.msft. Post upgrade, the new URL will be used for the Windows SharePoint Services 2.0 Web site and http://departments.contoso.msft will be used for the upgraded Windows SharePoint Services 3.0 Web site. You could use a new port number with the same host name for the new URL, such as http://departments.contoso.msft:8080, but usual practice is to create a new domain name.

13. Run the pre-upgrade scan tool, prescan.exe. To use this tool, you must be logged on as a member of the Administrators group on the local server. This tool is available as a separate download, the URL of which can be found at *http://technet2.microsoft.com/Office/en-us/library/3479e99e-0734-4237-a412-9fc42bf8bd251033.mspx?mfr=true*, and is part of the Windows SharePoint Services 3.0 setup program. It should be run prior to the upgrade process and again during the upgrade process, but before the SharePoint Products And Technologies Wizard is run. (See the "Task 2: Run the Prescan Tool" section later in this chapter.) Prescan.exe has two purposes:

    1. Parses and saves list definitions with the associated lists. After you apply Windows SharePoint Services 2.0 SP2, whenever a list is created it contains its list definition. Prescan calls the Windows SharePoint Services 2.0 SP2 method to complete this process for all lists.

    2. Reports common issues that will result in a failed upgrade.

    Such issues reported by this tool are as follows:

    1. The presence of customized site templates. You can then verify the customizations after the upgrade.

    2. The presence of orphaned objects.

    3. The presence of custom Web Parts. These need to be identified prior to the upgrade process so that a decision can be made whether they are needed when the site is migrated to Windows SharePoint Services 3.0. Such custom Web Parts will need to be investigated because they might need to be rebuilt or redeployed after the upgrade. Most custom Web Parts will continue to work after the upgrade, but they need to be tested on an ASP.NET 2.0 Windows SharePoint Services Web site.

Orphan Objects

An *orphan object* is an entry in one SQL database table that points to a nonexistent entry in another SQL database table. The most common orphan is where there is an entry for a site in the sites table of the configuration database but no corresponding site entry in the content database sites table. Windows SharePoint Services 2.0 SP2 contained two fixes to prevent orphans, and it also contained an update to stsadm.exe that could be used to clean orphans from the database. You might notice that you have orphans if stsadm -o restore fails to restore the site, even with the -overwrite option when you know the URL exists, or stsadm -o deletesite fails to delete the site. Information on orphans can be found at the following locations:

- "Orphaned Sites - Part 1, Part 2, and Part 3": *http://blogs.msdn.com/krichie/archive/2005/10/25/484889.aspx*, *http://blogs.msdn.com/krichie/archive/2005/10/31/487365.aspx*, and *http://blogs.msdn.com/krichie/archive/2006/06/30/652453.aspx*
- "SharePoint Orphans and Twins – Gotta love the little guys": *http://blogs.msdn.com/joelo/archive/2006/06/23/644954.aspx*
- "Orphan KBs! How to remove your Windows SharePoint Services and SPS 2003 orphans in a supported way!" *http://blogs.msdn.com/joelo/archive/2006/07/12/663629.aspx*
- "Description of a new command-line operation that you can use to repair content databases in Windows SharePoint Services": *http://support.microsoft.com/kb/918744/*

The Upgrade Process

This section provides additional details on the three upgrade approaches. The first stage in the upgrade process is to install Windows SharePoint Services 3.0. Then you can upgrade or migrate your Windows SharePoint Services 2.0 Web sites. The upgrade process is broken into four tasks, as follows:

- Task 1: Install Windows SharePoint Services 3.0 binaries
- Task 2: Run the prescan tool
- Task 3: Run the SharePoint Products And Technologies Configuration Wizard
- Task 4: Upgrade and migrate your Windows SharePoint Services 2.0 Web sites

If you want to use the content database migration upgrade approach, you should install Windows SharePoint Services 3.0 on your new server or servers. (The process is detailed in Chapter 5, "Installing Microsoft Office SharePoint Server 2007." If you want to use the in-place or gradual upgrade approach, tasks 1 through 3 are detailed in this chapter. The first three tasks are similar for both upgrade approaches, and therefore, the details for these three tasks will detail both the in-place and upgrade approaches. Task 4 is upgrade/migration-specific and will be detailed separately.

You can also use the stsadm.exe tool to upgrade and migrate a Windows SharePoint Services 2.0 Web site.

Task 1: Installing Windows SharePoint Services 3.0 Binaries—In-Place/Gradual Upgrade Approach

To install the Windows SharePoint Services 3.0 binaries, complete the following steps:

1. Download Windows SharePoint Services 3.0 from the Microsoft download site, and run SharePoint_setup.exe.
2. If an Open File – Security Warning dialog box is displayed, click Run.
3. A Microsoft Windows SharePoint Services dialog box appears, asking if you want to proceed with the installation. Click Yes.
4. A dialog box displays the progress of the installation. This dialog box might disappear, but the installation is still progressing, so be patient.
5. When the Read The Microsoft Software License Terms page is displayed, review the terms. Select the I Accept The Terms Of This Agreement check box, and then click Continue.
6. If the setup program found an upgradeable product installed on the server, there will be an Upgrade tab with a title of Upgrade Earlier Versions, as shown in Figure 23-2. Choose one of the three following options:
   a. Select the Yes, Perform A Gradual Upgrade option button to initiate a gradual upgrade.
   b. Select the Yes, Perform An Automated In-Place Upgrade option button to initiate the in-place upgrade.
   c. Select the No, Do Not Upgrade At This Time option button to install Windows SharePoint Services 3.0 alongside the Windows SharePoint Services 2.0 implementation.

Note If your Windows SharePoint Services 2.0 implementation does not support one of the upgrade approaches, the appropriate option button will be unavailable. You can see this in Figure 23-2, where the Windows SharePoint Services 3.0 setup program was run on a Windows SharePoint Services 2.0 standalone implementation that used Microsoft SQL Server 2000 Desktop Engine (Windows) (WMSDE).

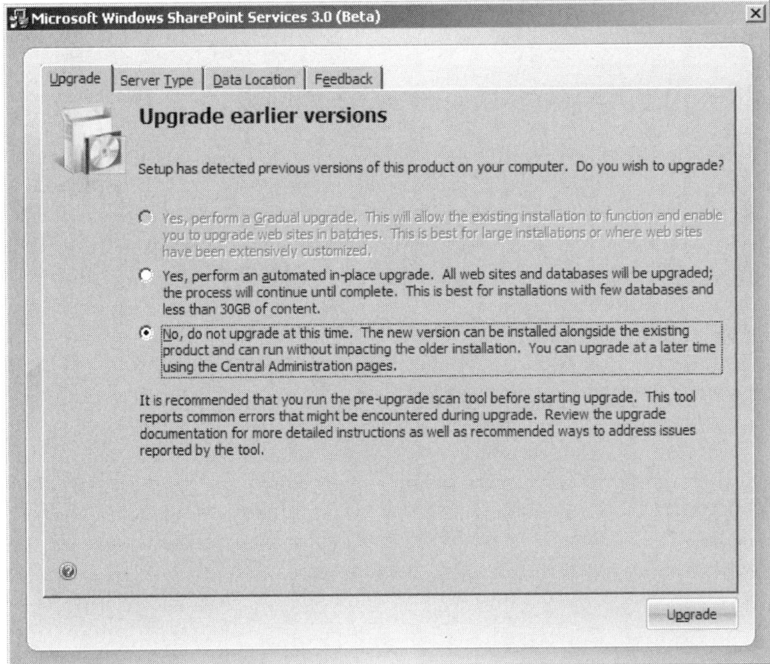

Figure 23-2 The Upgrade tab: Upgrade Earlier Versions

7. Click the Server Type tab, shown in Figure 23-3. Your choice here is dictated by your current Windows SharePoint Services 2.0 installation. Select the Web Front End option button if you have a Web farm or you use SQL Server 2000 or SQL Server 2005. Otherwise, select the Stand-Alone option button, which should be used only if your Windows SharePoint Services 2.0 implementation is a standalone installation that uses WMSDE—that is, you are not using SQL Server 2000 or SQL Server 2005. Using the Stand-Alone option installs Microsoft SQL Server 2005 Express Edition, also known as SQL Express.

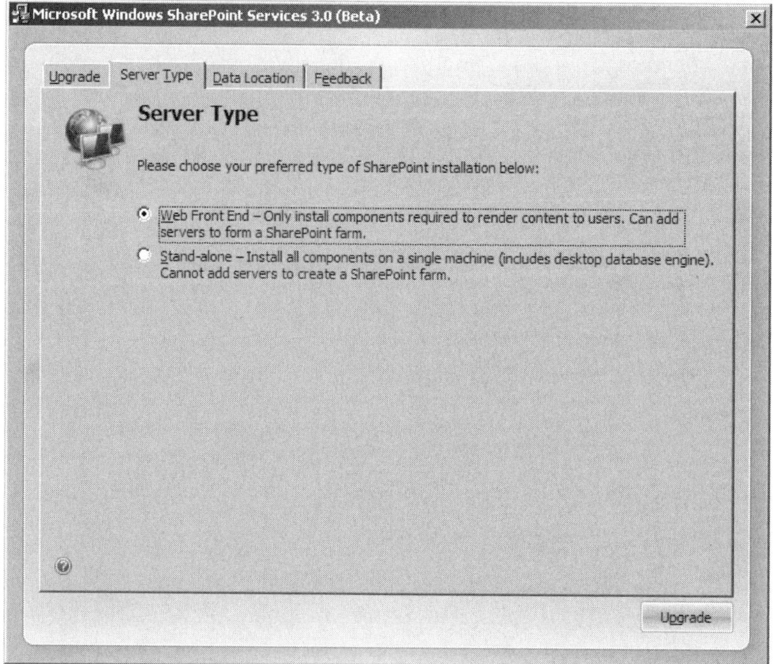

Figure 23-3 The Server Type tab showing the Web Front End and Stand-Alone options

Important This is an important step, which is very easy missed. Make sure this does not happen to you. Otherwise, you will need to uninstall Windows SharePoint Services 3.0 and reinstall it.

8. The remaining two tabs, Data Location and Feedback, can be used to customize your installation as described in Chapter 5. If you plan to use the server for search, you should choose a location with plenty of disk space available.
9. Click Upgrade. Setup runs and installs Windows SharePoint Services 3.0 binaries in the C:\Program Files\Common Files\Microsoft Shared\Web server extensions\12 directory—unless you changed the default location—and the following two links are added to the Administrative Tools menu:
   a. SharePoint 3.0 Central Administration
   b. SharePoint Products And Technologies Configuration Wizard

   During this portion of the upgrade process, no databases are created or upgraded and no modifications are made to IIS.

10. When the installation has completed, the completion Web page is displayed, as shown in Figure 23-4. Clear the Run The SharePoint Products And Technologies Configuration Wizard Now check box, and then click Close.

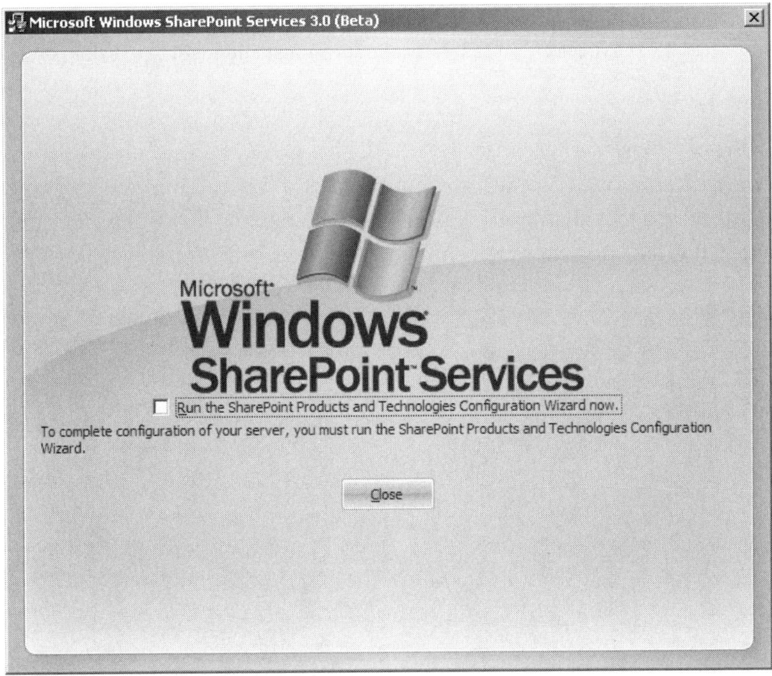

Figure 23-4 Windows SharePoint Services 3.0 binary installation complete

Task 2: Running the Prescan Tool

This should be the second time you have run this tool. The first execution of the prescan tool should be at the planning stage. The syntax of the prescan tool is as follows:

prescan [/c file] /All | [/v] urls

If you have your own custom site definitions (custom templates), you can use the prescan */C* parameter to specify a file path to the configuration files for custom templates. By adding custom templates to the configuration file, you tell prescan to mark them as custom templates. See Chapter 25 for more information on using this option. Other switches with this tool include the following:

- */All* scans the entire farm.
- */v* specifies Virtual Server scan mode; the default is SPSite scan mode.
- *Urls* specifies a list of one or more SPSite or virtual server URLs to scan.

To run the prescan tool, complete the following steps:

1. Run the pre-upgrade scan tool at this stage to be sure that you have identified and addressed any issues. To do this, open a command prompt and type the following commands:

```
CD C:\Program Files\Common Files\Microsoft Shared\Web server extensions\12\B
IN
prescan /All
```

2. Depending on the size of the installation, the pre-scan process can take some time. A percentage value will display showing progress. When complete, an "operation successful" message is displayed, followed by the names of two files–a log file and a summary file. The output looks similar to Figure 23-5.

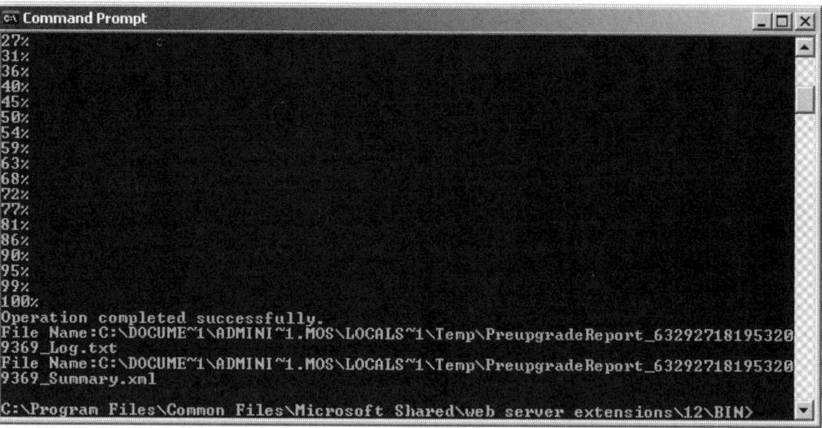

Figure 23-5 Prescan output

3. The _Log.txt file contains a list of all Web sites scanned, files that are unghosted, and any custom templates. A portion of the file can be seen in Figure 23-6.

PreupgradeReport_632942481807260832_Log.txt - Notepad

```
09/19/2006 07:36:32   Unghosted page: "http://social/CRCustom/Lists/Task List/duetoday.aspx".
09/19/2006 07:36:32   Unghosted page: "http://social/CRCustom/Lists/Task List/EditForm.aspx".
09/19/2006 07:36:32   Unghosted page: "http://social/CRCustom/Lists/Task List/MyItems.aspx".
09/19/2006 07:36:32   Unghosted page: "http://social/CRCustom/Lists/Task List/NewForm.aspx".
09/19/2006 07:36:32   Unghosted page: "http://social/CRCustom/Other/Forms/AllItems.aspx".
09/19/2006 07:36:32   Unghosted page: "http://social/CRCustom/Other/Forms/DispForm.aspx".
09/19/2006 07:36:32   Unghosted page: "http://social/CRCustom/Other/Forms/EditForm.aspx".
09/19/2006 07:36:32   Unghosted page: "http://social/CRCustom/Other/Forms/Upload.aspx".
09/19/2006 07:36:32   Unghosted page: "http://social/CRCustom/Other/Forms/WebFldr.aspx".
09/19/2006 07:36:32   Updating list schema in web.
09/19/2006 07:36:32 Scanning SPWeb: http://social/DocWkSpc
09/19/2006 07:36:32   Updating list schema in web.
09/19/2006 07:36:33 Scanning SPWeb: http://social/Social
09/19/2006 07:36:33   Updating list schema in web.
09/19/2006 07:36:34 Checking if any site has not been scanned
09/19/2006 07:36:34 Checking if any list has not been scrubbed
09/19/2006 07:36:34 Scan finished without failure.
09/19/2006 07:36:34 ===============================Logs===============================
09/19/2006 07:36:34 Log file: C:\DOCUME~1\ADMINI~1.MOS\LOCALS~1\Temp\PreupgradeReport_632942481807260832_Log.txt
09/19/2006 07:36:34 Summary file: C:\DOCUME~1\ADMINI~1.MOS\LOCALS~1\Temp\PreupgradeReport_632942481807360976_Summary.xml
09/19/2006 07:36:34 ==============================Totals==============================
09/19/2006 07:36:34 Number of sites skipped (already scanned):   0
09/19/2006 07:36:34 Number of sites scanned:   3
09/19/2006 07:36:34 Number of broken sites:   0
09/19/2006 07:36:34 Number of webs scanned:   22
09/19/2006 07:36:34 Number of broken webs:   0
09/19/2006 07:36:34 Number of webs using custom template:   0
09/19/2006 07:36:34 Number of pages scanned:   1317
09/19/2006 07:36:34 Number of unghosted pages:   931 (70.69% of total).
```

Figure 23-6 Preupgrade report _Log.txt file

The _Summary.xml file contains similar information, as shown in Figure 23-7.

```
<?xml version="1.0" encoding="utf-8" ?>
- <summary>
  - <sites>
    - <site url="http://departments" storage="33439298">
      - <webs>
        + <web url="http://departments/BoDBasic">
        + <web url="http://departments/BoDCustom">
        + <web url="http://departments/CMBasic">
        + <web url="http://departments/HDBasic">
        + <web url="http://departments/HDCustom">
        + <web url="http://departments/ProjectBasic">
        + <web url="http://departments/ProjectCustom">
        + <web url="http://departments/ResourceBasic">
        + <web
            url="http://departments/ResourceCustom">
        </webs>
      </site>
    - <site url="http://schools" storage="9486293">
      - <webs>
        + <web url="http://schools/CRBasic">
        + <web url="http://schools/CRCustom">
        </webs>
      </site>
    - <site url="http://social" storage="9486293">
      + <webs>
      </site>
    </sites>
  - <totals>
      <customTemplateCount value="0" />
      <unghostedPageCount value="931" />
    </totals>
  </summary>
```

Figure 23-7 Preupgrade report _Summary.xml file

Important Do not add any servers to your server farm after this point in the upgrade process, otherwise you could corrupt your installation. Wait until the upgrade process is complete.

Task 3: Running the SharePoint Products And Technologies Configuration Wizard

The SharePoint Products And Technologies Configuration Wizard creates a Windows SharePoint Services 3.0 Web application to host the SharePoint 3.0 Central Administration Web site. It creates a new configuration database to store configuration data for Windows SharePoint Services 3.0 and copies configuration data into this new database, from the Windows SharePoint Services 2.0 configuration database.

If you need language packs, install them now. In an in-place upgrade, if a particular Windows SharePoint Services 2.0 language pack is installed but its corresponding Windows SharePoint Services 3.0 language pack is not installed, at this point–that is, before the upgrade–the upgrade log records errors. However, the upgrade operation will still complete.

Run the SharePoint Products and Technologies Configuration Wizard using the following steps:

1. Click Start, point to All Programs, point to Administrative Tools, and then click SharePoint Products And Technologies Configuration Wizard.
2. In the SharePoint Products And Technologies Configuration Wizard, on the Welcome To SharePoint Products And Technologies page, click Next.
3. A message appears, notifying you that Internet Information Services (IIS), the SharePoint Administration Service, and the SharePoint Timer Service might need to be restarted or reset during configuration.
4. Click Yes to continue with the wizard.
   a. A message appears, as shown in the Figure 23-8, notifying you that you should download and install new language template packs for the new version. Click OK to confirm the message and continue with the wizard.

Figure 23-8 Installing Windows SharePoint Services Language Template Packs

5. If this is a gradual upgrade, perform the following steps:

   a. The Connect To A Server Farm page is displayed, as shown in Figure 23-9. Select the No, I Want To Create A New Server Farm option.

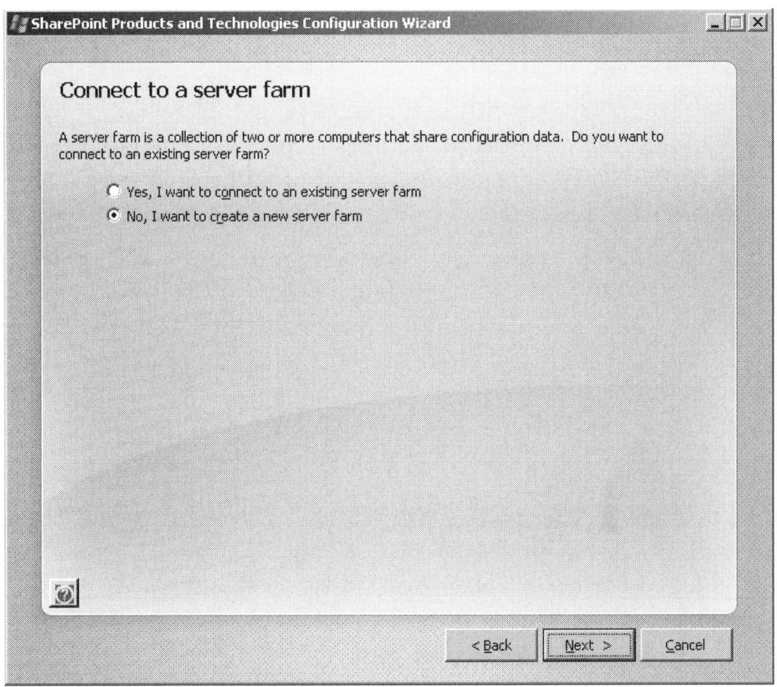

Figure 23-9 Connecting to a server farm

   b. On the Specify Configuration Database Settings page, perform the following actions:

      - In the Database Server text box, type the name of the server running SQL Server 2000 or SQL Server 2005.
      - In the Database Name text box, either except the default database name, SharePoint_Config, or type a database name.
      - In the Specify Database Access Account section, type the username and password that will be used to connect to the SQL server. The username should be entered in the format *domain\username*.
      - Click Next.

6. If you did not choose the Stand-Alone server type, you are presented with configuration screens for the SharePoint Central Administration Web application. Complete these screens as follows:

   a. On the Configure SharePoint Central Administration Web Application page, if you want to use a specific port number for SharePoint Central Administration, select the Specify Port Number check box and then type the port number to use.

   b. In the Configure Security Settings section, select either NTLM or Negotiate (Kerberos) as your authentication provider, depending on your environment, and then click Next.

      Important To enable Kerberos authentication, you must perform additional configuration. For more information about authentication methods, see Chapter 5.

   c. The Completing The SharePoint Products And Technologies Configuration Wizard page is displayed, as shown in Figure 23-10.

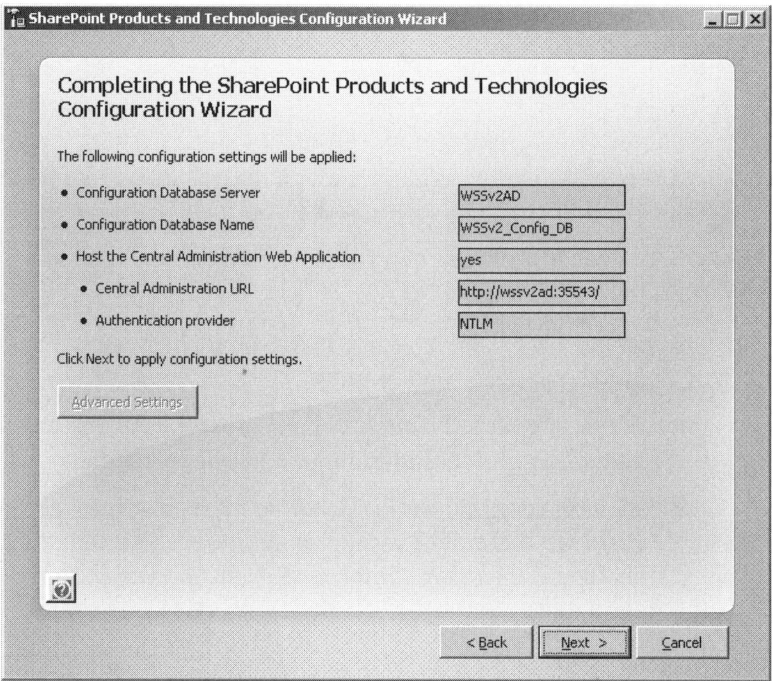

Figure 23-10 Completing the SharePoint Products And Technologies Configuration Wizard

   d. If this is a gradual upgrade, the Advanced Settings button will be active. Use this to enable Active Directory Account Creation Mode. This feature is unchanged in Windows SharePoint Services 3.0.

   e. Verify the settings, and then click Next.

7. The SharePoint Products And Technologies Configuration Wizard will now perform 10 configurations tasks for an in-place upgrade or 11 configuration tasks for a gradual upgrade approach. A clean Windows SharePoint Services 3.0 install usually consists of 9 configuration tasks. Task 1 commences, which initializes the upgrade and checks whether the pre-upgrade scan tool has been run.

8. If this is an in-place upgrade, a message appears notifying you that if you have a server farm with multiple servers, you must run setup on each server to install the new Windows SharePoint Services 3.0 binary files before running the configuration wizard and starting the upgrade process. Depending on your server farm configuration, and where you are in the process of installing and configuring Windows SharePoint Services 3.0, you have three choices:

   a. If this is the only server in your farm, no other actions are necessary. Click OK to continue with the wizard.

   b. If you have other servers in your farm, and you have not yet run setup and the configuration wizard on the other servers, leave this message open on this server–the designated server–and then run setup and the configuration wizard on the other servers in the farm. When all the other servers are at this same stage, you can return to this, the designated, server and click OK to continue with the SharePoint Products And Technologies Configuration Wizard. You can also run the SharePoint Products And Technologies Configuration Wizard from the command line. See Chapter 24 for more details on how to do this.

   c. If you have already run setup and the configuration wizard on all servers, the SharePoint Products And Technologies Configuration Wizard has completed on the designated server, and the Windows SharePoint Services 3.0 farm has no pending jobs, click OK to continue with the configuration wizard.

9. The upgrade process then continues with task 2, initiating the upgrade sequence. This task can take some time, after which the other tasks run.

10. The Configuration Successful page is displayed, as shown in Figure 23-11. Review the settings that have been configured, and then click Finish.

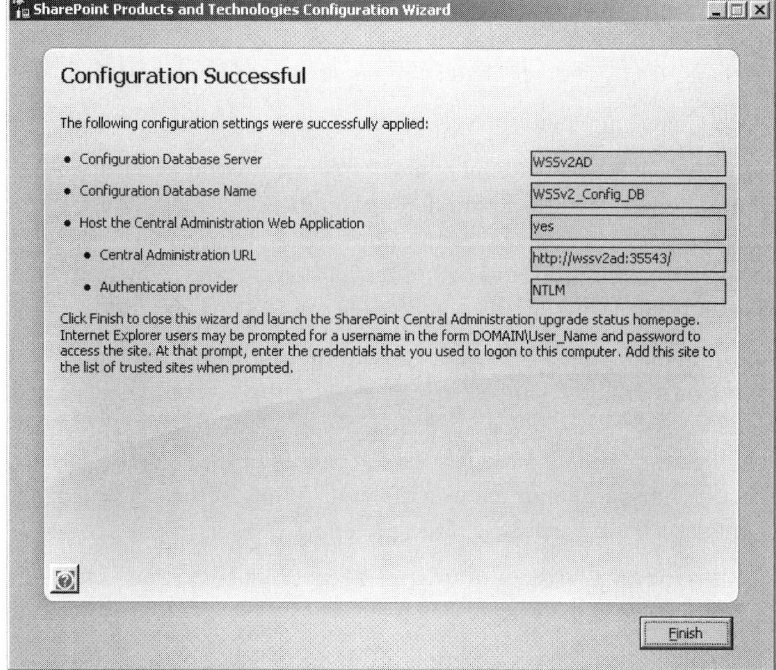

Figure 23-11 The Configuration Successful page

Task 4a: Upgrading and Migrating Windows SharePoint Services 2.0 Web Sites—In-Place Upgrade Approach

To complete an in-place upgrade process, following these steps:

1. The SharePoint Products And Technologies Configuration Wizard closes and the Upgrade Running page opens, as shown in Figure 23-12. You might be prompted to enter your username and password before the Upgrade Running page will open.

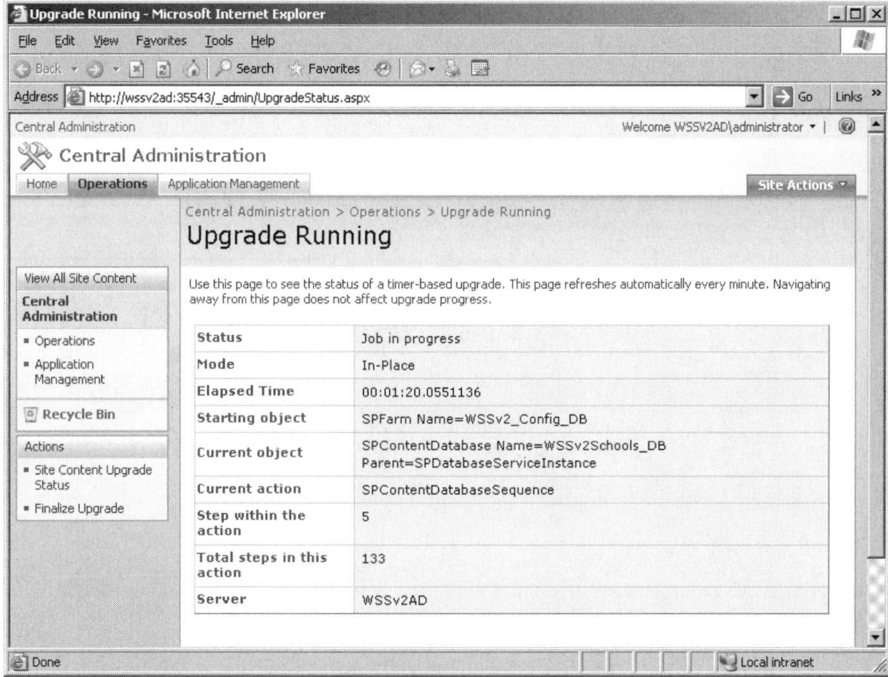

Figure 23-12 The Upgrade Running page

Important If the Upgrade Running page does not display or you get an error that the service is unavailable, this might be due to the excessive work that the server is undertaking, resulting in a timing issue. It does not mean that you have a failure. Do not reboot. Wait a while, and then click your browser's refresh icon. You can also check for error messages in the Upgrade.log and the trace log files, which are located at *%SystemDrive%\Program Files\Common Files\Microsoft Shared\Web server extensions\12\LOGS*. The trace log is named in the following format: Machine_name-YYYYMMDD-HHMM.log, where *YYYYMMDD* is the date and *HHMM* is the time.

2. The process of upgrading the Windows SharePoint Services 2.0 Web site is automatically started and consists of a number of scheduled timer jobs, which are started sequentially. These might take a while to complete. To check on the status of the upgrade process, click the browser refresh icon. You can monitor each timer job by opening the new SharePoint 3.0 Central Administration Web page. Then on the Operations tab, under Global Configuration, click Timer Job Status. The progress column shows the percentage complete for the current timer job, as

shown in Figure 23-13. This is not the progress for the whole upgrade progress–only for this particular timer job.

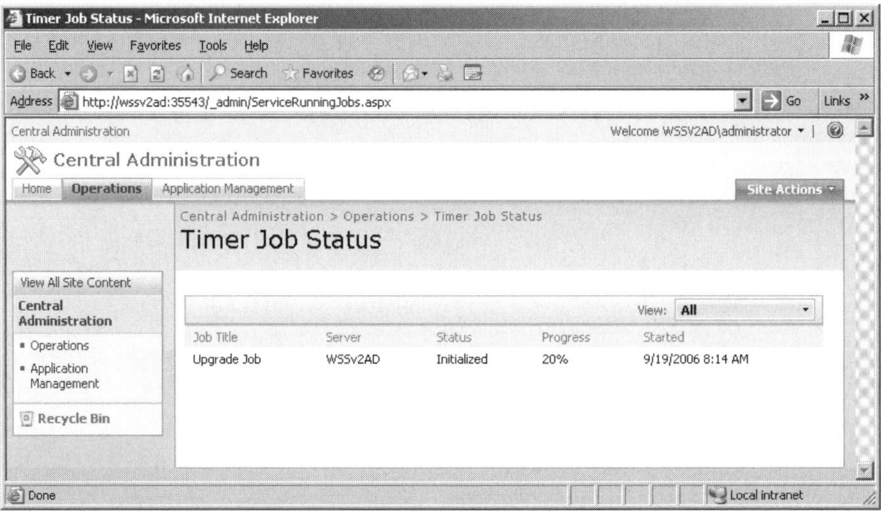

Figure 23-13 The Timer Job Status page

3. The upgrade is complete when the Status changes to No Job Pending, as shown in Figure 23-14.

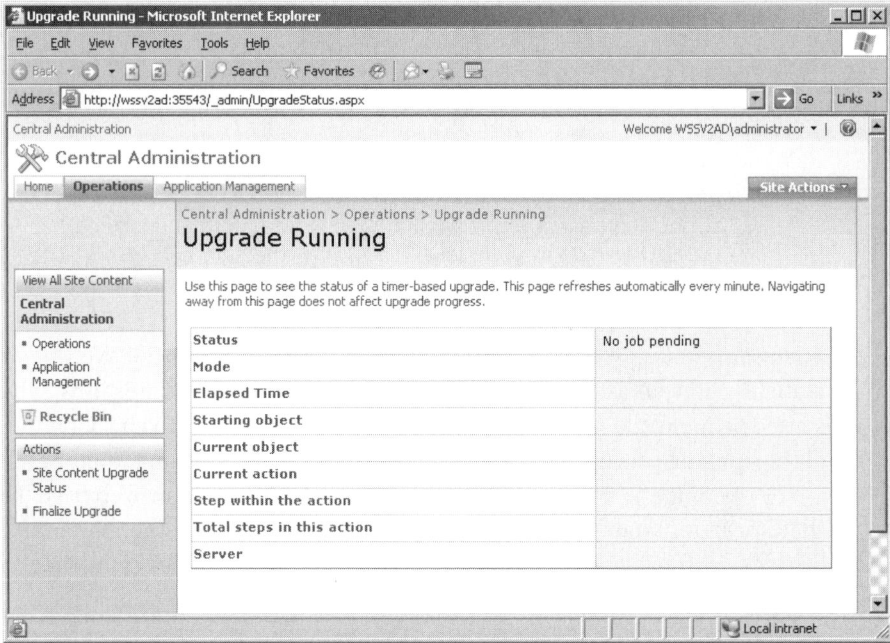

Figure 23-14 Status showing No Job Pending

Note If the upgrade fails or reports issues, refer to the Upgrade.log and Trace.log files.

4. On the Upgrade Running Web page, in the left navigation pane, under Actions, click Finalize Upgrade. The Finalize Upgrade Web page is displayed, as shown in Figure 23-15. This page shows an overview of known upgrade actions that you need to complete. Do not click Complete Upgrade until you have completed these actions and updated other servers in your farm.

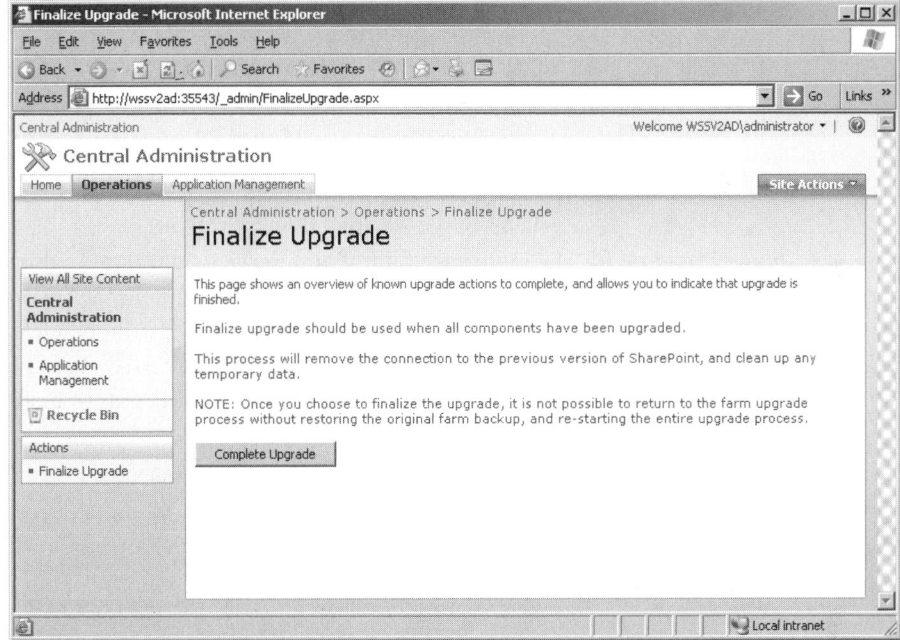

Figure 23-15 The Finalize Upgrade page

5. If there are any other servers in the farm, then on each server complete the SharePoint Products And Technologies Configuration Wizard as described in task 3.

6. When the configuration wizard has completed running on all servers on the farm, return to the SharePoint 3.0 Central Administration Web page. At the bottom of the home page in the Farm Topology Web Part, all servers should be listed together with the services they are running.

Task 4b: Upgrading and Migrating Windows SharePoint Services 2.0 Web Sites—Gradual Upgrade Approach

Unlike the in-place upgrade, the gradual upgrade does not automatically upgrade any Windows SharePoint Services 2.0 Web sites. You have to manually start this process, either using the Central Administration Web pages or using stsadm.exe. The following procedure details the Central Administration method. Details on using the command-line tool stsadm.exe to upgrade sites is covered in Chapter 24.

As a pre-upgrade task, you should have decided the names for the temporary URL domains for your Windows SharePoint Services 2.0 Web sites. For example, if the pre-upgrade URL for a Windows SharePoint Services 2.0 Web site is http://departments.contoso.msft, the new URL could be http://departmentsold.contoso.msft. Post upgrade, the new URL will be used for the Windows SharePoint Services 2.0 Web site and http://departments.contoso.msft will be used for the upgraded Windows SharePoint Services 3.0 Web site. You could use a new port number with the same host name for the new URL, such as http://departments.contoso.msft:8080, but usual practice is to create a host header. If this is your decision, at this point in the procedure create a CNAME entry on your DNS server if you haven't already done so.

If Kerberos is enabled for the Windows SharePoint Services 2.0 Web site, ensure that you have registered your service principal names (SPN) for the new URL. End-user applications ask for a Kerberos service ticket based on the URL of the Web service. Therefore, you need two SPNs–one for the Windows SharePoint Services 2.0 new URL (http://departmentsold.contoso.msft) and another for the Windows SharePoint Services 3.0 Web site (http://departments.contoso.msft). To register the SPN for the new URL, use the following command, where *contoso\Windows SharePoint ServicesAppPool* is the IIS application pool identity for the IIS Web site http://departmentsold.contoso.msft:

```
setspn -A http://
departmentsold.contoso.msft contoso\Windows SharePoint ServicesAppPool
```

More Info See Chapter 5 for more information on configuring Kerberos.

Important There are difficulties using the Kerberos protocol to connect to multiple Web applications that run on different ports under different identities. Therefore, when using Kerberos, it is recommended that for the new URL you use a different host name than the original URL for the Windows SharePoint Services 2.0 Web site. For more information, see Knowledge Base articles 899900 and 908209 found at *http://support.microsoft.com/default.aspx/kb/899900* and *http://support.microsoft.com/kb/908209* respectively.

Use the following steps to migrate Windows SharePoint Services 2.0 Web Sites using the gradual upgrade approach.

1. Open the SharePoint 3.0 Central Administration Web page if the SharePoint Products And Technologies Configuration Wizard did not automatically open it. Then

on the Operations tab, under Upgrade And Migration, click Site Content Upgrade Status.

2. The Site Content Upgrade Status Web page is displayed, as shown in Figure 23-16. In the Next Action column, click Begin Upgrade for the Web site you want to upgrade.

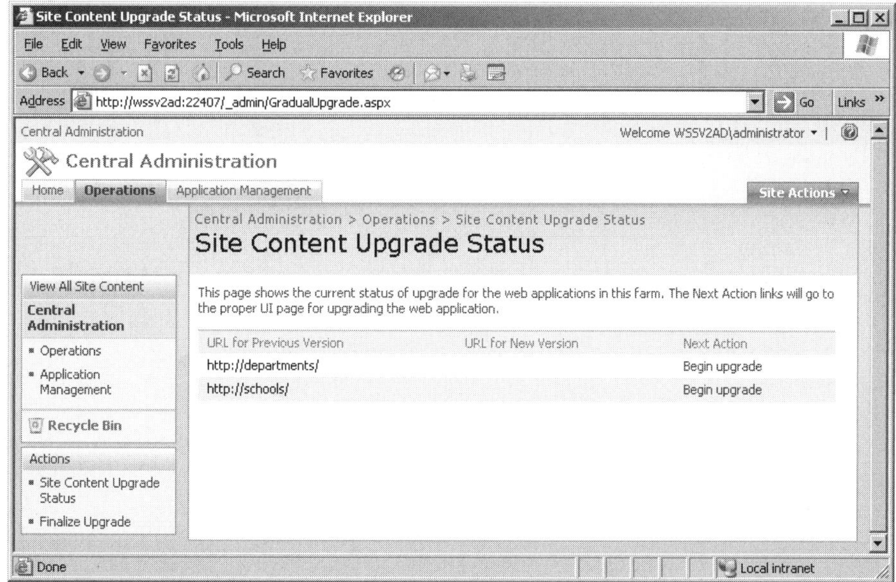

Figure 23-16 Site Content Upgrade Status page

3. The Set Target Web Application Web page is displayed, as shown in Figure 23-17. First, check that the Web application you want to upgrade appears in the Web Application To Upgrade section.

4. In the New URL For Original Content section, type a port number or host header name. This should match the new URL you created in step 1.

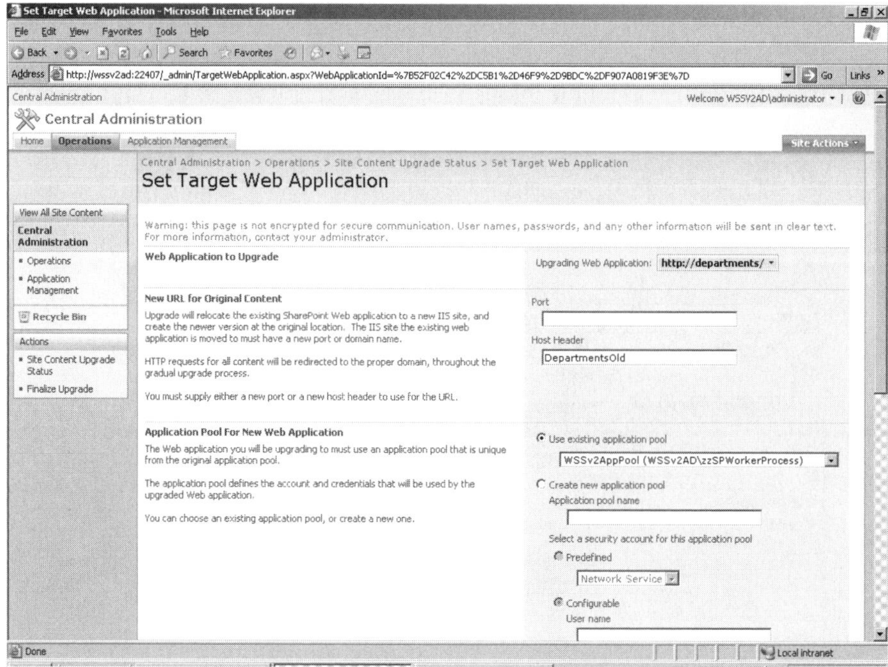

Figure 23-17 Set Target Web Application page

5. In the Application Pool For New Web Application section, either use an existing application pool or create a new application pool. If you do create a new application pool, it is recommended that you use the same IIS application pool identity (account) for the new URL as you used for the pre-upgraded URL. If the existing application pool used the IUSR_*ComputerName* or IWAM_*ComputerName* accounts, then to change or obtain the passwords for these accounts, refer to Microsoft Knowledge Based article 297989, found at *http://support.microsoft.com/kb/297989*.

6. In the Reset Internet Information Services section, select either Restart IIS Automatically or Restart IIS Manually depending on how you want to restart IIS on other farm servers.

7. In the Security Configuration section, select either Negotiate (Kerberos) or NTLM, depending on your environment.

8. In the Content Databases section, select either Automatic Database Name Selection or Manually Set Database Names. If you choose the Automatic database name option, a new database will be created using the naming convention *<old_database_name>_DB_Pair*.

9. Click OK. The Operations In Progress Web page is displayed while the following actions occur:

   a. The new host header or port is added to the existing Web application.

   b. The IIS application pool is created, if chosen.

   c. A new Web application is created. It is named <*original_web_application_name*>_Pair, whose home directory location is: c:\Inetpub\wwwroot\wss\VirtualDirectories\GUID, with the host header or port of the original Web application. The new Web application is created using the new application pool.

   > **Note** You must redeploy Web Parts in the bin directory of c:\Inetpub\wwwroot\wss\VirtualDirectories\GUID. You may need to create the bin directory if one does not already exist.

   d. A new database is created.

   When the Web application and database are created, the Site Collection Upgrade Web page is displayed, as shown in Figure 23-18.

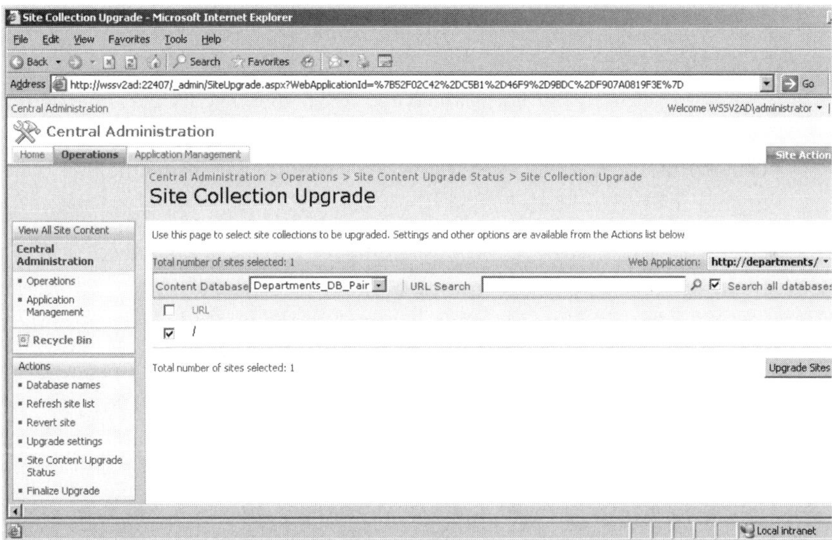

Figure 23-18 Site Collection Upgrade page

10. Open a new browser window, and type in the Address text box the original URL for your Windows SharePoint Service 2.0 Web site—for example, **http://departments.contoso.msft**. You should be automatically redirected to

http://departmentsold.contoso.msft, and your original Windows SharePoint Services 2.0 Web site should be displayed. If it is not, check that your DNS entry is set correctly. Do not progress further until you are able to successfully browse to your Windows SharePoint Service 2.0 Web site. If you need to administer the Windows SharePoint Services 2.0 Web site using the Windows SharePoint Services Central Administration Web pages, you need to use the new URL—that is, http://departmentsold.contoso.msft.

11. On the Site Collection Upgrade Web page, in the left navigation pane under Actions, click Upgrade settings.
12. The Upgrade Settings Web page is displayed. Select the check box if you want to reset your Web sites during the upgrade process, and then click Save.

> **Note** The default behavior is to keep your customizations during the upgrade process. This is the same default behavior as the in-place upgrade process. You can choose after the upgrade process to reset Web sites and pages to site definitions using the browser at a per-site level. However, with this setting, you can bulk reset all your Web sites within a content database, but only during the upgrade process.

13. On the Site Collection Upgrade Web page, select the check boxes next to the site collections you want to upgrade and then click Upgrade Sites.
14. The Sites Selected For Upgrade Web page is displayed, detailing the number of site collections, storage used originally, and the originating and target database names. Check that these details are correct by using the Web site analysis results obtained during the pre-upgrade tasks.
15. Click Continue. The Upgrade Running Web page is displayed, which is similar to the in-place upgrade process. A number of timer jobs are created. However, the mode is now Side-By-Side. Initially, the first job might be in a pending status. Once the job is in progress, it might take a while to complete.
16. The upgrade is complete when the Status has changed to No Job Pending. If the upgrade fails or reports issues, refer to the Upgrade.log and Trace.log files.

> **More Info** Information on troubleshooting configuration wizard failures and how to resume an upgrade can be found at *http://technet2.microsoft.com/Office/en-us/library/8c676788-f2bc-412b-b14e-6e13bee3e1301033.mspx?mfr=true*.

17. Open a new browser window, and type in the address text box the original URL for your Windows SharePoint Service 2.0 Web site—for example, **http://departments.contoso.msft**. You completed a similar exercise in step 10, where you were automatically redirected to http://departmentsold.contoso.msft. However, now that the upgrade is complete, you will not be redirected. Instead, you should now see the upgraded Web site. You can still browse to your original Windows SharePoint Services 2.0 Web site by using the new URL—that is, http://departmentsold.contoso.msft.

Task 4c: Performing a Content Database Migration

A content database can contain one or more site collections. Using the content database migration approach, you can gradually migrate the content databases you have created in your Windows SharePoint Services 2.0 installation. After you have installed and configured Windows SharePoint Services 3.0 on a new farm, complete the following steps:

1. Configure your new farm to match the settings of your old farm. There are no automatic method available that will take a Windows SharePoint Services 2.0 farm and create a similar Windows SharePoint Services 3.0 farm. You have to manually complete this task, which might include the following steps:

   a. Create IIS Web sites for each IIS Web site in your Windows SharePoint Services 2.0 installation. For each IIS Web site, use the properties dialog box to increase the connection timeout value on the Web Site tab and, using the Configuration button on the Home Directory tab, increase the ASP script timeout on the Options tab. Although you could leave the creation of the IIS Web site to the Application Management Web page in step 4 of this procedure, by creating it now you can create the bin and resource directories for custom code and assemblies. Ensure you do this on all Web front-end servers if you have a farm implementation.

   b. Copy customizations, such as custom Web Parts and site definitions, from your old farm to all Web front-end servers. It is important that these customizations be deployed prior to upgrading the content database so that they will be available during upgrade. Custom Web Parts must be deployed to the bin folder of the Web application or to the global assembly cache (GAC) of the server. Site definitions should be deployed either during the Windows SharePoint Services 3.0 setup or after setup using the command line. See Chapter 25 for more information on this.

   c. Re-apply farm configurations, such as outgoing e-mail server, security and permissions, quota templates using the SharePoint 3.0 Central Administration Web pages. This is a manually intensive and error-prone task, so take extra care during this task.

d. Ensure that all necessary services are started, by using the Services On Server link on the Operations Web page, as shown in Figure 23-19.

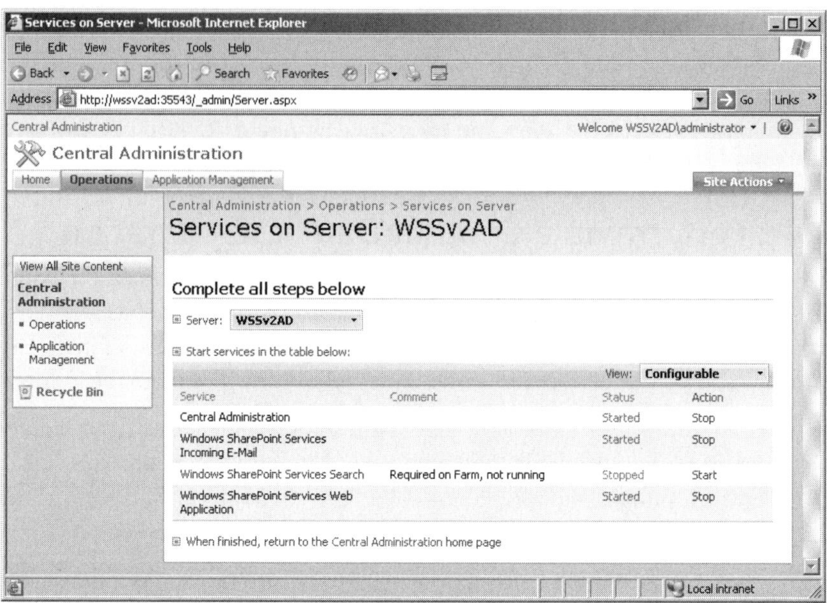

Figure 23-19 Services On Server page

2. Run prescan.exe on your Windows SharePoint Services 2.0 installation for content databases you plan to migrate.

3. Set the relevant Windows SharePoint Services 2.0 SQL content database as read-only. This will avoid the need to merge any updates post upgrade. Create a copy of the content databases on the SQL server that your Windows SharePoint Services 3.0 farm is configured to use. There are several options available, such as creating a backup of the SQL content database and then restoring it, using a different name if the SQL service is used by both the Windows SharePoint Services 2.0 and 3.0 farms, or copying the content database file and log file to the default database location on your SQL server and attaching it. The locations for a default SQL Server installation are as follows:

   - SQL Server 2000: C:\Program Files\Microsoft SQL Server\MSSQL\Data
   - SQL Server 2005: c:\Program Files\Microsoft SQL Server\MSSQL.1\MSSQL \Data

   To attach the database, you can use one of the following tools:

   - SQL 2000: Enterprise Manager

- ❑ SQL 2005: SQL Server Management Studio

Or you can use the SQL command-line tool, osql.exe. For more information, refer to SQL Server 2005 Books Online, which can be found at *http://www.microsoft.com/technet/prodtechnol/sql/2005/downloads/books.mspx.*

Note Users will see warning messages when the content databases are set to read-only. You must inform your users of this in your communications plan.

4. You can attach the content database that contains the root Windows SharePoint Services 2.0 Web site using either the SharePoint 3.0 Central Administration Web pages or stsadm.exe command, Use stsadm.exe to attach the content databases for large sites. The stsadm.exe command is detailed in step 9 of this procedure, and in Chapter 24. Otherwise, in the SharePoint 3.0 Central Administration, click the Application Management tab. Then in the SharePoint Web Application Management section, click Create Or Extend Web Application.
5. On the Create Or Extend Web Application Web page, click Create A New Web Application.
6. On the Create New Web Application Web page, complete the following actions:
   a. In the IIS Web Site section, click the Use An Existing IIS Web Site option button and select the IIS Web site you created in step 1.
   b. Alter the Security Configuration, Load Balanced URL, Application Pool, and Reset Internet Information Services sections, if appropriate. See Chapter 5 for more information on these options.
   c. In the Database Name And Authentication section, in the Database Name text box, enter the name of the content database you attached in step 3.
   d. In the Search Server section, select the appropriate Windows SharePoint Services search server and then click OK.
7. If you change the IIS Web site from Kerberos to NTLM authentication, a message is displayed. Click OK.
8. An Operation In Process Web page is displayed, after which the Application Created Web page is displayed. This states that there is no new SharePoint site collection created, which might lead you to believe that your content database was overwritten. This is not the case. Open a new browser, and type the address you created in step 1a.

Note If you did not complete step 2 before copying the Windows SharePoint Services 2.0 content database, you will get an error Web page stating that prescan.exe also was not run on this content database and the upgrade process will fail.

9. If the Web application contains more than one content database, you can use the stsadm.exe command-line tool to add the other content databases similar to the following command:

```
stsadm -o addcontentdb -url http://departments
-databasename Departments_DB -databaseserver SQLServer
```

   The content database for the root site must be added in step 4 and is the first to be upgraded. However, once the root content database is upgraded, there is no particular order for subsequent content databases.

Note If you try to use the Add A Content Database On The Manage Content Databases Web page, an error Web page is displayed stating that the database you are trying to attach requires an upgrade, which could time out the browser, and that you must use the stsadm.exe command. Using the command line allows you to batch the upgrade task and schedule it to run out of hours.

Post-Upgrade Tasks

After you have upgraded or migrated your Windows SharePoint Service 2.0 Web site, you should complete a number of post-upgrade tasks. One of these tasks is to review the log files, as previously mentioned, for any upgrade issues. The rest of this section details other tasks you should perform after the upgrade process is complete. You'll likely think of other ones to add to the list.

Completing the Windows SharePoint Services 3.0 Installation

The upgrade process might not have started all the services you require, and the installation might not be completely configured. For example, items such as the outgoing e-mail server, security, permissions, and quota templates might not have been configured.

You might also like to take advantage of some of the new features available in Windows SharePoint Services 3.0. You should review the installation and complete any outstanding tasks.

Confirming Upgraded Sites

You should check each Windows SharePoint Services 2.0 Web site that was migrated or upgraded. Address any discrepancies between the old site and the new site. Also, ensure that sites using custom Web Parts, site templates, and site definitions are functioning correctly, and redeploy them if necessary.

You should also check sites where you used the Content Editor Web Part (CEWP) to run JavaScript to alter the page layer or to add functionality, such as adding a tree view to the left navigation area to list subsites. Not only might such scripts not work after the upgrade, resulting in an error icon in the status bar of your browser, but they might not be necessary.

Review the upgraded versions of your customized sites—that is, those based on .stp files or sites customized using FrontPage. Determine whether they are acceptable to your users. You might need to reset them to the site definitions and then customize them with SharePoint Designer.

Windows SharePoint Services 3.0 manages permissions through role definitions, not site groups. This allows a consistent experience at the list, folder, and item level. After an upgrade, the Windows SharePoint Services 2.0 site groups are mapped to role definitions. For users or groups who were assigned specific list rights, the upgrade creates new roles with the appropriate list rights and assigns them to the new role. Familiarize yourself with these new settings, and change any operational procedures and end-user documentation to reflect the new environment.

Resetting Site Definitions

Microsoft released a number of application templates for Windows SharePoint Services 2.0 that were tailored to address requirements for specific business processes or sets of tasks for organizations of any size. (See *http://www.microsoft.com/technet/windowsserver/sharepoint/wssapps/default.mspx*.) These were site template files (.stp) and consisted mostly of ghosted pages. If you used them, you will be pleased to hear that they are mostly unaffected by the upgrade process. The content of these sites will usually migrate with no issues, but the look and feel is slightly altered and new functionality does not appear—for example, you can not use site settings to amend the lefthand navigation pane for the home page of the site, nor are the links on the home page security-trimmed. Most of the templates were provided in two formats: basic and custom. Custom templates not only include the additional lists and libraries, but the home page is customized. To reset a site, navigate to the Site Settings Web page, and in the Look And Feel column, click Reset To Site Definition. You can also reset using SharePoint Designer.

Deprecated Features

Windows SharePoint Services 3.0 has a number of new features, as well as ones that are significantly changed, deprecated, or removed. For example, the Calendar view type existed in Windows SharePoint Services 2.0 but has been upgraded for Windows SharePoint Services 3.0. It now includes a Year view in the left navigation pane that allows for easier navigation between months and also displays the current date.

Microsoft has aimed to make the upgrade as painless as possible, and most of your sites and the code you might have written for Windows SharePoint Services 2.0 will work in Windows SharePoint Services 3.0. However, there are differences, and you might not realize the affects of an upgrade until you have completed the upgrade process, which is why it is necessary for you to complete a trial upgrade as one of the pre-upgrade tasks. This section briefly covers the deprecated features but does not detail items in the object model that have been deprecated. You must refer to the Windows SharePoint Services 3.0 SDK for features that are still supported in Windows SharePoint Services 3.0. The three areas of particular interest are as follows:

- **Branding** The methods to use for branding your site have changed in the new version. For example, because Windows SharePoint Services 3.0 is based on ASP.NET 2.0, you can now use Master Pages to control the layout and structure of your pages. You should get your developer to reapply branding using the new methods. For more information, see the Windows SharePoint Services 3.0 SDK.
- **Themes** Themes have been reworked and redesigned based on ASP.NET 2.0 and are not kept during the upgrade process. Therefore, you need to either use the ones that come with Windows SharePoint Service 3.0 or create new themes. You can also design and apply themes using SharePoint Designer.
- **Form Libraries** Form libraries are now *form document libraries*. Therefore, if you created your own custom form libraries, you need to rework your form library definitions, create a new form library, and reapply the forms to the form libraries.

Revert Web Site

If you used the gradual upgrade approach, you have the ability to revert a Web site to the nonupgraded version 2.0 site. To do this, follow these steps:

1. Using SharePoint 3.0 Central Administration, on the Operations tab, under Upgrade And Migration, click Site Content Upgrade Status.
2. On the Site Content Upgrade Status Web page, on the same line as the URL that contains the site that you want to revert, click Continue Upgrade.
3. On the Site Collection Upgrade Web page, in the lefthand navigation pane, under Actions, click Revert Site.

4. On the Revert To Non-Upgraded Site Web page, ensure that the correct site collection is selected and then click Continue.
5. A message is displayed, warning you that all changes made to the upgraded site will be lost. Click OK.
6. The Operations In Progress page is displayed, after which the Site Collection Upgrade Web page is displayed (shown earlier in Figure 23-18), showing the reverted site collection as available to be upgraded.

Note You can also use stsadm.exe to revert the site. For information on how to do this, see Chapter 24.

Finishing the Upgrade Process

After you have completed all the upgrade actions and are satisfied with the upgrade process, complete the upgrade process as follows:

- If you used the gradual or content migration upgrade approach, delete upgraded Windows SharePoint Services 2.0 Web sites.
- Remove Windows SharePoint Services 2.0 language packs.
- Return to the Finalize Upgrade Web page (shown earlier in Figure 23-15), and click Complete Upgrade. A message appears, as shown in Figure 23-20. If you are certain that you have finished the upgrade process, click OK. When the Finish Upgrade process is complete, the Operations Web page is displayed. There is no longer an Upgrade And Migration section on this page. All temporary data that was used during the upgrade process is removed.

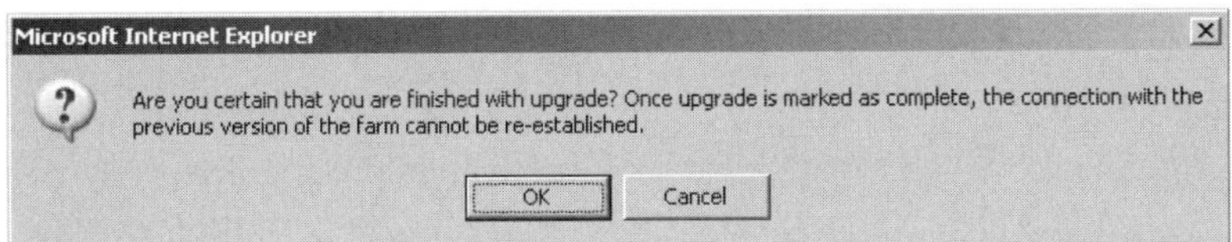

Figure 23-20 Finishing the upgrade

- For each Web front-end server, uninstall Windows SharePoint Services 2.0, uninstall WMSDE if appropriate, remove the Web sites from IIS, and delete the associated Web site files and any assemblies used by the Windows SharePoint Services 2.0 implementation from the GAC for each Web front-end server.

Important For an in-place or gradual upgrade, Windows SharePoint Services 3.0 tracks whether a Web site was created through Windows SharePoint Services 2.0 (\Web server extensions\60) or Windows SharePoint Services 3.0 (\Web server extensions\12) site definitions. After the upgrade process, any references to uncustomized (ghosted) front-end files are mapped from the \Web server extensions\60 directory to \Web server extensions\12. However, not every Web site is upgraded from \60 to \12. Any existing site definitions that do not have upgrade paths will still function but continue to point to their \60 pages. Before you uninstall Windows SharePoint Services 2.0, ensure you have checked all your customized site definitions. (See Chapter 25.)

- Delete the Windows SharePoint Services 2.0 configuration and content databases.
- If you used the content migration upgrade approach, decommission and reassign the Windows SharePoint Services 2.0 Web front-end servers.

Redistributing Content or Sites As Needed

After you have completed the upgrade process, you might want to redistribute content and sites. You might have completed some of this exercise as part of the pre-upgrade tasks. Windows SharePoint Services 3.0 provides additional options. Not only can you use stsadm.exe to redistribute site collections using the backup and restore options, you can also use the export and import options in stsadm.exe. These replace the use of smigrate.exe and use the new content migration application programming interfaces (APIs). For more information on the new APIs and stsadm.exe, see the Windows SharePoint Services 3.0 SDK and Administration Guide. After you have completed all the post-upgrade tasks, you cannot allow access to the Windows SharePoint Services 2.0 sites.

Summary

This chapter detailed how you might plan and implement an upgrade from Windows SharePoint Services 2.0 to Windows SharePoint Services 3.0. Both of these products have similar functionality, as well as a similar look and feel and, therefore, you may find that you and your users may need little or no training to use the new version, however they will need to be involved in the upgrade process. There are differences, Windows SharePoint Services 3.0 is based on ASP.NET 2.0, branding and customization is different; there is no longer an ISAPI filter; search uses SharePoint search and not SQL Server Full Text Search. You can upgrade your Windows SharePoint Services 2.0 Web sites to Windows SharePoint Services 3.0 Web sites using one of three upgrade approaches: in-place, gradual, or content database migration. Before you upgrade your environment, you must select the upgrade approach that best meets the needs of your organization and create a recovery plan for use if the upgrade process does not go as planned. For best results, follow these best practices:

- Back up your data before, during, and after the upgrade process.
- Determine the upgrade approach and how you will manage customizations.
- Design you Windows SharePoint Services 3.0 installation.
- Plan for additional storage, particularly on your SQL server.
- Test the upgrade in a non-production environment.
- Estimate the length of time the upgrade will take, and ensure you have a tested backout plan.
- Communicate your plan to managers, users, site owners, Web designers, and developers.

Chapter 24

Upgrading from Microsoft SharePoint Portal Server 2003

This chapter is designed for those of you who are planning to upgrade an existing Microsoft Office SharePoint Portal Server 2003 implementation. Office SharePoint Portal Server 2003 is built on Windows SharePoint Services 2.0. Microsoft Office SharePoint Server 2007 is built on top of Windows SharePoint Services 3.0, and therefore much of Chapter 23, "Upgrading from Microsoft Windows SharePoint Services 2.0," is relevant to the discussions in this chapter, as is Chapter 25, "Upgrading Site Customizations and Custom Site Definitions to Windows SharePoint Services 3.0." You should also refer to documents published by Microsoft. Good starting points are "Office Online Chapter Overview: Plan and prepare for upgrade available" on Microsoft TechNet, located at *http://technet2.microsoft.com/Office/en-us/library/53b8a28b-43c4-43aa-8854-d72d9b7b59c41033.mspx*, and "Migration and Upgrade Information for SharePoint Developers," a Microsoft Office Developer Center article located at *http://msdn.microsoft.com/office/server/moss/2007/migration/*.

The SharePoint Portal Server 2003 upgrade process is similar to the Windows SharePoint Services 2.0 upgrade process that was documented in Chapter 23. We will not repeat the detailed step-by-step procedures included in that chapter. However, in this chapter, we'll explore the use of the stsadm.exe command-line tool in the upgrade process and the effect of the upgrade process on a SharePoint Portal Server 2003 installation.

Note If you took part in the beta program and want to upgrade pilot environments to Release To Manufacturing (RTM) Office SharePoint Server 2007, you must first upgrade to Beta2 Technical Refresh (B2TR). For help doing this, refer to the Microsoft TechNet article "Installing Microsoft Office SharePoint Server 2007 for Beta 2 Technical Refresh," which is located at *http://technet2.microsoft.com/Office/en-us/library/f49862ab-e067-4723-bb90-7eb1182c65ce1033.mspx?mfr=true*. If your pilot environment included the Knowledge Network (KN) components, there is *no* straight upgrade path from Beta 2 to Knowledge Network Beta Technical Refresh. For more information on this issue, see *http://blogs.msdn.com/kn/archive/2006/09/22/Getting_Ready_for_KN_Technical_Refresh.aspx*.

There are not any tools provided to upgrade from SharePoint Portal Server 2001 to SharePoint Server 2007. If you have a SharePoint Portal Server 2001 deployment, you must migrate first to SharePoint Portal Server 2003 and then migrate again to SharePoint Server 2007.

The upgrade path from SharePoint Team Services is to upgrade to Windows SharePoint Services 2.0 and then to Windows SharePoint Services 3.0.

More Info To upgrade from Microsoft Content Management Server 2002, see Chapter 22, "Upgrading from Content Management Server 2002 to Microsoft Office SharePoint Server 2007."

Understanding Upgrade Options

You learned in Chapter 23, "Upgrading from Microsoft Windows SharePoint Services 2.0," that there are three options for upgrading a SharePoint Portal Server 2003 implementation to SharePoint Server 2007:

- In-place upgrade
- Gradual upgrade
- Content database migration

The Table 24-1 reconsiders these different approaches to help you find the one that works best for your implementation.

Table 24-1 Upgrade Alternatives and Tradeoffs

Upgrade option	Pros	Cons
In-Place	Simple. Uses existing hardware.	Entire farm is offline during the upgrade. No ability to easily revert.

Table 24-1 **Upgrade Alternatives and Tradeoffs**

Upgrade option	Pros	Cons
Gradual	Allows you granular control of the upgrade process at the site-collection level. Reduces the time a user is affected. You can revert to the original SharePoint Portal Server 2003 Web sites if needed. Uses existing hardware.	Requires SharePoint Server 2007 installation on the SharePoint Portal Server 2003 farm servers. Domain Name System (DNS) redirects for SharePoint Portal Server 2003 URLs during upgrade need to be created. Performance impact on SharePoint Portal Server 2003 servers can be significant because you're running two platforms side by side. This option is hardware intensive, requiring additional memory and extra Microsoft SQL Server storage.
Content database migration	Allows moving to a new farm or new hardware while retaining farm content. Allows "Web application by Web application" migration to new farm. The SharePoint Portal Server 2003 farm is not affected by the upgrade process. Better performance than the gradual upgrade method.	Much more complex migration design. Granularity is at the content-database level. Involves many manual steps, with a high level of administrative and developer effort. Requires a new farm and double the SQL Server storage capacity. Some features are not upgraded, such as Search and all customizations.

Whichever upgrade option you choose, you need to complete the following four stages for your upgrade to be successful:

- Planning the upgrade
- Pre-upgrade tasks
- The upgrade process
- Post-upgrade tasks

Planning the Upgrade

Because of the length of time your SharePoint Portal Server Web sites will be unavailable and the risk that the upgrade process might take longer than expected or that some portal sites might need some rework after upgrade, it is critical that the your organization plan the upgrade process and communicate this plan with site owners and users so that they know what to expect during the process. In a large organization, you will be only one of a team of people involved in this project.

Planning is important to any upgrade or migration scenario, and you can use the following list as a checklist to assist you during the planning process.

- Understand each upgrade approach.
- Understand the updated features and how the changes in the architecture affect your existing Windows SharePoint Services 2.0 and SharePoint Portal Server Web sites, and review the supported topologies. SharePoint Server 2007 has carried over a large number of features from SharePoint Portal Server 2003, such as user profiles, audience targeting, and personal sites. The sections following this checklist cover the effect of the upgrade on your SharePoint Portal Server 2003 environment, including the effects on areas, listings, search, shared services, My Site, and customizations.

> **More Info** There is a spreadsheet available on the Microsoft download site that compares Windows SharePoint Services 2.0, SharePoint Portal Server 2003, Windows SharePoint Server 3.0, and SharePoint Server 2007. This spreadsheet can be found at the following link: *http://download.microsoft.com/download/1/d/c/1dc632e8-71e1-466f-8a2f-c940f1438e0a/SharePointProductsComparison.xls*.

- Review the system requirements for SharePoint Server 2007. (See Chapter 5, "Installing Microsoft Office SharePoint Server 2007.")
- Identify portal Web applications that are actively used and need to be upgraded. You can back up and retire portal Web applications that you do not want to upgrade.
- Review all your portal areas and Windows SharePoint Services sites and workspaces that were created under any managed paths beneath your portal Web application, such as http://portal/sites/department. Doing so will help you know where your content is so that if you want to restructure the areas within your portal Web site, you can do so in advance of the migration. Or, if you are using the gradual migration method, you will know the location to which each site collection should

be migrated. This review can be completed either before or after the upgrade process and will not affect the time taken to upgrade your portal Web sites.

- Understand your current SharePoint Portal Server installation. Review and document your current environment, including all configuration settings—such as search scopes, audiences, content sources, and the Lightweight Directory Access Protocol (LDAP) query you used to import user profiles from Active Directory. Ensure you have up-to-date copies of files that you have used during the lifetime of the deployment, such as assemblies, Web Parts, site definitions, and image files. Be sure to include files you installed on the search and index servers, such as IFilters and file extension icons. Document any alterations that were made to web.config or any other files you might have altered for each virtual server, particularly those in the *%SystemDrive%*\Program Files\Common Files\Microsoft Shared\Web server extensions\60 directory. Review how the portal Web site is used and how content is added—in particular, the use of areas and listings. This list might seem excessive, especially if you are considering an in-place upgrade, but it will lead to a well-thought-out project plan and knowledge of the people who should be involved in the upgrade process. You should also ensure that users who administer the SharePoint Portal Server 2003 environment are configured explicitly with the correct level of access rights in your SharePoint Server 2007 deployment. Remember, SharePoint Server 2007 will not give access to members of the Local Administrators group by default.

> **Important** You need to contact software vendors whose products you have installed on your SharePoint Portal Server 2003 environment to see whether they have upgraded versions for SharePoint Server 2007. You might need to update these products for the new version. If you will be running the two environments side by side, as is the case in the gradual and in-place upgrade options, ensure you investigate the ability to run different versions of the products on the same server.

- Review your current SharePoint Portal Server 2003 infrastructure and decide if you want to modify it, such as reducing the size of your content databases, upgrading from SQL Server 2000 to SQL Server 2005, or using 64-bit technology. Do not upgrade your SQL Server as part of the upgrade process. Either complete this exercise well before you start the migration process or well after you have finished the upgrade process. As part of this task, create a diagram of your existing and post-upgrade architectures.
- Determine the order in which you plan to upgrade your servers in a Web farm implementation.

- Estimate the length of time the upgrade process will take and additional resources you might need, such as memory, storage, and backup media.
- Understand the URL redirection process in the gradual upgrade approach, and decide on your temporary domain names.

> **Important** When you create Web applications using either the SharePoint 3.0 Central Administration Web pages or the Internet Information Services (IIS) Manager, ensure you use different Web application pools than the SharePoint Portal Server 2003 Web sites. Use the same account for the identity of both sets of application pools.

- Use a test environment to perform a test upgrade of your production environment, with a view to finding the potential issues that you'll encounter during the production upgrade process.
- Identify the length of time the upgrade process will take and the amount of resources you will need. During the upgrade process you will run the prescan tool, which will help you identify issues you need to resolve before performing the upgrade process in production. The upgrade process also creates logs, and each entry is date and time stamped, allowing you to calculate the length of time the upgrade took. If you take note of the size of the content database—that is, the <portalname>_site database—prior to the upgrade and then obtain the time from the prescan.log, the calculation size_MB / time will provide you with an upgrade rate that you can use in your estimations. This upgrade rate will depend on your hardware resources and the available bandwidth between your SQL Server and your farm servers.
- Test custom Web Parts with ASP.Net 2.0.
- Determine how to handle customizations, including those made as the result of using Microsoft FrontPage 2003, custom site templates (.stp files), and custom site definitions. (See Chapter 25.)
- Create a communication plan for your organization so that everyone knows when their most important information will be upgraded to the new platform.
- Be sure that your users are trained and educated on the SharePoint Server 2007 software. Nothing will kill a great deployment like giving users a technology that they don't know how to use.

Real World Microsoft Office Web Components

If your environment included the Microsoft Office Web Components (OWC), which are available at *http://www.microsoft.com/downloads/details.aspx?displaylang=en&familyid=38BE67A5-2056-46A1-84B1-337FFB549C5C*, you should note that Microsoft has announced that these will be the discontinued. (see *http://blogs.msdn.com/excel/archive/2006/07/17/668544.aspx*.) However, these components will continue to work in Windows SharePoint Services 3.0 and SharePoint Server 2007 if you use the in-place or gradual upgrade approaches. If you choose the content migration option and therefore have a new server environment, they will not install by running ststpkpl.exe.

To install OWC in your new environment, follow these steps.

1. Copy the following three cab files from *%SystemDrive%*/program files\common files\Microsoft Shared\Web server extensions\6.0\wppacks in your Windows SharePoint Services 2.0 environment to a neutral directory, such as C:\temp, on each Web front-end in your new environment:
   - microsoft.sharepoint.solutions.greatplains.cab
   - microsoft.sharepoint.webparts.quickquote.cab
   - microsoft.office.dataparts.cab
2. On each Web front-end server, open a command prompt, navigate to *%SystemDrive%*\Program Files\Common Files\Microsoft Shared\Web server extensions \12.0\BIN and then type the following command for each cab file:

```
stsadm.exe -o addwppack -filename c:\temp\name_of_cab_file.cab
-globalinstall
```

Deprecated Features

You need to be aware of a number of deprecated features in SharePoint Server 2007. First, there is no longer a Topics Assistant that helps you categorize content in SharePoint Server 2007. Second, spsbackup.exe has been replaced by the Windows SharePoint Services 3.0 backup command-line tool, stsadm.exe. Third, unlike SharePoint Portal Server 2003, where each server in the farm hosted the Central Administration Web site, there is only one SharePoint Server 2007 Central Administration Web site, and it is hosted, by default, on the first server in the farm.

Similarly, the SharePoint Portal Server 2003 administrative object model has been deprecated in SharePoint Server 2007; therefore, any custom applications that rely on the administrative object model have to be rewritten to use the new object model in SharePoint Server 2007.

Other major features in SharePoint Portal Server 2003 that have been changed or deprecated are discussed in the following sections.

Areas

Once your SharePoint Portal Server 2003 portal Web site is upgraded, you will notice a different look and feel because your portal will be based on the Collaboration Portal site template. Figure 24-1 shows a portal before and Figure 24-2 shows a portal after the upgrade process.

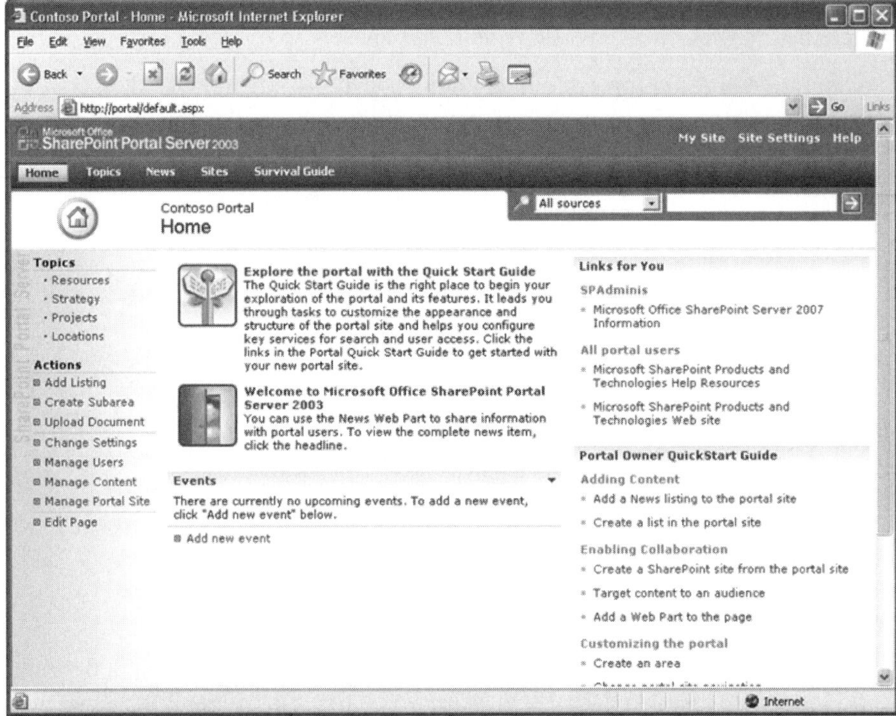

Figure 24-1 Portal prior to upgrade

The areas and their content are retained; however, the order on the top navigation bar has been altered. The Portal Owner QuickStart Guide Web Part is one of the depreciated Web Parts that you have to remove if it is on your home page.

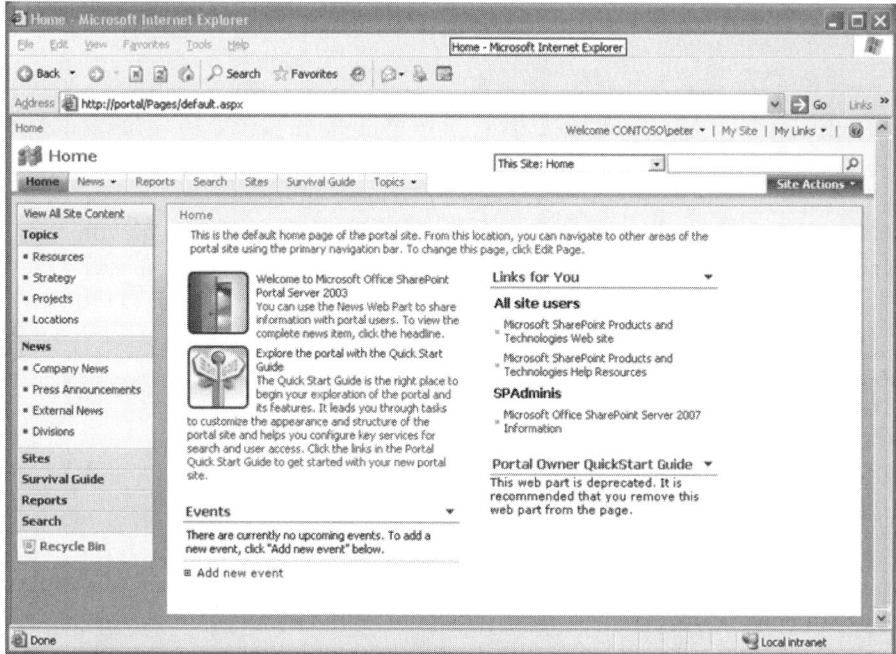

Figure 24-2 Portal upgraded to Collaboration Portal Web site

The portal no longer contains any application services, such as search and My Site. However, you still access these services (search and My Site) from the portal site, but they are now the responsibility of the Shared Services Provider (SSP)—that is, you cannot administer the application services using the portal administration pages; you must use the SharePoint 3.0 Central Administration pages.

In SharePoint Portal Server 2003, the area hierarchy that is visible through the browser on the top and left navigation bars and the Portal Site map is not reflected in the URLs of the areas. Each area is a heavily customized Windows SharePoint Services 2.0 subsite off the portal home Web page, and SharePoint Portal Server 2003 allows only 20 areas to appear under the portal root (home). When the root has 20 subsites, any new subsites are created in a Web directory, such as C1, C2, and so on. These Web directories are called *buckets*. This mechanism allowed you to reorganize your area taxonomy without breaking links. In Windows SharePoint Services 2.0, if you wanted to reorganize your site hierarchy, you needed to back up and delete the site from its current location and then restore it under a new parent site in the site hierarchy, using the smigrate.exe tool or FrontPage 2003. The need to dynamically reorganize the site hierarchy in SharePoint Portal Server 2003 was seen to be important. As a result, the need for buckets also caused some limitations. Not only did areas not inherit some of the basic Windows SharePoint

Services 2.0 features, but there was some loss of usability. Many organizations like to manage the naming conventions of their URLs, especially on intranet-facing Web sites.

Windows SharePoint Services 3.0 includes the ability to dynamically re-arrange a hierarchy of SharePoint sites, known as *re-parenting*, and SharePoint Server 2007 has removed the "buckets" concept. If any areas have a bucket URL, then, the bucket Web directory is removed in the upgrade process. The area is given a new URL using the logical site structure as a guideline. For example, http://portal.contoso.msft/C1/departments is upgraded to http://portal.contoso.msft/departments if departments is a top-level area. If departments is a subarea, say, of the topics area, then the URL is upgraded to http://portal.contoso.msft/topics/departments. The upgrade process checks for URL naming conflicts, and a number is appended to the URL, starting with zero, for URLs where duplicate names are found.

Listings

In SharePoint Portal Server 2003, whenever an area, subarea, or topic is created, a specialized link list, called *Portal Listings*, is created. The Group Listings Web Part allows you to display these links on pages throughout a portal Web site. The Group Listings Web Part also provides a roll up of links from areas below a specific branch of your area taxonomy and can be used with audiences. Both Portal Listings and the Group Listings Web Part are not included in SharePoint Server 2007. Web Parts based on the Group Listings Web Part—such as "News for You," "Latest News," and "Links for You"—are therefore not available. During the upgrade process, a new list (named *Listings*) is created and the upgrade moves listings in this list and the Group Listings Web Part to the Content Query Web Part.

Through a portal site, there were many links in the browser that allowed you to add link items to Portal Listings, such as Add Listing, Add Person, Submit To Portal Area, Select A Portal Area For This List, Select A Portal Area For This Document Library, and Add A Listing For This Document. These are all removed during the upgrade.

Although Portal Listings are a specialized link list and therefore you can point to data held elsewhere, they can also contain content. During an upgrade process, the area is converted to a Windows SharePoint Services Web site, a document library named Pages is created, and a page layout .aspx file is created in that document library for each listing that contains content. The page created is based on the page layout Article page, with an image of the page shown on the left side of the screen, as you can see in Figure 24-3.

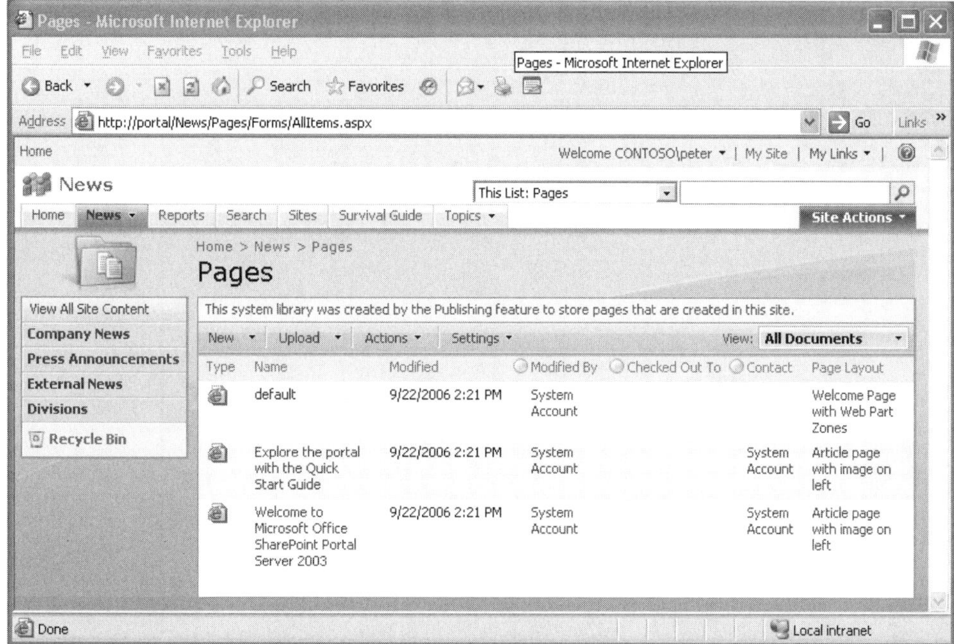

Figure 24-3 Page layout files for each upgraded Portal Listings that contains content

As a post-upgrade task, you should review the newly created list i.e. Listings, and the pages created during the upgrade process. Other features of SharePoint Server 2007 might suit your needs, for example, if the original listings are only referenced on one area and you do not need to use audiencing for displaying, sorting, and grouping links on a page, then consider using the Summary Link Web Part.

Sites Directory

The site directory has changed between the two versions and can be seen in Figure 24-4 and Figure 24-5. The site directory search box is removed, as the default search box now can search the site directory site and its subsites.

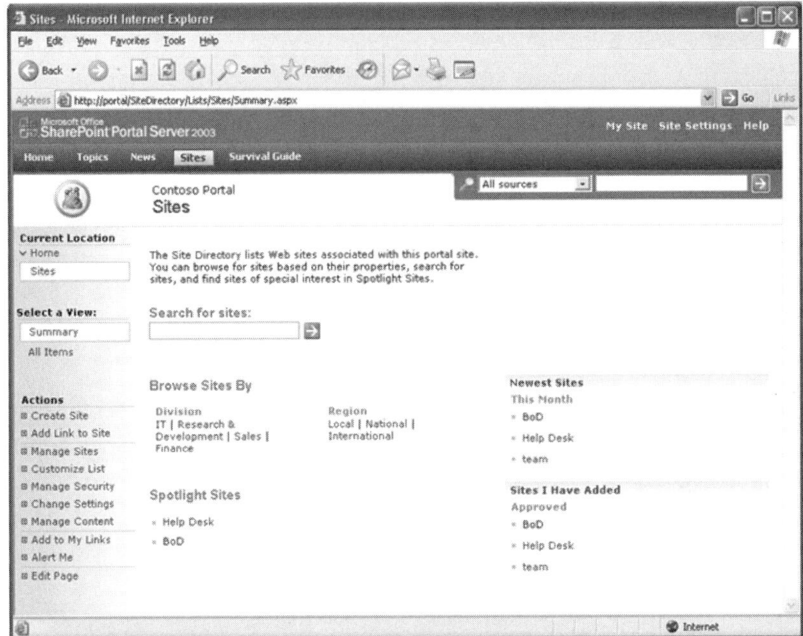

Figure 24-4 Site directory prior to the upgrade

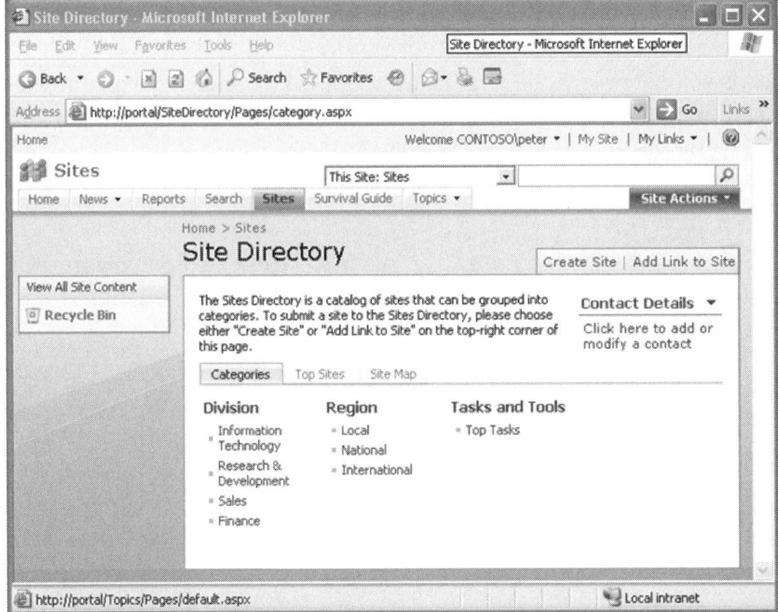

Figure 24-5 Upgraded site directory

By default, creating a site from the site directory does not create a new site collection, but creates subsites under the site directory. The default action can be changed by navigating to the top-level site settings for the portal Web site. Then, under Site Collection Administration, click Site Directory Settings. (This assumes you have enabled Self-Service Site Management for this Web application in Central Administration of your SharePoint Server 2007 deployment.) During the upgrade, any existing sites under the site directory remain as site collections and list items in the site directory list are migrated. For more information on the site directory, see Chapter 6, "Performing Central Administration and Operations Configuration," and Chapter 7, "Application Management and Configuration."

Search

During an in-place or gradual upgrade to SharePoint Server 2007, some search settings are upgraded. However, some elements are not upgraded, including the following ones:

- Index files
- Search scopes
- Search IFilters
- Word breakers
- Thesaurus files that you have installed

If you choose a database migration approach to upgrading, none of the search elements are upgraded, so you need to manually reconfigure these elements in the new environment.

Note If you have shared services, when you upgrade the parent portal, the settings from the parent portal's servers are added to the upgraded Search database.

A number of changes have been made to how SharePoint Server 2007 searches content compared to SharePoint Portal Server 2003. For example, there is no automatic propagation of indexes. There is no Advanced Search Administration mode, which allowed you to create multiple indexes. In SharePoint Server 2007, there is only one index, and the management of that index is very limited in the SSP interface.

There are changes to crawl rules and schedules. Crawl rules are no longer hierarchical; instead, they are a flat list. Crawl schedules are now completely tied in with content sources–that is, you cannot define a crawl schedule outside of a content source. The Query object model has been replaced, and the entire Search object model has been changed. Be sure to reference the new SharePoint Server 2007 Software Development Kit (SDK) found at *http://www.microsoft.com/downloads/details.aspx?FamilyId=6D94E307-67D9-41AC-B2D6-0074D6286FA9&displaylang=en* for specific information on how the object models have changed.

Shared Services

Shared services in SharePoint Portal Server 2003 was an optional feature that you could enable. In SharePoint Server 2007, it is mandatory to have an SSP. In SharePoint Portal Server 2003, you had to affiliate shared services with a portal in an environment where you had multiple portals and possibly over a number of farms. You had to have a specific parent/child style of portal topology to run shared services effectively.

If you use shared services in SharePoint Portal Server 2003, your upgrade process requires additional steps, unless you have one SharePoint Portal Server 2003 Web farm and are using the in-place upgrade option. Otherwise, you should upgrade the shared services portal first and then any child portals you want to upgrade. The upgrade process for shared services will result in the shared services portal being replaced by a new SSP Web application.

> **Note** If you need to upgrade a child portal first, for example, if you only want to upgrade a single child portal and not any others or the parent portal, create a temporary Shared Services Provider (SSP) in a new SharePoint Server 2007 environment and then upgrade the child portal and associate it with the temporary SSP for services.

In a gradual upgrade option, as long as the SharePoint Portal Server 2003 shared services portal has not been upgraded, this portal will continue to provide shared services to sites that have not been upgraded. The SSP in SharePoint Server 2007 will crawl everything that was crawled by SharePoint Portal Server 2003, and the SharePoint Portal Server 2003 shared services portal will continue to crawl the SharePoint Portal Server 2003 farm. This means that some content in your SharePoint Portal Server 2003 implementation will be crawled twice during the gradual upgrade process.

Therefore, you will see an increase in network bandwidth usage for crawling processes during a gradual upgrade process when shared services are involved in the overall upgrade process. To minimize the impact, you can reduce the scope of either the SharePoint Portal Server 2003 or SharePoint Server 2007 crawls, and as SharePoint Portal Server 2003 sites are upgraded, you can delete their start addresses from the SharePoint Portal Server 2003 search settings.

To ensure that you don't introduce duplicate user profile and audience data in your environment, be sure to first upgrade the Job Server in your SharePoint Portal Server 2003 farm to the SharePoint Server 2007 platform. This ensures that user profile and audience data is managed by the upgraded server. This also ensures that the data is pushed from SharePoint Server 2007 to a SharePoint Portal Server 2003 environment by way of a scheduled job run by the SharePoint timer service. Until the migration is completed, some of your SharePoint Portal Server 2003 portals will use the profile and audience data that is generated by the SharePoint Server 2007 server.

My Site

The in-place upgrade process takes the SharePoint Portal Server 2003 My Site and upgrades it to the improved SharePoint Server 2007 My Site, which is a Windows SharePoint Services 3.0 site from an architectural viewpoint. My Site is still a personal site that allows a user the opportunity to aggregate information "for me," "by me," and "about me." Significant enhancements include social networking, privacy controls, and Colleagues and Memberships Web Parts. Figure 24-6 and Figure 24-7 shows a My Site before and after the upgrade process.

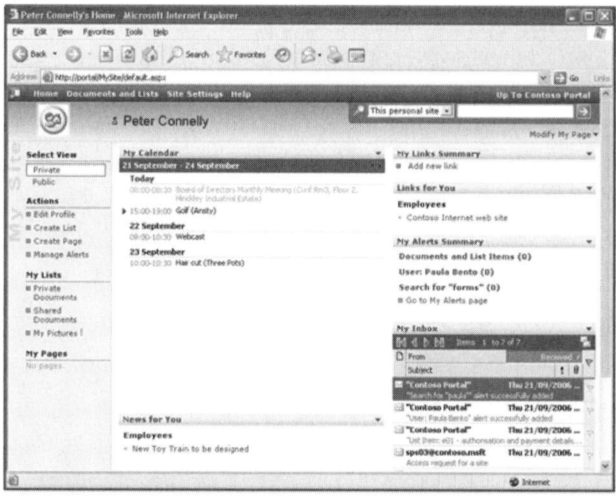

Figure 24-6 SharePoint Portal Server 2003 My Site

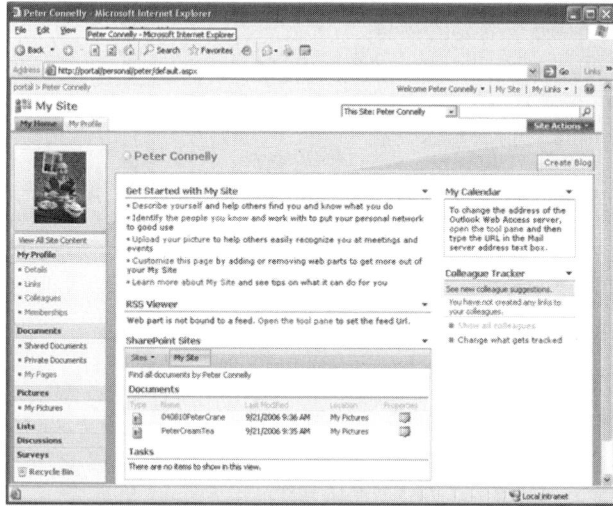

Figure 24-7 Upgraded My Site

The home page of My Site is now called My Home, which is your private page. Your public view is called My Profile, which you can use to share information with other users. Your new My Site will contain all content that your old My Site contained, including any details from the profiles database and any links you might have added, both private and shared. However, any modifications made to the SharePoint Portal Server 2003 private page will not appear on My Home. In SharePoint Portal Server 2003, the My Site functionality is based on one My Site area, plus a personal site collection for each user. The My Site area provides the private and profile pages, but all content and any subsites you create are part of your personal site collection, created under the personal managed path. During the upgrade, a managed path named *personal* is created and the personal site collections and the My Site area are upgraded. However, in SharePoint Server 2007 your private page is truly the home or default page of your personal site collection and not a redirection to a page in the My Site area. This is another reason why the private page is called "My Home" page. The old My Site area is still available, but it does not appear as a tab on your My Site. If you append MySite to the upgraded portal site's URL, such as http://portal.contoso.msft/MySite, the old My Site area is temporarily displayed (unpinned) as a tab, as shown in Figure 24-8.

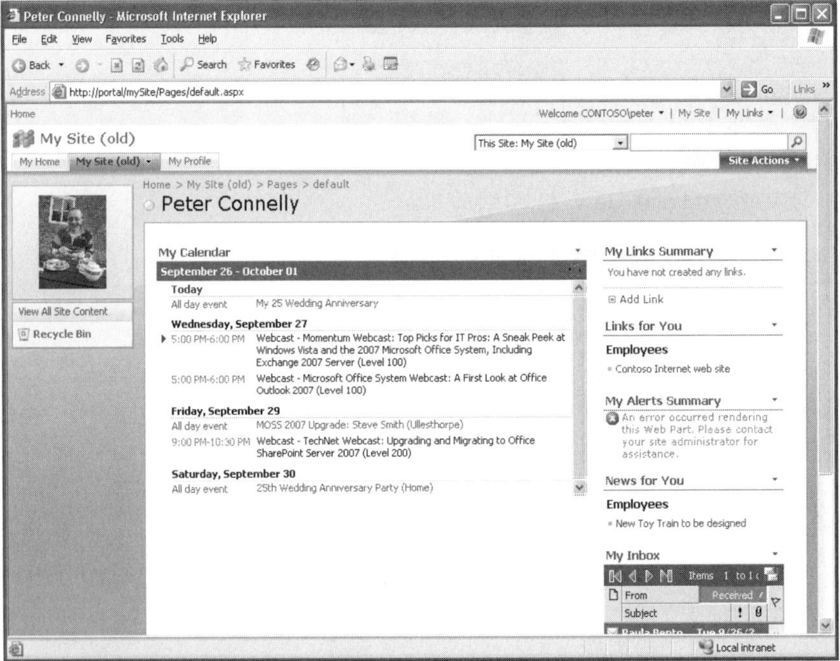

Figure 24-8 My Site (old)

The old My Site will contain Web Parts that will fail to render, as in the case of My Alerts Summary, which is not available in SharePoint Server 2007.

In a gradual upgrade, users continue to use the SharePoint Portal 2003 My Site until the user's personal site is upgraded. Also, once the SharePoint Portal Server 2003 shared services is upgraded, if a user makes changes to her user profile, those changes will not be reflected on the SharePoint Server 2007 environment until the user has upgraded her My Site to the SharePoint Server 2007 platform.

With a content database migration, where the SharePoint Portal Server 2003 and SharePoint Server 2007 environments are available at the same time, users are provided with two sets of profiles and My Sites. This can confuse users, so be sure to communicate clearly when the database that contains their SharePoint Portal Server 2003 My Site has been upgraded to the SharePoint Portal Server 2007 platform.

SharePoint Portal Server Alerts

In SharePoint Portal Server 2003, you could manage alerts through My Site and the My Alerts Summary Web Part. Now in SharePoint Server 2007, alerts are managed at the site level. To obtain a global view of your alerts, you must use the Microsoft Outlook 2007 client.

Some of the alerts a user has configured will be upgraded; however, the alerts mechanism in SharePoint Server 2007 will now revert to the Windows SharePoint Services 3.0 alerts. You can no longer add an alert on what was an area, which are now Windows SharePoint Services 3.0 sites. Alerts on people are replaced by the e-mail option for a colleague alert. If a user created an alert on keywords in search, these will need to be re-created.

User Profiles and Audiences

The in-place and gradual upgrade option retains user profiles and audiences. However, you need to reconfigure content database migration options. You should review both the managed properties list and the audiences you use. You might find that now you can target information based on SharePoint groups. You might no longer need all the audiences you have created.

Permissions

SharePoint Portal Server 2003 security model objects, such as *SPRole* and *SPList.PermissionsMask*, have been replaced by a new role-based security model. As a result, the user interface for permissions is different. The upgrade process will migrate the existing security settings to the new security model. If any custom applications use the old security model objects, on recompilation you will get warnings. Be sure to investigate these warnings and take appropriate action to ensure your users have access to all the information they need.

Single Sign-On

There are no schema changes to Single Sign-On (SSO) for SharePoint Server 2007. For a gradual upgrade, configure SharePoint Server 2007 to point to the SharePoint Portal Server 2003 SSO database. For the content database migration option, copy the SharePoint Portal Server 2003 SSO database to the SharePoint Server 2007 SQL Server and then configure the SharePoint Server 2007 servers to use this database.

E-Mail Enabled Document Libraries

In SharePoint Portal Server 2003, you could link a document library with a Microsoft Exchange 2000 or 2003 public folder so that files attached to messages posted to that public folder were automatically down-stepped into the e-mail-enabled document library. In SharePoint Server 2007, this functionality has been replaced with the incoming e-mail feature. Therefore, you need to configure incoming e-mail at the farm level to restore the ability to archive documents from e-mail messages. Document libraries, discussion boards, calendars, and announcements can be enabled to receive new postings via e-mail. In addition, extensible support is provided for custom e-mail handlers in Windows SharePoint Services 3.0.

Custom Branding and Cascading Style Sheets (CSS)

Custom branding and any references to cascading style sheets is lost during any of the upgrade options. You need to review and re-engineer your CSS solutions.

Performing Pre-Upgrade Tasks

Whichever upgrade approach you decide to use, you must perform a number of pre-upgrade steps or your upgrade process might fail. When you have completed these pre-upgrade tasks, you can commence your chosen upgrade approach. The pre-upgrade tasks that were detailed in Chapter 23 should be read in conjunction with the following list of tasks:

1. Ensure your SharePoint Portal Server 2003 installation is working correctly, and in a Web farm environment, ensure that all Web servers are configured identically. This requirement also includes drive letter names. The upgrade process will notice any inconsistencies and will fail if any inconsistencies exist. Use the following tools to check your installation:

    a. The SharePoint Configuration Analyzer can be used to check your SharePoint Portal Server 2003 server topology by using the SharePoint Portal Server Central Administration Web pages. Under the Server Configuration section, click Configure Server Topology. At the bottom of the Configure Server Topology Web page, check that it states, "There are no issues at this time. Your farm is fine.", as shown Figure 24-9. This does not indicate you do not have any issues, but it does state that you have a supported SharePoint Portal Server 2003 configuration.

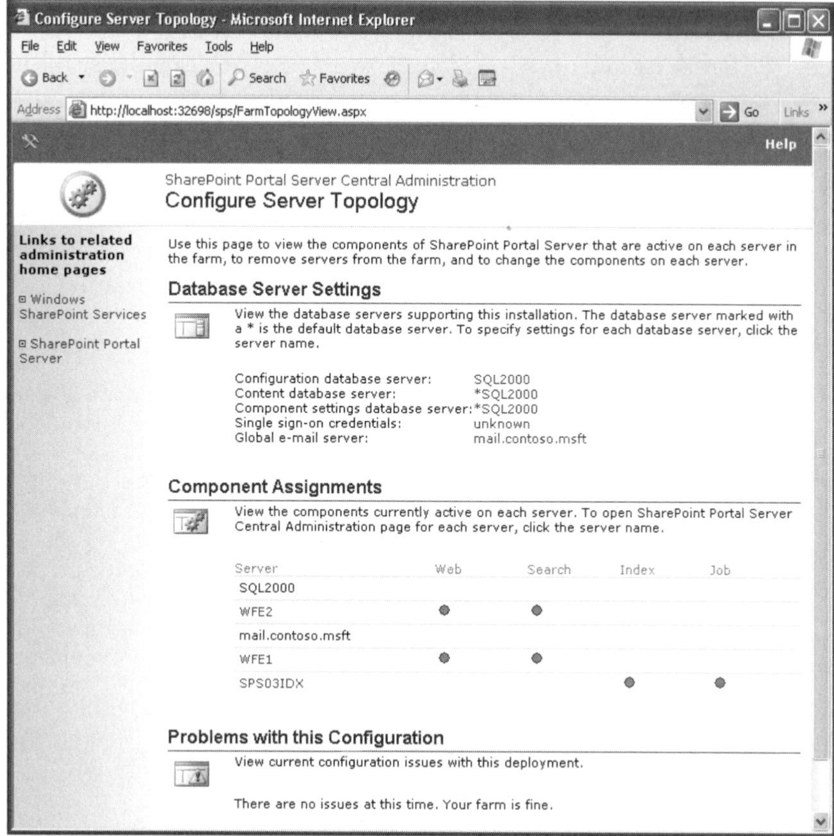

Figure 24-9 SharePoint Portal Server 2003 server topology

b. The prescan.exe tool, which you will run during the upgrade process, also indicates any issues it finds in your SharePoint Server 2007 installation, but again it might not find them all.

Important Prescan.exe cannot update locked, "over quota" sites or database orphans.

2. Run and test a full backup of your environment.
3. Install Windows SharePoint Services 2.0 Service Pack 2 (SP2), followed by SharePoint Portal Server 2003 SP2 whose features are described at *http://office.microsoft.com/en-gb/assistance/HA100806971033.aspx*. Be sure also to

read Microsoft Knowledge Base article KB 887623 found at *http://support.microsoft.com/default.aspx/kb/887623*. If you are updating a Web farm, update all Web servers to both service packs at the same time. Check that all IIS virtual servers are at the same service pack level. See Chapter 23 for details on how to check this.

4. Perform a backup of your updated environment. You cannot use the backups from step 1 to restore your environment because applying the service pack made database schema changes.

5. Install the Microsoft.Net Framework 3.0. When you do this, you will have side-by-side installations of .Net Framework 1.1 and 3.0. ASP.NET Web server extensions must be enabled in Internet Information Services (IIS). To do this, use IIS Manager or the aspnet_regiis -ir command from the .NET Framework directory (*%WinDir%*\Microsoft.NET\Framework\v2.0.50727).

> **Note** Although you can leverage ASP.NET 2.0 on Windows SharePoint Services 2.0 Web applications after you have installed SP2, SharePoint Portal Server 2003 Web applications do not support ASP.NET 2.0. This does pose a quandary for you on how you intend to check that custom Web Parts you have deployed on portal Web sites work correctly in an ASP.NET 2.0 environment. We suggest that, in a test environment, you change your portal Web site to ASP.NET 2.0 using IIS Manager to view the properties of the Web site. Then on the ASP.NET tab, choose 2.0.xxxx from the ASP.NET version drop-down list, as shown in Figure 24-10. However, if you do find issues, the real test will be in a SharePoint Server 2007 environment.

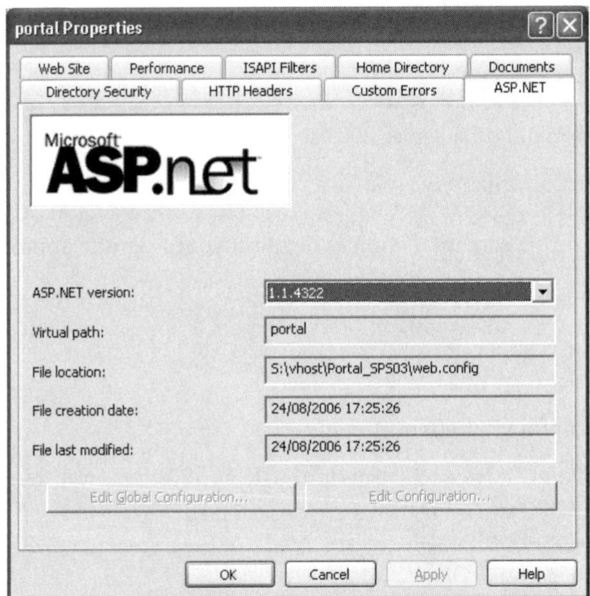

Figure 24-10 Web site properties—ASP.NET tab

6. Increase the ASP.NET runtime time out as detailed in Chapter 23, and use the IIS Manager to increase the Web sites' Connection time out on the Web Site tab to 65000 seconds.
7. Although you should have communicated and worked with site owners and users prior to this point in the process, you should once more detail the outage schedule to them.

Performing the Upgrade Process

This section provides additional details on the three upgrade approaches described previously in Chapter 23. The upgrade process can be divided into the following four tasks:

- Task 1: Install SharePoint Server 2007 binaries.
- Task 2: Run the prescan tool.
- Task 3: Run the SharePoint Products And Technologies Configuration Wizard.
- Task 4: Upgrade/Migrate your SharePoint Portal Server 2003 Web sites using one of the three approaches described previously.

We will detail, in this section, how these tasks are different than they were described in Chapter 23. In addition, we will detail the use of the stsadm.exe command line tool in the upgrade process. If you plan to use the content database migration approach, you should install the new hardware with SharePoint Server 2007 as detailed in Chapter 5, and then return to this chapter for details on the database migration task.

Task 1: Installing SharePoint Server 2007 Binaries—In-place/ Gradual Upgrade Approach

To install the SharePoint Server 2007 binaries, complete the following steps:

1. On the front-end Web server running Central Administration, install SharePoint Server 2007 from the CD by double-clicking on Setup.exe if the installation process does not automatically start. Setup will notice that you have an existing installation, and it will present you with a screen of choices to select your upgrade approach.
   a. Gradual Upgrade: Choose Yes, Perform A Gradual Upgrade.
   b. In-Place Upgrade: Choose Yes, Perform An Automated In-Place Upgrade (selected by default).
   c. Content Database Migration: No, Do Not Upgrade At This Time.

2. If you are upgrading a farm installation and this is the first server in the farm that you're upgrading, change the default server type on the Server Type tab from Standalone to Complete. Use Standalone only if your installation of SharePoint Portal Server 2003 uses the Microsoft SQL Server 2000 Database Engine (MSDE).

> **Note** The recommended upgrade option for a SharePoint Portal Server 2003 installation that uses MSDE is the in-place upgrade.

3. The remaining two tabs can be used to customize your installation, as described in Chapter 5. If you plan to use the server for search, you should choose a location with plenty of disk space available.
4. When Setup is complete, remember to clear the check box for starting the Post-Setup Configuration Wizard before you close the Microsoft Office SharePoint Server 2007 window.

   If you get a dialog box with the message, "In order to complete setup, a system reboot is necessary. Would you like to reboot now", click Yes and restart your computer.

Task 2: Running the Prescan.exe Tool

This should be the second time you have run this tool. The first execution of the prescan.exe tool should have been during the planning stage. (The syntax of the prescan.exe tool was described previously in Chapter 23.) Run the prescan.exe tool on one of your SharePoint Portal Server 2003 servers as explained in the following steps:

1. Open a command prompt, navigate to the Windows SharePoint Services 3.0 directory: *%SystemDrive%*\Program Files\Common Files\Microsoft Shared\Web server extensions\12\BIN, and type the following command:

```
Prescan /c preupgradescanconfig.xml /all
```

> **Note** In Chapter 23, you had to specify a configuration file only if your installation contained custom site definitions. SharePoint Portal Server 2003 depends on a number of site definitions that are used as templates to create areas within a portal Web site, such as Topics, News, Sites Directory, and My Site. If you do not specify the preupgradescanconfig.xml configuration file, the upgrade process will incorrectly identify these site definitions as custom templates, with the result that the upgrade process may not know how to handle area pages, which in turn may lead you to wrongly identify post upgrade tasks that need to be completed by your developer. The templates identified by the configuration file are those identified in the WEBTEMPSPS.XML located in the Windows SharePoint Services 2.0 directory *%SystemDrive%*\Program Files\Common Files\Microsoft Shared\Web server extensions\60\BIN, except for the STS template entry.

2. After the scan has completed, the names of the summary report and log files are displayed in the command-line window. These files should be reviewed for any outstanding issues, such as customized site definitions (templates) or customized Web Parts, as well as broken sites.

Task 3: Running the SharePoint Products And Technologies Configuration Wizard

Before running the configuration wizard, be sure to perform these actions:

1. Disable all antivirus software before trying to upgrade.
2. Deploy upgraded definition files and site definitions.
3. Upgrade custom Web Part packages. If you are using the content database migration upgrade option, redeploy all custom Web Parts to the new Web front-end servers. Similarly, if you are using the gradual upgrade option, you must redeploy your Web Parts to the \BIN folder of the new Web applications.
4. If you need language packs, install them now.
5. Ensure that all your SharePoint Portal Server 2003 Web applications are started on all Web front-end servers.

After performing these steps, it is time to run the configuration wizard. To successfully do this, follow these steps:

1. Run the SharePoint Products And Technologies Configuration Wizard on the first server in your farm. Choose the install type that matches the upgrade option you have chosen, and select a server type of Complete.
2. Progress through the rest of this task as detailed in Chapter 23, Task 3, steps 2 to 12.

> **Note** Your SQL Server will now include a new database named SharePoint_AdminContent_<GUID>. For a gradual upgrade, it will include a new configuration database, which if you accepted the default, is named SharePoint_Config.

In a Web farm environment, once SharePoint Server 2007 is successfully installed, either run the SharePoint Products And Technologies Configuration Wizard on the other servers or run the SharePoint Products And Technologies Configuration command-line tool (psconfig.exe) to upgrade the other servers to the SharePoint Server 2007 platform. To use the psconfig.exe command-line tool, follow these steps:

a. Open a command prompt, and navigate to *%SystemDrive%*\Program Files\Common Files\Microsoft Shared\Web server extensions\12\BIN.

b. For an in-place upgrade, use the following command:

```
PSCONFIG -CMD configdb -CONNECT -SERVER <SQLServerName>
-DATABASE <configDBname> -USER <Domain\username> -PASSWORD <pw>
-CMD installfeatures -CMD services -INSTALL -CMD secureresources
-CMD upgrade -INPLACE.
```

c. For a gradual upgrade, use the following command:

```
PSCONFIG -CMD configdb -CONNECT -SERVER <DBSERVERNAME>
-DATABASE <configDBname> -USER <user acct> -PASSWORD <pwd>
-CMD installfeatures -CMD services -INSTALL -CMD secureresources
-CMD upgrade -SIDEBYSIDE
```

Here is an explanation of the elements contained within the preceding commands:

- *<SQLServrName>* is the SQL Server that hosts your configuration database.
- *<configDBname>* is the name of your configuration database, which for an in-place upgrade is the name of the configuration database that you created for your SharePoint Portal Server 2003 installation. For a gradual upgrade, it is the name of the configuration database you created when you ran the SharePoint Products And Technologies Configuration Wizard on the first server of your farm. The default name for SharePoint Server 2007 is SharePoint_Config. The name of the configuration database can be found on the Configuration Successful screen as shown in Figure 24-11.
- *<Domain\username>* is the Server Farm administrator account. If you do not specify a valid username, psconfig returns an error message.

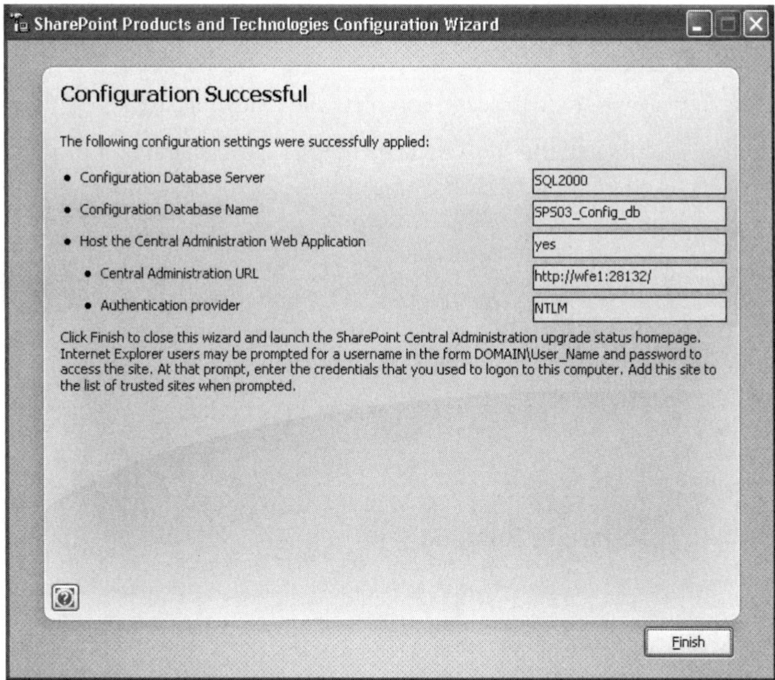

Figure 24-11 The Configuration Successful screen showing the name of the configuration database.

Note The psconfig command-line tool is a useful tool, and it has more parameters than those mentioned. For more information on the psconfig command-line tool, open a command prompt and type **psconfig -?**. To find more information on the configdb command, type **psconfig –help configdb**. If you have to repeat this process on multiple servers I recommend you create a batch file that contains this command.

Important If you use the SharePoint Products And Technologies Configuration Wizard to upgrade other servers in the farm, select to join an existing farm. Then on the Advanced Settings page, if the server is an application server, select Do Not Use This Machine To Host The Web Site or if the server is a Web front-end server, select Use This Machine To Host The Web Site.

Task 4a: Performing In-Place Upgrade of SharePoint Portal Server 2003 Web Sites

To complete the in-place upgrade process, complete the following steps:

1. After you have completed the steps detailed in task 3, the SharePoint Products And Technologies Configuration Wizard closes and the Upgrade Running page opens, as shown in Figure 24-12.

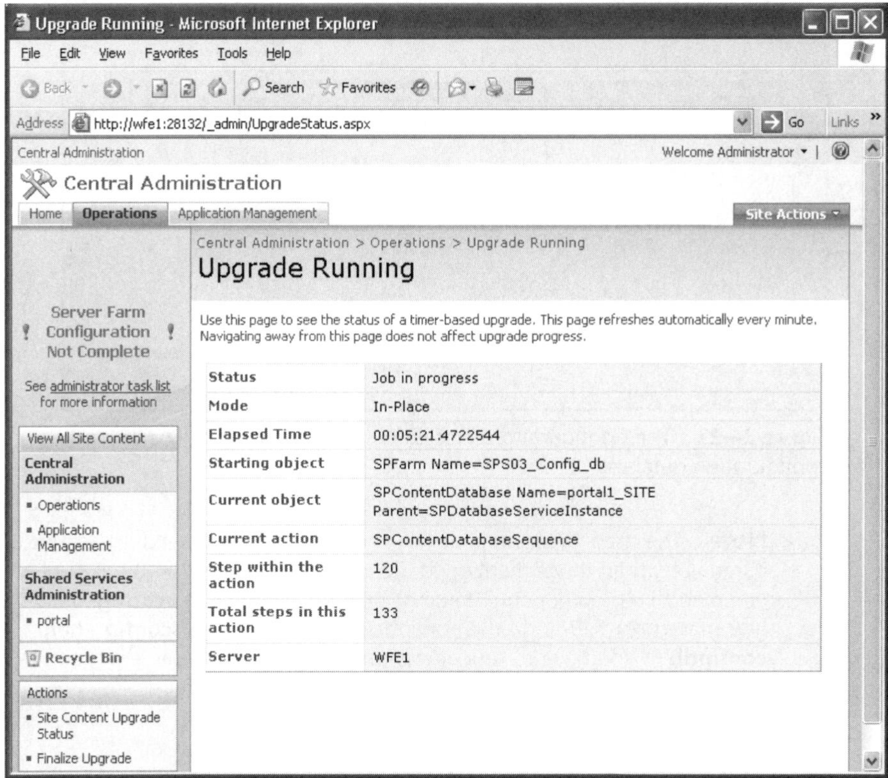

Figure 24-12 Upgrade Running page

If this is not a standalone implementation, in the left navigation pane you will see the words "Server Farm Configuration Not Complete" in red and a link to the administrator's task list below it. When you click the link, you are redirected to the home page of the Central Administration Web application, as shown in Figure 24-13.

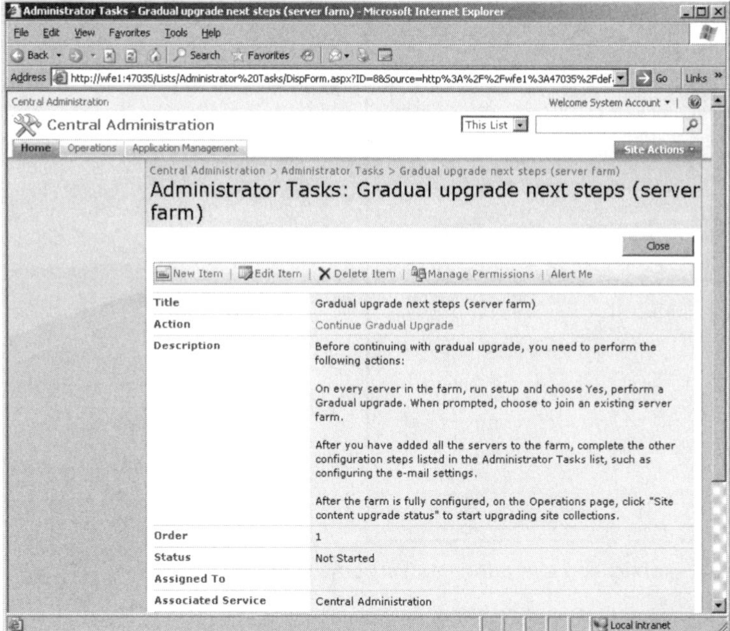

Figure 24-13 Central Administration—server farm configuration not complete

2. Once the upgrade process is complete on the first server in the SharePoint Server 2007 farm and the Upgrade Running page displays “No job pending,” click the Continue Gradual Upgrade link, and complete the upgrade process on the other servers.

3. If the upgrade fails or reports issues, check the event logs on the server and the messages in the Upgrade.log and the trace log files, which are located at *%SystemDrive%*\Program Files\Common Files\Microsoft Shared \Web server extensions\12\LOGS. An example of an event log entry is shown in Figure 24-14. This particular entry warns of internal name changes.

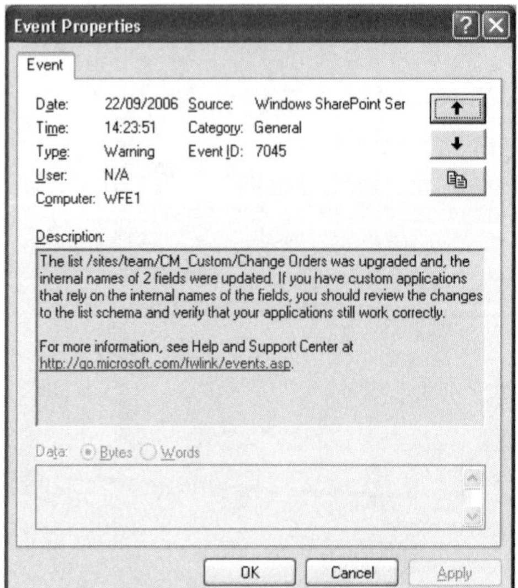

Figure 24-14 Application event log—List schema changes

Note You should review these resources even if the upgrade is a success, as they will inform you of changes made and the timing of the upgrade process. During the test pre-upgrade task, this information can be used in the planning stage of the upgrade process.

Task 4b: Performing a Gradual Upgrade

If your SharePoint Portal Server 2003 environment enabled shared services, you should upgrade the parent portal first. Once you have decided which portal to upgrade, you must upgrade the root of the portal—that is, http://portal.contoso.msft. Once the root is upgraded, you can then choose to upgrade other site collections. A SharePoint Portal Server 2003 portal Web site will consist of a number of site collections: the root, such as http://portal.contoso.msft; a site collection for each personal site, such as http://portal.contoso.msft/personal/<username>; and sites under the managed path, such as http://portal.contoso.msft/sites/<sitename>. You might have other managed paths with other site collections. Because areas are just Web sites under the root, you will upgrade all areas under a given portal. The granularity of the gradual upgrade process is the site collection.

Gradually upgrading your site collections, including the root, is similar to the gradual upgrade task detailed in Chapter 23. There will be slight differences. For example, on the Set Target Web Application Web page, you will be asked for the SSP and Search database names. However, the two processes are basically the same. This section summarizes the tasks you should complete.

1. Ensure you have a healthy SharePoint Server 2007 environment by completing the following tasks:
   a. Navigate to the SharePoint 3.0 Central Administration Web site, and complete the administrative tasks listed there. Ensure all services that are applicable for the servers in the Web farm are started. An SSP will be created when you upgrade your first portal site.
   b. Review the log files.
   c. Review the event logs.
   d. Resolve any issues.
2. Check that the site collection's SharePoint Portal Server 2003 Web application and the Windows SharePoint Services Web Application service are started on all Web front-end servers. This is required so that the Windows SharePoint Services 3.0 Timer service can create all the Web application pairs on all the required Web front-end servers. You can start this service using the following command line:

   ```
   stsadm -o provisionservice -action start -servicetype SPWeb
   ```
3. If this is your second attempt at upgrading a root Web application or a site collection that results in the addition of a content database, ensure that the databases created from the previous attempt no longer exist.
4. To upgrade your site collection, either use the SharePoint 3.0 Central Administration Web pages or use the stsadm.exe command-line tool. Use the following command as a model if you choose to use the stsadm.exe command-line tool:

   ```
   stsadm -o upgrade -sidebyside -url http://portal.contoso.msft
   -sitelistpath c:\sites.xml
   ```

   In this command, *sites.xml* is a file that contains a list of site collections to upgrade. The xml file should contain text similar to the following for each site collection:

   ```
   <WebApplication URL="http://portal.contoso.msft">
     <Database name="portal1_site">
      <sitecollection URL="http://portal.contoso.msft/personal/peter"/>
      <sitecollection URL="http://portal.contoso.msft/sites/team" />
      (more as needed)
     </Database>
   </WebApplication>
   ```

Note To reduce the amount of typing and to ensure you don't miss any site collections when creating this XML file, open a command prompt, navigate to the Windows SharePoint Service 2.0 directory *%SystemDrive%*:\Program Files \Common Files\Microsoft Shared\Web server extensions\60\BIN, type **stsadm –o enumsites –url http://<name of your portal>**, and redirect the output to a text file. This will provide a URL to each site collection in the virtual server. You need to run this command for each virtual server in your SharePoint Portal Server 2003 farm.

Other parameters that you can use with the upgrade option are as follows:

- -forceupgrade
- -quite
- -farmuser <Domain\userid>, which specifies the userid to use during the upgrade
- -farmPassword <password>

The upgrade process will create one target database for each original content database, plus a single temporary database used during the upgrade process. You can change the names of these databases, but the default names are <Portalname>_SITE_Pair and WSSUP_TEMP_<GUID>. These databases will be created on the same SQL server as the original content database. You should check the settings of these databases and include them in your maintenance and backup procedures.

To revert a site collection to SharePoint Portal Server 2003, use the SharePoint 3.0 Central Administration pages, as detailed in Chapter 23. Before you revert a site, ensure that the site still exists in your SharePoint Portal Server 2003 environment. We recommend you take a copy of the site collection before you revert it by using the stsadm –o export command. See Chapter 30, "Microsoft Office SharePoint Server 2007 Disaster Recovery."

Task 4c: Performing the Content Database Migration

Once you have installed and configured SharePoint Server 2007 on a new farm, complete the following steps:

1. On one of the servers on your SharePoint Portal Server 2003 Web farm, open a command prompt and navigate to the Windows SharePoint Services 3.0 directory *%SystemDrive%*\Program Files\Common Files\Microsoft Shared\Web server extensions\12\BIN. Then type the following command:

   ```
   prescan /c preupgradescanconfig.xml /all
   ```

2. Set the relevant SharePoint Portal Server 2003 SQL content databases as read-only.
3. Copy the content databases to the SQL server that the SharePoint Server 2007 uses.

4. Migrate the content database by using the SharePoint 3.0 Central Administration pages or the stsadm –o addcontentdb command, as detailed in Chapter 23.

Performing Post-Upgrade Tasks

After you have upgraded your SharePoint Portal Server 2003 Web site, you should complete a number of post-upgrade tasks as described in this section. You'll likely think of other ones to add to this list.

- Verify that all Web front-end servers render the upgraded sites successfully.
- Perform a full crawl of any content you want to index.
- Re-create search scopes.
- For gradual upgrades, configure the profile, user profiles, and audiences.
- Install any IFilters, word breakers, and thesaurus files you required.
- Configure SharePoint Portal Server 2003 so that it does not crawl the same content as SharePoint Server 2007.
- Manually reconfigure all search settings in the new environment.
- Configure incoming e-mail to reinstate any e-mail-enabled document libraries you had in SharePoint Portal Server 2003 or Windows SharePoint Services 2.0.
- If you used the gradual or content migration upgrade approach, delete upgraded Windows SharePoint Services 2.0 Web sites.
- Update your SQL Server operational procedures to include the new database, and remove those no longer in use. Shrink the transaction logs to reclaim disk space.
- In the gradual and in-place upgrade approach, where you no longer require SharePoint Portal Server 2003 to run side by side with SharePoint Server 2007, perform the following tasks:
    - Remove Windows SharePoint Services 2.0 language packs.
    - Uninstall SharePoint Portal Server 2003.
    - Uninstall MSDE if appropriate.
    - Remove the Web sites from IIS, and delete the associated Web site files and any assemblies used by the SharePoint Portal Server 2003 implementation from the global assembly cache (GAC) for each Web front-end.

- [ ] Decommission index servers that are no longer in use. In SharePoint Server 2007, you need only one index per farm. When you upgrade, the indexes are stored on the job server and the configuration settings from other indexes in the farm are copied into the SSP database.

Note Along with Chapters 23, this chapter identified the extent of the task in front of you. Use the checklist at the end of Chapter 23 to review the major points. We cannot stress enough the importance of performing and testing your backup and restore procedures. It is strongly recommended that you read the SharePoint Server 2007 Installation Release Notes. Check the Office 2007 Web site frequently for the most current information on the upgrade process.

Summary

In this chapter and the previous one, you learned about the upgrade process. The implementation and installation of SharePoint Server 2007 and Windows SharePoint Services 3.0 requires significant forethought and planning to be successful, and the same amount of thought and planning is needed when upgrading your existing SharePoint Portal Server 2003 and Windows SharePoint Services 2.0 Web sites. The more effort and thought you expend in creating your upgrade strategy, the greater the likelihood that the upgrade will be a success—and with less stress.

Chapter 25

Upgrading Site Customizations and Custom Site Definitions to Microsoft Windows SharePoint Services 3.0

Site definitions have changed dramatically in Microsoft Windows SharePoint Services 3.0. The first thing that you will notice is that they are much smaller. If your organization's development team created custom site definitions in Windows SharePoint Services 2.0, they need to know how to upgrade them and map them to a new Windows SharePoint Services 3.0 site definition. This knowledge will enable you to retain customizations and also take advantage of the new functionality Windows SharePoint Services 3.0 has to offer.

Although this book is written primarily for administrators of Microsoft Office SharePoint Server 2007, we recognize that there is an increasing number of administrators who are also tasked with development-oriented activities in their job. Increasingly, in our contact with SharePoint Technologies administrators, we encounter administrators who maintain dual skill sets in both administration and development. Precisely because we know that customizing a Windows SharePoint Services 3.0 site at the site-definition level is a skill set many of the readers of this book will need, this chapter is development oriented.

Windows SharePoint Services 2.0 Site Definitions and Unghosting

SharePoint sites are different from standard Web sites that you might find on the Internet or on an intranet. Typically, when you create a Web site, you create a file for every page that you want to display. Each page in the Web site has a corresponding HTML page or an ASP.NET page (ASPX). Internet Information Services (IIS) Web sites point to the folder containing the files. But SharePoint sites are different. They are simply rows in a database table storing the metadata about each site, area, or workspace. Each site listed in the Docs table in the contents database contains the setup path to a Default.aspx file hosted on the file system of the Web server, allowing us to make a single change to one Default.aspx page that affects every site that uses the page. The Default.aspx file, along with some other XML files, make up a site definition. The 60 hive is where these site definitions live. Each site definition contains the following folders and files:

- **DOCTEMP folder** The DOCTEMP folder contains subfolders for each Office application. You will notice a folder for Word, Excel, PowerPoint, FrontPage, InfoPath, Blank Web Part Pages, and Smart Pages. (These have abbreviated names. For example, Excel is *XL*.) Each subfolder contains the templates that are used in the document libraries to create a document when you click the New Document button. Upon creation of a document library, a default template is chosen and copied from the DOCTEMP\application_name folder and to the Forms folder in the document library. You can view the template file in the Forms folder by using the Explorer view for a document library.
- **LISTS folder** The LISTS folder contains the list definitions that are used by the site definition. Each list contains a Schema.xml file and a collection of .aspx pages that are used to view, edit, and create the list items. The Schema.xml file describes the fields and views that the list will use.
- **XML folder** The XML folder contains the core Site Definitions File (ONET.XML), STDVIEW.XML, and VWSTYLES.XML. STDVIEW.XML describes the views that you can create, such as Standard View, Calendar View, and DataSheet View. The VWSTYLES.XML files describe the styles that you can apply to each view, such as the Newsletter, Newsletter No Labels, Boxed, Boxed No Labels, Shaded, and Default Views styles.
- **Default.aspx file** The Default.aspx file is referred to by the site in the docs table of the content database. This file is responsible for creating the table structure and Web Part zones of a site.

Figure 25-1 shows an image of the 60 hive folder and how you can access it, as well as where to find the site definitions.

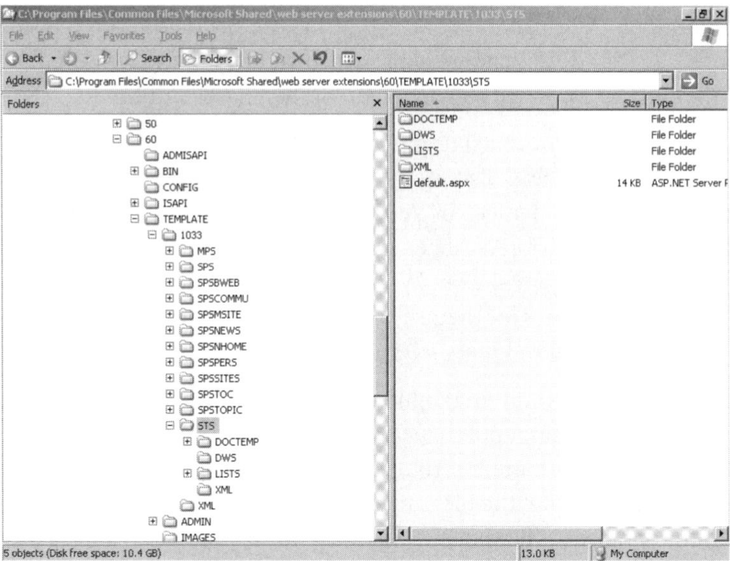

Figure 25-1 The 60 hive folder

> **Note** The term *60 hive* refers to a folder location of the SharePoint Web front-end server. It can be found by browsing to %SystemDrive%\Program Files\Common Files\Microsoft Shared\Web server extensions\60. Also, LCID is an acronym for Local Culture Identifier, and 1033 is the LCID for English (US).

IIS was modified in Windows SharePoint Services 2.0 to look in the Content database for the majority of the files it renders. If you look at the local path for the Virtual Servers Home directory, you will find a Web.config file, but you won't find any .aspx pages. These .aspx pages are accessed by IIS from the Content database. When a site is accessed, IIS looks in the Content database for the relevant site, which then references the Default.aspx in the site definition in the 60 hive. If you need to create some custom .aspx files or some user controls, you need to create an excluded managed path by using the Define Managed Paths option in the Virtual Server Settings page in SharePoint Central Administration. UserControl Virtual Directories were common in Microsoft SharePoint Products and Techologies 2003 if your developers created user controls that were loaded by a custom Web Part.

Team Sites, Blank Sites, and Document Workspaces are site definition configurations that are stored in the 60\TEMPLATE\LCID\STS folder. Meeting Workspaces—such as Basic

Meeting Workspace, Blank Meeting Workspace, Decision Meeting Workspace, Social Meeting Workspace, and MultiPage Meeting Workspace–are all configurations of the 60\TEMPLATE\LCID\MPS folder. STS and MPS contain a Default.aspx file and a collection of XML files, including the ONET.XML file, which forms the site definition. *Ghosted site* is the term used for a site that doesn't actually have its own copy of the Default.aspx and instead points to the Default.aspx on the file system of the SharePoint server.

Windows SharePoint Services 2.0 allows each user who has Contributor rights to modify her own personal view of each page, and also modify the personal properties of a Web Part. SharePoint keeps track of these changes by storing them in a Personalization table in the Content database. If the permission has been granted, users who have at least contributor rights can also create their own sites in Windows SharePoint Services 2.0. Site definitions empower users to create sites for themselves through the user interface, meaning they no longer need to ask Web developers to create a site for them.

Unghosted pages are the result of modifying a ghosted, or default, page in Microsoft FrontPage 2003 or any Web-page editing tool that can edit Windows SharePoint Services 2.0–based pages. *Unghosting* a page means that instead of saving changes to the Default.aspx file in the 60 hive, a copy of the file is made and stored as a customized page for that site in the content database. Microsoft, therefore, had to address this in SharePoint Server 2007 so that when we upgrade from Windows SharePoint Services 2.0 to version 3.0, the customized default.aspx pages that are in the Content database that require updating can be updated in such a manner to include the 2007 functionality.

The upgrade action on the SharePoint code base changes the default.aspx in the site definition, allowing ghosted sites to receive new functionality. If the default.aspx page is copied and stored in the content database, the unghosted page won't receive the new SharePoint Server 2007 functionality.

Microsoft has provided better ways of customizing sites in Windows SharePoint Services 3.0. Master pages are used across all Web sites, which means that developers can change a master page to effect changes across multiple Web sites from a single location instead of changing each site directly. SharePoint Designer 2007 is the replacement for Microsoft FrontPage 2003. It provides developers and power users with even more tools for customizing their sites, allowing them to perform such tasks as creating and applying workflows, using the Data Form Web Part, and customizing master pages. Although unghosting still occurs, it is less of a problem if the customization results are something you don't like because the site can be reset to its original site definition using the Site Settings option of Reset To Site Definition. Selecting this option will undo all the changes that have been made to the site in a single administrative action. This feature gives us a way to undo customizations that have been committed on the site.

Custom Site Definitions

In this section, you will learn about Windows SharePoint Services 2.0 custom site definitions so that you have a better understanding of how to upgrade them later in this chapter.

A custom site definition is usually created by a developer and involves an understanding of Collaborative Application Markup Language (CAML). The process usually involves heavily modifying XML files. In Windows SharePoint Services 2.0, custom site definitions are created so that you could incorporate the following:

- Custom cascading style sheet (CSS) files
- Additional or modified Web Part zones
- Custom list definitions
- Modified navigation
- Custom Web Parts
- Additional resources, such as ASPX pages
- Changes to the base types of the lists

In Figure 25-2, you can see how a custom list named Targets has been added into the ONET.XML file so that the Custom List can be created from the Create page in a team site.

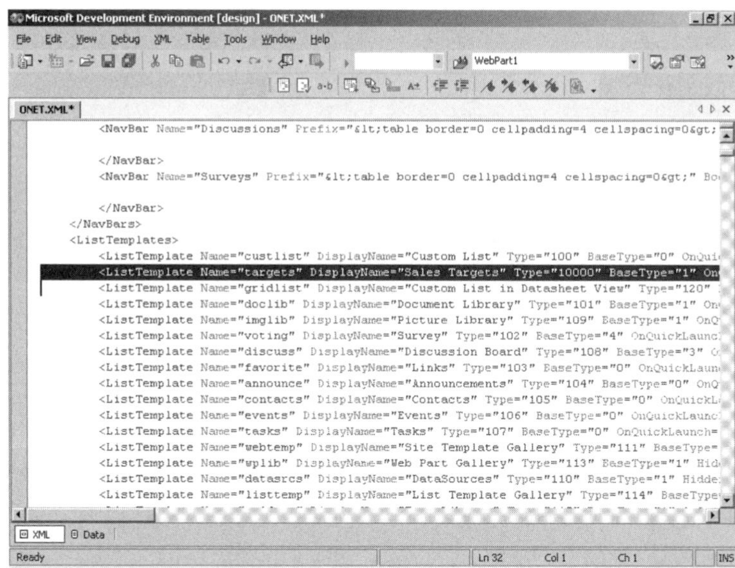

Figure 25-2 STSCONTOSOSALES Custom Site Definition ONET.xml file including a Custom List

Making these changes usually involves modifying the ONET.XML or Default.aspx file stored in each site definition, but it can also involve deploying extra .aspx pages, CSS files, XML files, and Web Parts.

Custom site definitions are created by copying and pasting an existing site definition, such as STS, to a neutral location and then making changes to the copy. For example, you can copy the STS folder in 60\TEMPLATE\LCID to 60\TEMPLATE\LCID \STSCUSTOM. This avoids overwriting the changes to the contents of the STS folder by Microsoft in the form of a service pack or upgrade. It also preserves the default site definition so that it can be copied to other locations and modified differently for different purposes.

The custom site definition is then made available to the Template Selection page by creating a copy of the WEBTEMP.XML file found in 60\TEMPLATE\1033\XML in 60\TEMPLATE\1033\XML\WEBTEMPCUSTOM.XML. Remember, it is the WEBTEMP.XML file that is responsible for making custom site definitions available to the Template Selection page. You can name it anything, as long as it is prefixed with "WEBTEMP" (without the quotation marks). SharePoint Portal Server 2003 has a similar file called WEBTEMPSPS.XML. Figure 25-3 is an illustration of a WEBTEMP.XML file. You can see the two site definitions that are referred to: STS and MPS. Note that each site definition has multiple configurations.

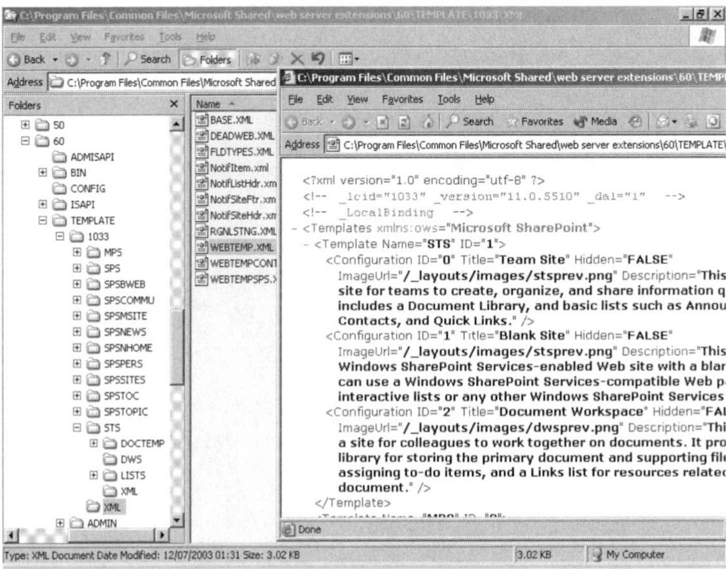

Figure 25-3 The WEBTEMP.XML file

Real World Using SharePoint Template Packages Instead of Site Definitions

In SharePoint Products and Technologies 2003, creating custom site definitions is a developer's responsibility, and rolling out custom site definitions is often an administrator's responsibility because it involves having access to the server and requires resetting IIS.

Custom site templates (STPs) are often created as an alternative to custom site definitions because they can be created using the SharePoint user interface and are basically a modification to the underlying site definition. The STP file is saved to the Site Template Gallery in the top-level site of a site collection. STP files can be made available globally using STSADM.exe (""C:\Program Files\Common Files \Microsoft Shared\web server extensions\60\BIN\STSADM.exe" -o addtemplate -filename "templatename.stp" -title "templatetitle" -description "templatedescription" ").

Custom site definitions will always perform better than a site template. However, using site templates doesn't involve heavy modification of XML files, and you don't need to be a programmer to create them. If you just want to make a small change to a site but reuse the changes for future sites, a site template can be an ideal solution.

Exploring Windows SharePoint Services 3.0 Site Definitions

In Windows SharePoint Services 3.0, site definitions are now streamlined. Lists, Document Library templates, and View styles are no longer part of a site definition. All these files have now moved to a more centralized location in the 12 hive. List definitions are now features and can be found in the Features folder under 12\TEMPLATE. List pages are in a Pages folder under 12\TEMPLATE, and the DOCTEMP folder is available in 12\TEMPLATE\1033\STS folder, even though the STS site definition itself is stored in the 12\TEMPLATE\sitetemplates folder. *Features* are reusable components that can be used to roll out list definitions, content types, workflow, custom actions, Web Parts, and even services such as the Excel Server Service. Rather than each site definition having its own copy of all the list definitions, each site definition simply installs and activates the required features for that particular type of site. This leaves a Site Definition folder with just the Default.aspx file and an ONET.XML file to form the STS site definition. Figure 25-4 displays some of the features in the FEATURES folder.

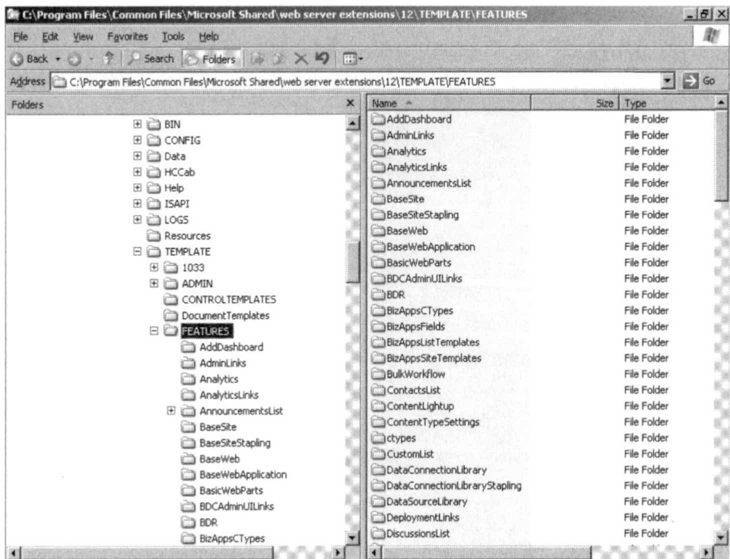

Figure 25-4 The FEATURES folder

Some site definitions do contain a LISTS folder. These site definitions include WIKI, BLOG, CENTRALADMIN, MPS, SPSMSITEHOST, SPSREPORTCENTER, SPSSITES, and SRCHCEN. However, site definitions do not duplicate any lists like they did in Windows SharePoint Services 2.0. They just add to the lists that are created as features, avoiding the duplication of files that occurred in Windows SharePoint Services 2.0.

Inside the ONET.XML file, there are many changes. For example, the *NavBars* element uses a resource for each navigation bar. The following *NavBars* element that has been taken from the STS site definition in Windows SharePoint Services 3.0 shows the reference to a resource for each navigation bar:

```
<NavBars>
  <NavBar Name="$Resources:core,category_Top;" ID="1002" />
  <NavBar Name="$Resources:core,category_Documents;" ID="1004" />
  <NavBar Name="$Resources:core,category_Pictures;" ID="1005" />
  <NavBar Name="$Resources:core,category_Lists;" ID="1003" />
  <NavBar Name="$Resources:core,category_Discussions;" ID="1006" />
  <NavBar Name="$Resources:core,category_Surveys;" ID="1007" />
  <NavBar Name="$Resources:core,category_Sites;" ID="1026" />
  <NavBar Name="$Resources:core,category_People;" ID="1027" />
</NavBars>
```

For site definitions that do have a LISTS folder, as mentioned above, a *ListElement* exists for each of the additional list definitions. Some Windows SharePoint Services 3.0 site definitions do contain a LISTS folder which is the same as all the Windows SharePoint Services 2.0 site definitions. The *ListTemplates* element isn't used in the STS site definition, as all of its lists are rolled out using features. The following example is taken from an SPS-SITES site definition in Windows SharePoint Services 3.0 and shows where the *ListTemplates* element registers the sites list, which is a list definition stored in SPSSITES\LISTS:

```
<ListTemplates>
  <ListTemplate Name="siteslst"
DisplayName="$Resources:spscore,SitesOnet_SitesListName;" FolderCreation="FALSE"
Type="300" BaseType="0" OnQuickLaunch="FALSE" SecurityBits="11"
Description="$Resources:spscore,SitesOnet_SitesListDescription;"
Image="/_layouts/images/itgen.gif" />
  <ListTemplate Name="Tabs"
DisplayName="$Resources:spscore,SitesOnet_TabsListName;" FolderCreation="FALSE"
Type="301" BaseType="0" OnQuickLaunch="FALSE" SecurityBits="11"
Description="$Resources:spscore,SitesOnet_SitesList_Description;"
Image="/_layouts/images/itgen.gif" />
  </ListTemplates>
```

Note You can create features to allow for customization of newly created and existing sites without having to completely create new Site Definition folders. Features are explained in more detail later in this chapter.

The purpose of the *DocumentTemplates* element is the same in the two versions. When you create a document library, the template that is used to create the library resides in the DOCTEMP folder. A copy of this template is then stored in a folder named Forms in the document library. The following example of the *DocumentTemplateFiles* element shows how the Wdtmpl.doc template is copied from the DOCTEMP folder in the 12 hive to the Forms folder in a document library and is renamed as part of the process to *Template.doc*:

```
<DocumentTemplateFiles>
  <DocumentTemplateFile Name="doctemp\word\wdtmpl.doc" TargetName="Forms/
template.doc" Default="TRUE" />
  </DocumentTemplateFiles>
```

The STS site definition has three configurations: Team Site, Blank Site, and Document Workspace. Regardless of which of the three configurations you select from the Template Selection page, your site will still use STS. However, each configuration receives different lists and Web Parts. A configuration element is shown below, displaying the use of features to roll out lists and Web Parts:

```
<Configurations>
  <Configuration ID="-1" Name="NewWeb" />
  <Configuration ID="0" Name="Default">
  <Lists>
 <List Title="$Resources:spscore,SitesOnet_SitesList_Title;"
Description="$Resources:spscore,SitesOnet_SitesList_Description;" Url="SitesList"
 Type="300">
```

```
  <Data>
  <Rows>
  <Row>
  <Field Name="Title">$Resources:spscore,SetupMySite;</Field>
  <Field Name="URL">~site/_layouts/
mysite.aspx?Redirect=1, $Resources:spscore,SetupMySite;</Field>
  <Field Name="TasksAndTools">
$Resources:spscore,SitesList_TopTasks_Text;
</Field>
  <Field Name="_ModerationStatus">0</Field>
  </Row>
  </Rows>
  </Data>
  </List>
  <List Name="Tabs"
Title="$Resources:spscore,SitesOnet_TabsList_Title;" Url="Tabs"
Description="$Resources:spscore,SitesOnet_TabsList_Description;"
Type="301">
  <Data>
  <Rows>
  <Row>
  <Field Name="TabName">$Resources:spscore,CategoriesTab;</Field>
  <Field Name="Page">category.aspx</Field>
  <Field Name="Comments">$Resources:spscore,CategoriesTabComment;
</Field>
  </Row>
  <Row>
  <Field Name="TabName">$Resources:spscore,CategoriesTab;</Field>
  <Field Name="Page">categoryresults.aspx</Field>
  <Field Name="Comments">$Resources:spscore,CategoriesTabComment;
</Field>
  </Row>
  <Row>
  <Field Name="TabName">$Resources:spscore,TopSitesTab;</Field>
  <Field Name="Page">topsites.aspx</Field>
  <Field Name="Comments">$Resources:spscore,TopSitesTabComment;
</Field>
  </Row>
  <Row>
  <Field Name="TabName">$Resources:spscore,SiteMapTab;</Field>
  <Field Name="Page">sitemap.aspx</Field>
  <Field Name="Comments">$Resources:spscore,SiteMapTabComment;
</Field>
  </Row>
  </Rows>
  </Data>
  </List>
  </Lists>
  <SiteFeatures>
  <Feature ID="F6924D36-2FA8-4f0b-B16D-06B7250180FA" />
  <!--  Base site feature
```

```
  -->
  <Feature ID="B21B090C-C796-4b0f-AC0F-7EF1659C20AE" />
  </SiteFeatures>
  <WebFeatures>
  <Feature ID="22A9EF51-737B-4ff2-9346-694633FE4416">
  <Properties xmlns="http://schemas.microsoft.com/sharepoint/">
  <Property Key="ChromeMasterUrl" Value="" />
  <Property Key="WelcomePageUrl"
Value="$Resources:cmscore,List_Pages_UrlName;/category.aspx" />
  <Property Key="PagesListUrl" Value="" />
  <Property Key="AllowedSubSiteTemplates" Value="" />
  <Property Key="AllowedPageLayouts" Value="" />
  <Property Key="EnableVersioningOnPages" Value="true" />
  <Property Key="EnableModerationOnPages" Value="true" />
  <Property Key="EnableApprovalWorkflowOnPages" Value="false" />
  <Property Key="RequireCheckoutOnPages" Value="true" />
  </Properties>
  </Feature>
  <Feature ID="8F15B342-80B1-4508-8641-0751E2B55CA6" />
  <Feature ID="541F5F57-C847-4e16-B59A-B31E90E6F9EA">
  <Properties xmlns="http://schemas.microsoft.com/sharepoint/">
  <Property Key="IncludePages" Value="false" />
  </Properties>
  </Feature>
  <Feature ID="00BFEA71-4EA5-48D4-A4AD-7EA5C011ABE5" />
  </WebFeatures>
  <Modules>
  <Module Name="Default" />
  </Modules>
  </Configuration>
```

In comparison to a Windows SharePoint Services 2.0 site definition, this file is now much smaller and can be changed more easily through the use of features.

Windows SharePoint Services 2.0 Site Definitions versus Windows SharePoint Services 3.0 Site Definitions

Table 25-1 lists some of the major differences between the Windows SharePoint Services 2.0 site definitions and the Windows SharePoint Services 3.0 site definitions.

Table 25-1 Comparison of Site Definitions in WSSv2 and WSSv3

Element	Windows SharePoint Services 2.0	Windows SharePoint Services 3.0
$Resources	No	Yes
NavBars element	Yes	Yes
ListTemplates element	Yes	Not STS
DocumentTemplate files	Yes	Yes
BaseTypes	Yes	No

Table 25-1 Comparison of Site Definitions in WSSv2 and WSSv3

Element	Windows SharePoint Services 2.0	Windows SharePoint Services 3.0
Configurations	Yes	Yes
Modules	Yes	Yes
Features	No	Yes

Other differences between the site definitions include the following items:

- The DOCTEMP folder is no longer stored as part of the STS site definition.
- Defaultdws.aspx is included in the STS folder beside Default.aspx. In version 2.0, it was stored as Default.aspx in a DWS folder.

> **Note** Defaultdws.aspx is the Document Workspace version of a team sites Default.aspx file.

- The Default.aspx file contains less code due to the use of master pages and placeholders. Every Default.aspx page is based on Default.master or mwsdefault.master, which can be found in 12\TEMPLATE\1033\Global.

> **Note** Mwsdefault.master is the master page file for the meeting workspaces.

Upgrading a site definition from Windows SharePoint Services 2.0 to Windows SharePoint Services 3.0 requires some work so that you can still incorporate your original customizations and inherit the new features of SharePoint Server 2007. In the next section, you will learn the possible methods of upgrading your site definitions.

Upgrading Your Customized Windows SharePoint Services 2.0 Site Definitions to Windows SharePoint Services 3.0

As you have learned, Windows SharePoint Services 3.0 site definitions are quite different from Windows SharePoint Services 2.0 site definitions, and therefore you must make many changes to a Windows SharePoint Services 2.0 customized site definition to make it function properly in Windows SharePoint Services 3.0.

When you upgrade your site definitions from Windows SharePoint Services 2.0 to Windows SharePoint Services 3.0, you have two options:

1. Create or copy your custom site definition changes into a new Windows SharePoint Services 3.0 site definition.
2. Take the functionality from Windows SharePoint Services 3.0 site definitions, and place it into your custom Windows SharePoint Services 2.0 site definition.

If you create a custom list and use a site definition to roll it out, the easiest option is to add your custom list to a new Windows SharePoint Services 3.0 site definition. However, a more advanced custom site definition might warrant adding the Windows SharePoint Services 3.0 functionality into your Windows SharePoint Services 2.0 custom definition. Keep in mind that you will have to incorporate features, content types, master pages, and the *SPWebPartManager* control into your version 2.0 custom site definition so that you can use ASP.NET 2.0 Web Parts and get the functionality and look and feel of the version 3.0 site definition.

In most cases, you'll end up choosing to upgrade your version 2.0 site definition to version 3.0 because overall, it will be easier to do this and result in you running on a version 3.0 platform. Table 25-2 lists the high-level steps involved in upgrading your Windows SharePoint Services 2.0 custom site definitions to Windows SharePoint Services 3.0 site definitions and the reasons for taking the steps.

Table 25-2 Steps for Upgrading WSSv2 Custom Site Definitions to WSSv3 Custom Site Definitions.

Step	Reason
Merge your Windows SharePoint Services 2.0 site definition customizations into a Windows SharePoint Services 3.0 site definition. There are two ways to do this: add your Windows SharePoint Services 2.0 changes to a Windows SharePoint Services 3.0 site definition, or add the new Windows SharePoint Services 3.0 features to your Windows SharePoint Services 2.0 site definition.	To incorporate your customizations and the new SharePoint Server 2007 functionality.
Transform your custom list definitions into features.	Windows SharePoint Services 3.0 rolls out list definitions as features. Users are then able to activate or deactivate the feature. Administrators are able to re-use the features throughout SharePoint.

Table 25-2 Steps for Upgrading WSSv2 Custom Site Definitions to WSSv3 Custom Site Definitions.

Step	Reason
Build a feature to roll out any custom Web Parts.	Features can be used to roll out lists and functionality across multiple sites. Features are an excellent way to make any type of new list or functionality available to your end users without having to touch each server in the farm or each client box that will connect to your SharePoint Server 2007 implementation.
Create a custom Upgrade Schema file to upgrade your existing sites and workspaces from the old Windows SharePoint Services 2.0 site definition to the new Windows SharePoint Services 3.0 site definition that you created previously.	Even though you have created a new site definition incorporating Windows SharePoint Services 3.0 functionality, you must upgrade existing sites so that they continue to use your new site definition. Without this step, they will continue to use the Windows SharePoint Services 2.0 site definition and will lack the new functionality and look and feel of a version 3.0 site.

Let's use an example to go through the process of upgrading your version 2.0 site definition to version 3.0. First you'll learn the steps involved when adding your customizations to a Windows SharePoint Services 3.0 site definition. This example assumes that you have added a custom list definition and a custom Web Part to a Windows SharePoint Services 2.0 site definition named STSCONTOSOSALES. The STSCONTOSOSALES site definition is very similar to the standard STS site definition, except that is has a Sales Targets list definition and a custom Web Part that displays Products data from the Contoso Sales database.

Windows SharePoint Services 3.0 site definitions no longer have a LISTS folder containing the list definitions. Therefore, there is no *ListTemplates* element to register the list definitions. All the lists are added as features within the STS list definition. Web Parts are also added as features in the STS Windows SharePoint Services 3.0 site definition.

In our example, a custom WebTemp.xml file is first created to populate the Template Selection page. The file is called WEBTEMPCONTOSO.XML and contained the following XML:

On the CD The following code example can be found on the book's companion CD, in the \Code\Chapter 25 folder in the Code1.txt file.

```
   <?xml version="1.0" encoding="utf-8" ?>
<!-- _lcid="1033" _version="11.0.5510" _dal="1" -->
```

```
<!-- _LocalBinding -->
<Templates xmlns:ows="Microsoft SharePoint">
 <Template Name="STSCONTOSOSALES"     ID="10001">
    <Configuration ID="0" Title="Contoso Sales Team Site"
Hidden="FALSE" ImageUrl="/_layouts/images/stsprev.png"
Description="CONTOSO Sales Team Site">   </Configuration>
</Template>
</Templates>
```

The ONET.XML file is then modified to register a custom list definition called Targets. Figure 25-5 shows the custom list definition in the LISTS folder of our custom site definition.

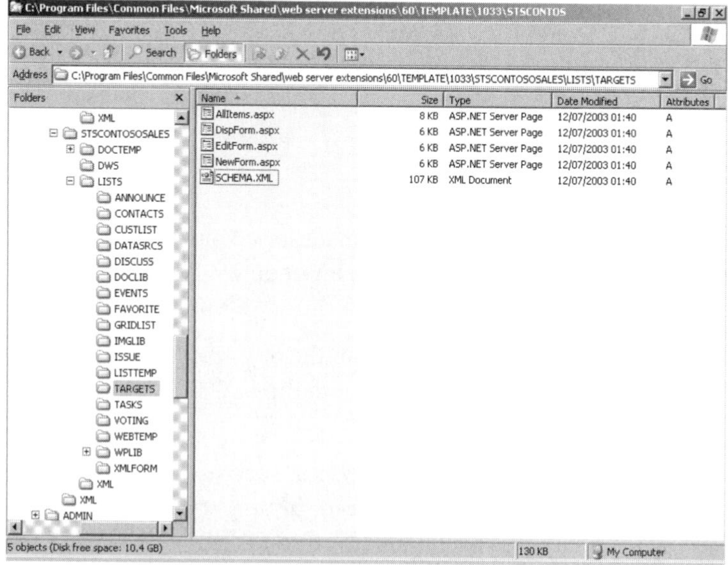

Figure 25-5 The Contoso Targets custom list

The following lines of XML code makes the Targets list available to the site definition and is created in the *ListTemplates* element:

On the CD The below code example can be found on the book's companion CD, in the \Code\Chapter 25 folder in the Code2.txt file.

```
<ListTemplate Name="Targets" DisplayName="Sales Targets"
Type="10000" BaseType="0" OnQuickLaunch="TRUE" SecurityBits="11"
Description="Create a Contoso Sales Target List"
Image="/_layouts/images/itgen.gif">
</ListTemplate>
```

A custom Web Part is also created and added to the right-hand Web Part zone on the Contoso Sales Team Site pages. The following lines of XML code makes the Web Part available on the page.

On the CD The following code example can be found on the book's companion CD, in the \Code\Chapter 25 folder in the Code3.txt file.

```
<AllUsersWebPart WebPartZoneID="Right" WebPartOrder="3">
<![CDATA[
<WebPart xmlns=http://schemas.microsoft.com/WebPart/v2version 2
   xmlns:iwp="http://schemas.microsoft.com/WebPart//Image">
     <Assembly>Contoso.WebParts, Version=1.0.0.0, Culture=neutral,
         PublicKeyToken=71e9bce111e9429c</Assembly>
     <TypeName>Contoso.WebParts.ProductsPart</TypeName>
     <FrameType>Standard</FrameType>
     <Title>Sales Products</Title>
     </WebPart>
   ]]>
</AllUsersWebPart>
```

Now that we've illustrated the customizations that were made in version 2.0, you can now follow the steps below to re-create your modifications for a Windows SharePoint Services 3.0 site definition:

1. Copy the Targets custom List Definition folder from the 60\TEMPLATE\1033 \STSCONTOSOSALES\LISTS folder, and paste it into the 12\TEMPLATE\FEATURES\TargetsList folder.
2. List definitions no longer have their own .aspx pages, such as AllItems.aspx, in Windows SharePoint Services 3.0. If you customized the .aspx pages in Windows SharePoint Services 2.0, leave them as they are. If you want to use the version 3.0 .aspx pages, change the SetupPath="pages\form.aspx" in the form tag of your list definition to use the new standard .aspx pages for all lists.
3. In the TargetsList folder, create a Feature.xml file, adding the following XML.

On the CD The following code example can be found on the book's companion CD, in the \Code\Chapter 25 folder in the Code4.txt file.

```
<?xml version="1.0" encoding="utf-8" ?>
<!-- _lcid="1033" _version="12.0.4017" _dal="1" -->
<!-- _LocalBinding -->
<Feature Id="00BFEA71-7E6D-4186-9BA8-C047AC7510000"
    Title="$Resources:core,targetslistFeatureTitle;"
    Description="$Resources:core,targetslistFeatureDesc;"
    Version="1.0.0.0"
```

```
    Scope="Web"
    Hidden="TRUE"
    DefaultResourceFile="core"
    xmlns="http://schemas.microsoft.com/sharepoint/">
    <ElementManifests>
        <ElementManifest Location="ListTemplates\targets.xml"/>
    </ElementManifests>
</Feature>
```

4. In the TargetsList folder, create a new folder called ListTemplates.

5. Inside the ListTemplates folder, create a targets.xml file and enter the following code.

On the CD The following code example can be found on the book's companion CD, in the \Code\Chapter 25 folder in the Code5.txt file.

```
<?xml version="1.0" encoding="utf-8" ?>
<!-- _lcid="1033" _version="12.0.4017" _dal="1" -->
<!-- _LocalBinding -->
<Elements xmlns="http://schemas.microsoft.com/sharepoint/">
    <ListTemplate
        Name="targets"
        Type="10000"
        BaseType="0"
        OnQuickLaunch="TRUE"
        SecurityBits="11"
        Sequence="330"
        DisplayName="$Resources:core,targetsList;"
        Description="$Resources:core,targetsList_Desc;"
        Image="/_layouts/images/itcontct.gif"/>
</Elements>
```

6. Create a copy of the STS folder in the 12\TEMPLATE\SiteTemplates folder, and name it STSCONTOSOSALES.

7. Add the following new entry for you new feature to the ONET.XML file in the *<Lists>* element under Configuration 0.

On the CD The following code example can be found on the book's companion CD, in the \Code\Chapter 25 folder in the Code6.txt file.

```
<List FeatureId="00BFEA71-7E6D-4186-9BA8-C047AC7510000"
Type="10000" Title="$Resources:core,TargetsList;" Url="$Resources:core,lists
_Folder;
/$Resources:core,Targets_Folder;" />
```

8. Create a new feature to roll out your custom Web Part, and add the new feature to the ONET.XML file as follows.

On the CD The following code example can be found on the book's companion CD, in the \Code\Chapter 25 folder in the Code7.txt file.

```
<SiteFeatures>
  <Feature ID="00BFEA71-7E6D-4186-9BA8-C047AC7510001" />
</SiteFeatures>
```

9. Copy the WEBTEMP.XML file from the 12\TEMPLATE\1033\XML folder, and paste it, naming the new copy WEBTEMPCONTOSO.XML.

10. Add a new entry as you did in the Windows SharePoint Services 2.0 WEBTEMPCONTOSO.xml file, making the new site definition (STSCONTOSOSALES) available to the Template Selection page. Figure 25-6 shows the Windows SharePoint Services 2007 Template Selection page.

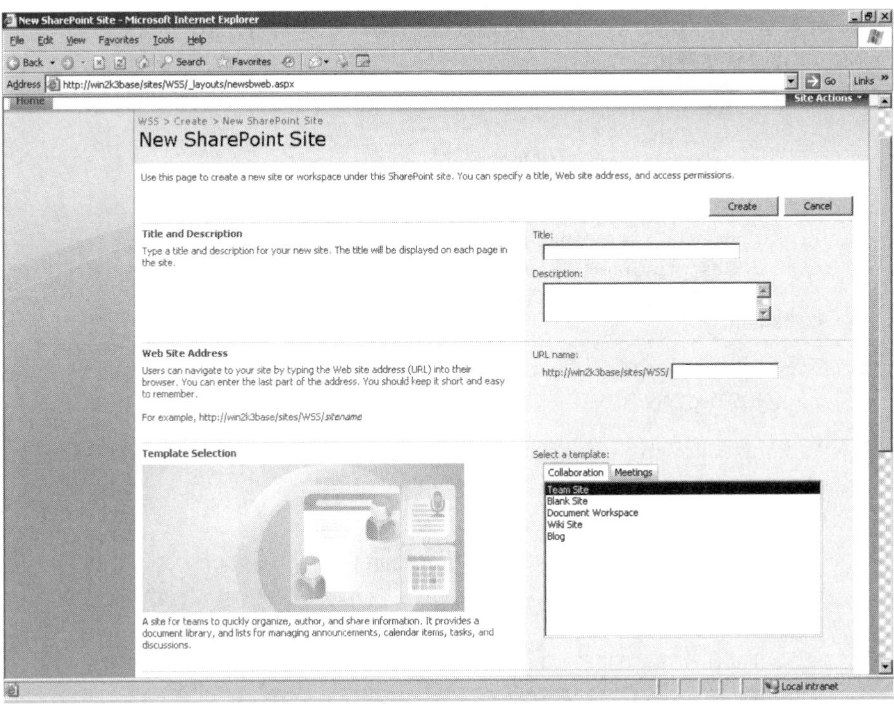

Figure 25-6 The Template Selection page

11. The last step is to create an upgrade definition file to map the Windows SharePoint Services 2.0 files to Windows SharePoint Services 3.0. This is explained later in this chapter.

Changing a Windows SharePoint Services 2.0 Site Definition to Incorporate Version 3.0 Functionality

This method is far more difficult and not recommended unless you are going to find it less work to change your Windows SharePoint Services 2.0 site definition and add in all the new Windows SharePoint Services 3.0 functionality. You need to carry out the following steps to make this happen:

1. Copy your Windows SharePoint Services 2.0 custom site definition to the sitetemplates folder in the 12 hive.
2. Add the SPWebPartManager to every page within your site definition. (This is required by ASP.NET 2.0 so that it can display Web Parts and Web Part zones.)
3. Remove the *<ListTemplates>* tags and contents from your ONET.xml if you are using a site definition that is based on STS. You need to remove the following list definitions from your site definition:
   - custlist
   - gridlist
   - doclib
   - imglib
   - voting
   - discuss
   - favorite
   - announce
   - contacts
   - events
   - tasks
   - xmlform
   - issue
4. In the *<Configurations>* tags, add a *<WebFeatures>* tag and add each feature that you want to deploy with that site. You need to deploy each list as a feature and deploy the basic Web Parts. At a minimum, the features you need to add are as follows:

Table 25-3 Features Required to Upgrade Your Custom Site Definition

Feature name	Feature GUID
AnnouncementsList	0BFEA71-D1CE-42de-9C63-A44004CE0104
ContactsList	FEA71-7E6D-4186-9BA8-C047AC750105
CustomList	BFEA71-DE22-43B2-A848-C05709900100
DataSourceLibrary	0BFEA71-F381-423D-B9D1-DA7A54C50110
DiscussionsList	0BFEA71-6A49-43FA-B535-D15C05500108
DocumentLibrary	0BFEA71-E717-4E80-AA17-D0C71B360101
EventsList	BFEA71-EC85-4903-972D-EBE475780106
GanttTasksList	0BFEA71-513D-4CA0-96C2-6A47775C0119
GridList	BFEA71-3A1D-41D3-A0EE-651D11570120
IssuesList	BFEA71-5932-4F9C-AD71-1557E5751100
LinksList	BFEA71-2062-426C-90BF-714C59600103
NoCodeWorkflowLibrary	00BFEA71-F600-43F6-A895-40C0DE7B0117
PictureLibrary	0BFEA71-52D4-45B3-B544-B1C71B620109
SurveysList	BFEA71-EB8A-40B1-80C7-506BE7590102
TasksList	BFEA71-A83E-497E-9BA0-7A5C597D0107
WebPageLibrary	0BFEA71-C796-4402-9F2F-0EB9A6E71B18
WorkflowProcessLibrary	00BFEA71-2D77-4A75-9FCA-76516689E21A
WorkflowHistoryList	0BFEA71-4EA5-48D4-A4AD-305CF7030140
XmlFormLibrary	0BFEA71-1E1D-4562-B56A-F05371BB0115

5. Add the Team Collaboration feature to *<WebFeatures>*. (This feature adds other required dependent features.)

6. Change the SetupPath="pages\form.aspx" in the form tag of your list definition to use the new standard .aspx pages for all lists.

7. (Optional) You might also want to take advantage of some of the new functionality in your list definition. This is optional but recommended so that your list definition gets the same functionality as all of the standard SharePoint lists. The new functionality includes the ability to work with content types and shared field definitions. To take advantage of this functionality, you need to use the *<Content Types>* tag to declare which content types to include in your list definition and a *<Field>* tag to include the GUIDs of the shared fields you are going to use. Without this step, users won't know why they can't add content types for your custom list definition although they can for other lists.

8. Test your new site definition by creating a new site from it. If it works as expected, you can continue to upgrade your existing sites to the new site definition.

Upgrading Existing Sites with an Upgrade Schema Definition File

Now that you have created your new site definition, you need to upgrade your sites from Windows SharePoint Services 2.0 to Windows SharePoint Services 3.0. Without this step, they will be accessible in SharePoint Server 2007 but continue to use the old site definition. As a result, they will have the look and feel of Windows SharePoint Services 2.0 sites. The purpose of the upgrade definition file is to move your version 2.0 sites to the version 3.0 platform so that those sites can take advantage of the SharePoint Server 2007 functionality.

In the 12 hive under the Config folder, you will find an UPGRADE folder consisting of multiple upgrade files, as shown in Figure 25-7.

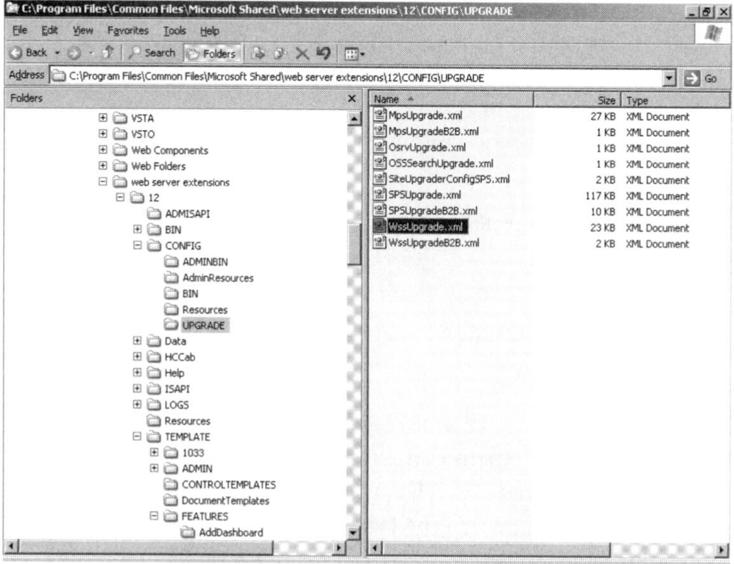

Figure 25-7 UPGRADE folder

One of the files is called WssUpgrade.xml. WssUpgrade.xml is the upgrade definition that SharePoint Server 2007 itself uses to upgrade existing SharePoint team sites, blank sites, and document workspaces to Windows SharePoint Services 3.0 from Windows SharePoint Services 2.0.

You can create your own upgrade definition file in this same folder by copying the WssUpgrade.xml file and giving it a unique name—for example, STSCONTOSOUpgrade.xml.

However, before you create your own upgrade definition, let's explore the existing WssUpgrade.xml file. Under the root element of *<Config>*, you will find a *<WebTemplate>* element. The *<WebTemplate>* element is telling the upgrade process which versions of SharePoint and which schemas you are upgrading from and to. If you upgrade the product version, you just specify *FromProductVersion*=2, and the process will upgrade the product to the most recent version. You can also upgrade from one schema to another schema, but not both the product version and the schema at the same time. You can also specify the locale so that you upgrade the correct site definition if you are using multiple language packs.

Note Windows SharePoint Services has a schema version for each site. The schema version is a number set by a developer. This number can be incremented by developers any time they make a significant enough change to a site definition to require using an upgrade template. This allows them to upgrade sites to use a new version of a site definition and to run two versions of the site definition side by side.

Following is a snippet from the WssUpgrade.xml file in the 12 hive showing the *<WebTemplate>* element:

```
<Config xmlns="urn:Microsoft.SharePoint.Upgrade">
    <WebTemplate
        ID="1"
        LocaleId="*"
        FromProductVersion="2"
        BeginFromSchemaVersion="0"
        EndFromSchemaVersion="0"
        ToSchemaVersion="1">
```

After this element will follow a *<Lists>* element containing multiple *<List>* elements. The purpose of the *<List>* elements is to upgrade each list, using its Type identifier (105 = contacts list, 104 = announcements, and so on), to the feature that implements the list definitions in Windows SharePoint Services 3.0.

Note The last three characters of the feature's GUID match that of the old list definition type IDs.

Following is the *<Lists>* element from the WssUpgrade.xml file:

```
<Lists>
   <List
       FromTemplateId="104"
       ToFeatureId="00BFEA71-D1CE-42de-9C63-A44004CE0104" />
   <List
       FromTemplateId="105"
```

```
        ToFeatureId="00BFEA71-7E6D-4186-9BA8-C047AC750105" />
    <List
        FromTemplateId="100"
        ToFeatureId="00BFEA71-DE22-43B2-A848-C05709900100" />
    <List
        FromTemplateId="110"
        ToFeatureId="00BFEA71-F381-423D-B9D1-DA7A54C50110" />
    <List
        FromTemplateId="101"
        ToFeatureId="00BFEA71-E717-4E80-AA17-D0C71B360101" />
    <List
        FromTemplateId="106"
        ToFeatureId="00BFEA71-EC85-4903-972D-EBE475780106" />
    <List
        FromTemplateId="120"
        ToFeatureId="00BFEA71-3A1D-41D3-A0EE-651D11570120" />
    <List
        FromTemplateId="1100"
        ToFeatureId="00BFEA71-5932-4F9C-AD71-1557E5751100" />
    <List
        FromTemplateId="103"
        ToFeatureId="00BFEA71-2062-426C-90BF-714C59600103" />
    <List
        FromTemplateId="109"
        ToFeatureId="00BFEA71-52D4-45B3-B544-B1C71B620109" />
    <List
        FromTemplateId="102"
        ToFeatureId="00BFEA71-EB8A-40B1-80C7-506BE7590102" />
    <List
        FromTemplateId="107"
        ToFeatureId="00BFEA71-A83E-497E-9BA0-7A5C597D0107" />
    <List
        FromTemplateId="115"
        ToFeatureId="00BFEA71-1E1D-4562-B56A-F05371BB0115" />
    </Lists>
```

Immediately after the *<Lists>* element is the *<Files>* element. This upgrades each list that exists on the upgraded team site. Rather than using the .aspx forms, such as AllItems.aspx and EditForm.aspx that live in the forms folder, the list will now use the standard forms stored centrally in the 12 hive. The location of some of these forms varies. In the next code block, you can see part of the *<Forms>* element. You will notice, by studying the WssUpgrade.xml file for yourself, that some of the entries don't move the location of the form at all.

```
<Files>
    <File
        FromPath="{LocaleId}\STS\Default.aspx"
        ToPath=  "SiteTemplates\STS\Default.aspx"
    />
    <File
```

```
        FromPath="{LocaleId}\STS\Lists\announce\AllItems.aspx"
        ToPath=  "pages\viewpage.aspx"
    />
    <File
        FromPath="{LocaleId}\STS\Lists\announce\DispForm.aspx"
        ToPath=  "pages\form.aspx"
    />
    <File
        FromPath="{LocaleId}\STS\Lists\announce\EditForm.aspx"
        ToPath=  "pages\form.aspx"
    />
    <File
        FromPath="{LocaleId}\STS\Lists\announce\NewForm.aspx"
        ToPath=  "pages\form.aspx"
    />
    <File
        FromPath="{LocaleId}\STS\Lists\contacts\AllItems.aspx"
        ToPath=  "pages\viewpage.aspx"
    />
    <File
        FromPath="{LocaleId}\STS\Lists\contacts\DispForm.aspx"
        ToPath=  "pages\form.aspx"
    />
```

The last element is the *<AppliedSiteFeatures>* element, which rolls out other functionality within the SharePoint team site. The following list shows the basic Web Parts, which make up the first feature rolled out by the *<AppliedSiteFeatures>* element:

- Content Editor Web Part
- Image Web Part
- XML Web Part
- Members Web Part
- Page Viewer Web Part
- Simple Form Web Part
- User Documents Web Part
- User Tasks Web Part

The second applied feature activates even more features. Features can have dependent features, so when you apply the feature in the following code block that ends in *BE5*, it activates all the list features that were listed in the preceding code block and is known as the Team Collaboration feature.

```
<AppliedSiteFeatures>
    <Feature ID="00BFEA71-1C5E-4A24-B310-BA51C3EB7A57" />
</AppliedSiteFeatures>
<AppliedWebFeatures>
    <Feature ID="00BFEA71-4EA5-48D4-A4AD-7EA5C011ABE5" />
</AppliedWebFeatures>
```

Note As well as having a WssUpgrade.xml, the upgrade folder also contains MpsUpgrade.xml to upgrade all multipage sites (MPS). The MPS site definition is the container of the meeting workspaces.

So to complete the upgrade of your sites, you need to create a new Upgrade Definition file that upgrades your existing sites to use your new site definition. Follow these steps to upgrade our STSCONTOSOSALES site definition.

1. Create a copy of the WssUpgrade.xml file, and call it STSCONTOSOSALES.xml.
2. The file will upgrade all the standard lists and files, as well as install all the required Web Parts and other functionality. We need to add to the file our customizations.
3. Create the following *<List>* element for our custom Targets list, ensuring that you use the same GUID as you did in your feature:

```
<List FromTemplateId="100"
      ToFeatureId="00BFEA71-7E6D-4186-9BA8-C047AC7510000" />
```

4. Create a *<File>* element for each file in the Forms folder of our Targets list, and point them to the standard forms, as shown in the following example:

```
<File FromPath="{LocaleId}\STSCONTOSOSALES\Lists\targets\AllItems.aspx"
                ToPath=  "pages\viewpage.aspx"/>
```

5. Create an *<AppliedWebFeatures>* element to roll out our custom Web Part, as shown in the following example:

```
<AppliedWebFeatures>
     <Feature ID="00BFEA71-7E6D-4186-9BA8-C047AC7510001" />
</AppliedWebFeatures>
```

6. Use the Installation And Configuration Wizard, as shown in Chapter 24.

Upgrading Customized Pages

Customized pages refers to pages that have been modified using Microsoft FrontPage 2003 and are stored in the content database. Customized pages were explained in detail earlier in this chapter. In general, you have two decisions to make. First, you can just leave the customized page as a customized page, and it will always look like a Windows SharePoint Services 2.0 page rather than a Windows SharePoint Services 3.0 page.

Unfortunately, though, when you go into Site Settings or into a list, you will receive a Windows SharePoint Services 3.0 page with the up-to-date look and feel. It is only the customized page of your site that will look out of date. If you think it will save you time and *if* you can lose the customizations you made in your version 2.0 page, you can reset the customized site back to the original site definition. Figure 25-8 illustrates this option in the interface.

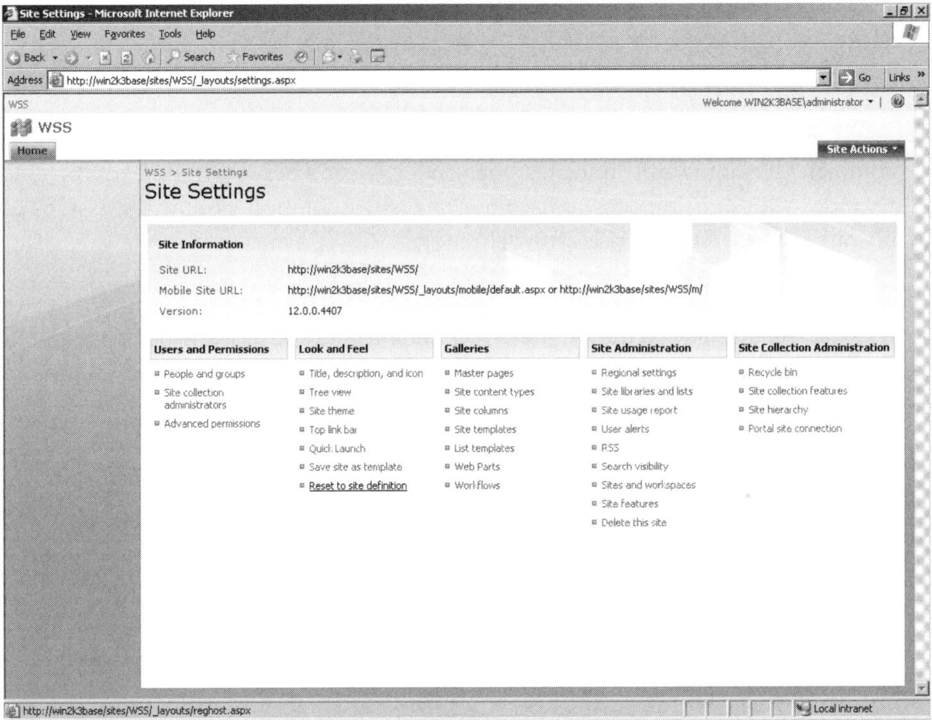

Figure 25-8 Reset To Site Definition option

Note If you used the Ghost Hunter Web Part (part of the Web Part Toolkit downloadable from *http://www.bluedoglimited.com*) in Windows SharePoint Services 2.0, you are already familiar with this process. You will lose some of the changes that you made in FrontPage, but others will remain. Navigation changes remain if you simply add a new link, but any new Web Part zones are lost and replaced with the original Web Part zones specified in the Default.aspx page in the site definition.

If your pages have any custom script or tags, SharePoint might have a problem with rendering. The SharePoint Parser automatically corrects certain known issues so that the page can be parsed. The issues that get corrected by version 3.0 are as follows:

- Invalid control IDs are not compliant with ASP.NET (such as when a name is invalid because the ID begins with a number or unsupported character), the ID is an empty string, or the ID is not unique with respect to other IDs on the page. This modification can break the page in a case where client-side script relies on the former ID names.

- Known attributes inserted in the page by Windows SharePoint Services (for example, __Preview, __Error, __Web PartId, Web Part) are handled by implementing the SharePoint *IAttributeAccessor* interface on Web Parts.
- Removal of *Trace* attributes.
- Addition of appropriate directives for registering tags such as *<WebPart:WebPartZone>* or *<SharePoint:Theme>*.

Windows SharePoint Services 3.0 does not attempt to fix the following breaking issues on pages:

- Unknown attributes on controls
- Presence of <object runat=server> tags
- Databinding expressions present inside attributes (<% ... %>).

Windows SharePoint Services stores a version integer for each customized page in the database. When a customized page is browsed, SharePoint checks the version number of the page. If the version number corresponds to a default page, SharePoint fixes these various issues and updates the page behind the scenes.

The _Layouts Virtual Directory

Any pages that are stored in the \Web Server Extensions\60\TEMPLATE\LAYOUTS\LCID setup directory, such as EditAlert.aspx, are automatically redirected to use the new /_layouts/Locale_ID/nameofoldpage.aspx or to /_layouts/newpage.aspx pages.

Upgrading Web Parts

Web Parts continue to function in Windows SharePoint Services 3.0, although they require a few changes in their configuration. If you create a new Web application to host a Windows SharePoint Services 3.0 installation, the web.config file for that Web application must be updated to include additional safe control and code access security (CAS) policy settings.

Although the general level of CAS restrictions remains the same in Windows SharePoint Services 3.0, the Windows SharePoint Services policy files have been updated to the ASP.NET 2.0 level and format. For this reason, it is not generally possible to reuse CAS policy files in Windows SharePoint Services 3.0.

Summary

In this chapter, you learned about what makes up a site definition and how to upgrade a custom site definition and any sites created using that site definition to Windows SharePoint Services 3.0. We also explored the concept of customized sites (unghosted sites) and how to upgrade them to Windows SharePoint Services 3.0.

Part VI
Extending Microsoft Office SharePoint Server 2007

Chapter 26

Introducing Features

New to the Microsoft Office SharePoint Server 2007 architecture, *Features* offer flexibility in terms of developing and deploying extended functionality–such as page templates, lists, content types, Web Parts, workflow, and events–to new and existing Office SharePoint Server 2007 sites. By default, SharePoint Server 2007 includes prepackaged Features as part of its base installation, such as a My Site Feature. The Feature framework has been extended to allow developers to create custom Features.

If you worked with site definitions in SharePoint Portal Server 2003, you'll appreciate the flexibility of Features! With SharePoint Portal Server 2003, if you wanted to add a list or document library to an existing site definition, you had to work with one large ONET.XML file to modify the XML code and then track each of those changes throughout the ONET.XML file. Likewise, if you wanted to add items to the SharePoint toolbars or menus, you had to work with complex Collaborative Application Markup Language (CAML). Features overcome the complexity of injecting such changes by chunking code into smaller, more manageable files, which can be more easily tracked, versioned, and deployed.

Both developers and administrators will benefit from using Features throughout a SharePoint Server 2007 deployment. Through Feature schemas, developers can scope and add simple changes, such as provisioning new pages to a SharePoint site, or registering and deploying complex solutions developed in Microsoft Visual Studio 2005, such as event handlers or workflows. Developers can also work with the SharePoint object model, which includes Feature classes to effect changes throughout the life cycle of Features. Examples of these changes include whether certain actions or events occur when a Feature is installed, activated, deactivated, or uninstalled. In addition, administrators can install and deploy Features with ease, using command-line tools, and will have at their fingertips the ability to switch Features on or off via the activate and deactivate options on administrative user-interface pages.

SharePoint Server 2007 includes a new form of deployment, namely Solution deployment. Solutions are custom packages, or redistributable CAB files, created by developers. Solutions can include Features, site definitions, template pages, global resources, and assemblies. Administrators can deploy Features to all Web front-end servers using Solution packages, and this will be demonstrated throughout this chapter, along with other Feature deployment options.

This chapter will look at defining the Feature schemas and configuring Feature elements. It will also demonstrate creating a custom event handler using Visual Studio 2005 and including that event handler as part of a Feature. You'll also gain some understanding of the Feature object model, with a walkthrough on creating a Web Part to show activated Features in a given scope within your SharePoint deployment. Finally, you'll learn how to include and deploy Features as part of a site definition.

Understanding the Default Feature Files

SharePoint Server 2007 includes a number of default Features that provide functionality offered as part of the base installation. The default Features are located under the 12 hive, where SharePoint Server 2007 puts all of its system files, at the following path:

%SystemDrive%\Program Files\Common Files\Microsoft Shared
\web server extensions\12\TEMPLATE\FEATURES

An example of one of the default Features is the document library (DocumentLibrary) Feature. This Feature is provisioned as part of the default STS site definition, or *Team Site template*, to create the default Shared Documents document library and also as the basis to create new document libraries within sites provisioned from the STS site definition.

The DocumentLibrary Feature is denoted by a globally unique identifier (GUID), which can be viewed in the browser URL when creating a new document library, such as http://server/_layouts/new.aspx?FeatureId={GUID}. This GUID is the Feature GUID, and if you open the Feature.xml file located in the DocumentLibrary folder under the

Features directory, you'll see the same GUID as that seen in the URL. Every Feature has its own GUID. As you create new Features, you generate a GUID for each of them. The next section looks at how to generate a GUID and include that in your Feature file, which is discussed in the "Creating Features in Visual Studio 2005" section in this chapter. Any custom Features you develop are added to the Features directory, where they are invoked by SharePoint.

Configuring Feature Components

A Feature can include any number of files, but it must include a Feature.xml file. The Feature.xml file, or *Feature manifest*, is the driver of the Feature, and this is the first file SharePoint looks at when invoking a Feature. It includes the high-level attributes, or *properties*, of the Feature, including Feature scope, references to other supporting Feature files, Feature dependencies, and assembly references deployed as part of a Feature.

Note If a Feature does not include a Feature.xml file, you receive an error message—such as "Value cannot be null"—when attempting to install or activate it.

Features are organized in folders under the Features directory on the Web front-end server. In addition to the Feature.xml file, Features can include subfolders and supporting files, such as element files that include, for example, event handler references, ASPX pages deployed as part of the Feature, ASCX files, dynamic-link libraries (DLLs), and RESX files.

In this section, you'll review the attributes and configuration of the Feature.xml file, as well as supporting element files. The upcoming sections will demonstrate how elements can be leveraged to make changes directly to your SharePoint sites.

Feature.xml File

The Feature.xml file is the core file of a Feature. It includes the identifying GUID, title, and scope of the Feature. This includes information such as whether the Feature will be made available to an entire SharePoint farm or a site collection. SharePoint uses the Feature.xml file to deploy the Feature and identify any supporting files, including any custom assemblies associated with the Feature. For example, a developer might have created a programming solution as part of the Feature that performs certain actions when the Feature is installed or activated. Such a solution is associated with the Feature.xml file in the *ReceiverAssembly* attribute by including the solution's assembly reference.

An example of a basic Feature.xml file, including its top-level attributes, is shown in the following code block:

```
<Feature xmlns=http://schemas.microsoft.com/sharepoint/
  Id="GUID"
  Title="Name of Feature"
  Description="Feature Description"
  Scope="Web"
  Hidden="FALSE">
  <ElementManifests>
    <ElementManifest Location="Elements.xml" />
  </ElementManifests>
</Features>
```

Table 26-1 provides an overview of Feature.xml attributes. You'll learn more about these attributes and how you can apply them in the "Creating Features in Visual Studio 2005" section of this chapter.

Table 26-1 Feature.xml Attributes

Feature attribute	Description
Id	The globally unique identifier (GUID) for the Feature, in Registry format.
Title	The name of the Feature. It's important because it makes the purpose of the Feature easily identifiable. It can be up to 255 characters in length.
Description	(Optional) Describes what the Feature does.
Version	Specifies the version of the Feature.
Scope	Specifies where the Feature will be deployed and made available—that is, server farm, Web application, site collection, or Web (site).
Hidden	Determines whether the Feature will be visible in the Feature administrative user interface. This option toggles between False and True. False is the default. Set this option to True to hide the Feature from administrative user interface.
AlwaysForceInstall	(Optional) If True, any updates to the Feature are installed within the given scope without manual intervention during updating. Removes the need to add the –force parameter to the stsadm.exe command line when redeploying a Feature.
DefaultResourceFile	(Optional) The resource file the Feature uses for additional configuration details.
ImageUrl	(Optional) The URL to an image you want to have associated with the Feature in the Feature administrative user interface.
ReceiverAssembly	(Optional) The strong name of the assembly that handles events for the Feature.*

Table 26-1 Feature.xml Attributes

Feature attribute	Description
ReceiverClass	(Optional) The fully qualified, case-sensitive name of the class that handles events for the Feature.
ActivationDependencies	(Optional) The Feature IDs of any dependent Features—that is, Features that depend on the Feature being activated before they can be activated.
ElementManifests	The relative path to associated element files for the Feature. This can include more than one element file.

*The *ReceiverAssembly* attribute in the Feature.xml file should not be confused with the Receiver element in the supporting element files. The *ReceiverAssembly* attribute names the assembly from which to load Feature events—that is, different events specified throughout a Feature life cycle, such as when a Feature is activated or deactivated, using special Feature classes through the SharePoint object model. The Receiver element in the element files associated with the Feature receives the assembly for a specific event handler assembly. Event handlers and Feature events will be demonstrated, respectively, in the "Creating an Event Handler Feature" and "Implementing Feature Events" sections in this chapter.

Element Files

Element files are supporting files for a Feature. They are referenced in the Features.xml file in the <ElementManifests> element tag—for example:

```
<ElementManifests>
    <ElementManifest Location="location\Elements.xml"/>
</ElementManifests>
```

Element files define the functionality of a Feature, such as including an additional button in a form, or list, toolbar, as shown in Figure 26-1, where an additional button named Site Help has been added.

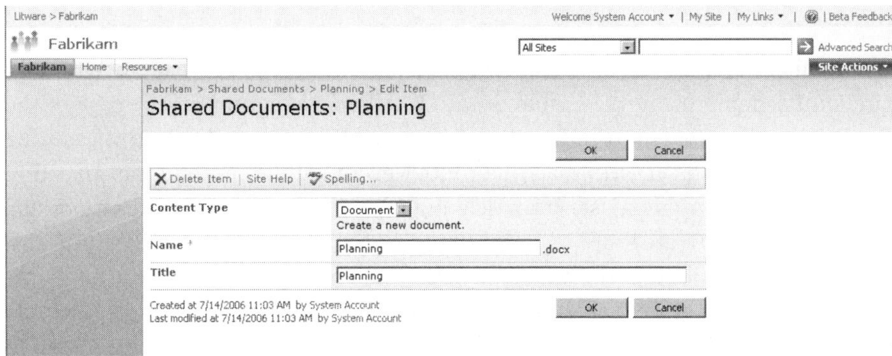

Figure 26-1 Example of Feature enhancement to list toolbar Site Help button

Functionality is included in element files via element tags. For example, you use the Receiver element to include, or register, a custom event handler as part of a Feature. Or you use the Custom Action element to include a URL on a page in a SharePoint site—for example, a URL to a special event, which you can remove at a later stage. The Module element is used to include pages as part of your Features, such as ASPX or HTML pages.

Throughout this chapter, examples may refer to element files as "Elements.xml". However, you do not need to use this name for the element files deployed as part of a Feature. For example, if you review the default Feature AnnouncementsList, you'll notice the ListTemplates subdirectory includes an element file named Announcements.xml. You can also have more than one element file per Feature. For example, you might want to devote one element file to defining the Custom Action elements and have another element file to define the workflow or Content Type elements for a Feature.

Element Examples

In the following example, the Receiver element is used in an element file to register the assembly and class for an event handler, which will be deployed as part of the Feature and applied to a specific list type in a SharePoint site:

```
<Receivers
<ListTemplateOwner="GUID"
ListTemplateId="101">
<Receiver>
    <Name>Event Handler</Name>
    <Type>ItemDeleting</Type>
    <SequenceNumber>1000</SequenceNumber>
    <Assembly>AssemblyName, Version=1.0.0.1, Culture=neutral,
PublicKeyToken=tokennumber</Assembly>
    <Class>ClassName</Class>
    <Data></Data>
    <Filter></Filter>
   </Receiver>
</Receivers>
```

Each element includes attributes to define the element; each attribute is exposed through the SharePoint schema using the Visual Studio IntelliSense feature. In the case of the Receiver element, the *<Type>* attribute defines the type of event handler. In this case, the event handler is of type *ItemDeleting*, a synchronous event handler used to trap an action as it occurs, such as stopping a user from deleting a file from a document library or list. The *<ListTemplateOwner>* attribute includes the GUID of the list template Feature, and the *<ListTemplateId>* attribute is the base type of the list. For example, *101* is the base type for document library, so the event handler will apply to the document library. A sample of an event handler included as part of a Feature deployment is included in the "Creating an Event Handler Feature" section of this chapter.

The Module element is used to provision files to a site. Here is an example of the Module element and its configuration:

```
<Module
  Name="HelloWorld" Path="" Url="">
  <File Url="HelloWorld.aspx"
   Type="Ghostable"
   IgnoreIfAlreadyExists="FALSE"
  </File>
</Module>
```

The <*File Url*> attribute refers to the location of the file when it is provisioned—for example, in the Feature folder. The <*File Type*> attribute can be *Ghostable*, *GhostableInLibrary*, or *Unghost*. This setting determines whether the changes are stored to the database or cached from the original template on the Web front-end server when customizations are made to the file or page using SharePoint Designer 2007.

Table of Elements

Table 26-2 lists the available elements for element files. Elements used in supporting element files are governed by the scope of the Feature—for example, Web or Farm. The available elements for each scope are described in this chapter in the "Administrating Feature Scope" section..

More Info For a more complete listing of element attributes, including details on Features schemas, visit the Windows SharePoint Services 3.0 Software Development Kit, which can be found on the Microsoft Download Center at *http://www.microsoft.com/downloads/details.aspx?FamilyId=05E0DD12-8394-402B-8936-A07FE8AFAFFD&displaylang=en*.

Table 26-2 Elements

Element name	Element description
Content Type	Contains a schema definition, for example to define metadata, templates and workflow, which you can reuse and apply to multiple list, and document library, definitions.
Content Type Binding	Content type binding enables you to provision a content type on a list, or document library, defined in the ONET.XML schema. Lists defined in the ONET.XML schema cannot be modified directly.
Control	A delegate control contains a registration controls installed on a Web page. This allows you to replace existing controls, such as the Windows SharePoint Services search control, with your own custom control.

Table 26-2 Elements

Element name	Element description
Custom Action	You can define custom actions in your Feature, such as: ■ Content type links for the content type settings page ■ Drop-down menu actions for the drop-down menu that appears for an item ■ Form toolbar buttons for New, Edit, or Display form toolbars ■ Site Settings link for the Site Settings page
Custom Action Group	A group of custom actions.
Document Converter	A *document converter* takes a document of one file type and creates a copy of that file in another file type, such as from a Microsoft Office Word 2007 Document to Web Page format.
Feature/Site Template Association	Binds a Feature to a site definition or template so that sites provisioned from that site definition or template include the Feature.
Field	Contains a field, or column, definition that can be reused in multiple lists.
Hide Custom Action	Hides a custom action that has been added through another custom action.
List Instance	Provisions a SharePoint site with a list which includes specific data.
List Template	A list definition or template, which defines a list that can be provisioned to a SharePoint site.
Module	Includes files which are included when provisioning sites, such as .aspx or .html files.
Receiver	Contains an item event handler receiver registration, such as a column, list or Web event handler.
Workflow	Defines a workflow for a list, or document library.

Resource Files

Resource files are essentially schema files that include XML elements to define and populate provisioned pages, Web Parts, and lists. They are installed as part of the default SharePoint installation on the Web front-end server at the following path:

%SystemDrive%\Program Files\Common Files\Microsoft Shared\web server extensions \12\Resources

Resource files further compartmentalize the SharePoint framework by placing key configuration details into smaller, pluggable files, and they afford developers the opportunity to further customize extensions such as custom lists by centrally defining custom data and value parameters.

The following example of using the default resource files includes the default DocumentLibrary Feature.xml file, which references the default resource file, core.en-US.resx, as its resource file. This is denoted in the *Title*, *Description*, and *DefaultResourceFile* attributes shown in the following code block:

```
<?xml version="1.0" encoding="utf-8" ?>
<!-- _lcid="1033" _version="12.0.4017" _dal="1" -->
<!-- _LocalBinding -->
<Feature Id="00BFEA71-E717-4E80-AA17-D0C71B360101"
    Title="$Resources:core,documentlibraryFeatureTitle;"
    Description="$Resources:core,documentlibraryFeatureDesc;"
    Version="1.0.0.0"
    Scope="Web"
    Hidden="TRUE"
    DefaultResourceFile="core"
    xmlns="http://schemas.microsoft.com/sharepoint/">
    <ElementManifests>
        <ElementManifest Location="ListTemplates\DocumentLibrary.xml" />
    </ElementManifests>
</Feature>
```

The core resource file in the Resources folder includes data and value tags for populating the Feature *Title* and *Description*:

```
<!-- DocumentLibrary Feature -->
  <Data Name="documentlibraryFeatureTitle">
    <Value>Document Libraries</Value>
  </Data>
  <Data Name="documentlibraryFeatureDesc">
    <Value>Provides support for document libraries for a site.</Value>
  </Data>
```

The DocumentLibrary Feature element file, DocumentLibrary.xml, includes the attributes *DisplayName* and *Description* as part of its ListTemplate definition. Corresponding data values in the core resource file are used to populate those attributes. The DocumentLibrary.xml file is shown in the following code block, with the reference to the core resource file for both *DisplayName* and *Description*:

```
<?xml version="1.0" encoding="utf-8" ?>
<!-- _lcid="1033" _version="12.0.4017" _dal="1" -->
<!-- _LocalBinding -->
<Elements xmlns="http://schemas.microsoft.com/sharepoint/">
    <ListTemplate
        Name="doclib"
        Type="101"
        BaseType="1"
        OnQuickLaunch="TRUE"
        SecurityBits="11"
        Sequence="110"
        DisplayName="$Resources:core,doclibList;"
```

```
        Description="$Resources:core,doclibList_Desc;"
        Image="/_layouts/images/itdl.gif"
        DocumentTemplate="101"/>
</Elements>
```

The core resource file populates *DisplayName* and *Description* from the data and value tags shown here:

```
<Data Name="doclibList">
    <Value>Document Library</Value>
  </Data>
  <Data Name="doclibList_Desc">
    <Value>Create a document library when you have a collection of documents or
other files that you want to share.  Document libraries support features such as
folders, versioning, and check out.</Value>
  </Data>
```

Developers can create custom resource files to add more configuration details to custom lists and document libraries, and then reference those custom resource files in custom Features.

> **Important** The default resource files should not be modified because this can destabilize existing, default functionality. Instead, create new resource files for any custom purposes. For example, you could copy the core resource file, rename it, and modify the XML parameters according to your needs.

For additional information on resource file configuration, refer to the .NET Framework 2.0 Software Development Toolkit (SDK) and search for Resources in RESX File Format. The SDK can be found on the Microsoft Download Center at *http://www.microsoft.com/downloads/details.aspx?displaylang=en&FamilyID=FE6F2099-B7B4-4F47-A244-C96D69C35DEC.*

Administering Feature Scope

There are two scope considerations when creating and deploying Features. The first consideration is the scope of the Feature itself—that is, whether the Feature is made available to a server farm, Web application, site collection, or site (or Web). The second consideration includes any elements you will use in the Feature and the scope of those elements. For instance, some elements, such as a Content Type element, can only be used in a site-scoped Feature whereas other elements, such as a Custom Action element, can be used across all Feature scopes..

Feature scope is defined in the Feature.xml file, using the *Scope* attribute. Once a Feature is installed, the SharePoint Server 2007 administrative user interface includes the ability to administer Features for given scopes, as shown in Table 26-3. This includes the ability to activate and deactivate Features.

Table 26-3 Administering Features Through the User Interface

Feature scope	Description	Administration UI path
Farm (denoted by *Farm*)	Specific to farm-level administrative tasks, such as application management. Farm-level Features are activated by default.	SharePoint Central Administration, Operations, Global Configuration, Manage Farm Features
Web Application (denoted by *WebApplication*)	Specific to Web application or virtual server requirements, such as Search	SharePoint Central Administration, Application Management, SharePoint Web Application Management, Manage Web Application Features
Site Collection (denoted by *Site*)	Specifies items that relate to an entire site collection, such as Web Parts or content types	Parent (or root) site of site collection, Site Settings, Site Collection Administration, Site Collection Features
Web or Site (denoted by *Web*)	Items that are specific to individual Web sites, such as list templates	Site, Site Settings, Site Administration, Site Features

Activation and deactivation of Features is not limited to the administrative user interface. You can also use Feature activation and deactivation through the stsadm.exe command-line tool, through the SharePoint object model, and by deploying the Feature as part of a site definition. The "Deploying Features" section of this chapter describes the deployment options. You will learn how to deploy a Feature as part of a site definition in the "Including Features in Site Definitions" section.

Figure 26-2 shows Features scoped at the farm level and visible in the administrative user interface page that can be activated and deactivated.

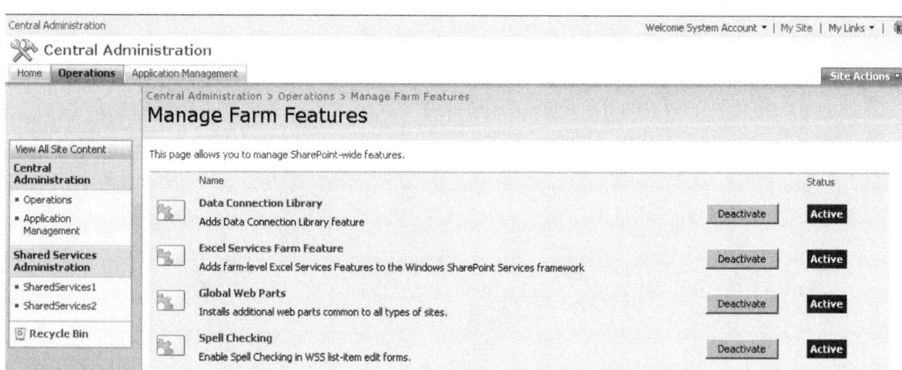

Figure 26-2 Farm-scoped Features shown in the administrative user interface

Note If a Feature is Hidden, it will not be visible in the administrative user interface. Farm-scoped Features, when installed, are activated by default.

Element Scoping

Not all elements are available at all scope levels. For example, the Custom Action element, which defines actions such as a link or additional toolbar button, is available at all Feature scope levels, whereas the Content Type element is available only within the scope of a site collection. A list of elements and respective scope allocation can be found in Table 26-4, and additional information concerning element scopes can be found in the Windows SharePoint Services 3.0 Software Development Kit on the Microsoft Download Center.

In addition, Table 26-4 lists elements available for a given Feature scope. For example, to deploy Content Types as part of your Feature, you need to scope your Feature for a site collection by using the *Scope* attribute in the Feature.xml file because deploying Content Types to a Web-scoped Feature is not supported. You would set the attribute as Scope="site", where *site* is the site collection.

Table 26-4 Element Scoping

Scope	Element
Farm	Control
	Custom Action
	Custom Action Group
	Document Converter
	Feature/Site Template Association
	Hide Custom Action
Web Application	Control
	Custom Action
	Custom Action Group
	Document Converter
	Feature/Site Template Association
	Hide Custom Action

Table 26-4 Element Scoping

Scope	Element
Site Collection	Content Type
	Content Type Binding
	Control
	Custom Action
	Custom Action Group
	Feature/Site Template Association
	Field
	Hide Custom Action
	List Instance
	Module
	Workflow
Web or Site	Content Type Binding
	Control
	Custom Action
	Custom Action Group
	Feature/Site Template Association
	Hide Custom Action
	List Instance
	List Template
	Module
	Receiver

An Example of a Site Collection-Scoped Feature

Here is an example of adding a simple site column to a site using a Feature. Both the Feature.xml and Elements.xml files are included. The Feature must be scoped to Site, as in a site collection, because this is the only scope to which you can deploy the Field element that is included in the associated Elements.xml file.

Feature.xml File

```
<?xml version="1.0" encoding="utf-8" ?>
<Feature xmlns="http://schemas.microsoft.com/sharepoint/"

  Id ="EA86643E-A8AF-4fa3-922A-94BF38C3E6B5"
  Title="Project Vision Field"
  Description =" A Field for Project Vision."
  Scope="Site">
  <ElementManifests>
    <ElementManifest Location="Elements.xml" />
  </ElementManifests>
</Feature>
```

Elements.xml File

```
<Elements xmlns="http://schemas.microsoft.com/sharepoint/">
  <Field ID="{32C5D7BB-BA83-48cc-BA7E-8600A5B669E0}"
   DisplayName="Project Vision"
   Type="Text"
   Required ="TRUE"
   Name="ProjectVision"
   RowOrdinal="0"
   ReadOnly="FALSE"
   Group="Project Field" />
</Elements>
```

Creating Features in Visual Studio 2005

Aside from the obvious development advantages, Visual Studio 2005 is the ideal environment for creating and developing Features. In creating the Feature.xml and element files, you can take advantage of the Visual Studio IntelliSense feature through associating the Windows SharePoint Services schema, as shown in Figure 26-3, or you can encompass your Feature in a Project Class Library and integrate other related files into your solution, such as a Feature event class.

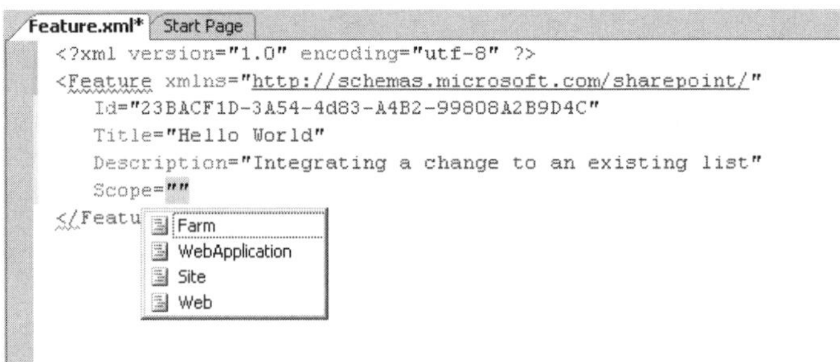

Figure 26-3 Visual Studio 2005 and IntelliSense association with Windows SharePoint Services schema

In this section, you'll learn how you can leverage the Visual Studio 2005 environment to create your Features, including adding the Windows SharePoint Services schema and uniquely defining your Feature using a GUID. You'll also include Feature elements to make changes to the SharePoint toolbar and menu items.

In the "Creating an Event Handler Feature" section of this chapter, you'll broaden your Visual Studio experience to include the SharePoint assembly reference and build an event handler using the SharePoint object model.

Creating the Project Class Library

To create your Feature, you create a Project Class Library, Visual Studio solution, where you can create your Feature folders hierarchy and later integrate some additional files and code into the same solution to add further functionality such as an event handler.

On the CD Throughout this chapter, coding examples other than XML are coded using C#. Coding examples, including Feature and element files, are included on the book's companion CD in the \Code\Chapter 26 folder.

To create your Visual Studio environment, complete the following steps:

1. Launch Visual Studio 2005 and click File, New Project.
2. Select the Visual C# Windows Project And Class Library template, and give the project a name, such as **SharePoint**, and identify a location to which to save your project, such as **[drive]\foldername**. Click OK.
3. In the Solution Explorer window, in your Visual Studio environment, right-click the project name, point to Add on the shortcut menu, and then select New Folder. Rename the folder to **Features**.
4. Under the Features folder, create a new folder and name it **LinkingExample**.

   This is where you add the Feature.xml and Feature element files you'll create as part of the examples in this section. Creating the Features folder hierarchy in Visual Studio categorizes your Features, allows you to add multiple Features to the one solution, and helps simplify the deployment process by having the Features and associated files already contained in folders that get copied to the Features directory on the Web front-end server.

Note SharePoint Server 2007 supports only low-order ASCII characters, and no spaces, for Feature folder and file names.

Creating the Feature.xml File

Create the Feature.xml file to define the scope of your Feature, and include references to the supporting Feature elements files. You will scope the Feature for Web, which means the Feature can be deployed and activated on all Web sites created on your server.

To create the Feature.xml file, complete the following steps:

1. Right-click the new Feature folder named LinkingExample, click Add, and then click New Item to open the Add New Item dialog box.
2. Under Visual Studio Installed Templates, click XML File.

3. In the Name text box, type **Feature.xml** and click the Add button to add the Feature.xml file under your LinkingExample folder.

You have created the basis from which to build your Feature. Next, you'll associate the SharePoint schema XML with the Feature.xml file so that you can use the IntelliSense feature to define the attributes for the Feature.

Associating Schema to a Feature

Associating the SharePoint schema to the .xml file allows you to use the IntelliSense feature in Visual Studio to add the attributes to your Feature.xml file. This process eliminates the need to manually enter each attribute. To associate the schema to your XML file, complete the following steps:

1. Double-click the newly created Feature.xml file to open it. Position your cursor in the Feature.xml file to activate the Properties window in Visual Studio.
2. In the Properties window of your Visual Studio solution, locate the Schemas field and click the Directory Path Expander to launch the XSD Schemas Locator dialog box.
3. In the XSD Schema dialog box, click the Add button.
4. In the Open XSD Schema dialog box, browse to the following path:

   %SystemDrive%\Program Files\Common Files\Microsoft Shared
   \web server extensions\12\TEMPLATE\XML

5. Click the wss.xsd file and then click Open to include the wss.xsd file in your Feature.xml file, which should now look like Figure 26-4, where the wss.xsd file is highlighted and selected. Click the OK button.

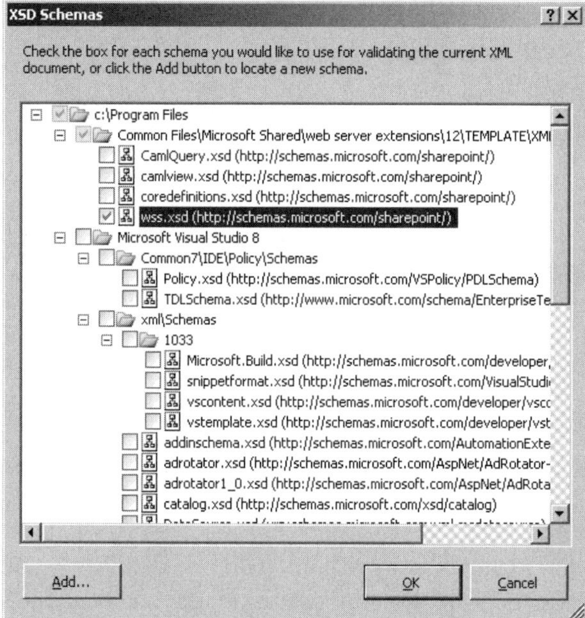

Figure 26-4 Adding the SharePoint schema to the Visual Studio .xml file

6. Verify that the schema file has been included in your Feature.xml file by ensuring that the path to the schema is included next to the Schemas option in the Properties window. Also verify that IntelliSense is active in your Feature.xml file.

7. Position your cursor at the top of your Feature.xml file and, using your keyboard, click the < key. If the SharePoint schema has been successfully added, you see a drop-down list with several options, including Feature, as shown in Figure 26-5.

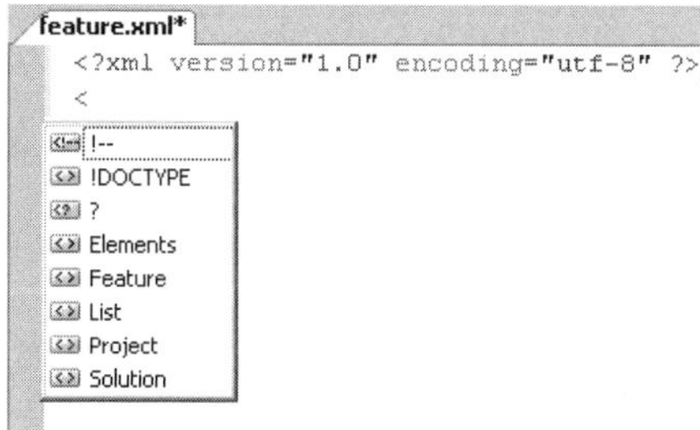

Figure 26-5 IntelliSense activated showing Feature selection

8. In the drop-down list, double-click Feature to instantiate and declare the Feature namespace.

9. Press Enter to start a new line, and then press your space bar to activate the IntelliSense drop-down list and access the Feature attributes.

10. On the drop-down list, double-click Id to add it to the Feature.xml file. As shown in Figure 26-6, this is the *Id* attribute for the GUID that will uniquely identify the Feature for your SharePoint deployment.

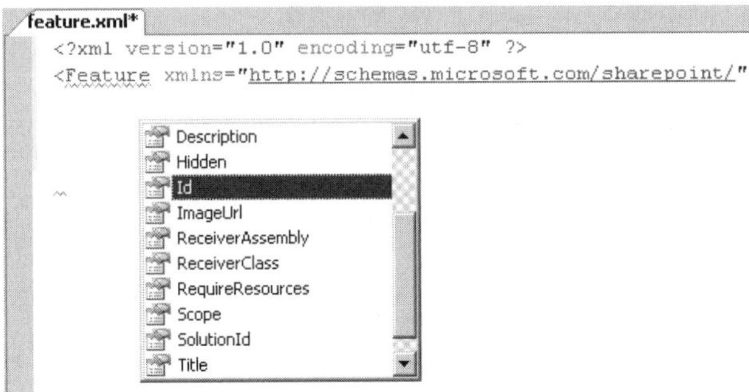

Figure 26-6 IntelliSense showing the Id attribute in a selection list

Generating the Feature GUID

Each Feature.xml file is uniquely identified using a globally unique identifier (GUID), formatted in Registry format. To add a GUID to your Feature.xml file, complete the following steps:

1. Open the Create GUID dialog box by using one of the following methods:
   - From the Visual Studio Tools menu, select Create GUID.
   - Browse to the Guidgen.exe file available in the Visual Studio Tools folder, and double-click the file. (This file is typically located in *%SystemDrive%*:\Program Files\Microsoft Visual Studio 8\Common7\Tools\guidgen.exe.)
2. Select the Registry Format option and then click the New GUID button to generate a GUID, as shown in Figure 26-7.

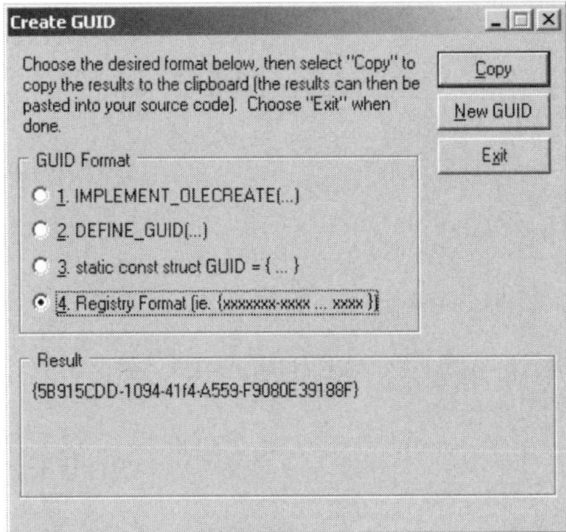

Figure 26-7 GUID generation

3. Still in the GUID dialog box, click the Copy button to copy the GUID and then paste it into your Feature.xml file next to the Feature *Id* attribute. Remove the braces from the GUID, and enclose the GUID in quotation marks, such as Id="GUID".

Note If the GUID Creation option does not appear on your Visual Studio 2005 Tools menu, you need to add the tool. Select External Tools from the Tools menu, type **Create GUID** in the Title box, and then browse to the Visual Studio tools location in the Command box. For example, browse to

%SystemDrive%\Program Files\Microsoft Visual Studio 8\Common7\Tools \guidgen.exe

Next, click Open, and then click OK. You should now have the Create GUID option available on your Tools menu.

Defining the Feature Scope and Other Feature Attributes

Once you've created your Feature.xml file and assigned the GUID to the Feature Id attribute, as described in the previous section, you can now proceed to populate the remaining attributes of the Feature.xml file, including the Feature scope. In this case, you will scope the Feature for Web, which means the Feature can be activated on all Web sites created on your server.

To add the Feature scope Web, position your cursor on a new line of your Feature.xml file and type the word Scope followed by the '=' sign. Following the '=' sign, you could either type in "Web" or select Web from the Visual Studio IntelliSense prompt. If you are not seeing IntelliSense prompts as you type, then go back to the section "Associating Schema to a Feature".

Populate the remaining attributes, including the Title for the Feature which will identify the Feature in the Site Features administrative page. This Feature will be entitled Toolbar and Menu Links. The Hidden attribute will be set to FALSE which means that when the Feature is installed, it will be visible on the Site Features administrative page. Your completed Feature.xml file should resemble that shown in Figure 26-8. Save the Feature.xml file.

```
Feature.xml*
<?xml version="1.0" encoding="utf-8" ?>
<Feature xmlns="http://schemas.microsoft.com/sharepoint/"

  Id="23BACF1D-3A54-4d83-A4B2-99808A2B9D4C"
  Title="Toolbar and Menu Links"
  Description="Adding links to toolbar and menu"
  Scope="Web"
  Hidden="FALSE"
  AlwaysForceInstall="TRUE">
 <ElementManifests>
   <ElementManifest Location="" />
   <ElementManifest Location="" />
 </ElementManifests>

</Feature>
```

Figure 26-8 Feature.xml file

At this point, leave the *<ElementManifests>* attributes as null values—that is, *<Element-Manifest Location="">*. This section explains how to create and configure two element files and then revisit the Feature.xml file to populate the ElementManifest Location with the location and names of the element files.

> **Note** If the *<AlwaysForceInstall>* attribute is set to True, you do not need to add the *–force* parameter to the stsadm.exe command line each time the Feature is updated and re-installed on the SharePoint server. If you do not want the Feature to be forcibly re-installed in the background during redeployments, remove this attribute or set it to False.

Creating Feature Element Files

With relative ease, you can add simple changes to your sites using Features and elements. In this section, you'll create two element files for your Feature in order to add custom toolbar and menu items to your site. The first element file, which we will name Toolbar.xml, will include a Site Help button on the edit toolbar of the document library forms page. The second file will demonstrate how to include an additional menu item in the SharePoint Site Action menu using an element file that we will name Menu.xml.

Adding Toolbar Items

You can use the <CustomAction> element to add a button to the Edit toolbar on the Document Library Form page within your site. To create the Toolbar.xml file, complete the following steps:

1. Create the element file by right-clicking the Feature folder (in this example, LinkingExample), point to Add, and select New Item.

2. In the Add New Item dialog box under the Visual Studio installed templates, click XML File and, in the Name box, type **Toolbar.xml**.
3. Click Add to add the Toolbar.xml file to your Feature and open the file ready for editing.
4. Position your cursor at the top of the Toolbar.xml file to activate the Properties window in Visual Studio. Browse to the Schemas field, and click the Directory Path Expander to launch the XSD Schemas locator dialog box.
5. In the XSD Schema dialog box, click the Add button.
6. In the Open XSD Schema dialog box, browse to the following path:

   %SystemDrive%\Program Files\Common Files\Microsoft Shared
   \web server extensions\12\TEMPLATE\XML

   > **Note** If you previously added the schema to the Feature.xml file in the same project, the wss.xsd file is already included in the XSD Schemas dialog box. You do not need to click Add and browse to the path containing the file.

7. Click the wss.xsd file, and then click Open to include the wss.xsd file in your Feature.xml file. Click the OK button.
8. Add the Elements and Custom Action elements and the element attributes, as shown in Figure 26-9, and save the file. This example includes a URL reference to the Mysite.aspx page in the SharePoint _layouts directory so that when a user clicks the Custom button on the Edit toolbar the user is directed to his My Site. But you can include links to other locations here, including internal and external links.

```
Toolbar.xml
<?xml version="1.0" encoding="utf-8" ?>
<Elements xmlns="http://schemas.microsoft.com/sharepoint/">
  <CustomAction Title="My Site"
     Sequence="10"
     RegistrationType="List"
     RegistrationId="101"
     Location="EditFormToolbar"
     Id="MySite Toolbar">
    <UrlAction Url="/_layouts/mysite.aspx" />
  </CustomAction>
</Elements>
```

Figure 26-9 Toolbar.xml file

> **Note** The *Title* attribute "Toolbar and Menu Links" is the name that will be displayed on the Site Features administrative page where you will be able to activate and deactivate the Feature.

Adding a Menu Item

You can create an additional menu item on the SharePoint Site Actions menu that displays the menu item User Guide. We will use the <Module> element to include an .aspx file as part of our Feature, and we will use the <CustomAction> element to display the additional menu item in the Site Actions menu using the URL to the .aspx file.

Creating the Menu File

To create the Menu.xml file and associated .aspx file, complete the following steps:

1. Right-click the LinkingExample Feature folder, point to Add, and select New Item to open the Add New Item dialog box.
2. Under Visual Studio Installed Templates, click XML File, and type **Menu.xml** in the Name box.
3. Click Add to add the Menu.xml file to your Feature folder, and open it ready for editing.
4. Follow the steps in the previous example to add the SharePoint schema reference to Menu.xml. Then add the <Elements>, <Module>, and <CustomAction> elements, and populate the attributes for each element as shown in Figure 26-10. Save the Menu.xml file.

Menu.xml

```
<?xml version="1.0" encoding="utf-8" ?>
<Elements xmlns="http://schemas.microsoft.com/sharepoint/">
  <Module
    Name=""
    Path=""
    Url="">
    <File
      Url="Help.aspx"
      Type="Ghostable"
      IgnoreIfAlreadyExists="FALSE">
    </File>
  </Module>
  <CustomAction
    Id="SiteActionsToolbar"
    GroupId="SiteActions"
    Location="Microsoft.SharePoint.StandardMenu"
    Sequence="1000"
    Title="User Guide"
    Description="A how to guide to help users understand how to use the features on
    <UrlAction Url="Help.aspx"/>
  </CustomAction>
</Elements>
```

Figure 26-10 Menu.xml file

Linking to a New Menu Item

You need to create the .aspx file that you'll provision as part of your Feature. You will link to this file from the new User Guide link on the Site Actions drop-down menu.

1. Right-click the LinkingExample Feature folder, point to Add, and then select New Item to open the Add New Item dialog box.

2. Under Visual Studio Installed Templates, click Text File, and type **Help.aspx** in the Name box. (Make sure you include the .aspx extension as part of the file name.) Then click Add.

3. In the open Help.aspx file, add some content. In keeping with ASP.NET 2.0 master pages, you could add a master page reference into the page to maintain consistency between your custom page and the default SharePoint pages. To do this, add the following directive to the top of the ASPX page, as shown in Figure 26-11:

```
<%@ Page Language ="C#" MasterPageFile="~masterurl\default.master" %>
```

```
Help.aspx*
Server Objects & Events        (No Events)
<%@ Page Language="C#" MasterPageFile="~masterurl\default.master" %>

<asp:Content ContentPlaceHolderID="PlaceHolderMain" runat="server" >

<h2>Hello, welcome to the Site User Guide</h2>

<b>Table of contents</b>
```

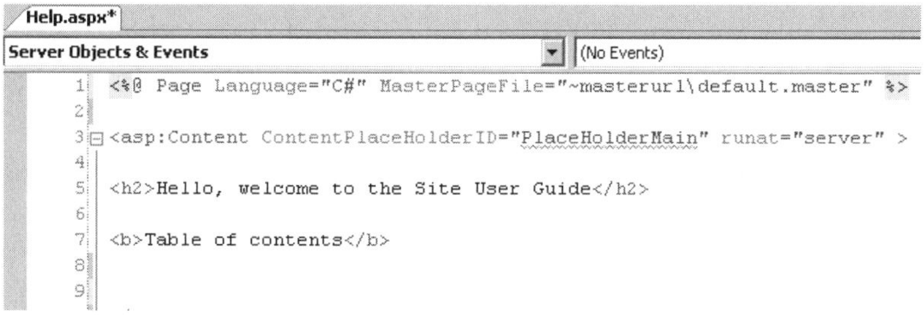

Figure 26-11 Help.aspx page format

Adding Element Files to the Feature.xml File

Now that you've created the element files for the Feature, you'll go back and reference those files in the Feature.xml file, using the <ElementManifests> attribute as explained next.

1. Open the Feature.xml file, and include the two element files you just created (Toolbar.xml and Menu.xml) in the <ElementManifest> Location attribute, for example:

```
<ElementManifests>
<ElementManifest Location="Menu.xml" />
<ElementManifest Location="Toolbar.xml" />
<ElementManifests>
```

2. Save the Feature.xml file, and close the Toolbar.xml, Menu.xml, and Help.aspx files if they are still open.

Installing and Activating a Feature

You'll install and activate the LinkingExample Feature you created. For a comprehensive explanation of the Feature deployment options, see the "Deploying Features" section.

To install and activate a Feature, complete the following steps:

1. Using Windows Explorer, navigate to the LinkingExample folder containing the Feature.xml, Toolbar.xml, Menu.xml, and Help.aspx files. Copy the folder, and paste it in the Features directory:

   %SystemDrive%\Program Files\Common Files\Microsoft Shared
   \web server extensions\12\TEMPLATE\FEATURES

2. Open your Windows command-line tool, and browse to the stsadm.exe command-line tool, which is located at

   %SystemDrive%\Program Files\Common Files\Microsoft Shared
   \web server extensions\12\BIN

3. Type the following command:

   ```
   stsadm.exe -o installfeature -name LinkingExample
   ```

4. Open your SharePoint Web site, and browse to the Site Settings page. (Remember that the Feature is scoped for "Web" so that it will be available for activation on your Web sites.)

5. On the Site Settings page, under Site Administration, click Site Features.

   You'll see the Feature in the list as Toolbar And Menu links, which is determined by its *Title* attribute. By default, the Feature status is set to Inactive, as shown in Figure 26-12. Note that the order in which the Features are listed on the Site Features page is alphabetical, based on Feature Title.

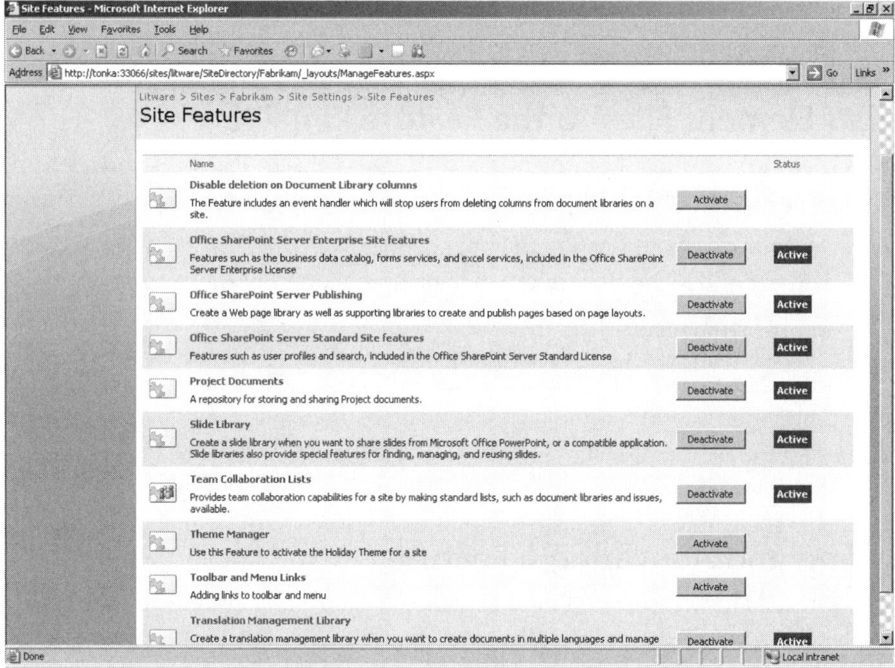

Figure 26-12 Site Features page showing the inactive Toolbar And Menu Links Feature

6. Click the Activate button to activate the Toolbar And Menu Links (LinkingExample) Feature.

7. By activating the Feature, the custom toolbar button is included on the document library Edit toolbar and the custom menu item is included on the Site Actions menu. Figure 26-13 shows the My Site custom toolbar button; Figure 26-14 shows the User Guide custom menu item.

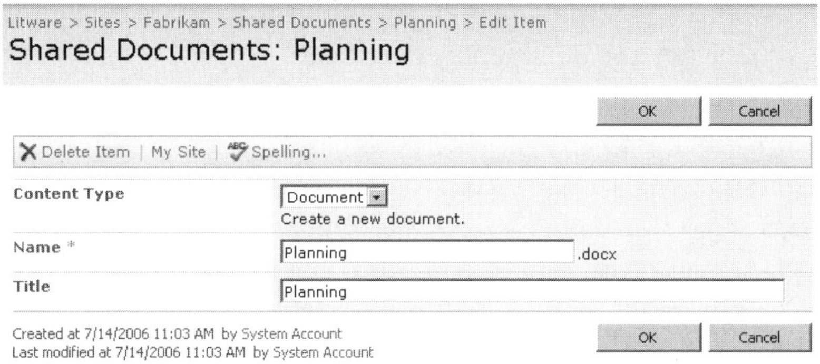

Litware > Sites > Fabrikam > Shared Documents > Planning > Edit Item
Shared Documents: Planning
OK Cancel
Delete Item | My Site | Spelling...
Content Type Document
Create a new document.
Name * Planning .docx
Title Planning
Created at 7/14/2006 11:03 AM by System Account
Last modified at 7/14/2006 11:03 AM by System Account
OK Cancel

Figure 26-13 Toolbar button shown when the Tool And Menu Links Feature is activated

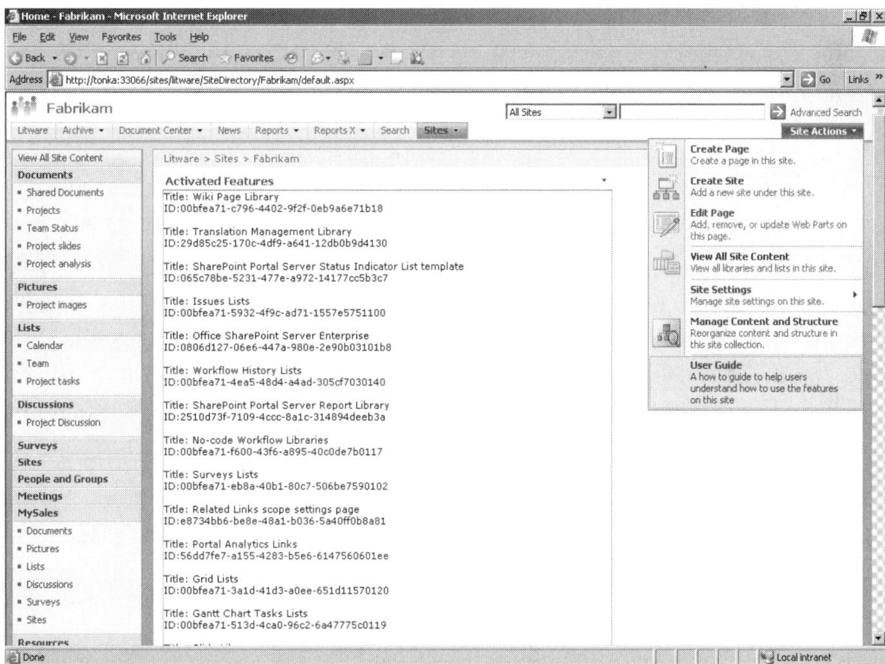

Figure 26-14 Menu item shown when the Tool And Menu Links Feature is activated

By using the <Module> element in the Menu.xml file, the Feature also includes the custom Help.aspx file, shown in Figure 26-15. Clicking the custom menu item, User Guide, in the drop-down Site Actions menu will redirect the user to the Help.aspx page. The redirection is a result of the <UrlAction> attribute of the <CustomAction> element in the Menu.xml file.

Figure 26-15 Help.aspx page shown in the user interface

Deploying Features

Once you've created your custom Feature and copied the Feature into the Features directory on your Web front-end server, you need to install that Feature before you can use it on your SharePoint sites. Installing a Feature is a two-step process. It includes both installing the Feature on the Web front-end server and activating the Feature to a given scope. However, developing and working with Features also necessitates removal or reinstallation of Features, or both, invoking the need to deactivate and uninstall Features.

This section looks at the methods for installing, activating, deactivating, and uninstalling Features, specifically by using the stsadm.exe command-line tool and the administrative user interface. Information about manipulating Feature deployment using the SharePoint object model can be found in the Windows SharePoint Services 3.0 SDK. Information on deploying Features via SharePoint site definitions is included in the "Including Features in Site Definitions" section of this chapter. Table 26-5 summarizes the methods for managing the Feature life cycle.

Table 26-5 Methods for Managing Feature Deployment and Life Cycle

Function	Methods
Install Feature	■ Stsadm.exe command-line tool ■ SharePoint Object Model
Activate Feature	■ Stsadm.exe command-line tool ■ Administrative User Interface ■ SharePoint Object Model ■ SharePoint Site Definition

Table 26-5 **Methods for Managing Feature Deployment and Life Cycle**

Function	Methods
Deactivate Feature	■ Stsadm.exe command-line tool ■ Administrative User Interface ■ SharePoint Object Model
Uninstall Feature	■ Stsadm.exe command-line tool ■ SharePoint Object Model

Using Stsadm.exe and Feature Commands

Features can be installed and managed using the stsadm.exe command-line tool, which is located at the following path:

%SystemDrive%\Program Files\Common Files\Microsoft Shared
\Web server extensions\12\BIN

For example, back in the "Installing and Activating a Feature" section, you installed the LinkingExample Feature by typing the stsadm.exe –o installfeature –name LinkingExample command at your Windows command prompt. Figure 26-16 shows the resultant output in the command window, which includes the parameters for installing a Feature using the command-line tool. In this case, the optional *-force* parameter is included in the command line because the Feature is being installed for a second time. The -force parameter is used where you have updated a Feature and then need to redeploy that Feature to push updates to existing instances of that Feature already activated throughout sites.

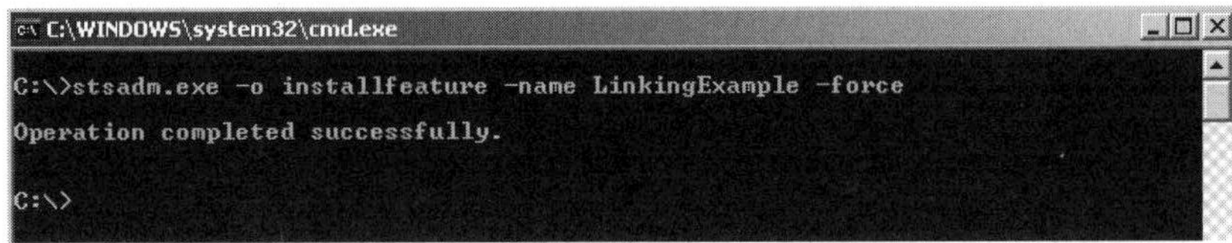

Figure 26-16 Stsadm.exe command to reinstall the LinkingExample Feature

More Info See the "Create System Path to stsadm.exe Command-Line Tool" sidebar to create a shortcut for accessing the stsadm.exe tool.

Table 26-6 summarizes the Feature commands available using the stsadm.exe command-line tool. The syntax for each command will be demonstrated in the upcoming sections. You can obtain the syntax for each command by using the stsadm.exe help command. For instance, to discover the syntax for the Activatefeature command, type in **stsadm.exe –help activatefeature** at your Windows command prompt then press the return key on your keyboard.

Table 26-6 Feature Stsadm.exe Commands

Command	Description
Installfeature	Installs the Feature to the specified scope, such as Farm or Web.
Activatefeature	Activates the Feature for the specified scope, or to a specific Web using the *–url* parameter.
Deactivatefeature	Deactivates a Feature from the existing scope.
Uninstallfeature	Completely removes the Feature from the specified scope.
Scanforfeatures	Displays a list of Features currently installed on the server.

The scanforfeatures command returns a list of installed Features on the Web front-end server, regardless of scope. For example, typing the stadam.exe –o scanforfeatures command returns a complete list of installed Features for the farm. This command also returns any failed Feature installations, including the name of the failed Feature, such as in the following command output:

```
Failed feature installations <Check the logs for more details>:
The Feature at 'folder\feature.xml' is corrupt.  Please re-install the Feature.
```

You can also save the scanforfeatures output to a text file, such as by specifying a text file to which to save the results to. For example, type the stsadm.exe –o scanforfeatures > filename.txt command to do this.

Real World Create System Path to Stsadm.exe Command-Line Tool

You can access the stsadm.exe command from any command prompt location on your server. You can also include a direct path to your stsadm.exe command by creating a system path. To do this, complete the following steps:

1. Click Start and then click Control Panel.
2. In the Control Panel window, double-click System.
3. In the System Properties dialog box, click the Advanced tab.
4. On the Advanced tab, click the Environmental Variables button.
5. In the System Variables section of the Environmental Variables window, browse to the Path Variable and click Edit.
6. In the Variable value box, scroll to the last entry, add a semi colon (;), and then add the path to the stsadm.exe command-line tool as follows:

   %SystemDrive%\Program Files\Common Files\Microsoft Shared
   \web server extensions\12\BIN

7. Click OK to save the new path, and then click OK on the Environmental Variables dialog box to save your changes. Click OK on the System Properties tab to exit.

You can now enter the stsadm.exe command prompt location on your server.

Permissions for Deploying Features

A server administrator is responsible for installing and uninstalling Features on the Web front-end server, using the stsadm.exe command-line tool. After Features are installed, they can be activated or deactivated at the given scope. Table 26-7 summarizes the required permissions for activating and deactivating Features through the administrative user interface.

Table 26-7 Permissions to Activate and Deactivate Features

Feature scope	Permission/role
Farm	Farm Administrator
Web Application	Farm Administrator
Site Collection	Site Collection Administrator
Web	Site Collection Administrator

Adding Feature Files to a Web Server File Location

After you've created your Feature and before you install it, you need to copy the folder containing your Feature to the Features directory on your Web front-end server, which can be found at the following location:

%SystemDrive%\Program Files\Common Files\Microsoft Shared
\web server extensions\12\TEMPLATE\FEATURES

Ensure that you include any files and subfolders belonging to a Feature as part of that parent folder, such as any pages or elements files being provisioned as part of the Feature. When you install the Feature using the *–name* parameter in the stsadm.exe command-line tool, SharePoint looks for the Feature in the Features directory by default.

Important There's a common scenario you might want to avoid. If, when using Windows Explorer,you create a new folder in the Features directory the new folder may not have inherited permissions. If you subsequently deploy a Feature in that new folder and permissions haven't correctly propagated, some SharePoint pages, such as site settings or list view pages, will throw an exception. To fix this problem, right-click the new folder, click Properties, click Security, and then click Advanced. On the Permissions tab, select the option "*Allow Inheritable Permissions from the parent to propagate to this object and all child objects. Include these with entries explicitly defined here*". Click OK. Alternatively, you can avoid this problem by creating the new folder at the command prompt by using the md command.

Installing Features

Before you can activate a Feature, you must install the Feature. To install the Feature using the stsadm.exe command-line tool, complete the following steps:

1. Launch the Windows command line, and browse to the location of the stsadm.exe command-line tool (if you haven't already created a system path for it).
2. Type the following command:

   ```
   stsadm.exe -o installfeature -name LinkingExample
   ```

   OR

   ```
   stsadm.exe -o installfeature -filename featurefolder\feature.xml
   ```

   If you are re-installing a Feature—for example, to include some changes or additional functionality—you need to include the *-force* parameter at the end of the command like this:

   ```
   stsadm.exe -o installfeature -name LinkingExample -force
   ```

Be sure to do an IISRESET after running this command.

For more information about re-installing and updating Features, see the "Updating an Existing Feature" section in this chapter.

Activating Features

In addition to installing a Feature, you must activate a Feature before it can be used in the target scope, such as Web or Site. By default, Features are set to a status of deactivated following installation. The one exception occurs when a Feature is deployed as part of a site definition, where it will be activated when a site is provisioned based on the site definition containing the Feature.

To activate Features using the stsadm.exe command-line tool, complete the following steps:

1. Launch the Windows command line, and browse to the location of the stsadm.exe command line tool (if you haven't already created a system path for it).
2. Type the following command:

   ```
   stsadm.exe -o activatefeature -name LinkingExample -url targetsite
   ```

> **Note** Farm-scoped Features are activated by default when installed.

To activate a Web-scoped Feature through the administrative user interface, complete the following steps:

1. Browse to the Web (or site) where you want to activate the Feature, and browse to the Site Settings page—for example, *http://server/sites/site/_layouts/settings.aspx*.
2. Under the Site Administration section on the Site Settings page, click the Site Features link.
3. On the Site Features page, locate the Feature you want to activate and click the Activate button in the Status column to activate the Feature.

For example, in Figure 26-17 the LinkingExample Feature has been activated on the Fabrikam site, denoted by the Name of Toolbar And Menu Links and the display of the Active Status button alongside the Feature.

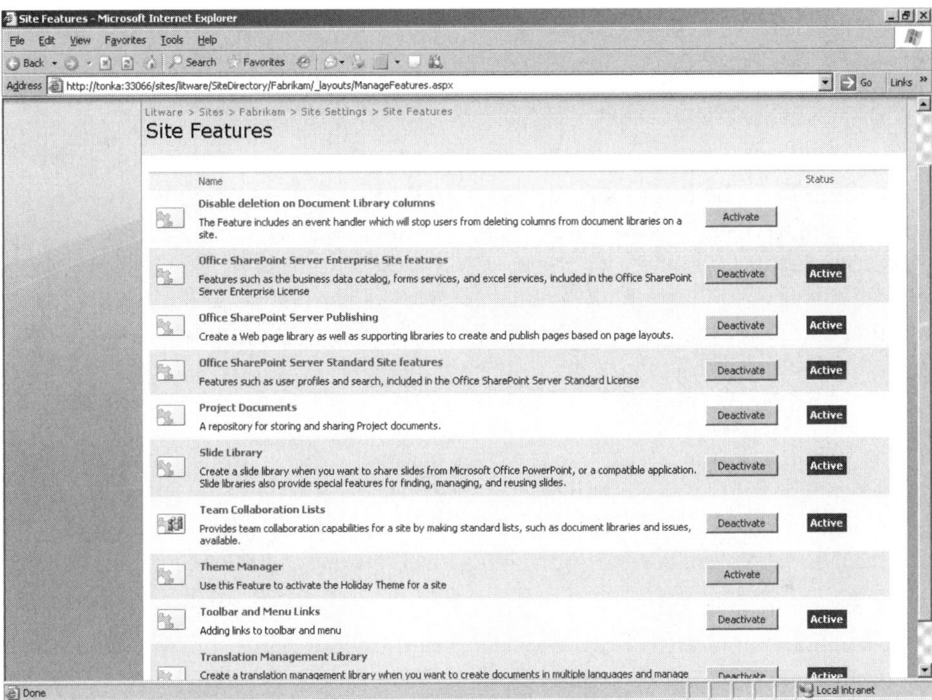

Figure 26-17 Feature activation through the administrative user interface

Features can also be activated through site definitions. This method is explained in the "Including Features in Site Definitions" section of this chapter.

Using Activation Dependencies and Scopes

Features can include *activation dependencies* on other Features, such as a Feature B being activated when Feature A is activated. Feature activation dependencies provide a means to streamline Feature activation throughout your SharePoint sites. Activation dependencies are included in the Feature.xml file by the <ActivationDependencies> attribute, such as:

```
<ActivationDependencies>
 <ActivationDependency FeatureId="GUID" /> <!-- name of Feature -->
</ActivationDependencies>
```

A Default Feature Activation Dependency

One example of a default Feature activation dependency is the Announcements List Feature, which is activated when the Team Collaboration Feature is activated. Open the Team Collaboration Feature Feature.xml file, which can be found at the following location:

%SystemDrive%\Program Files\Common Files\Microsoft Shared \web server extensions\12\TEMPLATE\FEATURES\TeamCollab

You should be able to see that there are a number of Features dependent on activation of the Team Collaboration Feature. The Team Collaboration Feature itself is automatically activated when new sites are provisioned from the STS site definition, such as the Team Site, where it is included as part of that site definition. If you deactivated the Team Collaboration Feature, you would also deactivate the dependent Features. See the "Including Features in Site Definitions" section to learn about enabling Feature activation through site definitions.

Hidden features are Features that have the *Hidden* attribute set to True in the Features.xml file. A dependent Feature, or a Feature depending on another Feature for activation, can be either hidden or visible if it is in the same scope as that Feature. However, a Feature, such as the Team Collaboration Feature, sponsoring other Feature activations cannot be hidden.

You can have *cross-scope* Feature activation dependencies, such as a Web-scoped Feature that is dependent on a site collection-scoped Feature. However, there are some general rules regarding cross-scope Feature activations. For example, when a Web-scoped Feature is dependent on activation of a site collection-scoped Feature, the Web-scoped Feature cannot be hidden. For details concerning Feature activation dependency cross-scope rules, see the Windows SharePoint Services 3.0 Software Development Kit.

Deploying Features by Using Solutions

In SharePoint Server 2007, Solutions are used to package and deploy Features, site definitions, Web Parts, template files, assemblies, and Code Access Security (CAS) policies to SharePoint Web front-end servers. Solutions supersede the wppackage deployment tool used in Windows SharePoint Services 2.0, and they eliminate manual deployment methods, such as the need to manually copy files and modify the Web.config files on Web front-end servers.

On the CD The sample Solution files used in this section are included on the book's CD in the \Code\Chapter 26 folder. This includes the Manifest.xml file, SharePointFeatures.DDF file, and Package folder, which includes the SharePointAC.wsp file.

Steps for Creating a Solution Package

The steps for creating a Solution package for deploying Features are as follows:

1. Create Manifest.xml file as part of the Visual Studio project containing the Features and associated files to be included in the Solution package.
2. Create the .ddf file as part of that same project. (The .ddf file contains information to compress files into a CAB file.)
3. Download and extract the Microsoft Cabinet Software Development Kit from *http://support.microsoft.com/kb/310618/en-us.*
4. In the Windows command line, run Makecab.exe on the .ddf file to generate a .wsp file. Include the path to the Makecab.exe file, or copy the Makecab.exe file into the same directory containing the Visual Studio project files, which includes the Manifest.xml and .ddf file.
5. Use the stsadm.exe command-line tool to add your .wsp file into the SharePoint Solution store.
6. Deploy the Solution package by using the stsadm.exe command-line tool, the SharePoint Solution Management administrative page, or the object model.

Creating the Manifest.xml File

To create the Manifest.xml file, complete the following steps:

1. Add a new file to the project containing your Features, and name the file Manifest.xml.
2. In the Manifest.xml file, include a reference to the SharePoint schema. This activates the IntelliSense feature and enables access to the Solution schema.
3. Populate the Manifest.xml file to include the Features you want to deploy as part of the Solution package. In the following example, two Features from the SharePoint project have been included as well as the project assembly reference, which is required for the event handler that is part of the SiteColumnHandler Feature:

```
<?xml version="1.0" encoding="utf-8" ?>
<Solution SolutionId="{C68719D0-18B7-4bf1-9E8B-B967BDDEF389}"
  xmlns=http://schemas.microsoft.com/sharepoint/>
  <FeatureManifests>
    <FeatureManifest Location="LinkingExample\Feature.xml"/>
    <FeatureManifest Location="SiteColumnHandler\Feature.xml"/>
  </FeatureManifests>
```

```
    <Assemblies>
      <Assembly DeploymentTarget="GlobalAssemblyCache"
            Location="SharePoint.dll">
        <SafeControls>
          <SafeControl
            Assembly="SharePoint, Version=1.0.0.0, Culture=neutral,
PublicKeyToken=ad7f6a147689147c"
            Namespace="SharePoint"
            TypeName="*" Safe="True" />
        </SafeControls>
      </Assembly>
    </Assemblies>
  </Solution>
```

Note You need to generate a GUID for your Solution Manifest file. Use the Guidgen.exe tool to do this. Unlike what you did for the GUID in the Feature.xml file, this time leave the surrounding braces intact.

Creating the Diamond Directive File (.ddf)

To create the Diamond Directive file, add a new file to the same project containing the Manifest.xml file and give it the .ddf extension–for example, SharePointFeatures.ddf. The following example .ddf file includes references to the Manifest.xml file, as well as the assembly and Features to be included as part of the CAB, and it provides Makecab.exe with the directives to compress the files into the CAB:

```
;*** SharePoint Features Example MakeCAB Directive file
;
.OPTION EXPLICIT ; Generate errors
.Set CabinetNameTemplate=SharePointAC.wsp
.set DiskDirectoryTemplate=CDROM ; All cabinets go in a single directory
.Set CompressionType=MSZIP ;** All files are compressed in cabinet files
.Set UniqueFiles="OFF"
.Set Cabinet=on
.Set DiskDirectory1=Package
;
; ** CAB Root
manifest.xml
SharePoint.dll
;
; ** LinkingExample Feature
.Set DestinationDir=LinkingExample
Features\LinkingExample\Feature.xml
Features\LinkingExample\Menu.xml
Features\LinkingExample\Toolbar.xml
Features\LinkingExample\Help.aspx
; ** SiteColumnHandler Feature
.Set DestinationDir=SiteColumnHandler
Features\SiteColumnHandler\Feature.xml
Features\SiteColumnHandler\Elements.xml
;*** End
```

Generate the CAB and WSP File

Open your Windows command-line tool, browse to the location of the project containing the Manifest.xml and .ddf files, and type the following command:

```
Makecab.exe -f sharepointfeatures.ddf
```

Upon successful execution, Makecab.exe generates a new folder, named Package. The Package folder contains a .wsp file, which is the file you will use to add the Solution to your SharePoint Solution store. The name of the .wsp file will be that name defined in the .ddf file's CabinetNameTemplate declarative, in this case SharePointAC.wsp.

Deploying the Solution

To deploy the Solution, you need to add the Solution to the SharePoint Solution store. To do this, complete the following steps:

1. Launch the Windows command-line tool, browse to the location containing the .wsp file, and type the following command:

   ```
   stsadm.exe -o addsolution -filename sharepointac.wsp
   ```

2. Browse to SharePoint Central Administration, and click the Operations tab. On the Operations page under the Global Configuration section, locate and click the Solution Management link.
3. On the Solution Management page, shown in Figure 26-18, click the Sharepointac.wsp Solution link.

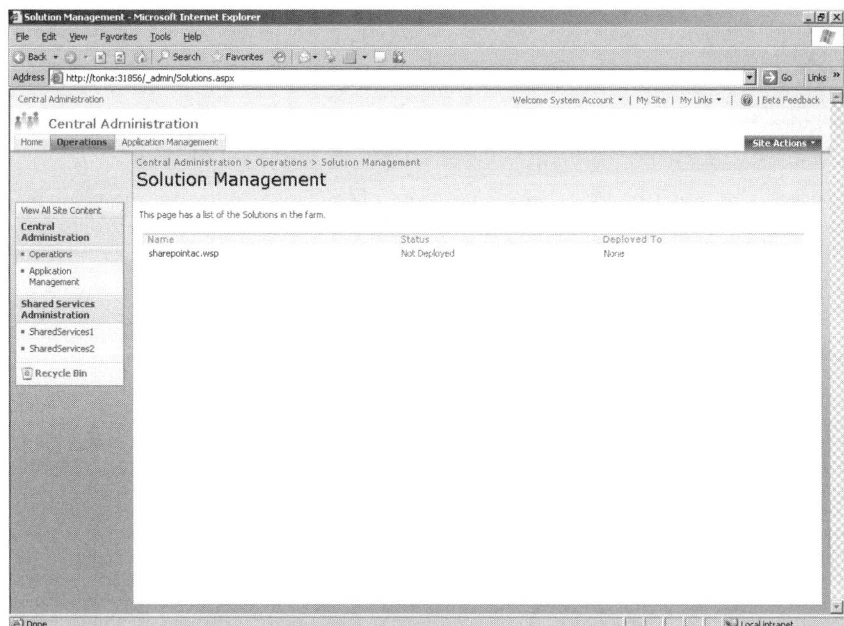

Figure 26-18 Added Solution shown on the Solution Management page

4. On the resultant Solution Properties page, click the Deploy Solution link in the toolbar.

5. On the Deploy Solution page, shown in Figure 26-19, configure the deploying options, including scheduling the Solution and choosing to deploy the Solution to all Web Applications or a specific Web Application.

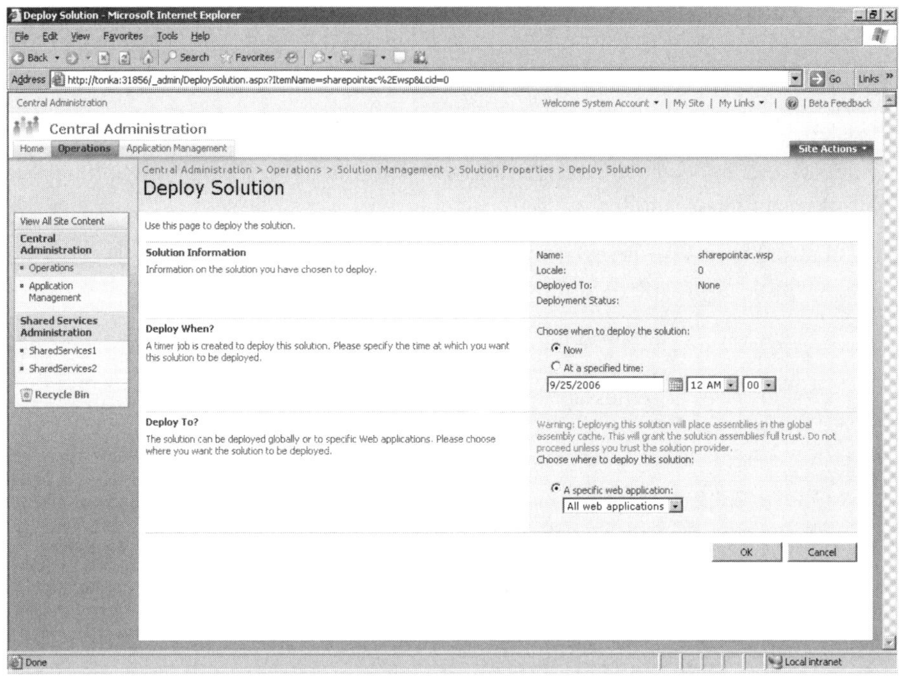

Figure 26-19 Deployment options for the Solution

Note The warning about the deployment of the Solution to the GAC appears on the Deploy Solution page because the value of the assembly *DeploymentTarget* attribute in the Manifest.xml file is set to "GlobalAssemblyCache".

Deactivating and Uninstalling Features

You can choose to deactivate instances of Feature. For example, you can turn off a particular functionality on your sites or a given site, or you can choose to uninstall a Feature, which completely removes the Feature from your SharePoint deployment. Features can be deactivated either through the administrative user interface or by using the stsadm.exe command-line tool.

To deactivate the Feature from a site using the administrative user interface, complete the following steps:

1. Browse to the site where you want to deactivate the Feature, click Site Actions, and under Site Administration, click Site Features.
2. On the Site Features page, locate the Feature you want to deactivate and click the Deactivate button to deactivate the Feature.

When you deactivate a Feature using the administrative user interface, you receive a warning message, as shown in Figure 26-20.

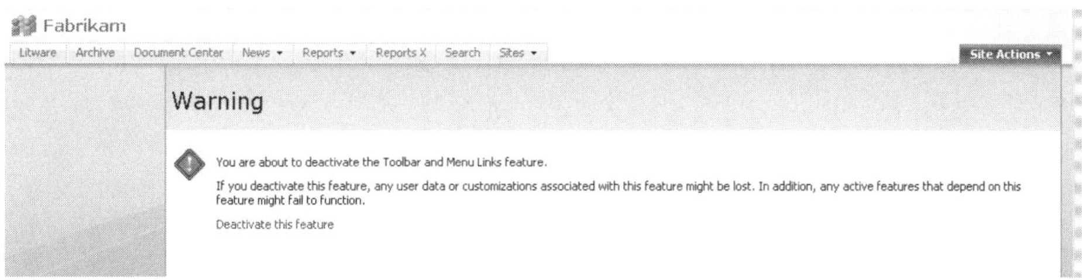

Figure 26-20 Warning message when deactivating Features through the administrative user interface

To deactivate the Feature using the stsadm.exe command-line tool, open the Windows command-line tool and type the following command:

```
stsadm.exe -o deactivatefeature -name LinkingExample -url
```

The URL parameter defines the URL of the site where you want to deactivate the Feature. Failure to enter the URL parameter results in a message notifying you the Feature was not deactivated, as shown in Figure 26-21.

```
C:\>stsadm.exe -o deactivatefeature -name Helloworld

Required parameter URL was not specified for feature '23bacf1d-3a54-4d83-a4b2-99
808a2b9d4c'.  The feature was not deactivated.

stsadm.exe -o deactivatefeature
           {-filename <relative path to Feature.xml> |
            -name <feature folder> |
            -id <feature Id>}
           [-url <url>]
           [-force]
```

Figure 26-21 Attempting to deactivate Features without the required URL parameter

To uninstall the Feature using the stsadm.exe command-line tool, open the Windows command line tool and type the following command:

```
stsadm.exe -o uninstallfeature -name LinkingExample
```

Important The stsadm.exe uninstallfeature command does not remove the Feature folder from the Features directory.

You should deactivate Features before uninstalling them, unless they are Web-scoped or farm-scoped Features. If you attempt to uninstall a site or Web-scoped Feature before deactivating that Feature, you receive a message notifying you that the Feature is still activated but you can optionally use the *-force* parameter to forcibly remove the Feature without deactivating it, as shown in Figure 26-22.

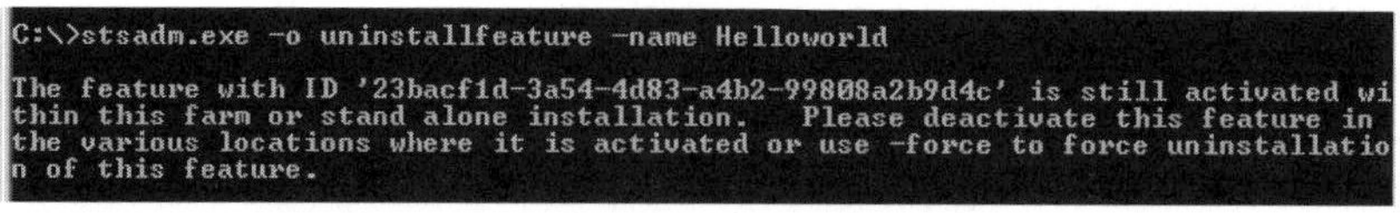

```
C:\>stsadm.exe -o uninstallfeature -name Helloworld

The feature with ID '23bacf1d-3a54-4d83-a4b2-99808a2b9d4c' is still activated wi
thin this farm or stand alone installation.  Please deactivate this feature in
the various locations where it is activated or use -force to force uninstallatio
n of this feature.
```

Figure 26-22 Attempting to uninstall an active Feature

Files deployed as part of the Feature <Module> element, such as an ASPX page, are not removed when a Feature is uninstalled. For example, if you deploy an ASPX page as part of a Feature and you then uninstall the Feature, you can still navigate to that ASPX page by typing the path to that page into the address line of your browser.

Updating an Existing Feature

You might find it necessary to update a Feature after installation. For example, you might want to modify a toolbar link or add a resource file, or you might add and deploy an event handler to existing instances of a Feature. To update an existing Feature, you must reinstall the Feature using the *-force* parameter and perform an IISRESET. You can do this by typing the following stsadm.exe command:

```
stsadm.exe -o uninstallfeature -name LinkingExample -force
```

Alternatively, you can include the *AlwaysForceInstall* attribute in the Feature.xml file and set the value to True, such as *AlwaysForceInstall="TRUE"*. This removes the need to enter the *-force* parameter in the command line during uninstall.

You should avoid changing the scope on an existing Feature in scenarios where that Feature has been activated within the given scope. For example, if you change the scope on an existing Feature from Web to Site, you need to reinstall the Feature, perform an IISRESET, and then attempt to deactivate the Feature from sites where the Web-scoped Feature was previously deployed and activated. Through the administrative user interface, you'll receive a warning message stating, "The Feature Is Not Currently Active," and you will not be able to deactivate the Feature from the previous scope.

Attempting to deactivate the same Feature through the stsadm.exe command-line tool also generates an error, as shown in Figure 26-23.

```
C:\>stsadm.exe -o deactivatefeature -name helloworld -url http://tonka:33066/sit
es/litware/SiteDirectory/Fabrikam/

The specified feature applies to the entire site collection, but the specified U
RL refers to a particular sub site.  To apply this feature to the entire site co
llection, use the root URL 'http://tonka:33066/sites/litware'.
```

Figure 26-23 Attempting to deactivate a Feature after a scope change

To deactivate Features from the previous scope, change the Feature back to the original scope, deactivate instances of the Feature from the original scope, uninstall the Feature, and then reinstall the Feature to the new scope.

Accessing Information with the Feature Object Model

SharePoint Server 2007 exposes a Feature object model that you can use to programmatically access Feature collections and extract information on Feature deployment, such as showing all activated Features within a given scope.

> **More Info** For full details about Feature classes, see the "Feature Object Model" topic in the Windows SharePoint Services 3.0 Software Development Kit.

The following example displays a list of activated Feature names and GUIDs on the root site of a site collection, using the Feature class *SPFeatureCollection*: The first section of code sets the context for the current site collection and specifies the root web of the site collection as the site against which to check for activated Features. The second part of the code renders the output and displays the results, which include the Title and ID for each activated Feature found within the root web of the site collection. Note, in the case of using the object model to detect activated Features, any hidden Features, that is those Features hidden from the Site Features administrative page, are also exposed.

> **On the CD** This code example is designed to be implemented as a Web Part. To implement and run the code, see the Active solution on the companion CD in the \Code\Chapter 26 folder. You need to recompile the project in Visual Studio, copy the DLL to the GAC, add the safe control to the Web.config file of the virtual directory to which you will deploy the Web Part, and populate the site collection Web Part Gallery with the Web Part.

```
protected override void RenderContents(HtmlTextWriter writer)
{
    SPSite siteCollection = SPControl.GetContextSite(Context);
    SPWeb site = siteCollection.RootWeb;
    SPFeatureCollection siteFeatures = site.Features;
```

```
    System.Globalization.CultureInfo cultureInfo = new System.Globalization.
CultureInfo(1033);

     foreach (SPFeature siteFeature in siteFeatures)
     {
         writer.Write("Title: " + siteFeature.Definition.GetTitle(cultureInfo) +
"<BR>ID:" + siteFeature.DefinitionId.ToString() + "<BR><BR>");

      }
   }
```

Figure 26-24 shows the resultant Web Part rendered on the Home page of the Fabrikam site.

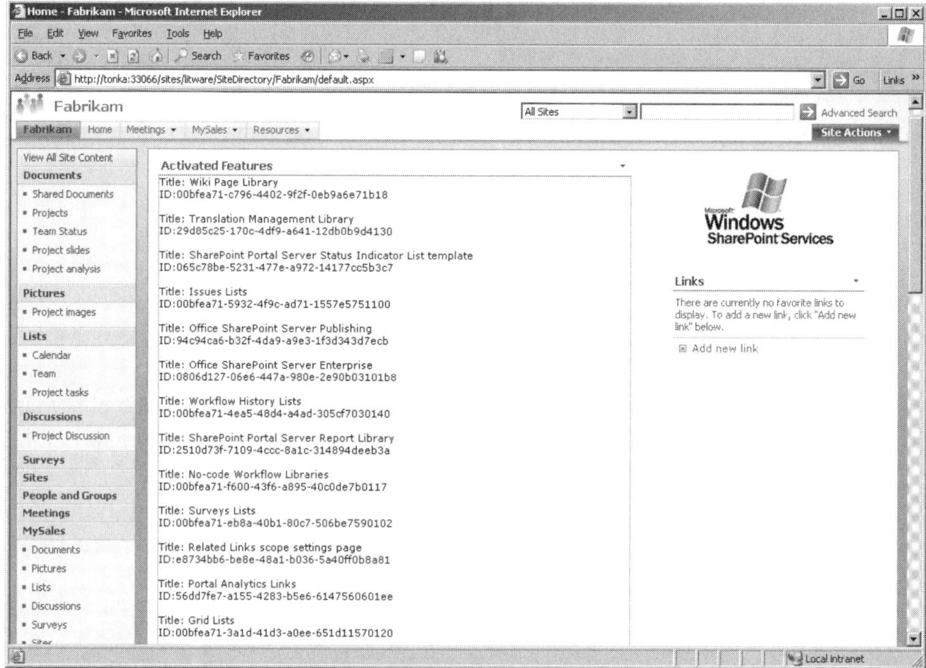

Figure 26-24 Deployed Web Part showing activated Features in site

Creating an Event Handler Feature

Event handlers are programs that enhance and add functionality throughout SharePoint sites and lists, manage events, and can be deployed to new and existing sites by using Features. The SharePoint object model includes several event classes that developers can use to develop and target event handlers specifically to items, lists, and sites.

In terms of deploying event handlers, in SharePoint Portal Server 2003 you can register event handlers through the administrative user interface, but this is no longer possible in SharePoint Server 2007. In SharePoint Server 2007, event handlers are deployed either by code, such as creating a Project Class to register an event handler, or as part of a Feature. Deploying event handlers with Features greatly simplifies the deployment process. You can use the Feature Receivers element to define the event handler assembly and provision the event handler as part of the Feature deployment. Add to this the ability to also activate and deactivate the event handler by toggling the Feature activation and deactivation settings, scope the event handler by using the Feature scope attribute, or targeting the Feature to a specific site during command-line activation, and you have a truly flexible solution.

This section demonstrates the steps involved in creating an event handler, using Visual Studio 2005, and deploying that event handler as part of a Feature. You'll review the type of events available to gain a better understanding of the type of functionality you can achieve by creating and deploying event handlers throughout your SharePoint sites.

Synchronous and Asynchronous Events

In addition to asynchronous events, SharePoint Server 2007 introduces *synchronous events*—that is, events that activate *before* the action occurs. An example of a synchronous event is one that can trap an item before it is deleted and remove the ability for users to delete an item, such as a file in a list or document library. Another example of a synchronous event is stopping users from adding columns to a custom list or document library. *Asynchronous events*, events that were possible in SharePoint Portal Server 2003, activate *after* an action occurs, such as appending an item to a list column or sending an e-mail after a file has been uploaded or a list entry has been made.

The SharePoint object model exposes several event classes, which ultimately inherit from the *Microsoft.SharePoint* assembly and directly inherit from the *Microsoft.SharePoint.SPEventReceiverBase* class. There are three main event classes:

- *SPItemEventReceiver*
- *SPListEventReceiver*
- *SPWebEventReceiver*

Each class includes both synchronous and asynchronous methods to work with events at the Item, List, or Web level. For instance, the *ItemDeleting* method, a synchronous member of the *SPItemEventReceiver* class, can be called to stop users from deleting files from a specific list or document library.

Table 26-8 shows examples of both synchronous and asynchronous event methods specific to each of the event class types: Item, List and Web. To view the full listing of events, launch the Visual Studio 2005 Object Browser, expand the Microsoft.SharePoint Assembly node, expand the Microsoft.SharePoint Namespace node, and then browse to each of the classes to view their respective event methods. You can also refer to the Windows SharePoint Services Software Development Kit (SDK) for an overview of the event classes.

Table 26-8 Examples of Synchronous and Asynchronous Events

Event class	Synchronous event	Asynchronous event
SPItemEventReceiver	*ItemDeleting*	*ItemDeleted*
SPListEventReceiver	*FieldDeleting*	*FieldDeleted*
SPWebEventReceiver	*SiteDeleting*	*SiteDeleted*

Building the Solution

In this example, you will use Visual Studio 2005 to create a Project Class Library and create an event handler to stop users from deleting columns from a list. Then you will deploy that event handler as part of a Feature. To build a Solution, complete the following steps:

On the CD The following example is included on the book's CD in the \Code\Chapter 26 folder in the Visual Studio SharePoint solution, and includes the cancelupdate.cs file and the SiteColumnHander Feature folder containing the Feature.xml and Elements.xml files.

1. Using Visual Studio 2005, create a new Project Class Library.
2. Add the references to the project, and code the solution.
3. Sign the assembly, build the Solution, and deploy Project DLL to the global assembly cache (GAC).
4. Create Feature.xml and Elements.xml files, and include the following:
   a. In the Elements.xml file, specify the list instance to which the event handler will apply.
   b. Add the Project Assembly to the Elements.xml file, and reference the Elements.xml file in the Features.xml file.
5. Deploy the Feature by copying the Feature files to the Features directory on the front-end server.
6. Test your event handler.

Creating a New Project Class Library

In this section, you'll create a new class file, cancelupdate.cs, for your event handler. To create the new class file, complete the following steps:

1. Launch Visual Studio 2005. On the File menu, click New Project to open the New Project dialog box.
2. Under Visual C# Templates, click Class Library.
3. In the Name text box, type the name of your project and then add the Location path. (This location, by default, is where your project will be built and DLLs will be output.) Click OK.
4. Change the name of the default Class1.cs file to cancelupdate.cs. This is the file where you will code your event handler. (In this example, the class file is named cancelupdate.cs.) Next, proceed to the "Adding a Reference" section.

Adding a Reference

You'll now add a reference to the Microsoft.SharePoint assembly so that you can access the necessary classes, methods, and properties for the project. To add a reference, complete the following steps:

1. On the Project menu, choose Add Reference to open the Add Reference dialog box.
2. Scroll down to Windows SharePoint Services. There are three references with the same name. Click the instance that references the following path:

   %SystemDrive%\Program Files\Common Files\Microsoft Shared
   \Web Server Extensions\12\ISAPI\Microsoft.SharePoint.dll
3. Click OK.
4. Add the *Microsoft.SharePoint* namespace at the top of the class file, and populate the remainder of the code as shown in the following code sample:

```
using System;
using System.Collections.Generic;
using System.Text;
using Microsoft.SharePoint;

namespace SharePoint
{
    public class cancelupdate : SPListEventReceiver
    {
        public override void FieldDeleting(SPListEventProperties properties)
        {
            properties.Cancel = true;
            properties.ErrorMessage = "You cannot delete columns from the " +
 properties.ListTitle + " list.";
        }
    }
}
```

5. Save the populated class file.

Signing the Project

Next, you'll sign the project assembly. This adds a strong name and allows you to add the project DLL into the GAC so that you can deploy the project to your SharePoint sites. It also generates a public key token that you'll embed into the Feature elements file when registering the assembly as part of the Feature deployment.

To sign the project, complete the following steps:

1. On the Project menu, choose *ProjectName* Properties to open the Properties dialog box.
2. Click the Signing option to open the Signing tab
3. Select the Sign The Assembly check box, and choose New from the Choose A Strong Name Key File list.
4. In the Create Strong Name Key dialog box, name the Key and optionally include a password to protect the key file. Click OK.

   Your project is now strongly named and ready to be deployed.
5. Close the Properties window to return to your project. The signed key file will be included under the Solution Explorer window, denoted by the extension .snk.
6. Right-click the project name, and click Build to build the project.

   Monitor the build status in the project Output window, and make sure the project built successfully.
7. Minimize Visual Studio, and browse to the location path you specified for the project.
8. Expand the Bin directory under the project folder, and then expand the Debug folder where the project DLL is located.
9. Launch a secondary instance of Windows Explorer, and browse to the following location:

   %SystemDrive%\WINDOWS\assembly
10. From the instance of Windows Explorer containing the Debug\Project DLL, select the DLL and drag and drop the DLL into the Assembly directory opened in the secondary instance of Windows Explorer.

Creating the Feature.xml and Elements.xml Files

Next, you'll create the Feature to deploy the event handler to your SharePoint sites. The Feature defines the list to which the event handler will apply and registers the project DLL to that list instance.

To create the Feature, complete the following steps:

On the CD These samples are also included on the companion CD in the \Code\Chapter 26 folder.

1. In the same project where you created the event handler, right-click the project name under the Solution Explorer window, click Add, and then click New Folder.
2. In the Name box, type **Features**.
3. Add another folder under the Features folder, and name that folder **SiteColumn-Handler**. Then add two new .xml files to the SiteColumnHandler folder by right-clicking the project name, clicking Add, clicking New Item, and selecting XML File. Name the files **Feature.xml** and **Elements.xml**, respectively.
4. Populate the Feature.xml file with the following code (optionally generate your own GUID for the *Id* attribute):

```
<?xml version="1.0" encoding="utf-8" ?>
<Feature
  Id="8E2C9B8A-A322-4956-8E72-5DDEBDAB5F37"
  Title="Disable deletion on Document Library columns"
  Description="The Feature includes an event handler which will stop users
from deleting columns from document libraries on a site."
  Scope="Web"
  Hidden="FALSE"
  ImageUrl=""
  xmlns="http://schemas.microsoft.com/sharepoint/">

  <ElementManifests>
    <ElementManifest Location="elements.xml"/>
  </ElementManifests>

</Feature>
```

5. Populate the Elements.xml file with the following code.

   The Elements.xml file defines on which list the event handler will work. In this case, the list is specified as type "101", which is the base type for the document library. But you can define another list type or create your own custom list and define that. The Elements.xml file also includes the assembly and class references for the event handler.

```
<?xml version="1.0" encoding="utf-8" ?>
<Elements xmlns="http://schemas.microsoft.com/sharepoint/">
```

```
    <Receivers ListTemplateId="101">
      <Receiver>
        <Name>cancelupdate</Name>
        <Type>FieldDeleting</Type>
        <SequenceNumber>1000</SequenceNumber>
        <Assembly>SharePoint, Version=1.0.0.0, Culture=neutral, PublicKeyToken
=ad7f6a147689147c</Assembly>
        <Class>SharePoint.cancelupdate</Class>
        <Data></Data>
      </Receiver>
    </Receivers>

</Elements>
```

> **Note** In the *Assembly* attribute, SharePoint is the name of the project. In the *Class* attribute, SharePoint is the name of the project, cancelupdate is the name of the class file including the event handler. The PublicKeyToken is the key that was generated when you signed the project assembly. You can get this key either by accessing the project DLL you added into the GAC and copying it, or you can use Lutz Roeder's Reflector for .NET tool, which will expose the project assembly information, including the public key token. Download the Reflector tool from *http://www.aisto.com/roeder/dotnet/*.

6. Save and close both files, and minimize Visual Studio.

Deploying and Testing a Feature

Now that you've created the project, deployed the DLL to the GAC, and created and configured the Feature, you can install and deploy the Feature.

To install and deploy the Feature, complete the following steps:

1. Open Windows Explorer, and browse to the Project Feature directory, which will be under the Project directory specified in the location path when you created the project.
2. Copy the SiteColumnHandler folder, and paste it into the Features directory.
3. To install the event handler Feature and make it available for activation on your SharePoint sites, open the Windows command-line tool, browse to the stsadm.exe location, and type the following command:

   ```
   stsadm.exe -o installfeature -name sitecolumnhandler
   ```
4. Browse to the SharePoint site where you want to activate the Feature.
5. On the Site Actions menu, choose Site Settings to open the Site Settings page.

6. Click Site Features under the Site Administration column to open the Site Features page.
7. Locate the new Feature, named Disable Deletion On Document Library Columns, and click the Activate button in the Status column to activate the Feature.
8. Test the Feature by going to one of your document libraries, such as Shared Documents. Go into the Document Library Settings and attempt to delete one of the existing columns. If your Feature has been successfully installed, you will receive an error page with the message, "You cannot delete columns from the <name of document library> list."

> **Note** If you update your event handler project class file, you need to rebuild the project, add the updated DLL to the GAC, and perform an IISRESET to make any changes to existing instances of the event handler throughout your SharePoint sites. Unless you've made changes to the Features files, such as Feature.xml or Elements.xml, you do not need to reinstall the Feature to make changes to an existing event handler instance.

Implementing Feature Events

You can use Feature events to manage a Feature life cycle by triggering events during Feature activation and Feature deactivation. Through Feature events, you can more succinctly manage the Feature life cycle by choosing to have certain events occur throughout each stage of Feature deployment, such as when one of the following actions are attempted for a Feature:

- Installed
- Activated
- Deactivated
- Uninstalled

For example, you might have dates of company events throughout the year that you want deployed to your SharePoint sites, but only for the period leading up to each event. You can create a Feature and use Feature events to deploy event details to sites or a specific site when that Feature is activated, and then remove those event details when the Feature is deactivated. Or perhaps you want the ability to turn on and turn off access to particular sites, such as granting a particular group of users access to a site for a given period, or maybe you want to activate a particular workflow but only at certain times during a month or a year. You can accomplish all of these tasks using Feature events.

Instantiating the *SPFeatureReceiver* Class Provisioning Callouts

Feature event provisioning callouts derive from the *Microsoft.SharePoint.SPFeatureReceiver* class. There are four provisioning callouts:

- *FeatureInstalled*
- *FeatureUninstalling*
- *FeatureActivated*
- *FeatureDeactivating*

The sample code shown in the "Creating the Feature Event File" section below shows a class that has been derived from the *SPFeatureReceiver* and the *FeatureActivated* and *FeatureDeactivating* callouts provisioned.

Creating the Feature Event File

This sample assumes two custom themes have been created: Holiday and Corporate. Using the *FeatureActivated* callout, the Holiday theme is applied to the targeted site or sites when the Feature is activated;using the *FeatureDeactivating* callout, the Corporate theme is applied when the Feature is deactivated.

Note You can just as easily use the default themes to demonstrate the functionality shown in this example. Default themes can be found at the following location:

%SystemDrive%\Program Files\Common Files\Microsoft Shared\web server extensions\12\TEMPLATE\THEMES

Choose two default themes and replace each Holiday and Corporate with the default themes.

To create the sample below, create a new class file in your Visual Studio project and name the class file HolidayTheme.cs. Populate the HolidayTheme.cs file with the code shown below.

On the CD The code in this example is included on the book's CD in the Visual Studio SharePoint solution. This includes the HolidayTheme.cs file and associated HolidayTheme Feature folder, which contains the Feature.xml file.

```
using System;
using System.Collections.Generic;
using System.Text;
using Microsoft.SharePoint;

namespace SharePoint
{
    class HolidayTheme : SPFeatureReceiver
```

```
    {
        public override void FeatureInstalled(SPFeatureReceiverProperties
properties){}

        public override void FeatureActivated(SPFeatureReceiverProperties
properties)
        {
            SPWeb site = (SPWeb)properties.Feature.Parent;
            site.ApplyTheme("Holiday");
            site.Update();
        }
        public override void FeatureDeactivating(SPFeatureReceiverProperties
properties)
        {
            SPWeb site = properties.Feature.Parent as SPWeb;
            site.ApplyTheme("Corporate");
            site.Update();
        }

        public override void FeatureUninstalling(SPFeatureReceiverProperties
properties){}
    }
}
```

Configuring the Feature.xml File for Feature Event

To install and deploy the Feature event demonstrated above, you need to create a Feature.xml file and reference the Feature event assembly and class using the *ReceiverAssembly* and *ReceiverClass* attributes, as shown in the following code sample.

Note This sample assumes you have created the *HolidayTheme* class file as part of the SharePoint project and deployed or updated the project DLL to the GAC. See the "Creating an Event Handler Feature" section for details on how to build and deploy project DLLs.

```
<?xml version="1.0" encoding="utf-8" ?>
<Feature xmlns="http://schemas.microsoft.com/sharepoint/"

  Id="F2493D50-8087-4cc4-9ACB-8D71F0325222"
  Title="Theme Manager"
  Description="Use this Feature to activate the Holiday Theme for a site"
  Version="1.0.0.0"
  Scope="Web"
  Hidden="FALSE"
  ReceiverAssembly="SharePoint, Version=1.0.0.0, Culture=neutral,
PublicKeyToken=ad7f6a147689147c"
  ReceiverClass="SharePoint.HolidayTheme"
  ImageUrl="" >

</Feature>
```

Copy the Feature to the Features directory on your SharePoint Web front-end server, install the Feature, and then activate and deactivate the Feature to trigger each of the Feature events. This Feature has been scoped for Web, which means you can activate and deactivate the Feature on sites throughout your SharePoint site collection.

Including Features in Site Definitions

Web-scoped and Site-scoped Features can also be deployed via site definitions. Site definitions form the basis from which to create SharePoint sites. For example, the default Team Site template is created from the default STS site definition. You can create your own custom site definitions to define specific functionality for sites, such as custom lists or content types, and you can add that functionality using Features.

In Windows SharePoint Services 2.0, a major advantage of creating site definitions as opposed to effecting change using FrontPage 2003 was the fact that sites provisioned from site definitions remained ghosted. With *ghosted* site definitions, the pages and templates in those sites were called directly from the Web front-end server rather than an unghosted version in the database, which resulted from FrontPage 2003 modifications. This resulted in better, overall server performance and end user experience.

Although ghosting and unghosting still exist in SharePoint Server 2007, you can now more easily reghost pages after they have become unghosted through customizations using SharePoint Designer 2007. But an added advantage to working with site definitions in SharePoint Server 2007 is the ability to more easily apply robust functionality using Features, to both new and existing site definitions. Features deployed via a site definition also become automatically activated on sites provisioned from the site definition. This removes the need for any manual or programmatic intervention to separately activate Features after Feature installation.

Note The terminology for ghosting and unghosting has changed for SharePoint Server 2007. In SharePoint Server 2007, ghosting is now referred to as uncustomized and unghosting is now referred to as customized.

This section covers how to create a custom site definition and include Web and Site-scoped Features to add a custom document library and content types and columns.

Note When sites are deployed based on a site definition containing your custom Features, those Features are automatically activated. However, you still need to have installed those Features *before* provisioning them as part of your site definition. If you attempt to create a site from a site definition containing a Feature where that Feature has not been installed, you will receive the following error during site creation: "Feature 'GUID' is not installed in this farm, and cannot be added to this scope."

Creating a Custom Site Definition

To demonstrate including and deploying Features as part of a site definition, you'll create a custom site definition named Projects which will be based on the default STS site definition. The default site definitions are located on the Web front-end server, at the following location:

%SystemDrive%\Program Files\Common Files\Microsoft Shared
\web server extensions\12\TEMPLATE\SiteTemplates

Note Avoid modifying the default site definitions, such as the default STS site definition. Changes made to the default site definitions are not supported by Microsoft, and you risk losing those changes during future upgrades, including service pack upgrades.

To create the new Projects site definition, complete the following steps.

On the CD The Projects site definition is included on the book's CD in the \Code\Chapter 26 folder.

1. In the SiteTemplates directory, locate the STS site definition folder. Copy and paste that folder to the SiteTemplates directory and rename it to Projects.

   Register the new Projects site definition by creating a Webtemp.xml, or template, file for the site definition. The Webtemp.xml file notifies SharePoint of the site definition and also enables you to configure additional information for the site definition, such as whether the site definition will be hidden or visible in the template picker when creating new sites, a description for the site definition and custom image to be displayed in the template picker when creating new sites. The default Webtemp.xml files are located at the following location:

   %SystemDrive%\Program Files\Common Files\Microsoft Shared
   \web server extensions\12\TEMPLATE\1033\XML

   Note The site definition template files must begin with Webtemp for SharePoint to recognize those files as site definition template files.

2. To create a Webtemp.xml file for the Projects site definition, create a new file named WebTempProject.xml and include the following code. The ID property in the Template Name attribute should be set to above 1000 to avoid any conflict with the default SharePoint templates. The Template Name value must exactly match the name of the site definition. You can also choose to include a *DisplayCategory* property as part of the configuration. The *DisplayCategory* value will be displayed as an

additional category from which to choose templates when creating sites—for example, in addition to the default categories of Collaboration, Meetings, and Enterprise.

```
<?xml version="1.0" encoding="utf-8" ?>
<!-- _lcid="1033" _version="12.0.4017" _dal="1" -->
<!-- _LocalBinding -->
<Templates xmlns:ows="Microsoft SharePoint">
 <Template Name="PROJECTS" ID="10001">
    <Configuration ID="0" Title="Projects Site" Hidden="FALSE"
     ImageUrl="/_layouts/images/stsprev.png" Description="This
     template creates a site for Project teams to create, organize,
     and share information quickly and easily. It includes a Document
     Library, and basic lists such as Announcements, Calendar, Contacts,
     and Quick Links." DisplayCategory="Projects" > </Configuration>
 </Template>
</Templates>
```

3. Save the WebTempProject.xml file, and then perform an IISRESET to deploy the new site definition and make it available as a template in the Template Selection section when creating new sites.

Note Any changes to the site definition .xml file and related template .xml file necessitate an IISRESET to have those changes implemented.

Adding a Feature to the Site Definition

You can customize sites provisioned from a new site definition by adding in new or custom Features. In this section, you'll add two custom Features to the new Projects site definition; one a Site-scoped Feature, including a ProjectXMeetings content type and columns, and the other a Web-scoped Feature, including a custom Project document library which also includes a custom Resource file.

Each SharePoint site definition includes an ONET.XML file, located in the XML folder under the site definition folder:

%SystemDrive%\Program Files\Common Files\Microsoft Shared
\web server extensions\12\TEMPLATE\SiteTemplates\<sitedefinitionfoldername>
\xml

The ONET.XML file includes functional directives for the site definition, including navigation, templates and views, references to default List Features, and custom Features, which will be provisioned to sites created from the site definition. You can include both Site Collection-scoped Features and Web-scoped Features in the ONET.XML file.

To reference a custom Feature in the Projects site definition ONET.XML file and have that Feature deployed and activated in sites provisioned from the Projects site definition, complete the following steps:

On the CD The following example assumes you have installed the ProjectContentTypes and ProjectDocumentLibrary Features included on the CD in the \Code\Chapter 26 folder in the Visual Studio SharePoint solution. It also assumes you have copied the Resource file, projectdocumentlibrary.en-US.resx, also included on the CD, to the Resources folder on your SharePoint server.

1. Using Visual Studio or Notepad, open the Projects site definition ONET.XML file and scroll to the section of the file that includes the <SiteFeatures> and <WebFeatures> tags, and the default Features, as shown in the following example:

```
<SiteFeatures>
  <!-- BasicWebParts Feature -->
  <Feature ID="00BFEA71-1C5E-4A24-B310-BA51C3EB7A57" />
</SiteFeatures>
<WebFeatures>
  <!-- TeamCollab Feature -->
  <Feature ID="00BFEA71-4EA5-48D4-A4AD-7EA5C011ABE5" />
</WebFeatures>
```

Note In this example, because you copied the ONET.XML file from the default STS site definition, the <SiteFeatures> and <WebFeatures> sections are already populated with the default BasicWebParts and TeamCollab Features. You can choose to remove these or leave them if you want to maintain the core functionality offered as part of the STS (Team Site) site definition. The <SiteFeatures> section denotes site collection Features, while the <WebFeatures> section denotes Web Features.

2. Add a new line to the SiteFeatures section and include the reference to the custom ProjectContentTypes Feature, as shown below:

```
<SiteFeatures>
       <!-- BasicWebParts Feature -->
       <Feature ID="00BFEA71-1C5E-4A24-B310-BA51C3EB7A57" />
       <! - - ProjectContentTypes - ->
       <Feature ID="11BBCF50-7847-4aa5-B422-1A0574670308"
</SiteFeatures>
```

In the case of the ProjectContentTypes Feature, we need to add this Feature to the SiteFeatures section of the ONET.XML file because the Feature includes the Content Type and Field Element which cannot be scoped to Web.

3. Next, add a new line to the WebFeatures section and include the reference to the custom ProjectDocumentLibrary Feature, as shown below:

```
<WebFeatures>
<!-- TeamCollab Feature -->
<Feature ID="00BFEA71-4EA5-48D4-A4AD-7EA5C011ABE5" />
<!- - ProjectDocumentLibrary - ->
<Feature ID="187EAD43-69B7-4142-8327-1D00FF75C681">
</WebFeatures>
```

4. Save the Projects ONET.XML file and then open the Windows command-line tool, and run an IISRESET.

The Projects site definition now includes two custom Features. When you provision a new site collection based on the Projects site definition, a new content type named ProjectXMeetings will be included in the Site Content Type Gallery of the root site of the site collection. If you click on the ProjectXMeetings content type you'll see that it includes two custom columns, Attendees and Highlights, as defined in the ProjectContentTypes Feature.

The custom Content Type Feature will have been activated during site provisioning but will not be visible on the site's Site Features administration page because this Feature is a hidden Feature, denoted by the Hidden="TRUE" attribute in the ProjectContentTypes Feature.xml file. The custom ProjectDocumentLibrary Feature will also be included on any new sites provisioned from the Projects site definition, as an additional Libraries template named Project Documents. The ProjectDocumentLibrary Feature will be also be visible on the Site Features administration page, which means you can optionally deactivate this Feature following deployment.

Note The Feature activation will fail if you included a Feature in your site definition that is dependent on another Feature being activated and that Feature is not activated. For example, if your site definition includes a Web-scoped Feature that is dependent on a Site Collection-scoped Feature being activated and the Site Collection-scoped Feature is not activated, the Web-scoped Feature activation will fail when deployed via the site definition.

Removing a Feature from ONET.XML File

If you remove a Feature reference or tag from the ONET.XML file, new sites provisioned from that site definition will continue to include an activated instance of the Feature *until* you perform an IISRESET. Once you've performed an IISRESET, after removal of the Feature reference from the ONET.XML file, the Feature remains installed and active on any *existing* sites created from that site definition as long as the Feature has not been deactivated or uninstalled.

Any sites created from the site definition *subsequent* to the removal of the Feature reference from ONET.XML and *following* an IISRESET still include the Feature if the Feature remains installed and scoped for the instance of the sites provisioned. But in this case, the Feature will not be automatically activated. You need to activate the Feature separately, either using the command-line tool or through the administrative user interface page, Site Features.

If you uninstall a Feature where the Feature is referenced in a site definition, the Feature will be uninstalled from all existing sites including those sites created from the site definition. Attempting to provision sites from that same site definition, which still contains the reference to the uninstalled Feature, generates the following error message: "Feature 'GUID' is not installed in this farm, and cannot be added to this scope."

If you subsequently reinstall the same Feature, it will be reinstalled to any existing sites provisioned from the site definition but will not be activated. Any new sites created from the site definition containing a reference to the Feature, once the Feature is reinstalled, will be automatically activated.

Summary

This chapter has demonstrated how to work with Features to enhance and extend your SharePoint sites. Features can be used to add small changes to sites, such as toolbar buttons and menu items right through to robust solutions, such as event handlers and Feature events.

In this chapter, you have learned about the core Feature components, including the Feature.xml file and also the associated element files through which you can define the Feature functionality, such as deploying files to a site or adding content types to sites. You have learned how to create a Feature, including how to integrate the SharePoint schema into your Visual Studio solutions and projects so you can easily generate and define your accompanying Feature elements and attributes.

The Feature object model has also been introduced and you have learned how you can leverage the Feature object model to access Feature collections within your site collections to perform administrative tasks. Synchronous and Asynchronous event handlers were also introduced and this chapter demonstrated how to provision an event handler using a Feature.

The chapter has also demonstrated how you can work with Features post-deployment by updating and redeploying Features, as well as manipulating Features through provisioning callouts to make certain events happen upon installing, activating, deactivating or uninstalling a Feature. In this chapter, we used an example of changing the site theme to a holiday theme upon activating a Feature, then changing the site theme to a corporate theme upon deactivating a Feature.

You have also learned how to administrate Features and the tools with which you can manipulate and deploy Features, such as the stsadm.exe command line tool. Finally, you have learned how you can dynamically provision Features by including them in site definitions.

In the next chapter, Chapter 27 “Using the Microsoft Office SharePoint Designer 2007 with Microsoft Windows SharePoint Services 3.0”, you’ll learn how you can change the appearance and functionality of SharePoint sites using SharePoint Designer 2007.

Chapter 27

Using Microsoft Office SharePoint Designer 2007 with Microsoft Windows SharePoint Services 3.0

Microsoft Office SharePoint Designer 2007 is a powerful tool for creating and customizing SharePoint Server 2007 sites. In fact, the feature set of Office SharePoint Designer 2007 is so powerful that you do not need to grant access to all features to every power user for them to be productive; most power users will be satisfied with access to a subset of all features. To address this issue, SharePoint Designer 2007 includes a Contributor Settings feature that you use to ensure that only selected users are able to make certain kinds of modifications. You'll find out more about this feature in this chapter.

Microsoft FrontPage 2003 is the predecessor of SharePoint Designer 2007. This chapter provides a comparison between FrontPage 2003 and SharePoint Designer 2007, as well as an introduction to the SharePoint Designer 2007 user interface. SharePoint Designer 2007 offers support for adjusting the user interface of SharePoint sites, and you will learn how to do this.

This chapter also explores the extensive support in SharePoint Designer 2007 for cascading style sheets, as well as how to work with data sources in SharePoint Designer 2007 and how to use the Data Form Web Part. In addition, this chapter covers the different usage reports that are included in SharePoint Designer 2007.

More Info The ability to create workflows is an important part of the SharePoint Designer 2007 feature set. Creating workflows using Windows Workflow Foundation and SharePoint Designer for Workflows is covered in depth in Chapter 28, "Implementing Microsoft Windows Workflow Services."

What Is Office SharePoint Designer 2007?

The 2007 Microsoft Office system offers two new products that are mostly based on Microsoft Office FrontPage technology: SharePoint Designer 2007 and Expression Web Designer. Both products address different usage scenarios.

Expression Web Designer is the next-generation tool for designing dynamic, standards-based Web sites. This product delivers a complete set of tools for Web design and development. Expression Web Designer is focused on the needs of professional Web designers seeking to build high-quality, standards-based Web sites for companies. It provides exceptional support for integrating XML, cascading style sheets (CSS), ASP.NET 2.0, XHTML, and other standard Web technologies into sites to make them more dynamic, interactive, and accessible.

SharePoint Designer 2007 is built specifically for information workers in an enterprise setting who are creating and customizing SharePoint Web sites and building workflow-enabled applications in Microsoft Office SharePoint Server 2007. SharePoint Designer 2007 provides these workers with versatile tools to produce more interactive Web pages that incorporate data from a wide variety of sources, as well as enable the support for existing business processes. SharePoint Designer 2007 also offers powerful reporting tools for the SharePoint platform. SharePoint Designer 2007 allows an enterprise's IT department to manage all these activities closely so that employees ultimately can be more productive in building and customizing SharePoint sites and applications.

Comparing SharePoint Designer 2007 and FrontPage 2003

The SharePoint Designer 2007 user interface closely resembles the user interface of FrontPage 2003. Microsoft has chosen to give the product a new name to emphasize that SharePoint Designer 2007 is now part of the SharePoint product family.

SharePoint Designer 2007 supports the same types of Web sites as FrontPage 2003 does. Examples of these types of Web sites are Web sites built with Windows SharePoint Services, disk-based Web sites, and Web sites that are managed via FrontPage Server Extensions.

When Do You Use SharePoint Designer 2007?

SharePoint Designer 2007 is ASP.NET 2.0–compliant and is targeted toward enterprise-solution creators and designers using SharePoint technology. SharePoint Designer 2007 supports technologies such as ASP.NET 2.0, cascading style sheets (CSS), and Windows Workflow Foundation (WWF). You can use SharePoint Designer 2007 to earily build no-code solutions. The following scenarios are examples of situations when using SharePoint Designer 2007 is useful:

- Tracking and reporting scenarios
- Designing lists and libraries to store data
- Making forms and views for presenting data
- Building application logic in the form of workflows
- Leveraging SharePoint Designer 2007 to aid in defining the user interface for the SharePoint platform
- Leveraging the SharePoint security system to define rights and roles for users of SharePoint Designer 2007

SharePoint Designer 2007 cannot be used to create custom Web Parts and controls, complex workflows, and custom form actions. If you want to do that, you need to use Microsoft Visual Studio 2005 Designer.

Working with SharePoint Designer 2007

SharePoint Designer 2007 is a product that contains a large feature set, which can be quite overwhelming when you start to work with SharePoint Designer 2007 for the first time. If you want to get to know the product, it helps to familiarize yourself with it gradually. To get you started with SharePoint Designer 2007, this section introduces you to working with the user interface. It covers some of the basics, including opening sites, working with task panes, configuring contributor settings, adding contributor settings to site templates, and creating new files.

Opening SharePoint Sites

Opening a SharePoint Server 2007 site by using SharePoint Designer 2007 is a simple operation. All you need is the URL of the SharePoint site and sufficient permissions to be able to interact with the SharePoint site. Administrators can use the Contributor Settings feature to determine the kind of changes members of a SharePoint group can make on a SharePoint site by using SharePoint Designer 2007. (You'll find more information about Contributor Settings in the "Configuring Contributor Settings" section.)

You can open a SharePoint site with SharePoint Designer 2007 in two ways:

- **Open SharePoint Designer 2007.** On the File menu, click Open Site. In the Open Site window, type the URL of your SharePoint site and then click Open.
- **Browse to the SharePoint site.** On the File menu, click Edit With Microsoft Office SharePoint Designer, or click the Edit toolbar button in the browser, as shown in Figure 27-1.

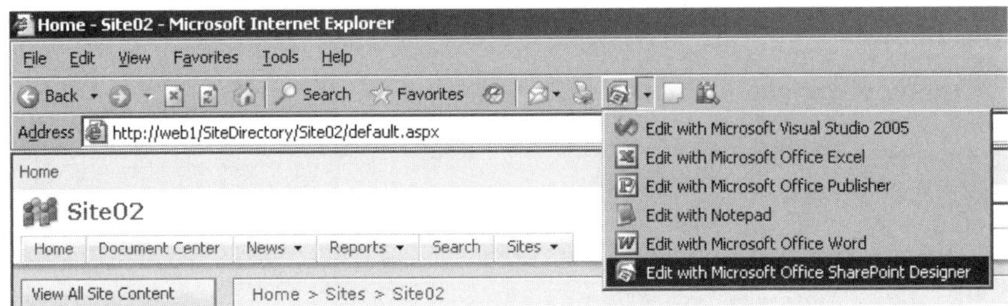

Figure 27-1 The Edit toolbar button

Getting to Know SharePoint Designer 2007

The first time you open a SharePoint site with SharePoint Designer 2007, you might be surprised by all the task panes and possibilities. This section introduces you to the user interface Task Panes.

By default, there are two task panes on each side of the middle of the screen, and the lower panes on each side contain two tabs each, as shown in Figure 27-2. The top left task pane is named Folder List, and the tabs in the lower left task pane are Tag Properties and CSS Properties. The top right task pane is named Toolbox, and the tabs in the lower right task pane are Apply Styles and Manage Styles. All task panes have two standard options: you can enlarge them and close them. Initially, the middle of the screen shows the contents of the SharePoint site; when you make a selection, the middle of the screen shows the page that is being edited.

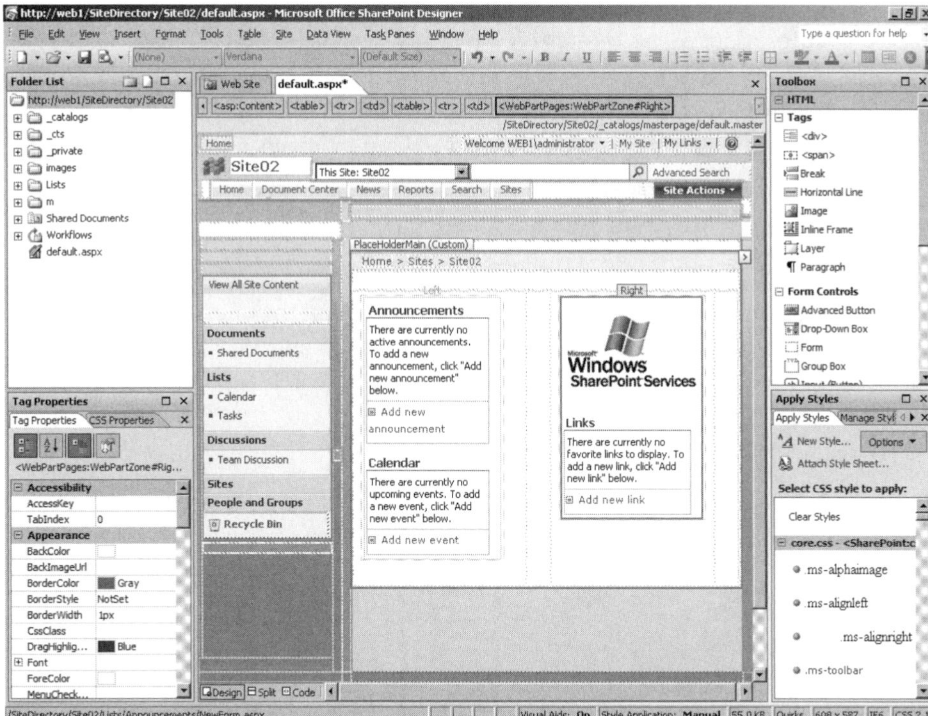

Figure 27-2 The default view of SharePoint Designer 2007

The task panes and tabs are described in more detail in the following list:

- **Folder List** This task pane displays all the folders and files in your site. You can remove and rename files or folders in this view. For example, in the _catalogs folder, you find the Master Page Gallery, where the master pages for your site are located. (Master pages are discussed later in this chapter, in the "About Master Pages" section.) When you right-click a folder, you can create a new HTML, CSS, or ASPX file; create a folder; or open the New SharePoint Content window. In the New SharePoint Content window, you can create a new list, document library, survey, or workflow.
- **Tag Properties** The Tag Properties tab provides an overview of all the attributes of a selected HTML tag in a page. You can select a tag either in design view or in code view.
- **CSS Properties** The CSS Properties tab shows all CSS properties available in a page.
- **Toolbox** The Toolbox task pane provides an overview of the HTML, ASP.NET, and SharePoint controls available for the current page.

> **Note** Controls are reusable components of a graphical user interface.

- **Apply Styles** The Apply Styles tab shows the CSS styles that are available for a certain page, and it allows you to create a new style and attach a new style sheet to the page.
- **Manage Styles** The Manage Styles tab interacts with the CSS Properties tab and shows a preview of the selected style.

SharePoint Designer 2007 has more task panes to offer than the ones shown by default. When you click the Task Panes menu, you can see all available task panes. (See Figure 27-3.)

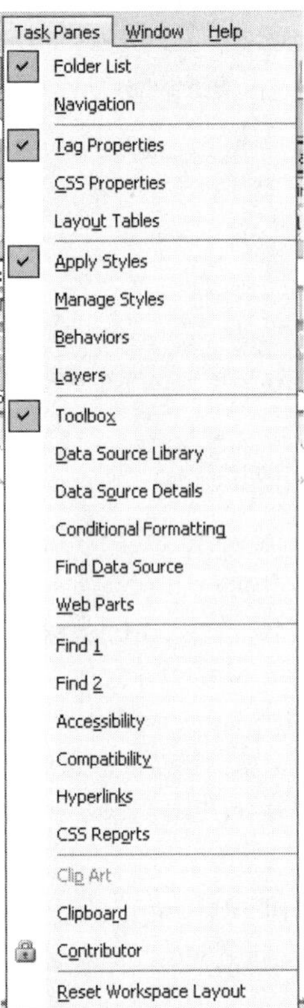

Figure 27-3 The Task Panes menu in SharePoint Designer 2007

In addition to the four default task pane locations shown in Figure 27-2, there are two other optional task pane locations that are not shown by default. The first one is located at the bottom in the middle of the screen. Please be aware of the fact that this task pane location is not shown in Figure 27-2. If you open one of the following task panes, that by default are shown in this task pane location: Accessibility, Compatibility, CSS, and Hyperlinks, and the Find 1 and Find 2 panes. The Clip Art, Clipboard, and Contributor task panes open, via the Task Panes menu, in a new task pane location on the right, next to the standard task panes. Be aware that the Clip Art, Clipboard, and Contributor task panes are not shown in Figure 27-2, as this figure displays only the task panes that are visible by default. You can use the Reset Workspace Layout option to reset the layout of SharePoint Designer 2007.

The Main Work Area

The middle of the screen contains an overview of the contents of a SharePoint site or the page that is currently being edited. If you open multiple pages, page tabs are added, so you can switch easily to other opened pages in your site. The one page tab that is always displayed is the Web Site tab; this tab shows you the contents of your site along with metadata such as the size of a file or the last modified date. The Web Site tab also gives you options for managing your Web site on the site level. To do this, right-click in the middle of the window and choose Site Settings to open the Site Settings window.

When you have selected the Web Site tab, you can see several new tabs at the bottom of your screen:

- **Folders** This is the default tab; it displays the folder structure of your Web site.
- **Copy Web Site** From this tab, you can click Remote Web Site Properties to set up a remote Web site. This allows you to copy SharePoint content to a remote location. The following remote Web server types are available:
  - FrontPage Server Extensions or SharePoint Services
  - WebDAV
  - File Transfer Protocol (FTP)
  - File System (You can use either a local folder or a location on the network.)
- **Reports** This tab shows the standard site summary report. Reports are covered in more detail in the section "Viewing Reports."
- **Navigation** This tab shows a graphical representation of your site.
- **Hyperlinks** This tab shows a graphical representation of the hyperlinks in your site.

Working with Views

When you select a page to edit, you can switch between different views of this page by using the tabs at the bottom of the screen. Table 27-1 shows the available views.

Table 27-1 Views in SharePoint Designer 2007

Name	Description
Design View	Design View is a what-you-see-is-what-you-get (WYSIWYG) editing mode. SharePoint Designer 2007 users often find this view the most convenient view because it allows you to easily create Web pages or add Web Parts to a page.
Split View	Split View allows you to see half the screen in Design View and the other half in Code View.
Code View	Code View shows you the HTML code and allows you to edit the page.

When you use Split View, any changes in the code do not appear automatically in Design View. Split View is implemented in this way for performance reasons, as it takes some time to render any code changes and update the Design View, thus interrupting the work process. However, you can use the key combination Alt+Page Down (or Page Up) to force Design View updates. If you want to swap views, press Ctrl+Page Down (or Page Up).

Note Preview View, which was available in FrontPage 2003, is not available in SharePoint Designer 2007 because, in Preview View, SharePoint pages are not rendered in a satisfactory manner. The resulting display did not come close to the way SharePoint pages actually look in a browser. The same was true for most ASP and ASP.NET pages. In SharePoint Designer 2007, there is a Preview In Browser view available from the File menu (or by pressing F12), which gives you the most accurate view possible. It shows you the page in Internet Explorer (or some other browser). You can choose which resolution you want to use to preview the page, and you can add browsers other than your default one. The only drawback is that you have to save your page first before you can preview it.

Configuring Contributor Settings

SharePoint Designer 2007 offers a great new feature called Contributor Settings. The Contributor Settings feature allows IT administrators to configure settings for members of SharePoint groups to control what they can do in SharePoint Designer 2007. You cannot manage users or groups via Contributor Settings; you do this using the SharePoint user interface.

Important FrontPage 2003 is a very powerful tool when it comes to editing SharePoint 2003 sites, but it also has drawbacks. For example, a user can unintentionally delete a SharePoint page by selecting Delete when right-clicking a SharePoint page.

To open the Contributor Settings window (shown in Figure 27-4), select Contributor Settings from the Site menu.

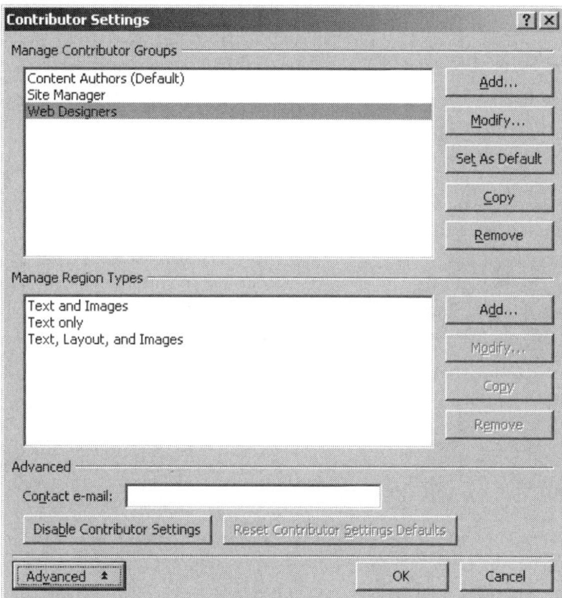

Figure 27-4 The Contributor Settings window

Note If you do not have administrator rights for a specified SharePoint site, you cannot modify the Contributor Settings of that site. SharePoint Designer 2007 displays a message indicating that you cannot modify the site settings. (See Figure 27-5.)

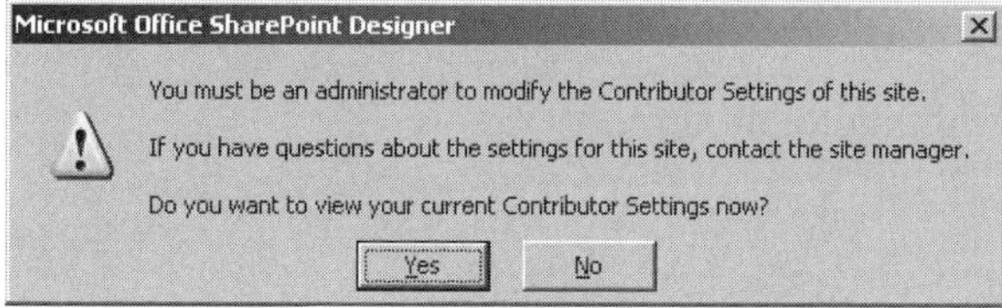

Figure 27-5 The Contributor Settings Alert message box

In the Manage Contributor Groups section of the Contributor Settings window, you can see the different contributor groups. By default, you cannot edit the contributor groups that are listed in the Contributor Settings window. You can change the list by clicking the Advanced button and clearing the Inherit Contributor Settings From Site Collection Or Defaults check box.

If you select a contributor group and then click Modify, the Contributor Group Properties window opens. Here you can specify a detailed set of constraints (as shown in Figure 27-6) by constraint type:

- General

- Folders
- Creating Pages
- Editing
- Formatting
- Images
- SharePoint

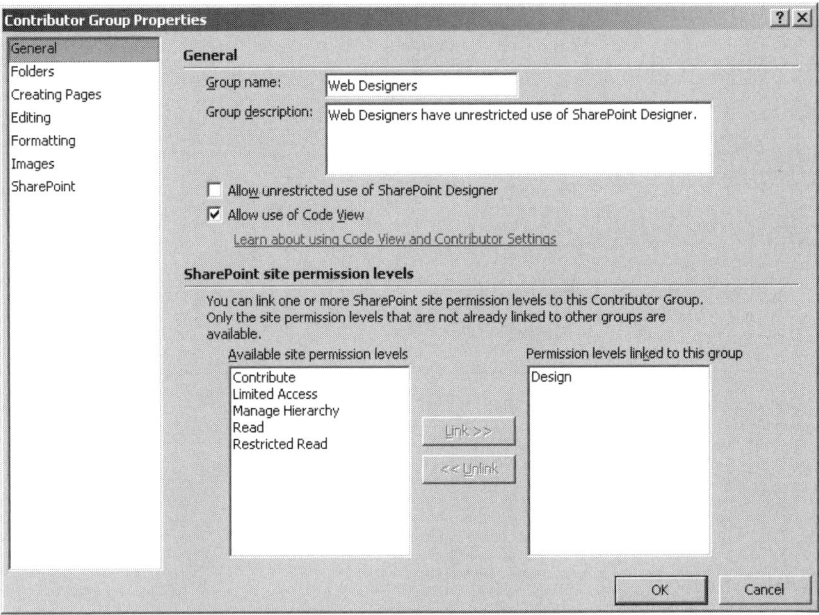

Figure 27-6 Setting constraints by contributor group

Real World Determining Contributor Setting

When determining contributor settings, typical SharePoint end users do not need to have access to SharePoint Designer and do not need to be able to perform design changes. Initially you could grant all permissions to farm, server, and site administrators and prohibit the use of SharePoint Designer to all other user groups. As time passes by, you can define which other user groups need to have access to SharePoint Designer and create fine-grained permission groups for them.

General

In the Contributor Group Properties window, with General selected in the task pane, you can determine whether you want to allow the use of code view or allow unrestricted use of SharePoint Designer 2007. Selecting the Allow Unrestricted Use Of SharePoint Designer check box allows a SharePoint group full use of SharePoint Designer 2007 for editing the SharePoint site. Selecting the Allow Use Of Code View check box determines whether a member of a SharePoint group is permitted to use the Code View option when editing pages in the SharePoint site.

On the left side of the Contributor Group Properties window, you can go to other windows that allow you to define fine-grained contributor settings. Fortunately, SharePoint Designer 2007 contributor settings do not introduce another user management system that you need to manage; contributor settings are built on top of the existing SharePoint user management features. Contributor settings allow you to create custom contributor groups in SharePoint Designer 2007 and link those to one or more SharePoint roles. As such, the feature is a security enforcement system dedicated to SharePoint Designer 2007.

Folders

The Folders window (shown in Figure 27-7) allows you to restrict folder access to specified contributor groups. You can specify the exact folders in which you allow certain contributor groups to edit existing pages. You can also specify the exact location where members of certain contributor groups are allowed to save new files and images.

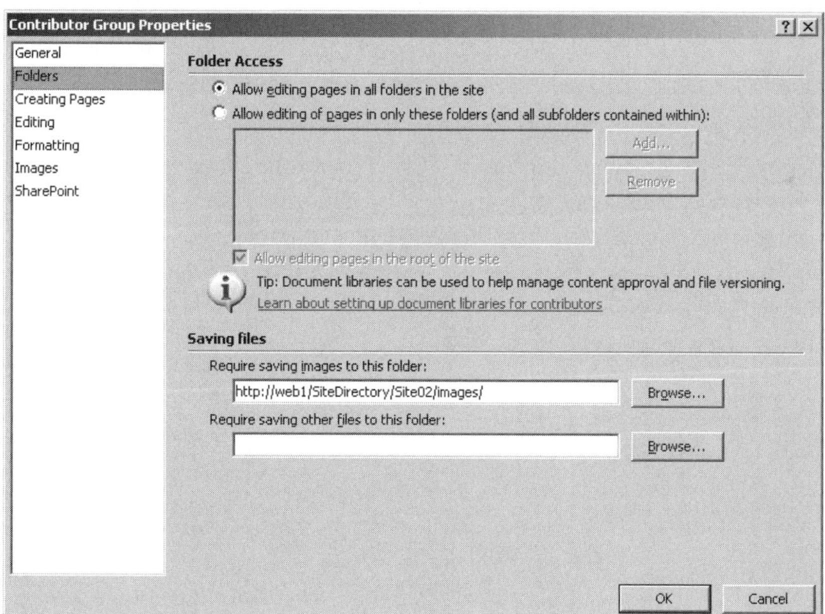

Figure 27-7 Setting folder access by contributor group

Creating Pages

In the Creating Pages window (shown in Figure 27-8), you can apply constraints on the type of pages a contributor group can create. You can also determine whether a contributor group is allowed to create new pages and whether the group can delete pages and folders. You also have the option to allow editing and deleting of master pages and content pages.

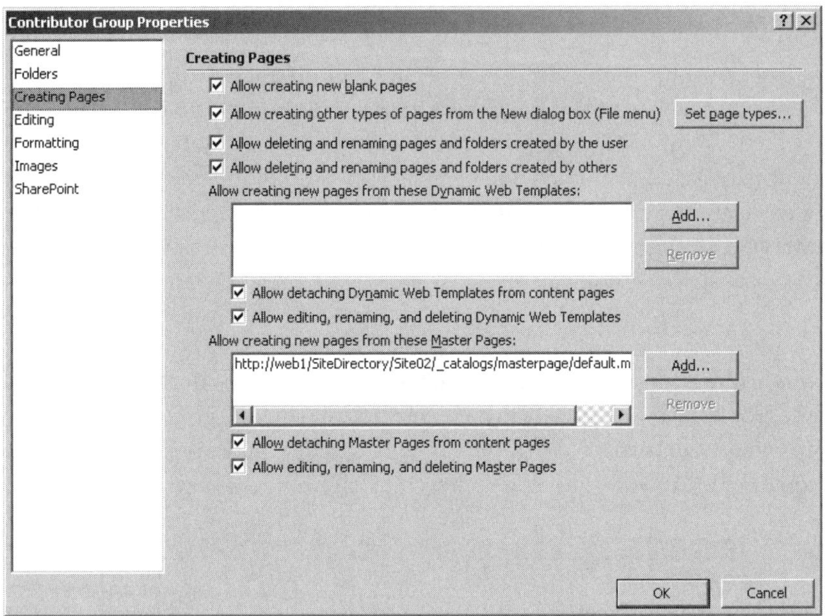

Figure 27-8 Setting page-creating constraints by contributor group

When you click the Set Page Types button, the Page Types dialog box opens (shown in Figure 27-9). The Page Types dialog box is where you define, for example, that a contributor group cannot create pages containing frames or master pages using File, New from the menu. The Page Types dialog box contains a Windows SharePoint Services Pages section that contains two types of SharePoint pages: List View Pages (pages containing lists) and Web Part Pages (pages containing Web Parts).

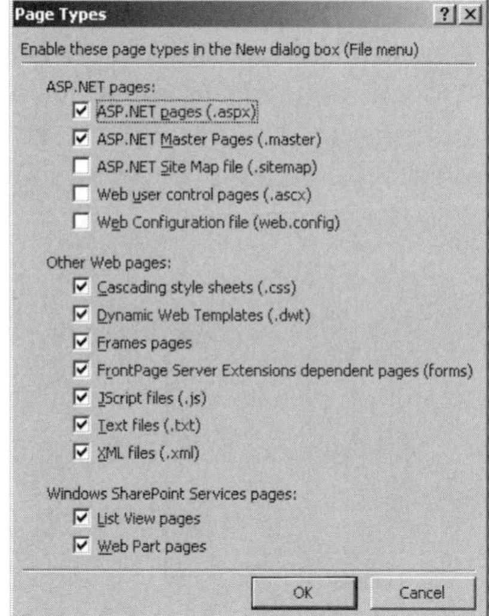

Figure 27-9 The Page Types dialog box

Editing

If you select Editing in the task pane of the Contributor Group Properties window (as shown in Figure 27-10), you can control whether a contributor group is only allowed to edit text or is also allowed to edit other page elements and properties. When you allow a contributor group to edit the page elements and properties, you can determine what kind of controls contributor group members can use in a page. For example, you might allow them to insert tables but not to insert interactive buttons.

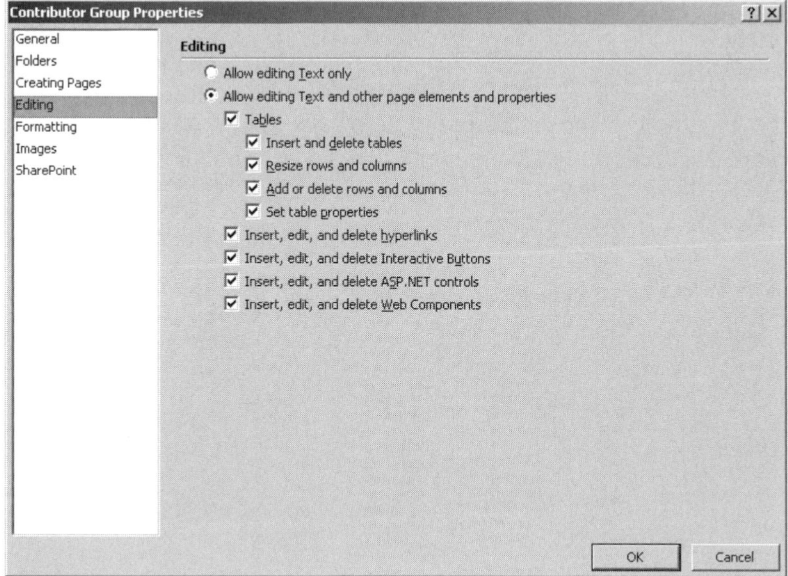

Figure 27-10 Setting editing rules by contributor group

Formatting

In the Formatting window (shown in Figure 27-11), you can specify whether the contributor group is allowed to change CSS styles settings. You can also specify that a group is allowed to apply CSS styles inline. You can use the Add button to specify that a contributor group can use only certain CSS files. You can decide to allow a group to change font properties and paragraph formatting, apply bullets and numbering, apply borders and shading, and edit page properties.

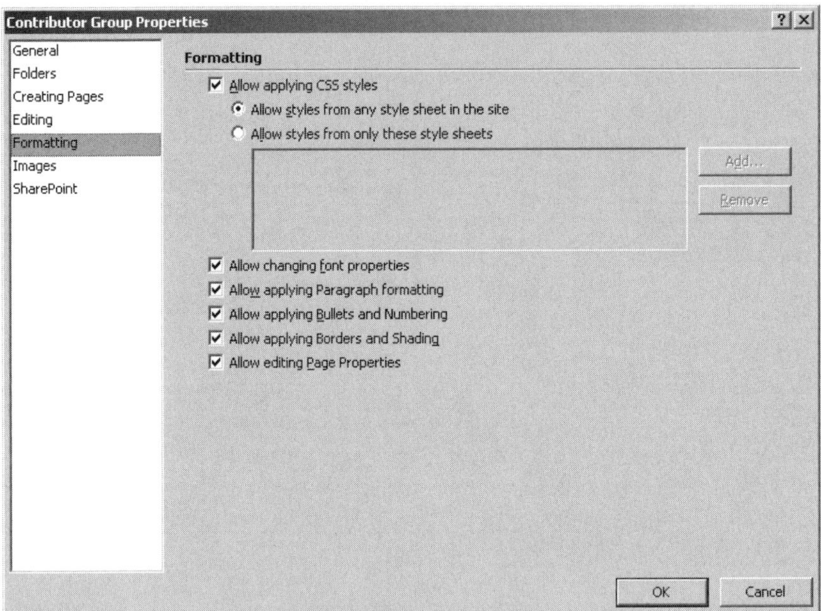

Figure 27-11 Setting formatting rules by contributor group

Images

Figure 27-12 shows the Images window. Here you can set constraints on the images that are used. For example, you can set the maximum size of images and allow the inserting and editing of photo galleries.

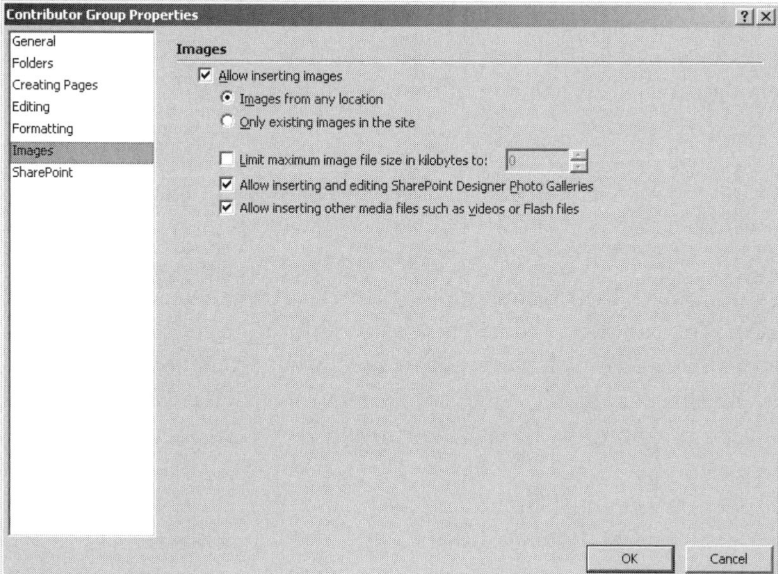

Figure 27-12 Setting constraints on image types by contributor group

SharePoint

The SharePoint window (shown in Figure 27-13) displays some SharePoint-specific settings. One important option you will find here is the ability to determine whether the contributor group is allowed to modify the home page. You can even restrict users from changing any page in the SharePoint site template.

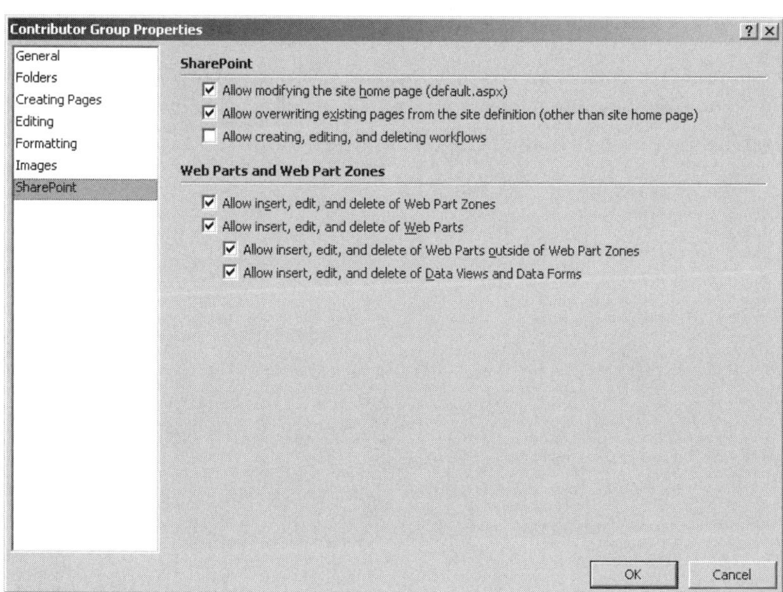

Figure 27-13 Setting SharePoint-specific constraints by contributor group

Adding Contributor Settings to Site Templates

Contributor settings are stored in the form of an XML file that is located on a SharePoint site. The contributor settings file is named Contributorsettings.htm.

Note Although the contributor settings file is an HTML content type, it is also valid XML. Because the contributor settings file mostly contains XML data instead of markup information, we call it an XHTML file instead of an HTML file.

The Contributorsettings.htm file is stored in the _contributor_settings folder in SharePoint Designer 2007. You can define contributor settings for a specific SharePoint site template that is located on a SharePoint server. A SharePoint site is an instance of a SharePoint site template. Any instance of the SharePoint site template that is created using a site template that contains contributor settings automatically uses the contributor settings defined in the template.

Note SharePoint Designer 2007 offers support for changing the default site template. You can import a site template in SharePoint Designer 2007 and copy the contributor settings file of such a template into your site template. This is a great way to define a default security policy for your SharePoint environments and deploy this The information in this chapter is based on the Microsoft Office SharePoint Server 2007 Beta 2 Technical Refresh release. At the time of writing this chapter, it is not yet possible to import a SharePoint site template. If you want to learn how to import a SharePoint site template, you should look at the Microsoft Office SharePoint Designer Help File.

Creating New Files

In SharePoint Designer 2007, it is very easy to create new files. When you click the File menu and choose New, the New window opens. In this window, you can create a page and choose between different kinds of pages, such as HTML, ASPX, and CSS. (See Figure 27-14.)

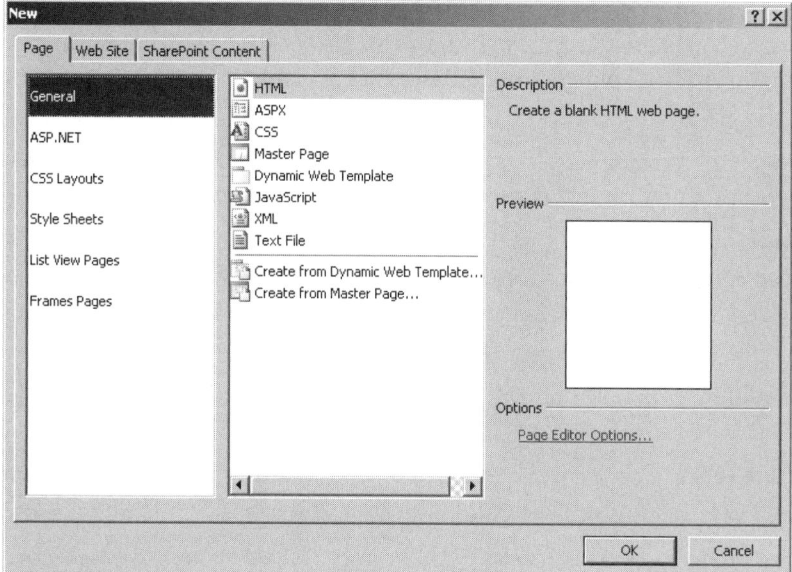

Figure 27-14 The Page tab of the New window

Using the New window, you can create specific ASP.NET items, such as a Web user control, Web configuration page, or sitemap. SharePoint Designer 2007 ships with a set of layout templates that are ready for you to use. You can choose between different kinds of cascading style sheets, List View Pages, Web Part Pages, and Frames Pages. You can also choose from a series of SharePoint Designer 2007 Server Templates that you can use to build, for example, a confirmation form or a guestbook form.

Understanding Master Pages

With master pages, you can easily change the look and feel for all the pages in a SharePoint site. Master pages provide a simple way to create a site template. They work by allowing you to design an HTML page with editable regions. These editable regions are called *content placeholders* and represent the parts of the template that will be customized on each page individually. The area outside the confines of content placeholders is identical for all the pages that are using the master page and is not editable on a page-by-page basis. By default, all pages in a SharePoint site use only one master page. The actual content of a content placeholder is defined by pages that use the master page: individual content pages, form pages, and application pages. The content in a content placeholder is also known as a *content placeholder definition*.

When rendered, the layout of a master page is automatically combined with the content of a page referring to such a master page to output a single HTML page. The way master pages work in Windows SharePoint Services 3.0 is identical to the way master pages work in ASP.NET 2.0.

The introduction of the concept of master pages into SharePoint technologies is a great new feature for ensuring uniformity between SharePoint sites. Master pages offer the following benefits:

- **An improved editing experience for Windows SharePoint Services pages** It is easier to make design changes in one place and propagate those changes to all the pages that use this master page.
- **Web-level editing** There is only one place to edit and change the master page elements.
- **User interface reuse** It is easy to create a page with a custom look and feel, and it is even easier to have all your pages adopt this look and feel.
- **Consistency** This includes consistency between pages and an improved end-user experience because of this consistent look and feel.

Content Pages

Content pages contain the definitions of content placeholders. All content pages share the same page structure: navigation, logos, search box, login controls, editing controls, CSS references, and the global breadcrumb. In Windows SharePoint Services 3.0, this shared page structure is placed in a master page called the *default.master*. The following SharePoint content pages use this default.master page:

- default.aspx
- The list pages
    - AllItems.aspx
    - DispForm.aspx
    - NewForm.aspx
    - EditForm.aspx
- The document libraries
    - Upload.aspx
    - Webfldr.aspx
- Newly created content pages in a SharePoint site

The standard set of content pages is initially located on the file system, in the same directory area as the rest of the template pages. For example, in the case of a SharePoint site, default.aspx is stored at [*drive letter*]:\Program Files\Common Files\Microsoft Shared\Web Server Extensions\12\TEMPLATE\SiteTemplates\sts. Form pages such as editform.aspx are stored in the [*drive letter*]:\Program Files\Common Files\Microsoft Shared\Web Server Extensions\12\TEMPLATE\Features folder.

SharePoint Hive

The location *%SystemDrive%*\Program Files\Common Files\Microsoft Shared\Web server extensions\12\ is also known as the SharePoint hive or SharePoint 12 hive. This is the starting place where all the files related to SharePoint are installed. For more details on the SharePoint hive, see Chapter 5, "Installing Microsoft Office SharePoint Server 2007."

A content page can have two states: customized or uncustomized. Once a content page is customized, it is stored in the content database. Uncustomized pages are stored on the file system. This is not a new concept; in SharePoint 2003, this was called unghosting (customized) and ghosting (uncustomized). One of the great new features in SharePoint Designer 2007 is the built-in ability to recognize customized pages and the option you have within the user interface to revert them to a template—in other words, to make them uncustomized again.

Content Placeholders

A master page consists of static text, controls, and one or more *ContentPlaceHolders* controls that define regions where customizable content can appear. Figure 27-15 shows a part of the default.master page containing *ContentPlaceHolders* controls.

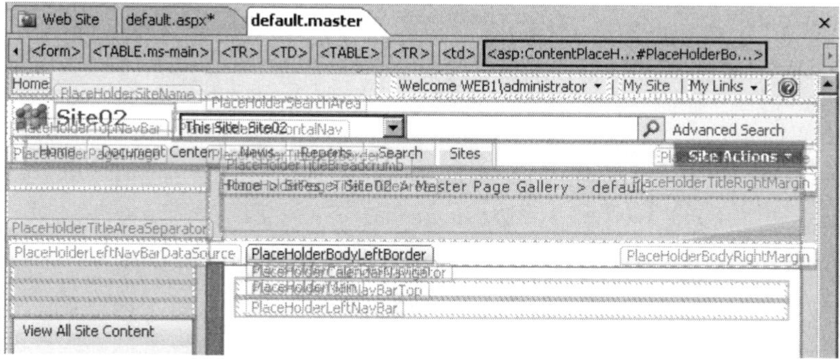

Figure 27-15 Default.master page with *ContentPlaceHolders* controls

Table 27-2 provides an overview of all content placeholders used by Windows SharePoint Services 3.0 pages.

Table 27-2 Overview of Content Placeholders

Name	Description
PlaceHolderBodyAreaClass	Additional body styles in the page header.
PlaceHolderBodyLeftBorder	Border element for the main page body.
PlaceHolderBodyRightMargin	Right margin of the main page body.
PlaceHolderCalendarNavigator	Shows a date picker for navigating in a calendar when a calendar is visible on the page.
PlaceHolderFormDigest	The "form digest" security control. The *FormDigest* control inserts security validation within a page, and its presence is required if you want to change data in the SharePoint content database.
PlaceHolderGlobalNavigation	The global navigation breadcrumb.
PlaceHolderHorizontalNav	The horizontal navigation area.
PlaceHolderLeftActions	Bottom of the left navigation area.
PlaceHolderLeftNavBar	Left navigation area.
PlaceHolderLeftNavBarBorder	Border element on the left navigation bar.
PlaceHolderLeftNavBarDataSource	*DataSource* element in the left navigation bar.
PlaceHolderLeftNavBarTop	Top element in the left navigation bar.
PlaceHolderMain	Page's main content.
PlaceHolderMiniConsole	A place to show page-level commands—for example, WIKI commands such as Edit Page, History, and Incoming Links.
PlaceHolderNavSpacer	The width of the left navigation area.
PlaceHolderPageDescription	Description of the contents of the page.
PlaceHolderImage	Image.
PlaceHolderTitleInTitleArea	Page title shown immediately below the bread-crumb.
PlaceHolderSearchArea	Search box area.
PlaceHolderSiteName	Site name.
PlaceHolderTitleAreaClass	Additional styles in the page header.
PlaceHolderTitleAreaSeparator	Separator in the page header.
PlaceHolderTitleBreadcrumb	Main content breadcrumb area.
PlaceHolderTitleLeftBorder	Left navigation area.

Table 27-2 **Overview of Content Placeholders**

Name	Description
PlaceHolderTitleRightMargin	Right margin of the title area.
PlaceHolderTopNavBar	Top navigation area.
PlaceHolderUtilityContent	Extra content at the bottom of the page.
SPNavigation	Empty by default in Windows SharePoint Services. *SPNavigation* can be used for additional page-editing controls.
WSSDesignConsole	The page editing controls when the page is in Edit Page mode (after clicking Site Actions, and then clicking Edit Page).

Master Page Tokens

When using master pages and content pages, you have to add an attribute to the Page directive of the content page. Windows SharePoint Services provides two kinds of tokens to reference the master page: dynamic and static tokens. These tokens apply only to Windows SharePoint Services master pages; they do not apply to ASP .NET 2.0 master pages.

- **Dynamic tokens** The value of a dynamic token is calculated at runtime, depending on the current instance of the *SPWeb* class. There are two types of dynamic tokens:
  - **~masterurl/default.master** This token is used by a Page Directive that is placed in a content page. The Page Directive looks like this:

    ```
    <%@ Page MasterPageFile="~masterurl\default.master"%>
    ```

    The token is replaced at runtime with the value of the *MasterUrl* property of the *SPWeb* class. This property contains the relative path to the master page. At installation time, all SharePoint content pages use this token and the *MasterUrl* property of the *SPWeb* class is set to the Windows SharePoint Services default.master. This value can be changed to point to a different master page.
  - **~masterurl/[custom].master** This token is used by a Page Directive that is placed in a content page. Replace *[custom]* with the name of your custom master page. The Page Directive looks like this:

    ```
    <%@ Page MasterPageFile="~masterurl\[custom].master"%>.
    ```

    The complete token is replaced at runtime by the value of the *CustomMasterUrl* property of the *SPWeb* class that contains the relative path to the master page. This token provides a way to define other custom master pages for a page.

- **Static tokens** You can use static tokens to link to a site-relative or site collection–relative master page. There are two types of static tokens:
  - **~site/default.master** If your content page is located at http://mySiteCollection/mySubSite/default.aspx and you use the token "~site/mypage.master", the content page uses the master page located at http://mySiteCollection/mySubSite/mypage.master.
  - **~sitecollection/default.master** If your content page is located at http://mySiteCollection/mySubSite/default.aspx and you use the token "~sitecollection/mypage.master", your content page uses the master page at http://mySiteCollection/mypage.master.

Instead of making use of dynamic or static tokens, you can change which master page a content page uses by directly changing the URL for the *MasterPageFile* attribute specified in the Page directive. Changing this attribute will influence which master page a specific content page uses. You can also use the *MasterUrl* property of the *SPWeb* class, which represents the entire SharePoint site, to change a master page. If you use the *MasterUrl* property of the current SharePoint site to change a master page, you will change the master page for all content pages in the SharePoint site.

When working with master pages in Windows SharePoint Services, you need to have a basic understanding of the meaning of page compilation mode and nested master pages. The *compilation mode* specifies how the ASP.NET engine compiles ASP.NET (.aspx) pages. The compilation mode for master pages is identical to the compilation mode for any other ASP.NET page. You can change the compilation mode whenever you want, and you can combine different compilation modes for master and content pages. There are three compilation modes: Always, Auto, and Never. The default compilation mode is Always, which means that a page will be compiled whenever a request to it is made. The Auto compilation mode means that the ASP.NET engine will not compile the page, if possible. The Never compilation mode means that the page will never be compiled dynamically. If the page contains a script block or code that requires compilation, ASP.NET will return an error and the page will not be run.

By default, master pages are uncustomized and are compiled when requested. Such master pages can contain inline script. However, you should be aware that once a master page is customized in SharePoint Designer 2007, the SharePoint SafeMode parser that prevents the execution of inline script parses the page.

By default, Windows SharePoint Services does not use *nested master pages*, but that does not block users from using them. You can create master pages at any level and have a master page that refers to another master page. For example, you can reference one master page from another master page using the following directive:

```
<%@ Master master=parent.master %>
```

You can add static Web Parts to a master page, but you cannot add dynamic Web Parts to master pages. Static Web Parts are Web Parts that are placed outside of a Web Part zone. A user cannot interact with a static Web Part or modify it within a browser. A dynamic Web Part is placed inside a Web Part zone, and a user can modify its properties. You can add zones to master pages and later add (dynamic) Web Parts to these zones in the browser. However, those Web Parts are associated to the content page, not to the master page.

The Difference Between Application, Content, and Form Pages

There are several types of pages in a portal site: application, content, and form pages. Customization of the site master page influences only the content pages for that specific site.

Application and form pages are pages that are used by Windows SharePoint Services itself and are shared across sites. Examples of such pages include the native SharePoint pages used to create new lists, document libraries, edit views, and so on. Application and form pages are stored at [*drive letter*]:\Program Files\Common Files\Microsoft Shared\Web server extensions\12\TEMPLATE\LAYOUTS. These pages run in direct mode, meaning that SharePoint does not intercept these pages but allows the pages to be executed normally by the ASP.NET engine. The contents of the layouts directory are considered to fall outside the scope of control of the Web site, and its pages are supplied directly by IIS as requested. Arbitrary code can be used within custom ASP.NET pages that are placed in this directory.

The master page applied to application and form pages is called *application.master*. If you want to use this master page, you must add an attribute to the Page directive of the application or form page. The token used to reference this master page is /_layouts /application.master. You can edit the application.master page and application and form pages in SharePoint Designer 2007.

Customize Master Pages

Windows SharePoint Services has one single master page built into it that applies to all content pages in a site. You can create your own master pages for a site and make them available for that site and the sites beneath it. There are two supported scenarios for customizing master pages:

- Make a copy of the default.master page, and remove the markup around placeholders.
- Start with a blank master page, and build it from the ground up. You can copy placeholders from the default.master page.

When creating custom master pages, developers must use the same set of content placeholders or a superset of these placeholders; otherwise, pages using the custom master page might fail to render. For custom applications, it is better to make your own custom master and to leave the default.master page alone.

SharePoint Designer 2007 has a safety net when you start customizing master pages. You can use the Version History command to roll back a page to a previous version. Alternatively, you could use the Revert To Template command to get the original master back from the site definition. The original master page is located at [*drive letter*]:\Program Files\Common Files\Microsoft Shared\Web server extensions\12.

Each page in a SharePoint site depends on a master page, and each SharePoint site has a Master Page Gallery. This Master Page Gallery contains all the master pages for all the pages in a SharePoint site. You can open a master page with SharePoint Designer 2007 via the browser. To open a SharePoint site in a browser, click Site Actions, click Site Settings, and in the Galleries section, click Master Pages. On the Master Page Gallery, you can click the drop-down menu and select Edit In Microsoft Office SharePoint Designer 2007.

The default master page is located at [*drive letter*]\Program files\Common Files\Microsoft Shared\Web Server extensions\12\Template\Features\MPLib. When this master page is uncustomized, its page definition is cached on the front-end Web server and shared across sites. If the master page definition in default.master is edited for a particular SharePoint site, an edited copy of the master page file is stored in the content database. This is called *customization*.

The Master Page toolbar is the key tool for customizing placeholders and creating new ones. The Master Page toolbar includes the functions listed in Table 27-3.

Table 27-3 Master Page Toolbar Functions

Image	Description
PlaceHolderBody	This drop-down list shows all the placeholders available in the master page.
	Click to open the Manage Content Regions dialog box.
	Click to show the Content Regions Labels in the page.

To create a new master page and add content placeholders, follow these steps:

1. From the Folder List task pane, open the _catalogs folder and right-click the masterpage folder. Select New, and then select SharePoint Content. The New SharePoint Content window opens.
2. Click the Page tab, click General, click Master Page, and then click OK. (See Figure 27-16.)

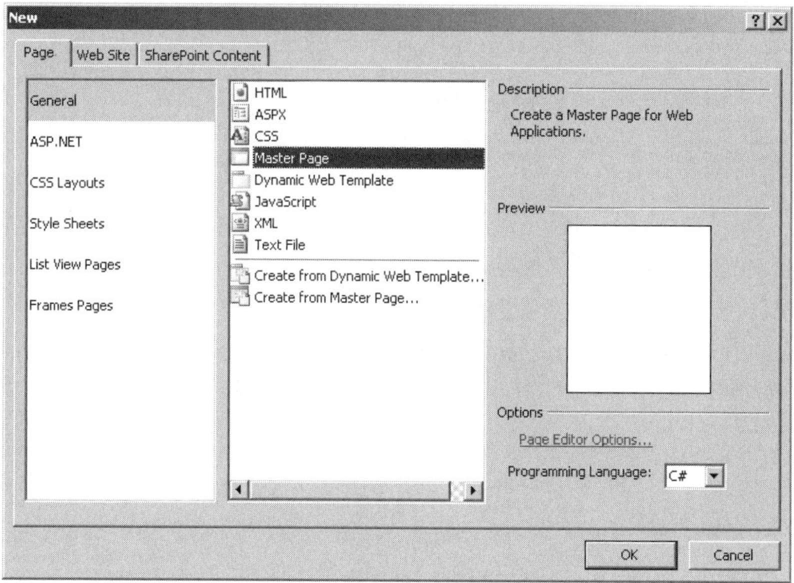

Figure 27-16 The Create A New Master Page window

3. To add new content regions, click Format, click Master Page, and then click Manage Content Regions or right-click the page in Design View and choose Manage Microsoft ASP.NET Content Regions. The Manage Content Regions window opens. Type a region name in the Region Name text box, and then click Add. The name of a region, also known as a placeholder, cannot contain any special characters or white spaces.
4. Select a region type for the content region. Click the region type of the new content region (by default, this is none). A drop-down list appears with the following three region types: Text And Images; Text Only; and Text, Layout, And Images.

After you create or customize a master page, you probably want to attach the master page to a content page. You can choose whether you want to set your master page as the default or as a custom master page. There are two ways to attach your master page:

- In the Folder List task pane, right-click the master page and choose either Set As Default Master Page or Set As Custom Master Page. If you choose Set As Default

Master Page, the default.master part of the master page token is replaced with the name of the new default master page. Make sure that you have included all the content placeholders that are used by the content pages in your master page.

- Click the Format menu (the main menu of SharePoint Designer 2007), select Master Page, and choose Attach Master Page. Doing this opens the Select A Master Page dialog box. Here you can set the default master page and the custom master page. (See Figure 27-17.)

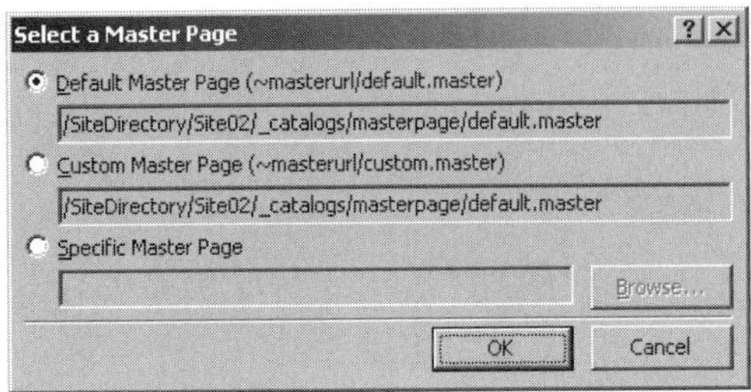

Figure 27-17 The Select A Master Page dialog box

In addition to being able to attach a master page to an existing content page, you can create a new content page based on your own master page. Right-click your master page in the Folder List task pane and choose New from Master Page. (See Figure 27-18). Doing this creates an .aspx file with all the content placeholders your master page contains.

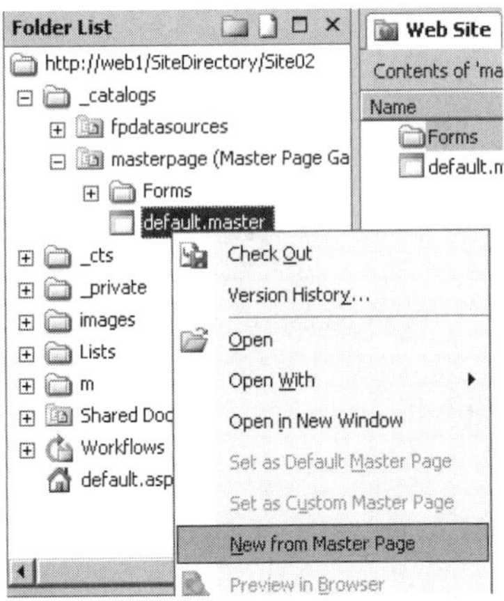

Figure 27-18 The New From Master Page link

Customizing a Web Site

Why would you want to customize a SharePoint site? Your reasons probably include the following: for visual differentiation reasons, for branding reasons, or you might want to build an entire and custom Web application altogether. There are three options for customizing a SharePoint site: via the browser, by editing a site definition, or by using SharePoint Designer 2007.

The main customization features of SharePoint Designer 2007 are the following:

- The ability to create and edit master pages
- The ability to modify default style sheets
- Deep support for ASP.NET controls
- The ability to create and edit publishing page layouts on Office SharePoint Server
- A built-in safety net that allows you to always revert a customized page or style sheet

In this section, we will discuss the SharePoint Designer 2007 features for customizing a site. We will look at customizing CSS pages, how to use SharePoint Designer 2007 to create the basic formatting of a page, and the Revert To Template feature.

Cascading Style Sheets, WYSIWYG, and Tools

Because SharePoint Designer 2007 is able to render CSS, CSS pages are shown in what-you-see-is-what-you-get (WYSIWYG) mode within SharePoint Designer 2007. SharePoint Designer 2007 includes several features to make creating styles a lot easier:

- **CSS design time preferences** Determine how CSS code is generated
- **CSS high fidelity rendering** Reproduces the end result of a page as displayed in a browser
- **CSS layout tools** Lets you choose between various page layouts
- **CSS property grid** Provides an overview of all CSS properties within a page or a specific style
- **CSS styles task pane** Allows you to apply and manage styles.
- **CSS reports** Allows you to generate reports that contain information about the styles used within a page or a set of pages.

With the CSS design-time preferences, you can set preferences that determine exactly how the CSS code is generated throughout an application to have complete control over SharePoint Designer 2007 code generation. To do this, from the Tools menu, click Page

Editor Options to open the Page Editor Options window. Click the CSS tab, and you will see the window shown in Figure 27-19.

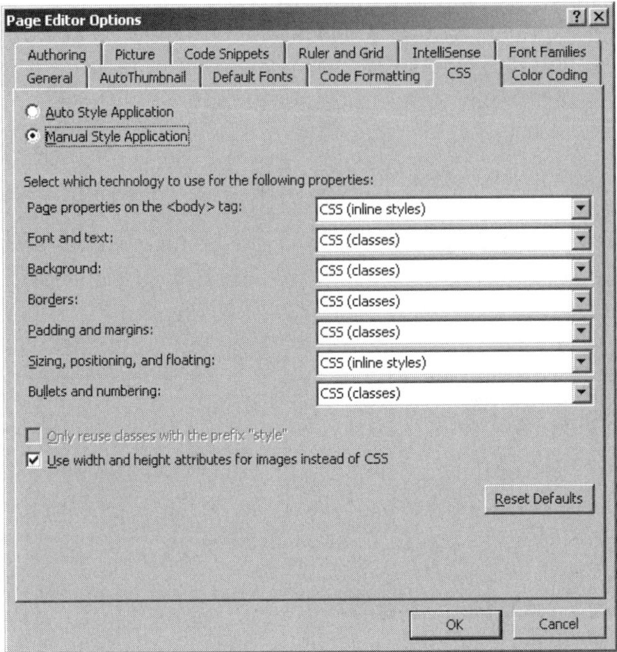

Figure 27-19 The CSS tab in the Page Editor Options window

On the CSS tab, you can select which CSS technology you want to use for a couple of properties. You can choose between inline CSS or styles in a page.

The CSS high fidelity rendering functionality in SharePoint Designer 2007 is able to produce a faithful representation of the look of the final browser-rendered page by making use of a powerful CSS rendering engine.

Auto Style Mode

In this section, you will see how to use SharePoint Designer 2007 to create the basic formatting of a page with the help of automatically generated CSS. This is called the Auto Style Mode.

SharePoint Designer 2007 makes it very easy to style a newly created page. To illustrate this, we will create a new HTML page by clicking the File menu, selecting New, and then choosing Page. Doing this opens the File New dialog box. Here you can choose a blank HTML page and click OK. Double-click the page to open it. Add a title, subtitle, and section with text to it while the page is in Design View by typing in three lines containing some words. This causes the creation of three paragraphs on the page. You can select one of those paragraphs—for example, the title paragraph—and change the size by using the Common toolbar. The Common toolbar also allows you to change the color of the paragraph. In this example (shown in Figure 27-19), we have changed the size of the title, changed the size of the subtitle, and made the color of the text block red and the title blue. While you are changing the formatting of the text, new CSS styles are created on the fly. Therefore, while you are busy applying basic formatting to your page in design view, you are also busy creating new CSS styles. If you want, these CSS styles can be reused within other pages.

If you change the title again—say, for example, that you make it bold this time—a new style is created. If you create a style that already exists, the old style is reused. The design surface is very efficient in reusing styles that are already generated in the page. Figure 27-20 shows what the page looks like.

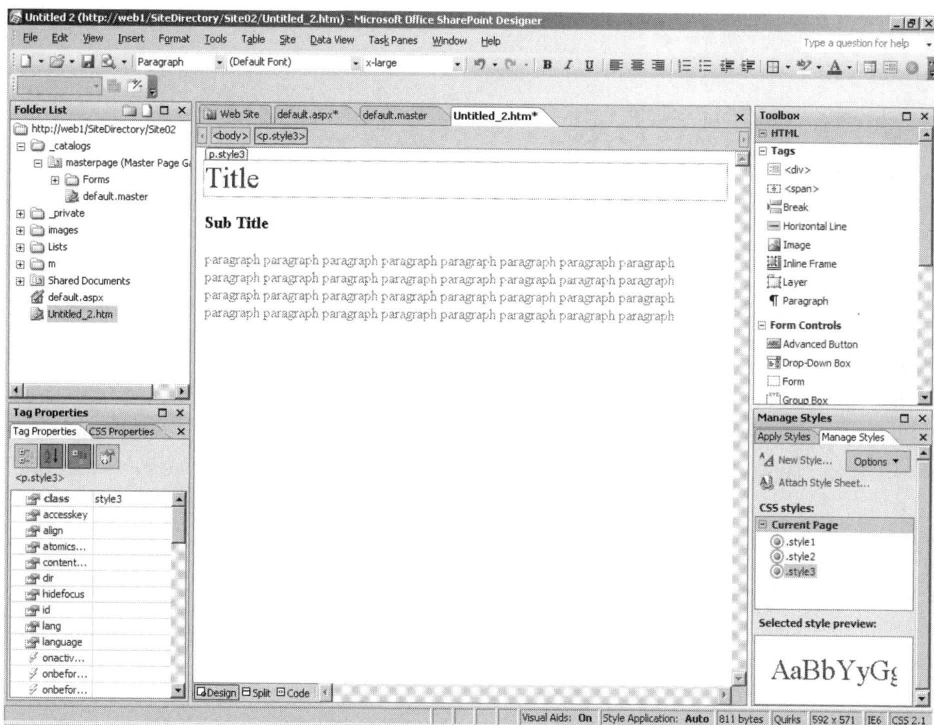

Figure 27-20 A new HTML page in SharePoint Designer 2007

When you go to the Code View of the HTML page, you will notice that the styles are included inline in the page as a style block. This appearance conforms with the design-time preferences that we set up in the Page Options dialog box. The following code block shows the code of the sample HTML page:

```
<!DOCTYPE html PUBLIC "-//W3C//DTD XHTML 1.0 Transitional//EN" "http://
www.w3.org/TR/xhtml1/DTD/xhtml1-transitional.dtd">
<html xmlns="http://www.w3.org/1999/xhtml">
<head>
  <meta http-equiv="Content-Language" content="en-us" />
  <meta http-equiv="Content-Type" content="text/html; charset=utf-8" />
  <title>Untitled 1</title>
  <style type="text/css">
    .style1
    {
      font-size: x-large;
      color: #0000FF;
    }
    .style2
    {
      color: #FF0000;
    }
    .style3
    {
      font-size: large;
    }
    </style>
</head>
<body>
<p class="style1"><strong>Title</strong></p>
<p class="style3">Sub Title</p>
<p class="style2">Paragraph paragraph paragraph paragraph paragraph
paragraph paragraph paragraph paragraph </p>
</body>
</html>
```

The Apply Styles and Manage Styles task panes in SharePoint Designer 2007 show the styles that we have created. At this point, there are three styles present. (See Figure 27-21.)

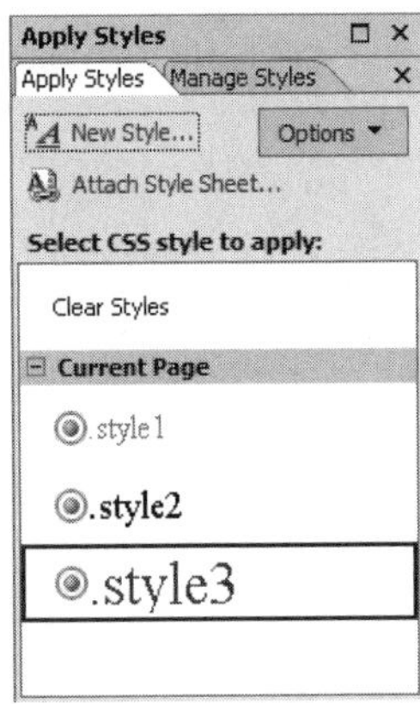

Figure 27-21 The Apply Styles task pane

This way of working is called the Auto Style Mode because you are automatically generating styles as you work. For example, when you are changing the color of a text, a style is generated to reflect this change. You can access and edit the styles directly.

Within the CSS Properties task pane, you can edit the CSS properties of a selected style. You can select a style and click on the *Color* property to select a new color for your style. Once you have selected a new color, the style changes immediately, which is also reflected in Design View.

The CSS Properties task pane is also useful when you create a new style. You can create a new style by using the Manage Styles tab in the Apply Styles task pane. Click the New Style link to open the New Style window. In the example shown in Figure 27-22, we have created an implicit CSS style for the HTML body element and have set its font-family to Broadway style.

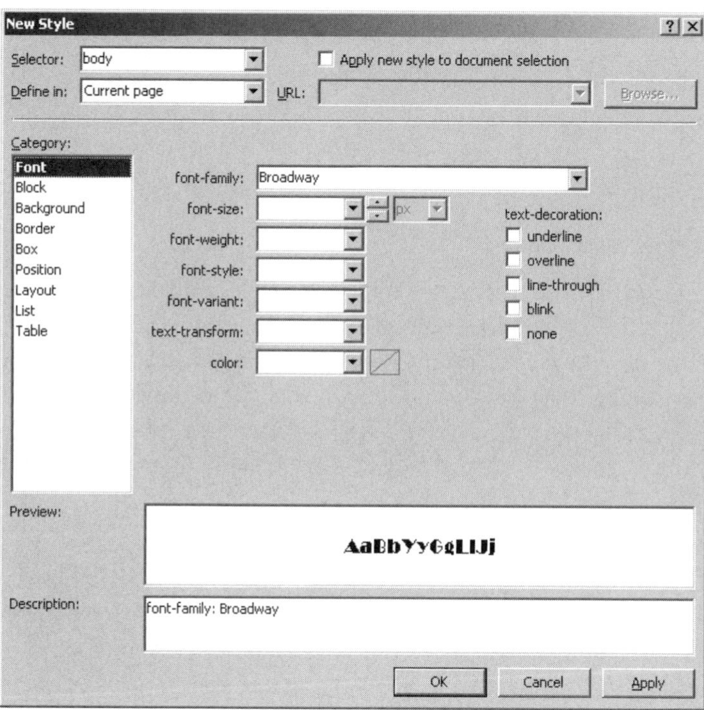

Figure 27-22 The New Style window

Because we have changed the font-family for the HTML body element, all items in the HTML page that inherit from the *<body>* element will have their font family changed accordingly. The CSS Properties task pane shows both the style and the body attributes of the selected paragraph. With this task pane, you can see exactly which attributes are set for each class.

A very cool feature of the CSS Properties task pane is the Summary button, which lets you roll up an overview of the properties that are changed. If you modify the body style and change the color, those changes are displayed in the CSS Properties task pane. First, you can see that two instances of the body style color property show up in the CSS Properties task pane. Then you should notice that one of those body styles is striked-out, signifying that this is the old body style that is replaced by the other, active body style. The active body style is the style that is applied to the body of the page. (See Figure 27-23.)

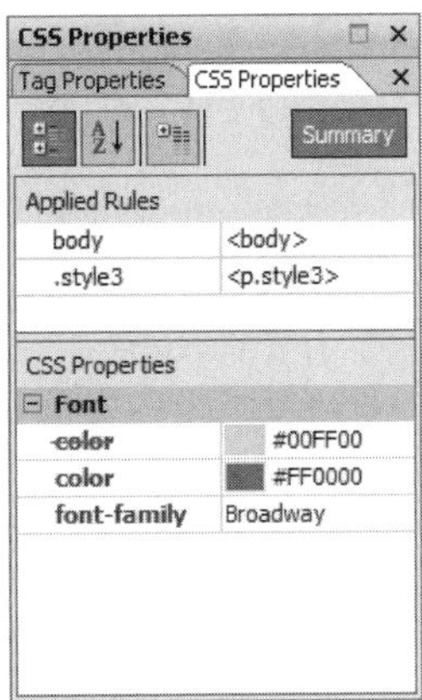

Figure 27-23 The CSS Properties task pane

Typically, you want to reuse a CSS style elsewhere. You can do this by moving CSS styles to an external file. You can create a new CSS file by clicking the File menu, selecting New, and choosing CSS. Save the new style sheet on the file system and name it Mystyles.css. Then go back to the Design View of our page, and look at the Manage Styles task pane that contains an option to attach a style sheet to the page by clicking the link Attach Style Sheet. Doing this opens the Attach Style Sheet dialog box, which lets you browse to your new style sheet.

After the style sheet is attached, you can see that the mystyles.css style sheet shows up in the Manage Styles task pane. Now you can move styles that were created earlier to the external style sheet by selecting them, and dragging and dropping them onto the external style sheet. The styles have now become part of the external style sheet, and our page is updated automatically so that it contains the following link to the mystyles.css style sheet:

```
<link rel="stylesheet" type="text/css" href="mystyles.css" />
```

As soon as you double-click a style in the Manage Styles task pane, you jump to the code definition of the style. When you click a style in the Manage Styles task pane, you are shown a preview of the selected style. (See Figure 27-24.)

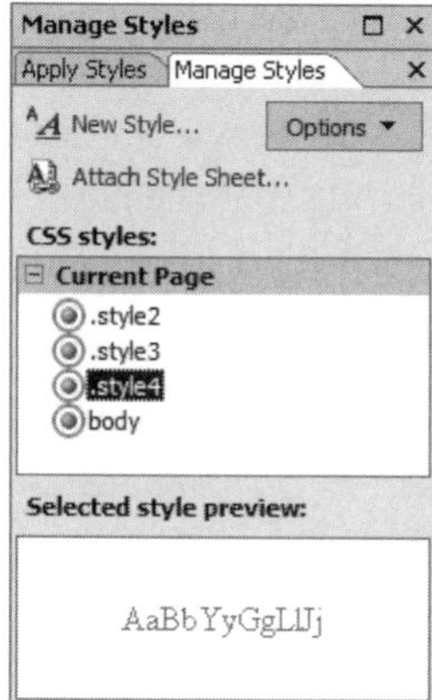

Figure 27-24 The Manage Styles task pane

Manual Style Mode

You can also manipulate the layout in the CSS manually, which is known as Manual Style Mode. You can do this using the Style Application toolbar. The Styles Application toolbar includes the functions listed in Table 27-4.

Table 27-4 **Style Application Toolbar Functions**

Image	Description
Style Application: Manual (Auto / Manual)	This drop-down list lets you choose between the two style modes: auto and manual. When you choose auto mode, all other functions of the toolbar are not available.
Target Rule: (New Inline Style)	This drop-down list shows the target rule you have selected. It also gives you the chance to create a new target rule by making use of the style builder.
Reuse Properties	Click to reuse exiting properties in the page.
Show Overlay	Click to show the overlay in the page.

If you use SharePoint Designer 2007 to click on several areas on a page that use different styles, you can see that the target rule shown in the Style Application toolbar changes to reflect the rule that is applied to the selected area. You can also create a new style rule and choose whether you want to create a new inline style rule or a style rule that is a part of a new style class altogether.

Note For reuse purposes, it is advisable to use external style sheets. Inline style sheets cannot be reused in other pages (unless you consider copy-and-paste reuse a form of reuse). In contrast, multiple pages are able to refer to a single external style sheet. This makes managing a single style much more convenient.

When you view a newly created HTML page in Split View and click the style of the paragraph, a highlighted square shows up around the edges of the style. (See Figure 27-25.)

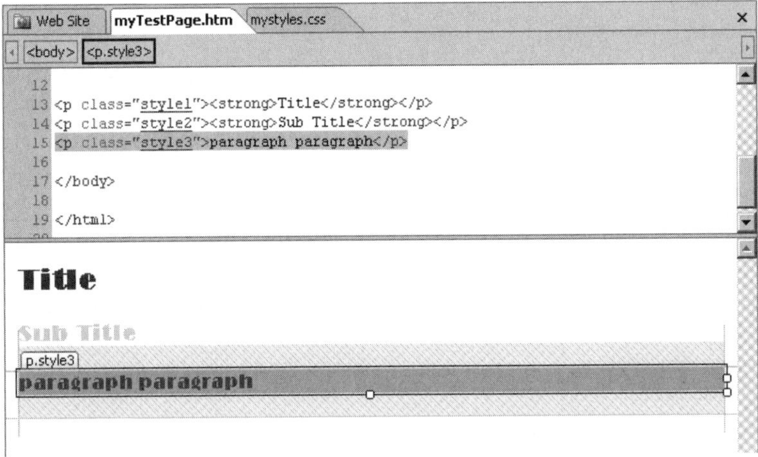

Figure 27-25 Square around the edges of a selected style

You can click the margin on the left and move it to the right to indent the text. The same can be done for the other margins to apply a change to a paragraph's margin. You can also make positional changes, including margins and padding, in Design View—a new feature in SharePoint Designer 2007. *Padding* refers to the ability to insert spaces between a page and its content or to the space between content elements.

CSS IntelliSense

If you are using SharePoint Designer 2007 for creating or editing styles, you reap the benefits of the new CSS IntelliSense feature. CSS IntelliSense can be used in Code View and gives you a much easier experience for designing a style. When you edit a style using CSS IntelliSense, the change is reflected immediately in the Design View of the page.

Note IntelliSense has been around for a long time in advanced development environments such as Microsoft Visual Studio. CSS IntelliSense makes it much easier to create CSS styles.

Figure 27-26 shows how to use CSS IntelliSense to set the background color for a style.

Figure 27-26 CSS IntelliSense in SharePoint Designer 2007

When you click the Tools menu and choose Page Editor Options, the Page Editor Options window opens. On the Authoring tab of this window, you can select which schema you want to use. This choice determines what is available in CSS IntelliSense. From a drop-down list, you can choose between the following options:

- CSS 1.0
- CSS 2.0
- CSS 2.1
- CSS IE6

CSS Link Server Control

The CSS Link server control is used in master pages and inserts a *<link>* element into the resulting HTML page to apply an external style sheet. Design View in SharePoint Designer 2007 recognizes the style sheets that are generated by this control. In code (which can be found in the master page), the CSS Link server control looks like this:

```
<SharePoint:CssLink runat="server"/>
```

You can find the style sheets that are used by the master page in the following location: [*drive letter*]:\Program Files\Common Files\Microsoft Shared\Web server extensions\12\TEMPLATE\LAYOUTS\1033\STYLES. The easiest way to create a new style sheet that is used by a master page is to create a copy of an existing style sheet.

CSS Layouts

SharePoint Designer 2007 is able to provide a preview of the way that a style will appear. You can have more than one layout per content type. You can create a page layout by clicking on the File menu and choosing New, which opens the New window. Then select Page and CSS Layouts. Here you can choose between the different layout options. For example, you can choose a page layout that contains only two columns or a page layout that contains a header, a logo, two columns, and a footer.

When you click each template in the New window, pay attention to the Description section at the top right of the window. Below this description, a preview of the page is shown. (See Figure 27-27.)

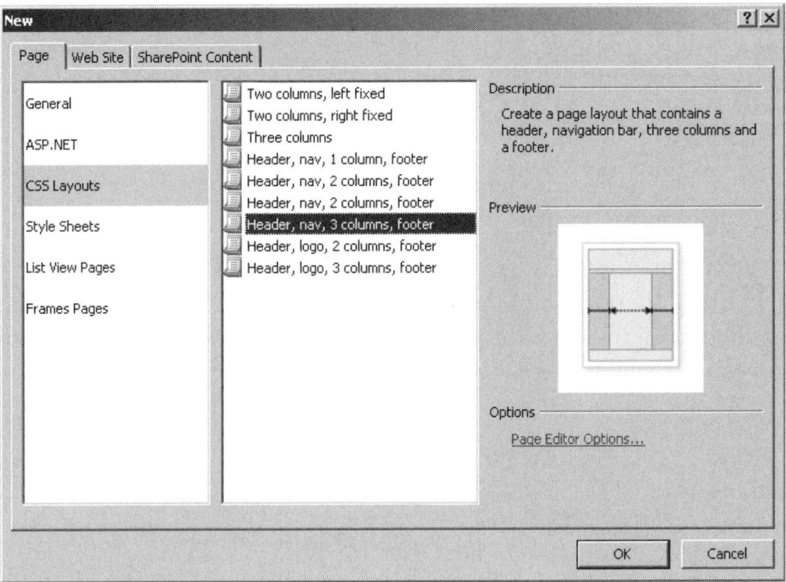

Figure 27-27 Page tab in the New window

Site Definition

A site definition is used to define a unique type of SharePoint site. Following is a list of the site definitions that are a part of a default Windows SharePoint Services installation:

- **Team site** Team sites help to create, organize, and share information quickly and easily.
- **Blank site** Blank sites are empty SharePoint sites.
- **Document workspace** Document workspaces allow team members to work together on documents.

- **Basic meeting workspace** Basic meeting workspaces contain the basic features that allow users to plan, organize, and track meetings.
- **Blank meeting workspace** Blank meeting workspaces are empty sites that are dedicated to managing team meetings. Such sites always need to be customized according to the specific requirements within a team.
- **Decision meeting workspace** Decision meeting workspaces are meeting workspaces that allow users to review relevant documents and keep track of decisions being made.
- **Social meeting workspace** Social meeting workspaces are planning tools for social occasions.
- **Multipage meeting workspace** Multipage meeting workspaces are identical to basic meeting workspaces in that they allow users to plan, organize, and track meetings. The difference is that a multipage meeting workspace, by default, consists of multiple pages.
- **Central admin template for central administration sites** Central administration sites allow power users to manage SharePoint.
- **Wiki template for Wikis** Wiki sites allow users to interact in an informal way. Wiki sites allow users add, edit, and link Web pages.
- **Blog template for blogs** Blog sites allow users to post information and allow other users to comment on this information.

Each site definition consists of a collection of files that are located within the [*drive letter*]:\Program Files\Common Files\Microsoft Shared\Web server extensions \12\template\sitetemplates subdirectories of a front-end Web server. Site definition files include .xml, .aspx (ASP.NET pages), .ascx (ASP.NET controls), .master page files, and document template files. Examples of document template files are .dot, .htm, and content files such as .gif and .doc files. You can edit the site templates in SharePoint Designer 2007 by clicking File menu and choosing Open. Browse to the site template you want to edit and click Open.

In SharePoint Designer 2007, you can also create a new SharePoint site based on these site templates. From the File menu, click New. Doing this opens the New dialog box. Click the Web Site tab and SharePoint Templates. Here you can choose which template you want to use. (See Figure 27-28.) The right side of the window contains a description of the template. At the bottom, you can specify the location of the new Web site. Selecting a template opens a new instance of SharePoint Designer 2007 and generates the site, which will take a few moments.

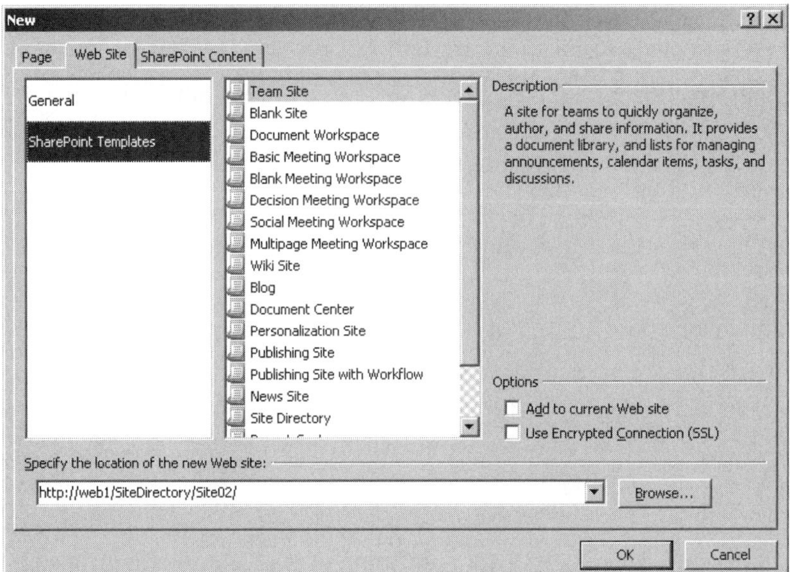

Figure 27-28 Web Site tab showing SharePoint Templates in the New window

Revert To Template

SharePoint Designer 2007 facilitates the configuration and customization of Web Parts. If you have edited a page but are not happy with the results, you can right-click that page in the Folder List task pane and choose Revert To Template Page. Doing this brings up a Site Template Page Warning with the following message: "Reverting to the template page will replace the contents of this page with the contents defined by the page template. A backup copy of the current page is created in the same folder." If you click Yes, the Folder List task pane shows that a backup copy is created. For example, if you revert the default.aspx page to its default page, the name of the backup copy becomes *default_copy(1).aspx.*

Note This is a much requested feature. A common complaint with SharePoint 2003 was the fact that FrontPage 2003 made it easy to unghost (customize) a page but impossible to ghost it again (uncustomize or revert to template).

Working With Data Integration

Microsoft made a couple of investments concerning data integration and SharePoint Designer 2007. The SharePoint Designer 2007 data access layer was a proprietary layer that was limited to accessing SharePoint, SQL Server, Simple Object Access Protocol (SOAP), and XML. It has moved to the ASP.NET data-model layer using data source controls. The data source controls that are available for SharePoint Designer 2007 are built for the same data sources as were supported by the previous data access layer, but the key value of the new model is that this is now a developer-supported model. Therefore, you can create custom data source controls, and if you implement the proper interfaces for those controls, they can be used with data-bound controls such as the data view and data form.

SharePoint Designer 2007 now supports read as well as write actions in data views. Data views used to be read only, only suitable for presenting data. Now SharePoint Designer 2007 also supports data forms: single record forms and multiple record forms. In addition, you can use data views to update data sources. Using data forms, you can update data stored in SharePoint, SQL Server, and XML files.

The third important improvement regarding data integration is a feature called the *aggregate data source*, which refers to the ability to take two data sources and aggregate them into a single data view. You can do things such as join related data from two tables in SQL Server, or you can concatenate or make a union of data coming from disparate data sources such as XML files.

The final new feature in SharePoint Designer 2007 data integration adds new ways to support the passing of parameters to a data view. In FrontPage 2003, you could have parameters originating from another Web Part and pass those to the data view via a Web Part connection. Alternatively, you could have parameters that came from query strings, although it was not very easy to get to those parameters. SharePoint Designer 2007 gives you a new user interface that lets you define parameters that originate ASP.NET controls located on the page, cookies, forms, query strings, or server variables.

Note The data integration possibilities of SharePoint Designer 2007 make creating overviews and simple Web forms applications so easy that creating such applications is achievable for site designers. Even developers will be surprised in a positive way with the development time it takes to create such applications.

The Data Source Library

The Data Source Library is the central repository of all your data sources. It is the location from where the data sources can be managed and accessed. There are different types of data sources that can be accessed using the Data Source Library in SharePoint Designer 2007:

- **SharePoint Lists** Here you find all lists that are available on the SharePoint site and the option to create a new SharePoint list.
- **SharePoint Libraries** Here you find all the libraries that are available on your SharePoint site.

- **Database Connections** You find all the database connections for the SharePoint site here.
- **XML Files** You find all the XML files that are used in the SharePoint site here.
- **Server-side Scripts** You find all the server-side scripts and Real Simple Syndication (RSS) feeds that are used in the SharePoint site here.
- **XML Web Services** You find all Web services that are used in the SharePoint site here.
- **Business Data Catalog** You find here all the Business Data Catalog (BDC) views that are created, and you will have the option to create a new view.
- **Linked Sources** You find all linked sources that are used in the SharePoint site here.

You can open the Data Source Library by clicking Insert Data View on the Data menu or Data Source Library on the Task Panes menu. Figure 27-29 shows the Data Source Library task pane.

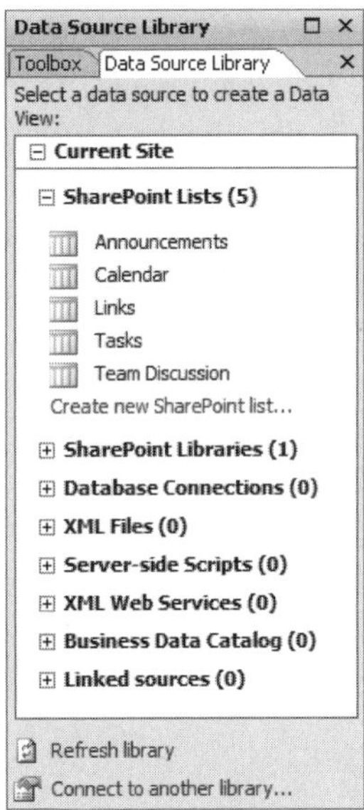

Figure 27-29 Data Source Library task pane

Adding a SharePoint List or Library

When you create a list data source using SharePoint Designer 2007, you can also specify columns, sorting, filtering, and grouping. The following steps show you how to add a SharePoint list as a data source:

1. In SharePoint Designer 2007, from the Data Source Library task pane, expand the SharePoint Lists folder by clicking the plus sign.

2. Click the Create New SharePoint List link to open the File New dialog box.
3. By default, SharePoint Designer 2007 shows the SharePoint Content tab of the File New dialog box containing all available SharePoint lists. The only thing you have to do here is to select the list that you want, specify a name for the new list in the Options section on the right side of the dialog box, and click OK. There is a description available for each one of the lists to make choosing lists easier.

If you want to add a SharePoint library as a data source, follow these steps:

1. In SharePoint Designer 2007, from the Data Source Library task pane, expand the SharePoint Libraries folder.
2. Click the Create New Document Library link to open the File New dialog box.
3. SharePoint Designer 2007 shows the SharePoint Contents tab of the File New dialog box containing all libraries of the SharePoint site. Please note that there is a description available for each library at the right of the window. Once you have selected a library, you can specify a name in the Options section on the right and then click OK.

Adding a Database Connection

Follow these steps to create a database connection:

1. Expand the Database Connections folder in the Data Source Library task pane, and click Connect To A Database. Doing this opens the Database Data Source Properties dialog box with the focus on the Source tab. (See Figure 27-30.)

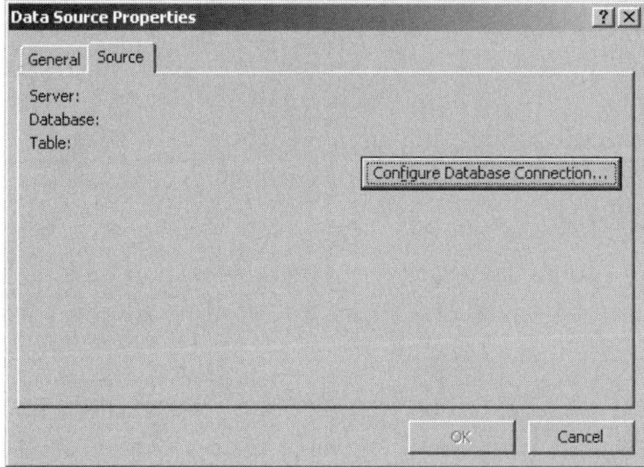

Figure 27-30 Database Data Source Properties dialog box

2. On the Source tab, click the Configure Database Connection button to open the Configure Database Connection Wizard. (See Figure 27-31.)

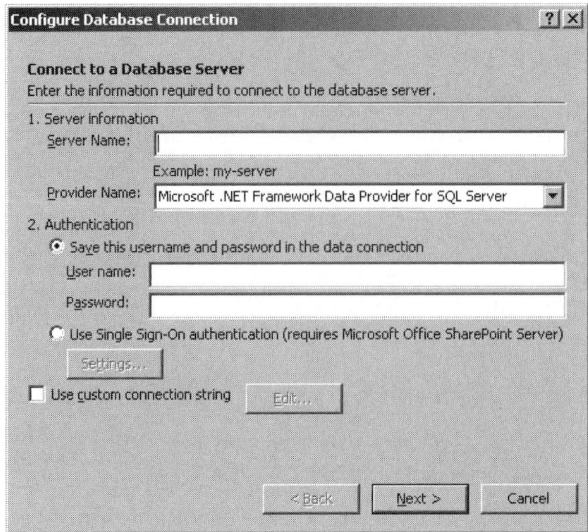

Figure 27-31 The Configure Database Connection Wizard

3. Enter the name of the database server you want to connect.
4. Choose the Provider Name you want to use. There are two options: Microsoft .NET Framework Data Provider For SQL Server or Microsoft .NET Framework Data Provider For OLE DB.
5. The next thing to choose is the authentication type. There are four options:
   a. Save This Username And Password In The Data Connection. You can specify a database user name and password to be saved in the connection string.
   b. Use Windows Authentication. This option requires integrated security to be supported by the data source because the Windows credentials of the client are used for authentication at the data source. This option is supported only when the data source is located on the same physical machine as the SharePoint server.
   c. Use Single Sign-On Authentication. You can use this option only when the SharePoint site is part of a SharePoint portal site and the administrator has enabled and configured Single Sign-On.
   d. Use Custom Connection String. When you want fine-grained control over the connection, you use this option. You can specify an OLE DB connection string that is used to connect to the database.

Note For most organizations, Windows authentication, if supported, will be the most appealing authentication model, as it is easy to configure and secure.

After finishing the specification of the authentication type you want to use, navigate to the next wizard page. On this page, you can select which database you would like to use from a drop-down list. After selecting the database, there are two options to proceed further:

- Select a table or view from that database. When you select a table or view displayed in the list and you click Finish, a window is displayed that lets you select the fields you want to display, specify filter criteria, and edit the sorting of the fields.
- Specify a custom select, update, insert, or delete command yourself by making use of SQL or stored procedures. After clicking Finish, you can make your own update, insert, select, and delete commands or edit a stored procedure.

Adding an XML File

You can connect to any given XML file, and SharePoint Designer 2007 automatically creates a data source for the XML file and imports it in the SharePoint site that is currently open in SharePoint Designer 2007. The following steps do not describe the creation of an XML file; you have to take care of that one yourself or choose an existing XML file location on your file system.

1. Go to the Data Source Library task pane, expand the XML Files folder, and click the Add An XML File link.
2. Completing step 1 opens the XML File Data Source Properties dialog box, where you can browse to your XML file.
3. If your XML file is not located on your Web site yet, you will see an alert message box that prompts you to import the file. (See Figure 27-32.)

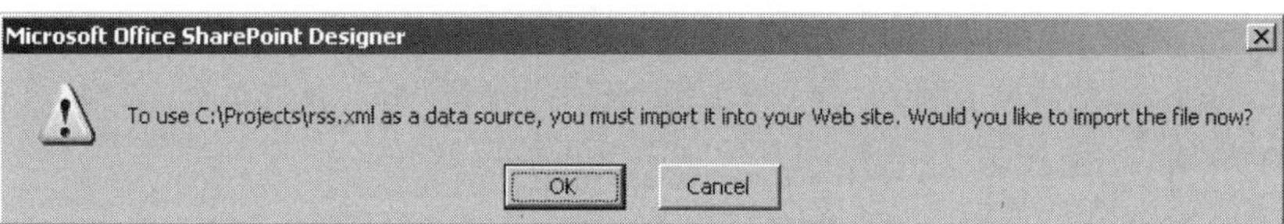

Figure 27-32 An alert message box

Adding a Server-side Script or RSS Feed

To add a server-side script or RSS feed data source, follow these steps:

1. Go to the Data Source Library task pane, expand the Server-side Scripts folder, and click the Connect To Script Or RSS Feed link. The server-side script Data Source Properties window opens. (See Figure 27-33.)

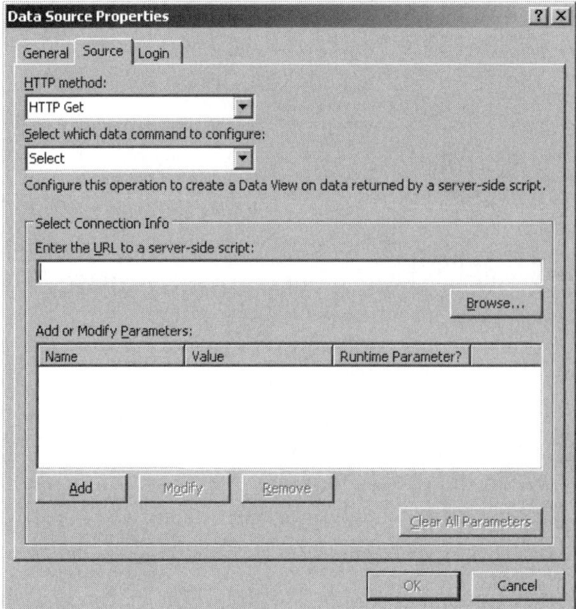

Figure 27-33 Server-side script Data Source Properties window

2. Select which HTTP method to use to run the script from the HTTP Method drop-down list. The default option is HTTP GET, and the other choice is HTTP POST.

3. Select which data command you want to configure. You can choose between the following commands: Select, Insert, Update, or Delete.

4. Type the path to the script in the Enter The URL text box.

5. If you want to add parameters that should be used when running the script from a Web page, click the Add button to open the Parameter dialog box.

Adding an XML Web service

To add a new XML Web service, follow these steps:

1. Go to the Data Source Library task pane, expand the XML Web Services folder, and click the Connect To A Web Service link. Doing this opens the XML Web Services Data Source Properties dialog box.

2. In the Service Description Location text box, type the URL of the Web service description file (.wsdl).

3. Click the Connect Now button to make a connection with the XML Web service. (See Figure 27-34.)

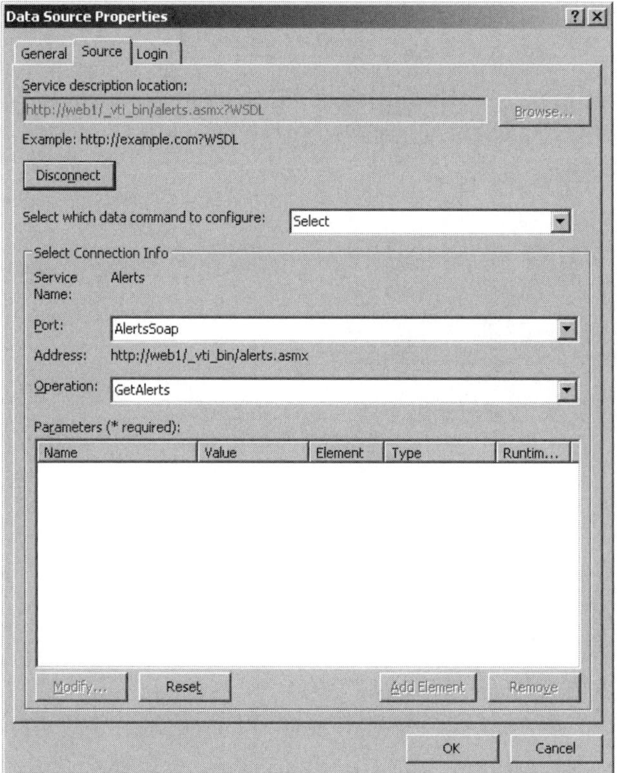

Figure 27-34 XML Web Service Data Source Properties window

Creating a New Business Data Catalog View

Although Business Data Catalogs are not discussed in detail in this chapter, you must be aware that there are different ways to create new views for a Business Data Catalog.

More Info For more details on Business Data Catalogs, see Chapter 12, "Administrating Data Connections."

The SharePoint Designer Data Source Catalog allows you to create a view by making use of a data source that is already available. You can create data views from a wide variety of data sources, such as RSS feeds, XML files, and Microsoft Office System 2007 documents. You can create a view of data located in Word 2007 documents by making use of the new Word XML-based file format and use such files as the data source. Later in this chapter, data views will be discussed in more detail.

Adding a Linked Source

Follow these steps to add a linked source data source:

1. Go to the Data Source Library task pane, expand the Linked Sources folder, and click the Create A New Linked Source link. Doing this opens the Data Source Properties dialog box, shown in Figure 27-35.

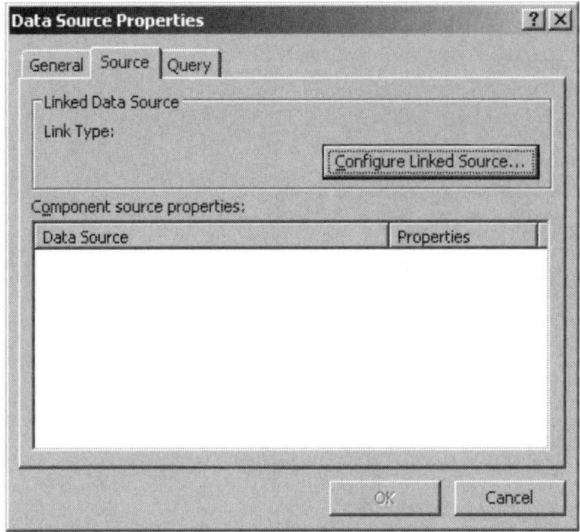

Figure 27-35 Data Source Properties dialog box

2. Click the Configure Linked Source button to open the Linked Data Sources Wizard. (See Figure 27-36.)

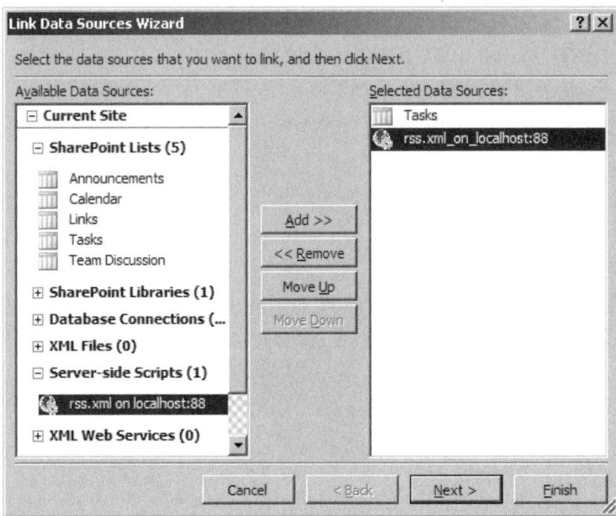

Figure 27-36 Linked Data Sources Wizard—step 1

3. In the Linked Data Sources Wizard, you see a list of all the data sources that are available for your SharePoint site, including the ones that you have added yourself via the Data Source Library task pane. Select a data source from the Available Data Sources list, and click Add. Click Next when you have finished selecting all data sources that you want to link together.
4. On the next wizard page, you can select the link type between the data sources. (See Figure 27-37.) There are two options:
   a. Merge The Content Of The Data Sources. Choose This Option If You'd Like To Sort, Group, And Filter The Data Sources As One Long List. (Recommended)
   b. Join The Contents Of The Data Sources By Using The Data Source Details To Insert Data Views And Joined Subviews.

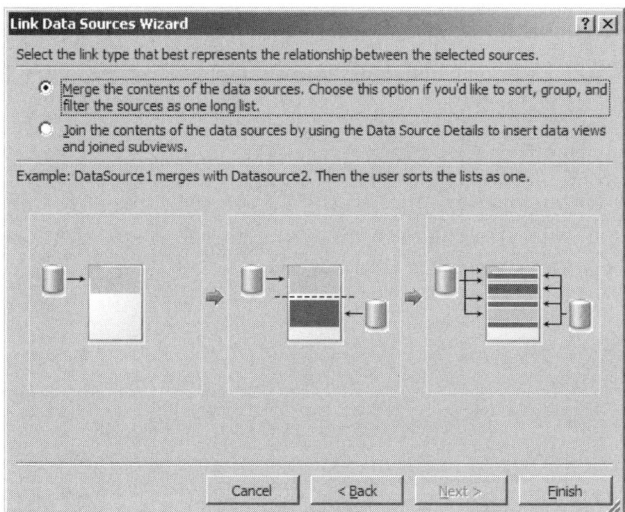

Figure 27-37 Linked Data Sources Wizard—step 2

Connecting to Another Data Source Library

A data source library consists of the lists and libraries that are available in the selected SharePoint site; in addition, you can add other data sources via the Data Source Library task pane. The Data Source Library task pane also makes it possible to connect to another Data Source Library from any SharePoint site. This way, you can share data sources.

Follow these steps to connect to another Data Source Library:

1. Go to the Data Source Library task pane, and click the Connect To Another Library link at the bottom of the task pane. Doing this opens the Manage Library dialog box.
2. Click the Add button to open the Collection Properties dialog box.
3. The Collection Properties dialog box contains two text boxes where you can type the display name and the location of the Data Source Library you want to add.

Using the Data Form Web Part

The Data Source Catalog is the central repository of all your data sources. It is the single location from which all your data can be accessed and managed. In the previous section, we showed the different data sources that are available. This section is dedicated to the use of these data sources via the Data Form Web Part.

The Data Form Web Part is not completely new; in SharePoint 2003, this it is called the Data View Web Part. Using the Data Form Web Part, you are able to use multiple data sources, including data coming from external data sources. The data presented in a Data Form Web Part is also known as a Data View. Follow the next steps to create a Data View.

1. Open your SharePoint site in SharePoint Designer 2007.
2. Go to the Data View menu, and click Insert Data View. Doing this opens the Data Source Library task pane, if it is not already open, and inserts a Data Form Web Part onto your Web Part page. (See Figure 27-38.)

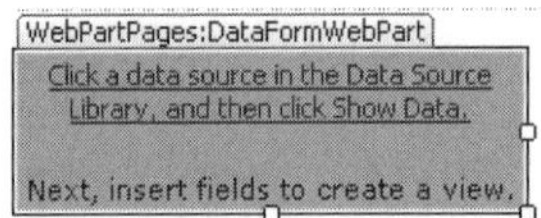

Figure 27-38 Data Form Web Part

The next step is to select a data source to create a data view. You can choose to select an already existing data source or to create a new data source, which was explained in the previous section. Select the data source you want, and choose Show Data from the drop-down list. Doing this opens the Data Source Details task pane containing all the fields that are available for that data source. (See Figure 27-39.)

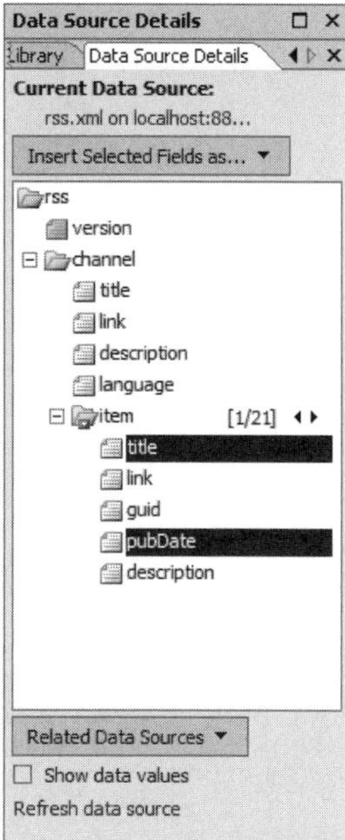

Figure 27-39 Data Source Details task pane

In the Data Source Details task pane, you can choose which fields you want to show in your data view. After selecting those fields, click the Insert Selected Fields As dropdown listbox. You can choose in what way you want to insert your selected fields. The following options are available:

- **Single Item View** This view shows one item per page, although you can customize paging to show more items at a time. This mode is read-only.
- **Multiple Item View** This view shows all the items that are available in the data source. This mode is read-only.
- **Single Item Form** This view shows one item per page, rendered as a form. In this mode, you can write data back to your data source.
- **Multiple Item Form** This view shows all items, rendered as a form. This mode allows you to write data back to your data source.

To make your data view exactly the way you want it to be, you can use the Common Data View Tasks action panel. Click on the arrow at the upper right corner of the Data View to open the Common Data View Tasks action panel, as shown in Figure 27-40.

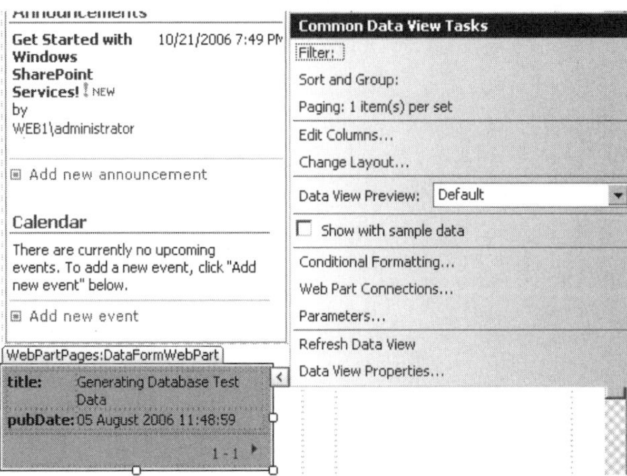

Figure 27-40 Common Data View Tasks action panel

In the Common Data View Tasks action panel, the following options are available:

- **Filter** Specify filter criteria to determine which list items are displayed.
- **Sort and Group** Specify how the data should be sorted and grouped.
- **Paging** Specify how many items you want to display per set.
- **Edit Columns** Specify which columns you want to display. A special kind of column is the Formula Column. Here you can build your own XPath expression to create a custom column. Figure 27-41 shows the XPath Expression Builder.

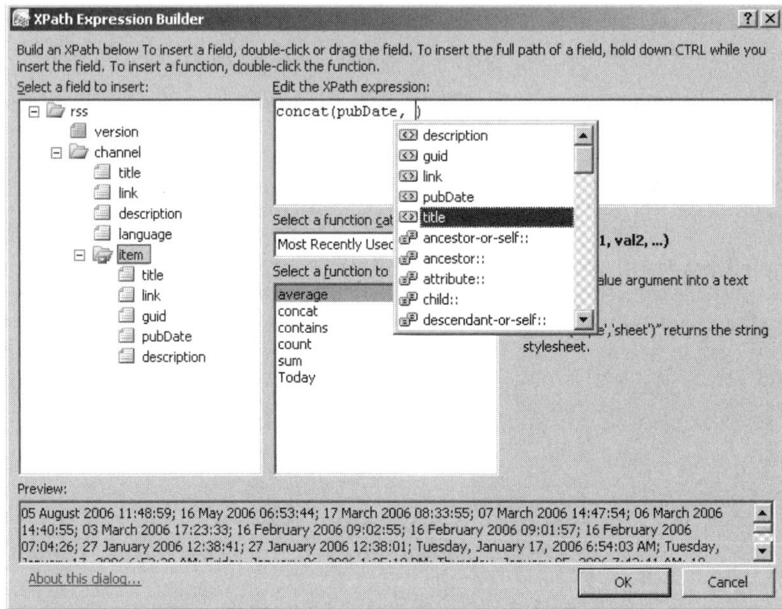

Figure 27-41 XPath Expression Builder dialog box

- **Change Layout** This option lets you specify which HTML view style or Datasheet view style you want to use for your data view.
- **Data View Preview** Here you can specify in what way you want to preview your Data View. You can choose between the following options from a drop-down list:
  - **Default** This option shows the default Data View.
  - **Hide All Filters** This options hides all filters that apply to a Data View.
  - **Limit To 1 Item** This option limits the items being shown in the Data View to 1 item.
  - **Limit To 5 Items** This option limits the items being shown in the Data View to 5 items.
  - **Limit To 10 Items** This option limits the items being shown in the Data View to 10 items.
  - **Show With Sample data. 'No Matching Items' Template** This option gives you a chance to write text that is displayed to the users when no matching items are found.
- **Conditional Formatting** If you click the Conditional Formatting link, the Conditional Formatting task pane is opened. This task pane allows you to specify conditions that are applied to fields. For example, you can make sure that items are shown only when the publish date equals today's date. Figure 27-42 shows the Conditional Formatting task pane.

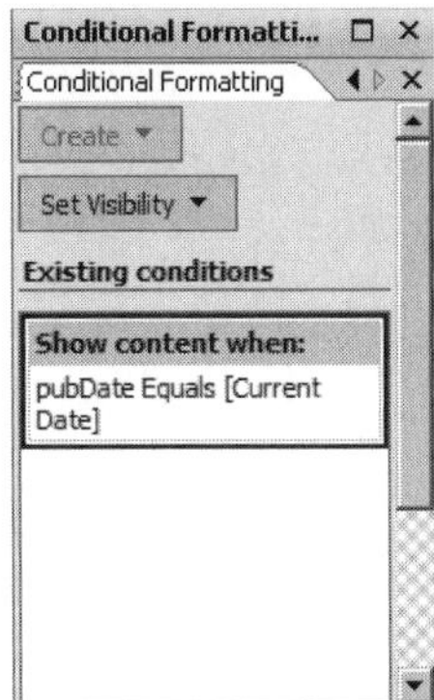

Figure 27-42 Conditional Formatting task pane

- **Web Part Connections** Clicking this link opens the Web Part Connections Wizard. This wizard lets you create new connections or manage existing connections between source and target Web Parts on the same page or another page (cross-page connections).

- **Parameters** Here you specify the source of your parameters. If the source is set to None, the default value is used. Figure 27-43 shows the Data View Parameters dialog box and all the available sources you can use.

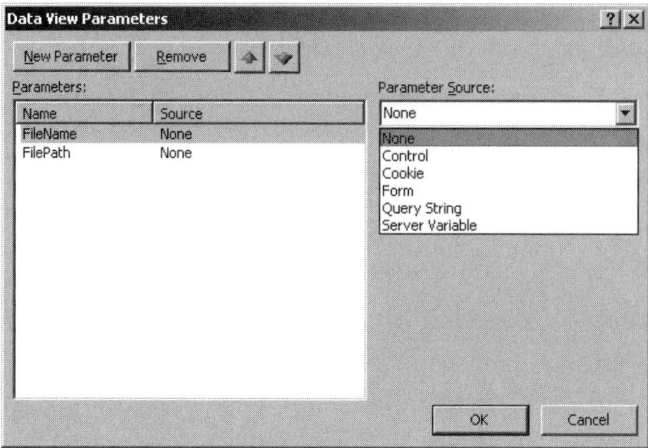

Figure 27-43 Data View Parameters dialog box

- **Refresh Data View** Clicking this link refreshes the data view.
- **Data View Properties** This opens the Data View Properties dialog box, where you can specify the toolbar, with or without sorting or filtering. You can also decide to show or hide the header or footer. The other tabs of this window let you define layout; the external xls file link source; how paging should be specified; and whether you want to add links to the current view to enable edit, delete, insert, and select modes.

The last feature of the data form Web Part that we will discuss in this chapter is field formatting. You will notice how easy it is to format fields by specifying XSL (eXtensible Stylesheet Language) code for a field. XSL is used to describe how XML content should be formatted or transformed. Clicking on the arrow next to a field opens the Common xsl:value-of Tasks action panel that lets you specify how the field must be formatted. (See Figure 27-44.)

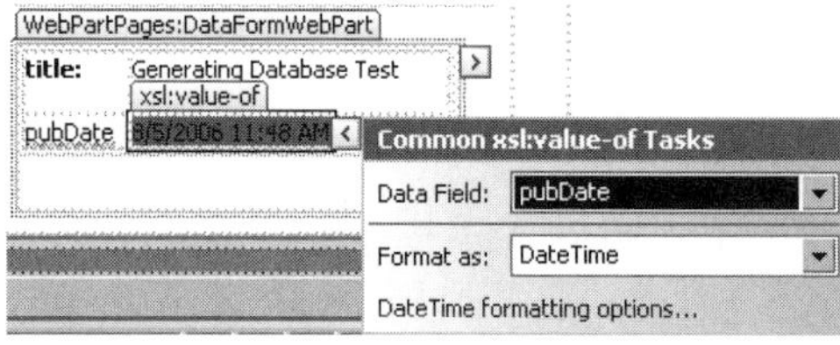

Figure 27-44 Common xsl:value-of Tasks action panel

Viewing Reports

SharePoint Designer 2007 is shipped with a number of reports that make it easy for an administrator to get an overview of the usage of a SharePoint site.

Note Before you can use the reports functionality in SharePoint Designer 2007, you have to make sure that usage analysis processing is configured on the SharePoint server. You can turn on usage analysis processing by going to SharePoint Central Administration, choosing the Operations tab and clicking Usage Analysis Processing in the Logging And Reporting section. The Usage Analysis Processing page lets you enable logging, choose a location to store the log files, and set the number of log files per Web application. You can also specify the time of day to run usage processing. The best moment to run usage processing is during off-peak hours, such as during the middle of the night.

If you click on the Site menu and choose Reports, you can choose between the following report categories:

- **Site Summary** Summary reports provide you with a quick overview of the statistics available for your SharePoint site. (This option is shown in Figure 27-45.)

Web Site

Site Summary

Name	Count	Size	Description
All files	47	165KB	All files in the current Web site
Pictures	0	0KB	Picture files in the current Web site (GIF, JPG, BMP, etc.)
Unlinked files	2	2KB	Files in the current Web site that cannot be reached by starting fro...
Linked files	45	164KB	Files in the current Web site that can be reached by starting from y...
Slow pages	0	0KB	Pages in the current Web site exceeding an estimated download tim...
Older files	0	0KB	Files in the current Web site that have not been modified in over 72...
Recently added files	47	165KB	Files in the current Web site that have been created in the last 30 d...
Checked out files	0	0KB	Files in Web site that are currently checked out.
Hyperlinks	199		All hyperlinks in the current Web site
Unverified hyperlinks	156		Hyperlinks pointing to unconfirmed target files
Broken hyperlinks	0		Hyperlinks pointing to unavailable target files
External hyperlinks	156		Hyperlinks pointing to files outside of the current Web site
Internal hyperlinks	43		Hyperlinks pointing to other files within the current Web site
Component errors	1		Files in the current Web site with components reporting an error
Style Sheet Links	0		All Style Sheet Links in the current web site.
Dynamic Web Templates	0		All files that are associated with a Dynamic Web Template.
Master Pages	41		All files that are associated with a Master Page.
Customized pages	44	163KB	Files from the SharePoint site definition that have been customized

Figure 27-45 Site Summary report in SharePoint Designer 2007

- **Files** Files reports display all the files in a SharePoint site and determine which ones are old, new, or recently changed. The Files reports also show who is working on a file, as well as the file creation and last modification dates.

- **Shared Content** Shared content reports display how shared content is used and by which pages shared content is used. Master pages are good examples of shared content.
- **Problems** Problems reports display potential problems with your Web site that can prevent visitors from wanting to return.
- **Workflow** Workflow reports let you monitor which workflows are used on a SharePoint site.
- **Usage** Usage reports display a detailed overview that provides insight into how your site is being accessed. They also display various pieces of information that can help you to improve your site and tailor it to the needs of your customers.

In addition to this default set of reports, more reports are available under the Tools section that is located on the menu. The Tools section contains the following reports:

- **Accessibility Reports** The accessibility reports give you a chance to check for compliance with the WCAG Priority 1, WCAG Priority 2, or Access Board Section 508 standards. You can choose what you want to see, Errors, Warnings, and a Manual Checklist. You can run this report for all pages, only the pages that are currently opened, selected pages, or the current page. The results pane of the accessibility report is shown in Figure 27-46.

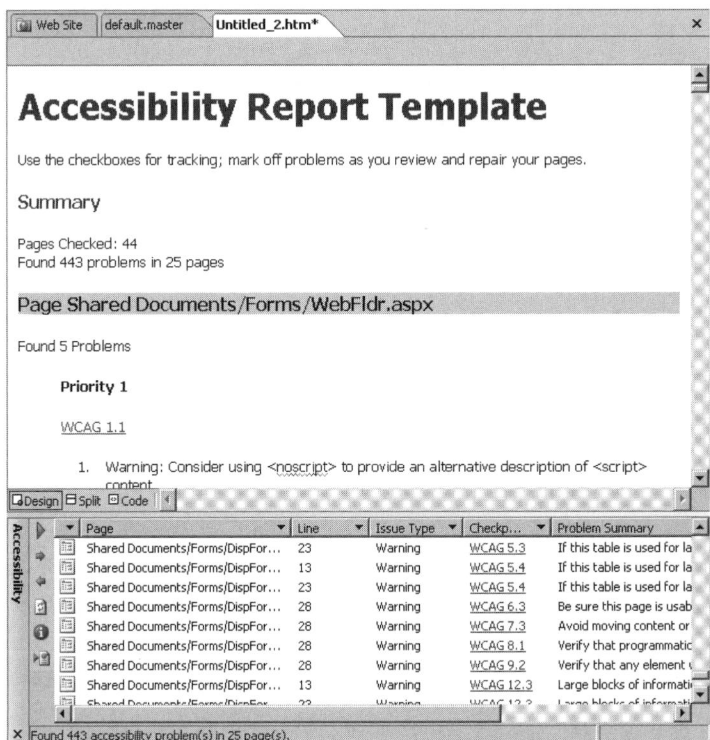

Figure 27-46 The accessibility report in SharePoint Designer 2007

Web Accessibility Standards

The intention of Web accessibility standards such as WCAG and Action Board Section 508 is to make Web content accessible to people with disabilities. These guidelines are intended for all Web content developers. WCAG stands for Web Content Accessibility Guidelines and is part of the Web Accessibility Initiative (WAI) that was formed by the Word Wide Web Consortium (W3C). Currently, WCAG can be subcategorized into three sections: priority 1 through 3. Priority 1 is the strictest form of the WCAG standard.

Section 508 refers to section 508 of the Rehabilitation Act of 1973 that requires federal agencies to provide information technology to the public that is accessible to people with disabilities. The Access Board (the Architectural and Transportation Barriers Compliance Board) was assigned the task of determining standards for accessible electronic and information technology.

Both standards try to accomplish the same goal, although both have a slightly different view on how to reach this goal.

- **Compatibility Reports** The compatibility reports check the HTML/XHTML compatibility of a page with HTML 4.01 Frameset/Strict/Transitional, all Internet Explorer versions, XHTML 1.0 Frameset/Strict/Transitional, and XHTML 1.1. The report also checks the CSS compatibility with CSS 1.0, CSS 2.0, CSS 2.1, or CSS IE6. The compatibility checker gives you the chance to check all pages, an open page or pages, selected pages, or the current page.
- **CSS Reports** The CSS reports dialog box contains two tabs. The first tab is the Errors tab, with which you can check for unused styles, undefined classes, and mismatched case. With the other tab, the Usage tab, you can check for Class Selectors, ID Selectors, and Element Selectors. For each tab, you can choose to check all pages, an open page or pages, selected pages, the current page, or style.

You can change some general settings for the way reports are shown. You can do this by going to the Tools menu, clicking Applications Options, and choosing the Reports View tab, as shown in Figure 27-47. You can make your own definition of recent, older, and slow files. For example, you can define that a slow file is a file that takes more than 40 seconds to download. You can also choose how much months of usage you would like to see in the report and whether you want to include a chart when you save the report.

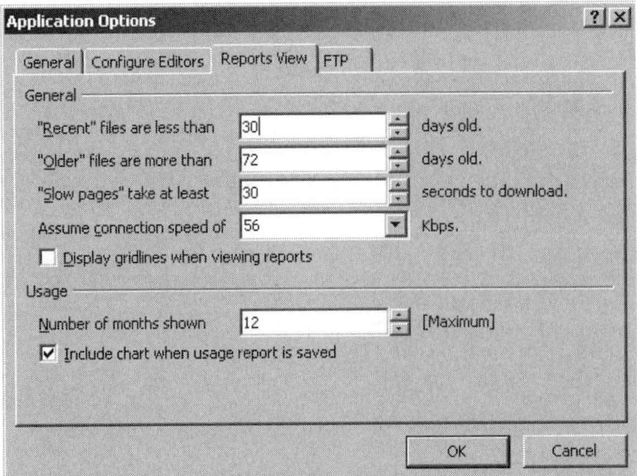

Figure 27-47 The Reports View tab in the Options dialog box

Summary

In this chapter, you saw how to use SharePoint Designer 2007. You also learned what Contributor Settings are and how you should use them. We explored the support for cascading style sheets in SharePoint Designer 2007. Next, the chapter discussed how to work with various data sources within SharePoint Designer 2007 and how to use those data sources within the Data Form Web Part. Finally, the chapter discussed the different reports that are included in SharePoint Designer 2007.

Chapter 28

Implementing Microsoft Windows Workflow Services

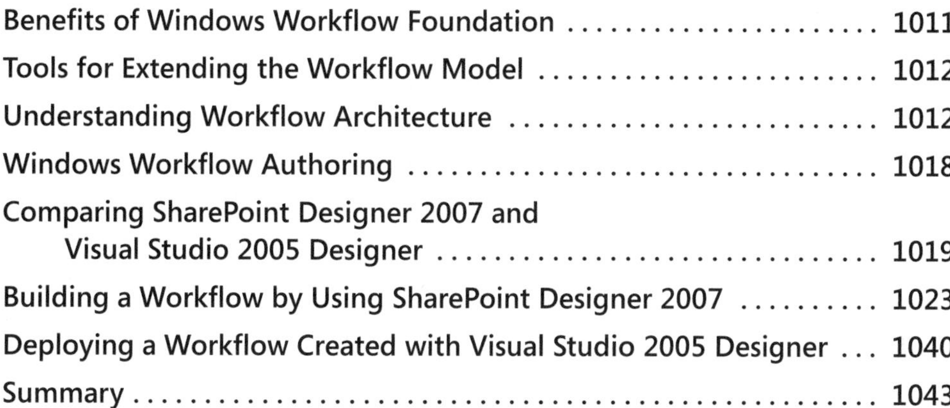

A *workflow* is a natural way to organize and run tasks, procedural steps, or activities, and it can involve people either within the same organization or belonging to multiple organizations. In software, a workflow can be seen as an executable representation of a work process.

Microsoft Windows Workflow Foundation provides a programming framework and tools for developing and executing a wide variety of workflow-based applications. Imagine, for example, an insurance company that wants to ensure that a request for proposal is handled efficiently from the draft version to the final version. A workflow can take care of this process and make certain that every person involved in handling the request for proposal uses the correct document and successfully completes their part in the process before allowing the workflow process to continue to the next step, to the next person.

Benefits of Windows Workflow Foundation

Windows Workflow Foundation makes the creation of applications that contain asynchronous, stateful, long-running, and/or persistent workflows a lot easier. The Windows Workflow Foundation *runtime engine* manages workflow execution and allows workflows to remain active for long periods of time and survive computer restarts. *Runtime services* offer functionality such as transactions and persistence to manage errors gracefully and correctly. By the way, the pricing model of Windows Workflow Foundation is rather attractive too: it is free of charge.

Windows Workflow Foundation provides a workflow model that allows developers to describe the processing required by their applications. The model increases developer productivity by creating a greater level of abstraction, and a natural separation of application and business logic from such details as flow control, state management, transactions, and synchronization.

Tools for Extending the Workflow Model

In a Microsoft Office SharePoint Server 2007 context, there are two development tools available for using and extending the workflow model. These are the Microsoft Visual Studio 2005 Designer for Windows Workflow Foundation and Microsoft Office SharePoint Designer 2007. Visual Studio 2005 Designer for Windows Workflow Foundation is a Visual Studio add-in; SharePoint Designer 2007 is a stand-alone application that is a successor of Microsoft FrontPage 2003. Refer to Chapter 27, "Using Microsoft Office SharePoint Designer 2007 with Microsoft SharePoint Services 3.0," to find detailed information about using SharePoint Designer 2007.

Note As an administrator, you probably will never work directly with Visual Studio 2005 to create workflows. Depending on your role, if you also act as a SharePoint site administrator, you are likely to use SharePoint Designer 2007 to create workflows.

The difference between Visual Studio 2005 Designer and SharePoint Designer 2007 is discussed extensively in this chapter in the "Comparing SharePoint Designer 2007 and Visual Studio 2005 Designer" section. You will learn the ins and outs of creating workflows using SharePoint Designer 2007. You will also learn how to extend existing SharePoint workflows and how to deploy workflows created using Visual Studio 2005.

Understanding Workflow Architecture

For workflow capabilities, the Microsoft Office system depends on Windows Workflow Foundation, which officially is a part of the Microsoft .NET Framework 3.0 (previously known as WinFX). This also means that the new workflow features in Office SharePoint Server 2007 are possible because of this new technology that facilitates the creation of workflows.

WinFX

WinFX is the code name for the .NET Framework 3.0 and builds on the previous release. The .NET Framework 3.0 adds four new components: Windows Workflow Foundation, Windows Presentation Foundation, Windows Communication Foundation, and Windows CardSpace. Currently, these four components are built on top of the .NET Framework 2.0.

Windows Communication Foundation is a component that supports building applications based on Service Oriented Architecture (SOA) and includes functionality such as Web services, remoting, enterprise services, queueing technologies, and Web Service Enhancements (WSE).

The Windows Presentation Foundation component of .NET 3.0 helps to create coherent user interfaces. Windows Presentation Foundation revolutionizes the development of user interfaces for Windows-based platforms by offering support for video, animation, two-and three-dimensional graphics, and various kinds of documents.

The final new component in the .NET Framework 3.0 is Windows CardSpace. Windows CardSpace offers a new approach to managing digital identities. To help people keep track of their digital identities, CardSpace represents each identity as a distinct information card that makes managing identities and passwords easier.

Windows Workflow Foundation is not a standalone application, as it always needs to be hosted by another application. The Microsoft Office system workflows use the Windows Workflow Foundation engine that is embedded inside SharePoint Server 2007 that acts as the workflow host. SharePoint Server 2007 does not use the set of pluggable services that is already included in the Windows Workflow Foundation engine, but it provides its own implementations of services for transactions, persistence, notifications, roles, tracking, and messaging.

SharePoint Designer 2007 is the most important tool when it comes to creating SharePoint workflows, as it makes creating workflows—whether they be simple, average, or complex—an appealing job. The Microsoft Office system client applications, such as Word 2007, start workflows by calling into the SharePoint Web services application programming interface (API).

Note Windows Workflow Foundation technology is an important part of the Microsoft strategy regarding workflow creation. Windows Workflow Foundation is the premier tool for creating workflows in Visual Studio 2005, so it is likely that third-party products will start to include this technology. Windows Workflow Foundation is embedded in all the Microsoft Office server products—such as SharePoint Portal Server, Project Server, Navision, and CRM. Other Microsoft products will use Windows Workflow Foundation as well. Microsoft BizTalk Server vNext (the one after BizTalk Server 2006) will also include Windows Workflow Foundation.

A workflow is executed on a SharePoint server, which in turn uses Windows Workflow Foundation as the foundation of the execution of a workflow process. SharePoint Server 2007 includes support for workflows in lists, libraries, and content types, and it provides queuing and management of lists and libraries to provide the necessary data to the Workflow Foundation runtime as demanded by the workflow's configuration.

Activity Management

SharePoint Server 2007 runs the workflow until it reaches a point at which it cannot proceed until a specific event occurs or the workflow ends. This leads to the persistence of such an activity to the database in a single SQL transaction. After that, the activity is discarded from memory. For example, a workflow process might halt until a document is approved.

If a workflow is not currently processing any activities, it can get into an idle state, which leads to the *hydration* of a workflow. As a result, the workflow is discarded from memory and persisted to a database. If a new event occurs that is targeted toward a hydrated workflow, the event handler extracts the workflow ID from the event and passes it into the SharePoint Server 2007 queue manager, which ensures that the correct workflow is started. In other words, SharePoint *dehydrates* the workflow as needed.

The context of workflow events is persisted to tables in the database. The two SQL Server database tables that are most important when it comes to storing information concerning workflows are Content DB.Workflow and ContentDB.WorkflowAssociation.

Important You should not create any application that programmatically accesses Content DB.Workflow and ContentDB.WorkflowAssociation directly. Microsoft does not support this, and using these tables in this way can cause severe performance problems. You cannot predict what load you will cause on the system when running this type of application. Instead, use the SharePoint Web services API and the SharePoint object model to accomplish tasks related to workflows.

Once workflow event information is stored in the database, it sits there waiting for an active thread of the SharePoint queue manager that is able to pick up the information and process it. Because of this, it is possible to start a workflow on a given Web front-end and continue to work on the workflow on another Web front-end.

If multiple workflow items are queued for processing by the Workflow Foundation runtime, one item per operating thread is processed until all items are done. If the SharePoint server runs out of bandwidth, the SharePoint Timer Service (also known as the Windows SharePoint Services Timer, or SPTimer) is used to queue items. The SharePoint Timer Service is a Windows service that handles scheduled jobs. For example, not only is the SharePoint Timer Services responsible for queueing workflow items, it is also responsible for handling workflow Delay activities. *Delay activities* are parts of a workflow that allow you to build delays in a workflow based on a time-out interval.

Workflow items are always processed by hydrated workflows. The decision to hydrate or dehydrate a workflow is made by SharePoint. Currently, it is not possible to influence this decision process and influence settings regarding queueing, load balancing, and time-based execution.

Storing Source Files in Document Libraries

Workflows designed with SharePoint Designer 2007 do not contain custom code and are not compiled and deployed as assemblies are. Rather, they are stored in the form of source files within Windows SharePoint Services and compiled into memory only when needed. For each SharePoint site, workflows of this type are stored in a separate document library. This document library contains a folder for each workflow designed in SharePoint Designer 2007. The folder contains all the source files necessary for the workflow, including the following ones:

- The workflow markup file, which contains markup that describes the activities included in the workflow. Workflow markup files have the .xoml file extension.
- The workflow rules file, which contains the business logic of the workflow in the form of declarative rules (instead of code). Workflow rules files have the .xoml.rules file extension.
- The workflow configuration file, which contains general workflow configuration information. Such files have the .xoml.wfconfig.xml file extension.
- ASP.NET Web Forms for any custom workflow forms necessary. Web Forms have the .aspx file extension.

As you can see in Figure 28-1, SharePoint Designer 2007 shows you all source files that are part of a workflow in the Folder List task pane.

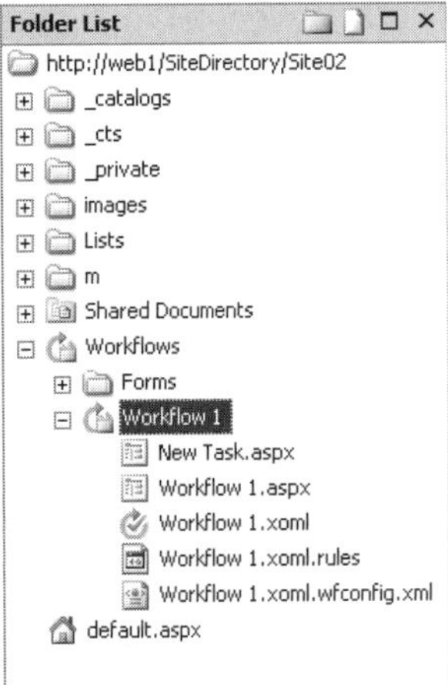

Figure 28-1 Source files of a workflow

Workflow Markup Language

Workflows are expressed in .xoml files containing workflow markup language. The .xoml file extension, shown in Figure 28-1, stands for eXtensible Object Markup Language (XOML) and is a serialization format for the Windows Workflow Foundation workflow objects. The schema for .xoml files is identical to the schema that is used for .xaml (eXtensible Application Markup Language) files. The only difference lies in the names of the file extensions.

Note The .xaml (pronounced "zammel") extension is the user interface markup language for Windows Presentation Foundation.

In principle, .xoml files can be created using any text or XML editor you choose, as long as such files adhere to the XOML schema. Nevertheless, it is advisable to use either SharePoint Designer 2007 or Visual Studio 2005 Designer because those products have built-in support for creating workflows.

Compiling Source Files

SharePoint Designer 2007 contains a just-in-time compiler that is able to compile the workflow source files into a workflow the first time that workflow is started. SharePoint Designer 2007 keeps the compiled workflow in memory to speed up future execution performance. Each time a workflow is started on a list or library item, SharePoint Designer 2007 needs to determine whether the workflow was deployed as an assembly or in the form of a collection of source files. The decision process contains the following steps:

- If a workflow assembly exists, SharePoint Designer 2007 calls that assembly to instantiate the workflow instance.
- If the workflow was deployed as a collection of source files, SharePoint Designer 2007 has to determine whether it already has a workflow loaded in memory that was compiled based on those source files.
  - If the workflow was previously compiled, SharePoint Designer 2007 calls the in-memory compiled workflow to instantiate the workflow instance.
  - If the workflow was not compiled earlier, SharePoint Designer 2007 uses its just-in-time compiler to compile source files into an in-memory workflow, which then will be called to instantiate the workflow instance.

How to Implement a Workflow

What choices do you have when it comes to implementing workflows? In SharePoint Portal Server 2003, sophisticated workflows were often implemented using third-party products. With the advent of strong support for workflow technology in SharePoint Server 2007, those third-party vendors will probably become less important in the near future. If you want to, you can also create your own workflows using the SharePoint event model.

For Windows and ASP.NET applications, developers can use the User Interface Process Application Block (UIPAB), which can be downloaded for free from *http://www.microsoft.com/downloads/details.aspx?familyid=98C6CC9D-88E1-4490-8BD6-78092A0F084E&displaylang=en* on the Microsoft Web site as a component that can be used in developing workflows.

Microsoft Exchange Server 2000 and 2003 and SharePoint Portal Server 2001 included a workflow engine that could be used to create workflows of medium complexity. (This workflow engine was a part of SharePoint Portal Server 2001 and was not supported officially.)

BizTalk Server 2006 includes Human Workflow Services (HWS), a technology intended to aid in creating human-oriented workflows, although Human Workflow Services is now considered to be deprecated technology. BizTalk Server includes a Windows SharePoint Services adapter that is able to communicate with SharePoint lists and libraries and can be used to build workflows, although this requires a considerable amount of work.

Currently, if you are building workflows using Microsoft technology, not just for SharePoint technology, the most appealing options are Windows Workflow Foundation and BizTalk Server 2006. Use Windows Workflow Foundation when you are creating workflows within an application (human-oriented workflows), and use BizTalk Server 2006 for creating workflows across applications (application-oriented workflows). Both products are suitable choices because they speed up the development time for creating workflows considerably and have a bright future.

Windows Workflow Authoring

Three important groups of users can be distinguished when it comes to creating workflows: knowledge workers, site administrators and Web designers, and developers. The following list describes the most likely division of responsibilities of these groups:

- **Knowledge workers** This group of users consists of people who will create ad hoc workflow solutions based on the predefined workflows already available in SharePoint Designer 2007. The complexity of these workflows will be low.
- **Site administrators and Web designers** This group will use SharePoint Designer 2007 to create custom workflows for a specific list or library. The complexity of such workflows will be average.
- **Developers** Developers will primarily use Visual Studio 2005 Designer to program their own workflows, custom code, and activities. Developers can use Visual Studio 2005 Designer to create highly complex workflows.

Workflows authored in SharePoint Designer 2007 differ from those created using the Visual Studio 2005 Designer for Windows Workflow Foundation in several important ways:

- In SharePoint Designer 2007, a workflow cannot be deployed to multiple lists. Such workflows are valid only for the list for which they were created.
- In SharePoint Designer 2007, you are authoring the workflow directly against a list and the workflow is associated with the list or library at design time. After the association is made, workflows are allowed to be run on items within the list or library. Workflows created using Visual Studio 2005 Designer have to be associated explicitly with a list or library through configuration. The advantage of the latter approach is that a workflow can be associated with multiple lists and libraries.
- You cannot modify workflows authored in SharePoint Designer 2007. Workflow modifications are explained in the "What Is Different" section later in this chapter.
- You cannot associate a workflow to a content type using SharePoint Designer 2007. Associating a workflow to a content type means that each list to which a content

type is added inherits the workflows associated to the content type at that time. Workflow associations update according to the rules of content type push down. In other words, if the administrator makes a change to a content type, he can choose to push down this change.

Comparing SharePoint Designer 2007 and Visual Studio 2005 Designer

SharePoint Designer 2007 workflows are also referred to as *no-code* workflows. All activities used within a SharePoint Designer 2007 workflow are well-known safely registered libraries that already have been deployed on the server.

Note A safely registered library is a .NET assembly that is registered as an entry on the SharePoint virtual server Web.config <SafeControls> list. Detailed information about this topic can be found in Chapter 31, "Administrating Code Access Security."

SharePoint Designer 2007 does not allow you to create your own activities, although it is able to generate raw XOML data, which is stored on the SharePoint server. During workflow execution time, the XOML data is interpreted by the runtime engine, which ensures that all activities used within a workflow are marked as safe. It is possible to use custom activities that are created using Visual Studio 2005, as opposed to using one of the predefined activities. Such activities have to be marked on the SharePoint virtual server as being safe.

What Is the Same

Visual Studio 2005 Designer and SharePoint Designer 2007 both offer the following capabilities:

- You can create workflows for SharePoint Designer 2007.
- A workflow markup file is generated. If you are using SharePoint Designer, a workflow markup file is generated after selecting and configuring the conditions and actions for a workflow. The workflow markup file is generated as soon as you click the Finish button of the Workflow Designer Wizard. Visual Studio 2005 Designer has a graphical tool that helps to create the workflow markup file. Visual Studio 2005 Designer lets you create a graphical model representing the workflow, and the workflow markup file is generated based on this representation.

- Workflows can be started based on certain events, such as the creation of a new document, and they can also be started manually. You can define multiple initiation forms that gather information from users. Initiation forms are displayed when users manually start a workflow on a SharePoint item.
- You can use custom forms for users to interact with SharePoint tasks.

The following three types of forms are used in SharePoint Designer 2007 workflows:

- *Association and initiation forms* are displayed to users and need to be filled out before the workflow itself is started.
- *Modification forms* present options to users that change the course of the workflow itself as it is running on an item. For example, a user might redirect the task of a document review to another person.
- *Task forms* are custom forms that help to create tasks that are the result of the workflow process, and they can be used to specify detailed information about a task. For example, if a user finishes a document review, this might lead to the creation of a new task. As a result, the original author needs to review the document. The reviewer might use the task form to write some additional comments directed to the author.

Note Windows SharePoint Services 3.0 workflows are forms agnostic. This means that you can use any forms technology you want, as long as the forms created are capable of invoking the Windows SharePoint Services object model, generating the data necessary to send to the Windows SharePoint Services object model, and receiving and parsing the required data from the Windows SharePoint Services object model. Currently, you can build workflow forms using ASP.NET or InfoPath.

What Is Different

The ways in which workflows authored in SharePoint Designer 2007 differ from those created using the Visual Studio 2005 Designer for Windows Workflow Foundation is described in the "Windows Workflow Authoring" section earlier in this chapter. Table 28-1 provides an overview of the differences between Visual Studio 2005 Designer for Windows Workflow Foundation and SharePoint Designer 2007 when it comes to creating workflows.

Table 28-1 Workflow Development Tools Differences

Visual Studio 2005 Designer for Windows Workflow Foundation	Office SharePoint Designer 2007
Code-behind files enable developers to write custom C# or Visual Basic code to express business logic.	No code-behind files; workflow rules files declaratively encapsulate business logic instead.

Table 28-1 Workflow Development Tools Differences

Visual Studio 2005 Designer for Windows Workflow Foundation	Office SharePoint Designer 2007
Workflow is authored as a template, which can be associated with multiple sites and lists.	Workflow is authored against a specific list and is data-bound to it at design time.
Workflow markup files, or markup and code-behind files, are compiled into a workflow assembly.	Workflow markup, workflow rules, and supporting files are not compiled into an assembly and are stored directly in a specific document library on a SharePoint site.
Workflow template must be associated with each list on which it is to be available.	Association happens when the workflow is authored against the specific list; no later association is necessary or possible.
You can use any forms technology. For Microsoft technology, this currently comes down to the ability to include ASP.NET and InfoPath forms in SharePoint workflows.	ASP.NET forms are automatically generated, and you can then customize them.
You can include workflow modifications.	Workflow modifications are not available. Workflow modifications are options that you present to your users to change the course of the workflow as it is running on an item. For example, you can allow a user to assign her tasks to another user.
You can author custom activities for inclusion in workflows.	You must use activities that are already provided on the SharePoint server.
Workflow assembly and workflow definition are packaged as a SharePoint Feature and deployed to a SharePoint site.	Deployment to a specific list or library happens automatically.
Microsoft Visual Studio debugging is available.	No step-by-step debugging is available.
You can author both sequential and state workflows.	You can author only sequential workflows.

Considerations

If you need to decide whether to create a workflow using SharePoint Designer or Visual Studio 2005 Designer, keep the following points in mind. If you are using Visual Studio 2005 Designer, you can create workflow templates and custom workflow activities, and you can also include code in your workflow and design forms. Also, when you use Visual Studio 2005 Designer, you are not programming a workflow against a specific SharePoint site. At a later time, you will be able to associate the newly created workflow with multiple SharePoint sites.

If you use SharePoint Designer 2007 to create a workflow, you are always designing a workflow for a specific SharePoint site. SharePoint Designer 2007 enables you to create declarative, rule-based workflows, and it lets you use pre-existing activities that are already deployed on the SharePoint server in your workflows. You cannot create your own activities or write code-behind pages. However, you can create new activities in Visual Studio 2005 Designer and use these to extend the set of activities located on the SharePoint server. After doing so, you can use those extended activities in SharePoint Designer 2007 workflows.

Code-Behind and Code-Beside Files

In the discussion about creating workflow applications so far, code-behind files have been mentioned now and then. As an administrator, you probably won't have to deal with this concept on a daily basis, but it might be useful to take a moment to elaborate on this topic.

Code-behind files are a concept best known from the ASP.NET world, where every .aspx page is compiled on request and ultimately inherits from a base class called *Page*. Code-behind files help to separate user interface code from page controller logic by forming an intermediate class that sits between the .aspx page and the ultimate *Page* base class. Code-behind files are usually compiled into assemblies and placed in the /bin directory of an ASP.NET application. Because the .NET common language runtime (CLR) automatically adds references to assemblies placed in the /bin directory, the .aspx page will have no trouble finding the code-behind class.

With the advent of ASP.NET 2.0, the code-behind model has changed to a *code-beside* model. Using the new concept of partial classes that allow one class to be defined in multiple source files, the .aspx file does not have to inherit from the code-behind file anymore. Instead, the .aspx file and the code-behind file are both partial classes that form a single class after compilation. The result of this is cleaner code.

Whenever this chapter refers to code-behind files, we are referring to partial classes that will be merged with other source files during compilation.

Building a Workflow by Using SharePoint Designer 2007

A custom workflow that is created using SharePoint Designer 2007 can be started in various ways: automatically after a file is created, automatically after a file is changed, or manually. Within workflows, you can use actions that are available out of the box, such as assigning a task to someone or sending an e-mail.

> **Note** Take some time to think about how the workflow should look before you grab SharePoint Designer 2007. Make sure you have, at the least, a clear picture of the workflow in your mind before you start creating one. Or better yet, create some kind of diagram to represent the workflow. Microsoft Office Visio is a suitable tool to create workflow diagrams.

The whole procedure of building a workflow with SharePoint Designer 2007 can be divided into four steps:

1. Create a workflow.
2. Customize the workflow initiation settings.
3. Configure the predefined conditions and activities.
4. Generate the workflow definition template and deployment.

In addition, the workflow designer should understand how SharePoint Designer 2007 controls custom activities but allows the extension of built-in workflows. Each of these topics is discussed in this section.

Creating a Workflow

To create a new workflow with SharePoint Designer 2007, complete the following steps:

1. Open the SharePoint site where you want to create a workflow using SharePoint Designer 2007.
2. Open the Workflow Designer Wizard by using one of the flowing methods:
   a. On the File menu, point to New and then select Workflow.
   b. On the File menu, select New.

      This will start the New dialog box, shown in Figure 28-2. Click on the SharePoint Content tab, and choose Workflow. Click Blank Workflow to create a new workflow.

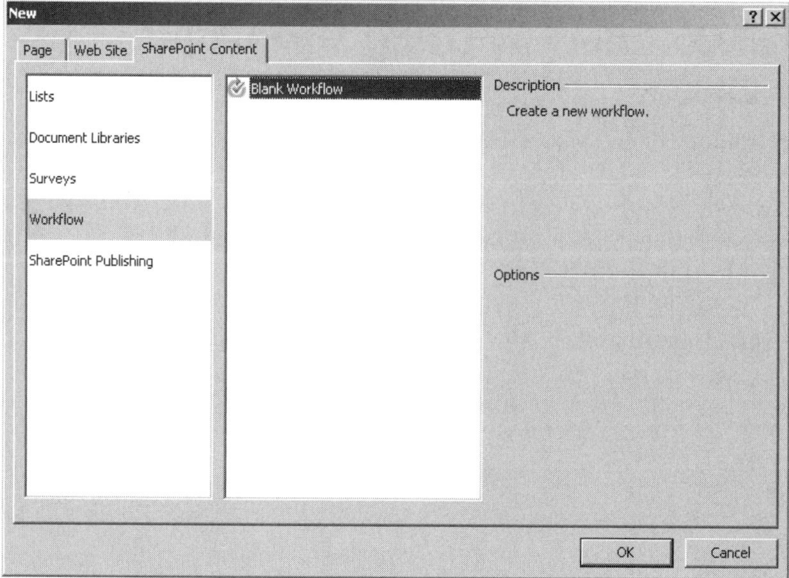

Figure 28-2 SharePoint Content tab in the New dialog box

3. On the Workflow Designer page shown in Figure 28-3, give the workflow a descriptive name and attach the workflow to a list that is available on your SharePoint site. A drop-down list shows all lists located on your SharePoint site.

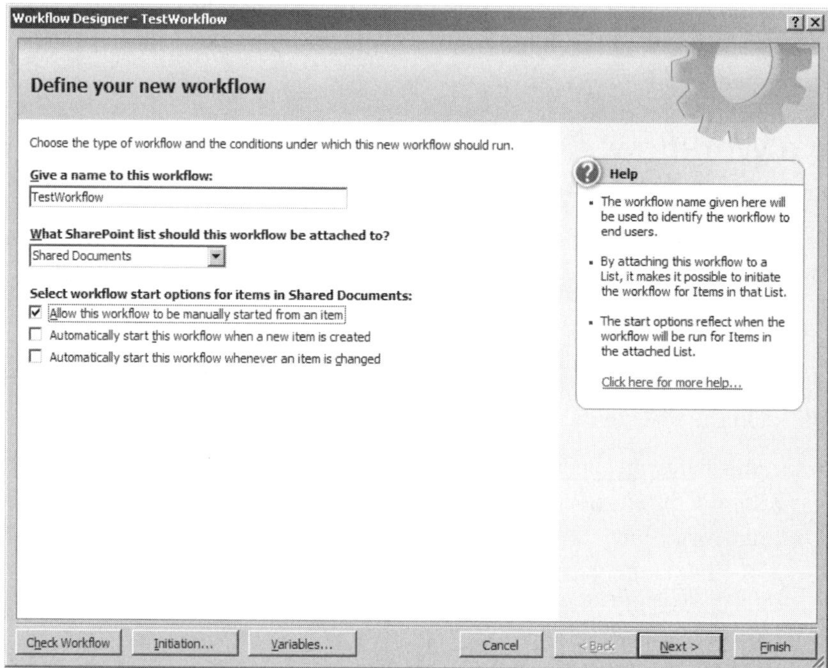

Figure 28-3 Defining your new workflow

You can also select one or more of the following workflow start options for items in the list you have chosen:

a. Allow This Workflow To Be Manually Started From An Item

b. Automatically Start This Workflow When A New Item Is Created

c. Automatically Start This Workflow Whenever An Item Is Changed

4. Click Next. This takes you to the configuration of the workflow steps, including the conditions and activities.

Customizing the Workflow Initiation Settings

A workflow uses initiation forms that are displayed to users as soon as they start a workflow that is associated with a given SharePoint item. You can use initiation forms to let users override or append the association parameters set by administrators, or specify additional parameters or information about the workflow as it applies to the given SharePoint item. Not all workflows require the use of initiation forms. You can create an initiation stage for your workflow in SharePoint Designer 2007. If you do, SharePoint Designer 2007 automatically generates an initiation form, using ASP.NET, according to your initiation specifications.

To create an initiation form according to your initiation specifications, complete the following steps:

1. Click the Initiation button at the bottom of the Workflow Designer Wizard. This opens the Workflow Parameters dialog box. (See Figure 28-4.)

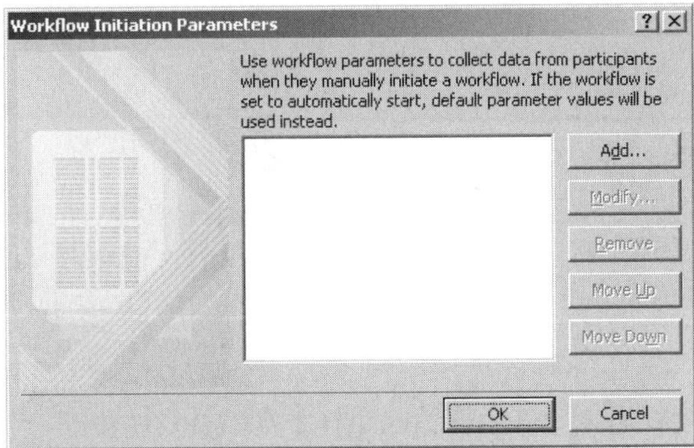

Figure 28-4 Workflow Parameters dialog box

2. Click Add to add workflow parameters. This opens the Add Field dialog box shown in Figure 28-5.

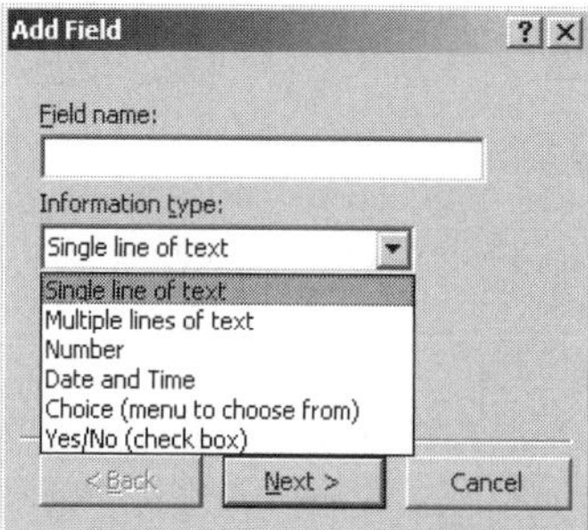

Figure 28-5 Add Field dialog box

3. The Add Field dialog box gives you the chance to add a field to specify a workflow parameter and choose an information type for that field. There is a range of types you can choose from. Depending on which type you choose, other contextual values will need to be defined. For example, if you create a new field called DateFinished and select the information type Date And Time, and click Next, a new window appears that shows you a range of options specifically concerned with date and time, as shown in Figure 28-6.

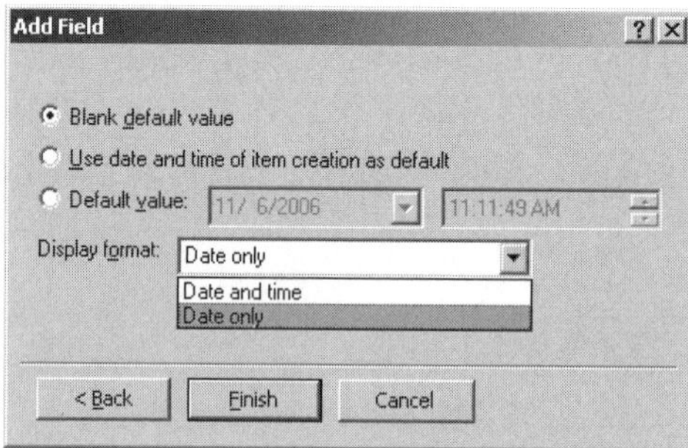

Figure 28-6 Defining date and time information type for a field

SharePoint Designer 2007 generates all ASP.NET forms that are required for workflow initiation. These .aspx files are stored on the SharePoint site, together with the workflow source files. They can be opened and customized in the same way as you would for any other .ASPX Web Form.

Configuring the Predefined Conditions and Activities

The next step of the workflow build process is to define the workflow steps. There is no practical limit to the number of workflow steps that can be added to a workflow; you can add as many as you want. You can add a workflow step by clicking on the Add Workflow Step link at the right of the wizard page under the heading Workflow Steps (see also Figure 28-15 later in this chapter). This Workflow Designer Wizard page lets you select conditions and activities.

Note Be sure to give the workflow step a descriptive name. This makes it easier to adjust the workflow once it is created.

Conditions

Conditions are configurable conditional clauses that direct the flow of the workflow. Conditions are represented by a sentence that contains variables that can be configured by the workflow designer using drop-down menus and dialog boxes. You can select conditions from a predetermined list and configure those conditions using the SharePoint Designer 2007 interface.

In SharePoint Designer 2007, you have nine standard conditions to choose from. The following list provides an overview of all available conditions:

- Custom Condition: *field* equals *value*. The *field* and *value* variables are variables that can be configured by you. For example, if you previously selected that the workflow applies to a document library, clicking *field* results in the display of a drop-down list containing all column names of that document library. Values in custom conditions are context-dependent. For example, you can choose a document library column that has the drop-down list data type. Once you click the *value* variable of a custom condition, a drop-down list is displayed that contains the values of the document library drop-down list column.
- Title Field Contains Keywords: title field contains *keywords*. The only part of a Title Field Contains Keywords condition that you can configure is the *keywords* variable. This variable is a text box that lets you type the keywords that you want to use. If you are unsure which keywords you are looking for, you can click the Display Data-Binding button next to the Keywords item to display the Define Workflow Lookup dialog box shown in Figure 28-7. This dialog box gives you the chance to select a list or library from a SharePoint site and look up which values it contains.

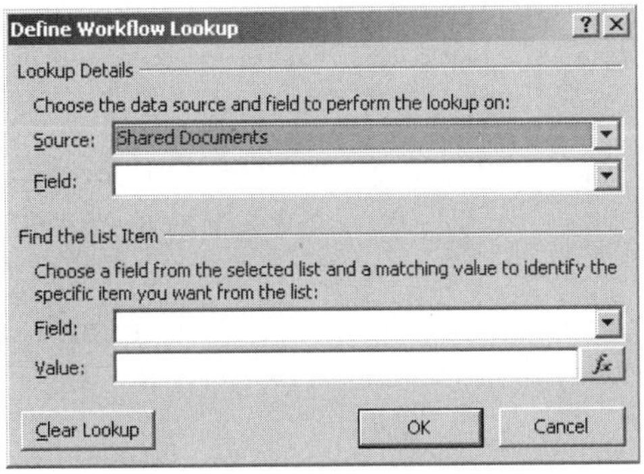

Figure 28-7 Define Workflow Lookup dialog box

- Modified In A Specific Date Span: modified between *date* and *date*. This condition lets you define two *date* variables. If you click one of the *date* variables, you can use the Date Value dialog box to choose a value. This dialog box is shown in Figure 28-8.

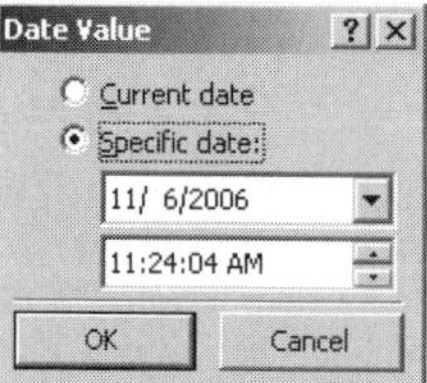

Figure 28-8 Date Value dialog box

- Modified By A Specific Person: modified by *specific person*. The *specific person* variable lets you configure a specific person via the Select Users dialog box shown in Figure 28-9.

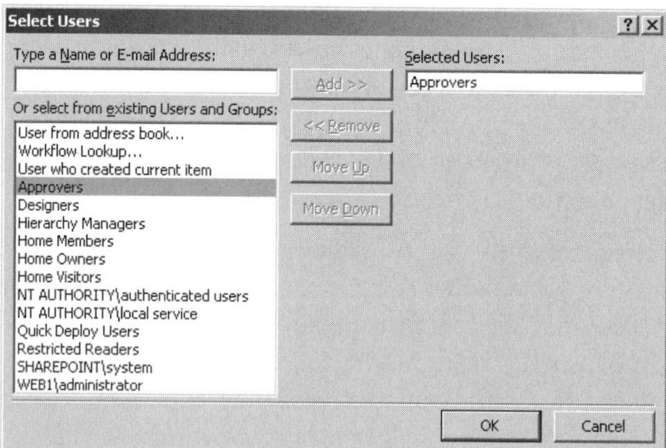

Figure 28-9 Select Users dialog box

- Created In A Specific Date Span: created between *date* and *date*. This condition contains two date variables. You can specify values for the *date* variables via the Date Value dialog box (shown earlier in Figure 28-8).
- Created By A Specific Person: created by a *specific* person. The value for the *specific person* variable can be configured via the Select Users dialog box (shown in Figure 28-9).
- The File Type Is A Specific Type: the file type is *specific type*. You can configure the *specific type* variable by typing the file type extension you expect in the text box that appears.
- The File Size In A Specific Range Kilobytes: the file size is between *size* and *size* kilobytes. The *sizes* variables are configurable via text boxes that will only let you type numerical values.

- Advanced Condition: *value* equals *value*. You can configure the *values* variables via the Display Data-Binding button, which is located next to the Keywords item. This opens a Define Workflow Lookup dialog box, which was shown earlier in Figure 28-7.

Activities

SharePoint Designer 2007 uses a wizard-driven interface that enables users to build sequential workflows that consist of predefined *activities*. Users can select activities from a predetermined list and configure those activities using the SharePoint Designer 2007 interface. These activities are essentially the same activities that are present in the Visual Studio 2005 Designer for Windows Workflow Foundation. There is a small difference, however, because SharePoint Designer 2007 hosts a user interface that is considerably more user friendly. In SharePoint Designer 2007, each activity appears in the form of an action, represented by a sentence that contains variables that the user can configure using drop-down menus and look-up dialog boxes. In Visual Studio 2005 Designer, you have to manipulate activities programmatically.

Core Actions

Out of the box, SharePoint Designer 2007 supports 17 different actions. Those actions can be divided into core actions, task actions, and list actions. The following list provides an overview of the *core* actions:

- Send An Email: send *this message*. Clicking the *this message* variable displays the Define E-mail Message dialog box shown in Figure 28-10. This dialog box lets you compose a message and makes extensive use of lookup variables to facilitate this process.

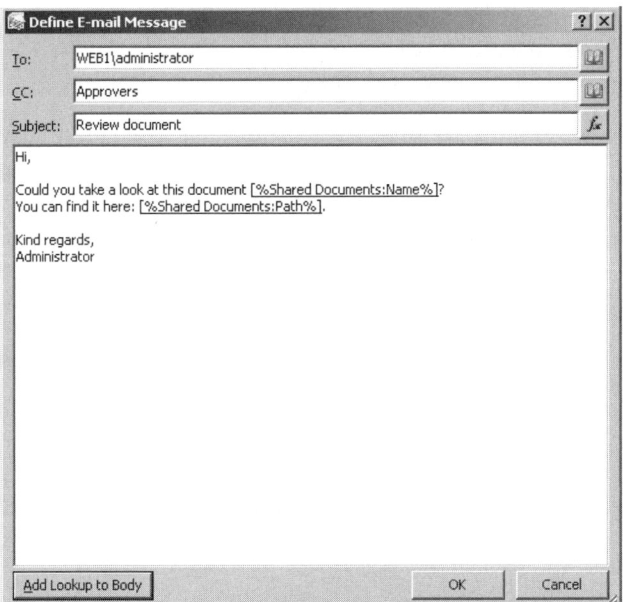

Figure 28-10 Define E-mail Message dialog box

- Set Field In Current Item: set *field* to *value*. Clicking the *field* variable results in the display of a drop-down list containing all the columns that are available for the list or library. The *value* variable can be configured by typing a value into a text box or by clicking the Display Data Binding button to open the Define Workflow Lookup dialog box (shown earlier in Figure 28-7).
- Wait For Field Change In Current Item: wait for *field* to equal *value*. Clicking the *field* variable displays a drop-down list containing all column names of the list or library that you have previously selected. The *value* variable is context-dependent. If the *field* variable you choose is a column that has the drop-down list data type, the values of this column are displayed as a drop-down list once you click the *value* variable.
- Set Workflow Variable: set *workflow* variable to *value*. Clicking the *workflow* variable displays a drop-down list containing all variables that are custom made for this particular workflow. If there are no workflow variables made yet, you get the option to create a new variable. You can also create a workflow variable by clicking the Variables button at the bottom of the Workflow Designer Wizard. This opens the Workflow Local Variables dialog box shown in Figure 28-11.

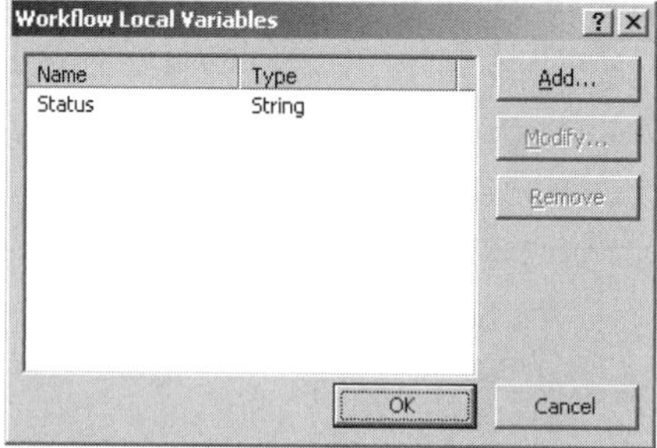

Figure 28-11 Workflow Local Variables dialog box

- Do Calculation: calculate *value* plus *value*, store in *variable*. Clicking the variable item displays a drop-down list containing all the workflow variables that you have made for this particular workflow. If there are no workflow variables present, you can create a new one by clicking the Variables button at the bottom of the Workflow Designer Wizard. This opens the Workflow Local Variables dialog box shown in Figure 28-11.
- Stop Workflow: stop the workflow and log *this message*. The *this message* variable can be configured to define a helpful message explaining why the workflow has stopped. This message will be logged in the history list.
- Log To History List: log *this message* to the workflow history list. You can define a message using the *this message* variable, which is logged in the workflow history list on the SharePoint site.

- Set Moderation Status: set moderation status to *this status* with *comments*. Clicking the *this status* variable displays a drop-down list containing the following status values: approved, rejected, and pending. Clicking the *comments* variable displays a text box that enables you to define additional comments.

Task Actions

The following list provides an overview of the three *task* actions that are available in SharePoint Designer 2007:

- Collect Data From A User: collect *data* from *this user*, store task ID in *0*. The *data* and *this user* variables can be configured by clicking them. If you click the *data* variable, the Custom Task Wizard dialog box opens, which offers you the chance to create a custom task for your workflow. SharePoint Designer 2007 automatically generates an ASP.NET form for such a task, according to the specifications defined in the wizard. Creating a task consists of giving the task a custom name, giving it a description, and defining fields (or questions) for the task. Please refer to the "Creating a Real World Workflow Example" section that demonstrates how to implement an example workflow. Each field is based on an information type (or data type). For example, you can create a drop-down list or a field that contains a single line of text. This option was shown earlier in Figure 28-5. Tasks are used to collect information from workflow users. The information will be stored in the Tasks list in the SharePoint site that contains the workflow. You can use custom task information later in the workflow by retrieving it via the Define Workflow Lookup dialog box.

  If you click the *this user* variable, you can select one person or more in the Select Users dialog box. (See Figure 28-9.) Each task has a unique task ID. By default, this is 0. Task IDs can be changed by assigning the value of a workflow variable to it. You can create a workflow variable by clicking the Variables button at the bottom of the Workflow Designer Wizard. This opens the Workflow Local Variables dialog box shown in Figure 28-11.

- Assign A Todo Item: assign *a todo item* to *these users*. Clicking on the *a todo item* variable opens the Custom Task Wizard dialog box. This dialog box lets you define *a todo item* that will be added to the task list for each specified user. With the *these users* variable, you can select one or more users in the Select Users dialog box (shown earlier in Figure 28-9).

- Assign A Group Survey: assign *a custom survey* to *these users*. Clicking the *a custom survey* variable opens the Custom Task Wizard dialog box. This dialog box lets you define a survey form for a group of users. With the *these users* variable, you can select one or more users in the Select Users dialog box (shown in Figure 28-9).

The following list provides an overview of the six list actions that are available in SharePoint Designer 2007:

- Update List Item: update item in *this list*. Clicking the *this list* variable opens the Update List Item dialog box shown in Figure 28-12.

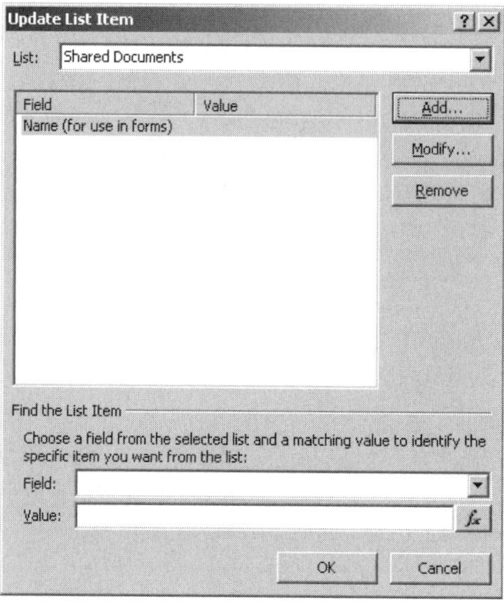

Figure 28-12 Update List Item dialog box

- Create List Item: create item in *this list*. Clicking the *this list* variable opens the Create New List Item dialog box shown in Figure 28-13. This dialog box gives you the chance to choose which list you want to create a new item in.

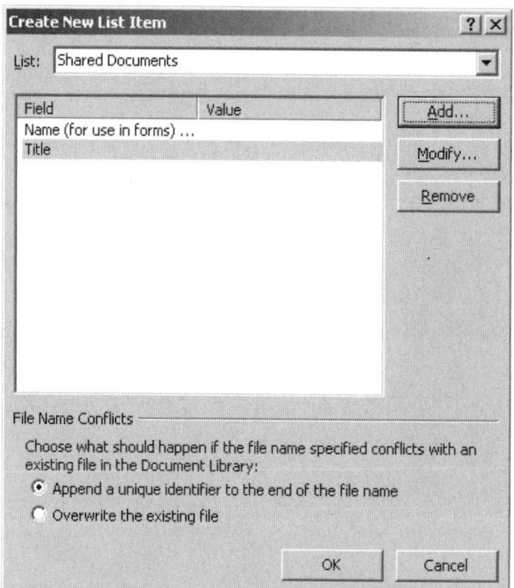

Figure 28-13 Create New List Item dialog box

- Copy List Item: copy item in *this list* to *this list*. Clicking the first *this list* variable opens the Choose List Item dialog box shown in Figure 28-14; clicking the second *this list* variable shows a drop-down list containing all available lists.
- Check Out Item: check out item in *this list*. Clicking the *this list* variable opens the Choose List Item dialog box (shown in Figure 28-14).
- Check In Item: check in item in *this list*. Clicking the *this list* variable opens the Choose List Item dialog box (shown in Figure 28-14).
- Delete Item: delete item in this list. Clicking the *this list* variable opens the Choose List Item dialog box (shown in Figure 28-14).

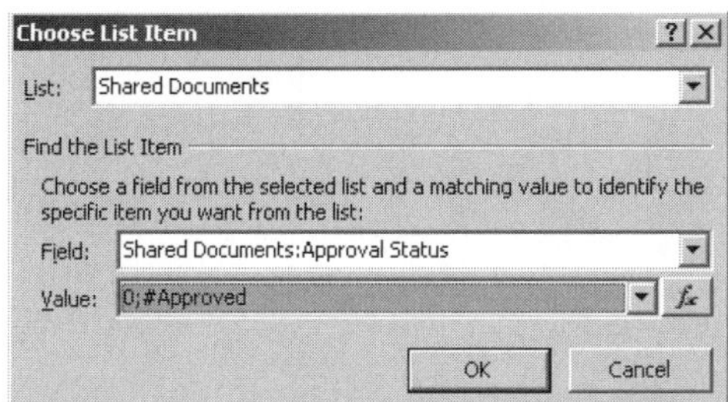

Figure 28-14 Choose List Item dialog box

While you are designing a workflow, you can click the Check Workflow button at the bottom of the Workflow Designer page (shown in Figure 28-15) at any time to check whether your workflow is correct. If the workflow is correct, a window appears that tells you the workflow does not contain any errors. If the workflow is not correct, asterisk signs (*) appear to indicate the problem areas of your workflow.

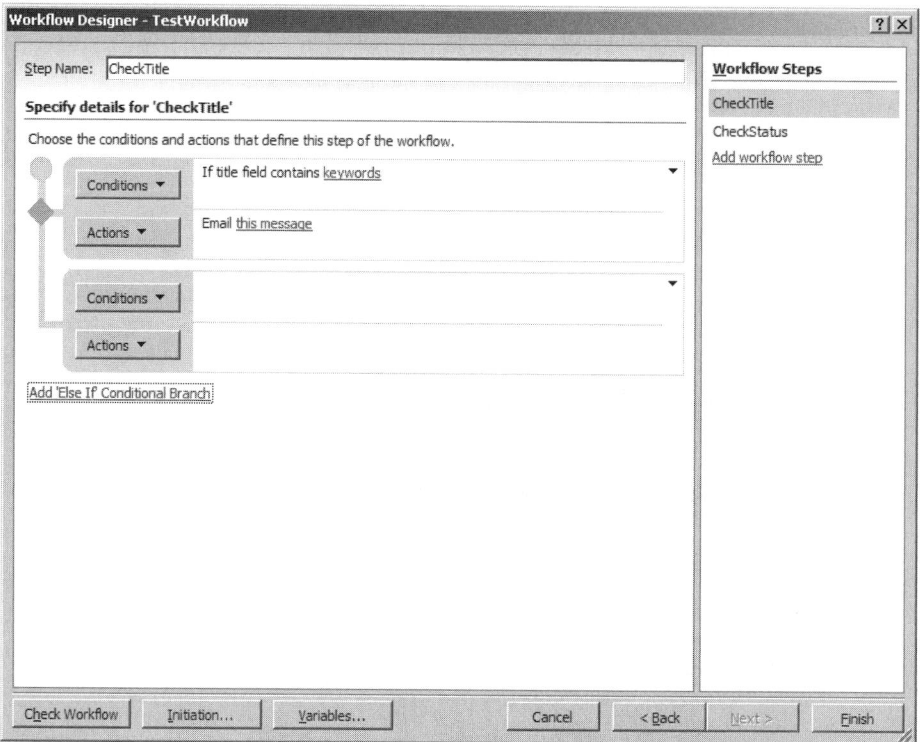

Figure 28-15 Workflow Designer page for verifying workflow details

Adding Conditional Branches to the Workflow

For each workflow step, you can add one or more conditional branches. A conditional branch can contain one or more conditions and one or more actions. You can add a conditional branch by clicking the link called Add 'Else If' Conditional Branch in the Workflow Designer page (shown in Figure 28-15). This adds another set of conditions and actions to the workflow.

Each conditional branch, consisting of a set of conditions and actions, can be moved up and down in the tree of conditional branches. For each conditional branch, you can also move the conditions and actions up and down. You can even specify whether you want your actions to be executed parallel or sequentially. If you choose to run actions in parallel, all actions that are a part of a particular conditional branch are run at once, simultaneously. If you choose to run actions in sequence, the first action in a particular conditional branch is run, followed by the next one and so on, until the last action of that branch has finished executing.

Generating the Workflow Definition Template and Deploying the Workflow

The next step in the workflow creation process is the generation of a workflow definition template and the deployment of the workflow. This is not hard to do because the workflow definition template is generated automatically by SharePoint Designer 2007, which is also responsible for handling the deployment of the workflow to the specified list. Clicking the Finish button in the Workflow Designer Wizard displays a window that shows an overview of the status of the workflow generation and its deployment.

Because you are designing a workflow against a specific list, and the deployment of workflows created in SharePoint Designer is taken care of for you, deployment is a much simpler process than the deployment of workflows created in the Visual Studio 2005 Designer for Windows Workflow Foundation.

Deleting a Workflow and Managing Source Files

Deleting a workflow from a list or library that was designed in SharePoint Designer 2007 does not delete the actual source files that are used to compile that workflow. Instead, the workflow is no longer associated with the list or library, although the source files remain stored in the workflow document library on the site.

You might find it useful to keep the source files around if you want to reuse items within the workflow in another workflow by copying them into the other workflow folder. Other than that, you can't do much with the source files of a deleted workflow. If you are not planning to reuse workflow items, you should remove the workflow from the workflow document library.

Real World Creating a Workflow Example

You have already learned how to employ SharePoint technology to create workflows. To illustrate the concepts discussed so far, you will now learn how to create a simple real-world workflow example.

Imagine, if you will, a company that gets regular requests from potential customers that are interested in purchasing a product. The potential customers want to learn more about the price of this product and want to receive extensive product details. The way our imaginary company deals with such requests is that it assigns an account manager that handles the request by writing a customized Request For Information (RFI) document. After writing this document, it needs to be reviewed by a colleague before sending it to the customer.

In this section, you will learn how to create a workflow that facilitates this process. To keep things simple, you will create a specific document library that contains documents that are relevant to our account managers. The SharePoint workflow springs into life as soon as a document is entered into this document library that contains the word Request in its title. As soon as that happens, a new task will be created indicating that such a document needs to be reviewed.

In order to support this workflow, you first need to go to a specific SharePoint site and create a new document library called RFI Documents. This document library will contain the documents created by account managers.

Once you have created this document library, start SharePoint Designer and open the SharePoint site that contains the RFI Documents document library. In the next procedure, you will start the creation of a new workflow.

1. Click File, select New, and choose workflow.
2. This opens the first step of the Workflow Designer wizard. Choose the following value for the workflow name: RFIWorkflow.
3. Select the RFI Document document library from the drop-down list.
4. Check the "Automatically start this workflow when a new item is created" check box.
5. Click Next.

Since you want to create a workflow that scans the title of documents and looks for the word Request, you are going to add a workflow condition. If this condition is true the workflow needs to create a new task indicating that a new RFI document is added that needs reviewing. You will add a workflow action that is responsible for this. The next procedure explains how to create a workflow condition and action to support our basic workflow process. This procedure continues where you left off, in the middle of the Workflow Designer wizard.

1. Click the Conditions button.
2. Select the following condition: Title field contains keywords.
3. Click keywords.
4. In the textbox that appears, type the following value: Request. This results in the addition of a condition to the workflow that states that some kind of action should happen if the title contains the keyword Request.
5. Click the Actions button.

6. Select the following action: Create List Item.
7. Select the "This list" variable. This opens the Create New List Item dialog box.
8. In the Create New List Item dialog box, select Tasks from the List drop-down list.
9. Click the Add button to add a field to the item that will be created in the Tasks list. Call this field Title and assign the following value to this field: Request. Click OK.

At this point, you have created a workflow. Click the Check Workflow button in the Workflow Designer wizard to validate the workflow and make sure that it does not contain any errors. Then, click Finish. After that, the SharePoint user interface displays a dialog box that indicates the workflow is being processed. When that is done, you can start testing the workflow by adding a new document to the RFI documents document library with the word Request in its title.

Using Custom Activities in SharePoint Designer 2007

Workflow designers cannot use SharePoint Designer 2007 to create custom activities that can be used in custom workflows. Instead, SharePoint Designer 2007 limits the use of activities and conditions to the set that has been included in the safe list that is included in the Web.config file of a SharePoint virtual server. Because of this, the workflow designer can rest assured that all activities and conditions have been pre-approved by a server administrator and thus should be safe to use. Conversely, server administrators can rest assured that workflow designers will not be able to create and deploy activities and conditions to the server without their approval.

Note The safe list provides a safety net: workflow designers and developers cannot deploy custom activities and conditions without the explicit consent and approval of a server administrator.

A condition consists of a custom .NET assembly containing a static method that evaluates some condition and returns a Boolean value when it is called. Developers can create custom activities and conditions that can be deployed to the server after including them within the safe list. To do this, complete the following steps:

1. Create the activity or condition in Visual Studio 2005 Designer, compile it as a strong-named assembly, and deploy it to the global assembly cache (GAC).

2. Add the activity or condition to the action safe list in the Web.config file of a SharePoint virtual server. The Web.config file can be found at the following location: [drive letter]:\inetpub\wwwroot\wss\virtualdirectories. Locate the *<SafeControls>* section in the Web.config file, and add another SafeControl element, which looks like this:

```
<SafeControl Assembly="[assembly name], Version=[version number],
Culture=neutral, PublicKeyToken=[public key token]"
Namespace="[namespace name]" TypeName="*" Safe="True" />
```

   Note .NET assemblies that contain code always have their *Culture* attribute set to *neutral*.

3. Go to the Wss.actions file that is located in the following folder: [drive letter]:\Program Files\Common Files\Microsoft Shared\web server extensions\12\TEMPLATE\1033\Workflow. In this file, you have to add an Action element, rules, and parameters before the action or condition appears in the SharePoint Designer 2007 user interface. The Action element provides Visual Studio 2005 with all the information it requires to appear and function correctly in the Visual Studio 2005 user interface. The following code listing shows a sample Action element:

```
<Action Name="MyTestActivity" ClassName="[class name]"
Assembly="[assembly name], Version=1.0.0.0, Culture=neutral,
PublicKeyToken=[public key token]" Category="Core Actions"
AppliesTo="all"></Action>
```

After completing all steps, the custom activity MyTestActivity is added to the Actions list of the Workflow Designer, as shown in Figure 28-16.

Note For more information about configuring web.config files and signing an assembly with a strong name, see Chapter 31 of this book.

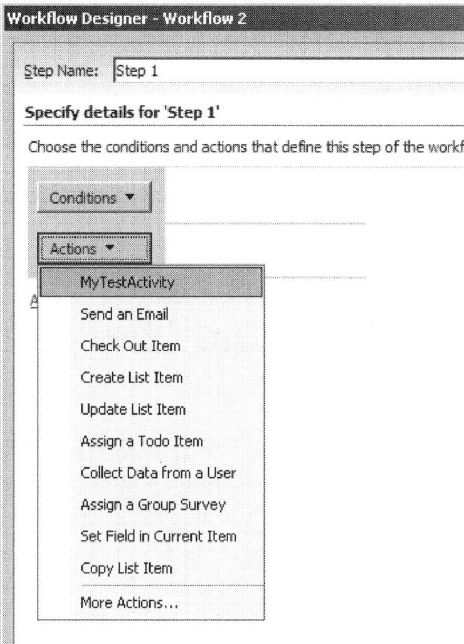

Figure 28-16 The custom activity MyTestActivity is added to the Actions list

Extending Built-in Business Document Workflows

In addition to creating custom workflows by using the Workflow Designer that is included in SharePoint Designer 2007, you can also extend the built-in business document workflows that are included in SharePoint Designer 2007. Chapter 9, "Document Management," explains which document workflows are available out of the box in SharePoint Designer 2007. You can use SharePoint Designer 2007 to edit the workflow tasks that are shipped with SharePoint Designer 2007. You can find these workflow tasks in the Workflow Tasks folder located in the root of the SharePoint site. The following list provides an overview of these workflow tasks:

- **Active.aspx** This file shows all active workflow items in the tasks list.
- **AllItems.aspx** This file shows all workflow tasks in the tasks list.
- **Byowner.aspx** This file shows all the workflow tasks that you own in the list.
- **DispForm.aspx** This file shows the contents of the workflow task after you click on a workflow task.
- **Duetoday.aspx** This file shows all the workflow tasks that are due today.
- **EditForm.aspx** This file shows the editable contents of the workflow task.

- **myGrTsks.aspx** This file shows all the workflow tasks assigned to your team in the tasks list.
- **MyItems.aspx** This file show all the workflow items assigned to you in the tasks list.
- **NewForm.aspx** This file shows the new item page that allows you to create a new task item.

Deploying a Workflow Created with Visual Studio 2005 Designer

If a workflow is created using the Workflow Designer of SharePoint Designer 2007, deployment is simple. If a workflow is created by using Visual Studio 2005 Designer for Windows Workflow Foundation, you have to deploy and activate the workflow before it can be used. For more information about using Visual Studio 2005 Designer for Windows Workflow Foundation to create workflows, see *http://msdn2.microsoft.com/en-us/library/ms441543.aspx*.

Pre-Deployment Tasks

Before you install and activate a workflow that is created using Visual Studio 2005 Designer, make sure the following tasks have been completed:

- The workflow must be compiled as a strongly named assembly. This is a developer task.
- A feature definition file (Feature.xml) must be present to provide SharePoint Designer 2007 with information that is necessary to deploy the workflow at the specified scope. This is also a developer task. It is advisable to open the feature definition file to check its contents. The following code listing shows a sample Feature.xml file:

```
<?xml version="1.0" encoding="utf-8"?>
<Feature Id="[guid]" Title="[workflow template title]"
  Description="[workflow description]" Version="1.0.0.0"
  Scope="Site"
  ReceiverAssembly="Microsoft.Office.Workflow.Feature, Version=12.0.0.0,
  Culture=neutral, PublicKeyToken=71e9bce111e9429c"
  ReceiverClass="Microsoft.Office.Workflow.Feature.WorkflowFeatureReceiver"
  xmlns="http://schemas.microsoft.com/sharepoint/">
  <ElementManifests>
    <ElementManifest Location="[workflow definition file]" />
  </ElementManifests>
  <Properties>
```

```
    <Property Key="GloballyAvailable" Value="true" />
    <Property Key="RegisterForms" Value="*.xsn" />
  </Properties>
</Feature>
```

- A workflow definition file (by default, called Workflow.xml) must be present to provide SharePoint Designer 2007 with information that is necessary to instantiate and run the workflow. The creation of a Workflow.xml file is a developer task. It is advisable to open the workflow definition file to check its contents. The following code listing shows a sample Workflow.xml file:

```
<?xml version="1.0" encoding="utf-8" ?>
<Elements xmlns="http://schemas.microsoft.com/sharepoint/">
  <Workflow
    Name="[workflow name]"
    Description="[workflow description]"
    Id="[guid]"
    CodeBesideClass="[workflow class]"
    CodeBesideAssembly="[namespace], Version=1.0.0.0, Culture=neutral,
    PublicKeyToken=[public key token]"
    >
    <Categories/>
    <MetaData/ >
  </Workflow>
</Elements>\
```

Note For more information about feature definition (Feature.xml) files, see *http://msdn2.microsoft.com/en-us/library/ms475601.aspx*, and for more information about workflow definition (Workflow.xml) files, see *http://msdn2.microsoft.com/en-us/library/ms439134.aspx*.

If the feature definition and workflow definition files are present and valid and the workflow assembly is strongly named, the workflow is almost ready to be deployed. Next, you need to customize the Install.bat file that is used in deployment to ensure that running this batch file will deploy the workflow files to the correct location, copy the workflow assembly to the Global Assembly cache, and activate the workflow in SharePoint Designer 2007. The Install.bat file is included in the Workflow Developer Starter Kit for Windows SharePoint Services 3.0. The developer who created the workflow should be able to provide this Install.bat file to you as well.

Note Solution providers, independent software vendors, value-added resellers, and other developers that want to write custom workflows for SharePoint Designer 2007 should download the Workflow Developer Starter Kit for Windows SharePoint Services 3.0 from *http://www.microsoft.com/downloads/details.aspx?familyid=5DDF902D-95B1-4640-B9E4-45440DC388D9&displaylang=en*. This starter kit contains Visual Studio project templates for building SharePoint sequential workflow libraries, SharePoint state machine workflow libraries, and samples. The starter kit requires that the following applications are installed: Visual Studio 2005, SharePoint Server 2007, the Windows Workflow Foundation Runtime components, and Visual Studio 2005 Extensions for Windows Workflow Foundation.

Performing Deployment and Activation

Open the Install.bat file, and replace the placeholder text with the information taken from the workflow project. This encompasses the following information:

- The feature directory name
- The feature XML file name
- The workflow definition XML file name
- The name and relative path of the compiled workflow assembly

During the deployment process, the Install.bat file will do the following things:

- Create a feature directory at the appropriate location on the server.
- Copy the feature definition file, workflow definition file, and InfoPath form files (if present) into the feature directory.
- Copy the compiled workflow assembly into the GAC.
- Activate the feature in SharePoint Designer 2007.

Post-Deployment Tasks

After deployment, you can associate this custom workflow with the lists and libraries that are located on the SharePoint site that contains the activated feature for the custom workflow. To accomplish this, follow these steps:

1. Browse to the SharePoint site, and go to a list or library.
2. Click List/Document Library settings and then click Workflow Settings in the Permissions And Policies section.
3. Choose the custom workflow that was created in Visual Studio 2005 Designer from the Select A Workflow Template check box.

Summary

This chapter starts with an explanation of the available tools for creating workflows in SharePoint 2007. Then, this chapter provided an overview of the architecture of Windows Workflow Foundation in a SharePoint Designer 2007 context. The chapter also discussed the workflow markup language (XOML). Also, the chapter describes the differences between Visual Studio 2005 Designer and SharePoint Designer 2007 when it comes to creating workflows. You have learned how to build a workflow step by step using SharePoint Designer 2007 and have seen which conditions and actions are available out of the box to be included in your workflows. You have also seen how to use custom activities and extend built-in document workflows. Finally, the chapter discussed how to deploy a workflow created with Visual Studio 2005.

In the next chapter, you will learn about the feature set comprised in the Web Parts that are available out-of-the-box in SharePoint Server 2007.

Chapter 29

Microsoft Office SharePoint Server 2007 Web Parts

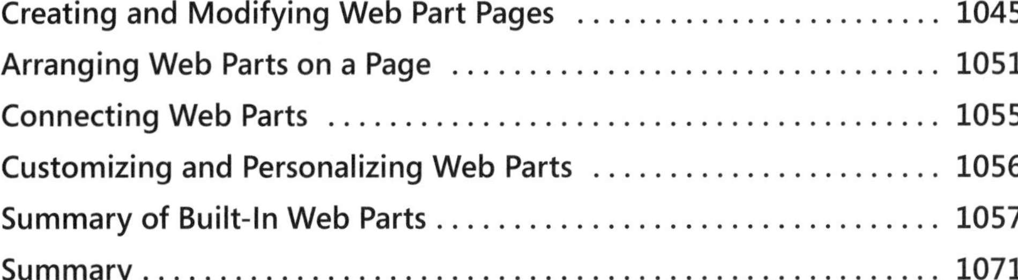

One of the most compelling reasons to purchase Microsoft Office SharePoint Server 2007 is the plethora of Web Parts that ship with this product. Some of these Web Parts form an overall feature that users will find very beneficial in their daily jobs.

A Web Part page is a special Web page that is configured with one or more Web Part zones that can host Web Parts. These zones can only be created on Web Part pages. You can think of Web Parts as individual units of code that are responsible for presenting data in customized views through the user's browser. A Web Part can be a prebuilt module or one of custom design. Either way, the modular structure of a Web Part allows simple manipulation and organization of information and functionalities on Web Part pages. This chapter will describe the individual functions and proper use of the Web Parts that come with Office SharePoint Server 2007.

Creating and Modifying Web Part Pages

When a site is created in SharePoint Server 2007, the home page is automatically a Web Part page. Each site template contains a set of default Web Parts. The most commonly used Web Part page template comes with the team site. A *Web Part page* is a content layout page that is used in conjunction with a master page to create the Web page that is rendered by the client's browser.

Some possible functions of Web Parts on pages and sites are as follows:

- To consolidate data
- To display text and images
- To promote collaboration and communication.

Note You can use Microsoft Office SharePoint Designer 2007 to create a Web Part page from scratch.

To understand how Web Parts work, you will create a blank Web Part page. Later, you will add and modify Web Parts on that page. To create a blank Web Part page, follow these steps:

1. Starting from a site, on the Site Actions menu, click Create.
2. In the Web Pages section, choose Web Part Page.
3. In the Name box, type a name for the new Web Part Page. This will become the file name, with an .aspx extension.
4. Select a layout template. There are eight templates to choose from, all with different Web Part zone layouts.

   More Info For more information about zones, see the "Arranging Web Parts on a Page" section later in this chapter.

5. In the Save Location section, choose a document library to save this new file in and click Create.

   Note If a document library does not already exist on the site, you will be prompted to create one.

The new Web Part Page is generated and appears in edit mode, which was referred to as *design mode* in SharePoint Server 2003.

Figure 29-1 is a team site with four Web Parts. The Web Parts are inside two Web Part zones that are labeled Left and Right. There is also an Add A Web Part button at the top of each zone. Notice the text at the top of the page that lets you know that you are editing the Shared Version of the page.

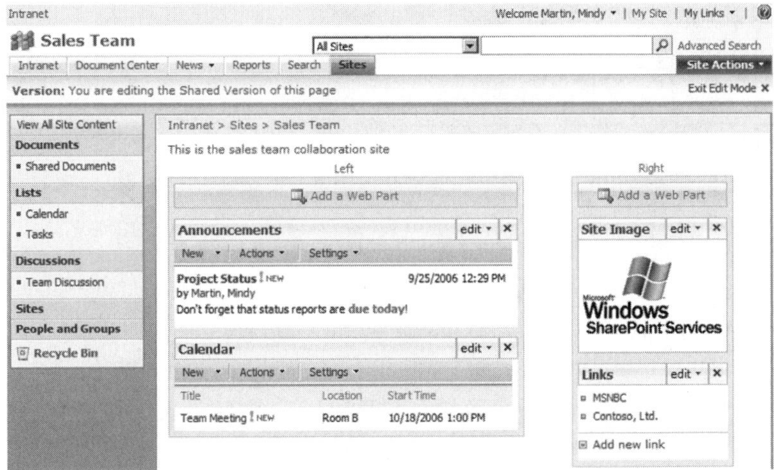

Figure 29-1 A Web Part page

More Info For more information about shared and personal versions, see the "Customizing and Personalizing Web Parts" section later in this chapter.

Adding Web Parts to a Page

A page must be in edit mode to add and modify Web Parts. You can enter edit mode by clicking Site Actions and then selecting Edit Page. Once you're in edit mode, there are two basic methods for adding Web Parts:

- The Add Web Parts dialog box
- Drag-and-drop from the Web Part tool pane

The following describes how to switch a page to edit mode and add a Web Part:

1. On the Site Actions menu, click Edit Page.
2. Edit mode is indicated by an Exit Edit Mode link under the Site Actions list.
3. Click the Add A Web Part button and the Add Web Parts dialog box appears. This box displays all Web Parts, listed in groups, and is shown in Figure 29-2.

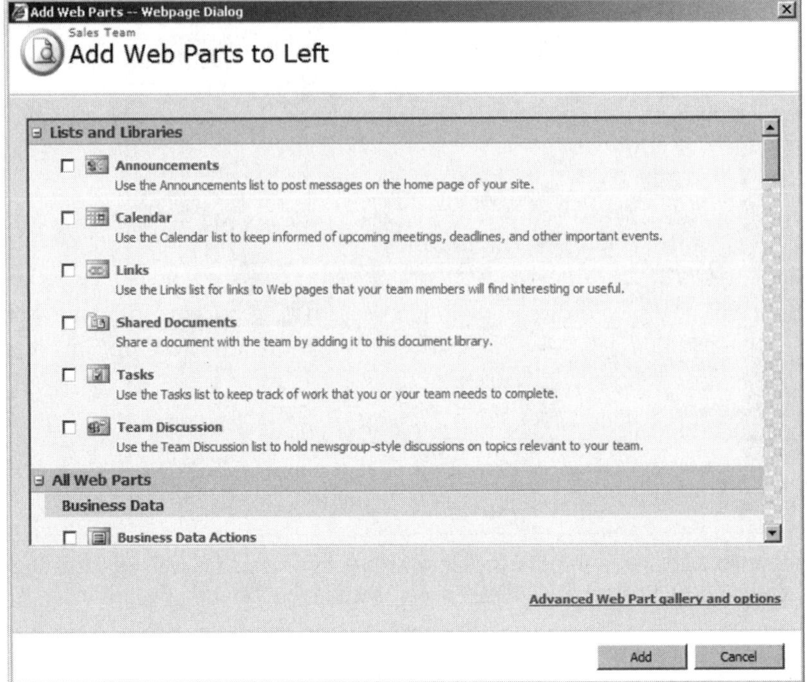

Figure 29-2 Add Web Parts dialog box

4. Select two Web Parts and click Add.

Figure 29-2 shows the Suggested Web Parts screen that automatically groups and filters the Web Parts the system interprets to be the most likely choices for the type of Web Part page with which you're working. Notice that you can get to the Web Part tool pane by clicking the Advanced Web Part Gallery And Options link. This Web Part tool pane is shown in Figure 29-3.

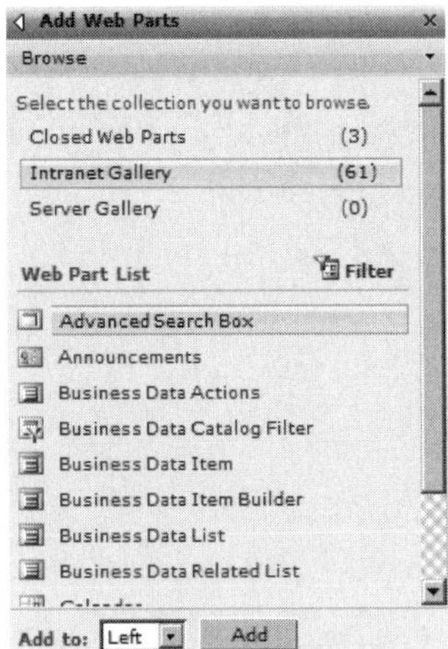

Figure 29-3 Web Part tool pane

The Web Part tool pane is the second way to add Web Parts to a Web Part page. In this tool pane, the Web Parts are listed alphabetically.

Note If the Add and Cancel buttons do not display at the bottom right of the Add Web Parts dialog box, collapse and expand the Lists And Libraries section. The Add button will appear at the bottom right of this screen.

Using the Web Part Gallery and Advanced Options

Other than the basic way of browsing for them, there are several ways to obtain Web Parts to add them to the page. This section will cover the more advanced options of adding Web Parts from the Web Parts tool pane.

Browse, Search, and Import are the three methods for finding a Web Part. In the top toolbar of the Web Part tool pane, click the down arrow, and a menu box for Browse, Search, and Import will appear.

Browse

The Web Part tool pane shows an alphabetical list of all Web Parts for the site collection, ten at a time. You can see the next 10 Web Parts in the list by clicking the Next link at the bottom of the tool pane.

Search

Besides scrolling through a long list of Web Parts, one page at a time, another way to find a Web Part is to use the Search feature. The titles and descriptions of all Web Parts in the site collection will be searched, with results displayed.

Import

This feature is useful when you need a Web Part that does not exist in the site collection. You can use this feature to import an existing Web Part from a file share into the Web Part gallery. The file extensions for Web Parts are .webpart or .dwp. Web Parts can be imported into the gallery by performing the following steps:

1. Navigate to the home page of the site collection by clicking the link at the top left of the screen.
2. Click the Site Actions menu, click Site Settings, and choose Modify All Site Settings.
3. In the Galleries section, select Web Parts. This page lists detailed file information about every Web Part.
4. To upload Web Parts for the site collection, click Upload on the toolbar, browse to .dwp or .webpart files, and click OK.

The Web Part you wanted to import should now appear in the list of Web Parts for the site.

Web Part Galleries

Web Part galleries are groups of Web Parts that are helpful in locating a specific Web Part. Referring back to Figure 29-3, three galleries are shown: Closed Web Parts, *Site Name* Gallery, and Server Gallery. There is a fourth gallery called the Online Gallery, which can be turned on or off in the Web application's properties in Central Administration. This gallery is not illustrated in Figure 29-3.

- **Closed Web Parts** This is a list of Web Parts that previously existed on the page but have been removed.
- ***Site Name* Gallery** The default location for all Web Parts in the site collection. The name is based on the site collection's name.
- **Server Gallery** This is a list of Web Parts available for all site collections in the Web application. Navigate to the virtual server in the SharePoint Server 2007 server's file system, create a new folder called "wpcatalog," and copy the .dwp and .webpart files to that folder.
- **Online Gallery** This is a collection of Microsoft MSNBC Web Parts located on the Internet. By default, this feature is enabled for each virtual server, but it can be turned off. To turn this feature off, go to SharePoint Central Administration and access the Application Management tab. Under Application Security, choose Security For Web Part Pages. In the Online Web Part Gallery section, choose the option to prevent access to it.

Managing the Online Web Part Gallery

An enabled online gallery will cause a performance hit on the server, which might be obvious when navigating the Web Part tool pane. This is due to the server trying to access the MSNBC online Web Part gallery. When the server tries to access this Web Part gallery, there is usually a 10 to 20-second delay in the Web Part tool pane appearing while the server tries to build the Web Part list in the online Web Part gallery.

If you want the MSNBC Web Parts for your deployment, best practice is to download them to your server and offer them as part of another, local gallery. Then go into Central Administration and turn off the online Web Part gallery for each Web application. This will increase performance and still allow your users to use these free Web Parts from MSNBC.

Web Part List Filtering

To access the Web Part list filter, click the Filter button in the Web Part tool pane, which was shown in Figure 29-3. This will elicit a new drop-down box, listing the different types of Web Part groups for filtering.

Exporting Web Parts

Exporting Web Parts is very useful when there is a need to copy a Web Part to another location. Web Parts can be exported in a couple of ways:

Note List View Web Parts cannot be exported because they are specific to the site.

- **Site-collection level** In the site collection's Web Part gallery, find the Web Part to be exported and click the edit icon. Next, click Export in the toolbar, and save the file to your hard drive. Then copy the Web Part to a file share from where the other site administrators can import the Web Part into their galleries.
- **Site/Page level** Exporting Web Parts at this level lets you retain Web Part settings or customizations. This allows an identical Web Part to be placed on another page. For example, this feature can be used in a case where a Content Editor Web Part has been customized with a lot of text and graphics and needs to be used "as is" on multiple pages. The following steps demonstrate how to export a Content Editor Web Part:
    1. Add the Content Editor Web Part to a page, and customize it with text and a table or image.
    2. On the Web Part menu, choose Export.
    3. Save this .dwp file to your computer's file system.

More Info For information on importing, see the "Import" section earlier in this chapter.

Arranging Web Parts on a Page

Web Part zones are storage units used to accommodate and organize Web Parts on a Web Part page. These are sections of the page layout where Web Parts can be placed. Multiple Web Parts can be positioned vertically in each zone.

Note Zones are pre-programmed within the page template that is used to create the page. The only way to modify the zones on a page is to edit the site using Microsoft SharePoint Designer 2007 or Visual Studio .NET.

Methods of Arranging Web Parts

Once Web Parts are added to a page, there are two methods for re-arranging them. The methods consist of performing a drag-and-drop operation or using the Web Part tool pane to modify the settings, as detailed in the following list:

- **Drag and drop** This is the quickest and most commonly used method. In edit mode, the cursor changes to a four-headed arrow when it hovers over a Web Part's toolbar. Drag and drop Web Parts from zone to zone, or up and down within the same zone.
- **Modify settings** On the Web Part toolbar, click Edit, which is a drop-down menu called the Web Part menu. Choose Modify Shared Web Part. Expand the Layout section in the Web Part tool pane. Modify the Web Part's location on the page by changing the Zone and Zone Index fields.

Removing Web Parts

Removing Web Parts is simple. While in edit mode, click the X at the top right of the Web Part, or choose Delete in the Web Part menu.

Modifying Web Part Settings

The edit menu options of a Web Part depend on the advanced settings of the Web Part. By default, the options are Minimize, Close, Delete, Modify Shared Web Part, Export, Connections, and Help.

Web Part Properties

To access the properties of a Web Part, click the Edit menu in the Web Part. Some properties are common throughout the various Web Parts, such as appearance, layout, and advanced. Besides the common properties, most Web Parts have custom properties that are listed either before or after the common properties.

List Views

The List View is a template using a standard set of Web Part tool pane settings. For example, lists and libraries use this template. In list views, you can edit the current view or select a view that already exists for that list.

Figure 29-4 shows the List Views tool pane. The Selected View field contains a drop-down list of choices of the user-defined views that exist for the library, plus Current View and Summary View. Use the Edit The Current View button to customize the current view within the Web Part. When an existing view is selected, edited, and saved, that edited version becomes the Current View.

Important Switching from the current view to another view listed in the drop-down list removes changes that have been made to the current view and might disable Web Part connections that depend on columns in the current view. If you are worried about losing your changes to the current view in the Web Part, you can create a named view in that list or library. This way, your custom view is named and saved, and it will be an option in the Selected View drop-down list.

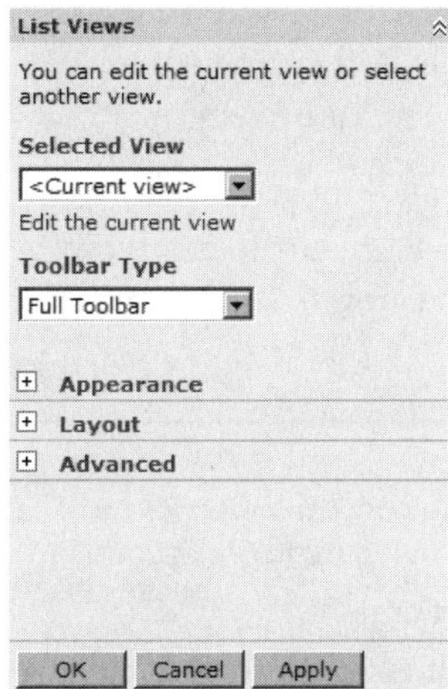

Figure 29-4 List View tool pane settings

The Toolbar Type is used to specify the manner in which the Web Part toolbar is displayed. Full Toolbar, Summary Toolbar, and No Toolbar are the options. Table 29-1 lists the available appearance properties of each Web Part in the Web Part tool pane.

Table 29-1 Appearance

Property	Description
Title	This is the text that shows in the Web Part title bar. Modifying this does not influence the name of the item, such as the document library name.
Height & Width	This specifies the number of pixels or allows the Web Part to adjust itself automatically to fit the zone.
Chrome State	The choices are Minimized or Normal. When the chrome state is minimized, only the title bar of the Web Part is displayed.

Table 29-1 Appearance

Property	Description
Chrome Type	This is the option that determines how the title bar and border are displayed. The border is a box around the entire Web Part.

What Is Chrome?

The term *chrome* refers to the Web Part frame elements. In the previous version of SharePoint Server, this was referred to as the Frame. For example, Chrome Type was previously referred to as Frame Style.

You can think of the chrome as the master page, whereas the content is displayed in the content page. Multiple content pages can be associated with a single master page. If you want to update the branding on your sites, most likely you'll use the master pages in the site collections to do this. You modify and customize these pages to include the look, feel, and functionality you want each site to enjoy.

The Web Part layout properties in Table 29-2 pertain to the Web Part location on the page, and the placement on the page in relation to other Web Parts.

Table 29-2 Layout Properties

Property	Description
Visible on Page	Hide the Web Part. This feature is often used to conceal a Web Part whose function is to feed data to other Web Parts via Web Part connections.
Direction	This option aligns the Web Part text to the left or right.
Zone	The zones are regions of the page such as Right, Left, Top, and Bottom. This drop-down box list shows the names of the zones on this page. This is an alternate to using the cursor to drag Web Parts to different zones.
Zone Index	The order of the Web Part compared to other Web Parts within a zone is the zone index. The lower the number, the higher on the page the Web Part will be within that zone. This option was previously referred to as "part order."

The advanced Web Part properties are listed in Table 29-3. When the personal version of a page is modified, these options are not available.

Table 29-3 Advanced Properties

Property	Description
Allow Minimize, Allow Close	Each Web Part menu has options to Minimize or Close. Close does not delete the Web Part from the page.
Allow Hide	Allows users the Visible On Page option for that Web Part.

Table 29-3 Advanced Properties

Property	Description
Allow Zone Change	This option determines whether Web Parts can be moved to different zones.
Allow Connections	When a page is in edit mode, the Web Part menu has an option to allow connections to other Web Parts.
Allow Editing in Personal View	To edit the personal view of a page, click Welcome [username] at the top of the page, and choose Personalize This Page.
Export Mode	Determines the level of data that can be exported from this Web Part. Options are Export All Data and Non-sensitive Data Only.
Title URL	When the title of the Web Part is clicked, this is the URL that users are directed to. Title URL was referred to as Detail Link in SharePoint Server 2003.
Description	This specifies the ScreenTip that appears when the cursor is hovered in the title area of the Web Part.
Help URL	If you click the Web Part menu and select the blue Help icon, the browser navigates to this link.
Help Mode	This option sets the method in which the help dialog box is displayed in the browser window. The functionality of this option also depends on whether the user's browser supports it.
Catalog Icon Image Url	Specifies the location of the optional 16 x 16 Web Part icon graphic.
Import Error Message	Specifies the text of the message that appears if there is an error importing the Web Part.
Target Audiences	This feature allows for target audiences to be specified.

Connecting Web Parts

The SharePoint Server 2007 Web Part infrastructure allows Web Parts to exchange information with each other at run time. The basic functionality of Web Part connections is that when an action is executed in one Web Part, it changes the displayed information in another Web Part.

Figure 29-5 shows two connected Web Parts. The Contacts Web Part shows a list of vendors. The Issue Tracking Web Part contains a list of assigned issues, with a column showing the vendor that each issue is associated with. To configure the Company field to connect the two Web Parts, that field must be displayed in the view of each Web Part. Once the connection has been established, when a user selects a contact in the list, the Issues list is filtered to display only issues associated with that company.

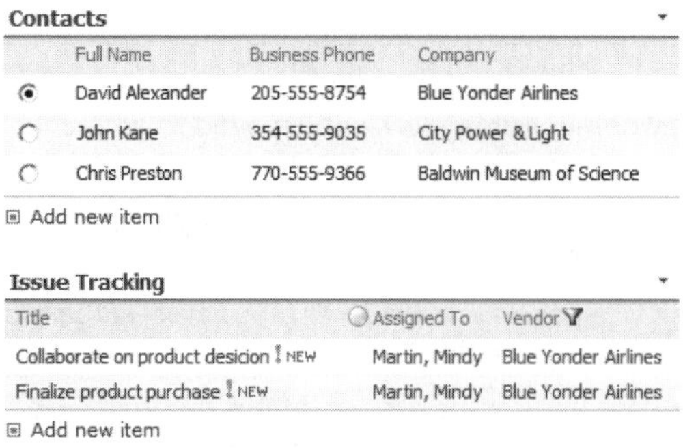

Contacts

	Full Name	Business Phone	Company
◉	David Alexander	205-555-8754	Blue Yonder Airlines
○	John Kane	354-555-9035	City Power & Light
○	Chris Preston	770-555-9366	Baldwin Museum of Science

Add new item

Issue Tracking

Title	Assigned To	Vendor
Collaborate on product desicion ! NEW	Martin, Mindy	Blue Yonder Airlines
Finalize product purchase ! NEW	Martin, Mindy	Blue Yonder Airlines

Add new item

Figure 29-5 Web Part connections

Web Parts can be connected only if they are compatible with each other. If the Web Parts are found to be incompatible, the Connection menu item in the browser will be dimmed and have a ToolTip explanation. Connections are not supported at all in some Web Parts, and a Web Part cannot be connected to itself, either directly or through a chain of connections. Some types of data, such as hyperlinks and multiple lines of text, are not supported.

Customizing and Personalizing Web Parts

Personalized Web Parts and Web pages filter or display information based upon the logged-in user's profile properties.

Security Alert There is a new way to view a page as a particular person in the organization, but it means that you have to log in to a page under that user's credentials. It is typically considered a security risk when users give their passwords to other users or even administrators. Click Welcome *Username* at the top of the page, and choose Sign In As A Different User.

When a Web Part page is modified, it is done so in one of two ways: through shared or personal versions. In SharePoint Server 2003, these were referred to as the shared and personal *views*. The shared version of the page is for all users of the site to see, and when changes are made in a shared version, they are intended for public consumption. When the personal version of a Web Part page is edited, any changes that are made are intended just for the logged-in user to see. To edit the personal version of a page, click the Welcome menu at the top of the screen, Welcome *Username*. Then choose Personalize This Page. Once a Web Part is modified in the personal version of the page, it becomes a personalized Web Part.

Web Part settings that can be modified on the personal version of a page include the following:

- **Layout and appearance** These common Web Part properties can be viewed and modified, but the Advanced ones cannot be.
- **Custom Web Part properties** The developer of the Web Part might have decided not to make some of these properties available for modification, or the permission level of the user could be a factor that determines what can be modified.
- **Deletion** Permissions of the Web Part determine whether it can be deleted.

As the owner or the administrator, you have several ways to customize your Web Part page. Customization applies when the modifications are to the shared version of the page or Web Part. Some examples of customization are editing the Web Part page title, changing the properties of individual Web Parts, and changing the layout of the page.

Summary of Built-In Web Parts

The following are the names and summaries of all the Web Parts that are included in SharePoint Server 2007. Web Part groups we will reference include Libraries, Communications, Tracking, Content Rollup, Dashboard, Filters, Miscellaneous, Outlook Web Access, and Site Directory. Within each group, two or more Web Parts are briefly discussed.

This is not an exhaustive list or discussion of each Web Part. Instead, the goal here is to generally inform you of the more common Web Parts that are included in Office SharePoint Server 2007. Web Parts that are discussed extensively in other parts of this book are not listed here, such as the Business Data Web Parts.

Libraries

All the Library Web Parts are List View Web Parts.

Document Library

A document library is a collection of files and folders for team members to collaborate on. Document libraries are an excellent replacement for network shared folders, and even Microsoft Exchange public folders.

More Info For more details on document libraries, see Chapter 9, "Document Management."

Form Library

A form library is a collection of XML-based business forms, such as status reports or purchase orders. This type of library requires Microsoft Office InfoPath. Form libraries should be created for each separate form your organization uses that needs to be filled out and submitted.

Wiki Page Library

A wiki page library is a collection of interconnected wiki pages. Wiki pages themselves support text, pictures, tables, hyperlinks, and wiki linking.

Real World Wiki Help

When a wiki library is created, wiki help information is automatically included in the library. This information includes details about the use, editing, and management of wiki pages. To create a new wiki, click View All Pages on the left side of the screen, and then click the New button.

Picture Library

Picture libraries are similar to document libraries, but they are written to host graphics and images. Picture libraries can be displayed and used in several ways. The pictures can be viewed as thumbnails or a slide show, and there are options to edit or download the pictures.

Data Connection Library

The purpose of a data connection library is to store, share, and manage data connection files. Connection files have an .odc extension. The .odc files contain parameters about where the data is stored, such as the database server and table name.

More Info For more details on data connection libraries, see Chapter 12 "Administrating Data Connections."

Translation Management Library

The purpose of the translation management library is to manage the translation of documents in several languages. The Translation Management Library feature must be enabled for a site in order to create this type of library. To learn more about Translation Management Library settings and administration, please consult Chapter 4, "Multilanguage Planning, Deployment, and Maintenance."

Slide Library

Slide libraries allow for sharing and collaboration on individual Microsoft Office PowerPoint slides. The Slide Library feature must be enabled for the site in order to create this type of library. At the top right of the site, click Site Settings and then Site Features. Next to Slide Library, click Activate.

Reports Library

The reports library allows the creation, management, and delivery of Web pages, documents, and key performance indicators. Report libraries communicate metrics, goals, and business intelligence information.

Communications

All the communications Web Parts are List View Web Parts.

Announcements

Announcements are usually placed at the top of Web sites. They are used to share news, project status, and other short bits of information. If announcements are time-sensitive, they can be set to expire on a certain date.

Contacts

A contacts list contains information about people who your team works with, such as vendors, customers, or partners. The data in a contact list is similar to what you see in Microsoft Outlook contacts lists, and they can be synchronized with Microsoft Outlook. This information can be collaborated on with teammates.

Discussion Board

The purpose of discussion boards is to conduct newsgroup-style discussions. These discussions can be viewed as a threaded list, and each individual post contains a photo of the user who last modified it. (This is, of course, if the users have set up their My Site and uploaded photos of themselves.)

Tracking

All the tracking Web Parts are List View Web Parts.

Links

The links list is simply a collection of Web site URLs that your team members will find helpful or interesting.

Calendar

The Calendar Web Part can be displayed as a list of events or as an actual calendar view. This appearance is similar to your Outlook calendar. Events and meetings can be shared with teammates, and they can also be synchronized with Microsoft Outlook.

Tasks

This Web Part displays a tasks list, similar to the tasks in Outlook. Tasks can be assigned to users, and they can also be synchronized with Outlook.

Project Tasks

A project tasks list allows the graphical viewing of a group of work items that you or your team needs to complete. The graphics view is actually a Gantt Chart, which displays the duration of project timelines in a calendar-based chart. This type of list can be synchronized with Outlook.

Issue Tracking

An issue tracking list is used to manage a set of issues or problems. You can assign issues to users, prioritize them, and even link issues that are related to each other.

Survey

Surveys are created to poll people, and they can be quickly created. They have also been enhanced in SharePoint Server 2007. The survey creator can now be very specific as to what questions are asked to certain users and how users' answers determine what questions are to be asked next. This advanced feature is called *branching logic*.

iView Web Part

This Web Part displays iViews from SAP portal servers. An iView is SAP's version of a Web Part because it is an encapsulated bit of functionality that was created for SAP's Web environment.

WSRP Consumer

WSRP stands for *Web Services for Remote Portlets*. This Web Part enables integration with other WSRP-compliant portal solutions. To use this Web Part, you need to modify some files on the server. This is a task you should pass on to the company's development or database team because it involves the creation of an XML file.

Content Rollup

Most of the Content Rollup Web Parts are available on My Sites only. Site Aggregator is the only content rollup Web Part that is available on other pages.

Colleague Tracker

The Colleague Tracker Web Part, shown in Figure 29-6, displays your list of colleagues and recent changes to their profiles or memberships.

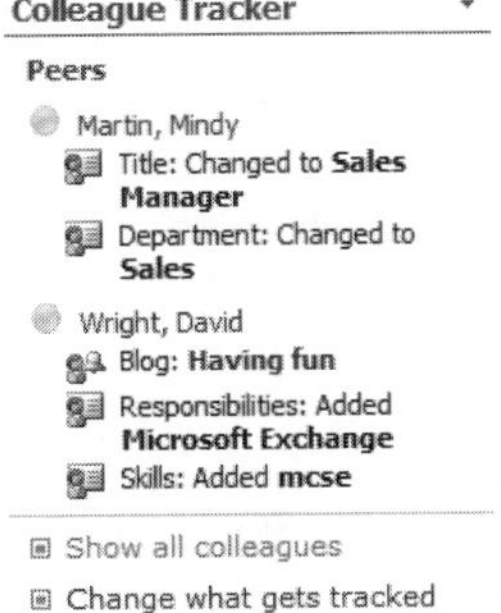

Figure 29-6 The Colleague Tracker Web Part

Alert settings for this list of colleagues can be customized. Colleague Tracker can be configured to show a visible alert according to the configuration in the Web Part tool pane.

Colleagues

The Colleagues Web Part displays a list of people in your own list of My Colleagues. It automatically tracks and suggests colleagues to add to your My Colleagues list, based on the frequency of e-mail interactions and common distribution list memberships. The online status of each colleague is displayed, and there is an option to create custom groups for them. Click the Manage Colleagues button for more advanced options. This Web Part differs from the Colleague Tracker in that the latter simply alerts you to changes in the profiles of colleagues in your Colleagues list.

In Common Between Us

When accessing another user's My Site page, this Web Part displays as "In Common With *Your Name*." The colleagues listed here are people who you and the user whose site you are visiting have both added to your My Colleagues lists.

Memberships

This Web Part displays your own distribution list memberships, along with a list of SharePoint Server 2007 sites that you have permissions to access.

My Links

The My Links Web Part displays your own My Links list. This is a list of favorite links that you create and manage. This list is also accessible at the top of the site, next to My Site.

SharePoint Documents

This Web Part allows you to look at a list of your own recent documents and tasks. This list contains documents and pictures that you've uploaded or edited and tasks that are assigned to you. There are tabs that contain your documents, pictures, and tasks for each respective site–across multiple document libraries and lists within each site.

Note This Web Part is security-trimmed and won't show links to items that you do not have access to. In addition, if you are logged into the site as the System Account, no information will display in this Web Part. This is by design.

My Workspaces

The My Workspaces Web Part displays sites created under your My Site. Contrary to the name of the Web Part, this is not limited to just workspaces. It displays any type of templated site that you created.

Recent Blog Posts

This Web Part displays recent posts to your blog. It is a Data View Web Part that obtains data from an Xsl file.

More Info For more information about My Sites, see Chapter 8, "Administrating Personalization and Portal Taxonomies."

Site Aggregator

Using this Web Part, users can easily and instantly go to each site in a set of Web sites of interest. Figure 29-7 shows the toolbar, where the sites name tabs are in a horizontal row. The Web Part itself can be likened to a window through which to view the Web sites, and the tabs at the top of the Web Part allow fast switching between them.

Figure 29-7 Site Aggregator Web Part

Dashboard

The dashboard Web Parts are used to display an overall view of business health. These are glimpses at critical enterprise data, with warnings and statuses displayed prominently.

Key Performance Indicators

The Key Performance Indicators (KPI) Web Part has a prerequisite. When adding this Web Part to a site, the Indicator List field in the Web Part tool pane requires the path to an existing KPI List. Figure 29-8 shows an example of this Web Part in edit mode.

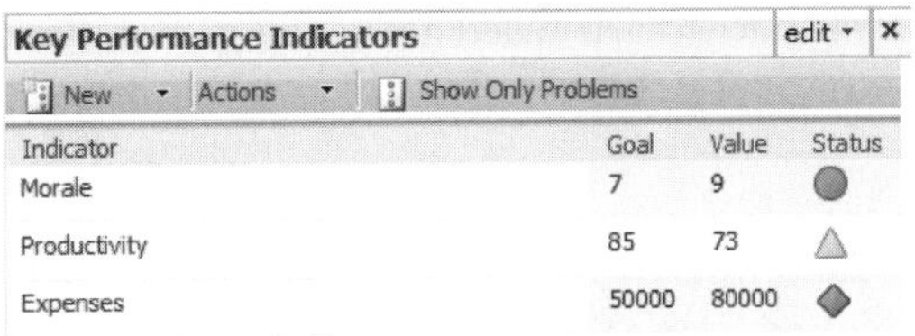

Key Performance Indicators edit ▾ ×

New ▾ Actions ▾ Show Only Problems

Indicator	Goal	Value	Status
Morale	7	9	
Productivity	85	73	
Expenses	50000	80000	

Figure 29-8 Key Performance Indicators Web Part

This Web Part displays the list of specified indicators, along with the goal value, actual value, and an icon displaying the status. For example, a green icon means that the indicator has met or exceeded its goal.

More Info For more information about key performance indicators, see Chapter 20, "Excel Services and Building Business Intelligence Solutions."

KPI Details

The KPI Details Web Part is similar to the KPI Web Part in that it must be configured to connect to an existing KPI list. This Web Part displays granular details about only one indicator, such as status numbers, the description, and comments.

Filters

Filter Web Parts are new to SharePoint Server 2007 and are a valuable asset when business-intelligence data is involved. Filter Web Parts are used to connect to data sources and are configured to display a dynamic filtered set of data. Some of these Web Parts can obtain their filter criteria from user input, and some can automatically filter data according to characteristics of the logged-in user, date, or other properties. This section will cover all the filter Web Parts and how they work. It also includes Table 29-5, which compares these Web Parts and their functions.

Filter Web Parts are designed to work with Microsoft SQL Server 2005 Analysis Services data, Microsoft Office SharePoint Server 2007 SharePoint lists, the Business Data Catalog, and data in a Microsoft Office Excel Web Access Web Part workbook.

Choice Filter

The Choice Filter Web Part is the most simple of the filter Web Parts. The page author simply types the list of values in, and there is no connection to any external source of data. Once this filter has been connected to other Web Parts, the values cannot be edited. Remove the connection to make changes.

Current User Filter

The Current User Filter Web Part automatically filters contents of Web Parts according to properties of the logged-in user. Any profile property can be used as the criteria for filtering data, such as the user's login name, city, or department.

Date Filter

The Date Filter Web Part allows you to filter data either by allowing users to choose a date or by filtering on a specific date that is configured by the page author. Figure 29-9 shows that, in edit mode, the Date Filter Web Part displays information on the name of the Web Part that it is connected to. This is a common feature among the Filter Web Parts.

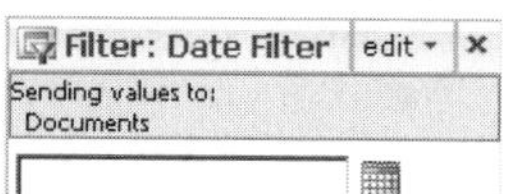

Figure 29-9 Date Filter Web Part

Filter Actions

This Web Part basically contains a button that acts as a Submit button when changes are made to any filter on the page. When there are connected Web Parts involved, this button is a useful addition to the page.

Page Field Filter

The Page Field Filter Web Part is for use on a Web Part page and not on a site. This filter uses a field from the properties of the page itself. The page field filter sends this data as criteria when connected to another Web Part on the page, and it filters the information in the Web Part according to that field.

Query String (URL) Filter

The Query String Filter allows filters to be added to a URL. This is useful when adding a link to a different page to a field in the dashboard KPI list. This filter passes a fixed value (or values) that is configured in the Web Part tool pane. Variables in the URL come from the linked Web Part.

SharePoint List Filter

The SharePoint List Filter Web Part is configured by the page author to obtain data from a specific SharePoint list.

SQL Server 2005 Analysis Services Filter

This filter allows the selection of a data connection from a Web Part on the current page, from a SharePoint data connection library, or from an Office data connection library.

Text Filter

The Text Filter Web Part can be configured to either require input from site users or provide a default value.

Filter Connections

The filter Web Parts functionality relies on Web Part connections. Each filter Web Part inherently needs to be connected to another Web Part. Otherwise, a yellow warning icon appears, indicating that the filter is not connected. The following are the data types for filter Web Parts:

- **Automatic** These data types are applied to Web Parts on a page automatically without any manual input from users viewing the page, and they are hidden unless in edit mode. For example, one of the automatic filters retrieves data from properties of the logged-in user's profile.
- **User** These data types rely on user-supplied values for data.
- **List** Data sources are configured by the site owner. List filters enable site users to select values from a list.

Not every type of Web Part can be connected to a filter. To view the list of Web Parts on the page that it can connect to, select the Web Part menu in edit mode, point to Connections, and then choose Send Filter Values To. The supported data types and Web Parts are listed in Table 29-5.

Table 29-4 Data Types

Data type	Selection format	Web part
Text	User	Text Filter Web Part
Number	User	Number Filter Web Part
Date	User	Date Filter Web Part
SharePoint list	List	SharePoint List Web Part
Business Data Catalog	List	Business Data Catalog Filter Web Part
SQL Server 2005 Analysis Services	List	Analysis Services Filter Web Part
Manually entered list	List	Any filter Web Part that uses a manually entered list in Web Part properties

Table 29-4 Data Types

Data type	Selection format	Web part
Values based on targeted Web Parts	List	Any targeted Web Part
Current User	Automatic	Current User Filter Web Part
Query string parameter	Automatic	Query String (URL) Filter Web Part
Fixed value	Automatic	Choice Filter Web Part
Page field value	Automatic	Page Field Filter Web Part

Miscellaneous

This section of Web Parts are grouped together because of their unique functions that don't fit neatly into the other groups we created. What follows is a brief discussion of each Web Part.

Content Query

In the past, the idea of propagating a list, such as contacts, from a main site down to subsites was not possible without performing custom coding. The Content Query Web Part allows you to display list information from other sites in the site collection. The data can even be filtered and grouped.

RSS Viewer

Really Simple Syndication (RSS) is a method of receiving various types of data from assorted types of data sources, but all in a standard, easily digestible format. Examples of RSS data sources are news headlines from a Web site, or blogs.

Summary Link

This Web Part is shown in edit mode in Figure 29-10. The Summary Link Web Part is used to display a set of URLs. The presentation of the list can be customized using grouping or styling. Items can be placed in a particular order by using the cursor to drag and drop them.

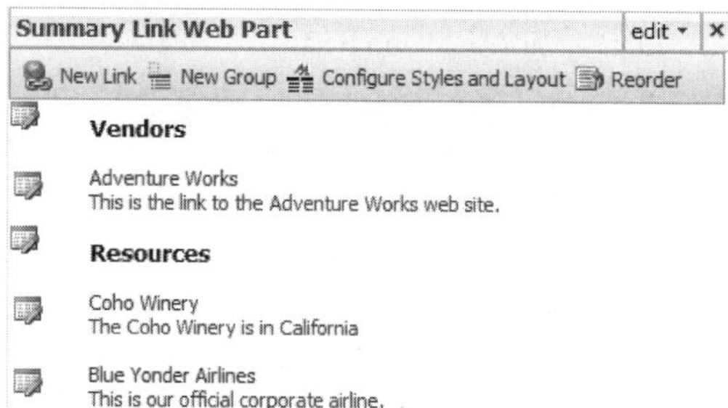

Figure 29-10 Summary Link Web Part

Table of Contents

The Table of Contents Web Part is a way to exhibit the navigational hierarchy of a Web site. This Web Part automatically produces a site map, beginning at the root level of the site collection, or at any other site level of your choosing.

Contact Details

This Web Part is used to display information about the contact person for a page or site.

Important Although this person might be designated as the contact for this particular site, this Web Part is in no way connected to the actual permissions for the site. Therefore, the contact for a site doesn't necessarily have administrator privileges (or any particular privileges at all) on the site.

Choose a user to be the contact person for this Web site, and their display name from Active Directory is shown in this Web Part. If that user has uploaded a photo to his My Site, this Web Part can also be configured to include it.

Content Editor

The Content Editor Web Part is a free-form editor. Text, tables, images, hyperlinks, and custom-formatted text can be included in this type of Web Part. Content can be edited using the Rich Text Editor that looks similar to Microsoft Word, as shown in Figure 29-11. The HTML source code can also be edited directly.

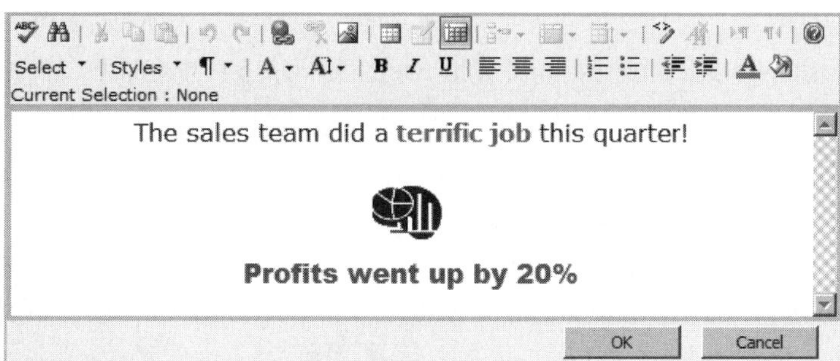

Figure 29-11 Content Editor Web Part

Form

The Form Web Part contains simple form controls. It is used in connections with other Web Parts to query or filter data. The default is one text box and a Go button.

Image Web Part

The Image Web Part is used to display a single image on a site. This is not to be confused with an Image Library, which is a collection of images.

Important Unlike the image in the Contact Details Web Part, if the original size of the image is too large, changing the size of the Web Part will not shrink the image down. The image must be manually edited to reduce the size as needed.

Page Viewer

The Page Viewer Web Part displays a window-like view to linked content, such as a Web page, folder, or file. When a file is displayed, it is shown correctly only if it is a certain kind of file. Microsoft documents and spreadsheets, forms, and .pdf files will not display at all. Images and text files do display correctly in the Web Part.

Relevant Documents

This Web Part displays documents that are applicable to the logged-in user. Query terms are defined in the Web Part tool pane in the Data section. Some options are "documents last modified by me" and "documents created by me."

Site Users

This Web Part shows a list of the site groups or users and their online status. This applies to users who have been assigned explicit permissions on the site, not those who are in groups that have been assigned permissions on the site. In SharePoint Server 2003, this was referred to as the Members Web Part.

User Tasks

This Web Part shows tasks assigned to the logged-in user. The User Tasks Web Part is very useful because now users can see a list of their tasks from anywhere in an entire site collection!

XML

The XML (Extensible Markup Language) Web Part allows you to display XML data. Use the XML and XSL Editors in the tool pane of this Web Part to create or modify XML and XSL source code.

Important The HTML FORM element cannot be included in an XML Web Part. The Form Web Part or the Page Viewer Web Part would be better suited for that element.

Outlook Web Access

The Outlook Web Access Web Part tool pane is shown in Figure 29-12. All of these Web Parts are compatible with Microsoft Exchange Server 2003 and newer. The tool pane for each of these Web Parts has a Mail Configuration section so that you can type the URL to Outlook Web Access (OWA), such as *http://mail.contoso.msft/exchange*. The Mailbox field requires the e-mail address prefix. For example, if Mindy Martin has an e-mail address of Mindy.Martin@contoso.msft, she would put "Mindy.Martin" in this field. Table 29-5 lists the OWA Web Parts and their descriptions.

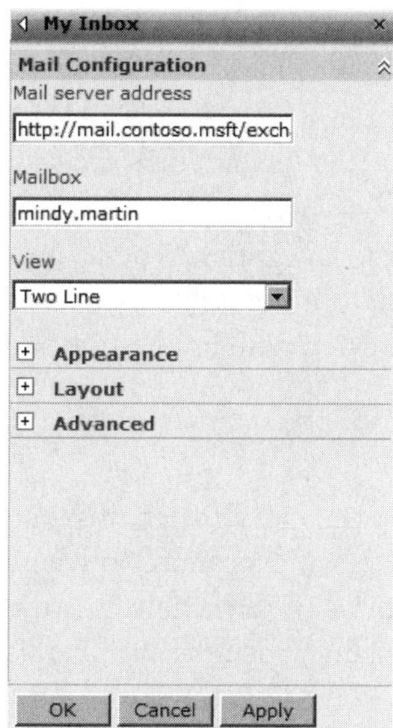

Figure 29-12 OWA Web Parts

Note When the "Outlook Web Access URL" user profile field is populated, users see a new My OWA link at the top of their screen. On the My Site page, the navigation at the top shows My OWA instead of My Site. Users who do not have this profile property populated will not see My OWA. Go to the User Profiles And Properties section in Shared Services to edit profile properties

Table 29-5 OWA Web Parts

Web Part	Description
My Calendar	Displays Outlook calendar
My Contacts	Displays Outlook contacts
My Inbox	Displays Outlook e-mail inbox
My Mail Folder	Displays a specific folder in Outlook
My Tasks	Displays Outlook tasks

The information in My Mail Folder and My Inbox looks exactly the same by default. Here is the difference between the two Web Parts:

- **My Inbox** This Web Part lists the contents of your inbox, and the Web Part tool pane allows for the selection of a view. These view selections are the same ones that exist in mail folders in Outlook.
- **My Mail Folder** This Web Part displays contents of a specific mail folder. For example, if there is a mail folder called SharePoint under the inbox, the Exchange Folder Name would be entered as Inbox\SharePoint.

Site Directory

The Sites Directory is a catalog of sites that can be grouped into categories. When a new site collection is created using the Collaboration Portal template, a site directory page is automatically included. Alternately, a site directory can be created with an existing site collection using the Site Directory template.

Categories

This Web Part displays categories from the site collection's Site Directory. When this Web Part is used properly, you can build a taxonomy of URL-addressable locations to where your users most often browse. You can modify both the categories and the choices within each category in this Web Part. The following options are available when the Web Part is in edit mode.

- **Create New Category** The user is prompted to select what type of information the column will contain, such as text, currency, date, and so on.
- **Edit Sites and Categories** This is a shortcut to the Sites list. Click Settings, and choose List Settings to edit and add categories (columns) and views.

Sites in Category

This Web Part displays the list of sites obtained from the site collection's Site Directory. This Web Part displays results after a category has been selected in the Categories Web Part.

Top Sites

This Web Part is simply a filter that shows only sites indicated as "Top Sites." The Top Sites field exists in the Sites List.

Note There is also a Site Map section on the Site Directory screen. This is similar to the Table Of Contents Web Part.

Summary

This chapter covered the basics of Web Parts and how to create Web Part pages. You learned about adding Web Parts to a page, the properties of them, and ways to arrange Web Parts on a page. Next, you learned about Web Part connections and looked at an example of two connected Web Parts.. Then you learned about customization and personalization, along with personal and shared views of a Web Part page. Finally, this chapter covered the detail about each individual Web Part and its function.

Chapter 30

Microsoft Office SharePoint Server 2007 Disaster Recovery

Many organizations have backup and restore procedures but yet are ill-equipped to handle any type of disaster recovery or continuity of operations. Don't make the mistake of being poorly prepared and having a catastrophic event destroy data without the possibility of recovery. Organizations that document and prepare can swiftly react and remain operational after a disaster. It is no accident that large banks and brokerage firms are able to access data following a major disaster; their disaster recovery plans are well documented and executed.

Disaster recovery in the modern IT professional's vocabulary has come to reference routine content recovery, recovery from accidental or natural disasters, and high availability. All the backup, restore, and continuity of operations procedures, along with thorough documentation, should be assembled into a disaster recovery plan. Your disaster recovery plan should be one of the most important document sets in your organization's process library.

Design your disaster recovery plan for a worst case scenario, and then use only the pieces required for data restores. For example, if you store your backup tapes offsite, it is a simple matter to retrieve those tapes for restores when a user deletes a document library. In this example, your data is protected for a disaster, but the same process is used for daily backups and restores. Design your disaster recovery plan to prevent duplication of effort by using the same processes for many types of events, whether man-made or natural. It is also important to understand that Microsoft Office SharePoint Server 2007 is a multitiered application, and traditional backup and restore methodologies might not be applicable.

This chapter will use typical backup and restore procedures as a foundation for discussing disaster recovery and business continuance for Office SharePoint Server 2007. In this chapter, you will learn how to do the following:

- Document your environment.
- Back up and restore SharePoint Server 2007.
- Design for high availability.

Understanding and Documenting Your Environment

When you begin to plan and design your disaster recovery plan, be sure to include all aspects of your implementation—not just the SharePoint Server 2007 servers. A medium-scale to large-scale SharePoint Server 2007 installation will have many infrastructure dependencies, along with the core components, such as Web front-ends, search servers, and database servers. It is nearly impossible to successfully execute a disaster recovery plan if you do not know all the dependencies in your environment. Your particular implementation might have dependencies in addition to those covered in the following section. Be sure to document and plan for all supporting components.

Documenting Your Infrastructure and Plan for Disaster

Begin your SharePoint Server 2007 disaster recovery plan by listing all hardware, software, and network components that support your installation. Talk to the administrators of these systems and identify any scheduled outages, such as maintenance windows, you need to take into account when planning. Unplanned outages can affect database mirroring or transaction log shipping, rendering your disaster recovery plan ineffective. Your disaster recovery plan is only as good as the weakest link, so involve the stakeholders early on and convince your peers that a good disaster recovery plan is a solid investment.

Network and System Administrators

Many disaster recovery plans adequately cover all hardware, software, and system components, but they leave out the most important part of the equation—you. For example, if the network administrator is on vacation when a disaster occurs, your restoration of your SharePoint Server 2007 server farm is of little help if the network is down. Many organizations keep a spreadsheet of all administrators that includes vacation and shift schedules. Using a list or Microsoft Office Excel spreadsheet in the browser are good ways to solve this problem. Include home telephone numbers, cell phone numbers, and any other relevant contact information that might be required for restoration of service.

Operating System

The most obvious component to SharePoint Server 2007 is the Microsoft Windows Server operating system. Several versions are available, so documenting your specific installation and having the installation media available is a great place to start.

Many organizations create snapshot images of all non-database servers for restores, and this is a recommended solution. Service packs, patches, or custom code might have to be applied after a server is restored from a system image. If you have large content indexes, you should restore the search server from an image and restore the indexes using native tools. The recommended approach is to use a freshly installed Windows Server image with SharePoint Server installed, all customizations installed, and patches applied. Keep a different image for each server because changing the security identifier (SID) of a single image to create multiple SharePoint Server 2007 Web front-end (WFE) servers and application servers has been proven to be a bad idea. Re-create the image every time service packs, patches, and site definition changes occur. This safeguard allows for rapid restoration of the server while retaining your Office SharePoint Server 2007 farm consistency.

Note The 12 hive is located at C:\Program Files\Common Files\Microsoft Shared\Web server extensions\12\.

You should also create a network share with all your system images, installation sources, patches, and third-party software additions. Doing this speeds recovery of systems by reducing media load times and version issues. You should back up this drive at least on a weekly basis.

Third-Party Software

Many organizations have third-party solutions running on their SharePoint Server 2007 server farms, including backup software, Web Parts, language packs, antivirus programs, and custom code. Document how these are installed, include installation keys, if necessary, and keep the installation media in a central location that is easily accessible. Remember to reinstall any third-party Web Parts and custom code before redeploying a WFE server. Not reinstalling all Web Parts on a load-balanced farm of WFE servers results in page errors and an inconsistent experience for the end user.

Network Components

Because SharePoint Server 2007 is primarily a Web service and is heavily network dependent, knowing all your connecting pieces is crucial to recovery or continuity of services. Include your network team early in your disaster recovery planning process and document all connected pieces. The following are examples of components to discuss with your network team:

- **Switches** Redundancy, virtual local area networks (LANS), Network Interface Card (NIC) teaming, port speed, duplex, dedicated backup LANs

- **Routers** Redundant paths, latency, hardware load balancing
- **Firewalls** Rules, redundancy, operating system version
- **Storage area network (SAN)** Compatibility, capacity, speed, Host Bus Adapter
- **Cabling and electrical topology** Redundant cabling, processes for working in your raised floor, redundant power, uninterruptible power supplies, generators

Note If you are using an Internet Service Provider (ISP), be sure to get a service-level agreement (SLA) that defines their strategies and obligations regarding these and all provided services.

Documenting Your Server Farm Configuration

When developing a disaster recovery plan for your installation, use a ground-up approach. This approach helps you to avoid missing components and to prepare for disasters. Be very methodical in documenting your configuration, beginning with your operating systems and SharePoint Server 2007–related services. The components discussed in the following sections are a good starting point for documenting your configuration.

Central Administration

With the exception of the SQL server, the server that hosts the Central Administration Web application is the most important component when recovering an SharePoint Server 2007 installation. In a complete loss of service, you need to bring up this server first and re-establish connections to your databases. It is important to completely document the installation of all servers, but this is especially true for your Central Administration Web application server. If the Central Administration server is the only failed component in your implementation, you can simply promote another server in the farm to the Central Administration server. This is done using the SharePoint Products and Technologies Configuration Wizard, but be sure to document this change if it will be permanent.

You will use your Central Administration server Web application console to access the Backup and Restore user interface (UI), or optionally, the command-line tool. Restoration of this server can be from a system image or by using the Windows Server *Backup Or Restore Wizard*.

WFE Servers

In an out-of-the-box SharePoint Server 2007 implementation, WFE servers are stateless servers, meaning they don't track client access and any WFE can serve SQL content data. This eases restoration of a WFE by allowing installation of the application binaries and then connecting to an existing SQL Server configuration database. The SQL Server configuration database populates any required information on the WFE to serve native SharePoint content. The exception to this is when you are customizing Web application content. As an example, many WFEs have branded images, custom pages, excluded managed paths, Web Parts, and specialized authentication mechanisms. All these components must be re-installed after a WFE system is rebuilt, reinforcing the importance of carefully documenting customized environments. The following is a list of items that must be documented to successfully back up and restore a customized WFE:

- Internet Information Services (IIS) configuration
- Customized authentication software
- Transmission Control Protocol (TCP) ports on Web applications and extended Web applications
- IIS-excluded managed paths and associated content
- Centrally located repository for IIS Metabase backups
- Secure Sockets Layer (SSL) certificate backups
- IIS Logs at *%systemroot%*\system32\LogFiles\w3svc<IIS Virt Server ID>
- Web Parts installed into the global assembly cache (GAC)
- Customized code in the 12 hive

Search Server

If your indexes are not large, rebuilding an index after a system image restore is a quick and simple way to return up-to-date search and query functionality. Alternatively, you can reinstall SharePoint Server to an existing farm and enable it as a Search server in Central Administration. If your index sizes are measured in gigabytes or terabytes, you should back up your indexes so that they can be restored, providing a reasonably timed return to service. The native backup and restore tools support backup and restore of the Shared Services Provider, and that includes the content indexes on the Index and Query servers, as well as the SQL databases containing the correlating metadata. If you do not back up large content indexes, the result is incomplete search results for hours or days, depending on the size of your content sources and speed of your hardware. Using the Index server as a dedicated WFE for indexing is recommended for most implementations, but in large implementations you should consider using all WFE servers for crawling (default). Doing so reduces the impact to end users when crawling large content sources. Document your index locations, and routinely monitor the size of your content indexes because your content sources can grow quickly. Figure 30-1 shows the traffic flow when using a dedicated WFE server for indexing SharePoint content in the same server farm.

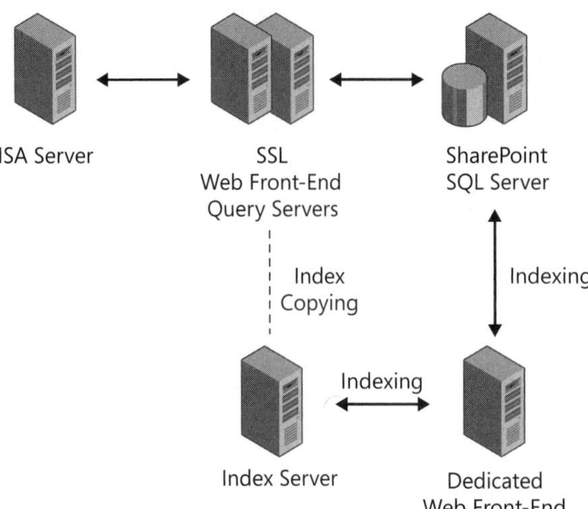

Figure 30-1 Using a dedicated WFE server for content indexing

Shared Services Provider

A Shared Services Provider (SSP) is simply another Web application in SharePoint Server 2007. For the most part, SSPs are backed up and restored using the same methods as any other Web application. However, there are a couple of differences. The first difference is when using a dedicated Web application for My Sites. This Web application and the associated IIS virtual server must be documented carefully, including IP addresses, TCP ports, and DNS entries as required. It is imperative that the namespace be exactly as it was before or the application will fail. If you are consuming My Sites hosted by a different Shared Services Provider, verify that your Trusted My Site Host Locations in Shared Services Administration is present and correct. The page that allows you to do this is shown in Figure 30-2, or refer to Chapter 18 for more information on My Site Trusted Host Locations.

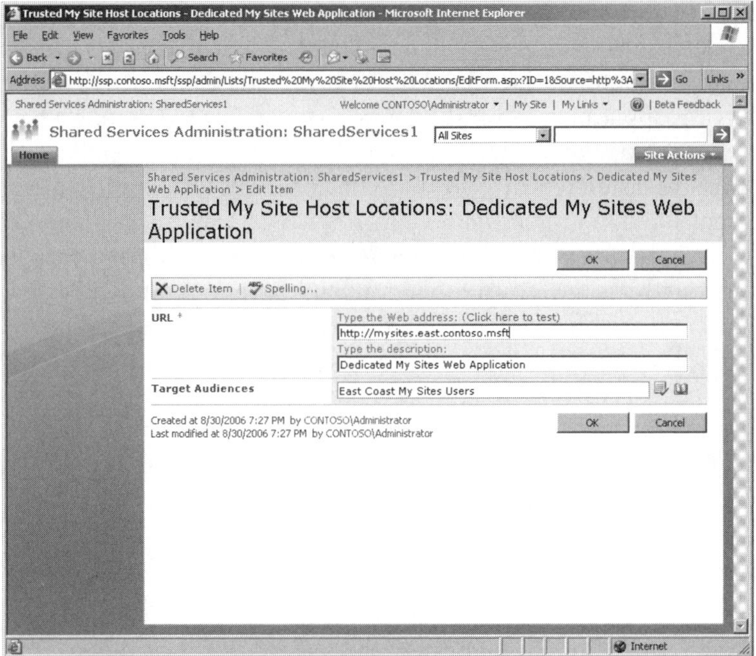

Figure 30-2 My Site Trusted Host Locations page

The second difference between SSPs and other Web applications occurs when using multiple SSPs in the same farm (that is, when you are using Intra-Farm Shared Services). If you lose multiple Intra-Farm SSPs, take your time and restore the first (default) SSP, and then continue restoring after successful testing of the first. Note that you cannot delete the only SSP in a farm if you make a mistake during data restoration. You must add another SSP, make it the default, and then delete the original. If you use multiple SSPs, you can benefit by creating detailed Microsoft Office Visio diagrams. These diagrams are a valuable asset when troubleshooting complex implementations before, during, and after disasters.

Best Practices When creating visual references of your farm structure, include the full names of your actual content databases and corresponding Web applications. This reduces confusion if you are forced to install your farm from SQL backups. Give your databases meaningful names (for example, *WSS_Content_SSP1* for the first SSP in a farm) during setup, because doing so aids in restoration.

Excel Calculation Services

Excel Calculation Services is backed up by a combination of a Shared Services Provider backup and a backup of the application server itself. The best method for backing up the Excel Calculation Services application server is creating a system image. Creating a new system image whenever major service packs or SharePoint Server 2007 application changes occur produces the fastest return to service. Remember this image needs to be a freshly installed copy of Windows Server, without a SID change. You can also back up ECS services using the Windows Server Backup Or Restore Wizard or third-party backup utilities. This method lengthens the return to service, but it works if insufficient disk space prevents you from creating full system images. Don't forget that the flexibility of SharePoint Server 2007 allows for easy reinstallation of an application server from scratch if one fails. If you must restore custom settings on the service, be sure to restore the SSP in which Excel Calculation Services was hosted under as well. If your organization heavily relies on Excel Calculation Services, you can benefit from having redundant application servers serving Excel Calculation Services.

> **Note** When restoring a SharePoint Server from an image, there is always the possibility the server account in Active Directory will not synchronize correctly. In this event, simply remove the server from Active Directory, reboot, and re-add the server to Active Directory. Remember to move the server to the correct organizational unit (OU) if required.

Documenting Your Farm Installation

Documenting your installation is a common theme throughout this chapter. A robust product such as SharePoint Server 2007 relies on many resources to provide its services. This section is an overview of how to document SharePoint Servers and related infrastructure.

Server Documentation

It is highly recommended to have detailed installation documentation defining every setting and keystroke required to build a server from scratch. This is a great way to document all the nuances with your servers, such as WFE 12 hive customizations, and it prevents you from missing configuration options and forgetting software when rebuilding servers. Create a separate document for each server that contains all relevant hardware information, such as the server name, BIOS and backplane versions, network interface cards, RAID controllers, and so on. Documenting your hardware configuration makes it easier to troubleshoot, download correct drivers, and effectively communicate with technical support in the event of failure. You should also document all service packs, hot fixes, antivirus, and any other software additions. When you have servers in a load-balanced cluster, it is very important that all machines have an identical configuration. If months have gone by since a server build without documentation, a Web Part or similar piece of software will definitely be forgotten when restoring the server. This creates an inconsistent, negative user experience that can be very difficult to troubleshoot.

It is wise to have these documents backed up to a source that is easily restored in a disaster. If you have them stored only on your SharePoint site and SharePoint fails, you cannot retrieve this documentation. Storing hard copies of all your disaster recovery documents onsite and offsite is a good idea. In addition, versioning this server documentation is an invaluable method of rolling back changes when patches or third-party software affect usability and performance.

Post-Installation Changes

After you have thoroughly documented your farm installation, continually update your server documents. This practice creates a "living" document set that is always current and can be used when restoring services. Create an appendix in your server documentation with version history, and note the reason for changing your specific installation. If possible, verify any changes you make with your peers.

Testing Your Disaster Recovery Plan

After you create a disaster recovery plan, you must test your plan. Having a plan that won't work is of little use, so execute a simulation of your disaster recovery plan annually, making sure to coordinate with your colleagues and stakeholders. Executing a disaster recovery plan on a production farm is generally a bad idea, but it's a good idea to test secondary server farms and system image restores. Build a lab with a mock-up of your production environment, if possible, and test your disaster recovery plan. Try things such as Search server failures, SQL content database corruption, IIS Metabase corruption, network card failures, hard drive failures, and any other common issues you might face. This type of testing provides valuable knowledge about how to bring back a failed server farm.

Backing Up and Restoring SharePoint Server 2007

There are several methods of backing up and restoring SharePoint Server 2007 content, and you should use a combination of these methods as needed for complete protection. You should test each of these in your environment and see what combination works best for you. Table 30-1 provides an overview of the methods available and their advantages and disadvantages.

Table 30-1 Disaster Recovery Methods for SharePoint Server 2007

Method	Ease of use	Operates on	Notes
Versioning	Document library feature	■ Documents ■ Lists ■ Web pages	Native functionality.

Table 30-1 Disaster Recovery Methods for SharePoint Server 2007

Method	Ease of use	Operates on	Notes
Recycle Bin	Easy end-user interface	■ Lists ■ List items ■ Document libraries ■ Documents	Not for disaster recovery.
Stsadm.exe	Requires script	■ Site collections ■ Sites	Best for restoring sites.
Central Administration backup ■ Farm ■ Web application ■ Content database	Graphical user interface (GUI) or command line	GUI is easy to use. Command line is required for scheduled backups.	
SQL backup	Complex, but complete	■ Databases only	Full fidelity. Must recrawl content.
Mirror farm	Very complex	■ Content only	Fastest disaster recovery failover.
Microsoft Volume Shadow Copy Service Writer	Server backup/ restore	■ Farm level ■ Individual restore	Requires Microsoft SQL Server 2005 and 'Longhorn' Server.

There are two primary methods of recovering content in SharePoint Server 2007: content recovery and disaster recovery. Content recovery should always be considered before resorting to disaster recovery methods. Content recovery methods are usually quick and easy, allowing faster return to service than disaster recovery methods. Examples of content recovery are using the native versioning and recycle bin functionality. Disaster recovery methods are used when all other options have failed, or there is a loss of hardware due to natural or man-made disasters. Disaster recovery usually means some loss of data, but this can be minimized with diligent preparation. Examples of disaster recovery are database restores and system rebuilds.

Performing Content Recovery

Content recovery refers to common activities performed to restore data, usually from accidental deletion or data corruption. Depending on the severity of the data loss, there are three standard methods for recovering data: document versioning, two-stage Recycle Bin, and the command-line tool stsadm.exe. There is also a custom option called Web Delete

Event, but it requires custom development. With this feature, you can automatically back up a site in the event of site deletion. Although this could be a great feature for critical sites, it is probably a bad idea to use it for enterprise-wide implementations because it doesn't scale well.

Document Versioning

The most common method for restoring corrupted content is the native versioning functionality available in all document libraries in SharePoint Server 2007. This functionality is disabled by default, but enabling this feature provides several improvements over the basic versioning in SharePoint Portal Server 2003. Examples of the improvements are limiting the number of minor and major versions, forcing approval and archival before deletion, and forced checkout. Document versioning is your first line of defense against data corruption and user changes. Be cautioned–if users have the ability to modify a document, they can delete it. Document versioning does not protect content; it only preserves history by saving a copy each time the content was saved. If a document is deleted, it must be recovered from the Recycle Bin.

Two-Stage Recycle Bin for Documents and Lists

One of the most anticipated features of SharePoint Server 2007 is the two-stage Recycle Bin, which is enabled by default. This should be your first method for restoring deleted files, and it is the easiest of the tools to use for recovering content. The Recycle Bin is envisioned to be primarily controlled by the end user, but site administrators can always restore files in the event of first-stage deletion. Remember–the Recycle Bin is a function of a Web application, not a site collection. You can modify the Recycle Bin settings by opening Central Administration, then Application Management, then Web Application Settings and scrolling down to the bottom of the page. You can modify the settings for both stages of the Recycle Bin, as shown in Figure 30-3

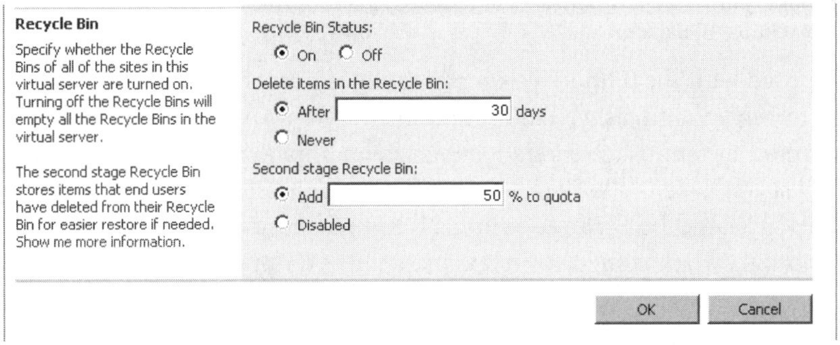

Figure 30-3 Two-stage Recycle Bin and configurable options

If you disable the Recycle Bin, as shown Figure 30-3, all Recycle Bins in that Web application are emptied, freeing up all disk space occupied by Recycle Bin content. This behavior is useful in an out-of-storage emergency, but otherwise it is best left alone. This should only be done when there are no other options, and should be re-enabled after your disk problem is resolved.

The Recycle Bin is a great content recovery tool, but it is not meant for disaster recovery. The Recycle Bin nearly eliminates the need for other restore methods when objects are deleted. By default, the second stage of your Recycle Bin is limited to 50 percent of your site quota, but it should be lowered to fit your storage needs. Raising this quota should be carefully considered given that incorrect stage configurations can waste large volumes of disk space. Keep in mind your site administrators have the ability to permanently delete objects in site collections. This is another reason to choose administrators for your critical sites carefully and provide all site administrators with adequate training.

Command-Line Tool stsadm.exe

In the directory *%SystemDrive%*\Program Files\Common Files\Microsoft Shared\Web server extensions\12\BIN resides the very powerful command-line tool stsadm.exe. Many SharePoint administrators include this directory in their system path for ease of use. Alternatively, you can create a batch file in *%SystemRoot%* that changes to that directory for you. The stsadm.exe command-line tool retains all the functionality from SharePoint Portal Server 2003 in addition to providing many of the new features in SharePoint Server 2007.

Site Migration

One of the new features of stsadm.exe is the replacement of smigrate.exe with stsadm.exe using the –o [import | export] options. Here is an example of exporting a site with stsadm.exe:

```
stsadm.exe -o export -url http://portal.contoso.msft/sites/HR
-filename c:\OSSBackups\HRBackup.bak
```

stsadm.exe, when used with the [import | export] option, is primarily a tool for developers moving or restoring content, as well as for administrators who might incrementally migrate sites. Monitor system usage carefully when frequently exporting or importing large sites because stsadm.exe is a very process-intensive application. Using this tool to consistently to back up large, busy site collections is not recommended. Here is a list of commonly used options when using the –o [export | import] option for exporting and importing sites:

- –url <URL to be exported>
- –filename <path and filename to export> (can append with –overwrite)

- –includeusersecurity (using this flag will include the permissions associated with object)
- (export only) –versions (1 = last major, 2 = current, 3 = last major and minor, 4 = all versions)
- (import only) –updateversions (1 = add new version to current, 2 = overwrite, 3 = ignore, 4 = terminate with conflicts)

Site Backup and Restore

You can also use stsadm.exe to back up and restore individual site collections when using the *–backup* option. Using this option creates full site backups that can be restored to any SharePoint server farm of the same version, with the added benefit of restoring the site with a different name. Having recent copies of site collections from stsadm.exe can dramatically decrease the amount of time required to restore object-level content when deleted. For example, items emptied from the second stage of the Recycle Bin, or Web pages deleted from a site collection, can be restored from a full-fidelity backup created with stsadm.exe –o backup. Be cautioned, backing up with this method is very processor intensive and might require large amounts of disk space. It does not scale well and should be used only on small farms or on your most critical sites. The following is an example of backing up a site using stsadm.exe:

```
stsadm.exe -o backup -url http://portal.contoso.msft/sites/HR -
filename c:\OSSBackups\HRBackup.bak
```

You can create a Microsoft Visual Basic script or batch file and use Scheduled Tasks in Control Panel to automate the process. The following options are commonly used when using the –o [backup | restore] option for backing up and restoring sites using stsadm.exe:

- –url <full URL> (for example, *http://portal.contoso.msft/sites/HR*)
- –filename (Include the path; this can be a drive letter or Universal Naming Convention name)
- –overwrite (using the overwrite flag will completely overwrite the destination)

The stsadm.exe backup and restore options are useful when restoring data that has been deleted, in spite of the protections offered by document versioning and the second-stage Recycle Bin. When this occurs, you must restore the entire content database containing the deleted items and restore the data to an alternate server farm.

Real World Restoring Content to an Alternate Server Farm

If you lose content that must be restored from farm-level backups, you have two choices: restore the content databases from the last backup and overwrite all current data, or restore content databases to a secondary farm and migrate them into the production farm. The first choice isn't generally acceptable, so this section will focus on restoring to an alternate server farm. Most organizations have a test environment, and this is the first logical location to use when attaching content databases and retrieving previously backed-up content. The following steps allow you to restore data from a farm-level or SQL Server database backup and restore it to the production server farm:

1. Restore the content database that held the deleted content to another SQL server or to a different database name if restoring to the same SQL server.
2. Attach the content database to a Web application by opening Central Administration, then Application Management, then SharePoint Web Application Management, and finally Content Databases, as shown in Figure 30-4.

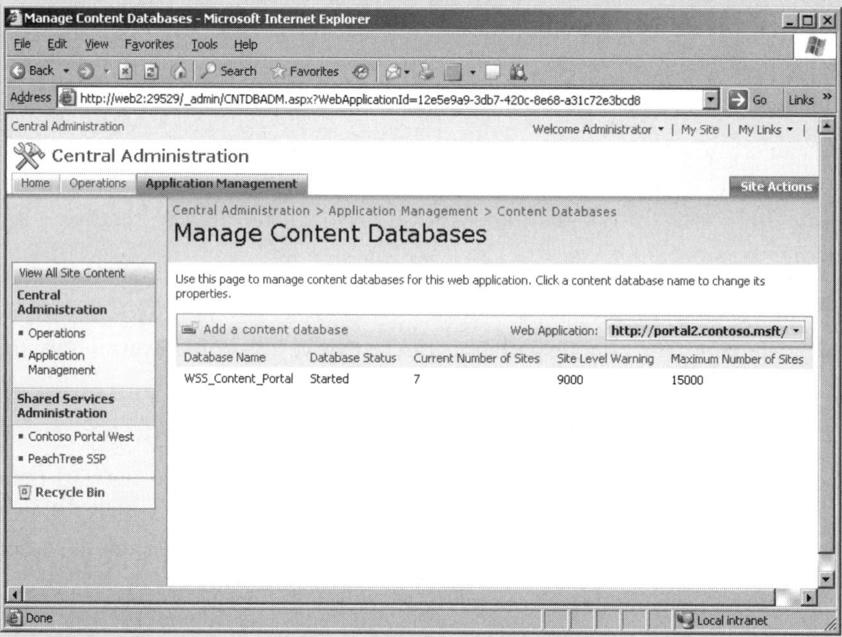

Figure 30-4 Attaching a content database to a Web application

3. When you attach a content database to an existing Web application, the sites are automatically populated in the configuration database.

4. If you need only a single file, retrieve the file using the same URL as for the production server, replacing the server namespace. For example, if the URL for the production server is http://portal.contoso.msft/sites/HR and the URL to your test server is http://test.portal.contoso.msft, browse to http://test.portal.contoso.msft/sites/HR to retrieve the file.

5. If you need to restore an entire site, use stsadm.exe to back up from the test server and restore to the production server. For example, if your disaster recovery name is *OSSBackups* and your test server is *http://test.portal.contoso.msft*, use the following command:

   ```
   stsadm.exe -o backup -url http://test.portal.contoso.msft/sites/HR -
   filename \\backupservername\OSSBackups\HRBackup.bak
   ```

   To restore the site with the original version history and permissions, run the following command from your production server:

   ```
   stsadm.exe -o restore -url http://test.portal.contoso.msft/sites/HR -
   filename \\backupservername\OSSBackups\HRBackup.bak
   ```

Both server farms must be in the same Active Directory domain. If they are not, you will lose all site-level and object-level permissions when restoring to the alternate server farm.

Performing Disaster Recovery

Many IT professionals today consider the entire methodology of backing up and restoring disaster recovery, but this section is specifically tailored to providing restoration of services after hardware failure, man-made disasters, or natural disasters. SharePoint Server 2007 now offers four methods of backing up data when preparing for disasters:

- Central Administration Backup/Restore utility
- Command Line Backup/Restore utility
- SQL Server backups and restores
- Volume Shadow Copy Service Writer in Windows Server "Longhorn"

This section will cover each of these methods and end with a section on backing up Microsoft Internet Information Services when using SharePoint Server 2007.

SharePoint Server Native Backup and Restore

A benefit of upgrading to SharePoint Server 2007 is that you gain the ability to back up and restore content directly from the Central Administration Web application. This is a very powerful tool, but it is primarily used when restoring content because it lacks the ability to schedule jobs from the user interface (UI). Administrators who want to schedule backups must create scripts using the command-line tool and schedule the script from Control Panel.

File Location

The native backup functionality in SharePoint Server does not provide a method of backing up data to tape. When using either the Central Administration UI or the command-line backup interface, you must back up data to a Universal Naming Convention (UNC) share. The backup process automatically creates subfolders in this share for each subsequent backup. It is very important that the SQL setup server account is using a domain account and that each farm server has direct access to this file share.

> **Note** If there are any errors when using the Central Administration UI, you must delete the timer job at http://<*adminsite:port*>/_admin/ServicejobDefinitions.aspx before successfully beginning any new backup/restore jobs. Otherwise, you receive the error, "The same item is already in the process of being backed up." You can find details of the associated errors in the Spsbackup.log file located in the root of the previously defined UNC.

The following accounts require Change and Read share permissions on the target file share, and all NTFS security permissions, with the exception of Full Control:

- The account authenticated to Central Administration when using the UI
- The logged-on account when manually running stsadm.exe
- The Run As account when scheduling scripted backups in Control Panel
- The Central Administration pool account in Internet Information Services, as shown in Figure 30-5

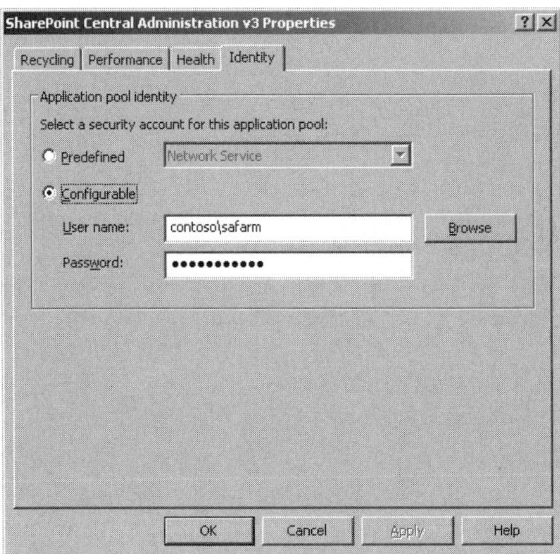

Figure 30-5 Verifying Central Administration IIS application pool account information

- SQL Server account, if Local System is the SQL service account
- The SPTimer service account, if using the Central Administration UI (by default, the same account used by the Central Administration application pool)

Best Practices It is best to use a centrally located file share for backups, and they should be accessible by all production and test servers and backed up on a regular basis. This can be the same file share used for SQL Server database dumps, but be careful of overloading storage spindles or network bandwidth if multiple backups are occurring simultaneously. Large organizations are best served by using a storage area network (SAN), with the UNC served from a Windows Server, for this purpose.

User Interface

Using the Central Administration UI is the easiest way to back up your farm for disaster recovery. Upon opening the Operations tab in Central Administration, you select Perform A Backup to begin the process. Figure 30-6 shows an example of components available for backup using the UI.

Start Backup Process | View History

Select	Component	Type	Description
☐	Farm	Farm	Content and configuration data for the entire server farm.
	SharePoint_Config	Microsoft.SharePoint.Administration.SPConfigurationDatabase	Configuration data for the entire server farm.
☐	Windows SharePoint Services Web Application	Windows SharePoint Services Web Application	Collection of Web Applications
☐	Portal	Web Application	Content and configuration data for this Web Application.
☐	WSS_Content	Content Database	Content for the Web Application.
	WSS_Administration	Central Administration	Collection of Web Applications
	Web Application	Web Application	Content and configuration data for this Web Application.
☐	SharePoint_AdminContent_ef586404-896a-44d7-adac-e72164b2af89	Content Database	Content for the Web Application.
☐	SharedServices1	Shared Services Provider	Database and Configuration Settings for this Shared Services Provider
	SSP	Web Application	Content and configuration data for this Web Application.
☐	WSS_Content_SSP	Content Database	Content for the Web Application.
	SharedServices1_DB	Shared Service Provider Database	Stores Configuration Settings for this Shared Services Provider
	SearchSharedApplication	Office SharePoint Server Search	Index content and/or serve search queries
	SharedServices1_Search_DB	SearchSharedDatabase	Search Index and Property Store
	UserProfileApplication	User Profile Application	User Profile Application
☐	SPSearch	Windows SharePoint Services Help Search	Index user and assistance content and serve search queries

Figure 30-6 Components available in the backup and restore UI

You can also specify a location for your file backups when using the Perform A Backup UI. If you need to change this location at a later time, be sure to leave your original backup location available for the length of time required to meet your SLAs. If you need to restore from a previously created backup source, change the location when viewing the backup and restore history.

Important You cannot perform a differential backup of the entire farm when a new Web application is created. You must perform at least one *full* backup before successfully completing a differential backup, whether using the UI or the command-line tool.

The downside to using the Central Administration Restore From Backup UI is the inability to restore items at the object level within site collections. Refer to the earlier sidebar on restoring content for a solution to use when restoring to an alternate server farm.

Farm-Level Backup and Restores with stsadm.exe

New in SharePoint 2007 is the ability to perform farm-level and Web application–level backup and restore from the command prompt. Farm-level backup and restore, also referred to as *catastrophic backup and restore*, is defined by using the *–directory* switch using stsadm.exe. The following is an example of a farm-level backup in its simplest form:

```
stsadm.exe -o backup -directory \\backupservername\backups\ -backupmethod full
```

Backups

Backing up using this method prevents SPTimer job errors and assures you that your backups won't fail. In addition, it provides a method for automated scripting and scheduling capabilities. The following are options when using stsadm.exe for farm-level backups.

- Mandatory
  - `-directory <UNC path>` The UNC path should be created on a server in the same domain, with share and security permissions set as previously defined.
  - `-backupmethod <Full | Differential>` At least one full backup should be performed on a new farm or when adding a new Web application. Be cautioned that all previous differential backups are required when restoring content. For this reason, best practices should be followed when using differential backups. More information can be found by going to *http://www.microsoft.com/technet/windowsserver/default.mspx* and searching for *disaster recovery*.
- **Optional**
  - `-item` This option allows the backup of a single Web application. Information must be entered *exactly* or the backup will fail. The following is an example of using *–item* if *Portal* is the Web application to back up:

    ```
    stsadm -o backup -directory \\backupservername\backups -
    backupmethod full -
    item "Farm\Windows SharePoint Services Web Application\Portal"
    ```

  - `-percentage` The percentage option controls the granularity of on-screen feedback as the operation progresses. If you are scripting, this is of no value.
  - `-backupthreads` If you have a large implementation and require significant throughput on your backups, this option can increase the amount of processing time allocated to backups. Be careful, increasing this on a production server can degrade the quality of service experienced by the end user.

- `-showtree` The showtree option is primarily used to define single items that you want to back up, but it is also useful for providing a comprehensive view of your server farm.
- `-quiet` This option suppresses output.

Restoring

Restoring from a previously created backup is accomplished by using one of the following two methods:

- Restoring to the same farm
- Restoring to an alternate farm

You need not change anything in your backup procedure—the same source media is used either way. The following options are available when using stsadm.exe for restoring to the same farm.

- **Mandatory**
  - `-directory <UNC path>` The directory that contains specific backup data you want to restore.
  - `-restoremethod <overwrite | new>` Using overwrite restores over existing data, and all content is lost. The new option allows you to back up to an alternate name, recovering data as required.
- **Optional**
  - `-backupid <ID from backuphistory>` This option can be found by using the following command:

    ```
    [stsadm.exe -o backuphistory -directory <UNC path> -backup]
    ```
  - `-item` This option restores a single Web application.
  - `-percentage` This option shows the granular process status of the restore.
  - `-showtree` This option shows content available for restores.
  - `-suppressprompt` This option uses the current username and password for username/password prompts.
  - `-username` This option assigns the username for the Web application process account.
  - `-password` This option assignes the password for the Web application process account.
  - `-quiet` This option suppresses output.

Restoring to an Alternate Server Farm

Restoring to an alternate farm using the command-line tool is similar to restoring to the same farm, but there are some differences. The first difference is the option to restore the configuration database. Restoring the configuration database to an existing server farm can cause severe failures, sometimes beyond repair. Use [–restoreconfigurationdatabase] only as the last option on the same farm. You use this primarily when installing or migrating to a new server farm. Note that all noncommitted configuration database transaction logs will be rolled back if this option is used, and all content in those transaction logs will be permanently lost. The following are additional options to use when restoring to an alternate server farm:

- `-restoreconfigurationdatabase` This option is particularly useful for complete farm restoration on an alternate server farm. Use this restore option in conjunction with an IIS Metabase backup and complete restoration of the farm. It can be used with the *–newdatabaseserver* option and requires that Named Pipes be enabled on the destination SQL Server.
- `-newdatabaseserver` This option is most likely used when restoring the entire farm to a different set of hardware. It can also be used for restoring to an alternate location when choosing not to use database mirroring, transaction log shipping, or SAN replication for business continuance.

The *–newdatabaseserver* option gives you the ability to restore to a new database server. Again, this option should be used only in worst case situations or when migrating content to a new database server.

SQL Server Backup and Restore

If you could back up only one server in your SharePoint Server 2007 server farm, it would be the SQL server that hosts your content databases. This can be accomplished by using the previously discussed farm-level backups, or through direct SQL Server backups. Although by backing up this server alone you would lose customizations on the WFE servers or content indexes in the event of a catastrophe, you would retain all your valuable content from site collections. Whichever combination of methods you choose to back up your server farm, complete SQL databases are the foundation.

Note Office SharePoint Server Central Administration backup and restore, along with stsadm.exe in catastrophic mode (catastrophic mode is when invoking farm-level backups with the *–directory* option), back up SQL databases *and* truncate transaction logs. This is a huge advancement from SharePoint Portal Server 2003 and negates the need to periodically back up databases, therefore truncating logs, with SQL Server.

Although the native backup tools now back up your databases, many large organizations might use SQL backups as their primary method for restoration in a disaster. Backing up using existing SQL Server procedures might allow for reuse of a pre-existing disaster recovery plan. If you decide to use SQL backups, be sure to verify all content databases using Central Administration.

In SharePoint Portal Server 2003, 50 gigabytes was the recommended maximum size for a database. The primary reason for this limit was the time it took to restore databases in the event of a disaster. With the improvements in SharePoint Sever 2007, there are no limits within the confines of SharePoint technologies. There are limits with SQL Server, however. An example is the 2-terabyte limit on databases when using Microsoft Clustering for fault tolerance. Before you let your databases grow larger than 50 gigabytes, determine the rate at which you can restore them and verify you will meet any SLAs in place. For example, a database size of 2 terabytes could take longer than seven hours to restore, even if you are using high-speed tape or backup to disk technologies. In these instances, using SAN snapshots or SQL Server transaction log shipping should be investigated.

Note If you have multiple, very large databases on a SAN, you could benefit from disk pivoting. *Disk pivoting* is when SQL Server backups are dumped to a SAN logical unit (LUN) attached to your SQL Server Active node in a cluster. Using SAN technology, this LUN is then moved to the Passive node and backups to media performed there. This approach uses the often wasted processing power of the passive node while increasing available resources on your active SQL Server node.

Internet Information Services Backup and Restore

The foundation of Internet Information Services (IIS) is the Metabase. The Metabase is a plain-text XML file that is usually modified via the IIS Manager application. The Metabase is the repository for IIS configuration data and is included in system-state backups selected from the Windows Server Backup Or Restore Wizard. The problem with this method of backing up the Metabase is that the entire system state must be restored, including the system registry. Although this is fine when a system is completely restored from bare metal, it is unacceptable when restoring only the Metabase. To overcome this limitation, you should back up all your IIS Metabases regularly and have them included in your backup routine. Create a batch file and schedule it as a weekly activity from Control Panel. The following is a sample batch file that backs up multiple IIS Metabases from a single location to their respective host's *%systemroot%*\system32\inetsrv\ directory:

```
cscript.exe %systemroot%\system32\iisback.vbs /backup /s Web1 /u administrator
/p password /b WeeklyBackup /v NEXT_VERSION /e backuppassword
```

In this example, *Web1* is the system being backed up, *administrator* is the username, *WeeklyBackup* is the name of the backup, and *NEXT_VERSION* defines how the backup file is incremented. You can add as many lines to this file as required for IIS servers in your environment. The resulting backups on multiple servers will be in their respective *%SystemRoot%*\System32\Inetsrv\ directories.

Note Back up the Metabase with a password. Doing so allows the Metabase to be restored to a different Windows Server if needed. Using the password option makes the Metabase portable, whereas not using the password means that the Metabase can be restored only to that particular instance of IIS. See *http://www.microsoft.com/technet/prodtechnol/WindowsServer2003/Library/IIS/21972953-44d3-4177-b0d2-f8e2cdef2efd.mspx?mfr=true* for complete details.

Another commonly overlooked component when planning for IIS disaster recovery is your Secure Sockets Layer (SSL) certificate. Many organizations use third-party certificate authorities for browser compatibility and verifiable security. If you lose a server and do not have the certificate backed up, interaction by the certificate vendor will be required if you cannot restore the IIS Metabase. Back up your SSL certificate whenever you are renewing or installing it. This can be done by viewing and exporting your certificate with the private key. Without the private key, you cannot reassign this certificate in the future. Use the same file location as your system images, patches, and other disaster recovery content.

More Info To export the private key, reference *http://www.microsoft.com/technet/prodtechnol/WindowsServer2003/Library/IIS/8d3bb71a-0a7f-443f-8084-908d0dab9caa.mspx?mfr=true* for more information.

Implementing Fault Tolerance

If days or weeks are too long to wait to recover from a disaster, consider implementing some form of fault-tolerance. Many organizations that serve critical functions from their SharePoint Server 2007 installations implement some form of fault tolerance. Many times the failover server farms are smaller and less expensive, albeit in a degraded state. This is an acceptable solution for most implementations, but verify that you don't have a requirement to build identical server farms. This section will assist you in planning and implementing several forms of fault tolerance with several levels to meet your needs and budget.

Web Application Load Balancing

The first step in creating simple and affordable disaster recovery is by scaling your WFE servers to handle hardware or service failure. Windows Server includes native functionality for load balancing servers and creating a virtual IP address (VIP) that is used for user connections. You can have up to 32 servers in a Network Load Balancing (NLB) configuration, but it is recommended that you have no more than eight WFE servers per SQL server, so this limitation shouldn't be applicable. Implementations larger than this can benefit by using multiple namespaces, SQL Server clusters, and possibly multiple server farms. If SSL is being used, Microsoft Internet Security And Acceleration Server can be used to terminate SSL connections, thereby reducing processor utilization on your WFE servers.

SharePoint Server 2007 also provides the option to make a WFE server a standalone server. This option allows WFE servers to be dedicated to serving Web content with no other SharePoint Server applications installed. This arrangement increases performance because application services, such as Excel Calculation Services or Search, are performed by other servers. Note that standalone WFE servers cannot be upgraded to accommodate application services in the event of a disaster. You need to uninstall and reinstall, choosing the *complete* option in the SharePoint Products and Technologies Configuration Wizard.

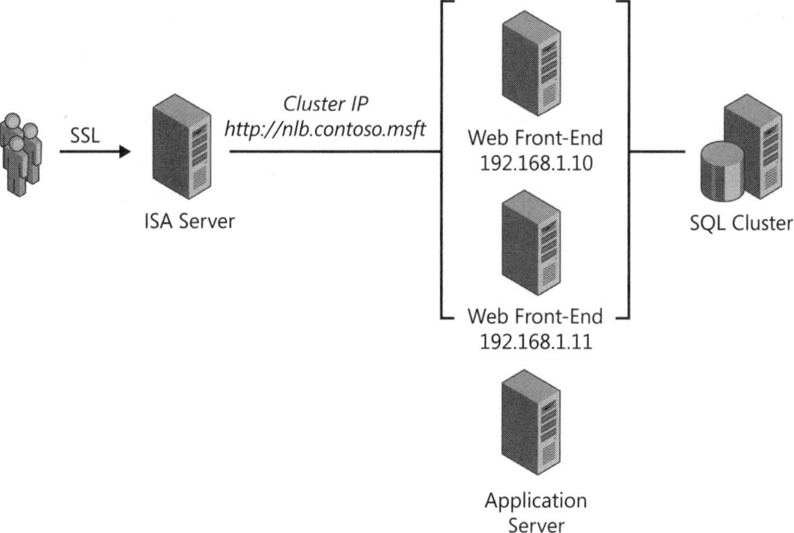

Figure 30-7 Using Windows Server Network Load Balancing

> **More Info** More information on Network Load Balancing can be found at *http://technet.microsoft.com/WindowsServer*. Search for *NLB* or *clustering* for detailed information for your implementation.

Application Server Load Balancing and Fault Tolerance

High availability for an Application Server is implemented differently than fault tolerance for a WFE. While WFEs use NLB to provide fault tolerance, the SPTimer service manages the traffic destined for application servers. Simply creating multiple Excel Calculation Services servers, for example, implements basic load balancing and fault tolerance for Excel Calculation Services in your farm. Query services are, by default, provided by the WFEs, so additional Query servers are not required unless you have specific search needs. You can have standalone Query servers, but this approach is not recommended unless it is driven by absolute business requirements.

SQL Server Clustering

Creating a load balanced Web front-end cluster is a great start, but having this cluster serve content from a standalone SQL server is of little use when the SQL Server hardware fails. Most medium scale and larger SharePoint 2007 implementations require a SQL Server cluster for fault tolerance.

In a basic two-server Active/Passive cluster configuration, a SQL Server cluster does not provide enhanced performance, only fault tolerance. This fault tolerance provided by SQL Server clustering can take several seconds to several minutes to fail over, depending on the size of your databases and transaction logs. Note that all transaction logs must be replayed when the passive node is made active. If you have large amounts of untruncated data, this failover could take several hours. Refer to SQL Server best practices at *http://www.microsoft.com/sql* for information on configuring and truncating transaction logs. Frequently truncating transaction logs increases SQL Server CPU and disk utilization, but it minimizes the failover time in the event of an SQL Server cluster active node failure. Figure 30-8 shows the configuration of a basic SQL cluster.

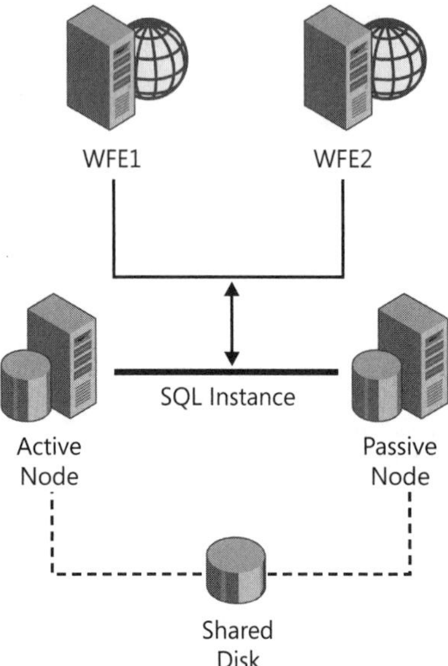

Figure 30-8 SQL clustering with SharePoint Server 2007

More Info For more information on clustering SQL servers, refer to *http://www.microsoft.com/technet/windowsserver/default.mspx* and search for *clustering*.

SQL Transaction Log Shipping

SQL transaction log shipping is a function of the SQL Server agent that backs up and restores transaction logs to a failover SQL server. The basic idea behind log shipping is that you have a "warm" failover farm introducing minimal delays in the event of a primary farm failure. All updates to your primary SQL Server content databases are replicated to a failover SQL server. This arrangement requires advanced SharePoint Server 2007 configuration of the failover farm. The following task list provides a starting point for doing this:

1. Make sure you are using the same domain and accounts for all similar processes (Farm, SSP, IIS processes, SQL SA account).
2. Make sure you are using the same version (including updates) of SQL Server on both farms.
3. Document content database to Web application mappings.
4. Create the failover farm using a second SQL server (not a second instance).
5. Make sure you are using identical, corresponding content database names when creating Web applications on the second farm.
6. Do not log ship config or Central Administration databases.
7. Ship logs to second SQL server, and verify integrity.
8. Take primary farm offline to test.
9. Bring failover farm content databases online.
10. Bring failover farm online.
11. Browse using a different namespace, change DNS, or purchase third-party software.
12. Use the same TCP port for both Central Administration Web applications for ease of configuration.

When using log shipping, it is important to overwrite the primary databases with the failover databases before bringing the primary server farm back online. Not doing so loses changes made on the failover farm when the primary farm is brought back online. Figure 30-9 is an example of log shipping when both farms are located at the same geographical location.

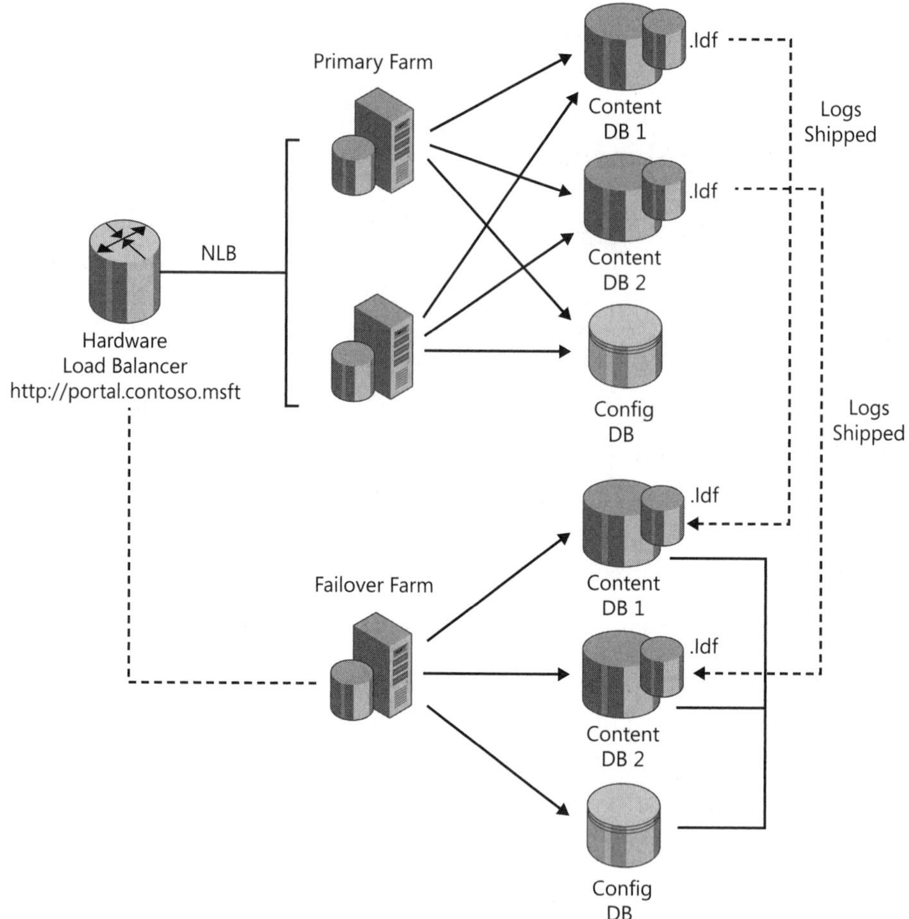

Figure 30-9 Using SQL Server transaction log shipping

As shown in Figure 30-9, transaction log shipping on a single local area network (LAN) can work quite well to provide a failover farm in the event of a catastrophic hardware failure. The downside to transaction log shipping is the manual intervention required on the failover server farm, because the databases will be in recovery mode and must be brought online manually. The failover server farm must also be taken out of quiesced mode in Central Administration. Remember to change any settings in your DNS servers to publish the new farm's IP address, or educate users of a second namespace that can be used in the event of a disaster.

Important When using SQL Server transaction log shipping or database mirroring, remember that any errors, such as file corruption or user mistakes, are replicated from the primary farm to the failover farm.

SQL Database Mirroring

A new feature in SQL Server 2005 Service Pack 1, database mirroring, has advantages over log shipping because it is a function of the SQL Server engine and can provide synchronous replication. Database mirroring is more expensive and complex to implement because it requires three SQL servers when configured in synchronous mode. The third server is a "witness" SQL server and provides automatic failover, which is the main advantage over transaction log shipping.

More Info For more information on using an SQL witness server, browse to *http://msdn2.microsoft.com/en-us/library/ms188712.aspx.*

When using database mirroring, you must manually intervene and bring the failover farm online, along with any namespace or DNS changes. Although database mirroring does not require the databases to be copied back to the primary farm (this is done automatically), it does not create secondary backups of databases on the failover farm. This is the main disadvantage compared to SQL Server transaction log shipping. With this in mind, you need to have current backups of your primary SQL Server cluster at your failover site.

More Info For detailed information on SQL Server database mirroring, visit *http://www.microsoft.com/technet/prodtechnol/sql/2005/dbmirror.mspx.*

Hardware Load Balancing

Some organizations find that the native load balancing provided by Windows Server is incapable of providing the granularity of services offered by hardware load balancing. Hardware load balancing can offer options such as session control, immediate failover, reporting, routing, VLAN trunking, and many other options. Keep in mind that hardware load balancing can introduce many complexities into your SharePoint Server 2007 environment because Windows Server is not aware that load balancing is occurring. Organizations that require hardware load balancing need to test for performance and compatibility in a lab before implementing.

Storage Area Networks

A storage area network (SAN) is a great addition to almost any SharePoint Server 2007 farm implementation. SANs vary from very simple frames using iSCSI technology to large, complex systems with multiple storage frames and fiber-channel fabrics. Whichever SAN solution you choose, be sure to check the Windows Server Catalog at *http://www.windowsservercatalog.com* to make sure your solution is supported.

Storage area networks provide a convenient way to provision and manipulate disk space for applications. Most storage frames add the benefit of intelligent software that manages bad blocks and sectors, as well as managing mirroring and parity. This offloads processing from the server hardware and minimizes the number of reboots required due to disk failures. With the storage frame software managing bad blocks, the days of waiting hours for chkdsk to run are over. SANs also provide for bit-level backups of your data for disaster recovery and can connect directly to tape subsystems, decreasing the amount of time and bandwidth required to back up your data. Be forewarned that bit-level copies require *all* information to be restored. The only way to restore object-level items from a bit-level backup is by attaching content databases to a secondary farm. Large enterprises should seriously consider a secondary farm for recovering production data, whether from SAN snapshots or by traditional backup methods.

Many SANs now include functionality to take snapshots of storage and replicate for quick failback of data. This method overwrites all data written from the time of the previous snapshot. You should consider using it only in an emergency, or you should restore data to an alternate location for content retrieval. SANs also provide for data replication that can be used to create warm server farms for business continuance.*Warm* server farms are powered on with all base software installed and ready to take the place of the primary farm. Before using this method, carefully test and verify that your installation is supported by Microsoft. Most organizations do well using SQL Server transaction log shipping or database mirroring to provide business continuance.

Summary

This chapter provided the basic information required to design and implement an SharePoint Server 2007 disaster recovery solution. Your organization might have extensive customizations, and the disaster recovery of that content must be documented and tested. As you have seen, there are many native tools you can use to back up your specific implementation. Remember to involve your stakeholders early on and understand the business requirements before designing your disaster recovery plan. Test multiple methods of disaster recovery for your installation, and make an informed decision about the best way to protect your valuable data.

Chapter 31

Administrating Code Access Security

The Trustworthy Computing initiative at Microsoft is a push toward greater security in Microsoft products and for Microsoft customers. The Trustworthy Computing initiative was launched in January 2002, when Bill Gates sent a memo to every full-time employee at Microsoft in which he introduced and stressed the importance of this strategy. Since then, all Microsoft product teams, including the SharePoint product team, have embraced the Trustworthy Computing initiative. It should come as no surprise that the echoes of the Trustworthy Computing initiative are felt clearly in the Microsoft Office SharePoint 2007 products and technologies, as will become clear in the rest of this chapter.

This chapter describes code access security (CAS), its role within the Trustworthy Computing initiative, and what code access security means in a SharePoint context. In addition, this chapter discusses how you can use code access security to achieve higher levels of security within SharePoint deployments.

Architecture and Terminology

To get the full benefit of this chapter, you need to be aware of the terminology and concepts related to CAS.

Identity-Based Security

When it comes to security paradigms, there are two different flavors: user identity-based security and code identity-based security. With *user identity-based security*, authentication takes place for particular user identities. During authorization, user credentials are mapped to specific resource access rights. The result of this security approach is that every code run on behalf of a user is executed with the same access rights. In the Microsoft .NET Framework, the implementation for this type of security is known as *role-based security*.

The other, newer security paradigm is code identity-based security. *Code identity-based security* is complementary to user identity-based security because it allows you to specify security settings based on the identity of code. For example, you can decide to allow the execution of any program located within your company's intranet.

Code Access Security

Code access security (CAS) is the .NET Framework answer to implementing code identity-based security and, as such, is the foundation of security in the .NET Framework. By combining user identity-based security and CAS, you can not only specify a set of privileges and restraints for a specific group or user, you can also assign different levels of trust to code with varying code identities executed by the same user.

Permissions

Permissions constitute the most fine-grained elements of CAS. A *permission* represents the fact that code is allowed to perform a specific operation. Every permission has a type and a scope. Permission types apply to different kinds of resources: Microsoft .NET defines 25 permission types—for example, the Registry permission type that grants permission to read, write, or create registry keys, and the Printing permission type that grants permission for printing operations.

Note You can find more information about the predefined permission types in Microsoft .NET at *http://msdn2.microsoft.com/en-us/library/h846e9b3.aspx*.

Permission scopes refer to the amount of freedom a permission provides. Permission scopes can vary from narrow (for example, the permission to read a file) to unrestricted (for example, permission to do anything with a file).

.NET assemblies typically require a collection of individual permissions to be able to function correctly. Such collections are called *permission sets*. .NET provides six predefined permission sets:

- Nothing
- Execution

- Internet
- LocalIntranet
- Everything
- FullTrust

These predefined permission sets are also known as the *named* permission sets. The FullTrust permission set is the most liberal of the named permission sets; it allows code to perform all operations.

Security Evidence

Code access security allows you to specify security settings based on the identity of .NET assemblies. The proof provided by .NET assemblies regarding their identity is called *security evidence*. Security evidence can be divided into two categories: origin-based evidence and content-based evidence.

Origin-based evidence is completely independent of the actual content of an assembly. The .NET common language runtime (CLR) only examines where the assembly is coming from. The standard locations known in origin-based evidence are current application directory, Global Assembly Cache (GAC), Site, URL, and Zone.

Content-based evidence examines the actual content of a .NET assembly. The .NET CLR looks for content-based evidence in the form of strong names, publisher identity, and assembly hash codes. Strong-named assemblies have fully qualified assembly names that include the assembly name, version number, culture (which always needs to be set to *neutral* for assemblies containing code), and the developer identity in the form of a public key token.

> **Note** In Visual Studio .NET 2003, strong-name key files consisting of public/private key pairs had to be created manually by using the strong-name tool (sn.exe). Next, a manual reference to the strong-name key file had to be included in the AssemblyInfo file of a .NET project. In Visual Studio 2005, the integrated development environment (IDE) makes it easy to sign assemblies with strong names. If you right-click the project file and choose Properties, you can click the Signing tab and generate a strong-name key file and sign the assembly from within the Visual Studio 2005 IDE. You can find more information about the strong name tool at *http://msdn2.microsoft.com/en-us/library/k5b5tt23.aspx*.

Assemblies that include *publisher evidence* are digitally signed with a certificate via the SignTool.exe command-line utility. *Hash evidence* is the most stringent form of evidence available. Hashes are calculated based on the contents of an assembly, so if a line of code in the assembly changes, the hash changes as well. Because of this, security policies based on hash evidence are very secure and very maintenance intensive.

As an administrator, you should use content-based evidence instead of origin-based evidence because content-based evidence is more accurate. Builders of frameworks, such as Microsoft itself, will typically prefer to specify default security policies based on origin-based evidence because they will never have enough insight into the solutions built using their framework to apply a meaningful security policy based on content-based evidence.

Security Policies

A code group associates a permission set with evidence. If a .NET assembly satisfies some kind of evidence, it is granted the rights in the permission set specified in the code group. A .NET security policy is a collection of code groups. The code groups within a security policy are completely independent of each other. The .NET CLR evaluates which code groups apply to a given assembly based on the evidence satisfied by the assembly and grants the union of the rights of all permission sets specified in the code groups. SharePoint defines two custom security policy files: WSS_Minimal and WSS_Medium. The SharePoint security policy files are discussed in the "Reading Security Policy Files" section of this chapter.

.NET allows administrators to provide multiple security policies, and multiple security policies can apply to the same assembly. The actual permissions that are granted to an assembly are the intersection of all permissions granted by all security policies.

There are four types of security policies:

- **Enterprise policy** Defines a policy that affects all computers within the entire enterprise.
- **Machine policy** Defines a policy for a specific computer.
- **User policy** Defines a policy for a specific user.
- **Application-domain policy** Defines a policy for all code running in a specific application domain. The default application-domain policy grants code full trust. The WSS_Minimal and WSS_Medium security policies are examples of application-domain policies.

Note Application domains are the fundamental scope for execution of code and ownership of resources in .NET. .NET objects always reside in exactly one application domain.

Calculating Permissions for Assemblies

In this section, you will learn about the process executed by the .NET common language runtime (CLR) to calculate which permissions apply to a .NET assembly.

When the .NET CLR loads an assembly, it computes the permissions the assembly is granted by calculating the permissions granted by all security policies. This set of permissions is calculated only once per application domain and is stored in memory for as long as the assembly remains loaded. If an assembly decides to invoke a class located in another assembly, that class might demand that the calling assembly have the required security permissions to access it. In such cases, to prevent luring attacks, it is not sufficient to check that the assembly that immediately invokes the class has the required permissions.

Note A *luring attack* occurs when code with a low level of trust attempts to get code with a high level of trust to do something on its behalf. This is also known as a *middleman attack*.

Not only do you need to know the permissions associated with the immediate caller, the .NET CLR must determine that every assembly up the call chain has the required permissions. This is also known as the *security permission stack walk*.

Stack Walks

In essence, a stack is just a list of data. New items added to the stack are placed on the top (push); items removed from the stack are also taken from the top (pop). The stack is used to keep track of different kinds of short-term data. A stack consists of different layers (or stack frames) that contain method arguments, local variables, and return addresses for each method that is executing within a program. The method stack frame can be used to trace the return path through nested method calls, which is required to determine the complete method call chain. This process occurs during the security stack walk.

Stack Walk Modifiers

In code, developers are allowed to modify the behavior of the stack walk via assertions, demands, denies, and permit only stack walk modifiers. As an administrator, you will not work with stack walk modifiers directly, although you must be aware of their existence if you want to understand all factors affecting code access security in general and the problems surrounding partially trusted callers in particular. Partially trusted callers are discussed in detail later in this chapter, in the "Partially Trusted Callers" section.

Developers can assert a security permission, which stops the stack walk in the stack frame doing the assertion. This is useful because stack walks can be quite expensive with regard to performance.

Note During the SharePoint 2007 beta phase, .NET performance profiling showed that the performance hit caused by complete stack walks ranged between 6.5 percent and 11 percent, illustrating that stack walks can have significant impact on performance.

One way to mitigate such performance hits is to assert security permissions. The downside of this approach is that callers further up the call chain might not have the required permissions to perform operations carried out by downstream objects. However, the assembly containing the assertion must be granted the permission it tries to assert, and only assemblies that are granted the Security permission are allowed to assert permissions.

A *security demand* triggers a stack walk demanding a given permission of all callers up the stack. In other words, during the stack walk, the complete method call chain is visited to determine if callers have sufficient permissions. If the .NET CLR discovers an assembly in the call chain that is not granted the demanded permission, the stack walk aborts and a security exception is raised. Security demands are useful in scenarios where the code is about to perform some sort of intensive operation that ultimately requires a specific permission. If the assemblies in the call chain do not have this permission, the operation will eventually fail. In such scenarios, it makes sense to ensure that the required set of permissions is granted before undertaking an intensive operation that takes up time and CPU processing power.

A *security deny* overrides administrative security policy and sets a stricter security policy programmatically. This is a technique often applied by third-party vendors, because they want to create secure components that are deployed in an environment that is not well known to them.

Permit only stack walk modifiers are the opposite of security denies. They are used to define which permissions are allowed, even if other permissions are granted administratively. Again, third-party vendors often use this technique.

Declarative Security

Code access security offers a mechanism to define security permissions programmatically as well as declaratively via security attributes. If you are an administrator, you are not likely to use programmatic or declarative forms of security permissions directly. However, it can be helpful to be aware of the concepts involved because you are likely to encounter .NET developers who make use of these security techniques. In addition, defining security permissions programmatically and declaratively helps Visual Studio 2005 to do a static analysis of the required permissions for a given assembly, which is helpful to administrators who want to determine the minimal permission set for a given assembly. Performing a static analysis of required permissions is discussed in the "Calculating the Required Assembly Permission Set" section of this chapter.

Best Practices Defining security permissions declaratively instead of programmatically helps to prevent cluttered code, which is a good thing for developers. Another advantage that is discussed less often is that using security attributes consistently makes it quite easy to determine the minimum set of permissions required to run code.

The following code listing shows examples of both models for defining security permissions. The *ProgrammaticSecurity()* method shows how to define the permission to read a file programmatically. The *DeclarativeSecurity()* method shows how to define the same permissions declaratively.

```
using System;
using System.Security.Permissions;

namespace MyNamespace
{
  class MyClass
  {
    private void ProgrammaticSecurity()
    {
      FileIOPermission permission = new FileIOPermission(
      FileIOPermissionAccess.Read, @"c:\test.txt");
      permission.Demand();
      // code that reads test.txt
    }

    [FileIOPermission(SecurityAction.Demand,
    Read = @"c:\test.txt")]
    private void DeclarativeSecurity()
    {
      // code that reads test.txt
    }
  }
}
```

For every permission attribute, you need to specify a security action. You already know four of them:

- Assert
- Demand
- Deny
- PermitOnly

The meaning of those security actions are identical to the meaning of stack walk modifiers that can be defined programmatically and that were discussed in the previous section.

In addition to those four security actions, you can choose from a wider range of security actions that is not available with programmatic security techniques:

- **DemandChoice** Choice actions allow you to combine permissions in a logical OR. If you want to demand that a method is granted either one of two or more permissions, you should use the DemandChoice security action. You can apply this action to classes and methods.
- **InheritanceDemand** This security action is used to demand a permission from any subclass of a given class. You can apply this action to classes and methods.
- **InheritanceDemandChoice** This security action is a combination between a choice action and an inheritance action. Please refer to DemandChoice for more information about choice actions. Please refer to InheritanceDemand for more information about inheritance actions. You can apply this action to classes and methods.
- **LinkDemand** This security action can be used to demand a permission at link time instead of call time, during Just-In-Time (JIT) compilation. This eliminates the stack-walk penalty, but you need to be aware that link time demands are calculated only during JIT compilation for the first caller up the call chain. Subsequent calls to the same method by other callers are not verified to have the required permissions. As a result, using LinkDemand leaves you more open for luring attacks. You can apply this action to classes and methods.
- **LinkDemandChoice** This security action is a combination between a choice action and a link demand action. Please refer to DemandChoice for more information about choice actions. Please refer to LinkDemand for more information about link demand actions. You can apply this action to classes and methods.
- **RequestMinimum** This security action indicates that a given permission is the minimum permission required for the target assembly to be able to execute. For example, if an assembly claims it needs to read a file via a RequestMinimum action, the assembly will not execute unless this permission is granted. You can apply this action only to an assembly.
- **RequestOptional** This security action specifies optional permissions that can be granted to an assembly. You can apply this action only to an assembly.
- **RequestRefuse** This security action specifies permissions that are not allowed to be granted to an assembly. You can apply this action only to an assembly.

Setting a Secure Default Policy

One of the results of the Trustworthy Computing initiative is that Microsoft products embrace a set of strategies called SD^3+C, a term coined by the Secure Windows Initiative team. *SD^3+C* stands for "secure by design, secure by default, secure in deployment and communications."

A product is *secure by design* when the overall design of a system takes security seriously. You can take several steps to accomplish this, such as security training for all personnel, adhering to design and coding guidelines, and developing regression tests for all previously fixed vulnerabilities.

A product is *secure by default* if it is secure enough out of the box. This goal can be achieved by taking steps such as these:

- Do not install a complete feature set. By default, install only features that your users regularly apply. In Office SharePoint Server 2007, you can choose to install advanced features such as Excel Services—a feature that is not installed by default.
- Make sure a product requires the least amount of privileges in order to execute correctly. Do not require code to run within the context of members of a local or domain administrators group when it does not require such capabilities. A good example of this is the fact that Web Parts executed in a SharePoint virtual server, by default, run under the WSS_Minimal trust level. This is covered in detail later in this chapter, in the "Configuring Security Settings in the Web.config File" section.

> **Note** As an administrator, you should be interested in the security privileges required by a piece of code, so that you know if the code is able to perform potentially dangerous operations. This is especially true when your company acquires software that is built by others. If you want to verify that the creators of a piece of software have put thought in determining how much privileges the code requires, you should demand detailed documentation regarding the minimum amount of privileges required to run the software. If you are buying a third-party product, you should always look for the presence of such documentation.

- Protect product resources. You must protect sensitive data and critical resources from attack. SharePoint Server 2007 includes a message digest (also known as the FormDigest) that you must include if you want to post a request to a SharePoint server that modifies the content database. The message digest contains security validation specific to a user, site, and time period.

A product is *secure in deployment* if the system is maintainable once it is installed. Following are steps you can take to achieve security in deployment:

- Make sure administrators can manage the security functionality of a product once it is installed.
- If a security vulnerability is found, make sure you have a mechanism in place so that you are able to create and apply a security patch as soon as possible.

Finally, *secure software in communications* means that software developers should be prepared for the discovery of application vulnerabilities and should communicate openly and responsibly with administrators (and/or end users) to help them take protective measures.

Note Of all the elements imposed by SD^3+C, secure by design and secure by default provide the most security benefit. They help to prevent the introduction of vulnerabilities in software and minimize the attack surface of software.

Configuring Security Settings in the Web.config File

The default security settings in the Web.config file of a SharePoint virtual server allow only a minimum amount of freedom—which makes a lot of sense considering the SD^3+C initiative. This section explains the security-related configuration settings in a SharePoint Web.config file.

The SafeControls Section

The first security-related setting is the <SafeControls> section. Before you can add Web Parts to Web Part pages, administrators have to make the server trust a Web Part. This is done by adding a <SafeControl> element to the <SafeControls> section. Each <SafeControl> entry identifies a trusted assembly.

Note In a typical SharePoint installation, many of the trusted assemblies found in the <SafeControls> section are Web Part libraries that contain one or more trusted Web Parts.

A <SafeControl> element has four attributes. The following code listing shows a <SafeControl> entry that allows all Web Parts belonging the *System.Web.UI.WebControls* namespace and are located in the *System.Web* assembly to be added to Web Part pages:

```
<SafeControls>
  <SafeControl Assembly="System.Web, Version=1.0.5000.0, Culture=neutral,
```

```
  PublicKeyToken=b03f5f7f11d50a3a" Namespace="System.Web.UI.WebControls"
  TypeName="*" Safe="True" />
</SafeControls>
```

The first attribute of a <SafeControl> entry is the *Assembly* attribute. This attribute identifies the assembly name of the assembly that contains the Web Parts. This name can be partially or fully qualified. If an assembly is partially qualified, this attribute contains only the name of the assembly. For example, this name is System.Web for an assembly that is named System.Web.dll. A fully qualified assembly name consists of four parts: the assembly name, version number, culture (which is always set to *neutral* for code assemblies), and the developer identity (a public key token). The following name is the name of the Microsoft.SharePoint assembly and is an example of a fully qualified assembly name: "Microsoft.SharePoint, Version=11.0.0.0, Culture=neutral, PublicKey Token=71e9bce111e9429."

Note Although you can add entries for partially qualified assemblies in the SafeControls list, it is recommended that you use fully qualified assembly names. This makes it easier to define security policies that are based on content-based evidence. In addition, if you choose to use strong-named assemblies consistently, the .NET Framework behaves consistently too. The .NET assembly resolver, which is responsible for deciding in which locations to look for a given assembly and decides which assembly version to load, acts quite differently when it comes to finding fully or partially qualified assemblies. In the real world, a lack of understanding of those differences now and then leads to problems where the assembly that is actually loaded differs from the one the administrator or developer expects.

Real World Establishing the Version Number of Referenced Assemblies

If you are not sure which version of an assembly is used by a .NET application, you can use the ILDASM (Intermediate Language Disassembler) .NET Framework tool. ILDASM is installed automatically as a part of every Visual Studio 2005 installation. If you open ILDASM, you can choose File, then Open and browse to the .NET application you want to investigate. This opens the .NET application in ILDASM. Double-click on the Manifest node to open the .NET assembly manifest. The assembly manifest contains information about the assemblies that are referenced within the .NET application. Assembly references are preceded by the *extern* keyword. The following code listing shows a part of a .NET assembly manifest containing a reference to the Microsoft.SharePoint assembly.

```
.assembly extern Microsoft.SharePoint
{
  .publickeytoken = (71 E9 BC E1 11 E9 42 9C )
  // q.....B.
  .ver 12:0:0:0
}
```

The second attribute of a <SafeControl> entry is the *Namespace* attribute. This contains the value for the .NET namespace for the Web Part. By convention, this name is often equal to the assembly name, although this does not have to be so. The correct value for this namespace can be retrieved by looking at the code itself. In C#, the namespace value is identified by the namespace keyword. The following code listing shows a code fragment with a namespace value of *MyNamespace*:

```
namespace MyNamespace
{
  class MyClass : WebPart
  {
    ...
  }
}
```

The third attribute of the <SafeControl> element is *TypeName*. The *TypeName* attribute specifies the Web Part class name. In C#, the class name is identified by the class keyword. The previous code listing shows a code fragment with the following type name: *MyClass*. You can also use an asterisk (*) to include all Web Part classes within the specified assembly and namespace.

The fourth attribute of the <SafeControl> element is *Safe*. By default, this attribute is set to *True*, so you can omit this attribute if you want. The *Safe* attribute needs to be set to *True* to make a Web Part trusted. Administrators can use this attribute and set it to *False* to ensure a Web Part is temporarily unavailable. This attribute is optional.

The final attribute of the <SafeControl> element is *AllowRemoteDesigner*. By default, this attribute is set to *True*. This optional attribute can be used to determine if a control can be manipulated via a remote designer such as Microsoft Office SharePoint Designer.

The securityPolicy Section

The <securityPolicy> section is located in the <system.web> section. The <securityPolicy> element defines a collection of mappings between security policy files and the trust level names for those security policy files. In ASP.NET, you can choose to use the special Full trust level. This trust level is equivalent to having full trust in the local machine zone; it allows ASP.NET applications to perform all operations. If you specify the Full trust level, the ASP.NET host does not apply any additional policies. Setting the trust level to Full on a SharePoint server is incompatible with the intentions of the SD^3+C initiative, making a SharePoint installation less secure by default.

Real World Web Part Permissions

Often a Web Part developer claims the trust level of the virtual server needs to be raised to Full because the Web Part requires additional permissions. Although doing so is easy, when it comes to securing your server, this is not the time to get lazy. If a Web Part does require additional permissions, make sure to obtain exact specifications of the permissions that are needed. Then create a custom security policy file to cater to these needs.

The <securityPolicy> section, a child of the <system.web> element, contains a collection of <trustLevel> elements that can be used to define custom security policy files. <trustLevel> elements are also used to define two security policy files that are shipped with SharePoint installations: WSS_Minimal and WSS_Medium. This is shown in the following code listing:

```
<securityPolicy>
  <trustLevel name="WSS_Medium" policyFile="
  C:\Program Files\Common Files\Microsoft Shared\
  Web Server Extensions\60\config\wss_mediumtrust.config" />
  <trustLevel name="WSS_Minimal" policyFile="
  C:\Program Files\Common Files\Microsoft Shared\
  Web Server Extensions\60\config\wss_minimaltrust.config" />
</securityPolicy>
```

The trust Element

The final Web.config setting that is important in specifying security settings is the <trust> element. The <trust> element configures the level of code access security applied to an application. By default, SharePoint applications run under the WSS_Minimal trust level. The following code listing shows the Web.config file of a SharePoint virtual server that runs under the default trust level of WSS_Minimal:

```
<trust level="WSS_Minimal" originUrl="" processRequestInApplicationTrust="false"
/>
```

The *level* attribute is used to set the name of the security policy file under which the application will run. The *originUrl* attribute can be used to define a well-formed URL that specifies the origin of an application. This attribute is useful in scenarios where origin-based evidence is important. The *processRequestInApplicationTrust* attribute specifies whether page requests are automatically restricted to the permissions that are configured in the trust policy file. If this attribute is set to *true*, the *Page* class uses the PermitOnly stack walk modifier on the ASP.NET permission set. In such scenarios, granting extensive permissions via a policy files is useless. If this attribute is set to *false*, only the security policy will be applied (instead of the intersection between the ASP.NET permission set and the security policy file). If you need more information about the PermitOnly stack walk modifier, refer to the "Stack Walk Modifiers" section.

Best Practices In SharePoint environments, always set the processRequestInApplicationTrust attribute to false. This is the default value for SharePoint environments; the default value for ASP.NET applications is true. If you do not set this attribute to false, creating custom security policy files is useless because the only permission set that will be applied to your code when the processRequestInApplicationTrust attribute is set to true is the ASP.NET permission set.

Understanding Security Policy Files

The easiest way to learn to read security policy files is by looking at existing security policy files. In this section, you will get a closer look at the custom SharePoint security policy files WSS_Minimal and WSS_Medium. You can find them by looking at the *policyFile* attribute of the <trustLevel> element of a SharePoint Web.config file. By default, the SharePoint policy files are located in the CONFIG folder of the SharePoint hive: [drive letter]:\Program Files\Common Files\Microsoft Shared\Web Server Extensions\12.

The SecurityClasses and CodeGroup Sections

The first interesting bit of a security policy file is the <SecurityClasses> section, which contains a collection of <SecurityClass> elements. <SecurityClass> elements have *Name* and *Description* attributes that are used to specify a friendly name and a fully qualified assembly name for permissions, membership conditions, and code groups that are used later on in the security policy file. The following code listing shows an example of a <SecurityClass> element:

```
<SecurityClasses>
  <SecurityClass Name="WebPartPermission"
  Description="Microsoft.SharePoint.Security.WebPartPermission,
  Microsoft.SharePoint.Security, Version=12.0.0.0, Culture=neutral,
  PublicKeyToken=71e9bce111e9429c"/>
</SecurityClasses>
```

Permissions

Permissions defined in the <SecurityClasses> section are used later in the security policy file to define permission sets. For example, the WSS_Minimal security policy file defines a permission set called SPRestricted that contains several permissions, one of them being a Web Part permission that allows Web Part connections. The following code listing shows a part of the SPRestricted permission set that is responsible for allowing Web Part connections:

```
<PermissionSet class="NamedPermissionSet" version="1" Name="SPRestricted">
...
<IPermission class="WebPartPermission" version="1" Connections="True" />
</PermissionSet>
```

Membership Conditions

Membership conditions are used within code groups, which are defined later in the security policy file. As you might remember, a code group associates a permission set with evidence. A membership condition is used to determine whether a certain assembly matches a code group by looking at content-based or origin-based evidence related to a .NET assembly. The WSS_Minimal and WSS_Medium policy files use the following membership conditions:

- **AllMembershipCondition** Matches all code.
- **StrongNameMembershipCondition** Determines whether an assembly matches a code group by looking at the strong name of the assembly.
- **UrlMembershipCondition** Determines whether an assembly matches a code group by looking at the complete URL (including the protocol) of the assembly.
- **ZoneMembershipCondition** Determines whether an assembly matches a code group by looking at the zone of origin. .NET defines the following five zones:
- **My Computer** Identifies code coming from the local machine.
- **Local Intranet** Identifies code coming from the intranet.
- **Internet** Identifies code coming from the Internet.
- **Trusted Sites** Identifies code coming from a list of trusted Internet sites, which can be defined via Internet Explorer (Tools > Internet options > Security tab > Trusted sites > click the Sites button).
- **Untrusted Sites** Identifies code coming from a list of untrusted Internet sites, which can be defined via Internet Explorer (Tools, Internet options, Security tab, Restricted sites, and click the Sites button).

The next code listing shows a sample membership condition that determines that the SPRestricted permission set will be applied to all assemblies located in the application directory of a SharePoint virtual server:

```
<CodeGroup class="UnionCodeGroup" version="1"
  PermissionSetName="SPRestricted">
  <IMembershipCondition class="UrlMembershipCondition"
  version="1" Url="$AppDirUrl$/*" />
</CodeGroup>
```

This permission associates the SPRestricted permission set to all assemblies located in SharePoint subdirectories. The default root folder for a SharePoint virtual server is located at [drive letter]:\inetpub\wwwroot\wss\virtual directories\[GUID]. The most interesting subdirectory of the SharePoint virtual server root folder is the Bin folder, where custom partially trusted assemblies containing Web Parts are stored.

> **Best Practices** A good starting point for implementing a security policy is to grant Microsoft assemblies, European Computer Manufacturing Association (ECMA) assemblies, and assemblies signed with the strong name of your company full trust and to grant all other assemblies no permissions at all.

You can grant specific permissions to assemblies based on the strong name they are signed with. To do this, you use the StrongNameMembershipCondition membership condition. The next code listing shows a code group that grants full trust to all assemblies that are signed with the Microsoft strong name:

```
<CodeGroup class="UnionCodeGroup" version="1"
PermissionSetName="FullTrust" Name="Microsoft_Strong_Name"
Description="grants code signed with the Microsoft strong
name full trust. ">
  <IMembershipCondition
  class="StrongNameMembershipCondition" version="1"
  PublicKeyBlob="[public key blob"/>
</CodeGroup>
```

The value of the *PublicKeyBlob* attribute of the <IMembershipCondition> element is not the same as the public key of the assembly. You need to use the Secutil.exe tool to retrieve the correct public key blob. To do this, open a Visual Studio command prompt (from the Start menu, select All Programs, point to Microsoft Visual Studio 2005, Visual Studio Tools, and then select Visual Studio 2005 Command Prompt) and issue the following command:

```
secutil.exe -hex -s [MyAssemblyName].dll
```

For example, you can use Microsoft.SharePoint.dll to retrieve the public key blob for all Microsoft assemblies.

Note You can find more information about the Secutil Tool at *http://msdn2.microsoft.com/en-us/library/akt2ytd6.aspx*.

Understanding Code Groups

A security policy file contains a collection of code groups. Code groups can have child code groups, thus forming a hierarchical tree of code groups. Each code group has a membership condition that determines whether a code group applies to a given assembly. The WSS_Minimal and WSS_Medium security policy files use two kinds of code groups: FirstMatchCodeGroup and UnionCodeGroup.

A FirstMatchCodeGroup code group tries to match its membership condition to an assembly. If the condition matches, the membership condition of every child code group is tested. The testing stops when the first match is made. The result of a FirstMatchCodeGroup code group is the union of the permissions granted by the root code group and the first child code group that matches.

The UnionCodeGroup code group is the most common type of code group. Such code groups result in a union of all permissions granted by the root code group and all child code groups that have matching membership conditions.

The next code listing shows a part of the <CodeGroup> section of the WSS_Minimal security policy file. The root code group is a FirstMatchCodeGroup, which returns the union of the permissions granted by itself and the first matching child code group. Because of its AllMembershipCondition membership condition, this root code group applies to all assemblies. The root code group itself grants code the Nothing permission set, which grants no permissions at all. The following code fragment shows that assemblies that are located in the application directory (represented by the $AppDirURL$ replacement token) will be granted the permissions defined in the SPRestricted permission set:

```
<CodeGroup class="FirstMatchCodeGroup" version="1"
PermissionSetName="Nothing">
  <IMembershipCondition class="AllMembershipCondition" version="1" />
  <CodeGroup class="UnionCodeGroup" version="1"
  PermissionSetName="SPRestricted">
    <IMembershipCondition class="UrlMembershipCondition" version="1"
    Url="$AppDirUrl$/*" />
  </CodeGroup>
</CodeGroup>
```

The NamedPermissionSets Section

A security policy file contains code groups that associate permission sets with evidence, as you have already seen. The <NamedPermissionSets> section in a security policy file determines which permission sets are allowed to be used in code groups. The WSS_Minimal and WSS_Medium policy files both refer to the FullTrust and Nothing permission sets that are predefined in .NET. You can also use the <NamedPermissionSets> section to create a new permission set, in which case you must specify which permissions are a part of such a permission set.

The following code listing shows the portion of the <NamedPermissionSets> section that defines that the FullTrust permission set can be used in the security policy file:

```
<NamedPermissionSets>
...
<PermissionSet class="NamedPermissionSet" version="1" Unrestricted="true"
Name="FullTrust" Description="Allows full access to all resources" />
</NamedPermissionSets>
```

Both of the SharePoint security policy files define a custom permission set called SPRestricted. The permissions granted by the WSS_Minimal SPRestricted permission set are more strict than the permissions granted by the WSS_Medium SPRestricted set. The following code listing shows a part of the <NamedPermissionSets> section that defines the SPRestricted permission set for the WSS_Minimal security policy file:

```
<PermissionSet class="NamedPermissionSet"
  version="1" Name="SPRestricted">
  <IPermission class="AspNetHostingPermission"
    version="1" Level="Minimal"/>
  <IPermission class="SecurityPermission"
    version="1" Flags="Execution" />
  <IPermission class="WebPartPermission"
    version="1" Connections="True" />
</PermissionSet>
```

Table 31-1 shows a complete overview of the permissions granted by the WSS_Minimal and WSS_Medium security policy files.

Table 31-1 Security Permissions Overview

Permission	WSS_Minimal	WSS_Medium
AspNetHosting	Minimal	Medium
Dns		Unrestricted
Environment		Read: TEMP;TMP;USERNAME;OS; COMPUTERNAME
FileIO		Read, Write, Append, PathDiscovery: $AppDir$

Table 31-1 Security Permissions Overview

Permission	WSS_Minimal	WSS_Medium
IsolatedStorageFile		Allowed: AssemblyIsolationByUser, UserQuota: 9223372036854775807
Printing		DefaultPrinting
Security	Execution	Assertion, Execution, ControlThread, ControlPrincipal, RemotingConfiguration
SharePoint		ObjectModel
Smtp		Connect
SqlClient		Unrestricted
Web		ConnectAccess: $OriginHost$
WebPart	Connections	Connections

Creating Policy Files

If you are not satisfied with the number or scope of permissions granted by the WSS_Minimal and WSS_Medium security policy files—which is normal for SharePoint implementations—you have three options. You can set the trust level of the SharePoint virtual server to Full, install assemblies in the GAC, or create your own custom policy file. Setting the trust level of the SharePoint virtual server to Full affects all assemblies used by the SharePoint virtual server and is the least secure option. Installing assemblies in the GAC grants a higher level of permissions to your assembly than necessary (because most assemblies do not require a full permission set) and is thus less secure. In addition, it makes assemblies installed in the GAC available to all virtual servers on the server. Although creating custom policy files requires the most work of all options, it is the most secure and recommended approach.

Security Alert Be cautious when buying third-party Web Parts that require a full permission set to execute successfully. This is a sign that the software has not been designed carefully. You can be more lenient when it comes to deciding whether to use Web Parts that were developed within your company.

Start creating a new policy file by customizing one of the SharePoint security policy files. This way, if anything goes wrong, it is easy to switch back to a valid state on your server. In the following procedure, you will create a new policy file based on the existing WSS_Minimal security policy file. Then you will modify the new policy file and add the permission to use the SharePoint object model and ensure it applies to assemblies that have a specific strong name (for example, your company strong name).

1. Go the location where the WSS_Minimal security policy file (wss_minimaltrust.config) is located. By default, this is [drive letter]:\Program Files \Common Files\Microsoft Shared\Web Server Extensions\12\config\.
2. Copy WSS_Minimal.config, and rename the file **[my policy].config**.
3. Open [my policy].config in Notepad.
4. Locate the <SecurityClasses> section, and add the following code:

```
<SecurityClass Name="SharePointPermission" Description="Microsoft.SharePoint
.Security.SharePointPermission,
Microsoft.SharePoint.Security, Version=12.0.0.0, Culture=neutral,
PublicKeyToken=71e9bce111e9429c"/>
```

5. Locate the <PermissionSet> element that has a *Name* attribute with the following value: SPRestricted.
6. Copy this element and all of its children, and paste it directly below the <PermissionSet> element.
7. Set the name attribute of the new <PermissionSet> element to [custom permission set].
8. Add the permission to use the SharePoint object model to the new permission set by adding the following code to the <PermissionSet> element:

```
<IPermission class="SharePointPermission" version="1"
  ObjectModel="True" />
```

The complete permission set looks like this:

```
<PermissionSet class="NamedPermissionSet" version="1"
  Name="[custom permission set]">
  <IPermission class="AspNetHostingPermission" version="1"
    Level="Minimal" />
  <IPermission class="SecurityPermission" version="1"
    Flags="Execution" />
  <IPermission class="WebPartPermission" version="1"
    Connections="True" />
  <IPermission class="SharePointPermission" version="1"
    ObjectModel="True" />
</PermissionSet>
```

At this point, you have defined a new permission set that grants code a number of permissions, such as granting code the permission to use the SharePoint object model. Next, you will create a new code group that specifies that this permission set is granted to assemblies that have a specific strong name by using the StrongNameMembershipCondition membership condition. Because the root code group in the security policy file is a FirstMatchCodeGroup, the .NET CLR will stop assigning permissions when the first match to a child code group is found. Therefore, to be sure that the new code group is applied, you must declare the new code group as the first child code group:

1. Add the following code directly below the root code group:

```
<CodeGroup class="UnionCodeGroup" version="1"
PermissionSetName="[custom permission set]">
  <IMembershipCondition class="StrongNameMembershipCondition"
  version="1" PublicKeyBlob="[public key blob]"
  Name="MyAssemblyName" />
</CodeGroup>
```

2. Retrieve the public key blob from an assembly by issuing the following command from the Visual Studio 2005 command prompt:

```
secutil.exe -hex -s [MyAssembly].dll
```

3. Copy the public key blob, and add the value to the *PublicKeyBlob* attribute of the <IMembershipCondition> element.

You have finished creating a custom security policy file.

In the next step, you need to adjust the Web.config file of your SharePoint virtual server so that it will use this custom security policy file. You can accomplish this by following these steps:

1. Open the Web.config file of your SharePoint virtual server, and locate the <SecurityPolicy> section.
2. Add the following code to this section:

```
<trustLevel name="MyCustomTrustLevel"
policyFile="[my policy].config" />
```

3. Locate the <trust> element, and let it refer to the new custom trust level, as shown in the following code listing:

```
<trust level="MyCustomTrustLevel " originUrl="" />
```

4. Open a command prompt, and type **iisreset** to apply the custom policy file to the SharePoint virtual server.

Note If you omit this last step, you might receive an error when accessing a SharePoint site, stating that the assembly security permission grant set is incompatible.

Partially Trusted Callers

If a strong-named assembly is added to the GAC, it is granted the FullTrust permission set and is available for use by any unknown and potentially malicious client. To prevent security problems, .NET enforces a rule specifying that strong-named assemblies can be called only by client assemblies that are granted the FullTrust permission set. By default, strong-named assemblies cannot be called by partially trusted assemblies, such as the assemblies located in the Bin folder of your SharePoint virtual directory. This is because the .NET JIT compiler adds link-time demands for the FullTrust permission set on every public or protected method on every public class in the assembly. If you need more information about link-time demands, refer to the "Declarative Security" section earlier in the chapter. The following code listing shows a sample method called *Test()*:

```
public void Test() {}
```

The .NET JIT compiler converts this method definition to the following code:

```
[PermissionSet(SecurityAction.LinkDemand, Name = "FullTrust")]
public Test() {}
```

If you do want to allow the calling of strong-named assemblies from within a partially trusted environment, you need to add the *AllowPartiallyTrustedCallersAttribute* assembly attribute located in the *System.Security* namespace to a strong-named assembly. This is also known as decorating a strong-named assembly with the *AllowPartiallyTrustedCaller-sAttribute* attribute. This attribute is also known as APTCA. In a C# project, you can do this by adding the following line of code to the *AssemblyInfo.cs* class of an assembly:

```
[assembly:AllowPartiallyTrustedCallers]
```

Calculating the Required Assembly Permission Set

Visual Studio 2005 can help to estimate the permissions an assembly requires. Although Visual Studio 2005 is a developer tool, as an administrator, you will find it helpful to get an idea of the permissions that a Web Part library requires. For example, if you are using a Weather Web Part that requires full permissions, something is definitely wrong with it. As an added bonus, Visual Studio 2005 can help you to retrieve the XML needed to define permissions in security policy files. If you want to try the techniques outlined in this section, you will need access to Visual Studio 2005, preferably installed on a test SharePoint server. This section does not assume you have any knowledge about Visual Studio 2005, and will guide you through the permission calculation process step by step.

During the first steps, you will create a test Web Part library. It will contain the minimal amount of code necessary to perform a successful calculation of the required permissions.

1. Start Visual Studio 2005. From the Start menu, point to All Programs, Microsoft Visual Studio 2005, and then select Microsoft Visual Studio 2005.
2. From the File menu, point to New, and then select Project.
3. In the left pane of the New Project window, expand the Visual C# node, under Project types, select the Class Library template.
4. Specify the following name: **MyWPLibrary**.
5. Specify the following location: **C:\projects**.
6. Leave the other default settings and click OK.

This creates a skeleton for a library file that can be used to contain Web Parts. During the next steps, you will use the *Microsoft.SharePoint.Security* assembly that contains SharePoint-specific permissions to demand the permission to use the SharePoint object model for the test Web Part library.

1. Right-click the References node and choose Add Reference to open the Add Reference window.
2. On the .NET tab, select Microsoft.SharePoint.Security.dll. Choose the second component name that is called Windows SharePoint Services. Verify that this component refers to Microsoft.SharePoint.Security.dll under Path.

   > **Note** The component name of this dll is Windows SharePoint Services. Because a default SharePoint installation contains multiple components with this name, picking the correct assembly is a bit more complicated than it should be.

3. Double-click Class1.cs. Replace the code in this file with the following code:

```
using System.Security.Permissions;
using Microsoft.SharePoint.Security;

namespace MyWPLibrary
{
  public class Class1
  {
    [FileIOPermission(SecurityAction.Demand, Read = @"c:\test.txt")]
    [SharePointPermission(SecurityAction.Demand, ObjectModel = true,
    Impersonate = true)]
    public void Test() {}
  }
}
```

This code creates a method called *Test()* and requires the presence of a couple of permissions; if the permissions are missing, this assembly will fail to execute. One of the permissions, FileIOPermission, requires the permission to read a file called test.txt and is not SharePoint-related at all. The other permission is SharePoint-related; SharePointPermission represents a custom permission that controls the ability to access SharePoint. This demand requires that the permission to use the SharePoint object model and impersonate code is granted to the assembly.

You cannot use Visual Studio 2005 to calculate the required permissions for libraries directly. Because .NET libraries cannot be executed without being hosted by another application, you first need to create a host application for it, and then you can calculate permissions for the test Web Part library. To do this, follow these steps:

1. Right-click the MyWPLibrary solution, point to Add, and then select New Project.
2. Expand the Visual C# section and choose the Windows Application template.
3. Specify the name **WPLibHost**, and then click OK.

At this point, you have created an application that can host a .NET library. Visual Studio 2005 will perform a static analysis of all method calls, so for the analysis to work, you need to call all the methods you want to analyze within the host application.

In this procedure, you will analyze the *Test()* method of the *MyWPLibrary* assembly. To do so, you must add a reference in the WPLibHost application host to this assembly and call this method.

1. Click the References node of the WPLibHost application, and choose Add Reference.
2. In the Add Reference window, click the Projects tab.
3. Ensure the MyWPLibrary project name is selected, and then click OK.
4. Double-click Form1.cs.
5. Press F7, or select View and then select Code, to open the code view for this class.
6. Add the code that calls the *Test()* method of the *MyWPLibrary* assembly to the *Form1()* constructor. The *Form1()* constructor should look like this:

   ```
   public Form1()
   {
     InitializeComponent();
     MyWPLibrary.Class1 testClass = new MyWPLibrary.Class1();
     testClass.Test();
   }
   ```

Because you have set up an application host that calls the test Web Part library, Visual Studio 2005 is now able to calculate the permissions the Web Part library requires to operate. Visual Studio 2005 will perform a static analysis of the current application and all referenced assemblies. The analysis involves all method calls, declarative attributes, and programmatic demands. This analysis provides only an estimate and might overestimate permissions because it analyzes all code paths including those that are never used. It might also underestimate permissions because it is not able to detect dynamic calls made using reflection. The correctness of the analysis is improved greatly if Web Part developers have taken the time and effort to demand permissions explicitly via declarative attributes.

In the next procedure, you learn how to calculate permissions for the test Web Part library.

1. Right-click WPLibHost and choose Properties.
2. Click the Security tab.
3. Select the Enable ClickOnce Security Settings check box.
4. Click the This Is A Partial Trust Application option.
5. Go to the Zone Your Application Will Be Installed From drop-down list and choose the following value: (Custom).
6. Click the Calculate Permissions button.

This starts the permission calculation. Ultimately, the permissions will appear in the Permissions Required By The Application section, as shown in Figure 31-1.

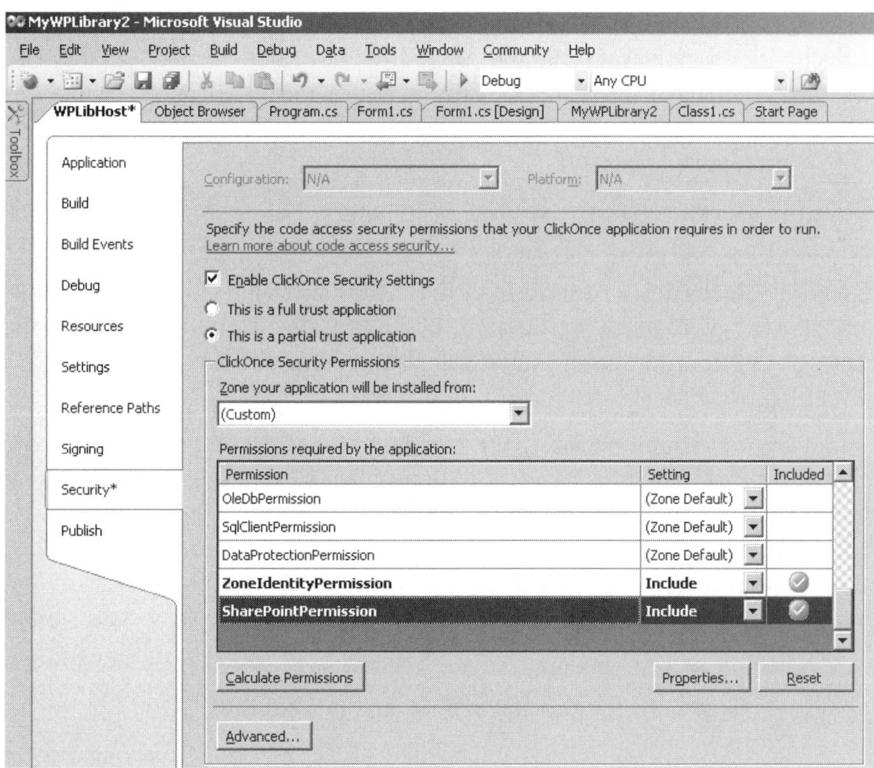

Figure 31-1 Calculated permissions

If you scroll down to the SharePointPermission permission and click Properties, you see the XML definition for this permission as shown in Figure 31-2. You can copy this XML definition and use it within a security policy file.

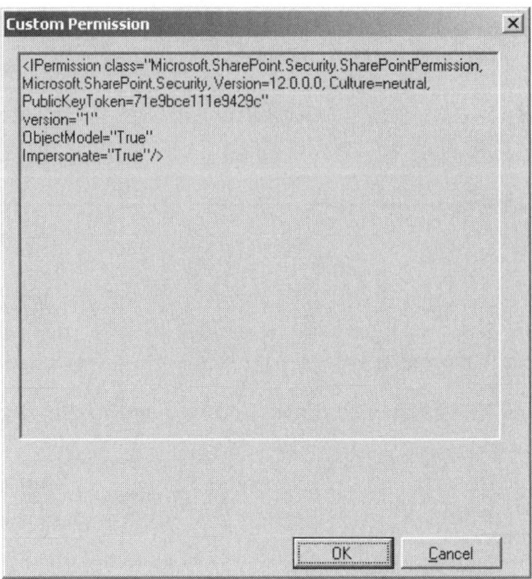

Figure 31-2 XML for a custom permission

As an alternative to using Visual Studio 2005, you can use the command-line tool Permcalc.exe, which is a part of the Visual Studio 2005 SDK, to calculate permissions for .NET assemblies. An advantage of Permcalc.exe is that it is also able to calculate permissions for library assemblies (.dll) directly. Open a Visual Studio 2005 command prompt, and type the following command:

```
permcalc.exe [myassembly].dll
```

As a result, Permcalc.exe starts to calculate the permissions required for the assembly and generates an XML file (by default, this XML file is called [myassembly].dll.PermCalc.xml) containing an overview of those permissions. By default, this XML file is saved in the folder where the assembly for which you are calculating permissions is located.

As was true for the Visual Studio 2005 tool, Permcalc.exe is accurate at calculating permissions that are demanded declaratively. It is less accurate when permissions are demanded programmatically, and even less accurate when it calculates permissions that are defined imperatively. *Imperative permissions* are permissions that are required because the code in a .NET assembly requires them, not because the permissions are demanded explicitly. For example, if someone writes a line of code that reads a given file, this is an imperative permission demand: the code will fail if it does not have the permission to read the file.

Best Practices In SharePoint scenarios, use the visual permission calculation tool included in Visual Studio 2005. Although Permcalc.exe might be useful for calculating permissions required for assemblies that do not require SharePoint permissions, currently this tool is useless in SharePoint scenarios. If you try to analyze an assembly that demands SharePoint permissions, you receive an error during XML output generation stating that SharePoint permissions are not marked as serializable.

Summary

In this chapter, you have learned about the concepts relevant to Code Access Security and have seen how the Code Access Security paradigm fits within the Trustworthy Computing initiative. You have learned about the difference between Identity-Based Security and Code Access Security. The chapter explains the basic building blocks that are important in Code Access Security, such as permissions, named permission sets, evidence, code groups, membership conditions, stack walk modifiers and security demands. You have also learned how to read and create SharePoint Server 2007 security policy files. Then the chapter discussed what partially trusted callers and APTCA are. The chapter concluded with an explanation of how to use Visual Studio 2005 to calculate the required security permissions for .NET assemblies.

About the Authors

Bill English

MCSE, MVP, President, Mindsharp, Minneapolis, Minnesota. An author and educator specializing in SharePoint Products and Technologies, Bill English is an industry leader on this exciting product set from Microsoft. Since 2000, Bill has authored 10 books on Exchange and SharePoint products. Bill is the co-owner of Mindsharp (*www.mindsharp.com*), a company that offers top-notch educational opportunities on the SharePoint platform. He has presented at Comdex, The Microsoft Exchange Conference, TechMentor, TechEd, Advisor Live, and Networld Interop. You can find his blog at *www.mindsharpblogs.com*. Bill lives in Minnesota with his wife and two children where he enjoys boating, photography, and golf.

Coauthors

Margriet Bruggeman Lois & Clark IT Services, Amsterdam, The Netherlands. Margriet is a software developer, architect, and consultant specializing in SharePoint and ASP.NET development. Margriet is co-owner of Lois & Clark IT Services and can be contacted via e-mail (*info@lcbridge.nl*) or by visiting the following Web site: *http://www.lcbridge.nl*.

Nikander Bruggeman Lois & Clark IT Services, Amsterdam, The Netherlands. Nikander is a software developer, architect, and consultant specializing in SharePoint and ASP.NET development. Nikander is co-owner of Lois & Clark IT Services and can be contacted via e-mail (*info@lcbridge.nl*) or by visiting the following Web site: *http://www.lcbridge.nl*.

Penelope Coventry MCSE, MCDBA, MCSD.NET, MCT, CTT+, MSF, ISEB IT Infrastructure Management, IT Project+, Hinckley, U.K. Penelope is an independent consultant who focuses on the design, implementation, and development of SharePoint Technology–based solutions. She co-authored the *Microsoft SharePoint Products and Technologies Resource Kit*, July 2004, and the two editions of *Microsoft Windows SharePoint Services Step-by-Step*, January 2005 and February 2007.

Milan Gross MCSD, MCSE, MCT, Solventis, Honolulu, Hawaii. Milan is a SharePoint architect and developer with over 10 years of experience designing and deploying Microsoft solutions. When not writing code, Milan teaches SharePoint training classes as a Mindsharp contract instructor. You can reach Milan at *http://solventis.com*.

Kathryn Hughes Kathryn works as a freelance SharePoint consultant and technical writer, and is based in Sydney, Australia. Kathryn is completing her Master's degree, majoring in interaction design and Web site usability. Kathryn blogs at *http://www.mindsharpblogs.com/kathy/*.

Steve Smith MVP SharePoint Portal Server, MCT , MCSE, Combined Knowledge, Lutterworth, U.K. Steve is co-owner and trainer of Combined Knowledge, a U.K.-based training and consultancy company based on Microsoft technologies but specializing in SharePoint. Steve began working heavily with Microsoft technologies in 1996 while based in India, and where he met his wife Sharon. Steve and Sharon now live in Leicestershire, England with their three great kids.

Daniel Webster MCT, MCSE: Security + Internet. Mindsharp, Senior Instructor, Kansas City, Missouri. Daniel has been a technical trainer since 1994, specializing in Microsoft Internet technologies and security.

Contributing Authors

Andrew Connell MVP, Senior Instructor/Developer, Mindsharp, Jacksonville, Florida. In 2005 and 2006, Andrew was awarded Microsoft Most Valuable Professional (MVP) for Microsoft Content Managemet Server for his contributions to the MCMS community. He co-authored *Advanced Content Management Server Development* by Packt Publishing (2005), *Developer's Guide to the Windows SharePoint Services v3 Platform* by Charles River Media (2006), and he specializes in content management solutions, including Web Content Management in Microsoft Office SharePoint Server 2007.

Ben Curry CISSP, MCP, CNE, CCNA, Huntsville, Alabama. Ben is an author and enterprise network architect specializing in knowledge management and collaboration technologies. Ben is a senior instructor and consultant for Mindsharp, a company focused on the next generation of Microsoft products. Ben has over fifteen years of experience designing, managing, implementing, and securing datacenter IT solutions.

Laura Derbes Rogers MCSE, HealthSouth Corporation, Birmingham, Alabama. Laura is a systems engineer on the Messaging and Collaboration Team in the Information Technology Group at the HealthSouth corporate office in Birmingham. Laura is a SharePoint administrator and trainer and is a native of Baton Rouge, Louisiana.

William Jackson NASA, Huntsville, Alabama. William is a senior computer engineer with a focus on myriad Microsoft products. He has 10 years experience in the IT industry, a BS in Computer Science, with an MCSE in NT4.0, Windows 2000, and 2003, as well as a CCNA. Will works at NASA for SAIC. He lives in Huntsville with his beautiful wife, Dana.

Brett Lonsdale MCT, MCSD.NET, Combined Knowledge, Lutterworth, U.K. Brett is a trainer of Microsoft technologies and a developer specializing in SharePoint Development and ASP.NET Web Applications. Brett is based in the U.K. and is a co-owner of Combined Knowledge.

Chris McCain CEO, National IT Training and Certification Institute, Tampa, Florida. Chris is a six-year veteran of the IT training and consulting field. Chris has worked with a variety of Microsoft features and products, such as Active Directory, DNS, DHCP, PKI, and IPSec. His work has helped him develop a specialization in architecting secure Microsoft networks on platforms like Windows Server 2003, Windows XP, and Windows Vista. Additionally, Chris has experience in training and deploying core server products such as SQL Server, SharePoint, and Virtual Server 2005. Chris has co-authored national publications, authored content for Microsoft Learning, and has been a portion of the brainshare behind ITCertMentor.com.

Mark Schneider PMI, VitalSkills, Minneapolis, Minnesota. Mark is a computer architecture, project management, and business process improvement consultant. He is currently on contract with Northwestern College and Radio as Director of Academic Computing.

Ken Sproule MCT, MCP, MCSD, MCSD.NET, Sproule Consulting, Minneapolis, Minnesota. Ken is an author, consultant, trainer, and developer with over 35 years of development and implementation experience spanning many platforms. Among other training and development endeavors, Ken developed the InfoPath and Forms Server Developer courses for Mindsharp. Ken is CEO of Open Resources, Inc. and Sproule Consulting, both of which are located in Minneapolis, MN.

Richard Taylor MCSE, MCT, Phoenix, Arizona, IGotIT Technical Services, LLC. Rick is a SharePoint architect and has assisted numerous, large companies in their implementations. He is a chemist, physicist, and an avid triathlete. You can visit Rick's blog at *http://slickrickistheman.spaces.live.com*.

Graham Tyler Graham Tyler works as a collaboration consultant for Microsoft Consulting Services in the U.K., where he designs and develops large-scale solutions for enterprise customers. Graham (BSc Hons. in Software Development) has been focused on SharePoint and Office technologies for five years, particularly in assisting early adopter customers to develop proof-of-concept and pilot projects using the beta versions of Microsoft Office SharePoint Portal Server 2003 and Microsoft Office SharePoint Server 2007. He has also spent several years working with government customers to architect large SharePoint deployments in challenging environments.

Index

A

G

J

K

L

N

O

P

Q

R

S

T

U

X

Z

What do you think of this book? We want to hear from you!

Do you have a few minutes to participate in a brief online survey? Microsoft is interested in hearing your feedback about this publication so that we can continually improve our books and learning resources for you.

To participate in our survey, please visit:
www.microsoft.com/learning/booksurvey

And enter this book's ISBN, 0-7356-2282-5. As a thank-you to survey participants in the United States and Canada, each month we'll randomly select five respondents to win one of five $100 gift certificates from a leading online merchant.* At the conclusion of the survey, you can enter the drawing by providing your e-mail address, which will be used for prize notification *only*.

Thanks in advance for your input. Your opinion counts!

Sincerely,

Microsoft Learning

Learn More. Go Further.

To see special offers on Microsoft Learning products for developers, IT professionals, and home and office users, visit: *www.microsoft.com/learning/booksurvey*

* No purchase necessary. Void where prohibited. Open only to residents of the 50 United States (includes District of Columbia) and Canada (void in Quebec). Sweepstakes ends 6/30/2007. For official rules, see: *www.microsoft.com/learning/booksurvey*